Handbook of Psychological Assessment in Primary Care Settings

Handbook of Psychological Assessment in Primary Care Settings

Edited by

Mark E. Maruish
United Behavioral Health
Minneapolis, MN

LEA
LAWRENCE ERLBAUM ASSOCIATES, PUBLISHERS
2000   Mahwah, New Jersey   London

Lawrence Erlbaum Associates, Inc., Publishers
10 Industrial Avenue
Mahwah, NJ 07430

Cover design by Kathryn Houghtaling Lacey

Library of Congress Cataloging-in-Publication Data

Handbook of psychological assessment in primary care settings / edited by Mark E. Maruish.
    p. cm
    Includes bibliographical references and index.
ISBN- 0-8058-2999-7 (cloth: alk. paper)
1. Psychodiagnostics—Handbooks, manuals, etc. 2. Primary care (Medicine)
I. Maruish, Mark E. (Mark Edward)
RC469 .H374 2000
61689′075—dc21   99-048451
CIP

Books published by Lawrence Erlbaum Associates are printed on acid-free paper, and their
bindings are chosen for strength and durability.

Printed in the United States of America
10 9 8 7 6 5 4 3 2 1

For my parents

Contents

Preface   xi
Mark E. Maruish

I: GENERAL CONSIDERATIONS   1

1. Introduction   3
Mark E. Maruish

2. Integrating Behavioral Health and Primary Care   43
C. J. Peek and Richard Heinrich

3. Integration of Behavioral Health Care Services in Pediatric   93
Primary Care Settings
Mary Evers-Szostak

4. Screening and Monitoring Psychiatric Disorder in Primary   115
Care Populations
Leonard R. Derogatis and Larry L. Lynn II

5. Integrating Behavioral Health Assessment   153
With Primary Care Services
Cori L. Ofstead, Diane S. Gobran, and Donald L. Lum

II: ASSESSMENT INSTRUMENTS   189

6. Evaluation of Mental Disorders With the PRIME–MD   191
Steven R. Hahn, Kurt Kroenke, Janet B. W. Williams, and Robert L. Spitzer

7. Directions and COMPASS–PC   255
Grant R. Grissom and Kenneth I. Howard

8. The Shedler QPD Panel (Quick PsychoDiagnostics Panel):   277
A Psychiatric "Lab Test" for Primary Care
Jonathan Shedler

 9. The SCL–90–R and Brief Symptom Inventory (BSI) in Primary Care   297
     Leonard R. Derogatis and Kathryn L. Savitz

10. Applications of the Symptom Assessment–45 Questionnaire (SA–45)   335
     in Primary Care Settings
     Mark E. Maruish

11. Daily Stress Inventory (DSI) and Weekly Stress Inventory (WSI)   373
     Phillip J. Brantley and Shawn K. Jeffries

12. The Beck Depression Inventory (BDI) and the Center for Epidemiologic   391
     Studies Depression Scale (CES–D)
     Phillip J. Brantley, Daniel J. Mehan, Jr., and Janet L. Thomas

13. The Hamilton Depression Inventory   423
     Kenneth A. Kobak and William M. Reynolds

14. Tools to Improve the Detection and Treatment of Depression   463
      in Primary Care
     Teresa L. Kramer and G. Richard Smith

15. Geriatric Depression Scale   491
     Forrest Scogin, Noelle Rohen, and Elaine Bailey

16. Using the Beck Anxiety Inventory in Primary Care   509
     Robert J. Ferguson

17. Self-Administered Alcoholism Screening Test (SAAST)   537
     Leo J. Davis

18. Screening for Cognitive Impairments in Primary Care Settings   555
     George J. Demakis, Michael G. Mercury, and Jerry J. Sweet

19. Using the SF–36 Health Survey in Primary Care   583
     Harry P. Wetzler, Donald L. Lum, and Dwana M. Bush

20. The Primary Care Assessment Survey: A Tool for Measuring,   623
     Monitoring, and Improving Primary Care
     Alison Murray and Dana Gelb Safran

21. The Difficult Doctor Patient Relationship Questionnaire   653
     Steven R. Hahn

              III: PRIMARY AND BEHAVIORAL HEALTH CARE   685
                      INTEGRATION PROJECTS

22. Improving Care for a Primary Care Population: Depression   687
     as an Example
     Patricia Robinson and Kirk Strosahl

23. A Case Study: The Kaiser Permanente Integrated Care Project   713
Arne Beck and Carolee Nimmer

24. The INOVA Primary Behavioral Health Care Pilot Project   735
Leonard Goldstein, Boris Bershadsky, and Mark E. Maruish

IV: FUTURE DIRECTIONS   761

25. Future Directions in Psychological Assessment and Treatment   763
 in Primary Care Settings
Kenneth A. Kobak, James C. Mundt, and David J. Katzelnick

Author Index   797

Subject Index   825

Preface

Here at the beginning of the 21st century we have witnessed major advances in the evolution of health care. Probably the most notable of these is the emergence and proliferation of managed health care. Resulting (for the most part) from out-of-control health care costs, it has changed the way health care is both financed and delivered. The impact of managed care has been both positive and negative, depending on whether the perspective taken is that of patient, provider, employer, or payer. Regardless of one's assessment of the situation, managed care is destined to continue in one form or another well into the 21st century.

As part of the evolution of managed care, a trend has begun relatively recently and is gaining momentum. This is the movement toward the integration of behavioral health care services into primary medical care practices. In a chapter appearing later in this book, Goldstein, Bershadsky, and Maruish very succinctly stated the factors supporting this movement:

1. A large proportion of patients who seek services from primary care providers experience significant psychological distress or symptomatology.
2. Primary care providers, in general, lack the specific training and skills they need to identify or provide appropriate treatment to these patients.
3. Consequently, patients with behavioral health problems consume a large proportion of the available primary care resources.
4. Identifying and adequately treating the behavioral health problems of primary care patients in the primary care setting has been shown to result in significant cost savings.
5. Consultation, liaison, and educational services offered by behavioral health professionals can be instrumental in ensuring the success of other health intervention efforts.

It is unlikely that the interest in what Goldstein et al. refer to as "primary behavioral health care" is just a passing fad. Aside from the potential direct and indirect cost savings that can be realized by providing adequate, efficient, cost-effective treatment to primary care patients with behavioral health problems, accreditation bodies such as the National Committee for Quality Assurance (NCQA) and the Joint Commission on Accreditation of Healthcare Organizations (JCAHO) are now requiring demonstration of health care organizations' efforts to integrate medical and behavioral health services. In addition, in the health domain as in other domains, consumers are expressing a desire for "one-stop shopping" for their health care needs. Thus, it would seem that the situation provides a new opportunity for behavioral health care professionals to become part of the solution to the health care crisis through the skills and training they have to offer to primary care providers. But the fact is that behavioral health care professionals have been providing these types of services for decades; it is the recognition of their value and the need to offer them through formalized programs that are recent advances. And it is this recognition that has served as the impetus for this handbook.

Several approaches could have been taken to develop a volume that would be useful to behavioral health practitioners who either are currently providing services in primary care settings or are considering such an undertaking. For example, the focus could have been on developing and implementing an integrated primary and behavioral health care program from the ground up; on providing brief, symptom-oriented therapies in primary care settings; or on describing models of consultation with primary care providers. Here, it is on using psychological screening and assessment instruments in primary care settings. My own experience lies in assessment, and I believe one of the most significant contributions behavioral health care can make to the more effective solution of mental health and substance abuse problems (and concomitant costs) in primary care settings is the tools and expertise it brings to the tasks of identifying and monitoring these problems.

There is a large audience for the type of information presented in this handbook which can be used not only by behavioral health care professionals, but also by primary care providers who may want to integrate into their practices the instruments (with additional, supervised training, as necessary) and/or other information discussed in the chapters that follow.

To facilitate readers' understanding, I have organized the book into four parts. Part I contains five chapters that deal with general topics and issues that provide a context for the information presented in the subsequent chapters. Chapter 1 discusses the prevalence of behavioral health disorders in primary care settings, their direct and indirect costs, and the concomitant need for better identification and treatment of mental health and substance use by primary care providers. Integrated primary and behavioral health care is identified as a solution to the existing problems—a solution that may take any of several forms, depending on the particular needs of the individual primary care setting. Chapter 1 also provides an overview of the potential contributions of various types of psychological assessment instruments for screening patients, planning an appropriate course of treatment, and assessing the outcomes of that treatment. The remaining four chapters in Part I address important issues and considerations related to the integration of primary and behavioral health care in general, with special attention being given to the integration of psychological assessment.

Part II presents a detailed discussion of each of a number of psychological instruments that I feel are useful for screening and/or monitoring primary care patients with significant behavioral health problems. The instruments considered as potential chapter topics were evaluated against several selection criteria, including the popularity of the instrument among behavioral health clinicians; recognition of its psychometric integrity; in the case of recently released instruments, the potential for the instrument to become widely accepted and used; the perceived usefulness of the instrument for screening and monitoring purposes; and the availability of a recognized expert on the instrument (preferably its author) to contribute a chapter to this book. In the end, the instrument-specific chapters selected for inclusion were those judged most likely to be of the greatest interest and utility to the majority of the book's intended audience.

The first three chapters of Part II deal with instruments developed specifically for use in primary care settings. These are the PRIME–MD, the COMPASS–PC, and the Shedler QPD Panel. Each of these multiscale instruments can be used to screen for the presence of significant behavioral health problems. Moreover, both the COMPASS–PC and the QPD Panel can be used to monitor the effects of treatment over time. Immediately following these are chapters on other multiscale instruments—SCL–90–R, BSI, and SA–45. Although not developed specifically for use in primary care settings, each of these three instruments has been found to be useful in assessing and/or monitoring primary care patients on nine psychological symptom domains.

Several of the other chapters in Part II present in-depth information on a number of instruments that are focused more on the assessment of specific types of behavioral health disturbance. Because of its prevalence in primary care patients, I have included a number of chapters dealing with some of the more commonly used and accepted depression instruments. These include the Beck, Hamilton, CES–D, GDS, and University of Arkansas depression measures. The BAI, SAAST, and DSI/WSI chapters provide information on instruments that address problematic anxiety, alcohol use, and stress, respectively. The importance of screening for cognitive impairments in primary care populations prompted the inclusion of a chapter addressing this issue. And with its widespread acceptance as the premier measure of overall health status in both medical and behavioral health care settings, it was imperative to discuss the use of the SF–36 in primary care settings.

In addition to chapters presenting discussions on instruments designed to assess the more obvious types of behavioral health problems faced in primary care settings, two other chapters were included in Part II. Each addresses an instrument used to assess two very important, but not always recognized, matters that have bearing on the treatment of *all* primary care patients. The Primary Care Assessment Scale, or PCAS, is an instrument that was developed to measure seven clinician–patient relationship-based domains that are said to define "primary care." In contrast, the Difficult Doctor–Patient Relationship Questionnaire, or DDPR–Q, was developed to assess a physician's response to a given patient, thus providing an estimate of how much the physician experiences the patient as "difficult."

Part III was developed to provide the reader with actual examples of how psychological assessment can be integrated into primary care settings. Each of the three chapters in this section presents a description of an integrated primary behavioral health care program offered in a managed care environment, with special emphasis on the use of psychological assessment in the program. Although one chapter describes a pilot program, the other two describe established, ongoing programs.

Finally, Part IV offers a prediction of future advances in psychological assessment that are likely to impact its use in primary care settings. Based on developing trends in both psychological assessment and the technology that is more and more relied on to support it, the reader will get a flavor for how assessment in primary care settings might be conducted in the 21st century.

The enterprise of primary behavioral health care service delivery has attracted a great deal of interest over the past few years. As a result, the body of literature addressing the relevant issues has grown significantly, and quite probably it will continue to grow as the benefits of integrated medical and mental health/substance abuse services become more evident to patient, providers, and payers. I hope that behavioral health clinicians and primary care providers who currently are involved or are contemplating involvement in integrated primary behavioral health care services find the chapters that follow to be helpful in maximizing the potential benefits that can result from such services.

ACKNOWLEDGMENTS

The development of this work was a significant undertaking, requiring the efforts and support from a number of people. First and foremost are the contributors to this work.

This project was successful only because of their commitment and willingness to share their knowledge, experience, and insights with this audience. In addition, I would like to thank Nancee Meuser who once again was kind enough to review and edit the chapters that I authored. Finally, I am grateful to those people who have supported me during this project.

—M.E.M.
Minneapolis, MN
January 2000

I

GENERAL CONSIDERATIONS

Introduction

Mark E. Maruish
United Behavioral Health, Minneapolis, Minnesota

That the cost of health care in the United States is staggering—and on the rise—should be of no surprise to anyone. U.S. Department of Commerce data (cited in Haber & Mitchell, 1997) indicate that in 1980, the per capita annual health care cost was $1,068. By 1993, this figure rose to $3,299. Selden (1997) noted that over the past four decades, the cost of health care has exceeded general inflation by 50%, whereas during 1995, health care price inflation was 60% higher than increases in prices generally. Ray (1996) reported that the cost of health care in 1995 was about $1 trillion, or 14.9% of gross domestic product, and that figure is expected to rise by 20% by the year 2000.

Fortunately, there also are indications that the rate of cost increases is slowing down. For example, data from the Watson Wyatt Worldwide Study (as cited in Selden, 1997) indicated that in 1995, health insurance cost increases were below that of inflation, likely reflecting the impact of the increasing limitations in service delivery owing to the proliferation of managed care. The 4.4% increase in total health care spending that occurred in 1996 was the lowest rate of increase in 37 years ("Health Care Spending," 1998). Total expenditures that year represented 13.6% of the gross national product, a proportion that thus remains unchanged since 1993. Moreover, a William M. Mercer, Inc., survey of nearly 4,000 employers (as cited in "Employers' Health Costs," 1998) indicated that health maintenance organizations' (HMO) per worker costs dropped from $3,385 in 1994 to $3,165 in 1997. At the same time, the results of the Mercer study also revealed that most employers expected higher health care costs in 1998.

Some of the unfortunate consequences of the managed care revolution have been restrictions on the behavioral health care services available to covered lives. These services are now typically provided through mental health "carve out" companies or HMOs "with an exclusive [provider] network and tight utilization controls" (Selden, 1997, p. 16). However, there are indications that positive changes related to the delivery of behavioral health care are taking place or on the horizon. Legislation has been enacted to eliminate the lack of parity that exists between general medical and behavioral health care benefits in health plans ("Mental Health Parity Act," 1998; "Millions with Mental Illnesses Benefit," 1997). In addition, Strosahl (1996) noted that managed behavioral health care is shifting its focus from cost containment and supply-side strategies to three other areas: evidence-based clinical services, a population-based care philosophy, and integration of services delivery systems that previously were independent. With regard to the latter, Lipsitt (1997) noted, "Those who govern managed care companies and administer large industries have discovered that health plans that fragment delivery of services are more costly and less likely to be given high 'satisfaction' ratings by patients than those that provide 'one-stop shopping'" (pp. 10–11).

The realization of the financial and patient-care benefits that can accrue from the integration of primary medical care and behavioral health care has resulted not only in professional and academic-level discussions and investigations, but also in actual implementation of integrated programs in primary care settings. The degree to which integrated service delivery is present in participating practices varies as a function of a number of factors (e.g., funding, third-party reimbursement criteria, staff interest and commitment to the program, availability of resources, office space limitations). Regardless of the extent to which these services are merged, efforts toward attaining this goal attest to the belief that any steps toward integrating behavioral health care services in primary care settings represent an improvement over the more traditional model of segregated service delivery.

The purpose of this chapter is to provide the reader with an overview of the impetus for, the current interest in, and the efforts toward the integration of behavioral health care in primary medical care settings. The intent is not to present a comprehensive exposition of endeavors in this area; rather, it is hoped that the information contained herein will create a context that facilitates an understanding of the detailed information presented in the chapters that follow.

DEFINITIONS

As is made clear in this and other chapters of this book, the reemergence of interest in the integration of primary and behavioral health care services has made it the focus of much discussion. Frequently, discussion of this topic—at conferences, in graduate classes, in the published literature—takes place without clarification of a few key terms. Thus, before proceeding further, clarification of terminology is warranted.

Primary Care

The Institute of Medicine (IOM; Donaldson, Yordy, Lohr, & Vanselow, 1996) offered a definition of *primary care* that is comprehensive and cuts to the core focus of this group of medical specialties. Thus,

> Primary care is the provision of integrated, accessible health care services by clinicians who are accountable for addressing a large majority of personal health care needs, developing a sustained partnership with patients, and practicing in the context of family and community. (p. 32)

The IOM (Edmunds et al., 1997) further explained that

integrated care refers to comprehensive, coordinated, and continuous services whose processes are seamless across different levels of care. Accountability refers to the responsibility for quality of care, patient satisfaction, efficient use of resources, and ethical behavior. The context of the family and community refers to an understanding of the importance of living conditions, cultural background, and the impact of family dynamics on health status and also recognizes the caregiving role of families. (p. 87)

Who are considered primary care providers? The answer probably will vary depending on who is asked. This author has adopted the inclusion criteria used in mid-1970s legislation that mandated training a larger number of primary care physicians. According to Borus (1985), primary care providers included the medical specialties of "family medicine, family practice, general internal medicine, and general pediatrics, seeing these physicians as most likely to meet patients' ongoing primary care needs" (p. 1302). In addition, there are the "nonmedical" primary care providers—"nurse practitioners, physicians' assistants, health aids, health ombudsman, and care managers—who work with primary care physicians to provide ongoing care and coordination of patients' care needs over time" (p. 1302). Note, however, that references to "primary care providers" in publications reported later in this chapter may not always be as inclusive as the definition just presented.

Primary Behavioral Health Care

Strosahl (1996) indicated that effective integration of primary medical care and behavioral health care requires behavioral health care to adopt a general model of service delivery "that is consistent with the goals, strategies, and culture of primary care" (p. 93). Accordingly,

> The *primary mental health care* [italics added] model involves providing direct consultative services to primary care providers and, where appropriate, highly condensed treatment services for patients that are tailored to the primary care culture. The guiding philosophy of this model is to provide behavioral health services to a population of primary care patients. Like primary medical care, consultative and/or condensed treatment services are delivered as a first-line intervention. If a patient fails to respond to this level of intervention (or is obviously in need of highly specialized services), a transfer of care to the mental health specialty system occurs. (p. 93)

A number of approaches to or models of primary mental health care can be developed and implemented. Models for an integrated system of primary medical care and behavioral health care and the options for service delivery within each are discussed in detail later in this chapter.

Consultation–Liaison Psychiatry

Primary behavioral health care is not to be equated with *consultation–liaison psychiatry*. According to the Academy of Psychosomatic Medicine (1997),

> *Consultation–liaison psychiatry* [italics added] is a subspecialty of psychiatry that deals with psychiatric disorders of the medically ill. "Consultation" refers to the process of evaluating and managing medical patients with psychiatric problems, while "liaison" refers to facilitating integrated care with a designated general medical provider or team.

... Psychiatrists with consultation–liaison experience and skill are uniquely equipped to
manage complex clinical problems that arise when mental disorders co-exist with medical conditions. . . . [They] are, therefore, well qualified to facilitate complex treatment
planning and collaboration with a multi-disciplinary medical healthcare team for management of mental disorders in the medically ill; to provide clinical leadership of the behavioral healthcare team; and to offer education on the psychiatric aspects of medical
care to general medical physicians and other providers. (pp. 286–287)

As later discussion shows, consultation–liaison psychiatry may be similar to one of
several options in various models of integrated primary and behavioral health care.
However, the degree to which it represents true integrated care is limited.

PREVALENCE OF BEHAVIORAL HEALTH DISORDERS

Mental health and substance abuse disorders, that is, *behavioral health disorders,* have a
significant presence in the population of the United States. The demands of those suffering from these disorders can have a substantial impact on health care resources — both behavioral and medical — and thus merit the attention of those who
are charged with their care as well as those attempting to control the cost of that care.

Prevalence in the General Population

The prevalence rates of mental health and substance abuse disorders reported in the
Substance Abuse and Mental Health Services Administration (SAMHSA) *Substance
Abuse and Mental Health Statistics Sourcebook* (Rouse, 1995) draw from the Kessler et al.
(1994) study of over 8,000 15- to 54-year-old noninstitutionalized U.S. civilians participating in the National Comorbidity Study, between the years of 1990 and 1992. A
structured interview was administered to each of the participants. The data from
those interviews were then used to assign both lifetime and past-year *Diagnostic and
Statistical Manual of Mental Disorders* (3rd ed., rev.; *DSM–III–R*) diagnoses. The
Kessler et al. findings indicated a past-year prevalence rate for any alcohol, drug
abuse, or mental health (ADM) disorder of 29.5%. Past-year (i.e., 1991) prevalence
rates for any mental disorder, any substance abuse/dependence disorder, and both
mental health and substance abuse disorders were 22.9%, 11.3%, and 4.7%, respectively. Past-year prevalence rates for any anxiety disorder and any affective disorder
were 17% and 11%, respectively, while lifetime prevalence rates for these conditions
were 25% and 19%, respectively. In addition, lifetime prevalence rate for any substance abuse/dependence disorder was 27%.

Prevalence in Primary Care Settings

Health care consumers present themselves to medical health care providers for any
number of reasons. Lipsitt (as cited in Locke & Larsson, 1997) reported that over 80
million physician visits account for eight common complaints: fatigue, back pain,
headaches, dizziness, chest pain, dyspnea, abdominal pain, and anxiety. Locke and
Larsson's review of the literature suggested that the most common of the somatic

complaints addressed by physicians could be placed into one of five symptom group-ings — gastrointestinal, neurological, autonomic, cardiovascular, and musculo-skeletal — and that many of these are commonly seen in anxious and depressed patients.

That physical complaints often belie the presence of an underlying behavioral health problem is most clearly illustrated in a 1991 national study of the prevalence of depressive symptoms reported by Zung, Broadhead, and Roth (1993). In this study, 765 family physicians from across the United States provided data from the Zung Self-rating Depression Scale (SDS) on nearly 76,000 adult patients, along with infor-mation related to the reason for their medical visit. The five most frequently reported reasons for seeing these physicians were checkups, upper respiratory infections, hy-pertension, throat symptoms, and problems with skin/nails/hair. Among the top 25 most common reasons for seeing their physician, depression ranked 24th (1.2% of the sample) and anxiety ranked 25th (1.1% of the sample). At the same time, using a pre-established cutoff of the Zung score (SDS $\geq$ 55), 20.9% of the total sample were found to be experiencing clinically significant depressive symptoms.

The literature is replete with data that attest to the high prevalence of patients that are seen in primary care settings with clinically significant behavioral health prob-lems. Table 1.1 presents only a small sample of the data that demonstrate the fre-quency with which primary care providers encounter these individuals. Supporting data can be found in Von Korff et al. (1987), Sato and Takeichi (1993), Skinner (1990), Hankin and Otkay (1979), Spitzer et al. (1994, 1995), Dreher (1996), Smith, Rost, and Kashner (1995), Barsky and Borus (1995), Tiemens, Ormel, and Simon (1996), Katon and Roy-Byrne (1989), Smith (1994), and Kessler et al. (1987).

Data on the prevalence of the comorbidity of behavioral health disorders and other illnesses, diseases, or disorders commonly seen in primary care settings pro-vide an even clearer picture of the situation. For example, Ciarcia (1997) reported sig-nificant comorbidity rates of depression with cancer (18–39%), myocardial infarction (15–19%), rheumatoid arthritis (13%), Parkinson's disease (10–37%), stroke (22–50%), and diabetes (5–11%), with overall medical outpatient and inpatient rates of 2–15%

TABLE 1.1
A Sample of Reported Prevalences for Behavioral
Health Disorders in Primary Care Settings

Study/Source	Disorder	Prevalence
Perez-Stable, Miranda, Munoz, and Ying (1990)	Major depression	6–16%
	Anxiety	10%
	Any	10–30%
Schulberg and Burns (1988)	Any	25%
Jenkins (1997)	Psychosocial problems (UK)	Approximately 33%
Johnson et al. (1995)	Alcohol abuse and dependence	5%
	Mood disorder	26%
	Anxiety disorder	18%
	Eating disorder	3%
	Somatoform disorder	14%
Ciarcia (1997)	Major depression	6%
Katon and Schulberg (1992)	Depression (outpatient)	5–10%
	Depression (inpatient)	6–14%
Locke and Larsson (1997)	Somatization	50%+
Institute for International Research (1997)	Anxiety disorders	20%

Note. Some listed prevalence rate data were extracted from secondary sources.

and 12%, respectively. In a 1988 study of a community sample of over 2,500 people, Wells et al. (cited in Academy of Psychosomatic Medicine, 1997) found that the 6-month, risk-adjusted prevalence rate of mental disorder was 24.7% and 17.5% for those with and without a chronic medical condition, respectively. The lifetime mental disorder prevalence rates were 42.2% and 33%, respectively. As for specific disorders, Wells et al. found prevalence rates of comorbid mental disorders to be 37.5% for neurologic disorders, 34.5% for heart disease, 30.9% for chronic lung disease, 30.3% for cancer, 25.3% for arthritis, 22.7% for diabetes, and 22.3% for hypertension.

It is especially important to note the extent to which comorbidity of behavioral health disorders with one another can occur in primary care settings. Johnson et al. (1995) found that among the 5% of the 1,000 primary care patients identified with alcohol abuse and dependence (AAD) using the PRIME–MD, 47% met the criteria for one or more *other* mental disorders. Thus, among those identified with AAD, 33% were also diagnosed with a mood disorder, 22% with an anxiety disorder, 6% with an eating disorder, and 14% with a somatoform disorder. Among the non-AAD patients, 35% were found to have one or more PRIME–MD-identified disorders. The rate of comorbidity of these disorders with one or more other PRIME–MD-identified disorders was 65% for mood disorders, 82% for anxiety disorders, 84% for eating disorders, and 73% for somatoform disorders.

All in all, Strosahl's (1996) summary of and conclusions about the situation are not surprising:

> The primary healthcare system is the de facto mental health system in the United States. General physicians provide fully half of all formal mental healthcare in the United States. They account for roughly 70 percent of all psychotropic prescriptions and fully 80 percent of antidepressants. Most studies suggest that somewhere between 50 and 70 percent of primary care medical visits have a psychosocial basis. Further, studies have suggested that as many as 50 percent of primary care patients have clinically elevated anxiety and/or depression. (p. 96)

THE COST OF BEHAVIORAL HEALTH DISORDERS

The costs attributed to behavioral health care disorders tend to vary, depending on the source of information. Table 1.2 presents just a sample of direct, indirect, and total costs that have cited for various disorders or groups of disorders. Note some discrepancies in identified costs associated with a given disorder or group of disorders (e.g., anxiety). Regardless, the costs are high, with the annual total exceeding $300 billion. A more detailed report of costs—financial and other—can be found in the SAMHSA *Substance Abuse and Mental Health Statistics Sourcebook* (Rouse, 1995).

One aspect of costs that bears mentioning, and that may or may not have been completely accounted for in the data presented in Table 1.2, is medical health care utilization. For instance, Zung et al. (1993), citing a 1988 article by Regier et al., indicated that the number of outpatient visits for patients with depressive disorders is three times that of the average patient. As part of Katzelnick, Kobak, Greist, Jefferson, and Henk's (1997) investigation, almost 30% of high utilizers of inpatient and outpatient medical services during a 2-year period at one HMO screened positive for depression; however, they were less likely to have a serious medical condition than those high utilizers without depression. Moreover, high utilizers were almost four

TABLE 1.2
Sample of Annual Cost Estimates for Behavioral Health Disorders

Study/Source	Disorder	Total Costs	Direct Costs[a]	Indirect Costs[b]
"Directions: Anxiety Costs Big Bucks" (1997)	Anxiety disorders	$65 billion	$15 billion	$50 billion
"NIMH Official Cites" (1996)	Schizophrenia	$65 billion	$19 billion	$46 billion
Burns (1997)	Depression	$44 billion	$12 billion	$32 billion
Rouse (1995)	Mental health disorders	$147.9 billion	$67 billion	$80.9 billion
	Alcohol disorders	$98.7 billion	$10.6 billion	$88.1 billion
	Drug abuse disorders	$66.9 billion	$3.2 billion	$63.7 billion
Rice and Miller (1996)	Anxiety disorders	$46.5 billion	$10.7 billion	$35.8 billion
	Schizophrenia	$32.5 billion	$17.3 billion	$15.2 billion
	Affective disorders	$30.4 billion	$19.2 billion	$11.2 billion
	Other disorders	$38.4 billion	$19.7 billion	$18.7 billion
"Nearly 40 Percent of Older Suicide Victims" (1997)	Depression in the elderly (65+)	[c]	$800 million	[c]
Stoudemire, Frank, Hedemark, Kamlet, and Blazer (1986)	Major depression	$16 billion	[c]	[c]

Note. Some of the listed prevalence rate data were extracted from secondary sources. Differences in costs associated with specific disorders reported by different sources may reflect differences in the years surveyed.

[a]Includes costs related to treatment (e.g., medical, administrative, support services, etc.).
[b]Includes costs incurred indirectly (e.g., loss of wages and productivity, incarceration, death, etc.).
[c]Not reported.

times more likely to be formally diagnosed as depressed by their primary care physicians. Katon and his colleagues (as cited in Academy of Psychosomatic Medicine, 1996) found that half of the high utilizers of health care in their HMO sample were psychologically distressed. The top 10% of health care utilizers ($n = 767$) accounted for 29% of all primary care visits and 52% of all specialty visits. Moreover, Smith and his colleagues (also cited in Academy of Psychosomatic Medicine, 1996) found that the medical costs for depressed patients were twice as high as those for non-depressed patients. These considerations are important because the comparison of inpatient and outpatient medical care utilized *before* behavioral health treatment to that utilized *after* treatment is the basis for claims of medical cost offset resulting from that treatment.

Behavioral Health Care Cost-Offset Findings

One of the major arguments in support of the integration of primary and behavioral health care services is related to the reports of overall, long-term medical cost savings that occur when patients with mental health and substance abuse problems who are seen in primary care settings are identified early on and receive appropriate treatment. Following is a sample of the data cited in the literature supporting this contention:

• Locke (1997) reported average annual savings of $428 for patients participating in an HMO's program to teach somaticizers appropriate means of dealing with their symptoms.

- A Southwest mental health program reported that a program of early diagnosis and treatment of depression led to an annual savings in charges of more than $2 million, or $749 per patient ("Lovelace, Patients Reap Rewards," 1997). These savings were realized primarily as a result of decreased utilization of medical visits rather than hospitalization.

- In a study conducted by the State of Ohio, the treatment of 741 chemical dependency patients yielded a per patient average savings of $370 in medical care costs during the 12 months after beginning treatment, as compared to the 12 months preceding care ("Ohio Study Documents Cost-Offsets," 1996). Additional average per-patient savings of $3,750 in criminal justice costs and $290 in motor vehicle accident costs also were realized.

- In one of two large-scale studies by Holder and Bloise (cited in the Sipkoff, 1995, report of a SAMHSA survey of cost-offset studies), family health care costs were reduced by an average of $60 per month over a 12-month period following mental health treatment of one family member. In the second cited study, health care costs of treated alcoholics were 24% lower than untreated alcoholics during the 48-month period following treatment. The same SAMHSA survey found a 12-month, 20% decrease in health care costs associated with mental health treatment.

- In one of two studies of primary care patients by Simon, Von Korff, and their colleagues (cited in Academy of Psychosomatic Medicine, 1997), the average annual health care costs for 6,000 patients with depression were $4,246 whereas the health care costs for the same number of patients without depression were $2,371. In a smaller study, the average annual costs of patients with either anxiety or depression was $2,390, as compared to $1,397 for patients without either disorder.

- Millman and Robertson and Staywell Health Management Systems (cited in Melek, 1996) conducted a study of the effects of health habits on auto workers' medical claims. The results indicated that the costs for individuals with "elevated mental health" risks were 13% higher than those individuals with low mental health risk. Similarly, the costs of elevated stress risk individuals were 24% higher than those of low stress risk individuals.

- Friedman, Sobel, Myers, Caudill, and Benson (1995) identified "six pathways by which psychosocial factors drive medical utilization and costs" (p. 510). For each of these pathways, they cited studies that support the contention that pathway-specific interventions can result in decreases of utilization and/or costs.

Another major area in which cost offset can be realized is related to workplace productivity. According to the American Psychological Association (1996), the health conditions most limiting the ability to work are mental disorders. It therefore is not surprising that major depression resulted in $23 billion in lost work days in 1990, and that in 1985, behavioral health problems resulted in over $77 billion in lost income. Also, the National Depressive and Manic-Depressive Association (as cited in "Depression Still Undertreated," 1997) reported that depression costs employers $4,200 per depressed worker, or $250 per employee, with only 28% of these costs going toward actual treatment. As indicated by Sturm and Wells (1996), also relevant to worker productivity is the importance of improving the *quality* of treatment currently being delivered by primary care practitioners:

> High-quality care leading to better health outcomes creates many benefits to other parties not involved in healthcare. These positive rewards are not realized by health plans

and providers but accrue to the employers of better-treated patients through reduced absenteeism and high productivity, to family members and friends through burdens of care for sick individuals, and to government agencies through fewer transfer payments (welfare, unemployment, disability). [Thus,] Improved functioning through better care increases family income over time by much more than the additional treatment costs. (p. 66)

Although Sturm and Wells were specifically addressing the need to improve the quality of treatment for depression, one can assume that the same conclusions may also be applicable to other behavioral health disorders.

These and several other similar findings have been used to support the assertions that money spent for the identification and treatment of behavioral health problems is money well spent. At the same time, it would appear that at least as far as *medical cost offset* is concerned, the case may not be as clear-cut as one might think. For example, Olfson and Pincus's (1994) study of data from the 1987 National Expenditure Survey of 40,000 people found that the average total medical expenditure for people who used psychotherapy was two times the average of the general population, even when the psychotherapy costs were excluded. Higgins's (1994) review of three "natural history" studies indicated that primary care patients with unrecognized psychiatric disorders used health care services less often than those with recognized disorders. In fact, based on their review of over 25 mental health offset cost studies published between 1965 and 1995, Sperry, Brill, Howard, and Grissom (1996) determined that

> The only conclusion to come from research on cost-offset due to mental health treatment is that this is no clear-cut indication of cost savings. Studies that claim such an effect are often methodologically flawed. The same design problems also cast doubt on the findings of studies that claim to find no cost-offset effect. Future research needs stronger methodology to be considered valid. Future studies should be prospective in design, and incorporate random assignment of patients with similar psychiatric diagnosis to different treatment groups. Also, direct efforts need to be made toward determining which disorders are likely to demonstrate cost-offset effects, as well as studying which specific cost-offset effects occur with particular disorders. (pp. 205–206)

Considering the issue from a more applied perspective, Melek (1996) acknowledged that medical cost offsets have been demonstrated. However, he also pointed out that medical providers have questioned the medical cost-offset effects of behavioral health care, and that this has impeded the integration of medical and behavioral health care. Factors that contribute to this problem include (a) a desire for isolated and fixed behavioral health care costs, (b) problems in identifying and measuring the cost offset of medical expenses, (c) the fact that some forms of behavioral health care are subjective, and (d) cost savings that can occur within behavioral health care organizations themselves. He concluded that "as new studies attempting to prove the interrelationship between behavioral and medical wellness and disease are completed, financial links should be developed to encourage the two groups to work together for the sake of complete wellness for their covered members" (p. 40)

Finally, there is a very practical aspect to the cost offset debate, that is, the time it takes to demonstrate cost offset. Frequently, medical cost savings resulting from the treatment of behavioral health care are revealed only over the course of several years. Thus, cost-offset evidence is meaningful to a payer only when its covered lives continue coverage with that payer for an extended period of time. As pointed out by one managed care company ("Managed Care Execs," 1997), "MCOs can't 'spend today to save tomorrow,' because they're probably going to lose that contract tomorrow to a lower bidder" (p. 2).

TREATMENT OF BEHAVIORAL HEALTH CARE PROBLEMS BY PRIMARY CARE PROVIDERS

As has been shown, the situation that exists in the United States today is one in which (a) behavioral health problems of various degrees of severity exist in significant number; (b) approximately half of the people with these problems seek treatment from their family physician or other primary care provider; and (c) a significant proportion of these same people are among the highest utilizers of medical resources. The question one must ask is: How is the primary care medical system performing as the de facto behavioral health care system (Regier, Narrow, Rae, Manderscheid, Locke, & Goodwin, 1993)? The answer is clear: Not well. The inadequacy of primary care providers in dealing effectively with patients with behavioral health problems has been recognized numerous times in the literature. This inadequacy exhibits itself in two general areas of service delivery: problem detection and appropriate treatment.

Inadequate Detection and Treatment of Behavioral Health Disorders

Detection of mental health and substance abuse/dependence symptoms and disorders is problematic for the primary care provider. Selden's (1997) and Burns's (1997) reviews of the literature suggested that anywhere between one third and one half of patients with behavioral health disorders seen in primary care settings go undetected. Higgins (1994) found the rate of unrecognized mental illness in primary care settings to be 33%–79% for adults and 44%–83% for children, based on the studies employing *DSM–III/DSM–III–R*-based structured interviews. Perhaps more important is the fact that the rates for the detection of particular disorders appear to vary considerably. The Academy of Psychosomatic Medicine's (1996) review of literature findings suggested that with inpatient populations, the rate of accurate diagnosis is 14–50% for depression, 14–37% for delirium and dementia, and 5–50% for alcohol-related disorders, with only 11% of patients with a mental disorder having a discharge diagnosis reflecting these disorders. A study conducted in the Netherlands by Tiemens, Ormel, and Simon (as reported in "Detection of Psychological Disorders," 1996) also found variability in detection accuracy with a sample of 340 primary care patients. The detection rates for patients receiving International Classification of Diseases, 10th Revision (ICD–10)-based diagnoses were approximately 60% for those with current depression, 54% for dysthymia, 59% for generalized anxiety disorder, 79% for agoraphobia, and 92% for panic disorder, with approximately 54% of those with *any* definite disorder being detected. Moreover, Sturm and Wells (1996) found that in the RAND Medical Outcomes Study, detection rates in prepaid and fee-for-service general medical practices differed, with detection in the latter being higher.

The seriousness of these problems is highlighted by Barraclough, Bunch, Nelson, et al. (as cited in Cole, Raju, & Barrett, 1997), who indicated that approximately 15% of patients with severe depression lasting 1 month or longer commit suicide, and that half of these patients see their physicians sometime during the month before their death. The problem seems to be particularly serious in geriatric populations. An NIH

Consensus Development Panel on Depression in Late Life (also cited in Cole et al., 1997) indicated that among elderly patients, 75% of those committing suicide had seen their primary care providers within a short period of time before their demise. Even more disconcerting is a report in *Decade of the Brain* (as cited in "Nearly 40 Percent of Older Suicide Victims," 1997) indicating that almost 40% of older persons who commit suicide visit primary care providers within 1 week of killing themselves.

Even if behavioral health problems are detected, the treatment that is provided to these patients frequently may be inadequate. For instance, the Tiemens et al. Netherlands study (as reported in "Detection of Psychological Disorders," 1996) indicated that there was no link between detection of a mental disorder and either improved outcome scores on the Comprehensive International Diagnosis Interview–Primary Care Version or improved occupational functioning. In addition, at 1 year post-detection, only one third of patients initially assigned a diagnosis recovered and half still met the criteria for a diagnosis. However, most of these data are related to the treatment of depressed patients. For instance, the National Depressive and Manic-Depressive Association (cited in "Depression Still Undertreated," 1997) reported that "up to half of depressed patients treated by primary care physicians receive no antidepressants, and only 10.7% of those who do receive medication are given adequate dosages over sufficient lengths of time" (p. 1). Rome (as cited in Burns, 1997) indicated that studies show that about 50% of those depressive patients who are accurately identified receive appropriate treatment. In addition, Wells's review of three large health policy studies of treatment of depression in the general medical sector (as cited in Academy of Psychosomatic Medicine, 1996) indicated that antidepressant treatment was prescribed 20% of the time and at suboptimal dosages; for 40% of these cases, the dosage was subtherapeutic.

Factors Related to Inadequacies in Identifying and Treating Behavioral Health Disorders in Primary Care Settings

The inadequacies in the care provided to patients with behavioral disorders patients in primary care settings are the result of multiple factors. First, there are those associated with the medical professions or the providers themselves. Primary care providers generally practice within what Cole and Raju (1996) termed the "biomedical model of illness," which is grounded in the philosophies of *dualism* (the distinction of mind and body) and *reductionism* (understanding health problems at a molecular level of physiology). This model promotes the idea that the only problems worth attending to are physical problems, thus perpetuating the stigma of mental illness. Adoption of this model is reflected in the type of training these providers have undergone and skills that they have (not) developed. As Lipkin (1996) indicated,

> It is not surprising that primary care physicians are poor diagnosticians of depression and other mental disorders. The average internal medicine program devotes less than 2 hours per year to teaching that is explicitly about psychiatric disorders. Family medicine programs spend about 12 hours, primary care internal medicine programs about 18 hours. (p. 52)

Lipkin went on to add that

> The failure of most primary care physicians is not because of a lack of knowledge about mental disorder and their diagnosis but rather a failure of the techniques of interviewing

and doctor–patient interaction to elicit the data needed to suspect the need for diagnosis. (p. 52)

Part of these communication problems is seen in what are termed "doorknob" questions, that is, questions asked by the provider at the end of an interview. Cole and Raju (1996) indicated that these "Oh, by the way . . ." questions occur in about 20% of all medical interviews. To some extent, these types of questions may reflect the provider's fear that exploring real or suspected behavioral health problems may open a Pandora's box of problems he or she may not be able to adequately attend to, given the financial and time constraints imposed by managed care or other forces. Hesitancy to explore potential problems also may reflect a fear that because of the associated stigma, this line of questioning may be considered intrusive and, consequently, result in patients seeking primary care services elsewhere (Lipkin, 1996).

Horst (1997) presented other provider-related factors that impede the detection and treatment of substance abuse patients in the primary care setting. He noted that the training of primary care providers does not expose them to the types of patients that they are likely to encounter in their practices. Although providers are more likely to have seen late-stage alcoholics and intravenous drug users during their training years, they are more likely to see the at-risk, nondependent substance abuser in day-to-day practice. The knowledge and experiences garnered, and the attitudes formed, during the training years may make the provider question one's own or the system's ability to adequately care for the patient; consequently, the provider may be reluctant to try.

Patient-related factors also play into the picture of inadequate services. Here, the most prominent factor is the stigma of mental illness. The fear or shame related to being diagnosed with a mental health disorder remains in American society. In fact, Lipkin (1996) noted that "More important than manpower issues is the continued lack of acceptance of the need for psychiatric and mental healthcare by the general population. Most people do not want to recognize, admit, or make public their mental infirmities and problems" (p. 49). Stelovich (1996) indicated that for this reason, many patients who have been diagnosed with major depression prefer to seek treatment in a primary care setting that views the problem (much as Cole & Raju, 1996, might predict) as a "chemical imbalance" or "a medical depression."

The third major set of factors has to do with the health care system in which primary and behavioral health care providers must operate. There are actually two sets of circumstances operating: one related to patients who have been identified as having behavioral health problems, and another in which such problems are yet to be identified by the patient or a health care professional. As for the former, Mitchell and Haber (1997) noted that in many instances the copayment for behavioral health services frequently is more than for primary care visits. This encourages the patient to seek either no treatment, or treatment that is less costly but provided by a less qualified health care professional (i.e., the primary care provider).

On the other hand, there also are disincentives for primary care providers to treat behavioral health problems, regardless of whether the patient is covered under an integrated service delivery system or a behavioral health care "carve out." As Edmunds et al. (1997, p. 88) indicated,

> The provision of care depends almost entirely on the fee and on the time needed to conduct the procedures that are reimbursed. When primary care clinicians are not paid for the time that they spend interviewing primary care patients about mental health and

substance abuse problems, the incentive structure works against the identification and treatment of mental health and substance abuse problems.

Moreover, even when identified in the primary care setting, there are disincentives for primary care providers to refer to mental health specialists when such would be the appropriate thing to do (Del Vecchio, 1996). Managed care and rationing strategies often result in poor continuity or coordination of care, or referral of patients to less appropriate systems of care.

Solutions to the Problem

Approximately half of the behavioral health care services in the United States today are delivered in primary care settings by professionals limited in their ability to accurately identify and appropriately treat individuals suffering from mental health or substance abuse problems. And the fact is, patients with behavioral health care problems will continue to turn to their primary care provider rather than a behavioral health care specialist for treatment, in spite of these well-intentioned professionals' frequent inability to provide the highest possible quality of service. Given this state of affairs, there are a number of steps that could be taken to improve the chances that patients needing behavioral health care services will receive appropriate, high-quality care.

Probably the most significant remedy for the current state of affairs is to improve the primary care provider's level of knowledge and skills in the area of behavioral health care. Lipkin (1996) identified the following areas in which primary care providers should become knowledgeable: diagnostic criteria; diagnostic tools; epidemiology; adaptations of their practice to the cultural beliefs of the patient population; and brief approaches to treatment, including relaxation and those treatments that are psychopharmacological, cognitive, and supportive in nature. Consistent with the recommendations of Higgins (1994), Lipkin also indicated that providers should develop interviewing skills that enable them to relate effectively to the patient, elicit the information necessary for the assignment of an appropriate diagnosis, and engage the patient in a plan of treatment. Being more culturally sensitive, educating patients, facilitating psychological and social support, and monitoring treatment also are important. Lipkin added, "Integration of knowledge, skills, and attitudes of the practitioner is critical for success in this area and requires practice. There is no quick fix" (p. 52).

Sperry et al. (1996) suggested that the implementation of more regular screening procedures would be beneficial, given the fact that less than half of patients with behavioral health problems in primary care settings are identified. In short,

> psychiatric illness is to medicine today what hypertension was 20 years ago: a major source of morbidity, disability, and mortality that could be prevented by earlier detection of disease, accomplished via mass screening by primary care providers. (p. 201)

Higgins (1994), however, did not advocate widespread screening; rather, he advocated the development of tools that will assist the primary care provider in identifying those patients who can benefit from behavioral health interventions. Consistent with Higgins and with Lipkin's (1996) assertions,

> Primary care physician recognition appears to be a necessary but not sufficient step to improve the outcome of psychiatric and psychological disorders in primary care settings. . . . To enhance outcomes, programs to improve screening for behavioral and psy-

chiatric disorders in primary care must be accompanied by interventions that increase the knowledge and skill of providers in treating these disorders. ("Detection of Psychological Disorders," 1996, p. 9 [Editor's Note])

There are two other major ways in which changes can come about through the provider. The first is by ensuring that only *appropriate* referrals are made to mental health specialists. Jenkins (1997) indicated that in order to ensure specialist services are well targeted, criteria for referrals need to be developed. These criteria should be based on epidemiological factors such as diagnosis, symptom severity, risk of danger to self or others, and the extent to which the care of the patient can be shared between the two providers. At the same time, frequently there is an issue of the availability of *affordable* behavioral health professionals to provide needed services. In a recent telephone survey of 5,100 primary care physicians conducted by the Center for Studying Health System Change (as cited in "Physicians Report Problems," 1998), 72% of the respondents indicated that they are not always able to find suitable outpatient mental health services for their patients. Sixty-eight percent responded similarly with regard to finding needed inpatient services.

Another means of improving care is through the implementation of guidelines for treatment of specific disorders. Both the Agency for Health Care Policy and Research (AHCPR) and the American Psychiatric Association have developed guidelines for the treatment of depression in primary care settings (as cited in "Depression Still Undertreated," 1997). According to Sturm and Wells (1996), cost savings would be realized if the quality of care provided to depressed patients were improved. They indicated that

> Spending the additional 20 to 30 percent for care that follows practice guidelines could quadruple the value of mental healthcare: The return on each dollar spent on care improves patients' ability to function on the job and around the house. The potential to improve the cost-effectiveness of care is especially great for depressed patients who visit general medical providers such as internists or family doctors. (p. 65)

Although Sturm and Wells's projections apply to the treatment of depression, it is likely that the appropriate and timely application of formal or informal "standard of practice" guidelines for the treatment of other behavioral health disorders will result in similar savings and/or improvement in functioning.

Educational efforts also should be directed to the patient/consumer as well as to the primary care provider. Certainly, making materials about the nature and treatment of behavioral health disorders available to patients, family members, and other significant people in the patients' lives (e.g., employers, friends) can help remove the stigma that simply perpetuates misunderstanding and impedes the delivery of needed treatment to those afflicted with behavioral health problems. In addition, supporting efforts such as the National Mental Illness Awareness Week, the National Depression Screening Day, National Institute for Mental Health Depression/Awareness, Recognition, and Treatment (DART) Program, and the National Public Education Campaign on Clinical Depression (NPECCD), as well as organizations such as the National Alliance for the Mentally Ill (NAMI), can further advance the public's knowledge of the nature and extent of mental health problems and substance abuse and treatment options ("Depression Still Undertreated," 1997).

Another form of patient/consumer education also should take place. That is, education should be geared toward helping those who need behavioral health care services make informed choices about the provider they choose and the treatment they receive (Del Vecchio, 1996). This knowledge leads to empowerment, which in turn can lead to increased care quality and decreased costs.

Possibly equal in importance to the provider- and patient-related changes toward improving primary care-delivered behavioral health care services are changes in the financial/incentive arrangements that play into the provider's day-to-day practice. Mitchell and Haber (1997) indicated that revision of the financial incentive structure to improve the recognition and treatment of mental health disorders will result in improvement in the patient's quality of life and possibly lowered overall medical costs (as was discussed earlier). Certainly, the move to create parity in benefits structures for medical and behavioral health services is a step in the right direction.

Implementation of any or all of the solutions just mentioned should improve the quality of services that primary care providers offer to their patients with mental health or substance abuse problems. However, as Edmunds et al. (1997) pointed out,

> the challenges in monitoring behavioral health care in primary care settings are magnified by the increased scope and complexity of the health conditions that are expected to be treated in the primary care settings, the wide variability in the extent of psychiatric training received by family physicians and other primary care practitioners, and the rapid development of new treatments that makes it increasingly difficult for practitioners to stay current. (p. 89)

Given this, the Edmunds et al. recommendations for maximizing the quality and benefits of treatment that patients with behavioral health problems can receive in the primary care setting are models of collaborative care between primary and behavioral health care professionals. Of particular interest among today's more forward thinkers are those models of *integrated primary behavioral health care.*

INTEGRATION OF PRIMARY AND BEHAVIORAL HEALTH CARE SERVICES

The integration of primary medical care and behavioral health care has existed in various forms for many years. However, only recently has it gained the attention and prominence of both the medical and behavioral health care professions as an effective and efficient means of attending to a significant portion of those patients suffering from mental health and substance abuse problems. The reasons for the growing interest in integrated primary and behavioral health care are as varied as the qualities that define it and the various options by which it can be provided.

Impetus for Integrating Primary and Behavioral Health Care

The current climate in both the primary and behavioral health care fields is probably more conducive to integration of services than ever before. In fact, some experts predict that integrated care as "a single, collaborative field" in health care systems will be a given in the 21st century ("Leaders Predict Integration," 1996). The factors that are helping to create this climate of openness to integration are numerous and range from the practical to the financial, to those related to external forces.

Practical Considerations.   There are a number of practical considerations that make integrated care a sensible solution to the problems that have been identified throughout this chapter. First, it is likely that primary care settings will remain key sources of behavioral health care service delivery. Strosahl (as cited in Burns, 1997, pp. 22, 24) noted that "There's no way the American healthcare system will be able to train enough behavioral healthcare providers to meet the increased demand existing in primary care." In the primary care setting, he saw the behavioral health care specialist as a consultant to the primary care provider, training that provider to recognize, treat, and manage patients with mental health or substance abuse problems.

Selden (as cited in "Efforts to Integrate with Primary Care," 1997) offered yet another consideration. Given the demands being placed on today's workforce, mental well-being is becoming a more prominent requisite for satisfactory job performance. As Selden indicated, "The abilities that are most severely affected by behavioral health disorders are exactly the skills you need to work with high-level data and people" (p. 2). Thus, the value associated with the identification and treatment of individuals with these disorders, wherever they may present themselves for care, is increasing.

Financial Factors.   As discussed earlier in this chapter, there is an increasing realization of the time demands and related costs that result from the provision of behavioral health care services in primary care settings. Sobel (as cited in "Collaborative Care Requires New Approaches," 1997) very succinctly stated the problem:

> The highest 10 percent of utilizers in general medical care . . . account for 29 percent of all primary care visits, 53 percent of all specialty visits, 40 percent of all hospital stays and 26 percent of all prescriptions. Meanwhile, 50 percent of high utilizers are psychologically distressed. (p. 4)

Moreover, 60% of medical visits have no biologic basis that can be confirmed, and the cost of treating patients with co-occurring medical and behavioral health disorders is disproportionate (Selden, as cited in "Efforts to Integrate with Primary Care," 1997). Thus, it is not surprising, as Sobel pointed out, that

> The effective use of behavioral health care in the primary care setting can:
>
> - Reduce outpatient utilization by 7 to 15 percent.
> - Reduce pediatric visits for acute illness by 25 percent.
> - Decrease acute asthma visits by one per year.
> - Reduce outpatient visits by somaticizing patients by 43 percents.
> - Decrease office visits by arthritis patients by 43 percent.
> - Decrease clinical utilization for chronic pain by 36 percent. (p. 4)

Thus, as Friedman et al. (1995) explained,

> Addressing the emotional distress or patients, whether because of psychological problems or medical illness, decreases utilization of costly medical services. It makes health and economic sense to offer high medical utilizers the benefits of focused mental health services through referral and outreach. Health care systems that make use of appropriate expertise directed at both medical and emotional distress can provide superior patient care and medical cost offset. (p. 514)

External Forces. The establishment of managed behavioral health care companies grew out of employers' dissatisfaction with the benefits and treatment that general health care organizations were providing to their employees with behavioral health disorders (Dixon, 1997). The result was the establishment of managed behavioral health "carve-out" companies. However, more recent cost-containment efforts are now moving the industry to consolidation of services under a "one-stop shopping" service delivery arrangement, at least for large health care customers (Freeman, 1997). These efforts have been supported by a broadening of the health care focus from the individual patient to populations, the removal of legal barriers to the merging of health care organizations, and a realization that the one-stop shopping paradigm is more likely to result in higher patient satisfaction ratings (Lipsitt, 1997).

Another external pressure to integrate services stems from the growing demands for accountability information surrounding behavioral health care services. This has led to the relatively recent development and implementation of the National Committee for Quality Assurance (NCQA) Managed Behavioral Health Accreditation Program (NCQA, 1997). Developed with input from various stakeholders—consumers, employers, health plans, policymakers, managed behavioral health care organizations (MBHOs), and providers—the program has three goals: (a) coordination of behavioral health care with medical care, (b) implementation of population-based, continuous quality improvement management systems, and (c) emphasis on preventive behavioral health.

Of most relevance to this discussion is NCQA's requirements for the coordination of behavioral health care with medical care and the establishment of preventive programs. According to Standard QI 6 of this program, "The organization ensures that the behavioral healthcare services provided to its covered population are coordinated and integrated with general medical care" (NCQA, 1997, p. 67). Meeting this standard requires the MBHO to: (a) exchange information throughout its continuum of care; (b) have the means of educating primary care physicians about the diagnosis, treatment, and referral of commonly seen mental health and substance abuse disorders; (c) review formularies and benefits related to medical and behavioral health care; (d) collaborate with medical practitioners with regard to the appropriate use of psychotropic medications; (e) ensure that behavioral health care patients receive needed medical care on a timely basis; (f) ensure that behavioral health care patients with comorbid medical problems receive timely, appropriate treatment; and (g) evaluate the coordination and continuity of patient care across settings and providers.

Moreover, according to Standard PH 1.2, "The organization must show evidence that it engages medical delivery systems or other health care practitioners in developing and adopting preventive behavioral health programs" (NCQA, 1997, p. 203). Both this and Standard QI 6 have particular relevance to managed care organizations (MCOs) that deliver behavioral services. Their services also will have to meet the MBHO standards to maintain their accreditation. Thus, NCQA standards for accredited MBHOs provide an incentive related to integrating primary and behavioral health care (NCQA, 1997).

Qualities of Integrated Care

The ideals and drive behind integrated primary care and behavioral health care are appealing to health care stakeholders—patients, payers, and providers. But if one were to ask members of each of these stakeholder groups to define integrated care, it is likely that there would be a lack of clear consensus about the meaning of the term. The models of integrated service delivery presented next bear this out. Before discussing these, it might be helpful to briefly review some of the general qualities or attributes that are thought to exemplify an integrated approach to primary and behavioral health care delivery.

First, a team approach to patient care lies at the core of the integrated service delivery. As Lipsitt (1997) noted.

> The secret of integrated systems lies in the ability of the parts to function interdependently in a dynamically complete context that is different and most likely more than the sum of the parts. . . . To function as a system, the parts must be able to interact without slavish adherence to disciplinary boundaries. In other words, consensus building must replace turf battles; participants must work for the benefit of the whole, not of individual parts. (p. 10)

Added to this are four elements to effective comanagement that were cited by Von Korff and colleagues (as cited in Locke & Larsson, 1997). These included: (a) collaboration on the development of the definition of the problem; (b) shared decision making as it applies to setting goals, planning treatment, and changing behavior; (c) developing a continuum of training and support for patient self-management; and (d) having a sustained program of active follow-up.

Two other important team-related considerations are noteworthy. Mitchell and Haber (1997) contended that the partnership between the service providers must be a "fluid system" in which the degree that each provider is active in the treatment process is a function of the needs of the patient. Thus, at one point in time, the primary care provider may take the lead in service delivery; on medical stabilization, the more prominent role may then shift to the behavioral health care provider. Compatible with this line of thinking is Peek's (1997) recommendation for building a "community of healthcare clinicians" that "articulate common ground for convening the diverse collaboration of clinicians on behalf of patients and families" (p. 10). Using a musician analogy, he wrote of the need for the health care professional to move from working as a soloist to working as an "ensemble-ist" with a shared sense of "providership." Without this providership, health care professionals are "left with divisive, competitive, self serving professional and guild interests that rob people of energy and work against everything [they] value for patients and families" (p. 10). (It is interesting to note that the Institute of Medicine [as cited in Edmunds et al., 1997] indicated that the relationship between the patient and the primary care provider should continue. In some cases, this may be in contradiction to the collaborative spirit espoused earlier.)

Moreover, an integral member of what Mitchell and Haber (1997) described as the *primary care partnership* is the patient. Patient involvement leads to a greater sense of mastery and self-control, and, consequently, a greater chance that the patient's treatment will be successful. Thus, the patient's role may move from one of a passive recipient of care to that of one actively making lifestyle changes to improve and maintain health. Indeed, the role of providers in educating and empowering patients to care for themselves has been identified as being a key component to a successful integrated system by many, including Von Korff and colleagues (as cited in Locke & Larsson, 1997; discussed earlier) and Sobel. Sobel (as cited in "Collaborative Care Requires New Approaches," 1997) noted that 80% of all illnesses are managed by patients themselves, and that a 10% decline in self-care would result in a 50% increase in demand for health care. By the same token, increasing self-care by 5% would result in a 25% reduction in health care demand.

Finally, Burns (1997) revealed a few other qualities that Strosahl identified as being defining of integral care: "[Strosahl's] definition of an integrated program requires that a health plan establish a system that is indiscernible to patients, that involves both types of providers working together in offices in close proximity and that reaches 40% of the primary care patients" (p. 2). Indeed, in the system that Strosahl describes, the behavioral health care specialists are considered primary care providers, and patients seeking behavioral health care are not distinguished from those seeking primary care. As is evident in later discussion, the degree to which these and related characteristics are key to integrated programs varies, depending on how broadly one wishes to consider care as "integrated."

Models of Integrated Service Delivery

The actual characteristics of any integrated program of primary behavioral health care service delivery will vary according to the degree to which the health care organization provides support—financial, infrastructure, and so on—for establishing and maintaining the program. Several authors have provided their conceptualizations of how cooperative delivery of medical/physical and behavioral health care services may be delivered. One major distinction that is important for understanding the integration paradigm is the contrast of *structural* versus *functional* integration drawn by Dixon (1997). A good example of structural integration would be the purchase of a carve-out company by an HMO for the purpose of managing its behavioral health benefit. Functional integration, on the other hand, would involve organization-wide changes in clinical practices and processes, yielding a better quality of service.

Following are three current views of the ways in which relationships between primary and behavioral health care services can be modeled. Others views probably exist, but they are likely to reflect only minor variations to those presented here. Although none of the following models have been identified as specifically exemplifying structural or functional integration, it would appear that most of the levels of integration within each are functional in nature.

The Biopsychosocial Care Continuum. Taking an "ecological" point of view, Peek (1997; see also Peek & Heinrich, 1995) conceived of health care as taking place in a three-dimensional space comprised of three continua. The *level and locus of the care continuum* reflects the intensity of care and the extent to which it removes the person from ordinary life, whereas prevention and illness care represent the two ends of the *wellness–illness (or disability prevention) continuum*. The third dimension, the *biopsychosocial care continuum*, recognizes that clinical problems range from being purely biomedical to purely psychosocial, with gradations or blends of the two components falling in between. Consequently, the continuum conveys the need for the patient to have access to a mix of psychosocial and biomedical components of care.

Constructed along the biopsychosocial care continuum is a "four-sector model" of service delivery (Peek, 1997). Here, the sector most appropriate for the patient largely depends on the patient's view of the presenting problem at a given point in time. *Free-standing medical care* is traditional medical care that is provided independent of behavioral health care. *Collaborative care: integration* is a type of service delivery that recognizes that the degree of the interplay of psychosocial and medical factors (such as is found in chronic illness or somaticizers with or without actual organic disease) requires management from a medical perspective using interdisciplinary medical care teams. The psychologist (or other behavioral health professional) is part of the medical care team, working under the patient's medical benefits. *Collaborative care: consultation* is used to provide separate but coordinated medical and behavioral health care to the same given problem. An example would be the service that is provided to facilitate both the medical and behavioral health care for an asthma patient who also is depressed. Lastly, *free-standing behavioral health care* represents the traditional behavioral health care that is provided independent of medical care.

In this model of service delivery, it is important to recognize that the sectors represent demarcations in practices, but *not* necessarily in people (Peek, 1997). It would not be unusual, and perhaps might even be expected, that a given professional would provide services across more than one sector. This would require behavioral health care professionals to develop a proficiency in collaborating with medical professionals — either in the role of a consultant or as a member of an integrated service delivery team — in order to function effectively within the provider organization.

Levels of Primary Mental Health Care. Strosahl (1996) discussed a somewhat different conceptualization of primary behavioral health care. The model described by Peek (1997) is more structurally based along a continuum of involvement of medical and behavioral health care factors, whereas Strosahl's model is based more on the degree of patient need.

Strosahl's (1996) primary behavioral health care delivery model includes three levels. At the *behavioral health consultation* level, physicians refer patients whom they think may have complicating psychosocial issues to the behavioral health care specialist. For the behavioral health specialist, "the aim of the consultation is to increase the impact of the physician's medication and psychosocial interventions" (p. 94). The patient may be seen alone or with the physician for a brief period, with the possibility of one or two follow-up visits. Face-to-face feedback is provided to the referring physician.

The *consultative case management* level is one best suited for patients with long-term physical and/or psychosocial problems requiring extended management in the primary care setting (Strosahl, 1996). The focus of the consultation includes case management, appropriate levels medical utilization, and assistance in meeting the patients' community needs and in their adaptation to their physical and/or psychosocial problems. Consultation takes place over long periods of time, although on a less frequent basis.

Strosahl's (1996) third level of service is *integrated specialty consultation*, which is intended for patients with high-cost and/or recurring problems commonly seen in primary care settings (e.g., panic attacks, major depression). This type of consultation employs a multifaceted approach, including planned visits with both the primary care provider and the consultant, thus enabling each provider to build upon the intervention of the other; patient education; the development of self-management skills; and feedback to the primary care provider regarding treatment strategies to be used during medical visits.

Regardless of the level of care, Strosahl (1996) saw primary behavioral health care as being provided through a consultative model in the primary care setting in a population-based care framework, with the primary care provider as the principal customer who remains in charge of the patient's care. Services are brief, limited in scope and duration, with feedback provided to the primary care provider on a same-day basis. Moreover, he noted that true integration involves more than just moving into the primary care setting and collaborating with the medical treatment team. The philosophies, strategies, and goals of the behavioral health care provider must be both feasible and consistent with those of the primary care provider if true integrated behavioral health care is to come about. As he indicated, "Integrated care will not be a tune-up, but a major overhaul in our philosophies and models of mental health services" (p. 95).

Levels of Systematic Collaboration Between Mental Health and Other Health Professionals. Doherty, McDaniel, and Baird (1996) provided yet another model for various degrees of collaboration and integration of primary and behavioral health care services. This model is generally consistent with that provided by Peek (1997). However, Table 1.3 reveals the hierarchical nature of this system, this hierarchy depending on both the physical proximity of behavioral health care and other health care providers, and the degree to which collaboration, communication, and a shared sense of vision and treatment paradigms exist. The higher the level of a given service delivery organization or program, the more integrated are the cultures and services of its medical and behavioral health care providers and, consequently, the better equipped it is to handle more demanding cases. A detailed description of each of these levels, where they generally can be found, and the types of cases that they are best and least suited to handle also are presented in Table 1.3.

Barriers to Integration

Implementation of any of the options described in the preceding models of primary and behavioral health care integration will likely require overcoming one or more obstacles. The types of obstacles that may present themselves are numerous; however, the literature suggests a few of them are fairly common. Although the more prominent of these have been discussed earlier in other contexts, it is helpful to briefly summarize them again here.

Cultural Differences. The dualistic and reductionistic attitudes that are prevalent in medicine today (Alter, Cole, & Raju, 1997; Cole & Raju, 1996; Friedman et al., 1995; Lipsitt, 1997) do not foster an atmosphere of understanding nor the administration of the most appropriate and effective treatment for patients presenting with behavioral health problems.

Patient Resistance. The stigma associated with behavioral health disorders appears to be on the wane. The availability of educational materials, new forms of treatment, and other efforts to dispel the myths of mental illness have been somewhat successful. However, the fact is that the stigma remains (Cole & Raju, 1996; Mitchell & Haber, 1997) and can present a formidable source of resistance to behavioral health intervention, even in the primary care setting where integrated services exist.

Reimbursement Issues. A major obstacle to the provision of appropriate, effective treatment for behavioral health problems has been reimbursement. This certainly is a problem when the patient presents himself or herself to a primary care pro-

TABLE 1.3

Levels of Systematic Collaboration Between Therapists and Other Health Professionals

Level	Description	Where Practiced	Handles Adequately	Handles Inadequately
I. Minimal collaboration	Mental health and other health care professionals work in separate facilities, have separate systems, and rarely communicate about cases.	Most private practices and agencies.	Cases with routine medical or psychological problems that have little biopsychosocial interplay and few management difficulties.	Cases that are refractory to treatment or have significant biopsychosocial interplay.
II. Basic collaboration from a distance	Providers have separate systems at separate sites, but engage in periodic communication about shared patients, mostly by telephone and letter. Communication is driven by specific patient issues. Mental health professionals view each other as resources, but operate on their own, with little sharing of responsibility and little understanding of each other's cultures. There is little sharing of power and responsibility.	Settings with active referral linkages across facilities.	Cases with moderate biopsychosocial interplay, for example, a patient has diabetes and depression, and management of both problems proceeds reasonably well.	Cases that have significant biopsychosocial interplay, especially when the medical or mental health management is not satisfactory to one of the parties.
III. Basic collaboration on site	Mental health and other health care professionals have separate systems but share the same facility. They engage in regular communication about shared patients, mostly by phone or letter, but occasionally meet face to face because of close proximity. They appreciate the importance of each other's roles, may have a sense of being part of a larger although somewhat ill-defined team, but do not share a common language or an in-depth understanding of each other's worlds. As in Levels I and II, medical physicians have considerably more power and influence over case management decisions than the other professionals, who may resent this.	HMO settings and rehabilitation centers where collaboration is facilitated by proximity, but there is no systemic approach to collaboration and misunderstandings are common. Also, medical clinics that employ therapists but engage primarily in referral-oriented collaboration rather that systemic mutual consultation and team building.	Cases with moderate biopsychosocial interplay that require occasional face-to-face interactions between providers to manage and coordinate complex treatment plans.	Cases with significant biopsychosocial interplay, especially those with ongoing and challenging management problems.

IV. Close collaboration in a partly integrated system	Mental health and other health care professionals share the same sites and have some systems in common, such as scheduling and charting. There are regular face-to-face interactions about patients, mutual consultation, coordinated treatment plans for difficult cases, and a basic understanding and appreciation for each other's role and culture. There is a shared allegiance to a biopsychosocial/systems paradigm. However, the routines are still sometimes difficult, team-building meetings are held only occasionally, and there may be operational discrepancies such as copays for mental health but not for medical services. There are likely to be unresolved but manageable tensions over medical physicians' greater power and influence on the collaborative team.	Some HMOs, rehabilitation centers, and hospice centers that systematically build teams. Also some family practice training programs.	Cases with significant biopsychosocial interplay and management complications.	Complex cases with multiple providers and multiple large systems involvement, especially when there is the potential for tension and conflicting agendas among providers or triangling on the part of the patient or family.
V. Close collaboration in a fully integrated system	Mental health and other health care professionals share the same sites, the same vision, and the same systems in a seamless web of biopsychosocial services. Providers and patients have the same expectations of a team offering prevention and treatment. All professionals are committed to a biopsychosocial systems paradigm and have developed an in-depth understanding of each other's roles and cultures. Regular collaborative team meetings are held to discuss patient issues and team issues. There are conscious efforts to balance power and influence among the professionals according to their roles and areas of expertise.	Some hospice centers and other special training and clinical settings.	The most difficult and complex biopsychosocial cases with challenging management problems.	Cases when the resources of the health care team are insufficient or when breakdowns occur in the collaboration with larger service systems.

Note. From Doherty, McDaniel, and Baird (1996). Reprinted with permission.

vider for treatment (e.g., see Cole & Raju, 1996; "Efforts to Integrate with Primary Care," 1997; Sperry & Brill, 1997), and the consequences of this are varied. For example, reimbursement issues related to the treatment of behavioral health problems in primary care settings may lead to inappropriate inpatient psychiatric treatment that *is* covered by the patient's benefit plan.

But the issue is a two-edged sword. Reimbursement also is a concern from the standpoint of the behavioral health care services provided outside of the primary care setting. For example, Mitchell and Haber (1997) noted that because of lower copayments, patients most in need of behavioral health care services may turn to their primary care provider instead of to a behavioral health care professional who is better trained to treat the problem. Moreover, Alter et al. (1997) suggested that patients referred by primary care providers may not be covered for the type of services that the behavioral health care professional offers; thus, there is little motivation to treat them.

Cost-Offset Ambiguities.   Proponents of the provision of behavioral health care services frequently point to medical cost-offset data as justification for including behavioral health care services in health care benefits packages. Selden (as cited in "Efforts to Integrate with Primary Care," 1997) suggested that employers purchasing coverage for their workforce require more definitive evidence of the cost advantage of behavioral health treatment. Recall the Sperry et al. (1996) contention that there is no clear-cut indication of medical cost savings that will accrue from mental health treatment. They pointed to flaws in the research methodology, whereas Melek (1996) noted difficulties in identifying and measuring cost offset. The length of time that may be required to demonstrate the medical cost offset derived from the provision of behavioral health treatment may well impede its demonstration. Finally, Friedman et al. (1995) pointed out a very practical barrier to providing evidence for cost offset:

> it is . . . frequently the case that insurance coverage for medical problems is handled by one company, whereas coverage for mental health problems is handled by another. Trying to convince the latter to spend money so that the former would save money is problematic at best. Developing mechanisms for addressing these problems is critical if health policy and the delivering of health services is brought into better alignment with the underlying psychosocial and behavioral issues that determine overall medical utilization and cost. (p. 516)

A discussion of potential solutions to overcoming these barriers to integration is beyond the scope of this chapter. The interested reader is referred to the cited works for insights into the authors' solutions for overcoming these and other obstacles that may impede the establishment of integrated service delivery systems.

THE ROLE OF PSYCHOLOGICAL ASSESSMENT IN PRIMARY CARE SETTINGS

During the past few years, psychological assessment has come to be recognized for more than just its usefulness at the beginning of treatment. Its utility has been extended beyond being a mere tool for describing an individual's current state, to a means of facilitating the treatment and understanding behavioral health care problems throughout and beyond the episode of care. Generally speaking, several available commercial and public-domain psychological tests can be employed as tools (a) to assist in *clinical decision-making* activities, including screening, treatment planning, and treatment monitoring; (b) for *outcomes assessment* for the purpose measuring and monitoring the effects of treatment, and outcomes management; and (c) more directly, used as *treatment techniques* in and of themselves. These instruments are useful only in mental health and substance abuse treatment settings, but also in other settings in which the need to identify and provide services for behavioral health problems exists. One such setting is the primary care setting.

Following is an overview of considerations related to psychological test instruments and the potential roles that psychological assessment can play in primary care settings. Note that how and for what purpose psychological testing is applied in primary care settings is not necessarily dependent on the type or degree of behavioral health care integration that exists therein. Nor is its use necessarily dependent on who among the provider team administers the test or applies the results. *With proper training or under the supervision of a psychologist or other qualified professional formally trained and experienced in the use of these instruments,* primary care providers can appropriately administer most psychological test instruments and employ the results in their offices and facilities.

General Considerations

The introduction of psychological testing in primary care settings, either alone or as part of a package of behavioral health care services, can greatly enhance the diagnostic and treatment options offered by primary care providers. However, there are a few very important considerations to be mindful of if testing is to be fully accepted as a part of the services offered by primary care providers or provider organizations.

One consideration is related to the reimbursement issue that was previously discussed. Testing must be able to pay for itself. Ficken (1995) commented on how the advent of managed care has limited the reimbursement for (and therefore the use of) psychological assessment. In general, he saw the primary reason for this as being a financial one. In an era of capitated health care coverage, the amount of money available for behavioral health care treatment is limited. MCOs therefore require a demonstration that the amount of money spent for testing will result in a greater amount of treatment cost savings. This author is unaware of any published or unpublished research to date that can provide this demonstration. In addition, Ficken noted that much of the information currently provided by psychological assessments is not relevant to the treatment of patients within a managed care environment. Understandably, MCOs are reluctant to pay for gathering such information.

Another consideration relates to general concerns that primary care providers have expressed regarding the use of self-administered psychological tests. One concern is their belief that patients do not want providers to ask questions related to psychosocial problems. Sperry et al. (1996), however, believed that the literature does not bear this out and suggested that part of the problem may be the provider's own discomfort in asking about these matters. Sperry and Brill (1997) indicated that the use of screening tools can actually reduce the provider's discomfort in obtaining information of this nature, particularly if these tools are viewed as "lab tests." Moreover, Sperry and Brill noted that patients are more comfortable revealing problems on self-administered tests than to providers. Patients are even more apt to disclose pertinent information if the screening tools are presented to them as lab tests. For those still concerned with this matter, Haber and Mitchell (1997) suggested that a behavioral health questionnaire be combined with a physical examination and presented as an annual "personal health evaluation" to help reduce any stigma that the patient may feel about responding to questions pertaining to their mental health and substance use.

Lastly, a significant consideration related to the use of psychological tests (or other means) for screening or monitoring patients has to do with how the results are used. Recognition of the presence of a disorder "appears to be a necessary but not sufficient step to improve the outcome of psychiatric and psychological disorders in primary care settings" ("Detection of Psychological Disorders," 1996, p. 8). Particularly with screening, the practitioner must be able to provide appropriate intervention for whatever disease or disorder is being assessed by the instrument.

Instrumentation for Behavioral Health Care Assessment

The psychological test instrumentation required for any assessment — whether in primary medical care, behavioral health care, or other settings — will depend on (a) the general purpose(s) for which the assessment is being conducted and (b) the level of information that is required for those purpose(s). Generally, most psychological test instrumentation that would serve the purpose of psychological/behavioral health care assessment in a primary care setting falls into one of four general categories.

Psychological/Psychiatric Symptom Measures. Probably the most frequently used instrumentation for screening and treatment planning, monitoring, and outcomes assessment is measures of psychopathological symptomatology. These measures also are the type of instruments on which the majority of the behavioral health care clinician's psychological assessment training has likely been focused. These instruments were developed to assess behavioral health problems that typically prompt people to seek treatment.

There are several subtypes of these measures of psychological/psychiatric symptomatology. The first is the *comprehensive multidimensional measure*. This is typically a lengthy, multiscale, standardized instrument that measures and provides a graphical profile of the patient on several psychopathological symptom domains (e.g., anxiety, depression) or disorders (schizophrenia, antisocial personality). Also, summary indices sometimes are available to provide a more global picture of the individual with regard to his or her psychological status or level of distress. Probably the most widely used and/or recognized of these multidimensional measures is the restandardized version of the Minnesota Multiphasic Personality Inventory, the MMPI-2 (Butcher, Dahlstrom, Graham, Tellegen, & Kaemmer, 1989).

Multidimensional instruments can serve a variety of purposes that facilitate therapeutic interventions in primary and behavioral health care settings. They may be used on initial patient contact to screen for the need for service and, at the same time, yield information that is useful for treatment planning. These instruments might also be useful in identifying specific problems that may be unrelated to the patient's chief complaints (e.g., low self-esteem). In addition, they generally can be administered numerous times during the course of treatment to monitor the patient's progress toward achieving established goals and to assist in determining what adjustments (if any) must be made to the clinician's approach. Moreover, use of such instruments pre- and posttreatment can provide individual treatment outcomes data and, at the same time, can be analyzed with the results of other patients to evaluate the effectiveness of an individual provider, a particular therapeutic approach, or an organization.

Abbreviated multidimensional measures are quite similar to the MMPI–2 and other comprehensive multidimensional measures in many respects. First, by definition, they contain multiple scales for measuring a variety of symptom domains and disorders. They also may allow for the derivation of an index that can indicate the patient's general level of psychopathology or distress. In addition, they may be used for screening, treatment planning and monitoring, and outcomes assessment purposes, just like the more comprehensive instruments. The distinguishing feature of the abbreviated instrument is, of course, its length: By definition, these instruments are relatively short and easy to administer and score. Their brevity does not allow for an in-depth assessment of the patient and his or her problems, but this is not what these instruments were designed to do. Probably the most widely used of these brief instruments are Derogatis's family of symptom checklists. These include the revision of the original Symptom Checklist–90, the SCL–90–R (Derogatis, 1983), and the 45-item version of the SCL–90–R, the Brief Screening Inventory (BSI; Derogatis, 1992). These instruments contain checklists of 90 and 45 psychological symptoms, respectively, which score on each of the instruments' nine symptom domain scales. Each instrument also has three summary indices. Another such instrument is the SA–45 (Strategic Advantage, Inc., 1996), a 45-item symptom checklist derived from the original, public-domain SCL–90. Its items score on the same nine symptom domains as the SCL–90–R and the BSI, as well as on two summary indices.

The major strength of the abbreviated multiscale instruments is their ability to quickly and broadly survey psychological symptom domains and disorders. Their value is most clearly evident in settings where both the time and dollars available for assessment services are limited. These instruments provide a lot of information quickly and are much more likely to be completed by patients than their lengthier counterparts. This last point is particularly important if one is interested in monitoring treatment or assessing outcomes, both of which require at least two or more assessments to obtain the necessary information.

Finally, there are the *disorder-specific measures,* which are designed to measure one specific disorder or family of disorders (e.g., anxiety, depression, substance abuse, suicidality). These instruments are usually brief, requiring less than five minutes to complete.

Measures of Neuropsychological Functioning.   Neuropsychological tests are designed to provide information related to the presence and/or degree of cognitive impairment resulting from brain disease, disorder, or trauma. The results of these tests also are used to draw inferences about the extent to which this impairment interferes with the patient's daily functioning. There are many psychometrically sound tests of neuropsychological functioning. Some instruments assess only specific areas of functioning (e.g., immediate verbal memory); others assess broader areas of functioning (e.g., a battery of memorial measures, such as the Wechsler Memory Scale–III, assessing immediate, intermediate, and remote verbal and nonverbal memory); and others are part of a battery of measures that provide a more "comprehensive" assessment of neuropsychological functioning (e.g., batteries that include tests of memory, language, academic skills, abstract thinking, nonverbal auditory perception, sensorimotor skills, etc.).

Werthman (1995) suggested that neuropsychological testing can make a significant contribution in the primary care setting by assisting primary care providers in accurately assessing or ruling out neuropsychological impairments (e.g., dementias), particularly if there is a comorbid Axis I *DSM–IV* disorder. In discussing the current attitude of MCOs toward the use of psychological testing in general, Werthman indicated that the current emphasis in neuropsychological testing is on "the use of highly targeted and focused psychological and neuropsychological testing to sharply define the 'problems' to be treated, the degree of impairment, the level of care to be provided and the treatment plan to be implemented" (p. 15). Accordingly, Werthman specifically pointed to the utility of specific tests or parts of tests, rather than entire test batteries, as being the most appropriate for meeting the needs of MCOs. Werthman also suggested that the role of the psychologist should only be to "determine . . . which of the neuropsychological tests is appropriate . . . to assist the primary provider in managing the case" (p. 15). However, it is this author's opinion that the use of neuropsychological instruments — whether they be ability-specific tests or complete batteries of tests — in primary care and other settings requires training and experience that necessitates psychologist involvement that goes well beyond offering advice.

Measures of General Health Status and Role Functioning.   During the past decade, there has been an increasing interest in the assessment of health status in medical and behavioral health care delivery systems. Initially, this interest was shown primarily within those organizations and settings focused on the treatment of physical diseases and disorders. In recent years, behavioral health care providers have recognized the value of assessing the patient's general level of health.

It is important to recognize that the term *health* means more than just the absence of disease or debility; it also implies a state of well-being throughout the individual's physical, psychological, and social spheres of existence (World Health Organization [WHO] Interim Commission, 1997). Dickey and Wagenaar (1996) noted that this concept of health recognizes the importance of eliciting the patient's point of view in assessing health status. They also pointed to similar conclusions reached by Jahoda specific to the area of mental health. Here, *self-assessment relative to how an individual believes he or she should feel* is an important component of "mental health."

Measures of health status and physical functioning can be classified into one of two groups: *generic* and *condition-specific*. Probably the most widely used and respected generic health status measures is the 36-item Medical Outcomes Study Short Form Health Scale (SF–36; Ware & Sherbourne, 1992; Ware, Snow, Kosinski, & Gandek, 1993). The SF–36 assesses eight dimensions of health — four addressing mental health-related constructs and four addressing physical health-related constructs — that reflect the WHO concept of "health." A 12-item, abbreviated version of the SF–36 also has been developed. The SF–12 (Ware, Kosinski, & Keller, 1995) was developed for use in large-scale, population-based research where broadly monitoring health status is all that is required. The SF–12 is relatively new but to date, the data that have been gathered in support of its use are promising.

Condition-specific health status and functioning measures have been utilized for a number of years. Most have been developed for use with medical rather than behavioral health disorders, diseases, or conditions. However, condition-specific measures of behavioral health status and functioning now are beginning to appear.

Quality of Life Measures. In their brief summary of this area, Andrews, Peters, and Teesson (1994) indicated that most of the definitions of "quality of life" (QOL) describe a multidimensional construct encompassing physical, affective, cognitive, social, and economic domains. *Objective measures* of QOL focus on the environmental resources required to meet one's needs and can be completed by someone other than the patient. *Subjective measures* of QOL assess the patient's satisfaction with the various aspects of his or her life and thus must be completed by the patient. Andrews et al. indicated distinctions between *QOL* and *health-related quality of life*, or HRQL, and between *generic* and *condition-specific* measures of QOL. QOL measures differ from HRQL measures in that the former assess the whole "fabric of life," whereas the latter assesses quality of life as it is affected by a disease/disorder or by its treatment. Generic measures are designed to assess aspects of life that are generally relevant to most people; condition-specific measures are focused on aspects of the lives of particular disease/disorder populations.

Service Satisfaction Measures. Given the expanding interest in assessing the treatment outcomes for the patient, it is not surprising to see an accompanying interest in assessing the patient's (and in some instances, the patient's family's) satisfaction with the services received. Satisfaction should be considered a measure of the overall treatment process, encompassing the patient's (and at times, others') view of how the service was delivered, the capabilities and attentiveness of the service provider, the perceived benefits of the service (if any), and any of a number of other selected aspects of the service the patient received. Patient satisfaction surveys *don't* answer the question, "What was the result of the treatment rendered to the patient?"; they *do* answer the question, "How did the patient feel about the treatment he or she received?" Thus, they serve an important program evaluation/improvement function.

Computerized Psychological Assessment. Many clinicians and researchers have espoused the use of computer-assisted psychological assessment in behavioral and primary care settings (e.g., Kobak, Greist, Jefferson, & Katzelnick, 1996; Mitchell & Haber, 1997; Moreland, 1996). The use of computers for assessment purposes is an efficient and cost-effective means of eliciting information important for screening for the presence of behavioral health care disorders, planning and monitoring the effects of treatment, and assessing the outcomes of that treatment. Moreover, Kobak et al. (1996) viewed it as a solution to the barriers associated with clinician-administered rating scales and structured interviews, which typically require expertise and training in their use. Software for the administration and scoring of psychological test instruments generally provides an automated interpretation of the results, with the interpretive algorithms and accompanying text usually developed by an expert in the use of the instrument. These "expert systems" can be particularly valuable to primary care providers, because their professional education typically does not include extensive training in the interpretation of psychological test instruments.

In addition to those instruments that have applicability across settings, a few instruments have been developed specifically for use in primary care settings. The most notable is the PRIME–MD (Spitzer et al., 1994), for which Kobak et al. (1997) developed and demonstrated the validity of an interactive voice response technology application. In discussing computer-administered tests in general, Kobak et al. (1996) indicate the need for users to ensure that any computer-automated instrument is equivalent to the instrument in its original format. Drawing from Butcher's work, Kobak et al. (1996) also cited other caveats to the use of computer-assisted testing:

> Avoid a passive stance when using computerized assessments; clinical judgment is needed to use test results to understand patients. Overevaluation of computerized assessments could result in clinicians relying on test interpretations without knowing the basis of the interpretations. Empirical evidence on the validity and reliability of any test should be evaluated before its use. Assessment software that generates reports that are too general have inadequate clinical utility. As with clinician-administered tests, validity data generated by the test developer may not apply to the specific patient taking the test. (p. 28)

Psychological Assessment as a Tool for Screening

Among the most significant ways in which behavioral health care services can contribute to an effective primary care delivery system is through the ability to quickly identify individuals in need of behavioral health or substance abuse treatment. In the field of psychology, the most efficient and thoroughly investigated screening procedures involve the use of self-report psychological test instruments. The power or utility of a psychological screening test lies in its ability to determine, with a high level of confidence, whether or not the respondent has a particular disorder or condition and the degree of its severity, and/or whether or not he or she is a member of a population with clearly defined characteristics. The most commonly used psychological screeners in daily clinical practice are those designed to identify the presence of some specific type of psychological disturbance or some specific aspect of psychological dysfunction, or to provide a broad overview of the respondent's point-in-time mental status or level of distress.

Implementation of Screeners Into the Daily Flow of Service Delivery. The utility of a screening instrument is only as good as the degree to which it can be integrated into a primary care setting's daily regimen of service delivery. This, in turn, depends on a number of factors. The first is the ease and speed of administering and scoring of the screener, and the amount of time required to train the provider's staff to successfully incorporate the screener into their daily work flow. The second factor relates to the instrument's use. Generally, screeners are developed to assist in determining the likelihood that the patient does or does not have the specific condition or characteristic the instrument is designed to identify. Use for any other purpose (e.g., assigning a diagnosis based solely on screener results, determining the likelihood of the presence of other characteristics) only serves to undermine the integrity of the instrument in the eyes of staff, payers, and other parties with a vested interest in the screening process. The third factor has to do with the ability of the provider to act on the information obtained from the screener. It must be clear how the clinician should proceed based on the information available. The final factor is staff acceptance and commitment to the screening process. This comes only with a clear understanding of the importance of the screening, the usefulness of the obtained information, and how the screening process is to be incorporated into the organization's daily business flow.

Ficken (1995) provided an example of how screeners can be integrated into an assessment system designed to assist primary care physicians in identifying patients with psychiatric disorders. This system (which also allows for the incorporation of practice guidelines) seems to take into account the first three utility-related factors already mentioned. It begins with the administration of a screener that is highly sensitive and specific to *DSM-* or *ICD*-related disorders. These screeners should require no more than 10 minutes to complete and should identify frequently seen treatable conditions that are associated with significant disability. Also, "[screeners'] administration must be integrated seamlessly into the standard clinical routine" (Ficken, 1995, p. 13). Somewhat similar to the sequence described by Derogatis and DellaPietra (1994), positive findings would lead to a second level of testing. Here, another screener that meets the same requirements as those for the first screener and that affirms or rules out a diagnosis would be administered. Positive findings would lead to additional assessment for treatment planning purposes. Consistent with standard practice, Ficken recommended confirmation of screener findings by a qualified psychologist or physician.

Other Considerations for Screening.   Ficken (1995) suggested a screening scenario that includes the use of disorder-specific instruments. This certainly seems to be an acceptable approach in settings where screening instruments are administered only to those who are suspected of having a specific disorder, or if effort is being made to identify only those with one or only a few types of disorders. However, in both these and other situations, there are others that recommend a different approach. As Sperry et al. (1996) pointed out,

> A serious limitation of all of these [disorder-specific] scales is their focus on only one type of pathology. Studies have demonstrated high comorbidity among psychiatric disorders, and this also suggests that a focus on any single disorder is inappropriately narrow. Screening programs for psychiatric disorders in primary care settings should be broad-based, and not limited to any single disorder. (p. 206)

Similarly, in addressing the issue of screening for depression in primary care settings, Zimmerman et al. (1994) noted that

> Coexistence of depression with other forms of pathology seems to be the rule, not the exception. We would predict the same to be true of other disorders as well. . . . Consequently, even if the clinical evaluation that follows the screening questionnaire is limited to those disorders that are positive on the questionnaire, it will nevertheless often need to cover multiple psychiatric disorders. Proper case finding in primary care . . . requires attention to a range of illnesses. (p. 394)

Another important consideration related to the use of psychological screeners is their level of sensitivity, or the degree to which those taking the test are identified as having the behavioral problem(s) the instrument was designed to detect. The more sensitive the instrument is, the greater the number of test takers that will be mistakenly identified as having the assessed problem. These *false positives* will lead to unnecessary work and costs for the provider (Locke & Larsson, 1997). At the same time, instruments with lower sensitivity (and thus, higher specificity) will yield more *false negatives* that may result in the type of increased work and medical costs that some of the literature has associated with undetected behavioral health problems. Thus, unless one incorporates something like the two-staged screening described earlier, one must decide which type of identification error is more acceptable, and then carefully evaluate potential screening instruments for the psychometric characteristics.

Psychological Assessment as a Tool for Treatment Planning

Problem identification through the use of screening instruments is only one way in which psychological assessment can facilitate the treatment of behavioral health problems in primary care settings. When employed by a trained clinician, psychological assessment also can provide information that can greatly facilitate and enhance the planning of a specific therapeutic intervention for the individual patient. It is through the implementation of a tailored treatment plan that the patient's chances of problem resolution are maximized.

The role that psychological assessment can play in planning a course of treatment for behavioral health care problems is significant. Butcher (1990) indicated that information available from instruments such as the MMPI-2 not only can assist in identifying problems and in establishing communication with the patient, but it also can help ensure that the plan for treatment is consistent with the patient's personality and external resources. In addition, when using certain multidimensional tests, the assessment may reveal potential obstacles to therapy, areas of potential growth, and problems that the patient may not be consciously aware of. Moreover, both Butcher and Appelbaum (1990) viewed testing as a means of quickly obtaining a second opinion. Other benefits of psychological assessment identified by Appelbaum include assistance in identifying patient strengths, weaknesses, and the complexity of the patient's personality, and in establishing of a reference point during the therapeutic episode.

There are several ways in which psychological assessment can assist in the planning of behavioral health care treatment for patients seen in primary care settings. The more common and evident contributions can be organized into three general categories: problem identification and clarification, identification of important patient characteristics, and monitoring of treatment progress.

Problem Identification and Clarification. Perhaps the most common use of psychological assessment in the service of treatment planning is for problem identification. The value of psychological testing becomes apparent in those cases where the patient is hesitant or unable to identify the nature of his or her problems—a common occurrence in primary care settings. With a motivated and engaged patient who responds honestly to items on a well-validated and reliable test, the process of identifying what led the patient to seek treatment from a primary care provider may be greatly facilitated. Cooperation shown during testing may be attributable to the nonthreatening nature of questions presented on paper or a computer monitor (as opposed to those posed by another human being); the subtle, indirect qualities of the questions themselves (compared to those asked by the clinician); or a combination of these reasons. In addition, the nature of some of the more commonly used psychological test instruments allows for the identification of secondary, but significant, problems that might otherwise be overlooked, even with the most forthcoming of patients.

Note that the type of problem identification and clarification described here is different from that conducted during screening (discussed earlier). Screening is more focused on determining the presence or absence of one or more problems, whereas problem identification and clarification generally takes a more in-depth approach to specifying the problem(s) the patient is experiencing. At the same time, there also is an attempt to determine, to a greater degree of certainty, problem severity and complexity as well as the extent to which the problem area(s) affect the patient's ability to function. Information gained from testing can enhance both the patient's and clinician's understanding of the problem and lead to the development of the most appropriate treatment plan.

Identification of Important Patient Characteristics. The identification and clarification of the patient's problems are of key importance in planning a course of treatment. However, there are numerous other types of patient information not specific to the identified problem(s) that may be useful in planning treatment and easily identified through the use of psychological tests (particularly tests that are multidimensional in nature). Treatment plans may be developed or modified with consideration to at least some of these nonpathological characteristics. The exceptions are generally found with clinicians or programs that take a "one size fits all" approach to treatment.

Monitoring Progress Along the Path of Expected Improvement. Information from repeated testing during the treatment process can help the clinician determine if the treatment plan is appropriate for the patient at a given point in time. Thus, primary care providers can use psychological assessment to determine whether their patients are showing the expected improvement as treatment progresses. If not, adjustments can be made. These adjustments may reflect the need for: (a) more intensive or aggressive treatment (e.g., increased medication dosage, referral for inpatient treatment); (b) less intensive treatment (e.g., reduction or discontinuation of medication, transfer from inpatient to outpatient care); or (c) a different therapeutic approach (e.g., changing from humanistic therapy to cognitive-behavioral therapy). Regardless, any modifications require later reassessment of the patient to determine if the treatment revisions have impacted patient progress in the expected direction. This process may be repeated any number of times during treatment, ultimately providing information important for determining when to appropriately terminate treatment.

Psychological Assessment as a Tool for Outcomes Management

The 1990s have witnessed accelerating growth in the level of interest and development of medical and behavioral healthcare outcomes programs. In short, fueled by soaring health care costs, there has been an increasing need for providers to demonstrate that what they do is effective.

In considering the types of behavioral health care outcomes that might be assessed in primary care settings, it is likely that a substantial number of providers would identify symptomatic change in psychological status as being the most important. However important change in symptom status may have been in the past, medical and behavioral health care providers have come to realize that change in many other aspects of functioning, such as those identified by Stewart and Ware (1992), are equally important indicators of treatment effectiveness. As Sederer, Dickey, and Hermann (1996) noted,

> Outcome for patients, families, employers, and payers is not simply confined to symptomatic change. Equally important to those affected by the care rendered is the patient's capacity to function within a family, community, or work environment or to exist independently, without undue burden to the family and social welfare system. Also impor-

tant is the patient's ability to show improvement in any concurrent medical and psychiatric disorder. . . . Finally, not only do patients seek symptomatic improvement, but they want to experience a subjective sense of health and well-being. (p. 2)

Although these comments were made with regard to treatment provided in behavioral health care settings, they are equally applicable to treatment provided in primary care settings.

Outcomes Assessment: Measurement, Monitoring, and Management. It is important to clarify the three general purposes or outcomes assessment. The first is outcomes *measurement*. This involves pre- and posttreatment assessment of one or more selected variables to determine the amount of change (if any) that has occurred in these variables as a result of therapeutic intervention.

A more useful approach is that of outcomes *monitoring*. This refers to "the use of periodic assessment of treatment outcomes to permit inferences about what has produced change" (Dorwart, 1996, p. 46). Like treatment progress monitoring used for treatment planning (discussed earlier), outcomes monitoring involves the tracking of changes in the status of one or more outcomes variables at multiple points in time. Assuming a baseline assessment at the beginning of treatment, reassessment may occur one or more times during the course of treatment (e.g., weekly, monthly), at the time of termination, and/or during one or more periods of posttermination follow-up. Treatment progress monitoring is used to determine deviation from the expected course of improvement, whereas outcomes monitoring focuses on revealing aspects about the therapeutic process that seem to affect change and, potentially, the enduring qualities of that change.

The third and perhaps most useful purpose of outcomes assessment is that of outcomes *management*. Dorwart (1996) defined outcomes management as "the use of monitoring information in the management of patients to improve both the clinical and administrative processes for delivering care" (pp. 46–47). Although Dorwart appeared to view outcomes management as relevant to the *individual* patient, this author views it as a means to improve the quality of services offered to the *patient population(s)* served by the provider. For example, information gained through repeated assessment of depressed patients in primary care settings can provide the organization with indications of what works best, with whom, and under what set of circumstances, thus helping to improve the quality of services for all primary care patients suffering from depression. In addition, outcomes management can serve as a tool for those organizations interested in implementing a continuous quality improvement (CQI) initiative.

CONCLUSION

The U.S. health care industry has undergone dramatic changes during the past two decades. What once was a loosely monitored system of care with skyrocketing costs has been changed to one with tight controls providing only limited services and choice of providers. These and other efforts to keep costs down (e.g., carve-out behavioral health benefits, lack of parity between medical and behavioral health benefits) have been particularly detrimental to those seeking help for mental health and substance abuse problems. For these and other reasons (e.g., stigma associated with mental illness), a considerable number of individuals with behavioral health problems have turned to their primary care providers for help — help that is often not provided or does not adequately meet the patient's needs.

Fortunately, the winds of change are now blowing in the favor of behavioral health care proponents. The enactment of the Mental Health Parity Act of 1996, the industry's realization of the benefits of one-stop health care, NCQA accreditation standards, and the growing belief that potential long-term health care cost savings can result from the appropriate treatment of behavioral disorders — these and other circumstances bode well for greater access to more and/or better behavioral health care services. They also serve as the impetus for a more pervasive integration of primary and behavioral health care services throughout the United States.

The alliance of primary and behavioral health care providers is not a new phenomenon; it has existed in one form or another for decades. This is partially due to the fact that approximately 25% of the patients being seen in primary care settings suffer from behavioral health problems that require some form of intervention. Many such problems go undetected by and/or are treated inappropriately by primary care providers. Further, some data suggest that patients with undetected or inappropriately treated disorders utilize a disproportionate amount of services and drive costs up, and that early identification and treatment of these individuals can result in cost savings related to long-term medical care, lost income, and lowered productivity in the workplace. Yet, other data do not support the medical cost-offset conclusions. The reality of the situation most likely lies somewhere in between.

Regardless, the value the behavioral health care professional brings to the primary care setting — either as an off-site consultant or as an on-site collaborative member of the primary care team — is attested to daily in primary care settings throughout the country. Moreover, there is every indication that the picture of interdisciplinary cooperation in the primary care setting will become more commonplace as the move to integrate behavioral and primary care gains momentum. The extent to which these two services will become integrated will, of course, depend on any number of factors (e.g., funding, available office space, staff interest and motivation) that will vary from setting to setting.

Clinical psychologists and other trained behavioral health care professionals can uniquely contribute to efforts to fully integrate their services in primary care settings through the establishment and use of psychological assessment services. Information obtained from psychometrically sound self-report tests and other-report instruments (e.g., clinician rating scales, parent-completed instruments) can assist the primary care provider in several types of clinical decision-making activities, including screening for the presence of mental health or substance abuse problems, planning a course of treatment, and monitoring patient progress. Testing can also be used to assess the outcome of treatment that has been provided to patients with mental health or substance abuse problems, thus assisting in determining what works for whom.

The degree to which psychological testing and assessment services become part of the package of primary behavioral health care services will depend on the value they bring to the integrated service delivery system. The key to the success of this endeavor will be in the behavioral health care professional's ability to educate and demonstrate to primary care providers how assessment can be a cost-effective means of serving the needs of a significant portion of their patient population. It is hoped that this and the other chapters in this volume will assist in these efforts.

ACKNOWLEDGMENT

Portions of this chapter are adapted from M. E. Maruish, "Therapeutic Assessment: Linking Assessment and Treatment," in M. Hersen & A. Bellack (Series Eds.) and C. R. Reynolds (Vol. Ed.), *Comprehensive Clinical Psychology, Volume 4. Assessment* (1998), with permission from Elsevier Science Ltd., Kidlington, UK.

REFERENCES

Academy of Psychosomatic Medicine. (1996). Mental disorders in general medical practice: An opportunity to add value to healthcare. *Behavioral Healthcare Tomorrow, 5,* 55–72.

Academy of Psychosomatic Medicine. (1997). Mental disorders in general medical practice: Adding value to healthcare through consultation-liaison psychiatry. In J. D. Haber & G. E. Mitchell (Eds.), *Primary care meets mental health: Tools for the 21st century* (pp. 255–292). Tiburon, CA: CentraLink.

Alter, C. L., Cole, S., & Raju, M. (1997). Overcoming ecological barriers to integration. In J. D. Haber & G. E. Mitchell (Eds.), *Primary care meets mental health: Tools for the 21st century* (pp. 35–46). Tiburon, CA: CentraLink.

American Psychological Association. (1996). *The costs of failing to provide appropriate mental health care.* Washington, DC: Author.

Andrews, G., Peters, L., & Teesson, M. (1994). *The measurement of consumer outcomes in mental health.* Canberra, Australia: Australian Government Publishing Service.

Appelbaum, S. A. (1990). The relationship between assessment and psychotherapy. *Journal of Personality Assessment, 54,* 791–801.

Barsky, A. J., & Borus, J. F. (1995). Somatization and medicalization in the era of managed care. *Journal of the American Medical Association, 274,* 1931.

Borus, J. F. (1985). Psychiatry and the primary care physician. In H. I. Kaplan & B. J. Sadock (Eds.), *Comprehensive textbook of psychiatry/IV* (4th ed., pp. 1302–1308). Baltimore, MD: Williams & Wilkins.

Burns, J. (1997). Providing care for the mind, body and soul. *Managed Healthcare, ??,* 20–24.

Butcher, J. N. (1990). *The MMPI-2 in psychological treatment.* New York: Oxford University Press.

Butcher, J. N., Dahlstrom, W. G., Graham, J. R., Tellegen, A. M., & Kaemmer, B. (1989). *MMPI-2: Manual for administration and scoring.* Minneapolis, MN: University of Minnesota Press.

Ciarcia, J. J. (1997, September). *Major depressive disorder: The burdens and promise.* Paper presented at the annual retreat of the Council for Behavioral Group Practices, Washington, DC.

Cole, S., & Raju, M. (1996). Overcoming barriers to integration of primary care and behavioral healthcare: Focus on knowledge and skills. *Behavioral Healthcare Tomorrow, 5,* 30–37.

Cole, S., Raju, M., & Barrett, J. (1997). Depression in primary care: Assessment and management. In J. D. Haber & G. E. Mitchell (Eds.), *Primary care meets mental health: Tools for the 21st century* (pp. 139–153). Tiburon, CA: CentraLink.

Collaborative care requires new approaches, says internist. (1997, November 17). *Mental Health Weekly, 7,* 4.

Del Vecchio, P. (1996). Dialogue: How should primary care address the problem of psychiatric disorders? Demand-side analysis of mental health services in primary care. *Behavioral Healthcare Tomorrow, 5,* 48, 51, 54.

Depression still undertreated despite efforts to redress. (1997, June). *Behavior Health Outcomes, 2,* 1–11.

Derogatis, L. R. (1983). *SCL–90–R: Administration, scoring and procedures manual–II.* Baltimore, MD: Clinical Psychometric Research.

Derogatis, L. R. (1992). *BSI: Administration, scoring and procedures manual–II.* Baltimore, MD: Clinical Psychometric Research.

Derogatis, L. R., & DellaPietra, L. (1994). Psychological tests in screening for psychiatric disorder. In M. E. Maruish (Ed.), *The use of psychological testing for treatment planning and outcome assessment* (pp. 22–54). Hillsdale, NJ: Lawrence Erlbaum Associates.

Detection of psychological disorders unrelated to outcomes. (1996, September). *Behavioral Healthcare Outcomes, 1,* 7–9.

Dickey, B., & Wagenaar, H. (1996). Evaluating health status. In L. I. Sederer & B. Dickey (Eds.), *Outcomes assessment in clinical practice* (pp. 55–60). Baltimore, MD: Williams & Wilkins.

Directions: Anxiety costs big bucks. (1997, May). *Practice Strategies,* p. 10.

Dixon, K. (1997). The roles of the behavioral health professional in integrated systems. In J. D. Haber & G. E. Mitchell (Eds.), *Primary care meets mental health: Tools for the 21st century* (pp. 27–31). Tiburon, CA: CentraLink.

Doherty, W. J., McDaniel, S. H., & Baird, M. A. (1996). Five levels of primary care/behavioral healthcare collaboration. *Behavioral Healthcare Tomorrow, 5,* 25-27.

Donaldson, M. S., Yordy, K. D., Lohr, K. N., & Vanselow, N. A. (Eds.). (1996). *Primary care: America's health in a new era.* Washington, DC: National Academy Press.

Dorwart, R. A. (1996). Outcomes management strategies in mental health: Applications and implications for clinical practice. In L. I. Sederer & B. Dickey (Eds.), *Outcomes assessment in clinical practice* (pp. 45–54). Baltimore, MD: Williams & Wilkins.

Dreher, H. (1996). Is there a systematic way to diagnose and treat somatization disorder? *Advances: The Journal of Mind-Body Health, 12,* 50.

Edmunds, M., Frank, R., Hogan, M., McCarty, D., Robinson-Blake, R., & Weisner, C. (Eds.). (1997). *Managing managed care: Quality improvement in behavioral health.* Washington, DC: National Academy Press.

Efforts to integrate with primary care gaining momentum. (1997, November 17). *Mental Health Weekly, 7,* 1–2.

Employers' health costs held down in 1997; most firms expect bigger rise in 1998. (1998, January 20). *Minneapolis Star Tribune,* p. B7, B10.

Ficken, J. (1995). New directions for psychological testing. *Behavioral Health Management, 20,* 12–14.

Freeman, M. A. (1997). Foreword: Mind and body—The integration of behavioral healthcare and medicine. In J. D. Haber & G. E. Mitchell (Eds.), *Primary care meets mental health: Tools for the 21st century* (pp. xii–ix). Tiburon, CA: CentraLink.

Friedman, R., Sobel, D., Myers, P., Caudill, M., & Benson, H. (1995). Behavioral medicine, clinical health psychology, and cost offset. *Health Psychology, 14,* 509–518.

Haber, J. D. & Mitchell, G. E. (Eds.). (1997). *Primary care meets mental health: Tools for the 21st century.* Tiburon, CA: CentraLink.

Hankin, J., & Otkay, J. S. (1979). *Mental disorder and primary medical care: An analytical review of the literature.* No. 5. Washington, DC: National Institute of Mental Health.

Health care spending posts slowest increase in decades. (1998, January 9). *Mental Health Weekly, 8,* 7.

Higgins, E. S. (1994). A review of unrecognized mental illness in primary care. *Archives of Family Medicine, 3,* 908–917.

Horst, T. (1997). Clinical presentation, screening, and treatment of substance abuse in the primary care setting. In J. D. Haber & G. E. Mitchell (Eds.), *Primary care meets mental health: Tools for the 21st century* (pp. 167–177). Tiburon, CA: CentraLink.

Institute for International Research. (1997). [Announcement for the Integrating Behavioral Health Primary Care conference.]

Jenkins, R. (1997). Lifting the global burden of mental disorders: Services policy and planning using epidemiology and disability measurement. *Behavioral Healthcare Tomorrow, 6,* 26–31, 94–96.

Johnson, J. G., Spitzer, R. L., Williams, J. B., Kroenke, K., Linzer, M., Brody, D., deGruy, F., & Hahn, S. (1995). Psychiatric comorbidity, health status, and functional impairment associated with alcohol abuse and dependence in primary care patients: Findings of the PRIME MD-1000 study. *Journal of Consulting and Clinical Psychology, 63,* 133–140.

Katon, W., & Roy-Byrne, P. P. (1989). Panic disorder in the medically ill. *Journal of Clinical Psychiatry, 50,* 299–302.

Katon, W., & Schulberg, H. (1992). Epidemiology of depression in primary care. *General Hospital Psychiatry, 14,* 237–247.

Katzelnick, D. J., Kobak, K. A., Greist, J. H., Jefferson, J. W., & Henk, H. J. (1997). Effect of primary care treatment of depression on service use by patients with high medical expenditures. *Psychiatric Services, 48,* 59–64.

Kessler, L. G., Burns, B. J., Shapiro, S., Tischler, G. L., George, L. K., Hough, R. L., Bodison, D., & Miller, R. H. (1987). Psychiatric diagnoses of medical service users: Evidence from the Epidemiologic Catchment Area program. *American Journal of Public Health, 77,* 18–24.

Kessler, L. G., McGonagle, K. A., Shanyang, Z., Nelson, C. B., Hughes, M., Eshleman, S., Wittchen, H. U., & Kendler, K. S. (1994). Lifetime and 12-month prevalence of DSM-III-R psychiatric disorders. *Archives of General Psychiatry, 51,* 8–19.

Kobak, K. A., Greist, J. H., Jefferson, J. W., & Katzelnick, D. J. (1996). Decision support for patient care: Computerized rating scales. *Behavioral Healthcare Tomorrow, 5,* 25–29.

Kobak, K. A., Taylor, L. V., Dottl, S. L., Greist, J. H., Jefferson, J. W., Burroughs, D., Mantle, J. M., Katzelnick, D. J., Norton, R., Henk, H. J., & Serlin, R. C. (1997). A computer-assisted telephone interview to identify mental disorders. *Journal of the American Medical Association, 278,* 905–910.

Leaders predict integration of MH, primary care by 2000. (1996, April 8). *Mental Health Weekly, 6,* 1, 6.

Lipkin, M. (1996). Dialogue: How should primary care address the problem of psychiatric disorders? Can primary care physicians deliver quality mental healthcare? *Behavioral Healthcare Tomorrow, 5,* 49, 52–53.

Lipsitt, D. R. (1997). From fragmentation to integration: A history of comprehensive patient care. In J. D. Haber & G. E. Mitchell (Eds.), *Primary care meets mental health: Tools for the 21st century* (pp. 3–12). Tiburon, CA: CentraLink.

Locke, S. E. (1997). Treating somatization: An update. *Behavioral Health Management, 17,* 22–23.

Locke, S. E., & Larsson, K. M. (1997). Clinical presentation, screening, and treatment of somatization in primary care. In J. D. Haber & G. E. Mitchell (Eds.), *Primary care meets mental health: Tools for the 21st century* (pp. 179–191). Tiburon, CA: CentraLink.

Lovelace, patients reap rewards primary care intervention in depression. (1997, September). *Behavioral Disease Management Report, 1,* 1–2.

Managed care execs face the providers at AAMFT's convention. (1997, October). *Psychotherapy Finances, 23,* 1–2.

Melek, S. P. (1996). Behavioral healthcare risk-sharing and medical cost offset. *Behavioral Healthcare Tomorrow, 5,* 39–46.

Mental Health Parity Act to take effect at midnight; Landmark law to benefit millions of American families. (1998, January 2). *Behavioral Healthcare Bulletin.*

Millions with mental illnesses benefit from new federal rules. (1997, December 24). *Behavioral Healthcare Bulletin.*

Mitchell, G. E., & Haber, J. D. (1997). The future of primary care/behavioral health integration: Questions . . . and some answers? In J. D. Haber & G. E. Mitchell (Eds.), *Primary care meets mental health: Tools for the 21st century* (pp. 238–245). Tiburon, CA: CentraLink.

Moreland, K. L. (1996). How psychological testing can reinstate its value in an era of cost containment. *Behavioral Healthcare Tomorrow, 5,* 59–61.

National Committee for Quality Assurance. (1997). *1997 surveyor guidelines for the accreditation of managed behavioral healthcare organizations.* Washington, DC: Author.

Nearly 40 percent of older suicide victims visit doctor during week before killing themselves. (1997, July 30). *InfoConsultNews.*

NIMH official cites high cost of schizophrenia. (1996, May 20). *Mental Health Weekly, 6,* 7.

Ohio study documents cost-offsets of substance abuse treatments. (1996, September). *Behavior Health Outcomes, 1,* 1–2.

Olfson, M., & Pincus, H. A. (1994). Outpatient psychotherapy in the United States, I: Volume, costs, and user characteristics. *American Journal of Psychiatry, 151,* 1281–1288.

Peek, C. J. (1997, May). *Integrating medical and behavioral care: Clinical, cultural, operational and financial roadmaps* [syllabus materials]. Workshop presented in the How to Design and Implement Your Primary Care Behavioral Health Integration Program conference, San Francisco, CA.

Peek, C. J., & Heinrich, R. L. (1995). Building a collaborative healthcare organization: From idea to invention to innovation. *Family Systems Medicine, 13,* 327–342.

Perez-Stable, E., Miranda, J., Munoz, R., & Ying, Y. (1990). Depression in medical outpatients: Underrecognition and misdiagnosis. *Archives of Internal Medicine, 150,* 1083–1088.

Physicians report problems in finding mental health specialists for their patients. (1998, January). *APA Monitor,* p. 6.

Ray, C. G. (1996, April 8). Opening plenary address of the annual meeting of the National Community Mental Healthcare Council, Atlanta, GA. *Mental Health Weekly, 6*(15), 1–2.

Regier, D. A., Narrow, W. E., Rae, D. S., Manderscheid, R. W., Locke, B., & Goodwin, F. K. (1993). The de facto US mental and addictive disorders service system: Epidemiologic Catchment Area prospective 1-year prevalence rates of disorders and services. *Archives of General Psychiatry, 50,* 85–94.

Rice, D. P., & Miller, L. S. (1996, August). *Health economics and cost implications of anxiety and other disorders in the United States.* Paper presented at Satellite Symposium X: World Congress of Psychiatry, Madrid, Spain.

Rouse, B. A. (Ed.). (1995). *Substance abuse and mental health statistics sourcebook.* DHHS Publication No. (SMA) 95-3064. Washington, DC: Superintendent of Documents, U.S. Government Printing Office.

Sato, T., & Takeichi, M. (1993). Lifetime prevalence of specific psychiatric disorders in a general medicine clinic. *General Hospital Psychiatry, 15,* 224–233.

Schulberg, H. C., & Burns, B. J. (1988). Mental disorders in primary care: Epidemiologic, diagnostic, and treatment research directions. *General Hospital Psychiatry, 10*, 79–87.

Sederer, L. I., Dickey, B., & Hermann, R. C. (1996). The imperative of outcomes assessment in psychiatry. In L. I. Sederer & B. Dickey (Eds.), *Outcomes assessment in clinical practice* (pp. 1–7). Baltimore, MD: Williams & Wilkins.

Selden, D. R. (1997). Integration of primary care and behavioral health: The driving forces. In J. D. Haber & G. E. Mitchell (Eds.), *Primary care meets mental health: Tools for the 21st century* (pp. 13–25). Tiburon, CA: CentraLink.

Sipkoff, M. Z. (1995, August). Behavioral health treatment reduces medical costs. *Open Minds*, p. 12.

Skinner, H. (1990). Spectrum of drinkers and intervention opportunities. *Canadian Medical Association Journal, 143*, 1054–1059.

Smith, R. G., Jr. (1994). The course of somatization and its effects on utilization of health care resources. *Psychosomatics, 35*, 263–267.

Smith, R. G., Jr., Rost, K., & Kashner, M. T. (1995). A trial of the effect of a standardized psychiatric consultation on health outcomes and costs in somaticizing patients. *Archives of General Psychiatry, 52*, 238.

Sperry, L., & Brill, P. (1997). Computerized technology: Integrative treatment outcome technology in primary care practice. In J. D. Haber & G. E. Mitchell (Eds.), *Primary care meets mental health: Tools for the 21st century* (pp. 229–235). Tiburon, CA: CentraLink.

Sperry, L., Brill, P. L., Howard, K. I., & Grissom, G. R. (1996). *Treatment outcomes in psychotherapy and psychiatric interventions.* New York: Brunner/Mazel.

Spitzer, R. L., Kroenke, K., Linzer, M., Hahn, S. R., Williams, J. B., Verloin duGruy, F., Brody, D., & Davies, M. (1995). Health-related quality of life in primary care patients with mental disorders: Results from the PRIME–MD 1000 study. *Journal of the American Medical Association, 274*, 1511–1517.

Spitzer, R. L., Williams, J. B., Kroenke, K., Linzer, M., Verloin duGruy, F., Hahn, S. R., Brody, D., & Johnson, J. G. (1994). Utility of a new procedure for diagnosing mental disorders in primary care: The PRIME–MD 1000 study. *Journal of the American Medical Association, 272*, 1749–1756.

Stelovich. S. (1996). Dialogue: How should primary care address the problem of psychiatric disorders? Psychiatric treatment in primary care: Choice or requirement? *Behavioral Healthcare Tomorrow, 5*, 48, 50, 53.

Stewart, A. L., & Ware, J. E., Jr. (1992). *Measuring functioning and well-being.* Durham, NC: Duke University Press.

Stoudemire, A., Frank, R., Hedemark, N., Kamlet, M., & Blazer, D. (1986). The economic burden of depression. *General Hospital Psychiatry, 8*, 387–394.

Strategic Advantage, Inc. (1996). *Manual for the Symptom Assessment–45 Questionnaire (SA–45).* Minneapolis, MN: Author.

Strosahl, K. (1996). Mind and body primary mental health care: New model for integrated services. *Behavioral Healthcare Tomorrow, 5*, 93–96.

Sturm, R., & Wells, K. B. (1996). Health policy implications of the RAND Medical Outcomes Study: Improving the value of depression treatment. *Behavioral Healthcare Tomorrow, 5*, 63–66.

Tiemens, B. G., Ormel, J., & Simon, G. E. (1996). Occurrence, recognition, and outcome of psychological disorders in primary care. *American Journal of Psychiatry, 153*, 636–644.

Von Korff, M., Shapiro, S., Burke, J. D., et al. (1987). Anxiety and depression in a primary care clinic. *Archives of General Psychiatry, 44*, 152–156.

Ware, J. E., Kosinski, M., & Keller, S. D. (1995). *SF–12: How to Score the SF–12 Physical and Mental summary scales* (2nd ed.). Boston: New England Medical Center, Health Institute.

Ware, J. E., & Sherbourne, C. D. (1992). The MOS 36-Item Short Form Health Survey (SF–36). I. Conceptual framework and item selection. *Medical Care, 30*, 473–483.

Ware, J. E., Snow, K. K., Kosinski, M., & Gandek, B. (1993). *SF–36 Health Survey manual and interpretation guide.* Boston: New England Medical Center, The Health Institute.

Wells, K. B., Golding, J. M., Burnam, M. A., et al. (1988). Psychiatric disorder in a sample of the general population with and without chronic medical conditions. *American Journal of Psychiatry, 145*, 976–981.

Werthman, M. J. (1995). A managed care approach to psychological testing. *Behavioral Health Management, 20*, 15–17.

World Health Organization Interim Commission. (1997). Constitution of the World Health Organization. *Chronicle of the World Health Organization, 1*, 29–40.

Zimmerman, M., Lish, J. D., Farber, N. J., Hartung, J., Lush, D., Kuzma, M. A., & Plescia, G. (1994). Screening for depression in medical patients: Is the focus too narrow? *General Hospital Psychiatry, 16*, 388–394.

Zung, W. K., Broadhead, W. E., & Roth, M. E. (1993). Prevalence of depressive symptoms in primary care. *The Journal of Family Practice, 37*, 337–344.

Integrating Behavioral Health and Primary Care

C. J. Peek
Richard Heinrich
HealthPartners, Minneapolis, Minnesota

This chapter orients behavioral health professionals to realities, trends, concepts, literature, and challenges they are likely to encounter while embarking on work in primary care settings. Behavioral health clinicians who understand realities and aspirations in contemporary health care will be in a position to build common ground and good relationships with primary care clinics and physicians and jointly improve the care of patients and health care practice. We describe some of the many possible variations on the theme of integrated behavioral health care from the perspective of behavioral health professionals, because this is who we are and who the reader of this book is likely to be. This chapter is based on what we have read in the literature, heard in discussions with people across the country, or experienced directly as lessons learned in our own work to bridge the "mind–body split" in the care of patients. It is structured to address the following issues:

1. Health care delivery in the future. The larger context for behavioral health integration is set by describing some trends in health care and what health care is "trying to be" or "will need to be" in the future, according to several authors.

2. The importance of integrating medical and behavioral care. Given what health care needs to be in the future, the case for better integration of behavioral health is made in two ways. The first is a scan of relevant research findings about the epidemiology of behavioral disorders and their treatment in primary care settings that suggests that a more integrated approach is needed and is promising. This is followed by a summary of common dissatisfactions with the traditional separate and parallel medical and behavioral health care delivery systems, as expressed by patients, clinicians, care systems and employers.

3. Approaches to primary care/behavioral health integration: distinctions and concepts. Several distinctions and concepts characterize some of the clinical or organizational approaches to behavioral health integration, as described in the literature and elaborated by the authors. Some of the "vocabulary" and opportunities the reader may encounter in the broad area of behavioral health integration are outlined.

4. Engaging primary care clinics: selecting a focus for behavioral health integration. How does one engage primary care physicians and clinics in finding a practical focus for behavioral health integration efforts? Because each primary care clinic or physician experiences the problems associated with nonintegrated behavioral health in different ways, joint discovery of a common focus is necessary. The behavioral health provider can enter the scene in a way that helps the clinic articulate what it needs and is ready for, rather than in a way that prematurely inserts behavioral health people, tools, or techniques.

5. Integrating behavioral health and primary care: a theme with variations. People who are involved in a number of seemingly different and customized behavioral health integration projects (the variations) could begin to lose track of what is in common among them (the theme). Clinic-specific customized behavioral health integration plans are tied together with a generic clinical process that underlies them all. Examples of focal areas for improved behavioral health integration are described using this generic clinical process.

6. One story: the HealthPartners experience. Behavioral health integration is taking place in many different ways in many different care systems, and no single story could be representative of them all. But telling one story (the one the authors have lived) can help the reader see how improved medical/behavioral health collaboration and integration might take place over time. Clinical and organizational themes are interwoven in the still unfolding story in one organization.

IMPROVING THE CARE AND THE CARE SYSTEM: A CENTRAL THEME

Medical and behavioral factors are intertwined for most primary care patients, and all patients, clinicians, and caregivers are embedded in a much broader care system (or "nonsystem" of care) with its own characteristics and features. Clinicians and patients alike say that part of what makes care go well or not so well is not just the severity of the illnesses or conditions encountered, but the suitability of the care delivery processes and systems encountered. Some features of the care system you happen to be working in make certain things easier to achieve and other things harder to achieve. These are the practical (or impractical) effects of care system design. For example, traditional separate and parallel systems of medical and behavioral care introduce a whole set of difficulties in care delivery, to be described later. Behavioral health integration is a response to that particular design problem.

Disconnected medical and behavioral health care is one among many clinical, operational, or financial design problems in health care. Health care is undergoing rapid change, and the working environment in primary care is no exception. Some of these changes or experiments will later be seen as good, others not so good. But over the long haul, health care will move toward greater "system-ness" and conscious design of the total care process, as described shortly. Primary care/behavioral health integration is just one piece of that larger drama.

In this chapter, we are treating the reader as someone interested in assessment in the very broadest sense, and who is looking for the most powerful ways to use a process improvement mindset to support the goals of primary care and the redesign of health care practice. We are treating the reader as someone who is interested in extending the familiar concepts of "detection," "diagnosis," and "treatment" used for the care of individuals to the care of populations of patients (including those not coming in for care at all), and for care process, systems, and organizational problems.

We are treating the reader as someone interested in the larger drama that includes improving both the *care* and the care *system*, and who can bring a very broad clinical and process improvement mindset to both. Because there is little choice but to redesign the care process, systems, and organization while trying to take care of specific patients, improving care ends up meaning organizational change. Improving the care and improving the care system are done together, where they succeed at all. Behavioral health clinicians can tell a great deal about the strengths and weaknesses of the care system by observing the progress of patients in that system and the characteristic difficulties encountered while taking care of patients in that system. Moreover, clinicians have a responsibility to point out and help make changes in the care system that are needed to make improvements in the care.

We challenge behavioral health professionals to look at care system or organizational factors as part of their work, including care system readiness to assimilate behavioral health integration, people, and tools and to become effective change agents in the rough-and-tumble of organizational change, as well as behavioral health experts emerging from the order and quiet of the professional consulting room. We hope that such expanded roles, relationships, and such a range of concerns prove as rewarding to readers as it has for us.

HEALTH CARE DELIVERY IN THE FUTURE

The Rapidly Evolving Face of Health Care Delivery

Health care is increasingly done in organized systems of care delivery and practice environments. Health care as a cottage industry of small, unorganized, and unmonitored fee-for-service practices is rapidly disappearing. Most clinicians are working in or with some form of organized care, even if not practicing in an HMO or large care system. At the same time, there is huge variation in goals, methods, and maturity across organized care systems (Miller & Luft, 1994, 1997). Organized systems of care are not all at the same stage of development, nor are they trying to accomplish the same things. For example, we have heard it said, "when you know one HMO, you know one HMO," and this goes for other forms of organized care as well. To give a sense of common direction for the future, here are three views of what health care needs to be in the future.

An Enhanced Primary Care Model. Patient, provider, purchaser, and cost pressures mean primary care across all care systems will have to demonstrate new capabilities in order to survive. O'Connor, Solberg, and Baird (1998) argued that primary care will have to reconfigure itself, develop an "enhanced primary care model" in order to survive competition from specialists and "disease carve-outs" who would be very happy to develop the next generation of better performing approaches to care. They make the case that primary care needs to go beyond episodic care to improve preventive care and chronic disease care. This means developing proactive, rather than reactive, mindset and care management methods, and then performing very well on public measures of quality. In order to do this, primary care has to go beyond "first-order change" (rearranging what we already have) to radical innovation or "second-order change" (articulating a goal and then rethinking what is needed to achieve it).

O'Connor et al. went on to specify factors that will stimulate this "second-order change" in primary care. These include (a) capitated[1] rather than fee-for-service payment, (b) a legal environment that is expanding the bounds of nursing practice, (c) sophisticated information systems, (d) a capacity for investment of substantial resources, (e) a corporate rather than health care professional approach to timelines, and (f) new models tailored to their customers' needs (i.e., well-received by patients and purchasers). Paraphrasing O'Connor et al., this innovation, an "enhanced primary care model," must provide a more organized, more consistent approach to care, and assure that more patients who develop specific needs receive critical elements of care at the right times. Tools of this enhanced primary care model include clinical guidelines, patient registries, computerized tracking of patients, team care, targeting and triage tools, recall systems, flowsheets, telephone outreach, standing orders, patient self-monitoring technology, individualization of therapy and therapy based on clinical status, and efficient use of subspecialty expertise.

Distinctive Characteristics of Future Outstanding Health Care Organizations. Don Berwick, MD, a national figure in health care quality improvement, has his own list of "distinctive characteristics of the future outstanding healthcare organization" (Berwick, 1997) that he encourages care systems to develop. Paraphrased here from a 1997 presentation, these characteristics are:

1. Ambitious improvement aims: challenging answers to "How good could we get?"
2. Improvement as a core strategy: continuous improvement of performance as the unifying business strategy.
3. Idealized designs for systems: care systems led and operated from a vision of ideal design; what the operating designs of the "perfect" system are.
4. Broad patterns of search for ideas and examples: very broad searches for ideas and examples outside the organization to form the basis for improvement.
5. Broad bandwidths for cooperation: the exchange of ideas, even with competitors, as an asset for improvement and solving basic problems. "Disease, not competitors, is the enemy."
6. A sense of total relationship with patients: lifelong relationships with patients. Foregoing short-term aims for long-term goals, and episodes of care occurring within the context of those relationships.
7. Redefinition of production and throughput to reflect integrated thinking: goals and forms of compensation that reflect integrated thinking. Providers and provider organizations cannot claim to value total relationship and improvement and then manage and reward fragmentary events.
8. Visible performance monitors: Monitors of key variables of success are visible and constantly monitored and displayed and updated.

---

[1]Capitation is a form of payment in which a care system or clinic receives a prearranged amount of money per month to take care of each patient or subscriber, rather than being paid separately for each service rendered.

9. Extremely high levels of trust in staff and patients: Patients are not blamed for their expectations, and staff members are supported in a manner that enables them to exercise pride in work and in improvement.

10. Commitment to justice and equity: justice and equity as reflected in health status and comfort, and through avoidance of selective marketing to those who need services least.

11. Deep knowledge of waste in all its forms: The greatest opportunities for revenue increase often lie within the care system's own operations.

12. Expansion of inquiry to matters of design and improvement: Academic organizations will define their research agendas on systems and their improvement as well as disciplinary knowledge.

Characteristics of Successful and Solvent Health Care Delivery in the Future. Keeping in mind such "futurist" views, direct experience, organizational mission and philosophy, and local market demands, a number of health care systems are designing themselves for a future that will call for the following characteristics or capabilities.

1. Population health. The future will require improving the health of an identified population of patients, with an emphasis on primary and secondary prevention. It means being concerned about patients who are not receiving treatment or coming in for their care, as well as those who are. The success of a health plan or delivery system will reside not only in the quality and cost of care for individuals who come in, but in terms of the health of entire populations and good stewardship of resources entrusted by that population. For example, a health plan will be concerned with diabetic control for its entire population of diabetics, not just for a few motivated individuals who consistently come in (Gilmer, O'Connor, Manning, & Rush, 1997; Pronk, O'Connor, Isham, & Hawkins, 1997). A total systems approach to care (Pronk & O'Connor, 1997), and healthy behavior change will be increasingly important aspects of reaching population health goals (Boyle, O'Connor, Pronk, & Tan, 1998; Prochaska, Norcross, & DiClemente, 1994; Pronk, Boyle, & O'Connor, 1998).

2. Good resource stewardship. Wise use of resources is essential if the goal is to responsibly take care of individuals, families, and populations who have entrusted a great deal of money (usually through employers or the government) to health plans and delivery systems. This usually means providing care for a prearranged amount of money (capitation) or a cost target based on a benefits package and actuarial experience. Good resource stewardship is not merely cost containment, but rather the most effective and judicious use of limited resources for ambitious care and health improvement goals. A complete system of health management and financial models that reward results and support good resource stewardship is required if quality and population health goals are to be met (Halvorson, 1993).

3. Use of evidence-based best practices wherever possible. Ambitious care and health improvement goals with good resource stewardship mean not wasting time and money on billable services, procedures, prescriptions, or care plans that don't really make a difference to illness care or health improvement. This in turn means finding out what makes a difference and what doesn't. The evidence basis for what is effective, more effective, equally effective but cheaper, or effective under what circumstances becomes very important. Unwanted, subjective variation between

providers undermines quality and resource stewardship goals. But no one provider can possibly stay completely up to date on all the evidence. Hence, clinical practice guidelines based on best available evidence become very important and can become a practical tool (Mosser, 1996; Rolnick & O'Connor, 1997). What is considered a best practice can and does change as new studies come in, but the point is that a mindset and practical emphasis on what is demonstrably effective are necessary if good value in health care is to be achieved.

4. Focus on the entire care process. People's lives, health problems, and healthy behavior efforts do not neatly sort themselves into "boxes" defining the traditional professional specialties or subdivisions. (Common "boxes" that subdivide the care process are described later.) Good quality, good service, and good resource steward-ship require improving the whole care process, not asking the patient to bridge gaps in care plans and communication that too often occur between professional special-ties, venues for care, or over the passage of time. As much as possible, evi-dence-based best practices will guide the entire care process—not just today's piece of it or one provider's piece of it. The basic "unit of analysis" for care will no longer be "today's problem," "my setting," or a particular organ system or disease. The nat-ural history of disease processes, healthy behavior change, and the interplay between various biological and psychosocial conditions and situational factors will become increasingly important in planning care. Continuity of care ("longitudinality") and integration of care across professions and care venues are a major goal, necessary to improve outcomes, resource stewardship, and patient satisfaction. Improved sys-tems for chronic care are another goal for care systems that are traditionally designed for acute care (Von Korff, Gruman, Schaeffer, Curry, & Wagner, 1997; Wagner, Aus-tin, & Von Korff, 1996).

5. Information systems and processes to help clinicians with care management and clinical decision making. Information systems aren't just for business purposes anymore. For example, information is a key tool for tracking health status of individ-uals and populations over time or across specialties and care venues. Registries or "risk lists" can be developed to alert clinics and clinicians for the need for interven-tions (O'Connor, Rush, & Pronk, 1997; Pronk et al., 1997). Automated medical rec-ords or more rudimentary clinical information systems can help clinicians maintain up-to-date care plans, refresh them with clinical data in real time, or even permit cli-nicians to "click" on their screens for clinical practice guidelines and best practices. Because clinicians and care systems will increasingly try to maximize quality for in-dividuals and populations while conserving limited resources, they will need better information and more practical information tools. The future of health care involves "flying by instruments" as well as "by the seat of your pants."

6. The right team to get the job done. Along with more comprehensive and better integrated care plans comes the practical necessity to establish care teams. No one per-son is in a position to do everything well in a comprehensive and well-integrated care plan. Team-based care delivery means every provider has the right role, doing the right part of the work, within every unfolding case. This entails developing collabo-rative practice across professions and care venues and preserving that teamwork and communication over time. Consistent teamwork must remain even as care plans, dis-ease processes, or healthy behavior changes evolve for a given patient or family, es-pecially for care of chronic conditions (Von Korff et al., 1997). As discussed at length later, primary care and behavioral health collaboration or integration is a key part of building care teams capable of the ambitious care, health improvement, and resource

stewardship goals required by the future. For example, the National Committee for Quality Assurance (NCQA) guidelines call for increasing evidence of care coordination between primary care and behavioral health (NCQA, 1998, 1999 editions).

7. Public measurement and competition as a system on quality, service, and cost. The public, purchasers, and public policymakers are increasingly expecting health care organizations to be accountable for results, and want to pay for results, not just for services. This requires a set of specific and public performance measures by which various health plans or care systems are evaluated (e.g., Health Plan Employer Data and Information Set; HEDIS, 1998). Such measures can enable patients and purchasers to track improvement or decline in the performance of a health plan over time and help patients and purchasers make informed judgement and choices among health plans. Such measures are also needed to confirm or restore public confidence in organized health care systems and to separate public relations and advertising claims from documented achievements. Public measurement of patient satisfaction with care systems (e.g., "State of Minnesota Employees Consumer Satisfaction Survey Results," 1997) will also become more common.

The Future Calls for Systems of Care Delivery That Actually Function Like Systems

The future will require building care systems out of what usually started out as "nonsystems" of individuals and groups, each doing their best to provide one aspect of patient care while able to see only one part of the bigger picture. This is largely due to the practical need to divide the knowledge, labor, professional accountability, geographic distribution, and financial responsibility for health care. The divisions we now live with developed for good reasons. But these divisions, as necessary as they have been, have often led to a fragmented nonsystem, defined by subdivisions of the care system or the professions rather than by how these components are linked as an entire care process for improving health. The total care process is often subdivided (and fragmented) along several lines, including:

1. By care venue. Each venue (specialty hospital, general hospital, emergency room, critical care unit, transitional care center, outpatient clinic, after-hours care center, nursing home, home care, community services) is too often a world unto itself, with the transitions for a given patient between venues fragmented, with gaps or redundancies.

2. By profession or specialty. Each health care discipline, department, or specialty often focuses on the care of one organ system, disease process, or set of techniques, with the whole picture too often remaining unclear, and coordination of care too often fragmented. Referral processes and communication methods usually go only so far in knitting back together care that has been fragmented along professional or organ-system lines. The medical/behavioral health "split" is a major source of such fragmentation.

3. By disease. For example, diabetes care may be provided through one program, specialty, or "carve-out" organization, asthma through another, heart disease through another, industrial injury through another, behavioral health problems through another. Separate programs or "carve-outs" for each disease may leave the patient who has multiple conditions in multiple programs, qualifying for none of them, or shifting back and forth as the person's condition changes or the balance be-

tween different conditions changes. The whole picture can easily be lost, and transitions between the pieces are easily fragmented.

4. By stage in disease process or degree of risk for disease. Health promotion, health education, or preventive services for a patient with risk factors for a condition may be housed or delivered in one division or program, disconnected from the primary physician or hospital who treats that same patient with that same condition once the risk or symptoms have escalated. The right balance and coordination of preventive care and illness care is often difficult to achieve.

5. By insurance coverage or care delivery contract. A person may have medical coverage with one medical group or network and behavioral health coverage with another group or network. Patients may be eligible for care with one clinician for one thing and a different clinician for another thing. This adds an additional challenge for clinicians who want to clearly see the whole picture. The individual patient may be covered by one insurance or care system but the spouse or children by another. The whole care picture, especially for families with interrelated health issues, can disappear. Seeking care is too often like navigating a maze, as if the health problem itself weren't enough of a challenge.

The challenge is to develop care systems that actually function like systems, in which the various care system components are not only on the map, but are actually interconnected so that a patient's or family's care remains integrated as it moves through various stages, venues, conditions, or providers, who all work within a larger "ecology of care" (Peek & Heinrich, 1995). A care system needs to be able to formulate a comprehensive care plan and then keep it visible and intact wherever the patient happens to show up. It must also reach out proactively, providing prevention and chronic care services where required to improve health and conserve limited health care resources.

This need for greater systemness is widely recognized, and necessary if care organizations are to move beyond a stage marked by preoccupation with cost control and collecting care system components under one business roof through acquisitions, mergers, and network building. A consolidation stage often seeks business or financial integration but by itself does little for clinical integration. The common term *integrated delivery system* usually means business integration that takes place before the much more challenging task of *clinical* integration. Some major care systems in "mature markets" such as the Twin Cities have already gone through much basic consolidation and are focusing more on effectively connecting up the pieces that now exist under one roof.

New Forms of Care Delivery Present Significant Practice Changes for Physicians

Behavioral health professionals need to understand the changes and strains in medical practice as they consider engaging primary care physicians in behavioral health integration. Many primary care physicians already report that they are staggering under the load of change, even those who believe it will ultimately be a good thing. In that environment, it is easy for behavioral health issues to be seen as "just one more thing" in the middle of those other changes, such as these four:

1. Adapting to new business entities and organizational cultures. New business entities, mergers, and consolidations bring new colleagues, new systems, and new

cultures. Even when positive, these add "transition stress" and can give a primary care setting the feel of a "construction site" replete with mess, sidewalk superintendents, and awkward temporary solutions. Reconstruction of the business and organizational environment means living with a layer of personal and professional adjustment superimposed on the already challenging task of patient care.

2. Becoming increasingly mindful of the whole care process. As care systems become more systematic, clinicians have greater opportunity to develop increased mindfulness of the whole patient, the whole population of patients, and the whole care process. There is more to keep in mind as "the bar" is raised. This precipitates an often painful awareness of the limitations of individual, one-on-one health care where the doctor does everything and has to remember and think of everything. This intensifies a felt need either for escape from the pressure or for collaboration and role differentiation between doctors, nurses, nurse practitioners, health educators, behavioral health professionals, and others on an expanded care team. But most physicians are not trained in collaborative practice, and it more often takes the form of a "good idea" than actual practice. The felt need for better or wider teamwork often seems very difficult to achieve during the press of the usual day to day, and this is a frustration to many primary care physicians.

3. Increasing public measurement of quality and service. As standards for demonstrated clinical quality and outcomes become more rigorous and more public, clinics, care systems or individual physicians become more interested in tracking their own performance (e.g., immunization, Pap smear, and mammography rates, diabetic control, lipid control, and incidence of heart attack). Population health goals can be quite public and quite aggressive, such as at HealthPartners (Isham, 1997), and all require proactive, population-based interventions, clinical practice guidelines, improved databases, and improved systems to help physicians and clinics manage individual patients. This shift in emphasis toward rewarding outcomes rather than just procedures is often perceived by physicians as positive, but it also represents more change and redirection of a finite amount of energy.

4. Increasing demand for good resource stewardship. Increased financial pressures and competition for business mean that good patient service and good stewardship of limited resources have also become much more important than in the era when providers billed and were automatically paid for services with no questions asked. Physicians not only have to deliver quality care to individuals and populations, with an emphasis on prevention as well as illness care, but increasingly must do so with an eye to the "most bang for the buck" in their choice of medications, tests, and clinical pathways. Good resource stewardship is a growing part of the basic professional perspective and obligation for physicians and clinics, even where rules, limits and utilization review methods are not imposed on clinicians from outside.

All these changes, even when felt to be positive, create a primary care environment where behavioral health integration, behavioral health professionals, and their tools may be experienced as competing for attention with a whole array of major changes and developments. To avoid entering primary care as a "competitor" for time and attention, it is crucial to understand the goals of contemporary primary care and the changes primary care physicians are undergoing. It is essential to engage primary care physicians and clinics in areas where they are *already* working for improvement and to find ways to help them carry these efforts forward. Behavioral health professionals need to become associated with a net improvement in care, and a net simplification in clinic life. If behavioral health professionals and tools are seen as "complicating clinic life," they won't go far in this high-pressure environment.

WHY INTEGRATE MEDICAL AND BEHAVIORAL HEALTH CARE: A BRIEF REVIEW OF RELEVANT FINDINGS

The knowledge base about how behavioral health factors play out in health care care is growing (for more extensive reviews of this growing literature see Klinkman & Oakes, 1998; Miranda, Hohmann, Attkinson, & Larson, 1994; Simon & VonKorff, 1997; Strosahl, 1997, 1998). The following sections touch on some of the developing research literature that suggests why a more integrated approach to behavioral health in primary care is promising. These findings are also intended to orient the behavioral health professional to important aspects of working with primary care patients in the primary care environment.

Primary Care Is the de Facto Mental Health Care Delivery System

Primary care is the de facto mental health care delivery system, or at least the "front end" of the mental health care delivery system for most people (Regier, Goldberg, & Taube, 1978; Regier et al., 1993). This conclusion is based on a much better understanding of the epidemiology mental disorders gained over the past 30 years (Narrow, Regier, Rae, Manderscheid, & Locke, 1993; Regier et al., 1978, 1993; Shapiro et al., 1984). Spurred on by the 1978 Presidential Commission on Mental Disorders, funding streams and programs were developed, such as the National Institutes of Mental Health Epidemiological Catchment Area study (NIMH ECA), to study the epidemiology of mental disorders (Burns, 1994). One of the central findings of NIMH ECA research was that primary care is where the majority of patients with mental disorders have contact with care delivery systems. Thus primary care becomes the major player in the de facto mental health care delivery system. It is where most patients with mental disorders receive their care now and will do so into the foreseeable future (deGruy, 1997).

This assessment is based on several lines of epidemiological research. First, of the patients who actively seek care for mental disorders, 50% of the care is provided by primary care physicians (Regier et al., 1978, 1993). However, only 50% of patients with mental disorders actively seek care for their disorders (Regier et al., 1993). Yet, as Strosahl reported in a recent review of this literature, approximately 70% to 80% of patients will make at least one primary care visit annually (Strosahl, 1997). From a population-based perspective, primary care will manage, directly or indirectly, 80% of the patients with mental disorders. Other patients with emotional distress but without a *DSM–IV* diagnosis will also present in primary care. Only a small percentage of the population of patients with mental disorders or emotional distress will ever see a mental health specialist.

From a population-based perspective as well as from the first-hand experience of primary care practitioners, primary care is the "somatic symptom superhighway," a phrase coined by Sobel (1997). Patients take their symptoms to primary care without regard to their medical or psychological origins. Primary care is the final common pathway for presentations of medical illness, psychiatric disorders, and emotional distress. Emotional distress is of particular importance to primary care practices. Some 70% of office visits to primary care physicians do not lead to a diagnosable medical illness (Strosahl, 1997). Patients present with a wide range of psychosocial or emotional distress, which, if codable at all, are nonillness codes (e.g., "stress," marital discord, job dissatisfaction, financial duress, working two jobs, crime in the neighborhood, family problems, lack of social support). Even though "nondiagnosable" and excluded from financial reimbursement as mental conditions, unaddressed stressors such as these can and do alter physiology and can lead to significant pathology (Dunman, Heninger, & Nestler, 1997; Holmes & Rahe, 1968). They may lead to depression and anxiety and/or may precipitate and alter the course of major mood disorders (Goodwin & Jamison, 1990). They are also associated with significant disability and high utilization of medical services (Strosahl, 1997; Von Korff, Ormel, & Katon, 1992).

It comes then as no surprise that primary care physicians prescribe more psychotropic medications than psychiatrists in all psychopharmacological categories, including antidepressants, antianxiety agents, hypnotics, and psychostimulants (Pincus et al., 1998).

Challenges for Primary Care Functioning as the "Front End" of Behavioral Health Care Delivery

Behavioral health providers should understand (as shown by the epidemiological studies) that primary care physicians are called on daily to diagnose and manage a broad range and severity of medical illnesses, psychiatric disorders, and emotional distress. This takes place in a care system designed primarily to manage acute, episodic, and often self-limiting medical problems. Most primary care visits occur in 15-minute blocks of time, often punctuated by interuptions to take phone calls, respond to nurses' or receptionists' questions, read lab reports, refill prescriptions, handle emergencies, and so on.

Given the importance of the medical sector in delivering mental health care, what do we know about how mental disorders surface in this setting and the quality of the care provided? The clinical and research literature in the past 20 years has raised and begun to answer important questions and concerns about the evaluation and treatment of mental disorders in the medical sector. This literature is complex and has been reviewed elsewhere (Miranda et al., 1994; Simon & VonKorff, 1997; Strosahl, 1997, 1998). Themes from this literature that are useful in preparing behavioral health professionals for work in primary care are included next.

Behavioral Health Problems Are Often Presented in a Medical Frame of Reference. The emerging literature on mental disorders in primary care suggests that patients with emotional distress and mental disorders present their symptoms in this medical frame of reference (Hellman, Budd, Borysenko, McClelland, & Benson, 1990; Kroenke & Mangelsdorff, 1989; Sobel, 1995). Depressive disorders, especially in the elderly, present more with somatic symptoms than cognitive symptoms (Blazer, 1993; Caine, Lyness, King, & Connors, 1994). This could be predicted, as there is frequent coexistence (comorbidity) with chronic medical illnesses such as strokes, cardiovascular disease, Parkinson's disease, rheumatoid arthritis, and diabetes mellitus (Blazer, 1993). The prevalence of depression with these medical conditions varies from 10% to 50% depending on the study (Robinson, Starr, & Price, 1984; Starkstein & Robinson, 1989). With each of these conditions that often present in elderly patients with multisystem disease, differentiating the symptoms of depression versus the symptoms of the medical illness is a daunting task. Many of these clinical presentations represent an inextricable mix of biomedical and psychosocial factors for which teasing out a referrable psychiatric diagnosis is logically and practically impossible.

If comorbid medical, psychiatric, and emotional distress weren't enough of a challenge, primary care patients themselves may not recognize mental health factors in their medical complaints, nor recognize that their somatic symptoms represent emotional distress and/or depression and anxiety (Barsky, 1988; Lipowski, 1988). Patients usually bring to the medical setting an expectation that at the end of the visit some action will be taken, most often in the form of further testing and/or a prescription for a medication that will solve a physical or medical problem. Symptoms are most often understood to be biological in nature, reflecting an underlying alteration in normal functioning that needs to be addressed. Physicians, as biomedically trained professionals, often have a similar expectation for themselves. The tacit message often is that when the physical problem is addressed, the patient will probably return to his or her previous level of functioning and well-being. When the physician recognizes psychiatric disorders or emotional distress, it may take significant relationship building and many visits before a patient is ready to accept psychosocial factors as part of the cause for symptoms or as part of the care plan. This is particularly true of elderly patients who were raised to manage their psychological problems on their own and would not ever bring a psychological problem to their physician. Especially for elderly patients, psychological or emotional distress is to be managed stoically (e.g. "you just have to accept these things as part of aging!").

Detection of Behavioral Health Problems in Primary Care Is a Complex Issue. Without full account of the complex issues of comorbidity, the huge range of severity, and concerns about coding and confidentiality, much of the early literature on recognition and treatment of mental disorders in primary care led to characterization of the primary care physician as an inferior species of mental health practitioner. A number of studies highlighted widespread nondetection and undertreatment of depression and other mental disorders (Ormel, Koeter, Brink, & Williege, 1991). But more recent studies of primary care physician ability to detect and treat mental disorders are more positive (Coyne, Schwenk, & Fechner-Bates, 1995; Simon & VonKorff, 1997). Recent literature suggests that depressive and anxiety disorders present differently in primary care than in traditional mental health settings, are generally milder, are associated with less disability, and occur in higher functioning individuals (Simon & Von Korff, 1997).

At the other end of the spectrum, many patients with mental disorders in primary care have comorbid medical and psychiatric illness (Ford, 1994). In such patients, the mental illness is less responsive to traditional treatments (Schulberg & Pajer, 1994). Overall, the more recent studies have demonstrated that primary care physician detection and management of anxiety and depressive disorders was considerably better with moderate and severe depressive illness than with mild symptoms. (Coyne et al., 1995; Simon & VonKorff, 1997).

Patients belief in medical explanations for symptoms may discourage diagnosis and documentation of mental disorders but not necessarily their actual recognition or treatment, especially when the patient presents with physical symptoms and physicians have legitimate concerns about how psychiatric diagnoses and information might affect the privacy or insurability of their patients. As mentioned earlier, the culture of primary care usually prepares patients and providers to see and deal with *physical* symptoms, causes, diagnoses, and treatments. Many primary care patients with psychiatric illnesses or psychological distress will not accept a mental health diagnosis (or even accept psychological contributing factors) and are managed and treated for their behavioral health disorder within a medical frame of reference. This is particularly true of patients who somatize or qualify for somatization disorder (Hellman et al., 1990; Kashner, Rost, & Cohen, 1995; Lipowski, 1988; Smith, Monson, & Ray, 1986). Integration provides clinicians an alternative to an "either-or" approach to negotiating explanatory stories and care plans acceptable to these patients.

The care of behavioral health disorders can also become a reimbursement challenge for physicians where insurance contracts will not reimburse primary care physicians for their treatment (some contracts specify that "behavioral health" is contracted out to a separate behavioral health provider). This may also affect coding and documentation but not the ability to recognize, detect, or treat. In many cases a physician who is uncomfortable for one reason or another about coding a mental health diagnosis such as depression can legitimately code an acceptable medical diagnosis such as fatigue or headache.

Finding useful approaches to detection of mental illness in primary care presents another set of challenges for behavioral health clinicians and researchers. In an interesting review of studies on screening for depression in primary care, Simon and VonKorff (1997) speculated that screening interventions for depressive disorders in primary care do not result in improved treatment outcomes because patients with less severe illness have self-limiting episodes and patients with severe depressive disorders do not get better without systematic, structured psychopharmacological and psychotherapeutic treatments. Given such findings and opinions, behavioral health professionals will be called on to help sort out a variety of detection and recognition issues, interacting comorbidities, and complex interactions between clinical, operational, and resource issues in program design.

Treatment of Mental Disorders in Primary Care

Challenges for a Young and Developing Research Literature.   The previous sections underscore some of the complexities of behavioral health disorders and factors as they present in primary care, especially its unique culture, the prevalence of comorbid conditions, and the vast range of condition severity. This has made it difficult to characterize and report consistent and general statements about the treatment of mental disorders or behavioral health problems in this setting. Early studies of the treatment of depression in primary care were guided by a "screening–detect–treat–improve" clinical paradigm that did result in improved outcomes (see Klinkman & Okkes, 1998, for a review). However, a second wave of studies that focused on improved detection and referral found no differences in outcomes than from the usual care. A notable exception is the demonstration of improved treatment outcomes for depression in primary care in the Katon et al. study (1996), where primary care physicians and behavioral health professionals comanaged patients with depression.

Klinkman and Okkes (1998) interpreted the inconsistencies in this still young and developing literature in the following way. In addition to the typical problems with case definition (comorbidity), inadequate outcome measures, and inadequate description of concurrent treatments that may have influenced the results, they contended that most of the treatment studies misunderstand and fail to scientifically address the fundamentally different phenomena of mental disorders in primary care including the epidemiology, comorbidity, subthreshold conditions, emotional distress, and styles of practice. They advocated and supported the new research trends in developing alternative diagnostic approaches to *DSM–IV* to adequately capture and document the reality of mental health problems as they present in primary care practice. They also highlighted the importance of studying other key variables, such as the patient–physician relationship, that can affect treatment outcomes in these complex disorders.

The Value of Long-Term Collaborative Relationships. Our own reading of the literature has been biased by our experience over the past 15 years in collaborating with physicians and integrating care within primary care clinics. We think that in addition to developing specific interventions, new programs, and enhanced training for physicians, two critical variables need sustained attention and continued study. One is the quality and primacy of the patient–physician relationship and its effect on treatment outcomes. The second is the development of successful long-term collaborative relationships between primary care physicians and behavioral health professionals.

We are convinced that treatment approaches that build long-term relationships between primary care physicians and behavioral health clinicians will bring better satisfaction and outcomes than approaches based on referral, stand-alone treatments, or treatments imported from specialty mental health settings. The value to providers and patients of a well-developed long-term relationship between a physician and a behavioral health clinician is described in Lucas and Peek (1997). The developing research also points in this direction. For example, in a well-defined research program at Group Health Cooperative of Puget Sound and the University of Washington Department of Psychiatry, over the past decade, Katon, Simon, VonKorff, and their colleagues have demonstrated the impact that such collaborative/integrative models can have in managing depression in primary care (Katon et al., 1996). Other researchers have found similar positive outcomes with collaborative/structured interventions in primary care (Mynors-Wallis, Gath, Lloyd-Thomas, & Tomlinson, 1995; Schulberg & Pajer, 1994).

Our own experience with medical/behavioral health collaboration and integration of care within medical clinics has led to creation of flexible and long-term working relationships that employ gradations of integration depending on the needs of the specific patient, couple, or family. Although not a prospective or outcome study, a retrospective utilization review of 1,063 high-utilizing patients treated in this model showed a reduction in physician visits and medical hospitalizations during a 1-year postintervention period, with increased referrals to hospice and mental health professionals (Davis et al., as reported in Peek & Heinrich, 1998). Overall, such collaborative relationships have been well received by our medical colleagues and patients (Fischer et al., 1998). Although primary care and behavioral health professionals will have to await further research that systematically documents effective interventions, collaborative approaches, programs, and best practices, the emerging literature and our own experience suggest there is much fertile ground for collaboration, experimentation, and application of behavioral health skills and approaches adapted to the primary care setting.

Behavioral Health Interventions and Reduced Medical Morbidity and Mortality. Behavioral health interventions have more recently captured the public's and the scientific community's attention in studies that showed reduced morbidity and mortality in heart disease and cancer (Fawzy et al., 1993; Linden, Stossel, & Maurice, 1996). Patients with heart attacks and untreated depression had 3.5 times the likelihood of dying from another heart attack within 6 months post heart attack compared to patients without depression (Frasure-Smith, Lesperance, & Talajic, 1993). It may be that the increased platelet stickiness associated with untreated depressive illness is the mechanism that accounts for the increased risk of dying post heart attack (Glassman & Shapiro, 1998). Fawzy et al. (1993) found that patients with malignant melanoma who attended a 6-week coping skills group had enhanced survival 6 years later. Spiegel, Bloom, and Kraemer (1989) also found enhanced survival for patients with advanced breast cancer who attended a support group, compared to a control group. Given the increased visibility and awareness of the direct and indirect impact of lifestyle and psychosocial variables on preventing complications in chronic medical illnesses and improving medical treatment outcomes, the behavioral health professional in primary care settings can be expected to be called on to help manage the care of patients with a variety of medical disorders including diabetes, rheumatoid arthritis, cancer, heart disease, and hypertension.

Behavioral Health and Stewardship of Health Care Resources. In addition to the value of behavioral health interventions to health outcomes, an important relationship exists between behavioral health interventions and stewardship of health care resources. The literature on medical cost offset has explored the impact of behavioral health disorders on the use of medical services and the relationship between behavioral health interventions and utilization of health services (Simon, Von Korff, & Barlow, 1995; Unutzer et al., 1997). Simon et al. (1995) found large cost differences in the care of primary care patients with anxiety and depressive disorders, even when controlling for medical comorbidity. Cummings in the Hawaii Medicaid project has published a number of papers to demonstrate that focused treatment rather than traditional psychotherapy can effectively manage patients referred from primary care, resulting in significant cost effects (Cummings, 1997). As mentioned earlier, simple retrospective utilization surveys of HealthPartners patients who received interventions from health psychologists in medical settings showed decreases in hospital utilization and physician visits that offset the increases in mental health visits, an encouraging if not scientific finding.

Research Makes a Strong Case for Redesigning Primary Care/Behavioral Health Practice. The literature on mental disorders in primary care makes a strong case for rethinking and redesigning primary care practice. From a population-based perspective, the primary care setting is where most patients with behavioral health disorders will present themselves for treatment. The growing literature on the effectiveness of collaborative treatment approaches between primary care physicians and behavioral health professionals is beginning to set a practice standard for medicine in the future, also suggested by the recent explosion of articles, books, conferences, and "how-to" workshops in this area. Given the traditional separate and parallel systems of mental and medical care that most clinicians work in and most patients receive their care in, the organizational redesign challenges of integrating behavioral health services should not be underestimated. Fundamental organizational design and professional changes are called for (deGruy, 1997; Peek & Heinrich, 1995, 1998).

WHY INTEGRATE MEDICAL AND BEHAVIORAL CARE: DISSATISFACTION WITH THE STATUS QUO

The literature on the care of patients with behavioral health problems in primary care is growing, and so is dissatisfaction with the traditional separate and parallel behavioral health and medical care delivery structures. Many people experience dissatisfaction while providing, receiving, or purchasing care in the traditional separate and parallel structures for medical and behavioral health care delivery.

Separate and Parallel Medical and Behavioral Health Delivery Offers a "Forced Choice." These separate and parallel structures often function like disconnected "boxes" that force providers and patients to choose between medical and behavioral health care, even when the clinical picture calls for a *blend* of biomedical and behavioral care. This structure often forces a choice between:

- Two kinds of problems.
- Two kinds of providers.
- Two kinds of care plans.
- Two kinds of clinics.
- Two kinds of covered benefits.

This either-or delivery structure exists even though most clinical presentations result from an interplay of biomedical and psychosocial factors that require a service blend. The basic problem with separate and parallel design is fragmented care that results when an either-or delivery structure is superimposed on the fluidly interacting clinical factors in health problems and health improvement as they actually play out. The phenomena of human health and illness do not neatly break down into these traditional "either-or" delivery structures. Therefore, providers, patients, care systems, and employers all experience major dissatisfactions stemming from fragmented care in unrealistic "separate and parallel" care delivery systems.

Common Dissatisfactions With the Traditional Separate and Parallel Care Delivery Systems. Tables 2.1–2.4 present examples of what the authors have heard over the years while doing clinical and managerial work, and while doing consultations with patients, clinicians, clinics, and care systems over complex casework and systems redesign involving the interplay of biomedical and psychosocial factors.

Dissatisfaction Is More About Flaws in the Care Model Than Mental Illnesses. The root problem giving rise to the dissatisfactions presented in Tables 2.1–2.4 is the "either-or" delivery structure, not behavioral health disorders per se. That is, most of these dissatisfactions are not so much about behavioral health disorders as they are about delivery system problems encountered while trying to take care of patients with behavioral health factors in the picture. These dissatisfactions are the symptoms of a system poorly suited to the clinical realities it confronts daily. The traditional separate and parallel approach to care delivery is so unrealistic that symptoms are sure to follow for everyone. Put another way, when available services don't meet the clinical needs, unhappiness, confusion, and misutilization result. On the other hand, when the health care system is designed to handle mental illnesses or behavioral health factors as a normal part of health care, these dissatisfactions begin

TABLE 2.1
Examples of Common Clinician Dissatisfactions With Separate
and Parallel Medical and Behavioral Health Care Systems

---

1. You don't know enough about the complex patient sitting in front of you.
   - There are several charts, all with just a piece of the story.
   - One of the charts is not available, but you need information that's in it.
   - The one person who knows the whole case well is on vacation.
2. Contacting other clinicians for more information is laborious or impractical.
   - Efforts to contact another provider results in "phone tag."
   - If you are a primary care doctor, the therapist can't talk to you due to confidentiality issues.
   - Practices and schedules are set up to expedite referrals, not to expedite talking about cases first.
3. Making referrals between primary care and behavioral health care can be an adventure. If you are a primary care doctor,
   - You find it difficult to engage patients about behavioral health factors in their physical problems.
   - You have to "sell" behavioral health referrals to patients who see their problems as medical.
   - You don't know the behavioral health providers, what they do, or who to refer to (as you do with the other specialists you use)
   - "Behavioral health is like a black hole my patients disappear into": You get little feedback. If you are a behavioral health professional,
   - Some patients come in saying, "I don't know why I'm here—my doctor sent me."
   - Some patients come in saying, "My doctor said you will do X with me," but the referral "order" doesn't sound right and you don't want to unsettle the patient or undermine the doctor.
4. Many patient problems don't fit neatly into "medical" or "behavioral health" domains.
   - If you are a primary care physician, it's a challenge to address emotional factors in headache or low back pain in a 15-minute visit.
   - Somatization is common and very difficult to address effectively using an "either-or" approach to medical and behavioral health care.
   - Distress and adjustment problems frequently arise for families coping with chronic illnesses.
   - "Thick charts" and unfocused high utlization result when services don't match clinical needs.
   - If you are a primary care doctor: (a) Some patients keep coming back even when you feel you don't have anything left to offer. (b) You find yourself ordering another test or referral but have the feeling you aren't getting to the real issues.
   - If you are a behavioral health provider and the patient focuses on physical problems, you don't really know what to make of it (and it's not so easy to find out).
5. Complex situations that don't fit separate behavioral health/medical systems "can ruin your day."
   - Some patients complain about their physician to the therapist, and complain about their therapist to the physician.
   - It takes much less time to refill the pain, tranquilizer, or time-off prescription than to confront the problem with the patient (but you know you have to).
   - You see a certain name on the schedule and want to go home.
   - You really need a team for some of your cases but it is laborious to push uphill to invent a team for every new situation that arises, so you just "tough it out alone."

---

to recede. It is a mistake to conclude that mental illnesses are the problem; the main problem lies in the design of our delivery system.

Bringing behavioral health and medical care together is a move in the right direction. But approaches based on merely detecting mental disorders and referring them out of the primary care system have only limited effect on those dissatisfactions. A "detect and refer" model, by itself, leaves the separate and parallel delivery structure intact by attempting to root out mental illness and substance abuse in primary care for separate behavioral health treatment. Although this may provide some short-term relief, in the long run this approach does not ease those dissatisfactions enough to carry us into a successful future.

In this larger context that includes care system design as well as clinical care, *detection* means detection of all sorts of care process and organizational problems, not just

TABLE 2.2

Examples of Common Patient Dissatisfactions With Separate
and Parallel Medical and Behavioral Health Care Systems

1. "I'm physically ill but they think its all in my head."
   - "I don't need to receive behavioral health care. I have a medical problem (and I'll prove it!)."
   - "I realize my life and my emotions affect my health, but I don't like the implication that my physical problem is only a psychological symptom."
2. "When will someone ask about how our family life and problems are affecting our health?"
   - "Living like this must have something to do with our physical problems."
3. "I have a family doctor, a specialist, a psychiatrist, a therapist, and a group therapist, and the left hand doesn't know what the right hand is doing."
   - "They keep sending me from one person to the next!"
   - "I repeat the same story over and over to every new person."
   - "Why can't they talk to each other!"
   - "No wonder health insurance is so high!"
4. "It seems like I'm at various doctors all the time and still not getting better."
   - "I get the feeling I'm not being a good patient."
   - "I get the feeling no one wants to see me anymore."
   - "It seems like they are trying to cut me off."
   - "I get the feeling everything is my fault."
   - "I get the feeling everything is their fault, and my lawyer is looking into it!"

TABLE 2.3

Examples of Common Care System Dissatisfactions With Separate
and Parallel Medical and Behavioral Health Care Systems

1. "Thick charts": High and unfocused utilization of outpatient physician and behavioral health care visits.
   - When delivery services don't match clinical needs, lots of "searching" and unnecessary visits result.
   - Disability management is a major, but often underaddressed, behavioral issue across most medical diseases.
2. Unnecessarily high hospital and referral costs.
   - Narrower understanding of the patient and family leaves clinicians and families with fewer options
   - Patient is referred or hospitalized when a break in continuity or coordination of care occurs at the wrong time.
3. Patients who are often unhappy with care, even though they get a lot of it.
   - Some of these become "difficult" patients: "Most difficult patients started out merely as complex."
   - A sizable group of patients get to be known as "crabby" or "noncompliant."
   - A group of patients are "searching," "doctor-shopping," or writing letters trying to secure help.
   - Patients whose behavior splits the team (if there is one), or who employ difficult behavior to force teamwork and a care plan.
4. Misunderstandings occur between primary care and behavioral health care providers.
   - There exists limited understanding of what the different professions can contribute to the entire care of patients and families.
   - "Culture clash" is based on different ways of training, knowing, talking, thinking, and working.
   - Pejorative mutual stereotypes are based on limited contact and opportunity to work out problems.
5. The problems of separate and parallel medical and mental health are no longer acceptable as "a normal cost of doing business."
   - Care systems can no longer postpone redesigning basic care processes to improve total system quality.
   - Care systems can no longer afford the satisfaction and service penalties associated with fragmented care along the medical–behavioral health split.
   - Care systems can no longer absorb unnecessary financial costs associated with fragmented care and hidden behavioral health problems played out in medical clinics.
   - Care systems must meet new NCQA standards for primary care/behavioral health integration.

TABLE 2.4
Examples of Employer Dissatisfaction With Separate and
Parallel Medical and Behavioral Health Care Systems

1. Traditional behavioral health care is often seen as an expense of dubious value.
   - It is a "black hole" employees and benefits dollars can disappear into.
   - Therapies often don't emphasize the value to patients of good work adjustment; instead, they are often preoccupied with abstract and impractical psychological matters.
   - Therapies don't appear to have the needs of employers in mind, such as getting people back to work or being more productive and less absorbed with their personal problems.
2. Employers experience productivity or citizenship problems with some employees who have mental health or substance abuse problems but who will have nothing to do with behavioral health care.
   - Employers are aware that employee distress and health problems don't sort themselves neatly into traditional behavioral health and medical categories.
   - Employers already know that primary care is the de facto mental health system.
   - Employers already know that psychologically distressed patients are not only more expensive employees, but also more expensive to provide health care benefits for.
   - Employers know that most primary care is not geared up well for the psychosocial dimension of health care problems that employees routinely present with.
3. Employers experience productivity problems attributable to family and marital distress not covered by benefits, but that play out in medical and employer costs anyway.
   - Ordinary family and marital distress are usually excluded from covered benefits but often adversely affect productivity, other employees, supervisors, and other employer and health care costs.
   - Many employers are already paying additional costs for employee assistance programs (EAPs) to handle noncovered psychosocial problems of employees.
4. Employees with complex cases complain about fragmentation in the care system.
   - Benefits managers hear employees complain about fragmentation or poor service in the care system.
   - Benefits managers are asked to intervene for employees asking for exceptions to benefits, additional services, noncovered or alternative services, or extended numbers of sessions or dollar limits, all because the available covered services don't match the clinical needs.

detection of psychiatric disorders or substance abuse. Detection of systems problems, commonplace fragmentation of care, and hidden psychosocial factors in care of medical illness may be as important or more important to the big picture in primary care than detection of mental illnesses per se.

APPROACHES TO PRIMARY AND BEHAVIORAL HEALTH CARE INTEGRATION: DISTINCTIONS AND CONCEPTS

Behavioral health integration isn't just one thing, and not all behavioral health has to be integrated with medical care. The following sections outline concepts and draw distinctions useful in understanding alternative forms of integration or possible relationships between behavioral health care and medical care. These concepts and distinctions are commonly encountered in the field, with many variations and shadings, and the following rendition is not produced as a definitive version of these concepts and distinctions.

Horizontal and Vertical Integration

This frequently drawn distinction, used in many industrial and health care contexts (e.g., Strosahl, 1997, 1998), refers to two approaches to integrating behavioral health: by an *overall population* of patients, whatever their health conditions, or by a *condition* suffered by a subset of the population.

Horizontal Integration. Horizontal integration means behavioral health services are designed as part of the primary care function, providing care to the broad primary care population, whatever the needs of that population. This is consistent with primary care's vision for itself. The unit of physician responsibility is the whole patient, or family, across health problems or stage in life. In administrative terms, a primary care physician has a "panel" of patients to take care of rather than a particular disease or organ system to take care of. Similarly, a primary care clinic is responsible for the care of its population of patients, whatever their diseases or health status.

With horizontal integration, the behavioral health component is woven into the generalist approach to the health care of patients, regardless of the combination of biomedical, psychosocial, or emotional factors that is presented. Patients are not required to present with or articulate explicit behavioral health agendas or a defined medical condition in order to qualify for help. This is especially important considering that it is very common for patients to hold their entire suffering in a medical frame of reference, even when a purely medical approach is only part of the story or has little left to offer them. These patients are very unlikely to seek behavioral health referral on their own and are often quite reluctant to accept behavioral health referrals even when urged to do so. Horizontally integrated behavioral health does not force patients and providers to accept a "mental" explanation for the problems in order to involve behavioral health factors and providers in the care.

Vertical Integration. Vertical integration means the entire care process *for a particular condition* is mapped out, with behavioral health expertise "designed in" at the right places from start to finish. This represents a standardized process of care tailored to the target condition and anchored in evidence-based best practices.

Although a special condition-specific process of care is mapped out, this does not necessarily mean that the care is "carved out" to a new set of providers or clinic. Vertical and horizontal strategies are both primary care strategies that can be carried out by primary care providers with the appropriate help from specialty medical and behavioral health care providers. At HealthPartners, most vertically integrated behavioral health has up to now taken place within medical specialties (e.g., endocrinology, oncology, neurology, and dental for chronic temperomandibular disorder) that were closely allied with primary care in the first place. At the same time, there is increasing focus within primary care settings on vertically integrated care of common problems encountered in primary care, such as diabetes (O'Connor & Pronk, 1998) and depression (DIAMOND Project[2]).

----

[2]The DIAMOND Project (1998), named as an acronym from "Depression Is A MANageable Disease," was a study of the feasibility of systematizing primary care for treatment of depression, by the HealthPartners Research Foundation, funded by MacArthur Foundation, with L. I. Solberg (principal investigator), L. R. Fischer (co-principal investigator), T. F. Davis, D. S. Alter, M. A. Baird, R. L. Heinrich, S. F. Lucas, C. J. Peek, and R. P. Power.

Specialty Behavioral Health Care and Integrated Behavioral Health Care

This distinction helps us think about care system design and developing the team-work of various kinds required in health care. In baseball, there are important spots on the field where players need to be positioned (because the ball often goes there). The duties and skills of ballplayers occupying the various positions differ in some predictable ways, but underneath it all, they all know baseball and act as ballplayers. Similarly, specialty and integrated behavioral health care represent two complementary approaches to the deployment of behavioral health clinicians and their tools within a complete health care system. The most basic distinction here is between the practice of behavioral health care as a *specialty*, positioned in the care system like the medical and surgical specialties, and the practice of behavioral health care positioned within a medical clinic or care team as a standard, integrated, and permanent function of the medical team. Many different variations and terms for this are in present use, with no single language pattern yet in widespread use. The following distinctions and terms therefore represent what the authors have found useful.

Behavioral Health as a Specialty. This is sometimes called *specialty behavioral health, specialty mental health,* or simply *traditional mental health*. Medical specialties (e.g., neurology, endocrinology, gastroenterology) are oriented around a single constellation of diseases or an organ system. Specialty care is usually delivered in a separate clinic bearing the name of the focal disease or organ system (e.g., oncology or cardiology), and patients reach specialists on a referral basis from primary care. As a generalization, specialty behavioral health follows a similar pattern: It is oriented around mental health and substance abuse illnesses and problems, care is delivered in separate behavioral health clinics, and care plans are more or less focused on behavioral health disorders rather than general health care and are carried out more or less independently by behavioral health professionals. Specialty behavioral health is one of many specialties that surround primary care and is linked via consults and referrals. Although most health plans or insurance permits direct patient self-referral to behavioral health care, referral is the main pathway primary care physicians follow to get mental health or substance abuse assessment or therapy for their patients.

Specialty behavioral health care services may include inpatient and intensive outpatient services, psychiatric consultation and treatment, plus group and individual therapies focused on covered mental illnesses and conditions. These are critical functions of any care system. But a traditional "behavioral health as a specialty" model, if forced to cover all care system needs for behavioral health care, leaves the care system with the separate and parallel delivery structures described earlier, with all the problems that go with it.

As a generalization, the specialty behavioral health care model tends to view behavioral health care work in terms of psychiatric diagnoses and diseases more than as behavioral, emotional, or comorbid contributing factors to other health problems and symptomatic distress. In the traditional context of behavioral health as a specialty service, the idea of *integration* might be seen as screening for psychiatric disorders and referral for behavioral health treatment, or colocating a specialty behavioral health care practice in a medical clinic. *Collaboration*, in this model, might be seen as coordinating separate and parallel medical and behavioral health care plans where the behavioral health portion might consist of hospitalization or medication for mental illnesses, programmatic group or individual therapies for serious mental health or substance abuse conditions, or taking over the behavioral health work from primary care providers during periods when mental health or substance abuse conditions become severe or unusual.

Improved consultation and coordination between medical providers and mental health/substance specialists is no doubt a big improvement over completely disconnected systems. But these adjustments to the traditional specialty referral model for behavioral health care do not get to the heart of a big portion of what is needed for primary care patients and physicians. Using the baseball analogy, there are at least two positions on the field that need to be filled by behavioral health clinicians, and making one player cover both positions is a big stretch that leads to dissatisfaction and a competitive disadvantage.

One difficulty that goes with using specialty behavioral health care (even when "attached" to a primary care site) to handle all the problems that surface in primary care is a higher threshold for patient eligibility for reimbursable behavioral health care: The patient usually must have a diagnosable behavioral health disorder (i.e., a *DSM–IV* diagnosis). If the patient has a chronic headache or stress-linked symptoms without a diagnosable mental condition, it may be difficult for the behavioral health care professional to find a reimbursable behavioral health care code, particularly if the patient is adamant that he or she has no behavioral health problems. Many subclinical states of distress or *DSM–IV* "V" code conditions (e.g., marital problems) are not covered by insurance, even though they play a large part in many difficult and costly cases in primary care (Simon et al., 1995; Von Korff et al., 1992). Although the *DSM–IV* code for "psychological factors affecting physical condition" can apply broadly to these situations, the basic (and totally unnecessary) strain here is the need to legitimize behavioral health care on the basis of a separate behavioral health care benefit rather than a comprehensive health care benefit that allows flexible use of various kinds of providers on the extended medical team.

From a patient service perspective, a specialty behavioral health care model requires the patient to be able and willing to articulate a mental health or substance problem (or at least go along with the physician's view of it) in order to go to a mental health or chemical health professional to get help. This is just fine for patients who can pick up the phone and say why they are calling. But many patients struggling with symptoms for which they go to their primary care physician cannot initially see a behavioral health connection and "won't go." Even if they do reach a therapist, complaining of aches and pains or denying behavioral health problems is often a quick route back to the physician. Forcing a behavioral or "mental" explanation on a patient who cannot see it yet is very poor service, or even a disservice.

From a patient access perspective, if all primary care patients with a behavioral health problem were referred to specialty behavioral health care, there wouldn't be enough psychiatrists or behavioral health clinicians to handle the load (Katzelnick, 1997). Furthermore, many patients wouldn't know why they were there ("I don't know why I am here—my doctor sent me"), and the problems of separate and parallel service delivery would remain. Because primary care is the de facto mental health system, it is unfair to patients (as well as providers) to expect the traditional specialty behavioral health care model, all by itself, to serve the behavioral health needs of a population. Specialty treatment (e.g., hospital, day treatment, and other therapies) for mental health and substance abuse disorders is essential, but cannot be expected to effectively cope with the volume and range of psychosocially related presentations in primary care.

From a teamwork perspective, a specialty mental health model, if left to do it all, tends to reinforce mutual stereotypes and misunderstandings between primary care and behavioral health care providers, because they usually relate at a distance and work from quite different philosophies and culture (McDaniel, Campbell, & Seaburn, 1995). With little opportunity to routinely discuss and resolve problems that do arise, misunderstandings may linger and mutual stereotypes flourish. Colocating specialty behavioral health care and primary care may improve this somewhat, but building up good teamwork, mutual trust, and rapid recovery from problems requires people to interact more routinely and more personally than usually takes place through referrals, phone calls, or even chats on the way to the parking lot.

Integrated Behavioral Health.   Integrated behavioral health refers to behavioral health care positioned in the care system as a normal part of the basic medical care function. Behavioral health clinicians are positioned within a medical clinic or care team as a standard, integrated, and permanent function of the medical team, including its culture and systems. There are two closely related variations on this:

- Behavioral health integrated in primary care (sometimes referred to as *primary care mental health* or *primary mental health care*). Behavioral health clinicians and functions are integrated into primary care functions, clinics, and teams.
- Behavioral health integrated in specialty medical care (i.e., medical or surgical specialties). Behavioral health clinicians and functions are integrated into medical and surgical specialty functions, clinics, and teams. (We don't call this *specialty behavioral health* in parallel with *primary care behavioral health* because of confusion with *behavioral health as a specialty* described earlier.)

Because this is a book about primary care, the rest of this section describes behavioral health as integrated in primary care. But most of what follows also applies to behavioral health integration in medical or surgical specialties. Keep in mind the following generalizations on the difference between the focus of primary care and specialty care:

- Primary care is oriented around care of specific *people* (or populations) across all the conditions they suffer from. A patient goes to their primary doctor for help with *whatever*, "because you're my doctor and you know *me*."
- Specialty care is oriented around care of specific *conditions* across all the people who suffer from them. A patient goes to a specialist for help with a *condition*, "because you're my doctor's expert and you know my *disease*."

Such differences in mission or focus between primary and specialty care apply to the integrated behavioral health providers in both settings as well. Integrated behavioral health providers in both primary care and specialty care take their cues from the basic mission of the setting they work in.

As stated earlier, "behavioral health integrated with primary care" is behavioral health care positioned as a normal part of the basic primary care function. The integrated behavioral health provider helps with whatever behavioral, emotional, or behavioral health-related factors emerge as important in the care of primary care patients. Common areas in which integrated behavioral health providers are involved at HealthPartners are chronic illnesses, headaches and other pain complaints, somatization or multiple vague complaints, industrial injury or worker's compensation, and with comorbid mental illnesses that complicate medical treatment and adherence. The behavioral health provider comes to the primary care clinic as a long-missing member of the primary care team, and shares the same broad population-based or "public health" mission of primary care, rather than being focused on a particular disease. The work crosses almost all medical conditions and is not characterized only by (or even primarily by) treatment for diagnosable mental disorders. Integrated behavioral health clinicians typically work out of medical exam rooms in the medical hallways, schedule with the same receptionists and scheduling system as the physicians, use the same waiting room, write in the medical chart, and have their name and picture on the wall and appear in the staff directory along with the other primary care clinicians.

Primary care behavioral health providers work within the primary care culture, systems, space, practice patterns, and philosophy, rather than importing an island of "behavioral health as a specialty" culture to the primary care clinic. The behavioral health clinician accepts and adapts to the medical culture without trying to change it or become insulated from it. Over a period of years, integrated behavioral health care people often have an important effect on primary care culture, particularly in a change toward greater acceptance and openness regarding difficult clinician–patient relationships and how to form care teams and plans that make clinic practice more satisfying and lead to better outcomes (see Lucas & Peek, 1997, for case examples).

Integrated behavioral health providers are willing and able to engage and work within a patient's medical explanation for their problems, without insisting that the patient be able to articulate a behavioral health care agenda. They do not press the patient to come out with the "underlying issues" or say "what's really going on." This is important because many primary care patients have significant behavioral health issues factored into their overall health concerns but are not aware of it at the outset. It is common for patients to hold their entire suffering in a medical frame of reference, even when a purely medical approach has little more to offer them. These patients are unlikely to seek psychotherapy on their own, and are often reluctant to start off talking about personal issues. They fear being "written off" as "it's all in your head," and are reluctant to begin psychologically when they believe a medical problem is the real issue. Only when they consider that the way they are living or feeling may have something to do with their suffering will they move into the personal, psychological, or behavioral areas.

Integrated behavioral health providers refrain from thinking of such a patient as "not a good therapy candidate," nor do they complain that "all the patient could think about was headache and fatigue." Instead, the clinicians realize that the situation calls for something besides application of traditional psychotherapy or psychological assessment. The situation calls for the therapist to help a patient distill a personal agenda out of a whole pot of physical suffering and anger at life or medical people while allowing the patient to retain the medical frame of reference for the suffering. This does not necessarily look or sound like psychological assessment or therapy to the patient or to the therapist. We suggest that behavioral health care clinicians who have developed this part of their professional repertoire have expanded their profession beyond the traditional techniques of mental health and substance abuse therapy into a broader profession of primary health care. Hence, at HealthPartners this new and expanded behavioral health role is called *primary care mental health* or *behavioral health integrated in primary care*. (See Strosahl, 1997, 1998, for similar description of "primary mental health care" at Group Health Cooperative of Puget Sound.)

Primary care patients are not the only "customers" for integrated behavioral health. Consultation to physicians and nurses (rather than the therapist taking over the care) is very common. The goal of such consultation is to help these care providers to broaden their repertoire and increase the effectiveness of their interventions and to help them manage their reactions to "difficult" patients. It is not uncommon for the integrated behavioral health providers to help the medical clinic physicians and staff recognize and constructively deal with personal "buttons" pushed by particularly challenging patients in the clinic (Lucas & Peek, 1997). Behavioral health providers also consult with primary care providers to keep patients being treated for chronic pain, anxiety, or industrial injury from falling into "disability ruts."

In addition to consultation, behavioral health providers participate in the ongoing care of patients with chronic medical illnesses such as diabetes, asthma, or cancer when depression, anxiety, coping skills, or psychosocial factors complicate medical management, patient morale, or family coping. When the behavioral health care provider does ongoing care, it is in the context of the overall medical care plan carried out by the medical team as managed by the physician rather than as a part of an independent behavioral health care plan. A few primary care patients have both significant medical illnesses and serious behavioral health diagnoses such as depression or personality disorder. When these patients do not engage well in specialty behavioral health care clinics, they are treated by the primary care team over a period of years, with the integrated behavioral health provider as a major figure on that care team.

Integrated behavioral health providers help make accurate, timely, and successful referrals to specialty behavioral health care when patients present with those needs, or as they begin to recognize specialty behavioral health care agendas within their physical suffering (e.g., incest survivors with chronic pain). It is very important to work with somatically preoccupied patients in the medical clinic until they are able to see how their personal situations affect their health or begin to accept behavioral health factors as part of the explanation for their symptoms. Only if and when such patients can articulate a need for the kind of therapy provided through specialty behavioral health care should they be referred. This process of distilling a behavioral health care agenda out of a pot of physical suffering could be called "pretherapy therapy" and is typically done by the integrated behavioral health provider. Specialty mental health referrals succeed only when both the patient and the clinician can articulate the purpose of the referral.

In capitated care systems, the cost of integrated behavioral health tends to be thought of as part of medical cost, rather than only as behavioral health care cost. There is far more emphasis on deploying the behavioral health care providers to exert leverage on overall health status and costs than on finding a way to generate billable behavioral health care codes or to reduce utilization of behavioral health services. Financial models for integrated behavioral health are probably simplest in a capitated environment, but creative ways to achieve the integrated clinical goal can be found in fee-for-service systems as well.

Acute and Chronic Care

Acute Mental Health and Substance Abuse Care. Acute episodes may well need specialty mental health care such as intensive therapy, groups, or hospital. But with acute episodes, the traditional practice of referring out at once to distant specialty behavioral health care may introduce delays, add strain to what may already be a stressed-out patient and family, reduce the amount or accuracy of general background knowledge of the case, and remove patients from what may be the familiar support of their primary care clinic. Integrated behavioral health providers can help primary care clinics assess and manage acute episodes of behavioral health disorders that might otherwise have to be referred out, even for assessment or triage. An integrated behavioral health therapist working closely with physicians can help with such acute episodes, but this is not the only alternative. For example, several HealthPartners primary care clinics have added a psychiatric nurse to their medical nursing triage function for this purpose, and to ensure accurate and timely specialty behavioral health assessment and referral when necessary.

Some patients with acute behavioral health conditions (e.g., panic attacks or depression) may exhibit physical symptoms that lead to referral to several specialists or repeated testing before a positive behavioral health care diagnosis is made (e.g., referrals or emergency-room visits for "heart attacks" or "asthma attacks" with patients with pronounced panic disorder, some of whom may also have organic factors in play). This pattern is common, expensive, and very poor patient service. Without behavioral health integration, primary care physicians tend to "diagnose mental health problems by exclusion," but with it they are able to more quickly reach positive diagnoses with behavioral health expertise on the primary care team.

Chronic Illness Care. Ongoing management of chronic illness tends to fall heavily on the patients and families themselves, giving rise to the need for what is often called *patient activation.* Healthy behaviors, self-care, and appropriate family involvement are key to effective chronic care. Primary care physicians can maintain ongoing treatments, an explanatory framework, structure, guidance, support, and other routine care, but cannot themselves "make it happen" for patients and families. Integrated behavioral health providers can help primary care clinics prevent exacerbations, complications, or delayed recovery associated with psychosocial problems such as depression, family or marital dysfunction, or social isolation that physicians might not be as aware of, have time for, or be nearly as effective at doing.

An example of the potential in addressing behavioral risk factors in chronic illness is the dramatic finding (previously cited in the literature section) that depression in patients with heart disease better predicts better predicts future cardiac events than coronary artery damage, high cholesterol, and smoking (Carney et al., 1988). Professional- and nonprofessional-led psychoeducational and therapy groups can be a helpful part of the primary care clinic's overall approach to chronic care management. An integrated behavioral health provider can help the clinic take advantage of findings such as these.

Healthy Behavior Change

Unhealthy behaviors such as chemical abuse, smoking, fatty diet, low fitness, and overweight are strongly associated with increased incidence of chronic illnesses such as diabetes and heart disease, and with increased health care costs. Modifiable health risks from unhealthy behaviors affect illness and health care cost expenditures across multiple chronic illnesses. (Goetzel et al., 1998). Key behavioral factors (weight control, lipid control, blood pressure control, and "readiness to change") affect risk across multiple chronic illnesses (Pronk, Tan, & O'Connor, 1999). Behavioral factors are strongly predictive of the total burden of illness and costs in a population. Although it is possible to stratify populations and care programs by disease, the interventions used may be essentially the same, because the serious behavioral risk factors are common across so many chronic conditions. Prochaska et al. (1994) proposed a systematic process with stages for healthy behavior change applicable across diseases. These findings suggest that addressing a core group of behavioral risk factors may provide the best clinical and financial leverage for the behavioral portion of chronic care management.

Primary care clinics and physicians traditionally have not been well equipped to systematically deal with the difficult area of healthy behavior change. Physicians have often relied on education (in the form of lectures, exhortation, or admonishment) and orders to patients who are not yet ready for that particular change but would benefit from healthier behaviors. The perceived inability of patients to adopt healthier behaviors and provider inability to "make it happen" is a serious frustration for physicians. Work in the area of healthy behavior change (Prochaska et al., 1994) has shown that tailoring patient, physician, or care system intervention to the change stage that a given patient is currently in greatly increases the likelihood of healthy behavior change. This should improve patient and provider satisfaction along with health status.

Although this is not traditional "mental health" or "chemical health" care, there is increasing sensitivity to the importance of "behavioral health" in this broader sense within primary care. Integrated behavioral health providers may become increasingly concerned with helping primary care physicians effectively address unhealthy behaviors, especially those related to substance abuse and unhealthy behaviors often related to depression.

ENGAGING PRIMARY CARE CLINICS: SELECTING A FOCUS FOR BEHAVIORAL HEALTH CARE INTEGRATION

Clinician, patient, care system, and employer "dissatisfactions" with separate and parallel medical and behavioral health care delivery were presented earlier. Although fragmented care and systems problems characterize these lists, every primary care clinic or practice group experiences these problems in a somewhat different way, and has somewhat different opportunities for taking advantage of the benefits of integrated behavioral health. As said earlier, actual primary care clinics are in the midst of a great many pressures and changes already, and behavioral health integration projects are very likely to face stiff competition from many other priorities in an already rushed primary care practice. As a practical matter, a clinic's particular behavioral health care integration strategies must clearly and squarely address the clinic's own dissatisfactions around behavioral health care; otherwise, the effort won't engage people. Successful integration strategies appeal to what already matters to patients and primary care clinicians, and this varies from place to place, and over time.

Helping Clinics Identify Their Own Problems and Articulate Their Own Visions

We have found it useful to help clinics discover their own needs and identify where they already have sufficient readiness for change before suggesting an integration approach or focal area. It is very common for primary care clinics to feel distress, dissatisfaction, and pressures regarding behavioral health factors in their practice, but not so common for a clinic to be able to clearly articulate those problems or a realistic alternative. For many, the problems of separate and parallel medical and behavioral health care systems are like background noise in a room: You habituate to it.

When people are thoroughly habituated to the problems of separate and parallel systems, it can be difficult for them at first to articulate just what the problem really is. Problems accepted for years and years as a "normal cost of doing business" still affect people, but may at first escape clear description. Therefore, we have found it helpful to precipitate this exploration by using a "hip-pocket" consultation process that consists of helping the clinic answer several questions regarding the psychosocial or behavioral health aspects of its practice. These are:

1. What kinds of important recurring problems or dissatisfactions with the psychosocial aspect of giving care is the clinic experiencing?
2. What kind of "preferred future" vis-à-vis behavioral health would the clinic or physicians like?
3. What should the clinic find out about its patient population before selecting a focus for integration?
4. Because the clinic has to start somewhere, what does the first integration project or pilot have to focus on and demonstrate?
5. What kind of help from behavioral health care clinicians does the clinic think it needs?
6. How do behavioral health providers need to be prepared for roles in the clinic?
7. How will the clinic learn enough to decide whether and how to move its pilot toward the mainstream?

Helping the clinic begin to answer these questions brings the integration project and its goals into sharper focus, and moves it from "ideology," "another good idea," or a "should," to something that truly engages people with what already matters to them where they live.

Common Things That Already Matter to Primary Care Physicians and Clinics

Such consultative discussions with primary care physicians and clinics reveal that improving quality and service is always a priority. But underneath that high-level goal, here are several examples of common focal areas that already matter to physicians and are good candidates for behavioral health integration:

- "Thick charts" reflecting somatization and/or high and unfocused outpatient utilization.
- "Difficult patients" that are emotionally draining to physicians and clinic staff.

- Unnecessary physician visits that reduce physician appointment availability.
- An alternative to the problems of traditional behavioral health referrals.
- Better medical clinic triage of behavioral health disorders and better consultation over medications and psychiatric emergencies.
- Reduction of unnecessary hospital and referral costs.
- Promotion of healthy behavior change for patients with chronic illnesses or risk factors.
- Help with a particular disease or condition (e.g., depression, chronic pain, industrial injury).

Each of these and other focal areas represents a potential starting point for behavioral health integration. The goal for early discussions is to get to the point where the clinic can clearly articulate one or two such practical goals for which behavioral health integration can be part of the solution.

Focus the Effort on One or Two Areas That Strongly Matter to the Clinic

The initial consultation task is to find the one or two practical goals that are synergistic with everything else that matters and is going on in the clinic. As said earlier, don't make a behavioral health proposal that ends up merely competing with the clinic's other priorities! It is a failure path for behavioral health people to go into a medical clinic recommending something that doesn't fit the clinic's situation or culture. For example, without having worked through a clear priority and reason for doing psychological screening with its patients as part of a larger plan, a clinic is very unlikely to tolerate another piece of paper, procedure, thing to remember, or disconnected piece of data to which members have to respond. Avoid creating a behavioral health care integration project that appears to complicate clinic life or that merely adds a new layer of work. All new elements and changes proposed have to address felt needs and then improve the practice in a very practical way, or they will fail. This means that well-intentioned behavioral health providers with an armful of studies, good ideas, and new tools are in for disappointment unless they go through a clinic-by-clinic process of understanding true needs and readiness for change, and are willing to engage clinics in what already matters to them (not just to the behavioral health providers). We have written more on how to help both behavioral health and primary care clinicians and clinics move toward behavioral health integration, using HealthPartners as an example (Peek & Heinrich, 1998).

INTEGRATING PRIMARY AND BEHAVIORAL HEALTH CARE: A THEME WITH VARIATIONS

We just said that primary care clinics and clinicians experience the problems of separate and parallel medical and behavioral health care in several different ways, and that different goals for behavioral health integration speak to different clinics at different times. We suggested that practical realities of care system change mean putting the consultant "hat" on and finding out what matters to clinics, one by one, and helping them design an approach to behavioral health integration that works for them. But if there are no off-the-shelf solutions that work for everyone, what ties it all together? How does a person make sense of all the local variations? What about "best practices", or is it all just a subjective matter of "what works for me"?

A Theme With Variations

We think of the multiplicity of possible local approaches as a "theme with variations," rather than as as a grab bag of unrelated and subjectively conceived projects. The top-level theme is better integration of care (less fragmentation) along the traditional "mind–body split" in health care. Subthemes emerge, such as using local data to help select a local clinical focus; using published literature to flag promising approaches; developing long-term collaborative relationships between physicians and therapists; training therapists to work within a medical culture; involving families; harmonizing the clinical, operational, and financial aspects of behavioral health integration; and taking a developmental approach to organizational change. Themes such as these can pull local variations together in one larger picture and help distinguish promising ideas from known pitfalls. Such underlying themes and design principles for improving medical/behavioral health integration have been described elsewhere in books (e.g., Blount, 1998; Cummings, Cummings, & Johnson, 1997; Doherty & Baird, 1983, 1987; Haber & Mitchell, 1998; Seaburn et al., 1996), and in many articles, such as deGruy (1997), McDaniel et al. (1995), and others cited in this chapter that were published in *Families, Systems, and Health*, an interdisciplinary journal devoted to this field.[3] We make no attempt to summarize all the unifying concepts, principles, and findings that could tie local variations together, but we offer a device here to help tie together the assessment and intervention approaches for some of the common focal areas that interest primary care clinicians.

A Generic Care Process for Organizing Local Variations in Behavioral Health Integration

To keep from being "lost in the trees" in the midst of designing local variations, it is helpful to keep "the forest" in view while working out the specifics for any number of different clinical targets. This can be especially important if a person or organization has several customized initiatives in several focal areas going on at once. Under these conditions, people can lose the "theme" in the midst of the "variations." Fortunately, it is possible to construct a generic care process that can be used across conditions or focal areas. We have found the following generic care process useful as a conceptual tool for planning integrated behavioral health programs across focal areas (adapted from a care process for depression in primary care used in the DIAMOND Project of 1998 at HealthPartners). The following stages are written to be generic and applicable across clinical conditions.

1. *Recognition.* Proactive identification of developing problems that may need attention in an individual or family. Here, the provider or clinic is alert for signs and in-

---

[3]*Families, Systems, and Health* is the peer-reviewed journal of collaborative family health care (S. McDaniel and T. Campbell, editors, PO Box 20838, Rochester, NY 14602). This journal is a benefit to members of the Collaborative Family Healthcare Coalition, an interdisciplinary professional community for those working in this broad area (40 West 12th St., New York, NY 10011).

dications that there may be something important going on that requires further investigation and possibly initiation of an episode of care or prevention. Recognition may stem from a population-based risk stratification, individual clinical data that providers see directly, or utilization patterns associated with a developing problem.

2. *Engagement.* Next, the provider engages the patient in exploring a possible agenda that he or she may not have recognized, or if recognized has not brought forward. The goal is to assess the patient's readiness to hear about a possible problem, negotiate with the patient an acceptable way of understanding such a problem, and help the patient become an informed participant in further evaluation and a possible episode of care.

3. *Evaluation.* This involves discovering what is really going on—collecting and synthesizing the wide range of clinical facts, problems, diagnoses, history, patient and family resources, and whatever else is going on in the overall case. The patient is assessed for readiness for the various clinically appropriate treatment options or care plans.

4. *Management.* The most efficient and effective care plan that ensures the appropriate level and kind of treatment is created and systematically carried out. The care plan is developed in the context of all the evaluation data and of everything else going on in the overall case, and in terms of patient and family readiness (and ability) to participate in various kinds of care plans.

5. *Maintenance.* This last step involves ongoing monitoring, tracking, and communication (e.g., phone or mail followup, chart and progress note sharing, proactive coordination of care). When an episode of care is completed, the question is, "What now?" What does the patient do to prevent relapse, maintain his or her "regimen," or participate in a long-term follow-up plan, as characteristic in chronic illnesses? If care is needed over an extended period, use an explicit framework of roles and goals (that includes the part played by patient and family) with systems for reliable coordination and communication.

This five-step generic care process is a more spelled-out version of the common "detection, treatment, maintenance" process. The main difference is in explicitly including the first two steps, recognition (scanning proactively for possibly necessary episodes of care) and engagement (negotiating patient acceptance of the possible need for some kind of care plan). These steps are featured here because they are often underplayed in actual care settings in a way that leaves the care system in a reactive (rather than proactive) position, and with too many patients who don't understand or want to participate in the care plan their doctor has ordered. This is especially true for conditions and care plans with major behavioral health components.

Application of the Generic Care Process: A Few Examples

This generic process can be used to plan clinical interventions for target areas (e.g., depression, the use for which it was orginally created). It can be applied to interventions for individual patients, for populations of patients, or aimed at operational or "systems" problems connected with the traditional separate and parallel systems of care. For example, in the DIAMOND Project of 1998, the *care process* for depressed patients and the *change process* for clinics wishing to systematize the care of depression were described using the same five-stage process (Table 2.5). Using the same

TABLE 2.5
A Five-Stage Model: Care Process and Change Process

	Care Process	*Change Process*
Recognition	System to identify patients with depression in its various forms	Identify and recruit clinics who want to systematize the identification and care of depressed patients
Engagement	System to facilitate discussion between providers and patients	Establish clinic-based process improvement team and leadership support
Evaluation	System to assess clinical problems and care options	Assess problems and options with current ways of providing depression care
Management	System to assure the just-right level of care	Develop and implement practical and systematic approach to depression care
Maintenance	System to track ongoing care	Monitor and reevaluate systems to improve depression care

Note. From the 1998 DIAMOND Project.

five-stage process description for improving the care and the care system and then studying both as part of the same project demonstrates acting on the insight that organizational or systems change is required for any significant and durable improvement in the care process.

It is not too difficult to adapt this same five-stage process description to other focal areas of interest as well. Table 2.6 contains examples of common focal areas "that already matter" to primary care clinics:

- Depression.
- Somatization or "thick charts."
- "Difficult" patients.
- Hospital and referral costs.
- Better behavioral health triage and referral.

Underneath the focal areas in Table 2.6 are examples of steps that could be taken in planning interventions for them. Reading down the table, examples of what could be done appear within each stage of the generic care process. Reading across the table, note the parallel thinking and similarities of approach to various clinical and operational or "systems" matters at each stage of the process.

This table illustrates how a keeping a generic clinical process in mind (the "theme") can assist in formulating specific interventions for a given focal area (the "variations"). The focal areas and steps offered here are merely examples. They are not intended as a prescription, and there are no doubt many more possibilities. The point in suggesting a tool like this is to encourage people to give a consistent structure to the many possible local variations on behavioral health integration, so that the "theme" is not lost in the "variations." Not only that, a tool like this can demonstrate that clinical process thinking can be applied to organizational issues as well. The same kind of thinking that it takes to understand and intervene with a clinical condition can be adapted for understanding and intervening with an organizational "condition" as well. Applying clinical concepts to organizational problems makes it much easier to engage clinicians in changing "systems problems" and then "owning" the solutions.

TABLE 2.6

Examples of a Generic Process Used for Planning Behavioral Health Interventions in Primary Care Settings

Focal Areas for Primary and Behavioral Health Care Integration

Process Elements	Depression	"Thick Charts"/Somatization	Difficult Patients	Hospital/Referral Costs	Better Behavioral Health Care Triage
Recognition	• Profile common signs of depression in clinic population and identify high-risk individuals • Screen for delayed recoveries from other problems • Identify patients whose physical symptoms are commonly caused by depression	• Determine utilization distributions • Stratify clinic population by visits, number of doctors, etc. • Identify patients with common somatization-related symptoms or diagnoses • Identify psychological distress • Devise early detection methods for somatization or thick charts in the making	• Physicians list "heart-sink" patients • Nurses and receptionists list unhappy patients • Profile of what makes patients difficult for the clinic	• Identify incidence of panic patients with repeat ER visits for chest pain or shortness of breath • Identify incidence of repeated CAT and MRI scans in patients with pain symptoms • Identify incidence of repeat visits to specialists in patients with multiple vague complaints • Profile the situations that lead to unnecessary hospitalization or referral	• Review patterns of delayed or inadequate triage or acute, chronic, or disguised behavioral health problems • Review patterns of unrecognized, non-referable, failed referral patients • Describe and diagnose the clinic's triage/referral problems
Engagement	• Engage patient in dialog about the pattern of symptoms and fit with dx of depression • Help patient develop understanding of depression in its various forms, incl. relationship to physical symptoms, chronic illnesses • Negotiate a provisional agenda for further assessment and planning	• Engage patients in welcome dialog about the nature of their suffering and their search for help • Negotiate a provisional agenda for further assessment or treatment planning • Engage integrated behavioral health professional as part of the medical team when the patient is ready and accepting	• Engage provider in non-pejorative dialog about the nature of patients suffering with the patient • Engage clinicians in nonpejorative dialog about their own distress in treating those patients • Negotiate a provisional agenda for further exploration and planning • Engage behavioral health as part of this if needed and welcome	• Engage clinic staff and leaders in nonpunishing dialog about the nature of unnecessary behavioral health-related hospitalization and referral costs and magnitude • Negotiate a provisional agenda for further assessment or planning for the issue • Engage behavioral health as part of the clinic team	• Engage clinic staff in nonpejorative dialog about the nature of behavioral health triage in medical clinics and the kind and magnitude of the problems • Negotiate a provisional agenda for further assessment or planning for the issue • Engage behavioral health as part of the clinic team

(Continued)

TABLE 2.6
(Continued)

Focal Areas for Primary and Behavioral Health Care Integration

Process Elements	Depression	"Thick Charts"/ Somatization	Difficult Patients	Hospital/Referral Costs	Better Behavioral Health Care Triage
Evaluation	Evaluate: • History, facts, findings, test results, and patient's own theory • Diagnosis/assessment • Kinds of care plan patient is willing to accept • How patient will talk about findings and plan to family		Evaluate: • Understand what makes this a difficult patient–clinician relationship • Kinds of relational or clinical shifts provider is willing and able to make • How provider will talk about the learnings and shift with self and others		Evaluate: • Facts, findings, resources and hypotheses so far • Where more study is needed, then do it • Care or triage process description and "diagnosis" • Kinds of changes in care or triage process the clinic is ready to make • How staff will talk about the findings and plan to each other and other clinics
Management	• Specify the care plan, including roles for the behavioral health care provider • Carry out the care plan, taking into account everything else going on with the patient		• Develop a care plan for the patient–clinician relationship in addition to that for the patient's health problems • Engage behavioral health provider in either care plan as needed		• Specify the plan to improve triage/referral process, including roles for behavioral health care • Operationalize the plan, taking into account everything else going on
Follow-up	• Monitor and track results and modify plan • Long-term plan (if needed) • Relapse prevention		• Monitor provider and patient satisfaction with care • Engage in relapse prevention		• Test, monitor results, and modify plan if necessary • Continuously improve care/triage/referral process • Test, monitor results, and modify plan if necessary

Note. ER, emergency room; CAT, computerized axial tomography; MRI, magnetic resonance imaging.

ONE STORY: THE HEALTHPARTNERS EXPERIENCE

Historical Context[4]

Separate and parallel systems of mental health and medical care delivery have left their imprint on care systems, medical groups, clinics, and individual practitioners around the country. Our experience with integrating medical and behavioral health care began in the mid 1980s at what was then called Group Health, Inc., a nonprofit, member-governed, staff model health maintenance organization (HMO), founded in 1957 with roots in the cooperative movement. Now part of HealthPartners, Group Health began as a single clinic in 1957, and by 1990 it had become a multisite, multispecialty clinic system staffed by 350 physicians and over 100 mental health clinicians practicing in 19 medical clinics, serving approximately 300,000 members. In the turbulent Twin Cities health care environment, Group Health merged in 1991 with another health plan and in 1994 with an academic physician–hospital group to become HealthPartners.[5]

The HealthPartners mental health benefit and care delivery department was established in the mid 1970s. Before that time, mental health care was done as a normal part of primary care medicine, occasional specialty referral, or in some cases was excluded from covered benefits. Most subscribers to the health plan had unformed views and expectations of mental health care at that time. At the department's beginning, referral to mental health was done by physicians who detected mental health conditions in need of evaluation. Physicians served a detection, agenda-setting, or "gatekeeping" function. Mental health visits were entered in medical charts like any other patient visit.

As a large mental health department emerged, the gatekeeping function for physicians was lifted, and direct patient access to mental health appointments was established. Members began more and more to see mental health services as a normal and directly accessible part of the health plan benefit. By 1983, a separate and confidential mental health chart was created, along with a confidentiality statement that reinforced the separation of mental health and medical records. The view that medical health care and mental health care are fundamentally different or separate became widespread not only among patients but also among clinicians and adminstrators. Medical staff rarely ordered and read mental health charts, and mental health providers usually did not read medical charts. "Phone tag" (this was before e-mail and voice mail) between medical and mental health clinics made routine coordination of care more challenging. Gradually, distance between medical and mental health staff increased, and mutual stereotypes between physicians and psychotherapists flourished at times when misunderstandings lingered without routine opportunities to discuss and resolve problems.

---

[4]A more detailed version of these events can be found in Peek and Heinrich (1998), a chapter in Blount (1998).

[5]HealthPartners is a member-governed, nonprofit health plan and care system with almost 800,000 members in the Twin Cities area. The integration projects described here took place within HealthPartners Medical Group and Clinics, part of the HealthPartners care delivery system consisting of a medical group of 550 physicians and 20-plus clinics serving approximately 240,000 members and patients. HealthPartners Medical Group and Clinics is the product of what were formerly known as Group Health Inc., founded in 1957 as a nonprofit HMO, and the clinics of St. Paul Ramsey Medical Center, a nonprofit hospital-based medical center and teaching institution founded decades earlier.

The mental health department fulfilled the traditional specialty behavioral health function, with the mental health benefit more or less independent of the medical benefit. As time went on, this specialty mental health function became less well adapted for the task of serving medical patients with disguised mental health problems or serving physicians whose patients had mental health problems disguised as or contributing to medical complaints. At the same time, tremendous member demand and expectation for traditional mental health and counseling services had developed, and handling this became the main challenge. A great deal of high-quality, and often inspired, behavioral health work went on behind the closed doors of the department, often invisible to medical providers, who sometimes experienced the doors being closed on *them*. Physicians often characterized referral to mental health as sending their patients to "a black hole."

This kind of historical background is not at all unusual. Very similar stories are heard all across the country. Parallel and distant medical and behavioral health services have been the rule, not the exception. HealthPartners' pilot projects were based on the organization's practical need to solve the problems of separate and parallel care delivery systems and on a clinical commitment to developing a better model of care, especially for complex patients whose problems straddle the traditional "mind–body" split in health care.

The First Pilot

In the 1980s, HealthPartners, like other care systems, had experienced the familiar dissatisfactions associated with the separate and parallel delivery systems, especially for complex patients such as those with chronic pain. One local and national response to fragmented care of chronic pain patients was the development of independent, fee-for-service integrated pain programs. The medical director became concerned that some complex chronic pain patients appeared to require higher than the usual level of teamwork or integration available internally, and needed referrals to integrated chronic pain programs in the community. These referrals were not only quite expensive, but also carried the additional challenge of incorporating the new care plan into the patient's regular care once the patient completed the program. Referral to external programs brought this other kind of integration problem, and the overall "system" problem in the care of chronic pain patients was still not fully addressed. Believing that considerable improvement should be achieved internally, with or without the use of outside pain clinic referrals, the medical director and dental director jointly sponsored a pilot project in 1984 to improve the care one such group of patients, those with chronic temporomandibular disorders (TMD).

TMD is a common cause of jaw pain, ear pain, headache, and problems with jaw function. TMD patients often clench or grind their teeth and have other habits of muscle bracing, as well as a range of possible structural problems of the jaw. Prior to this pilot, these patients often received disconnected trials of dental therapy, physical therapy, and sometimes mental health therapies. These components were typically *sequential and independent* rather than *simultaneous and integrated*. Clinicians often found the sequential approach to care less than satisfactory, often saw this as a "difficult" patient group, and the patients themselves appeared to complain about their care and ask for referrals to outside specialists or programs more than the average group of patients with a particular condition. These complaints and requests tended to find their way to the desks of the dental director or the member services director, where good internal solutions were not easy to find.

Based on an integrated approach developed at the University of Minnesota,[6] a health psychologist (the first author), two dentists, a physical therapist, a dental assistant, and a receptionist built up a similar integrated team within a dental clinic for especially complex TMD patients referred by physicians and dentists from across the entire care system. The TMD program was designed to integrate care in a way that addressed the clinical, operational, and financial problems inherent in separate and parallel systems of medical, dental, and behavioral health care for that population of patients. A number of design features helped achieve this result, such as:

• The dentist, psychologist, physical therapist, and receptionist worked as a team in the same space and waiting room in the same clinic for "one-stop shopping" and rapid, natural communication.

• New patients (those already known to be complex) saw all three providers sequentially during the first evaluation visit. Immediately afterward, the providers met together to pool their results and create a provisional care plan that integrated the dental, physical therapy, and behavioral factors. The patient (and sometimes spouse or other family members) then joined the providers and the actual care plan was negotiated, written down, and started.

• Patients were scheduled for all visits through the dental scheduling system within the dental clinic. Service coding and billing information was captured through the medical or dental service record. Progress notes for all three providers were kept in one chart, with periodic updates and summaries inserted in the general medical and dental charts.

• The primary care physician and primary dentist were made aware of the findings and care plan, and in many cases were made part of its negotiation and the follow-up care. This prevented the problem of creating specialized care plans that primary providers didn't understand or support well enough to follow through on.

• Visit copays were equalized across team members to avoid creating an incentive for patients to avoid the providers who might otherwise have higher copays (e.g., behavioral health), thus distorting the teamwork. This equalized copay was set at a level that would not discourage patients from following through with the entire team, especially early in care, when they might see two or three providers on the same trip to the clinic.

• Coverage for integrated care of TMD was shared by the medical and dental divisions of the care system, in recognition that this problem crosses the medical and dental areas. For these purposes, behavioral health was considered part of medical coverage.

Although these improvements are the obvious ones to make, for the sake of comparison imagine what would more likely be encountered in a traditional separate and parallel care delivery system:

• A patient who was told by the primary doctor or dentist that the patient needed help from a dentist, physical therapist, and behavioral health professional would

---

[6]Thanks to James Fricton, DDS, and Kate Hathaway, PhD, of the University of Minnesota for their initial guidance in establishing the HealthPartners TMD program. See Fricton (1989) and Fricton and Olson (1996) for more on myofascial pain and interdisciplinary care of temporomandibular disorders.

have to read three separate referral slips, make three separate phone calls, repeat personal information three times, schedule three separate appointments, drive to three separate locations, and pay three separate and different copays. These appointments would probably have been spread out over a period of days or weeks, and the patient would have to wait even longer for any synthesis of the results, and wonder when, how, and if those providers would be talking to each other.

• The referring provider would have to fill out three referral slips, later on read three reports, and then try to coordinate that care as well as possible, whereas the dentist, physical therapist, and behavioral health provider (who probably wouldn't know each other) would do their best to communicate with each other across distance and separate charts.

• Separate medical, dental, or behavioral health service records would be filled out at each visit, and progress notes would be filed in three separate charts. None of these systems would have supported these three providers making an integrated team effort.

• The patient might well have to negotiate for coverage because separate and parallel medical, dental, and behavioral health care systems and covered benefits don't neatly fit what it takes to care for TMD, and each area would probably have some contractual basis for thinking of the cost as belonging elsewhere.

By all accounts, the TMD program was a major success. The patients got better, were highly satisfied, and valued getting all of their care in one place from a consistent team of clinicians. After the TMD team began to take care of chronic patients from all across the care system, complaints and requests for referrals to outside specialists and programs dried up. The medical and dental directors were satisfied that internal improvements had improved quality of care and service, that the costs of treating these patients were reduced, and that continuity with primary medical and dental care was better than when addressing the issue by making outside referrals.

The TMD team worked well together (and is still in place with most of the original clinicians after 15 years), supporting each other with very complex and initially "difficult" and sometimes demanding patients. What started out as a particularly "troublesome patient group" became for these providers a particularly satisfying professional activity. This illustrates how strong feelings about "difficult patients" or "hard-to-manage conditions" can have as much to do with chronic problems in care system design as with the patients or conditions themselves. If the care system is not designed well for the clinical presentations it encounters, some patients and conditions will appear much more "difficult" than they really are. It turned out that previous patient and provider dissatisfactions with TMD care had more to do with flaws in care system design than in the TMD condition itself.

A Theme Deserving of Variations

The success of the TMD program began a gradual process of generalizing its key features to other parts of the care system. The goal was to formulate and demonstrate within HealthPartners clinics much improved clinical operational and financial practices for integrating the psychosocial dimension of health care. Over a 6-year period, the first author (C. J. Peek) recruited a small group of health psychologists to do similar work in the primary care and specialty clinics of the care system. The mission was to create within HealthPartners an innovation in health care services marked by:

- A biopsychosocial model of human health.
- Methods for synergizing the work of behavioral health and medical professionals.
- Integration of medical and mental health care at clinics with integrated behavioral health.
- Improved systems of care for complex patients for whom separate medical and mental health care leads to unsatisfactory clinical, systems, and financial outcomes.

From 1986 to about 1991 this group gradually established "placements" in about 14 primary care and specialty clinics. This pilot stage was characterized by variations on the basic theme of "integrated behavioral health" (described earlier). Of the many possible primary care and specialty clinics, only the ones most interested and ready became pilot sites with integrated behavioral health on site. These were variations on a theme, because each clinic or specialty experienced the problems of separate and parallel medical and behavioral health services in a different way and needed a locally customized approach. A consulting process for helping clinics articulate their own needs and goals for integrated behavioral health is described elsewhere (Peek & Heinrich, 1998) and was summarized earlier in this chapter. Several primary clinics showed great interest and went forward with integrated behavioral health, using a strategy of "horizontal integration." Early examples of behavioral health integrated in specialty care included oncology, pediatric and adult endocrinology, orthopedic surgery, and pediatric obesity. At this stage, these demonstrations were loaded for success by placing them in motivated clinics and staffing them with a highly dedicated and mutually supportive group of health psychologists. Salaries and leadership energies for this small group were funded, and tracked separately, by the mental health department as part of its contribution to the organization's overall effort to build a better care system.

These variations on the integrated behavioral health theme were also considered successful—valuable to physicians, patients, and the care system. Clinical, operational, and financial paradigms for integrated care were demonstrated well enough and broadly enough that by 1991, the time was approaching to begin moving the experiments into the mainstream. This occurred at about the same time the second author (Richard Heinrich) joined the organization as head of the Mental Health Department.

The Need to Move From Pilot to Mainstream

Between 1986 and 1995, the successes of the pilot projects created significant physician demand for such approaches in more and more primary care and specialty care settings. But this success itself carried risks to the project. The following signs indicated the need to begin to move past the pilot stage:

1. Integrated behavioral health services became popular among physicians, and the demand far exceeded the time available from the small group of health psychologists. Mainstream demand began to fall on pilot programs, leading to physician and patient concerns about access. This was confirmed later in a qualititative study of the

early health psychology demonstrations (Fischer, Heinrich, Davis, Peek, & Lucas, 1998).

2. The demonstrations were considered successful, but they were having about as much effect on the care system as a whole as could be expected, given their pilot status, functioning in only a portion of the care system. If a system-wide effect was desired, then a more mainstream approach would be required.

3. After 1991, the increasingly competitive environment in health care and the need to reduce unnecessary costs brought the integrated behavioral health pilots under new scrutiny and pressed for a new financial model. Up to 1991 the mental health department had provided the personnel at no cost to the medical clinics. This had been a fairly easy internal agreement about a fairly small amount of money within a system capitated for the total cost of care. But with the prospect of mainstreaming these demonstrations and the need for every department and clinic to be more conscious of resource stewardship, the financial model that fit well at the pilot stage appeared inadequate for mainstream application. As the financial realities of the 1990s began to sink in, the mental health and medical leaders began discussions about developing a mainstream financial model for integrated behavioral health as well as the most basic question of all: whether the 10-year-old project should be adapted for the mainstream as an innovation in the care model or be terminated.

4. If integrated behavioral health were to continue, it would have to take place in more clinics, using a broader range of behavioral health providers, working with mainstream systems, no "experimental" resource budget, no protection from greatly intensified market pressures clinics were experiencing, and an increased expectation for hard data on results. This meant subjecting the idea to mainstream forces and conditions, with much less of the "hand-built" attention, protection, and control of the early days.

5. About all that could be learned from the demonstrations in their present form had already been learned. They were popular with patients, physicians, clinics, and the health psychologists who worked in them, and were regarded by participating physicians as an improvement in quality, service, and access (Fischer et al., 1998). Although there were no scientific studies of outcomes, a utilization survey (previously mentioned) of about a thousand patients who had had a health psychology intervention was very favorable (Davis et al., as reported in Peek & Heinrich, 1998). This survey showed that patients seen by health psychologists had many more diagnoses and much higher health care utilization than other patients. In the year following health psychology intervention, there was greater behavioral health utilization but greater than 9% reduction in physician visits and a 27% reduction in hospital days. These figures tended to confirm what people already felt was going on—it was better care and appeared to be a good use of resources. It was time to act on the information generated from the pilots, as little new information would likely come from them in their form at that time.

Integrated Behavioral Health and the Wider Organization

At the same time when the health psychology pilots were being examined, the larger organizational context was being transformed. The two mergers that resulted in HealthPartners were taking place. This brought in a new mix of medical leadership and resulted in a medical group almost twice the size (going from 350 physicians to

550) as the original "Group Health" within which the pilots were started. In addition to dramatically increasing in size, HealthPartners Medical Group and Clinics served a more diverse group: about 60% capitated care with employed populations and about 40% fee-for-service work from self-insured employers, government programs, indemnity insurance, private pay, and indigent populations. Medical education and research also became much more prominent features of the new medical group's mission. These events created a whole new organizational context for integrated behavioral health, and this called for a conversation about the role of behavioral health in the new medical group.

This conversation took place in 1995 when specialty care and primary care work groups were outlining what the basic structure and philosophy of the new medical group should be. These work groups, composed of physicians and medical leaders from the two merging medical groups, each formulated a set of guiding principles for the role of behavioral health in the care system. It turned out that these principles were strongly supportive of the integrated behavioral health demonstrations and in effect amounted to an endorsement of the work done so far. Some of the elements included incorporation of on-site behavioral health providers, working from a model of collaborative care, maintaining the primacy of physician–patient relationships while working on behavioral health problems, timely access for provider-to-provider phone consults as well as patient appointments, rapid sharing of information from consultations and ongoing care, continuing education of physicians by behavioral health professionals regarding behavioral health problems in medical care, and a recognition that behavioral health is a big part of health care.

With agreement on such basic principles, reinforced by the experience and momentum from the early pilots, the HealthPartners Medical Group and Clinics decided to transform the pilot programs into a mainstream integration project. In 1996, this became a major feature of the long-range plan for primary care, with the medical director for primary care as its sponsor. The project became "The Primary Care Mental Health Project," led by primary care leaders, behavioral health leaders (including the second author), researchers, and operations leaders. The initial goal was to integrate behavioral health in four more primary care clinics. The longer term goal of the project was to make it possible, practical, and desirable for primary care clinics to actually function as the front end of the behavioral health care delivery system. This is not a "detect and refer" model, where the main thrust is screening patients for mental disorders and referring them to behavioral health providers for therapy or to physicians for medication. Instead, the project focuses heavily on overall care processes, care system redesign issues, and collaborative practice models, clinic by clinic. Behavioral health as a specialty (sometimes referred to as "traditional mental health" that takes place in separate mental health clinics) is an important part of this overall care system design because there will always be a need for specialized behavioral health care done outside the primary care setting. But the primary care mental health project does not merely colocate therapists in primary care clinics or create islands of specialty mental health practice in primary care. (The goal is horizontally integrated behavioral health as described in earlier sections.)

This project, with its 1996 endorsement and new name, expanded considerably in 1998. Today, 25% of the HealthPartners Medical Group and Clinics behavioral health professionals work in primary care clinics, and 16 of 22 its primary care clinics now have integrated behavioral health on site. Financing was worked out by agreement between the Primary Care and Behavioral Health Divisions. The behavioral health division provides the professional salaries and the primary care division supports the on-site overhead (office space, reception services, dictations, medical charting, etc.). Primary care also has provided additional funds to support behavioral health professionals as part of the startup for this project. The financial model and the leadership philosophy at the highest levels increasingly reflect collaboration and partnership between medical and behavioral health services in improving the health of a population of patients. The financial model, like the rest of the project, is a work in progress.

Mainstreaming the Pilots: Appealing to What Mattered at Each Clinic

It is one thing to reach an organizational decision to mainstream integrated behavioral health, and another thing to make it real in actual clinics. Although separate and parallel medical and behavioral health care leads to a set of common dissatisfactions, each clinic experiences these in different ways and to different degrees. Hence there is a need for local variations on the central theme. Therefore, a consulting process (described earlier) was developed to get at what matters to each clinic. Clinic-by-clinic behavioral health integration takes place on the basis of what is discovered to be important and "ready to happen" at each clinic. For this, it helps to put on the consultant's hat and find out, rather than prescribing a certain solution to everyone (Peek & Heinrich, 1998). This might vary from interest in a particular condition such as depression, to complex high-utilizing patients, "difficult patients," or better behavioral health evaluation and triage (such as described in Table 2.6). These are all reasonable variations on the theme.

Although the long-range vision of the Medical Group and Clinics includes system-wide integrated behavioral health, when to participate in the Primary Care Mental Health Project is up to each clinic, based when it is ready to move forward. To participate, some basic expectations have to be met (e.g., being able to articulate goals and commit to assembling an implementation team willing to meet regularly during startup because this is ultimately *their* project). Initial meetings typically include the behavioral health professionals, clinic leaders, and physicians and nurses from adult and pediatric medicine, as well as key people from operations areas (reception, chart room, and transcription). Such "locally owned" implementation teams have been key to successful integration of behavioral health professionals in the medical culture and practice, which is the basic objective. Such implementation teams help physicians and behavioral health professionals get to know each other, discover each other's skill areas, and begin to define how they can optimally work together prior to actually seeing patients. People are not thrown into the fray with full schedules on the first day. Instead, they have the opportunity to envision what meaningful and smooth consultation, collaboration, or referral (both formal and informal) would look like, what kinds of information to pass back and forth, and what sort of patients or situations should be the main focus of collaboration at that clinic.

Implementation also requires deliberate use of gradations of collaboration and integration. Although many complex patients need a team, the degree of collaboration required varies a great deal from case to case, and long-term success requires getting just the right amount of collaboration for each case (not too much, not too little). We described such a "four-sector model" elsewhere (Peek & Heinrich, 1995), and Doherty, McDaniel, and Baird (1996) offered a model of "five levels of primary care/behavioral healthcare collaboration" that helps clinicians envision gradations of collaboration and seek the right level for the particular situation they face. Clinically effective and resource-responsible collaboration can range from more or less solo treatment of a patient, through consultation or coordination of separate care, to deeply integrated team approaches where everyone works off one tightly integrated common care plan. The Primary Care Mental Health Project emphasizes the need to work at these various levels of collaboration, depending on the case.

Behavioral health professionals also learn to work as consultants to primary care physicians in addition to the more familiar path of taking referrals. This supports physicians in the ongoing care of patients with significant behavioral health factors rather than automatically meaning referral to the behavioral health provider. This "consultation" model is consistent with the guiding principles developed by the Medical Group during the merger.

Tasks for the Future

Behavioral health integration at HealthPartners began with the modest goal of improving the care of a specific group of complex chronic pain patients, but is increasingly one strand in a larger fabric of changes and integrations being woven together to build the "characteristics of successful and solvent health care of the future," as we described them at the beginning of this chapter. Some of the tasks that remain are:

1. Complete mainstreaming of behavioral health integration. Although HealthPartners has made significant progress moving its demonstration projects to the mainstream, it takes several years to turn good ideas into "hand-built" prototypes, test them, and then complete the major task of mainstreaming the demonstrations in the entire system. This developmental sequence, "from idea to invention to innovation" (Peek & Heinrich, 1995), has been unfolding since 1984 and will likely continue for several more years. This will probably continue as "variations" linked by a common "theme" of integrated care and the end of care fragmented along the "mind–body split."

2. Continue harmonizing the clinical, operational, and financial aspects of behavioral health integration. Although the clinical view of integrated behavioral health and its place in the care system has become increasingly clear, the operational and financial structures needed to support it are still a work in progress and need to be designed so they harmonize with the clinical view (see "three-world view" in Peek & Heinrich, 1995, 1998). Whenever an improvement is made in the care, a corresponding improvement will no doubt need to made in the care system in order to support it. Drawing the operational and financial views to match an evolving clinical vision is an ongoing task, and requires partnership between clinician and administrative leaders. The task is a total system task, not merely a clinical task.

3. Use the new capacities created by integrated behavioral health to advance initiatives in chronic care and population health (e.g., diabetes care, cardiac care, depression care, care of the frail elderly, and care of complex and distressed high-utilizing patients). Develop more advanced skill sets and clinical support systems for medical and behavioral health professionals who jointly face a full spectrum of chronic conditions, because patients with chronic illnesses often have comorbid medical and psychiatric conditions, and nearly all have significant psychosocial factors that can complicate (or help with) their care. Behavioral health integration is an important strand

in HealthPartners overall goals in chronic care and improving the health of the population, goals shared by more and more health plans and care systems.

4. Develop improving habits of collaborative practice and patient/clinician communication. Team care and effective collaborative relationships between providers, patients, and families are considered essential for quality of care, good service, and good resource stewardship, especially for the growing area of chronic care. Collaborative practice involves shifts in professional identity and practice among the various stripes of clinicians, and a shift of role for patients and families. It means building a common culture of "good providership" among all the different stripes of clinicians it takes to care for a population of patients (Peek & Heinrich, 1995, 1998). This takes time to accomplish in actual care settings, where the ideas, models, and demonstrations are often ahead of actual practice. Behavioral health integration, as demonstrated at HealthPartners, has featured long-term collaborative practice models. But this is not the only area in health care where a need for better teamwork and communication between clinicians and with patients and families has been identified. Better teamwork and communication is a care system goal, not just a behavioral health integration goal.

5. Systematically evaluate the impact of collaborative working relationships and integrated systems of care. Quality of care, quality of service, patient and provider satisfaction, and effective resource stewardship will be monitored as a guide to gradual and ongoing improvement of the care and of the care system. Some of this will be evaluated through formal research (e.g., the DIAMOND Project), and some will be evaluated through process improvement or program evaluation methodology. Systematic evaluation is required for development of best practices in the area of behavioral health integration, and some of the most important of these will be organizational best practices required to support clinical best practices. Different stakeholders (e.g., patients and families, clinicians, purchasers, and care system leaders) all have different needs for data and for different kinds of "proof" on which to base action. Hence a broad slate of evaluation measures that speak to what matters to this broad range of stakeholders is necessary.

CONCLUSION

The HealthPartners story is no doubt itself a variation on a theme. Although everyone faces similar challenges and can read the same literature base, different clinicians, provider groups, care systems, and health plans will all have to make their own way through the difficulties in delivering and receiving care across the traditional "mind–body split" in health care. Therefore, clinicians preparing themselves for work in this area should be prepared to (a) become very familiar with the "theme" — the common environment, pressures, problems, challenges, learnings, concepts, and literature of primary care and behavioral health that face people everywhere — and (b) become part of customized local "variations" on the theme of primary care integration. These local variations need to engage primary care providers and clinics with what is already important to them and will be most helpful in the long run if they improve the care and also support those gains by improving the care system.

Behavioral health clinicians who enter this field conscious of the greater primary care mission, and who search a very broad horizon for what needs to be done to accomplish it, what can be done in a practical world, and what they themselves can help primary care providers do in a particular place, will likely find themselves being heartily welcomed by primary care providers and clinics. Behavioral health and primary care providers, once starting down the path together, linked by a common mission that includes both medical and behavioral health functions and people, can develop long-term and effective collaborative relationships that have so rarely developed in the traditional separate and parallel systems of care.

These collaborative relationships can be harnessed not only for better patient care, but for transformation of the care system in regards to behavioral health. This is the greater task, as the clinical insights about integrated care most often exceed the organizational capacities to carry it out. It takes partnership between primary care and behavioral health clinicians and leaders who see themselves as part of a larger professional community with a mission that includes them both, and who see themselves working on the same side of a larger struggle to transform health care in this important way. The energy that flows between people when this partnership begins to take hold can carry the work through the inevitable adversity and challenge in this tumultuous environment, and sustain the sense that "this is an idea whose time has finally come."

ACKNOWLEDGMENTS

Many people at HealthPartners have helped make behavioral health integration a reality over the past 15 years. We acknowledge the contributions of physicians, dentists, health psychologists, nurses, psychotherapists, receptionists, clinic chiefs and managers, medical department heads, physician and administrative leaders and "champions" from throughout the organization, program evaluators and funders, all of whom have contributed to the goal of taking better care of patients by improving integration, collaboration, and the cooperation of people and perspectives. It is impossible to list all the individuals from across the organization who have contributed as collaborators, co-creators, co-consultants, or "early adopters" of the many ideas and demonstrations outlined here.

We are also indebted to the many colleagues outside HealthPartners who have enriched the field and our lives with articles, books, conference presentations, encouragement, and consults, such as through the Collaborative Family Healthcare Coalition, a special forum that has become a "home" for us and our work.

REFERENCES

Barsky, A. J. (1988). *Worried sick: Our troubled quest for wellness*. Boston: Little, Brown.
Berwick, D. M. (1997, October). *The ingredients of world class: Distinctive characteristics of the future outstanding healthcare organization*. Paper presented at the conference Putting Clinicians in the Cockpit, Institute for Clinical Systems Integration, Minneapolis, MN.
Blazer, D. G. (1993). *Depression in late life*. St. Louis, MO: Mosby.

Blount, A. (Ed.). (1998). *Integrated primary care: The future of medical and mental health collaboration*. New York: W. W. Norton.

Boyle, R. G., O'Connor, P. J., Pronk, N. P., & Tan, A. (1998). Stages of change for physical activity, diet, and smoking among HMO members with chronic conditions. *American Journal of Health Promotion, 12*(3), 170–175.

Burns, B. J. (1994). Historical considerations of mental disorders in primary care. In J. Miranda, A. A. Hohmann, C. C. Attkisson, & D. B. Larson (Eds.), *Mental disorders in primary care* (pp. 16–33). San Franciso: Jossey-Bass.

Caine, E. D., Lyness, J. M., King, D. A., & Connors, L. (1994). Clinical and etiological heterogeneity of mood disorders in elderly patients. In L. S. Schneider, C. F. Reynolds, B. D. Lebowitz, & A. J. Friedhoff (Eds.), *Diagnosis and treatment of depression in late life: Results of the NIH Consensus Development Conference* (pp. 21–54). Washington, DC: American Psychiatric Press.

Carney, R. M., Rich, M. W., Freedland, K. E., Saini, J., TeVelde, A., Simeone, C., & Clarke, K. (1988). Major depressive disorder predicts cardiac events in patients with coronary artery disease. *Psychosomatic Medicine, 50*, 627–633.

Coyne, J., Schwenk, T., & Fechner-Bates, S. (1995). Nondetection of depression by primary care physicians reconsidered. *General Hospital Psychiatry, 17*, 3–12.

Cummings, N. A. (1997). Behavioral health in primary care: Dollars and sense. In N. A. Cummings, J. L. Cummings, & J. N. Johnson (Eds.), *Behavioral health in primary care: A guide for clinical integration* (pp. 3–22). Madison, WI: Psychosocial Press.

Cummings, N. A., Cummings, J. L., & Johnson, J. N. (Eds.). (1997). *Behavioral health in primary care: A guide for clinical integration*. Madison, WI: Psychosical Press.

deGruy, F. V. (1997). Mental healthcare in the primary care setting: A paradigm problem. *Families, Systems and Health 15*: 3–26. Also appears in slightly modified form in Donaldson, M. S., Yordy, K. D., Lohr, K. N., & Vanselow, N. A. (Eds.). (1996). *Primary care: America's health in a new era* (pp. 285–311). Washington, DC: National Academy Press.

Doherty, W. J., & Baird, M. A. (1983). *Family therapy and family medicine*. New York: Guilford Press.

Doherty, W. J., & Baird, M. A. (Eds.). (1987). *Family centered medical care: A clinical casebook*. New York: Guilford Press.

Doherty, W. J., McDaniel, S. H., and Baird, M. A. (1996). Five levels of primary care/behavioral healthcare collaboration. *Behavioral Healthcare Tomorrow, 5*(5), 25–27.

Dunman, R. S., Heninger, G. R., & Nestler, E. J. (1997). A molecular and cellular theory of depression, *Arch Gen Psychiatry, 54*, 597–606.

Fawzy, F. I., Fawzy, N. W., & Hyun, C. D. (1993). Malignant melanoma. Effects of an early structured psychiatric intervention, coping, and affective state on recurrence and survival 6 years later. *Archives of General Psychiatry, 50*, 681–689.

Fischer, L. R., Heinrich, R. L., Davis, T. F., Peek, C. J., & Lucas, S. F. (1998). Mental health and primary care in an HMO. *Families, Systems, and Health, 15*, 4.

Ford, E. D. (1994). Recognition and underrecognition of mental disorders in primary care. In J. Miranda, A. A. Hohmann, C. C. Attkisson, & D. B. Larson (Eds.), *Mental disorders in primary care* (pp. 186–205). San Franciso: Jossey-Bass.

Frasure-Smith, N., Lesperance, F., & Talajic, M. (1993). Depresion following myocardial infarction: Impact on 6-month survival. *JAMA, 270*, 1819–1825.

Fricton, J. R. (1989). Myofascial pain syndrome. *Neurologic Clinics, 7*(2), 413–27.

Fricton, J. R., & Olsen, T. (1996). Predictors of outcome for treatment of temporomandibular disorders. *Journal of Orofacial Pain, 10*(1), 54–65.

Gilmer, T. D., O'Connor, P. J., Manning, W. G., & Rush, W. A. (1997). The cost to health plans of poor glycemic control. *Diabetes Care, 20*, 12.

Glassman, A. H., & Shapiro, P. A. (1998). Depression and the course of coronary artery disease. *American Journal of Psychiatry, 155*, 4–11.

Goetzel, R. Z., Anderson, D. R., Whitmer, R. W., Ozminkowski, R. J., Dunn, R. L., Wasserman, J., and the Health Enhancement Research Organization (HERO) Research Committee. (1998). The relationship between modifiable health risks and health care expenditures: An analysis of the multi-employer HERO health risk and cost database. *Journal of Occupational and Environmental Medicine, 40*(10), 1–12.

Goodwin, F. J., & Jamison, K. R. (1990). *Manic-depressive illness*. New York: Oxford University Press.

Haber, J. D., & Mitchell, G. E. (Eds.). (1998). *Primary care meets mental health: Tools for the 21st century*. Providence, RI: Behavioral Health Resource Press.

Halvorson, G. (1993). *Strong medicine*. New York: Random House.

HEDIS. (1998). Health Plan Employer and Data Information Set, 1998 report. Washington, DC: National Committee on Quality Assurance. [Available online: www.ncqa.org]

Hellman, C. J., Budd, M., Borysenko, J., McClelland, D. C., & Benson, H. (1990). A study of the effectivness of two group behavioral medicine interventions for patients with psychosomatic complaints. *Behavioral Medicine, 16*, 165–173.

Holmes, T. H., & Rahe, R. H. (1968). The social readjustment rating scale. *Journal of Psychosomatic Research, 11*, 213–218.

Isham, G. (1997, November/December). Population health and HMO's: The Partners for Better Health experience. *HealthCare Forum Journal*, pp. 36–39.

Kashner, T. M., Rost, K., & Cohen, B. (1995). Enhancing the health of somatization disorder patients: Effectiveness of short-term group therapy. *Psychosomatics, 36*, 462–470.

Katon, W., Robinson, P., Von Korff, M., Lin, E., Bush, T., Ludman, E., Simon, G., & Walker, E. A. (1996). Multifaceted intervention to improve treatment of depression in primary care. *Archives of General Psychiatry, 53*, 924–932.

Katzelnick, D. (1997, May). Integrated care and cost offset services for depressed and somaticizing high utilizers. *Proceedings of How to Design and Implement your Primary Care Behavioral Health Integration Program* (pp. 81–148), sponsored by the Institute for Behavioral Healthcare, San Francisco.

Klinkman, M. S., & Okkes, I. (1998). Mental health problems in primary care: A research agenda. *Journal of Family Practice, 47*, 379–384.

Kroenke, K., & Mangelsdorff, D. (1989). Common symptoms in abmulatory care: Incidence, evaluation, therapy and outcome. *American Journal of Medicine, 86*, 262–266.

Linden, W., Stosssel, C., & Maurice, J. (1996). Psychosocial interventions for patients with coronary artery disease: A meta-analysis. *Archives of Internal Medicine, 156*, 745–752.

Lipowski, Z. J. (1988). Somatization: The concept and its clinical application. *American Journal of Psychiatry, 145*, 1358–1368.

Lucas, S. F., & Peek, C. J. (1997). A primary care physician's experience with integrated behavioral health care: What difference has it made? In N. A. Cummings, J. L. Cummings, & J. N. Johnson (Eds.), *Behavioral health in primary care: A guide for clinical integration* (pp. 371–398). Madison, WI: Psychosocial Press.

McDaniel, S., Campbell, T., & Seaburn, D. (1995). Principles for collaboration between health and mental health providers in primary care. *Family Systems Medicine, 13*(3/4), 283–298.

Miller, R. H., & Luft, H. S. (1994). Managed care plan performance since 1980. *JAMA, 271*, 1512–1519.

Miller, R. H., & Luft, H. S. (1997). Does managed care lead to better or worse quality of care? *Health Affairs, 16*, 7–25.

Miranda, J., Hohmann, A. A., Attkisson, C. C., & Larson, D. B. (1994). *Mental disorders in primary care*. San Franciso: Jossey-Bass.

Mosser, G. (interviewed by S. Davidow). (1996). Developing and implementing health care guidelines for group medical practices: An interview with Gordon Mosser. *Joint Commission Journal on Quality Improvement, 22*, 4.

Mynors-Wallis, L. M., Gath, D. H., Lloyd-Thomas, A. R., & Tomlinson, D. (1995). Randomized controlled trial comparing problem solving treatment with amitriptyline and placebo for major depression in primary care. *British Medical Journal, 310*, 441–445.

Narrow, W. F., Regier, D. A., Rae, D. S., Manderscheid, R. W., & Locke, B. Z. (1993). Use of services by persons with mental and addictive disorders: Findings from the National Institute of Mental Health Epidemiologic Catchment Area Program. *Archives of General Psychiatry, 50*, 95–107.

National Committee on Quality Assurance. (1998). *NCQA standards for managed care organizations*. Washington, DC: Author.

National Committee on Quality Assurance. (1999). *NCQA standards for managed care organizations*. Washington, DC: Author.

O'Connor, P. J., Rush, W. A., & Pronk, N. P. (1997). Database system to identify biological risk in managed care organizations: Implications for clinical care. *Journal of Ambulatory Care Management, 20*, 4.

O'Connor, P. J., & Pronk, N. P. (1998). Integrating population health concepts, clinical guidelines, and ambulatory medical systems to improve diabetes care. *Journal of Ambulatory Care Management, 21*(1), 170–175.

O'Connor, P. J., Solberg, L. I., & Baird, M. (1998). The future of primary care: The enhanced primary care model. *Journal of Family Practice, 47*(1), 62–67.

Ormel, J., Koeter, M., Brink, W., & Williege, G. (1991). Recognition, management, and course of anxiety and depression in general practice. *Archives of General Psychiatry, 48*, 700–706.

Peek, C. J., & Heinrich, R. L. (1995). Building a collaborative healthcare organization: From idea to invention to innovation. *Family Systems Medicine, 13*(3/4), 327–342.

Peek, C. J., & Heinrich, R. L. (1998). Integrating primary care and behavioral health in a healthcare organization: From pilot to mainstream. In A. Blount (Ed.), *Integrated primary care: The future of medical and
mental health collaboration* (pp. 167–202). New York: Norton.

Pincus, H. A., Tanielian, T. L., Marcus, S. C., Olfson, M., Zarin, D. A., Thompson, J., & Zito, J. M. (1998).
Prescribing trends in psychotropic medications: Primary care, psychiatry, and other medical specialties. *JAMA, 279*, 526–531.

Prochaska, J. O., Norcross, J. C., & DiClemente, C. C. (1994). *Changing for good.* New York: Avon.

Pronk, N. P., Boyle, R. B., & O'Connor, P. J. (1998). The association between physical fitness and diagnosed
chronic conditions in health maintenance association members. *American Journal of Health Promotion,
12*(5), 300–306.

Pronk, N., & O'Connor, P. (1997). Systems approach to population health improvement. *Journal of Ambulatory Care Management, 20*(4).

Pronk, N., O'Connor, P., Isham, G., & Hawkins, C. (1997). Building a patient registry for implementation of
health promotion initiatives: Targeting high-risk individuals. *HMO Practice, 11*, 1, 43–46.

Pronk, N. P., Tan, A. W. H., & O'Connor, P. J. (1999). Obesity, fitness, willingness to communicate and
health care costs. *Medicine and Science in Sports and Exercise, 31*(11), 1535–1543.

Regier, D., Goldberg, I., & Taube, C. (1978). The de facto US mental health services system. *Archives of General Psychiatry, 35*, 685–693.

Regier, D. A., Narrow, W. E., Rae, D. S., Manderscheid, R. W., Locke, B. Z., & Goodwin, F. K. (1993). The de
facto US mental and addictive disorders service system: Epidemiologic catchment area prospective
1-year prevalence rates of disorders and services. *Archives of General Psychiatry, 50*, 85–94.

Robinson, R. G., Starr, L. B., & Price, T. R. (1984). A two year longitudinal study of post-stroke mood disorders: prevalence and duration at six months follow-up. *British Journal of Psychiatry, 144*, 256–262.

Rolnick, S. J., & O'Connor, P. J. (1997). Assessing the impact of clinical guidelines: research lessons learned.
Journal of Ambulatory Care Management, 20(4), 47–55.

Roter, D. L., Hall, J. A., Kern, D. E., Barker, L. R., Cole, K. A., & Roca, R. P. (1995). Improving physicians' interviewing skills and reducing patients' emotional distress. *Archives of Internal Medicine, 155*,
1877–1884.

Schulberg, H. D., & Pajer, K. A. (1994). Treatment of depression in primary care. In J. Miranda, A. A.
Hohmann, C. C. Attkisson, & D. B. Larson (Eds.), *Mental disorders in primary care* (pp. 259–286). San
Franciso: Jossey-Bass.

Seaburn, D. B., Lorenz, A. D., Gunn, W. B., Gawinski, B. A., Mauksch, L. B. (1996). *Models of collaboration.*
New York: Basic Books.

Shapiro, S., Skinner, E. A., Kesler, L. G., Von Korff, M., German, P. S., Tischler, G. L., Leaf, J., Benham, L.,
Cottler, L., & Regier, D. A. (1984). Utilization of health and mental health services: Three epidemiological catchment area sites. *Archives of General Psychiatry, 41*, 971–978.

Simon, G., Von Korff, M., & Barlow, W. (1995). Health care costs associated with depressive and anxiety
disorders in primary care. *Archives of General Psychiatry, 52*, 850–856.

Simon, G. E., & Von Korff, M. (1997). Is the integration of behavioral health into primary care worth the effort? A review of the evidence. In N. A. Cummings, J. L. Cummings, & J. N. Johnson (Eds.), *Behavioral
health in primary care: A guide for clinical integration* (pp. 145–162). Madison, WI: Psychosocial Press.

Smith, G. R., Monson, R. A., & Ray, D. C. (1986). Psychiatric consultation in somatization disorder. A randomized controlled study. *New England Journal of Medicine, 314*, 1407–1413.

Smith, G. R., Rost, K., & Kashner, T. M. (1995). A trial of the effect of a standardized psychiatric consultation on health outcomes and costs in somatizing patients. *Archives of General Psychiatry, 52*, 238–243.

Sobel, D. S. (1995). Rethinking medicine: Improving health outcomes with cost-effective psychosocial interventions. *Psychosomatic Medicine, 57*, 234–244.

Sobel, D. S. (1997, November). *Improving health outcomes through collaborative care: "Out of the box" healthcare
strategies.* Paper presented at the Third National Primary Care Behavioral Healthcare Summit, sponsored by the Institute for Behavioral Healthcare, Chicago.

Spiegel, D., Bloom, J. R., & Kraemer, H. C. (1989). Effect of psychosocial treatment on survival of patients
with metastatic breast cancer. *Lancet, 2*, 888–891.

Starkstein, S. E., & Robinson, R. G. (1989). Affective disorders and cerebral vascular disease. *British Journal
of Psychiatry, 154*, 170–182.

State of Minnesota Employees Consumer Satisfaction Survey Results. (1997). Sponsored by the State of Minnesota Joint Labor–Management Committee on Health Plans and the Dept. of Employee Relations, St.
Paul.

Strosahl, K. (1997). Building primary care behavioral health systems that work: A compass and a horizon. In N. A. Cummings, J. L. Cummings, & J. N. Johnson (Eds.), *Behavioral health in primary care: A guide for clinical integration* (pp. 37–60). Madison, WI: Psychosocial Press.

Strosahl, K. (1998). Integrating behavioral health and primary care services: The primary mental health model. In A. Blount (Ed.), *Integrated primary care: The future of medical and mental health collaboration* (pp. 139–166). New York: W. W. Norton.

Unutzer, J., Patrick, D. L., Simon, G., Grembowski, D., Walker, E., Ruter, C., & Katon, W. (1997). Depressive symptoms and the cost of health services in HMO patients age 65 years and older: A 4 year prospective study. *JAMA, 277,* 1618–1623.

Von Korff, M., Gruman, J., Schaeffer, J., Curry, W., & Wagner, E. (1997). Collaborative management of chronic illness. *Annals of Internal Medicine, 127,* 12.

Von Korff, M., Ormel, J., Katon, W., & Lin, E. H. (1992). Disability and depression among high utilizers of health care: A longitudinal analysis. *Archives of General Psychiatry, 49,* 91–100.

Wagner, E., Austin, T., & Von Korff, M. (1996). Organizing care for patients with chronic illness. *Milbank Quarterly, 74,* 4.

Integration of Behavioral Health Care Services in Pediatric Primary Care Settings

Mary Evers-Szostak
Durham Pediatric Psychology
Durham, North Carolina

One goal of current health care reform has been to reverse the trend toward specialization and fragmented care by bolstering primary care services as a foundation for more effective and cost-efficient care (Miranda, Hohmann, Atkinson, & Larson, 1994). This has led to an increasing interest in the development of integrated health care delivery systems in the past few years, and it now seems likely that we will see larger numbers of behavioral health care providers working alongside physicians and other medical personnel in primary health care settings to more thoroughly address the complex interaction between physical illness and psychological factors. This chapter addresses these developments in the area of children's health care, specifically in pediatric primary care settings. Several topics will be addressed: the justifications for integrating behavioral health care into pediatric primary care settings, current trends in identifying behavioral issues in these settings, and the issues and concerns that are important to consider in providing integrated care in pediatric primary care settings. The focus of the chapter also emphasizes the potential role of pediatric psychologists in these settings.

JUSTIFICATIONS FOR INTEGRATING BEHAVIORAL HEALTH CARE INTO PEDIATRIC PRIMARY CARE SETTINGS

The challenges facing U.S. children and families in the 1990s are alarming. About 20% of children live in poverty, and that number increases to about 25% for children under 6 years of age. The infant mortality rate in this country is higher than in 19 other developed nations. There has been a resurgence of preventable childhood diseases, due in part to inadequate rates of immunizations for infants and toddlers in urban areas. Families are under stress from a high divorce rate, difficulties finding adequate child care, and large numbers who lack health insurance and access to appropriate medical care.

Recently the American Psychological Association (APA) Task Force on Comprehensive and Coordinated Psychological Services for Children 0–10 released a call for service integration to better meet the needs of children (APA, Task Force, 1994). Members of the task force reported that there is an increasing consensus that the current service delivery system is not meeting the needs of children and families and that it will be necessary to make fundamental changes in how the system operates to ensure that services are comprehensive, responsive, and integrated. They encouraged psychologists to broaden their role in these systems to provide advocacy, prevention, consultation, assessment, and treatment for children and families. An emphasis on promoting psychological competence and self-sufficiency rather than focusing on dysfunction and pathology was also recommended. This would, of course, require a balance between prevention, early intervention, and treatment modalities. Finally, the task force members identified pediatric primary health care settings as a natural entry point for providing integrated care to address children's mental health needs.

Marketplace issues are also creating a move toward integrated systems of care, particulary the tendency for private insurers to eliminate or severely restrict mental health benefits (Illback, 1997). In addition to pressures from private insurers, many states have converted their Medicaid programs into managed care systems and many of these have also added a behavioral health "carve-out" (Paster, 1997). As financial resources shrink, integrated systems are likely to present the most efficient means of meeting the increasingly serious needs of children and families.

The high frequency with which children present with behavioral needs in pediatric primary care settings provides another justification for integrating psychological care into them (Goldberg, Roghman, McInerny, & Burke, 1984). Pediatricians have long recognized the importance of psychological issues in medical care (Richmond, 1967), and the field has expanded its boundaries to include addressing emotional, educational, and social aspects of children and their development (Haggerty, 1972, 1974; Yancy, 1975). Prevalence studies have found that children can present with developmental, emotional, and behavioral problems throughout their developing years and that the incidence of these problems increases over time. Zill and Schoenborn (1990) reported that 5.3% of 3- to 5-year-olds, 12.7% of 6- to 11-year-olds, and 18.5% of 12- to 17-year-olds have these kinds of problems. It also has been estimated that 20% of pediatric primary care patients have biosocial or developmental problems (American Academy of Pediatrics, 1978). This prevalence rate is similar to other community studies (Costello, 1990). It is no surprise, then, that care for behavioral and psychological problems has been referred to as "the new morbidity" in pediatrics (Costello, 1986; Haggerty, Roghmann, & Pless, 1975), and pediatricians tend to be the first professionals parents talk to about their children's behavior and development (Clarke-Stewart, 1978).

Problems in Traditional Pediatric Service Delivery

Although there are clearly demands for addressing biopsychosocial and developmental problems in pediatric primary care settings, it is increasingly difficult for pediatricians and other medical health care providers to meet them. For example, the demand to see increasing numbers of patients has had a dramatic effect on the time they can spend with each child. If pediatricians are asked to see four to six children each hour, they simply have very little time available to address developmental anticipatory guidance or to identify and manage psychological problems (Christophersen, 1983). For example, one observational study of pediatricians found that the time spent on anticipatory guidance averaged a high of 97 seconds for babies under 5 months of age and a low of 7 seconds for adolescents (Reisinger & Bires, 1980).

There are also concerns about pediatricians' training to meet these needs. In 1978 a survey conducted by the American Academy of Pediatrics Task Force on Pediatric Education found that large numbers of pediatricians thought that biosocial and developmental issues had been under emphasized in their training (American Academy of Pediatrics, 1978). It is unclear how much improvement has been made in this area since the Task Force's report. Weinberger and Oski (1984) surveyed 29 pediatric residency training programs and found no trend indicating an increased emphasis in training on biopsychosocial issues. In a more recent study, Wender and her colleagues (Wender, Bijur, & Boyce, 1992) did a follow-up survey of pediatricians trained after 1978 and found that many still rated their training in these areas as insufficient, although Wender et al. noted less dissatisfaction among those trained after 1984 and an increased interest in developmental and behavioral pediatrics as subspecialties.

Pediatricians' concerns about their abilities to identify behavioral and developmental concerns appear to be well founded. Costello and her colleagues (Costello et al., 1988) found that while pediatricians seldom misdiagnosed children as having a significant psychiatric disturbance (84% of those they identified as nondisturbed had no psychiatric disorder), they often failed to identify children with psychiatric disorders (only 17% of the children with significant problems were identified). One difficulty in identifying problems may be parents' apparent tendency to not talk to their pediatricians about these issues. Various studies have found that 40% to 80% of parents have questions or concerns about their children's behavior and development but few discuss these issues during office visits (Lynch, Wildman, & Smucker, 1997; Richardson, Keller, Selby-Harrington, & Parrish, 1996; Young, Davis, Schoen, & Parker, 1998).

Even when problems are identified, they are often not adequately addressed by the provider (Sharp, Pantell, Murphy, & Lewis, 1992). Sharp et al. (1992) found that 60% of psychosocial concerns expressed by parents resulted in no response or only a passive response (acknowledgment of the problem by asking more questions, but no information or reassurance offered) from pediatric and family medicine residents. Although parents may fail to report their concerns about psychological issues, they appear to expect that pediatricians will address behavioral issues when they are raised. One study found that 41.3% of parents who had changed or were strongly considering changing their pediatrician cited the doctor's lack of interest in the child's behavior as a primary reason for dissatisfaction (Hickson, Stewart, Altemeier, & Perrin, 1988). Another study (McClelland, Staples, Weisberg, & Berger, 1973) found that 37% of all well child visits to pediatricians involved support and counseling for issues related to parenting and behavior management, with an additional 19% of questions concerning school performance.

Pediatricians also express concern about parents' compliance with recommendations to obtain mental health services for their children. One study found that pediatricians referred 16% of the children they identified as having significant problems to specialty services (Horwitz, Leaf, Leventhal, Forsyth, & Speechley, 1992), whereas another study found that only 53% of children referred for counseling received the prescribed therapy (Joost, Chessare, Schaeufele, Link, & Weaver, 1989). Tuma (1989) estimated that 70% to 80% of children needing mental health services do not receive them. Having behavioral health care providers available in pediatric primary care settings would certainly help to ensure that more children in need of services would be identified and that the appropriate services would be more likely to be obtained.

Integration as a Solution to the Problems

Some evidence also suggests that parents like this model of care and are very comfortable using mental health care services provided in this way. Hurley, McIntire, and Evers-Szostak (1994) surveyed 320 parents to study parent satisfaction with the pediatric psychology services provided within two private pediatric offices — one in Fort Worth, Texas, and the other in Durham, North Carolina. They found that parents who had seen the psychologist in the pediatrics office were overwhelmingly positive about their experience. Even parents who had not seen the psychologist responded very positively. Although only 16% of the parents had actually used the psychologists' services, 94% of those responding thought that it was a good or excellent idea to provide these services within the pediatric office. Most parents (75%) thought there were no disadvantages to having a pediatric psychologist in the office. Of those who indicated at least one disadvantage, 42% thought parents might feel pressured to use the psychologist in the practice rather than one of their own choosing, 36% were concerned about confidentiality with the front office staff, and 27% were concerned about confidentiality with the pediatrician. The general impression held by parents was that having a pediatric psychologist in the primary care pediatric setting was beneficial, and most stated that they would use this service if they ever needed it. Most (84%) felt their child would be more comfortable in the familiar setting, and 80% felt there would be better communication between the psychologist and pediatrician. Another 63% stated that parents would be more comfortable in the familiar setting, 56% felt the psychologist would be child-oriented in that setting, and 45% would trust the psychologist if their pediatrician trusted him or her. Parents especially appreciated the opportunity to get some input about their children's development or minor concerns with a free phone call. Finney, Riley, and Cataldo (1991) also measured a high level of parental satisfaction with behaviorally oriented psychological services in a primary care setting.

Pediatricians and child psychologists certainly seem to be likely to collaborate well because both disciplines share interests in children's health and development. In fact, Lightner Witmer wrote about these common interests a hundred years ago (Witmer, 1896). Wilson (1964) recognized the potential benefits of including pediatric psychologists in primary care settings more than thirty years ago in his presidential address to the American Academy of Pediatrics. He said, "One of the things I would do if I could control the practice of pediatrics would be to encourage groups of pediatricians to employ their own clinical psychologists." Not long after Wilson (1964) made his remarks, Logan Wright (1967) began describing a new breed of psychologists — pediatric psychologists — who would have the skills necessary to work in pediatric medical settings rather than traditional psychiatric settings. An early description of collaboration in pediatric primary care settings also appeared at about the same time (Smith, Rome, & Freedheim, 1967). LeBaron and Zeltzer (1985) also argued that pediatrician–psychologist collaboration can result in significant improvements in children's primary health care.

Although the initial interest in this collaboration may have included some emphasis on primary care, pediatric psychology has developed since the late 1960s, largely as a specialty area focusing on psychological issues related to chronic physical illnesses mainly treated in tertiary care settings, usually large university medical centers. During this period, pediatric psychology developed a unique set of characteristics, including clinical practice based in medical settings, a medically based referral mechanism, an orientation toward health promotion and prevention to enhance normal development, an emphasis on developmental considerations, familiarity with consultation to physicians and parents, and a practical orientation to treatment techniques that are effective, time-efficient, and economical (Roberts, 1986). Given current changes in the health care system, it seems likely that pediatric psychologists will begin to become more involved in primary care settings. This is particulary true when one considers that most children receive their medical care in some sort of primary care setting (frequently a pediatric office or clinic) and that many children access the behavioral health care system in these settings. This also will likely prove to be a "natural fit" because the types of problems seen by pediatric psychologists tend to involve primary and preventive mental health care and often involve collaboration with pediatric medical care providers.

CURRENT TRENDS IN IDENTIFYING BEHAVIORAL ISSUES IN PEDIATRIC PRIMARY CARE

Although pediatricians clearly struggle to identify children with psychiatric disorders (Costello, 1986; Goldberg et al., 1984; Horwitz et al., 1992; Lavigne et al., 1993; Merritt, Thompson, Keith, Johndrow, & Murphy, 1993), there has been some evidence to suggest that they may be better suited to identify subthreshold problems that do not meet the criteria for a formal psychiatric diagnosis. For example, Horwitz et al. (1992) found that the pediatricians in their study identified 27.3% of 4- to 8-year-old children with problems that could be identified using a 13-point checklist of psychosocial and developmental problems based on a triaxial classification system developed by Burns, Burke, and Regier (1982). Although this represented an improvement over identification rates for psychiatric diagnoses, it must be noted that this classification system included social problems, which are usually viewed as risk factors in other prevalence and identification studies (Costello & Shugart, 1992).

Pediatricians have also reported that large numbers of children present with mental health problems that cause distress but fail to reach the level of severity required for a diagnosis using the rules in the American Psychiatric Association's *Diagnostic and Statistical Manual of Mental Disorders–IV* (American Psychiatric Association, 1994). Their concerns about children with subthreshold problems have not been heavily studied, but have received some support in research findings. Costello and Shugart (1992) found that 42% of children seen in a pediatric primary care setting had these kinds of problems. They also found that most disruptive behavior problems of this severity were associated with significant functional impairment and concluded that intervention for these problems may be needed to avoid more serious levels of impairment.

Pediatricians' efforts to treat children with psychological problems have also been thwarted by a reimbursement system that has often arbitrarily reserved *DSM–IV* (APA, 1994) diagnostic codes and psychiatric current procedural terminology (CPT) codes for use only by mental health providers. The organizational structure of managed care, in particular its emphasis on mental health "carve-outs," has also led to a separation of mental disorders from medical disorders at a time when research findings have increased our understanding of the interplay between mind and body. The current classification system clearly needs some additional work to make it possible for pediatricians to provide care for psychological concerns and to enhance communications between primary care providers and mental health clinicians (Wolraich, 1997). To better meet the needs of children, an addition to the classification system would have to include information about the common, but less severe psychosocial problems that primary care pediatricians frequently manage.

Development of a Useful Classification Scheme

In 1989 the National Institute of Mental Health sponsored two meetings between primary care practitioners in internal medicine, family practice, pediatrics, and obstetrics/gynecology and representatives of the American Psychiatric Association. Those meetings concluded that primary care providers did not find the *DSM–IV* (APA, 1994) useful and ended with a recommendation to develop a more appropriate system for use in primary care. Although the American Psychiatric Association assumed responsibility for development of a system to be used with adults, pediatricians expressed a need for a system that would not only address disorders but would also emphasize developmental changes and environmental factors. A collaborative effort led by the American Academy of Pediatrics and including the American Psychiatric Association, the American Psychological Association (primarily the Society for Pediatric Psychology), the Society for Developmental and Behavioral Pediatrics, the American Academy of Child and Adolescent Psychiatry, the American Academy of Family Physicians, the Canadian Pediatric Society, the Zero to Three/National Center for Clinical Infant Programs, the Maternal and Child Health Bureau, and the National Institute of Mental Health then began to develop a classification system for use with children in primary care settings (Wolraich, 1997).

This effort resulted in the development of the *Diagnostic and Statistical Manual for Primary Care (DSM–PC) Child and Adolescent Version* (Wolraich, Felice, & Drotar, 1996). Several assumptions were made in constructing the system (Wolraich, 1997):

1. Children demonstrate symptoms that vary along a continuum from normal variations to mental disorders, and this continuum can be grouped into normal developmental variations, problems, and disorders.
2. Environment has an important impact on the mental health of children, and if stressful situations are addressed, more severe mental health problems can be prevented later.
3. Children vary in how they manifest symptoms or respond to situations, depending on their age and development.
4. A useful system must remain compatible with existing systems such as *DSM–IV* (APA, 1994).
5. The system must be clear, concise, and user-friendly for primary care physicians.

6. The system must be based on objective information as much as possible, with consensus when this is not possible, and organized so that it can be verified or revised by subsequent research.

The *DSM–PC* (Wolraich et al., 1996) is divided into two major sections. The first section addresses the issue of the child's environment and allows the clinician to consider the impact of situations and stressors on the child's mental health. This section also includes information about potentially adverse situations and key risk and protective factors. A summary of common behavioral responses to stressful events for children of various ages is also provided.

The second section describes child manifestations that are organized into behavioral clusters. A clinician can begin by using an index of presenting complaints. Each cluster was developed to help the clinician evaluate the spectrum of the child's symptoms, common developmental presentations, and the differential diagnosis. The classification system is based on the assumption that most behavioral manifestations reflect a spectrum from normal to disordered behavior and each cluster has three categories: *developmental variations, problems,* and *disorders.* Developmental variations are behaviors that may raise some concern, but are within the range of expected behaviors for the child's age. Problems reflect behavioral manifestations that are serious enough to disrupt the child's functioning with peers, in school, and/or in the family but are not severe enough to warrant the diagnosis of a mental disorder. The disorders are those defined in the *DSM–IV* (APA, 1994). Although pediatricians may often manage developmental variations and problems, most children presenting with disorders would be referred to mental health clinicians. In a primary care setting that includes the integration of a pediatric psychologist, the psychologist or the pediatrician might manage developmental variations and problems. The psychologist would likely manage the care for children with disorders either directly or by referral to another mental health clinician in the community.

The section on childhood manifestations also includes developmental guidelines broken into four age periods: infancy (birth to 2 years of age), early childhood (3 to 5 years of age), middle childhood (6 to 12 years of age), and adolescence (13 years of age and older). These guidelines are designed to help the clinician recognize the differences in presentation of various problems or disorders in various age groups. The system is also designed to allow for the identification of alternative causes and differential diagnoses. Moreover, it addresses the issue of comorbidity of disorders. Finally, the manual provides general guidelines to determine the severity of a child's condition by considering symptoms, functioning, burden of suffering, and risk/protective factors. It suggests using the three categories of mild, moderate, and severe to describe severity.

Although the *DSM–PC* (Wolraich et al., 1996) is certainly a welcome addition to the tools available to primary care pediatricians, it remains to be seen whether it will, in fact, see much use. Widespread utilization of this manual will certainly depend on its usefulness in securing reimbursement for services. Most insurers have confined reimbursement for mental health services to a short list of psychiatric CPT codes linked to *DSM–IV* (APA, 1994) diagnoses. Rappo (1997) provided a list of current medical CPT codes that could be used along with *DSM–PC* diagnoses. Although pediatricians may find these codes useful, they have generally not been recognized for use by mental health clinicians. Therefore, it will also be necessary for third-party reimbursement to allow mental health clinicians working in pediatric primary care settings to link *DSM–PC* diagnoses with Rappo's list of CPT codes. Finally, mental health clinicians in other settings will need to become familiar with the *DSM–PC* (1996) if it is to help improve communication with pediatricians regarding children's mental health conditions.

Aids to Pediatric Classification

If pediatricians are to efficiently identify children with significant psychosocial problems, it seems likely that they will need good instruments to assist in the process. Although the development of behavior rating scales like the Child Behavior Checklist (CBCL) (Achenbach, 1991) and structured interviews like the Diagnostic Interview Schedule for Children (DISC; Shaffer et al., 1993) have helped with the identification of children with psychiatric diagnoses, there is some question about their utility in primary care settings. This is a particular concern when children with subthreshold problems are considered because psychiatric measures are unlikely to identify children with less severe but still significant problems. Psychiatric measures also tend to be more lengthy and could prove cumbersome for primary care clinicians to use. For example, the CBCL has 113 questions and is scored on eight clinical subscales. Structured interviews like the DISC are even more labor-intensive. Primary care clinicians clearly need simpler instruments that can be used quickly and are best described as screening tools (Jellinek, Murphy, & Burns, 1986).

Pediatricians should probably also remain flexible about screening (Christophersen, 1994). Some children are in obvious need of mental health care services and screening would be of little help to them. Children who are clearly developing normally probably also do not require much screening. To solve these problems, it has been suggested that screening be done in two stages (Frankenburg, 1983; Squires, Nickel, & Eisert, 1996). The first stage is done in the pediatrician's office and involves quick, simple testing that would preferably overestimate the number of children in need of further screening, thus resulting in a relatively high number of false positives. The second stage of screening would utilize instruments that take longer to administer but would yield more information for the clinician. It would likely be most efficient for this screening to be done by a pediatric psychologist in the office. Children could also be referred to other mental health care providers who do not operate with the same time pressures as do pediatricians.

Screening questionnaires to be used in the first stage should be valid, reliable, and select the correct children for further evaluation. They should also be brief, understandable, easily completed, and scored quickly. Finally, they should require a minimum of professional time unless the results indicate a problem. Eisert, Sturner, and Mabe (1991) have provided a helpful review of the issues involved in selecting screening tools for pediatricians. Their guidelines are also applied to several behavioral questionnaires.

Some instruments have been developed that are appropriate for use in the first stage of screening and two will be reviewed here. The Eyberg Child Behavior Inventory (Eyberg, & Ross, 1978; Robinson, Eyberg, & Ross, 1980) has been used widely in research and is well validated. It is a 36-item questionnaire that parents can complete in about 5 minutes and that pediatricians can review quickly. It includes questions about child behavior during bedtime and mealtime and is particularly helpful in identifying children at risk for disruptive behavior problems. It yields two scores that reflect the number of problems a child is having and their intensity.

Another instrument that has been used widely in research is the Pediatric Symptom Checklist (PSC) (Jellinek & Murphy, 1990; Jellinek et al., 1986). The PSC was designed specifically for psychosocial screening in pediatric office settings. It is a 35-item questionnaire that measures the presence of behavioral and/or emotional symptoms. Scoring is quick and yields a single total score. Cutoff scores of 24 for 4- and 5-year-old children (Little, Murphy, Jellinek, Bishop, & Arnett, 1994) and 28 for children 6–12 years of age (Jellinek et al., 1986) have been empirically established.

It should be noted that several other questionnaires are available to screen for psychosocial concerns in younger children. These include the Behavior Checklist (Richman & Graham, 1971), Behar's Pre-school Behavior Questionnaire (Behar, 1977), and the Toddler Behavior Screening Inventory (Mouton-Simien, McCain, & Kelley, 1997).

Although there has been increasing interest in first-stage screening among pediatricians, several problems have been identified. First, it appears that many primary care physicians are interested in screening but only a small percentage actually implement these procedures. One study followed up on 201 pediatricians and family practitioners who had requested information about the PSC and found that only 23% of those who responded reported that they had used the measure (Bishop, Murphy, Jellinek, & Dusseault, 1991). Second, a recent review of the current status of behavior screening methods concluded that it is unclear whether screening will cause a significant change in physician behaviors necessary to improve child functional outcomes (Stancin & Palermo, 1997). Jellinek and Murphy (1990) noted that screening is just one step in a process that raises additional questions about the pediatrician's ability to follow up on the results of the screening, family acceptance of referral to mental health clinicians, time devoted to psychosocial issues in light of time constraints and problems with reimbursements, and the effectiveness of interventions. Finally, most of the efforts to develop screening tools have focused on identifying children with psychiatric disorders. Although this is certainly necessary, use of these tools fails to identify many of the more common problems that pediatricians are likely to encounter and manage (Long, Hendon, & Henard-Zolten, 1993).

PROVIDING INTEGRATED CARE IN PEDIATRIC PRIMARY CARE SETTINGS

Pediatricians will continue to be called on for anticipatory guidance, advice about common behavior problems, early detection of problems, and referral for more serious disorders. Interested pediatricians can find a good deal of helpful information in the behavioral pediatrics literature. In fact, behavioral pediatricians have assumed a good deal of the responsibility for training current pediatric residents in the management of the "new morbidity." Several techniques for managing common behavior problems can be found in an article by Christophersen (1982). These ideas have been further expanded to address behavioral problems, medical/behavioral problems, educational intervention strategies, advanced intervention techniques, and office management strategies (Christophersen, 1994). Both of these publications include numerous examples of handouts that can be given to parents during office visits.

Additional attention has also recently been given to the idea of including behavioral health care professionals in the pediatric primary care office. Pediatric psychologists already have a strong history of successful collaboration with pediatricians in tertiary care settings and are probably extremely well suited to making the transition into working in pediatric primary care settings. In particular, the emphasis within pediatric psychology on preventive care and a focus away from psychopathology matches well with the issues to be managed in primary care settings.

Models of Integrated Pediatric Care

Several qualities of successful collaboration between pediatricians and pediatric psychologists have been identified. Psychologists who practice effectively in tertiary care hospitals or in primary care do not just transfer their training in traditional clinical psychology to these medical settings (Drotar, 1993, 1995). They take the time to understand and adapt to the special characteristics of the settings, populations, and providers. Most effective psychologists in medical settings have a strong personal and professional identity. A high level of professional commitment is common in this group, and they tend to be thorough, work hard, and go beyond minimal expectations. They are also flexible and know when to stick up for things and when to let things go. They know how to advocate for themselves without being overly aggressive or demanding. This comes in handy when one is dealing with the competing expectations that can go along with any collaboration. Most are comfortable developing plans and taking action. The best ones easily make psychological knowledge very user-friendly. It is important to remember that the psychologist's relationship with the pediatricians will be a long-term one. Therefore, appreciation and respect for pediatricians are important. The successful psychologist will understand the demands that pediatricians face, respect their expertise, and understand and tolerate their limits. This appreciation for colleagues is particularly important for pediatric psychologists working in primary care settings, because their frequent interactions with the pediatricians are likely to have an effect on the setting as well as on all the professionals involved. In other words, the pediatrician is likely to learn from the psychologist and the psychologist is likely to learn from the pediatrician throughout the course of their collaboration. Hamlett and Stabler (1995) described a developmental process that takes place in these collaborations that moves in higher degrees of complexity from clinical case management to long-term collaboration, and eventually on to program and policy development.

The model for integrated care in pediatric primary care settings is generally a collaborative one. The partners in this collaboration are the pediatricians, pediatric psychologists, nurses, lab personnel, and support staff within the office or clinic. Community contacts are also important and can include school personnel, developmental therapists, public sector providers, psychiatrists, and other therapists. There are some disadvantages to this approach, such as the need to negotiate with colleagues, some loss of control, and additional demands on the psychologist's time. The advantages are the input from colleagues with different areas of expertise, a broader range of activities, and not having to carry the entire load alone.

This type of collaboration is well known to pediatric psychologists because they have often functioned in tertiary care settings as behavioral health care consultants to their medical colleagues. Several conceptual models of pediatric consultation have been advanced (Burns & Cromer, 1978; Drotar, 1978; Stabler, 1979). Roberts and Wright (1982) discussed a three-part model of consultation. Effective psychology practice in pediatric primary care settings features aspects of all three parts.

In the *independent functions model*, the consultant provides independent diagnosis and treatment of the patient. This model has also been called noncollaborative (Drotar, 1978), the resource consultation model (Stabler, 1979), and the client-centered model (Burns & Cromer, 1978). The main information exchanges between the pediatrician and the consultant happen at the point of the referral and at the completion of care. The pediatrician and the consultant have very little contact with each other and do not work collaboratively. This model is very familiar to most pediatricians because it characterizes the majority of consultation they receive from their medical colleagues. An example for a pediatric psychologist in a pediatric primary care setting would be if the pediatrician referred a child with a learning disability for an evaluation and family support for appropriate educational planning. In that case, the psychologist would take over the responsibility for helping the child and family and would keep the pediatrician informed of plans and important developments.

The second type of consultation is the *indirect functions model*, which has also been called the process-educative model (Stabler, 1979). In this model, the consultant functions as a teacher or informed colleague, providing advice, teaching, or protocols for patient management. The pediatrician retains responsibility for patient care. In this model, the consultant has little or no direct contact with the patient. An example would be if a pediatrician were managing stimulant medication for attention deficit hyperactivity disorder (ADHD) and asked the psychologist for help in interpreting feedback from parents and teachers in determining whether the medication was helpful for a child.

The *collaborative team model* is similar to process consultation (Stabler, 1979) and collaboration as defined by Burns and Cromer (1978). In this model the consultant and the pediatrician truly collaborate and share responsibility and decision making for patient care. This model is employed more often in teaching/research centers and less in private practice settings because it is time-intensive and often requires team meetings. An example in a primary care setting would be if the psychologist and the pediatrician were collaborating in the care of a child with complicated encopresis that required medical management as well as behavioral interventions.

Effective integrated care models involve more than just providing traditional mental health services in primary care settings. This level of integration relies on using the indirect functions model and the collaborative teams model when appropriate and requires frequent communication between the pediatricians and the pediatric psychologist. This kind of collaboration allows the pediatric psychologist to have some input into a child's medical care as well as for the pediatrician to influence the child's behavioral health care. As such, it provides a more holistic approach to children's health care.

Although interest in integrating pediatric psychologists into primary care settings has increased recently, several earlier works described some of the aspects of this work (Fischer & Englen, 1972; Ottinger & Roberts, 1988; Schroeder, 1979; Walker, 1979). It may now be more common for pediatric offices and clinics to include a pediatric psychologist, but the trend has been slow to develop. One reason for this has been psychologists' lack of familiarity with the characteristics and demands of pediatric primary care settings. Students are not usually exposed to these settings during their training, and relatively few publications are available to guide psychologists interested in entering this area of practice (Christophersen, 1982, 1994; Evers-Szostak, 1998; Hurley, 1995; Routh, Schroeder, & Koocher, 1983; Schroeder, 1979, 1997; Schroeder & Gordon, 1991; Schroeder, Gordon, Kanoy, & Routh, 1983). Another reason is that many pediatric primary care offices are private practices, and psychologists moving into these areas must take on many business issues. Most pediatric psychologists are better prepared to confront practice in more academic settings, like university medical centers. Finally, private practice pediatricians are often so busy with patient care and their own business issues that it is difficult for them to take on the additional job of recruiting pediatric psychologists to work with them. There is some suggestion that the effort necessary to integrate a pediatric psychologist into a pediatric primary care office or clinic results in a positive experience for the psychologist. A recent survey of 261 pediatric psychologists found that 21% of them were working in private practice or outpatient pediatric settings and also found that the group in private practice reported the highest levels of job satisfaction (Drotar, Sturm, Eckerle, & White, 1993).

Although some information is available for pediatric psychologists working in these settings, it must be recognized that a shift in the focus of research and training will be necessary if more of them are going to be integrated into this kind of care. Although the clinical areas of psychology have emphasized pathology and dysfunction, truly integrated work in primary care settings requires a shift toward normal development and common, less severe problems. Pediatric psychologists working in primary care will be in a unique position to demonstrate treatments and management techniques that work with normally developing children in much the same way that many psychologists working in traditional mental health specialties have moved toward empirically validating treatments for psychiatric disorders. Holden and Schumann (1995) pointed out that little research has been done to evaluate the integration of pediatric psychology services into primary care, but it seems likely that more pediatric psychologists will have to move into these settings before this research can be done. Because many of these practices are not affiliated with university departments and rely heavily on fee-for-service work, it may prove difficult to complete these studies unless pediatric psychologists in academic departments and those working in these practices collaborate on this work. There are some indications that these studies would find positive results. Finney et al. (1991) found that 74% of the children served in an outpatient health care setting improved. They also noted some medical cost offset for some diagnoses with outpatient psychological interventions.

If psychologists are to be effective members of primary care teams, it is critical that they have a good understanding of these settings as well as the ways in which pediatricians approach their own work. In other words, psychologists must adapt their own thinking and approaches to be successful. Drotar (1993) identified ways in which pediatricians' and psychologists' expectations about how the other should perform their duties may differ. For example, pediatricians' familiarity with medical consultation may lead them to expect that a psychologist will provide prompt and specific feedback following a referral, as well as any necessary follow-up care for a patient. Psychologists who are more familiar with traditional mental health care settings may expect that pediatricians will supply them with comprehensive information about each patient they refer and be available to discuss the results of an evaluation in great detail. Because pediatric psychologists are trained in medical settings and are familiar with their demands and expectations, it should be expected that these kinds of conflicts are less likely to occur when they collaborate with pediatricians in primary care settings.

Pediatric psychologists accustomed to the work in tertiary care settings will have to become familiar with the demands of primary care. Pediatric primary care practices are very busy and are results oriented. A fast pace and a heavy workload are the norm. Work in these settings requires the quick recognition of problems and their solutions as well as the timely implementation of effective plans. The pace for pediatricians in primary care settings is much faster than that of their medical colleagues working in specialty clinics and tertiary care settings. In short, there is no time for the discussion of interesting diagnostic dilemmas or power struggles over psychological treatment plans. The focus is more likely to be on what the psychologist plans to do to solve a child's problems. Because pediatricians are often the first providers to identify developmental and psychological problems but may not have the time and skills to fully address them, a pediatric psychologist can play a valuable role in providing necessary patient care. Pediatricians can also be quite helpful to the pediatric psychologist. For example, they can frequently provide useful background information about children and families because they often have very long-term relationships with them. They may know things about children and families that it may be difficult for the psychologist to find out early in an evaluation.

At any given time, the pediatrics office is mostly full of babies and young children. These age groups have more frequent visits for preventive care and also are the ones more likely to be sick. It is important that a psychologist working in primary care pediatrics be comfortable working with infants, toddlers, preschoolers, and their parents. Most of the children seen in primary care settings are also developing normally, so it is necessary for the psychologist to become familiar with the problems common to most children. It also helps to be comfortable working with seasonal demands. The increased demand for medical care for acute illness in the winter means that the pace around the office or clinic is much more hectic at that time of year.

Finally, parents rely heavily on telephone contact with pediatricians and nurses, and it is important for the psychologist to develop strategies to be available this way as well. For example, it can be helpful to have a parent hotline that allows parents to call for advice on handling common behavior problems their children might be having that do not warrant an office visit. Work by Schroeder and her colleagues provides some guidance about parental concerns that are likely to be encountered in telephone calls and advice that parents find helpful (Kanoy & Schroeder, 1985; Mesibov, Schroeder, & Wesson, 1977). These studies have found that parents called most frequently with concerns in the following areas: negative behavior, toileting, personality or emotional problems, school problems, sleeping problems, developmental delays, sibling/peer problems, and divorce/separation. Parents who used a come-in/call-in service expressed high degrees of confidence in the counselors they talked with, and the vast majority of them rated the service as good.

The heavy workloads and quick pace of these settings require that psychologists manage stress well. Managing the workload can be difficult because it is unpredictable, so it is important to help the pediatricians, patients, and parents develop realistic expectations for the psychologist. It is also important that psychologists in these settings have realistic expectations for themselves. For example, it is critical for a pediatric psychologist working in a primary care setting to be absolutely clear about how many patients can be seen in a week and stick to that limit, particularly when things are more hectic in the office. It is also important to be clear about the types of problems the pediatric psychologist will manage. Although it may be tempting to become the mental health care provider for all the children in a pediatrics practice, doing so will quickly interfere with the psychologist's ability to take care of the more common, less severe problems that are more frequently the focus of the pediatrician's care.

CHARACTERISTICS OF PEDIATRIC PSYCHOLOGY
PRACTICE IN PRIMARY CARE SETTINGS

It is clear that the emphasis on prevention, intervention, and care for normally developing children in pediatric primary care has an effect on the practice of psychology in these settings. Much of the discussion here is based on experiences in the author's practice in Durham, North Carolina (Evers-Szostak, 1992, 1998; Evers-Szostak, Schroeder, & McClure, 1991; Evers-Szostak & Voegler, 1997). This pediatrics practice has seven full-time pediatricians and one full-time pediatric nurse practitioner, who care for about 35,000 patients. The pediatric psychology practice was started in 1988. A full-time pediatric psychologist and a half-time pediatric psychologist have now seen about 1,900 children. The average is about five new referrals per week, and the pattern of referral sources has remained very stable. Some parents in the pediatric practice view pediatric psychology as another part of their health care services, so 58% of referrals come from parents themselves. The pediatricians refer 31% of the psychologists' patients, and other physicians in the community refer an additional 2%. The remaining 9% of referrals come from a number of other sources. Many come from the nursing staff and sometimes from the receptionists. Other referrals come from teachers, school counselors, attorneys, and managed care companies.

As in most clinical situations, more boys than girls (63% vs. 37%) are seen. Because most of the children seen in the pediatrics office are younger, the psychologists' patients also tend to be younger, with 76% of them being 10 years old or younger. The age groups are as follows: 29% are 1–5 years of age, 47% are 6–10 years old, 20% are 11–15 years old, and 4% are 16 or older.

Presenting complaints have been tracked over the years. It should be noted that the percentages reported here reflect the fact that some children present with multiple complaints. The most common presenting problems (73%) involve negative behavior, attention deficit hyperactivity disorder (ADHD), and school concerns. Anxiety, divorce/separation, and depression are concerns for another 25% of the patients. Concerns that are quite familiar to pediatric psychologists (developmental delays, chronic illness, physical complaints, toileting problems, sleep disturbances, and grief issues) are involved in 14% of the presenting complaints. Other frequent concerns include child abuse/sex abuse (3%), peer problems/self-esteem (3%), fears/phobias (2%), and parent–child conflict (2%). When the data are examined further, some other patterns emerge. Boys tend to be seen more often for negative behavior and ADHD, and girls are more evenly spread out among the various categories of presenting complaints. Younger children are seen most frequently for negative behavior, and children in elementary school are frequently seen for ADHD. Adolescents continue to be seen for negative behavior and ADHD, but also begin to present with complaints about depression.

As can be seen, the psychologist in a pediatric primary care setting is confronted with the demand to address the needs of a very large number of children. This volume requires that the psychologist maintain a constant availability to new patients. This is critical to ensure that parents and children make appointments and keep them. Pediatricians in these settings value the increased likelihood of parents' following through on referrals to the psychologist in the office, but long waits to be seen can create problems with compliance and the timeliness of interventions. This demand leads to the necessity of referring children with certain types of problems out to other providers. These include complicated child abuse cases, eating disorders, major conduct disorders, substance abuse, and severe psychopathology. Children with these problems tend to slow down the flow of patients for the pediatric psychologist because they require a very large number of visits and the services of teams of providers that are not available in the pediatrics office. Thus, it is clearly necessary for pediatric psychologists practicing in pediatric primary care settings to maintain relationships with other mental health care clinicians in the local community who can be available to care for children and adolescents with more complicated and severe problems. It is particularly important to identify child psychiatrists who can be helpful in managing the pharmacological care for these patients and who may also have admitting privileges at local psychiatric units. Finally, these patients may also require referral to therapists who are more familiar with severe psychopathology.

As in most pediatric settings, the workload in primary care can be quite heavy and requires that the pediatric psychologist play several roles, including consultant, educator, clinician, and case-manager/advocate. A full-time pediatric psychologist can expect to average 25 patient hours per week with a range throughout the year of 15 to 35 patient hours per week. Typical clinical services include interviewing, testing, and psychotherapy. This is in addition to administrative time, consultation time, and phone calls. The emphasis on collaboration and integration of services means that the psychologist must be prepared to give away some services, such as consultations with the pediatricians and phone calls with parents. The advantage of providing these services is an increase in the visibility and perceived value of pediatric psychology in the practice.

Most children (60%) are seen for treatment only, and 29% are seen for evaluation only. The additional 11% are seen for evaluation and treatment. The number of visits in the author's practice ranges from 1 to 112, but the heaviest emphasis is on brief treatment. The modal number of visits is 1 and the median is 3 visits. Twenty-six percent of the children are seen for 1 visit, 75% are seen for 5 visits or less, and 86% are seen for 10 visits or less. Children seen for more visits tend to come for evaluation and treatment. Many of them also present with multiple problems.

This information easily leads to conclusions about the types of services that are effective in pediatric primary care settings. First, evaluations that quickly lead to appropriate developmental and educational interventions are important. These should mesh well with the efforts of special educators, speech/language therapists, occupational therapists, and physical therapists. Second, interventions must be problem-focused and brief. As a result, short-term behavioral approaches combined with long-term intermittent work are most effective. The psychologist in these settings must be also be comfortable with behavior management/parent training techniques, psychoeducational approaches, and early intervention. Third, because this is primary care, the psychologist must also be familiar with many community resources in order to be prepared to provide appropriate referrals for children and their parents. This work can include referrals to developmental therapists, school personnel, and other mental health professionals.

In a broad sense, services also include the psychologist's communication with the pediatricians and community physicians. They place a very high value on prompt feedback about their patients and often complain that mental health professionals frequently fall short in this regard. In the author's practice, parents are informed that the pediatric psychologists will be working collaboratively with the pediatricians and are told that this might limit their confidentiality. Parents' reactions to this approach tend to be very positive, and only a handful have expressed any concerns about it. In addition to providing prompt feedback, psychologists in these settings must communicate in the style of medical settings. This means that the message must be brief, accurate, and thorough. Good psychological consultants can take complicated concepts and present them in ways that are clear and seem sensible and pragmatic to physicians. It is critical in primary care to think from healthy, normal models rather than from pathology-oriented models.

Several methods of communication can be helpful. Within the office the pediatric psychologists and pediatricians rely most heavily on short curb-side consults, informal notes, and chart notes. Written feedback tends to be very brief and emphasizes conclusions and recommendations. There is usually little need to include much historical information because the pediatricians already know this. Recommendations for things the pediatricians should do in caring for a patient are particularly important and must be communicated clearly. It is also helpful to include something about how the psychologist plans to intervene. Communications outside the office are more variable. For example, the local schools want only full psychological reports. Local physicians tend to prefer letters they can use for chart documentation and sometimes request that these be faxed to improve the speed of response. A few physicians also ask for brief e-mail messages to keep them updated on progress.

SETTING UP A PEDIATRIC PSYCHOLOGY PRACTICE IN A PEDIATRIC PRIMARY CARE OFFICE

Truly integrated care requires that the psychologist be available in the pediatrics practice on a full-time basis. There are certainly other models that allow for close cooperation between pediatricians and pediatric psychologists, including part-time practice in the pediatrics office and strong referral relationships between pediatricians and pediatric psychologists in the community. This section provides information on setting up a full-time practice within a primary care pediatrics office to achieve a model of truly integrated care.

A good background in clinical child psychology is absolutely critical and a strong background in pediatric psychology is even better. Familiarity with interdisciplinary care models is also helpful. Pediatric psychologists have an advantage in these settings because of their skills in diagnosis and treatment, their familiarity with medical consultation–liaison models, their commitment to prevention and early intervention, and the emphasis in their training on working with physicians and medical patients. Experience in psychiatric settings or mental health centers is not as valuable to the psychologist in a pediatric primary care setting as is experience in a tertiary medical hospital or developmental disabilities center. A successful primary care pediatric psychologist must know how to work with infants, preschoolers, and elementary age children. Experience working with adolescents is helpful, particularly if it has emphasized normal adolescents rather than those with more severe psychological problems. The author's experience suggests that severely disturbed adolescents access the mental health system somewhere other than the private pediatrics office. In general, it is critical to have a good grounding in normal child development and common childhood problems. A strong understanding of ADHD, learning disabilities (LD), and developmental disabilities is also necessary.

Finally, the psychologist must have a firm grasp of behavioral and cognitive-behavioral treatments that are effective in individual work with children and in parent training. Long-term insight-oriented approaches are not appropriate in these settings, and children requiring them should be referred to other providers in the community. Although some of the children and parents seen in primary care might benefit from family therapy, formal training in this area is not necessary for the pediatric psychologist in these settings, because these needs can be addressed by other providers in the community.

The first step in the process of establishing a practice is, of course, identifying a pediatrics practice interested in having a psychologist in the office or clinic. In some instances, the pediatricians might approach a psychologist to join them. If this happens, the psychologist should listen carefully to what they are asking for. Once they have explained their reasons for looking for a psychologist, it will be possible to add to the list of things they could expect by describing other skills and interests that would mesh well with their practice.

It is more likely that a psychologist wishing to work in a primary care pediatric setting will have to actively look for a group of pediatricians to join and that it will be necessary to contact several groups before finding one that seems truly interested. In looking, it is important to first determine the pediatricians' general level of interest in mental health issues and their tendency to refer to mental health professionals. The psychologist's chances of joining a pediatrics practice obviously increase when the pediatricians themselves are psychologically minded. Although the pediatrics group is likely to be a private practice, possibilities also include ambulatory clinics at medical centers and public health clinics. The author's experience suggests that a pediatrics practice should have at least 10,000 and preferably at least 15,000 patients to support a full-time psychologist. That probably means three or four full-time pediatricians. It will also be important to be aware of changes in the local health care market. Many pediatric primary care practices are being considered for mergers and buyouts, and this could mean that a psychologist looking to join them could end up left out in the end.

There are two models for finding a group to join. First, the psychologist could approach a group he or she already knows. When doing this, it will be helpful to talk to the member of the group most likely to be open to the idea and to be willing to help sell the other members of the group on it. If possible, try to do a brief (10–15 minutes) presentation on having a psychologist in the office for all the pediatricians in the group at a convenient time. Follow up mainly with one member of the group, and keep in mind that it could take several months to convince the group to add a psychologist. Another way to find a pediatrics practice to join is to contact groups unfamiliar with the psychologist but possibly interested in having a psychologist in the office. To do this, begin by sending out an introductory letter and a curriculum vitae. The psychologist can then follow-up in much the same way as for a group he or she knows.

To establish a strong practice, the psychologist must be clear on setting up the appropriate business arrangements. It may be best to first be an independent contractor with the pediatricians, because they may not be interested in hiring the psychologist as an employee or as a partner. If there is more than one psychologist involved, it may be necessary to incorporate. Unless the pediatricians have a collection rate in excess of 95%, the psychologist will do better financially to handle his or her own billing. The financial arrangements between the psychologist and the pediatricians generally follow one of two patterns—either the psychologist pays a fixed cost for overhead, or the pediatricians collect a set percentage of the psychologist's collections.

Negotiating for space will be another critical area. Medical practices tend to be squeezed for space, so the psychologist will probably have to take whatever space the pediatricians can offer, provided that patients can be reasonably comfortable there and privacy can be assured. At a minimum, this means a door and enough room to seat a few people. These are busy settings, so expect this space to be noisy. It will be necessary sometimes to protect this space, and the psychologist should probably not expect to be able to get more space later unless the practice or clinic moves to a bigger building. When calculating overhead, the psychologist should include something for the use of the waiting room, but not for space like the lab and the nurses' station, which are not used for psychological services.

The psychologist will need access to telephones. It may be best at first to use the same phones as the pediatricians do and to ask for the receptionists to answer calls for the psychologist. Phone messages can be a problem, so a voice-mail system is good to add. The psychologist will also need to have a pager for emergency coverage. A computer to handle billing, word processing, and Internet access will also be necessary. Office furniture will be required, including a desk, chairs, a small table and chairs, a larger table for testing, and locked filing cabinets. The psychologist will also have to provide the appropriate tests and equipment.

It is important that the psychologist establish an appropriate niche in the office. The power structure of a medical office basically has two levels—the physicians and the support staff. To ensure an effective collaborative relationship, the psychologist should function at the level of the physicians. Several strategies are helpful in this regard. First, settle the issue of names. Call the physicians by their first names. In many settings, it will also be necessary for the psychologist to ask that the support staff address him or her as "Doctor." Second, follow the dress code of the office. For most pediatric primary care settings, this is fairly comfortable and informal. Third, if possible, the psychologist should ask for his or her name to be on the door and on the pediatricians' letterhead. Arrangements should also be made to do minimal but effective charting in the medical charts. Fourth, the psychologist should attend physician meetings and some staff meetings. It will be necessary to push for this in some instances. Finally, joining informal conversations around the office is also important, but remember to keep it short. At first, when the practice is getting established, it is vital for the psychologist to be in the office even when there are no patients to see. In general, times without patients are good for the psychologist to use to increase the visibility of psychological services in the office. Marketing efforts should focus most heavily on the pediatrics practice, because most referrals will come from parents in the practice and from the pediatricians.

It is probably necessary for pediatric psychologists in pediatric primary care settings to be prepared to work with managed care. Families with young children tend to favor this type of health insurance, and these settings are highly penetrated by managed care. Because the psychologist's availability to see the pediatricians' patients is critical to the functioning of this model of practice, it may be very difficult to avoid being on panels. If there is any good news in this, it is that the focus on brief treatment in these settings can be compatible with the demands of managed care. The bad news is the same as it is for other psychologists—more work in return for reduced reimbursements.

In closing, it is important to point out why a pediatric psychologist wants to practice psychology in a pediatric primary care setting and confront the various demands and complications involved with it. First, the collaboration between the psychologist and the pediatricians can be very supportive. Second, this model allows for very effective patient care that really can include prevention and early intervention. Third, the children are in these settings and it just makes sense to go to them. Fourth, the pediatrics office provides instant credibility and a steady referral base if the collaboration works well. Finally, this kind of work can be interesting and fun. Because things are so child focused, there are very few dull moments. No two days are quite alike in these settings, and new challenges constantly present themselves.

REFERENCES

Achenbach, T. M. (1991). *Manual for the Child Behavior Checklist/4-18 and 1991 Profile.* Burlington: University of Vermont, Department of Psychiatry.

American Academy of Pediatrics, Task Force on Pediatric Education. (1978). *The future of pediatric education.* Evanston, IL: American Academy of Pediatrics.

American Psychiatric Association. (1994). *Diagnostic and statistical manual of mental disorders* (4th ed.). Washington, DC: Author.

American Psychological Association, Task Force on Comprehensive and Coordinated Psychological Services for Children: Ages 0-10. (1994). *Comprehensive and coordinated psychological services for children: A call for service integration.* Washington, DC: American Psychological Association.

Behar, L. B. (1977). The Pre-school Behavior Questionnaire. *Journal of Abnormal Child Psychology, 5,* 265-275.

Bishop, S. J., Murphy, J. M., Jellinek, M. S., & Dusseault, K. (1991). Psychosocial screening in pediatric practice: A survey of interested physicians. *Clinical Pediatrics, 30,* 142-147.

Burns, B. J., Burke, J. D., Jr., & Regier, D. A. (1982). A child-oriented psychosocial classification system. In M. Lipkin & K. Kupka (Eds.), *Psychosocial factors affecting health* (pp. 185-208). New York: Praeger.

Burns, B. J., & Cromer, W. W. (1978). The evolving role of the psychologist in primary health care practitioner training for mental health services. *Journal of Clinical Child Psychology, 7,* 8-12.

Christophersen, E. R. (1982). Incorporating behavioral pediatrics into primary care. *Pediatric Clinics of North America, 29,* 261-296.

Christophersen, E. R. (1983). Behavioral analysis of well-baby and well-child care. In M. L. Wolraich & D. K. Routh (Eds.), *Advances in developmental and behavioral pediatrics* (Vol. 4, pp. 109-123). Greenwich, CT: JAI Press.

Christophersen, E. R. (1994). *Pediatric compliance: A guide for the primary care physician.* New York: Plenum Press.

Clarke-Stewart, K. A. (1978). Popular primers for parents. *American Psychologist, 33,* 359-369.

Costello, E. J. (1986). Primary care pediatrics and child psychopathology: A review of diagnostic, treatment, and referral practices. *Pediatrics, 78,* 1044-1051.

Costello, E. J. (1990). Child psychiatric epidemiology. In B. Lahey & A. Kazdin (Eds.), *Advances in clinical child psychology* (Vol. 13, pp. 53-90). New York: Plenum Press.

Costello, E. J., Edelbrock, C., Costello, A. J., Dulcan, M. K., Burns, B. J., & Brent, D. (1988). Psychopathology in pediatric primary care: The new hidden morbidity. *Pediatrics, 82,* 415-424.

Costello, E. J., & Shugart, M. A. (1992). Above and below the threshold: Severity of psychiatric symptoms and functional impairment in a pediatric sample. *Pediatrics, 90,* 359-368.

Drotar, D. (1978). Training psychologists to consult with pediatricians: Problems and prospects. *Journal of Clinical Child Psychology, 7,* 57-60.

Drotar, D. (1993). Influences on collaborative activities among psychologists and physicians: Implications for practice, research, and training. *Journal of Pediatric Psychology, 18,* 159-172.

Drotar, D. (1995). *Consulting with pediatricians: Psychological perspectives.* New York: Plenum Press.

Drotar, D., Sturm, L., Eckerle, D., & White, S. (1993). Pediatric psychologists' perceptions of their work settings. *Journal of Pediatric Psychology, 18,* 237-248.

Eisert, D. C., Sturner, R. A., & Mabe, P. A. (1991). Questionnaires in behavioral pediatrics: Guidelines for selection and use. *Journal of Developmental and Behavioral Pediatrics, 12,* 42-50.

Evers-Szostak, M. (1992, April). *A model for providing pediatric psychology services in a private pediatrics office.* Paper presented at the North Coast Regional Pediatric Psychology Conference, Buffalo, NY.

Evers-Szostak, M. (1998). Psychological practice in pediatric primary care settings. In L. VandeCreek, S. Knapp, & T. L. Jackson (Eds.), *Innovations in clinical practice: A source book* (Vol. 16, pp. 325–335). Sarasota, FL: Professional Resource Press.

Evers-Szostak, M., Schroeder, C. S., & McClure, S. Y. (1991, April). *Pediatric psychologists in private pediatric practices.* Paper presented at the Third Florida Conference on Child Health Psychology, Gainesville, FL.

Evers-Szostak, M., & Voegler, M. E. (1997, April). *Current issues in pediatric psychology practice in primary care.* Poster presented at the Sixth Florida Conference on Child Health Psychology, Gainesville, FL.

Eyberg, S. M., & Ross, A. W. (1978). Assessment of child behavior problems: The validation of a new inventory. *Journal of Clinical Child Psychology, 7,* 113–116.

Finney, J. W., Riley, A. W., & Cataldo, M. R. (1991). Psychology in primary care: Effects of brief target therapy on children's medical care utilization. *Journal of Pediatric Psychology, 16,* 447–462.

Fischer, H. L., & Englen, R. G. (1972). How goes the marriage? *Professional Psychology, 3,* 73–79.

Frankenburg, W. K. (1983). Infant and pre-school developmental screening. In M. D. Levine, W. B. Carey, A. C. Crocker, & R. T. Gross (Eds.), *Developmental-behavioral pediatrics* (pp. 927–937). Philadelphia: W. B. Saunders.

Goldberg, I. D., Roghman, K. J., McInerny, T. K., & Burke, J. D., Jr. (1984). Mental health problems among children seen in pediatric practice: Prevalence and management. *Pediatrics, 73,* 278–293.

Haggerty, R. J. (1972). The boundaries of health care. *Pharos of Alpha Omega Alpha, 35,* 106–111.

Haggerty, R. J. (1974). The changing role of the pediatrician in child health care. *American Journal of Diseases of Children, 127,* 545–549.

Haggerty, R. J., Roghman, K., & Pless, I. B. (1975). *Child health and the community.* New York: John Wiley and Sons.

Hamlett, K. W., & Stabler, B. (1995). The developmental progress of pediatric psychology consultation. In M. C. Roberts (Ed.), *Handbook of pediatric psychology* (2nd ed., pp. 39–54). New York: Guildford Press.

Hickson, G., Stewart, D., Altemeier, W., & Perrin, J. (1988). First step in obtaining child health care: Selecting a physician. *Pediatrics, 81,* 333–338.

Holden, E. W., & Schumann, W. B. (1995). The detection and management of mental health disorders in pediatric primary care. *Journal of Clinical Psychology in Medical Settings, 2,* 71–87.

Horwitz, S. M., Leaf, P. J., Leventhal, J. M., Forsyth, B., & Speechley, K. N. (1992). Identification and management of psychosocial and developmental problems in community-based, primary care pediatric practices. *Pediatrics, 89,* 480–485.

Hurley, L. K. (1995). Developing a collaborative pediatric psychology practice in a pediatric primary care setting. In D. Drotar (Ed.), *Consulting with pediatricians: Psychological perspectives* (pp. 159–171). New York: Plenum Press.

Hurley, L. K., McIntire, D. D., & Evers-Szostak, M. (1994, April). *Parent perceptions of pediatric psychology in primary care.* Poster presented at the Gulf Coast Regional Pediatric Psychology Conference, New Orleans, LA.

Illback, R. J. (1997). Creating responsive systems of care: Professional and organizational challenges. In R. J. Illback, C. T. Cobb, & H. M Joseph, Jr. (Eds.), *Integrated services for children and families: Opportunities for psychological practice* (pp. 281–301). Washington, DC: American Psychological Association.

Jellinek, M. S., & Murphy, J. M. (1990). The recognition of psychosocial disorders in pediatric practice: The current status of the Pediatric Symptom Checklist. *Journal of Developmental and Behavioral Pediatrics, 11,* 273–278.

Jellinek, M. S., Murphy, J. M., & Burns, B. (1986). Brief psychosocial screening in outpatient pediatric practice. *Journal of Pediatrics, 109,* 371–378.

Joost, J. C., Chessare, J. B., Schaeufelle, J., Link, D., & Weaver, M. T. (1989). Compliance with a prescription for psychotherapeutic counseling in childhood. *Journal of Developmental and Behavioral Pediatrics, 10,* 98–102.

Kanoy, K. W., & Schroeder, C. S. (1985). Suggestions to parents about common behavior problems in a pediatric primary care office. *Journal of Pediatric Psychology, 10,* 15–30.

Lavigne, J. V., Binns, H. J., & Christoffel, K., et al. (1993). Behavioral and emotional problems among preschool children in pediatric primary care: Prevalence and pediatricians' recognition. *Pediatrics, 91,* 649–655.

LeBaron, S., & Zeltzer, L. (1985). Pediatrics and psychology: A collaboration that works. *Journal of Developmental and Behavioral Pediatrics, 6,* 157–161.

Little, M., Murphy, J. M., Jellinek, M. S., Bishop, S. J., & Arnett, H. L. (1994). Screening 4- and 5-year-old children for psychosocial dysfunction: A preliminary study with the Pediatric Symptom Checklist. *Journal of Developmental and Behavioral Pediatrics, 15,* 191–197.

Long, N., Hendon, A., & Henark-Zolten, K. (1993, April). *Screening for common childhood behavior problems: A measure for use in the primary care setting.* Poster presented at the Fourth Florida Conference on Child Health Psychology, Gainesville, FL.

Lynch, T. R., Wildman, B. G., & Smucker, W. D. (1997). Parental disclosure of child psychosocial concerns: Relationship to physician identification and management. *Journal of Family Practice, 44,* 273–280.

McClelland, C. Q., Staples, W. P., Weisberg, I., & Berger, M. E. (1973). The practitioners' role in behavioral pediatrics. *Journal of Pediatrics, 82,* 325–331.

Merritt, K. A., Thompson, R. J., Keith, B. R., Johndrow, D. A., & Murphy, L. B. (1993). Screening for behavioral and emotional problems in primary care pediatrics. *Journal of Developmental and Behavioral Pediatrics, 14,* 340–343.

Mesibov, G. B, Schroeder, C. S., & Wesson, L. (1977). Parental concerns about their children. *Journal of Pediatric Psychology, 11,* 13–17.

Miranda, J., Hohmann, A. A., Atkinson, C. C., & Larson, D. B. (Eds.). (1994). *Mental disorders in primary care.* San Francisco: Jossey-Bass.

Mouton-Simien, P., McCain, A. P., & Kelley, M. L. (1997). The development of the Toddler Behavior Screening Inventory. *Journal of Abnormal Child Psychology, 25,* 59–64.

Ottinger, D. R., & Roberts, M. C. (1980). A university-based predoctoral practicum in pediatric psychology. *Professional Psychology, 11,* 707–713.

Paster, V. S. (1997). Emerging perspectives in child mental health service. In R. J. Illback, C. T. Cobb, & H. M. Joseph, Jr. (Eds.), *Integrated services for children and families: Opportunities for psychological practice* (pp. 281–301). Washington, DC: American Psychological Association.

Rappo, P. D. (1997). Use of the *DSM–PC* and implications for reimbursement. *Journal of Developmental and Behavioral Pediatrics, 18,* 175–177.

Reisinger, K. S., & Bires, J. A. (1980). Anticipatory guidance in pediatric practice. *Pediatrics, 66,* 889–892.

Richardson, L. A., Keller, A. M., Selby-Harrington, M. L., & Parrish, R. (1996). Identification and treatment of children's mental health problems by primary care providers: A critical review of research. *Archives of Psychiatric Nursing, 10,* 293–303.

Richman, N., & Graham, P. J. (1971). A behavioural screening questionnaire for use with three-year old children: Preliminary findings. *Journal of Child Psychology and Psychiatry, 12,* 5–33.

Richmond, J. B. (1967). Child development: A basic science for pediatrics. *Pediatrics, 39,* 649–658.

Roberts, M. C. (1986). *Pediatric psychology: Psychological interventions and strategies for pediatric problems.* New York: Pergamon Press.

Roberts, M. C., & Wright, L. (1982). Role of the pediatric psychologist as consultant to pediatricians. In J. M. Tuma (Ed.), *Handbook for the practice of pediatric psychology* (pp. 251–289). New York: John Wiley & Sons.

Robinson, E. A., Eyberg, S. M., & Ross, A. W. (1980).The standardization of an inventory of child conduct problem behaviors. *Journal of Clinical Child Psychology, 9,* 22–29.

Routh, D. K., Schroeder, C. S., & Koocher, G. P. (1983). Psychology and primary health care for children. *American Psychologist, 38,* 95–98.

Schroeder, C. S. (1979). Psychologists in a private pediatric practice. *Journal of Pediatric Psychology, 4,* 5–18.

Schroeder, C. S. (1997). Conducting an integrated practice in a pediatric setting. In R. J. Illback, C. T. Cobb, & H. M Joseph, Jr. (Eds.), *Integrated services for children and families: Opportunities for psychological practice* (pp. 221–255). Washington, DC: American Psychological Association.

Schroeder, C. S., & Gordon, B. N. (1991). *Assessment and treatment of childhood problems: A clinician's guide.* New York: Guilford Press.

Schroeder, C. S., Gordon, B. N., Kanoy, K., & Routh, D. K. (1983). Managing children's behavior problems in pediatric practice. In M. L. Wolraich & D. K. Routh (Eds.), *Advances in developmental and behavioral pediatrics* (Vol. 4, pp. 25–86). Greenwich, CT: JAI Press.

Shaffer, D., Schwab-Stone, M., Fisher, P., Cohen, P., Piacentini, J., Davies, M., Conners, C. K., & Rieger, D. (1993). The Diagnostic Interview Schedule for Children–Revised Version (DISC-R). I. Preparation, field testing, interrater reliability, and acceptability. *Journal of the American Academy of Child and Adolescent Psychiatry, 32,* 643–650.

Sharp, L., Pantell, R. H., Murphy, L. O., & Lewis, C. C. (1992). Psychosocial problems during child health supervision visits: Eliciting, then what? *Pediatrics, 89,* 619–623.

Smith, E. E., Rome, L. P., & Freedheim, K. D. (1967). The clinical psychologist in the pediatric office. *Journal of Pediatrics, 21,* 48–51.

Squires, J., Nickel, R. E., & Eisert, D. (1996). Early detection of developmental problems: Strategies for monitoring young children in the practice setting. *Journal of Developmental and Behavioral Pediatrics, 17,* 420–427.

Stabler, B. (1979). Emerging models of psychologist–pediatrician liaison. *Journal of Pediatric Psychology, 4,* 307–313.

Stancin, T., & Palermo, T. M. (1997). A review of behavioral screening practices in pediatric settings: Do they pass the test? *Journal of Developmental and Behavioral Pediatrics, 18,* 183–194.

Tuma, J. M. (1989). Mental health services for children. *American Psychologist, 44,* 188–199.

Walker, C. E. (1979). Behavioral intervention in a pediatric setting. In J. R. McNamara (Ed.), *Behavioral approaches to medicine: Application and analysis* (pp. 227–266). New York: Plenum Press.

Weinberger, H. L., Oski, F. A. (1984). A survey of pediatric resident training programs five years after the task force report. *Pediatrics, 74,* 523–526.

Wender, E. H., Bijur, P. E., & Boyce, W. T. (1992). Pediatric residency training: Ten years after the task force report. *Pediatrics, 90,* 876–880.

Wilson, J. L. (1964). Growth and development in pediatrics. *Journal of Pediatrics, 65,* 984–991.

Witmer, L. (1896). The common interests of child psychology and pediatrics. *Pediatrics, 2,* 390–395.

Wolraich, M. L. (1997). *Diagnostic and statistical manual for primary care (DSM–PC) child and adolescent version:* Design, intent, and hopes for the future. *Journal of Developmental and Behavioral Pediatrics, 18,* 171–172.

Wolraich, M. L., Felice, M. E., & Drotar, D. (Eds.). (1996). *The classification of child and adolescent mental diagnoses in primary care: Diagnostic and statistical manual for primary care (DSM–PC) child and adolescent version.* Elk Grove Village, IL: American Academy of Pediatrics.

Wright, L. (1967). The pediatric psychologist: A role model. *American Psychologist, 22,* 323–325.

Yancy, W. S. (1975). Behavioral pediatrics and the practicing pediatrician. *Pediatric Clinics of North America, 22,* 685–694.

Young, K. T., Davis, K., Schoen, C., & Parker, S. (1998). Listening to parents: A national survey of parents with young children. *Archives of Pediatric and Adolescent Medicine, 152,* 255–262.

Zill, N., & Schoenborn, C. A. (1990, November). *Developmental learning and emotional problems: Health of our nation's children, United States, 1988.* Advance data (No. 190). National Center for Health Statistics.

Screening and Monitoring Psychiatric Disorder in Primary Care Populations[1]

Leonard R. Derogatis
Larry L. Lynn II
Clinical Psychometric Research, Inc.,
and
Loyola College of Maryland

The data from recent comprehensive epidemiologic studies make it dramatically clear that psychiatric disorders represent a highly prevalent phenomenon in contemporary society. The benchmark NIMH Epidemiologic Catchment Area (ECA) Study (Meyers et al., 1984; Regier, Boyd, et al., 1988; Robins et al., 1984) demonstrated conclusively that psychiatric disorder is pervasive throughout the United States. Similar rates of disorder were observed in Europe and in Australia (Regier, Boyd, et al., 1988). Estimates of occurrence in medical populations place prevalence rates substantially higher than community estimates. Barrett, Barrett, Oxman, and Gerber (1988) reported rates of between 25% and 30% in their research, whereas Derogatis and Wise (1989) in their review summarized overall rates at between 22% and 33%. Similar rates were reported more recently by Hansson, Nettelbladt, Borgquist, and Nordstrom (1994) and Olfson et al. (1993). The large majority of these conditions are comprised of anxiety and depressive disorders (Derogatis et al., 1983; Von Korff, Dworkin, LeResche, & Kruger, 1988), which can be difficult to identify and diagnose.

Psychiatric disorders represent a significant and serious public health problem in their own right; however, when they exist in a comorbid fashion with primary medical disorders, the health care liability associated with them grows dramatically. Such comorbid conditions have a long list of undesirable features associated with them, including atypical responses to treatment, high side effects rates, increased numbers of medical events, longer durations of hospital stay, failure to adhere to treatment regimens, increased utilization rates, and significantly higher costs (Allison et al., 1995; Katon et al., 1990; Saravay, Pollack, Steinberg, Weischel, & Habert, 1996). In addition, because patients with comorbid conditions, when identified, are undergoing multiple treatment regimens simultaneously, the possibility of undesirable drug interactions is increased.

The latter issue, concerning complications arising from multiple treatment regimens, logically rests on the assumption that comorbid psychiatric disorders are rou-

---

[1]SCL-90-R and BSI are registered trademarks of Leonard R. Derogatis, PhD.

tinely identified, an assumption that is not supported by the facts. A vexing feature of these comorbid disorders is that this assumption is only sometimes met, because the identification of psychiatric disorders in primary care is extremely problematic, often hampering their effective treatment and disposition.

RECOGNITION OF PSYCHIATRIC DISORDERS IN PRIMARY CARE

The incentive for the development and systematic implementation of effective psychiatric screening in primary care derives not only from the increases in morbidity and mortality associated with undetected psychiatric disorders (Hawton, 1981; Kamerow, Pincus, & MacDonald, 1986; Regier, Roberts, et al., 1988), but also from several additional considerations. First, it is well established that between two-thirds and three-quarters of individuals with psychiatric disorders either go completely untreated or are treated by nonpsychiatric physicians; these individuals are never seen by a mental health professional (Dohrenwend & Dohrenwend, 1982; Regier, Goldberg, & Taube, 1978; Weissman, Myers, & Thompson, 1981; Yopenic, Clark, Aneshensel, 1983). Second, although a significant comorbidity exists between physical illness and psychiatric disorder (Barrett et al., 1988; Fulop & Strain, 1991; Rosenthal et al., 1992), the detection by primary care physicians of the most prevalent psychiatric disorders (i.e., anxiety and depressive disorders) is far less than comprehensive (Nielson & Williams, 1980; Linn & Yager, 1984). It is not rare to find recognition rates in medical cohorts falling below 50%. Third, given the documented increases in rates of health care utilization and health care costs attendant on undetected cases of psychiatric disorder, the implementation of systematic psychiatric screening in primary care would almost certainly result in a significant savings in health care expenditures. Finally, and perhaps most importantly, those individuals in our communities who are currently afflicted with undetected psychiatric disorders would be identified earlier in the course of their illnesses, enabling the initiation of effective treatment before the pervasive morbidity associated with chronicity sets in.

Problems Unique to Psychiatric Disorders

The prototypic psychiatric disorder is a hypothetical construct, with few if any pathognomonic clinical or laboratory signs and a pathophysiology and etiology that are only vaguely discernible. For these reasons, unique problems arise in the detection of psychiatric disorders, particularly in medical patients. The most prominent confound arises from the fact that the highly prevalent anxiety and depressive disorders often present with complaints of multiple somatic symptoms, which are difficult to differentiate from those arising from verifiable physical causes. Schurman, Kramer, and Mitchell (1985) indicated that 72% of visits to primary care doctors resulting in a psychiatric diagnosis present with somatic symptoms as the primary complaint. Katon et al. (1990) and Bridges and Goldberg (1984) both indicated that presentation with somatic symptoms as primary complaints is a key reason for misdiagnosis of psychiatric disorders in primary care. In their study of high health care utilizers, Katon et al. (1990) reported that the high health care utilization group had elevated SCL–90–R scores of almost a standard deviation, not only on the anxiety and depression subscales, but on the somatization subscale as well.

A second problem has to do with the misperception of clinical depressions as demoralization reactions (Derogatis & Wise, 1989). The courses of many chronic illnesses, particularly those that inevitably result in mortality, are characterized by a period of disaffection and demoralization. These negative affective responses are a natural reaction to the loss of vitality and well-being associated with being chronically ill and, in some instances, with the anticipated loss of life itself. Physicians familiar with caring for such patients (e.g., cancer, emphysema, renal diseases) can often misperceive true clinical depressions (for which effective treatments are available) as reactive states of demoralization that are a natural part of the illness. They subsequently fail to initiate a therapeutic regimen because they view such mood states as an aspect of the primary medical condition. There is good evidence that such reactive states can be reliably distinguished from major clinical depressions (Snyder, Strain, & Wolf, 1990), and patients suffering such painful comorbid conditions are done a substantial disservice by our failure to diagnose and treat them adequately.

Because most physicians have limited training in psychiatric nosology and diagnosis, a third impediment to the accurate identification of these cases is an incomplete diagnostic workup. Already responsible for an immense amount of information concerning the diagnosis and effective treatment of the patient's principal medical condition, it is not surprising that many primary care physicians do not feel highly confident about their skills in diagnosing comorbid psychiatric disorders. Also, although not readily prone to admit to such attitudes, some primary care physicians tend to minimize the importance of concomitant psychiatric problems relative to the primary medical disorder. Table 4.1 lists a series of factors found to often underlie the failure to detect anxiety and depressive disorders in primary care patients.

Physician Recognition of Psychiatric Disorder

There is no longer much debate concerning the fact that primary care physicians represent a de facto mental health care system in the United States (Burns & Burke, 1985; Regier et al., 1978, 1982). Evidence suggests that one-fifth to one-third of the primary care population suffer from at least one psychiatric condition (typically an anxiety or depressive disorder), underscoring the fact that primary care physicians' proficiency in recognizing psychiatric disorders is an significant health care issue. Current evidence suggests that only a fraction of prevalent psychiatric disorders are detected in primary care, a deficiency that unfortunately has considerable implications for the physical and psychological health of our patients (Seltzer, 1989).

TABLE 4.1
Factors Responsible for Physicians' Failure to Detect Anxiety
and Depressive Disorders in Primary Care

1. Affective syndrome masked by predominantly *somatic symptoms*.
2. Affective syndrome judged to be a *demoralization reaction*.
3. Affective syndrome missed because of *incomplete diagnostic workup*.
4. Affective syndrome *minimized* relative to medical disorder.
5. Affective syndrome *misdiagnosed as dementia* in elderly patient.
6. Affective syndrome misunderstood as *negativistic attitude*.

Unaided Physician Recognition. In recent years, a substantial number of studies documented both the magnitude and nature of the problem of undetected psychiatric disorder in primary care (Davis, Nathan, Crough, & Bairnsfather, 1987; Jones, Badger, Ficken, Leepek, & Andersen, 1987; Kessler, Amick, & Thompson, 1985; Schulberg et al., 1985). The data from these studies establish rates of accurate physician diagnosis of psychiatric conditions that range from a low of 8% (Linn & Yager, 1984) to a high of 53% observed by Shapiro et al. (1987). In a more recent primary care study, Yelin et al. (1996) observed that 44% of over 2,000 primary care patients who screened positive for clinical anxiety on the SCL–90–R (Derogatis, 1994), had been previously assigned a mental health diagnosis. Although this is an improvement, these data also underscore the fact that 56% of these patients went undiagnosed. Although the methodology and precision of studies of this phenomenon continue to improve (Anderson & Harthorn, 1989; Rand, Badger, & Coggins, 1988), rates of accurate physician diagnosis have remained for the most part unacceptably low. A summary of these investigations along with their characteristics and accurate detection rates appear in Table 4.2.

Aided Physician Recognition. The data from the investigations outlined previously highlight the need to intervene proactively to facilitate the recognition of psychiatric conditions among primary care doctors. This is particularly so in light of the strong consensus that in the future, primary care physicians will be playing even more of a gatekeeper role. If these health care professionals cannot accurately identify psychiatric conditions, they can neither adequately treat them personally nor refer them to appropriate mental health professionals. Such a situation will ultimately serve to degrade the quality of our health care systems further, and will act to deny effective treatment to those who in many ways need it most.

There is some evidence that primary care physicians can accurately identify both the prevalence of psychiatric disorders and the nature of these conditions. They estimate prevalence to be between 20% and 25% in their patient populations, and perceive anxiety and depressive disorders to be the most prevalent conditions they encounter (Fauman, 1983; Orleans, George, Haupt, & Brodie, 1985). In an effort to

TABLE 4.2
Recent Research on Rates of Accurate Identification
of Psychiatric Morbidity in Primary Care

Investigator	Study Sample	Criterion	Correct Diagnosis
Andersen and Harthorn (1989)	120 Physicians, primary care	DKI	33% — Affective disorder 48% — Anxiety disorder
Davis et al. (1987)	377 Family practice patients	Zung SDS	15% — Mild symptoms 30% — Severe symptoms
Jones et al. (1987)	20 Family physicians/ 51 patients	DIS	21%
Rand et al. (1988)	36 Family practice residents/ 520 patients	GHQ	16%
Kessler et al. (1985)	1,452 Primary care patients	GHQ	19.7%
Linn and Yager (1984)	150 Patients in a general medical clinic	Zung	8%
Schulberg et al. (1985)	294 Primary care patients	DIS	44%
Shapiro et al. (1987)	1,242 Patients at university internal medical clinic	GHQ	53%
Zung et al. (1983)	41 Family medicine patients	Zung SDS	15%

identify and overcome the psychiatric diagnosis problem in primary care, a number of investigators have studied the effects of introducing a diagnostic aid in the primary care setting, in the form of results from a psychological screening test. Although far from unanimous, the studies to date have concluded that in the appropriate situation, screening tests can significantly improve physician detection of psychiatric conditions.

Linn and Yager (1984) used the Zung Self-rating Depression Scale (SDS) and found an increase of from only 8% correct diagnosis to 25% in a cohort of 150 general medical patients. Similarly, Zung, Magill, Moore, and George (1983) reported an increase in correct identification rising from 15% to 68% in family medicine outpatients with depression using a similar intervention. Likewise, Moore, Silimperi, and Bobula (1978) observed an increase in correct diagnostic identification from 22% to 56% working with family practice residents. Not all studies have shown such dramatic improvements in diagnostic accuracy, however. Hoeper, Nyczi, and Cleary (1979) found essentially no improvement in diagnosis associated with making General Health Questionnaire (GHQ) results available to doctors, and Shapiro et al. (1987) reported only a 7% increase in accuracy when GHQ scores were made accessible. The issue of aided recognition of psychiatric disorders is a complicated one, with numerous patient and doctor variables having an effect. Nonetheless, the results of the studies on aided recognition appear promising, and an excellent contemporary review of the issues involved has been published by Anderson and Harthorn (1990).

To summarize this issue, the complex of problems inherent in identifying psychiatric cases in primary care is having a highly regressive impact on our overall health care system. As it is now structured, the preponderance of psychiatric disorders are seen by primary care physicians, who leave a majority of these conditions undiagnosed. Of the cases correctly identified, only a small minority are ever referred to mental health specialists, even though such conditions are known to be of a chronic and recurrent nature, and primary care "gatekeepers" admit that they feel less than fully competent to treat them. Undetected or improperly treated, anxiety and depressive disorders are frequently associated with substance abuse, alcoholism, suicide, excessive utilization of the health care system, and spiraling health care costs (Derogatis, DellaPietra, & Kilroy, 1992). Faced with these data, we should make a concerted effort to facilitate the proficiency of primary care physicians in the detection of psychiatric disorders.

OVERVIEW OF SCREENING

The Concept of Screening

Screening has been defined traditionally as "the presumptive identification of unrecognized disease or defect by the application of tests, examinations or other procedures which can be applied rapidly to sort out apparently well persons who probably have a disease from those who probably do not" (Commission on Chronic Illness, 1957, p. 45). Screening is a procedure conducted in an ostensibly well population in order to identify occult instances of the disease or disorder in question. Some authorities make a distinction between *screening* and *case finding*, which is defined as the ascertainment of disease in populations comprised of patients with other disorders.

Under such a distinction, the detection of psychiatric disorders among primary care patients would more precisely fit the criteria for case finding than for screening. In actual implementation, there appears to be little real difference between the two processes, so we have chosen to use the term *screening* for both methods.

Regardless of its specific manifestation, the screening process represents a relatively unrefined sieve, designed to segregate the cohort under assessment into "positives," who presumptively have the condition, and "negatives," who are ostensively free of the disorder. Screening is not a diagnostic procedure per se. Rather, it represents a preliminary filtering technique that identifies those individuals with the highest probability of having the index disorder for subsequent specific diagnostic evaluation. Typically, those screened "negative" are usually not involved in further evaluation.

The conceptual foundation for screening rests on the premise that the early detection of unrecognized disease in apparently healthy individuals carries with it a discernable advantage in achieving effective treatment and/or cure of the condition. Although logical, this assumption is not always justified. In certain conditions, early detection does not measurably improve our capacity to alter morbidity or mortality, either because diagnostic procedures are unreliable, or because effective treatments for the condition are not yet available.

In an attempt to facilitate a better appreciation of the particular health problems that lend themselves to effective screening systems, the World Health Organization (WHO) has published guidelines for effective health screening programs (Wilson & Junger, 1968). A version of these criteria is listed here.

1. The condition should represent an important health problem that carries with it notable morbidity and mortality.
2. Screening programs must be cost-effective; that is, the incidence/significance of the disorder must be sufficient to justify the costs of screening.
3. Effective methods of treatment must be available for the disorder.
4. The test(s) for the disorder should be reliable and valid, so that detection errors (i.e., false positives or false negatives) are minimized.
5. The test(s) should have high cost-benefit; that is, the time, effort and personal inconvenience to the patient associated with taking the test should be substantially outweighed by its potential benefits.
6. The condition should be characterized by an asymptomatic or benign period, during which detection will significantly reduce morbidity and/or mortality.
7. Treatment administered during the asymptomatic phase should demonstrate significantly greater efficacy than that dispensed during the symptomatic phase.

Some authorities do not believe that psychiatric disorders, and the screening systems designed to detect them, conclusively meet all of these criteria. For example, the efficacy of our treatments for certain psychiatric conditions (e.g., schizophrenia) is arguable, and in some conditions we have not definitively demonstrated that treatments initiated during asymptomatic phases (e.g., "maintenance" period of antidepressant treatment) are more efficacious than treatment initiated during acute episodes of the disorder. Nevertheless, it is generally accepted that psychiatric conditions and the screening models designed to identify them do meet the WHO criteria in the large majority of instances, and that the consistent implementation of screening systems in primary care populations can substantially improve the quality and cost-efficiency of our health care.

The Epidemiologic Screening Model

Because many readers do not possess detailed familiarity with screening paradigms, we briefly review the basic epidemiologic screening model. Essentially, a cohort of individuals who are apparently well, or, in the instance of case finding, who present with a condition distinct from the index disorder, are evaluated by a "test" to determine if they are at high risk for the particular disorder or disease. As outlined earlier, the disorder must have sufficient incidence or consequence to be considered a significant public health problem, and be characterized by a distinct early or asymptomatic phase during which it is anticipated that detection will substantially improve the results of treatment.

The screening test itself (e.g., Pap smear, Western blot) should be both *reliable*, that is, consistent in its performance from one administration to the next, and *valid*, that is, capable of identifying those with the index disorder and eliminating individuals who do not have the condition. In psychometric terms this form of validity has been traditionally referred to as *predictive* or *criterion-oriented* validity. In epidemiologic models, the predictive validity of the test is apportioned into two distinct partitions: the degree to which the test correctly identifies those individuals who actually have the disorder, termed its *sensitivity*, and the extent to which those free of the condition are correctly identified as such, its *specificity*. Correctly identified individuals with the index disorder are referred to as *true positives*, and those accurately identified as being free of the disorder are termed *true negatives*. Misidentifications of healthy individuals as affected are labeled *false positives*, and affected individuals missed by the test are referred to as *false negatives*. It should be noted that each type of prediction error carries with it a socially determined value or significance, termed its *utility*, and that utilities need not be equal. The basic fourfold epidemiologic table and the algebraic definitions of each of these validity indices are given in Table 4.3.

Sensitivity and specificity are a screening test's most fundamental validity indices; however, they are not the only parameters that can markedly affect a test's performance. In particular, the *prevalence* or *base rate* of the disorder in the population under evaluation can have a powerful effect on the results of screening. Two other indicators

TABLE 4.3
Epidemiologic Screening Model

Screening Test	Actual	
	Cases	*Noncases*
Test positive	*a*	*b*
Test negative	*c*	*d*

Note. Sensitivity (Se) = $a/(a + c)$
False negative rate $(1 - Se) = c/(a + c)$
Specificity (Sp) = $d/(b + d)$
False positive rate $(1 - Sp) = b/(b + d)$
Positive predictive value (PPV) = $a/(a + b)$
Negative predictive value (NPV) = $d/(c + d)$

of test performance, *predictive value of a positive* and *predictive value of a negative*, reflect the interactive effects of test validity and prevalence. These indices are also defined in Table 4.1, although their detailed discussion is postponed until a later section.

Psychometric and Evaluative Principles in Screening

Basic to a realistic appreciation of the psychometrics underlying psychiatric screening is the realization that we are involved in *psychological measurement*. The principles underlying psychological assessment are no different from those that govern any other form of scientific measurement; however, a major distinction that characterizes psychological measurement concerns the fact that the object of measurement is usually a *hypothetical construct*. In contrast, measurement in the physical sciences usually involves tangible entities, which are measured via ratio scales with true zeros and equal intervals and ratios throughout the scale continuum (e.g., weight, distance, velocity). In quantifying hypothetical constructs (e.g., anxiety, depression, impulsivity), measurement occurs on ordinal-approaching interval scales, which by their nature are less sophisticated and have substantially larger errors of measurement (Luce & Narens, 1987). Psychological measurement is no less scientific due to this fact; however, it is less precise than measurement in the physical sciences.

Reliability.   All scientific measurement is based on consistency or replicability. Reliability concerns the degree of replicability inherent in measurement. To what degree would a screening test provide the same results upon re-administration? To what extent do two clinicians agree on a psychiatric rating scale? Conceived differently, reliability can be thought of as the converse of measurement error. It represents that proportion of variation in measurement that is due to true variation in the attribute under study, as opposed to random or systematic error variance. Reliability can be conceptualized as the ratio of *true score variation* to the total measurement variance. It specifies the precision of measurement and thereby sets the theoretical limit of measurement validity.

Validity.   Just as reliability indicates the consistency of measurement, validity reflects the *essence* of measurement: the degree to which an instrument measures what it is designed to measure. In the context of screening, it specifies how well an instrument discriminates those who possess the attribute being screened from those in whom it is absent. Establishing the validity of a screening instrument is more complex and programmatic than determining its reliability, and rests on more elaborate theory. Although the validation process involves many types of validity experiments, the most explicitly applicable to the screening process is *predictive validity*.

The predictive validity of an assessment device pivots on its degree of correlation with an external reference criterion—some sort of gold standard. In the case of screening tests, the external criterion usually takes the form of a comprehensive laboratory and/or clinical diagnostic evaluation that definitively establishes the presence or absence of the index disorder. Central to a genuine appreciation of the concept of predictive validity is the realization that it is highly specific in nature. To say that a particular screening test is "valid" has little or no scientific meaning; tests are valid only for specific purposes. Psychological tests employed in screening for psychiatric disorder(s) must be validated empirically in terms of the diagnostic assignments they are designed to predict. For example, a particular unidimensional test for depression should be validated specifically in terms of its ability to accurately predict clinical depressions. The fact that it may also be valid for other purposes extends the overall utility of the test, but does not contribute to its validation as a screening measure.

Generalizability.   Like reliability and validity, *generalizability* is a fundamental psychometric characteristic of test instruments used in psychiatric screening paradigms. Many clinical disorders and manifestations of disease are systematically altered as a function of characteristics such as age, sex, race, and the presence or absence of a comorbid medical illness. When validity coefficients (i.e., sensitivity and specificity) for a screening test are established relative to a specific diagnostic condition, they may vary considerably if the demographic and health characteristics of the cohort on which they were established are altered significantly. To the extent that the test's validity is sustained across such shifts, its validity is considered highly generalizable, or robust.

For example, it is well established that men are more constrained than women in reporting emotional distress. Well-constructed tests measuring symptomatic distress develop distinct sets of norms for the two genders to deal with this effect (Nunnally, 1978). Another illustration resides in the change of the phenomenologic characteristics of depression across age: Depression in the very young tends toward less dramatic affective display, and progresses through the classic clinical delineations of young and middle adult years, to the geriatric depressions of the elderly, which are more likely to be characterized by dementia-like cognitive dysfunctions. Any single test is unlikely to perform with the same degree of validity across shifts in relevant parameters; therefore, generalizability must be established empirically and cannot merely be assumed. In a recent treatise on modernizing our conceptualization of validity in psychological assessment, Messick (1995) explicitly integrated generalizability, along with external criterion validity, as one of six discriminable aspects of construct validity.

The Problem of Low Base Rates

Over 40 years ago, psychologists were sensitized to the problem of low base rates and their dramatic impact on the predictive validity of psychological tests through the publication of a now classic paper by Meehl and Rosen (1955). The authors demonstrated that attempts to predict rare attributes or events, even with highly valid tests, would result in substantially more misclassifications than correct classifications if the prevalence of the event was sufficiently low. Unfortunately, knowledge and understanding of this important but obscure fact remained limited to a few specialists at that time. However, 11 years later, Vecchio published a report in the medical literature (Vecchio, 1966) dealing with essentially the same phenomenon. In Vecchio's paper, the substantive aspects of the report focused on screening tests in medicine, and the information reached a much wider audience. As a result, knowledge of the special relationship between low base rates and the predictive validity of screening tests has since become well recognized.

To be precise, low prevalence does not affect all aspects of a test's validity equally; its impact is felt primarily in the validity partition that deals with correctly classifying positives or "cases." Predictive validity concerning negatives, or "noncases," is minimally impaired because with extremely low prevalence, even a test with moder-

TABLE 4.4
Predictive Values of Positive and Negative Tests at Varying
Prevalence (Base) Rates (Sensitivity and Specificity = 95%)

Prevalence or Base Rate (%)	Predictive Value of a + (%)	Predictive Value of a − (%)
1	16.1	99.9
2	27.9	99.9
5	50.0	99.7
10	67.9	99.4
20	82.6	98.7
50	95.0	95.0
75	98.3	83.7
100	100	−

Note. Synopsis of data originally presented by Vecchio (1996).

ate validity will perform adequately in this regard. This relationship is summarized in Table 4.4, which is a synopsis of data originally given by Vecchio (1966).

In the example developed by Vecchio, the sensitivity and specificity of the screening test are given as .95, values that, although characteristic of laboratory-based screening tests, do not represent realistic validity coefficients for psychological screening tests. Table 4.5 provides a more realistic example of the relationship between prevalence and positive predictive value, based on a hypothetical cohort of N = 1,000, with validity coefficients (i.e., sensitivity and specificity) more consistent with those that might be genuinely anticipated for such tests.

The data of Tables 4.4 and 4.5 make it clear that as prevalence drops below 10%, the predictive value of a positive declines precipitously. In the first example, when prevalence reaches 1%, the predictive value of a positive is only 16%, which means in practical terms that in such situations five out of six positives will be false positives. The predictive value of a negative remains extremely high throughout the range of base rates shown and is essentially unaffected by low-prevalence situations. The example from Table 4.5 is more realistic in that the validity coefficients are more analogous to those commonly reported for psychological screening tests. In the screening situation depicted here, the predictive value of a positive drops from 77% when prev-

TABLE 4.5
Relationship of Prevalence (Base Rate) and Positive Predictive Value

Assumed Test Sensitivity = 0.80

Assumed Test Specificity = 0.90

Prevalence = 0.30 Actual Disorder			Prevalence = 0.05 Actual Disorder			Prevalence = 0.01 Actual Disorder		
Test	Pos.	Neg.	Test	Pos.	Neg.	Test	Pos.	Neg.
+	240	70	310	+	40	95	135	+	8	99	107
−	60	630	690	−	10	855	865	−	2	891	893
Sum	300	700		Sum	50	950		Sum	10	990	

Pos. predict. value = 240/310 = 77%	Pos. predict. value = 40/135 = 30%	Pos. predict. value = 8/107 = 7.5%

alence is 30% (e.g., the approximate rate of psychiatric disorders among medical cohorts) to 7.5% when prevalence falls to 1%. In the latter instance, 12 out of 13 positives would be false positives.

Sequential Screening: A Technique for Low Base Rates

Although screening for psychiatric disorders in general is not usually affected by problems of low base rates, there are specific mental health problems (e.g., suicide) and certain diagnostic categories (e.g., panic disorder) that have low community prevalence rates. In addition, as Baldessarini, Finklestein, and Arana (1983) noted, the nature of the population being screened can markedly affect the quality of screening outcomes. A good example of this distinction is provided by the dexamethasone suppression test (DST) when used as a screen for major depressive disorder (MDD). The DST functions as a relatively effective screen for MDD on inpatient affective disorders units where the prevalence of the disorder is quite high. In general medical practice, however, where the prevalence of MDD is estimated to be about 5% to 6%, the DST results in unacceptable rates of misclassification. The validity of the DST is insufficient to support effective screening performance in populations with low base rates of MDD.

A method designed to help overcome low base rate problems is commonly referred to as *sequential screening*. In a sequential screening paradigm, there are two phases to screening and two screening tests. Phase I involves an initial screen, whose primary purpose is to correctly identify individuals without the condition and eliminate them from consideration in Phase II evaluation. The initial screening also has the important effect of raising the prevalence of the index condition in the remaining cohort. Subsequently, in Phase II, a separate test of equal or superior sensitivity is then utilized. Because the base rate of the index condition has been significantly raised by Phase I screening, the performance of the Phase II screen will involve much lower levels of false positive misclassification. A hypothetical example of sequential screening is given in Table 4.6.

In Phase I of the hypothetical screening, a highly valid instrument with sensitivity and specificity equal to .90 is used in a large population cohort ($N = 10,000$) with a prevalence of 4% for the index condition. Because of the low base rate, the predictive

TABLE 4.6
Hypothetical Example of Sequential Screening as a
Strategy for Dealing With Low Base Rates

Phase 1
$N = 10,000$; Sensitivity = .90; Specificity = .90
Prevalence (Base Rate) = 4%
Predictive Value of a Positive =
$$\frac{360}{360 + 960} = 0.272 \text{ or } 27.2\%$$

Phase II
$N = 1,320$; Sensitivity = .90; Specificity = .90
Prevalence (Base Rate) = 27.2%
Predictive Value of a Positive =
$$\frac{(.272)(.90)}{(.272)(.90) + (.728)(.10)} = 0.77 \text{ or } 77\%$$

value of a positive is only 27.2%, meaning essentially that less than one out of every three positives will be true positives. The 1,320 individuals screened positive from the original cohort of 10,000 subsequently become the cohort for Phase II screening. With an equally valid, independent test (sensitivity and specificity = .90) and a base rate of 27.2%, the predictive value of a positive in Phase II rises to 77%, representing a substantial increase in the level of screening efficiency.

Sequential screening evaluates a high-risk subgroup of the population of interest by virtue of a series of consecutive sieves. These have the effect of eliminating from consideration individuals with low likelihood of having the disorder, and simultaneously raising the base rate of the condition in the remaining sample. Sequential screening can become costly because of the increased number of screening tests that must be administered. However, in specific circumstances where prevalence is low (e.g., HIV screening in the general population) and the validity of the screening test is already at a maximum, it may be the only method available to minimize errors in classification.

ROC Analysis

Although some screening tests operate in a qualitative mode, depending on the presence or absence of a key indicator, psychological screening tests function, as do many others, along a quantitative continuum. The individual being screened must obtain a probability or "score" above a criterion threshold or "cutoff" to be considered a "positive" or a "case." The cutoff value is usually determined to be that value that will maximize correct classification and minimize misclassification of the index disorder. If the relative consequences of one type of error are considered more costly than the other (i.e., the consequences have dramatically different utilities; e.g., false negative = missed fatal but potentially curable disease), the cutoff value will often be adjusted to take the differential utility into account. Although quantitative methods exist to estimate optimal threshold values (e.g., Weinstein et al., 1980), conventionally, they have simply been selected by inspection of cutoff tables and their associated sensitivities and specificities.

The selection of a cutoff value automatically determines both the sensitivity and specificity of the test because it defines the rates of correct identification and misclassification. Actually, for any given population, an entire distribution of cutoffs exists, with corresponding sensitivities and specificities. Further, as mentioned in the previous section, test performance (i.e., the error rates associated with a particular cutoff value) is highly affected by the prevalence or base rate of the disorder under study. Viewed from this perspective, a test should not be characterized by *a* sensitivity and specificity; rather it should be perceived as possessing *distributions* of sensitivities and specificities associated with the distribution of possible threshold values and the distribution of prevalences.

Receiver operating characteristic (ROC) analysis is a method that enables the visualization of the entire distribution of sensitivity/specificity combinations for all possible cutoff values and prevalences. As such, it enables the selection of a criterion threshold based on substantially more information and represents a much more sophisticated clinical decision process. ROC analysis was first developed by Swets (1964) in the context of signal detection paradigms in psychophysics. Subsequently, applications of the technique were developed in the areas of radiology and medical imaging (Hanley & McNeil, 1982; Metz, 1978; Swets, 1979). Madri and Williams

(1986) and Murphy et al. (1987) introduced and applied ROC analysis to the task of screening for psychiatric disorders. More recently, Somoza and his colleagues (Somoza, 1994, 1996; Somoza & Mossman, 1990b, 1991; Somoza, Steer, Beck, & Clark, 1994) published an extensive series of in-depth reports integrating ROC analysis with information theory to optimize the performance of diagnostic and screening tests. In their comprehensive series, these investigators reviewed the topics of test construction (Somoza & Mossman, 1990a), the effects of prevalence (Mossman & Somoza, 1991), optimization of information yield (Somoza & Mossman, 1992a), and maximization of expected utility (Mossman & Somoza, 1992), relative to ROC analysis and optimal screening strategies.

Typically, an ROC curve is generated by plotting corresponding values of a test's sensitivity (true positive rate) on the vertical axis, against the compliment of its specificity (false positive rate) on the horizontal axis, for the entire range of possible cutting scores from lowest to highest. A number of computer programs (e.g., Somoza & Mossman, 1991) are available to generate and plot ROC curves. The ROC curve demonstrates the discriminative capacity of the test at each possible definition of threshold (cutoff score) for psychiatric disorder. If the discriminative capacity of the test is no better than chance, the curve will follow a diagonal straight line from the origin of the graph (lower left) to its uppermost right corner. This line is termed the *line of no information*. The ROC curve rises from the origin (point 0,0) to its termination point (1,1) on a plane defined as already described. To the extent that a test possesses discriminative validity, the curve will bow in a convex manner toward the upper left corner of the graph. The greater the deviation in this manner, the greater discriminative capacity the test has for the application at hand. Examples of ROC curves are presented in Fig. 4.1.

An ROC summary statistic describing the discriminative capacity of a test is referred to as the *area under the curve* (AUC). The AUC may be thought of as a probability estimate that at each cutoff score a randomly chosen positive (or "case") will demonstrate a higher score than a randomly chosen negative. When the ROC curve follows the line of no information, the AUC = .50. In the situation of an optimal discrimination, the ROC curve would follow the outline of the ordinate of the graph from point 0,0 to point 1,0, and then move at right angles to point 1,1. In this situation the AUC would equal 1.0.

Although ROC analysis has been implemented in the area of psychiatric screening only within the past decade, investigators have found numerous imaginative applications for the technique. In addition to simply describing the distribution of validity coefficients for a single test, ROC analysis has been used to compare screening tests'

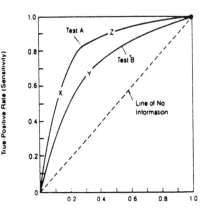

FIG. 4.1. ROC curves for two hypothetical psychiatric screening tests. From "Performance of Screening and Diagnostic Tests" by J. M. Murphy et al., 1987, *Archives of General Psychiatry, 44*, pp. 550–555. Copyright 1987 by American Medical Association. Reprinted by permission.

performances (Somoza et al., 1994; Weinstein, Berwick, Goldman, Murphy, & Barsky, 1989), aid in the validation of new tests, compare different scoring methods for a given test (Birtchnell, Evans, Deahl, & Master, 1989), contrast the screening performance of a test in different populations (Burnam, Wells, Leake, & Landsverk, 1988; Hughson, Cooper, McArdle, & Smith, 1988), and assist in validating a foreign-language version of a standard test (Chong & Wilkinson, 1989). ROC analysis has also been effectively integrated with paradigms from information theory to maximize information yield in screening (Somoza & Mossman, 1992b), and with decision-making models to optimize expected utilities of screening outcomes (Mossman & Somoza, 1992). Although ROC analysis does not represent a definitive solution for the complex problems of psychiatric screening, it does significantly increase the information available to the decision maker and provides a relatively precise and sophisticated method for making decisions.

SCREENING TESTS FOR PSYCHIATRIC DISORDERS

A History of Psychiatric Screening Measures

The predecessors of modern psychological screening instruments date back to the late 19th and early 20th centuries. Sir Francis Galton (1883) created the prototype psychological questionnaire as part of an exposition for the World's Fair. The first self-report symptom inventory, the *Personal Data Sheet*, was developed by Robert Woodworth (1918) as part of the effort to screen American soldiers entering World War I for psychiatric disorders. At approximately the same time, the psychiatrist Adolph Meyer constructed the first psychiatric rating scale, the Phipps Behavior Chart, at Johns Hopkins University (Kempf, 1914–1915). Since these pioneering efforts, hundreds of psychological tests and rating scales have been developed, and a number of the well-validated instruments have become widely used. In the current chapter we briefly review a small number of these instruments in an effort to familiarize the reader with the nature of screening measures available. This chapter is not the appropriate place for a comprehensive review of psychological screening tests (see Maruish, 1999; Sederer & Dickey, 1996; Spilker, 1996; Zalaquett & Wood, 1997), particularly given the number of excellent detailed reviews presented in the accompanying chapters of this book.

Assessment Modality: Self-Report Versus Clinician Rating

Although advocates and adherents argue the differential merits of self-report versus clinician ratings, a great deal of evidence suggests that the two techniques have strengths and weaknesses of roughly the same magnitude. Neither approach can be said to function more effectively overall in screening for psychiatric disorder. Each screening situation must be assessed independently, and the circumstances of each must be objectively weighed to determine which modality is best suited for any particular screening implementation.

Traditionally, self-report inventories have been more frequently used as screening tests than clinical rating scales, probably because the self-report modality has much to recommend it to the task of screening. Self-report measures tend to be brief, inexpensive, and are tolerated well by individuals being screened. These features lend the important attributes of cost efficiency and cost benefit to self-report. Self-report scales are also transportable; they may be used in a variety of settings, and minimize professional time and effort. In addition, their administration, scoring, and evaluation require little or no professional input. Recently, self-report tests have been adapted for use on personal computers, enabling test administration, scoring, evaluation, and storage of results entirely by computer, reducing both professional and technical time. Finally, perhaps the most significant advantage of self-report resides in the fact that in this modality, the test is being completed by the only person experiencing the phenomena — the respondent him- or herself. A clinician, no matter how skilled, can never know the actual experience of the respondent; rather, he or she must be satisfied with an apparent or deduced representation of the experience.

This last feature of self-report tests can also represent their greatest potential source of error — that is, patient bias in reporting. Because the test respondent is providing the test data, there exists the opportunity to consciously or unconsciously distort the responses given. Although patient bias does represent a potential difficulty for self-report, empirical studies have indicated that such distortions represent a problem only in situations where obvious personal gain is associated with response distortions. Otherwise, this problem usually does not represent a major source of bias (Derogatis, Lipman, Rickels, Uhlenhuth, & Covi, 1974a). There is also the possibility that response sets such as acquiescence or attempts at impression management may result in systematic response distortions, but such effects tend to add little error variance in most realistic clinical screening situations.

Probably the greatest limitation of most self-report arises from the inflexibility of the format: A line of questioning cannot be altered or modified depending on how the individual responds to previous questions. In addition, only denotative responses can be appreciated; facial expressions, tones of voice, attitudes and postures, and cognitive/emotional status of the respondent are not integral aspects of the test data. This inflexibility extends to the fact that the respondent must also be literate in order to read the questions.

The psychiatric rating scale or interview is a viable alternative to self-report instruments in designing a screening paradigm. The clinical rating scale introduces professional judgement into the screening process, and is inherently more flexible than self-report. The clinician has both the expertise and freedom to delve in more detail into any area of history, thought, or behavior that will deliver relevant information on the respondent's mental status. The clinician also carries the capacity to clarify ambiguous answers and probe areas of apparent contradiction. In addition, because of the clinician's sophistication in psychopathology and human behavior, there is the theoretical possibility that more complex and sophisticated instrument designs may be utilized in developing psychiatric rating scales.

On the negative side, just as self-report is subject to patient bias, clinical rating scales are subject to equally powerful interviewer biases. Training sessions and videotaped interviews may be utilized in an attempt to reduce systematic errors of this type; however, interviewer bias can never be completely eliminated. Furthermore, the very fact that a professional clinician is required to make the ratings significantly increases the costs of screening. Lay interviewers have been trained to do such evaluations in some instances, but they are rarely as skilled as professionals, and the costs of their training and participation must be weighed into the equation as well. Finally, the more flexibility designed into the interview, the more time it is likely to take for the clinician to complete the ratings. At some point, the "test" will no longer resemble a screening instrument, but begin to take on the characteristics of a comprehensive diagnostic interview.

Both self-report and clinical interview modalities are designed to quantify the respondent's status in such a way as to facilitate a valid evaluation of his or her "caseness." Both approaches lend themselves to actuarial quantitative methods, which allow for a normative framework to be established within which to evaluate individuals. Most importantly, both approaches "work." The nature of the screening task, the resources at hand, and the experience of the clinicians or investigators involved determine which method will work best in any particular situation.

Table 4.7 provides summary data on seven such instruments frequently employed as screening tests: SCL–90–R, BSI, GHQ, BDI, BASIS-32, CES–D, HAS, and HRDS. Five of the screening tests mentioned here are self-report, and the remaining two are clinician rated. Because many of the chapters in this book are devoted to detailed reviews of these tests, and a test overview would be highly redundant, Table 4.7 provides only a very brief summary of instrument characteristics.

Widely Used Psychological Screening Instruments

SCL–90–R/BSI. The SCL–90–R (Derogatis, 1977, 1983, 1994) is a 90-item, multidimensional, self-report symptom inventory, derived from the Hopkins Symptom Checklist (Derogatis, Lipman, Rickels, Uhlenhuth, & Covi, 1974b) and first published in 1975. The inventory measures symptomatic distress in terms of nine primary dimensions and three global indices of distress. The dimensions include somatization, obsessive-compulsive, interpersonal sensitivity, depression, anxiety, hostility, phobic anxiety, paranoid ideation, and psychoticism. Several matching clinician rating

TABLE 4.7
Psychiatric Screening Tests in Common Use With
Medical and Primary Care Populations

Instrument	Author and Date	Mode	Description	Time	Application	Sensitivity (Se)/ Specificity (Sp)
BASIS-32	Eisen 1965	Self	32 Items Multidimensional	5–20 min	3, 5, 7	Se NA Sp NA
BDI	Beck 1961	Self	21 Items Unidimensional	5–10 min	2, 3, 4	Se .76–.92 Sp .64–.80
BSI	Derogatis 1975	Self	53 Items Multidimensional	10–15 min	1, 2, 3, 4, 7	Se .72 Sp .90
CES–D	Radloff 1977	Self	20 Items Unidimensional	10 min	1, 2, 3, 4	Se .83–.97 Sp .61–.90
GHQ	Goldberg 1972	Self	60, 30, 12 Items Multidimensional	5–15 min	1, 2, 3, 4, 5	Se .69–1.0 Sp .75–.92
HAS	Hamilton 1959	Clin. Rat.	14 Items Bidimensional	20 min	1, 2, 3, 4, 6	Se .91 Sp .94
HRDS	Hamilton 1960	Clin. Rat.	21 Items Unidimensional	30+ min	1, 2, 3, 4, 5, 7	Se .94–1.0 Sp 1.0
SCL–90–R	Derogatis 1975	Self	90 Items Multidimensional	15–20 min	1, 2, 3, 4, 7	Se .73 Sp .91

Note. Applications are (1) community adults, (2) community adolescents, (3) inpatient/outpatient, (4) medical patients, (5) elderly, (6) children, and (7) college students.

scales, such as the Derogatis Psychiatric Rating Scale and the SCL–90 Analogue Scale, which measure the same nine dimensions, are also available. Norms for the SCL–90–R have been developed for adult community nonpatients, psychiatric outpatients, psychiatric inpatients, and adolescent nonpatients.

The Brief Symptom Inventory (BSI) (Derogatis, 1993; Derogatis & Melisaratos, 1983; Derogatis & Spencer, 1982) is the brief form of the SCL–90–R. The BSI measures the same nine symptom dimensions and three global indices using only 53 items. Dimension scores on the BSI correlate highly with comparable SCL–90–R scores (Derogatis, 1993), and the brief form shares most psychometric characteristics of the longer scale. Most recently, an 18-item version of the BSI has been developed and normed (Derogatis, 1997).

Both the SCL–90–R and the BSI have been used as outcome measures in an extensive array of research studies, among them a number of investigations focusing specifically on screening (Derogatis et al., 1983; Kuhn, Bell, Seligson, Laufer, & Lindner, 1988; Royse & Drude, 1984; Zabora, Smith-Wilson, Fetting, & Enterline, 1990). To date, the SCL–90–R has been utilized in over 1,000 published research studies, with over 500 available in a published bibliography (Derogatis, 1990). The BSI has also demonstrated sensitivity to psychological distress in a numerous clinical and research contexts (Cochran & Hale, 1985; O'Hara, Ghonheim, Heinrich, Metha, & Wright, 1989; Piersma, Reaume, & Boes, 1994). Both the SCL–90–R and the BSI have been translated into over two dozen languages.

General Health Questionnaire (GHQ). The GHQ was originally developed as a 60-item, multidimensional, self-report symptom inventory by Goldberg (1972). Subsequent to its publication (Goldberg & Hillier, 1979) four subscales were factor-analytically derived: somatic symptoms, anxiety and insomnia, social dysfunction, and severe depression. The GHQ is one of the most widely used screening tests for psychiatric disorder internationally, with its popularity arising in part from the fact that several brief forms of the test are available (e.g., the GHQ30 and GHQ12). The more recent brief forms retain the basic four-subscale format of the longer parent scale, but avoid including physical symptoms as indicators of distress (Malt, 1989). The GHQ has been validated for use in screening and outcome assessment in numerous populations, including the traumatically injured, cancer patients, geriatric populations, and many community samples (Goldberg & Williams, 1988).

Center for Epidemiologic Studies–Depression Scale. The Center for Epidemiological Studies Depression Scale (CES–D) was developed by Radloff and her colleagues (Radloff, 1977). It is a brief, unidimensional self-report depression scale comprised of 20 items that assess the respondent's perceived mood and level of functioning within the past 7 days. Four fundamental dimensions — depressed affect, positive affect, somatic problems, and interpersonal problems — have been identified as basic to the CES–D. The CES–D also has a total aggregate score.

The CES–D has been used effectively as a screening test with a number of community samples (Comstock & Helsing, 1976; Frerichs, Areshensel, & Clare, 1981; Radloff & Locke, 1985), as well as medical (Parikh, Eden, Price, & Robinson, 1988) and clinic populations (Roberts, Rhoades, & Vernon, 1990). Recently, Shrout and Yager (1989) demonstrated that the CES–D could be shortened to 5 items and still maintain adequate sensitivity and specificity, under the constraint that prediction be limited to traditional two-class categorizations. Generally, an overall score of 16 has been used as a cutoff score for depression, with approximately 15% to 20% of community populations scoring ≥16.

Beck Depression Inventory (BDI). The BDI is a unidimensional, self-report, depression inventory that employs 21 items to measure the severity of depression. Pessimism, guilt, depressed mood, self-deprecation, suicidal thoughts, insomnia, somatization, and loss of libido are some of the symptom areas covered by the BDI. The BDI was developed by Beck and his colleagues (Beck et al.) in 1961. A short (13-item) version of the BDI was introduced in 1972 (Beck & Beck, 1972), with additional psychometric evaluation accomplished subsequently (Reynolds & Gould, 1981). Recently, a revised version of the BDI has been published (Beck & Steer, 1993).

The BDI is characterized by the author as being most appropriate for measuring severity of depression in patients who have been clinically diagnosed with depression. It has been utilized to assess depression worldwide, with numerous community and clinical populations (Steer & Beck, 1996). Each of the items represents a characteristic symptom of depression on which the respondent is to rate him- or herself on a 4-point (i.e., 0–3) scale. These scores are then summed to yield a total depression score. Beck's rationale for this system is that the frequency of depressive symptoms is distributed along a continuum, from "nondepressed" to "severely depressed." In addition, *number* of symptoms is viewed as correlating with intensity of distress and severity of depression.

The BDI has been used as a screening device with renal dialysis patients, as well as with medical inpatients and outpatients (Craven, Rodin, & Littlefield, 1988). More recently, Whitaker et al. (1990) used the BDI with a group of 5,108 community adolescents and noted that it performed validly in screening for major depression in this previously undiagnosed population. In screening community populations, scores in the range of 17–20 are generally considered suggestive of dysphoria, whereas scores greater than 20 are felt to indicate the presence of clinical depression (Steer & Beck, 1996).

Behavior and Symptom Identification Scale (BASIS–32). The BASIS–32, otherwise known as the Behavior and Symptom Identification Scale, was designed and developed by Eisen, Grob, and Klein (1986) to evaluate the outcome of mental health interventions from the perspective of the patient. It is a 32-item, self-report inventory that assesses current "difficulty in the major symptom and functioning domains that lead to the need for inpatient psychiatric treatment" (Eisen, 1996, p. 65). A 1-week time window is typically utilized with the BASIS–32, and respondents rate the degree of difficulty they have been experiencing on each item via 5-point (0–4) scales. The BASIS–32 contains five cluster analysis-derived subscales: relation to self and others, daily living and role functioning, anxiety and depression, impulsive and addictive behavior, and psychosis. The five domains are not consonant with diagnostic entities, but reflect problems and manifestations of mental illness that are central aspects of the majority of psychiatric illnesses.

The BASIS–32 has been utilized primarily with psychiatric hospital inpatients, and to a lesser degree with psychiatric outpatients and day-hospital patients. Fundamental psychometric characteristics of the scale are quite respectable (Eisen, 1996), and its sensitivity to change has been demonstrated in large sample improvement profiles (Eisen & Dickey, 1996). Although developed and validated within psychiatric inpatient populations, research on the use of the BASIS–32 with outpatient cohorts is in progress, and may confirm its utility for psychiatric populations in general. By integrating items reflecting problems in daily living and functional status with those representing formal psychiatric symptoms, the BASIS–32 could fulfill a long-standing need for a brief outcomes measure focused on psychosocial integration.

Hamilton Anxiety Scale (HAS).   The HAS is a 14-item clinician rating scale published in 1959 by Hamilton. Each item represents a clinical feature of anxiety, requiring the clinician to rate the client on a 5-point scale from 0 (*not present*) to 4 (*very severe*). The items reflect both somatic (e.g., cardiovascular, respiratory, gastrointestinal, and genitourinary), and psychic/cognitive (e.g., memory and concentration impairment) manifestations of anxiety. The HAS was designed to yield two separate subscores for "psychic anxiety" and "somatic anxiety." The HAS has been used with children as well as adults (Kane & Kendall, 1989), coronary artery bypass patients (Erikkson, 1988), general medical/surgical patients (Bech et al., 1984), psychiatric outpatients (Riskind, Bech, Brown, & Steer, 1987), and many other groups. In addition to these applications, the HAS has become accepted as a standard outcome measure in clinical anxiolytic drug trials.

Hamilton Rating Scale for Depression (HRDS)/(HAM–D).   The HRDS is similar to the HAS in that both provide quantitative assessments of the severity of a clinical disorder. The HRDS was developed in 1960 by Hamilton, and later was revised in 1967 (Hamilton, 1967). It consists of 21 items, each measuring a depressive symptom. Hamilton recommended using only 17 items when scoring because of the uncommon nature of the remaining items (e.g., depersonalization).

Hedlung and Vieweg (1979) reviewed the psychometric and substantive properties of the HRDS in two dozen studies and gave it a very favorable evaluation. More recently, Bech (1987) completed a similar review and concluded that the HRDS is an extremely useful scale for measuring depression. A *Structured Interview Guide for the HRDS (SIGH–D)* also is available (Williams, 1988). It provides standardized instructions for administration, and has been shown to improve interrater reliability. Like the HAS with anxiety, the HRDS has also become a standard outcome measure in antidepressant drug trials.

SPECIAL SCREENING ISSUES

As mentioned previously, there is a high comorbidity between medical and psychiatric disorders, and physicians often have difficulty identifying the latter. Anfinson and Kathol (1992) go as far as to recommend laboratory screening for psychiatric patients because of a high prevalence of untreated medical disorders, and suggest that physicians are likely to miss both physical and psychiatric diagnoses in patients who need psychiatric hospitalization. Because of limited diagnostic training, physicians will probably continue to have difficulty with psychiatric disorders, and could greatly benefit from the introduction of efficient psychiatric screening methods. Examples of psychiatric screening for a variety of the most prevalent medical conditions are reviewed next. The emphasis here is on sensitive and efficient screening methods that will help enable the identification of comorbid psychiatric disorders in a variety of primary care settings.

Psychiatric Screening in Cancer Patients

Psychological distress is common among cancer patients due to the effects that the disease has on the patient, the patient's family, and the inherent difficulty in coping with a life-threatening illness. The initial diagnostic phase can be very stressful and can cause a great deal of psychological turmoil, including feelings of depression, anxiety, anger, and denial (Zabora et al., 1997). Other difficult issues arise from the fact that cancer is potentially a terminal disease that often requires invasive treatment and has a high rate of recurrence. Zabora et al. (1997) noted that there is about a 30% prevalence of elevated psychological distress at diagnosis of cancer and at recurrence. There is mixed evidence concerning whether patients who experience recurrence of symptoms may be less distressed and cope better with future treatment. Some may react more favorably because they have a familiarity with the medical system, whereas others may experience greater distress due to the symptom recurrence. Many experts suggest that psychological treatment should be available for highly distressed individuals first diagnosed with cancer, noting that patients' levels of pre-existing distress may be exacerbated by the diagnosis and become progressively worse if left unchecked.

Recently, Gotay and Stern (1995) published a review of the *Journal of Psychosocial Oncology* for the years 1986 to 1993 with a focus on the most common measures used to screen for patient psychological status. The authors further reviewed how these measures were applied with cancer patients. Seven instruments measuring depression, anxiety, mood, or other indices of psychological integration were found to be used most frequently. They included the Beck Depression Inventory (BDI), Center for Epidemiological Studies–Depression Scale (CES–D), State-Trait Anxiety Inventory (STAI), Symptom Checklist–90–R (SCL–90–R), Brief Symptom Inventory (BSI), Profile of Mood States, and Psychological Adjustment to Illness Scale (PAIS/ PAIS–SR).

Psychiatric Screening in Patients
With Coronary Artery Disease

Psychological distress is also a common experience of individuals with coronary artery disease and can adversely affect outcomes in these patients. More profound psychological conditions such as formal psychiatric disorders, particularly depressions, carry with them an even greater risk for adversely affecting cardiac morbidity and mortality. In this situation, screening systems can efficiently and effectively distinguish individuals who are at risk for comorbid psychopathology and, having identified such patients, possibly point the way toward effective interventions.

An outstanding example of the potential utility associated with screening in this patient population is provided in a report by Allison et al. (1995). These investigators studied 381 cardiac rehabilitation patients who were partitioned into "distressed" and "nondistressed" categories on the basis of scores on the SCL–90–R. Evaluation across a 6-month postdischarge interval disclosed that the distressed group had dramatically higher rates of cardiovascular rehospitalization and recurrent cardiac problems than the nondistressed patients. In addition, the mean rehospitalization costs for the distressed patients were approximately five times those for the low-distress group. The authors concluded that high levels of psychological distress not only increase the morbidity and risk of mortality of cardiac patients, but also substantially increase the costs of treating these patients.

Screening for Alcoholism

Alcoholism is a disease that many physicians feel unprepared to diagnose and treat. Israel et al. (1996) noted that 30% to 40% of physicians feel unprepared to diagnose alcoholism, whereas Chang (1997) reported that only 19% of physicians felt they had adequate preparation for treating alcohol-related disorders. Physicians often lack knowledge about the disorder and its symptoms, which often impedes treatment and may contribute to further medical problems. Hopkins, Zarro, and McCarter (1994) observed that physicians identified only 37% of problem drinkers appropriately. These authors believe that it is necessary to increase awareness about referral and screening procedures in medical school curricula and through the continuing education of practicing physicians. In these instances, the routine use of alcohol screens would help primary care doctors identify these conditions quickly and accurately so that they can initiate appropriate treatment or referrals.

Although there are a number of alcohol screening tests available, one of the simplest tools physicians can use is the CAGE questionnaire. This instrument consists of four questions that have sensitivity and specificity that range from 60% to 95% in identifying problem drinking (Israel et al., 1996). The four questions of the CAGE are:

1. Have you ever felt the need to Cut down on your drinking?
2. Have you ever felt Annoyed by someone criticizing your drinking?
3. Have you ever felt Guilty about your drinking?
4. Have you ever felt the need of an Eye opener (a drink first thing in the morning)?

Ford, Klag, Whelton, Goldsmith, and Levine (1994) noted that although 45% of physicians had heard of the CAGE, only 14% could recite all four questions needed. This research suggests that general knowledge about screening for alcoholism requires some enhancement in the training curricula for primary care physicians.

Several studies have addressed the differences in presentation, identification, and treatment needs for women with alcoholism (Amodei, Williams, Seale, & Alvarado, 1996; Chang, 1997; Cyr & Moulton, 1993). Alcoholism research has predominately focused on male treatment approaches, and few studies have addressed the distinct drinking behavior of women. Cyr and Moulton (1993) noted that problem drinking in women often goes unrecognized and untreated by primary care physicians. The authors feel there is a further need to educate physicians about female drinking problems so that they can educate their female patients about dysfunctional drinking behavior. Differential metabolism, higher blood alcohol levels, and higher alcohol-related morbidity and mortality are characteristic of females with an alcohol problem.

Screening for Depression

Depression is the most common psychological disorder seen in primary care and is the underlying basis for many symptoms reported to primary care doctors. Obviously, an accurate diagnosis of depression is needed for effective treatment, an accomplishment that often proves difficult due to the high overlap of depressive symptoms with the symptoms of concomitant medical disorders. Primary care physicians are most likely to see depressed patients who present with a variety of somatic complaints as well as fatigue and irritability. The addition of one of the many well-validated depression screening measures can make a significant contribution to the physician's ability to recognize clinical depressions in his/her patients.

As an example of effective screening, Callahan et al. (1994) implemented a screening program for depression using the Centers for Epidemiologic Studies Depression Scale (CES-D) and the Hamilton Depression Rating Scale (HAM–D) along with physician training that included education on depression. The investigators found that physicians who were educated about depression, had access to the screening instruments data, and were encouraged to make a diagnosis of depression were significantly more likely to diagnose depression and prescribe antidepressant medication. Rapp, Smith, and Britt (1990) also noted that use of the Extracted Hamilton Depression Rating Scale (XHDRS) substantially helped to correctly identify depression in an elderly cohort. The authors concluded that the XHDRS is a reliable and valid instrument with substantial utility for detecting depression in the elderly, and provides primary care physicians with a quick assessment tool that can aid the diagnosis of depression in their patients.

On a related issue, Wyshak and Barsky (1995) evaluated a subset of depressed and anxious clinic patients concerning the effectiveness of their medical care. In general, patients appeared satisfied, but there was little correlation between physician ratings of treatment effectiveness and patient satisfaction ratings. Patients who reported significant depressive symptoms were more likely to be dissatisfied with their medical care. Physicians tended to rate themselves as more effective with older, male patients who were not significantly depressed.

Screening in elderly patients is addressed more fully in a later section. However, the need for effective screening for depression in the elderly cannot be overemphasized. Depression is often mistaken for dementia or delirium in elderly patients, and multiple medical problems, typical of older patients, also decrease the likelihood of recognition of a depressive disorder (Rapp et al., 1990).

Screening for Suicidal Behavior

Chiles and Strosahl (1995) defined suicidal behavior as a "broad spectrum of thoughts, communications, and acts . . . ranging from the least common completed suicide . . . to the more frequent suicidal communications . . . and the most frequent suicidal ideations and verbalizations" (p. 7). They report that the rate of suicide has remained stable in the United States for the past 20 years at approximately 12.7 deaths per 100,000 and ranks as the eighth leading cause of death in the general population. Suicide ranks as the third leading cause of death for individuals 18–24 years old, and the suicide rate in the elderly is approximately double the rate of suicide in the population 18–24 years old.

Lish et al. (1996) noted that 82% of the people who commit suicide have visited primary care physicians within the past 6 months, 53% within 1 month, and 40% within 1 week prior to the suicide. This realization makes it imperative for primary care physicians to recognize the risk factors involved in suicidal behavior. As noted previously, one risk factor for suicide is the presence of a medical illness, which makes primary care physicians more likely to see cases of suicidal behavior earlier, as opposed to other professionals such as psychologists or psychiatrists. Unfortunately, it is likely that practitioners may miss the warning signs associated with imminent suicide.

Chiles and Strosahl (1995) noted that suicidal behavior can be broken down into three subtypes. The first type is suicidal ideation, which involves thoughts about suicidal behavior. Little is known about the predictive value of suicidal ideation, or how often it is followed by legitimate suicide attempts. The second subtype involves a suicide attempt, which tends to be more common in females and younger individuals. It is enlightening to note that 50% of those individuals who attempt suicide have no formal mental health diagnosis. The final category of suicidal behavior is completed suicide, which is more common in males and older individuals who often have diagnoses of depression, schizophrenia, alcoholism, or panic disorder. Lish et al. (1996) also reported that Whites and divorced or separated individuals are at increased risk for suicide. In contrast to suicide "attempters," between 50% and 90% of those who complete suicide do have some form of psychiatric diagnosis. Other risk factors include loss of a spouse (increased risk for up to 4 years), unemployment, physical illness, bereavement, and physical abuse. Certain personality traits have also been associated with an increased risk for suicide.

Clearly, a clinical interview with a detailed medical history that includes any psychiatric history and previous suicidal behavior is currently the most effective method for identifying suicide risk. Unfortunately, such interviews are quite time-consuming and not cost-effective, given the low base rate of completed suicide. This being the case, the most frequently utilized measures in screening for suicide are self-report inventories. Several inventories have been found useful in screening for suicidal behavior, including the Beck Hopelessness Scale (Beck, Kovacs, & Weissman, 1975) and the Beck Depression Inventory. Westefeld and Liddel (1994) noted that the 21-item Beck Depression Inventory is often used for screening in college students, and has been found to be very useful. Derogatis and Derogatis (1996) reported that the SCL–90–R and the BSI also showed utility in screening for suicidal behavior. Several investigators have reported that both the primary symptom dimensions and the their global scores were able to distinguish suicidal positives versus negatives, in a cohort diagnosed with depression and panic disorder (Bulik, Carpenter, Kupfer, & Frank, 1990; Noyes, Christiansen, Clancy, Garvey, & Suelzer, 1991). In addition, Swedo et al. (1991) found that all SCL–90–R subscales distinguished suicide attempters in an adolescent population. Throughout these studies, investigators observed that both adolescents and adult suicide attempters perceived themselves as more distressed and hopeless than individuals designated "at risk."

Another instrument that has been used to screen for suicidal behavior is the SCREENER. Lish et al. (1996) used this brief self-report inventory to screen for psychiatric disorders in a group of possibility suicidal individuals. The SCREENER screens for *DSM–IV* Axis I conditions and is available in a 96-item long form and a 44-item short form. Three questions address death or suicide, and an additional item addresses suicidal ideation directly. The authors recommend that clinicians should screen for substance abuse, panic disorders, and major depression, because these disorders all increase the risk of suicidal behavior in primary care settings.

Screening for Cognitive Impairment

Screening for cognitive impairment, particularly in geriatric populations, is extremely important because it is estimated that up to 70% of patients with an organic mental disorder (OMD) go undetected (Strain et al., 1988). Because some OMDs are reversible if discovered early enough, screening programs in high-risk populations (such as the elderly) can have a very high utility. Even in conditions found to be irreversible, early detection and diagnosis can help in the development of a treatment plan and the education of family members. Although the prevalence of cognitive disorders in the general population is fairly high, it is even more dramatic in the elderly. Furher and Ritchie (1993) noted a 6% prevalence of dementia in the general population, but indicated that the rate may rise to as much as 14% to 18% in the elderly. In terms of a specific cognitive impairment such as delirium, Hart et al. (1995) noted a prevalence of 10% to 13% in the general medical population, with a rate between 15% and 30% among elderly patients. Because the prevalence of cognitive disorders is so high in the elderly, it is necessary to have effective screening tools to facilitate early detection and timely treatment. Because cognitive decline is manifest disproportionately in this group, we limit our current review to work associated with elderly or geriatric patients.

Screening the geriatric patient can often be a challenging enterprise for a number of diverse reasons. First, these patients often present with sensory, perceptual, and motor problems that seriously constrain the use of standardized tests. Poor vision, diminished hearing, and other physical handicaps can undermine the appropriateness of tests that are dependent upon these skills. Similarly, required medications can cause drowsiness or inalertness, or in other ways interfere with optimal cognitive functioning. Illnesses such as heart disease and hypertension, common in the elderly, have also been shown to affect cognitive functioning (Libow, 1977). These limitations require screening instruments that are flexible enough to be adapted to the patient with handicaps or illnesses, and yet sufficiently standardized to allow normative comparisons.

Another difficulty in assessing cognitive impairment in this population is distinguishing cognitive impairment from aging-associated memory loss. This distinction requires a highly sensitive screening instrument, because the differences between these conditions are often subtle. Normal aging and dementia can be differentiated through their differential effects on language, memory, perception, attention, information-processing speed, and intelligence (Bayles & Kaszniak, 1987). An example of an instrument designed specifically for this purpose is the Global Deterioration Scale (GDS). The GDS is a screening test that has the capacity to describe the magnitude of cognitive decline, and to predict functional disability (Reisberg, Ferris, deLeon, & Crook, 1988).

An additional important issue encountered in screening geriatric populations involves comorbid depression. Depression is one of a number of disorders in the elderly that may imitate dementia, resulting in a syndrome referred to as "pseudodementia." These patients lack a discernable degenerative organic process underlying their conditions, and their dementia-like symptoms usually remit once the underlying affective disorder is effectively treated. Variability of task performance quality can often distinguish these patients from truly demented patients, who tend to have an overall lowered performance level on all tasks (Wells, 1979). If depression is suspected, it should be the focus of a distinct diagnostic work-up.

One of the most demanding diagnostic discriminations in this population is often that between dementia and the patient with acute confusional states, or delirium. This is particularly important, not only because of the increased occurrence of delirium in elderly medical patients, but because if left untreated delirium can progress to an irreversible condition. Delirium can have multiple etiologies, such as drug intoxication, metabolic disorders, fever, cardiovascular disorders, or effects of anesthesia. The elderly are particularly susceptible to misuse or overuse of prescription drugs, as well as metabolic or nutritional imbalances. Hypothyroidism, hyperparathyroidism, and diabetes are some of the medical conditions that can be mistaken for dementia (Albert, 1981). Fortunately, three cardinal characteristics enable us to distinguish dementia from delirium. The first of these is *rate of onset of symptoms*. Delirium is marked by acute or abrupt onset of symptoms, while dementia is a more gradual progression. Second is *impairment of attention*. Delirious patients have special difficulty sustaining attention on tasks such as serial sevens, and digit span. Finally, *nocturnal worsening* is a frequent feature characteristic of delirium, but not dementia (Mesulam & Geschwind, 1976). Collectively, these three cognitive markers usually enable an competent and accurate discrimination.

Recently, a number of measures were designed specifically to aid in the differentiation of delirium from dementia and depression in the elderly. One of these instruments is the Cognitive Test for Delirium (CTD), which is a nine-item examiner-administered scale that evaluates the cognitive components of orientation, attention span, memory, comprehension, and vigilance (Hart et al., 1995). The CTD is completely nonverbal and can be administered in 10 to 15 minutes. Using ROC analysis the authors found an optimal cutoff of <19 to distinguish delirium from other disorders. Overall, the CTD achieved 100% sensitivity and 95% specificity when the optimum cutoff score was used with demented ICU patients.

It is not uncommon for cases of cognitive impairment go undetected. This may be due to the fact that the early stages of cognitive dysfunction are often quite subtle, and that many cases first present to primary care physicians who have their principal focus on other systems (Mungas, 1991). Also, many physicians are unfamiliar with the available procedures for detecting cognitive impairment, whereas others are reluctant to add a formal cognitive screening to their schedule of procedures. Although relatively brief, the 10 to 30 minutes required by screening instruments may remain a formidable impediment, considering that, on average, family practice physicians spend 7 to 10 minutes with each patient. The solution to this problem may rest in training nurses and other health care professionals to administer cognitive screening instruments. Such an approach would not increase the time burden on the physician, and would enable him or her to evaluate the screening data in an abbreviated format.

Instruments With a General Versus Specific Focus

There are now quite a few instruments available that provide quick and efficient screening of cognitive functioning. Most of these address the general categories of cognitive functioning covered in the standard mental status examination, including attention, concentration, intelligence, judgment, learning ability, memory, orientation, perception, problem solving, psychomotor ability, reaction time, and social intactness (McDougall, 1990). However, not all instruments include items from all of these categories. These general instruments can be contrasted with another class of cognitive screening measures characterized by a more specific focus. For example, the Stroke Unit Mental Status Examination (SUMSE) was designed specifically to identify cognitive deficits and plan rehabilitation programs for stroke patients (Hajek, Rutman, & Scher, 1989). Another example of an instrument with a specific focus is the Dementia of Alzheimer's Type Inventory (DAT), designed to distinguish Alzheimer's disease from other dementias (Cummings & Benson, 1986). A more recent example of a specific measure is the Cognitive Test for Delirium (CTD), which screens specifically for delirium in intensive care units (Hart et al., 1995). In recent years, use of specific types of measures in combination with broader measures, has become more common.

Unlike other screening tests, the great majority of cognitive impairment scales are administered by an examiner. Of the instruments to be reviewed in this chapter, none are self-report measures. There are no pencil-and-paper inventories that can be completed by the respondent alone. Instead, these screening measures are designed to be administered by a professional and require a combination of oral and written responses. Most of the tests are highly transportable, however, and can be administered by a wide variety of health care workers.

Cognitive Screening Instruments

This section provides a brief summary of nine popular cognitive impairment screening measures. This is not intended to be an exhaustive review, but rather to provide some data on the nature of each measure and its psychometric properties (see Table 4.8).

Mini-Mental State Examination (MMSE). The MMSE was developed by Folstein, Folstein, and McHugh (1975) to determine the level of cognitive impairment. It is an 11-item scale measuring six aspects of cognitive function: orientation, registration, attention and calculation, recall, language, and praxis. Scores can range from 0 to 30, with lower scores indicating greater impairment.

The MMSE has proved successful at assessing levels of cognitive impairment in many populations, including community residents (Kramer, German, Anthony, Von Korff, & Skinner, 1985), hospital patients (Teri, Larson, & Reiffler, 1988), residents of long-term care facilities (Lesher & Whelihan, 1986), and neurological patients (Dick et al., 1984). Escobar et al. (1986) suggested using another instrument with Spanish-speaking individuals, as the MMSE may overestimate dementia in this population. Roca et al. (1984) also recommended other instruments for patients with less

TABLE 4.8
Screening Instruments for Cognitive Impairment

Instrument	Author	Description	Application	Sensitivity/ Specificity
MMSE	Folstein et al. (1975)	11 Items; designed to determine level of cognitive impairment	1, 3, 4	.83/.89
CCSE	Jacobs et al. (1977)	30 Items; designed to detect presence of organic mental disorder	2, 3, 4, 5	.73/.90
SPMS	Pfeiffer (1975)	10 Items; designed to detect presence of cognitive impairment	1	.55–.88/.72–.96
HSCS	Faust and Fogel (1989)	15 Items; designed to estimate presence, scope, and severity of cognitive impairment	2	.94/.92
MSQ	Kahn et al. (1960)	10 Items; designed to quantify dementia	1, 4, 5, 6	.55–.96/NA

Note. Applications are as follows: 1, community populations; 2, cognitively intact; 3, hospital inpatients; 4, medical patients; 5, geriatric; 6, long-term care patients.

than 8 years of schooling for similar reasons. In contrast, the MMSE may underestimate cognitive impairment in psychiatric populations (Faustman, Moses, & Csernansky, 1990). Finally, the MMSE has lower sensitivity with mildly impaired individuals, who are more likely to be labeled as demented (Doyle, Dunn, Thadani, & Lenihan, 1986). As such, the MMSE is most useful for patients with moderate to moderately severe dementia. Fuhrer and Ritchie (1993) also found that the MMSE was more discriminating for moderate dementia rather than mild dementia, but they did not find a significant difference between those who had less than 8 years of education versus those who had more than 8 years of education. The authors noted, however, that cutoff scores for the MMSE need to be adjusted when comparing clinical samples of dementia with higher prevalence than the 6% prevalence in the general population. Furher and Ritchie (1993) disagreed with cutoff points (18/19 for moderate dementia and 22/23 for mild dementia) presented by Jagger, Clark, and Anderson (1992) because they believe the latter's prevalence numbers were inflated due to the increased age of their sample. Both groups of authors supported the use of ROC analysis as a means for assessing the utility and cutoff scores for screening instruments.

Cognitive Capacity Screening Examination (CCSE).   The CCSE is a 30-item scale designed to detect diffuse organic disorders, especially delirium, in medical populations. The instrument was developed by Jacobs, Berhard, Delgado, and Strain (1977) and is recommended if delirium is suspected. The items include questions of orientation, digit recall, serial sevens, verbal short-term memory, abstractions, and arithmetic, all of which are helpful in detecting delirium (Baker, 1989).

The CCSE has been used with geriatric patients (McCartney & Palmateer, 1985), as well as hospitalized medical-surgical patients (Foreman, 1987). In comparisons of the MMSE, SPMSQ (discussed later), and CCSE, the CCSE was shown to be the most reliable and valid (Foreman, 1987). Like the MMSE, the CCSE is also influenced by the educational level of the subject. However, unlike the MMSE, the CCSE cannot differentiate levels of cognitive impairment or types of dementias and is most appropriate for cognitively intact patients (Judd et al., 1986).

Short Portable Mental Status Questionnaire (SPMSQ).   The SPMSQ (Pfeiffer, 1975) is a 10-item scale for use with community and/or institutional residents. This scale is unique in that it has been used with rural and less educated populations (Baker, 1989). The items assess orientation, and recent and remote memory; however, visuospatial skills are not tested. The SPMSQ is a reliable detector of organicity (Haglund & Schuckit, 1976) but should not be used to predict the progression or course of the disorder (Berg, Edwards, Danziger, & Berg, 1987).

High Sensitivity Cognitive Screen (HSCS).   This scale was designed to be as sensitive and comprehensive as lengthier instruments while still being clinically convenient. It was developed by Faust and Fogel (1989) for use with native English-speaking subjects 16–65 years old with at least an eighth-grade education who are free from gross cognitive dysfunction. The 15 items include reading, writing, immediate and delayed recall, and sentence construction, among others. The HSCS has shown adequate reliability and validity and is best used to estimate presence, scope, and severity of cognitive impairment (Faust & Fogel, 1989). The HSCS cannot pinpoint specific areas of involvement, and, as for most of these scales, should represent a first step toward cognitive evaluation, not a substitute for a standard neuropsy-chological assessment.

Mental Status Questionnaire (MSQ).   The MSQ is a 10-item scale developed by Kahn, Goldfarb, Pollock, and Peck (1960). It has been used successfully with medical geriatric patients (LaRue, D'Elia, Clark, Spar, & Jarvik, 1986), community residents (Shore, Overman, & Wyatt, 1983), and long-term care patients (Fishback, 1977). Disadvantages of this measure include its sensitivity to education and ethnicity of the subject, its reduced sensitivity with mildly impaired individuals, and its omission of tests of retention, registration, and cognitive processing (Baker, 1989).

Other Instruments.   Four additional measures have been developed that are particularly appropriate for primary care use because their main function is to simply rule out or detect the presence of dementia. FROMAJE (Libow, 1981) classifies individuals into normal, mild, moderate, and severe dementia groups and has been used successfully with long-term care patients (Rameizl, 1984). The Blessed Dementia Scale (Blessed, Tomlinson, & Roth, 1968) measures changes in activities and habits, personality, interests, and drives, and is useful for determining presence of dementia, though not its progression. The Global Deterioration Scale (GDS; Reisberg, Ferris, DeLeon, & Crook, 1982) can be used to distinguish between normal aging, age-associated memory impairment, and primary degenerative disorder (such as Alzheimer's disease). The GDS is useful for assessing the magnitude and progression of cognitive decline (Reisberg, 1984). In terms of diagnosing Alzheimer's disease, Steffens et al. (1996) have proposed using the Telephone Interview for Cognitive Status along with a videotaped mental status exam to improve diagnostic accuracy. The authors state that gathering information over the phone from Alzheimer's patients shows some promise and may limit physician time constraints.

A final instrument worth mentioning is the Chula Mental Test (CMT), developed by Jitapunkul, Lailert, Worakul, Srikiatkhachorn, and Ebrahim (1996) for use with the elderly in underdeveloped countries. The CMT was developed in response to a major problem with standard screening measures, which arises from the fact that they are based on Western concepts of cognitive dysfunction and may not be culturally or linguistically relevant in other countries. The CMT is a 13-item test that is less biased toward education and literacy, in order to minimize the number of false positives when screening in underdeveloped countries. The 13 items on the CMT test for remote memory, orientation, attention, language, abstract thinking, judgment, and general knowledge. The recommended cutoff score is 80% of the maximum score attainable. When this score is used, the CMT achieves a sensitivity of 100% and specificity of 90%, values that are quite good in this context.

MONITORING PSYCHIATRIC DISORDERS IN PRIMARY CARE

Once a diagnosis has been made and a treatment regimen implemented, the next major consideration involves establishing a mechanism to evaluate the effectiveness of treatment. What degree of symptom control has been achieved? What is the patient's subjective sense of well-being? How are family relations? Is the patient adjusting well at work? These questions all address major dimensions of response to treatment. Without becoming involved in formal outcomes studies, the practitioner can nonetheless introduce a systematic program of treatment monitoring to establish the nature and extent of the patient's treatment response.

As indicated elsewhere (see Derogatis & Savitz, chap. 9, this volume), the cardinal characteristic of a psychological monitoring measure is that it be sensitive to treatment-induced change. The latter may be thought of as a central effect that is imbedded in an array of diverse alternative effects, which requires separation and elucidation. An instrument selected to achieve treatment monitoring must have the capacity to represent response to treatment as "figure" against the collective "ground" of alternative effects. This means that in addition to having high *discriminative* potential (i.e., the ability to distinguish "functional" from "dysfunctional" individuals), instruments chosen for treatment monitoring must also possess powerful *evaluative* capacities that enable them to accurately represent changes in patient's status across time.

Time of Monitoring

The time frame for monitoring is obviously an important parameter that must be considered in designing a treatment monitoring system. Fundamentally, the nature of the condition being monitored and the characteristics of treatment response are major determinants of the optimal assessment schedule (i.e., days, weeks, months). Monitoring acute conditions calls for a different schedule of assessments than does the assessment of chronic disease states. Likewise, the variables or attributes being assessed (e.g., drug side effects, patient's mood, services utilization) also play a role in determining the most effective monitoring schedule. Initially, a baseline assessment must be done; however, "baseline" can be defined in myriad ways. Ideally, baseline measurement is established prior to the introduction of the treatment(s) under evaluation, but in close temporal contiguity to treatment initiation. Subsequently, additional follow-up assessments should be routinely done (monthly, semiannually, annually), with scheduling depending on the configuration of the parameters just discussed. Typically, a follow-up evaluation at 6 months post baseline enables an evaluation of the success of both acute treatment and continuation treatment phases. A further evaluation at 12 months enables an assessment of any maintenance treatment regimens initiated, and also serves to determine any signs of relapse or recurrence. Familiarity with the nature and course of the condition under assessment, along with an understanding of typical patterns of episodes of illness and episodes of care, usually serves as the most useful guide for establishing a monitoring schedule.

Domains of Monitoring

Treatment effects can be measured via a multitude of potential outcomes variables, from various indicators of clinical status (symptoms, side effects, complications) and measures of functional health status (e.g., physical capacity, cognitive functioning), to global well-being (e.g., affects balance) and measures of services utilization. At present, there are numerous well-validated psychological tests, rating scales, and standardized interviews to accurately quantify and assess the majority of these characteristics.

First and foremost, measures of *morbidity* should be integrated into the monitoring system. Evaluations of symptomatic distress, side effects of treatment, and concurrent medical events should be primary components of the monitoring package. The system must also be designed to register signs of relapse or recurrence should they occur, and to effectively communicate them to the treating physician.

Quality-of-life variables, including measures of functional health status, have become increasingly important, as we progress from traditional biomedical approaches to a more biopsychosocial model in viewing illness and treatment outcomes. Cognitive functioning, physical capacity, interpersonal and social relations, and vocational performance require assessment periodically to determine the effects treatment(s) are having on these important expressions of health status. Subjectively perceived *well-being* is also frequently included within the broad rubric of quality of life, and refers essentially to how the patient currently "feels" about the quality of his or her life experience. For measurement purposes, well-being is often construed as the nature and degree of balance between positive and negative emotional experiences (i.e., affects balance), with a positive affects balance being associated with good health and constructive engagement with the environment, and a negative affects balance being associated with psychological distress and loss of vitality. Measures of well-being are brief and simple to administer and have been shown to have strong empirical relationships with health status, in medical as well as in psychiatric populations. A number of well-designed instruments of this type are currently available (Derogatis, 1996; Derogatis & Rutigliano, 1996; Watson, Clark, & Tellegen, 1988).

Monitoring Change

Although seemingly rudimentary, the assessment and evaluation of changes in health status is often exceedingly complex. The answer to the fundamental question, "Did the patient improve as the result of treatment?" is frequently confounded by multiple mitigating issues. First, psychiatric disorders (e.g., anxiety, depression) are hypothetical constructs, which means that they must be operationally defined to be measured. Because the scales used to conduct such measurement possess no "ostensive" characteristics (e.g., distance, weight), the resulting measurements are relatively crude compared to those of the physical sciences. Although magnitude and direction of change are the most basic parameters of treatment efficacy, in the case of psychiatric conditions the magnitude of change required to define clinical improvement is a relative rather than an absolute number. Depending on where in the distribution (on the outcomes test) the patient scored at baseline, a 10-point score reduction could be interpreted as anywhere from "dramatic" to "minor" clinical change. This difficulty is due in part to the fact that overlap almost always exists between "normal" and "patient" score distributions, which means there is no definitive score or value at which clinical status ends and normal status begins.

In spite of these problem, well-designed instruments, with standardized norms possessing actuarial properties, do provide sufficient information to make reasonable clinical judgments comfortably. Such test instruments usually publish norms for both "patient" and "community" groups, which enable comparisons of where in each distribution treatment induced change places the patient. Recently, relatively elegant models have been proposed to ascertain the "clinical significance" of change (Jacobsen & Truax, 1991). However, a simple examination of the patient's pre–post treatment movement in the context of well-established norm sets will usually provide a satisfactory answer to the question, "Did the patient improve significantly?"

CONCLUSION

Currently, there is little doubt that psychiatric disorders qualify as conditions appropriate for the development of effective health screening programs (Wilson & Junger, 1968). The magnitude of the health problem they represent is extensive, and the morbidity, mortality, and costs associated with these conditions are imposing. We currently possess valid, cost-efficient mechanisms to effectively identify these conditions in medical and community settings, and the efficacy of our treatment regimens for most psychiatric conditions has improved substantially (Regier et al., 1988). It is unquestionably time to systematically implement psychiatric screening systems in primary care. This is particularly so when one considers the alternative, where compelling evidence exists that left to their natural courses, such conditions will result in chronic, compound morbidities of both a physical and psychological nature (Derogatis & Wise, 1989; Katon et al., 1990; Regier et al., 1988). Ultimately, it is of little consequence to develop effective systems of treatment planning and outcomes monitoring, if the majority of individuals who would benefit from these exercise are lost to the health care system.

REFERENCES

Allison, T. G., Williams, D. E., Miller, T. D., Patten, C. A., Bailey, K. R., Squires, R. W., & Gau, G. T. (1995). Medical and economic costs of psychologic distress in patients with coronary artery disease. *Mayo Clinic Proceedings, 70,* 734–742.

Albert, M. (1981). Geriatric neuropsychology. *Journal of Consulting and Clinical Psychology, 49,* 835–850.

Amodei, N., Williams, J. F., Seale, J. P., & Alvarado, M. L. (1996). Gender differences in medical presentation and detection of patients with a history of alcohol abuse or dependence. *Journal of Addictive Diseases, 15,* 19–31.

Anderson, S. M., & Harthorn, B. H. (1989). The recognition diagnosis, and treatment of mental disorders by primary care physicians. *Medical Care, 27,* 869–886.

Anderson, S. M., & Harthorn, B. H. (1990). Changing the psychiatric knowledge of primary care physicians: The effects of a brief intervention on clinical diagnosis and treatment. *General Hospital Psychiatry, 12,* 177–190.

Anfinson, T. J., & Kathol, R. G. (1992). Screening 2laboratory evaluation in psychiatric patients: A review. *General Hospital Psychiatry, 14,* 248–257.

Baker, F. (1989). Screening tests for cognitive impairment. *Hospital and Community Psychiatry, 40,* 339–340.

Baldessarini, R. J., Finklestein, S., & Arana, G. W. (1983). The predictive power of diagnostic tests and the effect of prevalence of illness. *Archives of General Psychiatry, 40,* 569–573.

Barrett, J. E., Barrett, J. A., Oxman, T. E., & Gerber, P. D. (1988). The prevalence of psychiatric disorders in a primary care practice. *Archives of General Psychiatry, 45,* 1100–1106.

Bayles, K., & Kaszniak, A. (1987). *Communication and cognition in normal aging and dementia.* Boston: Little, Brown.

Bech, P. (1987). Observer rating scales of anxiety and depression with reference to DSM-III for clinical studies in psychosomatic medicine. *Advances of Psychosomatic Medicine, 17,* 55–70.

Bech, P., Grosby, H., Husum, B., & Rafaelson, L. (1984). Generalized anxiety and depression measured by the Hamilton Anxiety Scale and the Melancholia Scale in patients before and after cardiac surgery. *Psychopathology, 17,* 253–263.

Beck, A. T., & Beck, R. W. (1972). Screening depressed patients in family practice: A rapid technic. *Postgraduate Medicine, 52,* 81–85.

Beck, A. T., Kovacs, M., & Weissman, A. (1975). Hopelessness and suicidal behavior: An overview. *Journal of the American Medical Association, 234,* 1146–1149.

Beck, A. T., & Steer, R. A. (1993). *Manual for the Beck Depression Inventory.* San Antonio, TX: Psychological Corporation.

Beck, A. T., Ward, C., Mendelson, M., Mock, J., & Erbaugh, J. (1961). An inventory for measuring depression. *Archives of General Psychiatry, 4,* 53–63.

Berg, G., Edwards, D., Danzinger, W., & Berg, L. (1987). Longitudinal change in three brief assessments of SDAT. *Journal of the America Geriatrics Society, 35,* 205–212.

Birtchnell, J., Evans, C., Deahl, M., & Master, N. (1989). The Depression Screening Instrument (DSI): A device for the detection of depressive disorders in general practice. *Journal of Affective Disorders, 16,* 269–281.

Blessed, G., Tomlinson, B., & Roth, M. (1968). The association between quantitative measures of dementia and of senile change in the cerebral gray matter of elderly. *British Journal of Psychiatry, 114,* 797–811.

Bridges, K., & Goldberg, D. (1984). Psychiatric illness in in-patients with neurological disorders: Patient's view on discussions of emotional problems with neurologists. *British Medical Journal, 289,* 656–658.

Bulik, C. M., Carpenter, L. L., Kupfer, D. J., & Frank, E. (1990). Features associated with suicide attempts in recurrent major depression. *Journal of Affective Disorders, 18,* 27–29.

Burnam, M. A., Wells, K. B., Leake, B., & Landsverk, J. (1988). Development of a brief screening instrument for detecting depressive disorders. *Medical Care, 26,* 775–789.

Burns, B. J., & Burke, J. D. (1985). Improving mental health practices in primary care. *Public Health Reports, 100,* 294–299.

Callahan, C. M., Hendrie, H. C., Dittus, R. S., Brater, D. C., Hui, S. L., & Tierney, W. M. (1994). Improving treatment of late life depression in primary care: A randomized clincal trial. *Journal of American Geriatric Society, 42,* 839–846.

Chang, G. (1997). Primary care: Detection of women with alcohol use disorders. *Harvard Review of Psychiatry, 4,* 334–337.

Chiles, J. A., & Strosahl, K. D. (1995). *The suicidal patient: Principles of assessment, treatment, and case management* (pp. 50–105). Washington, DC: American Psychiatric Press.

Chong, M., & Wilkinson, G. (1989). Validation of 30- and 12-item versions of the Chinese Health Questionnaire (CHQ) in patients admitted for general health screening. *Psychological Medicine, 19,* 495–505.

Cochran, C. D., & Hale, W. D. (1985). College students norms on the Brief Symptom Inventory. *Journal of Clinical Psychology, 31,* 176–184.

Commission on Chronic Illness. (1957). *Chronic illness in the United States, 1.* Cambridge, MA: Commonwealth Fund, Harvard University Press.

Comstock, G. W., & Helsing, K. J. (1976). Symptoms of depression in two communities. *Psychological Medicine, 6,* 551–564.

Craven, J. L., Rodin, G. M., & Littlefield, C. (1988). The Beck Depression Inventory as a screening device for major depression in renal dialysis patients. *International Journal of Psychiatry in Medicine, 18,* 365–374.

Cummings, J., & Benson, F. (1986). Dementia of the Alzheimer Type: An inventory of diagnostic clinical features. *Journal of the American Geriatrics Society, 34,* 12–19.

Cyr, M. G., & Moulton, A. W. (1993). The physician's role in prevention, detection, and treatment of alcohol abuse in women. *Psychiatric Annals, 23,* 454–462.

Davis, T. C., Nathan, R. G., Crough, M. A., & Bairnsfather, L. E. (1987). Screening depression with a new tool; Back to basics with a new tool. *Family Medicine, 19,* 200–202.

Derogatis, L. R. (1977). *SCL–90–R: Administration, scoring and procedures manual–I.* Baltimore, MD: Clinical Psychometric Research.

Derogatis, L. R. (1983). *SCL–90–R: Administration, scoring and procedures manual–II.* Baltimore, MD: Clinical Psychometric Research.

Derogatis, L. R. (1990). SCL–90–R: *A bibliography of research reports 1975–1990.* Baltimore, MD: Clinical Psychometric Research.

Derogatis, L. R. (1993). *BSI: Administration, scoring & procedures manual for the Brief Symptom Inventory–Third edition.* Minneapolis, MN: National Computer Systems.

Derogatis, L. R. (1994). *SCL–90–R: Administration, scoring & procedures manual–Third edition.* Minneapolis, MN: National Computer Systems.

Derogatis, L. R. (1996). *Derogatis Affects Balance Scale (DABS): Administration, scoring, and procedures manual.* Baltimore, MD: Clinical Psychometric Research.

Derogatis, L. R. (1997). *The Brief Symptom Inventory–18 (BSI–18).* Minneapolis, MN: National Computer Systems.

Derogatis, L., DellaPietra, L., & Kilroy, V. (1992). Screening for psychiatric disorder in medical populations. In M. Fava, G. Rosenbaum, & R. Birnbaum (Eds.), *Research designs and methods in psychiatry* (pp. 145–170). Amsterdam: Elsevier.

Derogatis, L. R., & Derogatis, M. F. (1996). SCL–90–R and the BSI. In B. Spilker (Ed.), *Quality of life and pharmacoeconomics* (pp. 323–335). Philadelphia: Lippincott-Raven.

Derogatis, L. R., Lipman, R. S., Rickels, K., Uhlenhuth, E. H., & Covi, L. (1974a). The Hopkins Symptom CheckList (HSCL): A self-report symptom inventory. *Behavioral Science, 19*, 1–15.

Derogatis, L. R., Lipman, R. S., Rickels, K., Uhlenhuth, E. H., & Covi, L. (1974b). The Hopkins Symptom Checklist (HSCL). In P. Pinchot (Ed.), *Psychological measurements in psychopharmacology* (pp. 79–111). Basel: Karger.

Derogatis, L. R., & Melisaratos, N. (1983). The Brief Symptom Inventory: An introductory report. *Psychological Medicine, 13*, 595–605.

Derogatis, L. R., Morrow, G. R., Fetting, J., Penman, D., Piasetsky, S., Schmale, A. M., Henrichs, M., & Carnicke, C. L. M. (1983). The prevalence of psychiatric disorders among cancer patients. *Journal of the American Medical Association, 249*, 751–757.

Derogatis, L. R., & Rutigliano, P. J. (1996). Derogatis Affects Balance Scale: DABS. In B. Spilker (Ed.), *Quality of life and pharmacoeconomics in clinical trials* (2nd ed., pp. 169–178). Philadelphia: Lippincott-Raven.

Derogatis, L. R., & Spencer, P. M. (1982). *BSI administration and procedures manual I.* Baltimore, MD: Clinical Psychometric Research.

Derogatis, L. R., & Wise, T. N. (1989). *Anxiety and depressive disorders in the medical patient.* Washington, DC: American Psychiatric Press.

Dick, J., Guiloff, R., Stewart, A., Blackstock, J., Bielawska, C., Paul, E., & Marsden, C. (1984). Mini-Mental State Examination in neurological patients. *Journal of Neurology, Neurosurgery, and Psychiatry, 47*, 496–499.

Dohrenwend, B. P., & Dohrenwend, B. S. (1982). Prepsectives on the past and future of psychiatric epidemiology. *American Journal of Public Health, 72*, 1271–1279.

Doyle, G., Dunn, S., Thadani, I., & Lenihan, P. (1986). Investigating tools to aid in restorative care for Alzheimer's patients. *Journal of Gerontological Nursing, 12*, 19–24.

Eisen, S. V. (1996). Behavior and Symptom Identification Scale (BASIS-32). In L. I. Sederer & B. Dickey (Eds.), *Outcomes assessment in clinical practice* (pp. 65–69). Baltimore, MD: Williams & Wilkins.

Eisen, S. V., & Dickey, B. (1996). Mental health outcome assessment: The new agenda. *Psychotherapy, 33*, 181–189.

Eisen, S. V., Grob, M. C., & Klein, A. A. (1986). BASIS: The development of a self-report measure for psychiatric inpatient evaluation. *Psychiatric Hospitalization, 17*, 165–171.

Erikkson, J. (1988). Psychosomatic aspects of coronary artery bypass graft surgery: A prospective study of 101 male patients. *Acta Psychiatrica Scandinavica, 77*(Suppl.), 112.

Escobar, J., Burnam, A., Karno, M., Forsythe, A., Landsverk, J., & Golding, J. (1986). Use of the Mini-Mental State Examination (MMSE) in a community population of mixed ethnicity: Cultural and linguistic artifacts. *Journal of Nervous and Mental Disease, 174*, 607–614.

Fauman, M. A. (1983). Psychiatric components of medical and surgical practice, II. Referral and treatment of psychiatric disorders. *American Journal of Psychiatry, 140*, 760–763.

Faust, D., & Fogel, B. (1989). The development and initial validation of a sensitive bedsider cognitive screening test. *Journal of Nervous and Mental Disease, 177*, 25–31.

Faustman, W., Moses, J., & Csernansky, J. (1990). Limitations of the Mini-Mental State Examination in predicting neuropsychological functioning in a psychiatric sample. *Acta Psychiatrica Scandinavica, 81*, 126–131.

Fishback, D. (1977). Mental status questionnaire for organic brain syndrome, with a new visual counting test. *Journal of the American Geriatrics Society, 35*, 167–170.

Folstein, M., Folstein, S., & McHugh, P. (1975). Mini-Mental State. *Journal of Psychiatric Research, 12*, 189–198.

Ford, D. E., Klag, M. J., Whelton, P. K., Goldsmith, M., & Levine, D. (1994). Physician knowledge of the CAGE alcohol screening questions and its impact on practice. *Alcohol and Alcoholism, 29*, 329–336.

Foreman, M. (1987). Reliability and validity of mental status questionnaires in elderly hospitalized patients. *Nursing Research, 36*, 216–220.

Frerichs, R. R., Areshensel, C. S., & Clark, V. A. (1981). Prevalence of depression in Los Angeles County. *American Journal of Epidemiology, 113*, 691–699.

Fulop, G., & Strain, J. J. (1991). Diagnosis and treatment of psychaitric disorders in medically ill inpatients. *Hospital and Community Psychiatry, 42*, 389–394.

Furher, R., & Ritchie, K. (1993). Re: C. Jagger et al.'s article 'Screening for dementia — A comparison of two tests using Receiver Operating Characteristic (ROC) analysis' 1992 7 659–665. *International Journal of Geriatric Psychiatry, 8*, 867–868.

Galton, F. (1883). *Inquiries into human faculty and its development.* New York: Macmillan.

Goldberg, D. (1972). *The detection of psychiatric illness by questionnaire.* Oxford: Oxford University Press.

Goldberg, D., & Hillier, V. F. (1979). A scaled version of the General Health Questionnaire. *Psychological Medicine, 9,* 139–145.

Goldberg, D., & Williams, P. (1988). *A user's guide to the General Health Questionnaire.* Windsor: Nfer-Nelson.

Gotay, C. C., & Stern, J. D. (1995). Assessment of psychological functioning in cancer patients. *Journal of Psychosocial Oncology, 13,* 123–160.

Haglund, R., & Schuckit, M. (1976). A clinical comparison of tests of organicity in elderly patients. *Journal of Gerontology, 31,* 654–659.

Hajek, V., Rutman, D., & Scher, H. (1989). Brief assessment of cognitive impairment in patients with stroke. *Archives of Physical Medicine and Rehabilitation, 70,* 114–117.

Hamilton, M. (1959). The assessment of anxiety states by rating. *British Journal of Medical Psychology, 32,* 50–55.

Hamilton, M. (1967). Development of a rating scale for primary depressive illness. *British Journal of Social and Clinical Psychology, 6,* 278–296.

Hanley, J. A., & McNeil, B. J. (1982). The meaning and use of the area under a Receiver Operating Characteristic (ROC) curve. *Diagnostic Radiography, 143,* 29–36.

Hansson, L., Nettlebladt, P., Borgquist, L., & Nordstrom, G. (1994). Screening for psychiatric illness in primary care. *Social Psychiatry & Psychiatric Epidemiology, 29,* 83–87.

Hart, R. P., Levenson, J. L., Sessler, C. N., Best, A. M., Schwartz, S. M., & Rutherford, L. E. (1995). Validation of a cognitive test for delerium in medical ICU patients. *Psychosomatics, 37,* 533–546.

Hawton, K. (1981). The long term outcome of psychaitric morbidity detected in general medical paitents. *Journal of Psychosomatic Research, 25,* 237–243.

Hedlund, J. L., & Vieweg, M. D. (1979). The Hamilton Rating Scale for Depression: A comprehensive review. *Journal of Operational Psychiatry, 10,* 149–165.

Hoeper, E. W., Nyczi, G. R., & Cleary, P. D. (1979). Estimated prevalence of RDC mental disorders in primary care. *International Journal of Mental Health, 8,* 6–15.

Hopkins, T. B., Zarro, V. J., & McCarter, T. G. (1994). The adequacy of screening, documenting, and treating diseases of substance abuse. *Journal of Addictive Diseases, 13,* 81–87.

Hughson, A. V. M., Cooper, A. F., McArdle, C. S., & Smith, D. C. (1988). Validity of the General Health Questionnaire and its subscales in patients receiving chemotherapy for early breast cancer. *Journal of Psychosomatic Research, 32,* 393–402.

Israel, Y., Hollander, O., Sanchez-Graig, M., Booker, S., Miller, V., Gingrich, R., & Rankin, J. G. (1996). Screening for problem drinking by the primary care physician-nurse team. *Alcoholism: Clinical and Experimental Research, 20,* 1443–1450.

Jacobs, J., Berhard, M., Delgado, A., & Strain, J. (1977). Screening for organic mental syndromes in the medically ill. *Annals of Internal Medicine, 86,* 40–46.

Jacobson, N. S., & Truax, P. (1991). Clinical significance: A statistical approach to defining meaningful chnage in psychotherapy research. *Journal of Consulting & Clinical Psychology, 59,* 12–19.

Jagger, C., Clarke, M., & Anderson, J. (1992). Screening for dementia — A comparison of two tests using Receiver Operating Characteristic (ROC) analysis. *International Journal of Geriatric Psychiatry, 7,* 659–665.

Jitapunkul, S., Lailert, C., Worakul, P., Srikiatkhachorn, A., & Ebrahim, S. (1996). Chula Mental Test: A screening test for elderly people in less developed countries. *International Journal of Geriatric Psychiatry, 11,* 715–720.

Jones, L. R., Badger, L. W., Ficken, R. P., Leepek, J. D., & Anderson, R. L. (1987). Inside the hidden mental health network: Examining mental health care delivery of primary care physicians. *General Hospital Psychiatry, 9,* 287–293.

Judd, B., Meyer, J., Rogers, R., Gandhi, S., Tanahashi, N., Mortel, K., & Tawaklna, T. (1986). Cognitive performance correlates with cerebrovascular impairments in multi-infarct dementia. *Journal of the American Geriatrics Society, 34,* 355–360.

Kahn, R., Goldfarb, A., Pollack, M., & Peck, A. (1960). Brief objective measures for the determination of mental status in the aged. *American Journal of Psychiatry, 117,* 326–328.

Kamerow, D. B., Pincus, H. A., & MacDonald, D. I. (1986). Alcohol abuse, other drug abuse, and mental disorders in medical practice: Prevalence, cost, recognition, and treatment. *Journal of the American Medical Assocation, 255,* 2054–2057.

Kane, M. T., & Kendall, P. C. (1989). Anxiety disorders in children: A multiple-baseline evaluation of a cognitive-behavioral treatment. *Behavior Therapy, 20,* 499–508.

Katon, W., Von Korff, M., Lin, E., Lipscomb, P., Russo, J., Wagner, E., & Polk, E. (1990). Distressed high utilizers of medical care: DSM-III-R diagnoses and treatment needs. *General Hospital Psychiatry, 12,* 355–362.

Kempf, E. J. (1914–1915). The behavior chart in mental diseases. *American Journal of Insanity, 7,* 761–772.

Kessler, L. G., Amick, B. C., & Thompson, J. (1985). Factors influencing the diagnosis of mental disorder among primary care patients. *Medical Care, 23,* 50–62.

Kramer, M., German, P., Anthony, J., Von Korff, M., & Skinner, E. (1985). Patterns of mental disorders among the elderly residents of eastern Baltimore. *Journal of the American Geriatrics Society, 11,* 236–245.

Kuhn, W. F., Bell, R. A., Seligson, D., Laufer, S. T., & Lindner, J. E. (1988). The tip of the iceberg: Psychiatric consultations on an orthopedic service. *International Journal of Psychiatry in Medicine, 18,* 375–378.

LaRue, A., D'Elia, L., Clark, E., Spar, J., & Jarvik, L. (1986). Clinical tests of memory in dementia, depression, and healthy aging. *Psychology and Aging, 1,* 69–77.

Lesher, E., & Whelihan, W. (1986). Reliability of mental status instruments administered to nursing home residents. *Journal of Consulting and Clinical Psychology, 54,* 726–727.

Libow, L. (1977). Senile dementia and pseudosenility: Clinical diagnosis. In C. Eisdorfer & R. Friedel (Eds.), *Cognitive and emotional disturbance in the elderly* (pp.). Chicago: Year Book Medical.

Libow, L. (1981). A rapidly administered, easily remembered mental status evaluation: FROMAJE. In L. S. Libow & F. T. Sherman (Eds.), *The core of geriatric medicine* (pp. 85–91). St. Louis, MO: C. V. Mosby.

Linn, L., & Yager, J. (1984). Recognition of depression and anxiety by primary care physicians. *Psychosomatics, 25,* 593–600.

Lish, J. D., Zimmerman, M., Farber, N. J., Lush, D. T., Kuzma, M. A., & Plescia, G. (1996). Suicide screening in a primary care setting at a Veterans Affairs medical center. *Psychosomatics, 37,* 413–424.

Luce, R. D., & Narens, L. (1987). Measurement scales on the continuum. *Science, 236,* 1527–1532.

Madri, J. J., & Williams, P. (1986). A comparison of validity of two psychiatric screening questionnaires. *Journal of Chronic Disordres, 39,* 371–378.

Malt, U. F. (1989). The validity of the General Health Questionnaire in a sample of accidentally injured adults. *Acta Psychiatrica Scaninavica, 80,* 103–112.

McCartney, J., & Palmateer, L. (1985). Assessment of cognitive deficit in geriatric patients: A study of physician behavior. *Journal of the American Geriatrics Society, 33,* 467–471.

McDougal, M. (1990). A review of screening instruments for measuring cognition and mental status in older adults. *Nurse Practitioner, 15,* 18–28.

Meehl, P. E., & Rosen, A. (1955). Antecedent probability and the efficiency of psychometric signs, patterns, or cutting scores. *Psychological Bulletin, 52,* 194–216.

Messick, S. (1995). Validity of psychological assessment: Validation of inferences from persons' responses and performances as scientific inquiry into score meaning. *American Psychologist, 50,* 741–749.

Mesulam, M., & Geschwind, N. (1976). Disordered mental status in the postoperative period. *Urologic Clinics of North America, 3,* 199–215.

Metz, C. E. (1978). Basic principles of ROC analysis. *Seminars in Nuclear Medicine, 8,* 283–298.

Moore, J. T., Silimperi, D. R., & Bobula, J. A. (1978). Recognition of depression by family medicine residents: The impact of screening. *Journal of Family Practice, 7,* 509–513.

Mossman, D., & Somoza, E. (1991). Neuropsychiatric decision making: The role of disorder prevalence in diagnostic testing. *Journal of Neuropsychiatry and Clinical Neurosciences, 3,* 84–88.

Mossman, D., & Somoza, E. (1992). Balancing risks and benefits: Another approach to optimizing diagnostic tests. *Journal of Neuropsychiatry and Clinical Neurosciences, 4,* 331–335.

Mungas, D. (1991). In-office mental status testing: A practical guide. *Geriatrics, 46,* 54–66.

Murphy, J. M., Berwick, D. M., Weinstein, M. C., Borus, J. F., Budman, S. H., & Klerman, G. L. (1987). Performance of screening and diagnostic tests. *Archives of General Psychiatry, 44,* 550–555.

Nielson, A. C., & Williams, T. A. (1980). Depression in ambulatory medical patients. *Archives of General Psychiatry, 37,* 999–1009.

Noyes, R., Christiansen, J., Clancy, J., Garvey, M. J., & Suelzer, M. (1991). Predictors of serious suicide attempts among patients with panic disorder. *Comprehensive Psychiatry, 32,* 261–267.

Nunnally, J. (1978). *Psychometric theory.* New York: McGraw-Hill.

O'Hara, M. N., Ghonheim, M. M., Hinrich, J. V., Metha, M. P., & Wright, E. J. (1989). Psychological consequences of surgery. *Psychosomatic Medicine, 51,* 356–370.

Orleans, C. T., George, L. K., Houpt, J. L., & Brodie, H. (1985). How primary care physicians treat psychiatric disorders: A national survey of family practitioners. *American Journal of Psychiatry, 142,* 52–57.

Parikh, R. M., Eden, D. T., Price, T. R., & Robinson, R. G. (1988). The sensitivity and specificity of the center for epidemiologic studies depression scale in screening for post-stroke depression. *International Journal of Psychiatry in Medicine, 18,* 169–181.

Pfeiffer, E. (1975). A short portable mental status questionnaire for the assessment of organic brain deficit in elderly patients. *Journal of the American Geriatrics Society, 23,* 433–441.

Piersma, H. L., Reaume, W. M., & Boes, J. L. (1994). The Brief Symptom Inventory (BSI) as an outcome measure for adult psychiatric inpatients. *Journal of Clinical Psychology, 50,* 555–563.

Radloff, L. S. (1977). The CES–D scale: A self report depression scale for research in the general population. *Applied Psychological Measurement, 1,* 385–401.

Radloff, L. S., & Locke, B. Z. (1985). The community mental health assessment survey and the CES–D Scale. In M. M. Weissman, J. K. Myers, & C. G. Ross (Eds.), *Community survey of psychiatric disorder* (pp.). New Brunswick, NJ: Rutgers University Press.

Rameizl, P. (1984). A case for assessment technology in long-term care: The nursing perspective. *Rehabilitation Nursing, 9,* 29–31.

Rand, E. H., Badger, L. W., & Coggins, D. R. (1988). Toward a resolution of contradictions: Utility of feedback from the GHQ. *General Hospital Psychiatry, 10,* 189–196.

Rapp, S. R., Smith, S. S., & Britt, M. (1990). Identifying comorbid depression in elderly medical patients: Use of the Extracted Hamilton Depression Rating Scale. *Psychological Assessment: A Journal of Consulting and Clinical Psychology, 2,* 243–247.

Regier, D. A., Boyd, J. H., Burke, J. D., Rae, D. S., Myers, J. K., Kramer, M., Robins, L. N., George, L. K., Karno, M., & Locke, B. Z. (1988). One month prevalence of mental disorders in the United States. *Archives of General Psychiatry, 45,* 977–986.

Regier, D. A., Goldberg, I. D., Burns, B. J., Hankin, J., Hoeper, E. W., & Nyez, G. R. (1982). Specialist/generalist division of responsibility for patients with mental disorders. *Archives of General Psychiatry, 39,* 219–224.

Regier, D., Goldberg, I., & Taube, C. (1978). The defacto US mental health services system: A public health perspective. *Archives of General Psychiatry, 35,* 685–693.

Regier, D. A., Roberts, M. A., Hirschfeld, Goodwin, F. K., Burke, J. D., Lazar, J. B., & Judd, L. L. (1988). The NIMH depression awareness, recognition, and treatment program: Structure, aims, and scientific basis. *American Journal of Psychiatry, 145,* 1351–1357.

Reisberg, B. (1984). Stages of cognitive decline. *American Journal of Nursing, 84,* 225–228.

Reisberg, B., Ferris, S., deLeon, M., & Crook, T. (1982). The Global Deterioration Scale for assessment of primary degenerative dementia. *American Journal of Psychiatry, 139,* 1136–1139.

Reisberg, B., Ferris, S., deLeon, M., & Crook, T. (1988). Global Deterioration Scale (GDS). *Psychopharmacology Bulletin, 24,* 661–663.

Reynolds, W. M., & Gould, J. W. (1981). A psychometric investigation of the standard and short form Beck Depression Inventory. *Journal of Consulting Clinical Psychology, 49,* 306–307.

Riskind, J. H., Beck, A. T., Brown, G., & Steer, R. A. (1987). Taking the measure of anxiety and depression: Validity of the reconstructed Hamilton scales. *Journal of Nervous and Mental Disorders, 175,* 474–479.

Roberts, R. E., Rhoades, H. M., & Vernon, S. W. (1990). Using the CES–D Scale to screen for depression and anxiety: Effects of language and ethnic status. *Psychiatry Research, 31,* 69–83.

Robins, L. N., Helzer, J. E., Weissman, M. M., Orvaschel, H., Greenberg, E., Burke, J. D., & Regier, D. A. (1984). Lifetime prevalence of specific psychiatric disorders in three sites. *Archives of General Psychiatry, 41,* 949–958.

Roca, P., Klein, L., Kirby, S., McArthur, J., Vogelsang, G., Folstein, M., & Smith, C. (1984). Recognition of dementia among medical patients. *Archives of Internal Medicine, 144,* 73–75.

Rosenthal, T. L., Miller, S. T., Rosenthal, R. H., Sadish, W. R., Fogleman, B. S., & Dismuke, S. E. (1992). Assessing emotional interest at the internist's office. *Behavioral Research & Therapy, 29,* 249–252.

Royce, D., & Drude, K. (1984). Screening drug abuse clients with the Brief Symptom Inventory. *International Journal of Addiction, 19,* 849–857.

Saravay, S. M., Pollack, S., Steinberg, M. D., Weinschel, B., & Habert, B. A. (1996). Four-year follow-up of the influence of psychological comorbidity on medical rehospitalization. *American Journal of Psychiatry, 153,* 397–403.

Schulberg, H. C., Saul, M., McClelland, M., Ganguli, M., Christy, W., & Frank, R. (1985). Assessing depression in primary medical and psychiatric practices. *Archives of General Psychiatry, 42,* 1164–1170.

Schurman, R. A., Kramer, P. D., & Mitchell, J. B. (1985). The hidden mental health network. *Archives of General Psychiatry, 42,* 89–94.

Sederer, L. I., & Dickey, B. (1996). *Outcomes assessment in clinical practice.* Baltimore, MD: Williams & Wilkins.

Seltzer, A. (1989). Prevalence, detection and referral of psychiatric morbidity in general medical patients. *Journal of the Royal Society of Medicine, 82,* 410–412.

Shapiro, S., German, P., Skinner, E., Von Korff, M., Turner, R., Klein, L., Teitelbaum, M., Kramer, M., Burke, J., & Burns, B. (1987). An experiment to change detection and management of mental morbidity in primary care. *Medical Care, 25,* 327–339.

Shore, D., Overman, C., & Wyatt, R. (1983). Improving accuracy in the diagnosis of Alzheimer's disease. *Journal of Clinical Psychiatry, 44,* 207–212.

Shrout, P. E., & Yager, T. J. (1989). Reliability and validity of screening scales: Effect of reducing scale length. *Journal of Clinical Epidemiology, 42,* 69–78.

Snyder, S., Strain, J. J., & Wolf, D. (1990). Differentiating major depression from adjustment disorder with depressed mood in the medical setting. *General Hospital Psychiatry, 12,* 159–165.

Somoza, E. (1994). Classification of diagnostic tests. *International Journal of Biomedical Computing, 37,* 41–55.

Somoza, E. (1996). Eccentric diagnostic tests: Redefining sensitivity and specificity. *Medical Decision Making, 16,* 15–23.

Somoza, E., & Mossman, D. (1990a). Introduction to neuropsychiatric decision making: Binary diagnostic tests. *Journal of Neuropsychiatry and Clinical Neurosciences, 2,* 297–300.

Somoza, E., & Mossman, D. (1990b). Optimizing REM latency as a diagnostic test for depression using ROC analysis and information theory. *Biological Psychiatry, 27,* 990–1006.

Somoza, E., & Mossman, D. (1991). Biological markers and psychiatric diagnosis: Risk-benefit analysis using ROC analysis. *Biological Psychiatry, 29,* 811–826.

Somoza, E., & Mossman, D. (1992a). Comparing and optimizing diagnostic tests: An information-theoretic approach. *Medical Decision Making, 12,* 179–188.

Somoza, E., & Mossman, D. (1992b). Comparing diagnostic tests using information theory: The INFO-ROC technique. *Journal of Neuropsychiatry and Clinical Neurosciences, 4,* 214–219.

Somoza, E., Steer, R. A., Beck, A. T., & Clark, D. A. (1994). Differentiating major depression and panic disorders by self-report and clinical rating scales: ROC analysis and information theory. *Behavioral Research and Therapy, 32,* 771–782.

Spilker, B. (1996). *Quality of life and pharmacoeconomics in clinical trials* (2nd ed.). Philadelphia: Lippincott-Raven.

Steer, R. A., & Beck, A. T. (1996). Beck Depression Inventory. In L. I. Sederer & B. Dickey (Eds.), *Outcomes assessment in clinical practice* (pp. 100–104). Baltimore, MD: Williams & Wilkins.

Steffens, D. C., Welsh, K. A., Burke, J. R., Helms, M. J., Folstein, M. F., Brandt, J., McDonald, W. M., & Breitner, J. C. (1996). Diagnosis of Alzheimer's disease in epidemiologic studies by staged review of clinical data. *Neuropsychiatry, Neuropsychology and Behavioral Neurology, 2,* 107–113.

Strain, J. J., Fulop, G., Lebovits, A., Ginsberg, B., Robinson, M., Stern, A., Charap, P., & Gany, F. (1988). Screening devices for diminished cognitive capacity. *General Hospital Psychiatry, 10,* 16–23.

Swedo, S. E., Rettew, D. C., Kuppenheimer, M., Lum, D., Dolan, S., & Goldberger, E. (1991). Can adolescent suicide attempters be distinguished from at-risk adolescents? *Pediatrics, 88,* 620–629.

Swets, J. A. (1964). *Signal detection and recognition by human observers.* New York: John Wiley & Sons.

Swets, J. A. (1979). ROC analysis applied to the evaluation of medical imaging techniques. *Investigatory Radiology, 14,* 109–121.

Teri, L., Larson, E., & Reifler, B. (1988). Behavioral disturbance in dementia of the Alzheimer type. *Journal of the American Geriatrics Society, 36,* 1–6.

Vecchio, T. J. (1966). Predictive value of a single diagnostic test in unselected populations. *New England Journal of Medicine, 274,* 1171.

Von Korff, M., Dworkin, S. F., LeResche S. K., & Kruger, A. (1988). An epidemiologic comparison of pain complaints. *Pain, 32,* 173–183.

Watson, D., Clark, L. A., & Tellegen, A. (1988). Development and validation of a brief measure of positive and negative affect: The PANAS scales. *Journal of Personality and Social Psychology, 54,* 1063–1070.

Weinstein, M. C., Fineberg, H. V., Elstein, A. S., H. S., Neuhauser, D., Neutra, R. R., & McNeil, B. J. (1980). *Clinical decision analysis.* Philadelphia: W. B. Saunders.

Weinstein, M. C., Berwick, D. M., Goldman, P. A., Murphy, J. M., & Barsky, A. J. (1989). A comparison of three psychiatric screening tests using Receiver Operating Characteristic (ROC) analysis. *Medical Care, 27,* 593–607.

Weissman, M. M., Myers, J. K., & Thompson, W. D. (1981). Depression and its treatment in a U.S. urban community. *Archives of General Psychiatry, 38,* 417–421.

Wells, C. (1979). Pseudodementia. *American Journal of Psychiatry, 136,* 895–900.

Westefeld, J. S., & Liddell, D. L. (1994). The Beck Depression Inventory and its relationship to college student suicide. *Journal of College Student Development, 35,* 145–146.

Whitaker, A., Johnson, J., Shaffer, D., Rapoport, J., Kalikow, K., Walsh, B., Davies, M., Braiman, S., & Dolinsky, A. (1990). Uncommon trouble in young people: Prevalence estimates of selected psychiatric disorders in a nonreferred adolescent population. *Archives of General Psychiatry, 47,* 487–496.

Williams, J. B. (1988). A structured interview guide for the Hamilton Depression Rating Scale. *Archives of General Psychiatry, 45,* 742–747.

Wilson, J. M., & Junger, F. (1968). *Principles and practices of screening for diseases*. Public Health Papers 34. Geneva: WHO.

Woodworth, R. S. (1918). *Personal data sheet*. Chicago: Stoelting.

Wyshak, G., & Barsky, A. (1995). Satisfaction with and effectiveness of medical care in relation to anxiety and depression: Patient and physician ratings compared. *General Hospital Psychiatry, 17*, 108–114.

Yelin, E., Mathias, S. D., Buesching, D. P., Rowland, C., Calucin, R. Q., & Fifer, S. (1996). The impact of the employment of an intervention to increase recognition of previously untreated anxiety among primary care physicians. *Social Science in Medicine, 42*, 1069–1075.

Yopenic, P. A., Clark, C. A., & Aneshensel, C. S. (1983). Depression problem recognition and professional consultation. *Journal of Nervous and Mental Disorders, 171*, 15–23.

Zabora, J. R., Blanchard, C. G., Smith, E. D., Roberts, C. S., Glajchen, M., Sharp, J. W., BrintzenhofeSzoc, K. M., Locher, J. W., Carr, E. W., Best-Castner, S., Smith, P. M., Dozier-Hall, D., Polinsky, M. L., & Hedlund, S. C. (1997). Prevalence of psychological distress among cancer patients across the disease continuum. *Journal of Psychosocial Oncology, 15*, 73–87.

Zabora, J. R., Smith-Wilson, R., Fetting, J. H., & Enterline, J. P. (1990). An efficient method for psychosocial screening of cancer patients. *Psychosomatics, 31*, 1992–1996.

Zalaquett, C. P., & Wood, R. J. (1997). *Evaluating stress: A book of resources*. Lanham, MD: Scarecrow Press.

Zung, W., Magill, M., Moore, J., & George, D. (1983). Recognition and treatment of depression in a family practice. *Journal of Clinical Psychiatry, 44*, 3–6.

Integrating Behavioral Health Assessment With Primary Care Services

Cori L. Ofstead
Diane S. Gobran
Ofstead & Associates, Inc.
St. Paul, Minnesota

Donald L. Lum
River Valley Clinic–Northfield,
Northfield, Minnesota

> The general medical sector is the only source of care for at least half of all depressed patients, but primary care clinicians do not recognize depression in about one-half of the affected patients in this sector. Even when general medical providers recognize the presence of a mental health problem, they may be hesitant to report it in the medical record out of concerns about confidentiality and stigmatization or lower reimbursement rates for care of psychiatric, compared with physical, conditions. (Wells, Sturm, Sherbourne, & Meredith, 1996, p. 24)

Wells et al. spoke to a common experience in general medical settings, and adeptly identified several of the reasons primary care providers may shy away from the behavioral health arena. Indeed, addressing depression and other mental and behavioral health conditions in a primary care setting can be very challenging.

However, there are compelling reasons to face this challenge head-on. According to Zung, Broadhead, and Roth, "Left untreated, depression can be lethal" (1993, p. 337). In fact, 15% of all patients with major depressive disorder eventually commit suicide (Zung et al., 1993). These researchers point out that depression also has economic ramifications for providers, because undiagnosed patients with depression are high utilizers of health care services, and visit outpatient facilities at three times the rate of all users. According to Zung et al., "Annual costs for major depression, including both direct costs (e.g., hospitalization, health care provider services, drugs) and indirect costs (e.g., lost productivity), are estimated to total over $16 billion" (p. 338).

This chapter addresses many of the issues that primary care providers (PCPs) face when integrating behavioral health assessment services with routine medical care. Throughout this chapter, PCP is used to refer to primary care providers, including physicians, physician assistants (PAs), nurse practitioners, and other clinicians working in a primary care setting.

IMPACT OF BEHAVIORAL HEALTH CONDITIONS

PCPs are accustomed to providing care for patients with both acute and chronic conditions. Many PCPs are aware that some patients seem anxious or depressed, or may be drinking too much alcohol. Because a patient's feelings may seem reasonable given the medical circumstances, the PCPs may disregard their intuitive understanding that the patient is suffering emotionally. However, the patient's feelings or symptoms may be just the "tip of the iceberg," and the patient may be severely affected by an underlying behavioral health condition.

For example, depression often coexists with other chronic conditions, such as diabetes and asthma. In our experience, patients with diabetes and other chronic conditions who are also suffering from untreated depression have significantly worse outcomes, especially with regard to functional status, symptoms, and the need for urgent care. In diabetics, these poor outcomes may be related to a diminished ability to follow dietary and exercise recommendations, monitor and manage their blood glucose levels, or seek lab tests and other care when needed. In severe cases, depressed patients may not be able to follow the basic self-care regimens that are essential to managing chronic physical conditions; they may not even get out of bed.

Our experience parallels the findings from two major outcomes studies that have been widely published and discussed. The Medical Outcomes Study, a pioneering effort to utilize self-administered assessment tools to evaluate functional status and quality of life, measured the health status of over 20,000 patients. This study demonstrated that major depression alone impacts patient quality of life and functional status as much as serious medical conditions, such as arthritis, heart disease, and diabetes (Stewart et al., 1989).

More recently, the Primary Care Evaluation of Mental Disorders (PRIME–MD) study utilized a derivative of the SF–36 (a general health status questionnaire) and the PRIME–MD (a behavioral health diagnostic tool) to evaluate 1,000 primary care patients (Spitzer et al., 1995). This study established that behavioral health conditions can affect patients' functional status and quality of life even more than most medical conditions.

For example, the PRIME–MD authors found significant impairment in health-related quality of life for patients with depression, anxiety, somatoform, and eating disorders (Spitzer et al., 1995). In this study, common mental disorders were associated with greater impairment (on scales measuring mental health, social functioning, general health, role function, and bodily pain) than several common medical disorders, such as cardiac disease, arthritis, hypertension, and diabetes. The only scale showing less impairment by patients with mental disorders than those with medical disorders was the physical functioning scale, which measures the patient's ability to perform a variety of physical tasks such as bathing and dressing, walking, and climbing steps (Spitzer et al., 1995).

The PRIME–MD study also revealed that there was "considerable impairment present in patients who only had subthreshold mental disorder diagnoses," which the authors said "adds to the growing body of evidence that primary care patients with subthreshold conditions also merit clinical attention" (Spitzer et al., 1995, p. 1515). The authors concluded that "mental disorders, particularly depressive disorders, accounted for considerably more of the impairment than did common medical disorders on all of the domains of HRQL [health related quality of life]" (Spitzer et al., 1995, p. 1515).

Other studies have found that over 80% of primary care patients with psychiatric disorders present with somatic complaints (Lieberman, 1997). Because of this, and the fact that more than half of the patients with psychiatric disorders receive their only care in a primary care setting (Wells et al., 1996), implementing a screening and diagnostic assessment process for behavioral health within the primary care clinic is very important.

Clearly, there is reason to be concerned about medical patients who also suffer from behavioral health conditions, and about the barriers to providing assessment, diagnostic, and treatment services for those conditions. But how prevalent are these problems in society? A number of studies have attempted to assess the prevalence of these kinds of comorbidities in general medical settings.

PREVALENCE OF BEHAVIORAL HEALTH CONDITIONS

Behavioral health conditions are very common in the general population, and are even more prevalent in persons being seen for medical conditions. Table 5.1 reports the prevalence of several common behavioral health conditions in primary care settings. The rates of expected prevalence in this table represent a range established by

TABLE 5.1
Prevalence of Behavioral Health Conditions

Condition	Rate	Source
Lifetime history of:		
Any psychiatric disorder	48%	1
Any anxiety disorder	25%	1
Generalized anxiety disorder	5–10%	2
Major depressive disorder	17%	1
Current or 1-year prevalence of:		
Any psychiatric disorder	10–39%	1, 6, 7, 9
An anxiety disorder	17–18%	1, 9
Generalized anxiety disorder	2–12%	2
Phobia	11%	4
Major depressive disorder	5–22%	1, 4, 6, 8
Alcohol use disorder	5–10%	4, 5, 9
Psychotic symptoms	4%	3
Failure to detect psych disorders in primary care	35–90%	1, 7

Note. Sources:
1 = Lieberman (1997, p. 145)
2 = Roy-Byrne & Katon (1997, p. 34–35)
3 = Olfson et al. (1996, p. 481)
4 = Wells et al. (1996, p. 30)
5 = Bien et al. (1993, p. 315)
6 = Zimmerman (1993, p. 479)
7 = Eisenberg (1992, p. 1080–1081)
8 = Olfson & Klerman (1992, p. 627)
9 = Spitzer et al. (1995, p. 1512)

taking the lowest and the highest prevalence rates documented in the referenced studies.

The Underrecognition of Behavioral Health Conditions

Lieberman (1997) cited a study by Kessler and coworkers that found that as many as 48% of primary care patients had a psychiatric disorder during their lifetime. Other studies have confirmed that up to 39% of patients seen in primary care have a psychiatric disorder (Eisenberg, 1992; Spitzer et al., 1995; Zimmerman, 1993).

Researchers have also found that psychiatric disorders remain undetected in 35% to 90% of patients who have these conditions and are treated in primary care settings (Eisenberg, 1992; Lieberman, 1997). Their work suggests that this holds true even for conditions such as depression, where the diagnostic criteria have been clearly delineated and treatment is effective for 80% of patients with the condition (Agency for Health Care Policy and Research [AHCPR], 1993). The problem of untreated mental illness was addressed in a 1997 consensus statement published by the National Depressive and Manic-Depressive Association. The statement concluded:

> There is overwhelming evidence that individuals with depression are being seriously undertreated. Safe, effective, and economical treatments are available. The cost to individuals and society of this undertreatment is substantial. Long suffering, suicide, occupational impairment, and impairment in interpersonal and family relationships exist. (Hirschfeld et al., 1997, p. 333)

The Prevalence of Depressive and Anxiety Disorders

Taken together, the preceding findings indicate that at least 20% of the patients seen in a primary care setting may be at risk for a range of depressive and/or anxiety disorders. Estimates of the percentage of primary care patients specifically having major depressive disorder vary from 5% to 9% (Wells et al., 1996) to as high as 26% (Spitzer et al., 1995), with most researchers concurring that at least 10% of primary care patients have a depressive disorder. In addition, Wells et al. found that 15% to 30% of patients presented with "clinically meaningful depressive symptoms" requiring treatment.

Along with depression, a number of other conditions are found to be highly prevalent in primary care. Wells et al. (1996), Roy-Byrne and Katon (1997), and Lieberman (1997) stated that anxiety disorders, including phobias and panic disorder, are common in the general medical population. Lieberman found that 17% of patients have a 12-month history of anxiety disorder. Wells et al. found that 11% of patients have phobias, and Roy-Byrne and Katon concluded that over 5% of patients have generalized anxiety disorder. Roy-Byrne and Katon's study showed that anxiety disorders are much more prevalent in patients with other psychiatric conditions, such as depression or dysthymia. They found that 35% to 50% of patients with major depressive disorder also have generalized anxiety disorder.

The prevalence findings just discussed were confirmed by the landmark PRIME–MD study. In 1995, Spitzer et al. reported that when 31 PCPs used the PRIME–MD instrument to evaluate 1,000 primary care patients, they found that 39% had a behavioral health disorder. Mood disorders were found in 26% of these patients, anxiety disorders were found in 18%, and somatoform disorder in 14% of the patients.

The Prevalence of Alcohol Abuse

With regard to alcohol abuse, Bien, Miller, and Tonigan (1993) and Wells et al. (1996) found that with proper evaluation, 7% to 10% of a general population would be found to have an alcohol-use disorder. Bien et al. (1993) said that "within populations seeking healthcare or other social services, the rate of alcohol problems is likely to be higher than in the general population (Royal College of Physicians, 1987), and problem drinkers more frequently seek consultation in such settings than from specialist alcohol treatment services (Institute of Medicine, 1990)" (p. 315).

The Prevalence of Psychotic Symptoms

Despite the belief that psychoses are rarely seen in primary care settings, Olfson, Weissman, Leon, Farber, and Sheehan (1996) found that almost 4% of patients being seen for medical conditions present with psychotic symptoms. Olfson et al. defined such symptoms as auditory and visual hallucinations, grossly disorganized speech, and delusions (such as thought broadcasting, a belief that others can hear the patient's thoughts). Patients reporting psychotic symptoms report more functional impairment than patients without such symptoms, and they are more likely to report that they are in fair or poor physical health. Furthermore, in the study by Olfson et al., almost 22% of the patients with psychotic symptoms reported feeling suicidal. Psychotic symptoms are much more common in patients presenting with anxiety, depression, or substance abuse than in other patients.

The Prevalence of Domestic Abuse

There is new awareness that many medical and behavioral health problems are related to violence (both domestic and street violence). Although men are frequently victims of street violence, women are the victims in the vast majority of domestic assaults. According to a researcher at Johns Hopkins University, physical abuse of women by their husbands may occur in over 10% of couples (Plichta, 1992). Another researcher asserts that between 1.8 and 4.0 million women are abused in their homes each year in the United States, and that 95% of the perpetrators are male (Attala, 1996). This abuse is associated with grave consequences for both the victim and the health system:

> Victims of abuse are much more likely than non-victims to have poor health, chronic pain problems, depression, suicide attempts, addictions, and problem pregnancies. Abused women use a disproportionate amount of health care services, including emergency room visits, primary care, and community mental health center visits. Despite its high prevalence and the disproportionate use of health care services it causes, woman abuse is rarely recognized by health care providers. (Plichta, 1992, p. 154)

Family violence often begins or worsens during pregnancy and in the postpartum period. In Amaro, Fried, Cabral, and Zuckerman's prospective study (1990) of 1,243 pregnant women in Boston, 7% of women reported physical or sexual violence during pregnancy. A recent review of the literature by Gazmararian et al. (1996) suggested that the occurrence of physical abuse during pregnancy could be as high as 20%.

Medical and Behavioral Health Comorbidity

A confounding factor in recognizing and diagnosing behavioral health conditions is the high level of both medical and mental health comorbidity. For example, patients with depression are more likely to have anxiety or alcohol disorders than are other medical patients, and their primary complaints may be fatigue or chest pain rather than bothersome mental health symptoms. Patients with depression, anxiety, or substance use disorder frequently have other behavioral health comorbidities, and are much more likely to be victims of violence or suicide (Olfson et al., 1996; Plichta, 1992; Roy-Byrne & Katon, 1997). These comorbidities may "muddy the waters," but they increase the potential gravity of any coexisting conditions and provide a compelling reason for PCPs to be alert for these conditions.

Summary

In summary, depression, anxiety, and substance abuse, as well as other behavioral health conditions, are likely to be highly prevalent in primary care, and to have untoward effects on patient outcomes. Research demonstrates that many primary care patients have behavioral health conditions, and a majority of these cases remain unrecognized and untreated. Because most patients receive their only care from a PCP, detecting behavioral health conditions in the primary care setting is absolutely critical.

BENEFITS AND COSTS

Benefits of Assessment for Patients with Behavioral Health Conditions

A major benefit associated with patient assessment is the probable recognition and treatment of patients with undiagnosed or undertreated behavioral health conditions. Determining the cause of these patients' symptoms and discomfort may provide considerable relief for the patients and their families. Appropriate treatment could also alleviate symptoms and provide significant improvement in psychosocial situations for patients and their families. In patients with serious behavioral health conditions, such treatment may prevent tragic outcomes (such as fatal accidents, suicide, homicide, domestic abuse, and death due to severe neglect).

In addition, assessment and treatment for behavioral health problems could be essential to the successful management of comorbid medical conditions. This is particularly true for patients with chronic conditions, such as diabetes and asthma, which require a great deal of self-management. For example, a severely depressed patient with diabetes may not be able to follow rigorous recommendations for self-care. Addressing any comorbid behavioral health conditions could significantly improve the patient's medical status.

Benefits of Assessment for Patients without Behavioral Health Conditions

On the other hand, behavioral health assessments may allow the PCP to rule out the existence of a behavioral health component in some patients with vague or unremitting symptoms. This process may facilitate the determination of an accurate diagnosis as well as the provision of appropriate treatment. The assessment may also ease patient concerns about their condition. For example, many patients experience symptoms of depression when having thyroid or other hormonal problems, or as a result of certain medications. Ruling out a psychological origin of these symptoms could be very helpful in the care process.

Because primary care is the first and often the only resource available to patients, behavioral health assessment in the primary care setting can improve patient outcomes and reduce the risks associated with behavioral health conditions. This assessment can work to the lasting benefit of patients and their families. The next section discusses ways that integration of these services benefits organizations and providers as well.

Benefits of Assessment for Organizations and Providers

Preparing for Managed Care, Accreditation, and Competition. In the current era of managed care and intensifying competition among provider groups, PCPs and health plans are struggling to remain financially viable, and are being held accountable for patient outcomes in new ways. The ability to compete may depend on the group's capacity to demonstrate its superior quality of care and patient outcomes.

Increasingly, patient surveys and other assessment tools are utilized to evaluate the quality of care. These tools have become more important as outside organizations are performing patient satisfaction surveys and monitoring patients' clinical and functional outcomes. Information gleaned from assessment tools is now being used by accrediting organizations, advocacy groups, and those contracting for health care services to measure the quality of care. The availability of such data exerts new pressure on providers to strive for satisfied patients and better outcomes, and to do whatever it takes to accomplish those goals.

Nationally, governmental and quasi-governmental organizations have begun to recommend or mandate the use of specific measures to assess the quality of health care. In the late 1990s, these organizations include the National Committee on Quality Assurance (NCQA), which accredits managed care organizations and publishes health care accountability standards; the Foundation for Accountability (FACCT), which develops accountability measures to guide health care decision making; the Health Care Financing Administration (HCFA), which administers the federal Medicare and Medicaid programs and oversees the provision of patient care under these programs; and the Joint Commission on Accreditation of Healthcare Organizations (JCAHO), which monitors the quality of care and provides accreditation to hospitals and long-term-care organizations. These organizations have begun to include clinical indicators, as well as patient outcomes and satisfaction surveys, in their gamut of assessment tools.

Surviving Financially. In provider groups that have accepted capitated contracts, the pressure to manage care and minimize preventable crises is felt internally, and is fiscally tangible. The compensation package for many PCPs now incorporates a structure based on the financial success of the group. This arrangement forces the PCP to accept the responsibility for patient care management, and carries some financial risk for the provider if the group is unable to manage patients within budgetary constraints. In these "managed care" environments, poor patient outcomes are very costly to the group's financial viability (frequently referred to as the "bottom line"), as well as to the PCPs' own incomes.

The financial success of a group can be compromised in small increments if PCPs prescribe unnecessary tests or treatments in an effort to diagnose and manage patients complaining of vague or unremitting symptoms. The clinic's bottom line takes a much greater hit when patients require emergency care, fail at self-management, become medical catastrophes ("train wrecks"), or are victims of accidents or violence. As noted earlier, these situations can evolve when patients who are medically ill also have behavioral health comorbidities that may exacerbate their conditions and limit their ability to care for themselves. Potential financial losses accrued by caring for such patients can be devastating to a clinic or health plan.

Reducing Liability Risks. Furthermore, in this litigious society, disregarding a patient's mental illness or substance abuse can place a PCP or clinic at risk of malpractice claims and third-party liability suits. Because the adverse effect of comorbid mental health conditions is well known, and there are screening and diagnostic tools available for use in the primary care setting, PCPs may be held accountable for *not* knowing or acting, when they should have.

Improving Job Satisfaction. Furthermore, taking care of such patients can be frustrating and demoralizing for the PCP. This may be especially true in cases where the patient is not participating in recommended self-management (commonly referred to as *noncompliance*) or is having preventable adverse clinical outcomes (e.g., those associated with diabetes, asthma, or a cardiac condition). Having behavioral health information about patients can give the PCPs new perspectives, and may allow them to address barriers to good outcomes. Such knowledge can be very empowering, and can release the PCP from sole responsibility for providing care and support to patients with comorbid behavioral health conditions (by involving other caregivers).

Alleviating Time and Resource Constraints. Most PCPs are very busy taking care of a large number of patients, often seeing more than 30 patients per day. A PCP's patient contact time can be eroded quickly when dealing repeatedly with patients whose recovery does not progress as expected or who continue to move from crisis to crisis. If a patient's central problem is actually an undiagnosed behavioral health condition, the patient is likely to continue having problems until this condition is addressed. Unnecessary clinic visits, diagnostic tests, and ineffective treatments all compromise the financial bottom line.

To the extent possible, providing assessment in the primary care setting allows the integration of medical and behavioral health services, which may result in better overall care plans and outcomes for patients. In addition, integrated services may be less costly for patients, providers, and third-party payors.

Time and resource constraints in most primary care settings preclude the performance of a comprehensive behavioral health assessment for all patients. Therefore, the primary care practice should consider the benefits and costs of patient assessment prior to determining criteria for patient selection and enrollment in the assessment process.

Costs of Patient Assessment

The costs associated with patient assessment include patient, staff, and clinician time, as well as the direct cost of questionnaires, technology, and reports. By far the most significant of these costs is the burden of additional duties on the PCPs and their staff in the clinic.

The identification of a large number of new cases could place stress on the primary care system, which may already be struggling with demands to increase "productivity" by seeing more patients per day. This increased patient volume could be difficult to manage in areas without community or specialty resources available for patient referral (where the sole responsibility for patient support and treatment may be held by PCPs and their staff). Even in areas that have behavioral health care resources, many behavioral health specialty groups are so busy that they are not able to provide immediate care for new patients. At some clinics, patients must wait for 4 to 6 weeks to get an appointment. Current systems may not easily absorb the time needed to perform diagnostic interviews and provide behavioral health counseling and other treatment to the volume of primary care patients potentially needing such services.

In addition to the time and resources used in assessing patients, there may be other costs associated with providing information and support to primary care patients. Patients found to have a current diagnosis need information about their condition. PCPs may also need to recommend appropriate resources to patients requiring support or choosing to pursue treatment. Providing information and patient education services requires the procurement of materials (such as pamphlets or videotapes) and could add a significant amount of time to the patient encounter.

Furthermore, the PCP may need to provide un-reimbursed patient care services for some patients. Therefore, the availability of primary care, community, and behavioral health specialty resources should be evaluated prior to initiating patient assessment. Then each clinic must determine how many patients can be assessed and responded to, given practical limitations in time, technology, and expertise.

DESIGNING THE INTEGRATION PROCESSES

There are four basic components involved in health assessment programs: assessment instruments (usually questionnaires); protocols for selecting patients and administering the questionnaire; a means to score and interpret the patient responses; and the application of the results to patient care. The process of integrating behavioral health assessments into primary care can be simple and inexpensive, or quite complex, depending on the goals and the methods used.

Many assessments are done by the PCPs to provide comprehensive care for patients they see in their practice. Specific goals for assessing individuals include screening symptomatic patients for the risk of behavioral health conditions; diagnosing behavioral health conditions in "at-risk" patients; and tracking patients with known behavioral health conditions to understand the impact of the condition and/or the treatment.

In some cases, assessments are done by the clinic or health plan to better understand groups of patients. One goal may be screening targeted groups of patients (e.g., high utilizers or patients with certain diagnoses, such as back pain, headaches, or diabetes) to identify "at-risk" individuals so that additional services can be offered. Another goal may be screening entire populations to evaluate the prevalence of behavioral health symptoms or conditions, so that the clinic or health plan can predict utilization and manage the financial risk associated with caring for the population. A third potential goal of many organizations is to document the prevalence and impact of behavioral health conditions and/or treatments on patient populations for accreditation, research, or marketing and contracting purposes.

Clinics have taken many different approaches to the task of integrating assessments with primary care. Programs range from very basic, qualitative assessments by the PCP, to complex screening processes utilizing advanced software and computer technology. A case study is presented later in this chapter to highlight the experiences of a PCP who pioneered the integration of patient health assessment with primary care services in his clinic.

Major Steps Toward Integration of Behavioral Health Assessment Services

No matter what approach best meets the needs of an individual clinic or PCP, five basic steps are required to design and implement a behavioral health assessment program. These steps are:

1. Design the behavioral health assessment process.
2. Delegate roles and responsibilities for PCPs, staff, and specialists.
3. Obtain information and resources from other organizations.
4. Educate staff and providers.
5. Implement, evaluate, and redesign the assessment process.

The remainder of the chapter discusses the most complex aspects of the implementation process in detail.

The Value of Patient Questionnaires

In a typical primary care environment, PCPs see patients who are generally healthy, as well as those with various physical and mental health problems. Using health assessment questionnaires can make the patient evaluation process more efficient for PCPs and staff. Such questionnaires can readily identify behavioral health components that may be contributing to a patient's overall condition.

Some of these instruments identify patients at risk of poor outcomes, as well as those with functional limitations, severe symptoms, and other health concerns. Other questionnaires provide symptom profiles or even behavioral health diagnoses. To be accepted in a clinical setting, the questionnaires should be easy for the patients, staff, and providers to use; provide good information quickly; and not add significant cost to the encounter.

Criteria for Selecting Assessment Instruments

Table 5.2 provides a list of questions to consider when evaluating behavioral health assessment questionnaires. A discussion of the major issues is given next.

How Easy Is the Instrument to Use?   Ease of use is directly related to questionnaire length. In most cases, shorter is better. Before selecting an assessment tool for behavioral health, the clinic should start by reviewing any forms already in use at the clinic. In many primary care settings, patients complete medical history forms, health risk appraisals, health status questionnaires, and administrative forms. This paperwork may already be placing a significant burden on the patient. The last thing a busy clinic needs is to reduce patient satisfaction by requiring patients to complete too many forms!

TABLE 5.2
Evaluating Behavioral Health Assessment Tools

The following questions were designed to guide the process of evaluating assessment tools:
1. The assessment tool should provide *good* information, given the PCPs' goals for the assessment program.
   a. What are the primary reasons for conducting the assessment?
   b. What is the purpose of the tool being considered?
   c. Is it appropriate for a primary care setting?
   d. Does it cover the *range* of behavioral health conditions commonly seen in the clinic, or does it have a more narrow target?
   e. Is it a *screener* or a *diagnostic* tool?
   f. Which specific conditions can it diagnose?
   g. Are other instruments or interviews needed to make a diagnosis?
   h. Does the instrument reflect the diagnostic criteria in the *Diagnostic and Statistical Manual of Mental Disorders–Fourth Edition (DSM–IV)*?
   i. Is it sensitive to changes in patient status over time (e.g., are the questions worded to distinguish "recovering" from "using" alcoholics)?
   j. What are the statistical merits (validity, reliability, specificity) of the tool?
   k. Is comparative data available?
2. The questionnaire should be easy for the provider and clinic staff to use.
   a. How long is the questionnaire?
   b. Is a special paper form or computer interface required for administration?
   c. Is the clinician required to provide input?
   d. What training is suggested to use the instruments and interpret the data?
   e. Is the scoring process easy and efficient?
   f. How frequently do errors occur in form completion, data entry, or scoring?
   g. Do such mistakes lead to serious consequences?
3. The questionnaire should be acceptable to most patients.
   a. How much time will it take the patient to complete the forms?
   b. Are the questions easy to understand?
   c. Is the form easy to complete? (Is the type font big enough for patients with vision problems? Are the check boxes or bubbles easy to fill in?)
   d. Are there too many questions about certain topics?
   e. Will the questions make the patient angry or defensive?
   f. Is the questionnaire available in other languages?
4. The assessment should not add significant cost to the patient encounter.
   a. Are there any copyright issues regarding the use of the instrument itself?
   b. What is the per unit cost for paper copies of questionnaires and reports?
   c. What is the availability and cost for software and hardware?
   d. Is there a per patient usage fee for the assessment tool?
   e. What are the charges for individual patient reports or aggregate analyses?
   f. How much staff and clinician time is required to administer and interpret the form?

Determining the number of items on a questionnaire may seem like an elementary process, but it can be difficult to ascertain. This is particularly true with automated assessment tools administered via direct patient input. Some of these tools utilize automated skips in response to patient input. For example, if a patient replies that she does not drink any alcohol, the system would automatically skip all of the alcohol abuse items. In these types of systems, some patients may be prompted to answer only a few questions. Other patients, particularly those indicating that they have multiple symptoms or behavioral health problems, may be prompted to answer many more questions. Therefore, we recommend that the range of potential items be carefully examined as part of the instrument evaluation process. Table 5.3 provides information about selected features for a sample of assessment instruments (to illustrate potential comparisons).

In addition to being brief, the questionnaires must be easy to read. Readability depends on the grade level of the vocabulary used, as well as the test's structure and visual layout. For example, small fonts are much more difficult to read, and the questions and response options on scannable bubble forms may be difficult to follow.

Finally, ease of use depends on the process required to score the questionnaire and summarize the responses. Preferably, the assessment will not add more than a few minutes to a patient visit, and should provide results for immediate use. Some questionnaires and data input devices do not allow the calculation of a score if there are any errors or missing items. Other tools allow score calculation, with an indication of the errors or missing items. Understanding this feature is important because some patients inadvertently make errors, whereas others purposefully skip items they prefer not to answer.

If the assessment tool relies on staff to score the items or perform manual data entry, then the scoring process depends on the skills and availability of staff. The data entry process may be simplified when scannable or faxable forms are used. However, these technologies generally do not work when the form is completed improperly (a common occurrence). If the patient is required to interact directly with data input technology (by using a touch screen, a keypad entry device, or even by completing scannable forms), the scores will depend entirely on the quality of patient responses.

How Useful Is the Information Provided?   Assessment tools are very attractive if they help PCPs establish what is wrong with a patient more efficiently. The value of information derived from an instrument depends on its ability to help PCPs diagnose and manage patients with conditions commonly seen in the primary care setting. Some instruments are intended to be used as screening tools that simply call attention to at-risk patients. Screening tools are usually very brief questionnaires administered to most or all patients, regardless of the reason for the appointment or primary complaint. The PCPs receive reports that "flag" any patient found to be at risk, alerting them of the need for further evaluation.

Other instruments are capable of providing condition-specific symptom profiles, or even diagnoses. These screening or diagnostic tools are given to only those patients the PCP believes are at risk for the targeted conditions. For example, a patient complaining of general fatigue, malaise, or loss of appetite could be asked to complete a depression screener; a patient with heart palpitations, headaches, or jaw pain could be asked to complete an anxiety screener. Patients presenting with several vague complaints or mysterious symptoms may require assessment using a more

TABLE 5.3

Features of Selected Assessment Instruments

| Instrument Name | Patient Component | | Clinician Component | Covers[a] | Use[b] | Ownership |
	Number of Items	Time (min)				
PRIME-MD	26		Y	D, A, Alc, +	B	Pfizer
COMPASS-PC	87	15	Y	D, A, Alc, +	S	Bristol Myers Squibb
Quick PsychoDiagnostic Panel	59–125	6–10	N	D, A, Alc, +	S	Shedler
Symptom Checklist-90–Revised	90	15–20	N	D, A, P, +		NCS
Brief Symptom Inventory (BSI)	53			D, +	S	NCS
Primary Care Assessment Survey	51	7	N	Other		Health Institute
Symptom Assessment-45 Questionnaire	45		N	D, A, P, +	S	Strategic Advantage
CAGE (Alcohol Assessment)	4	2	Y	Alc	S	Public Domain
BDI (Beck Depression Inventory)	21	<10	N	D	S	The Psychological Corp.
BDI-PC (Beck)	7	<5	N	D	S	The Psychological Corp.
HDI (Hamilton Depression Inventory)	17–21		N	D, +		
UAMS–D-Ark	11		N	D	D	CORE/UAMS
UAMS Depression Module	115+	25	Y	D, Alc	B	CORE/UAMS
GDS (Geriatric Depression Scale)	30		N	D	S	
GDS-Short	15, 10, 4		N	D	S	
CS-GDS	0		Y	D	S	
BAI (Beck Anxiety Inventory)	21	5–10	N	D, A	S	
SAAST (Self Admin. Alcohol Screening Test)	37	5–10	N	Alc	S	Public Domain
SF-36	39	5–8	N	D, A, +	S	Public Domain
MH-5	5	2	N	D, A, +	S	Public Domain
Basis-32	32		N	D, A, P, +		McLean Hospital
SCREENER	44 or 96	10	N	D, A, Alc, +	S	Compas
SIS–Q (Suicidal Ideation)	0		Y	D, +	S	UpJohn
SDDS-PC	16	5	Y	D, A, Alc	B	UpJohn
CES-D	20		Y	D	S	NIH

Note. The sources for this table are detailed in Appendix A by instrument.

[a]D, depression; A, anxiety; Alc, alcohol; P, Psychosis; +, additional conditions.

[b]S, screener; D, diagnostic; B, both.

broadly focused, multidimensional tool capable of identifying several behavioral health conditions.

A third strategy involves using a general health status measurement tool to assess the whole patient, because both physical and mental health play a role in symptoms and patient functioning. Such instruments shed light on many aspects of patient wellness. Patients found to be functioning poorly, highly symptomatic, or having mental health problems are asked to complete a more targeted assessment tool, as indicated by the situation.

How Valid and Reliable Are the Instruments?   When evaluating a questionnaire, PCPs should review any available evidence regarding the tool's validity and reliability. In many cases, this determination may be difficult because there is little published information about the questionnaire, or the only available information has been published by the instrument's author. In any case, when the distributor of an instrument claims that it is valid and reliable, PCPs should inquire about the numbers and types of patients used to test the instrument. Some instruments may provide value even in the absence of validity data; however, PCPs should be aware of the validation status prior to using them.

Is Data Management Technology Available?   Vendors have begun to design automated data management and reporting systems to support behavioral health assessment, making questionnaires more practical to use. The new technologies allow data from patient questionnaires to be entered and processed very efficiently, so that the clinician can review the results and take action during the patient visit.

Many clinicians want to purchase "off-the-shelf" products to support the management of health assessment data. Unfortunately, automated solutions may not always be viable. Some existing instruments have not yet been selected by vendors for product development, so there may not be any data management products to buy. In other cases, a preferred instrument may be copyrighted or supported by a single vendor, which limits flexibility regarding product features and cost. Much of the technology currently available for clinical use is in the early stages of development compared to other applications, such as word processors, and may require significant enhancement to function in the desired manner. Clinics need to consider these issues when selecting questionnaires if they hope to automate data management and reporting.

How Expensive Is the Assessment?   Finally, PCPs should carefully evaluate the costs associated with each assessment tool. Total cost includes the price of forms and technology, as well as the staff and clinician time involved. During the instrument selection process, PCPs and staff should experiment with competing assessment tools by completing and scoring them, and weighing the time and effort involved against the value derived from the scores or reports.

Defining the Assessment Process

Simple Assessments Performed by the PCP.   Many PCPs prefer to utilize behavioral health assessments the same way they use medical lab tests. They perform an assessment after taking a medical history and doing a physical exam when they have found signs or symptoms indicative of a potential behavioral health problem. Their main goal is to identify or rule out a behavioral health component in individual patients they believe are "at risk."

In the least complicated scenario, interested PCPs can simply start using behavioral health assessment tools in their own practice. This could be very inexpensive and straightforward, especially if the PCP does not require significant resources or the involvement of any staff. Many PCPs already incorporate some assessments, such as the four-item alcohol abuse screener known as "CAGE." This assessment tool is named for the first letter of four key words in questions often administered through a brief interview (Have you ever: needed to Cut down; felt Annoyed by criticism of your drinking; felt Guilty about drinking; needed an "Eye-opener"?). Others have memorized the diagnostic criteria for common conditions, such as depression or panic disorders, so that they can perform rudimentary assessments during routine office visits. These types of assessments are based on clinician interviews, and depend on the PCP's memory and intuition to obtain a diagnosis. Because of their brevity and simplicity, they are effective in a primary care setting, and they can work well for a motivated PCP who has the time to interview selected patients.

Processes That Involve Questionnaires and Staff Time. On the other hand, some PCPs prefer not to interview patients about behavioral health issues, and seek different approaches. One option is to have other staff, such as nurses, interview selected patients. Another option is to utilize questionnaires that are completed by individuals selected by the PCP or nurse, based on clinical criteria or the intuition that the patient's condition may have a behavioral health component. Standard questionnaires may allow the collection of more detailed information from patients, which could assist the PCP in making a diagnosis. Some questionnaires are easy to use and score, and require little or no training or technical support.

Processes Requiring Technology. Many clinics and PCPs prefer automated processes for collecting and managing assessment data. Most automated systems are capable of generating individual patient reports, as well as aggregate summaries for various groups of patients. These systems facilitate the use of long and more complicated assessment tools that may provide valuable information to the clinician during a patient visit. PCPs contemplating the installation of an automated system should carefully evaluate the cost and effectiveness of the technology, and arrange for training.

Population Screening Performed by the Health Care Organization. Some health care organizations are interested in assessing the prevalence of behavioral health conditions in the populations under their care. These assessments may be required by accrediting organizations. They also facilitate the calculation of financial risk and enhance the ability to manage utilization (by identifying individuals or groups needing further assessment). Aggregate information is also useful in determining the efficacy of various treatments or the effectiveness of various providers in managing patient care.

Most population assessments are coordinated by staff other than PCPs. Performing behavioral health assessments on populations can be very time-intensive, unless patient-completed questionnaires are used. Data aggregation is most efficient when technology is used to support data entry (e.g., forms that can be scanned into the database, or direct data input devices that are easy for patients to operate).

Criteria for Patient Selection

There are several methods of selecting patients for behavioral health assessment. Each primary care organization serves a unique population and responds to its own set of external and internal pressures. Therefore, before determining the scope of the assessment program, each organization should assess its financial and quality management pressures, define immediate and long-term goals, identify the populations of interest, and take stock of available resources. This preparatory work will facilitate the resolution of difficult issues involved in developing a patient eligibility and enrollment plan for behavioral health assessment.

Assessing Every Patient. Because the prevalence of behavioral health conditions in primary care patients is high, one model of patient assessment could involve screening every primary care patient. This model would provide a comprehensive evaluation of the population of patients seeking treatment at the clinic, and would undoubtedly reveal that many patients have previously unrecognized mental health conditions.

If a clinic is considering this model (assessing every primary care patient), comparing current claims data and scheduling records with expected prevalence statistics would aid in predicting the number of new cases. For example, if the clinic sees 1,000 patients and only 30 patients (three percent) are currently being treated for depression, then it is likely that an additional 70 to 170 patients (10%–20% of the population) would need diagnostic assessment and treatment. Understanding the potential for new cases is essential in allocating appropriate resources for the program.

A potential drawback to this model would be the assessment of many medical patients who are not at risk for current behavioral health diagnoses, while neglecting to assess persons who do not come to the clinic for medical care (who may be at risk for behavioral health problems). These persons may be at risk for both medical and mental health conditions that may benefit from early recognition and treatment, but they would not be afforded assessment unless they sought treatment.

Of course, this quandary could be addressed by assessing all health plan members or entire communities, rather than focusing on "patients" who come to the clinic for care. However, this strategy would consume considerable time and resources without a guarantee that it would provide benefit.

Assessing Selected Populations. Another model, based on clinical or administrative priorities, could involve the assessment of patients with specific diagnoses, complaints, or other characteristics that place them at higher risk for behavioral health problems. For example, assessment could be targeted to individual patients meeting clinical or administrative criteria, such as those outlined in Table 5.4. The early recognition of behavioral health conditions in these patients would be beneficial to both patient outcomes and the clinic's bottom line.

The best approach may be to have an automatic assessment process for defined populations, such as patients undergoing annual or preoperative physicals, plus an ad hoc assessment process for the PCP to use with any patient felt to be "at risk" due to one or more of the reasons detailed in Table 5.4. We recognize that some practice environments may not directly reimburse the PCP for behavioral health services. However, the provider may choose to assess and treat an "at-risk" patient anyway, because mental health comorbidities result in poor medical outcomes and make the

TABLE 5.4
Examples of Potential Criteria for Patient Selection

1. Patients with a history of one or more mental health conditions.
2. Patients who are "high utilizers" with certain characteristics or diagnoses (e.g., patients who visit the emergency room more than once a year with injuries, asthma attacks, diabetic crises, or heart palpitations; or patients who have extended or repeated hospitalizations for medical conditions).
3. Patients complaining of vague symptoms with no clear medical cause, such as fatigue, insomnia, change in appetite, or pain.
4. Patients with complex or frustrating conditions that are difficult to diagnose or are not responding to treatments that are usually effective.
5. Patients with severe functional limitations (e.g., who are not working, are sleeping all day, or are not able to perform their usual daily activities).
6. All patients with specific chronic conditions, such as those with diabetes, asthma, low back pain, or coronary artery disease. These conditions require patient self-management and can be quite costly to manage, especially if the patient has poor outcomes. A behavioral health problem can greatly hinder the patient's ability to adhere to recommended treatments.
7. All patients being seen for annual physicals. Generally, these patients would undergo a fairly comprehensive history and physical exam at this time. Providing behavioral health assessments during the visit would allow the PCP to integrate care for these patients, and may identify behavioral health problems that could exacerbate other medical conditions.

clinician's job very difficult, especially if multiple attempts to assist the patient are not resulting in the expected improvement.

Exclusion Criteria. When defining patient selection criteria, many clinics choose to exclude specific groups of patients from the assessment process. The exclusions are generally based on the patient's inability to complete self-administered questionnaires without assistance. For example, some clinics exclude patients who are blind, acutely ill, cognitively impaired, initially resistant to completing questionnaires, illiterate, or do not speak English.

Repeat Assessments. If PCPs expect to demonstrate the outcomes of care (such as the change in behavioral health status following treatment), they must develop a mechanism for reassessing patients at various times. These protocols should clearly define which patients are eligible for only an initial evaluation, and which patients will be assessed repeatedly. The time frames for patient follow-up should be designated based on the clinical condition and the average time required for the patient to experience some improvement (with proper care). In any case, the elapsed time between assessments should be short enough that the clinician can utilize the information to manage patient care.

RESOURCES REQUIRED

PCPs and clinics that implement models based on patient or clinician questionnaires need to allocate appropriate resources to the program. Table 5.5 summarizes specific resources we recommend for the successful integration of these assessments in medical settings, and a detailed discussion follows.

In most environments, there will be some initial startup costs, as well as ongoing overhead expenses associated with a program. The initial costs for purchasing prod-

TABLE 5.5
Overview of Required Resources

Tangible resources:
   1. Assessment tools (questionnaires).
   2. Technology for managing data and generating reports.
   3. Interpretation guides for reports.
   4. Trained personnel and tracking mechanisms for patient follow-up.
   5. Space for program activities and materials.
   6. Office supplies for mailing surveys or reminders.
Resources for dealing with "at-risk" patients:
   1. Brief guidelines or action protocols.
   2. Behavioral health specialists and community resources.
   3. Educational materials for patients.
Support and information from administration:
   1. Educational seminars and coaching for providers and staff.
   2. Coding and reimbursement information.
   3. Legal opinion and utilization review recommendations.

---

ucts and startup services can be estimated and managed as a one-time, fixed cash output. Each clinic should estimate expenses and budget for the initial startup and long-term implementation.

Ongoing costs relate directly to the number of providers and patients anticipated to be involved in the assessment process. Although assessment services may be charged to some patients to offset their cost, some providers choose not to charge directly for this service. In addition, in most practices, there will be some patients who need assessment services but cannot pay for them (via cash or insurance coverage). Finally, several resources usually must be purchased or arranged for to allow successful service integration.

Assessment Tools

Many assessment programs rely on patient questionnaires for initial screening and diagnostic evaluation. Other approaches are clinician based or include a clinician-derived component. The assessment tools may be paper questionnaires or the automated equivalent. Many automated product vendors charge a per-administration fee for the use of the instruments and/or for reports.

Regardless of the format (i.e., paper or automated data collection), the practice should estimate the volume of patients to be assessed and should estimate the cost for the first year of initial patient evaluation, follow-up assessment, and reporting. The need for separate follow-up questionnaires should also be determined, because some approaches utilize a slightly different format for patient follow-up. If the PCPs intend to utilize paper forms, they should inquire about discounts for high-volume purchases. We recommend that organizations pilot test questionnaires and associated data management systems before making any major purchases.

Technology for Managing Data

Although some paper questionnaires can be scored visually, automated scoring systems are often more efficient. They can reduce the staff time required to score the questionnaires manually, and they assure accuracy in calculating scores. In addition, many automated report generators can quickly provide an easy-to-interpret graphical representation of the assessment results for the clinician to use during the patient encounter. Automation also allows the aggregation of data for further analysis and the generation of summary reports.

Automated systems require equipment for data entry, data analysis, report generation, and data aggregation. Data entry can be accomplished through a variety of means, most of which involve computers connected to data input devices such as keyboards, scanners, touchscreen monitors, pen-based entry devices, voice recognition modules, or even fax machines. Data analysis and report generation are typically achieved through a computerized scoring algorithm, which can quickly process patient responses. A printer is also needed to generate written reports. Data aggregation can be done using an on-site database, or by submitting completed forms or data to a central repository for aggregate reports and comparisons with other organizations and providers. Most data repositories charge a fee for data analysis and report generation.

Selecting Hardware and Software.   Most behavioral health assessment tools are long or complex, and require a scoring algorithm to convert patient responses into useful information. Therefore, clinicians often need efficient and economical methods for scoring instruments.

There are many data management vendors selling products that support these instruments. The vendors have varying levels of practical experience in behavioral health assessment, but not all have had direct experience integrating these assessments into primary care. Thus, some features of their products may be particularly appealing to PCPs, whereas other features may be less useful, or even counterproductive in some settings. Finally, every software product has room for improvement.

Defining Data Management Goals.   A written list of assessment goals can serve as an informal "Request for Proposal" (RFP) by which available data management products can be compared. The discussion of goals should cover the purpose of the assessment program, instruments to be used, preferences for data entry, desired timing for report generation, the need for an aggregate database and statistical analyses, and the availability of skilled staff to support the technology. In addition, the availability of the hardware needed to run specific programs must be addressed, because many vendors assume that customers have in place computer systems that meet their software requirements, or that the customer will purchase whatever hardware is needed.

Evaluating Data Input Technology.   In the past, mainly due to technology limitations, patient-completed questionnaires required manual data entry. This process was time-consuming and cumbersome, and often precluded the generation of reports for clinician use *during* a visit. Data entry has evolved dramatically since the late 1980s. Although the technology is likely to continue changing and improving, there are currently a variety of options for automated entry. These options are listed in Table 5.6.

Evaluating Data Analysis and Reporting Technology.   Before selecting an instrument or data management product, PCPs should consider whether they desire reports on each individual patient or at the aggregate level, or both. They should also decide whether comparative norms or benchmarks are needed. Next, providers should determine the content they hope will be included in the standard report pack-

TABLE 5.6
Data Entry Options

---

1. Optical *mark* recognition scanners capable of reading written *marks* in the designated "bubble" areas on special forms.
2. Optical *character* recognition scanners capable of reading written *text* in designated areas on special forms.
3. Touchscreen monitors.
4. Standard keyboards.
5. Keyboards with only limited keys.
6. Push button data entry boxes.
7. Pen-based systems which allow direct input of written marks or text.
8. Automated telephone surveys.

---

age, and consider the preferred layout or design (e.g., tabular vs. graphical, black and white vs. colored). In addition, the PCPs should contemplate the potential need for customized analyses or reports, and inquire about the capabilities of the system to analyze data and generate reports. Lastly, clinic staff should participate in assessing the processes involved in data management and report generation to accurately estimate the time and effort needed to perform the behavioral health assessment. Table 5.7 lists broad issues that should be considered by various stakeholders when selecting a data management vendor.

TABLE 5.7
Questions to Consider When Selecting a Data Management Product

---

Issues important to clinicians:
1. Does the system support the instruments you want to use?
2. Can your existing staff handle the data management and report generation tasks without much hassle?
3. Does the system provide meaningful output (reports) in a timely fashion?
4. Does the system allow the addition of questions or other customization?
5. Can the system support longitudinal patient records, so that the clinician can assess change over time?
6. Will patients find the assessment tools and processes "user-friendly"?

Issues important to staff:
1. Is the technology simple and reliable to use?
2. Are manuals and adequate technical support readily available?
3. Is there a training program, or are people expected to learn the system on their own?
4. How much time does it take to enter data for each patient?
5. How are errors corrected?
6. How are reports generated?
7. What type of assistance will most patients require?
8. How flexible is the data collection for patients with special needs (e.g., those with vision problems, motor control problems, computer phobia, language/literacy issues, etc.)?

Additional issues important to administration:
1. Does the vendor have a good track record *in this line of business*?
2. Does the system require the user to perform extensive setup or design?
3. What are the hardware and space requirements needed to run the system?
4. Will the system be integrated with other programs or used on a network?
5. Do staff need special training?
6. Is continuing oversight by an MIS professional required?
7. Who has control of and ownership of the data?
8. How much does it *really* cost to make it work in your practice for the volume of patients needing assessment (including software, hardware, forms, per-patient charges, telephone/fax fees, technical support, training, data analysis, and customization)?

Interpretation Guides for Data and Reports.   Many PCPs are unfamiliar with behavioral health assessments and associated reports. Therefore, they may need an interpretation guide or access to comparative data in order to make sense of the patient assessment reports. When selecting instruments and vendors, the PCPs should also inquire about the availability and usability of such guides. In addition, the PCPs may arrange for someone knowledgeable about the assessments to coach them on the interpretation of patient reports and comparative data before incorporating such assessments into their practice.

Tracking Mechanisms for Patient Follow-Up.   Once patients have undergone behavioral health assessments, it is appropriate for the PCP to track their status over time. The best tracking mechanisms incorporate information about the dates of initial and subsequent assessments, as well as the findings or diagnoses. The information about diagnoses is important, because the desirable time frames for follow-up may be different depending on the patient's condition.

For example, patients found to be free of behavioral health conditions may be flagged so that they are not frequently required to undergo similar assessments. On the other hand, patients found to have subthreshold, acute, or chronic conditions may be good candidates for periodic reassessment so that the effects of treatment can be monitored and any exacerbation of the condition can be identified and rectified as soon as possible.

There are various manual and automated methods for tracking patients over time. For example, a simple manual tracking system could be designed using a card file organized by month so that patients are contacted according to a preestablished schedule. Dentists perfected this type of system long ago and are quite adept at contacting patients every 6 months to remind them to come in for a checkup!

Automated tracking systems can be as simple as computerizing the basic card-file system, or they can be rather sophisticated. The more sophisticated systems are tied to the patient assessment data system so that they recognize the dates of previous patient assessments and diagnoses, and automatically enroll the patient in an appropriate follow-up protocol (generally established or customized for the client). Such systems can be prompted to periodically generate lists of patients needing follow-up. They can also generate reminder letters, mailing labels, and reports on the current status of data collection.

Pilot Testing the System.   Before deciding to purchase anything, the clinic should pilot test the complete system thoroughly. Most providers are surprised by the features and functionality of software packages when they perform the initial pilot. Often, the pilot experience with a specific product allows the staff to discover several unexpected aspects of the data collection, data entry, and reporting processes that will have to be addressed before full implementation.

Any forms and devices should be tested for usability with the clinic's patient population prior to purchase. This is especially important if the technology relies heavily on patients to complete scannable forms or enter data directly. For example, older or less educated patients may have difficulty using *any* computer technology, and patients with visual or motor problems have difficulty seeing and/or responding to questionnaires administered using small-print scannable forms, touchscreens, or pen-based systems.

During the pilot testing, the staff should closely monitor and document patient and staff experience with the technology. This evaluation should address the training required to begin using the product; its overall ease of use; the amount of time it takes a patient to complete the assessment form; the frequency of patients requesting assistance from staff; the reasons for patient refusal to participate; the frequency of errors in form completion and/or data entry; and any technology failures or breakdowns. The pilot findings will be critically important in determining which package best meets the clinic's needs and in finalizing negotiations with the vendor.

Appropriate Space

The clinic should anticipate the potential need for additional space within participating departments or care areas. To begin with, patients will need a place to sit while completing forms. Sometimes the patient can be handed a form on a clipboard and can comfortably complete the assessment in the waiting room. In cases where the assessments will be performed at a computer workstation, additional space will be required for this equipment. If feasible, the place for completing forms should be quiet, offer few distractions, and feel fairly private to the patient. Because many forms take 15 to 20 minutes to complete, patients undergoing assessment may spend more time in the waiting room than usual, which could affect patient flow through the clinic.

There should also be a place where PCPs or staff can discuss sensitive behavioral health issues with patients without compromising confidentiality, privacy, or patient safety. Clinics may also need space for new equipment (such as a computer, scanner, fax machine, and/or printer), and storage for forms and other materials.

ROLES AND RESPONSIBILITIES FOR PROVIDERS AND STAFF

In environments where the PCPs plan to integrate behavioral health assessment on a limited scale, the participating providers may be able to perform all of the steps involved in patient assessment. Organizations planning a more comprehensive program should consider building an integration team charged with program design and oversight. The participation of this team in designing and implementing the assessment processes will be essential to the program's success. Support by the clinic's leadership is also critical for success.

The Integration Team

The integration team should include at least one representative from each staff area expected to play a role in patient assessment, triage, treatment, or referral. In many care settings, the members of the team include a receptionist, a nurse or medical assistant, a PCP, a behavioral health care provider, a pharmacist, an information systems specialist, and a patient advocate or community services liaison. Ideally, these team members will represent the opinions and concerns of their colleagues, and act as liaisons with other staff and clinicians in their areas. They will also share responsibility for educating and supporting their colleagues as the program is designed and implemented.

The involvement of PCPs and clinic staff in the planning process is essential for a successful program, and greatly improves the commitment of team members to integrating assessment into care. The team should meet regularly to design the integration strategy and develop processes for implementing it at the clinic. Processes may need to be customized for each participating clinical area. During pilot testing, a member of the integration team should be present to observe the actual processes, so that any barriers or challenges can be addressed. After the processes have been developed and tested, teams benefit from continued meetings to discuss any issues or concerns that arise.

Suggested Roles and Responsibilities for PCPs and Staff

Key activities involved in behavioral health assessment are outlined in Table 5.8. Specific plans for delegating these activities vary depending on the organization's size, available staff, other resources, and clinical priorities. This section outlines one model for a division of labor among clinicians and staff involved in an assessment program.

Primary Care Providers. PCPs identify patients for screening; review findings from patient screeners; prescribe additional assessments, if necessary; discuss assessment findings with patients; develop a treatment plan; provide treatment or refer the patient; obtain quick consultations with specialists, as needed; monitor patients; and provide follow-up care for patients undergoing treatment in the primary care setting. If a comprehensive program is being designed to integrate assessment services, PCPs play an essential role in program development.

Nursing Staff. The nursing staff members follow protocols to identify patients for assessment; review the results of patient screening; administer additional questionnaires, as indicated; provide information to patients; monitor patients being treated in primary care; triage and handle patients in crisis; and keep clinical records. In larger organizations, or those with comprehensive assessment programs, nursing staff members also participate in the program design.

Support Staff. The support staff members (such as receptionists and medical assistants) administer the screening questionnaires; perform or oversee data entry (when patients are inputting data); generate reports; update and monitor patient

TABLE 5.8
Key Activities Required for Behavioral Health Assessment

1. Identifying patients for assessment.
2. Administering and scoring the initial assessment tools (screeners).
3. Reviewing the results of screeners.
4. Administering additional *diagnostic* questionnaires or interviews for patients identified as "at risk" by the screeners.
5. Utilizing the results in the care process for any presenting *medical* condition.
6. Consulting with a behavioral health specialist or pharmacist, as indicated (for patient assessment and/or treatment).
7. Providing appropriate treatment for the *behavioral health* problem (or referring the patient, if appropriate or desired).
8. Monitoring the patient over time through additional assessments.
9. Adjusting the care plan, if necessary.

tracking logs; handle telephone calls from patients in crisis or experiencing medication side effects; provide information to patients; and make appointments with specialists, as directed by the PCPs.

Consulting Pharmacists.   These medication specialists provide clinicians and patients with information about psychotropic medications (e.g., basic features, potential contraindications, drug interactions, and side effects); recommend pharmaceuticals for medically ill patients, as requested by PCPs; monitor patient adherence to prescribed medications; educate patients about their medications; and discuss side effects with both patients and PCPs. They may also play a critical role in program design.

Information Systems Staff.   In most organizations, computer system professionals are involved if software and hardware will be used to manage data or score instruments. They may be responsible for setting up and maintaining software and hardware; providing basic training to staff; arranging for the routine backup of critical data; performing initial troubleshooting when problems occur; and arranging for technical support from the vendor, when necessary.

Patient Advocate.   Depending on the size of the organization, this role could be filled by a social worker, clergy person, nurse, or paraprofessional. Advocates refer patients to community resources; direct patients who do not have financial resources for behavioral health care to appropriate services; and provide support for patients in crisis. The person in this role may also offer unique perspectives during the program design phase.

Support From the Leadership

Upper management can provide financial support, human resources, assistance negotiating with outside organizations, and conceptual guidance to support the success of the integration process. For example, management may purchase equipment, materials, and training, or may arrange for outside support of the program (such as grant funding or the donation of educational materials). The clinic's leadership may also negotiate with payors for appropriate reimbursement, and develop referral arrangements with specialty providers and community service organizations.

In larger organizations, management often charters a clinical advisory board to develop a comprehensive program integrating behavioral health assessment with primary care services. Their role is to act as a liaison to the organization's leadership. They provide guidance; arrange for educational seminars; build enthusiasm and buy-in among staff and providers; and promote accountability for integrating the assessments. Ideally, participants on this board include the medical director, a behavioral health care specialist, a PCP, a nurse or medical assistant, an administrator, and a pharmacist. Unlike the integration team, this board is generally not responsible for the daily implementation of the program, but has a continuing advisory role.

Coding and Reimbursement Policies.   The PCPs and nursing staff will need information from administration about appropriate ways to code services for reimbursement. In addition, administration should articulate policies for handling the care of patients without behavioral health coverage.

Legal Opinion.   Administration should procure opinions from the utilization review staff and legal counsel regarding the risks associated with behavioral health assessment and treatment. This opinion should also cover the risks associated with *not* assessing certain patients or groups of patients.

ADDITIONAL BEHAVIORAL HEALTH RESOURCES

Given the current workload of many PCPs, it may be difficult for them to embrace any new program that requires the devotion of significant additional time. The development of clear and simple processes for responding to the results of behavioral health assessment may facilitate its integration (because PCPs will not have to "reinvent the wheel" with each patient, and can delegate specific responsibilities to nursing staff or other professionals). Access to behavioral health specialists, community resources, and educational materials will provide the PCPs with additional support.

Behavioral Health Referral Resources

In most cases, PCPs will need access to qualified behavioral health specialists who are committed to responding to referrals in a timely fashion. PCPs may also need access to these specialists or knowledgeable pharmacists for quick consultations, particularly in complicated cases or for patients needing medication immediately.

Selecting Specialists and Building Relationships.   Referral relationships and expectations for service should be clarified prior to the initiation of patient assessment. The clinic should identify providers with the desired skills and credentials, including various types of providers, such as psychiatrists (who can prescribe medications), psychologists, and social workers or family therapists. The PCPs should then meet with several potential referral sources to discuss the processes being developed to integrate behavioral health assessment into the primary care setting. They should inquire about the behavioral health specialists' philosophy of patient care, treatment options, and availability to support the PCPs in caring for patients. Both groups should agree on the model of integration (consultative, collaborative, or truly integrated) for providing behavioral health care services. In addition, the PCPs should review the methods the specialists utilize to manage patient satisfaction and outcomes. PCPs should clarify their expectations for the provision of services to referred patients (in regard to the timeliness of visits and communication with the referring PCP). Payment options for referred patients should also be reviewed, and a copy of the rate structure and list of accepted insurance carriers should be procured. In addition, the PCPs should discuss the arrangement for reimbursement when they need a quick consultation (e.g., by telephone).

After discussing these issues, the PCP should select behavioral health specialists for inclusion on a referral list and obtain a supply of business cards or brochures to give to referred patients. They can then collaborate on the management of several patients, and work together to evaluate and improve the processes and outcomes of care. The PCP should have a backup plan for situations where the referral resource is not immediately available, especially in areas where there are long waiting times for initial appointments.

Guidelines and Pathways

If patients are assessed for behavioral health problems, some of the patients will be found to need further assessment, diagnosis, and treatment. The frequency of such findings should not be underestimated. As noted earlier, previous studies of primary care patients indicate that PCPs should expect that 20% of their patients have a current behavioral health condition requiring further assessment and treatment.

The planning process should include the development of guidelines for further assessment, diagnosis, and treatment or referral. Comprehensive guidelines are available through a variety of specialty associations, governmental agencies, and academic institutes. A partial list of resources for behavioral health guidelines is included in Appendix B. However, the available guidelines tend to be quite lengthy and academic and may not be suitable for implementation in primary care settings.

Therefore, we suggest that PCPs review available guidelines and distill out the essential ingredients for inclusion in a set of customized guidelines appropriate for their setting. To facilitate acceptance and use, these guidelines should be short (i.e., one or two pages) and simple to follow. They should outline the process for diagnosis and treatment (including recommended medications and psychological or behavioral support), and define situations requiring specialty referral. In addition, the guidelines should clearly delineate the responsibilities of both clinicians and staff. Customized guidelines are attractive because they are very clear about the processes to be followed. Comprehensive guidelines may permit ancillary personnel, such as nurses or social workers, to perform essential tasks. These health care professionals could administer diagnostic assessments for patients found to be "at risk," educate patients about their condition, and monitor patients' status after the PCP makes the initial diagnosis and recommendations for treatment. Shifting some responsibilities to staff can reduce the time that PCPs must dedicate to the program.

Developing several disease-specific pathways (e.g., for depression, alcohol abuse, anxiety, etc.) may be desirable, because different behavioral health conditions have strikingly different treatment approaches. For example, some cases of depression can be successfully treated with medications, whereas phobias and substance abuse generally require behavioral change for successful outcomes. In cases where the PCP may be prescribing medication, the guideline should include recommended agents and dosages, as well as contraindications and side effects. At a minimum, there should be a protocol for triaging and handling suicidal patients, as well as patients who may harm themselves or others. All members of the care team should be aware of this protocol.

Educational Materials

The PCP should be prepared to provide educational materials to patients undergoing behavioral health assessment. Many of these patients will be found to be "at risk" or will have a behavioral health diagnosis. They and their families will need information about the condition. Other patients who have subthreshold conditions or are simply struggling to cope with life's challenges also may benefit from supportive information. Educational materials are available through mental health associations, specialty treatment providers, and pharmaceutical companies (many of which provide pamphlets free of charge without mention of specific pharmaceutical agents).

Community Resources

In addition, the clinic should develop a comprehensive list of community resources for patients needing extra support or those without financial resources or insurance coverage for behavioral health care. A sample of the types of local resources often available for patients is included in Table 5.9.

EDUCATING PROVIDERS AND STAFF

Clinic administration should be prepared to offer educational seminars for all providers and staff who will have roles and responsibilities in the behavioral health assessment program. This should include cognitive skills development for PCPs, nursing staff, pharmacists, behavioral health specialists, and patient advocates about the processes of patient assessment, diagnosis, and treatment. We recommend that organizations include the components detailed in the sample agenda shown in Table 5.10 when designing educational programs for use with PCPs and clinic staff.

CASE STUDY: INITIATING A BEHAVIORAL HEALTH ASSESSMENT PROGRAM

Since 1995, the River Valley Clinic in Northfield, Minnesota, has been doing pioneering work in primary care behavioral health screening. River Valley Clinic is a group practice with 12 family physicians, an internist, general surgeon, obstetrician-gynecologist, four nurse practitioners and physician assistants, and a complement of secondary specialists including ENT (ear, nose, and throat), urology, podiatry, and orthopedics. The clinic serves 12,000 patients in Northfield, a small college town in

TABLE 5.9
Organizations to Include on a Community Resource List

1. Community mental health services (e.g., government or grant-supported programs available free or at a reduced cost).
2. Suicide prevention services.
3. Alcohol and drug treatment centers.
4. Child protection and "vulnerable adult" services.
5. Domestic abuse programs and shelters.
6. "12-Step" support groups (e.g., Alcoholics Anonymous (A.A.), Al-Anon, Narcotics Anonymous (N.A.), Overeaters Anonymous (O.A.), Emotions Anonymous).
7. Situation-specific support groups (e.g., those dealing with grief, cancer, parenting).
8. Educational seminars (e.g., workshops on stress management, caring for aging parents or small children, smoking cessation).

TABLE 5.10
Sample Agenda for a Primary Care Educational Seminar

1. How the use of patient assessment will improve patient care.
2. Roles and responsibilities for patients, providers, and clinic staff.
3. The patient assessment process (selecting patients for screening and diagnosis, administering the instruments, interpreting the results).
4. Data management and reporting (software/hardware training).
5. Patient tracking (maintaining log sheets and other records).
6. Communicating with patients about behavioral health issues.
7. Guidelines for diagnosis and patient management.
8. Deciding whether to treat or refer to specialty care.
9. Using medications to treat behavioral health problems in otherwise *healthy* patients (selection of agents and doses; features of various classes and brands of drugs; side effects; drug interactions; etc.).
10. Using medications to treat behavioral health problems in *medically ill* or fragile patients (e.g., the appropriate selection of medications for patients with diabetes, heart disease, or other chronic conditions).
11. Providing brief counseling or support to patients.
12. Referring patients to supplemental psychotherapy or drug/alcohol "treatment."
13. Managing crises (related to the condition or its treatment).
14. Handling patients who refuse treatment, are especially "at risk," or who have other special situations (e.g., homeless, suicidal, medically compromised).
15. Coding for reimbursement.
16. Confidentiality, record keeping, and legal issues.

southern Minnesota. The clinic has had a tradition of separate, affiliated mental health services with psychiatry and clinical psychologists.

Goals for the Assessment Program

The clinic's initial interest in collecting health status information was to improve the care of defined populations of patients with chronic diseases, such as asthma. However, a compelling secondary goal was for clinicians to be able to use data to weave quality improvement, care redesign, and outcomes management into the activities of daily clinical decision making.

Support and Leadership

Organizational support for the program was provided by the clinic's parent organization, Allina Health System, Office of Medical Policy. A system-level clinical innovation team, the Living Lab, was formed to implement health status assessment in a consortium of group practices. The health system provided a part-time project manager for participating sites and financial support to cover resource costs. Local sponsorship by the clinic management and the physician leadership resulted in funding for a physician champion and the allocation of staff time to implement the project.

Implementation Team and Advisory Board

At the clinic level, a small team consisting of a physician, nurse, and receptionist was used to implement the program. A larger, coordinating interdisciplinary team met only several times, primarily to enhance clinic-wide communication. The small team approach was new to the clinic, and significantly different than the highly formal continuous quality improvement efforts that had been the standard at the clinic. It was hoped that utilizing a small team would help meet the aggressive implementation timelines established for the project.

Assessment Processes and Tools

The Living Lab selected the Health Status Questionnaire (HSQ, a variation of SF–36), because it emphasizes "whole health," that is, the mutual contribution of physical and mental health functioning to personal health and well-being. Velocity Healthcare Informatics, Inc., was chosen as a vendor because their OPFax product was a low-cost, fax-based technology that could be used to scan answer sheets, process data, and create patient assessment graphs without requiring the purchase of special hardware or software.

During the second phase of the program, the physicians decided to supplement the HSQ with a depression-specific tool (the Zung Self-Rating Depression Scale) for patients at risk of depression (based on a low mental health score or positive answers on the depression screening questions). Recently, clinicians tested the use of the D–ARK (Depression Arkansas Scale, a short instrument which aids in diagnosing depression) for confirmation of depressive disorder and suicide risk, and the SAAST (Self-Administered Alcohol Screening Test, a short, self-administered survey) for assessing potential alcohol abuse. (Both the D–ARK and SAAST are addressed in detail in later chapters of this volume.)

Typically, patients were identified for participation by the physician. If the patient was identified before the visit, an HSQ was mailed to the patient's residence. The patient would mail it back or bring it to the clinic. If the patient was identified at the time of the office visit, the nurse or receptionist gave the questionnaire to the patient. The patient completed the 39-item HSQ in 5 to 10 minutes on a bubble answer sheet. The receptionist quickly reviewed the bubble sheet for missing or multiple answers and corrected errors. The receptionist then fed the sheet into a fax machine. The fax image was collected and processed by OPFax at the vendor's location. Then a graph was generated and faxed back, usually in less than 5 minutes, and placed on the chart by the nurse.

Pilot Testing the Assessment Process

In the first phase, July through September 1995, the clinic conducted a pilot to test the generation of health status graphs for use by the provider during the office visit. This phase was focused on data collection and report generation. The pilot demonstrated that the technology worked to produce point-of-service health status graphs. However, the graphs had little impact on care. It is important to note that participating clinicians had not been specifically trained to interpret health status findings.

Implementing Assessment and Graph Interpretation

After the pilot test, the HSQ was formally selected as the health status measurement tool to be utilized in a chronic disease management program. The second phase of the program focused on data collection and report generation, and included targeted training for health care providers. The clinic chose to implement a standardized, scripted "graph assessment" interview technique and a clinical coaching program developed through the collaborative efforts of Dr. Dwana Bush, from Atlanta, Georgia, and Dr. Donald Lum (the coauthor of this case study). The interview technique and coaching program were employed to facilitate clinician interpretation of "abnormal" graphs and use of health status information in support of clinical actions. Dr. Bush was invited in May 1996 to kick off this second phase of the project. Subsequently, training was provided to all clinic health care providers in Northfield in late 1996.

Education and Coaching for Providers. The clinical mentoring and coaching program consisted of several components: educational materials; a self-assessment experience (whereby the participants completed and interpreted their own HSQ graphs); a half-day educational session with intensive one-on-one coaching; and continued guidance in health status graph interpretation and patient interview techniques for several weeks after the initial training.

Patient Response. Generally, patients responded positively to the HSQ, and believed that it assisted the clinician in better understanding their needs or health problems. Patients who indicated that they saw no value from the health status tool or that it was "a hassle" were often those who received little or no feedback from the clinician regarding their health status.

Provider Response. Provider reaction to the training and the outcomes program depended on a variety of factors. Favorable reaction was based on a positive coaching experience, sufficient cases to adequately appreciate the value of the HSQ, and the timely availability of individual patient's health status graphs. Unfavorable provider reactions were often due to the additional time required by the assessment process, a dislike of forms, delays in getting graphs, or discomfort in managing psychological problems.

Challenges Encountered and Lessons Learned

Through the implementation process, the clinic staff became aware of a need for further clinician training, as well as enhancement of the available tools, processes and technology. Initially, the project manager had provided the staff with only minimal training regarding the operation of OPFax. In retrospect, more time investment in training, including troubleshooting, would have accelerated the learning curve for successful fax transmission. Although the fax technology worked well for data capture and production of graphs for the low volumes associated with startup, higher patient volumes require more efficient data input devices and methods. These could eliminate the rework associated with human review of answer sheets for incomplete responses, double entries, or other errors.

In addition, and as anticipated, there were other challenges encountered during the implementation process. For example, although key constituencies at the health system level were aware of the project activities, often ordinary clinic staff members were oblivious about our objectives and progress. We are now keenly aware that internal communication and marketing at all levels are important components for any successful clinical innovation project.

Findings and Results

In addition to depression, several other problems were commonly identified, including anxiety, acute and chronic stress, sleep disorders, and overwork. Typical treatment for depressed patients included brief counseling and medication. Occasionally, providers made referrals to mental health specialists for patients with serious symptoms or in need of longer term management.

Overall, implementation of the health assessment has been a success. There is growing sensitivity to the presence of depression and other behavioral health problems in primary care. In particular, the participating clinicians have realized the importance of screening for behavioral health problems in defined populations of patients such as those with chronic diseases, high utilizers, and patients with multiple and/or vague somatic complaints, and for health maintenance exams.

Next Steps

Currently, a clinic team is planning health assessment of the entire population of diabetes patients to determine behavioral health problems as comorbidity. The initiative at the clinic continues to grow based on the personal commitment of the physician champion, the medical director, and a core of primary care providers and staff who actively use, derive great value from, and have substantially improved patient care through the use of these health assessment tools.

CONCLUSION

There are compelling reasons to integrate behavioral health assessment with primary care services. Providers and health care organizations will benefit greatly from the successful integration of services, because the costs associated with poor patient outcomes are high in today's health care environment, and the benefits derived from good patient outcomes can be so remarkable. Indeed, integration of services may be essential to continuing financial viability.

More importantly, patients and their families greatly benefit from the integration of services, because their lives can be significantly impacted by undiagnosed or untreated behavioral health conditions. Recognizing and managing these conditions can improve the treatment of comorbid medical conditions and can provide considerable psychosocial relief.

The integration process requires commitment of substantial time and resources and can be quite challenging. However, thoughtful planning and collaborative program design can alleviate many of the challenges faced by the original pioneers who sought to integrate these services in primary care (as discussed earlier, in the case study). Incorporation of the information and suggestions provided in this chapter will facilitate the acceptance of behavioral health assessment by providers and clinic staff, and will expedite integration of the assessment process.

ACKNOWLEDGMENTS

The authors wish to recognize and express appreciation to several people who made meaningful contributions to this chapter. We first thank Cindy Ofstead, PhD, for her outstanding insights regarding the chapter's content and organizational structure. Don Lum, MD, was the provider of the case study. Special thanks to Harry Wetzler,

MD, MSPH, for always sharing his wisdom and enthusiasm. Finally, we thank LuWanna LaPole for invaluable research and administrative support.

APPENDIX A: CITATIONS FOR TABLE 5.3
(Features of Selected Assessment Instruments)

PRIME-MD
Spitzer, R. L., Williams, J. B. W., Kroenke, K., Linzer, M., deGruy, F. V., III, Hahn, S. R., Brody, D., & Johnson, J. G. (1994). Utility of a new procedure for diagnosing mental disorders in primary care: The Prime-MD 1000 study. *Journal of the American Medical Association, 272,* 1749–1756.

COMPASS-PC
Grant Grissom (personal communication, May 20, 1998)

QPD PANEL
Jonathan Shedler (personal communication, April 6, 1998)

SCL-90-R
Katon, W., Von Korff, M., Lin, E., Walker, E., Simon, G. E., Bush, T., Robinson, P., & Russo, J. (1995). Collaborative management to achieve treatment guidelines: Impact on depression in primary care. *Journal of the American Medical Association, 273,* 1026–1031.
Mitchell, J. V. (Ed.). (1985). *The ninth mental measurements yearbook.* Lincoln, NB: The University of Nebraska Press.
Von Korff, M., Ormel, J., Katon, W., & Lin, E. H. B. (1992). Disability and depression among high utilizers of health care. *Archives of General Psychiatry, 49,* 91–100.

BSI (Brief Symptom Inventory)
Piersma, H. L., & Boes, J. L. (1995). Agreement between patient self-report and clinician rating: Concurrence between the BSI and the GAF among psychiatric inpatients. *Journal of Clinical Psychology, 51,* 153–157.

PCAS (Primary Care Assessment Survey)
Crotty, M. T. (1997). *Medical Outcomes Trust: Monitor* (Vol. 2, Issue 1). Boston, MA: Medical Outcomes Trust.

SA-45
Mark Maruish (personal communication, May 22, 1998)

BDI and BDI-PC (Beck Depression Inventory)
Beck, A. T., Guth, D., Steer, R. A., & Ball, R. (1997). Screening for major depression disorders in medical inpatients with the Beck Depression Inventory for primary care. *Behaviour Research and Therapy, 35*(8), 785–791.
Kramer, J. J., & Conoley, J. C. (Eds.). (1992). *The eleventh mental measurements yearbook.* Lincoln, NB: The University of Nebraska Press.

HDI (Hamilton Rating Scale for Depression)
Coulehan, J. L., Schulberg, H. C., Block, M. R., Madonia, M. J., & Rodriguez, E. (1997). Treating depressed primary care patients improves their physical, mental, and social functioning. *Archives of Internal Medicine, 157,* 1113–1120.

UAMS – Depression Outcomes Module and D-ARK
Rost, K., Smith, G. R., Burnam, M. A., & Burns, B. J. (1992). Measuring the outcomes of care for mental health program: The case of depressive disorders. *Medical Care, 30, 5,* 266–273.

GDS (Geriatric Depression)

Burke, W. J., Rangwani, S., Roccaforte, W. H., Wengel, S. P., & Conley, D. M. (1997). The reliability and validity of the collateral source version of the Geriatric Depression Rating Scale administered by telephone. *International Journal of Geriatric Psychiatry, 12,* 288–294.

Lyness, J. M., Noel, T. K., Cox, C., King, D. A., Conwell, Y., & Caine, E. D. (1997). Screening for depression in elderly primary care patients. *Archives of Internal Medicine, 157,* 449–454.

Rovner, B. W., & Shmuely-Dulitzki, Y. (1997). Screening for depression in low-vision elderly. *International Journal of Geriatric Psychiatry, 12,* 955–959.

BAI (Beck Anxiety Inventory)

Enns, M. W., Cox, B. J., Parker, J. D. A., & Guertin, J. E. (1998). Confirmatory factor analysis of the Beck anxiety and depression inventories in patients with major depression. *Journal of Affective Disorders, 47,* 195–200.

Impara, J. C., & Plake, B. S. (1998). *The thirteenth mental measurements yearbook.* Lincoln, NB: The University of Nebraska Press.

SAAST (Self-Administered Alcoholism Screening Test)

Davis, L. J., & Morse, R. M. (1980). Self-Administered Alcoholism Screening Test: A comparison of conventional versus computer-administered formats. *Alcoholism: Clinical and Experimental Research, 15,* 155–157.

Hurt, R. D., Morse, R. M., & Swenson, W. M. (1980). Diagnosis of alcoholism with a self-administered alcoholism screening test. *Mayo Clinic Proceedings, 55,* 365–370.

SF-36 and MH-5

Beusterien, K. M., Steinwald, B., & Ware, J. E. (1996). Usefulness of the SF–36 Health Survey in measuring health outcomes in the depressed elderly. *Journal of Geriatric Psychiatry and Neurology, 9,* 1–9.

BASIS-32

Eisen, S. V., Dill, D. L., & Grob, M. C. (1992). Reliability and validity of a brief patient-report instrument for psychiatric hospital care. *Hospital Community Psychiatry, 42,* 1120–1126.

SIS-Q (Suicidal Ideation)

Cooper-Patrick, L., Crum, R. M., & Ford, D. E. (1994). Identifying suicidal ideation in general medical patients. *Journal of the American Medical Association, 272,* 1757–1762.

SDDS-PC (Symptom Driven Diagnostic System for Primary Care)

Olfson, M., Weissman, M. M., Leon, A. C., Sheehan, D. V., & Farber, L. (1996). Suicidal ideation in primary care. *Journal of General Internal Medicine, 11,* 447–453.

CES-D (Center for Epidemiology Studies Depression Scale)

Olfson, M., Gilbert, T., Weissman, M., Blacklow, R. S., & Broadhead, E. (1995). Recognition of emotional distress in physically healthy primary care patients who perceive poor physical health. *General Hospital Psychiatry, 17,* 173–180.

APPENDIX B: RESOURCES FOR BEHAVIORAL HEALTH GUIDELINES

Contact Information

Guidelines Available in 1999

Agency for Health Care Policy & Research (AHCPR)
Publications Clearinghouse
P.O. Box 8547
Silver Spring, MD 20907-8547
(800) 358-9295

Depression in Primary Care

Institute for Clinical Systems Integration   Major Depression
  (ICSI)   Generalized Anxiety Disorder
The ARDEL Group   Panic Disorder
13355 10th Avenue North, Suite 108   Attention Deficit Disorder
Minneapolis, MN 55441-5510   Domestic Violence
(612) 545-1919
(612) 545-0335 fax

FACCT - The Foundation for Accountability   Major Depression
520 SW 6th Avenue, Suite 700
Portland, OR 97204
(503) 223-2228

American Psychiatric Press, Inc. (APA)   Adult Psychiatric Evaluation
1400 K Street NW, Suite 1101   Major Depressive Disorder
Washington, DC 20005   Panic Disorder
(800) 368-5777   Bipolar Disorder
                                                    Eating Disorders
                                                    Nicotine Dependence
                                                    Substance Abuse Disorders

REFERENCES

Agency for Health Care Policy and Research. (1993). *Depression in primary care: Vol. 1. Detection and diagnosis* (AHCPR Publication No. 93-0550). Washington, DC: U.S. Government Printing Office.

Amaro, H., Fried, L. E., Cabral, H., & Zuckerman, B. (1990). Violence during pregnancy and substance use. *American Journal of Public Health, 80*, 575–579.

Attala, J. M. (1996). Detecting abuse among women in the home. *Home Care Provider, 1*(1), 12–18.

Bien, T. H., Miller, W. R., & Tonigan, J. S. (1993). Brief interventions for alcohol problems: A review. *Addiction, 88*, 315–336.

Eisenberg, L. (1992). Treating depression and anxiety in primary care. *New England Journal of Medicine, 326*, 1080–1084.

Gazmararian, J. A., Lazorick, S., Spitz, A. M., Ballard, T. J., Saltzman, L. E., & Marks, J. S. (1996). Prevalence of violence against pregnant women. *Journal of the American Medical Association, 275*, 1915–1920.

Hirschfeld, R. M. A., Keller, M. B., Panico, S., Arons, B. S., Barlow, D., Davidoff, F., Endicott, J., Froom, J., Goldstein, M., Gorman, J. M., Guthrie, D., Marek, R. G., Maurer, T. A., Meyer, R., Phillips, K., Ross, J., Schwenk, T. L., Sharfstein, S. S., Thase, M. E., & Wyatt, R. J. (1997). The national depressive and manic-depressive association consensus statement on the undertreatment of depression. *Journal of the American Medical Association, 277*, 333–340.

Lieberman, J. A. III. (1997). Recognizing depression in primary care patients. *Hospital Practice, 32*, 145–148.

Olfson, M., & Klerman, G. L. (1992). The treatment of depression: Prescribing practices of primary care physicians and psychiatrists. *Journal of Family Practice, 35*, 627–635.

Olfson, M., Weissman, M. M., Leon, A. C., Farber, L., & Sheehan, D. V. (1996). Psychotic symptoms in primary care. *Journal of Family Practice, 43*, 481–488.

Plichta, S. (1992). The effects of woman abuse on health care utilization and health status: A literature review. *Women's Health Issues, 2*, 154–163.

Roy-Byrne, P. P., & Katon, W. (1997). Generalized anxiety disorder in primary care: The precursor/modifier pathway to increased health care utilization. *Journal of Clinical Psychiatry, 58*(Suppl. 3), 34–40.

Spitzer, R. L., Kroenke, K., Linzer, M., Hahn, S. R., Williams, J. B. W., deGruy, F. V. III, Brody, D., & Davies, M. (1995). Health-related quality of life in primary care patients with mental disorders. *Journal of the American Medical Association, 274*, 1511–1517.

Stewart, A. L., Greenfield, S., Hays, R. D., Wells, K., Rogers, W. H., Berry, S. D., McGlynn, E. A., Ware, J. E., Jr. (1989). Functional status and well-being of patients with chronic conditions: Results from the Medical Outcomes Study. *Journal of the American Medical Association, 262*, 907–913.

Wells, K. B., Sturm, R., Sherbourne, C. D., & Meredith, L. S. (1996). *Caring for depression*. Cambridge, MA: Harvard University Press.

Zimmerman, M. (1993). A five-minute psychiatric screening interview. *Journal of Family Practice, 37,* 479–482.

Zung, W. W. K., Broadhead, E., & Roth, M. E. (1993). Prevalence of depressive symptoms in primary care. *Journal of Family Practice, 37,* 337–344.

ASSESSMENT INSTRUMENTS

Evaluation of Mental Disorders With the PRIME-MD

Steven R. Hahn
Albert Einstein College of Medicine and Jacobi Medical Center

Kurt Kroenke
Regenstrief Institute for Health Care and Indiana University School of Medicine

Janet B. W. Williams
Robert L. Spitzer
New York State Psychiatric Institute and Columbia University

The Primary Care Evaluation of Mental Disorders (PRIME–MD) is a two-stage case-finding and diagnostic instrument that was designed specifically for primary care clinicians in the general medical setting (Spitzer et al., 1994). Half of individuals with psychopathology who receive any medical care do so exclusively from primary care providers. Although one quarter of adult primary care patients have mental disorders, half or fewer of those disorders are detected, and those that are detected often receive suboptimal treatment. Admittedly, primary care patients with mental disorders may have fewer and milder symptoms and less impairment than patients seen by mental health specialists. On the other hand, mental disorders encountered in primary care are associated with more functional impairment than most of the physical disorders that are typically the principal focus of general medicine.

Primary care physicians' failure to detect and treat mental disorders has many causes. Deficiencies in both what physicians know how to do and how they use that knowledge contribute. Unlike new procedures or tests that supplant less efficient versions of what physicians already understand and use, the PRIME–MD was designed from the outset to change physicians' practice patterns and to remedy a knowledge deficit. This perspective dictated that the PRIME–MD had to be, on the one hand, a self-guiding, user-friendly educational tool that could effectively provide the knowledge of diagnostic criteria that primary care physicians lack. On the other hand, it also had to be a rapid, cost-effective procedure whose application would be consistent with the existing milieu of the primary care encounter.

The generation of case-finding tools antecedent to the PRIME–MD, such as the Zung Self-rating Depression Scale (Zung, 1965), the General Health Questionnaire (GHQ) (Goldberg & Hillier, 1978), and the Center for Epidemiological Studies Depression Scale (CES–D) (Radloff, 1977), identified patients likely to have some mental disorder but did not make specific diagnoses. On the other hand, diagnostic tools capable of making specific diagnoses, such as the Structured Clinical Interview for *DSM–III–R* (SCID; Spitzer, Williams, Gibbon, & First, 1992) and Diagnostic Interview Schedule (DIS; Robins et al., 1985), were far too complicated and time-consuming to be compatible with primary care practice. In contrast, the PRIME–MD was developed as a single procedure to both screen populations to determine who was at risk *and* to guide the clinician all the way to a specific DSM criteria-based diagnosis. Further, ease and efficiency of administration in the primary care setting was a major aim.

BACKGROUND

Prevalence and Health-Related Consequences of Mental Disorders

Mental disorders in primary care are common and associated with significant health and quality of life impairment. Knowledge of prevalence and associated morbidity served as both rational for and guide to the design of the PRIME–MD.

Prevalence. A number of studies dating from the late 1970s through the 1980s examined the prevalence of common mental disorders in the primary care setting. Data from these studies converged on the conclusion that major depressive disorder is present in 6% to 10% of primary care patients (Katon & Schulberg, 1992), and mental disorders meeting *DSM–III* or Research Diagnostic Criteria (RDC) are present in 20% to 26%. An important international study found a worldwide mean prevalence of eight common International Classification and Diagnosis System, Version 10 (ICD–10), mental disorders of 21%, but also demonstrated considerable cross-cultural variability (8% in Shanghai, 53% in Santiago, Chile: Ormel et al., 1994; Sartorius et al., 1993; Ustun & Sartorius, 1996). The few studies that have examined psychiatric comorbidity demonstrated that patients frequently have more than one mental disorder (Coyne, Fechner-Bates, & Schwenk, 1994; Ormel et al., 1994; Zimmerman et al., 1994). The National Comorbidity Survey concluded that half of all lifetime mental disorders are accounted for by the 14% of the population having three or more disorders (Kessler et al., 1994).

Health-Related Outcomes. There is ample documentation that mental disorders have an adverse effect on health-related outcomes. Depression is associated with more impairment in health-related quality of life than most chronic medical diagnoses (Turner & Noh, 1988; Von Korff, Ormel, Katon, & Lin, 1992; Wells et al., 1989). Patients with psychopathology use more health services in the primary care setting than patients without mental disorders (Henk, Katzelnick, Kobak, Greist, & Jefferson, 1996; Karlsson, Lehtinen, & Joukama, 1995; Regier et al., 1988; Shapiro et al., 1984; Von Korff et al., 1992), and are less satisfied with care (Cherkin, Deyo, Street, & Barlow, 1996; Hansson, Borgquist, Nettelbladt, & Nordstrom, 1994; Hueston, Mainous, & Schilling, 1996; Wyshak & Barsky, 1995).

Detection of Mental Disorders

Measuring Physician Detection. Assessment of clinicians' ability to detect mental disorders in primary care must overcome several methodological challenges. The criteria for "detection" used in most studies have been inconsistent and lack diagnostic precision and rigor. Psychopathology has been labeled as detected if physicians believed any psychopathology was present, or if they identified broad categories of disorder such as depression (Katon & Von Korff, 1990; Kessler, Cleary, & Burke, 1985). In some studies, the prescription of any psychotropic medication or provision of "counseling" was used as a surrogate for detection. In no study was specific diagnostic labeling required as a criteria of detection. Methods of assessing physician detection also vary: Some studies have used chart review, which tends to underestimate rates of detection (Jenks, 1985; Katon & Von Korff, 1990), and others have employed physician questionnaires, which alerts physicians to the purpose of the study and therefore tends to overestimate detection.

Rates of Detection. Despite these methodological problems, studies of physician detection converge on the conclusion that 30% to 60% of patients with mental disorders are not detected as having a mental disorder. Depression has been the most intensively studied of the mental disorders. Using several criteria for detection of depression, Kirmayer, Robbins, Dworkind, and Yaffe (1993) found that rates ranged from 24% to 67% depending on the rigor of the criterion used. Coyne, Schwenk, and Fechner-Bates (1995) discovered that family physicians endorsed a diagnosis of depression in 35% of patients with major depression and 28% of patients with any depressive disorder. Simon and von Korff's (1995) study of 2,000 patients found that two-thirds of depressed patients were recognized as distressed and half were prescribed medications.

Physician Factors Influencing Detection. Physician interviewing style has been shown to influence detection of mental disorders. Both the content of the interview and the communication process have an impact on the likelihood of detection. In the Badger et al. (1994a) study of physician interviewing, inquiry regarding specific symptoms of depression was positively correlated with detection of depression. However, elicitation of specific depressive symptoms was generally low. Most physicians elicited only three symptoms, and physicians never made their diagnosis on the basis of complete *DSM* criteria (i.e., depressed mood or anhedonia and a total of five symptoms). Failure to elicit information regarding all the symptoms relevant to the diagnosis of psychopathology is presumed to be due in part to deficits in physicians' knowledge of these criteria. Indeed, studies have demonstrated that primary care physicians have incomplete knowledge in the diagnosis and management of mental disorders (Cohen-Cole et al., 1982; Penn, Boland, McCartney, Kohn, & Mulvey, 1997). Robbins, Kirmayer, Cathébras, Yaffe, and Dworkind (1994) demonstrated that physicians who acknowledge that psychological problems influence physical illness detect mood and anxiety disorders more effectively.

Physicians' skills have also been associated with detection. Skills in using "patient-centered" communication and in gathering a lot of information in general, as well as sensitivity to nonverbal communication, are positively associated with detection (Badger et al., 1994a, 1994b; Goldberg, Jenkins, Millar, & Faragher, 1993; Robbins et al., 1994; Roter et al., 1995).

Although interview content and process are consistently related to detection, the effect of physicians' attitudes is less clear. In one study, self-rated interest in psychosocial issues did not correlate with desirable interviewing style (Badger et al., 1994b). In another study, sensitivity to patients' emotions correlated negatively with detection of mental disorders (Robbins et al., 1994). A tendency to blame depressed patients for causing their illness has been shown to correlate with nondetection (Rob-bins et al., 1994). Main, Lutz, Barrett, Matthew, and Miller (1993) confirmed that clinicians' perceptions of the importance of detecting depression in their practice were related to a multitude of attitudes, including physicians' emotional discomfort dealing with depression, their perception that patients would be uncomfortable dis-cussing depression, perceived self-efficacy and satisfaction in treating depression, and the perceived time and effort required for treatment.

Patient Factors Influencing Detection. Few studies have examined patient char-acteristics associated with physician detection of mental disorders in primary care, and virtually all have examined only mood disorders. Unsurprisingly, the most con-sistent observation has been that detection is better when psychiatric symptoma-tology is overt and more severe (Badger et al., 1994a; Coyne et al., 1995; Freeling, Rao, Paykel, Sireling, & Burton, 1985; Schwenk, Coyne, & Fechner-Bates, 1996). Three studies using *DSM–IV* Global Assessment of Functioning scores (GAF; Spitzer, Gib-bon, Williams, & Endicott, 1996) demonstrated that undetected depressed patients have milder impairment (Coyne et al., 1994, 1995; Schwenk et al., 1996). Because the GAF relies heavily on symptom severity in assessing functional status, the associa-tion between functional impairment and detection may be confounded by symptom severity.

It has commonly been taught that underlying depression is often missed when anxiety, which may be more obvious, is present (Bridges & Goldberg, 1987; Paykel & Priest, 1992; Rodin, Craven, & Littlefield, 1991). Coyne et al. (1994) demonstrated the opposite: comorbid anxiety was twice as prevalent in detected than in undetected (58% vs. 27%) depressed patients. The presence of multiple physical symptoms and comorbid physical illness has also traditionally been described as a barrier to detec-tion of mental disorders, resulting in so-called "masked" depression. The true rela-tionship between physical symptoms and detection probably depends both on the number of symptoms and patients' willingness to accept psychological explanations for their symptoms and distress. Kirmayer et al. (1993) demonstrated that the likeli-hood of detection in patients with anxiety or mood disorders increased with total number of unexplained physical symptoms and hypochondriacal worry, but was de-creased and delayed in patients reluctant to attribute their symptoms to psychologi-cal distress. Several studies suggest that patients' resistance to psychiatric labeling decreases detection and stems from fear of stigmatization and confusion about the implications of the diagnosis (Dew, Dunn, Bromet, & Schulberg, 1988; Olfson, 1991; Paykel & Priest, 1992).

Kirmayer et al. (1993) found that age had no effect on recognition, male gender de-layed detection initially but had no effect over a 12-month period, and detection cor-related positively with level of education. Other studies have suggested that female patients are more likely to have mental disorders diagnosed, but with some risk for false positive attribution (Cleary, Burns, & Nycz, 1990).

Systems Factors. Physicians frequently cite lack of time as one of the most im-portant obstacles to detection (Main, Lutz, Barrett, Matthew, & Miller, 1993; Orleans, George, Houpt, & Brodie, 1985; Rost, Humphrey, & Kelleher, 1994). The adequacy and availability of mental health specialists and services may also affect primary care physicians' efforts to detect mental disorders (Klinkman, 1997). Moreover, the ad-verse effect of payment policies that preclude reimbursement for the treatment of mental disorders in the primary care setting is a major disincentive to detection and treatment (Glass, 1995; Hirschfeld et al., 1997), and will be more important for economically disadvantaged patients who have greater difficulty obtaining mental health services from specialists. Rost, Smith, Matthews, and Guide (1994) documented nonreimbursement for care of mental disorders as a reason for deliberately misdiagnosing depression in primary care.

Summary: Epidemiological Foundation of the PRIME-MD Project.   The epidemiological studies and investigations of primary care provider behavior just described supported the rationale for developing the PRIME-MD and guided its design. The demonstrated morbidity and underdetection of mental disorders established the need for enhanced primary care evaluation of mental disorders. The overall prevalence and common co-occurrence of multiple mental disorders dictated the need to evaluate a spectrum of disorders, not depression exclusively. Finally, demonstrated deficiencies in physicians' knowledge of diagnostic criteria and interviewing skills determined the need for an efficient and explicitly structured guide to the assessment of specific diagnostic criteria.

OVERVIEW OF THE PRIME-MD

The PRIME-MD was developed by a team of investigators headed by Robert Spitzer and Janet Williams, whose previous accomplishments included pioneering work as senior editors of the American Psychiatric Association's *Diagnostic and Statistical Manual* (*DSM*) versions III and III-R. This work established fundamental principles of psychiatric nosology and classification used today. In addition, Spitzer and Williams developed the Structured Clinical Interview for *DSM* (SCID), a comprehensive diagnostic procedure designed to be used by a trained mental health provider (Spitzer et al., 1992).

Other members of the PRIME-MD investigatory team were primary care internists and family physicians working in academic primary care training programs. In addition to being themselves representative of the end users of the PRIME-MD, members of the PRIME-MD team had extensive experience as clinical investigators of topics related to the epidemiology, diagnosis, and management of mental disorders in primary care settings and in teaching psychiatric and behavioral science to medical trainees.

Initial Development of the PRIME-MD

Development of the PRIME-MD incorporated the following assumptions based on the epidemiological and educational research already summarized:

1. Mental disorders are common.
2. Many patients have more than one type of mental disorder.
3. Mental disorders often are undetected.
4. Case-finding that identifies patients at high risk for a mental disorder has an inadequate impact on diagnosis and treatment; the procedural endpoint should be a diagnosis.

5. Physician acceptance requires an instrument that is quick, easy to use, and focused on common and important disorders.

The first version of the PRIME–MD was developed over an 8-month period of administering preliminary versions of the PRIME–MD to 450 patients at seven primary care sites. Tested instrument items were discussed and revised at weekly conference calls, resulting in the final version of the PRIME–MD that was validated in the PRIME–MD 1000 Study (Spitzer et al., 1994). Further minor modifications, described later, were made after the validation study to reflect differences in *DSM–IV* criteria and to streamline application.

General Considerations and Description of the PRIME–MD

Design of the PRIME–MD began with a two-stage "screen/case-find and diagnose" procedure. This design was based on the expectation that, in contrast to screening or case-finding procedures, the specific diagnostic endpoint of the PRIME–MD would be the beginning of a self-sustained process of evaluation and treatment of the diagnosed condition. Although the objective of achieving a specific diagnosis determined the minimum length and complexity of the procedure, the need to create an acceptably brief instrument set limits on the level of diagnostic detail included, and on the extent to which evaluation of diagnosed disorders could be included.

The *screening/case-finding component* was to be a self-administered, paper-and-pencil self-report that could be administered in the waiting room prior to the clinical encounter. The screen needed to both identify patients in need of further evaluation and enhance efficiency by limiting further evaluation to specific categories of disorder. The PRIME–MD *diagnostic component* was conceived as a branching-logic, physician-administered interview subdivided into modules addressing the categories of disorder screened by the patient self-report.

Criteria for the inclusion of a diagnosis in the PRIME–MD should ideally follow those established for screening or case-finding in general (Campbell, 1987; Frame, 1986; Schwenk, 1996):

- The condition must be sufficiently common and have an important impact on health-related quality of life or mortality.
- The case-finding/screening procedure must be accurate and have an acceptable risk and cost.
- Screening or case-finding must improve outcomes compared to waiting for the disorder to become more apparent.
- Treatment of the condition at the stage of screening or case-finding must be available, acceptable, and effective.

In addition to excluding uncommon or trivial conditions, and in the interest of producing an acceptably brief and efficient instrument, the PRIME–MD would *not* include:

- Protocols for subtypes of conditions or the secondary evaluation of the diagnosed conditions.

- Diagnoses that would be detected in the course of the evaluation of comorbid conditions already included in PRIME–MD (e.g., posttraumatic stress disorder, which is usually accompanied by one of the included mood or anxiety disorders).
- Conditions that are readily detected (if not accurately diagnosed) by means already routinely employed in primary care practice (e.g., conditions producing thought disorders that are apparent in the course of an ordinary medical interview).

The resulting instrument addresses five categories of mental disorders (listed in Table 6.1). The first component of the PRIME–MD is a one-page Patient Questionnaire (PQ), completed by the patient before seeing the physician (see Fig. 6.1). The second component is the Clinician Evaluation Guide (CEG), a structured interview administered by the physician (see Fig. 6.2). The PQ is used by the physician to determine which if any of the five "modules" of the CEG should be administered to the patient.

Patient Questionnaire (PQ). The Patient Questionnaire consists of 25 yes–no questions about symptoms and signs present during the previous month and a single question about the patient's overall health. The questions are divided into five

TABLE 6.1
Prevalence of Selected Psychiatric Disorders Detected
by PRIME–MD in 1,000 Primary Care Patients

Mental Disorder	Total Sample Number (%)		Site Range (%)
Any psychiatric diagnosis	386	(39)	30–52
Any *DSM–IV* threshold diagnosis	257	(26)	18–38
Subthreshold only	129	(13)	10–14
Any mood disorder	260	(26)	19–35
Major depressive disorder	115	(12)	7–19
Dysthymia	78	(8)	5–15
Partial remission or recurrence of major depression	63	(6)	4–9
Minor depressive disorder	64	(6)	2–9
Rule out depressive disorder due to physical disorder, medication, or other drug	24	(2)	2–4
Rule out bipolar disorder	8	(1)	<1–1
Any anxiety disorder	178	(18)	10–25
Anxiety not otherwise specified	90	(9)	7–13
Generalized anxiety disorder	70	(7)	2–13
Panic disorder	36	(4)	1–6
Rule out anxiety disorder due to physical disorder, medication, or other drug	19	(2)	1–3
Any somatoform disorder	139	(14)	9–29
Multisomatoform disorder	82	(8)	4–18
Somatoform disorder not otherwise specified	42	(4)	2–9
Hypochondriasis	22	(2)	<1–5
Somatoform pain disorder	8	(1)	1–1
Probable alcohol abuse	51	(5)	3–7
Any eating disorder	30	(3)	1–7
Binge eating disorder	30	(3)	1–7
Bulimia nervosa	1	(<1)	0–<1
Eating disorder not otherwise specified	1	(<1)	0–<1

Note. From Spitzer et al. (1994). Utility of a new procedure for diagnosing mental disorders in primary care: The PRIME-MD 1000 Study. *Journal of the American Medical Association, 272,* p. 1751. Copyright © 1994. Reprinted with permission.

PATIENT QUESTIONNAIRE

Updated for DSM-IV™

NAME: _____   AGE: _____

SEX: ☐ Male ☐ Female   TODAY'S DATE: _____

INSTRUCTIONS: This questionnaire will help your doctor better understand problems that you may have. Your doctor may ask you more questions about some of these items. Please make sure to check a box for every item.

During the PAST MONTH, have you been bothered A LOT by...		*During the PAST MONTH...*

	YES	No		YES	No		YES	No
1. stomach pain	☐	☐	12. constipation, loose bowels, or diarrhea	☐	☐	21. have you had an anxiety attack (suddenly feeling fear or panic)	☐	☐
2. back pain	☐	☐						
3. pain in your arms, legs, or joints (knees, hips, etc)	☐	☐	13. nausea, gas, or indigestion	☐	☐	22. have you thought you should cut down on your drinking of alcohol	☐	☐
4. menstrual pain or problems	☐	☐	14. feeling tired or having low energy	☐	☐			
5. pain or problems during sexual intercourse	☐	☐	15. trouble sleeping	☐	☐	23. has anyone complained about your drinking	☐	☐
6. headaches	☐	☐	16. your eating being out of control	☐	☐	24. have you felt guilty or upset about your drinking	☐	☐
7. chest pain	☐	☐	17. little interest or pleasure in doing things	☐	☐	25. was there ever a single day in which you had five or more drinks of beer, wine, or liquor	☐	☐
8. dizziness	☐	☐						
9. fainting spells	☐	☐	18. feeling down, depressed, or hopeless	☐	☐			
10. feeling your heart pound or race	☐	☐	19. "nerves" or feeling anxious or on edge	☐	☐	Overall, would you say your health is: Excellent ☐ Very good ☐ Good ☐ Fair ☐ Poor ☐		
11. shortness of breath	☐	☐	20. worrying about a lot of different things	☐	☐			

FIG. 6.1.   The PRIME–MD Patient Questionnaire (PQ). Copyright © 1996 Pfizer Inc. All rights reserved. Reproduced with permission. PRIME-MD® is a trademark of Pfizer Inc.

groups corresponding to the five categories of mental disorder assessed in the PRIME–MD. The PQ is designed as a paper-and-pencil self-report but can also be administered by clerical or nursing personnel, or by the physician.

The first group of PQ items addresses 15 of the most common physical symptoms (excluding upper respiratory symptoms) encountered in primary care (Kroenke, Arrington, & Mangelsdorff, 1990; Schappert, 1992). The PQ begins with physical symptoms, in the belief that patients visiting their primary care provider would be most comfortable with these items and would perceive the provider as being inter-

MOOD MODULE

MAJOR DEPRESSION

For the last 2 weeks, have you had any of the following
problems <u>nearly every day</u>?

1.	Trouble falling or staying asleep, or sleeping too much?	**Yes**	**No**
2.	Feeling tired or having little energy?	**Yes**	**No**
3.	Poor appetite or overeating?	**Yes**	**No**
4.	Little interest or pleasure in doing things?	**Yes**	**No**
5.	Feeling down, depressed, or hopeless?	**Yes**	**No**
6.	Feeling bad about yourself — or that you are a failure or have let yourself or your family down?	**Yes**	**No**
7.	Trouble concentrating on things, such as reading the newspaper or watching television?	**Yes**	**No**
8.	Being so fidgety or restless that you were moving around a lot more than usual? **If No:** What about the opposite — moving or speaking so slowly that other people could have noticed? **Count as Yes if Yes to either question, or if psycho-motor agitation or retardation observed during interview.**	**Yes**	**No**
9.	In the last 2 weeks, have you had thoughts that you would be better off dead or of hurting yourself in some way? **If Yes:** Tell me about it.	**Yes**	**No**
10.	**Are answers to five or more of #1 to #9 Yes (one of which is #4 or #5)?**	Yes → *Major Depressive Disorder* Go to #12	**No**

FIG. 6.2. The first page of the PRIME–MD Clinician Evaluation Guide (CEG) Mood Module. Copyright © 1996 Pfizer Inc. All rights reserved. Reproduced with permission. PRIME–MD® is a trademark of Pfizer Inc.

ested in their overall health, both physical and emotional. Originally, three or more symptoms from this group were used to trigger administration of the somatoform module of the CEG. However, a seven-symptom threshold has recently been shown to identify most patients with a clinically significant somatoform disorder (Kroenke, Spitzer, deGruy, & Swindle, 1998). The original PQ contained a 16th item in this group screened for hypochondriacal concerns, a diagnosis eliminated in the final version.

The somatoform PQ items are followed by a single screening question for eating disorders; a positive response triggers administration of the eating disorders module of the CEG. Mood disorders are addressed in two items that ascertain the presence of depressed mood or anhedonia, the two *DSM* "A criteria" for the diagnosis of mood disorders. A positive response to either of these items triggers the mood module of the CEG. Anxiety disorders are addressed in three items: one each for the cognitive and the physical symptoms of generalized anxiety, and a single item screening for panic attacks. A single positive response to any of these items is an indication that the anxiety module should be administered.

Four items address alcohol use, the first three of which are taken from the CAGE Questionnaire (Ewing, 1984). The fourth alcohol screening item substitutes a more sensitive question about consuming more than five drinks in one day for the least sensitive CAGE question (taking an "eye-opener," i.e., consumption to counteract symptoms of withdrawal or hangover). Again, a positive response to any one of the four items triggers the alcohol module of the CEG.

In answering most PQ items, patients are instructed to answer yes only if they have "OFTEN been bothered during the last month" (capitalization in the PQ). The only exceptions are the anxiety attack item, and the four alcohol items that do not require that the symptom be present "often."

The last question on the PQ addresses the patient's perception of his or her health. This item was included because a discrepancy between patient and physician perception of health status can be a clue to hidden psychopathology (Olfson, Gilbert, Weissman, Blacklow, & Broadhead, 1995).

The Clinician Evaluation Guide (CEG). The CEG is a structured interview guide, divided into five modules addressing each category of mental disorder. The diagnostic data and decisions are based on *DSM–IV* criteria. The sequence in which the modules should be administered, indicated by their position in the CEG, was established to maximize efficiency by capitalizing on the redundancy of some items in the mood and anxiety modules. The chosen sequence — mood, anxiety, eating, alcohol, and somatoform — also makes it possible to determine if physical symptoms are due to a mood or anxiety disorder so that they are not also counted when considering somatoform disorders (as per *DSM–IV* criteria). In each module entered, the physician continues from item to item unless instructed to skip items or exit from the module. The anxiety module consists of two subsections: The items pertaining to the diagnosis of panic disorder are addressed only if the PQ question about panic attacks was endorsed; otherwise, the anxiety module begins with questions designed to determine if generalized anxiety disorder is present. The CEG takes an average of 8.5 min to administer.

Languages. Versions of the PRIME–MD are available in several languages, including four Philippine dialects, Afrikaner, Spanish, French, and Chinese (Pang, Chao, Fabb, Lai, & Leung, 1997; Pang, Chao, Fabb, Leung, & Yeung, 1997).

Disorders Included in the PRIME–MD

Although there may be some debate regarding the extent to which mood, anxiety, and alcohol disorders meet all the indications for screening (Schwenk, 1996; U.S. Preventive Services Task Force, 1996), their inclusion in the PRIME–MD was justified by their prevalence, associated morbidity, and potential for treatment.

Mood Disorders. Major depressive disorder, major depression in partial remission or recurrence, dysthymic disorder, bipolar disorder, and minor depression were selected for inclusion in PRIME-MD. A qualifying diagnosis of secondary mood disorder can be appended to any of these. Subtypes of major depressive disorder and bipolar disorder were not included, based on a consensus that the two more general diagnoses were appropriate endpoints for a diagnostic process that would still require an evaluation extending beyond the objectives of the PRIME-MD as a case-finding and diagnostic tool.

Anxiety Disorders. Among the anxiety spectrum disorders, panic and generalized anxiety disorders, anxiety not otherwise specified (NOS), and a qualifying diagnosis of secondary anxiety disorder were included. Posttraumatic stress disorder (PTSD) and obsessive-compulsive disorder (OCD) were not included in PRIME-MD because they are relatively less common, and should be detected during the evaluation of the already included mood and anxiety disorders that are typically comorbid with PTSD and OCD.

Alcohol Abuse. The endpoint selected for the alcohol abuse/dependence module was a conditional diagnosis, that is, "probable alcohol abuse or dependence." Although the administration of the PRIME-MD alcohol module represents a more intensive evaluation than is typically employed by the small group of primary care providers who do ask more than one or two quantitative questions about alcohol consumption, the task of reaching definitive conclusions about alcohol abuse or dependence and distinguishing between the two goes beyond what can be accomplished with the PRIME-MD. Alerting the physician and patient to the presence of a potential problem with alcohol, even if it is not known whether full criteria for dependence or abuse are present, is probably worthwhile despite the potential adverse effect of labeling the patient. It is now believed that even lower levels of alcohol use, so-called "problem drinking," may warrant physician intervention in the form of counseling about the dangers of excess alcohol use and consideration of referral for self-help or other treatment.

Somatoform Disorders. Despite confusion regarding appropriate diagnostic criteria in the primary care setting and less consensus about effective management strategies, somatoform disorders were included in the PRIME-MD for several reasons. First, somatoform disorders are important in explaining many physical symptoms encountered in primary care patients for which there is no adequate organic explanation (Kroenke et al., 1990; Schappert, 1992). Second, somatoform disorders, by some definitions such as Escobar's abridged somatization disorder, have been demonstrated to have a significant prevalence and impact on health-related quality of life (Escobar, Burnman, Karno, Forsythe, & Golding, 1987). Third, somatization has been demonstrated to present a serious challenge to the doctor–patient relationship and is one of the principle causes of physician-experienced distress (Hahn, Thompson, Stern, Budner, & Wills, 1994). Fourth, interventions with somatizing patients have been demonstrated to have an impact on health care costs, utilization of resources, and possibly functional status (Smith, Monson, & Ray, 1995; Smith, Rost, & Kashner, 1995). Fifth, an effective case-finding and diagnostic procedure for somatoform disorders would be of value in investigating the epidemiology, diagnosis, and management of these disorders, even in the absence of current consensus on management strategies.

The choice of which specific somatoform disorders to be included was one of the most challenging in the development of the PRIME–MD. Somatization disorder is relatively rare in primary care (1% to 4%) and fails to capture many patients with clinically significant somatization. In addition, the diagnosis of somatization disorder requires the assessment of the lifetime prevalence of 35 symptoms and a complex decision algorithm considered to be far too cumbersome, especially for so low a yield. On the other hand, undifferentiated somatoform disorder (and somatoform pain disorder, a minor variation) requires the presence of only one unexplained symptom and was therefore felt to be too inclusive. Escobar's abridged somatization disorder was closer to the kind of diagnosis felt to be useful, but it too required assessment of lifetime prevalence of many symptoms and had different diagnostic criteria for males and females (Escobar et al., 1987). It was decided to use "multisomatoform disorder" despite the fact that it is not an official *DSM* diagnosis. A diagnosis of multisomatoform disorder is made when three or more current symptoms whose presence or severity is not explained by organic disease are associated with disability and a pattern of unexplained symptoms for 2 or more years. This diagnosis has the advantages of not requiring the assessment of lifetime incidence of symptoms from a lengthy list, identical criteria for male and female patients, and the likelihood of identifying the group of patients whose health-related quality of life and medical care is influenced by somatoform symptoms (Kroenke et al., 1997).

Somatoform pain disorder and somatoform disorder NOS were included in the original version of the PRIME–MD to assess the prevalence and impact of lower levels of somatization. Hypochondriasis as a distinct preoccupation with specific diseases whose absence cannot be accepted by the patient despite adequate testing and evidence was also included. Because their prevalence was low, hypochondriasis and somatoform pain disorder are not included in the current version of the PRIME–MD.

Eating Disorders. Recent studies have indicated that eating disorders are common in the general population. Primary care providers have an important role to play in detecting and managing these conditions (National Institute of Mental Health, 1993; Spitzer et al., 1993). PRIME–MD includes the diagnoses of binge eating disorder (not a *DSM* diagnosis), bulimia nervosa, and eating disorder, NOS.

Patient Self-Report Forms of the PRIME–MD

The Patient Problem Questionnaire (PPQ): A Self-Administered Version of the PRIME–MD. The PRIME–MD was designed to be a cost-efficient method of diagnosing mental disorders, and in most respects it meets that objective admirably. However, the quest for greater efficiency in the primary care setting has become relentless in the current health care marketplace. Although the 8.5 min per patient required on average to administer the PRIME–MD does not seem like a lot of time to invest in the detection and diagnosis of mental disorders, it represents one half to one third of the time typically allocated for the routine primary care encounter in internal medicine. It is also the case that half of the CEG interviews performed will not be rewarded with a diagnosis. Furthermore, administering the PRIME–MD is just the beginning of a process that includes evaluation, treatment planning, and patient education, all of which also take time. The use of midlevel providers to administer the PRIME–MD on behalf of the primary physician as described later is one strategy for enhancing the efficiency of the PRIME–MD. Another strategy is to administer not only the PQ screen but the CEG itself as a patient self-report. A newly developed Patient Problem Questionnaire, or PPQ, has been designed to do just that (Spitzer, Williams, & Kroenke, 1997).

The PPQ is three pages long and contains questions similar to those found in the CEG. To simplify administration, several mood and anxiety disorders have been combined into single categories. Dysthymia, major depression in partial remission or recurrence, and minor depression have been combined into "other depression." Generalized anxiety disorder and anxiety not otherwise specified are combined into a single category, "other anxiety disorder." Because the PPQ relies on self-report, diagnoses must be confirmed by the physician. However, instead of taking an average of 8.5 min of physician time to take an inventory of symptoms, the PPQ enables the physician to accomplish the symptom-focused part of the interview much more rapidly, allowing more time for patient-centered evaluation and treatment intervention. Base rates of diagnoses obtained using the PPQ in preliminary evaluations are similar to those obtained using the PRIME–MD (Spitzer et al., 1997). In addition, the PPQ provides for a graded symptom severity reporting rather than simple yes–no responses.

Computer-Administered Telephone PRIME–MD. Kobak and his colleagues developed a version of the PRIME–MD that uses interactive voice response (IVR) technology to administer a computerized version of the PRIME–MD by telephone (Kobak et al., 1997). In their validation study, a convenience sample of 200 subjects selected to ensure high prevalence of PRIME–MD disorders was interviewed by a computer-driven system that enables patients to record their responses to questions using a touch-tone phone. The IVR–PRIME–MD uses the same branching structure as the PRIME–MD, but includes questions for social phobia and obsessive-compulsive disorder, and excludes the somatoform module.

The operating characteristics and the validity of the IVR–PRIME–MD were compared to the PRIME–MD administered by a primary care physician during a clinical encounter, and to the SCID administered by a trained mental health practitioner during a phone interview. Using the SCID as the diagnostic standard, the IVR–PRIME–MD demonstrated high specificity (79%), sensitivity (88%), and overall accuracy ($\kappa = .66$) for the presence of any diagnosis. These operating characteristics were comparable to those of the PRIME–MD administered face to face by a trained primary care clinician (83%, 88%, and .70, respectively). The IVR–PRIME–MD diagnosed more alcohol abuse and obsessive-compulsive disorder, but yielded lower rates of panic disorder than did the clinician-administered PRIME–MD. Comparative data on patient and physician acceptance and satisfaction with the three different procedures were not reported.

VALIDATION: THE PRIME–MD 1000 STUDY

The PRIME–MD 1000 Study was designed to test the utility and validity of the PRIME–MD by answering the following questions:
As to criterion validity:

1. Are the frequencies of mental disorders found by PRIME–MD comparable to those observed in other primary care samples using structured but much lon-

ger diagnostic interview schedules administered by mental health professionals?

2. Do diagnoses made by primary care providers using PRIME–MD agree with
   those made independently by mental health professionals?

Regarding convergent validity:

1. Do patients with PRIME–MD mental disorders have significant functional impairment and greater health care utilization compared with patients without
   PRIME–MD diagnoses?
2. Is there a substantial relation between physician-generated PRIME–MD diagnoses of mood, anxiety, and somatoform disorders and the patient scores on
   corresponding self-rated symptom severity scales?

And with regard to utility:

1. What is the average amount of time required by the primary care provider to
   complete the PRIME–MD evaluation?
2. Does the use of PRIME–MD increase recognition of mental disorders by primary care providers?
3. Do primary care providers find the information obtained with the PRIME–MD
   of value in understanding and treating their patients, and does this affect their
   treatment?
4. Are patients comfortable having their primary care providers ask them questions about psychological symptoms, and do they believe their answers will be
   helpful to their physicians in understanding and treating their problems?

Methods

Sites and Selection of Subjects.   The study was conducted at the four primary care
sites shown in Table 6.2. To ensure accurate estimates of true prevalence for the rarer of
PRIME–MD diagnoses whose frequencies were approximately 4% during the development phase, a sample size of 1,000 subjects was enrolled in the study (this sample
size would allow the prevalence estimates to have a narrow 95% confidence interval of
±1%). From January 1992 to March 1993, 1,360 patients were approached in order to
obtain the desired sample size. Reasons for nonparticipation included: The patient had
already been evaluated with PRIME–MD during the developmental phase ($n = 109$),
did not desire to participate ($n = 89$), was unable to speak English ($n = 81$), was too ill or
frail ($n = 53$), or other reasons ($n = 28$). The first 369 patients were selected by convenience but independently of the participating physicians' suspecting or knowing that
a patient had any psychopathology. The remaining 631 patients were selected using
site-specific methods to avoid sampling bias (see Table 6.2). The convenience sample
did not differ significantly from the systematically sampled subjects in age, sex, ethnicity, education, functional status, or the frequency of PRIME–MD diagnoses.

A total of 31 primary care providers participated in the study (including four of
the authors). Their mean age was 40 years ($SD \pm 9.1$), 60% were male, and the average
number of years of practice since residency was 10 ($SD \pm 9.5$). Physicians at three of
the sites (76% of the 31 physicians) were trained in internal medicine. The remaining
physicians, all at the University of South Alabama, were trained in family medicine.

TABLE 6.2
PRIME–MD 1000 Study Sites

Site (N)	Description	Sampling Method[a]
New England Medical Center General Medical Associates, Boston (228)	Hospital-based group practice	All patients during a selected clinic session
Jacobi Medical Center/Albert Einstein College of Medicine (formerly Bronx Municipal Hospital Center), Bronx, New York (293)	City Hospital clinic	Every third patient until physician's quota reached
Walter Reed Army Medical Center General Medicine Clinic, Bethesda, Maryland (303)	Clinic for both active-duty and retired military personnel and their families	Consecutive patients during a clinic session until physician's quota reached
University of Alabama College of Medicine, Mobile, Alabama (176)	Family practice clinic	Two consecutive patients per session, the first one chosen at random from among the first five patients

[a]First 369 subjects sampled by convenience; remaining 631 using method indicated to avoid sampling bias.

All physicians participated in a 1- to 3-hr training session on the use of PRIME–MD led by one of the authors.

Data Collection.   Prior to the clinical encounter, patients completed the PQ as well as measures of symptom severity, functional status, and utilization of health care services (see Tale 6.3). Physicians received the PQ at the beginning of the visit and examined it during the visit at a time of their choice. They administered any CEG modules triggered by positive responses. Before examining the PQ, physicians indicated whether they believed the patient to be currently suffering from a mood, anxiety, alcohol abuse/dependence, eating, or somatoform disorder based on their prior knowledge of and interaction with the patient up to that point.

After completing any CEG modules to be administered, physicians indicated which of eight physical illnesses (plus a write-in "other") the patient had, their assessment of the value of the PRIME–MD, and the time they began and ended the PRIME–MD assessment. After one third of the patients were entered, the 10-item Difficult Doctor Patient Relationship Questionnaire (DDPRQ–10) was added to the protocol and completed after the PRIME–MD CEG. The DDPRQ–10 evaluates the physician's subjective response to the patient and the process of care, assessing the extent to which the patient is experienced as "difficult" by the provider (Hahn et al., 1994). Midway through the study, two items assessing current and planned treatment with psychotropic medications and referral were added.

Approximately 8% of the items on the patient validation study questionnaires and 3% of the CEG nondiagnostic items were not completed. For each SF–20 scale and for the three symptom severity scales, total scores were estimated if information was available for more than 60% of the scale items. After these estimates, results remained missing on 7% to 12% of subjects for different scales.

To assess whether primary care providers using PRIME–MD make diagnoses that conform to *DSM–III–R* criteria, a telephone interview was conducted at three of the four study sites within 48 hr of the PRIME–MD visit. Telephone assessments were performed by a PhD clinical psychologist or senior psychiatric social worker who

TABLE 6.3
Data Collected in the PRIME–MD 1000 Study

Instrument/Item	Description (Ref.)
Patient Completed	
PRIME–MD Patient Questionnaire (PQ)	27-Item[a] case-finding/screening self-report for mood, anxiety, alcohol, eating and somatoform disorders
Medical Outcomes Study Short-Form General Health Survey (SF–20)	20-Item health-related quality of life on six dimensions rated 0 to 100; 100 = best health (Stewart, Hays, & Ware, 1988)
Zung Depression Scale	20-Item self-report depression screen (Zung, 1965)
Zung Anxiety Scale	20-Item self-report anxiety screen (Zung, 1971)
Somatic Symptom Inventory	20-Item self-report somatoform symptom assessment (Wyshak, Barsky, & Klerman, 1991)
Health care utilization	3-Item self-report: 2 on number of recent visits, 1 on satisfaction with care during last 3 months
Disability days	Number of days in last 3 months
Physician Completed	
PRIME–MD Clinician Evaluation Guide (CEG)	Modular structured interview for diagnosis of mood, anxiety, alcohol, eating and somatoform disorders
Familiarity with patient	1 Item: "not at all," "somewhat," and "fairly well"
Knowledge of patient's mental disorders before PRIME–MD	5-Item yes/no assessment of the presence of mood, anxiety, alcohol, eating and somatoform disorders, *completed prior to examining PQ*
Time for the PRIME–MD	Time required to examine PQ and complete CEG
Comorbid physical disorders	9-Item yes/no assessment of hypertension, arthritis, cancer, and heart, diabetes, liver, renal, pulmonary, and "other" diseases.
Perceived value of PRIME–MD	1-Item, 5-point Likert (1 = not at all valuable to 5 = very valuable)
Treatment, current and planned	Added midway through the study
Difficult Doctor–Patient Relationship Questionnaire–10	10-Item self-report assessing physician's subjective response to patient and process of providing care; administered to last 627 subjects (Hahn et al., 1994)
Self-assessed interest and training in psychiatric diagnosis	2 Self-report Likert items (collected once for each participating physician).
Mental Health Professional Telephone Interview	Telephone interview at 3 of the 4 study sites within 48 hr of PRIME–MD; initiated midway through study, completed by 431 of the 539 eligible
Repeat of PRIME–MD CEG mood, anxiety, alcohol, and eating disorders modules	Modular structured interview for diagnosis of mood, anxiety, alcohol, and eating disorders; somatoform module eliminated from phone assessment because data on physical illness unavailable to phone interviewer
SCID open-ended probes	Open-ended questions assessing functioning, mood, psychosocial stressors; ambiguous responses systematically explored (Spitzer et al., 1992)
Patient's comfort with and perceived value of the CEG	2 Items, administered to patients who were asked questions from the CEG by their provider

[a]The version of PRIME–MD PQ used in the validation study had 26 symptom-related items and 1 self-report assessment of general health; the current version of the PRIME–MD PQ contains 25 symptom items and 1 general health item.

were unaware of the results of the PRIME–MD evaluation, using a semistructured interview that included the CEG questions and several open-ended questions about overall functioning, mood, recent stressors, and problems with work or family. The open-ended questions, taken from the SCID (Spitzer et al., 1992), were used to screen and probe for psychopathology that might not otherwise be elicited, and as in the standard administration of the SCID, interviewers were specifically instructed to explore ambiguous responses. Somatoform diagnoses were not assessed because the interviewer did not have access to information regarding possible physical illness as a cause of physical symptoms. Because the mental health practitioners had special training in evaluating psychopathology, and the interview, compared with the CEG, was more like a psychiatric clinical interview, the mental health practitioner assessment can be regarded as a diagnostic criterion standard for assessing the validity of the primary care providers' PRIME–MD diagnoses. The mental health practitioner telephone interview initiated midway through study was completed by 431 of the 539 eligible subjects. Nonparticipation in the telephone reinterview was due to failure to reach the subject within 48 hr ($n = 44, 8\%$), not providing informed consent for a reinterview ($n = 29, 5\%$), too ill, hard of hearing or other communication problem ($n = 20, 4\%$), and no phone ($n = 15, 3\%$).

Results

Description of Patients. Patients in the PRIME–MD 1000 Study ranged in age from 18 to 91, with a mean age of 55 ($SD \pm 16.5$ years). The mean age range across the four sites was 43 to 64 years. Sixty percent were female (site range 50%–73% female); 58% were white (site range 30% to 75% white); 28% were college graduates (site range 4%–45% college graduates); and 77% were established clinic patients, the remainder were being seen for the first time. The most common types of physical disorders were hypertension (48%), arthritis (23%), diabetes (17%), heart disease (15%), and pulmonary disease (8%).

Prevalence of PRIME–MD Diagnoses. The prevalence rates for patients in four broad categories of severity were: (a) 19% for those who had so few symptoms on the PQ that no CEG module was triggered (symptom screen-negative), (b) 42% for patients who had symptoms but who did not meet criteria for any diagnoses, (c) 13% for those who met criteria for a mild or "subthreshold" mental disorder, and (d) 26% for patients who met criteria for a *DSM–III–R* diagnosis. The prevalence of the 18 specific diagnoses assessed in the PRIME–MD 1000 Study are displayed in Table 6.1. Most subjects with psychopathology had multiple disorders: Of the 386 patients with a disorder, 56% had more than one, and 29% had three or more.

Agreement With Mental Health Practitioner Diagnoses. Agreement between diagnoses made by primary care physicians using the PRIME–MD and mental health practitioners using the telephone interview protocol was generally good. Analysis of specific disorders and categories of disorders that were made at least 10 times by either group (regardless of agreement) are presented in Table 6.4. Sensitivity (the proportion of patients given a diagnosis by the mental health practitioner correctly identified by the primary care provider) was very good for any psychiatric diagnosis and at least satisfactory for the diagnostic modules. Sensitivity ranged from poor in subthreshold diagnoses to very good for more severe disorders. Specificity (the proportion of patients found to be free of the diagnosis by the mental health practitioner that were also noted to be disease free for that diagnosis by the primary care provider) was excellent for all diagnostic modules and for specific diagnoses, indicating a low frequency of false-positive diagnoses by primary care providers using PRIME–MD. Overall accuracy rates across modules and specific categories were generally excellent. The κ (kappa) coefficient for chance corrected agreement was good for any diagnosis (.71), and satisfactory to good for specific modules; κ values for both major depressive and panic disorders also were good (.61 and .60).

TABLE 6.4

Indexes of Agreement Between PRIME-MD Diagnoses Made by Primary Care Physicians (PCPs) and Mental Health Professionals (MHPs) and Their Prevalence ($n = 431$)

Diagnosis	Sensitivity (%)	Specificity (%)	Positive Predictive Value (%)	Overall Accuracy Rate (%)	κ	Prevalence (%) PCP	Prevalence (%) MHP
Any psychiatric diagnosis	83	88	80	86	0.71	37	36
Any mood disorder	67	92	78	84	0.61	26	30
Major depressive disorder	57	98	80	92	0.61	10	14
Partial remission or recurrence of major depressive disorder	26	96	41	89	0.26	6	10
Dysthymia	51	96	56	92	0.49	8	9
Minor depressive disorder	22	94	19	89	0.15	7	6
Any anxiety disorder	69	90	60	86	0.55	21	19
Panic disorder	57	99	68	96	0.60	4	5
Generalized anxiety disorder	57	97	55	94	0.52	7	7
Anxiety disorder not otherwise specified	33	91	31	84	0.23	12	11
Probable alcohol abuse/dependence	81	98	65	98	0.71	5	4
Any eating disorder	73	99	80	98	0.73	5	5

Note. From Spitzer et al. (1994). Utility of a new procedure for diagnosing mental disorders in primary care: The PRIME-MD 1000 Study. *Journal of the American Medical Association, 272,* p. 1753. Copyright © 1994. Reprinted with permission.

Operating Characteristics of the PQ.   Although clinicians are explicitly instructed to follow their own clinical impressions in choosing to administer a CEG module even if the PQ screen item(s) are negative, the overall sensitivity of the PRIME–MD procedure will be limited by the sensitivity of the PQ. Similarly, the efficiency of the PRIME–MD will be determined to a great extent by the specificity of the PQ. The operating characteristics of the PQ are reported in Table 6.5 using both the PRIME–MD result obtained by the primary care provider and the mental health practitioner evaluation as criteria. Sensitivity (using the mental health practitioner's diagnoses) was good to excellent for the anxiety, eating, and alcohol modules. The sensitivity of the two PQ depression items for major depression was 86%, identical to that of the 20-item Zung Self-rating Depression Scale (using the cutoff score of 50 on the Zung in the same sample; Magruder-Habib, Zung, & Feussner, 1990). Specificity for major depressive disorder was also virtually identical to the 20-item Zung (75% for the two-item PQ, and 74% for the Zung). Specificity was particularly good for mood, alcohol, and eating modules using either the mental health practitioner or primary care PRIME–MD diagnoses as the criterion standard. The PQ anxiety and somatoform disorders screens were the least specific, and thus the least efficient.

Symptom Severity and PRIME–MD Diagnoses.   The correlation between PRIME–MD diagnoses and symptom severity as measured by symptom checklists was examined to assess convergent validity. Partial correlations between scores on the Zung Self-rating Depression Scale (Zung, 1965) and any PRIME–MD mood disorders was 0.58; between the Zung Anxiety Scale (Zung, 1971) and any anxiety disorder, 0.53; and between the Somatic Symptom Inventory (Wyshak, Barsky, & Klerman, 1991) and any somatoform disorder, 0.44.

Health-Related Quality of Life.   Mental disorders are associated with functional impairment and increased health care utilization. Evaluation of these health-related outcomes was therefore performed using the Medical Outcomes Study Short Form–20 (SF–20) (Stewart, Hays, & Ware, 1988) as an additional assessment of construct or convergent validity of PRIME–MD diagnoses. Results of the SF–20 confirm that health-related quality of life (HRQL) is impaired proportionally to the severity of psychopathology diagnosed on the PRIME–MD (Spitzer et al., 1994, 1995). Figure 6.3 shows the means of the six SF–20 scales, grouped by severity of psychopathology into four groups: patients who were symptom screen-negative, patients who had symptoms but no diagnosed disorder, patients with a subthreshold diagnosis, and patients with a threshold mental disorder. The mean SF–20 scores have been adjusted for number of physical disorders, gender, age, minority status, educational level, and study site. Group main effects for severity of pathology were all significant ($p < .001$), and all paired comparisons among the four groups were significant at p less than .05 with the exception of differences between symptom screen-negative patients and those with symptoms but no diagnosis on the role and social functioning scales.

The four groups of patients already described were kept from their usual activities because of not feeling well for 2.2, 3.2, 4.3, and 11.0 days, respectively. Overall group effect as well as pairwise differences between those with threshold diagnoses and each of the other three groups were all significant at p less than .001 (values adjusted for number of physical disorders, gender, age, minority status, educational level, and study site).

In order to isolate the unique contribution of each disorder or class of disorders, the decrements in individual SF–20 scales were adjusted for the effects of demo-

TABLE 6.5
Operating Characteristics of the Patient Questionnaire (PQ)

PQ Screen-Positive Module	Number[a]	Criterion Standard: Diagnoses by Primary Care Physician (N = 1000)				Criterion Standard: Diagnoses by Mental Health Professional (N = 431)			
		Sensitivity (%)[b]	Specificity (%)	Positive Predictive Value (%)	Overall Accuracy Rate (%)	Sensitivity (%)	Specificity (%)	Positive Predictive Value (%)	Overall Accuracy Rate (%)
Any module	805	100	32	48	58	92	48	50	64
Mood	325	100	91	80	94	69	82	62	78
Anxiety	486	100	63	37	59	94	53	31	60
Alcohol	124	100	92	41	93	81	91	27	91
Eating	139	100	89	23	89	86	88	28	88
Somatoform	681	100	37	20	46	–	–	–	–

Note. From Spitzer et al. (1994). Utility of a new procedure for diagnosing mental disorders in primary care: The PRIME-MD 1000 Study. *Journal of the American Medical Association, 272,* p. 1953. Copyright © 1994. Reprinted with permission.

[a]Number of subjects from the total sample of 1,000 who screened positive for that module.

[b]Sensitivity is 100% because a primary care physician module diagnosis was made only when the PQ was screen-positive for that module.

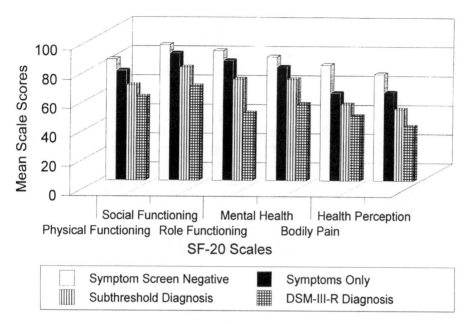

FIG. 6.3.   Relationship of PRIME–MD results to functional status. All paired comparisons between the four groups were significant at p less than .05, using Bonferroni's correction for type I errors, with the exceptions of the differences between the symptom screen-negative patients and patients with symptom screen-positive but no psychiatric diagnoses on the role and social functioning scales (both $p < .10$). SF–20 indicates Short-Form General Health Survey. From Spitzer et al. (1994). Utility of a new procedure for diagnosing mental disorders in primary care: The PRIME–MD 1000 Study. *Journal of the American Medical Association, 272,* p. 1754. Copyright © 1994. Reprinted with permission.

graphic characteristics and the presence or absence of other mental and physical disorders by multiple regression analysis (Spitzer et al., 1995). To permit comparisons across all six scales, results were expressed as an effect size (difference between those with and without the disorder on each scale divided by the standard deviation of the scale in the total sample). The PRIME–MD 1000 Study confirmed the results of previous studies that mood disorders are associated with substantial impairment in HRQL that exceeds that associated with nearly all physical disorders across all domains of HRQL, including pain and physical functioning. The PRIME–MD 1000 Study also established that significant and unique patterns of functional impairment are associated with other mental disorders. In contrast to mood disorders producing impairment in all dimensions of HRQL, anxiety disorders were found to be associated specifically with impaired social functioning and mental health. Somatoform disorders have a profound effect on role functioning, bodily pain, and general perception of health, but no impairment in mental health. (Somatizers reported insignificantly *better* mental health functioning than did patients with no mental disorder. This finding is both interesting and consistent with the theory that somatizing patients experience psychological distress as physical symptoms.)

It is important for primary care providers to appreciate, as an incentive for improving the detection and treatment of mental disorders in their practices, that much of the suffering borne by their patients is secondary to mental disorders rather than the physical conditions that all too often are exclusively the focus of physician attention. Mental disorders accounted for a substantially larger percentage of the variance in all domains of HRQL, including physical functioning and bodily pain, than did all of patients' physical disorders combined. Results from the PRIME–MD 1000 Study demonstrated that even minor mental disorders such as minor depression, anxiety disorder NOS, and somatoform disorder NOS are associated with significant impairment.

Utilization of Health Care Services. Observed differences in self-reported health care utilization between the four groups of patients distinguished by the presence and severity of PRIME–MD diagnosed mental disorders conform to the expected positive correlation between psychopathology and utilization. Figure 6.4 shows self-reported visits to physicians and the emergency department during the previous 3 months. The group main effect was significant both for number of visits to the physician ($p < .005$) and for visits to the emergency room ($p < .001$). Pairwise differences between those with threshold disorders and all three other groups were also significant with the exception of the difference in physician visits between those with threshold and those with only subthreshold diagnoses.

Time, Perceived Value, and Acceptability of PRIME–MD. The PRIME–MD CEG took an average of 8.4 min, and less than 20 min in 95% of cases. In patients without a PRIME–MD diagnosis the CEG required an average of 5.6 min, and 95% of those cases required less than 11 min. The PRIME–MD procedure took an average of 11.4 min for those with a PRIME–MD diagnosis, and less than 24 min in 95% of cases. As expected, the PRIME–MD CEG took longer to administer in patients who had more mental disorders.

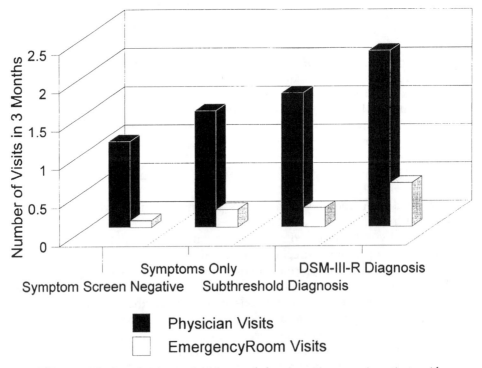

FIG. 6.4. Number of visits to physicians and the emergency room in patients with *DSM–III–R* mental disorders, subthreshold mental disorders, positive Patient Questionnaire (PQ) results but no mental disorder, and negative PQ results.

After administering the CEG, physicians rated the value of the PRIME–MD using a 5-point Likert scale to respond to the following question: "Considering the time that you spent doing the CEG, how valuable was the information that you obtained in helping you understand and treat this patient?" Physicians found the PRIME–MD to be somewhat or very helpful for 61% of patients given the CEG, and for 83% of those who met criteria for a PRIME–MD diagnosis. Surprisingly, the PRIME–MD was perceived to be more valuable the longer it took to administer (partial $r = .36$, controlling for number of physical disorders, gender, age, minority status, educational level, and study site), undoubtedly due to the fact that longer interviews produced more diagnoses. Of equal interest is the observation that physicians found the PRIME–MD to be just as valuable in evaluating patients whose psychopathology had already been suspected as in diagnosing previously unknown cases. These results suggest that use of the PRIME–MD enhanced diagnostic clarity or certainty even when patients had recognized psychiatric caseness, supporting the contention that a procedure resulting in a diagnosis will be more valuable than one limited to case-finding as its endpoint. It was rare for physicians to find that the PRIME–MD was of no value; they did so for only 7% of patients administered the CEG and only 1% of patients who received a PRIME–MD diagnosis.

During the mental health specialist telephone interview, those patients who had been asked questions from the CEG during their PRIME–MD assessment were asked how comfortable they were answering those questions. Almost all (96% of the 252) were "very" or "somewhat" comfortable. Almost all (90%) also said that they believed that the CEG questions were "very" or "somewhat" valuable in helping their physicians better understand or treat the problems they had been having.

Detection of Mental Disorders.   Despite the high self-assessed interest in psychiatric diagnosis reported by the study physicians, previously undetected psychiatric cases were diagnosed in approximately one half (48%) of the 287 patients with mental disorders who were previously known to their physicians. In about a third of patients who had been recognized as psychiatric cases, the PRIME–MD result indicated a category of disorder that differed from the physicians' pre-PRIME–MD assessment. Administration of PRIME–MD generated plans for new treatments in 60 of the 105 with mental disorders who were currently receiving no treatment. Planned treatments were as common in previously detected as they were in newly diagnosed patients.

Conclusions of the PRIME–MD 1000 Study

The validity and utility of the PRIME–MD are supported by the results of the PRIME–MD 1000 Study. The prevalence of threshold mental disorders diagnosed by the PRIME–MD are similar to those found in previous studies that used longer structured interviews administered by mental health providers (Barrett, Barrett, Oxman, & Gerber, 1988; Katon & Schulberg, 1992; Schulberg & Burns, 1988; Von Korff et al., 1987). The agreement between PRIME–MD diagnoses made by primary care providers and those made by the mental health provider during the blinded telephone interview approaches that observed among mental health practitioners using diagnostic interview schedules (Andreasen, Flaum, & Arndt, 1992; Williams et al., 1992). The high specificities observed across CEG modules indicates that physicians using the PRIME–MD seldom made false positive diagnoses. Although PRIME–MD sensitivity is modest for some disorders compared to mental health practitioners using a longer interview, it is double what the physicians themselves achieve when unaided by the PRIME–MD procedure. The sensitivity of primary care physicians using PRIME–MD is also better than that achieved by lay interviewers using a longer structured diagnostic interview in a study that evaluated that approach compared to psychiatrists as the standard (Helzer et al., 1985). The observed level of agreement between primary care provider PRIME–MD and mental health practitioner diagnoses was achieved despite the difficulties inherent in the diagnosis of the relatively mild cases of psychopathology encountered in the primary care setting (Robins, 1985). Measures of psychiatric symptoms, health-related quality of life, satisfaction with care, and utilization of health care services all demonstrated the adverse effect of psychopathology on these health-related outcomes, strongly supporting the convergent validity of PRIME–MD diagnoses.

The component of the PRIME–MD for which the best comparative data exist, the PQ depression screen, measures up extremely well against other screening approaches. Using the PRIME–MD 1000 Study database, the two-item PQ depression screen had essentially the same sensitivity and specificity as the 20-item Zung Self-Rating Depression Scale. In a meta-analysis comparing nine depression case-finding instruments, the two-item PQ depression screen compared favorably to its much longer predecessors (Mulrow et al., 1995). Whooley et al. conducted a head-to-head comparison of the two-item PRIME–MD PQ depression screen with six other depression case-finding instruments including the CES–D, the Beck Depression Inventory, and the SDDS–PC (Whooley, Avins, Miranda, & Browner, 1997). Their results indicated that the all of these instruments had comparable ROC curves (range 0.82–0.89), and the PRIME–MD PQ two-item depression screen had a sensitivity of 96%.

The relatively brief time required to administer the PRIME–MD and physicians' rating of its value in management support the conclusion that the PRIME–MD can be integrated into the time-pressured primary care environment in some settings. The multidiagnostic scope of the PRIME–MD is congruent with the demonstrated high levels of comorbidity found in patients with mental disorders in primary care, and provides information important in the evaluation and management of patients with multiple disorders. At the same time, the modular construction of the physician interview enhances efficiency by focusing the physician's attention on disorders that have a high probability of being present.

USE OF THE PRIME–MD FOR SCREENING BEHAVIORAL HEALTH DISORDERS

In every primary care encounter, patients and physicians must respond to multiple competing agendas. In 25% to 40% of patients, a mental disorder will be among those agendas, and in many of those instances the mental disorder will be the proximate cause of the most impairment of health-related quality of life. Nevertheless, addressing a patient's mental disorders will not always be the first priority among competing demands. Different patient agendas, the variety of clinical encounters, the history of the doctor–patient relationship, changes in life situation and comorbid medical problems, and the resources of the care environment all affect the way in which the PRIME–MD can and should be used. The following discussion addresses considerations in the application of the PRIME–MD.

Candidates for Evaluation With the PRIME–MD:
General Considerations

In Primary Care.   The recommendations of expert panels on case-finding, screening, and prevention in the primary care management of mental disorders can be taken as a point of reference for consideration of appropriate use of the PRIME–MD in clinical practice. The U.S. Preventive Services Task Force is perhaps the most influential of consensus groups, and has developed recommendations regarding mood disorders, alcohol abuse, and suicide risk. The Task Force has not recommended the routine screening of persons who are "asymptomatic" for mood disorder, but has encouraged case-finding through maintaining a high index of suspicion among patients with risk factors, which they list as "adolescents and young adults, persons with a family or personal history of depression, those with chronic illnesses, those who perceive or have experienced a recent loss, and those with sleep disorders, chronic pain, or multiple unexplained somatic complaints" (U.S. Preventive Services Task Force, 1996, pp. 544–545). The Agency for Health Care Policy and Research clinical practice guidelines for depression in primary care are more explicit in their recommendation to use case-finding self-report instruments, but also favor their administration to a subset of patients with risk factors (Depression Guideline Panel, 1993a, 1993b). The U.S. Preventive Services Task Force reached the conclusion that there was "insufficient evidence to conclude that routine depression screening is indicated in unselected patients, because it has not been shown that the early detection and treatment of depression in primary care leads to improved outcome when compared to routine diagnosis and treatment of this disorder when symptoms appear and are detected" (p. 543).

Although the PRIME–MD 1000 Study does not provide the direct outcome evidence that the Preventive Services Task Force requires to recommend universal case-finding, it does provide presumptive evidence that such a recommendation may be appropriate. Furthermore, the task force recommendations were based on the assumption that the first generation of long depression screening instruments rather than a two-item screen were the only methods available for case-finding. Indeed the task force, specifically citing the PRIME–MD as an example, advised that approaches such as that embodied in the PRIME–MD may change their assessment of the utility of "routine use of screening tools."

Another caveat that the task force applied to its own recommendations is the fact that the clinical action being considered is not, strictly speaking, "screening" because the disorders being searched for cannot be "asymptomatic." From this perspective, the PRIME–MD PQ is not so much a screening tool that detects asymptomatic patients as it is a procedure that corrects a deficiency in physicians' clinical practice. Although the risk factors mentioned in the task force recommendations should raise the providers' index of suspicion, the presence of a mood disorder in 26% and of some mental disorder in 39% of unselected patients suggests that the clinician's index of suspicion should already be raised to a level sufficient to trigger case-finding when the patient walks in the door. The cost benefit of such an approach seems justified by the operating characteristics and efficiency of the PRIME–MD Patient Questionnaire. It is hard to argue that physicians should not ask two questions to determine whether a patient is depressed or anhedonic if they do not already know. In the case of depression in particular, even without the added efficiency of self-administration featured by the PRIME–MD PQ, answers to the two PQ depression items can be ascertained faster and have better predictive power than an assessment of the risk factors that the Preventive Services Task Force and the AHCPR recommend be used to trigger case-finding.

These observations suggest that the PRIME–MD might play a useful role in the routine care of primary care patients. When the PRIME–MD is administered to an unselected group of primary care patients, 80% will trigger at least one module of the Clinician Evaluation Guide. In half of those evaluations, the physician will be rewarded by the confirmation of a mental disorder. Two-thirds of these disorders will meet criteria for a *DSM–IV* diagnosis, and the remaining third will have a minor or "subthreshold" disorder. If the physician is familiar with the patient, the yield of new diagnoses will still double the number of patients whose psychopathology is detected. Finally, there is strong evidence that even previously detected disorders will be more specifically and precisely identified.

The timing of administration of the PRIME–MD to established patients and readministration to previously screened patients should be guided by clinical judgement. In this regard, "risk factors" such as those identified by the Preventive Services Task Force should trigger use of the PRIME–MD. Other characteristics of patients that should prompt evaluation with the PRIME–MD are discussed later.

In Episodic Care. The investment of time required to administer the PRIME–MD, however brief, is nevertheless easier to justify in a long-term primary care relationship with the physician. The utility of the PRIME–MD in episodic care deserves separate consideration. In the episodic or "walk-in" encounter, patients may be seen by their own physician, someone other than their own physician, or they may not (yet) have a personal physician. Patients may be seen for relatively simple, administrative problems such as medication renewals, or for relatively straightforward medical problems, such as upper respiratory infections. Although PRIME–MD might still reveal undiagnosed mental disorders, its addition to an unscheduled episodic visit is usually not consistent with the time allocated for episodic visits. On the other hand, episodic visits are often the mode of presentation for the mental disorders that the PRIME–MD was designed to detect (Kroenke et al., 1990, 1994; Kroenke & Mangelsdorf, 1989). In these presentations, the PRIME–MD will facilitate greater understanding of the patient's true needs, and may lead to greater patient and physician satisfaction. In a recent study employing the PRIME–MD with 500 patients presenting for evaluation of a physical symptom, Jackson et al. demonstrated that use of the PRIME–MD coupled with a means to quickly identify symptom-related expectations decreased patients' unmet expectations and residual illness concerns, as well as physicians' experience of patients as difficult (Jackson, Chamberlin, & Kroenke, 1996).

In Medical Subspecialty Care. Every medical subspecialist frequently confronts one or more conditions that are recognized to be caused in part by or reactive to psychological factors. Pulmonologists treat asthmatics whose symptoms vary dramatically with current life stressors, as do symptoms in irritable bowel disease, various headache syndromes, low back pain, and other general medical disorders. In some cases, underlying organic disease treated by the subspecialist may be absent altogether despite the presence of highly suggestive symptoms. For example, the most common medical presentation of panic disorder in the primary care setting is chest pain, and panic disorder is one of the most common diagnoses eventually made in patients who undergo cardiac catheterization and are found to have normal coronary arteries (Beitman et al., 1989). Ideally, patients should have been evaluated for mental disorders by a primary care physician prior to referral. However, evaluation of psychopathology prior to referral for subspecialty care is currently not the rule for several reasons. In fee-for-service systems, patients often self-refer to specialists. In the primary care setting, 40% to 60% of mental disorders are undetected unless a procedure like the PRIME–MD is routinely employed. For these reasons it would be useful for subspecialists to incorporate the PRIME–MD into their evaluation of some of their patients, particularly those with unexplained symptoms.

Use in Consultation–Liaison Psychiatry. The PRIME–MD was designed for use by primary care providers and tested in the outpatient primary care setting. Its raison d'être was the documented insensitivity of unaided primary care providers to the mental disorders present in their patients. Presumably, liaison psychiatrists would not suffer from this deficit. However, the growing familiarity of primary care providers with the PRIME–MD and the PRIME–MD's capacity to make the diagnostic criteria of mental disorders explicit in an easy-to-understand format suggest that it could be used by mental health specialists consulting on medical patients as a method of communicating the results of the psychiatric evaluation. For similar reasons, behavioral health clinicians should consider using the PRIME–MD when working in multidisciplinary and liaison settings.

Who Should Administer the PRIME–MD?

The PRIME–MD was developed for and validated with primary care physicians. Experience with more extensive structured psychiatric interviews in the hands of trained lay interviewers has demonstrated adequate validity and reliability compared to mental health professionals. It is therefore reasonable to expect that, with the exception of the somatoform module which requires reaching conclusions regarding the relationship between symptoms and physical illness, nurses or midlevel providers such as nurse practitioners, physician assistants, and social workers could administer the PRIME–MD accurately on behalf of physician providers. Adoption of this strategy could result in a significant increase in the efficiency of the PRIME–MD for the primary provider because half of patients who are interviewed with the CEG do not have a PRIME–MD mental disorder. Instead of interviewing 80% of patients and achieving a diagnosis half the time, the midlevel provider would interview the 80% of patients who trigger at least one module of the CEG and report the results to the primary care physician. The primary care physician could then devote more time to reviewing the PRIME–MD results and evaluating and treating the diagnosed conditions and less time performing interviews that do not alter the course of treatment. Behavioral health clinicians, including psychologists and social workers, can also use the PRIME–MD when working in collaboration with primary care providers in the medical setting.

Candidates for Administration: Patient Characteristics

Among those characteristics that should raise the clinician's index of suspicion and trigger administration of the PRIME–MD, the three most strongly substantiated by the PRIME–MD 1000 Study were:

1. The presence of multiple unexplained physical symptoms.

2. Functional impairment out of proportion to the patient's nonpsychiatric medical problems.
3. Physician-experienced difficulty in caring for the patient.

Physical Symptoms.   The PRIME–MD 1000 Study confirmed previous studies that have demonstrated that physical symptoms in medical patients are associated with mental disorders and frequently cannot be accounted for by medical diagnoses (Kroenke et al., 1994). Patients in the study endorsed a mean of four out of the 15 physical symptoms on the PRIME–MD PQ. Physicians determined that 16% to 33% of those symptoms were somatoform. The presence of any physical symptom more than doubled the likelihood of an anxiety or mood disorder, and somatoform symptoms had a particularly strong association with psychopathology. Figure 6.5 shows the dramatic increase in the prevalence of mood and anxiety disorders associated with increasing numbers of physical symptoms. These data strongly support the argument that any patient with multiple physical complaints or somatoform symptoms (i.e., symptoms that cannot be accounted for by physical disease) should be assessed for mental disorders.

Functional Impairment.   As previously discussed, the impairment in health-related quality of life produced by mental disorders is so substantial that functional impairment should trigger an evaluation for mental disorders in any patient who has not already been assessed. The PRIME–MD 1000 Study demonstrated that mental disorders produced more degradation of HRQL than did physical conditions, even in those patients who had significant physical disorders.

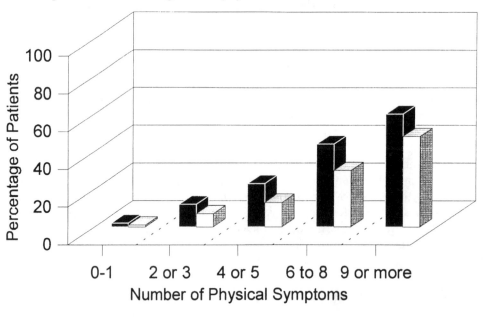

FIG. 6.5.   Relationship between the number of physical symptoms and the prevalence of mood and anxiety disorders.

Physician-Experienced Difficulty in the Doctor–Patient Relationship. One dramatically notable characteristic of patients that should trigger evaluation with the PRIME–MD is the physician's subjective experience of difficulty in caring for the patient. Variously referred to as difficult or frustrating patients, "heart-sink" patients (i.e., your heart sinks when you know you have to see them), or with even more pejorative terms such as "crock," these patients have long been thought to be difficult to care for in part because of the presence of mental disorders. The recent development of the Difficult Doctor Patient Relationship Questionnaire (DDPRQ), the 10-item version of which was used in the PRIME–MD 1000 Study, has for the first time enabled empirical study of patients who are experienced as difficult (Hahn et al., 1994, 1996). A subsequent chapter on the DDPRQ presents a detailed description of this instrument's development, use, and related findings from empirical studies (chap. 6).

Administration of Individual PRIME–MD Components

The PRIME–MD PQ. In standard practice, the PRIME–MD PQ is given to the patient to complete prior to seeing the physician. During the PRIME–MD 1000 Study, it was given to patients in the waiting room by clerical staff. It might also be mailed to the patient's home. Although the PQ requires minimal reading skills, a few patients will have difficulty due to problems with visual acuity or literacy. Patients have accepted having the PQ read to them, although the loss of confidentiality may influence response bias, particularly with the alcohol abuse section. The decision to give the patient the PRIME–MD PQ may be made by clerical staff following a protocol; for example, it may be automatically administered to all patients who are new to the office or provider, scheduled for periodic health maintenance, or making unscheduled visits with particular presenting complaints. Alternatively, the physician may decide to ask a patient to complete the PQ before seeing them because mental disorders are suspected, or for any of the range of problems associated with mental disorders (e.g., the patient seems dissatisfied or is experienced as difficult, has multiple physical symptoms, is a "high utilizer" of health care services, etc.).

Clinicians might also elect to administer the PQ orally to the patient during the visit. The PRIME–MD's modular design allows the physician to administer only those PQ items that seem relevant, although the high rates of undetected comorbid mental disorders from different categories of mental disorder should lead to caution about skipping sections of the PQ. In practice, when physicians are familiar with certain patients, they may already know whether the patient has multiple physical complaints. In fact, the presence of multiple physical symptoms should prompt administration of the nonsomatoform PQ items and subsequently triggered CEG modules. Therefore, it is common for physicians to administer the ten PQ items that address mood, anxiety, eating, and alcohol disorders during the clinical encounter. When the PQ is administered orally, the physician can move directly to the corresponding CEG module as soon as one mood, generalized anxiety, or alcohol item is endorsed because the remaining symptoms on the PQ in these sections are also addressed by the CEG. The eating disorders and panic disorder PQ sections already consist of only one item.

The PRIME–MD CEG. If patients have completed the PQ, they typically hand it to the physician at the beginning of the visit. A quick glance will inform the physician whether or not any modules have been triggered by the patient's responses. Even if

CEG modules have been triggered, the physician should nonetheless begin the encounter with an appropriate "patient-centered" assessment of the patient's concerns and negotiate an agenda for the visit (Cohen-Cole, 1991; Putnam & Lipkin, 1995; Smith & Hoppe, 1991). The decision as to when, or even whether, to administer the CEG should be made in the context of that negotiated agenda.

The PRIME–MD CEG provides the structure for a "physician-centered" or symptom-driven assessment of the patient's symptoms. The issues addressed by the PRIME–MD typically have great significance to the patient and the PRIME–MD interview often evokes strong emotional responses. It is important to address the patient's emotional response to the diagnoses and underlying psychosocial issues, and the proper method for doing so is a patient-centered interaction. Patient-centered interviewing is characterized by the use of open-ended questions that elicit the patient's emotional response as well as factual information (Cohen-Cole, 1991; Putnam & Lipkin, 1995; Smith & Hoppe, 1991). Open-ended questions are followed by "directive" questions that focus the patient's attention on more circumscribed areas while leaving decisions about how to discuss those areas primarily up to the patient. In the overall process of the medical encounter, closed-ended questions used in the PRIME–MD CEG would ideally be integrated in a patient-centered interview.

The physician should be sensitive to emotional reactions evidenced by the patient's tone of voice, facial expression, or additional comments made to elaborate on the yes/no responses that the CEG asks for. In such instances, the physician should acknowledge the patient's emotional responses and promise to return to them shortly, while suggesting that completion of a few more questions might lead to a better understanding of the patient's mood or anxiety disorder. This approach offers the advantage of allowing the physician to formulate therapeutic recommendations such as medication or referral for therapy based on specific diagnoses when talking to the patient about the life situations that underlie their emotional distress and mental disorders.

On the other hand, the physician may want to move to a patient-centered interviewing style as soon as an emotional response is evident, returning to the remaining PRIME–MD CEG items later to complete the assessment of the patient's mental disorders. The PRIME–MD item inquiring about suicidal ideation is so likely to evoke the kind of emotional distress that requires attention that the PRIME–MD itself employs a patient-centered "directive question" as a follow-up to a positive response.

The CEG modules should be administered in the order in which they are arranged in the PRIME–MD, that is, mood, anxiety, eating, alcohol, and finally somatoform. This sequence maximizes efficiency and allows symptoms secondary to mood and anxiety disorders to be identified prior to administering the somatoform module so that those symptoms are not also counted toward a somatoform diagnosis. When responding to CEG items it is important to ensure that the patient understands the duration and severity criteria that are the "frame" for each symptom. For example, symptoms of depression are counted toward a diagnosis only if they have been present nearly every day for at least 2 weeks. Within each module, the items are addressed sequentially until an instruction to skip to a subsequent item, or exit the module (and begin the next module triggered by the PQ) is encountered. The CEG indicates the diagnoses present as the criteria are met.

The PRIME–MD CEG alcohol abuse and dependence module requires the greatest skill in administration. Although the agreement between mental health practitioner interview and primary care provider assessment using the PRIME–MD was good for alcohol disorders (κ = 0.71), a recent study comparing a computer-driven, interactive voice recognition PRIME–MD interview administered by telephone demonstrated twice the prevalence of alcohol problems discovered by face-to-face interview with either the PRIME–MD administered by a primary care provider or the SCID administered by a mental health practitioner (Kobak et al., 1997; Spitzer et al., 1994). Detection of alcohol abuse in patients is complicated by the patient's desire to conceal a socially undesirable behavior, physicians' collusion in avoiding detection of a problem that is difficult to treat and evokes strong reaction in the caregiver, and the denial that is a cardinal feature of alcoholism (Clark, 1995; Moore et al., 1989; Ness & Ende, 1994).

Documentation. The final page of the PRIME–MD CEG package is a checklist of PRIME–MD diagnoses with ICD–9–CM codes that can be used as a summary of the diagnostic findings and placed in the chart. The summary sheet also includes the current procedural terminology (CPT) and evaluation management (EM) codes that can be used for visits during which the PRIME–MD has been administered. Alternatively, the entire PRIME–MD CEG and/or PQ can be placed in the patient's record.

Use With Other Evaluation Data

All of the diagnoses obtained by the PRIME–MD require further evaluation before treatment can be planned and initiated. Methods used to accomplish this evaluation can be structured or unstructured, but in actual practice the PRIME–MD has not commonly been followed by secondary structured protocols. The PRIME–MD has implicit indications for such evaluation in several places.

For example, if the mood module reveals suicidal ideation, the physician is directed to ask the open-ended question, "Tell me about it." Several approaches to the assessment of suicide risk based on demographic characteristics and the presence, lethality, and availability of a suicide plan have been described (Brody et al., 1995; Depression Guideline Panel, 1993a, 1993b). The presence of significant suicidal ideation or intent is generally considered to be an urgent indication for consultation with a mental health specialist. Although 75% of patients with an anxiety disorder and half of those with alcohol abuse have a comorbid mood disorder, and thus will be assessed for current suicidal ideation when the mood module is administered, patients with anxiety and alcohol-related disorders who did not trigger the mood module may also benefit from assessment for suicidal ideation.

Both the mood and anxiety modules direct the physician to assess whether disorders diagnosed in those modules are secondary to "physical disorder, medication, or other drug." The PRIME–MD does not provide guidance regarding specific evaluations to rule out a secondary disorder, but strategies for accomplishing this are well discussed in the medical literature. The essential task of the somatoform module is for the primary provider to "rule out" physical explanations for the presence or severity of the patient's symptoms. The PRIME–MD does not provide specific guidance for this task either, relying instead on the knowledge and expertise of physicians to accomplish this process.

One of the basic steps in the evaluation of patients with any one mental disorder is to determine whether other mental disorders are present. Because the PRIME–MD assesses the most common of mental disorders in primary care, this important step is intrinsic to the PRIME–MD. Assessment of mental status, psychosis, and drug abuse other than alcohol are not included in the PRIME–MD and should be addressed in any patient with a PRIME–MD diagnosis. Other mental disorders such as obsessive-compulsive disorder, posttraumatic stress disorder, and social phobia might also be considered in selected patients in whom suggestive symptoms are detected during the PRIME–MD evaluation.

One measure of the severity of mood disorders—the number of the nine symptoms of depression present—is intrinsic to the PRIME–MD. Severity of mood and other disorders should also be assessed in terms of associated functional impairment. The simplest classification scheme would characterize the disorder as *mild* if activities have become more difficult for the patient but are still being performed in an acceptable fashion. Patients with *moderate* disorders will have lost the ability to perform some important activities, whereas those with *severe* disorders will have substantial loss of functional capacity. Patients with mild disorders will rarely need to be hospitalized, those with moderate disorders may if their support system is not robust, and those with severe disorders will generally require hospitalization unless they have a very strong social support system. Although structured methods for assessing functional capacity exist, primary care clinicians generally perform an unstructured assessment. Self-administered HRQL instruments that can be computer-scored are available for use in outpatient settings (Parkerson, Broadhead, & Tse, 1995; Ware, 1993). Data obtained using structured assessments of patients' health-related quality of life can assist physicians in managing mental disorders, and they could be used to target the specific areas of deficit revealed on multidimensional HRQL instruments such as the SF–20 or SF–36 (Rubenstein et al., 1995).

Assessment of the patient's social system (i.e., family, job, friends, and other sources of support and causes of life stress) is an important component of the evaluation of patients with mental disorders. Primary care providers usually perform an unstructured assessment of these factors. There is a growing body of literature describing semistructured, efficient, and sophisticated methods of assessing the patient's social system and applying that perspective to primary care (Hahn, 1997).

Guidelines for Decision Making

As discussed in greater detail later in this chapter, one of the most significant accomplishments of the PRIME–MD, distinguishing it from the previous generation of case-finding tools, is its capacity to aid the physician in reaching the critical third step of the continuum of care: diagnosis. Because making a specific diagnosis is the point of departure for making decisions about treatment, this feature of the PRIME–MD is of paramount importance. Use of the PRIME–MD in a primary care setting will produce a dramatic increase in the need to make management decisions about mental disorders that is unique for two reasons: First, the decision makers, that is, primary care providers, have not been as extensively trained in the evaluation and management of mental disorders as have mental health specialists. Second, although the foundation for managing PRIME–MD-diagnosable conditions has been well established in general psychiatric patients, the spectrum of disease and symptom severity, comorbid organic pathology, use of medications for organic disease, and the personality (*DSM* Axis II) profiles of patients in primary care differ from those found in the psychiatric population, in which most of the evidence for treatment efficacy has been obtained. Recommendations for applying PRIME–MD results to management decisions are broadly based on standard psychiatric approaches to specific PRIME–MD diagnoses, tempered by these unique features of the primary care provider and patient.

Determining the Need for Behavioral Health Care Intervention. *DSM* diagnostic criteria for mental disorders are intended to identify conditions that cause clinically significant impairment. Although some *DSM* diagnoses may have poor or no treatment, many are amenable to some therapeutic intervention. On these grounds, any "threshold" PRIME–MD diagnosis should be considered for a behavioral health care intervention. The urgency, intensity, and type of intervention will depend on the severity of the condition, assessed as previously described. In comparison to psychiatric populations with similar diagnoses, the proportion of primary care patients whose symptom syndromes only meet the minimum criteria for a *DSM* diagnosis is larger. For example, in the PRIME–MD 1000 Study, roughly 40% of patients with major depressive disorder (MDD) had only five of the nine symptoms of depression present at the required intensity and duration, the minimum number need to make the diagnosis. An additional 20% of patients with MDD had six symptoms. Primary care patients may have less functional impairment than psychiatric patients with the same diagnoses and symptoms counts. Although the milder spectrum of disease intensity observed in primary care has implications for specific treatments, it does not obviate the need for some attention when diagnoses are made. In fact, data from the PRIME–MD 1000 Study demonstrated that even "subthreshold" diagnoses made with the PRIME–MD are associated with significant functional impairment, increased health care utilization, and decreased satisfaction with care. Whether or not specific behavioral health care interventions are available for a specific diagnosis, the presence of even the mildest PRIME–MD diagnosis has some impact on the patient, and should be acknowledged explicitly in the physician's communications with the patient.

Determining the Most Appropriate Intervention. Although guidelines for treating the mental disorders diagnosed by PRIME–MD are beyond the scope of this discussion, the factors influencing choice of intervention can be identified. The first question is: Who should be responsible for treatment decisions once mental disorder(s) are detected, the primary care provider or the mental health specialist? There is no single answer to this question, but rather it depends on the primary care provider's comfort with assessment and treatment; the availability of mental health resources in the community and reimbursement system; the specific mental disorder(s); and the severity of the patient's illness, comorbidities, and attitudes about seeing mental health specialists.

As discussed later, primary care providers currently demonstrate tremendous heterogeneity in the skills and knowledge required to diagnose and evaluate mental disorders, and a corresponding spectrum of comfort in doing so. Studies that have compared the outcome of usual care of depression in primary care with either care received in mental health settings or primary care enhanced by collaboration with mental health professionals or protocols for management of depression have consistently shown better outcomes for the more intensively treated patients (Katon et al., 1995, 1996; Schulberg et al., 1996, 1997; Schulberg, Katon, Simon, & Rush, 1998; Simon et al., 1996). Furthermore, the proven deficits in primary care providers' ability to detect mental disorders suggests that they may not always be adequately equipped to evaluate and treat psychopathology. Although these observations suggest a substantial need for improvement in primary care management, it does not follow that all patients with mental disorders should be referred to mental health professionals.

As a practical matter, the resources for evaluating all patients with mental disorders in the mental health setting are not available. In fact, managed care reimbursement systems effectively restrict access to mental health services with the assumption, founded or not, that primary care providers can and should treat a significant proportion of their patients with common mental disorders. To some extent our knowledge of physician performance is already outdated, and almost certainly fails to appreciate the potential of emerging educational, diagnostic, and therapeutic technologies: It is generally believed that the skills and knowledge of primary care providers have been steadily improving during the last 10 to 20 years as a result of the dissemination of behavioral sciences training in graduate medical and continuing medical education programs. The PRIME–MD itself facilitates the evaluation required to make decisions. Although the parameters have not been adequately delineated, there certainly exists a subset of patients who can be evaluated effectively by a subset of primary care providers, and treated for their conditions without referral to mental health specialists.

Still, many primary care patients with PRIME–MD-diagnosable mental disorders might benefit from care provided by a mental health specialist. Engagement in treatment with a mental health specialist will of necessity involve review of diagnostic conclusions and management decisions made by the primary care provider. For this reason, many primary care providers defer to a psychiatrist decisions about pharmacotherapy that they might otherwise make themselves when they anticipate an expeditious referral to a mental health setting that includes psychiatric evaluation and pharmacological treatment. Conversely, delay in effecting a referral, whether due to patient resistance or insufficient resources for rapid referral, will often necessitate initiating pharmacotherapy while awaiting mental health specialty services. One common pattern that has emerged, particularly in managed care settings, is allocating pharmacological decisions to the primary care physician while reserving referral to mental health professionals (often nonphysician) when psychotherapeutic intervention is required.

Although no single answer will suit all patients, physicians, or clinical settings, a truly integrated delivery system with both mental health and primary care services present as part of a unified health care team offers the considerable advantage of being able to flexibly adapt to the needs of the majority of participants. Such systems, developed and evaluated by Katon et al. (1995, 1997) among others, have shown demonstrably better care than those that retain a structural boundary between mental health and primary care services.

In addition to health care delivery systems issues such as the relative roles of primary care provider versus mental health specialists, a number of patient-specific factors are critical to determining appropriate treatment. These include:

1. Comorbid general medical conditions, and current medications.
2. Co-occurring mental disorders.
3. Patient attitudes toward treatment modalities.
4. The patient's social and family system.
5. Personality style and physician experienced difficulty in the doctor–patient relationship.

Comorbid physical illness is a critical factor in determining appropriate treatment for mental disorders. Included in the PRIME–MD decision tree is a step requiring the clinician to consider whether a symptom syndrome, such as major depression, is secondary to a medical disorder rather than a primary psychiatric disorder. For example, a medical disorder may occasionally be a biological cause of a depressive syndrome (e.g., hypothyroidism). More commonly, general medical disorders are a risk factor for a primary psychiatric diagnosis (e.g., major depression is nearly twice as likely in patients with a variety of types of cancer, cerebrovascular disorders, and cardiac disease). In either case, recognition and appropriate treatment of the comorbid physical condition is necessary to optimize treatment of the mental disorder. Finally, comorbid physical conditions may have a dramatic effect on the patient's vulnerability to adverse drug reactions and interactions, and therefore will influence the choice of medications.

As previously noted, it is common for patients with mental disorders to have more than one type of disorder. Treatment decisions must be based on the relative severity and primacy of the co-occurring conditions. When alcohol or other substance abuse is present, successful treatment of any other mental disorder usually requires treatment and control of the substance abuse problem. Medications should be chosen to treat as many of the co-occurring conditions as possible.

Patient preferences for treatment of mental disorders can vary widely. In rare instances, mental disorders interfere with patients' decisional capacity and justify depriving patients of their autonomy. In most circumstances, however, the patient's preferences regarding alternative treatments, or the use of any treatment at all, play a central role. For certain diagnoses there is good evidence that one modality of treatment is more effective than another, whereas in many situations different modalities are likely to have equal efficacy. For example, pharmacotherapy is more effective than psychotherapy alone in severe major depression whereas the two modalities have similar efficacy in mild and moderate depression (Depression Guideline Panel, 1993b; Gelenberg & Delgado, 1998). When no clear advantage has been demonstrated for one treatment over another, patients' preferences may play a major role in determining the choice of treatment. On the other hand, patients' preferences are often based on incomplete or inaccurate information, and intensely held because of the fear and anxiety generated either by misperceptions or inappropriate generalization from past experience. Therefore, although the patient's preferences must always be respected and understood, they need not be taken at face value, nor should the patient's initial responses be taken as final if the health care provider thinks it is in the patient's best interests to employ a different approach. Indeed, it is part of the art of caring for patients to develop a collaborative model of decision making. When a difference of opinion persists, clinicians should employ the kind of staged behavioral change approach described by Prochaska and DiClemente to help patients accept the need for intervention (Prochaska, DiClemente, & Norcross, 1992).

The patient's family and social system may also play an important role in decisions about treatment. Severe functional impairment may lower the threshold for mental health specialist intervention, medication, and hospitalization, as well as the urgency for intervention. However, the presence of a strong family or social support system may mitigate the urgency of treatment. Family members can play an important role in watching patients with suicidal ideation, ensuring adherence to medication and scheduled visits, and monitoring adequate self-care for patients who might otherwise require hospitalization. Patients with milder illness whose families can be organized to respond to their distress might be spared the need for medication or psychotherapy altogether. Finally, the family system's response to somatization is almost always critical in the management of somatoform disorders. Unfortunately, dysfunctional families and mental disorders frequently go hand in hand. Family problems can worsen the prognosis for disorders presenting in early or milder forms. Therefore, a family assessment that reveals significant dysfunction may justify more aggressive and intensive interventions.

Most of the mental disorders diagnosable by the PRIME–MD dramatically increase the difficulty clinicians experience in the doctor–patient relationship (Hahn et al., 1994, 1996). This difficulty in turn is associated with higher utilization of services, increased dissatisfaction with care, and greater impairment in health-related quality of life. In addition to the Axis I disorders diagnosable with the PRIME–MD, the presence of multiple physical symptoms and an abrasive personality style characterize the patient who is experienced as difficult. The presence of difficulty in the doctor patient relationship, discussed in greater detail in the chapter on the Difficult Doctor Patient Relationship Questionnaire, elsewhere in this volume, should trigger (a) an assessment of the three characteristics of difficult patients — Axis I disorders, somatization, and abrasive personality style — and (2) an introspective assessment of the physician's subjective emotional response and subsequent behavior toward the patient. The treatment for clinician-experienced difficulty lies more in the management of negative emotional experience than in the treatment of the patient per se.

Specific Treatment Recommendations

The management of the *mood disorders* diagnosable with the PRIME–MD has been well researched and discussed in a large and growing literature on the management of depression in the primary care setting. The majority of patients with diagnosable mood disorders encountered in primary care have milder forms of their disorder and are thus more suitable for treatment in the primary care setting. The introduction of new, effective, and safe medications for mood disorders has led to a dramatic increase in their use. Major depressive disorder is clearly one indication for the use of antidepressant medication, although psychotherapy may be as effective in patients with mild to moderate major depression. Additional benefit has been demonstrated from the use of psychotherapy, specifically cognitive and interpersonal psychotherapy, in combination with medication. Dysthymic disorder may also respond to antidepressant medication. A history of past mania, a family history of mania, or the presence of manic symptoms should lead to consideration of bipolar disorder, which may require not only mood-stabilizing medication but also psychiatric referral or consultation for this more complicated diagnosis.

Patients with major depressive disorder in partial remission or recurrence should be treated as though they have current major depression in order to achieve a complete remission or prevent further deterioration of their mood disorder. It is therefore important to distinguish depression in partial remission or recurrence from minor depression. Although the number of current symptoms of depression may be the same, the functional impairment associated with partial remission or recurrence of major depression is substantially greater than that of minor depression, and the prognosis if untreated is poorer.

The choice of initial medication should take into consideration a variety of factors including common side effects and past experience with antidepressants. Selective serotonin reuptake inhibitors (SSRIs) and tricyclics seem to be equally efficacious when taken in adequate doses, but the former appear to be better tolerated, and therapeutic doses more easily achieved. The conventional wisdom suggesting that sedating anti-depressants be used for patients with prominent insomnia has been challenged by the observation that insomnia generally responds concurrently with the other symptoms of depression when successfully treated with nonsedating medications. Therefore, a more reasonable approach to insomnia in the depressed patient is to treat with an ad-junctive hypnotic until the antidepressant relieves the insomnia along with the other symptoms of depression, rather than commit a patient to 9–12 months of medica-tion-induced sedation for a symptom that often resolves in 4–6 weeks.

The goal in treatment of depression should be complete remission of symptoms. Response to antidepressant medication will usually require 2 to 3 weeks, and the maximal effect of an antidepressant may not be achieved for 6 to 8 weeks (Depression Guideline Panel, 1993b; Gelenberg & Delgado, 1998). In the treatment of major de-pression, medication should be maintained at the dose required to produce remis-sion for a minimum of 4–5 months after complete remission of symptoms is achieved. Treatment should be more prolonged if remission of symptoms has been difficult to achieve or unstable. Although clinical trials have not confirmed the practice, it is rec-ommended that patients with recurrent episodes of major depression be treated with full-dose antidepressant medication to prevent recurrence for a duration of two or more times the intraepisode interval. Chronic prophylactic treatment, at remis-sion-producing doses, should be considered for patients who have three or more epi-sodes of depression. The duration of treatment for dysthymic disorder has not been established but is likely to be as long as or longer than the 4–5 months after remission recommended for major depressive disorder. Whether psychotherapy might shorten the optimal duration of pharmacotherapy or the risk of relapse has not been studied.

Potential indicators for psychiatric referral include the presence of psychosis, sig-nificant suicidal ideation or intent, functional deterioration, and past or current treat-ment failure. Additionally, failure to respond to adequate doses of first- or sec-ond-line antidepressant medications should prompt consideration of mental health referral. In refractory cases of profound depression, electroconvulsive therapy (ECT) is sometimes warranted. Patients with bipolar disorder requiring mood-stabilizing medications and patients using monoamine oxidase inhibitors require careful medi-cation monitoring by experienced physicians, typically psychiatrists. These medica-tions are used infrequently in the primary care setting, making it unlikely either that the primary care physician will have the necessary experience or that the health care delivery system will have the specialized surveillance and patient education pro-grams necessary to safely manage these medications. Finally, mental health referral may be required when there is need for interpersonal or cognitive psychotherapy or marital or family counseling.

Comorbidity is a particularly important consideration in the treatment of *anxiety disorders*. Three-quarters of patients with a PRIME–MD-diagnosable anxiety disorder have a comorbid mood disorder, and 84% of patient with an anxiety disorder have more than one diagnosable mental disorder. Decisions about the primacy of the anxi-ety disorder(s) present versus other disorders as well as the quest for parsimony in pharmacotherapy are therefore important clinical challenges. In addition to treating co-occurring mood disorders, antidepressant medications including SSRIs have demonstrated effectiveness for panic disorder, and may be useful in generalized anx-iety disorder. In treating patients with anxiety disorders, the activating effect of the

SSRIs may require lower initial doses and slower titration to avoid increasing agitation, particularly in panic disorder (Reiman, 1998).

Adjunctive hypnotics are often needed in initial treatment. High-potency, long-acting benzodiazepines (e.g., clonazepine) can be effective in panic disorder with relatively low risk for abuse or dependency. The shorter acting, lower potency benzodiazepines (e.g., alprazolam, lorazepam) have proven more difficult to use and are often suboptimally effective in treating the generalized anxiety that often prompts their use. Buspirone is uniquely effective in the treatment of generalized anxiety disorder, and does not present the risk of central nervous system depression, sedation, or dependency that is present with the benzodiazepines. It is often not effective, however, in patients who have chronically used benzodiazepines.

Treatment of *eating disorders* requires multidisciplinary intervention. PRIME–MD includes criteria for the diagnosis of the purging and nonpurging types of bulimia nervosa, and binge eating disorder. In patients with anorexia nervosa (a rarer and less occult diagnosis not included in PRIME–MD), physicians may have to consider involuntary hospitalization when patients' behavior constitutes an immediate risk to their lives. Dental evaluation and treatment and continued monitoring for medical complications of purging are important in patients with bulimia and patients with anorexia nervosa who purge. Comorbid depression should be treated with appropriate medication and psychotherapy; however, antidepressant medications may be helpful in patients with bulimia independent of comorbid depression. Patients with anorexia or bulimia nervosa as well as those with binge eating disorder may benefit from psychotherapy and/or self-help support groups. Weight loss treatment should be considered for obese patients with binge eating disorder.

Treatment of *alcohol abuse and dependency* is particularly challenging because patients' desire and readiness for changing their alcohol abusing behavior is the major determinant of outcome and is seldom an unambivalent desire and readiness to change when the problem is first diagnosed using the PRIME–MD or other screening instrument. Prochaska and DiClemente (Prochaska et al., 1992) outlined a model for understanding the stages of behavioral change that is crucial to determining the role and action of the primary care provider when the diagnosis of alcohol abuse or dependence has been made. These authors identified five stages (see Table 6.6): precontemplative, contemplative, decision, action, and maintenance. Because relapse so often occurs after initial efforts to change behaviors, it is frequently added explicitly as a sixth stage. These stages are common to all behavioral change, and the model is particularly useful in addressing health-related habitual behaviors including other forms of substance abuse, dietary change, adherence to medication or exercise regimens, and home monitoring of disease parameters such as blood pressure or glucose levels.

TABLE 6.6
Prochaska–DiClemente Model of Stages of Readiness for Change

Stage of Change	Description
Precontemplative	Unaware that the problem exists, or that they have it.
Contemplative	Aware of the problem, but ambivalent about changing behavior(s).
Preparation	Has decided to change the behavior.
Action	Acts to change behavior.
Maintenance	Adjusts life patterns to maintain new behavior.
Relapse	Fails to maintain new behavior.

Assessing the stage of readiness to change alcohol use behavior may help target the interventional strategy that is most appropriate for a particular patient. The patient's stage of change may also influence the clinician's ability to detect alcohol abuse. In the PRIME–MD 1000 Study, the half of alcohol abusing patients who were undetected by their primary care provider claimed to have a higher level of functioning on the health-related quality of life measure than patients with no psychopathology whatever. This observation suggests that denial, indicative of the precontemplative and contemplative stages, may have been present, making detection of their problem less likely. Systematic screening with the PRIME–MD can overcome this barrier to detection to some extent, but higher rates of alcohol abuse detected when the PRIME–MD is used anonymously suggest that detection is harder in patients who are precontemplative and contemplative even with a structured screen (Kobak et al., 1997).

Once alcohol abuse or dependence is diagnosed, it is common for primary care providers to tell patients that they should stop drinking and enter an alcohol treatment program. This approach seems obvious but will not succeed if the patient is in any stage other than that of "decision" or "action." It is understandable that clinicians often fail to consider the patient's readiness to act on their problem because the desirable next step for the patient seems so self-evident. However, the majority of patients will be precontemplative, contemplative, or in relapse. It is important that physicians not be in denial themselves regarding the need to work with patients at the stage of change in which they find them.

The key intervention with precontemplative patients is education: both in general, and about their own behavior and medical condition. With precontemplative patients whose failure to think about their problem is sustained by denial, more individualized education about the health and interpersonal consequences of their behavior, combined with techniques to address their ambivalence, will be required. These techniques, central to working with patients in the contemplative stage, focus on shifting the patient's ambivalence in the direction of positive change. One key to addressing the ambivalent contemplative patient is to avoid lecturing on what the clinician thinks the patient should do. The alternative to this almost unavoidable interventional reflex is to explore the patient's assessment of the pros and cons of both changing and staying the same, providing educational correction and amplification only in the context of the patient's own unique understanding and situation.

Once patients have decided that they should act, the clinician's task is to help patients identify the remaining barriers to taking action. An essential task in the decision or preparation phase is to assemble information about resources necessary to take action. Detailed practical information about alcohol treatment programs, Alcoholics Anonymous (AA), Al-Anon, employee assistance programs, and the financial, legal, and vocational consequences of taking action is essential.

The action phase of treating alcohol abuse and dependence can take many forms, such as inpatient treatment with medical detoxification, outpatient detoxificiation, AA without medical supervision, and changing alcohol use without any specific or formal assistance. Decisions about the need for detoxification depend on the amount of alcohol being used and evidence of tolerance and withdrawal with decreased use of alcohol. Because the medical consequences of alcohol withdrawal can be life-threatening, a careful assessment by an experienced clinician is essential. Although success in achieving and maintaining sobriety has been assessed for a variety of alcohol treatment modalities, data about AA are of necessity incomplete because the anonymity of AA programs generally precludes formal evaluation. Nevertheless, a general consensus in the medical community that success correlates positively with the intensity of the intervention guides most clinical efforts.

The skills, strategies, and resources required during the maintenance phase of behavioral change differ from those required to make an initial change in behavior. Achieving sobriety in the context of an intensive inpatient detoxification and rehabilitation program is different from maintaining sobriety in daily life. Clinicians should be able to assess the patient's strategy for maintaining new behavior; in the case of alcohol abuse this will often require assessing the patient's use of AA. It is important to become familiar with the essential features of 12-Step programs such as "home meetings," use of a telephone list, sponsors, and "working the steps," so that effective use of the program can be assessed. Often patients will be reluctant to accept the need for maintenance treatment, and the Prochaska–DiClemente model can be applied again by assessing whether the patient is in a precontemplative or contemplative stage of accepting the need for maintenance treatment, and educating and exploring ambivalence accordingly. One important task for the maintenance phase is to anticipate a possible relapse, and proactively discuss a strategy for coping with relapse.

Relapse is the most common outcome in the treatment of alcohol abuse and dependence. It adds an additional burden of shame and a decreased sense of self-efficacy when it occurs. Although condoning relapse is not a good idea, normalizing and destigmatizing relapse in a limited way can mitigate the deleterious effects of failure. It is very common for the therapeutic relationship to deteriorate when relapse occurs because patients are concerned about experiencing their physician's disapproval. It is therefore useful to anticipate these concerns and to promise and preview a supportive and positive response to the possibility of a relapse.

The management of *somatoform disorders* in the primary care setting has received considerable attention but to less satisfying effect than most of the other PRIME–MD diagnosable disorders. This state of affairs has several causes, one of which is the lack of an effective pharmacological treatment. Another, perhaps more important cause is the fact that recommended interventions require the physician to change as much as the patient. Table 6.7 lists the accepted principles that can assist in developing the empathic trusting doctor–patient relationship that is considered to be the key to managing somatization.

Most of these suggestions explicitly or implicitly direct the physician to behave in ways that are contrary to the behaviors typically induced in physicians by a patient's

TABLE 6.7

Managing Somatization

1. Don't dispute the reality or severity of the patient's physical complaints.
2. Use understandable and mutually acceptable language to explain the patient's symptoms.
3. Establish appropriate goals and expectations for both yourself and the patient.
4. Schedule follow-up visits at regular intervals, independent of symptoms.
5. Set limits on phone calls and drop-in visits.
6. Respectfully evaluate each symptom, with careful interview, physical examination, and judicious use of diagnostic tests.
7. Use medications to treat defined disorders (e.g., depression, anxiety, etc.) or to reduce (not remove) specific target symptoms, particularly chronic pain.

Note. From Kaplan (1997). Somatization. In M. D. Feldman & J. F. Christensen (Eds.), *Behavioral medicine in primary care: A practical guide* (p. 208). Stamford, CT: Appleton & Lange. Adapted with permission from The McGraw-Hill Companies.

somatization. For example, physicians are tempted to minimize the importance or severity of the patient's symptoms, and justify long intervals between visits because of the perceived absence of "real pathology." Somatoform disorders are among the most distressing encountered by primary care providers (Hahn, 1997; Hahn et al., 1994). The lack of apparent physical cause for the symptoms as well as the patient's lack of response to treatment (or worse, the production of new complaints that are side effects of prescribed treatments) make the provider feel as if the patient "wants to be ill" or "doesn't want to get better." Physicians are only partially aware that they have reached this conclusion about the patient's behavior, and patients definitely do not experience this attitude consciously. "Wanting to be ill" or "not wanting to get better" violates the basic contract of the sick role, as described by Talcott Parsons and others (i.e., that the patient is supposed to want to get better). This transgression plays an important role in producing the negative feelings generated by somatization. The patient's somatization initially evokes frustration and a sense of failure that generates anger. The anger in turn produces feelings of guilt and shame because doctors are not "supposed" to feel angry toward patients. It is therefore understandable that these negative feelings lead to physician behaviors that are virtually the opposite of the therapeutic ones enumerated earlier. The reflex countertherapeutic behaviors that are typically evoked in the provider compound the difficulties in the doctor–patient relationship when the patient experiences the rejection, disdain, and avoidance implicit in the physician's frustrated and angry behavior.

The list of suggested management behaviors is therefore useful as an aid to recognizing and altering the physician's manifest behavior in the face of inevitable emotional pressures to act otherwise. However, the list of suggestions does not offer an alternative model for understanding or working with somatization Such an alternative may be provided by using a different paradigm to understand somatization: a paradigm that places the somatization in the context of the patient's family and social system, and allows the physician to understand that somatization serves a purpose in the patient's life (Hahn, 1997).

A family-systems analysis of somatization will usually reveal that patients' somatization is an unconscious response to family dysfunction and painful interpersonal problems. Patients somatize because their roles and the responses of others to them are altered to the extent that the somatization confers on them the status of the sick role. The need for this role alteration is inevitably the result of family dysfunction, and the somatization is the best that the patient and the family can do under the circumstances to stabilize the family and cope with the dysfunction or adverse circumstances. Viewed from this perspective, the physician can feel empathy for both the patient's and family's pain and their attempt to cope and adapt, even while feeling frustration and anger about the patient's (and the family's) use of somatization as a method for solving problems. More importantly, this understanding of the function of somatization enables the physician to take four steps in its management.

1. Analyze the family system. Identify the family conflicts and problems, and while doing so encourage the patient to reveal and relate the emotional pain produced by the family dysfunction. In short, "bring the pain into the room."

2. Reframe: Identify the family problem as worthy of attention *in addition to, not instead of* the somatoform symptoms. Use the magnitude of the pain witnessed during the first step to reinforce the reframing of attention to the family issues. For example, "It seems to me that these very painful family problems you are describing are

worth looking at in addition to your headaches and other physical symptoms." Identify and endorse the objective the patient is pursuing while separating it from the somatoform symptom. For example, "Even if you were the picture of good health, and didn't have your (somatoform symptoms), I could understand why you would want these family issues resolved."

3. Empathically witness. Acknowledge the patient's and family's attempts to deal with their problems: "I am truly impressed with how well you are doing despite everything you have to deal with." Acknowledge the patient's positive and altruistic motivations: "You really care about your family members despite the difficulties you are having with them." Empathic witnessing is a powerful healing act that can be accomplished by helping patients tell their story in the context of the relationships that are important to them in their lives.

4. Refer to a family therapist or mental health specialist. When family dysfunction producing significant disability and distress is encountered, referral for further intervention is indicated. A referral to a therapist or mental health specialist is more likely to be completed and successful when it is preceded by the kind of family history, reframing, and empathic witnessing described, for example, "Because these family problems are so painful, and because everything you have tried so far has failed to change these problems, and because you care so much about your family, it might be a good idea for you and maybe some of your family members to see a therapist who has special expertise in helping families." Referral to mental health specialists should be accompanied by assurances that the primary care provider will continue to maintain a supportive partnership with the patient and will continue to evaluate and manage all physical complaints and problems. The referral must be articulated in terms of the underlying psychosocial problems, not as a treatment for somatization or the patient's physical symptoms.

Prediction of Treatment Outcome

The PRIME–MD is not designed to make prognostic assessments. Our understanding of probable treatment outcome is based on current knowledge about the efficacy of treatment for the different PRIME–MD diagnoses in general. Formal clinical trials of treatment for PRIME–MD diagnoses in the primary care setting are relatively sparse because most treatment studies have been done with psychiatric patients. Advances in pharmacological treatment, and improved recognition and treatment of mental disorders in the primary care setting should lead to cautious optimism that the true potential for successful treatment of PRIME–MD disorders is underestimated by data published to date.

Providing Feedback of Results

The administration of the PRIME–MD CEG is intrinsically a form of feedback to the patient. The physician's administration of each module is cast as an explicit response to the patient's responses on the PQ: "I see that you indicated that you have been bothered by feeling down or depressed during the last month. Let me ask you some questions about other problems you might have that could be related to feeling depressed." As patients observe the physician administering the PRIME–MD CEG they become aware that a series of symptoms that go together and constitute a syndrome is being evaluated. A recognizeable coherence to the pattern of responses to the questions being asked can make a powerful impression even though patients may have no more sophisticated an understanding of the psychiatric syndrome than they do of many of the laboratory results that physicians discuss with them, such as a "spot" on a chest x-ray or the value of a "TSH" (thyroid-stimulating hormone) test.

As the PRIME–MD CEG is administered, physicians can either report diagnoses to the patient as they are made or after all CEG modules have been administered. Although additional data need to be gathered to complete evaluation of potential diagnoses, giving feedback to the patient about those diagnoses is the first stage of intervention. Patients' knowledge of and attitudes about the diagnosed mental disorders should be ascertained, as well as their preferences regarding different treatment options. Although the results of a PRIME–MD evaluation do require explanation, the fact that they are diagnoses rather than scale or symptom scores makes the physician's efforts to educate the patient more straightforward.

USE OF THE PRIME–MD IN TREATMENT MONITORING

The purpose of monitoring the treatment of conditions diagnosable with the PRIME–MD is to assess symptom severity and the persistence of the diagnosis. The PRIME–MD is designed to detect when patients have the criteria required for diagnosis and can be used to determine whether conditions persist. However, it is not designed for the graduated assessment of symptom severity or response to treatment. Nonetheless, the PRIME–MD can be used at any time to determine if the criterion symptoms are still present, and the PQ physical symptom checklist and the symptom lists in the mood and anxiety modules can be administered at sequential visits as part of the process of monitoring treatment. The self-administered version of the PRIME–MD, the Patient Problem Questionnaire (PPQ) described previously, does provide for graded symptom severity reporting rather than simple yes–no responses. Thus serial completion of the PPQ can be used for assessment of individual symptom's response to treatment.

DISEASE-SPECIFIC CONSIDERATIONS

Considerable attention has been given to the concern that diagnosis of mental disorders may be confounded by comorbid physical conditions because both types of disorders cause and are diagnosed by the presence of physical symptoms. Two kinds of problems have been addressed: Mental disorders may be overdiagnosed when physical symptoms related to physical disorders are misattributed to a mental disorder. This concern has been most carefully addressed in the diagnosis of mood disorders, where a number of studies have examined the effect of comorbid general medical conditions on the specificity of symptom rating scales and diagnostic criteria (Rodin et al., 1991). The second problem is to determine whether a mental disorder that can be caused by a physical disorder (e.g., major depression secondary to hypothyroidism) is in fact exclusively due to that disorder when it is present or whether the depression is instead comorbid with, but independent of, the physical disorder. In the case of both these problems, the concern is that an incorrect understanding of the relationship between physical and mental disorders may lead to overlooking and/or failure to treat one or the other. These diagnostic distinctions are also important because different social values are attached to diagnoses depending on whether they are understood as being caused by physical versus psychological pathology. In general, the social bias lies in the direction of considering the dispensations of the sick role as being more valid in the case of physical rather than psychological diagnoses. Chronic fatigue syndrome, premenstrual dysphoric disorder, and multiple chemical sensitivity disorders are conditions in which the controversial nature of this distinction has become evident.

The correct attribution of an individual symptom will be more difficult in the case of vegetative/physical rather than cognitive/emotional symptoms. In administering the mood, anxiety, eating, and alcohol modules of the PRIME–MD clinicians are not explicitly instructed to distinguish whether individual symptoms are due to a physical disorder or to the mental disorder being considered. By adhering to the intensity and duration criteria of the individual question frames, the impairment criteria for each diagnosis, and the total symptom threshold, the likelihood that a patient will falsely meet criteria for a mental disorder appears to be low. However, when a patient's symptom count places the person over but close to the diagnostic threshold for a specific disorder, clinical judgment should be employed if one or more of the symptoms contributing to the diagnosis is clearly due to an unrelated physical disorder, such as difficulty sleeping because of nocturia due to obstructive uropathy. Reinterpretation of the PRIME–MD result in such a case might result in withholding the diagnostic label, or employing less aggressive management strategies. However it is worth noting that both sleep and appetite disturbance were among the four symptoms most predictive of major depression in the PRIME–MD study; therefore, the presence of a physical disorder that could cause either of these symptoms does not mean that the symptom is in fact caused by that physical disorder (Brody et al., 1998).

On the other hand, clinicians are explicitly instructed to consider whether mood or anxiety disorders are secondary to a physical illness, medication, or drug, and to attach the qualifier "secondary" to the mood and anxiety disorders diagnosed. It is important to understand that mood and anxiety disorders may be the end result of multiple stressors, including physical illness, and that the concept of a secondary disorder should not be invoked because a physical illness is experienced as a life stress contributing to depression, such as depression following the diagnosis of a terminal illness such as AIDS or metastatic cancer. The concept of secondary depression or anxiety should be reserved for those relatively rare situations where the symptom syndrome can be wholly or largely attributed to a single disorder (e.g., anxiety in hyperthyroidism or excessive caffeine use; or depression in hypothyroidism or as a side effect of a centrally acting antihypertensive medication). The temporal relationship between the onset of the illness or the use of the medication or drug is an important clue to the secondary nature of the mental disorder. It would be rare for depression to be caused by the use of a centrally acting antihypertensive that had been taken for a substantial period of time before the onset of the depression. A causal relationship is also strongly supported when remission of the mental disorder follows treatment of the physical illness or withdrawal of the medication or drug. The attribution of a secondary disorder would be confirmed by relapse upon rechallenge, a criterion that is rarely employed for obvious reasons. In keeping with the desired parsimonious use of a designation of secondary disorder, the prevalence of secondary mood and anxiety disorders in the PRIME–MD 1000 Study was low: 2%–4% and 1%–3%, respectively (Spitzer et al., 1994). In the case of somatoform disorders, distinguishing between symptoms caused by comorbid physical illness and somatoform symptoms per se is the essence of the diagnostic challenge. It is also rife with difficulty. The diagnosis of multisomatoform disorder is based on a pattern of multiple complaints over time in addition to three current symptoms and is therefore something of a judgment call. It is also important to note that under current diagnostic criteria, symptoms that have been attributed to mood or anxiety disorders cannot also contribute to a diagnosis of multisomatoform disorder. This hierarchical decision rule has been challenged on the grounds that the presence of multisomatoform disorder has a large effect on impairment in health-related quality of life that is independent of the presence of other mental disorders (Kroenke, Spitzer, et al., 1997).

IMPROVING DETECTION OF BEHAVIORAL HEALTH DISORDERS IN PRIMARY CARE SETTINGS

The PRIME–MD was developed to remedy a perceived deficit in physicians' detection and treatment of mental disorders. However, in critiquing the performance of primary care clinicians, it is only fair to point out the many barriers that interfere with detection and management, including limited time, somatic presentations of depressed patients, stigmatization that can inhibit open discussion, competing medical problems, and inadequate reimbursement (Kroenke, 1997). Klinkman (1997) offered a "competing demands model" that argues that given the complex and multiple agendas patients and physicians bring to each clinical encounter, nondetection is neither surprising nor necessarily "inappropriate." He suggested that four domains will influence the priority of those agendas and the likelihood that detection of mental disorders will get adequate attention: (a) physician characteristics, including skills, knowledge, and attitudes about psychosocial issues; (b) patient characteristics; (c) the structure of the health care "ecosystem"; and (d) the public policy environment.

The ability of a case-finding and diagnostic tool such as the PRIME–MD to change clinical practice will depend on its effect in all four of these domains. The PRIME–MD must correct deficiencies in physicians' clinical skills and knowledge, and be instrumental in changing attitudes that influence the priority of detection and diagnosing mental disorders. The PRIME–MD should detect disorders despite patient characteristics that contribute to nondetection and be useful in educating patients and enhancing their disposition to accept treatment for mental disorders. The PRIME–MD must be consistent with the structural elements of the primary care setting, such as time constraints and reimbursement policies, that constitute barriers to detection. Ideally, a detection and diagnostic procedure should be instrumental in changing the practice system's incentive structure in favor of giving diagnosis of mental disorders a higher priority. Finally, a case-finding diagnostic tool can be instrumental in influencing public policy by generating population-based data about unmet needs and structural barriers to detection and treatment.

Previous Efforts to Change Physician Practice in Detection of Mental Disorders

The management of mental disorders can be described as a sequence of steps that constitute a continuum of care common to virtually all medical problems. Clinicians must:

1. Maintain an appropriate index of suspicion.
2. Screen (asymptomatic) or case-find (symptomatic but hidden) patients to identify patients at risk.
3. Diagnose the condition when present.
4. Evaluate patients with the diagnosis.
5. Initiate and monitor treatment.

Four strategies have been employed to improve management of mental disorders
and can be distinguished by the stages of the continuum of care they address and the
extent to which they alter the structure of the health care delivery system. These include:

1. Educational interventions to enhance skills and knowledge in any or all of the
   stages, with no structural interventions.
2. Structured use of instruments for case-finding alone, without diagnostic, evaluation, or treatment interventions.
3. Liaison psychiatry collaborative-care and referred-care interventions that include the diagnostic, evaluation, and treatment stages of the continuum, with
   or without a case-finding intervention.
4. Structured use of a two-stage case-finding and diagnostic instrument such as
   the PRIME–MD.

Impact of Educational Interventions on Detection, Treatment, and Outcome.
Several studies have evaluated the effect of educational interventions on physicians'
ability to make accurate diagnoses of mental disorders. Most have assessed the impact of the educational intervention using written case vignettes or videotaped cases
and have demonstrated improvement in physician skill and knowledge (Andersen &
Harthorn, 1990; Bowman, Goldberg, Millar, Gask, & McGrath, 1992; Gask, Goldberg,
Lesser, & Millar, 1988; Penn et al., 1997). Goldberg, Steele, Smith, and Spivey (1980)
demonstrated improved diagnostic accuracy in actual clinical practice in the poorest
performing physicians. Other assessments of the impact of physician education on
actual clinical practice have yielded more discouraging results (Shapiro et al., 1987).
In a follow-up study of collaborative-care intervention that included intensive physician education, Lin et al. (1997) found that rates of antidepressant medication prescription and patient adherence declined to preintervention levels after termination
of the structural changes implemented during the active study period.

Impact of Case-Finding on Detection, Treatment, and Outcome. Structured methods to aid the physician are an obvious solution to the underdiagnosis of depression
and other mental disorders in the primary care setting. The first generation of instruments designed to enhance care of mental disorders in the primary care setting focused on the second step of the continuum of care: case-finding. The General Health
Questionnaire (Goldberg & Hillier, 1978), for example, was designed to measure the
symptoms and distress associated with any mental disorder. The Zung Depression
Inventory (Zung, 1965), the Beck Depression Inventory (Beck, Ward, Mendelson,
Mack, & Erbaugh, 1961), and the Center for Epidemiological Studies Depression
Scale (Radloff, 1977) were designed to detect a population of patients with a high
probability of having a mood disorder, but did not purport to make specific *DSM* cri-

teria-based diagnoses. For the most part, although sensitive for psychiatric "case-ness," these self-report questionnaires are not very specific for specific categories of disorder; rather, they measure the generalized distress or "demoralization" associated with all mental disorders (Dohrenwend & Dohrenwend, 1965; Katon & Von Korff, 1990; Mulrow et al., 1995).

A number of studies have evaluated the effect of providing feedback from case-finding instruments to physicians on the detection and management of depression, and the results are inconclusive. Several case-finding/feedback studies have demonstrated increased notation of depression and levels of treatment (Linn & Yager, 1980; Magruder-Habib et al., 1990; Moore, Lilimperi, & Bobula, 1978). Two studies showed that disclosure of depression had some beneficial effect on severity and duration of depression (Johnstone & Goldberg, 1976; Zung, Magill, Moore, & George, 1983). Other studies failed to show significant changes in detection (Hoeper, Nycz, Kessler, Burke, & Pierce, 1984; Shapiro et al., 1987), and in one study that examined depression status as an outcome, disclosure of undetected depression had no impact on patients' depression status at 12 months (Dowrick & Buchan, 1995).

Impact of Collaborative-Care and Referred-Care Interventions. The failure of enhanced case-finding alone to consistently improve outcomes led to interventions that enhance or supplement physician performance in the remaining stages of the continuum of care (i.e., diagnosis, evaluation, and treatment). Two series of studies have demonstrated that supplementing primary care providers' usual care approach to post-case-finding management can lead to better depression related outcomes than interventions that stop at the case-finding stage.

Schulberg et al. (1996) conducted a study in which the benefit of feedback from case-finding was compared to on-site pharmacotherapy administered by specially trained primary care physicians, or to on-site psychotherapy delivered by mental health specialists. In this study, the CES–D was used as a case-finding tool with 7,652 patients in clinic waiting rooms, the DIS was used to establish a diagnosis, and patients with depression were evaluated by a consultation–liaison psychiatrist. Ultimately, 276 subjects agreed to randomization to one of three treatments: pharmacotherapy, interpersonal therapy, or feedback to and care from their primary provider (i.e., "usual care" plus feedback). Patients randomized to either pharmacotherapy or interpersonal therapy (standardized treatment) did significantly better over the 8 months of the study in terms of severity of depressive symptoms and recovery from depression. Among treatment completers, 70% of the patients receiving standardized treatment had recovered at 8 months compared to 20% of usual care patients. Among all patients (intent to treat analysis), recovery was seen at 8 months in approximately half of those receiving standardized treatment and in 18% of those in the usual care wing.

The Schulberg et al. (1996) study used a referral model in which pharmacotherapy as well as psychotherapy was taken out of the hands of the primary care provider, although the services were provided in the primary care site. In contrast, Katon et al. (1995) evaluated a collaborative model in which patients were seen by both primary care provider and consultation–liaison (C/L) psychiatrist, the C/L psychiatrist actively consulted with the primary care provider, and both primary care providers and patients received educational interventions. Significant improvements in depression-related outcomes were observed. The Katon et al. study differs from the Schulberg et al. study in that no case-finding intervention was included. Subjects in the study had all been recognized as depressed by their provider without the aid of a protocol for detecting previously unrecognized depression. Thus, although this study, and a subsequent one that added psychotherapy to the treatment program (Katon et al., 1996), demonstrates the utility of a "collaborative" intervention for patients with recognized depression, the potential impact on the 40% to 60% of depressed patients that probably remained undetected cannot be assessed.

Structured Use of PRIME–MD: Case-Finding and Diagnosis. The positive impact of PRIME–MD on rates of detection and treatment demonstrated in the PRIME–MD 1000 Study support the conclusion that a two-stage, case-finding and diagnostic instrument may have more impact on diagnosis and the initiation of treatment than case-finding alone. A study performed by Valenstein et al. (1997) further supports the conclusion that use of PRIME–MD will result in improved detection and higher rates of treatment. In contrast to the PRIME–MD 1000 Study in which the use of PRIME–MD was initiated and monitored by research coordinators and incentives for participation were provided to a group of self-selected physicians, Valenstein et al. examined rates of PQ and CEG use by unselected physicians under three "realistic (i.e., economically and logistically feasible) support conditions," and a no-support control:

1. Nonclinical staff support condition (NCSS): The PQ was distributed to patients, collected, and placed in each patient's chart prior to the visit by nonclinical research staff.
2. Nursing support condition (RN): The PQ was distributed, collected, and placed in the chart by nursing staff already working in the clinic (i.e. no additional personnel were added to the clinic staff).
3. Physician "prompt" condition (Prompt): PQs were distributed by both RNs and nonclinical staff and reviewed by research staff, who placed brightly colored written prompts in the chart, indicating which modules were triggered by the PQ.
4. No-support condition: Physicians were made aware that the PRIME–MD was available but initiation and completion was left entirely up to the provider.

After instructing all providers in the use of the PRIME–MD, the three active support conditions and no-support condition were employed during rotating weeks of the 15-week study period. The study was performed in a Veterans Administration (VA) clinic, and 2,263 patients were enrolled and eligible for evaluation. All three active support conditions significantly increased the use of the PQ (11% in no-support vs. 80%–81% in the active support conditions). Although physicians were selective in which PQ-positive patients received a CEG interview, all active support conditions produced much higher rates of CEG use than the no-support condition. Compared to no support, the odds ratio (O.R.) for CEG use in the NCSS condition was 9.7, 95% confidence interval (C.I.) 2.8–33.3; for RN support, O.R.= 14.2, C.I. 3.9–52.6; and for Prompt, O.R. = 24.7, C.I. 7.5–81.7. The use of written physician prompts was significantly more likely to result in CEG completion than the NCSS or RN support conditions. Compared to no support, all three active support conditions resulted in significantly more new diagnoses (O.R.s ranged from 4.1 to 3.2), and the RN and Prompt conditions resulted in significantly more provider actions (O.R. = 1.7, C.I. 1.1–2.6, and O.R. = 1.8, C.I. 1.2–2.7 respectively).

Differential Impact of Education, Case-Finding and Diagnostic Tools, and Structural Intervention

One conclusion that can be drawn from evaluation of these four kinds of interventions (i.e., physician education, feedback from case-finding alone, collaborative care or referred care, and structured use of two-stage case-finding and diagnostic tools) is that physician education and/or case-finding interventions that fall short of diagnosis are not enough to change care patterns. On the other hand, in the two other intervention strategies where changes in patterns of care were demonstrated, the task of diagnosis (as opposed to case-finding) was targeted with a structural intervention.

The collaborative-care or referred-care strategy has the best evidence for change in outcome, is the most effective, and makes the greatest change in the structure of the delivery system. In the Schulberg et al. (1996) study, initiation and delivery of care along the entire continuum from case-finding to treatment monitoring was taken out of the hands of the primary care provider and became an independent part of the structure of the health care delivery system. In the Katon et al. (1995) studies, the diagnosis, evaluation, and treatment phases of care were structurally changed in the treatment environment. The conclusion that change in system structure, not improvement in physician skills and knowledge, is the necessary condition for improvement in mental disorders-related care is consistent with the "competing demands" model discussed earlier. That model anticipates that physician skill and knowledge are easily overshadowed, for better or for worse, by other and more potent determinants of physician behavior.

The Schulberg et al. and Katon et al. studies evaluate the impact of interventions that include all stages of the continuum of care. The PRIME–MD 1000 Study and Valenstein et al. study are early efforts to assess the impact of the PRIME–MD's ability to help the physician make specific diagnoses. It remains to be seen whether the change in process observed in these studies results in commensurate change in outcome, and how the type of intervention studied by Valenstein et al. compares in cost and effect to the collaborative-care and referred-care model. As described later, the PRIME–MD can also serve as a tool in collaborative-care or referred-care interventions.

STRENGTHS AND LIMITATIONS OF THE PRIME–MD

The PRIME–MD measures up well to many of the criteria established for evaluating outcome measures (Newman & Ciarlo, 1994). These same criteria are also appropriate for evaluating this and other instruments for screening and treatment monitoring purposes in primary care settings.

Relevance

Epidemiologic data from the PRIME–MD 1000 Study and previous studies of psychopathology in primary care clearly establish the relevance of the disorders targeted by the PRIME–MD. The prevalence, associated morbidity, and low rates of unaided detection in the primary care setting all support the conclusion that results obtained from the PRIME–MD will be relevant to the intended population. The use of situational or patient characteristic triggers for the administration of the PRIME–MD might further increase the likelihood that the result will be relevant to patient care.

Procedures

Results of the PRIME–MD 1000 Study demonstrate the feasibility of training primary care physicians to use the PRIME–MD. Both the PQ and CEG are self-guiding instruments that require little additional documentation or instruction to use. Aside from the PRIME–MD forms, no other equipment is needed. Minimal clinical support staff effort is required to initiate the PRIME–MD procedure with literate patients, and the clerical staff time required to assist patients with the PQ who cannot read is brief. The Patient Problem Questionnaire, an entirely self-report form of the PRIME–MD, requires greater patient sophistication but is easy for the majority of patients to complete. The computer-driven interactive voice recognition PRIME–MD will require investment in suitable telephone and computer systems.

Objective Referents

Individual items and the diagnoses evaluated by the PRIME–MD are scored dichotomously as present or absent. Each item is scored according to specific intensity and duration of the symptom as relevant for the specific diagnosis. Results of the PRIME–MD are thus comparable between patients and populations.

Use of Multiple Respondents

The PRIME–MD was not designed to be completed by evaluators or respondents other than the patient and provider. Certain symptoms such as psychomotor agitation or retardation can be judged by the physician as well as the patient's self-report. It is not unusual for other family members to be present during primary care encounters, and their input to the questions being addressed can contribute to the assessment. The PRIME–MD has no specific mechanism for identifying the source of data when other informants are used, and relies on the clinician's judgment in incorporating the data into the assessment. Data from the PRIME–MD 1000 Study would suggest that obtaining information regarding alcohol use from other informants might be particularly useful in that subset of patients whose self-report may be distorted by denial and social desirability reporting bias.

Treatment Linkage

Compared to unaided clinicians' general impressions that patients with mental disorders have some kind of psychological problem, the specific diagnoses generated by PRIME–MD are an essential step in determining the range of treatments from which the patient may benefit. However, the PRIME–MD is not designed to evaluate the severity of diagnoses in a way that can be used to identify which of the treatments available for the diagnoses is more likely to be useful. To the limited extent that the instrument can be used to monitor the patient during treatment, it can be of assistance in determining if a chosen treatment is working.

Psychometric Strength

The PRIME–MD 1000 Study (Spitzer et al., 1994) has established that the PRIME–MD is a reliable and valid instrument when used in the primary care setting. It has provided a rich data set from which we have learned much about mental disorders in primary care, including health-related quality of life (Linzer et al., 1996; Spitzer et al., 1995), gender differences (Kroenke & Spitzer, 1998; Linzer et al., 1996; Williams et al., 1995), patient difficulty (Hahn et al., 1996), somatization (Kroenke et al., 1994, 1998; Kroenke, Spitzer, et al., 1997; Kroenke & Spitzer, 1998), and alcohol disorders (Johnson et al., 1995).

A literature review (Mulrow et al., 1995) and prospective study (Whooley et al., 1997) show that the PRIME–MD is as good or better than other measures designed to detect depression. Two studies have demonstrated that PRIME–MD performs as well as a longer structured, criteria-based diagnostic interview (Kobak et al., 1997; Spitzer et al., 1994). Agreement between PRIME–MD and standardized diagnostic interviews administered by mental health professionals approaches that observed between mental health professional in psychiatric research studies. Construct validity is strongly supported by convergence with other validated measures of health-related quality of life and psychiatric symptomatology.

The greater sensitivity of the PRIME–MD to alcohol abuse when administered by phone using a computer-guided interactive voice response interview suggests that mode of administration may introduce some social desirability and other response biases. The PQ screen for alcohol problems is as susceptible to conscious withholding and unconscious denial as are other alcohol screens. It remains to be seen how new self-report versions of the PRIME–MD vary in performance from the physician-administered version and vary depending on whether administration is by paper and pencil, interactive computer in the office, or interactive voice response methods.

It is well known that prevalence of psychopathology is strongly and negatively correlated with socioeconomic status (SES). This association was observed in the PRIME–MD 1000 Study, where intrasite variability in rates of psychiatric caseness could be explained for three of the four sites using the limited demographic indicators of SES available. It is therefore likely that the physician-administered PRIME–MD will give stable results across different medical practices.

Valenstein et al. (1997) investigated the use of the PRIME–MD by unselected physicians under several realistic clinical support conditions. Increasingly, PRIME–MD is becoming a criterion standard itself for primary care research, including recent studies in special populations (Parker et al., 1997; Philbrick, Connelly, & Wofford, 1996) and primary care patients with physical complaints (Kroenke, Jackson, & Chamberlin, 1997; O'Malley et al., 1998). However, a great deal still needs to be learned regarding the utility of the PRIME–MD as a treatment planning and monitoring tool. In particular, sensitivity to treatment-related change in patient status has not yet been evaluated.

Low Measure Costs Relative to Its Uses

Costs for administration of the PRIME–MD are limited to the cost of the forms and the time required for distribution and administration. No additional costs are incurred in analyzing or processing the results. As a structured and validated psychiatric assessment, the PRIME–MD may qualify for reimbursement from third-party in-surance payers, covering the cost of administration and generating revenue.

The PRIME–MD has been cited as an example of the kind of case-finding diagnos-tic tool appropriate for programs targeted to improve the health and cost of care of populations (Katon et al., 1997). It can be used for cost containment to determine or justify eligibility for treatments or services. In one author's clinic site, prescriptions for the SSRI that is supplied at low cost to patients require completion of the PRIME–MD mood module. Administration to high utilizers of medical care may identify many patients with otherwise unidentified mental disorders, enhance the di-agnostic precision in those who were previously known to have psychopathology, and lead to lower long-term costs of care.

Understanding by Nonprofessional Audiences

PRIME–MD results are specific diagnoses and thus are relatively easy for the patient or lay audience to understand. Educating patients about their diagnosis is an essen-tial first step in the process of treatment and evaluation, and explaining the results of the PRIME–MD thus does not add to the burden of patient education, but rather facil-itates it. In presenting PRIME–MD results, there is no need to explain psychological constructs that are secondary to the central diagnostic description of the patient's problem, nor do the ranges, anchors, and significance of particular values of score scales need to be explained.

One of the challenges inherent in presenting psychiatric diagnoses to the many pa-tients who are reluctant to accept that they have a mental disorder is the absence of a true laboratory test that can "prove scientifically" that the disorder is present. An ex-ception is the powerful effect often observed when abnormal laboratory tests indicat-ing pathology produced by alcohol abuse are presented to patients. In some respects, the PRIME–MD resembles a "test." In contrast to an interview gathering the same data but without use of the PRIME–MD forms, when the PRIME–MD is adminis-tered, patients are impressed that the questions they are being asked constitute a rec-ognized diagnostic pattern because the instrument exists as a physical form. Indeed, one author compares the PRIME–MD to an electrocardiogram or chest x-ray: In this case, it is a "physical" tracing of the psyche rather than the heart or the lungs. The PRIME–MD's existence reinforces the point that mental disorders are well under-stood by the medical community and common enough to warrant the development of a standardized procedure. The effect of the procedure not only enhances patient understanding but contributes to the kind of confidence that individual patients need in order to adhere to regimens and that families need in order to be supportive. Patients themselves can refer to the PRIME–MD procedure when explaining the na-ture of their problems to others in their social system.

For the same reasons that the PRIME–MD may facilitate communication with pa-tients and their families, data about populations can be easily communicated to fund-ing agencies, administrators, and other clinical personnel. The PRIME–MD is ideal for efficiently determining the prevalence and persistence of indicator psychiatric di-agnoses in populations in program outcomes research and evaluation (Katon et al., 1997). In the short period of time that the PRIME–MD has been available, it has al-ready become one of the most popular instruments for epidemiological and out-comes studies in the primary care setting.

Easy Feedback and Uncomplicated Interpretation

The PRIME-MD requires no further "interpretation" after administration because the results are presented as diagnoses. Although the diagnoses require explanation in their application, no scale constructs or values need to be interpreted. The summary sheet for diagnoses made during the procedure is a convenient and readily understood reporting format.

Usefulness in Clinical Services

The diagnoses derived from the PRIME-MD serve as the foundation for clinical action and communication. PRIME-MD diagnoses are the foundation for choosing further evaluations, treatments, and services. The PRIME-MD results can be used to justify reimbursement for assessment and treatment of mental disorders. The PRIME-MD was designed to accomplish these objectives in the most efficient, least costly, and least burdensome fashion. The high perceived benefit of the PRIME-MD reported by physicians and especially the positive correlation between perceived benefit and the amount of time required to administer it support the conclusion that the goal of cost-effectiveness has been adequately achieved.

Compatibility With Clinical Theories and Practices

The theoretical foundation of the PRIME-MD is the almost universally accepted *DSM-IV* diagnostic model. The PRIME-MD has utility across the broad spectrum of clinical theories and practices because it makes no presumptions, other than in choice of included conditions, regarding treatment approach or etiological model. The PRIME-MD detects and diagnoses conditions that all primary care services need to attend to, regardless of the services they offer or their approach to treatment.

CASE STUDY

The following case study is based on the management of representative patients seen in our clinic.

A.G. was seen for the first time by a third-year medical resident who presented the patient to a supervising attending physician. A.G. had been a patient of the clinic for 10 years and had made an average of 15 visits per year for the last several years to her previous primary care provider, to the walk-in clinic, and to the emergency room. In the previous year alone she had made 40 visits. Her record was filled with notes recording multiple physical complaints that had been vigorously investigated with persistently negative results. Although she complained of shortness of breath, and asthma was on her problem list, her lung exams and pulmonary function tests were consistently normal. She also reported diarrhea, but stool tests and colonoscopy were normal. Symptoms suggestive of an ulcer led to gastroscopy, which was unremarkable. She complained of severe pain in multiple joints, but on examination there was no evidence of inflammation, and x-rays and serological tests were negative.

The resident described A.G. as presenting her current symptoms ("a flare up of her diarrhea, and joint pains") with an innocent but earnest request that the physician would resolve the problem. The resident found it striking that the history of past failures to diagnose and treat her problems had no effect on her current expectations.

The resident was at a loss as to how to manage the situation, and more than a little frustrated and annoyed by the perceived unreasonableness of the patient's expectations. Although the resident reported that the patient seemed somewhat anxious and agitated, she could not characterize the patient's affect or psychiatric symptoms more specifically. The attending physician pointed out that the patient's pattern of multiple physical complaints was consistent with a somatoform disorder, that mood and anxiety disorders commonly occurred in association with somatoform disorders, and that all of these diagnoses were commonly undetected unless formally assessed. The attending physician requested that the resident use the PRIME–MD.

On the Patient Questionnaire (PQ), A.G. endorsed 10 of the 16 physical symptoms, triggering the somatoform module of the Clinician Evaluation Guide (CEG); the "feeling depressed" item triggered the mood module; and the "panic attack" and "worried about a lot of things" items, triggered the anxiety module. The eating disorders and alcohol abuse and dependence screens on the PQ were negative. She rated her health as "poor."

The resident then administered the PQ-triggered modules in their sequence in the CEG: the mood module, the anxiety module, and the somatoform module. In the mood module the patient endorsed five symptoms—impaired sleep, low energy, poor concentration, depressed mood, and low self-esteem—which fulfills the criteria for major depressive disorder. Confirming 2 years of impairment-causing depressed mood at least half of the time, her presentation also fulfilled criteria for dysthymia. In the panic section of the anxiety module she initially admitted to rare attacks of "nerves." However, when the panic questions were applied to what the patient called "asthma attacks," which always had a prominent component of anxiety, the patient's symptoms met criteria for panic disorder. In the remaining sections of the anxiety module, the patient admitted to being nervous, anxious, and on edge, had many physical symptoms associated with generalized anxiety disorder (some of which had already been detected on the mood module), and acknowledged that these symptoms caused functional impairment. However, she said that her only worries were her medical conditions, and that otherwise she did not worry about many different things. Her symptoms therefore met criteria for anxiety disorder not otherwise specified but not generalized anxiety disorder. In the somatoform module her symptoms met criteria for multisomatoform disorder by confirming many years of multiple, impairment-causing physical symptoms that doctors could not adequately explain or treat.

The mood and anxiety disorders diagnosed using the CEG were presented to the patient, who accepted them as an accurate description of her emotional state and as among her many medical problems. She was interested in trying medication to relieve her emotional distress and a tricyclic antidepressant was begun.

As anticipated, A.G. did not believe that her physical symptoms were due to a mood or anxiety disorder, nor was the diagnosis of multisomatoform disorder used explicitly in offering a new explanatory model for her illness experience. Instead, a family-systems assessment was performed (Hahn, 1997), which revealed lifelong failure and frustration in establishing a marital relationship, and a compensatory and overly close relationship with the patient's mother. The relationship between A.G. and her mother was complicated by the mother's unusually great need for assistance in caring for A.G.'s chronically ill and dependent 35-year-old sister. The patient's physical symptoms enabled her, on the one hand, to compete with her sister's illness in obtaining her mother's attention, and on the other hand to excuse herself from obligation with minimal guilt when her mother's requests for help with the sister became excessive. In the course of several family and individual meetings with the patient, the resident and attending physician empathically acknowledged the distress caused by the patient's family problems and difficulty establishing a satisfying marital relationship. It was suggested to A.G. that she would be entitled to impose limits on her involvement with her mother and sister "even if she was in perfect health." Finally, A.G. was encouraged to accept that these family issues were as worthy of attention as her physical symptoms (not the cause of them), and individual and/or family therapy was recommended. The patient accepted the rationale for referral but was skeptical about its usefulness and more skeptical about her family's willingness to participate.

On subsequent visits the patient's antidepressant medication was gradually increased to a full dose, and her symptoms of depression and the frequency of panic attacks decreased. Repeat administration of the PRIME–MD revealed that she no longer had current dysthymia, and her major depression was in partial remission. Her unscheduled visits decreased over the next year and the intensity of her somatization diminished somewhat. When she did complain of physical symptoms, the physician responded by inquiring about the situation with her mother and sister, and the patient was able to ventilate her frustration and receive some empathic support. When the resident completed her training, the attending physician became the primary care provider.

Initially the patient did not follow through with the referral for psychotherapy, but 2 years later when she initiated another relationship, she began weekly psychotherapy. The patient's somatization decreased further, and on the occasions that she did report a "flare-up" of one of her complaints, a recent perturbation in the family system could usually be easily identified. She has chosen to remain on the antidepressant medication and has been free of all but brief episodes of depressed mood.

This case demonstrates a number of important features related to the utility of the PRIME–MD. The patient had severe psychopathology, with four concurrent distinguishable mental disorders. Mean health-related quality of life scores for patients with this combination of diagnoses were in the lowest decile and health care utilization rates and physician-experienced difficulty in the highest decile of patients in the PRIME–MD 1,000 Study. Although physicians had previously suspected that mental disorders were present in this patient, they had never made a specific diagnosis or initiated diagnosis-specific treatment. The PRIME–MD enabled the physician to identify specific diagnoses and reframe both the physician's and the patient's understanding of the cause of the patient's morbidity (although their respective explanatory models were not identical). Establishing specific diagnoses led to initiation of effective treatment and substantial improvement of the patient's health-related quality of life while at the same time decreasing inappropriate utilization of health care services and the physician's frustration. Repeated administration of the PRIME–MD enabled the physician to track the patient's illness over time. This case also illustrates the utility of the PRIME–MD as an educational instrument facilitating supervision and training of clinicians in the clinical setting.

SUMMARY AND CONCLUSIONS

The PRIME–MD is a two-stage psychiatric case-finding and diagnostic tool designed specifically for use in primary care. In contrast to older "first-generation" mental disorder case-finding instruments, the PRIME–MD's unique contribution was to be the first primary care instrument that takes the critical step of determining a specific psychiatric diagnosis after finding an undifferentiated psychiatric case. The PRIME–MD contains separate modules addressing the five most common categories of psychopathology seen in primary care: mood disorders, anxiety disorders, alcohol abuse and dependence, eating disorders, and somatoform disorders. The PRIME–MD is valid and reliable when used by primary care providers, acceptable to patients, and perceived as valuable to primary care providers (Spitzer et al., 1994). The PRIME–MD has increasingly been selected as a research tool by clinical investigators. When the PRIME–MD is initiated by clerical or nursing staff, primary care providers will in fact employ the PRIME–MD, make new psychiatric diagnoses, and initiate new treatments without additional incentive (Valenstein et al., 1997). PRIME–MD's use of a preliminary case-finding screen, separate modules for each category of disorder, and use of branching logic with timely exits in the clinician-administered diagnostic component account for its demonstrated temporal efficiency. The recently developed and entirely self-administered Patient Problem Questionnaire and interactive voice response versions of the PRIME–MD promise even greater efficiency.

The central function of the PRIME–MD is in detection and treatment planning. It has an obvious and prominent role to play in continuous-care settings, but can also be of benefit when applied judiciously in episodic care, in subspecialty consultations, and as an educational tool and facilitator of communication in consultation-liaison psychiatry. It may be particularly useful to behavioral health clinicians working in primary care settings. Although evidence suggests some role for the PRIME–MD as part of routine health maintenance with most if not all primary care patients, those with many physical symptoms, unexplained functional impairment, and patients that are experienced as difficult by their provider are most certain of benefiting from its use.

The PRIME–MD has proven easy to use. Administration of the PRIME–MD is flexible: It may be used in its entirety or in parts. Use of the PQ may be initiated by the provider or clerical staff in the waiting room or begun during the visit by administering the PQ orally. The CEG is designed to be administered by the physician, but may also be administered by a nurse or midlevel provider, by phone using an interactive voice response system, or self-administered as the Patient Problem Questionnaire. The biggest challenge in administering the PRIME–MD is to incorporate the PRIME–MD's symptom-driven questions into a patient-centered clinical encounter.

The PRIME–MD is unique among psychological tools in that it was designed to change clinicians' behavior in a domain of practice that has been refractory to modification despite numerous previous efforts. Our understanding of this dilemma has been enhanced by the recently articulated "competing demands" model described by Klinkman (1997), which argues that because there are always more agendas than can be addressed, attention to those that are not obvious, immediately compelling, and/or reinforced by structural mandate or incentive will always be deferred in favor of agendas that are. Undetected mental disorders remain undetected because they are not obvious and immediately compelling, and the health care delivery system currently provides little structural incentive or mandate for detection. Initiating the PRIME–MD procedure by protocol immediately changes the priority given to mental disorders because the PRIME–MD case-finding Patient Questionnaire is designed to make mental disorders obvious, and the diagnostic Clinician Evaluation Guide is designed to make them compelling. Although individual clinicians may choose to use the PRIME–MD with individual patients or more generally in their own practices, changing the mental health of primary care populations will undoubtedly require more general modification of the health care system. The PRIME–MD is ideally suited for this task. However, further study of patient and encounter characteristics that should trigger the PRIME–MD, the resources required to support its administration and manage resulting diagnoses, and evaluation of changes in health outcomes remain to be done.

ACKNOWLEDGMENT

The development of the PRIME–MD was underwritten by an unrestricted educational grant from the Roerig and Pratt Pharmaceuticals divisions of Pfizer, Inc., New York, NY.

REFERENCES

Andersen, S. M., & Harthorn, B. H. (1990). Changing psychiatric knowledge of primary care physicians: Effects of a brief intervention on clinical diagnosis and treatment. *General Hospital Psychiatry, 12,* 177–190.

Andreasen, N. C., Flaum, M., & Arndt, S. (1992). The Comprehensive Assessment of Symptoms and History (CASH): An instrument for assessing diagnosis and psychopathology. *Archives of General Psychiatry, 49,* 615–623.

Badger, L. W., deGruy, F. V., Hartman, J., Plant, M. A., Leeper, J., Anderson, R., Ficken, R., Gaskin, S., Maxwell, A., Rand, E., & Tietze, P. (1994a). Patient presentation, interview content, and the detection of depression by primary care physicians. *Psychosomatic Medicine, 56,* 128–135.

Badger, L. W., deGruy, F. V., Hartman, J., Plant, M. A., Leeper, J., Ficken, R., Maxwell, A., Rand, E., Anderson, R., & Templeton, B. (1994b). Psychosocial interest, medical interviews, and the recognition of depression. *Archives of Family Medicine, 3,* 899–907.

Barrett, J. E., Barrett, J. A., Oxman, T. E., & Gerber, P. D. (1988). The prevalence of psychiatric disorders in a primary care practice. *Archives of General Psychiatry, 45,* 1100–1106.

Beck, A. T., Ward, C., Mendelson, M., Mack, J., & Erbaugh, J. (1961). An inventory for measuring depression. *Archives of General Psychiatry, 4,* 561–571.

Beitman, B. D., Mukerji, V., Lamberti, J. W., Scmid, L., DeRosear, L., Kushner, M., Flaker, G., & Basha, I. (1989). Panic disorder in patients with chest pain and angiographically normal coronary arteries. *American Journal of Cardiology, 63,* 1339.

Bowman, F. M., Goldberg, D. P., Millar, T., Gask, L., & McGrath, G. (1992). Improving the skills of established general practitioners: The long-term benefits of group teaching. *Medical Education, 26,* 63–68.

Bridges, K., & Goldberg, D. (1987). Somatic presentation of depressive illness in primary care. In P. Freeling, L. J. Downey, & J. C. Malkin (Eds.), *The presentation of depression: Current approaches* (pp. 9–11). London: Royal College of General Practitioners.

Brody, D. S., Thompson, T. L., Larson, D. B., Ford, D. E., Katon, W. J., & Magruder, K. M. (1995). Recognizing and managing depression in primary care. *General Hospital Psychiatry, 17,* 93–107.

Brody, D. S., Hahn, S. R., Spitzer, R. L., Kroenke, K., Linzer, M., deGruy, F. V. III, & Williams, J. B. W. (1998). Identifying depressed patients in the primary care setting: A more efficient method. *Archives of Internal Medicine, 158,* 2469–2475.

Campbell, T. L. (1987). Is screening for mental health problems worthwhile in family practice? An opposing view. *Journal of Family Practice, 25,* 184–187.

Cherkin, D. C., Deyo, R. A., Street, J. H., & Barlow, W. (1996). Predicting poor outcomes for back pain in primary care using patients' own criteria. *Spine, 21,* 2900–2907.

Clark, W. (1995). Effective interviewing and intervention for alcohol problems. In M. Lipkin, Jr., S. M. Putnam, & A. Lazare (Eds.), *The medical interview: Clinical care, education and research* (pp. 284–293). New York: Springer Verlag.

Cleary, P. D., Burns, B. J., & Nycz, G. R. (1990). The identification of psychiatric illness by primary care physicians: The effect of patient gender. *Journal of General Internal Medicine, 5,* 355–360.

Cohen-Cole, S. A. (1991). *The medical interview: The three function approach.* St. Louis, MO: Mosby-Yearbook.

Cohen-Cole, S. A., Bird, J., Freeman, A., Baker, J., Hain, J., & Shugerman, A. (1982). An oral examination of the psychiatric knowledge of medical housestaff: Assessment of needs and evaluation baseline. *General Hospital Psychiatry, 4,* 103–111.

Coyne, J. C., Fechner-Bates, S., & Schwenk, T. L. (1994). Prevalence, nature and comorbidity of depressive disorders in primary care. *General Hospital Psychiatry, 16,* 267–274.

Coyne, J. C., Schwenk, T. L., & Fechner-Bates, S. (1995). Nondetection of depression by primary care physicians reconsidered. *General Hospital Psychiatry, 17,* 3–12.

Depression Guideline Panel. (1993a). *Depression in primary care: Vol. 1. Detection and diagnosis* (Clinical Practice Guideline No. 5). Rockville, MD: Department of Health and Human Services, Public Health Service, Agency for Health Care Policy and Research. (Publication No. 93-0550)

Depression Guideline Panel. (1993b). *Depression in primary care: Vol. 2. Treatment of major depression* (Clinical Practice Guideline No. 5). Rockville, MD: Department of Health and Human Services, Public Health Service, Agency for Health Care Policy and Research. (Publication No. 93-0551)

Dew, M. A., Dunn, L. O., Bromet, E. J., & Schulberg, H. C. (1988). Factors affecting help-seeking during depression in a community sample. *Journal of Affective Disorders, 14,* 223–234.

Dohrenwend, B. P., & Dohrenwend, B. S. (1965). The problem of validity in field studies of psychological disorders. *Journal of Abnormal Psychology, 70,* 52–69.

Dowrick, D., & Buchan, I. (1995). Twelve month outcome of depression in general practice: Does detection or disclosure make a difference? *British Medical Journal, 311,* 1274–1276.

Escobar, J. I., Burnman, M. A., Karno, M., Forsythe, A., & Golding, J. M. (1987). Somatization in the community. *Archives of General Psychiatry, 44,* 713–718.

Ewing, J. A. (1984). Detecting alcoholism: The CAGE questionnaire. *Journal of the American Medical Association, 252,* 1905–1907.

Frame, P. S. (1986). A critical review of adult health maintenance. Part 4. Prevention of metabolic, behavioral and miscellaneous conditions. *Journal of Family Practice, 23,* 29–39.

Freeling, P., Rao, B. M., Paykel, E. S., Sireling, L. I., & Burton, R. H. (1985). Unrecognized depression in general practice. *British Medical Journal, 290,* 1880–1883.

Gask, L., Goldberg, D., Lesser, A. L., & Millar, T. (1988). Improving the psychiatric skills of the general practice trainee: An evaluation of a group training course. *Medical Education, 22,* 132–138.

Glass, R. M. (1995). Mental disorders: Quality of life and inequality of insurance coverage [Editorial]. *Journal of the American Medical Association, 274,* 1557.

Gelenberg, A. J., & Delgado, P. L. (1998). Depression. In A. J. Gelenberg & E. L. Bassuk (Eds.), *The practitioner's guide to psychoactive drugs* (pp. 19–97). New York: Plenum Publishing Corporation.

Goldberg, D. P., & Hillier, V. F. (1978). A scaled version of the General Health Questionnaire. *Psychological Medicine, 9,* 139–145.

Goldberg, D., Jenkins, L., Millar, T., & Faragher, E. (1993). The ability of trainee general practitioners to identify psychological distress among their patients. *Psychological Medicine, 23,* 185–193.

Goldberg, D. P., Steele, J. J., Smith, C., & Spivey, L. (1980). Training family doctors to recognize psychiatric illness with increased accuracy. *Lancet, 2,* 521–523.

Hahn, S. R. (1997). Working with specific populations: Families. In M. D. Feldman & J. F. Christensen (Eds.), *Behavioral medicine in primary care: A practical guide* (pp. 57–71). Stamford, CT: Appelton & Lange.

Hahn, S. R., Kroenke, K., Spitzer, R. L., Brody, D., Williams, J. B. W., Linzer, M., & deGruy, F. V. III (1996). The difficult patient: Prevalence, psychopathology, and functional impairment. *Journal of General Internal Medicine, 11,* 1–8.

Hahn, S. R., Thompson, K. S., Stern, V., Budner, N. S., & Wills, T. A. (1994). The difficult doctor–patient relationship: Somatization, personality and psychopathology. *Journal of Clinical Epidemiology, 47,* 647–658.

Hansson, L., Borgquist, L., Nettelbladt, P., & Nordstrom, G. (1994). The course of psychiatric illness in primary care patients: A 1-year follow-up. *Social Psychiatry & Psychiatric Epidemiology, 29,* 1–7.

Helzer, J. E., Robins, L. N., McEvoy, L. T., Spitznagel, R. L., Soltzman, R. K., Farmer, A., & Brockington, I. F. (1985). A comparison of clinical and diagnostic interview schedule diagnoses: Physician reexamination of lay-interviewed cases in the general population. *Archives of General Psychiatry, 42,* 657–666.

Henk, H. J., Katzelnick, D. J., Kobak, K. A., Greist, J. H., & Jefferson, J. W. (1996). Medical costs attributed to depression among patients with a history of high medical expenses in a health maintenance organization. *Archives of General Psychiatry, 53,* 899–904.

Hirschfeld, R. M. A., Keller, M. B., Panico, S., Arons, B. S., Barlow, D., Davidoff, F., Endicott, J., Froom, J., Goldstein, M., Gorman, J. M., Guthrie, D., Marek, R. G., Maurer, T. A., Meyer, R., Phillips, K., Ross, J.,

Schwenk, T. L., Sharfstein, S. S., Thase, M. E., & Wyatt, R. J. (1997). Consensus statement: The National Depressive and Manic-Depressive Association consensus statement on the undertreatment of depression. *Journal of the American Medical Association, 277,* 333–340.

Hoeper, E. W., Nycz, G. R., Kessler, L. G., Burke, J. D., & Pierce, W. E. (1984). The usefulness of screening for mental illness. *Lancet, I,* 33–35.

Hueston, W. J., Mainous, A. G., & Schilling, R. (1996). Patients with personality disorders: Functional status, health care utilization, and satisfaction with care. *Journal of Family Practice, 42,* 54–60.

Jackson, J. L., Chamberlin, J., & Kroenke, K. (1996). A controlled trial to assess the value of recognizing mental disorders and concerns and expectations. *Journal of General Internal Medicine, 11*(Suppl. 1), 134.

Jenks, S. F. (1985). Recognition of mental distress and diagnosis of mental disorder in primary care. *Journal of the American Medical Association, 253,* 1903–1907.

Johnson, J. G., Spitzer, R. L., Williams, J. B. W., Kroenke, K., Kroenke, K., Linzer, M., Brody, D., deGruy, F. V. III, & Hahn, S. (1995). Psychiatric comorbidity, health status, and functional impairment associated with alcohol abuse and dependence in primary care patients: Results from the PRIME-MD 1000 study. *Journal of Consulting and Clinical Psychology, 63,* 133–140.

Johnstone, A., & Goldberg, D. (1976). Psychiatric screening in general practice. *Lancet, I,* 605–608.

Kaplan, C. (1997). Somatization. In M. D. Feldman & J. F. Christensen (Eds.), *Behavioral medicine in primary care: A practical guide* (p. 204–211). Stamford, CT: Appleton & Lange.

Karlsson, H., Lehtinen, V., & Joukama, M. (1995). Psychiatric morbidity among frequent attender patients in primary care. *General Hospital Psychiatry, 17,* 19–25.

Katon, W., Robinson, P., Von Korff, M., Lin, E., Bush, T., Ludman, E., Simon, G., & Walker, E. (1996). A multifaceted intervention to improve treatment of depression in primary care. *Archives of General Psychiatry, 53,* 924–932.

Katon, W., & Schulberg, H. C. (1992). Epidemiology of depression in primary care. *General Hospital Psychiatry, 14,* 237–247.

Katon, W., & Von Korff, M. (1990). Caseness criteria for major depression: The primary care clinician and the psychiatric epidemiologist. In C. C. Attkinson & J. M. Zich (Eds.), *Depression in primary care: Screening and detection* (pp. 43–62). New York: Routledge.

Katon, W., Von Korff, M., Lin, E., Walker, E., Simon, G. E., Bush, T., Robinson, P., & Russo, J. (1995). Collaborative management to achieve treatment guidelines: Impact on depression in primary care. *Journal of the American Medical Association, 273,* 1026–1031.

Katon, W., Von Korff, M., Lin, E., Unützer, J., Simon, G., Walker, E., Ludman, E., & Bush, T. (1997). Population-based care of depression: Effective disease management strategies to decrease prevalence. *General Hospital Psychiatry, 19,* 169–178.

Kessler, L. G., Cleary, P. D., & Burke, J. D. (1985). Psychiatric disorders in primary care: Results of a follow-up study. *Archives of General Psychiatry, 42,* 583–587.

Kessler, R. C., McGonagle, K. A., Zhao, S., Nelson, C. B., Hughes, M., Eshleman, S., Wittchen, H. U., & Kendler, R. S. (1994). Lifetime and 12-month prevalence of DSM–III–R psychiatric disorders in the U.S. *Archives of General Psychiatry, 51,* 8–19.

Kirmayer, L. J., Robbins, J. M., Dworkind, M., & Yaffe, M. J. (1993). Somatization and the recognition of depression and anxiety in primary care. *American Journal of Psychiatry, 150,* 734–741.

Klinkman, M. S. (1997). Competing demands in psychosocial care: A model for the identification and treatment of depressive disorders in primary care. *General Hospital Psychiatry, 19,* 98–111.

Kobak, K. A., Taylor, L. H., Dottl, L., Greist, J. H., Jefferson, J. W., Burroughs, D., Mantel, J. M., Katzelnick, R., Norton, H. J., Henk, H. J., & Serlin, R. C. (1997). A computer-administered telephone interview to identify mental disorders. *Journal of the American Medical Association, 278,* 905–910.

Kroenke, K. (1997). Discovering depression in medical patients: Reasonable expectations. *Annals of Internal Medicine, 126,* 463–465.

Kroenke, K., Arrington, M. E., & Mangelsdorff, A. D. (1990). The prevalence of symptoms in medical outpatients and the adequacy of therapy. *Archives of Internal Medicine, 150,* 1685–1689.

Kroenke, K., Jackson, J. L., & Chamberlin, J. (1997). Depressive and anxiety disorders in patients presenting with physical complaints: Clinical predictors and outcome. *American Journal of Medicine, 103,* 339–347.

Kroenke, K., & Mangelsdorf, A. D. (1989). Common symptoms in ambulatory care: Incidence, evaluation, therapy, and outcome. *American Journal of Medicine, 86,* 262–266.

Kroenke, K., & Spitzer, R. L. (1998). Gender differences in the reporting of physical and somatoform symptoms. *Psychosomatic Medicine, 60,* 150–155.

Kroenke, K., Spitzer, R. L., deGruy, F. V. III, Hahn, S. R., Linzer, M., Williams, J. B. W., Brody, D., & Davies, M. (1997). Multisomatoform disorder: An alternative to undifferentiated somatoform disorder for the somatizing patient in primary care. *Archives of General Psychiatry, 54,* 352–358.

Kroenke, K., Spitzer, R. L., deGruy, F. V., & Swindle, R. (1998). A symptom check list to screen for somatoform disorders in primary care. *Psychosomatics, 39,* 263–272.

Kroenke, K., Spitzer, R., Williams, J. B. W., Linzer, M., Hahn, S. R., deGruy, F. V. III, & Brody, D. (1994). Physical symptoms in primary care: Predictors of psychiatric disorders and functional impairment. *Archives of Family Medicine, 3,* 774–779.

Lin, E. H., Katon, W., Simon, G., Von Korff, M., Bush, T. M., Rutter, C. M., Saunders, K. W., & Walker, E. A. (1997). Achieving guidelines for the treatment of depression in primary care: Is physician education enough? *Medical Care, 35,* 831–842.

Linn, L. S., & Yager, J. (1980). The effect of screening, sensitization, and feedback on notation of depression. *Journal of Medical Education, 55,* 942–949.

Linzer, M., Spitzer, R., Kroenke, K., Williams, J. B., Hahn, S., Brody, D., & deGruy, F. (1996). Gender, quality of life, and mental disorders in primary care: Results from the PRIME–MD 1000 study. *American Journal of Medicine, 101,* 526–533.

Magruder-Habib, K., Zung, W. W. K., & Feussner, J. R. (1990). Improving physicians' recognition and treatment of depression in general medical care: Results from a randomized clinical trial. *Medical Care, 28,* 239–250.

Main, D., Lutz, L., Barrett, J., Matthew, J., & Miller, R. S. (1993). The role of primary care clinician attitudes, beliefs, and training in the diagnosis and treatment of depression. *Archives of Family Medicine, 2,* 1061–1066.

Moore, J. T., Lilimperi, D. R., & Bobula, J. A. (1978). Recognition of depression by family medicine residents: The impact of screening. *Journal of Family Practice, 7,* 509–513.

Moore, R. D., Bone, L. R., Geller, G., Mamon, J. A., Stokes, E. J., & Levine, D. M. (1989). Prevalence, detection and treatment of alcoholism in hospitalized patients. *Journal of the American Medical Association, 261,* 403–407.

Mulrow, C. D., Williams, J. W., Jr., Gerety, M. B., Ramirez, G., Montiel, O. M., & Kerber, C. (1995). Case-finding instruments for depression in primary care settings. *Annals of Internal Medicine, 122,* 913–921.

National Institute of Mental Health. (1993). *Eating disorders* (NIH Publication No. 93-3477). Bethesda, MD: National Institutes of Health.

Ness, D. E., & Ende, J. (1994). Denial in the medical interview: Recognition and management. *Journal of the American Medical Association, 272,* 1777–1781.

Newman, F. L., & Ciarlo, J. A. (1994). Criteria for selecting psychological instruments for treatment outcome assessment. In M. E. Maruish (Ed.), *The use of psychological testing for treatment planning and outcomes assessment* (pp. 98–110). Hillsdale, NJ: Lawrence Erlbaum Associates.

Olfson, M. (1991). Primary care patients who refuse specialized mental health services. *Archives of Internal Medicine, 151,* 129–132.

Olfson, M., Gilbert, T., Weissman, M., Blacklow, R. S., & Broadhead, W. E. (1995). Recognition of emotional distress in physically healthy primary care patients who perceive poor physical health. *General Hospital Psychiatry, 17,* 173–180.

O'Malley, P. G., Wong, P. W. K., Kroenke, K., Roy, M. J., & Wong, R. K. H. (1998). The value of screening for psychiatric disorders prior to upper endoscopy. *Journal of Psychosomatic Research, 44,* 279–287.

Orleans, C. T., George, L. K., Houpt, J. L., & Brodie, H. K. H. (1985). How primary care physicians treat psychiatric disorders: A national survey of family practitioners. *American Journal of Psychiatry, 142,* 52–57.

Ormel, J., Von Korff, M., Ustun, T. B., Pini, S., Korten, A., & Oldehinkel, T. (1994). Common mental disorders and disability across cultures: Results from the WHO collaborative study on psychological problems in general health care. *Journal of the American Medical Association, 272,* 1741–1748.

Pang, A. H. T., Chao, D. V. K., Fabb, W. E., Lai, K. Y. C., & Leung, T. (1997). Validation study of the Chinese version of the Primary Care Evaluation of Mental Disorders (cPRIME-MD) Part I — Translation and reliability. *Supplement to the Journal of the American Medical Association, Southeast Asia, 13,* 16–18.

Pang, A. H. T., Chao, D. V. K., Fabb, W. E., Leung, T., Ng, F. S., & Yeung, O. C. Y. (1997). Validation study of the Chinese version of the Primary Care Evaluation of Mental Disorders (cPRIME-MD). Part II — Validity. *Supplement to the Journal of the American Medical Association, Southeast Asia, 13,* 19–22.

Parker, T., May, P. A., Maviglia, M. A., Petrakes, S., Sunde, S., & Gloyd, S. V. (1997). PRIME–MD: Its utility in detecting mental disorders in American Indians. *International Journal of Psychiatry and Medicine, 27,* 107–128.

Parkerson, G. R., Broadhead, W. E., & Tse, C. K. (1995). Health status and severity of illness as predictor of outcomes in primary care. *Medical Care, 33,* 53–56.

Paykel, E. S., & Priest, R. G. (1992). Recognition and management of depression in general practice: consensus statement. *British Medical Journal, 305,* 1198–1202.

Penn, J. V., Boland, R., McCartney, J. R., Kohn, R., & Mulvey, T. (1997). Recognition and treatment of depressive disorders by internal medicine attendings and housestaff. *General Hospital Psychiatry, 19,* 179–184.

Philbrick, J. T., Connelly, J. E., & Wofford, A. B. (1996). The prevalence of mental disorders in rural office practice. *Journal of General Internal Medicine, 11,* 9–15.

Prochaska, J. O., DiClemente, C. C., & Norcross, J. C. (1992). In search of how people change. Applications to addictive behaviors. *American Psychologist, 47,* 1102–1114.

Putnam, S. M., & Lipkin, M., Jr. (1995). The patient-centered interview: Research support. In M. Lipkin, Jr., S. M. Putnam, & A. Lazare (Eds.), *The medical interview: Clinical care, education and research* (pp. 530–537). New York: Springer-Verlag.

Radloff, S. L. (1977). The CES-D scale: A self-report depression scale for research in the general population. *Applying Psychological Measurement, 1,* 385–401.

Regier, D. A., Hirschfeld, R. M. A., Goodwin, F. K., Burke, J. D., Jr., Lazar, J. N., & Judd, L. L. (1988). The NIMH depression awareness, recognition and treatment program: Structure, aims and scientific bases. *American Journal of Psychiatry, 145,* 1351–1357.

Reiman, E. M. (1998). Anxiety. In A. J. Gelenberg & E. L. Bassuk (Eds.), *The practitioner's guide to psychoactive drugs* (pp. 213–264). New York: Plenum.

Robbins, J. M., Kirmayer, L. F., Cathébras, P., Yaffe, M. J., & Dworkind, M. (1994). Physician characteristics and the recognition of depression and anxiety in primary care. *Medical Care, 32,* 795–812.

Robins, L. N. (1985). Epidemiology: Reflections on testing the validity of psychiatric interviews. *Archives of General Psychiatry, 42,* 918–924.

Robins, L. N., Helzer, J. E., Orvaschel, H., Anthony, J. C., Blazer, D. G., Burnam, A., & Burke, J. D., Jr. (1985). The Diagnostic Interview Schedule. In W. W. Eaton & L. G. Kessler (Eds.), *Epidemiologic field methods in psychiatry: The NIMH Epidemiologic Catchment Area Program* (pp. 285–308). New York: Academic Press.

Rodin, G., Craven, J., & Littlefield, C. (1991). *Depression in the medically ill: An integrated approach.* New York: Brunner/Mazel.

Rost, K., Humphrey, J., & Kelleher, K. (1994). Physician management preferences and barriers to care for rural patients with depression. *Archives of Family Medicine, 3,* 409–414.

Rost, K., Smith, R., Matthews, D. B., & Guide, B. (1994). The deliberate misdiagnosis of major depression in primary care. *Archives of Family Medicine, 16,* 267–276.

Roter, D. L., Hall, J. A., Kern, D. E., Barker, L. R., Cole, K. A., & Roca, R. P. (1995). Improving physicians' interviewing skills and reducing patients' emotional distress: A randomized clinical trial. *Archives of Internal Medicine, 155,* 1877–1884.

Rubenstein, L. V., McCoy, J. M., Cope, D. W., Barrett, P. A., Hirsch, S. H., Messer, K. S., & Young, R. T. (1995). Improving patient quality of life with feedback to physicians about functional status. *Journal of General Internal Medicine, 10,* 607–614.

Sartorius, N., Ustun, T. B., Costa e Silva, J. A., Goldberg, D., Lecrubier, Y., Ormel, J., Von Korff, M., & Wittchen, H. U. (1993). An international study of psychological problems in primary care: Preliminary report from the WHO Collaborative Project on Psychological Problems in General Health Care. *Archives of General Psychiatry, 50,* 819–824.

Schappert, S. M. (1992). National Ambulatory Medical Care Survey: 1989 Summary. *Vital Health Statistics, 13*(110).

Schulberg, H. C., Block, M. R., Madonia, M. J., Scott, C. P., Rodriguez, E., Imber, S. D., Perel, J., Lave, J., Houck, P. K., & Coulehan, J. L. (1996). Treating major depression in primary care practice: Eight-month clinical outcomes. *Archives of General Psychiatry, 53,* 913–919.

Schulberg, H., Block, M., Madonia, M., Scott, C., Lave, J., Rodriguez, E., & Coulehan, J. (1997). The "usual care" of major depression in primary care practice. *Archives of Family Medicine, 6,* 334–339.

Schulberg, H. C., & Burns, B. J. (1988). Mental disorders in primary care: Epidemiologic, diagnostic, and treatment research directions. *General Hospital Psychiatry, 10,* 79–87.

Schulberg, H. C., Katon, W., Simon, G. E., & Rush, A. J. (1998). Treating major depression in primary care practice: An update of the Agency for Health Care Policy and Research Practice Guidelines. *Archives of General Psychiatry, 55,* 1121–1127.

Schwenk, T. L. (1996). Screening for depression in primary care: A disease in search of a test. *Journal of General Internal Medicine, 11,* 437–439.

Schwenk, T. L., Coyne, J. C., & Fechner-Bates, S. (1996). Differences between detected and undetected patients in primary care and depressed psychiatric patients. *General Hospital Psychiatry, 18,* 407–415.

Shapiro, S., German, P. S., Skinner, E. A., Von Korff, M., Turner, R. W., Klein, L. E., Teitelbaum, M. L., Kramer, M., Burke, J. D., & Burns, B. J. (1987). An experiment to change detection and management of mental morbidity in primary care. *Medical Care, 25,* 327–339.

Shapiro, S., Skinner, E. A., Kessler, L. G., Von Korff, M., German, P. S., Tischler, G. L., Leaf, P. J., Benham, L., Bottler, L., & Regier, D. A. (1984). Utilization of health and mental health services: Three epidemiologic catchment sites. *Archives of General Psychiatry, 41,* 971–978.

Simon, G. E., & Von Korff, M. (1995). Recognition, management, and outcomes of depression in primary care. *Archives of Family Medicine, 4,* 99–105.

Simon, G., Von Korff, M., Heiligenstein, J. H., Revicki, D. A., Grothaus, L., Katon, W., & Wagner, E. H. (1996). Initial antidepressant selection in primary care: Effectiveness and cost of fluoxetine vs tricyclic antidepressants. *Journal of the American Medical Association, 275,* 1897–1902.

Smith, G. R., Monson, R. A., & Ray, D. C. (1986). Psychiatric consultation in somatization disorder. *New England Journal of Medicine, 314,* 1407–1413.

Smith, G. R., Rost, K., & Kashner, T. M. (1995). A trial of the effect of a standardized psychiatric consultation on health outcomes and costs in somatizing patients. *Archives of General Psychiatry, 52,* 238–243.

Smith, R. C., & Hoppe, R. B. (1991). The patient's story: Integrating the patient and physician centered approaches to interviewing. *Annals of Internal Medicine, 115,* 470–477.

Spitzer, R. L., Gibbon, M., Williams, J. B. W., & Endicott, J. (1996). Global assessment of functioning (GAF) scale. In L. I. Sedere & B. Dickey (Eds.), *Outcomes assessment in clinical practice* (pp. 76–78, 182). Baltimore, MD: Williams and Wilkins.

Spitzer, R. L., Kroenke, K., Linzer, M., Hahn, S. R., Williams, J. B. W., deGruy, F. V. III, Brody, D., & Davies, M. (1995). Health-related quality of life in primary care patients with mental disorders: Results from the PRIME–MD 1000 Study. *Journal of the American Medical Association, 274,* 1511–1517.

Spitzer, R. L., Williams, J. B. W., Gibbon, M., & First, M. B. (1992). The Structured Clinical Interview for DSM–III–R (SCID), I: History, rationale, and description. *Archives of General Psychiatry, 49,* 624–629.

Spitzer, R. L., Williams, J. B. W., & Kroenke, K. (1997). *Quick guide to the patient problem questionnaire.* Available from R. L. Spitzer, Biometrics Research, New York State Psychiatric Institute.

Spitzer, R. L., Williams, J. B. W., Kroenke, K., Linzer, M., deGruy, F. V. III, Hahn, S. R., Brody, D., & Johnson, J. G. (1994). Utility of a new procedure for diagnosing mental disorders in primary care: The PRIME–MD 1000 Study. *Journal of the American Medical Association, 272,* 1749–1756.

Spitzer, R. L., Yanovski, S., Wadden, T., Wing, R., Marcus, M. D., Stunkard, A. D., Devlin, M., Mitchell, J., Hasin, D., & Horne, R. L. (1993). Binge eating disorder: Its further validation in a multisite study. *International Journal of Eating Disorders, 13,* 137–153.

Stewart, A. L., Hays, R. D., & Ware, J. E. (1988). The MOS Short-Form General Health Survey: Reliability and validity in a patient population. *Medical Care, 26,* 724–732.

Turner, R. J., & Noh, S. (1988). Physical disability and depression: A longitudinal analysis. *Journal of Health and Social Behavior, 29,* 23–37.

U.S. Preventive Services Task Force. (1996). *Guide to clinical preventive services* (2nd ed.). Baltimore, MD: Williams & Wilkins.

Ustun, T. B., & Sartorius, N. (Eds.). (1996). *Mental illness in primary care: An international study.* New York: John Wiley & Sons.

Valenstein, M., Dalack, G., Blow, F., Figueroa, S., Standiford, C., & Douglass, A. (1997). Screening for psychiatric illness with a combined screening and diagnostic instrument. *Journal of General Internal Medicine, 12,* 679–685.

Von Korff, M., Ormel, J., Katon, W., & Lin, E. H. B. (1992). Disability and depression among high utilizers of health care: A longitudinal analysis. *Archives of General Psychiatry, 49,* 91–100.

Von Korff, M., Shapiro, S., Burke, J. D., Teitelbaum, M., Skinner, E. A., German, P., Turner, R. W., Klein, L., & Burns, B. (1987). Anxiety and depression in a primary care clinic: Comparison of Diagnostic Interview Schedule, General Health Questionnaire, and practitioner assessments. *Archives of General Psychiatry, 44,* 152–156.

Ware, J. E. (1993). *SF–36 Health Survey: Manual and interpretation guide.* Boston: Health Institute, New England Medical Center.

Wells, K. B., Stewart, A., Hays, R. D., Burnam, M. A., Rogers, W., Daniels, M., Berry, S., Greenfield, S., & Ware, J. (1989). The functional status and well-being of depressed patients: Results form the Medical Outcomes Study. *Journal of the American Medical Association, 262,* 907–913.

Whooley, M. A., Avins, A. L., Miranda, J., & Browner, W. S. (1997). Case-finding instruments for depression: Two questions are as good as many. *Journal of General Internal Medicine, 12,* 439–445.

Williams, J. B. W., Gibbon, M., First, M. B., Spitzer, R. L., Davies, M., Borus, J., Howes, M. J., Kane, J., & Pope, H. G., Jr. (1992). The Structured Clinical Interview for DSM–III–R (SCID), II: Multisite test-retest reliability. *Archives of General Psychiatry, 49*, 630–636.

Williams, J. B. W., Spitzer, R. L., Linzer, M., Kroenke, K., Hahn, S. R., deGruy, F. V., & Lazev, A. (1995). Gender differences in depression in primary care. *American Journal of Obstetrics and Gynecology, 173*, 654–659.

Wyshak, G., & Barsky, A. (1995). Satisfaction with and effectiveness of medical care in relations to anxiety and depression: Patient and physician ratings compared. *General Hospital Psychiatry, 17*, 108–114.

Wyshak, G., Barsky, A. J., & Klerman, G. L. (1991). Comparison of psychiatric screening tests in a general medical setting using ROC analysis. *Medical Care, 29*, 775–785.

Zimmerman, M., Lish, J. D., Farber, N. J., Hartung, J., Lush, D., Kuzma, M. A., & Plescia, G. (1994). Screening for depression in medical patients: Is the focus too narrow. *General Hospital Psychiatry, 16*, 388–396.

Zung, W. W. K. (1965). A self-rating depression scale. *Archives of General Psychiatry, 12*, 63–70.

Zung, W. W. K. (1971). A rating instrument for anxiety disorders. *Psychosomatics, 12*, 164–167.

Zung, W. W. K., Magill, M., Moore, J. T., & George, D. T. (1983). Recognition and treatment of depression in a family medicine practice. *Journal of Clinical Psychiatry, 44*, 3–6.

Directions and COMPASS–PC

Grant R. Grissom
PsyberMetrics

Kenneth I. Howard
Northwestern University

COMPASS for Primary Care (COMPASS–PC) was developed by Compass Information Services, Inc. in collaboration with the Advanced Healthcare Services Division of the Bristol-Myers Squibb Company. It was subsequently purchased by Bristol-Myers for use in Directions, its behavioral health care disease management system for primary care settings.

This chapter describes COMPASS–PC and its role within the broader Directions framework, including:

- Developmental history.
- Psychometric properties.
- Basic interpretive strategy.
- Usefulness as a screener and confirmatory test.
- Usefulness in treatment monitoring.
- Risk adjustment.
- Potential as a "learning system," capable of continual improvement in its contribution to clinical decision support.

Finally, a case study is presented to illustrate the use of COMPASS–PC and its potential as a tool to help physicians identify, and to provide the most cost-effective and appropriate care to patients suffering from a behavioral disorder.

OVERVIEW

Developmental History

COMPASS–PC is grounded in basic research and theory development accomplished primarily by Dr. Kenneth Howard and colleagues at Northwestern University since the early 1980s. It also reflects the vision of Dr. Peter Brill, the founder of Compass Information Services.

Outcomes Management. Every day there are hundreds of thousands of behavioral health care treatment interventions delivered to the public. Each represents the potential for learning, that is, the opportunity to better understand which types of interventions are most effective for which types of patients. However, the opportunity to learn from clinical experience is squandered in the absence of data and with a lack of theoretical models relating treatment to clinical change. In the large majority of treatment episodes, no standardized measures of clinical status are collected. In the rare instances when data are collected, the absence of a theoretical framework precludes the type of learning and development that is essential for determining the best treatment for particular patients.

Tremendous advances in the effectiveness of behavioral health care would be possible through theory-based measurement systems made practical by the proliferation of increasingly affordable computers. The goal would not be merely the assessment of treatment outcomes (*outcomes measurement*), but the systematic collection, analysis, and reporting of treatment information to support both clinical decision making at the level of the individual patient and continual "learning" at the level of the treatment system (*outcomes management*).

In the early 1980s, Dr. Philip Friedman developed a method for monitoring patient status during treatment. Specifically, Dr. Friedman periodically collected questionnaire data from patients, combined the patients' responses to derive clinical scale scores, and compared those scores to benchmarks (normative data) in order to evaluate patient progress (Friedman, 1982). Our initial efforts to adapt Dr. Friedman's methods involved the construction of a battery of scales considered by therapists to be clinically meaningful-symptom checklists, self-esteem questionnaires, marital relationships scales, and so on. However constituted, use of these batteries consistently produced the same three responses from therapists: (a) "The battery takes too long to complete"; (b) "You need to add a measure of _____" (the measure suggested usually reflected the treatment theory favored by the therapist, with wide variation among analysts, Rogerians, behaviorists, etc.); and (c) "We don't know what these data mean."

Clearly, a guiding theory was required to select measures and to provide a useful interpretive framework. Fortunately, much of the necessary theory development was well advanced. Dr. Howard and his associates had made good progress toward determining the key phases of effective treatment (and the clinical measures corresponding to each), and demonstrating a lawful relationship between "doses" of treatment and patient improvement. The former (*phase theory*) could be used to guide the development of an instrument to assess clinical change concurrently with treatment. The latter (*dose-response theory*) suggested a method for establishing an interpretive framework, enabling clinicians to monitor a patient's progress in relation to an expected (normative) improvement curve and quickly determine what the data "mean."

Phase Theory and Dose-Response Theory. Phase theory (Howard, Lueger, Maling, & Martinovich, 1993) posits three phases in the course of successful outpatient mental health treatment. During the first phase, *remoralization*, the patient comes to feel more hopeful and able to mobilize personal coping resources. Once remoralization occurs, the patient experiences symptomatic improvement during the *reme-*

diation phase. Finally, the third phase, *rehabilitation*, involves unlearning maladaptive, long-standing psychological or behavioral patterns and finding more constructive ways to cope with various areas of life (e.g., relationships, work).

Phase theory research has demonstrated that these phases are sequential, and causally dependent. Its importance to COMPASS–PC lays in providing an answer to the question: What should we measure? COMPASS–PC scales were constructed to measure subjective well-being (SWB), current symptoms (CS), and current life functioning (CLF), which correspond to remoralization, remediation, and rehabilitation, respectively. Assessment of changes in these areas (both their sequence and rate) can provide useful and actionable information to the practitioner as to the effectiveness of treatment for a given patient.

Dose-response theory (Howard, Kopta, Krause, & Orlinsky, 1986) documented a relationship between the amount of treatment provided and the probability of patient improvement. The relationship proved to be different for different clinical syndromes. Dose-response theory has been extended in subsequent research that suggests that the likely extent and rate of improvement for a specific patient is predictable from patient characteristics, symptom severity, and the type of treatment provided (see Howard, Moras, Brill, Martinovich, & Lutz, 1996). Thus, dose-response theory provides a foundation for use of COMPASS–PC as a predictive or "learning" system (see later discussion).

Development Criteria. Having identified a scientifically strong and clinically useful foundation for COMPASS–PC, it was necessary to establish the criteria that would guide development of a broader outcomes management system. COMPASS–PC would require not only psychometrically strong scales and items, but a method for collecting, analyzing, and reporting data and a plan for implementation as a learning system. Successful implementation in a treatment system would require the establishment of a "culture of measurement" in which administrative and clinical staff genuinely understood, valued, and embraced outcomes management (Sperry, Grissom, Brill, & Marion, 1997). These considerations suggested the following development criteria/system characteristics:

- Grounded in established theory.
- Psychometrically strong.
- Yielding clinically actionable information concurrent with treatment.
- Low administrative burden.
- Low respondent burden.
- Responsive to the needs of multiple stakeholders: payers, clinicians, administrators, patients.
- Risk ("case mix") adjusted.
- Involving a learning system: continual improvement in performance of the measurement system as data accumulate.
- Data collection from both patients and clinicians.

From these criteria, it was possible to devise a set of product features that were essential for COMPASS–PC. First, the *core scales* were established as subjective well-being, symptoms, and functioning. These were dictated by phase theory, the need for clinical actionability, and focus-group feedback from payers.

Second, *length, reading level, and structure/formatting* of the instrument were important to minimizing respondent burden. The challenge is familiar: how to cover the required measurement domains with scales of acceptable reliability and validity without imposing excessive demands on the patient's time and reading skills. The design
goals for COMPASS–PC were an average vocabulary/reading level of fifth grade,
and an average completion time of less than 15 min.

Third, *administrative efficiency* was considered the sine qua non of staff acceptance.
The requirements associated with managed care, coupled with heightened cost consciousness, have dramatically increased the paperwork demands on both clinical and
administrative staff in health care settings. COMPASS–PC would have to require the
absolute minimum of staff involvement; it would need to fit seamlessly into routine
clinic procedures. Additionally, there would need to be alternative methods for data
collection appropriate to varying operational and budgetary constraints.

Fourth, *responsiveness to the needs of multiple stakeholders* requires that those needs
be made explicit and drive the system design/performance objectives. The success of
any outcomes management system is directly linked to its clinical utility. Primary
care physicians rarely have objective, timely, and relevant information that could
help them to treat behavioral health care problems. COMPASS–PC was designed to
help physicians decide:

- Does this patient have a mental health or chemical dependency problem that requires attention?
- If so, which course of action (e.g., referral to a specialist, treatment with medication, monitoring) would be most appropriate?

Further, if a decision is made to prescribe a medication, COMPASS–PC helps the
physician to determine the choice of medication and whether the treatment is working:

- Is there overall improvement in mental health status (i.e., feelings of well-being,
  reduced symptoms, improved life functioning)?
- Has there been a reduction in specific symptoms of concern (e.g., depression,
  anxiety)?
- Is the patient experiencing side effects of the medication?
- Has the patient recovered to the point where the medication can safely be discontinued?

COMPASS–PC provides third-party payers with documentation of treatment effectiveness and assurance that data are used at all system levels (see outcomes management vs. measurement, discussed later) to provide cost-effective, high-quality
care. In addition to utility for managing individual care, COMPASS–PC data can
help system administrators to:

- Establish clinical pathways and treatment guidelines.
- Identify clinicians who are unusually effective (e.g., to help train their col-
  leagues).
- Identify clinicians who regularly deviate from treatment guidelines (i.e., who
  may require additional training).
- Assess overall system performance and changes over time.

Eventually (see patient profiling, discussed later), as the "learning" capability develops, administrators will be able to evaluate overall system performances in relation to expectations that are empirically based and risk adjusted (i.e., that take into account clinical characteristics, such as diagnosis, chronicity, and severity).

Outcomes Measurement Versus Management. Outcomes assessment is new to behavioral health care, and the distinction between *measurement* and *management* is poorly understood. The two types of systems vary markedly in their functionality/utility (Sperry, Brill, Howard, & Grissom, 1996). The requirements that outcomes management systems be integrated into routine care and serve a clinical decision support function create additional challenges for developers. Issues of instrument length, administrative and respondent burden, and the "turnaround time" required to produce a patient report are more critical for management than for measurement systems.

Creation of COMPASS–PC: The Need for Behavioral Health Care Outcomes Management in Primary Care. The decision to create a version of COMPASS specific to the needs of primary care physicians was based on findings presented in an article by Dr. Jennifer Lish (1996). Its main points were:

- Most people with common psychiatric disorders seek care from general medical physicians (rather than mental health professionals; Regier, Narrow, & Rae, 1993).
- Primary care physicians recognize fewer than half of the psychiatric disorders in their practice (Wells, Hays, Burnam, Rogers, Greenfields, & Ware, 1989).
- Costs associated with behavioral health disorders (impairment, disability) exceed those due to physical disorders such as cardiovascular disease, hypertension, diabetes, and arthritis (Wells, Stewart, Hays, et al., 1989).
- Anxiety and depression are associated with greater medical care utilization in all age groups (Klerman et al., 1991). Alcoholism is associated with a tremendous number of medical sequelae (Miller, Belkin, & Gold, 1991).
- Half (53%) of all adults who commit suicide visit their physicians in the month prior to their death (Van Casteren, Van der Veken, Tafforeau, & Van Oyden, 1993).
- Assisting primary care physicians in the diagnosis and treatment of depression has been found to reduce the rate of suicide in their patients by 30% (Rutz, von Knorring, & Walinder, 1989).

In short, there is overwhelming evidence that an effective behavioral health care outcomes management system for primary care settings would have a substantial "payoff" in reduced costs and suffering.

Psychometric Properties

COMPASS–PC provides for patient self-report and physician ratings. The core patient scales are Subjective Well-Being (SWB: 6 items); Current Life Functioning (CLF: 17 items), and Current Symptoms (CS: 51 items). Scores on these scales are combined to derive the patient's Mental Health Index (MHI). The patient's need for treatment is evaluated by comparing these scores to norms for a nontreatment ("normal") population; treatment progress is evaluated by monitoring changes over time.

Results of numerous analyses of the reliability, validity, and sensitivity to change of these scales have been published by Dr. Howard (Howard et al., 1996). Generally, studies have found reliability in the good to excellent range, and have documented convergent, content and "known group" validity. The following is a summary of their findings.

Content sampling for the SWB scale includes both positive and negative affect, and health and contentment. In a sample of 197 adult psychotherapy patients assessed prior to treatment, internal consistency reliability (alpha) for SWB was .79, and test–retest reliability was .82. Alpha for a sample of primary care patients ($N = 1,320$) was .74. In a sample of 108 nonpatients, SWB correlated at .79 with the General Well-Being Scale at .73 with the total score of the SF–36, and at .76 with its 5-item mental component score. The distributions in Fig. 7.1 show excellent discrimination between scores for 1,320 primary care patients and a community sample ($N = 981$) on the SWB scale.

The SWB, CS, CLF, and MHI scores shown in Figs. 7.1–7.4 were normed on the primary care sample. Thus, the mean and standard deviation of the T-scores for the primary care sample are 50 and 10, respectively, for each of the four scales. The mean

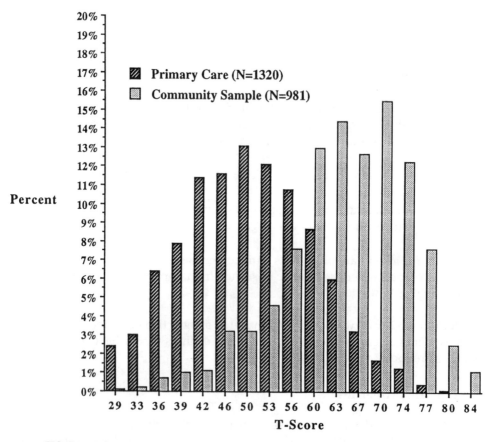

FIG. 7.1. Subjective Well-Being score distributions for screened primary care patients and a general community sample.

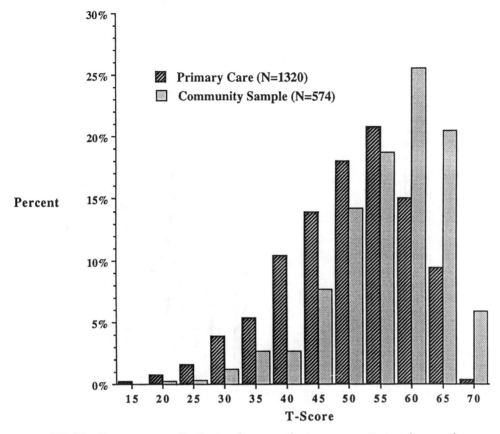

FIG. 7.2. Symptoms score distributions for screened primary care patients and a general community sample.

and standard deviation of the SWB scores for the community sample were 64.5 and 9.45.

The COMPASS–PC symptoms scale (CS) was constructed using the signs and symptoms of six Axis I diagnoses described in the *Diagnostic and Statistical Manual for Mental Disorders*, third edition revised (*DSM–III–R*; American Psychiatric Association, 1987): adjustment disorder, anxiety, bipolar, depression, phobia, and obsessive-compulsive. Of adult outpatients who seek treatment in behavioral health settings and qualify for an Axis I diagnosis, approximately 90% present with one of these six. Construction of the CS section was completed by the addition of a screener for chemical dependency and several items to detect common side effects of psychotropic medications, but these do not contribute to the CS scale score.

In a sample of 160 adult psychotherapy patients assessed at intake, the internal consistency reliability (alpha) of CS was .94, and the test–retest reliability ($N = 53$; 3- to 4-week interval) was .85. Alpha for a sample of 1,320 adult primary care patients was .93. Table 7.1 shows reliabilities for CS subscales for the primary care sample.

Criteria validity was assessed using psychotherapy patient samples. The CS total score correlates at .91 ($N = 249$) with an abbreviated, 47-item version of the SCL–90–R. The Depression subscale, of particular importance to COMPASS–PC, correlates at .68 ($N = 272$) with the Center for Epidemiologic Studies of Depression Scale (CES–D) and at .87 ($N = 44$) with the Beck Depression Inventory. Finally, the mean Depression

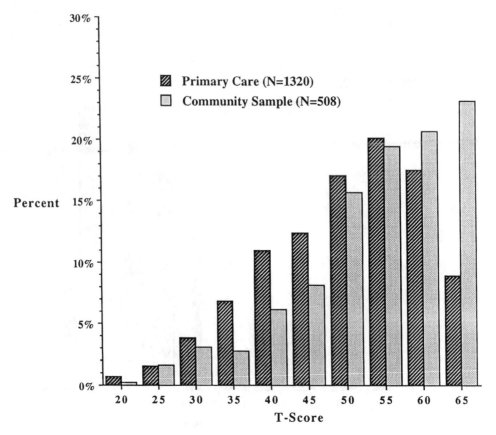

FIG. 7.3. Life Functioning score distributions for screened primary care patients and a
general community sample.

subscale score for 13 patients diagnosed with depression using the Structured Clinical Interview for Diagnosis (SCID) was nearly a full standard deviation higher than
that of 15 patients with other SCID Axis I diagnoses. Figure 7.2 shows the distributions of CS scores for primary care patient ($N = 1,320$) and community ($N = 574$) samples. The mean and standard direction of the CS scores for the community sample
were 56.3 and 8.77.

The CLF scale was developed to assess the degree of disability caused by the patient's psychological condition. Scale items were generated primarily from the Social
Security Disability Guidelines. In a sample of 70 adult psychotherapy patients assessed prior to treatment, the internal consistency reliability (alpha) for CLF was .93
and the test-retest ($N = 48$; 3–4 weeks interval) reliability was .76. Table 7.2 shows the
reliabilities for all CLF subscales in a primary care patient sample, and Fig. 7.3 shows
the distribution of CLF scores for patient ($N = 1,320$) and community ($N = 508$) samples. The mean and standard deviation of the CLF scores for the community sample
were 54.0 and 9.81.

The MHI — a combination of SWB, CS, and CLF total scores — had an internal consistency (alpha) of .87 in a sample of 163 adult psychotherapy patients and a test–retest reliability of .82 ($N = 213$). In an adult primary care sample ($N = 1,320$), alpha was
.88. As shown in Fig. 7.4, MHI scores for a primary care patient population ($N = 1,320$)
are normally distributed and distinct from the distribution for a community sample

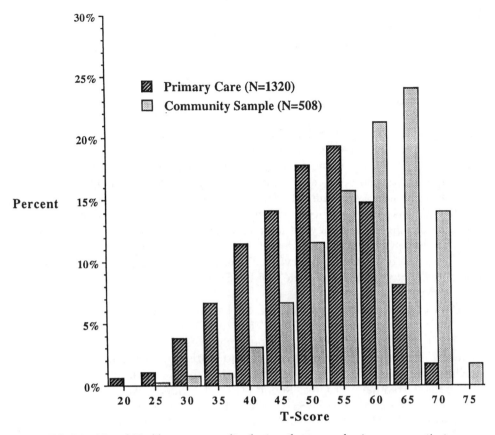

FIG. 7.4. Mental Health status score distributions for screened primary care patients and a general community sample.

TABLE 7.1
Reliabilities of Current Symptoms Subscales ($N = 1,320$)

Subscale	Internal Consistency
Adjustment Disorder	.73
Anxiety	.68
Bipolar	.59
Depression	.89
Obsessive-Compulsive	.77
Phobia	.69
Substance Use	.79

TABLE 7.2
Current Life Functioning ($N = 1,320$)

Subscale	Internal Consistency
Family Functioning	.61
Health and Grooming	.64
Intimate Relationships	.69
Self-Management	.70
Social Relationships	.79
Work, School, Household	.85

($N = 508$). The mean and standard deviation of the MHI scores for the community sample were 58.6 and 8.92.

Basic Interpretive Strategy

In the Directions program, Bristol–Myers Squibb has paired COMPASS–PC with an anxiety/depression screener (FOCUS) to provide an integrated outcomes management system. All new patients in the primary care setting complete FOCUS, a symptom checklist consisting of general medical symptoms and 34 symptoms of anxiety and/or depression. When the patient returns the FOCUS form, office staff slip it into a jacket that has a transparent column highlighting the anxiety and depression symptoms, permitting rapid review. If the patient endorses "constant worry" plus three other anxiety symptoms, or six depression symptoms, the screen is positive and a note is recorded for physician review. Patients who screen positive on FOCUS are asked by the physician to complete COMPASS–PC to evaluate the need for treatment for the psychological condition.

At the clinic's option, COMPASS–PC can be administered to the patient through a hand-held computer called a Point-of-View (POV) box, or by pencil and paper. POV administration allows for immediate, on-site processing and reporting of patient responses. The paper version must be faxed to a Bristol–Myers Squibb facility, where the form is processed and a report provided to the clinic via return fax.

A patient Treatment Progress Report (TPR), described next, is generated after every administration of COMPASS–PC. The TPR includes tables and graphs showing changes in the MHI, SWB, CS, and CLF scores over the course of treatment, interpreted using percentile scores showing the relationships of patient scales to a normative sample of over 10,000 patients entering outpatient mental health treatment. This normative sample provides for evaluation of a patient's status and progress in relation to individuals who seek treatment for similar behavioral health care problems. Trends in these scale scores indicate changes in global patient well-being, symptoms, and functioning. The TPR also shows changes for each symptom over time.

The TPR is the interpretive tool used by the physicians to determine:

- If treatment is necessary. Generally, MHI scores below 65 suggest the need for treatment, particularly if the Anxiety and/or Depression subscale scores are also below 65.
- If the patient should be referred to a mental health specialist. An MHI score below 17 normally suggests the need for a referral, particularly if suicidal ideation is present.
- If the patient is suicidal. A notation appears in the "Critical Signs" section of the TPR if the patient reports suicidal thoughts or attempts.
- If the patient is making progress. The MHI trend line is a global indicator, whereas subscale scores and item-level data allow the physician to "drill down" to more detailed information.
- If there is evidence of serious side effects of medication. The symptom list includes known side effects of frequently prescribed medications.
- If the patient has recovered. The TPR graph for the MHI trend line shows a "normal range" of scores characteristic of nontreatment populations. MHI scores in this range suggest that treatment may no longer be necessary.

COMPASS-PC thus helps the physician to confirm whether treatment is necessary, decide on a treatment plan, evaluate patient progress, and determine when to stop treatment. We turn now to the role of COMPASS-PC within the broader Directions program.

DIRECTIONS AND COMPASS-PC

Office Procedure

The procedures for implementing Directions are summarized in Fig. 7.5. Generally, all patients seeking treatment (i.e., other than those seeking routine physicals) are asked to complete the FOCUS screener already described. Those screening positive for anxiety and/or depression symptoms (typically 10%–15%) are asked to complete COMPASS-PC. (As noted earlier, in some settings, a POV box is used, allowing for immediate production of a TPR for physician review; in others, a pencil/paper version is faxed to a processing center and the TPR is made available by return fax within 48 hr.)

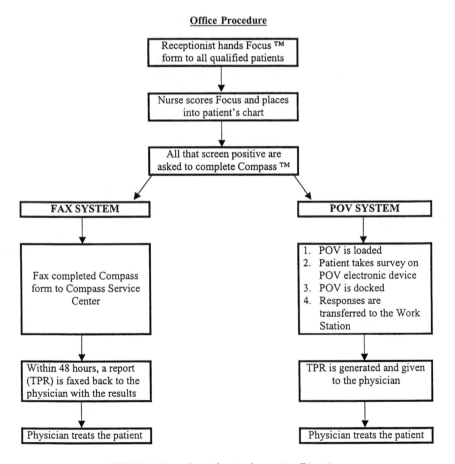

FIG. 7.5. Procedures for implementing Directions.

The Treatment Progress Report

The TPR features a "drill down" design with global progress indicators (i.e., MHI) and the MHI subscales presented on the first page, and detailed information about changes in the severity of reported symptoms on a second page. The major components of the TPR are the MHI trend chart; Critical Signs; MHI Components Table; Symptoms Checklist; and Medication Information.

Figure 7.6 illustrates an MHI trend line for a patient who completed COM-PASS–PC each month (except August) from April through September 1997. The April testing showed relatively mild problems: An MHI of approximately 75 usually does not require treatment; it does, however, require monitoring. Indeed, the scores from May through July are in the "normal range," characteristic of individuals who do not require mental health treatment. By September, a significant deterioration to the 50th percentile indicates that the patient's mental health status has become worse than half of the patients entering outpatient treatment for psychological problems. Scores at this level suggest that medication or psychotherapy may be beneficial; further deterioration (e.g., approaching the "severe" range) would suggest referral to a mental health specialist.

The face page of the TPR also includes any critical clinical signs that should be immediately brought to the physician's attention. These include suicidal thoughts, indicators of substance abuse, and potential dangerousness ("Wanting to hit someone or something"). Also, if the patient's responses are suggestive of the *DSM–IV* criteria for a major depressive episode, a note appears on the face page.

Table 7.3 presents an MHI Components table. The MHI and its component scales and subscales are presented here as percentile scores — for the initial administration and for the two most recent administrations, each of which are presented with their respective dates. Change Since Initial shows the difference (in percentile points) between the initial (baseline) administration of COMPASS–PC and the most recent administration. The contents of Well-Being, Symptoms Alleviation, and Life Functioning scales were discussed in the previous section, as was the meaning of Normal and Severe. Data for the Symptoms Alleviation scale and its subscales (Adjustment Disorder, Anxiety, Bipolar, Depression, Obsessive-Compulsive, Phobia, Substance Abuse) reflect symptom remission, so that patient improvement moves in the same upward direction on all three scales.

Patients completing COMPASS–PC report their recent (past 2 weeks) symptoms using a 6-point scale to indicate how frequently they have experienced each symp-

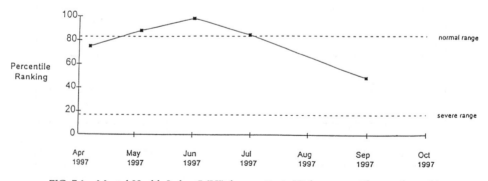

FIG. 7.6.   Mental Health Index (MHI) for a patient. Higher percentiles are favorable.

TABLE 7.3
MHI Components

	Initial Administration 4/7/97	Administration 7/2/97	Administration 9/2/97	Change Since Initial
Well-Being				
(Normal >83; severe <17)	37	46	93	56
Symptoms Alleviation				
(Normal >83; severe <17)	31	73	79	48
Adjustment Disorder	41	63	69	28
Anxiety	10	92	95	85
Bipolar	37	93	93	56
Depression	9	27	47	38
Obsessive-Compulsive	32	88	77	45
Phobia	34	83	83	49
Substance Abuse	No substance abuse reported	No substance abuse reported	No substance abuse reported	
Life Functioning				
(Normal >83; severe <17)	51	27	58	7
Mental Health Index (MHI)				
(Normal >83; severe <17)	41	48	84	43

Note. The table reflects symptoms as reported by the patient that may or may not meet *DSM–IV* criteria for the corresponding diagnosis. Higher scores indicate improvement.

tom. Each symptom rated 3 ("several times") or higher on either the initial or most recent administration is shown in the Symptom Checklist section of the TPR.

As shown in Table 7.4, the symptoms are grouped into those that have improved, become worse, or remained unchanged over the course of treatment. For each, the checklist table shows the rating when COMPASS–PC was first administered (Initial), the rating from the most recent administration, and the change from initial to most recent. The physician can readily identify symptoms that are problematic (e.g., possible side effects of medication) and those that have improved (e.g., in response to medication). The example shown in Table 7.4 suggests an overall deterioration in patient symptoms.

Finally, Medication Information displays the information provided by the physician on COMPASS–PC (prescription and dosage), as well as common side effects of the medications prescribed.

Guidelines for Decision Making

The types of decisions that can be informed by COMPASS–PC were discussed earlier. Administration of COMPASS–PC at strategic intervals during treatment enhances the usefulness of the TPR.

How Often Should One Monitor?   The initial administration occurs when a patient screens positive on FOCUS. Subsequent administrations might be scheduled when:

- A new medication is started.

TABLE 7.4
Symptom Checklist

	Initial	Most Recent	Change
Improved			
Feeling guilty	4	1	3
Fatigue	3	1	2
Thoughts over and over again—can't get rid of	5	2	3
Feeling ill or run down	3	2	1
No change			
Change in my weight	3	3	0
Trouble falling asleep	5	5	0
Worse			
Difficulty concentrating	4	6	-2
Feeling restless	4	6	-2
Feeling sad most of the day	3	5	-2
Tension or aches in my muscles	2	4	-2
Feeling like life is not worth living	2	4	-2
Difficulty making decisions	2	4	-2
Troubling events in my daily life	1	3	-2
Being sluggish or without energy	4	5	-1
Not enjoying things as much as I used to	4	5	-1
Decreased sex drive	3	4	-1
Trying to push thoughts out of my head	2	3	-1

Note. Positive change indicates improvement. Symptoms in the past 2 weeks: 1 = not at all, 2 = once or twice, 3 = several times, 4 = often, 5 = most of the time, 6 = all of the time.

- The physician wishes to assess the effects of a medication or nonpharmacological treatment.
- Dosage is adjusted.
- The patient reports no improvement (change of medication may be appropriate).
- The patient reports marked improvement, and the physician is considering discontinuing a medication or reducing dosage.

Patients whose MHI is subnormal but not low enough to warrant treatment should be monitored if they report feeling worse, or at 4- to 6-week intervals.

Reliable Change.   All measures are subject to error; the standard error of measurement for a scale is a function of its reliability and the variability of scores in the population. In the case of COMPASS–PC, the error of measurement associated with the MHI yields an index of reliable change of 5 *T*-score points. That is, two observed MHI scores must differ by at least 5 *T*-score points before it can be concluded with a high degree of confidence that the difference is real (i.e., not due to measurement error). The correspondence between *T*-score and percentile points is variable, but 5 *T*-score points approximately equals 15 percentile points.

The uncertainty associated with a single score greatly favors instruments that are designed for treatment monitoring. Collecting multiple measures over time enhances the usefulness of the data. For example, three MHI scores in the "normal" range (83 and above) provides very high confidence that the patient no longer requires treatment, even though each of these scores taken separately is subject to the 15-point error range and should be understood to indicate a true score that could be as low as 68 (i.e., 83 − 15).

Disease-Specific Considerations

COMPASS–PC is quite comprehensive in its scope. As discussed elsewhere, the COMPASS–PC Symptoms scale includes a broad range of symptoms representing seven disorders. These seven diagnoses account for more than 90% of patients who seek outpatient behavioral health care and qualify for a DSM diagnosis. The symptom subscale scores are, in effect, screens for their corresponding disorders: adjustment, depression, general anxiety, obsessive-compulsive, phobia, bipolar, and substance abuse.

COMPASS–PC has particular strengths as both a screen and monitoring tool for depression, one of the disorders of most concern in primary care. First, the elements necessary to diagnose a major depressive episode are included among the Symptoms items. When a patient's responses meet criteria, a message ("Patient may have experienced a Major Depressive Episode") appears on the Treatment Progress Report. Second, the high reliability of the depression subscale (.89) means that the measurement error associated with depression scores is small. Thus, the subscale can be appropriately used both as a screen and as a measure of change in the severity of depressive symptoms during the course of treatment.

Risk Adjustment.   Comparisons of outcomes across settings, providers, and so forth require that the data are risk adjusted to take into consideration patient characteristics (e.g., demographics, diagnosis, symptom severity) that affect the degree or rate of improvement. Risk-adjustment procedures for COMPASS–PC are established using multiple regression.

Strengths and Limitations of Use in Primary Care Settings

COMPASS–PC, with its implementation within the Directions program, was designed to satisfy the information needs of the physician while allowing easy integration into routine office procedures.

A major strength of Directions and COMPASS–PC is the system's accommodation to the requirements of the work flow in primary care facilities. During focus groups, both physicians and administrators stressed the need for accurate, timely, and easily understood reports within a system that made the absolute minimum of administrative demands on doctors and office staff. The POV option for collecting, storing, analyzing, and reporting COMPASS–PC data satisfies this need, making it possible to implement the system with negligible impact on staff.

A second important strength is the ability to quickly evaluate the patient's condition using the composite MHI score, while accessing more detailed information through review of the subscales that comprise the MHI.

The usefulness of COMPASS–PC in clinical decision support, discussed elsewhere, is a third strength of the system. The ability to screen for a broad range of disorders, to monitor the impact of treatment (e.g., using the MHI and depression scores), and to evaluate patient status against clinically meaningful benchmarks (e.g., the "normal line") provides the functionality desired by most physicians.

Finally, the scope of COMPASS–PC measurement extends beyond symptoms to subjective well-being and life functioning. These domains are known to be important in behavioral health care treatment. They also provide a framework that is very familiar to the physician, who is accustomed to seeing patients who feel ill (poor subjective well-being), complain of specific symptoms, and describe the limitations their illness imposes on their daily lives (functioning). COMPASS–PC allows the doctor to assess behavioral health problems within the context of a familiar model of illness.

A limitation of COMPASS–PC within primary care settings is its length, which makes it inappropriate for administration to all patients. The FOCUS screener was developed for Directions so that all patients could be quickly screened for depression and anxiety symptoms, with only those who screen positive being administered the COMPASS–PC.

Future Directions: Learning Systems and Patient Profiling

Among the most important features of COMPASS–PC is its potential to continually enhance its usefulness as it "learns" from past history, that is, as data accumulate to support ever greater refinements in its capacity to adjust for patient characteristics and project expected path of treatment. Preliminary research on patient profiling (Howard et al., 1996) has demonstrated the feasibility of a method for using COMPASS–PC data to predict the likely change in MHI that would result from various treatments (e.g., medications, psychotherapy). Associated with each predicted path is a "failure boundary" useful for identifying ineffective treatments.

It will one day be possible to select the most promising treatment for a patient by examining the predicted paths associated with various treatment options. Then, as treatment progresses, the actual MHI data can be compared with the predicted path to determine whether the treatment is "working" as well as expected. A patient whose score falls below the failure boundary is unlikely to recover unless the treatment is modified.

Patient profiling is illustrated in Fig. 7.7. This case was selected from the sample used by Dr. Howard in his initial work on patient profiling. The "actual MHI" trend line shows the treatment experience of a 36-year-old man who sought psychotherapy for a marital problem and was diagnosed with an adjustment disorder.

The profiling procedure is still under development, so the clinician did not have the "Expected MHI" or the "Failure Boundary" line available to him. With access to this information, he may have questioned whether psychotherapy was the treatment of choice, in view of the very modest improvement indicated by the "Expected MHI" line. Furthermore, he would have been alerted in session 12, when the patient's score dipped below the "Failure Boundary," that a successful outcome from individual psychotherapy was unlikely. Discussion of these data might have encouraged the patient to accept a medication, or to join his wife in marriage counseling.

CASE STUDY

The case of Donna R. demonstrates the use of Directions and COMPASS–PC in identifying, treating, and monitoring the course of treatment in an underlying behavioral health condition.

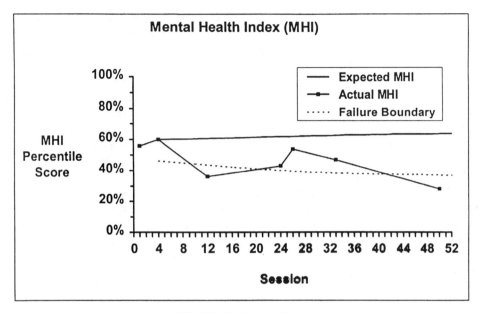

FIG. 7.7. Patient profiling.

History

Donna is a 32-year-old, white, female, customer service representative. She is divorced, with two children. She sustained a contusion to her left hip in September 1995 when she slipped on a greasy spot in her employer's parking lot. Treated conservatively by an orthopedist, Donna returned to work in November, 2 months after the injury. She met subsequently with her primary care physician, Dr. B., on four occasions during the month of December.

Course of Treatment

Donna was seen by Dr. B. in December some 3 months after the injury, at which time she complained of intermittent back pain, tension headaches, fatigue, and hypersomnia. Dr. B. examined Donna at that time. Except for slight tenderness in the left sacral region, the examination was unremarkable. Donna was asked to fill out the FOCUS screening form, and was prescribed ibuprofen 600 mg BID and warm compresses. She was instructed to call if the pain was not noticeably improved within a week. Donna called a week later to be seen by Dr. B.

Because she reported continued pain without physical signs to account for it, increased lethargy and difficulty getting up in the morning, and had a FOCUS score indicating mixed depression–anxiety, Donna was administered a COMPASS–PC (1/5/96). The Treatment Progress Report (TPR) indicated the possibility of a major depressive episode, severe level with prominent anxiety symptoms, and possible alcohol/drug abuse.

When Dr. B. saw Donna the following week, he determined that, although she had not previously been diagnosed with major depression, she had felt like this several times before in her life. Upon questioning, Donna indicated that her two to three glasses of wine per week had, during the past month, become two to three per day.

He learned as well that Donna's mother had a lifelong weight problem and often spent days on end in bed, and that a maternal uncle had been diagnosed with depression and had responded well to one of the new selective serotonin reuptake inhibitor (SSRI) antidepressants.

Dr. B. told Donna that she was suffering from major depression, that she had most likely inherited a vulnerability to this disorder, that each successive episode lowered her threshold to yet another episode, and that her use of alcohol seemed to be a way of self-medicating her depression but, given her family history, was something that needed to be addressed. Donna agreed to a trial of the antidepressant that her uncle used, and to a referral for an alcohol evaluation—and treatment if warranted. She also agreed to refrain from alcohol use in the meantime.

The antidepressant medication was started at a low dosage and gradually increased, although to a level still below the average daily dosage range. Donna called the office in 3 weeks to indicate that she was tolerating the medication, was oversleeping less, and had somewhat more energy; however, she was still feeling just as depressed, self-critical, sad, weepy, and not enjoying her life. Dr. B. therefore doubled the dosage of the antidepressant (bringing it to the lower limit of the average daily dosage range).

When seen a week later (2/5/96) for her scheduled 1-month follow-up appointment, Donna repeated the list of symptoms she had mentioned in the previous week's phone call. She also noted that after a couple of days of increasing the medication, she began to have great difficulty getting to sleep, and often felt "wired," quite agitated, and rather irritable with her children and coworkers. Dr. B. ordered a second administration of COMPASS–PC. This substantiated that there had been no overall improvement, some shifting in depressive symptoms, and some worsening of anxiety symptoms. Because Donna reported that she was compliant with medication and continued to abstain from alcohol, Dr. B. decided to discontinue the first antidepressant and start Donna on a different SSRI antidepressant that specifically addresses anxiety symptoms.

One month later, Donna reported resolution of all symptoms, continued abstinence from alcohol, and increased energy and productivity. A third administration of COMPASS–PC (3/4/96) indicated marked overall improvement. Medications were continued and a 2-month medication-monitoring appointment was scheduled.

The final TPR (3/4/96) for Donna's case is provided in Fig. 7.8.

SUMMARY

The Directions program provides an administratively efficient method to screen (FOCUS) for psychological disorders in a Primary Core setting, to confirm the need for treatment and monitor progress (COMPASS–PC). The instruments are psychometrically sound and grounded in an established theory of mental health treatment.

COMPASS–PC is unique in its potential as a "learning system." Initial research suggests that it will be possible to predict the path of patient progress for various treatments. This would provide a breakthrough in the physician's ability to select a treatment or referral option and evaluate its effectiveness. Most importantly, the performance of COMPASS–PC will continually improve as data accumulate and the prediction/failure boundary algorithms are refined. For the first time, a mechanism

Administration Number: 2 Patient Name: Physician ID:
Administration Date: 02/01/96 Patient ID: Physician Name:

Mental Health Index - Patient Report

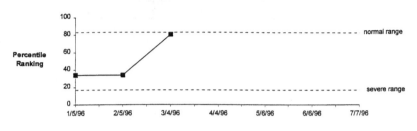

Critical Signs

None.

MHI components - Higher scores indicate improvement

The chart below reflects symptoms as reported by the patient that may or may not
meet DSM IV criteria for the corresponding diagnosis.

	Initial 01/05/96	02/05/96	Most Recent 03/04/96	Change Since Initial
WELL-BEING (NORMAL >83; SEVERE <17)	26	36	73	+47
SYMPTOMS ALLEVIATION (NORMAL >83; SEVERE <17)	43	43	81	+38
Adjustment Disorder	47	47	79	+32
Anxiety	34	34	78	+44
Mania/Hypomania	50	50	65	+15
Depression	26	25	48	+22
Obsessive Compulsive	53	53	60	+7
Phobia	50	50	72	+22
Substance Abuse	31	30	90	+59
LIFE FUNCTIONING (NORMAL >83; SEVERE <17)	32	32	80	+48
MENTAL HEALTH INDEX (MHI) (NORMAL >83; SEVERE <17)	34	34	81	+47

This report reflects only the information supplied by the patient and physician on the COMPASS PC form. The information in this report is not intended
to replace clinical judgment, the physician has full responsibility for the care and well being of his/her patients.

FIG. 7.8.   Donna's final TPR.

Symptom Checklist - Positive change indicates improvement

	Initial 01/01/96	Most Recent 03/03/96	Change
Improved			
Headaches	6	1	+5
Back pain	6	1	+5
Chest pain or discomfort	6	1	+5
Feeling sad most of the day	6	1	+5
Feeling ill or run-down	6	1	+5
Difficulty concentrating	6	2	+4
Not enjoying things as much as I used to	6	2	+4
Being sluggish or without energy	6	2	+4
Being irritable and easily angered	6	2	+4
Experiencing a great deal of stress	6	2	+4
Decreased sex drive	6	2	+4
Worrying too much about unimportant things	5	1	+4
Feeling worthless	5	1	+4
Feeling hopeless about the future	5	1	+4
Restless sleep, out of my normal pattern	5	1	+4
Troubling events in my daily life	4	1	+3
Crying or weeping spells	4	1	+3
Difficulty making decisions	4	1	+3
Shortness of breath or rapid	4	1	+3
Trouble falling asleep	3	0	+3
Feeling restless	4	2	+2

No Change
None

Worse
None

Symptoms in the past two weeks (prior to assessment date):

3 = several times
4 = often
5 = most of the time
6 = all of the time

Current Medication Information
(as reported on the COMPASS PC form)

Prescription Name	Current Dose	Top Three Side Effects *
Effexor (venlafaxine)	100 mg.	1. nausea 2. somnolence 3. dizziness

*Side effects and minimum and maximum dosage recommendations, if present, were supplied by the medical director of "your healthcare system".

This report reflects only the information supplied by the patient and physician on the COMPASS PC form. The information in this report is not intended to replace clinical judgment, the physician has full responsibility for the care and well being of his/her patients.

FIG. 7.8. *(Continued)*

will exist to benefit from the experience — the successes and failures alike — of previous patients. COMPASS–PC brings a scientific tool to the art of treatment.

ACKNOWLEDGMENT

The authors are pleased to acknowledge the work of Dr. Jennifer Lish, a codeveloper of COMPASS-PC and respected colleague.

REFERENCES

Friedman, P. H. (1982). Assessment tools and procedures in integrative psychotherapy. In A. Gurman (Ed.), *Questions and answers in the practice of family therapy* (Vol. II, pp. 46–49). New York: Brunner/Mazel.

Howard, K. I., Lueger, R., Maling, M., & Martinovich, Z. (1993). A phase model of psychotherapy: Causal mediation of outcome. *Journal of Consulting and Clinical Psychology, 61*, 678–685.

Howard, K. I., Kopta, S. M., Krause, M. S., & Orlinsky, D. E. (1986). The dose-effect relationship in psychotherapy. *American Psychologist, 41*, 159–164.

Howard, K. I., Moras, K., Brill, P. L., Martinovich, Z., & Lutz, W. (1996). Evaluation of psychotherapy: Efficiency, effectiveness and patient progress. *American Psychologist, 51*(10), 1059–1064.

Lish, J. (1996). Primary care and behavioral medicine treatment outcomes. In L. Sperry, P. L. Brill, K. I. Howard, & G. R. Grissom (Eds.), *Treatment outcomes in psychotherapy and psychiatric interventions* (pp. 199–215). New York: Brunner/Mazel.

Miller, N. S., Belkin, B. M., & Gold, M. S. (1991). Alcohol and drug dependence among the elderly: Epidemiology, diagnosis and treatment. *Comprehensive Psychiatry, 32*, 153–165.

Regier, D. A., Narrow, N. E., & Rae, D. S. (1993). The de facto U.S. mental and addictive disorders service system: Epidemiological Catchment Area prospective 1-year prevalence rates of disorders and services. *Archives of General Psychiatry, 30*, 85–94.

Rutz, W., von Knorring, L., & Walinder, J. (1989). Frequency of suicide on Gotland after systematic post-graduate education of general practitioners. *Acta Psychiatrica Scandinavica, 80*, 151–154.

Sperry, L., Brill, P. L., Howard, K. I., & Grissom, G. R. (Eds.). (1996). *Treatment outcomes in psychotherapy and psychiatric interventions.* New York: Brunner/Mazel.

Sperry, L., Grissom, G., Brill, P., & Marion, D. (1997). Changing clinicians practice patterns and managed care culture with outcomes systems. *Psychiatric Annals, 27*(2), 127–132.

Van Casteren, T., Van der Veken, J., Tafforeau, G., & Van Oyden, P. (1993). Suicide and attempted suicide reported by general practitioners in Belgium, 1990–91. *Acta Psychiatrica Scandinavica, 87*, 451–455.

Wells, K. B., Stewart, A., Hays, R. D., et al. (1989). The functioning and well-being of depressed patients. Results from the Medical Outcomes Study. *Journal of the American Medical Association, 262*(7), 914–919.

Wells, K. B., Hays, R. D., Burnam, M. A., Rogers, W., Greenfields, S., & Ware, J. E. (1989). Detection of depressive disorder for patients receiving prepaid or fee-for-service care: Results from the Medical Outcomes Study. *Journal of the American Medical Association, 262*(23), 3298–3302.

The Shedler QPD Panel
(Quick PsychoDiagnostics Panel):
A Psychiatric "Lab Test" for Primary Care

Jonathan Shedler
Harvard Medical School and Digital Diagnostics, Inc.

Approximately 60% of patients with diagnosable psychiatric disorders never make it to psychiatrists, psychologists, or other mental health professionals. Instead, they go to their primary care doctors. For better or worse, primary care is the de facto mental health services system in the United States (Regier, Goldberg, & Taube, 1978). Unfortunately, it is a mental health services system that often fails. Primary care physicians fail to diagnose 50% to 70% of patients with depression and other psychiatric disorders (e.g., Andersen & Harthorn, 1989; Borus, Howes, Devins, Rosenberg, & Livingston, 1988; Katon, 1987; Nielson & Williams, 1980; Ornel, Koeter, van den Brink, & van de Willige, 1991; Rydon, Redmon, Sanson-Fisher, & Reid, 1992; Schulberg & Burns, 1988; Schulberg, Saul, & McClelland, 1985; Kessler, Cleary, & Burke, 1988). These patients often suffer needlessly. They are also high utilizers of medical services and contribute to rising health care costs (Franco et al., 1995).

Many health care experts agree there is need for improved mental health screening in primary care. Nevertheless, physicians rarely use mental health screening tests. Around 1991, I began a program of research to find out why. The answer was straightforward: Existing mental health screening tests were not practical in primary care and did not meet physicians' needs.

This research led to the development of the Shedler Quick PsychoDiagnostics Panel (QPD Panel), a psychiatric "lab test" designed to meet the special needs of primary care physicians. The test is fully automated. Patients self-administer the test in approximately 6 min using hand-held computer tablets (Fig. 8.1). There is no need to score the test or tabulate responses. Instead, physicians receive a computer-generated "lab report" that resembles a familiar blood chemistry report. The QPD Panel screens for the following nine disorders, and makes specific diagnoses based on *DSM–IV* diagnostic criteria (American Psychiatric Association, 1994):

1. Major depression.
2. Dysthymic disorder.
3. Bipolar disorder.
4. Generalized anxiety disorder.

FIG. 8.1.   The Shedler QPD Panel.

5. Panic disorder.
6. Obsessive-compulsive disorder (OCD).
7. Bulimia nervosa.
8. Alcohol and/or substance abuse.
9. Somatization.

The QPD Panel also identifies patients with clinically significant disorders who do not meet formal *DSM–IV* diagnostic criteria (e.g., patients who would be diagnosed with depressive disorder NOS or anxiety disorder NOS [not otherwise specified]), and it screens for suicide risk.

This chapter discusses the special needs of primary care physicians; explains why the QPD Panel has gained physician acceptance where other tests have not; presents data on the reliability and validity of the QPD Panel; presents findings on both physician acceptance and patient acceptance; and finally, discusses the use of the QPD Panel for treatment monitoring and outcome assessment.

WHY DOCTORS DON'T USE MENTAL HEALTH SCREENING TESTS

To find out why physicians rarely use mental health screening tests, I conducted interviews and focus groups with primary care physicians in several states. I began the interviews by telling the physicians about the high prevalence of psychiatric disorders in primary care (studies show that psychiatric disorders are present in at least 20% of medical outpatients; e.g., Barrett, Barrett, Oxman, & Gerber, 1988; Kessler et al., 1987). Then I asked the physicians if they really wanted to know whether a patient suffered from a psychiatric disorder. Most said they did.

However, when I asked the physicians if they would be willing to conduct a brief structured psychiatric interview to get this information, they said "no." When I asked if they would be willing to have their patients complete a pencil-and-paper questionnaire, they also said "no." The physicians, as a group, were concerned about their patients' welfare. Nevertheless, there was formidable resistance to the use of any mental health screening tool.

In some cases, the physicians felt personally uncomfortable delving into emotional matters, or believed (incorrectly) that their patients would be uncomfortable. Some physicians felt their training in psychiatry was inadequate. But the biggest concern, by far, was time. The physicians told me they felt overwhelmed with responsibilities and barely had enough time to address the medical issues that were their primary concern. The last thing they wanted was a screening procedure that took up still more of their time, or took up the time of their staff. Physicians who had prior experience with mental health questionnaires, like the Zung Depression Inventory (Zung, 1965) or Beck Depression Scale (Beck, Ward, Mendelson, & Erbaugh, 1961), said the tests did not really meet their needs. Some felt the tests had been pushed on them by administrators or researchers who did not understand the pressures of primary care practice.

I asked the physicians to describe the hypothetical, ideal psychiatric test—one they would want to use, and keep on using. From the interviews and focus groups, the following "wish list" emerged:

1. The test should require no time from physicians or office staff. (Physicians and staff were already overburdened.)
2. The test should require no special training to use.
3. The test should diagnose the full range of disorders commonly seen in primary care. (Tests that screened for only one disorder did not provide sufficient information.)
4. The test should make specific *DSM-IV* diagnoses. (Physicians did not want "cutoff" scores, they wanted diagnoses spelled out for them.)
5. The test should not involve forms or paperwork. (The physicians hated paperwork.)
6. The test should not interfere with office routines or patient flow.
7. The test should be liked and accepted by patients. (Physicians did not want their patients to feel they were being asked inappropriately personal questions, or being treated "like numbers.")

From the perspective of a test author, some of these requirements may seem unreasonable, but from a physician's frame of reference they make sense. That frame of reference is a medical lab test. Lab tests do not take up physician time, or staff time, or create excess paperwork. They do not disrupt office routines or interfere with patient flow. They require minimal time and effort: Physicians simply *order* lab tests, and get back the diagnostic information they want.

Existing mental health tests did not meet these requirements. An exhaustive review of available tests revealed that each one had significant limitations that would prevent it from gaining physician acceptance. For example, PRIME–MD (Spitzer et al., 1994) requires physicians to conduct face-to-face patient interviews that last 8 min on average, and can run to 15 min or more. Such an instrument is often out of the question in real-world medical settings, where physicians may have only 10 to 15 min to spend with a patient. Self-report questionnaires like the Beck and Zung depression scales are self-administered, but they still involve paperwork, and someone has to tabulate the scores. Also, they do not make specific *DSM–IV* diagnoses (they provide cutoff scores only), and they screen for one disorder only.

These findings may seem at odds with published reports describing the successful use of various mental health assessment tools in primary care settings. To resolve the apparent contradiction, it is necessary to distinguish between "studies" and real-world use. Studies are time limited, data collection is carefully monitored, extensive clerical support ("site management") is provided, and physicians or health care organizations are often paid for their participation. For these reasons, studies — especially well-funded studies — do not resemble real-world conditions. In nearly all cases, the physicians stop using the mental health screening test as soon as the study is completed, but this is not mentioned in the publications that follow. The litmus test for a successful screening test is, "Do physicians continue using the test, once artificial incentives are removed?" Despite favorable reports in prestigious medical journals, the answer has generally been "No."

The available mental health tests had been developed with little or no input from primary care physicians. The test developers decided what the tests should do and how they should do it, and they assumed primary care physicians would be satisfied with the result. They were mistaken. The interviews and focus groups made it clear that primary care physicians had special needs. These interviews and focus groups provided a foundation for development of the QPD Panel.

USE AS A SCREENER

The QPD Panel is self-administered on portable, hand-held computer tablets (see Fig. 8.1). These computer tablets have a large LCD (liquid crystal display) screen, and *True* and *False* response buttons. Patients can hold the units in their laps as they take the test.

The QPD Panel begins with the following instructions, displayed on the LCD screen:

> Your doctor is interested in both your physical and emotional health. This questionnaire will ask about physical and emotional problems you may be having. Your answers will help your doctor give you the best medical care possible.
>
> You will see a series of statements. If a statement applies to you, press the button labeled True. If a statement does not apply to you, press the button labeled False.
>
> Your answers are confidential, between you and your doctor, so please answer as honestly as you can. Most people finish the questionnaire in 5 to 10 minutes.

The QPD Panel then displays a series of diagnostic questions, all with a True/ False response format. Patients answer by pressing the True and False buttons. The initial questions are about physical symptoms, consistent with what a patient expects to be asked in a doctor's office. In fact, these symptoms are associated with anxiety or depression (e.g., "My hands and feet often feel cold and clammy," "My heart often pounds or races"). The test then leads gradually into questions that are more psychological in content. The questions are worded in simple language and require less than a sixth-grade reading level.

The test makes use of artificial intelligence (logic and branching), so not all patients are asked the same questions. Instead, questions are selected for presentation based on the patient's responses to previous questions. Thus, psychologically healthy patients are not asked irrelevant questions, and patients who may have psychiatric disorders are examined in depth. The use of artificial intelligence allows the test to screen for nine psychiatric disorders and make specific *DSM–IV* diagnoses, while requiring only 6.2 min (on average) to complete.

When the patient has finished answering the questions, the hand-held computer tablet is placed on a small stand (base unit) connected to a printer. The QPD Panel "lab report" is printed automatically, as soon as the hand-held unit is placed on the base. Additionally, the equipment stores all patient data electronically, and the resulting database can be downloaded to a computer for subsequent data analysis (e.g., to create aggregate reports).

The QPD Panel may be administered to all patients when they check in for their office appointment; alternatively, it may be administered in cases where the physician suspects a psychiatric disorder. If the test is administered at check-in, the typical procedure is as follows:

1. The receptionist hands the test unit to the patient.
2. The patient self-administers the test in the waiting room.
3. The patient returns the unit and a "lab report" is printed immediately.
4. The physician receives the "lab report" before examining the patient.

The QPD Panel integrates seamlessly into the workflow and requires virtually no time from physicians or office staff. The "lab report" is chart-ready and requires no transcription, and the entire screening process is accomplished effortlessly.

THE QPD PANEL LAB REPORT

The "lab report" is an essential feature of the QPD Panel diagnostic system, and was designed after extensive consultation with primary care physicians. The report resembles a standard blood chemistry report, familiar to all physicians. Because the report has a familiar "look and feel," physicians can begin using the QPD Panel without special training. Figure 8.2 shows a sample QPD Panel lab report.

Numeric scores indicate the severity of symptoms associated with depression, anxiety, panic disorder, obsessive-compulsive disorder, bulimia, alcohol or substance abuse, and somatization. Higher scores indicate more severe symptoms. Normal reference ranges are included on the report. A score outside the reference range indicates clinically significant symptoms.

If a score falls outside the normal reference range, a note appears on the lab report indicating whether the patient meets formal *DSM–IV* criteria for a specific psychiat-

```
                                                                                    (Page 1)
                    Shedler QPD Panel (Quick Psycho-Diagnostics Panel)
                                 Digital Diagnostics, Inc.

    _____Physician Copy_____

    Physician:     Dr. Joel Fleischman                                      Sex: M
    Patient:       Smith, John                                              Age: 37
    Ref No         123456789
    Date           7/19/98


    _____Diagnostic Report_____
    Test                              Results                         Reference Range
                            within range      out of range

    _____
    Depression                                    21                       0–10
    Anxiety                       8                                         0–10
    Panic Disorder                2                                         0–8
    OCD                           0                                         0–3
    Bulimia                       0                                         0–4
    Alcohol/Substance Abuse       1                                         0–2
    Somatization                  6                                         0–11



    Notes:
    Symptoms consistent with Major Depressive Episode.
    Suicidal ideation
```

```
                                                                                    (Page 2)
    Patient:       Smith, John
    Ref No:        123456789


    Depressive Symptoms

    _____

    —Depressed mood, nearly every day, 2 weeks or longer duration
    —Diminished interest or pleasure in activities
    —Appetite loss
    —Weight loss
    —Insomnia
    —Fatigue, loss of energy
    —Feelings of worthlessness or guilt
    —Poor concentration
    —Hopelessness
    —Suicidal ideation: answered true to "I have thoughts about killing myself"
```

FIG. 8.2. Sample lab report.

ric diagnosis. For example, if the depression score is out of range, a note may state that the patient meets *DSM–IV* criteria for major depressive episode or for dysthymic disorder. A note will also identify patients at risk for suicide. Finally, the lab report lists the specific symptoms that led to the diagnosis.

In the sample report in Fig. 8.2, the patient has a depression score of 21, well outside the reference range of 0 to 10. Notes inform the physician that the patient meets *DSM–IV* criteria for major depression, and that he has suicidal ideation (he answered *True* to "I have thoughts about killing myself"). The second page of the lab report lists the specific symptoms that led to the diagnosis of major depression. In this hypothetical case, the physician would do well to treat the patient for depression, or refer him to a psychologist or psychiatrist for treatment.

SUMMARY OF TEST DEVELOPMENT

Disorders were selected for inclusion in the QPD Panel based on (a) epidemiological data concerning their prevalence in primary care, (b) the preferences of primary care physicians, determined through interviews and focus groups, and (c) the author's judgment about the feasibility of diagnosing the disorder via an automated procedure.

The QPD Panel is a hybrid test, combining features of an inventory and a structured interview. All patients answer a core set of 59 questions. When responses suggest the possibility of a psychiatric disorder, the test branches into diagnostic modules that probe in depth. The QPD Panel contains more than 200 diagnostic questions, but no patient sees them all. Patients answer only the questions that are relevant to them.

The QPD Panel software contains the scoring algorithms. The software calculates numeric scores that quantify the severity of symptoms (e.g., the severity of depression) by summing *True* responses to relevant test items. Additionally, the QPD Panel uses pattern-matching algorithms to match the patient's symptom profile against *DSM–IV* diagnostic criteria. These algorithms allow the QPD Panel to make specific *DSM–IV* diagnoses such as major depressive episode, generalized anxiety disorder, and panic disorder, and so on.

Test development began with construction of a large initial item pool. The content of this item pool reflected the diagnostic criteria specified in *DSM–IIIR* and *DSM–IV*, theoretical writings on the included diagnoses, empirical findings pertaining to the included diagnoses, the clinical experience of the author, and the clinical experience of a panel of psychiatrists and psychologists expert in psychological assessment. An important consideration was that the questions could be answered quickly (a goal was that the entire test should require less than 10 min to complete). For this reason, questions were written in true/false format. Questions using this format require less cognitive processing time than questions using a multiple-choice or rating-scale format.

A series of studies helped determine which of the items would be included in the final QPD Panel. A pilot patient sample responded to all items, and also rated the items on dimensions relevant to patient acceptance or user-friendliness. A panel of expert psychologists and psychiatrists evaluated each item with respect to diagnostic import. The items were correlated with each other, and with scores on established, well-validated psychological tests.

Items selected from the item pool for inclusion in the QPD Panel met stringent criteria, with respect to both their psychometric properties and their user friendliness. The psychometric criteria were as follow:

1. The items showed acceptable correlations with established, well-validated tests.
2. The items showed acceptable intercorrelations with other QPD Panel items intended to assess the same construct.
3. The items increased the reliability (coefficient alpha) of their respective scales.
4. The items were statistically diagnostic (i.e., items with overly high or low endorsement rates were eliminated).
5. The items were judged high in diagnostic importance by the panel of experts.
6. The items covered the diagnostic criteria specified by *DSM–IV*.

With respect to user-friendliness, the items met the following additional criteria:

1. The items required no more than a grade school reading level.
2. Patients rated the items as clear and easy to understand.
3. Patients rated the items as appropriate for primary care (i.e., the questions were not perceived as inappropriate, offensive, or overly intrusive).
4. Patients could respond to the items without assistance.

The items, presentation sequence, branching rules, and diagnostic algorithms were incorporated into a computer software program. The initial plan was to administer the QPD Panel on desktop computers, but this proved impractical. Although the computer seemed a perfect solution in the drawing room, it was unworkable in the real world, for reasons that seem obvious in retrospect.

Why Computers Don't Work in Primary Care

Most physicians do not have spare computers in their offices. When we offered to provide computers, we discovered that physicians usually had no place to put them. Typically, there was insufficient space in the waiting room (and insufficient privacy), and there were no spare rooms available for setting up computer workstations. When we did place a computer in a primary care office, it interfered with patient flow. Often there were several patients in the waiting room but only one computer available, causing a backlog of patients waiting to take the test. Finally, there was an "intimidation" factor. Some patients did not feel comfortable working at a computer screen and keyboard, and they reacted negatively.

Ultimately we found the ideal hardware platform for the QPD Panel in the form of a hand-held computer tablet, originally designed for collecting survey data. The hand-held devices are about the size of a book (see Fig. 8.1). They are wireless and portable, and patients can hold them in their laps while they self-administer the test. The units are nonthreatening and patients seem to enjoy using them. A busy medical office can have several test units, so multiple patients can take the test at once. The QPD Panel software was rewritten to take advantage of this new hardware platform.

Field Testing and Refinement

The QPD Panel, on the new hardware platform, underwent approximately 1 year of field testing in busy primary care medical clinics. We created a feedback loop, so we could obtain ongoing feedback from physicians and patients who used the QPD Panel, make modifications based on that feedback, then receive additional feedback about the modified test. This process cycled through many iterations and led to numerous modifications of both the QPD Panel software and the hardware platform.

The modifications were aimed at maximizing both the validity and the user-friendliness of the QPD Panel. During the field-testing period, test questions were rewritten to make them clearer and simpler. Test administration times were monitored, and revisions were made in the QPD Panel branching and logic to make the test more time efficient. Changes were made in the formatting of the lab report to accommodate physician preferences. Approximately 90 patients participated in a pilot validation study, where QPD Panel diagnoses were validated against psychiatric diagnoses obtained through structured psychiatric interviews. These data were used to refine the QPD Panel diagnostic algorithms, to maximize sensitivity and specificity.

VALIDITY

The QPD Panel makes specific psychiatric diagnoses based on *DSM–IV* diagnostic criteria. For the mood and anxiety disorders, QPD Panel diagnoses were validated against diagnoses made by the *Structured Clinical Interview for DSM–IV* (SCID) (First, Spitzer, Gibbon, & Williams, 1995), widely regarded as the "gold standard" for psychiatric diagnosis. Validity of the Alcohol/Substance Abuse scale was established by demonstrating the scale's ability to differentiate abusers from control patients. Finally, the QPD Panel Depression and Anxiety scale scores (numeric scores) were correlated with established measures of depression and anxiety to establish convergent validity. The validity studies have been described in detail elsewhere (Shedler, Beck, & Benson, 1999) but are summarized here.

Mood and Anxiety Disorders

Research subjects were 203 health maintenance organization (HMO) patients who were referred by their physicians, or self-referred, for a first-time mental health consultation. None were receiving mental health treatment at the time of the study. The sample was approximately two-thirds female and one-third male, with a mean age of 41.39 years (*SD* = 11.69).

The patients completed an assessment protocol that included administration of the QPD Panel, the SCID structured interview, and the Hamilton Depression Inventory (Reynolds & Kobak, 1995). The order of the procedures was randomized. SCID interviews were conducted by MA- or PhD-level mental health professionals trained in the administration of the SCID, and blind with respect to all other study data.

Table 8.1 presents indexes of agreement between QPD Panel diagnoses and SCID structured interview diagnoses. To avoid reporting indexes that may be unreliable, findings are presented only for those disorders that were diagnosed a minimum of 12 times by both instruments.

TABLE 8.1
Indexes of Agreement Between QPD Panel Diagnoses and SCID Diagnoses ($n = 203$)

| | Sensitivity | Specificity | Positive Predictive Value | κ | Prevalence (%) | |
					QPD	SCID
Major depression	.81	.96	.90	.79	30.0	34.2
Generalized anxiety disorder	.79	.90	.72	.67	26.4	23.9
Panic disorder	.71	.97	.81	.72	12.4	13.5
Obsessive-compulsive disorder	.69	.97	.64	.64	8.3	7.6

The first three columns of Table 8.1 present the sensitivity (proportion of patients with a positive SCID diagnosis who were correctly identified by the QPD Panel), specificity (proportion of patients without a SCID diagnosis who were correctly identified by the QPD Panel), and positive predictive value (proportion of patients given a diagnosis by the QPD who were correctly identified) of the QPD Panel. Sensitivity was very good for all diagnoses, ranging from a low of .69 (for obsessive-compulsive disorder) to a high of .81 (for major depression). Specificities were uniformly excellent, ranging from .90 to .97, indicating that the QPD Panel seldom made false positive diagnoses (i.e., diagnoses not confirmed by the SCID interview).

The fourth column of Table 8.1 reports kappa (κ) coefficients, which provide an index of agreement between the QPD diagnoses and SCID diagnoses, correcting for agreement due to chance (Cohen, 1960). Kappa coefficients were good to excellent for all diagnoses, ranging from a low of .64 for OCD to a high of .79 for major depression.[1]

The last two columns of Table 8.1 show the prevalence rates for each of the diagnoses, as determined by the QPD Panel and by the SCID. Prevalence rates obtained by the two instruments were comparable for all diagnoses, suggesting that neither instrument had a systematic tendency to overdiagnose or underdiagnose any disorder.

Alcohol and Substance Abuse

The QPD Panel includes a 14-item alcohol and substance abuse scale. All patients answer 5 of the questions; the remaining questions are presented only when previous responses suggest abuse. The alcohol/substance abuse score is obtained by summing True responses to the scale items, so the scale has a possible range of 0–14.

The goals of the validation study were (a) to evaluate the diagnostic accuracy of the scale and (b) establish the optimum cut point for making a positive diagnosis. The study evaluated the QPD Panel's ability to distinguish between patients known to suffer from alcohol or substance abuse, and a healthy control sample.

Subjects were 159 patients enrolled in an HMO health plan. Forty-six of the patients had been diagnosed as alcohol or substance abusers by their physicians or by a mental health professional and had been referred to a chemical dependency clinic for treatment (chemical dependency sample). The remaining 113 patients were control patients selected from a primary care sample (control sample).

---

[1]The diagnostic module for OCD has since been revised, and we anticipate higher validity coefficients for OCD in future studies.

TABLE 8.2
Validity Indexes for QPD Panel Alcohol/Substance Module ($n = 159$)

Number of Items Answered True	Sensitivity	Specificity	Positive Predictive Value	κ
≥1	1.00	.83	.71	.74
≥2	.98	.92	.83	.86
≥3	.78	.96	.88	.76
≥4	.76	.96	.90	.76

Table 8.2 reports the sensitivity (proportion of chemical dependency patients correctly identified by the QPD Panel), specificity (proportion of control patients correctly identified by the QPD Panel), positive predictive value (proportion of patients given a diagnosis by the QPD who were correctly identified), and kappa (κ) coefficient, obtained using different scale cut points. The first row presents the validity coefficients when a scale score of 1 or greater was treated as a positive diagnosis, the second row presents the validity coefficients when a scale score of 2 or greater was treated as a positive diagnosis, and so on.

The scale achieved optimal diagnostic accuracy when a scale score of 2 or higher was treated as a positive diagnosis (Table 8.2, figures in bold). The resulting test achieves near-perfect sensitivity (.98) and excellent specificity (.92).

Convergent Validity of QPD Panel Depression and Anxiety Scales

Virtually all psychiatric disorders seen in primary care are characterized by the presence of anxiety or depressive affect, or both. Increases in anxiety or depression generally precede the emergence of a full-blown psychiatric disorder, and decreases accompany recovery. The QPD Panel includes scales that quantify the severity of depression and anxiety.

To establish convergent validity of the QPD Panel Depression and Anxiety scales, we examined correlations between these scales and several established, well-validated measures of depression and anxiety. The correlations were obtained in a variety of adult patient samples, with sample sizes ranging from $N = 131$ to $N = 203$ (Shedler, Beck, & Bensen, 1999). The QPD Panel Depression scale correlated highly with the Beck Depression Inventory (BDI; $r = .80$), the Hamilton Depression Inventory ($r = .87$), the Center for Epidemiological Studies Depression Scale (CES–D; $r = .79$), and the Zung Self-rating Depression Scale ($r = .78$). The QPD Panel Anxiety scale correlated highly with the Spielberger State-Trait Anxiety Inventory ($r = .67$), and the anxiety subscale of the Symptom Checklist–90 (SCL–90; $r = .76$). All correlations are statistically significant ($p < .001$) and near the upper limits permitted by the reliabilities of the scales.

Psychometric Characteristics of the QPD Panel Numeric Scales

The QPD Panel provides numeric scores that measure the severity of pathology in seven potential problem areas. In all cases, higher scores signify greater pathology. These numeric scores have three major uses:

1. Out-of-range scores identify clinically significant pathology, even when patients do not meet formal *DSM–IV* criteria for a psychiatric diagnosis.
2. Among patients with psychiatric diagnoses, the scores indicate the severity of the symptoms.
3. The scores are sensitive to change and can be used for treatment monitoring or outcome assessment (see Outcome Assessment section).

Table 8.3 lists psychometric characteristics of the seven QPD Panel scales. The first column indicates the possible range of the score, from minimum to maximum. The second column indicates the normal reference range; values outside this range indicate clinically significant pathology. The third column presents the reliability of the scale, assessed by coefficient alpha (a measure of internal consistency; Cronbach, 1951). Scale reliabilities are uniformly excellent, ranging from a low of .78 for somatization to a high of .95 for panic.

Finally, Table 8.3 lists the means (and standard deviations) observed in two reference samples. The control sample consists of 483 transit employees in the Denver area, who participated in a voluntary mental health screening program during an employee health fair. The clinical sample consists of 178 patients presenting for treatment at a community mental health agency that serves a relatively disturbed patient population. These scores are presented only as general reference points, to help familiarize readers with the characteristics of the QPD Panel scales. As one would anticipate, all scores are higher for the clinical sample than for the control sample, and all differences are statistically significant.

Limitations of the Validation Research

Because of the low prevalence rate in our patient sample, we were unable to calculate stable validity coefficients for two QPD Panel diagnoses, dysthymic disorder and bulimia nervosa. The diagnostic modules for these disorders have high face validity,

TABLE 8.3
Characteristics of the QPD Panel Scales

Scale	Scale Range	Normal Reference Range	Reliability (Alpha)	Mean (SD) for Control Sample (n = 483)	Mean (SD) for Clinical Sample (n = 178)
Depression	0–28	0–10	.89	3.86 (4.61)	15.54 (7.72)
Anxiety	0–27	0–10	.87	4.31 (4.47)	13.96 (7.67)
Panic	0–22	0–8	.95	0.50 (2.18)	6.15 (7.60)
OCD	0–20	0–5	.88	0.63 (2.19)	5.57 (7.05)
Bulimia	0–7	0–4	n/a[a]	0.53 (0.98)	1.21 (1.86)
Alcohol/subtance abuse	0–14	0–2	.94	0.33 (1.10)	1.97 (3.70)[b]
Somatization	0–15	0–11	.78	2.62 (2.73)	6.25 (4.17)

[a]Because of the design of the Bulimia module (involving extensive branching and "skip patterns"), coefficient alpha cannot be computed.

[b]In a chemical dependency sample (see Alcohol and Substance Abuse section), the mean Alcohol/Substance Abuse score was 8.78 (SD = 4.31).

and test development followed the same procedures used for the other diagnostic modules. For these reasons, we expect that the dysthymic disorder and bulimia nervosa modules will show similarly high validity coefficients in larger patient samples. Nevertheless, formal validation against a diagnostic criterion must await future research.

There was no attempt to validate the diagnosis of bipolar disorder against an external criterion. In the author's opinion, a definitive diagnosis of bipolar disorder should be made by a trained mental health professional with a thorough knowledge of the patient's history. For this reason, the QPD Panel is designed to screen for possible bipolar disorder, not make diagnoses. Patients with positive QPD Panel results for bipolar disorder should be referred to a psychiatrist for evaluation and treatment.

PHYSICIAN ACCEPTANCE

Authors of psychological tests routinely present data on reliability and validity, but rarely present data on physician acceptance. Such data are crucial because in primary care settings, physician acceptance is just as important as validity. Tests that are inconvenient for physicians, or do not meet physicians' needs, are likely to sit on the shelf. When this happens, validity findings become irrelevant, because *the validity of an unused test is exactly zero.*

If a psychological test is intended for use in medical settings, then test developers should report physician satisfaction data as routinely as they report validity data. The physician satisfaction data should be collected under "real-world" conditions — that is, in busy medical clinics where physicians have no artificial incentive to use the test.

Table 8.4 presents the results of a physician satisfaction survey for the QPD Panel. Data were provided by a sample of 26 primary care providers affiliated with one of two Kaiser Permanente medical clinics in the Denver area. Kaiser Permanente is a staff-model HMO; its primary care clinics are extremely busy, and physicians work under considerable time pressure. The physicians were offered no incentives to use the QPD Panel, financial or otherwise.

TABLE 8.4
Means for Physician Satisfaction Questionnaire

Item	Mean (SD)	Percent "agree" or "strongly agree"
The QPD Panel is convenient and easy to use.	4.8 (0.40)	100%
The QPD Panel integrates easily into the primary care clinic.	4.6 (0.90)	89%
The QPD Panel presents results in a clear, easy-to-understand format.	4.8 (0.51)	96%
The QPD Panel is well-accepted by patients.	4.6 (0.50)	100%
The QPD Panel helps me provide better patient care.	4.7 (0.60)	100%
The QPD Panel can be used immediately by any physician, without special training required.	4.6 (0.75)	100%

Note. Scoring: 1 = *strongly disagree*, 2 = *disagree*, 3 = *neither agree nor disagree*, 4 = *agree*, 5 = *strongly agree*, $N = 26$.

Physicians rated each of the statements listed in Table 8.4 using a 5-point rating scale, where 1 = *strongly disagree*, 2 = *disagree*, 3 = *neither agree nor disagree*, 4 = *agree*, and 5 = *strongly agree*. All the physicians had used the QPD Panel for at least a month prior to completing the survey (and at the time of this writing, all are still using it).

Means for the physician satisfaction items were uniformly high, and in all cases were near the scale maximum of 5.0 (*strongly agree*). As another way of presenting the data, the last column of Table 8.4 lists the percentage of clinicians who "agreed" or "strongly agreed" with the questionnaire statement (i.e., assigned scale ratings of 4 or 5). The data leave little doubt about the high level of physician acceptance achieved by the QPD Panel, or the value of the physician interviews and focus groups that guided the QPD Panel's development.

The results summarized in Table 8.4 are consistent with anecdotal data recently reported to the author. Kaiser Permanente conducted a study in one primary care clinic, which involved screening patients for mental disorders using the QPD Panel. The physicians received QPD Panel lab reports and treated or referred patients as they saw fit. The study was time limited, and the Kaiser Permanente researchers had intended to remove the QPD Panel when the study was completed, for use in another medical facility. At the completion of the study, however, the physicians refused to give up the QPD Panel. They found the test so clinically useful that they insisted on keeping it (indeed, they had to put up something of a fight, because management had not budgeted for the QPD Panel hardware). This is the opposite of what usually happens in primary care studies, where physicians stop using mental health screening tests at the earliest opportunity.

PATIENT SATISFACTION

The QPD Panel was developed with an eye to patient satisfaction as well as physician satisfaction. The goal was to create a test that would be easy for patients to use, that patients would perceive as relevant and appropriate in a primary care setting. The evidence indicates that we were successful. In over 2 years of use in busy primary care medical clinics, no patient has complained about the QPD Panel or objected to taking it. On the contrary, patients have spontaneously commented that the test made them feel good about the quality of care they were receiving, and led them to feel that their doctors cared about them.

In formal patient satisfaction surveys, we asked patients who had used the QPD panel to respond to four survey items using an agree/disagree response format. Table 8.5 shows the results for a sample of 77 primary care patients. Nearly 100% of the patients agreed that the QPD Panel was easy to use, that the questions were clear and easy to understand, and that the test asked about things that were important for their doctors to know. Nearly all disagreed that the questions were too personal or made them feel uncomfortable. We have replicated these findings several times.

OUTCOME ASSESSMENT

Ideally, a psychological test designed for primary care should be useful not only for patient screening, but also for treatment monitoring and outcome assessment. The

TABLE 8.5
Patient Satisfaction Questionnaire ($N = 77$)

Item	Percent "agree"
The questionnaire was easy to use.	97%
The questions were clear and easy to understand.	99%
The questionnaire asked about things that are important for my doctor to know.	96%
The questions were too personal and made me feel uncomfortable.	4%

QPD Panel Depression and Anxiety scales were designed for this purpose. Physicians can readminister the QPD Panel as often as desired. By comparing Depression and Anxiety scores with scores from earlier test administrations, physicians can monitor change or evaluate treatment outcomes. Changes of five points or more (approximately one standard deviation) may be regarded as clinically significant.

To formally evaluate the utility of the QPD Panel as a measure of change, we followed a sample of depressed patients longitudinally. Primary care physicians identified a sample of 113 patients suffering from depressive disorders. These patients completed the QPD Panel at the time of their initial primary care appointment (pretreatment) to establish baseline Depression scores. The patients were then treated for depression with antidepressant medication (an SSRI), brief psychotherapy, or a combination of both. The QPD Panel was readministered 4 weeks after initiation of treatment, and again at 12 weeks after initiation of treatment (for a detailed description of this study, see chap. 23 by Beck & Nimmer, this volume).

The mean QPD Panel Depression score was 14.8 at baseline. At 4-week follow-up the mean Depression score had dropped to 11.2, a decrease of approximately 25%. At 12-week follow-up, the mean Depression score had dropped to 7.7, a decrease of approximately 50% (or slightly more than one standard deviation) from baseline. Differences between pre- and posttreatment scores were statistically significant ($p <$ .001). A similar pattern was observed for the QPD Panel Anxiety scores. Figure 8.3

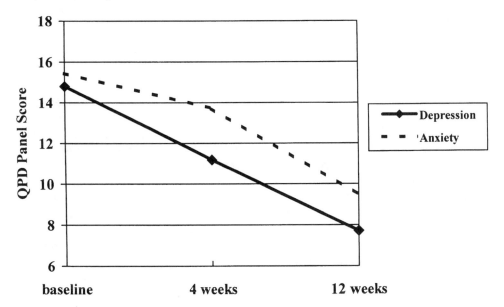

FIG. 8.3.   QPD Panel Depression and Anxiety scores, pre- and posttreatment.

charts changes in the QPD Panel Depression and Anxiety scores from baseline through 12-week follow-up. The findings speak both to the efficacy of the intervention and to the utility of the QPD Panel as a measure of change.

DATA REPORTING

The QPD Panel hardware stores patient data electronically. As patients complete the QPD Panel, their responses are added to the database automatically. This database can be downloaded to other computer systems for subsequent data analysis (the database file can be transferred in a variety of popular file formats). The database can be downloaded and managed locally, at the data collection site. Alternatively, Digital Diagnostics, Inc. can provide data management services, and can download the QPD Panel database to its central offices via modem. (QPD Panel units can be equipped with internal modems. When a unit is connected to a telephone line, data retrieval can be accomplished remotely).

Aggregate Reports

The QPD Panel database can be integrated with existing patient databases for research purposes, or can be used on a stand-alone basis to generate aggregate reports (e.g., monthly, quarterly, annually) on the patient population. For example, the database can be used to track the prevalence of psychiatric disorders, identify the most common symptoms, determine comorbidity of disorders, and so on. Figure 8.4 is an example of an aggregate report prepared for a community mental health agency. The report provides descriptive statistics for a sample of new patients presenting for treatment during a 1 month period. It should be noted that the agency serves a relatively disturbed patient population, and the prevalence of mental disorders is not representative of mental health populations generally.

Future Trends

As behavioral health organizations continue to use the QPD Panel for outcome assessment, Digital Diagnostics, Inc. is accumulating a database of outcome data. Such a database can provide performance benchmarks for health care organizations. For example, researchers will be able to compare the performance of alternative disease management programs, or compare the performance of different treatment facilities, relative to established norms. Figure 8.5 illustrates how this kind of data could be used to evaluate the effectiveness of two hypothetical treatment facilities, Clinic A and Clinic B, in treating major depression. The solid line represents normative improvements in mental health scores (i.e., changes from baseline) over 12 weeks of treatment (the mental health scores are computed by summing the Depression and Anxiety scale scores, then reflecting the resulting scale so that higher scores signify greater health). In this hypothetical example, Clinic A surpasses established norms, and its patients experience better than average outcomes. Clinic B lags behind the norms, and its patients appear to receive minimal benefit from treatment.

QPD Panel Aggregate Report
Aggregate data for 30-day period ending 1/9/98

Total patients tested: 178

Prevalence of psychiatric disorders in patient sample

Diagnosis	% of Patients Meeting Diagnostic Criteria	n
Mood Disorders		
Major Depression	55.6%	99
Dysthymic Disorder	0.6%	1
Depressive Disorder NOS	12.9%	23
Bipolar Disorder	26.4%	47
Anxiety Disorders		
Generalized Anxiety Disorder	7.9%	14
Panic Disorder	29.2%	52
Obsessive-Compulsive Disorder	29.2%	52
Anxiety Disorder NOS	13.5%	24
Other Disorders		
Bulimia Nervosa	3.4%	6
Alcohol/substance abuse	28.1%	50
Suicide Risk		
Patient expresses suicidal ideation	27%	48
Patient is imminent suicide risk	5.6%	10

QPD Panel items most often answered "True" (top 10 items)

QPD Item	Percent of Patients Answering "True"	Rank
I feel sad or depressed.	82%	1
I would say that being sad or depressed is making it difficult for me to work, take care of things at home, or get along with others.	82%	2
I have been having trouble falling asleep or staying asleep.	79%	3
I often regret things I did or said while I was under the influence of alcohol or drugs.	77%	4
I feel I cannot think or concentrate as well as I used to.	76%	5
I am usually worried about several things all at once.	76%	6
I often find that I want to continue drinking or taking drugs after my friends say they have had enough.	73%	7
I am often irritable.	72%	8
I find little or no interest or pleasure in my daily activities.	70%	9
I worry too long after an embarrassing situation.	69%	10

Comorbidity of selected diagnoses with alcohol/substance abuse:

Diagnosis	% of Patients With Comorbid Alcohol/Substance Abuse
Major Depression	32.3%
Depression NOS	30.4%
Bipolar Disorder	42.1%
Generalized Anxiety Disorder	35.7%
Anxiety NOS	20.8%

FIG. 8.4.   Sample aggregate report.

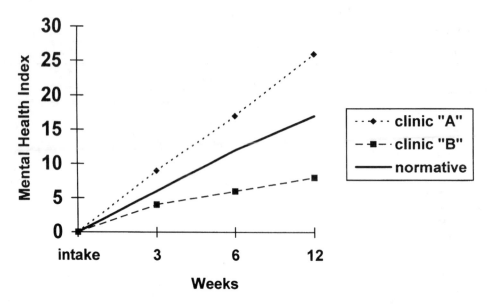

FIG. 8.5.   Comparing treatment efficacy of two clinics (hypothetical data).

SUMMARY

Most patients with psychiatric disorders seek treatment from primary care physicians, not from mental health professionals. Unfortunately, primary care physicians fail to diagnose 50% to 70% of patients with depression and other common psychiatric disorders. These undiagnosed patients suffer needlessly, experience considerable disability, and contribute to rising health care costs.

Although health care experts agree there is need for improved mental health screening in primary care, primary care physicians rarely use mental health screening tests. To determine why such tests have not gained physician acceptance, the author conducted interviews and focus groups with primary care physicians in several states. The interviews and focus groups revealed that the available mental health test did not meet physicians' needs. In general, they required too much time and effort from physicians, and did not present diagnostic information in a form useful to physicians.

The interviews and focus groups provided the foundation for development of the Shedler QPD Panel (an acronym for Quick PsychoDiagnostics Panel), an instrument designed to integrate seamlessly into busy primary care offices and clinics and to meet the special needs of primary care physicians. The QPD Panel is fully automated. Patients self-administer the test on portable, hand-held computer tablets that they hold in their laps. Diagnostic questions are presented in large, clear text on a video screen, and patients answer by pressing True and False response buttons. The test makes use of logic and branching, so healthy patients are not asked irrelevant questions, and patients who may have psychiatric disorders are examined in depth. The test screens for nine psychiatric disorders and makes specific diagnoses based on *DSM–IV* diagnostic criteria, yet requires only 6.2 min to complete, on average.

Physicians receive a computer-generated "lab report" that is printed immediately, on site. The lab report is chart-ready and has a "look and feel" that is familiar to physicians, resembling a standard blood chemistries report. Because the test provides results in a familiar format, physicians can begin using the QPD Panel without special training. The lab report provides three types of information: (a) numerical scores indicating the severity of disturbance, (b) a specific *DSM–IV* diagnosis, and (c) a list of the symptoms that led to the diagnosis.

QPD Panel diagnoses were validated against the SCID structured psychiatric interview, widely regarded as the "gold standard" for psychiatric diagnoses. Sensitivity and specificity are high. Equally important, the test achieves high ratings for both physician satisfaction and patient satisfaction. One hundred percent of physicians who participated in a formal physician satisfaction survey agreed that the QPD Panel is easy to use, helps them provide better patient care, and can be used immediately without special training. Patient acceptance is similarly high, with nearly 100% of patients agreeing that the QPD Panel is easy to use, asks questions that are clear and easy to understand, and asks about things that are important for their doctors to know.

The QPD Panel can be used not only for initial screening, but also for treatment monitoring and outcome assessment. The test can be readministered periodically. By comparing test results with results obtained from earlier test administrations, a physician can determine whether a patient's status has changed. In addition, the QPD Panel stores patient data electronically, and the resulting database can be used for research purposes, or to generate aggregate reports on the patient population (e.g., prevalence of psychiatric disorders, comorbidity, most prevalent psychiatric symptoms, etc.).

Psychiatric disorders are common in primary care, and most physicians report that they want to know when their patients suffer from psychiatric disorders. However, the lack of a practical screening instrument has been an obstacle to widespread mental health screening in primary care settings. The QPD Panel is designed to meet the need for a practical primary care screening tool. As mental health screening becomes more prevalent in primary care, more patients will receive effective treatment, and there will be less stigma associated with treatment. Psychiatric disorders have been referred to in the medical literature as the "hidden major illnesses," but there is no good reason for them to stay hidden.

ACKNOWLEDGMENTS

The author thanks Kevin Kearney and Alan Malik of Point-of-View Survey Systems, Denver, CO, for their work in developing the hardware platform for use in primary care settings. I also thank Stephen Bensen, PhD, Anne Samson, PsyD, and the entire medical staff of the Kaiser Permanente Aurora Centre Point medical facility for their invaluable feedback during the field testing phase.

REFERENCES

American Psychiatric Association. (1994). *Diagnostic and statistical manual of mental disorders* (4th ed.). Washington, DC: Author.

Andersen, S. M., & Harthorn, B. H. (1989). The recognition, diagnosis, and treatment of mental disorders by primary care physicians. *Medical Care, 27,* 869–886.

Barrett, J. E., Barrett, J. A., Oxman, T. E., & Gerber, P. D. (1988). The prevalence of psychiatric disorders in a primary care practice. *Archives of General Psychiatry, 45,* 1100–1106.

Beck, A. T., Ward, C. H., Mendelson, M., & Erbaugh, J. (1961). An inventory for measuring depression. *Archives of General Psychiatry, 4,* 561–571.

Borus, J. F., Howes, M. J., Devins, N. P., Rosenberg, R., & Livingston, W. W. (1988). Primary health care providers' recognition and diagnosis of mental disorders in their patients. *General Hospital Psychiatry, 10,* 317–321.

Cohen, J. (1960). A coefficient of agreement for nominal scales. *Educational and Psychological Measurement, 20,* 37–46.

Cronbach, L. J. (1951). Coefficient alpha and the internal structure of tests. *Psychometrika, 16,* 297–334.

First, M. B., Spitzer, R. L., Gibbon, M., & Williams, J. B. W. (1995). *Structured Clinical Interview for DSM–IV Axis I Disorders (SCID).* Washington, DC: American Psychiatric Press.

Franco, K., Tamburino, M., Campbell, N., Zrull, J., Evans, C., & Bronson, D. (1995). The added cost of depression to medical care. *Pharmacoeconomics, 7,* 284–291.

Katon, W. (1987). The epidemiology of depression in medical care. *International Journal of Psychiatry in Medicine, 17,* 83–112.

Kessler, L. G., Burns, B. J., Shapiro, S., Tischler, G. L., George, L. K., Hough, R. L., Bodison, D., & Miller, R. H. (1987). Psychiatric diagnoses of medical service users: Evidence from the Epidemiological Catchment Area Program. *American Journal of Public Health, 77,* 18–24.

Nielson, A. C., & Williams, T. (1980). Depression in ambulatory medical patients. *Archives of General Psychiatry, 37,* 999–1004.

Ormel, J., Koeter, M. W. J., van den Brink, W., & van de Willige, G. (1991). Recognition, management, and course of anxiety and depression in general practice. *Archives of General Psychiatry, 48,* 700–706.

Regier, D. A., Goldberg, I. D., & Taube, C. A. (1978). The de facto U.S. mental health services system. *Archives of General Psychiatry, 35,* 685–693.

Reynolds, W. M., & Kobak, K. A. (1995). *Hamilton Depression Inventory: A self-report version of the Hamilton Depression Rating Scale.* Odessa FL: Psychological Assessment Resources.

Rydon, P., Redmon, S., Sanson-Fisher, R. W., & Reid, A. L. A. (1992). Detection of alcohol related problems in general practice. *Journal of Studies on Alcohol, 53,* 97–202.

Schulberg, H. C., & Burns, B. J. (1988). Mental disorders in primary care: Epidemiologic, diagnostic, and treatment research directions. *General Hospital Psychiatry, 10,* 79–87.

Schulberg, H. C., Saul, M., & McClelland, M. (1985). Assessing depression in primary medical and psychiatric practices. *Archives of General Psychiatry, 12,* 1164–1170.

Shedler, J., Beck, A., & Bensen, S. (1999). *Practical mental health assessment in primary care: Validity and utility of the Shedler Quick PsychoDiagnostics Panel (QPD Panel).* Manuscript submitted for publication.

Spitzer, R. L., Williams, J. B. W., Kroenke, K., Linzer, M., deGruy, F. V., Hahn, S., Brody, D., & Johnson, J. G. (1994). Utility of a new procedure for diagnosing mental disorders in primary care: The PRIME–MD 1000 study. *Journal of the American Medical Association, 272,* 1749–1756.

Zung, W. W. K. (1965). A self-rating depression scale. *Archives of General Psychiatry, 12,* 63–70.

The SCL-90-R and Brief Symptom Inventory (BSI) in Primary Care*

Leonard R. Derogatis
Kathryn L. Savitz
Clinical Psychometric Research, Inc.,
and
Loyola College of Maryland

The National Institute of Mental Health (NIMH) Epidemiologic Catchment Area (ECA) study, an investigation of psychiatric disorders in the community involving nearly 20,000 individuals, is by far the most comprehensive research yet completed on the prevalence of psychiatric disorders in the community. These data make it clear that psychiatric disorders represent a highly prevalent phenomenon in our society (Robins et al., 1984; Myers et al., 1984; Regier et al., 1988).

In terms of specific diagnoses, the overall rate for affective disorders was 5.1%, whereas that for anxiety disorders was 7.3% (Regier et al., 1988). Six-month prevalence estimates for affective disorders ranged from 4.6% to 6.5% across the five ECA sites (Meyers et al., 1984). Comparable 6-month estimates for anxiety disorders revealed rates for panic disorder ranging from 0.6% to 1.0%, whereas the prevalence of agoraphobia varied from 2.5% to 5.8% across the various sites (Weissman & Merikangas, 1986).

MEDICAL SETTINGS

In medical populations, prevalence rates of psychiatric disorder are substantially elevated over community estimates. This is particularly true of anxiety and depressive disorders, which account by far for the majority of psychiatric diagnoses assigned to medical patients (Barrett et al., 1988; Derogatis et al., 1983; Von Korff, Dworkin, & Krueger, 1988). In recent reviews of psychiatric prevalence in medical populations, Barrett et al. (1988) observed overall prevalence rates of 25% to 30%, whereas Derogatis and Wise (1989) reported prevalence estimates which varied between 22% to 33%. The latter authors stated, "In general, it appears that up to one-third of medical inpatients demonstrate symptoms of depression, while 20 to 25% reveal more substantial depressive manifestations" (p. 101).

---

*SCL-90-R and BSI are registered trademarks of Leonard R. Derogatis, PhD.

Regarding anxiety disorders, Kedward and Cooper (1966) observed a prevalence rate of 27% in an early study of a London general practice, and Schulberg and his colleagues (1985) reported a combined rate of 8.5% for phobic and panic disorders among American primary care patients. Wise and Taylor (1990) concluded that 5% to 20% of medical inpatients suffer the symptoms of anxiety, while 6% receive formal anxiety diagnoses.

Clearly these data demonstrate that psychiatric disorders are a persistent and demonstrable set of problems that affect substantial numbers of our population, and represent vulnerabilities that are particularly exacerbated by the presence of medical illness.

PSYCHIATRIC DISORDERS AND PSYCHOLOGICAL DISTRESS

The formal assignment of a psychiatric diagnosis not only requires that psychological symptoms be present, but also demands that they be present in a certain designated configuration, often for a specified minimum period of time; that they not be the result of toxins or a primary medical disease process; and that certain exclusionary criteria be absent from the clinical picture (American Psychiatric Association, 1994). When dealing with patients with a primary medical disorder, the criteria for formal psychiatric diagnosis can often become blurred, in spite of the fact that the patient may have incurred substantial dysphoria and distress. This is because, as Derogatis and Wise (1989) pointed out, "symptoms of anxiety and depression can be independent concomitants of, reactions to, substitutes for, or integral aspects of an entire spectrum of medical disorders" (p. 81). Particularly in serious chronic medical conditions, where the patient's coping capacity and psychological integrity are severely tested, symptoms of anxiety and depression sometimes become indistinguishable features of the principal medical illness. These *psychological distress* states, although they do not formally qualify as diagnostic entities, nonetheless are associated with a substantial degree of discomfort and significantly reduce quality of life. A study lending dramatic support to this observation was recently reported by Johnson, Weissman, and Klerman (1992), who found that levels of service burden and health impairment were as high or higher for individuals with subdiagnostic levels of depressive symptoms as for individuals receiving a diagnosis of major depression or dysthymic disorder. When such states coexist with a medical disorder, they frequently serve to further undermine the patient's sense of well-being and can in some instances subvert adherence to medical treatment regimens.

This distinction is relevant to the current discussion because the SCL–90–R and Brief Symptom Inventory (BSI) are not confined to serving as screening measures for "caseness" (although they may be used in that capacity), but rather are outcomes measures designed to assess symptomatic distress across the entire psychopathologic continuum. The SCL–90–R and BSI are broadly sensitive to symptomatic manifestations, from levels of mild dysphoria in the community population, through morbid distress states, to levels of symptomatology characteristic of formal psychiatric disorders. These instruments are not limited to operationalizing diagnostic status, but in addition are sensitive to a comprehensive range of psychological distress states and to the effects of interventions designed to improve or alter these conditions.

THE IMPACT OF COMORBIDITY

The detection and characterization of psychiatric conditions comorbid with primary medical disorders are extremely important, because the evidence is very compelling that unidentified, and therefore untreated, psychiatric disorders have a spectrum of nonsalutary effects on the course and outcome of primary medical conditions. Derogatis and DellaPietra (1994) reviewed the array of problems intrinsic to the identification of anxiety and depressive disorders in primary care, and a number of authors (e.g., Bridges & Goldberg, 1984; Katon et al., 1990) emphasized that principal among these is the high rate of presentation with somatic symptoms among these patients. In addition to increases in morbidity and mortality associated with untreated comorbid psychiatric conditions (Kamerow, Pincus, & MacDonald, 1986; Regier et al., 1988), increased levels of health care utilization have been well documented (Katon et al., 1990). Also, high levels of psychological distress among medical patients have been associated with increased medical costs (Allison et al., 1995) and increased length of hospital stay (Saravay, Pollack, Steinberg, Weinschel, & Habert, 1996). Because primary care physicians are functioning increasingly as the "gatekeepers" for effective mental health treatment, identification and measurement of these comorbid conditions assume even greater consequence.

THE SCL-90-R AND THE BSI

The SCL-90-R (Derogatis, 1977, 1994) is a 90-item self-report symptom inventory. It evolved most directly from the Hopkins Symptom Checklist (HSCL) (Derogatis, Lipman, Rickels,Uhlenhuth, & Covi, 1974a, 1974b), which has roots in a number of earlier tests, such as the Cornell Medical Index (Wider, 1948).

A prototype version of the SCL-90-R was first described in 1973 (Derogatis, Lipman, & Covi, 1973), and the final version of the instrument was completed 2 years later (Derogatis, 1975). The inventory measures psychological symptoms and distress in terms of nine primary symptom dimensions and three global indices. The primary symptom dimensions of the SCL-90-R are somatization, obsessive-compulsive, interpersonal sensitivity, depression, anxiety, hostility, phobic anxiety, paranoid ideation, and psychoticism. The global measures were designed to provide summary measures of overall distress status, each from a slightly different perspective. The globals are termed the Global Severity Index (GSI), the Positive Symptom Distress Index (PSDI), and the Positive Symptom Total (PST).

The SCL-90-R and its companion instruments in the series were developed to be utilized with an extensive range of respondents. The inventory may be validly employed with community respondents, a broad spectrum of medical outpatients and inpatients, and the large majority of patients with psychiatric disorders. The SCL-90-R is currently available in over 26 languages, including Dutch, English, French, German, Italian, Russian, and Spanish. Microcomputer scoring, administration, and interpretation programs are also available for the SCL-90-R.

The Brief Symptom Inventory (BSI) (Derogatis, 1993; Derogatis & Melisaratos, 1983; Derogatis & Spencer, 1982) is comprised of 53 items, and represents the brief form of the SCL-90-R. It was also completed in 1975, and reflects psychological distress/disorder in terms of the same nine symptom dimensions and three global indices as its longer counterpart. The BSI was designed specifically for measurement situations in which the time constraints will not allow at least 15 min, the time typically required to complete the SCL–90–R. Scores on the SCL–90–R and the BSI are highly correlated, however, and very often the brief version of the test is preferred, even in the absence of time constraints. As with the SCL–90–R, the three global indices, nine principal symptom dimensions, and 53 individual items reflect the three basic levels of clinical interpretation of the test.

The SCL–90–R represents a psychological test that is broadly applied and highly utilized in its own right; however, it also serves as the centerpiece of a series of matched, multimodality tests. A major advantage of a multimodality approach rests in the fact that it enables assessment of clinical status through both self-report and expert clinical judgement, using comparable measuring devices. This goal was realized in the case of the SCL–90–R/BSI through the development of two matched "companion" clinical rating scales.

The Derogatis Psychiatric Rating Scale (DPRS) is a multidimensional clinical rating scale designed to be the clinician's version of the SCL–90–R. The first nine dimensions of the DPRS match the nine symptom constructs of the SCL–90–R. Eight additional dimensions, important to valid clinical interpretation but not amenable to reliable self-report, also comprise the scale. A brief form of the DPRS (termed the Brief Derogatis Psychiatric Rating Scale, BDPRS) is also available; it consists of only the nine matching SCL–90–R/BSI symptom constructs.

The SCL–90 Analogue Scale is a second companion scale to the SCL–90–R/BSI. It is designed for health professionals (e.g., physicians, nurses, social workers, lay interviewers) who have not received extensive training in psychopathology and psychiatric nosology. It is a graphic or analogue scale that represents the nine primary symptom dimensions of the SCL–90–R along 100-mm lines, extending from "not-at-all" at the minimum distress point to "extremely" at the maximum. Any of the three companion clinical observer's scales may be used in conjunction with either the SCL–90–R or the BSI.

NORMS AND NORMATIVE SAMPLES

In judging the clinical meaning of psychological test scores, just as in evaluating the clinical implications of a blood chemistry panel, reliable, meaningful standards must be available for comparison. No matter how well designed and validated a test is, without such standards (referred to as *norms* in psychological measurement), the test will have little utility in evaluating the individual patient's status. Norms provide an interpretive point of reference; they define the patient's status on the characteristic(s) being measured relative to a representative sample of like individuals. If norms are well constructed, they enable the clinician to make actuarial statements concerning the patient's status: for example, "Mr. Smith's level of depression is at the 98th percentile of the community norm, clearly suggesting a clinical level of disorder," or "Ms. Green's IQ score was more than a full standard deviation below the mean, placing her in the bottom 15% of the normative group."

Technical issues concerning the construction of norms are usually considered esoteric and arcane for all but psychometricians; however, there are several key properties that signal the quality of a norm. First, the norm must be based on a *representative sample* of individuals from the population to which comparisons are intended. If the comparison to be made is with "normals," then a representative cohort of community individuals free of discernable psychiatric disorder should comprise the normative group. If, on the other hand, a clinician wishes to compare the psychological distress profile of a Stage II breast cancer patient to like patients, then the normative cohort should be comprised of respondents diagnosed with a similar malignancy. Second, the norms should be *actuarial* in nature, allowing the clinician to appreciate the meaning of the patient's scores or values in terms of centile or probability equivalents. Third, the level of *generalizability* of the norm must be clearly stated. It is well established that distributions of many important biological and psychological characteristics are altered considerably as a function of parameters such as gender, age, and health status. Particularly in the area of psychological distress/disorder, normative inferences should be based on age- and gender-specific norms, with the added realization that the presence of an active medical illness or condition almost invariably inflates distress levels significantly.

Currently there are four formal norms for the SCL–90–R and BSI: (a) psychiatric outpatients, (b) community nonpatients, (c) psychiatric inpatients, and (d) community adolescents (Derogatis, 1994). All norms for the SCL–90–R/BSI are actuarial in nature and gender keyed. Gender keying represents an important normative refinement when attributes involving emotional expression or psychological distress are being assessed, because of well-established gender differences in reporting emotional distress.

The Psychiatric Outpatient Norm for the SCL–90–R (Norm A) is based on 1,002 heterogeneous outpatients who presented for treatment at the outpatient psychiatry departments of four major teaching hospitals located in the East and Midwest. The same sample was utilized in creating the Outpatient Norm for the BSI. Norm B, the Community Nonpatient Norm, was established on a cohort of 973 individuals who represent a stratified random sample from a diversely populated county in a major eastern state. Again, the Community Norm for the BSI was also developed based on this sample. The Psychiatric Inpatient Norms (Norm C) for both the SCL–90–R and BSI are based on a sample of 423 individuals who were a heterogeneous group of patients from the psychiatric inpatient services of three major eastern hospitals. The Adolescent Community Norm (Norm E) for the SCL–90–R is based on 806 adolescents who were enrolled in two geographically distinct midwestern high schools. Adolescent Community Norms for the BSI were developed from a sample of 2,408 adolescents, ranging in age from 13 to 19 years, who attended six different schools in two distinct states. Detailed demography for all published norms for the SCL–90–R may be found in the *SCL–90–R®: Administration, Scoring & Procedures Manual* (Derogatis, 1977, 1994). Similar data for the BSI is provided in *Brief Symptom Inventory (BSI®): Administration, Scoring & Procedures Manual* (Derogatis, 1982, 1993).

RELIABILITY AND VALIDITY

Reliability

Reliability essentially pertains to the consistency or replicability with which an instrument measures the characteristic(s) under observation. It is the converse of measurement error, and represents the proportion of variation in any measurement that is due to systematic variation of the attribute under study (e.g., depression, hardiness, impulsivity), as opposed to variance due to random or systematic error. Two formal types of reliability estimates are available for the symptom dimensions of the SCL–90–R: (a) *internal consistency*, and (b) *test–retest*. The former serves to reflect the homogeneity of the item sets developed to represent each symptom construct; test–retest reliability is much more of a measure of temporal stability, or score consistency across time.

SCL–90–R Reliability

Internal consistency coefficients for the nine dimensions of the SCL–90–R were calculated from the data of 209 "symptomatic volunteers" (Derogatis, Rickels, & Rock, 1976) in the form of coefficients alpha (α). Coefficient alpha treats within-form correlations among the items as analogous to correlations between alternate forms, and makes the assumption that the average correlation among actual items is equivalent to the correlation among items in the hypothetical alternate form (Nunnally, 1970). Coefficients in this assessment were quite satisfactory, ranging from a low of .77 for Psychoticism to a high of .90 for Depression. Internal consistency coefficients for the SCL–90–R were also developed more recently by Horowitz, Rosenberg, Baer, Ureno, and Villasenor (1988) based on 103 outpatients presenting for psychotherapy. Coefficients alpha in that study ranged from a low of .84 for Interpersonal Sensitivity to a high of .90 for Depression (see Table 9.1).

The test–retest coefficients presented in Table 9.1 were developed from a sample of 94 heterogenous psychiatric outpatients who presented for evaluation and treatment at the psychiatric outpatient department of a major eastern teaching hospital. One week elapsed between testings, and as is clear from the sizes of the coefficients, the SCL–90–R possesses very acceptable test–retest reliability. Coefficients ranged from a low of .78 on Hostility, to a high of .90 on the Phobic Anxiety dimension. All other stability coefficients fell in the middle of the range .80 to .90. In addition to these estimates of temporal stability, Horowitz et al. (1988) also evaluated the test–retest

TABLE 9.1
Internal Consistency and Test–Retest Reliability Coefficients for the SCL–90–R

Symptom Dimension	Internal Consistency (Coefficient α)		Test–Retest (r_{tt})	
	Derogatis (1976)[a]	Horowitz et al. (1988)[b]	Derogatis (1983)[c]	Horowitz (1988)[b]
I. SOM	.86	.88	.86	.68
II. O-C	.86	.87	.85	.70
III. INT	.86	.84	.83	.81
IV. DEP	.90	.90	.82	.75
V. ANX	.85	.88	.80	.80
VI. HOS	.84	.85	.78	.73
VII. PHOB	.82	.89	.90	.77
VIII. PAR	.80	.79	.86	.83
IX. PSY	.77	.80	.84	.77
GSI	—	—	—	.84

Note. Symptom dimension acronyms identified in Table 9.2. GSI, global severity index.
[a]N = 219 Symptomatic volunteers.
[b]N = 103 Psychiatric outpatients.
[c]N = 94 Heterogeneous psychiatric outpatients, with 1 week elapsed between tests.

reliability of the SCL–90–R in their sample of 103 psychiatric outpatients. Even across 10 weeks, coefficients were well within the acceptable range, with the coefficient for the GSI reported as .84, and subscale coefficients ranging from a low of .70 for Obsessive-Compulsive to a high of .83 for Paranoid Ideation.

BSI Reliability

Internal consistency reliability coefficients for the BSI were established based on a sample of 719 psychiatric outpatients, using Cronbach's coefficient alpha (α). The alpha coefficients for the nine dimensions of the BSI ranged from a low of .71 on the Psychoticism dimension to a high of .85 on Depression. Independent investigators have reported internal consistency coefficients in a comparable range for the BSI (Aroian & Patsdaughter, 1989; Croog et al., 1986).

As indicated previously, test–retest reliability is an indicator of the consistency of measurement across time. If untreated, psychological distress or psychopathology tends to endure for moderate to substantial periods of time; therefore, a test designed to measure symptomatic distress should register high test–retest coefficients over a span of 2 weeks. To address this issue, 60 nonpatient individuals were tested across a 2-week interval. Coefficients ranged from a low of .68 for Somatization to a high of .91 for Phobic Anxiety. The Global Severity Index also revealed an excellent stability coefficient of .90, providing assurance that the BSI represents consistent measurement across time. Internal consistency and test–retest reliability coefficients for the nine primary symptom dimensions and three global indices of the BSI are represented in Table 9.2.

Alternate forms reliability is a third form of reliability that is typically illustrated in correlation between score distributions from two different forms of a test. Although we do not have a pure alternate form of the BSI, the SCL–90–R is a test that measures identical symptom constructs. To evaluate the level of agreement between the two test forms, correlations were calculated based on a sample of 565 psychiatric outpa-

TABLE 9.2
Internal Consistency and Test–Retest Reliability Coefficients for the Nine
Primary Symptom Dimensions and Three Global Indices of the BSI

Dimension	Number of Items	Internal Consistency (α) (N = 719)	Test–Retest (r_{tt})
I. Somatization (SOM)	7	.80	.68
II. Obsessive-Compulsive (O-C)	6	.83	.85
III. Interpersonal Sensitivity (INT)	4	.74	.85
IV. Depression (DEP)	6	.85	.84
V. Anxiety (ANX)	6	.81	.79
VI. Hostility (HOS)	5	.78	.81
VII. Phobic Anxiety (PHOB)	5	.77	.91
VIII. Paranoid Ideation (PAR)	5	.77	.79
IX. Psychoticism (PSY)	5	.71	.78
Global Indices			
Global Severity Index (GSI)		—	.90
Positive Symptom Distress Index (PSDI)		—	.87
Positive Symptom Total (PST)		—	.80

TABLE 9.3
Correlations Between Symptom Dimensions of the SCL–90–R
and the BSI Based on 565 Psychiatric Outpatients

SOM	O-C	INT	DEP	ANX	HOS	PHOB	PAR	PSY
.96	.96	.94	.95	.95	.99	.97	.98	.92

tients. Coefficients across the nine primary symptom dimensions are given in Table 9.3.

The data demonstrate very high correlations between the BSI and the SCL–90–R on all nine symptom dimensions. At least for psychiatric populations, the two tests show high agreement on all nine of the symptom constructs.

Validity

Two major issues should be understood about the validation of psychological test instruments. The first issue involves the *specificity* of validity, and the second has to do with the *programmatic nature* of the validation process. The former refers to the fact that in order for the question "Is this test valid?" to have any scientific meaning, the conditional modifier "For what purpose?" must be introduced. Psychological tests are not "valid" in general; like all other scientific measuring instruments, they are valid for certain specific measurement purposes and invalid for most others.

The second issue reflects the fact that contemporary psychometric theorists have increasingly stressed construct validity as the principal criterion for the validation of psychological tests and the assignment of meaning to them (Messick, 1975, 1981). The validation process, when accomplished successfully, involves an extensive program of experiments and analyses that are highly analogous to the steps necessary to prove a scientific theory. Data from predictive, content, convergent-discriminant, and other types of validation experiments serve to contribute to the ultimate validation of the tests. The process of establishing the validity of a test is represented by a integrated series of studies that function to extend and redefine the limits of generalizability of the test as a definition of the construct (e.g., depression) being measured.

SCL–90–R Validity

Convergent-discriminant validation is a basic form of validity that is designed to demonstrate that the measure of interest correlates substantially with distinct measures of the same construct, and shows little or no correlation with measures of dissimilar constructs. Derogatis, Rickles, and Rock (1976) demonstrated good convergent-discriminant validity for the SCL–90–R in a study contrasting its dimensions with those of the Minnesota Multiphasic Personality Inventory (MMPI). In addition to the standard MMPI clinical scales, the MMPI was also scored for the Wiggins (1969) content scales and Tryon's (1966) cluster scales. Results illustrated that SCL–90–R dimensions had their highest correlations with like MMPI constructs in every case except Obsessive-Compulsive, which has no directly comparable MMPI scale. Boleloucky and Horvath (1974) reported a comparable study comparing SCL–90–R dimensions to the dimensions of the Middlesex Hospital Questionnaire (MHQ). In their study, there was high convergence between like scales on the majority of test dimensions, with respectable discrimination between dissimilar scales as well. Both of these studies are presented in detail in the SCL–90–R administration manual (Derogatis, 1994).

More recently, Koeter (1992) evaluated the convergent-discriminant validity of the Anxiety and Depression dimensions of the SCL–90–R in comparison with the General Health Questionnaire (GHQ) and concluded that both instruments showed good convergent and discriminant validity. Similarly, Wiznitzer et al. (1992) utilized receiver operating characteristic (ROC) analysis to contrast the SCL–90–R with the Young Adult Self-Report (YASR) and the GHQ-28. The SCL–90–R and the YASR performed at equivalent levels in this population, with both outperforming the GHQ-28. Choquette (1994) contrasted the Depression dimension of the SCL–90–R with the BDI and DIS criteria in identifying clinical depression in alcoholic patients, and concluded that the SCL–90–R and the BDI performed comparably, a finding similar to that of Moffett and Radenhausen (1983) with an analogous population.

Using a different approach to validation, Derogatis and Cleary (1977) cast the hypothesized dimensional structure of the SCL–90–R into a binary "hypothesis matrix" (i.e., each item was assigned a 1 for the factor it loaded on and a 0 for all others). Subsequently, data from the SCL–90–R evaluations of 1,002 psychiatric outpatients were factor analyzed and the solution was rotated toward the "target" matrix via the Procrustes method (Hurley & Cattell, 1962). Rotations were also accomplished via normalized varimax procedures (Kaiser, 1958). Comparisons of both solutions matched the hypothesized dimensional structure of the SCL–90–R cleanly, with only the Psychoticism dimension showing some scatter.

A rigorous and systematic series of validation experiments reflecting elements of concurrent, criterion-oriented, and construct validity for the SCL–90–R was reported by the British investigators Peveler and Fairburn (1990). They compared and correlated scores from the SCL–90–R with those from the Present State Examination (PSE) (Wing, Cooper, & Sartorious, 1974), a clinician-administered, detailed, structured interview. Two distinct samples were utilized in the study: a sample of diabetics ($n = 102$), representing a chronic medical disease group, and a cohort of bulimics ($n = 71$), exemplifying patients with high levels of "neurotic" symptoms. Three distinct validation experiments comprised the study. In the first investigation, the case-finding power of the SCL–90–R was evaluated via receiver operating characteristic (ROC) analysis and logistic regression analysis. In this experiment, the proficiency of the SCL–90–R to detect PSE-defined psychiatric "caseness" was evaluated. The instrument performed efficiently in each instance, with areas under the curve (AUC) of .90 + .03 in both cases. In the diabetic sample the optimum sensitivity was 88% with a specificity of 80%, whereas with the bulimic sample, sensitivity was 76% with a specificity of 92%. Logistic regression analysis relating the GSI from the SCL–90–R to the probability of being a PSE-defined case also characterized the instrument favorably. Sensitivity among diabetics was 72%, whereas specificity was 87%; among bulimics, values were 77% and 91%, respectively.

These investigators also evaluated the validity of the global indices of the SCL–90–R as accurate measures of general severity of psychopathology by correlating them with global indices from the PSE. Across both samples, all coefficients were statistically significant and ranged from approximately .60 to .82. In addition, the validities of the SCL–90–R subscales were tested by evaluating their capacities to predict the presence of PSE syndromes through discriminant function analysis. Appropriate subscales were revealed in 12 of 14 instances in the diabetic sample, and 11 of

14 cases in the bulimic cohort. A further concurrent validation exercise was conducted with the Depression subscale of the SCL–90–R by correlating it with two independent depression inventories, the BDI and the Asberg Rating Scale. Correlations were .80 and .81, respectively.

BSI Validity

A comprehensive review of criterion-oriented validity studies involving the BSI was recently made available by Derogatis (1993). Approximately 120 research reports on the BSI were reviewed involving an extensive range of substantive areas. In addition, Derogatis and Derogatis (1996) published a comprehensive review of research with both the SCL–90–R and the BSI. These studies collectively demonstrated the BSI to be broadly sensitive to the manifestations of psychological distress and interventions designed to ameliorate it across a broad range of conditions. As an illustration of the BSI's general sensitivity to psychological distress status, several of the more interesting of these studies are briefly reviewed here.

Evidence for the BSI's sensitivity in a screening paradigm is provided by a recent report that contrasted several methods for the psychosocial screening of newly diagnosed cancer patients (Zabora, Smith-Wilson, Fetting, & Enterline, 1990). These investigators reported an 84% "hit rate" for the BSI in identifying patients who were determined by independent criteria to be suffering from clinical levels of distress, both at time of initial diagnosis and subsequently at 1-year follow-up. Additionally, a comparative cost-benefit analysis resulted in a strong recommendation for the BSI.

Gift (1991) also reported on the sensitivity of BSI subscales, in this instance to differential respiratory status in a sample of adult asthmatics. In an attempt to determine the underlying causes of episodes of dyspnea (difficulty breathing) in these patients, she utilized the BSI and measured airway obstruction and oxygen saturation during periods of high and low dyspnea. Significant elevations were noted on Anxiety, Depression, Somatization, and Hostility during periods of high dyspnea.

Thompson, Gallagher, and Breckenridge (1987) demonstrated high sensitivity for the BSI in a study of treatment-induced change. These investigators compared the relative efficacy of three distinct psychotherapies in applications with depressed elderly patients. Although no substantial differences were observed between treatments, the BSI showed significant reductions in psychological distress for all three interventions across time, a finding that supported an alternate hypothesis.

Finally, in an intriguing study reported by Chiles, Benjamin, and Cahn (1990), the BSI was utilized with a random sample of 802 members of the Washington State Bar Association to contrast the psychological distress levels of smokers versus nonsmokers. Results showed that among male members of the Bar, almost all BSI subtests revealed smokers to be significantly more highly distressed than nonsmokers. Somatization, Anxiety, and Depression made the greatest contribution to discrimination, with the highly distressed group also showing significantly greater alcohol use. No comparable differences were observed among females, revealing a substantial interaction between gender and smoking status.

As has been noted previously, the type of validation of most interest to clinicians and researchers is the more tangible, pragmatic form, that is, predictive or criterion-oriented validity. Current estimates, based primarily on *SCL–90–R: A Bibliography of Research Reports, 1975–1990* (Derogatis, 1990), *SCL–90–R: Symptom Checklist–90–R Bibliography* (Derogatis, 1996a), and *Brief Symptom Inventory (BSI) Bibliography*

(Derogatis, 1996b), suggest that there are now between 800 and 1,000 published reports pertaining to SCL–90–R criterion-oriented validation, and approximately half that many associated with the BSI. Therapeutic intervention studies evaluating treatments as diverse as meditation (Carrington et al., 1980), multicenter psychotherapy protocols (Shapiro & Firth, 1987), and numerous psychotropic drug trials (Ballenger et al., 1988; Noyes et al., 1984) attest to the instrument's sensitivity to treatment-induced change. Characteristic SCL–90–R profiles for most major diagnostic groups have been established, including those for anxiety (Cameron, Thyer, Nesse, & Curtis, 1986), depression (Prusoff, Weissman, Klerman, & Rounsaville, 1980), panic disorder (Buller, Maier, & Benkert, 1986), and sexual dysfunctions (Derogatis, Meyer, & King, 1981). Such profiles have also been developed for recently delineated compound nosologic subtypes, for example, comorbid panic/depression (Wetzler, Kahn, Cahn, van Praag, & Asnis, 1990) and substance abuse (Steer, Platt, Ranieri, & Metzger, 1989). In addition, the SCL–90–R and BSI have been utilized as psychological distress measures with most major medical illness groups (e.g., cancer, cardiovascular, diabetes, renal diseases).

INTERPRETATION OF THE SCL–90–R AND THE BSI

The SCL–90–R and the BSI were designed to be interpreted in terms of three distinct but related classes of information: global scores, dimension scores, and individual test items. The optimal interpretation of the test protocol is dependent on integration of information from all three source levels. A significant advantage associated with the SCL–90–R/BSI concerns the fact that test scores are reported in terms of standardized area *T*-scores. Scores of this type possess considerable advantages because they are based on a normalizing area transformation of the raw score distribution. This gives the clinician the capacity to make actuarial statements concerning the test respondent's percentile status relative to the norm(s), and thereby to place him or her in an accurate normative position. As an example, regardless of the specific score under consideration, an area *T*-score of 60 will always assign the respondent to the 84th percentile of the referent norm. Similarly, an area *T*-score of 70 will place the individual in the 98th percentile. This feature enables the clinician to make not only accurate comparisons between his patient's status and various norms of interest, but also meaningful comparisons within individual profiles (e.g., comparison of levels of depression vs. anxiety), and, as a result, a more meaningful interpretation of potential therapeutic change.

Global Scores

The GSI represents the most sensitive single quantitative indicator concerning the respondent's overall psychological distress status on the SCL–90–R/BSI. It reflects information on both the *number* of symptoms of distress the individual is enduring, and the *intensity level* of his/her distress. By comparison, the PSDI is designed to be more of a "pure" intensity measure, adjusted for numbers of symptoms. The PSDI can also prove useful in communicating about the respondent's *distress style*, that is, whether he or she is apt to be an "augmenter," typically exaggerating distress, or a "minimizer," more likely to be stoic and understated. The PST reveals the number of symptoms the respondent has endorsed to any degree. It contributes to interpretation by conveying the breadth or array of symptoms that the individual is currently experiencing. Although there are no formal validity scales on the SCL–90–R/BSI, the PST can serve as a coarse indicator of whether or not the respondent is attempting to consciously misrepresent his/her status. Concerning symptom suppression, PST raw scores of 3 or less for adult normal females and 2 or less for adult normal males on the SCL–90–R are extremely uncommon and should be viewed with some misgivings. On the question of augmentation, PST scores greater than 70 for females and greater than 65 for males are rarely observed as valid scores outside of psychiatric inpatient populations. Analogous scores are available for the BSI, printed in its standard administration manual (Derogatis, 1993). Although crude indicators, these values can be useful in identifying individuals in the community population with extreme response styles.

Dimension Scores and the SCL–90–R/BSI Profile

A major advantage of the SCL–90–R/BSI resides in the fact that in spite of their relative brevity, they deliver multidimensional symptom profiles, which contain a considerable amount of information concerning the respondent's symptomatic distress. Multidimensional measurement significantly enhances the breadth of clinical assessment compared to unidimensional measurement by providing a syndromal context within which specific dimensional psychopathology may be more meaningfully evaluated. It delivers a symptomatic context against which to interpret scores on any specific symptom dimension. In conjunction with global scores and data on specific symptoms, it enhances the development of an integrated picture of the respondent's current clinical status and level of well-being.

Individual Symptoms

The third element in the interpretive strategy underlying clinical evaluation with the SCL–90–R/BSI involves the use of the discrete items or symptoms of the test. We make reference here not only to the items comprising the nine primary symptom dimensions, but also to the additional or "configural" items of the test. For example, an elevation on the Depression dimension plus a substantial score on suicidal ideation should be interpreted differently and with more immediate concern than an equivalent Depression score in the absence of evidence of suicidal ideation. In such an instance, suicidal ideation would be treated as a "symptom of note," the presence of which would clearly alter the clinical decision process. As another example, clinical levels of depression combined with early-morning awakening, loss of interest, and high levels of guilt may signal the emergence of a major affective disorder. The same Depression score with a dissimilar pattern of accompanying symptoms might be interpreted quite differently.

The configural items are not pure reflections of any one specific dimensional construct; they are designed to enhance specific predictions concerning the respondent's clinical status. They represent clinically significant symptom manifestations that are not unique to any of the SCL–90–R/BSI primary symptom dimensions. As examples, sleep and appetite disturbances represent potentially significant clinical manifestations. They do not occur solely in the context of a specific syndrome, but their presence in a particular case can be a significant aid in clinical decision making.

Caseness Criteria for the SCL-90-R/BSI

When the SCL-90-R, BSI, or any other psychological inventory or rating scale is utilized in a screening paradigm, an operational definition of *caseness* must be established. The caseness criterion essentially refers to the numerical value (i.e., a cutoff score) on a test indicator, at or above which the respondent is considered to be a "positive" or a case. The caseness criterion is a probabilistic value, chosen to maximize valid case identification (e.g., sensitivity and specificity) and minimize errors (i.e., false positives and false negatives). In psychiatric screening, it is difficult to develop a definitive caseness criterion value for a particular test, because other important parameters (e.g., gender, age, prevalence of the condition in the population being screened) can significantly affect the validity of any criterion value. Nevertheless, it is possible to establish a common criterion for caseness that has demonstrated generalizability across a range of populations and has proven useful in a number of screening contexts.

Such a general caseness criterion value is given next for the SCL-90-R and the BSI. It is not possible in the context of this monograph to provide complete supporting data for the general caseness criterion given here; however, this criterion has shown effectiveness in accurately discriminating individuals comprising the normative community nonpatient cohort from those comprising the psychiatric outpatient sample. Further, in a multicenter epidemiologic study of the prevalence of psychiatric disorder in newly admitted cancer patients, the predictive value of a positive was 86% using this criterion (Derogatis et al., 1983). According to this definition, a "case" is defined by:

$$\text{Positive Dx} = T_{\text{GSI}} \geq T_{63} \quad \text{or} \quad T_{2\text{DIM}} \geq T_{63}$$

The definition should be understood as, if the respondent has a GSI score (using Norm B, the community nonpatient norm) greater than or equal to a T-score of 63, or any two primary dimension scores are greater than or equal to a T-score of 63, then the individual shall be considered at high risk for a psychiatric diagnosis and therefore, a positive case. An optimal strategy would involve developing population-specific screening criteria for caseness, with attention to the significant demographic parameters of the population of interest. When this is not possible, the decision rule provided here has been shown to often serve as an effective general criterion.

THE SCL-90-R AND BSI IN PRIMARY CARE POPULATIONS

Screening for Psychiatric Disorder in Primary Care

Because an entire chapter of this volume is devoted to the topic of screening and monitoring psychiatric disorders in primary care (by Derogatis & Lynn, chap. 4), a detailed discussion of this important issue is not presented here. There are, however, intrinsic aspects of the screening process in primary care populations that should be highlighted. There is a clear consensus that the prevalence of psychiatric disorders in primary care populations is considerably higher than it is in the community (Derogatis & Wise, 1989). There is an equally strong consensus that most primary care physicians have substantial difficulty in identifying and diagnosing these comorbid psychiatric conditions. These facts lead to the unfortunate, but well-supported, conclusion that a large majority of psychiatric disorders in primary care go undetected, and therefore untreated (Regier et al., 1988).

This realization carries with it substantial negative implications for our health care system. Not only do psychiatric disorders represent a significant health care concern in their own right, but when they coexist undetected with primary medical disorders, they often substantially complicate effective treatment of the principal medical condition. Frequently, such patients (i.e., 20%–30% of primary care cohorts) adhere poorly to treatment regimens, demonstrate atypical responses to treatment, have high utilization rates, and display significantly higher costs associated with their treatment (Allison et al., 1995; Katon et al., 1990).

Effective screening systems, based on brief, reliable psychological instruments and standard screening principles, have been available for an extended period of time. The SCL–90–R and the BSI have both been used effectively in screening paradigms with medical patients (Derogatis et al., 1983; Kuhn, Bell, Seligson, Laufer, & Lindner, 1988; Royce & Drude, 1984; Zabora et al., 1990), as have a number of other tests. The costs of routinely implementing psychiatric screening systems represent a minute fraction of the expenses we now incur from unrecognized mental illness in primary care. We should move swiftly and decisively to correct this deficiency, because it represents a problem in contemporary health care that is both identifiable and easily remediable.

The BSI®-18.   More recently, in response to continued demands for greater economy of time and efficiency in assessment, the BSI–18 has been developed. The BSI–18 is a very brief, 18-item screening inventory designed to screen for psychiatric disorder in medical and community populations. It is essentially comprised of items selected from the Anxiety, Depression, and Somatization dimensions of the SCL–90–R/BSI, and is scored in terms of these three dimension scores and a Total score. Currently, two well-constructed norms have been developed for the BSI–18: the Community Norm, based on a well-stratified sample of approximately 1,200 community individuals, and the Cancer Norm, based on 1,500 individuals with a broad spectrum of diagnoses who were patients at a large regional cancer center in Baltimore, MD. The decision to concentrate test item composition on symptoms that are characteristic of somatization, depression, and anxiety disorders derives from the well-documented realization that between 75% and 80% of psychiatric diagnoses in primary care reflect these conditions. Also, because these dimensions are close derivatives of the analogous named dimensions of the SCL–90–R and BSI, the large body of information that has been developed from 25 years of the implementation of these tests can be generalized to the BSI–18. The BSI–18 has recently become available for general use, and we anticipate that it will make a significant contribution to psychiatric screening efforts in primary care.

Anxiety, Depressive, and Somataform Disorders

There is compelling evidence (Derogatis & DellaPietra, 1994; Derogatis & Wise, 1989) that anxiety and depressive disorders account for between 75% and 80% of the psychiatric conditions seen in primary care practices. Because many of the manifestations of these disorders are somatic in nature, they can be easily confused with medical disorders and somataform psychiatric conditions (Kirmayer, Robbins, Dworkin, & Jaffe, 1993; Simon & Von Korff, 1991). Because of their pervasive nature, and the fact that many authorities believe depressive disorder to be the most prevalent clinical problem in primary care (Katon & Sullivan, 1990), we have reviewed applications of the SCL-90-R/BSI in this area in some detail.

The SCL-90-R has been used as an outcome measure in many studies focused on depression. Weissman et al. (1977) used the instrument to characterize primary versus secondary depressions, and the same research group used the SCL-90-R in an epidemiologic study of depression in five distinct populations (Weissman, Sholomskas, Pottenger, Prusoff, & Locke, 1977). Quitkin et al. (1984) applied the test as an outcome measure in a treatment trial of *l*-deprenyl in atypical depressives, and found it sensitive to drug-placebo differences on a number of dimensions. Meanwhile, Wetzler et al. (1990) profiled differences between depressed and panic patients on the SCL-90-R, and Stewart, Quitkin, Terman, and Terman (1990) contrasted atypical depressions with seasonal affective disorders on the test. In addition, Bryer, Borelli, Matthews, and Kornetsky (1983) used the SCL-90-R in a depressed sample to predict suppressors versus nonsuppressors on the dexamethasone suppression test (DST). Employing discriminant function analysis, these investigators were able to correctly predict DST status in 73% of cases.

Working with a community cohort of young adults, Angst and Dobla-Mikola (1984) reported discriminating among three groups of depressives with the SCL-90-R, partitioned according to frequency and duration of episodes. Discriminations among groups were made at both dimension score and item levels. In an interesting predictive study, Robinson, Olmsted, and Garner (1989) found that they could predict from elevated SCL-90-R scores during the second trimester of pregnancy those women who would have difficulties adjusting at 1 year postpartum. In an informative review, Katon and Sullivan (1990) examined depression occurring among chronic medical populations, and enumerated a series of studies done with the SCL-90-R.

More recently, Wetzler, Khadivi, and Oppenheim (1995) compared the psychological assessments of bipolar versus unipolar depressives on the SCL-90-R as well as the MMPI and the MCMI. In spite of a great deal of clinical anecdote about phenomenologic differences between bipolar and unipolar depressions, no consistent differences were found in the mean profiles of the two groups on any of the three measures. McCullough and his colleagues (McCullough et al., 1994) replicated their study of an untreated sample of community dysthymics, and again included the SCL-90-R as a component of their assessment battery. Twenty-four dysthymics were followed for 1 year, with three showing spontaneous remission at the end of that period. At the completion of a subsequent 4-year follow-up, one of the three remissions had relapsed. SCL-90-R Symptom profiles were extremely constant over the study period, leading the authors to again conclude that dysthymia is an enduring chronic disorder with insidious onset and problematic social functioning and symptomatic distress.

The BSI has also been utilized in outcomes studies of depression. Amenson and Lewinsohn (1981) used the BSI in a longitudinal prevalence study. They observed, consistent with numerous other investigators, that the prevalence of depressive phenomena was higher for women than for men no matter which indicators they used. They also noted that women with previous histories of depression were much more likely to experience recurrences of their depression than were men with similar histories. Buckner and Mandell (1990) also utilized the BSI in a prospective study of young adult psychoactive drug users, in an attempt to establish their risk for developing depression. The results of their evaluation identified use of methaqualone as being a reliable predictor of depression, along with low self-esteem, and negative life events.

The Suicidal Patient

A prominent issue in the diagnosis and treatment of patients with depression concerns the reliable early identification of the potentially suicidal patient. Several contemporary studies have addressed this question using the SCL-90-R/BSI. Bulik, Carpenter, Kupfer, and Frank (1990) contrasted 67 patients suffering from recurrent major depression and a history of attempted suicide with 163 recurrent depressives without a history of suicidal behavior. Four subscales (Somatization, Interpersonal Sensitivity, Paranoid Ideation, and Psychoticism) as well as the global scores significantly discriminated attempters from nonattempters. A logistic regression analysis with these and other variables enabled 77% correct prediction of cases.

There is increasing evidence (Coryell, 1988) that panic disorder has an associated increased risk for suicide, as does a diagnosis of depression. In an analogous evaluation of panic patients who did and did not attempt suicide, Noyes et al. (1991) reported findings similar to those of Bulik and her colleagues (1990). Seven of the nine primary symptom dimensions of the SCL-90-R and the GSI successfully discriminated suicide attempters from those who did not make attempts. As did Bulik et al. (1990), these investigators found patients who made suicide attempts had greater severity of distress in general, with particular elevations on measures of inferiority feelings and self-deprecation.

Cohen, Test, and Brown (1990) employed the BSI among other measures to predict potential for suicide among schizophrenic patients being treated in a community treatment center. Eight of the 82 patients in the sample eventually committed suicide. In addition to greater dissatisfaction with their lives at the time of admission, these patients revealed significantly higher distress levels on the BSI.

Swedo and her associates (1991) extended the predictive value of the SCL-90-R in suicidal behavior to suicidal teenagers. These authors compared adolescents with a history of attempted suicide to adolescents judged to be at risk for suicide for a variety of reasons, and an adolescent control group. All SCL-90-R measures successfully discriminated suicide attempters from controls; the majority of subscales differentiated those designated "at risk" from controls; and the Obsessive-Compulsive subscore and the PSDI (measuring distress intensity) significantly discriminated the attempters from those at risk. These data suggest that like their adult counterparts, adolescents who actually attempt suicide tend to perceive themselves as more distressed and hopeless than other adolescents who are deemed at risk.

Concerning anxiety disorders, Cameron et al. (1986) used the SCL-90-R to profile patients with distinct *DSM-III* anxiety disorders. Additionally, they employed the instrument in a study to evaluate the influence of exercise on severity of anxiety in patients diagnosed with anxiety disorders (Cameron & Hudson, 1986). Thirty-one percent of patients with panic attacks were exercise sensitive, compared to only 7% of other patients. The SCL-90-R Anxiety and Phobic Anxiety subscales were particularly effective in making this discrimination. Ae Lee and Cameron (1986) evaluated the relationship between Type-A behavior, symptom distress patterns, and family history of coronary heart disease among males and females with anxiety disorders.

Significant correlations between SCL-90-R Anxiety and Hostility scores and Jenkins Activity Scale (JAS) Type-A scores were observed among males, but not among female patients. These same investigators (Ae Lee, Cameron, & Greden, 1985) also used the instrument to evaluate the relationship between caffeine consumption and the experience of anxiety in anxious patients. They discovered that severity of anxiety was not related to amount of caffeine consumption; however, the subset of patients who reported becoming anxious in response to drinking coffee had higher SCL-90-R Anxiety, Somatization, and Phobic Anxiety scores than those who did not. Caffeine consumption was equivalent in the two groups.

In their comprehensive review, Katon and Roy-Byrne (1991) posited a mixed anxiety–depression syndrome. They cited strong evidence to substantiate the existence of this nosologic entity, with studies involving the SCL-90-R contributing substantial confirmational data. Individuals afflicted with the condition are found to have a high incidence of medically unexplained problems, and be proportionally greater utilizers of health care. They also appear to be at increased risk for more severe anxiety and mood disorders. Similarly, Clark and Watson (1991) developed a tripartite model of anxiety and depression. They argued that at the clinical level, anxiety and depressive phenomena may be explained by a general distress factor and two specific factors of anxiety and depression. The authors mobilized an impressive body of data to support their theory, in particular noting that this pattern was very explicit in numerous studies with the SCL-90-R. Also examining the relationship between anxious, depressed and anxious/depressed states, Strauman (1992), working from a self-discrepancy model, utilized the Anxiety subscale of the SCL-90-R to predict specific vulnerabilities to emotional disorders. According to this theory, the hypothesized patterns of vulnerability (i.e., anxious vs. depressive symptoms and affects) are based in "actual-ideal" versus "actual-ought" self-discrepancies, and were strongly confirmed by the outcome of the study. In another discriminative study involving two anxiety disorders, Noyes and his associates (Noyes et al., 1992) contrasted SCL-90-R dimension and symptom scores between patients diagnosed with generalized anxiety disorder (GAD) versus those with panic disorder diagnoses (PD). The GAD patients revealed symptoms indicative of central nervous system (CNS) hyperarousal, whereas PD patients' profiles appeared more indicative of autonomic hyperactivity. Consistent with other reports, the GAD patients tended to manifest significantly lower scores on SCL-90-R Depression, Anxiety, and Phobic Anxiety, and to experience less overall psychological morbidity.

Because the SCL-90-R and BSI are multidimensional and contain a Somatization dimension as well as Depression and Anxiety subscales, they are well suited to the evaluation of somataform conditions. Consistent with this fact, Rief, Hiller, Geissner, and Fichter (1995) examined the course of pathology in 30 patients with somataform disorders. Patients were assessed using the SCID and the SCL-90-R and were assigned to a variety of treatment interventions. Results indicated that patients with somataform disorders and a comorbid affective disorder ($N = 24$) had somatoform symptoms that persisted through the 2-year follow-up period, whereas patients without a comorbid diagnosis were more likely to remit within this time period. Overall, significant symptom reduction was observed for somatoform patients over the 2-year period as indicated by the Somatization, Depression, Anxiety, and Phobic Anxiety subscales of the SCL-90-R.

Katon et al. (1990), focusing on the prognostic value of somatic symptoms, used the SCL-90-R to provide an operational definition of "high distressed–high utilizers" within two large primary care practices. The high-distress group was further divided into four subgroups on the basis of numbers of unexplained somatic symptoms. The investigators observed linear increases in SCL–90–R dimension scores of Somatization, Depression, and Anxiety, as well as independent diagnoses of psychiatric disorder, as they moved progressively through the somatic symptom subgroups from "low" to "high."

Kellner, Hernandez, and Pathak (1992) also reported an interesting study with the SCL–90–R with somaticizing patients. These researchers related distinct dimensions of the SCL–90–R to different aspects of hypochondriasis. In this study they observed high levels of the SCL–90–R Somatization and Anxiety dimensions to be predictive of hypochondriacal fears and beliefs, whereas elevations on Depression were not. Further, they observed that fear of disease correlated most highly with the SCL–90–R Anxiety score, but that the false conviction of having a disease was more highly correlated with somatization.

SEXUAL VICTIMIZATION

Sexual and physical abuse are often-overlooked factors associated with the onset and/or the persistence of medical problems. Victimized individuals experience significant emotional distress and personal devaluation, which can lead to a chronic vulnerability and compromise the effective treatment of their medical conditions. The experience often traumatizes victims, leaving them generically vulnerable to a broad spectrum of stressors. There is substantial evidence that many victims of sexual abuse exhibit clinical manifestations of anxiety or depressive disorders, without a clear understanding of the contribution made by their victimization experiences. For these reasons, it is very important for primary care providers to have an awareness of the pernicious effects on well-being that sexual and/or physical abuse can have, and how they can undermine the best designed plans for health intervention.

A number of investigators have established the utility of both the SCL–90–R and the BSI in work with sexually abused patients. Frazier and Schauben (1994) investigated the stressors experienced by college-age females in adjusting to the transition to college life. The most commonly reported problems were test pressure, financial problems, personal rejection, relationship dissolution, and academic failure. Significant correlations were found between the magnitude of stress and levels of psychological symptoms on the BSI. Survivors of sexual victimization had significantly higher total scores on the BSI. Interestingly, ethnic differences were observed such that Asian Americans revealed an increased number of stressors, higher levels of stress, and more psychological symptoms.

Bennett and Hughes (1996) attempted to develop normative data for the BSI with this population, by examining a cohort of female college students who were victims of sexual abuse. Results of their evaluation indicated that sexual abuse victims had significantly elevated BSI scores and increased adjustment problems compared to individuals without an abuse history. These researchers found that college females who had suffered sexual abuse demonstrated BSI symptom profiles essentially equivalent to individuals undergoing psychological treatment.

Williams, Borduin, and Howe (1991), working with a somewhat younger population, contrasted the symptomatic distress of physically and sexually abused adolescents with adolescents who had suffered neglect and with a control group of nonabused adolescents on the SCL-90-R. Their results showed the two abuse groups to be dramatically more distressed than controls, with the adolescents who suffered neglect revealing an intermediate position.

Chronic pain is another condition observed to be affected by earlier experiences with sexual victimization. Toomey, Seville, Mann, Abashian, and Grant (1995) assessed a heterogeneous group of chronic pain patients and observed that those patients with a history of sexual abuse scored higher overall on the SCL-90-R than did nonabused patients. This suggests that a previous history of abuse may sensitize individuals, who subsequently experience greater psychological distress than individuals without such experiences. Further, the authors suggested, this sensitization may become manifest in site-specific chronic pain syndromes. Results of this study argue for making inquiry concerning sexual abuse a standard aspect of the clinical workup with this group of patients.

Similar findings were reported by Walker et al. (1995), who found that female patients with chronic pelvic pain evidenced significantly higher symptomatic distress levels than a patient cohort (tubal ligation) without pain. The mean score for chronic pelvic pain sufferers was sufficiently high that it fell in the 60th percentile of a psychiatric outpatient norm on most SCL-90-R measures. The pain group also was found to have a more prevalent history of diagnosable psychiatric disorders, especially major depression. In addition, its members revealed a greater history of somatization disorder, drug abuse, phobia, and sexual dysfunction. Pertinent to this issue, they also revealed a significantly greater incidence of sexual abuse as compared to the nonpain group.

Coffey, Leitenberg, Henning, Turner, and Bennett (1996) also investigated the sequelae of sexual abuse in a sample of 192 women with a history of childhood sexual abuse. They also studied how effective various methods of coping with victimization were, and whether they resulted in healthy adult adjustment. Women who had been sexually abused revealed a higher total distress score on the BSI than women in a nonabused control group, and a greater proportion of their BSI subscale scores fell in the clinical range. In terms of coping strategies, most victims of sexual abuse utilized a variety of methods of disengagement, a strategy that apparently contributed to higher degrees of psychological distress. These findings tend to support the belief that women with a history of sexual abuse tend to experience greater difficulties with psychological adjustment in general. Further, the authors suggest it is important to appreciate how specific coping methods, especially disengagement, can be ultimately counterproductive and lead to poorer adjustment and unhappiness.

TREATMENT MONITORING

For a psychological test instrument to be useful and effective as a mechanism for monitoring treatment, it must be first and foremost sensitive to treatment-induced change. Treatment-induced change may be thought of as an effect that exists embedded in a context of many other effects, some random and others systematic. Because an extensive variety of factors will have a bearing on a patient's status at any moment, the task becomes a classic "signal-to-noise" detection problem. An instrument chosen to monitor treatment must possess the capacity to reflect the influence of therapeutic effects as "figure" against the collective "ground" of other variable effects.

Instruments chosen to monitor treatments must possess not only discriminative capacity (i.e., the ability to distinguish functional vs. dysfunctional individuals at some moment in time), but also a robust evaluative capacity to enable them to reveal changes within individuals across time. Thus, the time frame for monitoring, in terms of disease or disorder-appropriate increments (e.g., days, weeks, months), becomes an important monitoring design parameter. Monitoring acute treatment effects calls for a different schedule of assessments than does monitoring over a prolonged period of treatment, or for maintenance interventions. A thorough understanding of the nature and natural history of the disorder is probably the best guide to determining an appropriate monitoring schedule.

A standard model for monitoring treatment calls for an initial measurement at baseline, just prior to the initiation of treatment, followed by sequential assessments on a weekly, monthly, or quarterly basis, depending on the nature of the disorder. Typically, an assessment at 6 months postinitiation provides a means of assessing not only the acute phase of treatment, but continuation treatment as well. A follow-up evaluation at 12 months postinitiation provides a mechanism to evaluate the success of any maintenance regimen that has been instituted, and assess for the possibility of relapse.

Evaluation of Change

On the surface, the evaluation of change appears deceptively straightforward: the patient either responded favorably to the treatment or did not. However, not only is the question of whether or not change took place important, but also highly relevant are questions such as how much change took place, over what time period, in what direction, what was its nature, and the duration over which it was maintained. Another significant issue involves the dose-response relationship, that is, the dose of treatment(s) at which clinical improvement was observed (Kopta, Howard, Lowry, & Beutler, 1994). When "dose" is used in this context, it takes on a broader meaning than the traditional milligrams per time increment definition, and includes the total magnitude of therapeutic intervention (visits, hours, interventions) delivered to treat the patient.

Although in traditional clinical trials the "significance" of observed changes is defined through probabalistic statistical procedures, we have been aware for many years that there is often little unanimity between statistical significance and the "clinical" significance of observed changes. Irrespective of the level of significance (α level), statistical significance often contributes little to our appreciation of whether observed changes possess clinical meaning or significance (Cohen, 1992). Many nonclinical variables (e.g., sample size) play a role in determining the statistical significance of observed changes, and serve to undermine the possibility of any one-to-one relationship between statistical probability and clinical consequence.

Reliable Change Index: A Paradigm for Clinical Significance

In addressing this problem, a number of experts have suggested that the concept of *recovery*, or a return to normal functioning, could serve as an effective basis for a definition of clinically significant change. In such models, recovery is defined as movement from a clinical or dysfunctional level of symptoms into the normal or functional range, during or immediately subsequent to treatment. Dysfunctional versus functional levels of symptoms are operationally defined by score distributions or *norms* developed for both functional and clinical populations. Norms for the functional population are typically developed from community samples, whereas those for dysfunctional samples are taken from clinical cohorts (e.g., psychiatric outpatients). Recovery is then defined as a posttreatment test score that is more likely to come from the functional as opposed to the dysfunctional distribution.

Although logical and workable, assuming the outcomes measure in use has norms for both normal and clinical populations, this single-criterion model of clinically significant change suffers from a serious potential shortcoming. Certain patients might begin treatment only marginally dysfunctional, and would require only minimal movement toward normal to be defined as having changed significantly. Others, who initially manifested much more dramatic distress, would have to experience profound therapeutic change to arrive at the same distress level (within the normal range). Clearly, the latter patients would have experienced a much more clinically significant change than the former; nonetheless, both would be considered recovered according to the single-criterion model.

Recently, Jacobsen and his associates developed a dual-criterion paradigm for clinically significant change that effectively addresses this perplexing problem (Jacobsen, Follette, & Ravenstorf, 1986; Jacobsen & Truax, 1991). In the dual-criterion model, not only must a patient's test score move from the dysfunctional into the functional range during treatment, but in addition, the magnitude of change must be larger than a magnitude termed the *reliable change index* (RCI). The RCI is calculated using only the patient's pre- and posttreatment test scores and the standard error of the difference score. Application of the RCI criterion (which may be generated with liberal or conservative confidence intervals) substantially decreases the possibility that a trivial change in a marginally dysfunctional patient will be characterized as clinically significant.

With the adoption of an RCI model, not only do treatment comparisons provide estimates of statistically significant changes, but they also provide data on the relative proportions of patients who showed a significant positive response (i.e., improvement or recovery), a significant negative response (i.e., clinical deterioration), and those with negligible responses (i.e., clinically unchanged). These data will contribute to a much more rich and meaningful evaluation of the differential efficacy of treatments and other clinical interventions and will greatly expand our understanding of whether and for whom various treatments work.

APPLICATIONS IN SPECIALIZED MEDICAL SETTINGS

Psychological factors play a prominent role in the courses and etiologies of many medical conditions, an observation that has been historically well documented. Information on psychological status has infrequently been integrated into treatment plans for medical patients, however, in large measure because physicians in charge of these patients are unfamiliar with the methods of psychological assessment and the interpretation of psychological test data. From their inception, the SCL–90–R and the BSI were designed for use in primary care and specialized medical populations, as well as community and psychiatric cohorts. These medical populations contain the highest prevalence of occult psychiatric disorder (Derogatis & DellaPietra, 1994), an important fact given the knowledge that many medical treatment regimens can be dramatically affected by patients' psychological status. The studies cited next represent a small proportion of the published research done with the SCL–90–R/BSI in specialized medical cohorts, and underscore the potential value of brief measures of psychological status for treatment planning and monitoring in these medical populations.

Oncology

The SCL–90–R/BSI has been utilized extensively with oncology patients. Early in its development, Craig and Abeloff (1974) used the SCL–90–R to demonstrate clinical levels of psychological distress in cancer patients, and Abeloff and Derogatis (1977) used the scale to describe the distinctive psychological symptom picture of breast cancer patients. In addition, Derogatis, Abeloff, and Melisaratos (1979) employed the SCL–90–R to demonstrate that length of survival with metastatic breast disease was distinctly related to coping style, a finding also reported by Rogentine et al. (1979) with malignant melanoma patients.

In an earlier study, Derogatis, Abeloff, and McBeth (1976) used the SCL–90–R and its companion the SCL–90 Analogue Scale to compare oncologists' perceptions of their patients' psychological distress with those of the patients themselves. Evaluations were done shortly after admission, and once computed, scores were converted to standardized scores for each doctor–patient pair. Doctor–patient difference scores ($T\Delta$ values) were then calculated. Results showed that physicians' global ratings of psychological distress appeared to be a function of their perceptions of levels of interpersonal sensitivity (i.e., self-deprecation) and anxiety, but were independent of their perceptions of depression, which they minimized relative to patients' self-ratings. Analyses also revealed that the highest subscale correlations with physicians' independent global ratings of patient psychological distress occurred on Anxiety ($r = .50$) and Hostility ($r = .48$). Correlations between the physicians' global distress ratings and the patients' self-rated global scores were only marginal. These results were interpreted as suggesting that oncologists were basing their perceptions of psychological distress on selective indicators rather than on global manifestations or signs of depression.

Within the past decade, considerable work with the SCL–90–R and BSI has been done in patients with a variety of types and stages of cancer. Northouse and Swain (1987) examined the psychosocial adjustment of breast cancer patients and their husbands at 3 and 30 days postsurgery using the BSI. Patient distress at both assessments was significantly higher than the community normative sample, but significantly lower than that of psychiatric patients. Interestingly, there were no significant differences between patients' and husbands' levels of distress. Husbands experienced levels of distress equivalent to their wives who underwent mastectomies. Also, distress levels for both patients and their husbands did not decrease between assessment intervals. A similar study of spousal response to breast cancer was conducted by Hannum, Geiss-Davis, Harding, and Hatfield (1991), who evaluated breast cancer patients and their spouses within a year of diagnosis. These researchers found that spouses' coping skills and their ratings of marital quality were the best predictors of patients' levels of symptomatic distress, underscoring a biopsychosocial context within which to interpret the illness experience.

Familial involvement and metastatic cancer was also examined by Wellisch and his colleagues (1992). In a cross-sectional design, these researchers investigated psychological adjustment in daughters of breast cancer patients who learned of their mothers' disease in early childhood, adolescence, and adulthood. BSI scores were negatively correlated with comfort level of daughters being involved with their mothers' cancer. In addition, elevated scores on the GSI and the Depression subscale were associated with daughters' decreased satisfaction with sexual relationships.

In another study with breast cancer patients, Schleifer et al. (1991) used the SCL–90 Analogue to evaluate factors that affect oncologists' adherence to chemotherapy protocols. The sample consisted of 107 breast cancer patients who were followed for 26 weeks of treatment. Fifty-two percent of patients experienced an unjustified regimen modification. Physician perception of psychological distress was not a significant factor in modifying prescriptions in the majority of protocols; however, on a vincristine protocol, the patient global severity scores and several SCL–90 Analogue scale score elevations were significantly related to physician nonadherence.

The association between survival rate and psychological distress in women with Stage II breast cancer was assessed by Tross et al. (1996). Patients were divided into high-, medium-, and low-distress categories based on their SCL–90–R scores. After a 15-year follow-up period, GSI scores were not found to be significantly related to disease-free interval or overall survival effects across the three groups. Psychological distress levels were not effective predictors of survival rates in this patient cohort.

Most recently, Gilbar (1998) employed the BSI to determine whether having a family history of breast cancer is related to women's ability to cope with the threat of being diagnosed with the disease. Women with and without a family history were divided into four subgroups: first-time referral without a symptom, first-time referral with a symptom, regular check-up without a symptom, and regular check-up with a symptom. Results revealed that women with a family history of breast cancer who had a regular check-up with a symptom scored significantly higher on the Depression, Hostility, and Paranoid subscales, as well as the GSI, than all other groups. Findings confirm these authors' prediction that family history is an important factor in the level of psychological distress levels of women with symptoms of breast cancer.

In addition to breast cancer, research with the SCL–90–R and the BSI has been conducted in other cancer populations. Shover, Fife, and Gershenson (1989) utilized the BSI to assess psychological distress in women with cervical cancer. Results revealed a significant decrease of symptoms from pre-treatment baseline to the 6-month posttreatment evaluation. A significant decrease in scores was also revealed at 6-month and 12-month follow-up evaluations for the Interpersonal Sensitivity and Anxiety dimensions, and the BSI global scores. In addition, levels of Depression and Phobic Anxiety were lower during this 6- to 12-month posttreatment interval. Gilbar (1991) also used the BSI to compare a heterogeneous group of cancer patients who completed their chemotherapy regimen to a group who terminated therapy prior to completion. Among other findings, the patients who dropped out of chemotherapy scored significantly higher on Hostility and a number of other BSI scales.

Johnstone et al. (1991) reported a differential psychological response to treatment in two groups of cancer patients (testis vs. Hodgkins) on standard treatment protocols comparable in prognosis and treatment intensity. Although both patient cohorts showed elevated SCL–90–R profiles at the beginning of treatment, Hodgkins patients

revealed a marked reduction in psychological distress at the 3-month follow-up evaluation. No comparable reduction in distress was apparent among testis patients,
even though they had been informed that their chances for survival were quite good.
Interestingly, the partners of both patient groups showed a return to normal levels of
psychological distress following treatment.

In a study of leukemia survivors by Lesko, Ostroff, Mumma, Mashberg, and Holland (1992), the effects of bone marrow transplant and chemotherapy on long-term
psychological adjustment were examined. At a 5-year posttreatment assessment interval, male and female patients scored 0.5 to 1 standard deviation higher on all clinical scales, except the Hostility subscale, and on the global distress indices of the BSI
than a normative community sample. Leukemia survivors, in general, exhibited increased levels of distress compared to nonpatient counterparts, although levels of
symptomatology were lower than psychiatric outpatients.

Roberts, Rossetti, Cone, and Cavanaugh (1992) also used the SCL–90–R in a longitudinal study of posttreatment levels of psychological distress in gynecologic cancer
patients who had survived from 1 to 19 years. These researchers found, somewhat
surprisingly, that considerable symptomatology persisted after the acute episode of
illness. Mean levels on many subscale scores were observed over the 85th centile of
the community norm. Baider, Peretz, and DeNour (1992) evaluated a heterogeneous
group of cancer patients who had completed treatment, some of whom were also Holocaust survivors. Consistent with other research demonstrating the cumulative vulnerability associated with previous trauma, the Holocaust survivors revealed significantly greater symptomatic distress levels.

Levine, Raczynski, and Carpenter (1991) used the SCL–90–R in a study of weight
gain among breast cancer patients undergoing adjuvant treatment. They observed
significant relationships between a number of SCL–90–R measures and weight gain.
Global measures of distress showed a positive relationship to weight; however, both
Obsessive-Compulsive and Interpersonal Sensitivity subscales had significant negative coefficients in a regression equation. These findings suggest that although weight
gain in cancer patients is associated with overall psychological distress, when the patients feel that they have more control over their life as well as when they utilize their
social resources to a higher degree, they may decrease their risk for weight gain.

Grassi and Rosti (1996a) sought to determine the association between psychological disorder and the development of abnormal illness behavior in patients with a variety of oncological diseases (i.e., breast, lung, genito-urinary, gastrointestinal, lym-
phatic). The GSI of the SCL–90–R accounted for 19.4% of the variance in predicting
patient acknowledgment of the disease. Furthermore, most of the SCL–90–R subscales were significantly correlated with the Illness Behavior Questionnaire (IBQ)
main scales and second-order factors. Grassi and Rosti (1996b) also examined psychological adjustment of survivors of long-term and advanced cancer, with sites that
included breast, stomach, lymph, kidney, and other types, over a 6-year period. From
the time of initial assessment to their 6-year follow-up evaluation, patients' scores on
the Interpersonal Sensitivity, Paranoid Ideation, and Psychoticism subscales were
significantly lowered. Patients with a *DSM–III–R* diagnosis at follow-up were found
to score significantly higher on the majority of SCL–90–R subscales compared to patients without a diagnosis. These findings suggest patients with early psychological
maladjustment are more likely to sustain emotional difficulties later during a cancer
illness. For those with a particular interest in this area, Gotay and Stern (1995) provided a very useful review of SCL–90–R/BSI studies in oncology.

In light of the research conducted on the psychological distress of patients with cancer, it is also relevant to consider factors associated with behaviors that are known risk factors for cancer. In this light, Chiles et al. (1990) investigated the association between smoking and psychological symptomatology among 802 male and female lawyers in the state of Washington. Generally, these researchers found significant differences by gender on the majority of BSI subscale scores, with women scoring higher on those measures. However, male smokers reported significantly more psychological symptoms than did their nonsmoking cohorts, and were also more likely to abuse alcohol and experience higher levels of anger than their nonsmoking male counterparts. Interestingly, there were no significant differences in distress levels between smoking and nonsmoking females. Results of this study suggest that, for males, psychological distress may influence smoking behavior, which, in turn, increases their risks for cancer. Early identification and treatment of individuals, especially males, experiencing emotional difficulties could conceivably be considered a helpful intervention in the prevention of cancer.

Cardiology

In addition to being used extensively in oncology populations, the SCL–90–R and the BSI have also been widely used to evaluate patients' psychological integration in cardiology populations. For instance, Bohachick (1984) reported significant reductions in distress among a cohort of hypertensives exposed to a progressive relaxation paradigm in addition to standard exercise regimen, compared to an exercise only group.

Dew et al. (1994) sought to identify psychosocial factors associated with distress in cardiac transplant patients. Using the SCL–90–R at 2, 7, and 12 months postsurgery, these researchers found significantly elevated scores on the Anxiety subscale at 2- and 7-month follow-up assessments; however, levels returned to essentially normative levels by 12 months postsurgery. Depression levels were also significantly elevated at 2 months; however, at 7 and 12 months, depression decreased to normative levels. Overall, Anxiety and Depression scores significantly improved over time; however, patients whose scores were in the clinical range at the initial 2-month assessment retained elevated distress levels at later postsurgery evaluations. In considering other psychosocial variables, history of depression and/or anxiety disorder, low family caregiver support, and diminished feelings of self-worth and mastery were associated with greater susceptibility to depression and anxiety during the 12-month recovery period. In addition to these variables, high use of avoidance coping strategies as well as younger age were associated with elevated anxiety levels, whereas life events involving loss were found to predict depressive symptoms. Investigators concluded that psychosocial variables should be assessed prior to heart transplant surgery to ensure effective psychological treatment in emotionally vulnerable patients.

A similar study was performed by Hamer, Blumenthal, McCarthy, Philips, and Pritchett (1994), who investigated 69 male and female patients with paroxysmal atrial fibrillation (AF) and paroxysmal supraventricular tachycardia (SVT). These researchers studied patients' perceptions of their medical condition as well as their coping strategies. All subscale scores on the SCL–90–R, including Depression and state Anxiety, were within one standard deviation of those for normals. Overall, most patients with supraventricular arrhythmias appeared well adjusted and did not exhibit symptoms of psychological distress.

Perhaps the most dramatic study with cardiac patients was a 6-month follow-up study reported by Allison et al. (1995) with a sample of 381 cardiac rehabilitation patients referred for a variety of cardiovascular disorders and/or procedures. Using the SCL–90–R, these investigators partitioned their cohort into "high psychological distress" versus low distress groups. Comparisons across a 6-month interval postdischarge revealed that the high-distress group had significantly higher rates of cardiac rehospitalization and recurrent cardiac events compared to the low-distress group. More striking, however, was the fact that the mean rehospitalization costs for the high-distress patients were almost five times the mean cost of the low-distress group (i.e., $9,504 vs. $2,146). The authors concluded that psychological distress has an obvious adverse impact on coronary patients, and systematic assessment programs should be instituted to accomplish successful identification and appropriate intervention with these patients who are clearly at higher risk.

HIV/AIDS

Based on the increasing interest and awareness of the psychological factors associated with HIV and AIDS, many researchers have examined the levels of psychological distress in HIV/AIDS patients. Levine, Anderson, Bystritsky, and Baron (1990) used the SCL–90–R in a small sample of HIV patients with major depressive syndrome who were treated with fluoxetine (Prozac). These authors observed significant improvement on almost all SCL–90–R measures over the 4 weeks of active treatment, and treatment gains were sustained at 2-month follow-up. In an earlier study, Atkinson et al. (1988) investigated the prevalence of psychiatric disorders among homosexual men with AIDS, AIDS-related complex (ARC), non- or mild-symptomatic HIV, and those who tested negative for HIV. Compared to uninfected heterosexual males, homosexual males from all sample groups exhibited significantly higher levels of distress on the SCL–90–R Somatization, Obsessive-Compulsive, Depression, Anxiety, and GSI measures. Furthermore, those patients with ARC demonstrated the greatest psychological difficulty, as opposed to the heterosexual control group and most of their homosexual cohorts.

In a similar study, J. B. W. Williams et al. (1991) used the BSI to establish baseline rates of psychological symptomatology in homosexual men who were HIV positive and HIV negative. Results indicated that, overall, symptom levels of depression and anxiety were relatively low for both groups. However, men with HIV evidenced significantly higher levels of depression than did their non-HIV counterparts. Although this finding was only marginally significant, it does indicate that the disease has some measurable effect on the psychological integration of those affected.

Several more recent studies have employed the BSI to investigate psychological factors associated with HIV infection. Kennedy, Skurnick, Foley, and Louria (1995) examined psychological distress among heterosexual couples with at least one partner HIV positive. Contrary to prediction, family support was not found to play a significant role in differentiating emotional distress. Gender was the only variable found to significantly affect psychological well-being, such that females had higher elevations on all BSI subscales than males. This was true for both HIV-positive and HIV-negative females with HIV-positive male partners. It is assumed from these findings that women in a relationship affected by HIV express higher levels of symptomatic distress than men. Hopefully, awareness of these psychological vulnerabilities will influence clinicians to institute specific treatment for HIV patients and their partners.

Research on HIV-positive and -negative homosexual men with a diagnosable personality disorder was conducted by Johnson, Williams, Rabkin, Goetz, and Remien (1995). HIV-positive men with personality disorders indicated significantly more psychological distress on BSI Depression and Anxiety subscales, as well as the GSI, than HIV-negative men and men without a personality disorder. Furthermore, one third of those HIV positive men with personality disorders ($N = 21$) also had a comorbid Axis I clinical disorder. These authors concluded that the co-occurrence of both HIV and a personality disorder probably enhances vulnerability to concurrent Axis I clinical disorders, particularly anxiety and depressive syndromes.

More recently, Grassi, Righi, Sighinolfi, Makoui, and Ghinelli (1998) utilized the BSI in a study of coping styles in HIV patients. They observed that, compared to other tests, the GSI was most predictive of the effectiveness of patients' coping strategies. More specifically, higher GSI scores indicated patients' impaired ability to cope with their illness. In addition, the GSI was found to be negatively associated with amount of social support patients received and positively related to levels of anxiety, fatalistic attitudes, and degree of hopelessness.

Alcohol and Substance Abuse

It is well documented that alcohol abuse and substance abuse are often comorbid with anxiety and depressive disorders. Investigators have frequently used the SCL–90–R or the BSI to document the distress levels of these comorbid conditions. As examples, Steer and Hassett (1982) used the SCL–90 Analogue to identify the differential weights assigned various dimensions of psychopathology in arriving at staff judgments of global severity of illness. Over 1,000 patients were contrasted with 809 substance abuse clients. They found that Interpersonal Sensitivity and Psychoticism were the best predictors of global severity ratings in mental health patients, whereas Anxiety and Paranoid Ideation scores accounted for most variance among ratings of substance abusers. Because alcohol and substance abuse disorders have such high prevalence and prominent comorbidity with psychiatric disorders, evidence of the utility of the SCL–90–R/BSI in treatment planning with these classes of patients represents a significant step forward.

Desoto, O'Donnell, Allred, and Lopes (1985) completed a very informative study on the recovery from alcoholism over time. They compared the psychological symptomatology of 363 recovering alcoholics on the SCL–90–R across five temporal abstinence groups (<6 months; 6 months–2 years; 2–5 years; 5–10 years; >10 years). Results showed a slow but progressive reduction in symptomatic distress over the 10-year period (mean GSI = 1.04, 0.74, 0.56, 0.48, 0.37, respectively, for the five groups). Early in recovery, dramatic levels of distress were in evidence, followed by eventual reductions to normative levels. Community levels of distress were not reached for 5 to 10 years, however. The most prominent elevations occurred on Depression, Interpersonal Sensitivity, Obsessive-Compulsive, Psychoticism, and Anxiety subscales, with the symptom of guilt being predominant. Distress on these measures eventually fell to normal levels; however, the investigators noted a residual syndrome of cognitive dysfunction that remained present even after many years of abstinence.

Because alcoholism rarely occurs as a completely independent condition, it is important in developing optimal treatment strategies to identify subtypes of the disorder that have relevance for treatment course and outcome. A recent study by Liskow,

Powell, Nickel, and Penick (1991a) used both the SCL–90–R and the MMPI to discriminate four diagnostic subtypes among a sample of 360 male inpatient alcoholics. Twenty-nine percent of the sample were found to have a comorbid antisocial personality disorder (ASP). These were further discriminated into ASP and alcoholism, ASP and alcoholism plus drug dependence, and ASP and alcoholism plus depression. The SCL–90–R profiles for the four groups were highly discriminated, an important characteristic for treatment planning because these subtypes were observed to differ substantially in terms of onset, severity, course of alcoholism, and pattern of medical complications. In a 1-year follow-up study, these same authors (Liskow, Powell, Nickel, & Penick, 1991b) observed that the ASP plus drug dependence subgroup showed the poorest rate of improvement, whereas the ASP plus depression subgroup showed substantial improvement. They concluded that the presence of additional drug problems in ASP alcoholics was a poor prognostic sign, whereas the presence of clinical depression indicated a high probability of successful treatment.

In a study more oriented toward treatment evaluation per se, Dongier, Vachon, and Schwartz (1991) utilized the SCL–90–R to help evaluate the efficacy of bromocriptine as a treatment for alcohol dependence in an 8-week double-blind, randomized trial with ambulatory alcoholics. Results showed the SCL–90–R Interpersonal Sensitivity and Hostility subscales, and all three global measures, to significantly discriminate the bromocriptine versus placebo groups.

Turning to drug dependency, a number of researchers have published studies with the SCL–90–R that have high relevance for treatment design. Following on the work of Rounsaville, Glazer, Wilber, Weissman, and Kleber (1983), which showed a sensitivity of 89% for the SCL–90–R in detecting psychopathology among heroin addicts, Steer, Platt, Hendriks, and Metzger (1989) used modal profile analysis with Dutch and American cohorts of heroin addicts to identify three distinct subtypes based on the SCL–90–R: *anxious-depressed, hostile,* and *paranoid.* In addition to the observation that the paranoid subtype was much more likely to also use marijuana, the authors discussed a number of distinct treatment planning options that could hinge upon the availability of this information. The same group of investigators (Steer, Platt, Ranieri, & Metzger, 1989) conducted a similar analysis of SCL–90–R data from 458 methadone patients. They observed the same three modal subtypes, and in addition defined a fourth, the *somaticizing* subtype. The potential utility and impact on treatment planning of subtype membership in this group of chemical abusers was also discussed.

In demonstrating its sensitivity to differential levels of psychopathology in substance abusers, Kleinman et al. (1990) administered the SCL–90–R to three distinct groups of cocaine abusers: (a) those free of any additional *DSM–III–R* diagnosis, (b) those with an additional *DSM–III–R* Axis II personality disorder, and (c) those with an additional *DSM–III–R* Axis I (clinical) diagnoses. Mean GSI scores for the three groups were .53, .65, and .87, respectively, illustrating high levels of discriminative sensitivity. Using the BSI, Buckner and Mandell (1990) identified both a statistically and clinically significant increase in depression among drug abusers. More specifically, these investigators found that over a 1-year assessment period, drug abusers who were asymptomatic relative to depression at the initial evaluation tended to score at or above the 90th centile on the BSI depression subscale after 1 year. Similarly, Carey, Carey, and Meisler (1991) demonstrated the dual impact of comorbid conditions in a study contrasting a heterogeneous sample of psychiatric patients who also abused drugs with a matched sample of psychiatric outpatients with no history of drug abuse. The sample with additional drug abuse had significantly higher symptom distress scores on six of nine subscales and all three globals of the SCL–90–R.

More recently, Johnson, Brems, and Fisher (1996) compared psychopathology levels of drug abusers not receiving treatment with those in treatment. Using data from the Mercier et al. (1992) treatment sample, they found SCL–90–R scores to be significantly higher for the majority of subscales for the treatment versus the nontreatment sample. As predicted, drug abusers in treatment were found to evidence more psychological symptoms than those not in treatment, except on the Hostility and Paranoid Ideation scales, where the nontreatment group exhibited higher levels. Approximately 60% of male nontreatment abusers and 47% of female nontreatment abusers obtained GSI scores equal to or greater than the psychiatric cutoff for "caseness," warranting a dual diagnosis. This research suggests that the presence of a comorbid condition is associated with a greater likelihood that drug abusers will seek treatment.

Other Medical Populations

The SCL–90–R and the BSI have been employed with numerous other medical populations. To provide some examples, the SCL–90–R was used by Malec and Neimeyer (1983) to examine spinal-cord-injured (SCI) patients with the anticipation of predicting length of inpatient rehabilitation and quality of performance of self-care at discharge. Results of this study showed the Depression subscale to be the best predictor of length of stay, whereas the GSI had the highest (inverse) correlation with a discharge self-care rating. The authors recommended brief psychological measures as having substantial utility for treatment planning in SCI patients.

Sullivan et al. (1988) used the SCL–90–R to contrast patients suffering from tinnitus who were diagnosed as depressed, with tinnitus patients who were free of depression, and hearing-impaired controls. All SCL–90–R measures significantly discriminated the tinnitus plus major depression group from both of the other two samples. In an interesting predictive study, mentioned earlier, Robinson et al. (1989) found that they could predict from elevated SCL–90–R scores during the second trimester of pregnancy those women who would have difficulties adjusting at 1 year postpartum.

Fricchione et al. (1992) evaluated psychological distress patterns among patients with end-stage renal disease who had been identified as high and low deniers. Significantly reduced SCL–90–R scores were evidenced among high deniers compared to low deniers on the majority of measures. The treatment implications for the detection and handling of mood disorders among the high deniers were discussed and interpreted by the authors.

The SCL–90–R and the BSI have also been utilized effectively in studies with a health care systems orientation. Saravay, Steinberg, Weinschel, Pollack, and Alovis (1991) used it to evaluate the impact of psychological morbidity and length of stay (LOS) in the general hospital. SCL–90–R Depression, Anxiety, and global scores were significantly correlated with length of stay, whereas psychiatric diagnosis did not predict LOS. Saravay et al. (1996) also recently reported on a 4-year follow-up study of psychiatric comorbidity in medical patients. Among major findings, these investigators observed patients with elevated scores on the Interpersonal Sensitivity or Depression dimensions of the SCL–90–R at admission spent twice as many days rehospitalized, whereas patients with elevated Hostility scores experienced twice as many readmissions. Similarly, Katon et al. (1990) used the SCL–90–R to define "highly distressed" patients among 767 high health care utilizers in a large HMO. Fifty-one percent of the sample fit the criterion. Not only did these patients make disproportionate use of health care facilities, but they also revealed a high prevalence of chronic medical problems, experienced significant limitation of activities associated with their illnesses, and had substantially elevated prevalence of major depressive disorder, dysthymia, and anxiety disorders. In a somewhat analogous investigation, Drossman et al. (1991) evaluated the nature of health care behavior in a sample of almost 1,000 patients with inflammatory bowel disease. In this study, the SCL–90–R was found to have significant predictive value in a regression model predicting number of physician visits during the previous six months.

THE SCL–90 ANALOGUE AND DEROGATIS PSYCHIATRIC RATING SCALE (DPRS): MATCHING CLINICIAN RATING SCALES

A distinct advantage of the SCL–90–R/BSI concerns the fact that valid, matched clinician rating scales have been developed that may be used in conjunction with the self-report measures. If clinicians' judgments about the patient's psychological status are of interest or importance, evaluations on the same distress syndromes may be obtained, measured from both patient and clinician perspectives. Differences in patient–caregiver perceptions can then be evaluated by comparing clinician judgments with patient self-ratings.

As mentioned previously, the SCL–90 Analogue is a clinical observer's rating scale designed specifically for the health professional without detailed training in psychopathology or mental health. The SCL–90 Analogue is brief and uncomplicated, usually requiring less than 5 min to complete. In addition to representations for the nine SCL–90–R symptom dimensions, the rating scale also contains an analogue global distress scale.

An example of the use of the SCL–90 Analogue scale is provided by a study done by Derogatis, Abeloff, and McBeth (1976) with a small sample of cancer patients, also described in the Oncology section of this chapter. Shortly after admission, patients completed an SCL–90–R. Subsequently, the primary treating oncologist filled out an SCL–90 Analogue Scale on the patient based on a clinical interview. Raw scores were converted to standardized (area-T) scores for each patient on each measure, and doctor–patient difference scores ($T\Delta$ values) were calculated. Results showed that as physicians' ratings of global psychological distress rose, they tended to judge the patient to be increasingly distressed on Interpersonal Sensitivity and Anxiety dimensions, but viewed much less distress arising from depression than did the patient. Analyses also demonstrated that the highest subscale correlations with the physicians' independent global ratings of patient psychological distress were on Anxiety (r = .50) and Hostility (r = .48). Correlations between the physicians' global distress ratings and patients' self-rated global tended to be low and insignificant. This result suggested that oncologists were basing their judgments much more on selective indicators of distress rather than overall manifestations of distress.

The DPRS has also been utilized in a variety of interesting studies. For example, Winokur, Guthrie, Rickels, and Nael (1982) used the DPRS as a validating instrument for patients' self-ratings of psychological distress on the SCL–90–R. Approximately 60 medical patients from two settings participated in the trial. Two psychiatrists who were completely unaware of each others' or patients' self-rating completed DPRS ratings on the patients. Psychiatrist-patient correlations were generally high, with Depression ($r = .63$), Anxiety ($r = .63$), and Phobic Anxiety ($r = .72$) showing the highest agreement. The authors report sensitivities for the SCL–90–R Depression scale of .91 and .89 in the two groups of patients, with specificities of .78 and .85, respectively. In another study, Perconte and Griger (1991) used both the DPRS and the SCL–90–R to discriminate differential treatment responders among Vietnam veterans suffering from posttraumatic stress disorder. Although the investigators did not report on levels of agreement between the two instruments, both were highly accurate in discriminating successful, unchanged, and relapsing patients. Similarly, Fricchione et al. (1992) used the DPRS and the SCL–90–R to evaluate high versus low deniers among patients with end-stage renal disease. DPRS subscales of Interpersonal Sensitivity, Anxiety, and Sleep Disturbance were significantly elevated among the low deniers, as were numerous SCL–90–R scales.

ADVANTAGES AND LIMITATIONS OF THE SCL–90–R AND THE BSI

Fundamentally, the SCL–90–R/BSI are designed to provide accurate information on the psychological distress status of medical patients, and to do so in a rapid, easy-to-use, and cost-efficient manner. These brief inventories require very little patient time, and almost no time from medical professionals. Administration and scoring of the tests are simple and straightforward, and may be accomplished by nurses, physician assistants, or laboratory technicians. Much in the fashion of a "psychological laboratory test," SCL–90–R/BSI scores can serve a screening function, alerting the physician to abnormal symptom levels and helping to identify those patients who are suffering from clinical levels of psychological distress. Because the tests are multidimensional, the nature of distress patterns may be profiled (e.g., high Depression scores in the context of elevated Phobic Anxiety), adding additional useful information. Individual symptoms of note (e.g., suicidal ideation, early-morning awakening, difficulty sleeping) are also easily ascertained and highlighted.

Because the SCL–90–R and BSI possess well-constructed norms, they may also be efficiently used for treatment monitoring. Multiple administrations of the tests do not affect their validity, and because they are brief and easy to understand, patient compliance with test taking is not a problem. The normative library associated with these tests enables clinicians to appreciate patients' distress levels precisely, and thereby further enhances the quality of test-related clinical decisions. Low costs, ease of use, and efficiency in delivering information on patients' status are signature features of the SCL–90–R and the BSI, and recommend them highly for use in primary care.

As a caveat, it is important to remember that just as with all other self-report inventories, use of the SCL–90–R and BSI assumes the validity of the "inventory premise" — that the respondent can and will respond as honestly as possible to all test items. In instances of compromised cognitive function (e.g., delirium or dementia), dramatic psychopathology (e.g., acute toxic psychosis), compromised language ability, or willful misrepresentation, the validity of self-report assessment will be jeopardized to some degree. Also, in a large majority of situations, patients' perceptions of the value and merit of completing such inventories will mirror the opinions of treating physicians and their staffs. Those facilities that take the time and make the effort to explain the value and importance of such assessments and demonstrate a sincere interest in determining their patients' psychological status and well-being will observe a much greater commitment on the patients' part to do a conscientious job of completing the inventories.

SUMMARY

The SCL-90-R, BSI, BSI-18, and their matching clinical rating scales represent a unique set of brief, multidimensional psychological test instruments for the assessment of psychological symptoms and psychological distress. Their successful application in hundreds of published clinical studies, across an extremely broad spectrum of medical populations and contexts, provides confirmation of their validity and utility in the primary care setting. Sensitivity to pharmacotherapeutic, psychotherapeutic, and other treatment interventions, as well as to clinically significant changes in stress and distress levels, provides endorsement for these test instruments. The availability of matching clinician rating scales contributes the unique capability of obtaining comparable clinician ratings in addition to those of patients themselves. In addition, the SCL-90-R and BSI have been used extensively worldwide and are available in over two dozen languages.

REFERENCES

Abeloff, M. D., & Derogatis, L. R. (1977). Psychological aspects of the management of primary and metastatic breast cancer. In G. L. Stonesifer & E. F. Lewison (Eds.), *Breast cancer*. Baltimore: Johns Hopkins University Press.

Ae Lee, M., & Cameron, O. G. (1986). Anxiety, type A behavior and cardiovascular disease. *International Journal of Psychiatry in Medicine, 16,* 123-129.

Ae Lee, M., Cameron, O. G., & Greden, J. F. (1985). Anxiety and caffeine consumption in people with anxiety disorders. *Psychiatry Research, 15,* 211-217.

Allison, T. G., Williams, D. E., Miller, T. D., Patten, C. A., Bailey, K. R., Squires, R. W., & Gau, G. T. (1995). Medical and economic costs of psychological distress in patients with coronary disease. *Mayo Clinic Proceedings, 70,* 734-742.

Amenson, C. S., & Lewsinsohn, P. M. (1981). An investigation into the observed sex differences in prevalence of unipolar depression. *Journal of Abnormal Psychology, 90,* 1-13.

American Psychiatric Association. (1994). *Diagnostic and statistical manual of mental disorders* (4th ed.). Washington, DC: Author.

Angst, J., & Dobler-Mikola, A. (1984). The Zurich study: The continuum from normal to pathological depressive mood swings. *European Archives of Psychiatry and Neurological Sciences, 234,* 21-29.

Aroian, K. J., & Patsdaughter, C. A. (1989). Multimethod, cross-cultural assessment of psychological distress. *Image-Journal of Nursing Scholarship, 21,* 90-93.

Atkinson, H., Grant, I., Kennedy, C. J., Richman, D. D., Spector, S. A., & McCutchan, J. A. (1988). Prevalence of psychiatric disorders among men infected with human immunodeficiency virus. *Archives of General Psychiatry, 45,* 859-864.

Baider, L., Peretz, T., & DeNour, A. K. (1992). Effect of the holocaust on coping with cancer. *Social Science & Medicine, 34,* 11-15.

Ballenger, J. C., Burrows, G. D., Dupont, R. L., Lesser, I. M., Noyes, R., Pecknold, J. C., Rifkin, A., & Swinson, R. P. (1988). Alprazolam in panic disorder and agoraphobia: Results from a multicenter trial. I. Efficacy in short-term treatment. *Archives of General Psychiatry, 45*, 413–422.

Barrett, J. E., Barrett, J. A., Oxman, T. E., & Gerber, P. D. (1988). The prevalence of psychiatric disorders in a primary care practice. *Archives of General Psychiatry, 45*, 1100–1106.

Bennett, S. E., & Hughes, H. M. (1996). Performance of female college students and sexual abuse survivors on the Brief Symptom Inventory. *Journal of Clinical Psychology, 52*, 535–541.

Bohachick, P. (1984). Progressive relaxation training in cardiac rehabilitation: Effect on psychological variables. *Nursing Research, 33*, 283–287.

Boleloucky, Z., & Horvath, M. (1974). The SCL-90 rating scale: First experience with the Czech version in healthy male scientific workers. *Activitas Nervosa Superior, 16*, 115–116.

Bridges, K., & Goldberg, D. (1984). Psychiatric illness in in-patients with neurological disorders: Patient's view on discussion of emotional problems with neurologists. *British Medical Journal, 289*, 656–658.

Bryer, J. B., Borrelli, D. J., Matthews, E. J., & Kornetsky, C. (1983). The psychological correlates of the DST in depressed patients. *Psychopharmacological Bulletin, 19*, 633–637.

Buckner, J. C., & Mandell, W. (1990). Risk factors for depressive symptomotology in a drug using population. *American Journal of Public Health, 80*, 580–583.

Bulik, C. M., Carpenter, L. L., Kupfer, D. J., & Frank, E. (1990). Features associated with suicide attempts in recurrent major depression. *Journal of Affective Disorders, 18*, 27–29.

Buller, R., Maier, W., & Benkert, O. (1986). Clinical subtypes in panic disorder: Their descriptive and prospective validity. *Journal of Affective Disorders, 11*, 105–114.

Cameron, O. G., & Hudson, C. J. (1986). Influence of exercise on anxiety level in patients with anxiety disorders. *Psychosomatics, 27*, 720–723.

Cameron, O. G., Thyer, B. A., Nesse, R. M., & Curtis, G. C. (1986). Symptom profiles of patients with DSM-III anxiety disorders. *American Journal of Psychiatry, 143*, 1132–1137.

Carey, M. P., Carey, K. B., & Meisler, A. W. (1991). Psychiatric symptoms in mentally ill chemical abusers. *Journal of Nervous and Mental Disease, 179*, 136–138.

Carrington, P., Collings, G. H., Benson, H., Robinson, H., Wood, L. W., Lehrer, P. M., Woolfolk, R. L., & Cole, J. (1980). The use of meditation-relaxation techniques for the management of stress in a working population. *Journal of Occupational Medicine, 22*, 221–231.

Chiles, J. A., Benjamin, A. H., & Cahn, T. S. (1990). Who smokes? Why? Psychiatric aspects of continued cigarette usage among lawyers in Washington State. *Comprehensive Psychiatry, 31*, 176–184.

Choquette, K. A. (1994). Assessing depression in alcoholics with the BDI, SCL-90-R, and DIS criteria. *Journal of Substance Abuse, 6*, 295–304.

Clark, L. A., & Watson, D. (1991). Tripartite model of anxiety and depression: Psychometric evidence and taxonomic implications. *Journal of Abnormal Psychology, 100*, 316–336.

Coffey, P., Leitenberg, H., Henning, K., Turner, T., & Bennett, R. T. (1996). The relation between methods of coping during adulthood with a history of childhood sexual abuse and current psychological adjustment. *Journal of Consulting and Clinical Psychology, 64*, 1090–1093.

Cohen, J. (1992). A power primer. *Psychological Bulletin, 112*, 155–159.

Cohen, J. (1977). *Statistical power analysis for the behavioral sciences.* New York: Academic Press.

Cohen, L. J., Test, M. A., & Brown, R. L. (1990). Suicide and schizophrenia: Data from a perspective community treatment study. *American Journal of Psychiatry, 147*, 602–607.

Coryell, W. (1988). Mortality of anxiety disorders. In R. Noyes, M. Roth, & G. D. Burrows (Eds.), *Handbook of anxiety (Vol. 2): Classification, biological, and associated disturbances* (pp.). New York: Elsevier.

Craig, T. J., & Abeloff, M. (1974). Psychiatric symptomatology among hospitalized cancer patients. *American Journal of Psychiatry, 131*, 1323–1327.

Croog, S. H., Levine, S., Testa, M. A., Brown, B., Bulpitt, C. J., Jenkins, C. D., Klerman, G. L., & Williams, G. H. (1986). The effects of antihypertensive therapy on the quality of life. *New England Journal of Medicine, 314*, 1657–1664.

Derogatis, L. R. (1975). *The SCL-90-R.* Baltimore, MD: Clinical Psychometric Research.

Derogatis, L. R. (1977). *SCL-90-R: Administration, scoring, and procedures manual I.* Baltimore, MD: Clinical Psychometric Research.

Derogatis, L. R. (1982). *BSI: Administration, scoring, and procedures manual for the Brief Symptom Inventory–First edition.* Minneapolis, MN: National Computer Systems.

Derogatis, L. R. (1983). *SCL-90-R: Administration, scoring, and procedures manual–II.* Baltimore, MD: Clinical Psychometric Research.

Derogatis, L. R. (1990). *SCL-90-R: A bibliography of research reports 1975–1990.* Baltimore, MD: Clinical Psychometric Research.

Derogatis, L. R. (1993). *BSI: Administration, scoring, and procedures manual for the Brief Symptom Inventory-Third edition*. Minneapolis, MN: National Computer Systems.

Derogatis, L. R. (1994). *SCL–90–R: Administration, scoring, and procedures manual*. Minneapolis, MN: National Computer Systems, Inc.

Derogatis, L. R. (1996a). *SCL–90–R Bibliography*. Minneapolis, MN: National Computer Systems.

Derogatis, L. R. (1996b). *Brief Symptom Inventory Bibliography*. Minneapolis, MN: National Computer Systems.

Derogatis, L. R., Abeloff, M. D., & McBeth, C. D. (1976). Cancer patients and their physicians in the perception of psychological symptoms. *Psychosomatics, 17*, 197–201.

Derogatis, L. R., Abeloff, M. D., & Melisaratos, N. (1979). Psychological coping mechanisms and survival time in metastic breast cancer. *Journal of the American Medical Association, 242*, 1504–1508.

Derogatis, L. R., & Cleary, P. A. (1977). Factorial invariance across gender for the primary symptom dimensions of the SCL–90–R. *British Journal of Social & Clinical Psychology, 16*, 347–356.

Derogatis, L. R., & Dellapietra, L. (1994). Psychological tests in screening for psychiatric disorder. In M. Maruish (Ed.), *Psychological testing: Treatment planning and outcome assessment*. New York: Lawrence Erlbaum Associates.

Derogatis, L. R., & Derogatis, M. F. (1996). SCL–90–R® and the BSI®. In B. Spilker (Ed.), *Quality of life and pharmacoeconomics in clinical trials* (2nd ed., pp.). New York: Raven Press.

Derogatis, L. R., Lipman, R. S., & Covi, L. (1973). SCL–90: An outpatient psychiatric rating scale — Preliminary report. *Psychological Bulletin, 9*, 13–27.

Derogatis, L. R., Lipman, R. S., Rickels, K., Uhlenhuth, E. H., & Covi, L. (1974a). The Hopkins Symptom Checklist (HSCL): A measurement of primary symptom dimensions. In P. Pichot (Ed.), *Psychological measurements in psychopharmacology* (pp.). Basel: Karger.

Derogatis, L. R., Lipman, R. S., Rickels, K., Uhlenhuth, E. H., & Covi, L. (1974b). The Hopkins Symptom Checklist (HSCL): A self-report symptom inventory. *Behavior Science, 19*, 1–15.

Derogatis, L. R., & Melisaratos, N. (1983). The Brief Symptom Inventory: An introductory report. *Psychological Medicine, 13*, 595–605.

Derogatis, L. R., Meyer, J. K., & King, K. M. (1981). Psychopathology in individuals with sexual dysfunction. *American Journal of Psychiatry, 138*, 757–763.

Derogatis, L. R., Morrow, G., Fetting, J., Penaman, D., Piasetsky, S., Schmale, A. H., Hendrichs, M., & Carnicke, C. M. (1983). The prevalence of psychiatric disorders among cancer patients. *Journal of the American Medical Association, 249*, 751–757.

Derogatis, L. R., Rickels, K., & Rock, A. (1976). The SCL–90–R and the MMPI: A step in the validation of new self-report scale. *British Journal of Psychiatry, 128*, 280–289.

Derogatis, L. R., & Spencer, P. M. (1982). *BSI administration and procedures manual I*. Baltimore, MD: Clinical Psychometric Research.

Derogatis, L. R., & Wise, T. N. (1989). *Anxiety and depressive disorders in the medical patient*. Washington, DC: American Psychiatric Press.

DeSoto, C. B., O'Donnell, W. E., Allred, L. J., & Lopes, C. E. (1985). Symptomotology in alcoholics at various stages of abstinence. *Alcoholism, 9*, 505–512.

Dew, M. A., Simmons, R. G., Roth, L. H., Schulberg, H. C., Thompson, M. E., Armitage, J. M., & Griffith, B. P. (1994). Psychosocial predictors of vulnerability to distress in the year following heart transplantation. *Psychological Medicine, 24*, 929–945.

Dongier, M., Vachon, & Schwartz, G. (1991). Bromocriptine in the treatment of alcohol dependence. *Alcholism Clinical and Experimental Research, 15*, 970–977.

Drossman, D. A., Leserman, J., Mitchell, C. M., Zhiming, M., Zagami, E. A., & Patrick, D. L. (1991). Health status and health care use in persons with inflammatory bowel disease: A national sample. *Digestive Diseases and Sciences, 36*, 1746–1755.

Frazier, P. A., & Schauben, L. J. (1994). Stressful life events and psychological adjustment among female college students. *Measurement and Evaluation in Counseling and Development, 27*, 280–292.

Fricchione, G. L., Howanitz, E., Jandorf, L., Kroseslor, D., Zervas, I., & Woznicki, R. M. (1992). Psychological adjustment to end-stage renal disease and the implications of denial. *Psychosomatics, 33*, 85–91.

Gift, A. G. (1991). Psychologic and physiologic aspects of dyspnea in asthmatics. *Nursing Research, 40*, 196–198.

Gilbar, O. (1998). Coping with threat: Implications for women with a family history of breast cancer. *Psychosomatics, 39*, 329–339.

Gilbar, O. (1991). The quality of life of cancer patients who refuse chemotherapy. *Social Science and Medicine, 32*, 1337–1340.

Gotay, C. C., & Stern, J. D. (1995). Assessment of psychological functioning in cancer patients. *Journal of Psychosocial Oncology, 13*, 123–160.

Grassi, L., Righi, R., Sighinolfi, L., Makoui, S., & Ghinelli, F. (1998). Coping styles and psychosocial-related variables in HIV-infected patients. *Psychosomatics, 39*, 350–359.

Grassi, L., & Rosti, G. (1996a). Psychiatric and psychosocial concomitants of abnormal illness behavior in patients with cancer. *Psychotherapy and Psychosomatics, 65*, 246–252.

Grassi, L., & Rosti, G. (1996b). Psychosocial morbidity and adjustment to illness among long-term cancer survivors. *Psychosomatics, 37*, 523–532.

Hamer, M. E., Blumenthal, J. A., McCarthy, E. A., Philips, B. G., & Pritchett, E. L. C. (1994). Quality of life in patients with paroxysmal atrial fibrillation or paroxysmal supraventricular tachycardia. *American Journal of Cardiology, 74*, 826–829.

Hannum, A., Giese-Davis, J., Harding, K., & Hatfield, A. K. (1991). Effects of individual and marital variables on coping with cancer. *Journal of Psychosocial Oncology, 9*, 1–20.

Horowitz, L. M., Rosenberg, S. E., Baer, B. A., Ureno, G., & Villasenor, V. S. (1988). Inventory of Interpersonal Problems: Psychometric properties and clinical applications. *Journal of Consulting and Clinical Psychology, 56*, 885–892.

Hurley, J. R., & Cattell, R. (1962). The Procrustes program: Producing direct rotation to test a hypothesized factor structure. *Behavioral Science, 7*, 258–262.

Jacobson, N. S., Follette, W. C., & Ravenstorf, D. (1986). Toward a standard definition of clinically significant change. *Behavior Therapy, 17*, 308–311.

Jacobson, M. S., & Truax, P. (1991). Clinical significance: A statistical approach to defining meaningful clinical change in psychotherapy research. *Journal of Consulting and Clinical Psychology, 59*, 12–19.

Johnson, M. E., Brems, C., & Fisher, D. G. (1996). Self-reported levels of psychopathology and drug abusers not currently in treatment. *Journal of Psychopathology and Behavioral Assessment, 18*, 21–34.

Johnson, J., Weissman, M. M., & Klerman, G. L. (1992). Service utilization and service mobility associated with depressive symptoms in the community. *Journal of the American Medical Association, 267*, 1478–1483.

Johnson, J. G., Williams, J. B. W., Rabkin, J. G., Goetz, R. R., & Remien, R. H. (1995). Axis I psychiatric symptoms associated with HIV infection and personality disorder. *American Journal of Psychiatry, 152*, 551–554.

Johnstone, B. G. M., Silberfield, M., Chapman, J., Phoenix, C., Sturgeon, J., Till, J. E., & Sutcliffe, S. B. (1991). Heterogeneity in responses to cancer, part 1: Psychiatric symptoms. *Canadian Journal of Psychiatry, 36*, 85–90.

Kaiser, H. E. (1958). The Varimax criterion for analytic rotation in factor analysis. *Psychometrika, 23*, 187–200.

Kamerow, D. B., Pincus, H. A., & MacDonald, D. I. (1986). Alcohol abuse, other drug abuse, and mental disorders in medical practice: Prevalence, cost, recognition, and treatment. *Journal of the American Medical Association, 255*, 2054–2057.

Katon, W., & Roy-Byrne, P. P. (1991). Mixed anxiety and depression. *Journal of Abormal Psychology, 100*, 337–345.

Katon, W., & Sullivan, M. D. (1990). Depression and chronic medical illness. *Journal of Clinical Psychiatry, 15*, 3–11.

Katon, W., Von Korff, M., Lin, E., Lipscomb, P., Russo, J., Wagner, & Polk, E. (1990). Distressed high utilizers of medical care DSM–III–R diagnoses and treatment needs. *General Hospital Psychiatry, 12*, 355–362.

Kedward, H. B., & Cooper, B. (1966). Neurotic disorders in urban practice: A 3 year follow-up. *Journal of College of General Practice, 12*, 148–163.

Kellner, R., Hernandez, J., & Pathak, D. (1992). Hypochondriacal fears and their relationship to anxiety and somatization. *British Journal of Psychiatry, 160*, 525–532.

Kennedy, C. A., Skurnick, J. H., Foley, M., & Louria, D. B. (1995). Gender differences in HIV-related psychological distress in heterosexual couples. *AIDS Care, 7*, 33–38.

Kirmayer, L. J., Robbins, J. M., Dworkin, M., & Yaffe, M. J. (1993). Somatization and the recognition of anxiety and depression in primary care. *American Journal of Psychiatry, 150*, 734–741.

Kleinman, P. H., Miller, A. B., Millman, R. B., Woody, G. E., Todd, T., Kempt, J., & Lipton, D. S. (1990). Psychopathology among cocaine abusers entering treatment. *Journal of Nervous and Mental Disease, 178*, 442–447.

Koeter, M. W. (1992). Validity of the GHQ and the SCL–90–R anxiety and depression scales: A comparative study. *Journal of Affective Disorders, 24*, 271–279.

Kopta, S. M., Howard, K. I., Lowry, J. L., & Beutler, L. E. (1994). Patterns of symptomatic recovery in psychotherapy. *Journal of Clinical and Consulting Psychology, 62*, 1009–1016.

Kuhn, W. F., Bell, R. A., Seligson, D., Laufer, S. T., & Lindner, J. E. (1988). The tip of the iceberg: Psychiatric consultations on an orthopedic service. *International Journal of Psychiatric Medicine, 18*, 375–378.

Lesko, L. M., Ostroff, J. S., Mumma, G. H., Mashberg, D. E., & Holland, J. C. (1992). Long-term psychological adjustment of acute leukemia survivors: Impact of bone marrow transplantation versus conventional chemotherapy. *Psychosomatic Medicine, 54*, 30–47.

Levine, S., Anderson, D., Bystritski, A., & Barton, D. (1990). Eight HIV-seropositive patients with major depression responding to fluoxetine. *Journal of Acquired Immune Deficiency Syndrome, 3*, 1074–1077.

Levine, E. G., Raczynski, J. M., & Carpenter, J. T. (1991). Weight gain with breast cancer adjuvant treatment. *Cancer, 67*, 1954–1959.

Liskow, B., Powell, B. J., Nickel, E. J., & Penick, E. (1991a). Antisocial alcoholics: Are they clinically significant diagnostic subtypes? *Journal of Studies on Alcohol, 52*(1), 62–69.

Liskow, B., Powell, B. J., Nickel, E. J., & Penick, E. (1991b). Diagnostic subgroups of antisocial alcoholics: Outcome at 1 year. *Comprehensive Psychiatry, 31*, 549–556.

Malec, J., & Neimeyer, R. (1983). Psychologic prediction of duration of inpatient spinal cord injury rehabilitation and performance of self-care. *Archives of Physical and Medical Rehabilitation, 64*, 359–363.

McCullough, J. P., McCune, K. J., Kaye, A. L., Braith, J. A., Friend, R., Roberts, W. C., Belyea-Caldwell, S., Norris, S. W., & Hampton, C. (1994). One year prospective replication study of an untreated sample of community dysthymia subjects. *Journal of Nervous and Mental Diseases, 182*, 396–401.

Messick, S. (1975). The standard problem: Meaning and values in measurement and evaluation. *American Psychologist, 30*, 955–966.

Messick, S. (1981). Constructs and their vicissitudes in educational and psychological measurement. *Psychological Bulletin, 89*, 575–588.

Moffett, L. A., & Radenhausen, R. (1983, August). *Assessing depression in subtsance abusers: The SCL–90–R and Beck Depression Inventory.* Paper presented at the 91st Annual Convention of the American Psychological Association, Anaheim, CA.

Myers, J. K., Weissman, M. M., Tischler, G. L., Holzer, C. E. III, Leaf, P. J., Orvaschel, H., Anthony, J. C., Boyd, J. H., Burke, J. D., Kramer, M., & Stoltzman, R. (1980–1982). Six-month prevalence of psychiatric disorders in three communities. *Archives of General Psychiatry, 41*, 959–970.

Myers, J. K., Weissman, M. M., Tischler, G. L., Holzer, C. E. III, Leaf, P. J., Orvaschel, H., Anthony, J. C., Boyd, J. H., Burke, J. D., Kramer, M., & Stoltzman, R. (1984). Six month prevalence of psychiatric disorders in three communities. *Archives of General Psychiatry, 41*, 959–970.

Northouse, L. L., & Swain, M. A. (1987). Adjustment of patients and husbands to the initial impact of breast cancer. *Nursing Research, 36*, 221–225.

Noyes, R., Anderson, D. J., Clancy, J., Crowe, R. R., Slymen, D. J., Ghoneim, M. M., & Hinrichs, J. V. (1984). Diazepam and propranolol in panic disorder and agoraphobia. *Archives of Psychiatry, 41*, 287–292.

Noyes, R., Christiansen, J., Clancy, J., Garvey, M. J., Suelzer, M., & Anderson, D. J. (1991). Predictors of serious suicide attempts among patients with panic disorder. *Comprehensive Psychiatry, 32*, 261–267.

Noyes, R., Weissman, C., Garvey, M. J., Cook, B. L., Seuzler, M., & Clancy, J. (1992). Generalized anxiety disorder versus panic disorder. Distinguishing characteristics and patterns of comorbidity. *Journal of Nervous and Mental Disease, 180*, 369–379.

Nunnally, J. (1970). *Introduction to psychological measurement.* New York: McGraw-Hill.

Perconte, S. T., & Griger, M. L. (1991). Comparison of successful, unsuccessful, and relapsed Vietnam veterans treated for posttraumatic stress disorder. *Journal of Nervous and Mental Disease, 179*, 558–562.

Peveler, R. C., & Fairburn, C. G. (1990). Measurement of neurotic symptoms by self-report questionnaire: Validity of the SCL–90–R. *Psychological Medicine, 20*, 873–879.

Prusoff, B. A., Weissman, M. M., Klerman, G. L., & Rounsaville, B. J. (1980). Research diagnostic criteria subtypes of depression: Their role as predictors of differential response to psychotherapy and drug treatment. *Archives of General Psychiatry, 37*, 791–801.

Quitkin, F. M., Liebowitz, M. R., Steward, J. W., McGrath, P. J., Harrison, W., Rabkin, J. G., Markowitz, J., & Davies, S. O. (1984). *l*-Deprenyl in atypical depressives. *Archives of General Psychiatry, 41*, 777–780.

Regier, D. A., Boyd, J. H., Burke, J. D., Rae, D. S., Myers, J. K., Kramer, M., Robbins, L. N., George, L. K., Karno, M., & Locke, B. Z. (1988). One month prevalence of mental disorders in the United States. *Archives of General Psychiatry, 45*, 977–986.

Rief, W., Hiller, W., Geissner, E., & Fichter, M. M. (1995). A two-year follow-up study of patients with somatoform disorders. *Psychosomatics, 36*, 376–386.

Robbins, L. N., Helzer, J. E., Croughan, J., & Ratcliff, K. S. (1981). National institute of mental health diagnostic interview schedule. *Archives of General Psychiatry, 38*, 318–389.

Roberts, C. S., Rosetti, K., Cone, D., & Cavanaugh, D. (1992). Psychosocial impact of gynecologic cancer. *Journal of Psychosocial Oncology, 10,* 99–109.

Robins, L. N., Helzer, J. E., Weissman, M. M., Orvaschel, H., Greenberg, E., Burke, J. D., & Regier, D. A. (1984). Lifetime prevalence of specific psychiatric disorders in three sites. *Archives of General Psychiatry, 41,* 949–958.

Robinson, G. E., Olmsted, M. P., & Garner, D. M. (1989). Predictors of postpartum adjustment. *Acta Psychiatrica Scandinavica, 80,* 561–565.

Rogentine, D. S., VanKammen, D. P., Fox, B. H., Docherty, J. P., Rosenblatt, J. E., Boyd, S. C., & Bunney, W. E. (1979). Psychological factors in the prognosis of malignant melanoma: A prospective study. *Psychosomatic Medicine, 41,* 647–655.

Rounsaville, B. J., Glazer, W., Wilber, C. H., Weissman, M., & Kleber, H. D. (1983). Short-term interpersonal psychotherapy in methadone-maintained opiate addicts. *Archives of General Psychiatry, 40,* 620–638.

Royce, D., & Drude, K. (1984). Screening drug abuse clients with the Brief Symptom Inventory. *International Journal of Addiction, 19,* 849–857.

Saravay, S. M., Pollack, S., Steinberg, M. D., Weinschel, B., & Habert, M. (1996). Four year follow-up of the influence of psychological comorbidity on medical rehospitalization. *American Journal of Psychiatry, 153,* 397–403.

Saravay, S. M., Steinberg, M. D., Wienschel, B., Pollack, S., & Alovis, N. (1991). Psychological comorbidity and length of stay in the general hospital. *American Journal of Psychiatry, 148,* 324–329.

Schleifer, S. J., Bhardwaj, S., Lebovits, A., Tanaka, S., Messe, M., & Strain, J. J. (1991). Predictors of physician nonadherence to chemotherapy regimens. *Cancer, 67,* 945–951.

Schover, L. R., Fife, M., & Gershenson, D. M. (1989). Sexual dysfunction and treatment of early stage cervical cancer. *Cancer, 63,* 204–212.

Schulberg, H. C., Saul, M., McClelland, M., Ganguli, M., Christy, W., & Frank, R. (1985). Assessing depression in primary medical and psychiatric practices. *Archives of General Psychiatry, 42,* 1164–1170.

Shapiro, D. A., & Firth, J. (1987). Prescriptive vs. exploratory psychotherapy: Outcomes of the Sheffield Psychotherapy Project. *British Journal of Psychiatry, 151,* 790–799.

Simon, G. E., & Von Korff, M. (1991). Somatization and psychiatric disorders: The NIMH Epidemiologic Catchment Area Study. *American Journal of Psychiatry, 148,* 1491–1500.

Steer, R. A., & Hasset, T. (1982). Contributions of individual syndromes to global psychopathology ratings for mental health and substance abuse patients. *Journal of Clinical Psychology, 38,* 448–551.

Steer, R. A., Platt, J. J., Hendriks, V. M., & Metzger, D. S. (1989). Types of self-reported psychopathology in Dutch and American heroin addicts. *Drug and Alcohol Dependence, 24,* 175–181.

Steer, R. A., Platt, J. J., Ranieri, W. F., & Metzger, D. S. (1989). Relationships of SCL-90-R to methadone patients' psychosocial characteristics and treatment response. *Multivariate Experimental Clinical Research, 9,* 45–54.

Stewart, J. W., Quitkin, F. M., Terman, M., & Terman, J. S. (1990). Is seasonal affective disorder a variant of atypical depression? Differential response to light therapy. *Psychiatry Research, 33,* 121–128.

Strauman, T. J. (1992). Self-guides, autobiographical memory and anxiety and dysphoria: Toward a cognitive model of vulnerability to emotional distress. *Journal of Abnormal Psychology, 101,* 87–95.

Sullivan, M. D., Katon, W., Dobie, R., Sakai, C., Russo, J., & Harrop-Griffiths, J. (1988). Disabling tinnitus associated with affective disorder. *General Hospital Psychiatry, 10,* 285–291.

Swedo, S. E., Rettew, D. C., Kuppenheimer, M., Lum, D., Dolan, S., & Goldberger, E. (1991). Can adolescent suicide attempters be distinguished from at-risk adolescents? *Pediatrics, 88,* 620–629.

Thompson, L. W., Gallagher, D., & Breckenridge, J. (1987). Comparative effectiveness of psychotherapy for depressed elders. *Journal of Consulting and Clinical Psychology, 55,* 385–390.

Toomey, T. C., Seville, J. L., Mann, J. D., Abashian, S. W., & Grant, J. R. (1995). Relationship of sexual and physical abuse to pain description, psychological distress, and health-care utilization in a chronic pain sample. *Clinical Journal of Pain, 11,* 307–315.

Tross, S., Herndon, J., Korzun, A., Kornblith, A. B., Cella, D. F., Holland, J. F., Raich, P., Johnson, A., Kian, D. T., Perloff, M., Norton, L., Wood, W., & Holland, J. C. (1996). Psychological symptoms and disease-free and overall survival in women with stage II breast cancer. *Journal of the National Cancer Institute, 88,* 661–667.

Tryon, R. C. (1996). Unrestricted cluster and factor analysis with application to the MMPI and Holzinger–Harman problems. *Multivariate Behavioral Research, 1,* 229–244.

Von Korff, M., Dworkin, S. F., & Krueger, A. (1988). An epidemiologic comparison of pain complaints. *Pain, 32,* 173–183.

Walker, E. A., Katon, W. J., Hansom, J., Harrop-Griffiths, J., Holm, L., Jones, M. L., Hickok, L. R., & Russo, J. (1995). Psychiatric diagnoses and sexual victimization in women with chronic pelvic pain. *Psychosomatics, 36,* 531–540.

Walsh, B. T., Hadigan, C. M., Devlin, M. J., Gladis, M., & Roose, S. P. (1991). Long-term outcome of antidepressant treatment for bulimia nervosa. *American Journal of Psychiatry, 148,* 1206–1212.

Weissman, M. M., & Merikangas, K. R. (1986). The epidemiology of anxiety and panic disorder: An update. *Journal of Clinical Psychiatry, 47,* 11–17.

Weissman, M. M., Pottenger, M., Kleber, H., Ruben, H. L., Williams, D., & Thompson, W. D. (1977). Symptom patterns in primary and secondary depression: A comparison of primary depressives and depressed opiate addcits, alcoholics, and schizophrenics. *Archives of General Psychiatry, 34,* 854–862.

Weissman, M. M., Sholomskas, D., Pottenger, M., Prusoff, B. A., & Locke, B. Z. (1977). Assessing depressive symptoms in five psychiatric populations: A validation study. *American Journal of Epidemiology, 106,* 203–214.

Wellisch, D. K., Gritz, E. R., Schain, W., Wang, H., & Slau, J. (1992). Psychological functioning of daughters of breast cancer patients, Part II: Characterizing the distressed daughter of the breast cancer patient. *Psychosomatics, 33,* 171–179.

Wetzler, S., Kahn, R. S., Cahn, W., VanPraag, H. M., & Asnis, G. M. (1990). Psychological test characteristics of depressed and panic patients. *Psychiatry Research, 31,* 179–192.

Wetzler, S., Khadivi, A., & Oppenheim, S. (1995). The psychological assessment of depression: Unipolars versus bipolars. *Journal of Personality Assessment, 65,* 557–566.

Wider, A. (1948). *The Cornell Medical Index.* San Antonio, TX: Psychological Corporation.

Wiggins, J. S. (1969). Content dimensions in the MMPI. In J. N. Butcher (Ed.), *MMPI: Research developments and clinical applications* (pp.). New York: McGraw-Hill.

Williams, J. B. W., Rabkin, J. G., Remien, R. H., Gorman, J. M., & Ehrhardt, A. A. (1991). Multidisciplinary baseline assessment of homosexual men with and without human immunodeficiency virus infection. *Archives of General Psychiatry, 48,* 124–130.

Williamson, J. M., Borduin, C. M., & Howe, B. A. (1991). The ecology of adolescent maltreatment: A multilevel examination of adolescent physical abuse, sexual abuse, and neglect. *Journal of Consulting and Clinical Psychology, 59,* 449–457.

Wing, J. K., Cooper, J. E., & Sartorius, N. (1974). *The measurement and classification of psychiatric symptoms.* London: Cambridge University Press.

Winokur, A., Guthrie, M., Rickels, K., & Nael, S. (1992). Extent of agreement between patient and physician ratings of emotional distress. *Psychosomatics, 23,* 1141–1146.

Wise, M. G., & Taylor, S. E. (1990). Anxiety and mood disorders in mentally ill patients. *Journal of Clinical Psychiatry, 51,* 27–32.

Wiznitzer, M., Verhulst, F. C., Van den Brink, W., Koeter, M., van der Enoe, J., Griel, R., & Koot, H. M. (1992). Detecting psychopathology in young adults: The Young Adult Self-Report, the General Health Questionnaire, and the Symptom Checklist–90–R as screening instruments. *Acta Psychiatrica Scandinavica, 86,* 32–37.

Zabora, J. R., Smith-Wilson, R., Fetting, J. H., & Enterline, J. P. (1990). An efficient method for psychosocial screening of cancer patients. *Psychosomatics, 31,* 192–196.

Applications of the Symptom Assessment–45 Questionnaire (SA–45) in Primary Care Settings

Mark E. Maruish
United Behavioral Health
Minneapolis, Minnesota

In Maruish's (1999) overview of the current uses of psychological testing, the potential contributions of this tool for clinical decision making are discussed. With behavioral health care treatment limitations and other cost-control measures imposed by managed care and other health care stakeholders (e.g., employers), the use of brief, inexpensive, or public domain measures of symptom severity appears to be particularly suited to meeting the needs of marketplace (Maruish, 1994; Ficken, 1995). One such instrument is the recently developed Symptom Assessment–45 Questionnaire (SA–45; Strategic Advantage, Inc. [SAI], 1998). The value of the SA–45 has been demonstrated not only in behavioral health care settings, but also in primary care settings where approximately one quarter of the patients suffer from some form of behavioral health problem. The purpose of this chapter is to provide an overview of the development of the SA–45 as well as its potential applications in primary care settings.

DEVELOPMENT OF THE SA–45

Background

One way in which the need for brief psychological measures has been successfully addressed in the behavioral health care field is through a series of symptom checklists developed by Leonard Derogatis and his colleagues. This includes the original Symptom Checklist–90 (SCL–90; Derogatis, Lipman, & Covi, 1973), the Symptom Checklist–90–Revised (SCL–90–R; Derogatis, Rickels, & Rock, 1976; Derogatis, 1983, 1994), and a much shorter (by almost half) version of the revised checklist, the Brief Symptom Inventory (BSI; Derogatis, 1992, 1993). The utility of the BSI in behavioral health care settings is attested to by the number of organizations that have chosen it for internal use (e.g., Pallak, 1994). However, its cost can present a barrier to its use for many providers who wish to routinely administer tests to their clientele. With a need for an inexpensive, brief, multidimensional measure that could serve as a preliminary screener, treatment outcome indicator and general purpose research tool, Strategic Advantage, Inc. (SAI), a behavioral health care outcomes assessment and consultation group, set out to develop an alternative measure.

The SCL-90 was the logical source from which to derive and further develop a set of items to satisfy SAI's requirements. The professional literature supports the use of the SCL-90 as a valid and reliable measure of psychological distress that can be used for screening and the assessment of treatment outcomes. The SCL-90 is a public domain instrument that has demonstrated its suitability for use with both adults and adolescents and has gained widespread acceptance within the behavioral health care provider community. Moreover, as reported in the BSI manual (Derogatis & Spencer, 1982), Derogatis's earlier research with the SCL-90 (Derogatis & Cleary, 1977) demonstrated that only a limited number of items from each of its scales was necessary to maintain the definition of the construct purportedly measured by that scale. Finally, SAI had employed the SCL-90 in outcomes measurement consulting work for a number of years. Consequently, SAI was quite familiar with its strengths and limitations. SAI also had a large number of data sets containing SCL-90 and other collateral data that could facilitate the completion of key aspects of instrument development.

Using an approach different from that used by Derogatis and his colleagues, SAI researchers selected 45 items from the SCL-90 (five items to assess each of the nine SCL-90 symptom domains) for inclusion in the SA-45. Separate gender-based norms were developed for both adolescents and adults from both inpatient and nonpatient populations, and the requisite validity and reliability studies were completed. The SA-45 and its abbreviated version, the SA-24, have become key components of the instrumentation employed by SAI in its behavioral health care outcomes research. With its demonstrated psychometric properties and utility, the SA-45 is now commercially available to qualified behavioral health care providers.

The primary goal of SA-45 development efforts was to use the proven items and structure of the SCL-90 to create a brief, valid, and reliable measure of psychiatric symptomatology that could be used for the assessment of treatment outcomes. Also, it was hoped that the instrument would have additional utility for screening patients and tracking their progress during the course of treatment. As demonstrated in this and the following sections of this chapter, these goals were achieved.

Summary of Development

The approach taken in developing the SA-45 was that of cluster analysis. For the purpose of initial item selection, the SCL-90 results of an inpatient sample tested at the time of admission to a large system of private psychiatric hospitals were used. This sample was described in Davison, Bershadsky, Bieber, Silversmith, Maruish, and Kane (1997) as their inpatient *intake sample* but hereafter is referred to as the *development sample*. It consisted of 690 adult females, 829 adult males, 466 adolescent females, and 400 adolescent males.

To examine the structure of the symptom domains, items were intercorrelated and Ward's (1963) method of cluster analysis was applied to the correlation matrix. A nine-cluster solution was forced, with each cluster containing five items. Based on these findings, nine scales matching the symptom domain scales of the SCL-90 were constructed, each incorporating the five items from the respective SCL-90 parent scale that were identified through the cluster-analytic procedures. Subsequent cluster analyses were performed on five subgroups (adult inpatients, adolescent inpatients, combined adult and adolescent female inpatients, combined adult and adolescent male patients, and combined adult and adolescent nonpatients) in order to examine the degree to which items clustered according to expectations (Davison et al., 1997). The item response sets required for this study were extracted from existing SCL–90 data sets. The number of hits (i.e., items that clustered according to expectation) ranged from 35 (78%) of the 45 items using nonpatient data to 43 (96%) of the items using adult inpatient intake data. In comparison, cluster analyses of SCL–90 intake data and BSI item responses extracted from those same SCL–90 data yielded hits for 51 (61%) of the 83 scored SCL–90 items, and for 42 (86%) of the 49 scored BSI items.

SAI's experience with the SCL–90 and BSI indicated that two summary indices found on both instruments — the Positive Symptom Total (PST) and the Global Severity Index (GSI) — were useful as descriptors of overall level of psychopathology or symptomatology. Thus, SA–45 versions of these indices were incorporated into the instrument. The PST index is the total number of symptoms reported by the respondent to be present to any degree during the previous seven days. The GSI represents the sum of the item response values (ranging from 1 to 5) for all items on the SA–45 and thus provides a good indication of the respondent's overall level of distress or disturbance.

Normative Data

Nonpatient normative data for the SA–45 items were extracted from SCL–90 data sets gathered on groups of 748 adult females, 328 adult males, 321 adolescent females, and 293 adolescent males. These nonpatient samples included employees of a large, national behavioral health care company and their family members, along with approximately 300 adolescents from a midwestern suburban high school. In calculating the mean and standard deviation for each SA–45 scale and index, cases in which one or more item responses for a given scale or index were missing (i.e., omitted or for which more than one response was indicated) were not included in the data for that scale or index. Thus, means and standard deviations for the 11 scales and indices are based on 714 to 748 adult females, 312 to 328 adult males, 302 to 321 adolescent females, and 293 adolescent males, depending on the scale or index being considered.

Recognizing that being able to compare a patient's results to those of inpatients may enhance the interpretation of results, SCL–90 data sets for groups of adult and adolescent inpatients were rescored to arrive at raw scores for each of the 11 SA–45 scales and indices. The inpatient means and standard deviations for the scales and indices are based on 4,732 to 5,300 adult females, 4,753 to 5,276 adult males, 2,424 to 2,715 adolescent females, and 1,935 to 2,196 adolescent males. The SA–45 development sample was included in these samples.

Development of Area *T*-Score and Percentile Conversions

Standard scores were developed by first calculating the frequency of the score distributions of the SA–45's nine symptom domain scales and the PST and GSI indices for the four age-by-gender nonpatient samples. These calculations resulted in a total of 44 score distributions, which were then modeled using a quasi-Newtonian search algorithm and the maximum likelihood method. The resulting models were used to estimate a frequency distribution for each scale and index score for each age-by-gender sample. Using the estimated frequency distribution, the raw scores were transformed to area T-scores for the four nonpatient normative groups. This same procedure also was applied to the inpatient normative sample data to arrive at raw score-to-inpatient area T-score conversions.

Area T-scores, rather than linear T-scores, were selected for use in interpreting SA–45 results. Employment of the more commonly used linear T-scores assumes that the characteristic or construct being measured by the instrument is normally distributed—an assumption that one cannot make regarding psychopathological characteristics. Area T-scores have the effect of normalizing the distribution of scores and permitting accurate percentile determination. For example, an area T-score of 60 (i.e., one standard deviation above the mean) is equivalent to the 84th percentile. A linear T-score of 60 equates to the 84th percentile *only when the distribution is normal*; otherwise, it represents only a rough approximation.

Another way in which the SA–45's scored-data conversions differ from the standard is the manner in which percentiles have been computed. Although a percentile is frequently computed and interpreted to indicate the percentage of the normative sample that obtained a score *lower than* the score being referred to, an SA–45 percentile indicates the percentage of the normative sample that obtained scores *equal to or lower than* that score. Thus, 84% of the relevant age and gender-specific SA–45 normative group scored equal to or lower than anyone obtaining a scale or index raw score that equals a percentile of 84 (or area T-score of 60). At the same time, only 16% of that same normative group scored higher than that person on that particular scale or index.

Development of SA–45 online administration and scoring software required the transformation of the nonpatient normative conversion data from a tabular form to a more compressed form for economical storage. To accomplish this, polynomial functions of either five degrees for the nine domain scale scores and the PST score or seven degrees for the GSI score were developed to fit the area T-score for each nonpatient normative subsample. Quasi-Newtonian search algorithms that minimized the squared error were used to fit the polynomial functions, thus yielding a more efficient means of electronically storing the SA–45 nonpatient norms tables.

Corrections for Missing Item Responses

With scales comprised of only five items each, the omission of even one SA–45 item means that the corresponding item pool of the symptom domain scale is reduced by 20%. To correct for this, stepwise linear regression methods were used to develop an equation for predicting or estimating the value for each SA–45 item when it is the only item missing from its parent scale, thus permitting an accurate estimate of the total raw score for a given scale when only one response value for the scale is missing. Similarly, methods for estimating the total raw score for the PST and GSI indices were developed for use in those cases in which the total number of missing item response values is 10 or fewer for the PST index and 11 or fewer (approximately one quarter of the total SA–45 item pool) for the GSI. Here, the mean value replacement method was found to represent the optimal solution for arriving at the predicted total raw scores. These means of correcting for missing items were found to yield raw scores that generally correlate at about .98 with actual scores across age and gender groups.

Psychometric Considerations

The psychometric integrity of any psychological test, rating scale, or related measure or procedure is reflected in two broad constructs: reliability and validity. *Reliability* refers to the extent to which an instrument is consistent in what it measures. *Validity* refers to the degree to which an instrument measures what it purports to measure.

Reliability. The internal consistency reliability of each of the nine symptom domain scales was evaluated using Cronbach's coefficient alpha for each of four large adult samples and four large adolescent samples (Davison et al., 1997). The coefficients were computed from the results of samples of mental health or chemical dependency inpatients who took the SCL–90 at the time of treatment intake; those intake patients who took the SCL–90 again at treatment termination; those intake patients who took the SCL–90 again 6 months following treatment termination; and large samples of nonpatients. The alpha coefficients for the adult samples ranged from .71 for the Psychoticism scale for the follow-up sample to .92 for the Depression scale for the termination sample. For the adolescent samples, the alphas ranged from .69 for the Psychoticism scale for both the termination and follow-up samples to .90 for the Depression scale for the intake sample.

In another examination of internal consistency, each of the SA–45 item response values was correlated with the total raw score for each of the nine symptom domain scales. In those instances in which an item was correlated with the scale of which it is a member, that item was removed from the scale before the scale score and correlation were calculated. For the combined development sample (2,442 male and female adult and adolescent psychiatric inpatients), it was determined that the highest correlations of 42 of the 45 items (93%) were with the scale to which each item belongs. For 19 of these 42 items (45%), the correlations were at least .10 greater than the correlation of these items with any other scale. For a cross-validation sample (13,550 male and female adult and adolescent psychiatric inpatients), 43 of the 45 items (96%) correlated highest with their parent scales, with correlations for 18 (42%) of these 43 items being at least .10 greater than their correlation with any other scale.

Adult, nonpatient test–retest study data were gathered on 15 males and 42 females who were not receiving any behavioral health care services at the time of testing. The study employed a 1- to 2-week retest interval. The raw score-based correlations were generally in the .80 range, with notable exceptions for the Somatization scale (.69) and Anxiety scale (.42). One possible explanation for these findings is that the Anxiety scale items are sensitive to variations in common, everyday experiences (e.g., "Feeling tense or keyed up," "Feeling so restless you couldn't sit still"). Similar sensitivities might also be operating with some of the Somatization items (e.g., "Soreness in your muscles"). Generally, the *T*-score changes from first to second test administration were only slightly lower, averaging a drop of only 1.66 points for the nine symptom domain scales and 3.36 points for the PST and GSI.

In a similar study of 48 adolescent males and 16 adolescent females, the raw score-based correlations were quite variable, ranging from .51 for the Hostility scale to .85 for the Psychoticism scale. Consistent with the adult findings, the Anxiety scale coefficient (.58) was the next to the lowest of the coefficients. The area *T*-score-based correlation coefficients generally showed only slight variations from those reported for the raw scores. Area *T*-score changes from the first to second administrations were relatively stable, dropping on an average only 1.12 points for the nine symptom domain scales and 2.27 points for each of the two summary indices.

SA–45 test–retest reliability coefficients also were computed for combined-gender adult, adolescent, and combined age-group inpatient psychiatric samples retested at 1-, 2-, and/or 3-week intervals. Overall, moderate level correlations were obtained for all three age groups. In general, these correlations are consistent with what one might expect for a brief symptom measure that is administered to a psychiatric inpatient sample over the three time intervals.

Validity. The SA–45 construct validity has been demonstrated through various approaches. One approach was an investigation of the instrument's interscale correlations. Using the SCL–90 item responses of more than 1,300 adult inpatients, the SA–45 interscale correlations were found to range from .38 between the Phobic Anxiety and Hostility scales, to .75 between the Interpersonal Sensitivity and Depression scales, suggesting a substantial degree of shared variance (14%–56%) and a lack of clear independence among these nine scales. Similar analyses were conducted on the interscale correlations for the inpatient adolescent sample ($N = 770+$), resulting in findings that were similar to those for the adult sample. At the same time, additional analyses of the same SCL–90 data indicated that the SA–45 scales are statistically more distinct than those in the SCL–90 for both adults and adolescents; with one exception, the distinction between the SA–45 scales is equal to or better than that for the BSI for both age groups.

An instrument developed to assess the presence and/or intensity of normal personality or psychopathological constructs should yield results that differentiate groups with varying degrees of those constructs. In the case of psychiatric inpatients, one would expect them to report more severe symptomatology at the time of admission than at the time of discharge or several months thereafter. One also would expect nonpatients to report less symptomatology than psychiatric inpatients at the time of admission, and also to report a level of symptomatology that would be no more (and probably less) than inpatients at the time of their discharge and on postdischarge follow-up. Results reported by Davison et al. (1997) generally revealed the expected group differences for adults. The results were somewhat different for the male and female adolescent subsamples but generally supported the SA–45's ability to discriminate among groups of patients with different levels of symptom severity.

Related to the contrasted group comparisons is the SA–45's ability to accurately classify a respondent as belonging or not belonging to inpatient and nonpatient samples (i.e., sensitivity and specificity) using a single score or set of scores yielded by the instrument. In establishing cutoffs for maximized sensitivity and specificity, a 90% rate of correct classification of inpatients and nonpatients, respectively, was used in order to match the prevalence or base rate of inpatients within the total available sample. Preliminary findings reveal that the use of scores from a subset of the SA–45 scales in a derived logistic regression equation is superior to the GSI score alone for classification purposes. Analyses revealed relatively high sensitivity and specificity values for both adult gender samples, with the female values (.87 and .87, respectively) being somewhat higher than those for the males (.78 and .86, respectively) when optimized classification cutoffs are applied. For the two adolescent groups, the values for optimized classification showed a substantial drop, with the sensitivity and specificity values being .73 and .69, respectively, for the females and .57 and .68, respectively, for the males.

In order to cross-validate the item composition of the nine symptom domain scales, SA–45 item responses were extracted from SCL–90 intake data for four groups of psychiatric inpatients and submitted to the same cluster-analytic procedures used to derive the scales. The four samples consisted of 8,459 adults, 3,793 adolescents, 6,110 males, and 6,142 females. For each group, the number of correct classifications was as follows: 44 (98%) for the adult patient group; 32 (71%) for the adolescent patient group; and 43 (96%) for each of the male and female patient groups. Overall, the findings support the cluster solution originally derived for the SA–45. However, as has been found in other SA–45 investigations, the psychometric data for adolescents are not as strong as they are for adults.

Because the SA–45 items were derived from the SCL–90 in a manner that retained the structure and representativeness of the symptom domains of the parent instrument, the SA–45's scales and global indices should correlate highly with those of the SCL–90. In order to demonstrate this, the SCL–90 results of the adult and adolescent inpatient development samples were scored using standard SCL–90 scoring procedures and then rescored to obtain SA–45 data. The correlations between the scales and indices of the two instruments for these large samples of adult and adolescent inpatients generally were found to be .95 or higher. The notable exception is the correlation for the Psychoticism scale (.88–.90). These relatively low correlations are probably due to scale content differences. In considering these data, one should be mindful that the relationship between the two sets of scales was probably maximized owing to the fact that the SA–45 data were derived from the same SCL–90 data with which it was correlated.

With 35 of the SA–45's items being identical to items scored on the BSI, one would expect scales from these two brief symptom measures also to be highly correlated. Because all scored BSI items are contained in the SCL–90, scores for the nine BSI scales were derived from the SCL–90 data sets used for the SA–45 development. Results similar to those found for the SA–45/SCL–90 correlations were found for the SA–45/BSI correlations. Again, differences in content likely account for the relatively low correlation between the two Psychoticism scales, and the fact that SA–45 and BSI data were derived from the same SCL–90 data likely maximized the obtained correlations.

The SA–45's content validity can be examined through its item-total scale correlations. As indicated earlier, each of the SA–45 items demonstrates its strongest relationship with the scale to which it belongs. All of these correlations are higher than the .30–.50 range that Reynolds (1991) considered substantial when evaluating the content validity of an instrument. Two additional findings also support the content validity of the SA–45. First, the content of each scale's five items reflects symptoms that are pathognomonic or commonly associated with the broad group of disorders suggested by the scale's title. The possible exception lies with the Phobic Anxiety scale. Also, the high correlations between the SA–45 and SCL–90 scales and indices lend support for the content validity of the SA–45 for the purpose for which it was developed.

Comparability of the Stand-Alone and SCL–90-Extracted Versions of the SA–45

The majority of the data reported for the SA–45 were extracted from or based on SCL–90 data sets of adult and adolescent patient and nonpatient groups. Consequently, an important consideration in evaluating these data is the degree to which SA–45 results obtained from the administration of SA–45 items when presented by themselves are comparable to those that would be obtained if they were based on item responses given as part of an SCL–90 test administration.

One method of determining whether the "stand-alone" version and the SCL–90-extracted version of the SA–45 are comparable would be to examine the extent to which the psychometric characteristics of one version, derived from the results of one sample, are similar to those of the other version administered to a second sample from the same population. SAI used this approach because it had access to the first set of SA–45 stand-alone data on a large group of psychiatric inpatients being treated within the same hospital system from which the development and validation data were obtained. Despite the fact that the available data did not permit sample matching on the important demographic, diagnostic, and treatment variables, the data obtained from the administration of the stand-alone version yielded mean scale/index scores, interscale correlations, item-total scale correlations, and alpha coefficients that are quite consistent with those reported for the SCL–90-extracted version. However, caution in the use of the PST index is suggested, and results of the cluster analyses performed using stand-alone data were somewhat mixed, possibly owing to the particular sample used. Moreover, the alpha coefficients for nonpatient samples—particularly for the adolescent sample—generally were lower than those found using SCL–90-extracted data for similar samples. The reason for this is unclear, although the small size and/or particular composition of each of the two nonpatient samples may account for the differences.

Overall, preliminary comparisons of the SCL–90-extracted and stand-alone versions of the SA–45 support the comparability of the two versions, at least for adults. For adolescents, the initial findings suggest that the stand-alone version may not be as reliable as it is for adults. As with any other instrument for which an updated or alternate version has been developed, the exact degree of comparability of the stand-alone and SCL–90-extracted versions will become clear as the results of other investigations around this issue begin to appear in the professional literature.

Validity of the SA–45 in Primary Care Settings

Recently, a project designed to demonstrate the benefits of integrating behavioral health care services in primary medical care settings incorporated the use of the SA–45 with other measures. Preliminary data from this project (Goldstein & Maruish, 1997) provided an opportunity to further investigate the concurrent and construct validity of the SA–45 with a population of individuals seeking medical services in family practice setting. The participants for this investigation included 126 adults (18 years and older) seeking services at an outpatient family practice clinic. All were receiving services under capitated health care contracts, and all agreed to participate in a two-phase project designed to investigate the benefits of making available on-site psychological screening, consultation, and time-limited services in primary care settings.

Several instruments were selected for use in this study. However, for the purpose of this chapter, data from only three of the measures are presented. The first is the SA–45. The second is the SF–12 Health Survey (SF–12; Ware, Kosinski, & Keller, 1995), a 12-item abbreviated version of the SF–36 Health Survey (SF–36; Ware, Snow, Kosinski, & Gandek, 1993) developed to yield predicted T-scores for the SF–36 Mental Component Summary (MCS) and Physical Component Summary scales (PCS; Ware, Kosinski, & Keller, 1994). The third is a 6-item questionnaire on which the patient indicates his or her use of medical and psychiatric inpatient, outpatient, and emergency room services during the previous 3 months.

The SA–45 GSI, PST, and Somatization T-scores were correlated with the SF–12 T-scores for the Mental Component Summary (MCS–12) and Physical Component Summary scales (PCS–12; see Table 10.1). Correlations of the GSI with the MCS–12 and PCS–12 were both significant; however, as might be expected, the GSI/MCS–12 correlation (–.69) was greater than the GSI/PCS–12 correlation (–.27). Similar PST/MCS–12 and PST/PCS–12 correlations were found (–.64 and –.25, respectively). This same pattern of relationships between SA–45 and SF–12 variables was found in the correlations between the two SF–12 measures and (a) the number of SA–45 symptom domain scale scores greater than or equal to 60T (–.64 and –.21, respectively), and (b) the number of SA–45 symptom domain scale scores greater than or equal to 70T (–.43 and –.35, respectively). However, the reverse pattern was noted in the correlations between the T-scores of the SA–45 Somatization scale and each of MCS–12 and PCS–12 (–.25 and –.50, respectively). Note that all correlations were significant at the .01 level. Also, all correlations were negative because the SA–45 and SF–12 are keyed in opposite directions: High scores on the SF–12 indicate positive health status, whereas high SA–45 scores indicate increasing symptom severity.

Goldstein and Maruish (1997) also looked at the relationship between several SA–45 variables and medical and psychiatric resource utilization variables (see Table 10.2). Four different sets of comparisons were made. First, the average number of days/visits reported for those with a GSI T-score of 60 or greater was compared to that of those with a GSI T-score less than 60 on each of the three medical utilization variables and the three psychiatric utilization variables. This same type of comparison was then made for groups divided on the basis of (a) a PST T-score of 60 or greater, (b) one or more SA–45 symptom domain scales with a T-score of 60 or greater, and (c) two or more SA–45 symptom domain scales with a T-score of 60 or greater. In each of the four comparisons, the two groups differed significantly from each other (at at least $p < .05$) on the number of medical outpatient visits in the expected direction (e.g., patients with GSI ≥ 60 had more outpatient visits than those with GSI < 60). There were no significant group differences on any of the other five utilization variables.

TABLE 10.1
Intercorrelations of SA–45, SF–12, and Resource Utilization Variables

Variables	GSI	PST	Scales ≥60	Scales ≥70	SOM Scale
Positive Symptom Total	.97**				
SA–45 Somatization Scale	.70**	.66**			
Physical Component Scale	-.27**	-.25**	-.21**	-.35**	-.50**
Mental Component Scale	-.69**	-.64**	-.64**	-.43**	-.25**
Medical–Emergency Room	.02	.02	.03	-.08	.15
Medical–Hospitalization	-.05	-.07	-.08	-.05	.10
Medical–Outpatient	.31**	.29**	.33**	.38**	.21*
MH/SA–Emergency Room					
MH/SA–Hospitalization					
MH/SA–Outpatient	.00	-.01	.04	.11	-.01
Number of SA–45 Scales ≥60T	.89**	.85**			
Number of SA–45 Scales ≥70T	.58**	.47**			

*$p < .05$.
**$p < .01$.

TABLE 10.2
Mean Medical and Psychiatric Resource Utilization by SA-45 Symptom Domain Scale Elevations

Type of Service	GSI		PST		Symptom Domain Elevations ≥60T		Symptom Domain Elevations ≥60T	
	≥60	<60	≥60	<60	≥1	<1	≥2	<2
Medical—Emergency Room Visits	.06	.07	.07	.06	.08	.06	.08	.06
Medical—Hospitalization Days	.00	.15	.00	.15	.06	.19	.09	.15
Medical—Outpatient Visits	3.00	1.53*	2.94	1.52**	2.27	1.33*	2.39	1.46*
MH/SA—Emergency Room Visits	.00	.00	.00	.00	.00	.00	.00	.00
MH/SA—Hospitalization Days	.00	.00	.00	.00	.00	.00	.00	.00
MH/SA—Outpatient Visits	.56	.33	.44	.35	.35	.38	.36	.37

*$p < .05$.
**$p < .005$.

344

Basic Interpretive Strategy

The SA–45 was designed to serve as a measure of treatment outcome for psychiatric populations. It also can provide information that is important in identifying and monitoring significant psychological problems in primary care settings. However, one must be aware of the SA–45's limitations, particularly if it is used for diagnostic or treatment planning purposes. It is a brief instrument that is not inclusive of all possible psychiatric symptomatology. Thus, the SA–45 generally should be used as only one source of information about the patient. When combined with information obtained from other psychological tests, patient and collateral interviews, a review of medical records or other historical information, and/or (in some cases) medical/lab tests, the SA–45 can assist the clinician in screening for the need for behavioral health care services, arriving at a diagnosis, formulating a treatment plan, and monitoring patient progress during treatment. It also can serve as a tool for assessing the outcomes of behavioral health care interventions provided in the primary care setting.

Interpretation of an individual's SA–45 results begins with the assumption that the SA–45 is an appropriate instrument to administer to that individual. Factors related to the development of the SA–45 mandate that the instrument be administered only to those individuals who meet *all* of the following criteria:

- Are at least 13 years old.
- Read at the sixth-grade level or higher.
- Are not experiencing a level of distress or agitation that would likely impair their ability to indicate valid answers to all items. (Note that the SA–45 may be administered when an individual's distress has subsided to a level that will not interfere with his or her ability to provide an accurate assessment of current symptomatology.)

At the core of the SA–45 data are the area *T*-scores and percentiles derived from the nonpatient normative data for the 11 symptom domain scales and summary indices. The area *T*-score provides a measure that is useful in determining the presence of significant problem areas. Separate nonpatient norms are available for use with male and female adult and adolescent groups. As a general rule, an area *T*-score of 60 or greater on a given scale or index (i.e., one standard deviation above the nonpatient normative group's mean area *T*-score of 50) indicates a problem area warranting further investigation.

The SA–45 nonpatient percentiles can provide additional descriptive information. For example, an SA–45 percentile of 87 (i.e., 87th percentile) on the Depression scale means that 87% of the nonpatient age- and gender-matched normative sample obtained a score equal to or lower than that of the respondent. Conversely, it also means that only 13% of that same nonpatient normative sample scored higher.

With an understanding of this basic information, a four-step approach to the interpretation of the SA–45 is recommended for use in the primary care setting.

Step 1: Assess the General Validity of the Results. The nature of the SA–45 and other symptom checklists — "obvious" items with no "subtle" items — makes it relatively easy for the respondent to overreport ("fake bad") or underreport ("fake good") the presence of symptoms to just about any desired degree. And, like many symptom checklists, there currently are no empirically derived special scales or indices to detect the validity of the test taker's responses to the SA–45 items. However, on a rational basis, the presence of any of the following conditions should lead one to question the validity of SA–45 results:

• Unusually quick completion time. Three minutes, that is, an average time of 4 sec to read and respond to each of the 45 items, can probably serve as a useful, minimum completion time for the SA–45. Thus, completion of the instrument in less than 3 min suggests that the respondent likely has not carefully attended and/or responded to the SA–45 items.

• Unusually slow completion time. An SA–45 completion time of 30 min or more is much longer than is generally encountered in clinical settings. Long completion times may be the result of any of several factors, such as poor reading skills, obsessive rumination about the meaning of specific items and/or how to respond to them, or poor concentration, any of which may have interfered with the respondent's ability to accurately report how frequently they have recently experienced the listed psychological symptoms. Thus, completion of the instrument in more than 30 min should lead one to at least question whether the patient is capable of providing an accurate assessment of his or her symptoms.

• Missing items. The SA–45 *Technical Manual* (SAI, 1998) provides instructions for correcting (a) the raw score of any of the nine symptom domain scales for which only one response to that scale's five items is missing, (b) the PST raw score when 10 or fewer of the 45 responses are missing, and (c) the GSI raw score when 11 or less of the 45 responses are missing. Otherwise, depending on the number and scales to which the missing items belong, relevant symptom domain scales, the PST, and/or the GSI should not be interpreted.

• Patterned responding. Visual inspection of the SA–45 answer form or computer-generated report may reveal that the test taker entered their responses in a questionable manner. On the one hand, it would seem highly unlikely — particularly when the SA–45 is administered because of a care provider's suspicions — that a person would experience each of the SA–45 symptoms to the same degree during the past 7 days. On the other hand, consider the type of patterned responding in which the sequence of responses, beginning with item 1, was 1, 2, 3, 4, 5, 4, 3, 2, 1, 2 and so on, or was 1, 2, 1, 2, 1, 2 and so on, or something similar, through item 45. The probability that valid responding would yield these types of response patterns would seem to be very low. Their presence therefore should lead one to question the validity of the obtained profile.

• Results inconsistent with presentation. Other causes for concern are SA–45 profiles that appear inconsistent with the respondent's clinical presentation or with other evaluation data (e.g., results from other abnormal personality measures, currently taking antidepressant medication). For example, it would be highly unlikely that a suicidal person taking the SA–45 would obtain a profile in which *all* area *T*-scores — especially that for Depression — are below 60 (i.e., indicating no significant psychological distress). Similarly, it is improbable that a high-functioning chief executive officer (CEO) of a large corporation would obtain a profile in which the *T*-score for every scale and index is elevated above 70*T*.

Step 2: Evaluate Overall Level of Symptom Distress.   Assuming a valid profile, begin the interpretation of SA–45 results with an evaluation of the respondent's overall level of symptom distress or disturbance by noting the nonpatient area *T*-scores and percentiles for both the PST index and GSI. Each is a measure of the respondent's overall level of distress and disturbance: one through a count of the number of symptoms reported to have been present to any degree during the previous seven days (PST), and the other through the overall intensity level of the 45 listed symptoms (GSI). A nonpatient, norms-based GSI and/or PST area T-score of 60 or higher, or a percentile of 84 or higher, suggests that the number of symptoms the respondent is reporting (PST) and/or the intensity at which he or she is experiencing them (GSI) is significant and warrants further investigation. The investigation may take the form of a psychosocial or diagnostic interview with the respondent, collateral interviews, more extensive psychological testing, medical/lab tests, or a combination of approaches. In interpreting percentiles, one must keep in mind that an SA–45 percentile equivalent indicates the percentage of the normative sample who obtained a score equal to or lower than that score.

Step 3: Evaluate Area **T-Scores** *and Percentiles for the Nine Symptom Domain Scales.* The next step involves the examination of the nonpatient area T-scores and percentiles for each of the symptom domain scales. Scale elevations based on nonpatient norms, viewed either alone or in comparison with other scales, can be useful in identifying more specifically the problem areas that are present and that have contributed to any elevation on either or both the GSI and PST indices. Scale elevations also can help in the development of a treatment plan. Again, a symptom domain scale area T-score of 60 or higher, or a percentile of 84 or higher based on nonpatient norms, suggests a likely problem area and the need for further investigation.

In evaluating scale elevations, it is important to know exactly what each scale is assessing. Following is a summary of the content of each of the nine symptom domain scales.

Anxiety (ANX). Items from this scale inquire about symptoms related to fearfulness, panic, tension, and restlessness.

Depression (DEP). This scale consists of items asking about recent experiences with feelings of loneliness, hopelessness, and worthlessness. Other symptoms that are assessed include a loss of interest in things and feeling blue.

Hostility (HOS). A number of hostility-related symptoms are found on this scale. They include having uncontrollable temper outbursts, getting into frequent arguments, shouting, and feeling urges to harm others or to break things.

Interpersonal Sensitivity (INT). The respondent's symptomatic feelings about himself or herself in relation to others are assessed here. These include feeling inferior or self-conscious around others, feeling that others are unsympathetic or unfriendly, and feeling uneasy when others are talking with or watching the respondent.

Obsessive-Compulsive (OC). Difficulty in concentrating or making decisions, repetitive checking or doing tasks slowly to ensure correctness, and problems with one's mind "going blank" are obsessive-compulsive symptoms presented on this scale.

Paranoid Ideation (PAR). Some of the subtler forms of paranoid thinking are assessed on this scale, such as feeling that others take advantage of the respondent, cannot be trusted, are responsible for his or her troubles, fail to give credit for his or her achievements, and watch or talk about him or her.

Phobic Anxiety (PHO). On this scale, the respondent is asked to rate his or her recent experiences with fear or uneasiness when being in open spaces and crowds, using public transportation, and leaving home alone. Avoidance of specific places, things, and activities also is asked about.

Psychoticism (PSY). A number of symptoms of disordered thinking are queried here. These include auditory hallucinations, feelings that others know or are controlling one's thinking, and ideas that one should be punished for his or her sins.

Somatization (SOM). The presence of rather vague physical symptoms is assessed here, including hot or cold spells and feelings of numbness, soreness, tingling, and heaviness in various parts of the body.

Step 4: Evaluate Individual Item Responses. Evaluation of the domain scale scores should be followed by an examination of the individual items to which the respondent indicated a response other than "Not at all." This, along with scale composition information from the *Technical Manual* (SAI, 1998), will one enable one to determine which symptoms reported on the SA–45 contribute to each scale's overall score. In evaluating individual item responses, one will also obtain a more detailed picture of current symptoms, which can assist in developing specific goals for therapeutic work (if needed).

Individual item responses warrant special scrutiny in those cases in which the only "significant" scale elevations are either at or only slightly above a T-score of 60. This is particularly important if the results are being used to screen for or otherwise classify individuals as having psychological problems that require further evaluation. The metrics of the SA–45 are such that the report of relatively minor problems can result in these types of mild elevations on some of the scales. For example, a raw score of 8 on the Anxiety scale is transformed to an area T-score of 60 for adult males. Although the raw score indicates that the test taker may have responded "A little bit" to three of the five Anxiety scale items (and "Not at all" to the other two Anxiety scale items), identification of individuals with a relatively mild symptoms may not be of concern to the clinician. However, the individual who obtains an Anxiety scale raw score of 8 by indicating that he or she has been bothered "Quite a bit" by "Spells of terror and panic" during the past 7 days (and "Not at all" to the other four Anxiety scale items) would probably be an appropriate candidate for further evaluation or classification.

GENERAL CONSIDERATIONS FOR USE OF THE SA–45 IN PRIMARY CARE SETTINGS

The SA–45 was developed to serve as a brief, cost-effective instrument for measuring one aspect of the impact or effectiveness of the treatment (i.e., symptomatic improvement) in individual facilities and programs within a large behavioral health care provider organization. As such, it was primarily intended to be a low-burden tool for gathering a large amount of data during a given time period (e.g., monthly, quarterly), which later would be analyzed in aggregate form. However, with the demonstration of its psychometric integrity, the SA–45's potential as a real-time, clinical decision-making tool quickly became apparent. Although the SA–45 is a relatively straightforward instrument, using it as a clinical tool (as opposed to a performance measurement data-gathering tool) demands more in terms of both the knowledge of the instrument and how it can and cannot be used in the assessment and treatment of individual patients. This is the case regardless of the setting in which it is used or the professional who has integrated it into his or her armamentarium of assessment tools.

The prevalence of behavioral healthcare problems in primary care settings, the costs they impose on the health care system, the need for more effective means of identifying them, and the movement toward the integration of primary and behavioral health care services all have been discussed in earlier chapters of this volume. Psychologists and certain other trained behavioral health care professionals who consult with or have been integrated into primary care practices likely have the necessary training to use the SA–45 for clinical purposes already. However, with training, education such as that provided in the SA–45 *Technical Manual* (SAI, 1998) and this chapter, and/or supervised experience, other health care professionals — primary care physicians, physician assistants, social workers, nurse practitioners, and so forth — can gain the knowledge and skills that will enable them to use the SA–45 appropriately. As with any instrument that assesses abnormal personality or psychiatric symptomatology, a working knowledge of psychopathology obtained from formal or informal training is, of course, required for anyone using the SA–45 for clinical decision making.

This author recognizes that in integrated primary behavioral health care systems, primary medical care providers may be just as likely to treat certain types of psychological problems or disorders as behavioral health care professionals. Consequently, the diversity of medical and behavioral health care professionals who might employ the SA–45 in primary care settings has been considered during the development of the remainder of this chapter. Use of the term *primary/behavioral health care provider* acknowledges this diversity and implies no assumptions about the reader's profession; however, it does assume the possession of the previously specified qualifications for employing the SA–45 for clinical decision making.

USE OF THE SA–45 AS A SCREENER

One way in which psychological assessment can contribute to the development of an efficient integrated system of primary and behavioral health care is by using it to screen potential patients to determine the need for behavioral health care treatment, and/or to determine the likelihood that the problem being screened for is a particular disorder of interest. One of the most concise, informative treatments of the topic of the use of psychological tests in screening for behavioral health disorders is provided by Derogatis and DellaPietra (1994). In this work, these authors turned to the Commission on Chronic Illness (1987) to provide a good working definition of health care screening in general, that being

> the presumptive identification of unrecognized disease or defect by the application of tests, examinations or other procedures which can be applied rapidly to sort out apparently well persons who probably have a disease from those who probably do not. (p. 45)

Derogatis and DellaPietra (1994) further clarified the nature and the use of screening procedures, stating that

> the screening process represents a relatively unrefined sieve that is designed to segregate the cohort under assessment into "positives" who presumably have the condition, and "negatives" who are ostensibly free of the disorder. Screening is not a diagnostic procedure per se. Rather, it represents a preliminary filtering operation that identifies those individuals with the highest probability of having the disorder in question for subsequent specific diagnostic evaluation. Individuals found negative by the screening process are not evaluated further. (p. 23)

The most commonly used screeners in daily clinical practice are those designed to identify some specific aspect of psychological functioning or disturbance, or to provide a broad overview of the respondent's point-in-time mental status. The multidimensional nature of the SA–45 allows it to serve as a screener for both specific and more generalized psychopathology or distress.

Relevant Psychometric Support

The preceding section of this chapter provides an overview of the psychometric properties of the SA–45, including preliminary data supporting the validity of the instrument in primary care settings. Other data lend further support for use of the instrument for screening purposes in these settings.

Relevant Normative Data. Among the analyses performed by Goldstein and Maruish (1997) on their primary care data set were basic but important descriptive statistics. As shown in Table 10.3, all T-scores for the 11 SA–45 scales and indices fell within one standard deviation of the nonpatient normative sample mean. However, a wide degree of variability on these measures is indicated by the T-score standard deviations and ranges for each of the 11 measures. These data are not unexpected, given the prevalence of psychosocial distress or disorders that has been reported in primary care settings (see chap. 1 of this volume). That is, one would anticipate that a substantial portion of the primary care population would report the presence of symptoms suggestive of psychological distress or disturbance.

TABLE 10.3
SA–45 Scale and Index Mean T-Scores, Standard Deviations,
and T-Score Ranges for a Primary Care Sample

SA–45 Variables	N	Mean	SD	Range
Anxiety	126	54.56	7.82	44–81
Depression	125	53.05	6.64	47–74
Obsessive-Compulsive	126	51.52	7.63	42–72
Somatization	126	54.37	7.09	41–74
Phobia	126	59.32	2.89	51–74
Hostility	126	55.68	5.46	43–88
Interpersonal Sensitivity	125	52.05	5.45	38–73
Paranoid Thinking	126	51.20	7.35	39–76
Psychoticism	126	59.26	2.57	48–68
Positive Symptom Total	126	48.78	9.43	35–72
Global Severity Index	126	49.21	8.97	37–71

Of particular note are the relatively high mean area T-scores on the Phobia and Psychoticism scales (59.32 and 59.26, respectively) in Table 10.3. These probably reflect the structure of the norms tables for these scales: Endorsement of the presence of only one of either scale's five items to even the least degree ("A little bit") results in a T-score greater than 60 — the score range suggesting the need for further evaluation. Thus, a mildly elevated score on these or the other SA–45 symptom domain scales reinforces the importance of conducting the item analysis recommended in Step 4 of the four-step approach to interpretation presented earlier.

Consistency With DSM–IV and ICD–9 Criteria. The SA–45 was designed primarily to provide a brief, broad measure of a respondent's point-in-time level of psychological distress. Although providing information that may be useful in assigning a diagnosis, neither the items nor the results from the SA–45 were ever intended to be all-inclusive, or even necessarily consistent with any psychiatric classification system. Any attempt to achieve this consistency would result in a much lengthier, less efficient instrument.

Diagnostic Efficiency Statistics. An important aspect of any screening procedure is the efficiency with which it can provide information useful to clinical decision making. The power or utility of a psychological screener lies in its ability to determine, with a high level of probability, whether the respondent does or does not have a particular disorder or condition, or whether he or she is or is not a member of a group with clearly defined characteristics.

As part of its development (see SAI, 1998), an investigation was conducted to determine the SA–45's ability to accurately classify a respondent as belonging or not belonging to inpatient psychiatric and nonpatient samples (i.e., sensitivity and specificity, respectively) using a single score or set of scores yielded by the instrument. In establishing cutoffs for maximized sensitivity and specificity, a 90% rate of correct classification of inpatients and nonpatients, respectively, was used in order to match the prevalence or base rate of inpatients within the total available sample. Preliminary findings reveal that the use of scores from a subset of the SA–45 scales in a derived logistic regression equation is superior to the GSI score (i.e., a general measure of psychological distress or disturbance) alone for classification purposes. Analyses revealed relatively high sensitivity and specificity values for both adult gender samples, with the female values (.87 and .87, respectively) being somewhat higher than those for the males (.78 and .86, respectively) when optimized classification cutoffs were applied. For the two adolescent groups, the values for optimized classification showed a substantial drop, with the sensitivity and specificity values being 0.73 and 0.69, respectively, for the females and 0.57 and 0.68, respectively, for the males.

Other Supportive Data. Unfortunately, the reported efficiency statistics do not apply directly to the use of the SA–45 for discriminating those likely to need behavioral health intervention from those who likely do not. In addition, only the Goldstein and Maruish (1997) study provides data derived from a primary care sample — and these data are preliminary. However, the Goldstein and Maruish data do offer indirect support for the sensitivity of SA–45 in primary care settings. First, in looking at the sample in terms of whether they reported significant levels of distress on the symptom domain scales ($T \geq 60$), 46.8% were found to have one or more significantly elevated scales. This is consistent with the prevalence rates of psychosocial distress in primary care patients reported in some of the literature (see Maruish, 1999), lending indirect supportive evidence regarding the sensitivity of the SA–45 to psychological problems in this population.

Further indirect evidence of the SA–45's sensitivity was found in Goldstein and Maruish's (1997) comparison of the 3-month outpatient medical resource utilization of those primary care patients with (a) one or more significantly elevated symptom domain scales, and (b) two or more significantly elevated symptom domain scales, to the utilization of those who did not meet these respective criteria. The results revealed that the group with one or more elevated scales and the group with two or more elevated scales each had a significantly higher number of mean medical outpatient visits during the previous 3 months than their respective comparison groups. This is consistent with literature reporting the high resource utilization among those with behavioral health problems.

Implementation

In general, a couple of different tacks can be taken in implementing the SA–45 in the primary care setting. One involves the primary/behavioral health care provider using it as just another lab test or procedure, ordering it on an as-needed basis. Another approach is more systematic. Here, the SA–45 may be applied to all patients upon their first visit to the primary/behavioral health care provider and/or on a scheduled basis thereafter (e.g., yearly), regardless of the patient's primary complaint. Note that this latter approach does not preclude having the patient complete the instrument at other times either to regularly monitor progress during an episode of care, or on suspicion of developing psychological problems during the same or another episode of care.

Notwithstanding, successfully integrating the SA–45 into the primary/behavioral health care provider's psychological tests and procedures requires the type of work flow analysis and implementation planning that has been described in other chapters of this book. In addition, administration of the SA–45 or any other self-report measure, particularly in busy primary care practices, can be difficult from the standpoints of staff time, patient cooperation, and surrounding distractions. Moreover, there are other issues to be considered depending on the particular SA–45 administration and scoring format that will be applied. With the InfiniFax fax-in/fax-back version, immediate availability of a fax machine and communications line may be problematic. The PsychManager desktop computer version requires the availability of a personal computer for administration and/or scoring of the SA–45. Staff training and availability can be especially problematic in offices that opt to forgo automated scoring and reporting for the QuikScore hand-scored version of the SA–45.

Another important factor that must be considered is how the SA–45 should be used in the screening process. Should it be used by itself, or should it be used with one or more other psychological measures? The answer to that depends on a number of factors.

Use as a Stand-Alone Instrument. The SA–45 can provide a quick, high-level snapshot of the respondent's current level of distress. Its brevity, ease of use, low cost, and options for immediate scoring and reporting make it one of the most cost-effective and efficient means of screening for the presence of significant psychological disturbance in both psychiatric and nonpsychiatric settings. SA–45 results are not intended, nor should they ever be used, for assigning diagnoses or making definitive statements about the presence of significant psychological disturbance in the absence of additional, supporting information from other sources. At best, the results should be used to determine the likelihood that such disturbance is or is not present and to help guide the primary/behavioral health care provider's decision about whether to seek confirmatory evidence via clinical and/or collateral interview, further testing, referral for behavioral health consultation, or other sources.

Use With Other Instruments and Procedures.   The SA–45 is an abbreviated version of the original SCL–90 consisting of items selected for their ability to mirror the nine symptom domains of the parent instrument. Thus, it is limited in its ability to detect the presence or absence of symptoms that are not represented by the five items in each of the nine symptom domain scales. Consequently, it cannot be used to provide a comprehensive, detailed assessment of the psychological status of the test taker. Moreover, the manner and purpose for which the SA–45 was developed poses additional limitations to its use for treatment planning purposes. Like many other "abnormal personality" instruments, the SA–45 does not yield information relevant to psychological strengths or assets that can be used by the patient during therapeutic intervention.

As noted earlier, the SA–45 can be useful in the screening process, but only if it is used in conjunction with other sources of information (e.g., interview and collateral data, behavioral observations, information from medical records, other medical or psychological test data). On the one hand, it may serve as a source of hypotheses about patient needs and resources that should be verified by data from other sources. For example, a significantly elevated Anxiety scale area T-score ($T > 59$) obtained from the routine administration of SA–45 at intake should *not* lead to the assignment of an anxiety disorder diagnosis. Rather, it should lead the primary/behavioral health care provider to further evaluate the *possibility* of the presence of such a disorder and the need for treatment targeted at the alleviation of anxious symptomatology. Similarly, although a Depression scale area T-score less than 60 suggests that the respondent probably is not depressed, this factor by itself should not completely rule out the presence of depression, particularly if there is evidence to the contrary (e.g., clinical presentation).

Conversely, SA–45 results can be a source of confirmatory information for hypotheses generated by other means. For example, a primary/behavioral health care provider might use the SA–45 results to validate the results of another instrument or impressions of a patient derived from a clinical interview. Here, the SA–45 can provide data that may help verify impressions about the presence or absence of significant psychological distress or domain-specific symptomatology, and/or the level at which one or both are being experienced by the respondent.

Ficken (1995) provided an example of how the use of two screeners can be integrated into an assessment system designed to assist primary care providers in identifying patients with psychiatric disorders. Implementation of this system begins with the administration of a screener that is highly sensitive and specific to *DSM*- or *ICD*-related disorders. Ficken felt that these screeners should require no more than 10 min to complete, and "their administration must be integrated seamlessly into the standard clinical routine" (p. 13). Somewhat similar to the sequence describe by Derogatis and DellaPietra (1994), positive findings would lead to a second level of testing. Here, another screener that meets the same requirements as those for the first screener and also affirms or rules out a diagnosis would be administered. Positive findings would lead to additional assessment for treatment planning purposes. Consistent with standard practice, Ficken recommended confirmation of screener findings by a qualified psychologist. However, other health care professionals with the previously specified qualifications would also seem to have the necessary credentials for this task.

Potential Implementation Issues.   The utility of the SA–45 or any screening instrument is only as good as the degree to which it can be integrated into the primary care practice's daily regimen of service delivery. This, in turn, depends on a number of factors. The first is the degree to which the administration and scoring of the screener is quick and easy, and the amount of time required to train the primary/behavioral health care provider's staff to successfully incorporate the screener into the daily work flow.

The second factor relates to the instrument's use. Generally, screeners are developed to assist in determining the likelihood that the patient does or does not have the specific condition or characteristic the instrument is designed to identify. Use for any other purpose (e.g., assigning a diagnosis based solely on SA–45 results, determining the likelihood of the presence of other characteristics) only serves to undermine the integrity of the instrument in the eyes of staff, payers, and other parties with a vested interest in the screening process.

The third factor has to do with the ability of the primary/behavioral health care provider to act on the information obtained from the screener. It must be clear how they should proceed based on the information available.

The final factor is staff acceptance and commitment to the screening process. This comes only with a clear understanding of the importance of the screening, the usefulness of the obtained information, and how the screening process is to be incorporated into the daily work flow of the primary care practice.

Guidelines for Decision Making

The SA–45 can provide managed care organizations (MCOs) and their primary and behavioral health care providers with an efficient means of gauging a patient's overall level of distress and likely presence of disturbance in specific domains of symptomatology. This information can help determine the need for behavioral health care intervention, the appropriate kind or level of that intervention, and the patient's ability or willingness to profit from treatment.

Determining Need for Behavioral Health Intervention.   The SA–45 can assist in addressing level-of-care issues in two ways. First, it can help the primary/behavioral health care provider determine if the respondent's overall level of psychiatric distress or disturbance and/or level of domain-specific symptomatology are significant enough to warrant further evaluation and/or the need for behavioral health care services. When employed this way, the SA–45 is being used as a screener. As previously noted, a *T*-score of 60 or greater on either of the two summary indices (GSI and PST) or one or more of the nine symptom domain scales should prompt the clinician to consider this option.

Determining Appropriate Treatment.   The primary/behavioral health care provider also may find the tables and formulas for calculating SA–45 base rate-adjusted PPP and NPP statistics presented in the *Technical Manual* (SAI, 1998) useful in discriminating those who may be in need of inpatient psychiatric services from those not in need of any services. Because outpatient psychiatric normative data are not yet available, the information provided in the *Technical Manual* cannot assist in discriminating the likely need for inpatient versus outpatient services, nor the need for outpatient versus no services. Regardless, these statistics may provide clues to the appropriate level of care for individuals presenting with a wide range of psychological problems.

Similarly, the SA–45 may be useful in determining the appropriateness of certain adjuncts to care provided to psychiatric patients, including the use of psychotropic medication. Although there have been no studies designed to determine whether specific SA–45 indicators for the appropriateness of medication exist, the nonpatient normative data for the nine symptom domain scales may provide some direction. For example, a Depression scale area T-score of 70 or greater (based on nonpatient norms) indicates that 95% of the relevant age- and gender-specific normative group achieved a Depression scale score that was at or below the level achieved by the respondent. Conversely, only 5% of the normative group scored higher. Intuitively, this level of endorsement of the content of this scale—recent experiences with feelings of depression, loneliness, hopelessness and worthlessness, and a loss of interest in things—would suggest the presence of a condition that might benefit from the addition of antidepressant medication to the therapeutic regimen. Similarly, significantly high elevations on other SA–45 symptom domain scales (e.g., Anxiety, Psychoticism) should lead one to consider the use of other appropriate types of medications (e.g., antianxiety agents, major tranquilizers) as therapeutic adjuncts.

Determining Potential Treatment Problems. The treatment planning process assumes that the individual being seen in the primary care setting is experiencing one or more problems of sufficient concern to warrant their seeking help to ameliorate the problem(s), regardless of whether the presenting problem or its origin is organically or psychologically based. Interpretation of SA–45 results in the manner just described can assist the primary/behavioral health care provider in quickly determining if indeed there is a significant problem warranting a course of psychological/psychiatric intervention in addition to or in place of medical treatment.

Unfortunately, there are no specific SA–45 scales or indices that provide a direct measure of a respondent's ability or willingness to participate in medical or behavioral health treatment. However, there are a few indicators that can be derived from the administration of the test and that, if present, may suggest potential problems in engaging the patient in the therapeutic endeavor. One is the patient's overt reaction to the request to complete the SA–45. Because the test is relatively brief and contains straightforward items, the demands on the test taker are minimal. Complaints about item relevance or the time required to complete the instrument, failure to respond to several items, or any other negative reaction or form of resistance might be predictive of problems in eliciting the patient's full cooperation during more extensive evaluation and/or treatment. For the primary/behavioral health care provider, this may have implications regarding the likelihood of the patient benefiting from medical or behavioral health treatment.

In addition, for the treating behavioral health clinician, it may have implications for the approach taken with the patient (e.g., direct vs. indirect, behavioral vs. cognitive) and itself may become grist for the therapeutic mill. Moreover, a significantly elevated score on any of the Interpersonal Sensitivity, Hostility, and Paranoid Ideation scales may signal potential problems in forming a therapeutic bond. Additional effort in establishing rapport with patients such as these may be required if one is to expect meaningful therapeutic progress.

Prediction of Treatment Outcome. At the time of the writing of this chapter, no formal studies investigating the SA–45's ability to predict the outcome of behavioral health care intervention with effected primary care patients have been completed. However, as part of the project reported on by Goldstein and Maruish (1997), the investigators plan to investigate whether SA–45 results obtained on initial screening—either alone or with other variables (e.g., SF–12, client characteristics)—can be used to predict posttermination level of distress, psychological or medical resource utilization, or service satisfaction.

Provision of Feedback to the Patient

Providing patients with feedback about their test results is good practice. For psychologists, it also is now a requirement specified in the American Psychological Association's *Ethical Principles* (1992). According to Ethical Standard 2.09, "psychologists ensure that an explanation of the results is provided using language that is reasonably understandable to the person assessed or to another legally authorized person on behalf of the client" (p. 8).

The presentation of the results via the SA–45 profile allows the patient to easily see potential problem areas and his or her overall level of psychological distress in relation to age- and gender-appropriate reference groups. Finn and his associates (Finn, 1996a, 1996b; Finn & Martin, 1997; Finn & Tonsager, 1992) developed an excellent framework for providing feedback of the results of multidimensional instruments. Employing Finn's "therapeutic assessment" approach when providing the patient with feedback about his or her SA–45 results potentially has the additional benefit of turning the feedback session into a therapeutic intervention. It is the recommended approach for behavioral health care professionals when providing SA–45 feedback. Assuming a similar knowledge and skill level, it is also recommended for medical professionals in the primary care setting; otherwise, a more straightforward approach should be taken.

USE OF THE SA–45 FOR TREATMENT MONITORING

Planning a course of health care treatment does not end with the initiation of the therapeutic intervention. Verification of the appropriateness of the patient's individualized treatment regimen over time is required to ensure that what was initially thought to be "the best approach" continues to be just that. Periodic assessment of the patient's progress toward the achievement of established treatment goals is an important part of the verification process. Treatment planning also involves the modification of the prescribed treatment (if necessary) to maximize the patient's chances of achieving the established goals. In some cases, it also may involve modification of the goals themselves. Thus, monitoring patient progress during the episode of care is critical to the success of any therapeutic endeavor.

Treatment progress monitoring of both medical and behavioral health care patients is frequently conducted on an informal basis. Based on their impressions, care providers typically evaluate and document the patient's progress after each treatment intervention. Impressionistic evaluation of the patient (i.e., "clinical judgment") certainly is one means of gauging patient progress. However, the subjective nature of this process limits its utility, particularly for tracking patients over extended periods of time. Clinical judgment does not permit close comparison with normative referents, nor does it lend itself well to the statistical analysis needed to determine if changes are "significant." However, primary/behavioral health care providers now are beginning to move toward more structured means of tracking patient improvement over time. The brevity and content of the SA–45, along with its normative data and known psychometric properties, make it an ideal instrument to use for treatment monitoring in primary care settings. It can provide a sound, defensible means of measuring improvement, stagnation, or deterioration of general and domain-specific psychological disturbance as the patient progresses during the episode of care.

General Considerations

Monitoring changes in the level of psychological distress or disturbance should begin with the administration of the SA–45 at the time of treatment initiation. This will serve as the baseline against which the patient's status may be compared at any time thereafter. Although baseline measurement can be taken at any point during the episode of care, administering the SA–45 at the beginning of treatment has the added benefit of providing data for treatment planning purposes as described earlier. (In most cases, the results of an SA–45 administered for screening purposes by the primary/behavioral health care provider can be the best baseline measure of symptom status.) A decrease in the area T-score(s) of the GSI, PST, and/or relevant symptom domain indices and scales from one point in time to another would suggest that prescribed treatment is having a positive effect, and supports the continuation of the prescribed treatment. No change or an increase in relevant area T-scores would suggest that the patient's condition has not improved or has deteriorated. Assuming that symptomatic improvement should have taken place during the interval of time between testings, an evaluation of the appropriateness of the treatment would be warranted.

Relevant Psychometric Support

The SA–45 is a relatively new instrument; consequently, it cannot draw on the type of empirical support that typically accompanies more established instruments. However, data obtained during its development are relevant to its use as a treatment monitoring and outcomes measure, regardless of the setting in which it is administered. First, there are the test–retest reliability coefficients obtained from adult and adolescent nonpatient samples. Recall that adult raw score-based correlations generally were found to be in the .80 range, with the exceptions being Somatization scale (.69) and Anxiety scale (.42). This possibly was due to the fact that some of the items on each of these scales may be sensitive to variations in normal, everyday experiences. For adolescents, the raw score-based correlations are more variable, ranging from .51 for the Hostility scale to .85 for the Psychoticism scale. Somewhat similar to the adult findings, the Anxiety scale coefficient (.58) is the next to the lowest of the coefficients for adolescents. Thus, factors unrelated to treatment may influence the results on certain SA–45 scales from one point in time to another. At the same time, employing statistically sound methods such as the Reliable Change (RC) index (which takes into account the reliability of the scale or index; see later discussion) should lessen one's concern about use of the less reliable SAI scales.

In addition, Davison et al. (1997) compared the SA–45 scores of gender- and age-matched nonpatient and three psychiatric inpatient groups assessed at three points in time (intake, discharge, and 6-month follow-up). Generally, the findings were as one would hypothesize for an instrument designed to be sensitive to changes in level of psychological distress: The scores of patients at intake were greater than those at discharge, which, in turn, were greater than those at follow-up. Also, scores for the nonpatients were lower than those of all patient groups. There were some exceptions to this trend, particularly among the adolescent groups. This is consistent with other findings that suggest that the SA–45 is more sensitive to changes in the psychological status of adults than those of adolescents.

Implementation Issues

The use of the SA–45 for treatment monitoring may present challenges to many busy primary care practices — ones that are different from those that may arise when it is used for screening or outcomes assessment purposes. Perhaps the most significant challenges are (a) integrating the monitoring process into the work flow of the practice, (b) eliciting patient cooperation for repeated testing, and (c) determining how often to monitor patient progress.

Integration of Monitoring Into the Daily Work Flow. The busier the practice, the more difficult will be the integration of readministrations of the SA–45 into the daily office work flow. In fact, integrating a process for retesting patients may be even more difficult than integrating the administration of the SA–45 as an initial screening tool as a routine office procedure. Screening via the SA–45 or similar tests may become routine with new patients, or with existing patients according to a standard schedule (e.g., as part of a yearly health status assessment). Monitoring, however, is more likely to be sporadic and unpredictable. Consequently, the cooperation of the staff responsible for the administration and scoring of the test must be elicited in order to ensure that scheduled or on-request readministrations are completed in a smooth and timely fashion.

The importance of the primary care administrative/clerical staff's cooperation cannot be stressed enough. Staff buy-in to any system of psychological assessment is critical to the success of the system. Eliciting staff cooperation can be facilitated by explaining the value of the SA–45 in primary care practices, providing adequate training for the administration and scoring of instrument through whichever format the practice is using (i.e., fax, desktop computer, or hand scoring), and establishing priorities and procedures for ensuring that administering and scoring the test takes place with a minimum of disruption to the patient's and the staff's normal daily routine.

Eliciting Patient Cooperation. As in traditional behavioral health care settings, some primary care patients will be resistant to readministration of the SA–45 and similar types of psychological tests. The reasons for this resistance can be quite varied, ranging from a reluctance to having to disclose psychological problems once again, to being pressed for time by other commitments. Resistance to retesting may be particularly strong in patients who refuse to accept any psychological explanation for the symptoms they present.

Overcoming patience resistance to retesting may be difficult, and there are no clear-cut solutions to the problem. However, the probability of the primary/behavioral health care provider overcoming the patience's resistance or refusal sometimes may be increased by presenting the SA–45 as just another type of "lab test" that will yield additional information about the effectiveness of the treatment being offered. In other instances, cooperation might be easily elicited if the patient's real concern about retaking the SA–45 is identified and dealt with in a manner that is satisfactory to the patient. Thus, at the very least, the primary/behavioral health care provider should discuss resistance with the patient whenever it occurs.

Determining How Often to Monitor. The frequency at which one might use the SA–45 to monitor the psychological status of the patient is dependent on several factors. The first is the instrument itself. The demands of the SA–45 require the respondent to indicate, on a 5-point scale, "how much [each of the 45 listed symptoms] has bothered or distressed you during the past 7 days, including today." Responses elicited during a readministration that occurs less than 7 days after the first administration would include the patient's consideration of some portion of his or her status during the previously considered time period. This may make interpretation of the change in symptom status (if any) from one administration to another difficult if not impossible. Thus, it is recommended that the SA–45 not be readministered for at least 7 days.

Another consideration is the anticipated length of treatment. If the primary/behavioral health care provider expects that an episode of care will be relatively short, multiple administrations of the SA–45 may be of little value from a monitoring standpoint. For example, limitations in a patient's health care plan may mean that the patient cannot or will not be seen for behavioral health intervention after 10 visits, or it may be obvious that the presenting problem is, by its nature, likely to be time limited (e.g., bereavement after the death of a family member). In cases such as these, one may wish to monitor the patient only once or twice during the anticipated course of treatment to ensure that he or she is on track for the expected degree of psychological improvement, given the brevity of the intervention. On the other hand, the primary/behavioral health care provider may wish to plan for more regular and frequent readministrations of the SA–45 (e.g., bimonthly) to those who likely will be followed on a long-term basis (e.g., primary care patients who also are bipolar or personality-disordered).

Variables directly related to the patient may have some bearing on the frequency at which retesting should occur. It is probably safe to say that the chance of obtaining valid results from patients displaying resistance to medical or behavioral treatment in general, or to completing the SA–45 in particular, is inversely related to the frequency at which they are required to retake the test. For this reason, resistant/uncooperative patients should not be retested any more than is absolutely necessary. Similarly, the benefits of obtaining retest data for monitoring purposes must be weighed against the psychological cost to the patient. For some individuals, the completion of instruments like the SA–45 — particularly in primary care clinics and other nonbehavioral health care facilities — can be quite stressful and, consequently, may not yield any benefits for the patient; in fact, readministration may result in more harm than good. Thus, one must carefully determine the advisability of administering *any* instrument — even once — to patients such as these.

Finally, the primary/behavioral health care provider must consider the patient's symptomatology. Certainly, one needs to be aware of fluctuations in those symptoms — organically or psychologically based — that might impair the patient's ability to render valid responses to the SA–45 items. At the same time, the experienced primary/behavioral health care provider should be able to determine, by the type and severity of the patient's problem(s), the number of visits or points in time when significant or otherwise expected changes should occur, and then to plan for reassessment with the SA–45 accordingly. In this approach, the primary/behavioral health care provider essentially develops a nonempirical, clinically based expected path of improvement and uses monitoring via the SA–45 (and perhaps other means) to ensure that the patient is where he or she is supposed to be at predetermined points in time. The expected path of improvement likely would be problem or symptom specific, such that patients presenting primarily with a social phobia have different paths of improvement and points of expected change than patients presenting with major depression.

Use of SA–45 Data for Clinical Decision Making

There are basically two reasons for monitoring behavioral health care treatment progress. The first is to determine if the prescribed treatment is resulting in psychological symptom reduction. The other is to determine if the level of distress or disturbance has been reduced to a level that, in the primary/behavioral health care provider's judgment, requires no further treatment. Features of the SA–45 provide primary/behavioral health care providers with information that can assist him or her in these determinations.

Determining Statistically and Clinically Significant Change: Use of the Reliable Change (RC) Index. How much change in an SA–45 scale or index score should be considered "significant" and deserving of attention? The answer to the question depends on whether one prefers to base his or her judgment on *statistically significant* or *clinically significant* differences in test results. Recently, many behavioral health care clinicians and researchers have begun to apply Jacobson and Truax's (1991) Reliable Change (RC) index to determine the statistical significance of the differences between scores. The RC index is the difference between two scores at two points in time (i.e, time 2 minus time 1, or any score minus an earlier score), divided by the standard error of difference (S_{diff}). In the case of the SA–45, if the resulting value is less than -1.96, one can be 95% confident ($p < .05$) that real improvement has occurred. The minimum raw-score and area T-score differences required for statistical significance for each SA–45 scale and index computed from the RC index formula are presented in Table 10.4.

Jacobson and Truax's (1991) RC index allows clinicians to use instruments such as the SA–45 to demonstrate whether behavioral health care intervention has resulted in "statistically reliable" change from any two points in time. However, they and their colleagues (Jacobson, Follette, & Revenstorf, 1984) also acknowledged the importance of determining clinically significant change to clinicians, researchers, and patients. Accordingly, clinically significant change (i.e., improvement) may be described as change that is both statistically reliable and moves the patient either from the range of dysfunction into that of normal functioning or within the functional (normal) range. Movement occurs when the patient's level of functioning, however

TABLE 10.4
Minimum Raw-Score and *T*-Score Differences Required for Establishing Reliable
Change Between Two Test Administrations for SA–45 Scales and Indices

	Adults[a]		Adolescents[b]	
Scale	Minimum Raw Score Difference	Minimum T-Score Difference	Minimum Raw Score Difference	Minimum T-Score Difference
ANX	4.15	13.33	4.00	11.20
DEP	2.20	6.57	3.60	7.93
HOS	1.95	5.65	6.50	11.75
INT	2.90	7.73	4.30	8.70
OC	3.05	8.93	4.85	11.64
PAR	2.75	8.40	4.55	11.14
PHO	1.25	4.24	3.20	6.51
PSY	1.25	3.96	1.95	5.65
SOM	3.20	10.01	6.80	14.91
PST	9.95	10.39	11.20	10.62
GSI	13.50	8.09	21.15	10.92

Note. Change scores derived from application of Jacobson and Truax's (1991) procedures for computing the Reliable Change (RC) index using the test–retest reliability coefficients for nonpatient adult and adolescent samples reported in the SA–45 *Technical Manual* (SAI, 1998).

[a]Based on nonpatient test–retest reliability coefficients ($N = 57$) found in Table 6.2 of the SA–45 *Technical Manual*.

[b]Based on nonpatient test–retest reliability coefficients ($N = 64$) found in Table 6.3 of the SA–45 *Technical Manual*.

measured, falls either (a) two standard deviations from the mean of the dysfunctional population (in the direction of normal/unimpaired functioning), (b) within two standard deviations of the mean of the normal population, or (c) closer to the mean of the normal population than to the mean of the dysfunctional population. The raw-score-to-area *T*-score conversion tables in the *Technical Manual* (SAI, 1998) allow one to determine whether the patient meets criterion (b) or (c). Note, however, that the nature of the SA–45 symptom domain *T*-scores (i.e., no inpatient symptom domain *T*-scores ≤30) makes it impossible to determine improvement on the symptom domain scales using criterion (a). Not withstanding, according to Jacobson and Truax, criterion (c) is preferable to criterion (b) when the normal and dysfunctional distributions overlap, as is the case with the SA–45.

This approach for determining clinically significant improvement in the patient's status also can be used to determine if clinically significant deterioration has occurred. In this case, an SA–45 RC greater than +1.96 and movement from the range of normal functioning to that dysfunction or within the dysfunctional range would be required. Jacobson and Truax (1991) did not specify what the clinical criteria deterioration should be, as they did for determining improvement. However, based on the improvement criteria, one might surmise that deterioration has occurred if the patient's SA–45 score(s) move to fall either (a) two standard deviations from the mean of the normal population (in the direction of dysfunction), (b) within two standard deviations of the mean of the dysfunctional population, or (c) closer to the mean of the dysfunctional population than to the mean of the normal population. For the previously stated reason, one might also surmise that criterion (c) is the preferred standard.

When to Discontinue Treatment.   Regardless of who is treating behavioral health problems in the primary care setting, the care provider is frequently faced with the difficult decision of when to discontinue treatment. Certainly, one or more nonclinical factors (e.g., limits on behavioral health care coverage, staff availability) may play heavily into the primary/behavioral health care provider's decision to terminate the treatment for the behavioral health problem. In the absence of these external forces, this decision may or may not be made with consideration of the need for continued treatment for any comorbid medical problem.

There are no guidelines for discontinuing behavioral health intervention based on SA–45 results—nor should there be. As in other clinical applications, SA–45 scores should be used as only one source of information on which the provider should base his or her decision about whether to terminate behavioral health treatment. Here, attainment of established treatment goals, patient and/or collateral report of improved daily functioning, presentation during office visits, and perhaps other data should serve as the primary indicators of whether the patient has achieved optimum treatment benefit, with SA–45 findings providing support for the clinical decision. In general, a "normal-range profile" (i.e., no scales or indices 60T or greater) would certainly support clinical impressions and/or patient report of no significant psychological distress requiring further treatment. Similarly, one or more significantly elevated scales or indices would strengthen a conclusion that continued treatment is called for, with the strength of the support increasing with T-scores at the higher elevations. At the same time, SA–45 results that clearly contradict conclusions based on other sources of information should lead the primary/behavioral health care provider to at least consider seeking further support for the initial conclusion.

USE OF THE SA–45 FOR TREATMENT OUTCOMES ASSESSMENT

The SA–45 was developed to support the behavioral outcomes research work being conducted for a large, nationwide network of inpatient psychiatric facilities. Thus, features of the instrument—brevity, coverage of nine symptom domains, indexes for summarizing overall level of disturbance, low cost—make it more attractive than many other measures of psychological distress that were not developed specifically for outcomes assessment. Furthermore, its applicability for outcomes research extends to the primary care arena.

General Issues

Use of the SA–45 for outcomes assessment raises no special issues beyond those for similar instruments. Again, it was developed for use in behavioral health care outcomes research with adults and adolescents. Consequently, its use for this purpose is likely to be of much less concern than the use of other instruments that were not developed primarily for outcomes assessment purposes.

Clinical Applications of the SA–45 for Outcomes Assessment

There are several ways in which the SA–45 may be used to assess the outcomes of behavioral health care treatment. How it is applied in a specific health care setting depends a number of factors.

What to Evaluate. The SA–45 provides nine symptom-specific measures and two measures of overall level of psychological distress. The GSI score probably is more frequently used for outcomes assessment purposes than any other SA–45 variable. It not only reflects both pervasiveness (i.e., number of symptoms) and frequency psychological symptomatology in one score; it also is one of the most reliable of the SA–45 measures. At the same time, scores on one or more SA–45 symptom domain scales may prove to be equally valuable. For example, because many primary care patients present with depressive symptomatology, the score on the Depression scale may be as important a variable as the GSI to be evaluated in the provider organization's outcomes assessment program.

Intended Use. The SA–45 may serve multiple purposes related to an outcomes measurement initiative. The most obvious is that of providing an *outcomes variable*, that is, a direct measure of treatment outcomes in the domain of psychological functioning. This probably is the most common use of the SA–45 when employed for outcomes assessment. However, it also can serve other purposes. The SA–45 also may help ensure fair and meaningful comparisons of behavioral health or medical outcomes among primary/behavioral health care providers. When its results (GSI most frequently) are employed as a *risk adjuster*, it can help "level the playing field" by taking into account the fact that the patients of one provider typically may present with more severe psychological disturbance than the patients of the other providers. Risk-adjusting outcomes by SA–45 results, either alone or along with other relevant variables (e.g., age, gender, history of previous treatment), is particularly important when practices serving significantly different patient populations are being compared to each other or to a standard that represents the average of several practices.

SA–45 results also can be used as predictors of other outcomes or related variables. For example, SA–45 scores obtained at the time of screening might serve as either a predictor of other outcomes, such as medical resource utilization or work functioning 3 to 6 months posttreatment termination, or as a predictor of variables that may have a relationship to outcomes variables. This might include length of episode of care, number or type of medications prescribed, or other process variables.

When to Measure. When administered immediately before or at the beginning of treatment, the SA–45 provides a baseline measure of both overall and domain-specific psychological functioning. These results can then be compared with SA–45 results obtained at treatment termination to determine how much change (if any) has occurred as a result of the treatment intervention. Although important, this information is limited with regard to the effect that treatment has had on the patient's psychological status. If the SA–45 is readministered one or more times after the termination assessment (e.g., 3, 6, or 12 months postdischarge), the results from these follow-up assessments can be compared to those obtained at screening/intake, discharge, or both. This will permit the clinician to draw additional and possibly more important conclusions regarding the effectiveness of treatment, that is, whether treatment has resulted in lasting effects on the patient's level functioning.

Deciding whether to conduct follow-up assessment of patients with the SA–45 and/or any other assessment tool is not a simple matter. There are number of issues that should be addressed when considering the incorporation of a follow-up assessment component into a primary/behavioral health care provider's outcomes management program. Among the most important of these are: How useful would this type of information be to the primary/behavioral health care provider? How would the data be used? Who would be assessed (i.e., a sample of patients vs. all treated patients)? Should follow-up assessment be conducted by phone interview or mail-out survey? What financial and personnel resources would be available for this undertaking? What would be the likelihood of locating former patients months after the episode of care has ended? There is no question that SA–45 lends itself well to follow-up assessment and can provide valuable information; the major issue is whether this is an endeavor that the primary/behavioral health care provider can successfully undertake.

How to Analyze the Data. The preceding discussion of methods for determining statistical and clinical significant changes in SA–45 scores for treatment monitoring also applies to the use of the instrument to assess the treatment outcomes for the individual patient. Use of Jacobson and Truax's (1991) RC index to determine clinically significant change in psychological functioning is appropriate, regardless of whether one is assessing change from screening/intake to treatment termination, termination to follow-up, screening/intake to follow-up, or from one follow-up assessment to another. The analysis of aggregated SA–45 data requires a different approach that is beyond the scope of this chapter. The reader is referred to Newman and Tejeda (1999) for an excellent discussion of approaches to the analysis of group data.

Use of SA–45 Findings With Other Evaluation Data. The SA–45 can meet the need for a measure of current level of psychological functioning within a comprehensive outcomes assessment and management system in the primary care setting. Results of the SA–45 can easily be integrated with patient- or provider-reported data pertaining to other aspects of patient functioning — social functioning, occupational functioning, academic performance, well-being, substance use, medical resources utilization — to present a clear picture of changes that have occurred during the episode of care. SA–45 results are independent of findings from other functional measures and thus do not present the user with redundant information. In aggregate, the SA–45 results — particularly the GSI score — can be used as risk-adjustment variables and, possibly, predictors of outcomes in other domains of functioning.

Provision of Feedback Regarding Outcomes Assessment Findings

Treatment outcomes data is of potential interest to several stakeholders, including the patient, the primary/behavioral health care provider, and third parties with a vested interest in the patient (e.g., payers). The manner in which SA–45 findings are presented to illustrate changes in psychological functioning resulting from treatment will depend on the intended recipient of this information. The presentation of the results to the patients via the SA–45 profile of both pre- and posttreatment scores allows the patients to see their overall level of psychological distress in relation to age- and gender-appropriate nonpatient norms as well as how much they have improved. Depending on the level of interest and intellect of the patient, the provider also might wish to supplement this information with discussions of changes in specific SA–45 item responses and/or the statistical and clinical significance of scale and index changes. A version of Finn's "therapeutic assessment" approach to providing assessment feedback to patients (Finn, 1996a, 1996b; Finn & Martin, 1997; Finn & Tonsager,

1992), modified for the discussion of posttreatment data as opposed to pretreatment data, may provide qualified professionals an excellent framework for this process.

Providers and third parties are audiences that may require a different exposition of outcomes data. They are more likely to be interested in findings related to specific *groups* of patients rather than individual patients. A discussion of this type of exposition follows.

Use as a Data Source for Behavioral Health Care Service Report Cards

Health care report cards are common means of communicating aspects of an organization's effectiveness in treating the populations it serves. Among the types of report card information that might be conveyed by primary care practices/organizations is the degree of positive change in the level of psychological distress or disturbance of patients presenting with behavioral health problems. Because it provides this type of information, SA–45 data can be useful and informative for the intended report card audience. Moreover, it lends itself well to the types of analyses that are frequently employed for the purpose of these reports.

Generally, there are two ways in which the SA–45 can help provide evidence of a primary care practice/organization's ability to effectively treat patients with mental health or substance use problems, with or without comorbid medical problems. The first is by providing a direct measure of change in psychological status. Although any of several variables might be employed to show change, the single best and most useful SA–45 measure for this purpose is the GSI area T-score. This is because the GSI is more representative of the patient's general level of symptomatology than any other SA–45 measure. It is, in fact, a combination and representation of all nine symptom domain measures. In addition, this author's experience indicates that primary care providers and nonprofessional/lay audiences with no formal training in psychological testing can easily grasp the nature of what is being represented by the SA–45 GSI. Similarly, the nonpatient norms-based area T-score is a metric that is easily understood by most patient care stakeholders. Thus, using GSI nonpatient-based area T-scores enables a primary/behavioral health care provider to convey the most meaningful information about change in psychological status, in the most understandable form to all parties with an interest in treatment outcomes.

There are several ways in which aggregated GSI data can be used to represent a degree of improvement in a patient sample or population. The most obvious (and arguably the most useful) is a straightforward average GSI area T-score change from screening/intake to treatment termination. These data also may be delineated for subsamples based on diagnosis, age, number of outpatient visits, payer of services, service unit, individual primary/behavioral health care provider, another outcomes variable (e.g., change in occupational functioning), or any other variable(s) that would be meaningful for the intended audience. GSI data also can be presented in terms of the percent of patients who exhibited an area T-score change that is greater than a minimum standard set by the organization or another relevant party (e.g., accrediting body, payers). A useful minimum standard might be a decrease in the GSI area T-score by 10 or more points (i.e., one standard deviation), or a statistically significant GSI T-score decrease as defined by Jacobson and Truax (1991).

Another way in which the SA–45 can help provide evidence of an primary/behavioral health care provider's ability to effectively treat patients with behavioral health problems is by using it to risk adjust findings in other outcome domains. It is not uncommon for providers with less than favorable outcomes to complain that their patients' outcomes are worse because "My patients are sicker." As alluded to earlier, SA–45 results can assist in making fair outcomes comparisons across primary/behavioral health care providers, service units, and organizations by adjusting data that might have been influenced by the patients' level of psychological distress or disturbance. Further adjustment might be made based on other variables (e.g., length of episode of care, education, motivation to engage in treatment) that the primary care practice/organization has found to be related to the outcome domains of interest. There are a number of sophisticated statistical techniques that can be used for risk adjustment purposes. Discussion of these techniques is beyond the scope of this chapter; however, interested readers are referred to the work of Iezzoni (1994) for an excellent exposition on this topic.

DISEASE-SPECIFIC CONSIDERATIONS

Because it is a relatively new instrument, there have been no investigations of the effects of specific diseases or disorders on SA–45 results. Intuitively, it would not be surprising for patients with physical diseases or disorders that are commonly accompanied by symptoms that are similar to psychiatric symptoms assessed by the SA–45 (e.g., concentration difficulties, hot and cold spells, numbness/tingling sensations) to obtain elevated scores on the symptom domain scales to which the items assessing these symptoms belong (e.g., Depression, Somatization). Thus, in primary care and other medical settings, it is particularly important to conduct an item analysis of the SA–45 scales that are significantly elevated.

STRENGTHS AND LIMITATIONS OF THE SA–45 IN PRIMARY CARE SETTINGS

Although developed primarily for use in the assessment of treatment outcomes in behavioral health care settings, the SA–45 has a number of features that make it valuable for use in primary care settings. At the same time, the manner in which it was developed presents limitations for its use with primary care patients.

Strengths

The SA–45's brevity and ease of use make it well-suited for screening/intake assessment, treatment progress monitoring, and outcomes assessment in primary care settings. At the same time, as a multidimensional measure of psychological symptomatology, the SA–45 provides the clinician with a broad survey of various symptom domains and a better measure of overall psychological distress and disturbance than can be obtained from brief measures of single-symptom domains (e.g., depression screeners).

In conjunction with a report of the problem(s) in the patient's own words, the results of the SA–45 obtained during screening/intake can help the primary/behavioral health care provider immediately begin formulating and implementing a plan of treatment. Its low cost is an important consideration, given that readministration of any psychological instrument for treatment monitoring can be expensive in terms of both actual costs and lost opportunities for actual treatment. Readministration of the SA-45 at or about the end of the episode of care may provide data that do or do not support the need for continued treatment — an important consideration for patients with limited behavioral health care benefits. Moreover, with the availability of scoring and reporting via either hand scoring or automated products and services, most primary/behavioral health care providers can have immediate access to SA-45 findings.

Limitations

The SA-45 is an abbreviated version of the original SCL-90 consisting of items selected for their ability to mirror the nine symptom domains of the parent instrument. Thus, it is limited in its ability to detect the presence or absence of symptoms that are not represented by those broad domains; at the same time, amelioration of certain types of symptoms (e.g., those related to eating disorders, specific types of phobias, sexual dysfunction) may not be reflected in SA-45 results. Also, the SA-45 does not yield information relevant to psychological strengths or assets that can be used by the patient during psychological treatment, thus posing limitations to its use for treatment planning purposes. However, both of these characteristics are common among many other "abnormal personality" instruments and not specific to the SA-45.

As is the case with many other self-report, multidimensional measures of psychiatric symptomatology, the patient must have a certain minimum reading ability (sixth grade level), and his or her psychological state must permit valid, reliable responding to the SA-45 items. Barring the fulfillment of these requirements at the time of screening/intake, an objectively measured baseline of psychological distress may not be possible. However, although it is probably impractical in most primary care settings, one may consider reading the SA-45 items to the patient if his or her reading ability is the only issue. In this situation, having the patients indicate their answers on the SA-45 answer sheet rather than giving an oral reply to the examiner would probably lessen, but not eliminate, the common concerns about the effects of this nonstandardized form of administration on the psychometric integrity of the results.

Moreover, the test-retest reliability coefficients for the Somatization scale are relatively low for both adults and adolescents, as is the Anxiety scale coefficient for adults. Consequently, greater changes in area T-scores or raw scores from one point in time to another would be required to achieve clinically or statistically significant change on these scales than for the other symptom domain scales.

CASE STUDY

Ms. X is a 35-year-old African-American, married female with a 1-year-old daughter. She is college educated and does not work outside of the home. She cares for her daughter full time and occasionally cares for her mother, who suffers from multiple neurological problems. Ms. X was first seen by her primary care provider over a year ago, complaining of gastrointestinal problems that caused her to awaken in the middle of the night. She reported having experienced the problem since becoming sexually active while in her early twenties. Medical examination revealed neither medical problems that could be causing the problem nor the presence of any sleep disorder. She was prescribed medication during the visit, but because of changes in insurance coverage, she did not return for her follow-up visit.

Ms. X was seen again 10 months later, this time complaining of weight loss and problems in gaining weight. She also reported feeling anxious as a result of unspecified frustrations with her husband, having to provide care to her mother, and the demands placed on her by her young daughter. During the visit, she was administered the SA–45, the SF–12 Health Survey (Ware et al., 1994), and the Zung Self-rating Depression Scale (Zung, 1965).

Ms. X's GSI score suggested that she was experiencing a mild level of psychological distress ($T = 60$). This was reflected in the accompanying mild-to-moderate elevations on the Anxiety, Obsessive-Compulsive, Somatization, and Hostility scales (see Fig. 10.1). Of particular note was her Obsessive-Compulsive score ($T = 71$), resulting from a response of "Moderately" to each of the five items on that scale. The next highest elevations were on both the Anxiety and Somatization scales ($T = 62$). On the Anxiety scale, she indicated that during the past week she was bothered "A little bit" by feeling fearful and tense/keyed up, and "Moderately" by "Feeling so restless [she] couldn't sit still"; on the Somatization scale, she reported having been bothered "Moderately" by hot/cold spells and weakness in parts of her body, and "A little bit" by sore muscles. Although her Depression score was within acceptable limits ($T =$

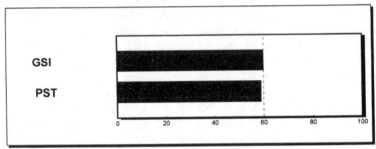

GRAPH OF T-SCORES FOR INDEXES
(Non-Patient Norms)

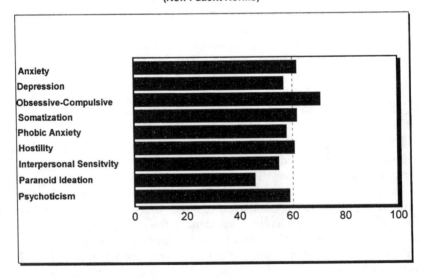

GRAPH OF T-SCORES FOR SYMPTOM DOMAIN SCALES
(Non-Patient Norms)

FIG. 10.1.   SA–45 case study profile, nonpatient comparison, Jane Doe.

57), Ms. X did respond "A little bit" to "Feeling blue," and "Moderately" to "Feeling no interest in things." The Depression scale findings were consistent with her score of 53 on the Zung, suggesting the presence of minimal to mild depression.

Finally, on the SF–12, she obtained normal-range scores on the Physical Component Summary (PCS) scale ($T = 51$). However, her Mental Component Summary (MCS) scale score was quite low ($T = 32$), suggesting the presence of emotional/psychological distress that was causing her significant role and social dysfunction. (Unlike SA–45 scores, low SF–12 scale scores indicate impaired physical and/or emotional health status.) A review of her MCS-related item responses revealed that during the previous four weeks, Ms. X neither accomplished as much she wanted nor performed tasks as carefully as usual. During that same period, she felt calm and peaceful only "A little of the time," while feeling downhearted and blue "Some of the time."

Her physician prescribed a selective serotonin reuptake inhibitor (SSRI) antidepressant and referred her to the in-office behavioral health care provider for further evaluation and therapy. She was described by the therapist a being "very private, a difficult person to do therapy with." Ms. X did not return for her follow-up appointment; however, the behavioral health care provider did reach her by phone a few months after the first visit. Ms. X reported that she had taken the SSRI for only 1 day, stating that for her, "it was not the way to go." At the same time, she reported that she had changed her diet, begun exercising every day, and generally felt the best she had felt in years. During the phone call, the therapist readministered the SF–12 along with the SA–24. The SA–24 is a 24-item version of the SA–45 that yields a predicted SA–45 GSI T-score along with the standard Depression scale score. The SA–45 developers designed the SA–24 for use in treatment outcomes studies where only a measure of overall psychological distress is needed. On the SA–24, Ms. X obtained a predicted GSI T-score of 46. According to Jacobson and Truax's (1991) RC index, this would indicate statistically reliable improvement in Ms. X's overall level of psychological distress from the time of the initial assessment. However, the drop of the Depression T-score from 57 to 51 would not be considered statistically reliable. On the SF–12, she obtained normal-range scores on both the MCS ($T = 55$) and the PCS ($T = 54$), indicating substantial improvement on the MCS as well.

This case illustrates the value of implementing the four-step approach to interpreting SA–45 results in primary care settings. It also shows the value of integrating instruments such as the SF–12 and the Zung into the evaluation process. For example, although the GSI and PST indicated that the overall level of distress to be almost normal limits, analysis of individual scale T-scores and item responses suggested potential problem areas. Also, the SF–12 MCS T-score indicated effects of Ms. X's psychological problems on her ability to function — something the SA–45 was not designed to do. Finally, although the behavioral health care provider did not really have an opportunity to assist the patient to any great degree, the use of the SA–45 (and SF–12) results from repeated administrations did indicate that Ms. X indeed appeared to show significant and reliable improvement (for one reason or another) over the 3 months between testings.

SUMMARY AND CONCLUSIONS

The development of the SA–45 provides those trained in the use of psychological tests with another useful tool for screening, treatment planning and monitoring, and outcomes assessment. Derived from the original SCL–90, the SA–45 was designed to assess the same symptom domains as the parent instrument using only half as many items. The development of nonpatient adult and adolescent gender-specific norms, the use of area T-scores instead of the more traditional (but less appropriate) linear T-scores, and the ability to employ sophisticated means for replacing missing responses are among the features that enable wide applicability in a variety of settings with various populations. Primary care patients are among those populations for whom the SA–45 is well suited.

Although relatively new, initial investigations into its psychometric characteristics support the SA–45 as a measure of psychiatric symptomatology. Cronbach's alpha coefficients and item-total correlations reveal acceptable levels of internal consistency reliability for the nine symptom domain scales. Test–retest correlations obtained from nonpatient adult and adolescent data are generally acceptable, with a few exceptions — most notably, those for the Anxiety scale — which warrant consideration when using the SA–45 for treatment monitoring or outcomes assessment purposes.

The validity of the SA–45 has been examined from a variety of perspectives. It has been shown to be sensitive to expected differences in nonpatient and psychiatric inpatient groups, as well as to changes in patient symptomatology over time as a result of behavioral health treatment. This sensitivity is not as pronounced with adolescent populations as it is with adult populations. The SA–45 scales have been found to correlate highly with their companion scales from the SCL–90 and BSI. To some extent, this reflects the fact that the SCL–90 data also served as the source of data for both the SA–45 and BSI data in those investigations. Also, the interscale correlations are quite similar to those found for the SCL–90 and the BSI; at the same time, the SA–45 scales appear to be more independent than their companion scales in these related instruments. Moreover, the finding of expected relationships between SA–45 variables and nontest variables in primary care populations provides specific concurrent validation related to its use in primary care settings. Finally, item-total scale correlations and the symptomatology assessed by each symptom domain scale's five items attest to the content validity of the instrument.

The availability of separate sets of nonpatient normative data and accompanying area T-score conversion tables for adults and adolescents facilitates the interpretation of SA–45 results. For all age and gender groups, the use of the nonpatient norms-based area T-score of 60 (i.e., one standard deviation above the mean) is the recommended cutoff for determining the likelihood of significant distress, regardless of whether one is evaluating symptom-domain or overall level of distress. Preliminary data from the reported primary behavioral health care study provide specific support for the use of the general nonpatient norms with primary care patients. Moreover, further interpretive information can be obtained by looking at individual responses to items comprising those scales with significant area T-score elevations.

In addition to helping identify specific symptom domains requiring intervention (and perhaps placing individuals into appropriate levels of care), the SA–45 can assist in other treatment planning purposes for the primary care patient. It can be used to confirm hypotheses generated by patient data obtained by other means. It also can provide information about the respondent's willingness to engage in treatment. Overall, its brevity, low cost, and symptom-focused orientation make it useful not only for screening and treatment planning, but also for monitoring change during the course of treatment by the primary/behavioral health care provider.

Finally, the SA–45 is well suited as a measure of psychiatric symptomatology for use as part of a health care outcomes system. It fares quite well when evaluated against standard criteria for outcomes measures (see Newman & Ciarlo, 1994), particularly with regard to considerations of cost, psychometric integrity, ease of us, and understandability by nonprofessionals. Also, it provides information that can be useful for the development of health care report cards from two perspectives. First, comparison of results from pretreatment testing to those from posttreatment and/or follow-up testing can yield data regarding the effectiveness of the primary/behavioral health care provider's intervention; it thus can serve as a direct measure of treatment outcomes. Second, SA–45 variables can be used to risk adjust other outcomes variables (e.g., work/school performance) or process variables (e.g., length of episode of care/number of outpatient visits) according to symptom severity, thus facilitating fair comparisons across service providers.

As would be the case with any new psychological test instrument, the full utility and value of the SA–45 for screening, treatment planning and monitoring, and outcomes assessment purposes in primary care settings will become evident only as psychologists, physicians, and other primary and behavioral health care professionals employ it in their clinical and research work. This obviously will take time, but the initial data are encouraging.

ACKNOWLEDGMENTS

Portions of this chapter were adapted from Strategic Advantage, Inc., *Symptom Assessment–45 Questionnaire (SA–45) Technical Manual* (1998), with permission from Strategic Advantage, Inc.; from M. E. Maruish, "Therapeutic Assessment: Linking Assessment and Treatment," in M. Hersen & A. Bellack (Series Eds.) and C. R. Reynolds (Vol. Ed.), *Comprehensive Clinical Psychology, Volume 4. Assessment* (1998), with permission from Elsevier Science Ltd.; and from M. E. Maruish, "Introduction," in M. E. Maruish (Ed.), *The Use of Psychological Testing for Treatment Planning and Outcomes Assessment* (2nd ed., 1999), with permission from Lawrence Erlbaum Associates.

REFERENCES

American Psychological Association. (1992). Ethical principles of psychologists and code of conduct. *American Psychologist, 47*, 1597–1611.

Commission on Chronic Illness. (1987). *Chronic illness in the United States, 1.* Cambridge, MA: Commonwealth Fund, Harvard University Press.

Davison, M. L., Bershadsky, B., Bieber, J., Silversmith, D., Maruish, M. E., & Kane, R. L. (1997). Development of a brief, multidimensional, self-report instrument for treatment outcomes assessment in psychiatric settings. *Assessment, 4*, 259–276.

Derogatis, L. R. (1983). *SCL–90–R: Administration, scoring and procedures manual–II for the revised version* (2nd ed.). Towson, MD: Clinical Psychometric Research.

Derogatis, L. R. (1992). *BSI: Administration, scoring and procedures manual–II.* Baltimore, MD: Clinical Psychometric Research.

Derogatis, L. R. (1993). *Brief Symptom Inventory (BSI) administration, scoring and procedures manual* (3rd ed.). Minneapolis, MN: National Computer Systems.

Derogatis, L. R. (1994). *SCL–90–R: Symptom Checklist–90–R (SCL–90–R) administration, scoring, and procedures manual.* Minneapolis, MN: National Computer Systems.

Derogatis, L. R., & Cleary, P. A. (1977). Confirmation of the dimensional structure of the SCL–90: A study in construct validation. *Journal of Clinical Psychology, 33,* 981–989.

Derogatis, L. R., & DellaPietra, L. (1994). Psychological tests in screening for psychiatric disorder. In M. E. Maruish (Ed.), *The use of psychological testing for treatment planning and outcome assessment* (pp. 22–54). Hillsdale, NJ: Lawrence Erlbaum Associates.

Derogatis, L. R., Lipman, R. S., & Covi, L. (1973). SCL–90: An outpatient psychiatric rating scale – Preliminary report. *Psychopharmacology Bulletin, 9,* 13–27.

Derogatis, L. R., Rickels, K., & Rock, A. (1976). The SCL–90 and the MMPI: A step in the validation of a new self-report scale. *British Journal of Psychiatry, 128,* 280–289.

Derogatis, L. R., & Spencer, P. M. (1982). *The Brief Symptom Inventory (BSI): Administration, scoring and procedures manual-I.* Towson, MD: Clinical Psychometric Research.

Ficken, J. (1995). New directions for psychological testing. *Behavioral Health Management, 20,* 12–14.

Finn, S. E. (1996a). Assessment feedback integrating MMPI-2 and Rorschach findings. *Journal of Personality Assessment, 67,* 543–557.

Finn, S. E. (1996b). *Manual for using the MMPI–2 as a therapeutic intervention.* Minneapolis, MN: University of Minnesota Press.

Finn, S. E., & Martin, H. (1997). Therapeutic assessment with the MMPI–2 in managed health care. In J. N. Butcher (Ed.), *Personality assessment in managed care* (pp. 131–152). Minneapolis, MN: University of Minnesota Press.

Finn, S. E., & Tonsager, M. E. (1992). Therapeutic effects of providing MMPI–2 test feedback to college students awaiting therapy. *Psychological Assessment, 4,* 278–287.

Goldstein, L., & Maruish, M. E. (1997, September). *Primary care marketing and linkage strategies for group practices.* Paper presented at the annual retreat of the Council of Behavioral Group Practices, Washington, DC.

Iezzoni, L. I. (Ed.). (1994). *Risk adjustments for measuring health care outcomes.* Ann Arbor, MI: Health Administration Press.

Jacobson, N. S., Follette, W. C., & Revenstorf, D. (1984). Psychotherapy outcome research: Methods for reporting variability and evaluating clinical significance. *Behavior Therapy, 15,* 336–352.

Jacobson, N. S., & Truax, P. (1991). Clinical significance: A statistical approach to defining change in psychotherapy research. *Journal of Consulting and Clinical Psychology, 59,* 12–19.

Maruish, M. E. (1994). Introduction. In M. E. Maruish (Ed.), *The use of psychological testing for treatment planning and outcome assessment* (pp. 3–21). Hillsdale, NJ: Lawrence Erlbaum Associates.

Maruish, M. E. (1999). Introduction. In M. E. Maruish (Ed.), *The use of psychological testing for treatment planning and outcome assessment* (2nd ed., pp. 1–39). Mahwah, NJ: Lawrence Erlbaum Associates.

Newman, F. L., & Tejeda, M. J. (1999). Selection of design and statistical procedures for progress and outcome assessment. In M. E. Maruish (Ed.), *The use of psychological testing for treatment planning and outcome assessment* (Vol. I, 2nd ed., pp. 225–266). Mahwah, NJ: Lawrence Erlbaum Associates.

Newman, F. L., & Ciarlo, J. A. (1994). Criteria for selecting psychological instruments for treatment outcome assessment. In M. E. Maruish (Ed.), *The use of psychological testing for treatment planning and outcome assessment* (pp. 98–110). Hillsdale, NJ: Lawrence Erlbaum Associates.

Pallak, M. S. (1994). National outcomes management survey: Summary report. *Behavioral Healthcare Tomorrow, 3,* 63–69.

Reynolds, W. M. (1991). *Adult Suicide Ideation Questionnaire professional manual.* Odessa, FL: Psychological Assessment Resources.

Strategic Advantage, Inc. (1998). *Symptom Assessment–45 Questionnaire (SA–45) technical manual.* Toronto, ON: Multi-Health Systems.

Ward, J. H. (1963). Hierarchical grouping to optimize an objective function. *Journal of the American Statistical Association, 58,* 236–244.

Ware, J. E., Jr., Kosinski, M., & Keller, S. D. (1994). *SF–12 Physical and Mental Health Summary scales: A user's manual* (3rd ed.). Boston: Health Institute, New England Medical Center.

Ware, J. E., Jr., Kosinski, M., & Keller, S. D. (1995). *SF–12: How to score the SF–12 Physical and Mental Health Summary scales* (2nd ed.). Boston: Health Institute, New England Medical Center.

Ware, J. E., Jr., Snow, K. K., Kosinski, M., & Gandek, B. (1993). *SF–36 Health Survey manual and interpretation guide.* Boston: Health Institute, New England Medical Center.

Zung, W. K. (1965). A self-rating depression scale. *Archives of General Psychiatry, 12,* 63–70.

Daily Stress Inventory (DSI) and Weekly Stress Inventory (WSI)

Phillip J. Brantley
Pennington Biomedical Research Center, Louisiana State University

Shawn K. Jeffries
Department of Psychology, Louisiana State University

Psychosocial stressors play a significant role in many of the presenting symptoms of primary care patients (Campbell, Seaburn, & McDaniel, 1994; Dalack & Zweifler, 1997; Sloane, 1998). Studies that analyze reasons for seeking medical services indicate that primary care patients frequently seek services secondary to stress-related symptoms and/or disorders, such as headache, gastrointestinal distress, and chest pain (Sobel, 1995). Meyer and Haggerty (1962) showed that chronic stress was positively associated with high rates of streptococcal pharyngitis, with up to one third of streptococcal infections preceded by a stressful family event. Katon (1985) estimated that 50% of primary care visits involve significant psychosocial concerns. Kroenke and Mangelsdorff (1989) analyzed 1,000 patients followed for 3 years in an internal medicine clinic. They targeted the 14 most common symptoms (e.g., fatigue, dizziness, headache, chest pain) for study. Of these symptoms, only 16% were found to be clearly attributable to organic etiologies. The authors concluded that although only 10% of these presenting complaints were identified by physicians as psychological in nature, many of the reported symptoms were likely due to psychosocial factors such as environmental stressors.

Researchers in the field of family systems medicine have long recognized the connection between psychosocial stressors and illness onset and exacerbation (McDaniel, 1992). Psychosocial distress has been implicated in the etiology and/or exacerbation of such conditions as chronic idiopathic prostatitis (Berghuis, Heiman, Rothman, & Berger, 1996), somatization disorder (Ford, 1997), and adverse pregnancy outcomes (Langer et al., 1996). In an international study of medically unexplained physical symptoms, the World Health Organization concluded that psychosocial stress may be specifically responsible for many of the multiple, persistent, and medically unexplained somatic symptoms seen by primary care physicians across multiple cultures and populations (Isaac et al., 1995).

The well-established connections between stress and both physical and psychological disorders have led researchers to suggest that assessing stressors can be helpful in identifying patients at risk for the development and/or exacerbation of medical and psychological disorders (Dalack & Zweifler, 1997). As early as the 1930s, Adolf Meyer advocated that family physicians monitor the life events of patients suffering from illnesses to assess possible psychosocial contributions to their medical illnesses (Lief, 1948). More recently, the importance of screening for psychosocial stressors by family medicine and internal medicine physicians has become an increasingly emphasized topic in the medical literature (Campbell et al., 1994; Gage & Leidy, 1991). Despite this increased awareness, Rosenberg, Commerford, and Driever (1991) found a relatively low concordance rate (60%) between physician identification of psychosocial distress and a well-validated screening test (General Health Questionnaire) among primary care patients. This suggests that primary care physicians may benefit from supplemental instruction and/or assistance in assessing their patients' psychosocial stressors, including specialized training in interviewing patients regarding psychosocial stressors, input from a consulting psychologist present during the interview, or an introduction to quick screening measures to identify those patients who might be at risk for stress-related illnesses.

Recent textbooks on family medicine have acknowledged the importance of recognizing the connections between stressful life events and physical symptoms for optimal patient care (Sloane, 1998). These texts have attempted to provide some direction for physicians assessing stress in their patients. For example, in the textbook *Family Medicine: Principles and Practice*, Campbell et al. (1994) outlined principles and guidelines for identifying family stress, assessing family functioning, and intervening with families. Sloane (1998) suggested that family medicine physicians encourage patients suffering from anxiety or adjustment disorders to recognize the relationship between physical symptoms and life stressors. Sloane (1998) also recommmended the use of life events inventories to help clarify patients' understanding of the role of life change and stress and the expression of physical symptoms.

The presence of health psychologists in a primary care setting can also facilitate identification and subsequent intervention with patients experiencing high levels of psychosocial distress. McDaniel (1995) emphasized the advantages of a collaborative relationship between family physicians and psychologists for assessment and treatment of stress-related disorders. However, it may not always be practical for a consulting psychologist to assess the majority of patients seen in a family medicine clinic, given that primary care physicians may see between 10 and 20 patients per day. Therefore, screening measures may assist the primary care physician in identifying stressful life situations.

Early identification appears to be optimal for a favorable prognosis for both physical and psychological disorders. In fact, accurate and early assessment of physical disorders such as hypertension and diabetes have been shown to be beneficial in long-term health outcomes such as disease severity, quality of life, length of treatment, and return to work (Brunton & Edwards, 1994; Smith, Sheehan, & Ulchaker, 1994). Early detection of psychological problems also appears to be beneficial. Undetected and untreated psychological disorders such as major depression have been shown to result in substantial amounts of physical and psychological impairment, as well as occupational interference (Public Health Service Agency for Health Care Policy and Research, 1993). Early detection of psychological problems involves assessment of psychosocial stressors to prevent stress-related physical symptoms and psychological disorders.

Much evidence exists to suggest that primary care populations are at risk for the development of adverse health-related outcomes as a result of psychosocial stressors.

Following long-term exposure to stressors, behavioral changes may occur that can negatively influence the primary care patient's health status in a number of adverse ways. For instance, chronically stressed individuals tend to engage in poor health practices such as increased cigarette smoking, excessive alcohol consumption, and sedentary life-style (Lovallo, 1997). In one study of primary care patients made up predominantly of low-income, minority females, a high prevalence of modifiable high-risk behaviors such as sedentary life-style, increased cigarette smoking, and high dietary fat intake was present (Brantley, Carmack, Boudreaux, & Scarinci, 1996). Specifically, 52% of subjects engaged in no leisure-time physical activity, 26% of subjects engaged in significant nicotine consumption, and 61% of subjects consumed greater than 30% of their calories from fat. In addition, 62% of the sample met criteria for obesity as defined by a Body Mass Index score of above 27.3 kg/m² for females and 27.8 kg/m² for males. The results of this descriptive study clearly show a population characterized by poor health outcomes and high rates of modifiable high-risk behaviors.

Similar to the prevalence of high-risk behaviors, the rates of psychological disorders have also been shown to be quite high in primary care populations. For example, the prevalence of major depressive disorder as defined by the *DSM–IV* (American Psychiatric Association [APA], 1994) is more than two times as great among primary care patients (5–10%) as it is among nonhospitalized individuals (2–4%; Katon & Schulberg, 1992). Brantley, Scarinci, Ames, and Jones (1998) found that stress added unique variance to the prediction of symptoms of major depression in a primary care population. Mazure (1998) emphasized the importance of chronic life stressors such as poverty, medical disability, and extended marital difficulties as risk factors for depression. He noted, however, that previous difficulties in the assessment of minor stressors plus a lack of research on their contribution to depression has limited the extent of findings in this area and highlighted the need for future research. Chronic stress was also theoretically linked by many researchers to the development and maintenance of various forms of psychopathology (Faravelli, 1985; Gillis, 1992).

Primary care individuals experiencing high levels of stress are therefore at increased risk for a number of adverse physical and psychological consequences. Taking the prevalence of high-risk health behaviors such as sedentary life-style into account, high rates of chronic illnesses among this population are not surprising. Given the inability of some primary care patients (e.g., low income) to control the occurrence of common chronic stressors such as poor living conditions and decreased financial resources, chronic stress may be an unavoidable part of their day-to-day existence. Brief psychological intervention with primary care patients referred by their physician has been shown to improve health outcomes compared to controls (Brantley, Veitia, Callon, Buss, & Sias, 1986; Mynors-Wallis, Gath, Lloyd-Thomas, & Tomlinson, 1995; Robinson et al., 1994). However, the ability of physicians to correctly identify those in need of specialized referrals has been called into question (Public Health Service Agency for Health Care Policy and Research, 1993; Wise, 1995.) Some have suggested that a life events inventory may be an effective tool in assisting physicians making this determination (Campbell et al., 1994). Moreover, although the involvement of psychologists in the management of primary care patients may represent optimal patient care, this situation may not be practical. For these reasons, the development of stress assessment techniques may be of great benefit in reducing poor health outcomes, reducing levels of chronic stress and resultant psychopathology, and assisting in the design of stress management programs specifically targeted for this population. Although the need for continued research in the area of stress and primary care is clear, the assessment of stress is primarily dependent on the way that stress is defined, as well as its relationship to physical health and illness.

ETIOLOGICAL MODELS OF STRESS

Research on stress and its relationship to physical health has a long history, dating back to Cannon's (1939) work on the "fight or flight" response, the concept of homeostasis, and the idea that an organism's steady state of existence could be disrupted by strong emotional reactions. Selye (1950) originally coined the term *stress*, and conceptualized stress as a general, nonspecific response to external demands. Alternatively, Lacey (1950) emphasized the importance of the specificity of the stress response. He maintained that different individuals will respond to external demands with varying physiological reactions (i.e., cardiovascular, muscular, gastrointestinal), depending on their dominant systemic response style. The popularity of specificity theories of stress and illness led to the development of Alexander's (1950) specific-conflict hypothesis, in which individuals with certain personality features were predisposed to develop certain physical disorders. Although empirical support for the specificity theory of stress response and the specific conflict hypothesis has been inconclusive, such theories did represent popular scientific opinion during the 1940s and 1950s.

Since then, there have been many new theoretical attempts to define the nature of stress and its effects on individuals. Some approaches have emphasized an individual's physiological "stress response," whereas other approaches have focused on the occurrence of stressful situations or life events and their resultant effect on an individual's well-being. Still others have emphasized stress as a process or transaction between external events and internal appraisals. Cohen, Kessler, and Gordon (1995) categorized the current major theories of stress into three broad categories: the biological perspective, the environmental perspective, and the psychological perspective. Figure 11.1 illustrates this categorization system, which serves as a framework to discuss current approaches to the definition of stress.

Biological Perspective

The biological perspective focuses on the responsiveness of physiological systems to both external stressors and psychological demands. This perspective explains stress as an overall physical response to a perceived environmental demand. Selye (1950, 1956) explored the role of stress in health through the development of the general adaptation syndrome (GAS). The GAS is defined as a response cycle in which an organism confronted with a noxious stressor cycles through a "biologic stress syndrome" including phases of alarm, resistance, and exhaustion. Stress as conceptualized by Selye (1956) originates from the environment, and results in a nonspecific bodily response affecting an individual's overall physiological functioning. Over time, extended activation of these systems leads to both psychological and physiological disorders. For example, continued exposure to environmental stressors results in the body developing "diseases of adaptation" such as arthritis and shock.

Two physiological systems believed to mediate the classic stress response are the sympathetic-adrenal medullary (SAM) system and the hypothalamic-pituitary-adrenocortical (HPA) axis (Cohen et al., 1995). Although a full discussion of the mecha-

BIOLOGICAL PERSPECTIVE **(RESPONSE THEORY)**

STRESS ──────────────────────────▶ ALTERATIONS IN PSYCHOLOGICAL
(major and minor life events)						FUNCTIONING

ENVIRONMENTAL PERSPECTIVE **(STIMULUS THEORY)**

DEMAND OR STRESSOR ──────────────────────────────▶ STRESS
										(Potentially pathognomic responses)

PSYCHOLOGICAL PERSPECTIVE **(TRANSACTIONAL THEORY)**

ENVIRONMENTAL EVENTS
	+			──────────────────▶ STRESS
PERSONAL APPRAISAL

FIG. 11.1.   Conceptualizations of stress.

nisms by which the SAM system and the HPA axis are proposed to moderate the experience of stress is beyond the scope of this chapter, Friedman, Charney, and Deutch (1995) provided a comprehensive review of this subject. Since the early 1980s, increased interest in the biological perspective of stress has given rise to the field of psychoneuroimmunology (Maier, Watkins, & Fleshner, 1994), which examines the interactions between behavior, the nervous system, and the immune system.

Environmental Perspective

The environmental perspective focuses on the role of stressful life events in the etiology and maintenance of illness and disease. This perspective had its origins in the 1930s with Adolf Meyer, who suggested that physicians fill out a life events chart as a standard part of the general examination of medically ill patients (Lief, 1948). Different areas of emphasis within this "stimulus" perspective include the controllability of the stressor, the harmfulness of the stressor, and the amount of change created by the stressor. Hawkins, Davies, and Holmes (1957) placed emphasis on the cumulative nature of stressful events and individual vulnerabilities that make some individuals more or less likely to contract "stressor-related" diseases. Stressful life events range from discrete to chronic, and emphasis is on the different intensity and temporal characteristics of the stressor.

Psychological Perspective

The psychological perspective emphasizes the perception of potential harm in the environment and the method by which a stimulus is appraised (Lazarus & Folkman, 1984). Lazarus and Folkman distinguished between primary appraisal (whether a stimulus is perceived as threatening or not) and secondary appraisal (evaluation of coping resources to determine the extent to which the effects of a stressor may be minimized). According to this viewpoint, should the perception of threat be perceived to exceed coping and/or avoidance strategies, a negative emotional state will result. The psychological perspective views stress as a transaction between the person and his or her environment. Stress is therefore defined by the individual's perception relative to the environment.

Cohen et al. (1995) integrated the biological, environmental, and psychological perspectives into a unifying definition of stress encompassing all three perspectives.

These researchers stated that stress involves "environmental demands [that] tax or exceed the adaptive capacity of an organism, resulting in psychological and biological changes that may place persons at risk for disease" (Cohen et al., 1995, p. 3).

ASSESSMENT OF STRESS

Different approaches to the conceptualization of the nature of stress and the stress response have consequently led to the development of differential assessment procedures. Three broad approaches to the measurement of stress include physiological assessment (biochemical methods), life events measurement, and measurement of stress appraisal.

Physiological assessments of stress have typically included three areas of measurement: measurements of stress hormones, cardiovascular assessment, and assessment of the level of immune system functioning (Baum & Grunberg, 1995). Common endocrine measures of stress include plasma and urinary levels of epinephrine and norepinephrine, as well as corticosteroids produced by the adrenal cortex, and endogenous opioid peptides. These hormones have been measured both in naturalistic settings and in response to a laboratory stressor such as aversive noise, a cold pressor, or a challenging cognitive task (Baum & Grunberg, 1995). Cardiovascular measures of the stress response include blood pressure, pulse, and peripheral blood flow through the skin capillary beds or to skeletal muscles (Krantz & Falconer, 1995). Examination of immune system responding is a much more recent method of assessing stress from a physiological standpoint, and includes the analysis of immunological assays such as blastogenesis and natural killer (NK) cell activity (Kiecolt-Glaser & Glaser, 1995).

The environmental perspective represents both a diverse and accessible method of measuring stress and the stress response. Often, this environmental perspective takes the form of life events measurement. Most stress research since the early 1980s has examined the effects of major life events, such as the death of a family member, a divorce, or change of a job (Brown, 1989). Several important scales have been developed in this regard, including the Schedule of Recent Experience (SRE; Hawkins et al., 1957) and the Social Readjustment Rating Scale (SRRS; Holmes & Rahe, 1967). Many studies suggest a modest but significant relationship between major life events and the occurrence of medical and psychological disorders (see Dohrenwend & Dohrenwend, 1974, for a review).

Although the concepts of appraisal and stressful events had been used informally by researchers such as Arnold (1960) and Grinker and Spiegel (1945), the assessment of perceived stress was popularized by Lazarus and Folkman (1984). Appraisal theory centers around the aforementioned concepts of primary and secondary appraisal, and has been measured by tools such as the Perceived Stress Scale (PSS; Cohen, Karmarck, & Mermelstein, 1983) and the Stress Appraisal Measure (SAM; Peacock & Wong, 1990). The PSS is one of the few empirically validated assessment instruments of perceived stress and measures the extent to which situations are viewed as stressful by the patient. Although appraisal is a useful and important concept in explaining individual differences in stress responses, relatively few adequate measures of appraisal have been developed in this area.

The frequency with which major life events occur makes them somewhat problematic as a daily or even weekly source of information. In addition, previous research comparing major and minor stressors has shown that minor stressors (e.g., driving in heavy traffic, argument with spouse) have a greater impact on overall well-being than major stressors (Brantley & Jones, 1993; Delongis, Coyne, Dakof, Folkman, & Lazarus, 1982; Holahan & Holahan, 1987). Therefore, measuring daily minor stress has become an increasingly popular line of research (Monroe, 1983; Thomason, Brantley, Jones, Dyer, & Morris, 1992).

The Daily Stress Inventory (DSI) and subsequently developed Weekly Stress Inventory (WSI) are two minor life events measures that were developed to assess the differential contributions of minor stress to the prediction of physical illness and other psychological symptomatology. The DSI and WSI contain not only a measure of life events, but also a measure of stress appraisal, thus combining both the psychological and environmental perspectives discussed earlier. These two measures are not limited by wide contiguous intervals, are relatively easy to administer, and have direct applications to primary care populations.

DAILY STRESS INVENTORY

Development

Preliminary development of the DSI began with the intention of developing a method of measuring the relationship between minor life events and historically "stress-related" or psychosomatic disorders such as tension headache or gastrointestinal distress. The DSI was developed with several other purposes in mind as well, such as quantifying naturally occurring stress-illness patterns, examining how these patterns may fluctuate over a daily or weekly period of time, and measuring the effectiveness of stress-management interventions (Brantley, Catz, & Boudreaux, 1997).

The Daily Stress Inventory is a 58-item questionnaire that assesses type and intensity of minor stressors. The DSI is designed for males and females over age 17 years with at least a seventh-grade reading level. Although the DSI does not yield formal diagnostic information, it does provide a quantifiable means of monitoring occurrence of minor stressors, elevations in stress responses, and the progress of stress-reduction interventions. Minor stressors are conceptualized as frequently occurring, annoying, or unpleasant events. The DSI samples the occurrence of minor stressors over a 24-hr period, and yields three scores: an Event Score, an Impact Score, and an Impact/Event (I/E) Ratio Score. The Event Score is calculated as the number of stressful items occurring during the day, or the frequency of stressful events. The Impact Score measures perceived stress on a scale of 1 (happened but not stressful) to 7 (caused me to panic). Higher Impact Scores indicate increased levels of perceived stress. The I/E Ratio Score is the average impact rating for a particular day.

The original item pool of the DSI consisted of 71 items generated from stress diaries of graduate students, volunteers, and psychology clinic attendees. These 71 items were narrowed to avoid closely related items as well as items too highly associated with actual physical or psychological conditions. In addition, target items were those that occurred many times in a short period of time and were considered stressful by a majority of individuals.

The 58 items retained on the DSI were grouped into five content areas: Interpersonal Problems, Personal Competency, Cognitive Stressors, Environmental Hassles, and Varied Stressors. Content areas were developed for the purpose of quantifying the amount of stress associated with relatively minor events that have a relatively high potential for occurring on any given day. Scale development conducted primarily on adult community residents ensured that the DSI adequately sampled from domains of interest relative to this population. Respondents are also given the opportunity to generate stressors that are not included in the 58 items but cause significant amounts of stress. Examples of the items included in each of the 5 areas are:

1. Interpersonal Problems: "argued with another person"
2. Personal Competency: "performed poorly at a task"
3. Cognitive Stressors: "heard some bad news"
4. Environmental Hassles: "had car trouble"
5. Varied Stressors: "misplaced something"

Available Norms

Normative data on the DSI was collected from the following demographic groups: community adults, college students, medical patients, and nonpsychotic, psychiatric outpatients. Normative data were originally collected from 473 adults in the community surrounding a large state university in the southeastern United States (see Table 11.1). The sample was composed of 67% females and 33% males, 83% Caucasian individuals and 17% non-Caucasian individuals, and 47% of the sample had a college degree. DSI data were collected for 7 consecutive days and form the database from which T-scores and percentile scores were derived.

The medical patient sample was composed of 223 adults living in the southeastern portion of the United States. Medical disorders represented in the sample were asthma, Crohn's disease, chronic renal failure, angina, and chronic, recurrent headaches. Of the total sample, 58% were females, 42% were males, 73% of the sample was married, and non-Caucasian subjects comprised 45% of the sample. Fifty-one percent of the subjects were employed, 32% were unemployed, 16% were retired, and 1% were full-time students. Fifty-three percent of the medical sample had less than a high school education, 29% had a high school diploma, and 9% had a college degree. Mean age was 45.6 years. Results of one-way analysis of variance (ANOVAs) revealed no significant differences among the medical groups or employment status groups on any DSI scores.

TABLE 11.1
DSI Descriptive Statistics for the Adult Sample (N = 473)

Score	Mean	SD	Range
Event	12.18	8.75	0–58
Impact	30.95	27.88	0–188
I/E Ratio	2.32	1.01	0–5.45
Event$_{WK}$	88.28	52.93	4–405
Impact$_{WK}$	227.05	162.22	4–1032
I/E Ratio$_{WK}$	2.49	0.73	1–6.13

TABLE 11.2
DSI Descriptive Statistics for the Medical Patient Sample (N = 223)

Score	Mean	SD	Range
Event	8.48	7.12	0–34
Impact	20.24	20.96	0–131
I/E Ratio	2.09	1.23	0.00–5.57
Event$_{WK}$	66.92	48.95	0–304
Impact$_{WK}$	155.16	127.77	0–790
I/E Ratio$_{WK}$	2.35	0.98	1.00–5.78

Normalized T-scores and percentiles have been developed for the medical patient sample, and can be found in the DSI manual (Brantley & Jones, 1989). In general, most raw DSI scores in the medical patient sample were five T-scores lower than those in the adult normative sample. Lower Event Scores may represent the fact that medical patients have restricted activity levels or have reduced environmental demands compared to nonmedical patients. Table 11.2 displays descriptive statistics for the medical patient sample.

Psychometric Information

Preliminary reliability and validity data for the DSI were collected from a sample of 433 community adults (Brantley, Waggoner, Jones, & Rappaport, 1987). Mean age was 34.9 years, and although no sex differences were found among number of events endorsed, females were found to rate items as being more stressful than did males. Seven expert judges (clinical psychologists) independently categorized the 58 items into five content categories of 5 to 17 items each.

Reliability.   The DSI has previously been shown to have adequate reliability. Brantley and colleagues (1987) found the internal consistency of the DSI to be .83 for Event Scores and .87 for Impact Scores, suggesting acceptable reliability of domain sampling. Stability across time (28 days) was also examined for the DSI, yielding test–retest reliability coefficients of .72 and.41 for Event Scores and Impact Scores, respectively. These numbers suggest the following implications: daily event occurrence is moderately stable, daily impact is moderately variable, weekly event occurrence is highly variable, and weekly perceived impact is highly stable. Additionally, single Event Scores or Impact Scores of a given day do not appear to reliably predict scores on any other day. The DSI was found to be sensitive to stress level difference on weekdays versus weekends when administered to 70 adults (Brantley, Cocke, Jones, & Goreczny, 1988).

Validity.   Several studies have provided evidence for the DSI's convergent and discriminant validity with both physiological and self-report indices of stress (Brantley et al., 1987; Brantley, Dietz, McKnight, Jones, & Tulley, 1988). For example, Brantley et al. (1987) found that DSI scores were significantly correlated with two other daily measures of stress, namely, a global rating of stress and the Hassles Scale (Kanner, Coyne, Schaefer, & Lazarus, 1981). Further evidence of convergent validity is demonstrated by the fact that the DSI was positively related to changes in two endocrine measures of stress (cortisol and vanillylmandelic acid) when these endocrine measures were sampled for 10 consecutive days along with concurrent administra-tion of the DSI (Brantley, Dietz, McKnight, Jones, & Tulley, 1988). In terms of discriminant validity, the DSI was shown not to be related to daily hostility or a monthly index of daily uplifts (Brantley et al., 1987), showing that the DSI measures the perceived impact of minor events without being unduly influenced by variations in anger or positive event occurrence.

In addition to adequate convergent and discriminant validity, the DSI has also been shown to possess adequate construct validity in its ability to detect daily changes in symptoms of stress-related disorders. Goreczny, Brantley, Buss, and Wa-ters (1988) found that high-stress periods as identified by the DSI have been associ-ated with a higher number of self-reported asthma and anxiety symptoms among asthmatics. An examination of stress and diabetes showed that blood glucose levels were significantly elevated on high-stress days as measured by the DSI (Goetsch, Abel, & Pope, 1994; Goetsch, Wiebe, Veltum, & Van Dorsten, 1990). A clear associa-tion has also been demonstrated between DSI scores and exacerbation of bowel signs and pain symptoms in Crohn's disease patients (Garrett, Brantley, Jones, & McKnight, 1991). Other areas of symptom prediction/association in relation to the DSI include migraine and muscle-contraction headaches (Mosley, Penzien, & Johnson, 1991), symptom exacerbation among lupus patients (Adams, Dammers, Saia, Brantley, & Gaydos, 1994), physical and emotional symptoms of postconcussive syndrome (Gouvier, Cubic, Jones, Brantley, & Cutlip, 1992), and general somatic complaints and symptoms of autonomic arousal among both college students (Waters, Rubman, & Hurry, 1993) and paramedics (Boudreaux et al., 1995).

Administration/Interpretation

The DSI has three different administration periods: a single day, daily for 1 week, and daily over multiple weeks. For clinical purposes, the latter two formats are pref-erable in order to provide an adequate sample of data. Daily and weekly Impact Scores and Impact/Event Ratio Scores can be graphed on a Stress Tracking Chart available with the manual. Allowances are made for missing data during the 1-week measurement period.

After scoring the DSI, a percentile score is derived from the frequency distribution of the appropriate normative sample, and this provides information about the re-spondent's score relative to other scores in that sample. Normalized T-scores have a mean of 50 and a standard deviation of 10. Scores at or above 60 should generally be considered clinically significant and worthy of further review with the patient. It must be mentioned, however, that there is not a cutoff score on the DSI that can lead to the diagnosis of a formal stress disorder as defined by the *DSM–IV* (APA, 1994). However, there are several conditions that may be a focus of clinical attention in the *DSM–IV* for which psychosocial stressors play an integral part, such as relationship problems, academic problems, occupational problems, phase-of-life problems, and stress-related physiological responses affecting a general medical condition (APA, 1994).

Ratings over several days are usually necessary to establish a stable measure of stressful events and their impact. Therefore, caution must be used when interpreting the scores of a single day. When examining Event Scores over several days, higher scores may reflect a higher level of involvement in the environment, such as over-loaded daily schedules, an aggravating environment, or poor organization of time.

This is important when comparing primary care patients' scores to the appropriate normative sample. Lower Event Scores may reflect either lower stress or the extent to which the given individual is less able to interact with his or her environment due to mitigating factors such as increased age, number of chronic illnesses, or lack of mobility.

High Impact Scores on the DSI represent a reliable indicator of a person's appraisal of daily events and subsequent stress. High Impact/Event Ratio Scores are indicators of an individual's vulnerability to stressful events, or perhaps a temporary state of high sensitivity due to excessive environmental demands. Low Impact/Event Ratio Scores may reflect above-average stress management skills or the tendency to deny or to minimize the effect of stressful events experienced.

WEEKLY STRESS INVENTORY

As discussed previously, the DSI has been used for symptom monitoring with specific medical illnesses, and has been proposed for use as an outcome measure in the implementation of stress management interventions. However, for many research and clinical purposes, daily assessment may be too brief and monthly assessments may be too long. Therefore, to bridge this gap in assessment methodology, the Weekly Stress Inventory (WSI) was developed (Jones & Brantley, 1989). Brantley, Jones, Boudreaux, and Catz (1995) recommended the use of the Weekly Stress Inventory for specific medical disorders where stress may play a part in symptom exacerbation.

Development of the WSI

The WSI has several conceptual and practical advantages for examining the links between minor life events and disease processes. The relatively high workload placed on the respondents completing daily measures may restrict the amount of time given to the assessment period. Not only is weekly measurement is more conducive to longer, more extensive assessment periods, but it also allows for medical or psychological patients to complete this measure before or after their weekly appointments.

Item generation for the WSI was performed based on the contributions of the Daily Stress Inventory, the Hassles Scale (Kanner et al., 1981), the Inventory of Small Life Events (ISLE; Zautra, Guarnaccia, & Dohrenwend, 1986), and write-in items from persons completing the aforementioned measures. One hundred community-dwelling adults completed a pilot version of the WSI, and items were retained if they were endorsed by at least 10% of the population, were considered relevant to the population, and had an item-total correlation of .25 or greater. Based on this criteria, 87 items were retained.

For each of the 87 items, the respondent is asked to indicate whether the item occurred within the past week, to rate the perceived stressfulness of the experienced event on a scale from 1 (occurred, but was not stressful) to 7 (extremely stressful), and to indicate whether that event happened three or more times that week. The three scores derived from the WSI are identical to those from the DSI, namely, Impact Scores, Event Scores, and Impact/Event Ratio Scores. Directions for the WSI and selected sample items are included in Appendix A.

Standardization was performed on 522 community-dwelling adults matched to the 1980 census data in terms of race, age, and sex. Normative data for the WSI are presented in Table 11.3

In addition to normative data of community adults, data were collected on medical patient populations. Demographically, this sample was approximately 81% female, 75% African American, and 75% uninsured. Mean age was 45 years and mean level of education was approximately 11 years. Means and standard deviations for WSI Event Scores and Impact Scores were 22.85 (15.21) and 86.85 (75.90), respectively. Similar to the DSI, WSI scores for medical patients with chronic illnesses tend to be lower than those found in community adults. Mean Event Scores are typically five points lower, and mean Impact Scores average 10 points lower. As suggested earlier, these lower Impact Scores and Event Scores may represent restricted activity levels of individuals with chronic medical illnesses. This pattern of lower WSI scores has been observed in other medical samples, including headache patients (Mosley, Penzien, & Johnson, 1991) and male cardiac patients (Mosley et al., 1996).

Psychometric Properties

Reliability estimates for the WSI were conducted on the standardization sample, as well as on samples of headache patients and coronary heart disease patients (Mosley, Seville, Johnson, Brantley, Penzien, Wittrock, & Rubman, 1991; Mosley et al., 1996). High-reliability estimates were found for all three samples for the WSI Event subscale (.92–.96) and for the WSI Impact subscales (.93–.99). The WSI has been reported to have adequate test–retest reliability coefficients (>.83), both within the same week and across a 2-week period (Brantley et al., 1995; Mosley et al., 1996). Concurrent validity has also been established for the WSI, as it has correlated highly ($r =$ .61 to .69) with other measures of minor stress (i.e., the Hassles Scale).

Commonly Used Adjuncts

The WSI is often supplemented with measures of major life events, such as the Life Events Survey (LES; Sarason, Johnson, & Siegel, 1978), in order to comprehensively assess differential sources of stress over a given period of time. In fact, recent research has shown that when using both measures and controlling for the presence of major life events, minor stress adds unique variance to the prediction of subsequent development of depressive symptoms (Brantley, Scarinci, Ames, & Jones, 1998) and physical symptoms (Brantley & Jones, 1993).

In addition to other measures of life stress, there are many psychological inventories that assess psychological or physical symptomatology on a weekly basis and can be used in conjunction with the WSI. These inventories include the Beck Depression

TABLE 11.3
Normative Table: WSI Scores Stratified by Age for Adult Community Sample

Age (years)	n	WSI Event		WSI Impact	
		Mean	SD	Mean	SD
15–19	67	38.25	21.47	189.39	99.50
20–39	223	35.00	17.55	113.09	77.18
40–50	138	29.57	19.16	94.50	75.08
60	91	24.65	20.75	78.68	94.52
Total	519	32.16	19.46	105.38	84.74

Note. From Jones and Brantley (1989). Reprinted with permission.

Inventory for Primary Care (BDI–PC; Beck, Guth, Steer, & Ball, 1997; Beck, Steer, Ball, Ciervo, & Kabat, 1997), the Center for Epidemiological Studies of Depression Scale (CES-D; Radloff, 1977), and the Modified Wahler Physical Symptoms Inventory (Wahler, 1983).

CLINICAL IMPLEMENTATION OF THE DSI/WSI IN A PRIMARY CARE SETTING

The DSI and WSI have many implications for use with primary care patients. First, these measures could be used as methods for identifying populations at risk for developing stress-related disorders such as chronic headaches, irritable bowel syndrome, and arthritis exacerbation. Although both of these measures are able to identify highly stressed individuals, the WSI has been suggested by the authors as the preferred measure when a primary care physician wishes to obtain a discrete picture of amount and perception of minor stress over the recent past. The DSI is more useful for tracking symptoms and stress over time to determine whether stress plays a major role in a primary care patient's presenting physical symptoms and/or physical symptoms and/or physical disorders.

Other more anecdotal uses have been observed while conducting some of the already mentioned studies with the DSI. For example, many medical patients have reported that tracking their stressors allows them to become more aware of the daily activities in which they were choosing to engage, thus establishing a greater sense of control and predictability over their daily routine. Therefore, the DSI and WSI may have clinical uses as a therapeutic monitoring tool, although further research elaborating the specific nature of this potential benefit must still be conducted.

Finally, the DSI and WSI were designed with the intention of being used as an outcome variable in the implementation of stress-management interventions such as those suggested by Miechenbaum (1974) and Barlow and Rapee (1991). Given the high rate of chronic illnesses and unremitting stressors in primary care populations, studying the relationship between stress and illness is a logical objective. Use of the DSI and/or the WSI to accomplish this objective is both practical and efficient, as these measures can be completed in the time it takes for a patient to wait to see his or her doctor. Moreover, there are very few cost constraints, and if the respondent has at least a seventh-grade reading level, these measures are very easy to use. The DSI can be obtained from Psychological Assessment Resources Incorporated in Odessa, Florida. The WSI can be obtained by contacting the senior author.

SUMMARY

Both the Daily Stress Inventory and the Weekly Stress Inventory are psychometrically sound, nonintrusive measures of minor life stressors shown to have a great deal of predictive value in the occurrence and severity of many symptoms of chronic illnesses. Previous research has shown that psychosocial distress may have a higher impact on health status than many chronic illnesses (Kroenke & Mangelsdorff, 1989). The high rates of chronic illnesses in low-income, primary care patients suggest that both the DSI and WSI are appropriate screening devices for psychological symptomatology among these patients. Indeed, Brantley and Jones (1993) previously found an association between minor stress and exacerbation of illness symptomatology in disorders presumed to be "stress related," such as headaches, asthma, inflammatory bowel disease, and diabetes. In addition, when used in conjunction with a measure of major life events such as the LES, DSI, and WSI scores can be used by clinical researchers as outcome variables in psychological regimens such as stress management programs. Studies (e.g., Timmerman, Emmelkamp, & Sanderman, 1998) have shown that a stress management training program can improve outcomes in people at risk due to high stress secondary to life events. Timmerman and colleagues (1998) found that stress management resulted in significantly less distress and daily hassles, indicating the importance of measuring these variables in a clinical setting for primary care patients. Brown (1989) suggested that frequent assessments of stressful events and symptomatology may strengthen our understanding of the causal factors involved in the stress-disorder relationship.

In a primary care practice, the DSI and WSI can also help primary care practitioners to identify "at-risk" patients experiencing high levels of minor stress that may complicate their medical picture through symptom exacerbation of stress-related illnesses. Identification of these "at-risk" patients can also help to ensure their referral to stress management programs that will serve to decrease future unnecessary and costly primary care medical services, as well as to increase a patient's overall quality of life. Greater collaboration between physicians and psychologists was previously suggested as a method of increasing the quality of service delivery in primary care medicine (McDaniel, 1995), and both the DSI and WSI can be used as clinical tools to facilitate this increased collaboration for improved management of primary care patients.

APPENDIX A
Directions and Selected Items From the Weekly Stress Inventory

Directions:

Below are listed a variety of events that may be viewed as stressful or unpleasant. Read each item carefully and decide whether or not that event happened to you during **this past week**. If the event did not happen this week, circle the **X** to the right of that item. If the event **did** happen, show the amount of stress that it caused you by circling a number from **1 to 7** to the right of that item (see scale below). Additionally, if the event happened 3 or more times during this past week, put a check in the blank (__) to the right of that item.

Selected Items:

Had a job or assignment overdue

Argued with a coworker

Hurried to meet a deadline

Was graded or evaluated on performance

Had household chores (shopping, cooking, etc.)

Was lied to, fooled, or tricked

Had confrontation with someone of authority (police, boss)

Spoke or performed in public

Had too many responsibilities

REFERENCES

Adams, S. G., Jr., Dammers, P. M., Saia, T. L., Brantley, P. J., & Gaydos, G. R. (1994). Stress, depression, and anxiety predict average symptom severity and daily symptom fluctuation in systemic lupus erythematosus. *Journal of Behavioral Medicine, 17,* 459–477.

Alexander, F. (1950). *Psychosomatic medicine: Its principles and applications.* New York: Norton.

American Psychiatric Association. (1994). *Diagnostic and statistical manual of mental disorders* (4th ed.). Washington, DC: Author.

Arnold, M. B. (1960). *Emotion and personality* (Vols. 1 and 2). New York: Columbia University Press.

Barlow, D. H., & Rapee, R. M. (1991). *Mastering stress: A lifestyle approach.* Dallas, TX: American Health.

Baum, A., & Grunberg, N. (1995). Measurement of stress hormones. In S. Cohen, R. C. Kessler, and L. U. Gordon (Eds.), *Measuring stress: A guide for health and social scientists* (pp. 175–192). New York: Oxford University Press.

Beck, A. T., Guth, D., Steer, R., & Ball, R. (1997). Screening for major depression disorders in medical inpatients with the Beck Depression Inventory for Primary Care. *Behaviour Research and Therapy, 35,* 785–791.

Beck, A. T., Steer, R. A., Ball, R., Ciervo, C. A., & Kabat, M. (1997). Use of the Beck Anxiety and Depression Inventories for Primary Care with medical outpatients. *Psychological Assessment, 4,* 211–219.

Berghuis, J. P., Heiman, J. R., Rothman, I., & Berger, R. E. (1996). Psychological and physical factors involved in chronic idiopathic prostatitis. *Journal of Psychosomatic Research, 41,* 313–325.

Boudreaux, E., Brantley, P. J., Mandry, C., Adams, S., Springer, A., & Rabalais, J. (1995). The identification of stress responders: Differences in between- and within-subjects analyses. *Proceedings of the 29th Annual Association for the Advancement of Behavior Therapy Convention,* p. 333.

Brantley, P. J., Carmack, C. Boudreaux, E., & Scarinci, I. (1996). *High risk behaviors in low-income primary care patients in Louisiana.* Unpublished document, Division of Primary Care Research, Pennington Biomedical Research Center, Baton Rouge, LA.

Brantley, P. J., Catz, S. L., & Boudreaux, E. D. (1997). Daily Stress Inventory. In C. P. Zalaquett & R. J. Wood (Eds.), *Evaluating stress: A book of resources* (pp. 97–112). Lanham, MD: Scarecrow Press.

Brantley, P. J., Cocke, T. B., Jones, G. N., & Goreczny, A. J. (1988). The Daily Stress Inventory: Validity and effect of repeated administration. *Journal of Psychopathology and Behavioral Assessment, 10,* 75–81.

Brantley, P. J., & Jones, G. N. (1989). *The Daily Stress Inventory: Professional manual.* Odessa, FL: Psychological Assessment Resources.

Brantley, P. J., Dietz, L. S., McKnight, G. T., Jones, G. N., & Tulley, R. (1988). Convergence between the Daily Stress Inventory and endocrine measures of stress. *Journal of Consulting and Clinical Psychology, 56,* 549–551.

Brantley, P. J., & Jones, G. N. (1993). Daily stress and stress-related disorders. *Annals of Behavioral Medicine, 15,* 17–25.

Brantley, P. J., Jones, G. N., Boudreaux, E. D., & Catz, S. L. (1995). Weekly Stress Inventory. In C. P. Zalaquett & R. J. Wood (Eds.), *Evaluating stress: A book of resources* (pp. 405–420). Lanham, MD: Scarecrow Press.

Brantley, P. J., Scarinci, I. C., Ames, S. C., & Jones, G. N. (1998). Minor stressors as predictors of depression in a low-income primary care population. *International Journal of Psychiatry in Medicine, 27*(4), 304–305.

Brantley, P. J., Veitia, M. C., Callon, E. B., Buss, R. R., & Sias, C. R. (1986). Assessing the impact of psychological intervention on family practice clinic visits. *Family Medicine, 18,* 351–354.

Brantley, P. J., Waggoner, C. D., Jones, G. N., & Rappaport, N. B. (1987). A Daily Stress Inventory: Development, reliability, and validity. *Journal of Behavioral Medicine, 10,* 61–74.

Brown, G. W. (1989). Life events and measurement. In G. W. Brown & T. O. Harris (Eds.), *Life events and illness* (pp. 3–45). New York: Guilford.

Brunton, S. A., & Edwards, R. K. (1994). Hypertension. In A. K. David, T. A. Johnson, Jr., D. M. Phillips, & J. E. Scherger (Eds.), *Family medicine: Principles and practice* (4th ed., pp. 216–223). New York: Springer-Verlag.

Campbell, T. L., Seaburn, D. B., & McDaniel, S. H. (1994). Family stress and counseling. In A. K. David, T. A. Johnson, Jr., D. M. Phillips, & J. E. Scherger (Eds.), *Family medicine: Principles and practice* (4th ed., pp. 216–223). New York: Springer-Verlag.

Cannon, W. B. (1939). *The wisdom of the body* (2nd ed.). New York: Norton.

Cohen, S., Karmarck, T., & Mermelstein, R. (1983). A global measure of perceived stress. *Journal of Health and Social Behavior, 24,* 385–396.

Cohen, S., Kessler, R. C., & Gordon, L. U. (1995). Strategies for measuring stress in studies of psychiatric and physical disorders. In S. Cohen, R. C. Kessler, & L. U. Gordon (Eds.), *Measuring stress: A guide for health and social scientists* (pp. 3–26). New York: Oxford University Press.

Dalack, G. W., & Zweifler, A. J. (1997). Counseling for behavior change. In D. J. Knesper, M. B. Riba, & T. L. Schwenk (Eds.), *Primary care psychiatry* (pp. 77–92). Philadelphia: W. B. Saunders.

DeLongis, A., Coyne, J. C., Dakof, G., Folkman, S., & Lazarus, R. S. (1982). Relationships of daily hassles, uplifts, and major life events to health status. *Health Psychology, 1,* 119–136.

Dohrenwend, B. S., & Dohrenwend, B. P. (1974). *Stressful life events: Their nature and effects.* New York: Wiley.

Faravelli, C. (1985). Life events preceding the onset of panic disorder. *Journal of Affective Disorders, 9,* 103–105.

Ford, C. V. (1997). Somatization and fashionable diagnoses: Illness as a way of life. *Scandinavian Journal of Work and Environmental Health, 23*(Suppl. 3), 7–16.

Friedman, M. J., Charney, D. S., & Deutch, A. Y. (Eds.) (1995). *Neurobiological and clinical consequences of stress: From normal adaptation to PTSD.* Philadelphia: Lippincott-Raven.

Gage, L. W., & Leidy, N. K. (1991). Screening for psychosocial distress: Implications for prevention and health promotion. *Public Health Nursing, 8,* 267–275.

Garrett, V. D., Brantley, P. J., Jones, G. N., & McKnight, G. T. (1991). The relation between daily stress and Crohn's disease. *Journal of Behavioral Medicine, 14,* 87–95.

Gillis, J. S. (1992). Stress, anxiety, and cognitive buffering. *Behavioral Medicine, 18,* 79–83.

Goetsch, V. L., Abel, J. L., & Pope, M. K. (1994). The effects of stress, mood, and coping on blood glucose in NIDDM: A perspective pilot evaluation. *Behaviour Research and Therapy, 32,* 503–510.

Goetsch, V. L., Wiebe, D. J., Veltum, L. G., & Van Dorsten, B. (1990). Stress and blood glucose in Type II diabetes mellitus. *Behaviour Research and Therapy, 28,* 531–537.

Goreczny, A. J., Brantley, P. J., Buss, R. R., & Waters, W. F. (1988). Daily stress and anxiety and their relation to daily fluctuations of symptoms in asthma and chronic obstructive pulmonary disease (COPD) patients. *Journal of Psychopathology and Behavioral Assessment, 10,* 259–267.

Gouvier, W. D., Cubic, B., Jones, G. N., Brantley, P. J., & Cutlip, Q. (1992). Postconcussion symptoms and daily stress in normal and head-injured college populations. *Archives of Clinical Neuropsychology, 7,* 193–211.

Grinker, R. R., & Spiegel, J. P. (1945). *Men under stress.* New York: McGraw-Hill.

Hawkins, N. C., Davies, R., & Holmes, T. H. (1957). Evidence of psychosocial factors in the development of pulmonary tuberculosis. *American Review of Tuberculosis and Pulmonary Disorders, 75,* 768–780.

Holahan, C. K., & Holahan, C. J. (1987). Life stress, hassles, and self-efficacy in aging: A replication and extension. *Journal of Applied Psychology, 17,* 574–592.

Holmes, T. H., & Rahe, R. H. (1967). The social readjustment rating scale. *Journal of Psychosomatic Research, 11,* 213–218.

Isaac, M., Janca, A., Burke, K. C., Costa, J. A., Acuda, S. W., Altamura, A. C., Burke, J. D., Chandrashekar, C. R., Miranda, C. T., & Tacchini, G. (1995). Medically unexplained somatic symptoms in different cultures: A preliminary report from phase I of the World Health Organization International Study of Somatoform Disorders. *Psychotherapy and Psychosomatics, 64,* 88–93.

Jones, G. N., & Brantley, P. J. (1989). *The Weekly Stress Inventory.* Unpublished manuscript, Louisiana State University, Baton Rouge.

Kanner, A. D., Coyne, J. C., Schaefer, C., & Lazarus, R. S. (1981). Comparison of two modes of stress measurement: Daily hassles and uplifts versus major life events. *Journal of Behavioral Medicine, 4,* 1–39.

Katon, W. (1985). Somatization in primary care. *Journal of Family Practice, 21,* 257–258.

Katon, W., & Schulberg, H. (1992). Epidemiology of depression in primary care. *General Hospital Psychiatry, 14,* 237–247.

Kiecolt-Glaser, J. K., & Glaser, R. (1995). Measurement of immune responses. In S. Cohen, R. C. Kessler, & L. U. Gordon (Eds.), *Measuring stress: A guide for health and social scientists* (pp. 213–229). New York: Oxford University Press.

Krantz, D. S., & Falconer, J. J. (1995). Measurement of cardiovascular responses. In S. Cohen, R. C. Kessler, & L. U. Gordon (Eds.), *Measuring stress: A guide for health and social scientists* (pp. 193–212). New York: Oxford University Press.

Kroenke, K., & Mangelsdorff, A. D. (1989). Common symptoms in ambulatory care: Incidence, evaluation, therapy, and outcome. *American Journal of Medicine, 86,* 262–266.

Lacey, J. I. (1950). Individual differences in somatic response patterns. *Journal of Comparative and Physiological Psychology, 43*, 338–350.

Langer, A., Farnot, U., Garcia, C., Barros, F., Victora, C., Belizan, J. M., & Villar, J. (1996). The Latin American trial of psychosocial support during pregnancy: Effects on mother's well-being and satisfaction. Latin American Network for Perinatal and Reproductive Research (LANPER). *Social Science and Medicine, 42*, 1589–1597.

Lazarus, R. S., & Folkman, S. (1984). *Stress, appraisal, and coping.* New York: Springer.

Lief, A. (Ed.). (1948). *The commonsense psychiatry of Dr. Adolf Meyer.* New York: McGraw-Hill.

Lovallo, W. R. (1997). *Stress and health: Biological and psychological interactions.* Sage: Thousand Oaks, CA.

Maier, S. F., Watkins, L. R., & Fleshner, M. (1994). Psychoneuroimmunology: The interface between behavior, brain, and immunity. *American Psychologist, 49*, 1004–1017.

Mazure, C. M. (1998). Life stressors as risk factors in depression. *Clinical Psychology: Science and Practice, 5*, 291–313.

McDaniel, S. H. (1992). *Medical family therapy: A biopsychosocial approach to families with health problems.* New York: Basic Books.

McDaniel, S. H. (1995). Collaboration between psychologists and family physicians: Implementing the biopsychosocial model. *Professional Psychology: Research and Practice, 26*, 117–122.

Meyer, R. J., & Haggerty, R. J. (1962). Streptococcal infections in families: Factors altering individuals susceptibility. *Pediatrics, 29*, 539–549.

Miechenbaum, D. (1974). *Cognitive behavior modification.* Morristown, NJ: General Learning Press.

Monroe, S. M. (1983). Major and minor life events as predictors of psychological distress: Further issues and findings. *Journal of Behavioral Medicine, 6*, 189–205.

Mosley, T. H., Penzien, D. B., & Johnson, C. A. (1991). Time series analysis of stress and headache. *Cephalalgia, 11*, 306–307.

Mosley, T. H., Seville, J. T., Johnson, C. A., Brantley, P. J., Penzien, D. B., Wittrock, D. A., & Rubman, S. (1991, March). *Psychometric properties of the Weekly Stress Inventory.* Paper presented at the 12th annual meeting of the Society of Behavioral Medicine, Washington, DC.

Mosley, T. H., Payne, T. H., Plaud, J. J., Johnson, C. A., Wittrock, D. A., Sevile, J. L., Penzien, D. B., & Rodriguez, G. (1996). Psychometric properties of the Weekly Stress Inventory (WSI): Extension to a patient sample with coronary heart disease. *Journal of Behavioral Medicine, 19*(3), 273–287.

Mynors-Wallace, L., Gath, D. H., Lloyd-Thomas, A. R., & Tomlinson, D. (1995). Randomized controlled trial comparing problem solving treatment with amitriptyline and placebo for major depression in primary care. *British Medical Journal, 310*, 441–446.

Peacock, E. J., & Wong, P. T. P. (1990). The Stress Appraisal Measure (SAM): A multi-dimensional approach to cognitive appraisal. *Stress Medicine, 6*, 227–236.

Public Health Service Agency for Health Care Policy and Research. (1993). *Depression in primary care: Detection and diagnosis* (AHCPR Publication, No. 93-0551). Rockville, MD: U.S. Department of Health and Human Services.

Radloff, L. S. (1977). The CES-D scale: A self-report depression scale for research in the general population. *Applied Psychological Measurement, 1*, 385–401.

Robinson, P., Bush, T., Von Korff, M., Katon, W., Line, E., Simon, G. E., & Walker, E. (1994). Primary care physician use of cognitive behavioral techniques with depressed patients. *Journal of Family Practice, 40*, 352–357.

Rosenberg, M., Commerford, K., & Driever, M. (1991). Identification of psychosocial distress: A comparison of internal medicine and family medicine residents. *Journal of General Internal Medicine, 6*, 529–534.

Sarason, I. G., Johnson, J. H., & Siegel, J. M. (1978). Assessing the impact of life changes: Development of the Life Experiences Survey. *Journal of Clinical and Consulting Psychology, 46*, 932–946.

Selye, H. (1950). *The physiology and pathology of exposure to stress.* Montreal: Acta.

Selye, H. (1956). *The stress of life.* New York: McGraw-Hill.

Sloane, P. D. (Ed.). (1998). *Essentials of family medicine* (3rd Ed.). Baltimore, MD: Williams & Wilkins.

Smith, C. K., Sheehan, J. P. & Ulchaker, M. M. (1994). Diabetes mellitus. In A. K. David, T. A. Johnson, Jr., D. M. Phillips, & J. E. Scherger (Eds.), *Family medicine: Principles and practice* (4th ed., pp. 216–223). New York: Springer-Verlag.

Sobel, D. S. (1995). Rethinking medicine: Improving health outcomes with cost-effective psychosocial interventions. *Psychosomatic Medicine, 57*, 234–244.

Thomason, B. T., Brantley, P. J., Jones, G. N., Dyer, H. R., & Morris, J. L. (1992). The relation between stress and disease activity in rheumatoid arthritis. *Journal of Behavioral Medicine, 15*, 215–220.

Timmerman, I. G. H., Emmelkamp, P. M. G., & Sanderman, R. (1998). The effects of a stress-management training program in individuals at risk in the community at large. *Behaviour Research and Therapy, 36,* 863–875.

Wahler, H. J. (1983). *The Wahler Physical Symptoms Inventory manual.* Los Angeles: Western Psychological Service.

Waters, W. F., Rubman, S., & Hurry, M. J. (1993). The prediction of somatic complaints using the Autonomic Nervous System Response Inventory (ANSRI) and the Daily Stress Inventory (DSI). *Journal of Psychosomatic Research, 37,* 117–126.

Wise, R. N. (1995). Commentary: Underdiagnosis of depression in general practice. *Mind/Body Medicine, 1,* 23.

Zautra, A. J., Guarnaccia, C. A., & Dohrenwend, B. P. (1986). Measuring small life events. *American Journal of Community Psychology, 14,* 629–655.

The Beck Depression Inventory (BDI) and the Center for Epidemiologic Studies Depression Scale (CES-D)

Phillip J. Brantley
Pennington Biomedical Research Center,
Baton Rouge, Louisiana

Daniel J. Mehan, Jr.
Janet L. Thomas
Louisiana State University

Depressive disorders are among the most prevalent forms of psychopathology. Large-scale community studies have found a 17% to 24% lifetime prevalence rate for depressive symptomatology (Horwath, Johnson, Klerman, & Weissman, 1992; Kessler et al., 1994). Some have estimated that the point prevalence of the depressive illnesses approximates 6% to 10% of the population (Katon et al., 1996). The U.S. Department of Health and Human Services (1995) reported that the annual incidence of depressive disorders among adult Americans is higher than 10%. Analyses of data from all five sites of the Epidemiological Catchment Area (ECA) program of the National Institute of Mental Health (NIMH) indicate a 1-month prevalence rate of 2.2% for major depressive disorder and 3.3% for dysthymic disorder (Regier, Goldberg, & Taube, 1978).

The prevalence of major depressive disorder in the primary care sector is even greater. Estimates of prevalence rates for major depression in this population have ranged from 4.8% to 8.6% (Callahan et al., 1996). When dysthymic disorder and depression not otherwise specified (NOS) are included, nearly 25% of the primary care population is thought to have a depressive disorder. Katon (1982) found that more than 33% of consecutive primary care attendees reported substantial levels of psychological distress. In addition, approximately 15% to 25% met diagnostic criteria for an affective disorder. Zung, Broadhead, and Roth (1993) found that approximately 21% of a national survey of over 75,000 patients receiving medical care by a family practice physician described significant symptoms of depression. Moreover, approximately 50% of all patients who are treated for depressive illnesses are seen exclusively in primary care clinics. It is further estimated that an additional 20% to 30% of depressed patients are treated in both specialty and primary care settings (Katon et al., 1996).

The prevalence of depressive disorders in primary care is not likely to diminish in the near future. New health care policy is placing greater responsibility on primary care physicians regarding mental health issues. In response to rising cost pressures, insurance coverage of mental health treatment has grown more restrictive (Simon, Ormel, VonKorff, & Barlow, 1995). Proposals to reform health care financing often include stricter limits for mental health coverage than for general medical services. Consequently, third-party payers are attempting to shift mental health services to primary care generalists, whose costs are only 33% to 50% of those incurred by specialists (Schulberg et al., 1997).

The ramifications of depressive disorders are substantial. Research over the last decade has clearly demonstrated the burden that depressive illnesses have on individuals and on society as a whole (Simon, VonKorff, & Barlow, 1995). Depression has been shown to produce profound social and vocational disability (Schulberg et al., 1997). The Rand Medical Outcomes Study (Wells et al., 1989) and the PRIME–MD 1000 (Spitzer et al., 1995) concluded that the debilitating effects of depression equal or surpass those of many chronic physical illnesses. Several studies have demonstrated that the reduction in physical and mental functioning demonstrated by patients with depression was similar to the decrease in functioning demonstrated by patients with diabetes, arthritis, heart disease and low back pain (Coulehan, Schulberg, Block, Madonia, & Rodriguez, 1997; Schonfeld et al., 1997; Simon, VonKorff, & Barlow, 1995).

In addition to increased disability, a diagnosis of depression is associated with a generalized increase in the frequency of health care visits and health care costs (Simon, VonKorff, & Barlow, 1995). These researchers investigated the direct health care costs for a large sample of primary care patients with recognized depression. They found that patients diagnosed with depression had higher annual health care costs ($4,246 vs. $2,371, $p < .001$) than patients without a depressive diagnosis. In addition, depressed patients were found to have higher costs for every category of care including primary care, medical specialty, medical inpatient, pharmacy, and laboratory. The large cost differences persisted after adjustment for medical comorbidity and direct treatment costs for depression.

If left untreated, the consequences of depression can be lethal. According to a 1994 investigation of completed suicides, an estimated 62% of suicide victims had some form of mental disorder, most frequently depression. Moreover, 50% had consulted their general practitioner within 2 months of their suicide, (Matthews, Milne, & Ashcroft, 1994).

Negative consequences of depressive symptoms are even evidenced among primary care patients who do not meet full criteria for major depression. A recent study (Wells et al., 1989) discovered that poor physical, social, and role functioning of patients with depressive symptoms, whether or not they met full criteria for major depression, was equal to or greater than that of patients with chronic conditions, such as hypertension, diabetes, and arthritis. This point is particularly important because researchers estimate that up to 30% of all primary care patients experience some depressive symptoms.

The high prevalence rates and significant negative ramifications of depressive symptoms among primary care populations underscore the importance of detecting these symptoms among patients. However, research continues to suggest that primary care providers fail to detect and treat as many as 35% to 70% of patients with depressive disorders (Coyne, Schwenk, & Fechner-Bates, 1995; Mulrow et al., 1995). Additional studies have consistently found that primary care physicians identify only 20% to 35% of patients with major depressive disorder or dysthymic disorder (Coyne et al., 1995; Coyne & Schwenk, 1997; Schulberg et al., 1995; Zung, Broadhead, & Roth, 1993).

Recent studies have identified several possible reasons for the low rate of identification of mood disorders by primary care providers. First, time constraints often prevent physicians from providing an adequate review of depressive symptomatology. Second, funding policies that penalize primary care providers for making a diagnosis of depression (i.e., no reimbursement) may contribute to the low detection rates (Bruce, Takeuchi, & Leaf, 1991). Third, patients often attribute differential meaning to the malaise being experienced. Therefore, physicians confronted with a patient's ambiguous symptoms are likely to interpret them within diagnostic paradigms most familiar to their specialty and theoretical orientation.

One of the most common detection challenges facing the general practitioner is that ambulatory medical patients tend to present their depressive symptoms in a less direct form than is typically provided in a mental health facility. This tendency may be compounded by the presence of true medical symptomatology (Van Hook, 1996). As a consequence, physical and psychiatric illnesses with similar manifestations may be inaccurately labeled and inappropriately treated. Zung et al. (1993) reported that only 2% of primary care patients cited depression as the reason for their visit, although 21% were diagnosed with a clinical depressive episode. Coyne et al. (1995) found that patients who were more openly psychologically distressed and presented with a greater variety of depressive symptomatology were detected more frequently by primary care physicians than patients manifesting predominantly somatic symptoms.

Poor recognition of depression in primary care patients has prompted a demand for more effective and efficient methods of screening for depressive symptoms in primary care settings. Attempts to improve screening procedures have included the implementation of multiple measure inventories, observer rating scales, diagnostic interviews, and self-report symptom scales. Time and relative ease of administration have made self-report measures increasingly popular over the years. However, despite the practicality of these instruments, they are not without their limitations. This chapter reviews two of the most widely used self-report depression screening tools, the Beck Depression Inventory (BDI and its derivatives) and the Center for Epidemiologic Studies–depression Scale (CES–D), and comments on their utility within primary care settings.

BDI MEASURES

History of BDI Scales

Original BDI. The original BDI was developed to assess the severity of depression in adolescents and adults and was not intended to reflect any particular theory of depression. The scale was based on clinical observations and symptom descriptions that were reported frequently by psychiatric patients but infrequently by nondepressed psychiatric patients (Beck, Ward, Mendelson, Mock, & Erbaugh, 1961). The observations and descriptions were consolidated into 21 items, which assessed the following 21 symptoms and attitudes: mood, pessimism, sense of failure, self-dissatisfaction, guilt, punishment, self-dislike, self-accusations, suicidal ideas, crying, irritability, social withdrawal, indecisiveness, body image change, work difficulty, insomnia, fatigability, loss of appetite, weight loss, somatic preoccupation, and loss of libido. Each item consisted of four alternative response choices, organized according to the severity of their content. Selection of an individual response within each item corresponded to a severity rating that ranged between 0 and 3.

BDI–Short Form. A shorter, simplified version of the BDI was proposed in 1972 (Beck & Beck, 1972). This shortened form consisted of 13 items selected from the original BDI on the basis of the relation of each item to the overall score and to clinical ratings of depression (Vredenberg, Krames, & Flett, 1985). Although the short version of the inventory was designed to facilitate the use of the BDI in family practice, many researchers and clinicians began to utilize the short form as a substitute for the original BDI. The dangers of this practice were outlined in Vredenberg et al. (1985) and echoed by Steer and Beck (1985). Given that the BDI–Short Form is not a generally accepted substitute for the BDI at present, the measure's usefulness as a screening instrument in primary care is limited and it is not addressed further in this review.

BDI–IA. In 1979, a revised version of the original BDI was published (Beck, Rush, Shaw, & Emery, 1979). This version, the BDI–IA, eliminated alternative wordings for the same symptoms and avoided double negatives. Six items remained unchanged, and the wording of the other 15 items was altered. The number of statements per item was reduced from four to three. A technical manual for the BDI–IA was first published in 1987 and was followed by a 1993 edition that included only slight revisions of recommended score ranges for determining the severity level of depressive symptoms. Beck and Steer (1987) compared the psychometric characteristics of this revised BDI with the characteristics of the original version and found them to be comparable in psychiatric patients. Until that report, most individuals were unaware of the BDI–IA and the majority of the literature still employed the original measure. Even today, much of the cited literature regarding the BDI employed the original version.

BDI–II. As the American Psychiatric Association continued to revise its *Diagnostic and Statistical Manual of Mental Disorders* (*DSM*), the adequacy of the original BDI was questioned (Moran & Lambert, 1983; Vredenberg et al., 1985). Steer and Beck (1985) were confident that the changes in criteria initiated in both *DSM–II* and *DSM–III* did not warrant a change in the original BDI measures. However, the new criteria of *DSM–III-R* and *DSM–IV*, coupled with the fact that some symptoms typically observed in long-term hospitalized patients became gradually less useful in assessing the severity of depression in outpatients and short-term inpatients, highlighted the need for a new psychological measure of depression. This need was satisfied with the introduction of the Beck Depression Inventory–Second Edition (BDI–II). In this revised version, four items (weight loss, body image change, somatic preoccupation, and work difficulty) were replaced with four new items (agitation, worthlessness, concentration difficulty, and loss of energy), two items were changed in order to permit increases as well as decreases in both appetite and sleep, and only three items were not reworded (Beck, Steer, & Brown, 1996). The process of item development was conducted on a sample of psychiatric outpatients diagnosed with various psychiatric disorders. Unlike the BDI–IA, the BDI–II represented a substantial revision of the original BDI.

BDI–PC. Due to the high degree of overlap between the somatic and perform-ance symptoms of depression and the types of symptoms that occur in medical ill-nesses, many depression screening instruments tend to produce inflated estimates of depression in patients with medical problems. Consequently, a version of the BDI that focused on nonsomatic items was constructed in order to screen out medical pa-tients without affective and cognitive symptoms of depression. The resultant seven-item, self-report instrument was called the Beck Depression Inventory for Pri-mary Care (BDI–PC). This scale included an item that assessed sadness and an item that assessed loss of pleasure, as one of these two symptoms is necessary to establish a *DSM–IV* diagnosis of major depressive disorder. A suicidal wishes or thoughts item was selected because this symptom is an important clinical indicator of suicidal risk in depressed patients. The final four items (pessimism, past failure, self-dislike, and self-criticalness) were included because they loaded significantly on the cogni-tive dimension of the BDI–II (Beck, Steer, Ball, Ciervo, & Kabat, 1997).

Psychometric Characteristics of the Scale

Reliability and Validity of the BDI. The psychometric characteristics of the origi-nal BDI have been reviewed countless times with diverse samples of both psychiatri-cally diagnosed and normal populations. Two comprehensive reviews investigated the psychometric properties of the BDI across a wide range of both clinical and nonclinical populations and reported high indices of reliability regardless of clinical population (Beck, Steer, & Garbin, 1988; Steer, Beck, & Garrison, 1986). Split-half reli-ability coefficients between .58 and .93 were reported (Beck & Beamesderfer, 1974; Gallagher, Nies, & Thompson, 1982; Reynolds & Gould, 1981; Strober, Green, & Carlson, 1981), and item-total correlations have ranged between .22 and .86 (Strober et al., 1981). The value of test–retest reliability for depression screening instruments is debatable, given the fluctuations in symptom severity during depressive episodes and the tendency for episodes to represent a state rather than a trait. Nonetheless, high lev-els of test–retest reliability (.69 to .90) in both psychiatric and nonpsychiatric patients have been demonstrated (Beck et al., 1988; Gallagher et al., 1982; Strober et al., 1981).

Beck et al. (1988) reported that numerous studies have found strong evidence of concurrent validity for the BDI. The measure correlated highly with multiple, well-established measures of depression, including the Hamilton Rating Scale for De-pression (HRSD), the Zung Self-rating Depression scale, the Minnesota Multiphasic Personality Inventory Depression (MMPI–D) scale, and clinician ratings of depth of depression. The correlation was highest between the BDI and clinician ratings (.96) and lowest between the BDI and *DSM–III* major depression (.33). These findings are not surprising, given that the instrument was constructed based on clinical observa-tion of depressed patients but was not designed as a diagnostic instrument.

Reliability and Validity of the BDI–IA. The revised version of the BDI demon-strated similar evidence of strong psychometric characteristics with data collected from the following six normative samples: patients with major depression, single epi-sode; patients with major depression, recurrent episode; patients with dysthymic dis-order; patients with mixed diagnoses; alcoholics; and heroin addicts. The BDI–IA has shown high internal consistency in both clinical and nonclinical populations. As might be expected, nonpsychiatric samples have produced more stable scores on the

BDI–IA (test–retest correlations between .60 and .90) than psychiatric samples (test–retest correlations between .48 and .86). Beck et al. (1988) reviewed Pearson product-moment correlations between the BDI–IA and selected concurrent measures of depression presented in a variety of studies. Their meta-analysis produced a mean correlation of .72 between the clinical ratings of depression and BDI–IA scores for nonpsychiatric subjects. Schaefer et al. (1985) investigated correlations among the BDI–IA, the MMPI–D scale, and the Zung Self-rating Depression Scale in psychiatric inpatients and inpatient drug abusers and found all of the correlations to be above .55 for both groups. Beck and Steer (1987) also reported significant relationships between the BDI–IA and both the HRSD and the Symptom Checklist–90 (SCL–90) Depression-Dejection scale (Derogatis, 1975).

Reliability and Validity of the BDI–II. The psychometric characteristics of the BDI–II were investigated using one college-student group and a sample from four different psychiatric outpatient clinics. The coefficient alpha of the BDI–II for the college students was .93 and for the outpatient sample was .92. These coefficient alpha values are higher than the mean coefficient alpha (.86) reported by Beck et al. (1988) for the BDI–IA in their meta-analysis of nine psychiatric samples. Even after controlling for the familywise error rate in each sample using a Bonferroni adjustment, Beck et al. (1996) found that all corrected, item-total correlations for the 21 BDI–II items were significant beyond the .05 level (one-tailed test) for both the outpatient sample and the college-student sample. Moreover, a small subsample of outpatients tested during their first and second therapy sessions was used to gain an estimate of the stability of the BDI–II. The resultant test–retest correlation of .93 was significant.

The positive relationships between the BDI–II and the Beck Hopelessness Scale and between the BDI–II and the Scale for Suicidal Ideation have been cited as evidence of the convergent validity of the BDI–II. The instrument was more positively correlated with the Hamilton Psychiatric Rating Scale for Depression (scored with revised procedures) than it was with the Hamilton Rating Scale for Anxiety (scored with revised procedures). This finding was taken as evidence of discriminant validity by the authors of the BDI–II.

Preliminary Psychometric Data on the BDI–PC. Although the psychometric characteristics of the BDI–PC have not yet been extensively studied, preliminary evidence is encouraging. Weiss (1996) concluded that the BDI–PC could function as a stand-alone instrument because ratings of its seven items appeared to be independent of the other 14 BD–II items. The 26 psychiatric inpatients who were readministered the BDI–II by Beck et al. (1996) were used to determine the 1-week test–retest reliability of the BDI–PC. The reliability estimate obtained was .82. Finally, Beck, Guth, Steer, and Ball (1997) found that a BDI–PC cutoff score of 4 correctly classified medical inpatients with or without major depression 82% of the time. Another study concluded that a cutoff score of 6 yielded acceptable sensitivity (83%) and specificity (95%) rates for detecting medical outpatients with or without major depression (Beck, Steer, Ball, Ciervo, & Kabat, 1997). Although these initial results are promising, further research demonstrating strong psychometric characteristics of the BDI–PC are warranted.

Interpretive Strategy

BDI. The original BDI is scored by summing the ratings of the 21 items provided by the patient. If two statements were chosen for an item, the higher rating is used in the calculation. The maximum obtainable score is 63. The general guidelines for cutoff scores are as follows: scores from 0 to 9 are considered within the normal range, scores from 10 to 18 are indicative of mild to moderate depression, scores from 19 to 29 are indicative of moderate to severe depression, and scores from 30 to 63 are indicative of severe depression. These guidelines were derived from analyses of the original BDI and were based on the mean total BDI scores that corresponded to clinically determined classifications of minimal, mild, moderate and severe depression. Nonetheless, Beck and Beamesderfer (1974) suggested that alternative cutoff scores, based on the clinical decisions for which the scale is being administered, may be used. The BDI manual emphasized the importance of considering the administration sample and purpose in employing different cutoff scores. For example, researchers who wish to gain a pure sample of depressed patients should raise the cutoff scores; if the purpose is to detect the maximum number of depressed persons, the cutoff scores should be lowered to minimize false negatives. Several investigators have suggested that significantly higher cutoff scores be employed for primary care populations in order to reduce the number of false positives produced by cutoff scores established in community studies (Schulberg et al., 1985; Turner & Romano, 1984).

In addition to gauging the overall severity of depression, the interpretation process should also include an examination of specific item content. The symptoms relevant to suicide ideation (items 2 and 9) are especially important, as evidence suggests that they may be reliable predictors of eventual suicide (Beck, Weissman, Lester, & Trexler, 1974). Special attention should also be given to the weight loss item (item 19). If the examinee reports an intention to lose weight, the rating is not included in the total score. Finally, each patient displays a unique depressive syndrome, which may be addressed individually. Consequently, the examiner may wish to note the overall pattern of symptoms.

BDI-II. The BDI-II is scored by summing the highest ratings for each of the 21 items. The maximum total score is 63. Optimal cutoff scores for the assessing severity of depression among individuals with major depressive disorder were determined through the use of receiver operating characteristic (ROC) curves. The ROC analysis is a mathematical technique that calculates the true positive rates and false negative rates for a scale at various cutoff scores and plots the resultant rate pairs for the cutoff scores as a graph. From this graph, the levels of sensitivity and specificity for each possible cutoff score and an index of the accuracy of discrimination provided by the scale can be determined.

Based on the ROC analysis, the BDI-II manual recommends the following cutoff scores for persons diagnosed with major depression: Scores from 0 to 13 are indicative of minimal depression, scores from 14 to 19 are indicative of mild depression, scores between 20 and 28 are indicative of moderate depression, and scores from 29 to 63 are indicative of severe depression. In selecting these guidelines, greater importance was placed on sensitivity relative to specificity in order to minimize the probability of false negatives. This decision was based on the fact that the instrument was designed to screen for major depression for clinical purposes. As with the original

BDI, attention to item content is clinically important, and different cutoff scores may be used for the BDI–II depending on the unique characteristics of the individuals being examined or the purpose of administration. Researchers or clinicians who intend to utilize the scale may wish to consult the ROC curves for their particular sample.

BDI–PC. The BDI–PC is scored by summing the highest ratings for each of the seven items. The maximum total score is 21. As with the other BDI measures, respondents are asked to describe themselves for the "past 2 weeks, including today" in order to satisfy the minimum *DSM–IV* criteria for the presence of a major depressive disorder. Although the chosen cutoff may again be based on the administration sample and purpose, Beck, Steer, Ball, Ciervo, and Kabat (1997) found that a cutoff score of 6 on the BDI–PC yielded the highest simultaneous rates of sensitivity and sensitivity with respect to the diagnosis of major depressive disorder among family practice outpatients. Among medical inpatients, a cutoff score of 4 has been found to correctly classify individuals as being diagnosed with or without major depression 82% of the time (Beck, Guth, Steer, & Ball, 1997).

Screening for Depression With BDI Instruments

The rise in popularity of self-report inventories as screening devices for depression is not surprising. As previously mentioned, depression is highly prevalent in primary care, and physicians often fail to diagnose and treat a large percentage of these depressed patients. An additional factor leading to the development of this popularity is the demand for quantifiable assessment data and objective indices of treatment outcomes. Finally, the time and skill required to implement complex diagnostic instruments preclude the widespread use of such methods as an effective depression screen in primary care.

Consequently, researchers and clinicians have made standardized self-report inventories an increasingly popular tool in primary care settings. The BDI and its derivatives are among the inventories most widely implemented for this purpose. The popularity of these instruments has been aided by the ease with which the measures may be administered. For example, the original BDI, the BDI–IA, and the BDI–II take only 5 to 10 min to complete when self-administered. The BDI–PC is shorter in length than all of these measures. Accordingly, this instrument may take even less than 5 min to administer. In most cases, following proper instruction, the measures may be self-administered. Teri (1982) estimated the vocabulary of the BDI to be consistent with that of a fifth-grade reading level, and the vocabulary of the BDI–IA and BDI–II appears similar to that of the original measure. Even in cases where these tests must be administered orally, the estimated time of completion is still 15 min or less.

The Purpose of the BDI Instruments: Syndromal vs. Diagnostic Depression. Those who use BDI measures to screen for depression must understand the varied definitions of depression and must recognize the intended purpose of the instruments. The term *depression* has developed numerous connotations over the years. The term may be used to indicate everything from the presence of sad feelings to the presence of a clinically diagnosable disorder with multiple criteria. Beck (1967) suggested that, in professional circles, depression may be characterized as a symptom, a syndrome, or a nosologic disorder. This distinction is of critical importance. Although the clinical syndrome of depression may be appropriately characterized as a psychological dysfunction, it is not synonymous with the nosologic category of depression. In fact, a cluster of symptoms considered indicative of a depression syndrome may be present in individuals with diagnoses other than depressive disorders. Accordingly, unlike the nosologic category of depression, the syndrome suggests no unique etiological genesis, no differential prognosis, and no response to treatment. The BDI is a sensitive measure of syndrome depression, but, like many other self-report inventories (including the CES-D), was never intended to be a diagnostic screening device.

Consistency of the BDI Measures With *DSM-IV*

The BDI measures do not include the full coverage of *DSM-IV* criteria. For example, the original BDI does not contain questions regarding increased appetite, weight gain, hyposomnia, psychomotor agitation or retardation, nonsuicidal death wishes, and problems with concentration. The BDI-II corrected many deficiencies of the original version by addressing symptoms more consonant with *DSM-IV* criteria (Table 12.1). The BDI-PC, for reasons discussed later, completely eliminates somatic and performance items. Thus, the BDI-PC assesses a limited number of the *DSM-IV* symptoms required for a depressive episode (Table 12.2). Consistent with *DSM* criteria, all of these measures examine symptoms occurring over the course of the 2 weeks prior to administration. However, unlike in the *DSM-IV*, none of the inventories specify the need for specific criteria (e.g., sad mood or anhedonia) to be endorsed, The inventories cannot rule out the presence of other, contributing factors (i.e., substances, medical conditions) or disorders and provide no index of the level of impairment resulting from symptomatology.

Diagnostic Efficiency of BDI Measures

BDI.   Although the BDI was designed to assess the severity of syndromal depression in psychiatrically diagnosed patients rather than to screen for the presence of depressive disorders in normal adolescent and adult populations, the instrument has been widely implemented for the latter purpose. The usefulness of the measure for this purpose has been the subject of substantial debate (Dobson & Brieter, 1981; Sacco, 1981), and the authors of the BDI recommend caution in such practices. The BDI does appear to have positive predictive values between 2 and 4 times the estimated population base rate for major depression (Depression Guideline Panel, 1993). In addition,

TABLE 12.1
Consistency of the BDI-II With the *DSM-IV*

DSM-IV Criteria	BDI-II Items
Depressed mood	Sadness, crying (items 1 and 10)
Diminished interest or pleasure in most activities	Loss of pleasure (item 4)
Significant weight loss/gain or change in appetite	Changes in appetite (item 18)
Insomnia or hypersomnia	Changes in sleeping patterns (item 16)
Psychomotor agitation or retardation	Agitation (item 11)
Fatigue or loss of energy	Loss of energy, tiredness or fatigure (items 15 and 20)
Feelings of worthlessness or excessive guilt	Guilty feelings, worthlessness (items 5 and 14)
Diminished ability to think or concentrate	Concentration difficulty (item 19)
Recurrent thoughts of death	Suicidal thoughts or wishes (item 9)

TABLE 12.2
Consistency of the BDI–PC With the *DSM–IV*

DSM–IV Criteria	*BDI–II Item*
Depressed mood	Sadness (item 1)
Diminished interest or pleasure in most activities	Loss of interest (item 7)
Significant weight loss/gain or change in appetite	No items
Insomnia or hypersomnia	No items
Psychomotor agitation or retardation	No items
Fatigue or loss of energy	No items
Feelings of worthlessness or excessive guilt	No items
Diminished ability to think or concentrate	No items
Recurrent thoughts of death	Suicidal thoughts or wishes (item 6)

some researchers have found the BDI to be superior to primary care physicians in identifying depressed patients (Nielson & Williams, 1980). These researchers reported that recognition of depressed patients with the BDI nearly matched recognition by psychiatric interviewers. However, other researchers have suggested that high BDI scores may not necessarily be indicative of depression, but represent overall adjustment problems (Gotlib, 1984; Tanaka-Matsumi & Kameoka, 1986).

Recent findings indicate that the BDI is relatively sensitive, but only moderately specific, with respect to a single diagnostic category. In both community samples (Oliver & Simmons, 1984) and samples of college students (Deardorff & Funabiki, 1985; Hammen, 1980), a significant number of high scorers on the BDI do not have diagnosable disorders. Furthermore, many of those who do have disorders do not have current, primary affective disorders. This lack of specificity should come as no surprise, given that the BDI measures a depression syndrome rather than the presence of depressive disorders. This syndrome is characterized by symptomatology that may be present in other diagnostic categories or that may reflect transient events or personality variables inconsistent with known diagnostic categories. Moreover, unlike the "gold standard" for diagnosing depression (clinical interviews and the application of standardized, *DSM–IV* specified criteria), the BDI measures do not include the full coverage of *DSM–IV* criteria.

Although the research argues against using BDI measures in order to classify individuals according to specific diagnostic categories, the sensitivity of the instruments renders them valuable to primary care physicians. The BDI measures enable clinicians to decrease the number of persons who need more intensive diagnostic interviewing without missing persons who might benefit from a complete diagnostic interview. Mulrow et al. (1995) demonstrated that, in a group of 100 patients in a clinic with a 5% average prevalence rate of depression, the clinician would have to conduct only 31 diagnostic interviews to identify the 4 with major depression, and only 1 person with major depression would be missed. Moreover, these researchers estimated that about 20% of patients with depression would be missed using screening, compared to the 50% often missed in current practice.

BDI–PC.   As studies continued to examine the usefulness of the BDI with different populations, researchers began to notice that medical patients presented unique difficulties. This population produced high estimates of anxiety and depression. These elevated scores appeared to result from overlap between the types of symptoms that occur in medical illnesses and the somatic and performance symptoms of anxiety and depression. In other words, the somatic symptoms commonly used to make a diagnosis of depression may actually result from physical illness. Consequently, researchers have concluded that the cognitive/affective symptoms are the best indicators for severity of depression in medically ill populations. In response to these conclusions, the BDI–PC was developed to screen for depression among medically ill patients. The BDI–PC is a self-report measure based on nonsomatic symptoms that researchers have proposed might assist physicians in excluding medical patients without cognitive or affective symptoms from more elaborate diagnostic evaluations (Volk, Pace, & Parchman, 1993).

Initial studies have demonstrated the ability of the BDI–PC to discriminate among patients diagnosed with major depressive disorder, patients with other types of mood disorders, and patients without mood disorders (Beck, Steer, Ball, Ciervo, & Kabat, 1997). Moreover, employing a cutoff score of 6 for the BDI–PC yielded sensitivity and specificity rates of 83% and 95%, respectively, for detecting medical outpatients with and without major depression. Beck, Guth, Steer, and Ball (1997) reported that a slightly lower cutoff score of 4 correctly classified medical inpatients as diagnosed with or without major depression under varied estimates of underlying sample prevalence rates for the disorder (10% to 66%). The specificity rates obtained by these researchers represent a significant improvement over the 72% rate that Mulrow et al. (1995) reported in their review of nine instruments commonly used to screen for depression in primary care.

While these findings are encouraging, certain limitations should be noted. First, although the BDI–PC excludes somatic and performance symptoms for theoretical reasons, such symptoms are included in the *DSM–IV* criteria for depressive disorders and cannot simply be overlooked. The psychological origins of these symptoms can only be determined clinically. Future research regarding the clinical utility of the BDI–PC to screen for mood disorders in primary care patients should use an instrument like the Structured Clinical Interview for the *DSM* (SCID). Second, the samples used in the BDI–PC studies limit the generalizability of results. In one study, the sample reflected patients already suspected of having psychiatric diagnoses by their attending physicians (Beck, Guth, Steer, & Ball, 1997); the other study noted the need for an investigation of samples with a higher proportion of minorities and with varied socioeconomic backgrounds (Beck, Steer, Ball, Ciervo, & Kabat, 1997).

Implementation Issues

Use as a Stand-Alone Instrument Versus Multiple-Stage Assessment. Although the BDI measures have demonstrated high sensitivity and have value associated with their ease of administration, Kendall, Hollon, Beck, Hammen, and Ingram (1987) argued against the implementation of these self-report measures as stand-alone instruments. Rather, these authors maintain that the use of multiple methods of assessment is required to provide convincing diagnostic statements. Kendall et al. (1987) posited a multiple-gate strategy, consistent with classic, multimethod measurement methodology. Specifically, self-report syndromal assessment with a BDI measure would be utilized to identify potential cases for further assessment. Identification of cases warranting further attention would be performed through the use of predetermined cutoff scores. Cases that qualify for further assessment would then be administered the self-report measure a second time, accompanied by a structured diagnostic interview.

The benefits of utilizing multiple self-report measures within the initial stage is uncertain. Past research has suggested that different self-report inventories of depression may actually offer different measures of depression (Kerner & Jacobs, 1983). For example, factor analyses of the BDI and the Zung Self-rating Depression Scale have found factors specific to each scale. This finding indicates that the specific emphases of these scales may contribute specific depression indicators and that both may be important components of a thorough, objective measure of depression (Giambra, 1977). However, Fitzgibbon, Cella, and Sweeney (1988) examined the BDI, the Hamilton Depression Rating Scale, and the Depression Adjective Checklist and maintained that the correlations between these self-report measures of depression were sufficiently high to advocate the use of only one measure of depression when assessing a heterogeneous group. Kendall et al. (1987) echoed these findings, suggesting that the BDI alone was sufficient as a first-stage screening instrument. They reported that the inclusion of additional, self-report, syndromal measures (e.g., the MMPI–D or the Zung) might increase the clinician's confidence in the accuracy of the syndromal assessment, but would not provide the information necessary for assigning a diagnostic label. These additional measures would vary neither the method of assessment nor the level of assessment. Similarly, the addition of a clinician-rated assessment scale would not vary the level of assessment and thus would be of little value.

In order for strong diagnostic conclusions to be determined, the second level of assessment must yield self-report scale scores that meet a specified criteria and must yield ratings on structured interviews that meet diagnostic classification criteria. There are several structured interviews which may prove useful in this second level of assessment. The SCID, the Schedule for Affective Disorders and Schizophrenia (SADS), and the Diagnostic Interview Schedule are three such interviews.

Special Issues in Implementation

The Problems of High-End and Low-End Specificity. Concerns regarding both the high-end specificity and the low-end specificity of the BDI have been raised. As mentioned earlier, elevated syndrome depression scores may be indicative of dispositional qualities, transitory life events, or the presence of diagnosable disorders other than depressive disorders. On the opposite end of the spectrum, there are dangers in using low scores (i.e., 0–1) on the BDI as a strategy for identifying nondepressed individuals. Hammen (1983) noted that some individuals selected for their low scores may be characterized as "Pollyannas" or as individuals with other forms of psychopathology rather than, or in addition to, depression.

The Need for Appropriately Trained Administrators. Primary care professionals who choose to implement the BDI in their practice may have properly trained paraprofessionals administer and score the measure. However, the measure should only be used and interpreted by professionals with appropriate clinical training and experience (Beck & Steer, 1987). In particular, because depression may be associated with an increased risk of suicide in psychiatric patients, those who utilize the BDI should be familiar with appropriate referral mechanisms or appropriate psychotherapeutic assessment and intervention techniques for such situations.

Guidelines for Clinical Decisions Based on the BDI

Although there is extensive research on the utility of the BDI as a screening instrument for depression, there is relatively little information to guide clinicians in making decisions regarding appropriate interventions or treatments based on BDI scores. This may be due, in part, to the fact that actions taken may depend on the physician's experience and comfort level regarding psychotherapeutic treatments. The little guidance that is available is primarily restricted to actions based on scores obtained with the original version of the BDI. The authors suspect that many of these suggestions may be successfully applied to results obtained from the BDI–IA and the BDI–II. However, the construction of the BDI–PC is significantly different. Therefore, until the necessary research is conducted, this measure should probably be used solely as a screening device rather than as an indicator of any specific treatment strategies.

As mentioned earlier, Kendall et al. (1987) advocated the use of multiple measures of assessment. These researchers further suggested that the term *depression* be reserved for individuals with BDI scores greater than 20 and concurrent, interviewer-based diagnoses. One might infer from this suggestion that a cutoff of 20 is recommended to determine those individuals who should receive a full, more structured assessment for the presence of depressive disorders. When this further assessment yields an interviewer-based diagnosis, the initiation of an intervention or a referral to a mental health professional should be considered. Any intervention should be conducted by an individual with extensive and specific training in mental disorders and their treatment.

BDI scores that exceed 30 are typically considered indicative of severe depression. Studies that have chosen outpatients on the basis of meeting Feighner Research Diagnostic Criteria, or *DSM–III* criteria for primary unipolar depression generally report mean BDI scores around 30 (Beck, Hollon, Young, Bedrosian, & Budenz, 1985; Murphy, Simons, Wetzel, & Lustman, 1984; Rush, Beck, Kovacs, & Hollon, 1977) In these cases, the physician should strongly consider a referral to a mental health professional. Furthermore, the guidelines set forth by the Agency for Health Care Policy and Research (AHCPR) for the treatment of depression in primary care specify that severe depressions may be more likely to respond to medication therapy than mild or moderate levels of depression (Depression Guideline Panel, 1993). Accordingly, physicians who possess the expertise necessary to provide adequate pharmacotherapy may wish to consider the initiation of a trial of such therapy for patients with BDI scores greater than 30. However, physicians should refrain from making any treatment decisions based solely on the results of a single inventory. Rather, the inventory should be used as an indicator and as part of a more comprehensive and thorough assessment.

Particular attention should be paid to certain individual items on the BDI. For example, special attention should be given to items relevant to suicidal ideation. Patients who endorse suicidal ideation (item 2) and hopelessness (item 9) with ratings of 3 or 4 should be closely scrutinized for suicide potential. The AHCPR guidelines recommend that patients who are seriously suicidal be immediately referred to a mental health professional.

Using the BDI in Treatment Monitoring

Although the BDI has enjoyed popularity as a depression assessment instrument, Edwards et al. (1984) noted that many clinicians believe that the measure overreacts to patient halo effects and thus is an unsuitable index of treatment outcome. Moran and

Lambert (1983) reported that the BDI was more liberal than the Hamilton Rating Scale for Depression (HRS–D) in determining the effects that both drugs and psychotherapy had on depression. However, Edwards et al. (1984) argued that these results were based on crude statistical procedures and investigated the claims with more advanced methods. The use of meta-analysis techniques indicated that the BDI did not overestimate treatment effects relative to estimates obtained from the HRS–D and that the BDI was actually less liberal than the HRS–D.

Meta-analysis on the sensitivity of depression assessment scales to therapeutic change shows that the BDI is sensitive to drug treatment effects (McNair, 1974). Additional studies on the validity of the BDI in therapy control have tended to focus on proving sensitivity to changes (Beck et al., 1988). More recently, however, researchers have investigated the construct validity of the BDI in measuring treatment outcome (Richter et al., 1997). In other words, these researchers attempted to demonstrate that the BDI measures the same construct in repeated measurement and that the change in scores can be explained by treatment effects. This research confirmed the previously reported sensitivity of the BDI to therapeutic change in long-term intervals of several weeks. However, significant changes within an interval of 1 day in a group of dysthymic patients could not be explained by therapeutic effects or by temporary changes in mood. Based on these results, the BDI does not appear appropriate for frequently repeated measurements in short time intervals. Rather, it is appropriate only for the assessment of change in a time interval of several weeks.

The construct validity of the BDI in measuring treatment outcome and the fact that, contrary to previously held notions, the assessment tool does not appear to overestimate treatment effects make the BDI an attractive choice for assessing depression in situations where a more comprehensive assessment is impractical or impossible. However, Edwards et al. (1984) cautioned that the measure may be most appropriate only when investigators wish to utilize the most conservative index of treatment outcome available. Moreover, in such cases conservatism will be achieved at the expense of power.

As for exact directions regarding appropriate cutoff scores, most investigators are reluctant to offer rigid guidelines for identifying further assessment needs or for establishing different degrees of syndromal depression or clinically significant change. However, Kendall et al. (1987) offered some guidelines for consideration. In general, the range of scores from 0 to 9 on the BDI may be viewed as normal, although extremely low scores may be representative of fake-good response sets, transient life events, or other psychopathology. Scores of 10 to 20 are associated with mild levels of depression, with scores between 10 and 17 suggesting dysphoria and scores greater than 17 more closely associated with depressive states. Scores between 20 and 30 are indicative of moderate levels of depression, whereas scores greater than 30 reflect severe levels of depression. The recently published manual for the BDI–II included slightly different cut scores for patients diagnosed with major depression (Beck et al., 1996). Its authors recommended adherence to the following guidelines: 0–13 for minimal depression, 14–19 for mild depression, 20–28 for moderate depression, and 29–63 for severe depression. Finally, maximum clinical efficiency of the BDI–PC was obtained using cutoff scores of 4 for medical inpatients (Beck, Guth, Steer, & Ball, 1997) and 6 for medical outpatients (Beck, Steer, Ball, Ciervo, & Kabat, 1997). Whichever measure is used, it is clear that these suggested cutoff scores could be varied, depending on the administration sample and purpose. For example, if a primary care physician wishes to detect the maximum number of depressed persons, lower scores are recommended (Beck & Steer, 1987). Nielson and Williams (1980) found that, when using the BDI as a screen for depression with medical patients, a cutoff score of 10 was optimal. In choosing this score, greater weight was given to sensitivity relative to specificity because the cost of administering a test and follow-up interview was considered low compared to the cost of missing a case of depression.

Although past research investigated the utility of the BDI in assessing treatment outcome, little guidance was provided in the literature for when treatment may be discontinued. Kendall et al. (1987) suggested that clients with BDI scores of 0 to 9 after clinical intervention may be viewed as remitted. Based on this data, clinicians should consider the termination of treatment once scores in this range are achieved and maintained for a reasonable period of time.

CENTER FOR EPIDEMIOLOGIC STUDIES DEPRESSION SCALE (CES–D)

Development

The Center for Epidemiologic Depression Scale (CES–D) is becoming one of the most commonly used depression screening instruments in primary care practice (Schulberg et al., 1985). Although it was originally developed to measure self-reported depressive symptomatology in community samples, it is now predominantly a tool used by physicians in medical settings. The National Institute of Mental Health began development of the CES–D in 1971 to address the need for a self-report measure that would obtain information on depressive symptomatology in a nonpsychiatric, community sample. The selection of the original components from which the scale items were later drawn was based on factor-analytic studies, clinical judgment, and frequency of use in other depression questionnaires. The original components represented the symptoms most commonly associated with the clinical manifestation of depression, including depressed mood, guilt feelings, worthlessness, hopelessness, helplessness, appetite loss, decreased energy, and sleep disturbance (Markush & Facero, 1973; Radloff, 1977).

After the original components were chosen, specific items representing these components were selected from the Minnesota Multiphasic Personality Inventory (Hathaway & McKinley, 1943) and from established, self-rated depression scales developed by Zung (1965), Beck, Ward, Mendelson, Mock, and Erbaugh (1961), and Raskin (1965). Twenty items were compiled to assess the following depressive symptoms and attitudes: irritability, loss of appetite, "blues," just as good as others (not), decreased concentration, depressed mood, lethargy, hopeful (not), helplessness, anxiety, sleep disturbance, happiness (not), social withdrawal, loneliness, emotional sensitivity, enjoyed life (not), crying, sad mood, low self-esteem, and decreased energy.

Scale development proceeded with an evaluation of the items in a pretest given to a small sample of convenience. After minor revisions and item clarification, the CES–D pretest items were added to a 300-item NIMH structured interview. This NIMH interview was utilized in a large-scale study designed to measure depression, general psychopathology, well-being, and social desirability in a community population sample. Participants over the age of 18 were selected by independent probability sampling of households in the Midwest, and the structured interview was administered in the homes of selected participants by trained personnel. Adequate psychometric characteristics were subsequently confirmed in the original sample and later in a clinical sample of both psychiatric inpatients and individuals receiving treatment for depression in an outpatient mental health clinic (Radloff, 1977).

Radloff (1977) originally reported that a total score of 16 on the CES–D discriminated psychiatric patients from general population samples (Weissman, Sholomskas, Pottenger, Prusoff, & Locke, 1977). Specifically, she identified that 70% of the patient population scored above this cut score, whereas only 21% of the general population scored at or above this total. The CES–D cut score of 16 was further able to discriminate among patient groups with different levels of depression severity. Radloff (1977) also generated normative data for subgroups of different ages (under 25, 25–64, and over 64 years), for men and women, for both African American and White participants, and for subgroups representing three education levels (less than high school, high school, and greater than high school). The coefficient alpha for each subgroup was .80 or above. Furthermore, exploratory factor analysis validated that the factor structure did not differ between the subgroups, nor did it differ from the pattern generated by the total population sample.

Normative data for the CES–D were also collected in 1974–1975 as part of the National Health and Nutrition Examination Survey (NHANES–I). The CES–D was administered to a national probability sample of 3,059 persons ranging in age from 25 to 74 years. Sayetta and Johnson (1980) reported that findings from this study revealed a mean score of 7.1 (*SD* = 7.2) for men and 10.0 (*SD* = 9.1) for women. Additionally, age and racial subgroup patterns were not found to be statistically different from the total population sample.

Psychometric Characteristics of the CES–D

Reliability. Since the late 1970s the psychometric characteristics of the CES–D have been extensively evaluated across a diverse range of clinical and community population groups. The vast majority of studies support Radloff's original reliability and validity statistics, finding the CES–D to be highly internally consistent. The original analyses (Radloff, 1977) identified split-half correlations (Nunally, 1967) of .90 for the patient group and .85 for the community sample. Spearman–Brown correlation coefficient estimates were identified at .92 for patient groups and .87 for community samples. Coefficient alpha was measured at .85 for normal respondents and .90 for the patient sample. Interitem and item-scale correlations were found to be higher in the patient sample than in the nonpsychiatric community sample. Additionally, the correlation between the CES–D total score for the patient group and the severity of depression as rated by a psychiatric nurse was .56. Based on the high degree of internal consistency of the scale, Radloff (1977) proposed that a single, total score be used to estimate the degree of depression severity.

The value of test–retest reliability in self-report measures of depression is inherently questionable, given the potential for asymmetric regression toward the mean and the biasing effects of repeat testing (Radloff, 1977). Additionally, the temporal structure of a measure can further threaten the validity of test–retest measurement. The CES–D was designed to measure depressive symptomatology "during the past week." Given the nature of the individual items, a depressive reaction to an acute event can significantly influence the total score. Therefore, it is reasonable to predict that an individual may be relatively free of symptoms during an initial rating period yet have a high score during a subsequent retest administration. Taking this factor into account, Radloff (1977) anticipated moderate levels of test–retest correlation when the CES-D was administered at 3, 6, or 12 months following the initial interview.

Test–retest correlation results were as predicted. Longer test–retest intervals resulted in moderate levels of correlation, whereas shorter time intervals between the original test and the retest produced higher correlation coefficients. Additionally, subjects who reported no acute life events at either testing were found to have the highest test–retest reliability; the lowest correlation was found for participants with significant stressful life events surrounding both test administrations. Respondents with no life events at either administration, representing the fairest estimate of test–retest reliability, obtained a correlation estimate of .54 (Radloff, 1977).

Validity. Feightner and Worrall (1990) concluded that studies examining the psychometric properties of the CES-D in community and clinical samples have shown correlation coefficients between .51 and .89 with other measures of depressive symptomatology, including the Hamilton Rating Scale (Hamilton, 1967), the Symptom Checklist-90 (SCL-90; Derogatis, 1975), and the Raskin Rating Scale (Raskin, 1965). Additionally, Santor, Zuroff, Ramsay, Cervantes, and Palacios (1995) reported that the CES-D correlated highly with the Beck Depression Inventory (Beck et al., 1961). Tests of concurrent validity, based on interviewer ratings of depression and the CES-D, have found lower correlation coefficients, from .46 to .53 (Radloff, 1977). These lower correlation coefficients are not surprising, given the predilection of the CES-D to detect the presence of distress rather than a diagnosable clinical depression.

Radloff (1977) originally identified a four-factor structure model following principle-components factor analysis with varimax rotation. The original four factors were interpreted as follows:

1. Depressed affect (blues, depressed, lonely, cry, sad).
2. Positive affect (good, hopeful, happy, enjoy).
3. Somatic and retarded activity (bothered, appetite, effort, sleep, get going).
4. Interpersonal (unfriendly, dislike).

Subsequent confirmatory factor analytic studies have validated the four-factor structure in a wide variety of clinical and community population samples. A review by Knight, Williams, McGee, and Olaman (1997) concluded that Radloff's four-factor model has been confirmed in younger and older age subjects (Hertzog, Van Alstine, & Usala, 1990), urban populations (Clark, Aneshensel, Frerichs, & Morgan, 1981), English and Spanish-speaking psychiatric inpatients (Roberts, Vernon, & Rhoades, 1989), Mexican Americans (Roberts, 1980), elderly African Americans (Jones-Webb & Snowden, 1993), and comorbidly medically ill Caucasian females (Knight et al., 1997). However, several minority researchers have found that either a three-factor model (Guarnaccia, Angel & Worobey, 1989) or a five-factor solution (Thorson & Powell, 1993) better fit their data. Thomas, Applegate, Scarinci, Jones, and Brantley (1998) were unable to confirm the four-factor model in a sample of low socioeconomic status (SES), African American, primary care patients. Therefore, it has been hypothesized that the ethnicity of the sample may account for the variability in factor structure. Knight et al. (1997) theorized that the original four-factor model may best describe population samples who are highly acculturated and have a good command of the English language. Therefore, cautious interpretation should be exercised when the CES–D is used in a minority population.

Short Form of the CES–D

Several researchers have demonstrated that the 20-item CES–D could be reduced in number with minimal impact on the psychometric properties of the instrument. Andresen, Malmgren, Carter, and Patrick (1994) evaluated a 10-item version of the CES–D in an community sample consisting of persons age 65 years and older. The shortened CES–D consisted of items measuring irritability, concentration, depressed mood, anhedonia, hopelessness, anxiety, sleep disturbance, loneliness, lethargy, and unhappiness. When compared to the original 20-item version, the 10-item CES–D was found to have good predictive validity at .97. Test–retest correlation was also good at .71. Shrout and Yager (1989) found that neither sensitivity nor specificity was compromised when a five-item version of the CES–D (felt depressed, hopeless, crying spells, people disliked me, and felt unhappy) was administered to a population of adults ranging in age from 17 to 60.

Most recently, Santor and Coyne (1997) investigated combinations of individual items that would effectively differentiate depressed from nondepressed individuals. Nine items from the original CES–D were found to produce the greatest distinction between depressed and nondepressed persons. The nine-item CES–D included irritability, depressed mood, "blues," sleep disturbance, unhappiness, amotivation, lack of concentration, sadness, and anhedonia. The nine-item version was highly correlated (.93) with the original CES–D. However, the positive predictive value of the revised scale was poor when compared to an SCID diagnosis of depression. Given that the usefulness of the shorter versions of the CES–D have not been generally accepted as a substitute for the original 20-item scale, these versions are not addressed further in this review.

Interpretive Strategy

The CES–D is scored by summing the participant response ratings to 20 brief statements following the question, "How often have you felt this way during the past week?" Respondents record the frequency/duration of occurrence of each symptom on the following 4-point scale: 0 (rarely or none of the time/less than 1 day), 1 (some or a little of the time/1–2 days), 2 (occasionally or a moderate amount of the time/3–4 days), or 3 (most or all of the time/5–7 days). Prior to summing the overall total score, reverse scoring is used to calculate the rating of each of the four positively worded items (4, 8, 12, 16). Thus, total summary scores can range from 0 to 60, with a higher score indicating a higher frequency of symptoms occurring and/or more symptoms present during the previous week. As previously reviewed, a cut score of 16 is typically employed to indicate a significant elevation in depressive symptomatology (Radloff, 1977).

When interpreting the meaning of the total score of the CES–D, the interviewer is first advised to consider the purpose for which the measure was originally designed. Santor and Coyne (1997) emphasized that the detection of a clinical diagnosis was never the original goal. The scale items and temporally focused response choices were chosen to detect the presence of depressive symptoms experienced in the past week in a nonclinical community sample. Hence, the detection of the full criteria for a diagnosable depressive disorder according to the fourth edition of the *Diagnostic and Statistical Manual of Mental Disorders* (American Psychiatric Association [APA], 1994) was never the intention.

The total CES–D score represents an estimation of the amount of time the individual experienced a group of depressive symptoms during the previous week. This may or may not correspond to a diagnosable depressive disorder. An elevated total score does not communicate whether the depressive symptoms are secondary to an acutely stressful situation, the somatic presentation of a comorbid medical disorder, a medication or recreational drug reaction, or a clinically relevant depressive disorder. In addition, a high total score may reflect strong endorsement of a few items or low rating of a larger number of items (Fechner-Bates, Coyne, & Schwenk, 1994). Therefore, to improve the efficiency of the measure in detecting a clinically significant degree of impairment, a preeminent goal is to establish an efficient cut score that best identifies a clinically significant degree of distress.

Cut Score.   Radloff (1977) originally proposed that a total score of 16 provided the best discriminative ability to detect significant depressive symptomatology in both community and patient samples (Weissman, Sholomskas, Pottenger, Prusoff, & Locke, 1977). However, several researchers subsequently identified higher scores to be more predictive of depression in specific populations samples. Lyness et al. (1997) reported that a cut score of 21 was the most efficient score to detect depression in elderly primary care patients. Husaini, Neff, Harrington, Hughes, and Stone (1980) proposed increasing the cut score to 17 to indicate "possible" depression and to 23 for "probable" depression when evaluating rural, community residents. Schulberg et al. (1985) reported that raising the cut score to 27 in primary care samples resulted in a higher degree of predictability (89%), while maintaining good specificity (70.4%). However, several investigators have determined that specificity is sacrificed when the cut score is increased, resulting in an increase in false-negative cases (Berwick et al., 1991; Schulberg et al., 1985; Zich, Attkisson, & Greenfield, 1990). In summary, although the standard cut score of 16 may be preferred for screening high-risk groups for which overdetection is preferred, higher cut scores may prove optimal for depression screening in a general medical population, which may have inflated scores secondary to comorbid medical complaints.

Screening for Depression

General Considerations.   The popularity of the CES–D has been influenced by the ease with which the measure may be utilized. Although the CES–D was originally designed to be administered as a self-report measure, subsequent research has utilized it as an interviewer-assisted measure, a telephone assessment tool, and a computerized screening instrument (Weissman et al., 1975). Whether the scale is self-rated or completed with oral assistance, administration of the scale can be achieved in under 10 min. The CES–D has the advantage over many depression screening inventories in several areas. The CES–D is quite concise in wording, shorter in length (20 items), limited in the number of response choices (0–3), unidimensional (frequency of symptom occurrence between none of the time and all of the time), and temporally specific (last week). Additionally, according to the Flesch–Kincaid readability level (Flesch, 1948), the CES–D can be used in populations with a grade-school reading level of 3.4 years.

The CES–D was designed to be used by the public domain. Therefore, the scale can be administered, duplicated, and published without permission (see Appendix A). The following address can be used to secure an original copy of the measure: Public Inquiries, National Institute of Mental Health, Room 7C-02, 5600 Fishers Lane, Bethesda, MD 20892.

Diagnostic Efficiency of the CES–D. The primary purpose of self-report screening measures in the primary care setting is to identify patients who will benefit from additional assessment and possible treatment of their depressive symptomatology (Santor & Coyne, 1997). It is therefore essential that a self-report measure accurately predict the presence of a possible depressive disorder if it is to be considered a reliable screening instrument. Recent studies, however, have indicated that less than one-third of populations with scores above standard cut points on self-report screening inventories meet criteria for a depressive disorder (Coulehan, Schulberg, & Block, 1989; Fechner-Bates et al., 1994; Myers & Weissman, 1980).

Sensitivity and specificity statistics refer to the relationship between an elevated score on a measure and a corresponding clinical diagnosis. A measure that is highly *sensitive* will correctly identify a high proportion of individuals with a particular diagnosis. *Specificity* refers to the proportion of individuals who are correctly classified as not suffering from the disorder. Although the sensitivity and specificity of self-report measures vary according to diagnostic criteria and population characteristics, established cutoff scores generally provide good sensitivity but poorer specificity in nonpsychiatric populations (Fechner-Bates et al., 1994).

Breslau (1985) concluded that the prevalence rate of elevated scores on self-report depression measures is often two to six times higher than the population base rates for depressive disorders. With little exception, researchers who rely on the CES–D as a first-stage screening instrument contend that the use of the standard cut score yields a sample of patients in which only a minority meet diagnostic criteria for a major depressive disorder. Boyd, Weissman, Thompson, and Myers (1982) reported that less than one third of persons scoring above the CES–D cut score of 16 were diagnosed as depressed according to the Research Diagnostic Criteria (RDC) (Spitzer, Endicott, & Robins, 1978). When the CES–D was compared to the Schedule for Affective Disorders and Schizophrenia (Endicott & Spitzer, 1978), both Lewinsohn and Teri (1982) and Roberts and Vernon (1983) found that although the standard score of 16 detected a diagnosable depression in approximately 80% of the cases, 36% and 40%, respectively, were "misdiagnosed."

Thomas, Scarinci, Mehan, Jones, and Brantley (1998) conducted a recent analysis to evaluate the predictive validity of the CES–D in determining a depressive spectrum diagnosis as indicated by the Diagnostic Interview Schedule for the *DSM–IV* (DIS–IV). Using the standard cut score of 16, the CES–D correctly classified 95% with a current depressive disorder using a weighted classification system based on a 10% baserate. However, specificity (69%) and overall accuracy (72%) were sacrificed. Raising the cut score to 27 significantly improved the overall accuracy (89.4% correctly classified) of the measure. Similarly, Schulberg et al. (1985) found that increasing the cut score to 27 resulted in increased diagnostic efficiency based on the DIS–III–R. In summary, attempts to improve the diagnostic efficiency of the CES–D in the primary care sector may require an elevation in the cut score utilized.

Other Diagnoses.   Several investigators have examined the relationship between an elevated CES–D score and the presence of other forms of psychopathology. Fechner-Bates et al. (1994) found that a score above the standard cut point of 16 was as likely to predict a *DSM–III–R* diagnosis of a depressive disorder as it was an anxiety disorder. Additionally, Breslau (1985) reported that an elevated score on the CES–D was as strongly associated with a diagnosis of generalized anxiety disorder (according to the *DSM–III–R*) as it was with major depressive disorder. In another study conducted by Myers and Weissman (1980), 33% of community respondents with elevated CES–D scores had a current diagnosis of a major depressive disorder, 14% had another depressive diagnosis, 18% had a diagnosis other than depression, and 33% met no diagnostic criteria. These results support the Kirmayer et al. (1993) conclusion that the CES–D may be best conceptualized as a measure of the demoralization or distress that often accompanies clinically significant depression and anxiety disorders (Kirmayer et al., 1993). Therefore, the expectation that the CES–D will provide diagnostic differentiation is unrealistic (Roberts & Vernon, 1983). The amount of skill and information required to discern one affective disorder from another limits the diagnostic utility of all screening measures. Although many studies continue to rely on self-report measures to substantiate the presence of a diagnosable depressive disorder, Haaga and Soloman (1993) concluded that there appears to be a trend away from applying the label *depression* to an elevated score on a self-report measure.

Consistency With *DSM–IV* Criteria

The CES–D was designed for use as a screening measure to detect depressive symptomatology; however, it cannot be considered a true diagnostic tool as it does not assess several *DSM–IV* criteria. Although the measure contains questions regarding appetite, sleep disturbance, psychomotor retardation, problems with concentration, and hopelessness (Table 12.3), it does not contain specific items that address increased appetite and weight gain, hypersomnia, psychomotor agitation, or suicidal ideation. Second, the CES–D examines symptoms occurring during the past week, whereas, the *DSM* requires the presence of symptoms of at least a 2-week duration in order to satisfy diagnostic criteria. Third, the CES–D is unable to ascertain current level of impairment and whether the symptom manifestation represents a significant change in functioning. Fourth, the *DSM–IV* specifies the need for either sad mood or anhedonia; however, the CES–D total score does not indicate specific item endorse-

TABLE 12.3
Consistency of the CES–D With the *DSM–IV*

DSM-IV Criteria	*CES-D Items*
Depressed mood	I felt depressed/I could not shake the blues/ Happy (not)
Diminished interest or pleasure in most activities	I enjoyed life (not)
Significant weight loss/gain or change in appetite	Didn't feel like eating
Insomnia or hypersomnia	My sleep was restless
Psychomotor agitation or retardation	I could not get going
Fatigue or loss of energy	I felt that everything I did was an effort
Feelings of worthlessness or excessive guilt	I felt I was as good (not) as others/life failure
Diminished ability to think or concentrate	I had trouble keeping my mind on what I was doing
Recurrent thoughts of death	I felt hopeful (not) about future

ment. Fifth, the CES–D has not been found to effectively discriminate symptomatology present that is secondary to comorbid pathology (i.e., medical problems, substance abuse, psychopathology) from symptoms reflecting transient, stressful life events. Although an elevated score on the CES–D may not definitively indicate a clinically diagnosable depressive disorder, the detection of distress in a primary care patient may warrant timely recognition, as even mild forms of distress may affect medical utilization and adherence.

Implementation Issues

The use of the CES–D as a stand-alone screening instrument for preventive purposes has been aided by the measure's ease of administration, high sensitivity in detecting the presence of depressive symptomatolgy, and relative lack of false negatives. However, the CES–D has not been supported as a clinically relevant diagnostic tool to determine treatment eligibility. The high percentage of false positives identified when using the standard cut score would prove costly if the CES–D were used as the sole method to determine treatment appropriateness (Roberts et al., 1989). Fechner-Bates et al. (1994) cautioned researchers not to rely solely on a CES–D total score as the criterion for depression, as the individual items represent the symptoms most typical of depression and the common manifestations of general psychological distress common to many psychiatric disorders and stressful situations.

Several alternatives have been suggested to enable the CES–D to have increased diagnostic efficiency in the primary care setting. The first suggestion is to use a higher cut score. As previously mentioned, several studies (Schulberg et al., 1985; Thomas et al., 1998) have shown adequate diagnostic specificity and sensitivity by increasing the cut score to 27 (Schulberg et al., 1985). This practice maintains a high rate of sensitivity while successfully reducing the false-positive rate. Another alternative is to utilize the CES–D as part of a two- or three-stage screening process.

Shrout and Fleiss (1981) suggested establishing intervention eligibility by using a two-stage screening process that includes a validated structured or semistructured diagnostic interview. In the first stage, assessment eligibility is determined by using the CES–D as a screening test. Participants who score above the established cut score on the CES–D should receive a further evaluation using an established diagnostic instrument or interview. Schulberg et al. (1995) used the CES–D as a screening measure in a three-phase assessment study. During the first assessment phase, a CES–D cut score of 22 was used to maximize test sensitivity. The DIS was utilized to determine a depressive diagnosis during the second phase. The third phase included further analysis by comparing the DIS-positive patients with those given a diagnosis as assessed by a psychiatrist. Although a two-stage screening and interview procedure is valid and economical, researchers are cautioned that substantial numbers of patients who score above the standard cut score on the screening measure will not have a diagnosable disorder (Fechner-Bates et al., 1994).

Issues in Implementation. The diagnosis of clinical depression is based on a number of clinical criteria, including the presence of a constellation of symptoms for which alternative explanations (e.g., organic, substance-related causes) have been ruled out (APA, 1994). In contrast, psychological research commonly categorizes respondents as depressed or nondepressed on the basis of scores on self-report measures of distress such as the CES–D. As previously mentioned, this is a dangerous practice, as summary scores on these measures may reflect strong endorsement of a few items or weak endorsement of many items. Moreover, such self-report scales do not rule out alternative explanations of elevated scores. Finally, given the content of items, it is possible to have a score above the CES–D cut score without having a single symptom that would count toward a diagnosis of major depressive disorder (Coyne, Schwenk, & Smolinski, 1991; Schulberg et al., 1985).

Duncan-Jones and Henderson (1978) reported a substantial decrease in the correlation between screening scores and clinical diagnoses as the interval between measurements increased beyond a week. They concluded that a significant proportion of psychiatric morbidity may be acute in nature and will diminish over time. This finding is extremely relevant when examining the usefulness of two-stage screening efforts. It indicates that the lack of "fit" between the CES–D and the diagnostic interview employed (SCID, DIS, SADS) may be attributable, in part, to the assessment interval employed.

Use as an Instrument for Treatment Monitoring

Although the CES–D has risen in popularity as a screening measure, few studies have evaluated its use as a treatment monitoring instrument. In the New Haven Clinical Study, Weissman et al. (1975) found that the CES–D was responsive to treatment-induced change in a clinical sample following 4 weeks of treatment. The mean CES–D score in the "recovered" group declined by 20 points, whereas those patients with continued symptomatology evidenced only a 12-point decrease. Additionally, the decrease in score on the CES–D correlated highly with the decreases found on the SCL–90, the Hamilton Depression Rating Scale, and the Raskin measure of depression. Based on the limited data evaluating the CES–D as a treatment monitoring instrument, clinicians are advised to assess for treatment efficacy utilizing additional measures and clinical interviews.

CONCLUSION

Strengths and Limitations of the BDI and the CES–D in Primary Care

If primary care physicians wish to utilize either the CES–D or the BDI (or its derivatives) in their practices, they should be aware of the strengths and limitations of the measures when employed in such settings. Many of these strengths and weaknesses have been mentioned, either directly or indirectly, earlier in this chapter. The key strengths and limitations are summarized in this section.

Strengths. The most obvious strengths of these measures are the ease of administration, the low cost of administration, and the amount of time required to administer and score the tests. For primary care physicians, who are burdened with heavy work loads and who are often restricted to shorter patient visits and lower costs of treatment in managed care environments, time is of the essence. The BDI and the CES–D, although they may not conclusively identify the specific disorder of a patient, do provide the physician with a tool to rapidly determine those patients who warrant further assessment for depressive disorders. This is particularly useful for primary care physicians. After all, research has demonstrated that a large percentage of visits to primary care physicians are psychological in nature and that primary care physicians are not particularly effective at recognizing the psychological problems of their patients on their own. The low reading level necessary for completing the instruments allows for a large percentage of properly instructed patients to fill out the measure on their own, perhaps in the office waiting area. Even when the tests must be administered orally, the time of administration is relatively short.

Although strong evidence of improved clinical outcomes subsequent to implementing case-finding instruments is still lacking, several studies maintain that using the instruments does improve the recognition and treatment of depression among primary care physicians. These measures may assist clinicians in decreasing the number of patients who warrant more intensive psychological assessment while not missing those individuals who might benefit from further assessment. With regard to specific treatment strategies, a very much-elevated BDI score (i.e., 30 or higher) is generally recognized as an indication of severe depressive symptomatology and thus may suggest an immediate referral to a mental health professional and/or the initiation of a trial of antidepressant medication. On the opposite end of the spectrum, some researchers have reported that very low BDI scores (i.e., 0–9) in previously depressed patients may signal a remission of symptoms and thus may suggest that termination of treatment be considered. Although the severity of depressive symptoms based on an elevated CES–D total score has not been evaluated, it is generally agreed that a score above 27 (Schulberg et al., 1985) in a primary care patient warrants further evaluation. Although no single, self-report measure should serve as the sole basis for treatment decisions, these measures may assist physicians in making determinations by providing useful information regarding the presence and/or severity of symptoms. Further improvements in the rates of recognition and treatment of depression represent a positive step toward the most appropriate, efficient, and effective treatment of patients.

The BDI–PC deserves special attention here as it may be particularly relevant to primary care professionals. Preliminary evidence suggests that this measure may be the most appropriate of the BDI measures for use with medically ill patients. Many of the patients who visit primary care clinics may suffer from medical illnesses, the sequalae of which may overlap with somatic and performance symptoms of depression. The BDI–PC shows promise as a method of assessing the presence of depression in medically ill patients by focusing on the cognitive/affective symptoms of depression.

Limitations. Perhaps the most important limitation of both the BDI measures and the CES–D in primary care settings is their inability to provide conclusive nosologic information. In other words, although the measures may alert physicians to the likely presence of significant depressive symptoms, they cannot identify the specific diagnostic category to which a patient may belong and they are not a substitute for clinical interviews or diagnostic criteria. Because the recommended, first-line treatments for depression are generally based on the specific disorder present, the most appropriate and effective treatment may not be evident from BDI or CES–D scores.

Some researchers have suggested that these measures also have problems regarding both high-end specificity and low-end specificity. They argue that high scores may represent broadly distressed or dysthymic individuals rather than individuals who are specifically depressed. In addition, there is evidence to suggest that low scores may reflect symptom denial (a fake-good response style) rather than an absence of depressive symptoms. Each of these potential problems could have significant ramifications on both research and clinical practice, and both demand further investigation.

Finally, there are some potential limitations associated with the content of the measures. First, these self-report inventories do not include full coverage of the *DSM-IV* diagnostic criteria, the application of which is considered the "gold standard" for the diagnosis of depression. Second, at least one study suggests that the BDI may be particularly susceptible to defensive or malingering response sets due to the lack of subtle item content and the consistency in the ordering of items from least to most pathological (Dahlstrom, Brooks, & Peterson, 1990). Finally, in those instances when the patient is uneducated or severely affected, the advantages of greater practicality and lesser demands on the physician's time may be canceled out by the fact that the patient needs assistance in completing the scale.

Summary

There is a clear need for improvement in the recognition of depression by primary care physicians. Recent literature suggests that major depression occurs in approximately 5% to 10% of primary care patients and that as many as two to three times as many patients in these settings have depressive symptoms that fall short of the criteria for major depression (Katon & Schulberg, 1992). Moreover, estimates indicate that 60% of all health care visits involving mental health issues occur in the general practitioner's office (Magil & Garret, 1988), and that a larger percentage of community residents with major depression are seen by primary care physicians (over 50%) than by mental health professionals (20%) (Katon & Schulberg, 1992). Unfortunately, studies also indicate that primary care physicians are not particularly good at recognizing these depressed patients. As many as 50% of patients with either major or minor depression do not receive an accurate diagnosis (Eisenberg, 1992; Simon & VonKorff, 1995).

Efforts to improve the recognition of depression by primary care physicians have included the utilization of self-report measures, such as the CES-D and the BDI. Although these measures were originally developed to assess the severity of depressive symptoms, they have gained popularity as screening devices for depression in primary care. Those who argue against this practice cite several common limitations of the measures in this capacity. The most frequently voiced criticisms include the limited specificity of the measures and their resultant inability to yield conclusive statements regarding nosologic classification. In addition, some have pointed to content issues, noting that the measures do not offer exhaustive coverage of *DSM-IV* symptomatology.

Despite these limitations, implementing the CES-D or the BDI as part of depression screening procedures in primary care appears to have significant potential benefits. The psychometric properties of the original BDI, the BDI-II, and the CES-D have been extensively studied and the measures have demonstrated good reliability and validity. Preliminary results on the newer measures, the BDI-I and the BDI-PC, are also promising.

Although the literature does not support using these measures to identify specific diagnoses, the instruments are sensitive to the presence of depressive disorders. The inventories may be used to assist physicians in the determination of those patients who may benefit from additional assessment. Consequently, recognition rates may improve and the overall number of individuals who will need a more thorough, time-consuming psychological assessment would be reduced. In addition, the measures provide information on the severity of symptomatology, which may be a useful component in decisions regarding referrals to mental health professionals and/or the initiation of particular treatment strategies.

APPENDIX A

Center for Epidemiologic Studies–Depression Scale

Using the scale below, indicate the number which best describes
How often you felt or behaved this way during the past week:

0	Rarely or none of the time	(less than 1 day)
1	Some or a little of the time	(1–2 days)
2	Occasionally or a moderate amount of the time	(3–4 days)
3	Most or all of the time	(5–7 days)

1. I was bothered by things that usually don't bother me.	0	1	2	3
2. I did not feel like eating, my appetite was poor.	0	1	2	3
3. I felt that I could not shake the blues, even with help from my family and friends.	0	1	2	3
4. I felt that I was just as good as other people.	0	1	2	3
5. I had trouble keeping my mind on what I was doing.	0	1	2	3
6. I felt depressed.	0	1	2	3
7. I felt that everything I did was an effort.	0	1	2	3
8. I felt hopeful about the future.	0	1	2	3
9. I thought my life had been a failure.	0	1	2	3
10. I felt fearful.	0	1	2	3
11. My sleep was restless.	0	1	2	3
12. I was happy.	0	1	2	3
13. I talked less than usual.	0	1	2	3
14. I felt lonely.	0	1	2	3
15. People were unfriendly.	0	1	2	3
16. I enjoyed life.	0	1	2	3
17. I had crying spells.	0	1	2	3
18. I felt sad.	0	1	2	3
19. I felt that people disliked me.	0	1	2	3
20. I could not get "going."	0	1	2	3

REFERENCES

American Psychiatric Association. (1994). *Diagnostic and statistical manual of mental disorders* (4th ed.). Washington, DC: Author.

Andresen, E. M., Malmgren, J. A., Carter, W. B., & Patrick, D. L. (1994). Screening for depression in well older adults: Evaluation of a short form of the CES-D. *American Journal of Preventive Medicine, 10*(2), 77–84.

Beck, A. T. (1967). *Depression.* Philadelphia: University of Pennsylvania Press.

Beck, A. T., & Beamesderfer, A. (1974). Assessment of depression: The Depression Inventory. In P. Pichot (Ed.), *Modern problems in pharmacopsychiatry* (pp. 15–169). Basel: Karger.

Beck, A. T., & Beck, R. W. (1972). Screening depressed patients in family practice: A rapid technique. *Postgraduate Medicine, 52,* 81–85.

Beck, A. T., Guth, D., Steer, R. A., & Ball, R. (1997). Screening for major depression disorders in medical inpatients with the Beck Depression Inventory for Primary Care. *Behaviour Research and Therapy, 35*(8), 785–791.

Beck, A. T., Hollon, S. D., Young, J. E., Bedrosian, R. C., & Budenz, D. (1985). Treatment of depression with cognitive therapy and amitriptyline. *Archives of General Psychiatry, 42,* 142–148.

Beck, A. T., Rush, A. J., Shaw, B. F., & Emery, G. (1979). *Cognitive therapy of depression.* New York: Guilford Press.

Beck, A. T., & Steer, R. A. (1987). *Manual for the Beck Depression Inventory.* San Antonio, TX: Psychological Corporation.

Beck, A. T., Steer, R. A., Ball, R., Ciervo, C. A., & Kabat, M. (1997). Use of the Beck Anxiety and Depression Inventories for Primary Care with medical outpatients. *Psychological Assessment, 4*(3), 211–219.

Beck, A. T., Steer, R. A., & Brown, G. K. (1996). *Manual for the Beck Depression Inventory–II.* San Antonio, TX: Psychological Corporation.

Beck, A .T., Steer, R. A., & Garbin, M. G. (1988). Psychometric properties of the Beck Depression Inventory: Twenty–five years of evaluation. *Clinical Psychology Review, 8,* 77–100.

Beck, A. T., Ward, C. H., Mendelson, M., Mock, J. E., & Erbaugh, J. (1961). An inventory for measuring depression. *Archives of General Psychiatry, 4,* 561–571.

Beck, A. T., Weissman, A., Lester, D., & Trexler, L. (1974). The measurement of pessimism: The Hopelessness Scale. *Journal of Consulting and Clinical Psychology, 42,* 861–865.

Berwick, D. M., Murphy, J. M., Goldman, P. A., Ware, J. E., Barsky, A. J., & Weinstein, M. C. (1991). Performance of a five-item mental health screening test. *Medical Care, 29,* 169–176.

Boyd, J. H., Weissman, M. M., Thompson, D., & Myers, J. K. (1982). Screening for depression in a community sample: Understanding the discrepancies between depressive symptom and diagnostic scales. *Archives of General Psychiatry, 39,* 1195–1200.

Breslau, N. (1985). Depressive symptoms, major depression, and generalized anxiety: A comparison of self-reports on CES–D and results from diagnostic interviews. *Psychiatric Research, 15,* 219–229.

Brown, C., Schulberg, H. C., Madonia, M. J., Shear, M. K., & Houck, P. R. (1996). Treatment outcomes for primary care patients with major depression and lifetime anxiety disorders. *American Journal of Psychiatry, 153*(10), 1293–1300.

Bruce, M. L., Takeuchi, D. T., & Leaf, P. J. (1991). Poverty and psychiatric status. *Archives of General Psychiatry, 48,* 470–474.

Callahan, E. J., Bertakis, K. D., Azari, R., Robbins, J., Helms, L. J., & Miller, J. (1996). The influence of depression on physician-patient interaction in primary care. *Family Medicine, 28*(5), 346–351.

Clark, V. A., Aneshensel, C. S., Frerichs, R. R., & Morgan, T. M. (1981). Analysis of effects of sex and age in response to items on the CES–D scale. *Psychiatric Research, 5,* 171–181.

Coulehan, J. L., Schulberg, H. C., Block, M.R. (1989). The efficiency of depression questionnaires for case fining in primary medical care. *Journal of General Internal Medicine, 4,* 541–547.

Coulehan, J. L., Schulberg, H. C., Block, M. R., Madonia, M. J., & Rodriguez, E. (1997). Treating depressed primary care patients improves their physical, mental, and social functioning. *Archives of Internal Medicine, 157,* 113–1120.

Coyne, J. C., & Schwenk, T. L. (1997). The relationship of distress to mood disturbance in primary care and psychiatric populations. *Journal of Consulting and Clinical Psychology, 65*(1), 161–168.

Coyne, J. C., Schwenk, T. L., & Fechner-Bates, S. (1995). Nondetection of depression by primary care physicians reconsidered. *General Hospital Psychiatry, 17*(1), 3–12.

Coyne, J. C., Schwenk, T. L., & Smolinski, M. (1991). Recognizing depression: A comparison of physicians ratings, self-report, and interview measures. *Journal of the American Board of Family Practice, 4,* 207–215.

Dahlstrom, W. G., Brooks, J. D., & Peterson, C. D. (1990). The Beck Depression Inventory: Item order and the impact of response sets. *Journal of Personality Assessment, 55*(1&2), 224–233.

Deardorff, W. W., & Funabiki, D. (1985). A diagnostic caution in screening for depressed college students. *Cognitive Therapy and Research, 9,* 277–284.

Depression Guideline Panel. (1993). *Depression in primary care: Volume 1. Detection and diagnosis* (Clinical Practice Guideline, No. 5). Rockville, MD: U.S. Department of Health and Human Services, Public Health Service, Agency for Health Care Policy and Research. (AHCPR Publication No. 93-0550)

Derotatis, L. R. (1975). *Symptom Checklist-90.* Minneapolis, MN: National Computer Systems, Inc.

Dobson, K. S., & Breiter, H. J. (1981). Cognitive assessment of depression: Reliability and validity of three measures. *Journal of Abnormal Psychology, 92,* 107–109.

Duncan-Jones, P., & Henderson, S. (1978). The use of a two-phase design in a prevalence survey. *Social Psychiatry, 13,* 231–237.

Edwards, B. C., Lambert, M. J., Moran, P. W., McCully, T., Smith, K. C., & Ellingson, A. G. (1984). A meta-analytic comparison of the Beck Depression Inventory and the Hamilton Rating Scale for Depression as measures of treatment outcome. *British Journal of Clinical Psychology, 23,* 93–99.

Eisenberg, L. (1992). Treating depression and anxiety in primary care: Closing the gap between knowledge and practice. *New England Journal of Medicine, 326,* 1080–1084.

Endicott, J., & Spitzer, R. (1978). A diagnostic interview: The Schedule for Affective Disorders and Schizophrenia. *Archives of General Psychiatry, 35,* 837–834.

Fechner-Bates, S., Coyne, J. C., & Schwenk, T. L. (1994). The relationship of self-reported distress to depressive disorders and other psychopathology. *Journal of Consulting and Clinical Psychology, 62*(3), 550–559.

Feightner, J. W., & Worrall, G. (1990). Early detection of depression by primary care physicians. *Canadian Medical Association Journal, 142*(11), 1215–1221.

Fitzgibbon, M., Cella, D. F., & Sweeney, J. A. (1988). Redundancy in measures of depression. *Journal of Clinical Psychology, 44*(3), 372–374.

Flesch, R. A. (1948). A new readability yardstick. *Journal of Applied Psychiatry, 23,* 221–233.

Gallagher, D., Nies, G., & Thompson, L. W. (1982). Reliability of the Beck Depression Inventory with older adults. *Journal of Consulting and Clinical Psychology, 50,* 152–153.

Giambra, L. M. (1977). Independent dimensions of depression: A factor analysis of three self-report depression measures. *Journal of Clinical Psychology, 33*(4), 928–935.

Gotlib, I. H. (1984). Depression and general psychopathology in university students. *Journal of Abnormal Psychology, 93,* 19–30.

Guarnaccia, P. J., Angel, R., & Worobey, J. L. (1989). The factor structure of the CES-D in the Hispanic health and nutrition examination survey: The influences of ethnicity, gender and language. *Society of Scientific Medicine, 29*(1), 85–94.

Haaga, D. A., & Solomon, A. (1993). Impact of Kendall, Hollon, Beck, Hammen, and Ingram (1987) on treatment of the continuity issue in "Depression" research. *Cognitive Therapy and Research, 17*(4), 313–324.

Hamilton, M. (1967). Development of a rating scale for primary depressive illness. *British Journal of Medical Psychology, 32,* 50–55.

Hammen, C. L. (1980). Depression in college students: Beyond the Beck Depression Inventory. *Journal of Consulting and Clinical Psychology, 48,* 126–128.

Hammen, C. L. (1983, May). *Cognitive and social processes in bipolar affective disorders: A neglected topic.* Paper presented at the convention of the American Psychological Association, Anaheim, CA.

Hathaway, S. R., & McKinley, J. C. (1943). *The Minnesota Multiphasic Personality Inventory manual.* Minneapolis, MN: University of Minnesota Press.

Hertzog, C., Van Alstine, J., & Usala, P. D. (1990). Measurement properties of the Center for Epidemiological Studies Depression Scale (CES-D) in older populations. *Journal of Counseling and Clinical Psychology, 2*(1), 64–72.

Horwath, E., Johnson, J., Klerman, G. L., & Weissman, M. M. (1992). Depressive symptoms as relative and attributable risk factors for first-onset major depression. *Archives of General Psychiatry, 49,* 817–823.

Husaini, B. A., Neff, J. A., Harrington, J. B., Hughes, M. D., & Stone, R. H. (1980). Depression in rural communities: Validating the CES-D scale. *Journal of Community Psychology, 8,* 20–27.

Jones-Webb, R. J., & Snowden, L. R. (1993). Symptoms of depression among blacks and whites. *American Journal of Public Health, 83*(2), 240–244.

Katon, W. (1982). Depression: Somatic symptoms and medical disorders in primary care. *Comprehensive Psychiatry, 23,* 274–287.

Katon, W., Robinson, P., Von Korff, M., Lin, W., Bush, T., Ludman, E., Simon, G., & Walker, E. (1996). A multifaceted intervention to improve treatment of depression in primary care. *Archives of General Psychiatry, 53,* 924–932.

Katon, W., & Schulberg, H. C. (1992). Epidemiology of depression in primary care. *General Hospital Psychiatry, 14,* 237–247.

Kendall, P. C., Hollon, S. D., Beck, A. T., Hammen, C. L., & Ingram, R. E. (1987). Issues and recommendations regarding use of the Beck Depression Inventory. *Cognitive Therapy and Research, 11*(3), 289–299.

Kerner, S. A., & Jacobs, K. W. (1983). Correlation between scores on the Beck Depression Inventory and the Zung Self-Rating Depression Scale. *Psychological Reports, 53,* 969–970.

Kessler, R. C., McGonagle, K. A., Zhao, S., Nelson, C. B., Hughes, M., Eschleman, S., Wittchen, H., & Kendler, K. S. (1994). Lifetime and 12-month prevalence of DSM-III-R psychiatric disorders in the United States. *Archives of General Psychiatry, 51,* 8–19.

Kirmayer, L. J., Robbins, J. M., Dworkin, M., & Yaffe, M. J. (1993). Somatization and the recognition of depression and anxiety in primary care. *American Journal of Psychiatry, 150*(5), 734–741.

Knight, R. G., Williams, S., McGee, R., & Olaman, S. (1997). Psychometric properties of the Center for Epidemiologic Studies Depression Scale (CES-D) in a sample of women in middle life. *Behaviour Research and Therapy, 35*(4), 373–380.

Lewinsohn, P., & Teri, L. (1982). Selection of depressed and nondepressed subjects on the basis of self-report data. *Journal of Consulting and Clinical Psychology, 50,* 590–591.

Lyness, J. M., Noel, T. K., Cox, D., King, D. A., Conwell, Y., & Caine, E. D. (1997). Screening for depression in elderly primary care patients: A comparison of the Center for Epidemiologic Studies–Depression Scale and the Geriatric Depression Scale. *Archives of Internal Medicine, 157*(4), 449–454.

Magil, M. K., & Garrett, R. W. (1988). Behavioral and psychiatric problems. In R. B. Taylor (Ed.), *Family medicine* (3rd ed., pp. 534–562). New York: Springer-Verlag.

Markush, R. E., & Favero, R. V. (1973). Epidemiologic assessment of stressful life events, depressed mood, and psychophysiological symptoms: A preliminary report. In B. S. Dohrenwend & B. P. Dohrenwend (Eds.), *Stressful life events: Their nature and effects.* (pp. 171–190). New York: John Wiley & Sons.

Matthews, K., Milne, S., & Ashcroft, G. W. (1994). Role of doctors in the prevention of suicide: The final consultation. *British Journal of General Practice, 44,* 345–348.

McNair, D. M. (1974). Self-evaluation of antidepressants. *Psychopharmacologica, 37,* 281–302.

Moran, P. W., & Lambert, M. J. (1983). A review of current assessment tools for monitoring changes in depression. In M.S. Lambert, E. R. Christensen, & S. DeJulio (Eds.), *The assessment of psychotherapy outcome* (pp. 263–303). New York: Wiley.

Mulrow, C. D., Williams, J. W., Gerety, M. B., Ramirez, G., Montiel, O. M., & Kerber, C. (1995). Case-finding instruments for depression in primary care settings. *Annals of Internal Medicine, 122,* 913–921.

Murphy, G. E., Simons, A. D., Wetzel, R. D., & Lustman (1984). Cognitive therapy and pharmacotherapy: Singly and together in the treatment of depression. *Archives of General Psychiatry, 41,* 33–41.

Myers, J. K., & Weissman, M. M. (1980). Use of a self-report symptom scale to detect depression in a community sample. *American Journal of Psychiatry, 137*(9), 1081–1084.

Nielson, A. C., & Williams, T. A. (1980). Depression in ambulatory medical patients. *Archives of General Psychiatry, 37,* 999–1004.

Nunnally, J. C. (1967). *Psychometric theory.* New York: McGraw-Hill.

Oliver, J. M., & Simmons, M. E. (1984). Depression as measured by the DSM–III and the Beck Depression Inventory in an unselected adult population. *Journal of Consulting and Clinical Psychology, 52,* 892–898.

Radloff, L. S. (1977). The CES-D Scale: A self-report depression scale for research in the general population. *Applied Psychological Measurement, 1*(3), 385–401.

Raskin, A. (1965). *NIMH Collaborative Depression Mood Scale.* Rockville, MD: National Institute of Mental Health.

Regier, D. A., Goldberg, I. D., & Taube, C. A. (1978). The de facto US mental health services system: A public health perspective. *Archives of General Psychiatry, 35,* 685–693.

Reynolds, W. M., & Gould, J. W. (1981). A psychometric investigation of the standard and short-form Beck Depression Inventory. *Journal of Consulting and Clinical Psychology, 49,* 306–307.

Richter, P., Werner, J., Bastine, R., Heerlein, A., Kick, H., & Sauer, H. (1997). Measuring treatment outcome by the Beck Depression Inventory. *Psychopathology, 30,* 234–240.

Roberts, R. E. (1980). Reliability of the CES-D scale in different ethnic contexts. *Psychiatric Research, 2,* 125–134.

Roberts, R. E., & Vernon, S. W. (1983). The Center for Epidemiologic Studies–Depression Scale: Its use in a community sample. *American Journal of Psychiatry, 140*(1), 41–46.

Roberts, R. E., Vernon, S. W., & Rhoades, H. M. (1989). Effects of language and ethnic status on reliability and validity of the Center for Epidemiologic Studies–Depression Scale with psychiatric patients. *Journal of Nervous and Mental Disease, 177*(10), 581–592.

Robins, L. N., Helzer, J. E., Croughan, J., & Ratcliff, K. S. (1981). The National Institute of Mental Health Diagnostic Interview Schedule: Its history, characteristics, and validity. *Archives of General Psychiatry, 38,* 381–389.

Rush, A. J., Beck, A. T., Kovacs, M., & Hollon, S. D. (1977). Comparative efficacy of cognitive therapy and pharmacotherapy in the treatment of depressed outpatients. *Cognitive Therapy and Research, 1,* 17–37.

Sacco, W. P. (1981). Invalid use of the Beck Depression Inventory to identify depressed college-student subjects: A methodological comment. *Cognitive Therapy and Research, 5,* 143–147.

Santor, D. A., & Coyne, J. (1997). Shortening the CES-D to improve its ability to detect cases of depression. *Psychological Assessment, 9*(3), 233–243.

Santor, D. A., Zuroff, D. C., Ramsay, J. O., Cervantes, P., & Palacios, J. (1995). Examining scale discriminability in the BDI and CES-D as a function of depressive severity. *Psychological Assessment, 7,* 131–139.

Sayetta, R. B., & Johnson, D. P. (1980). Basic data on depressive symptomatology, United States 1974–75. *Vital and Health Statistics* (Ser. 11, No. 216, DHEW Publication No. 80-1666). Washington, DC: US Government Printing Office.

Schaefer, A., Brown, J., Watson, C. G., Plemel, D., Demotts, J., Howard, M. T., Petrik, N., Balleweg, B. J., & Anderson, D. (1985). Comparison of the validities of the Beck, Zung, and MMPI depression scales. *Journal of Consulting and Clinical Psychology, 53*, 414–418.

Schonfeld, W. H., Verboncoeur, C. J., Fifer, S. K., Lipschutz, R. C., Lubeck, D. P., & Buesching, D. P. (1997). The functioning and well-being of patients with unrecognized anxiety disorders and major depressive disorder. *Journal of Affective Disorders, 43*, 105–119.

Schulberg, H. C., Block, M. R., Madonia, M. J., Scott, C. P., Lave, J. R., Rodriguez, E., & Coulehan, J. L. (1997). The usual care of major depressive disorder in primary care practice. *Archives of Family Medicine, 6*, 334–339.

Schulberg, H. C., Madonia, M. J., Block, M. R., Coulehan, J. L., Scott, C.P., Rodriguez, E., & Block, A. (1995). Major depressive disorder in primary care practice: Clinical characteristics and treatment implications. *Psychosomatics, 36*(2), 129–137.

Schulberg, H. C., Saul, M., McClelland, M., Ganguli, M., Christy, W., & Frank, R. (1985). Assessing depression in primary medical and psychiatric practices. *Archives of General Psychiatry, 42*, 1164–1170.

Shrout, P. E., & Fleiss, J. L. (1981). Reliability and case detection. In J. Wing, P. Babbington, & L. N. Robbins (Eds.), *What is a case? The problem of definition in psychiatric community surveys* (pp. 117–128). London: Grant, McIntyre.

Shrout, P. E., & Yager, T. J. (1989). Reliability and validity of screening scales: Effect of reducing scale length. *Journal of Clinical Epidemiology, 42*(1), 69–78.

Simon, G., Ormel, J., Von Korff, M., & Barlow, W. (1995). Health care costs associated with depression and anxiety disorders in primary care. *American Journal of Psychiatry, 152*(3), 352–357.

Simon, G. E., & Von Korff, M. (1995). Recognition, management, and outcomes of depression in primary care. *Archives of Family Medicine, 4*, 99–105.

Simon, G., Von Korff, M., & Barlow, W. (1995). Health care costs of primary care patients with recognized depression. *Archives of General Psychiatry, 52*, 850–856.

Spitzer, R. L., Endicott, J., & Robins, E. (1978). RDC: Rationale and reliability. *Archives of General Psychiatry, 35*, 773–782.

Spitzer, R., Kroenke, K., Linzer, M., Hahn, S., Williams, J., deGruy, F., & Davies, M. (1995). Health-related quality of life in primary care patients with mental disorders. *Journal of the American Medical Association, 274*, 1511–1517.

Steer, R. A., & Beck, A. T. (1985). Modifying the Beck Depression Inventory: A reply to Vredenberg, Krames and Flett. *Psychological Reports, 57*, 625–626.

Steer, R. A., Beck, A. T., & Garrison, B. (1986). Applications of the Beck Depression Inventory. In N. Sartorius & T.A. Ban (Eds.), *Assessment of Depression* (pp. 121–142). New York: Springer-Verlag.

Strober, M., Green, J., & Carlson, G. (1981). Utility of the Beck Depression Inventory with psychiatrically hospitalized adolescents. *Journal of Consulting and Clinical Psychology, 49*, 482–483.

Tanaka-Matsumi, J., & Kameoka, V. A. (1986). Reliabilities and concurrent validities of popular self-report measures of depression, anxiety, and social desirability. *Journal of Consulting and Clinical Psychology, 54*, 328–333.

Teri, L. (1982). The use of the Beck Depression Inventory with adolescents. *Journal of Abnormal Child Psychiatry, 10*, 277–284.

Thomas, J. L., Applegate, B. W., Scarinci, I. C., Jones, G. N., & Brantley, P. J. (1998, November). *Confirmatory factor analysis of the CES–D in a low-SES primary care population.* Poster session presented at the annual meeting of the Association for the Advancement of Behavior Therapy, Washington, DC.

Thomas, J. L., Scarinci, I. C., Jones, G. N., Mehan, D. J., & Brantley, P. J. (1998). [Predictive validity of the CES–D for depressive disorders in low SES primary care females.] Unpublished raw data.

Thorson, J. A., & Powell, F. C. (1993). The CES–D: Four of five factors? *Bulletin of the Psychonomic Society, 11*, 577–578.

Turner, J. A., & Romano, J. M. (1984). Self-report screening measures for depression in chronic pain patients. *Journal of Clinical Psychology, 40*(4), 909–913.

Van Hook, M. P. (1996). Challenges to identifying and treating women with depression in rural primary care. *Social Work in Health Care, 23*(3), 73–92.

Vredenberg, K., Krames, L., & Flett, G. L. (1985). Reexamining the Beck Depression Inventory: The long and the short of it. *Psychological Reports, 57*, 767–778.

Volk, R. J., Pace, T. M., & Parchman, M. L. (1993). Screening for depression in primary care patients: Dimensionality of the short form of the Beck Depression Inventory. *Psychological Assessment, 5,* 173–181.

Weiss, L. (1996, March). *A progress report on the development and validation of the Beck Depression Inventory–Primary Care version prepared for Smith-Kline Beecham Pharmaceuticals by the staff of the Psychological Corporation.* Unpublished manuscript.

Weissman, M. M., Prusoff, B., & Newberry, P. (1975). *Comparison of the CES–D with standardized depression rating scales at three points in time.* (Tech. Rep. Contract ASH-74166). Yale University. Rockville, MD: National Institute of Mental Health.

Weissman, M. M., Sholomskas, D., Pottenger, M., Prusoff, B. A., & Locke, B. Z. (1977). Assessing depressive symptoms in five psychiatric populations: A validation study. *American Journal of Epidemiology, 106,* 203–214.

Wells, K. B., Stewart, A., Hayes, R. D., Burnam, A., Rogers, W., Daniels, M., Berry, S., Greenfield, S., & Ware, J. (1989). The functioning and well-being of depressed patients: Results from the Medical Outcomes Study. *Journal of the American Medical Association, 262,* 914–919.

Zich, J. M., Attkisson, C. C., & Greenfield, T. K. (1990). Screening for depression in primary care clinics: The CES–D and the BDI. *International Journal of Psychiatry in Medicine, 20(3),* 259–277.

Zung, W. W. K. (1965). A self-rating depression scale. *Archives of General Psychiatry, 12,* 63–70.

Zung, W. W., Broadhead, W. E., & Roth, M. E. (1993). Prevalence of depressive symptoms in primary care. *Journal of Family Practice, 37,* 337–344.

13

The Hamilton Depression Inventory

Kenneth A. Kobak
Dean Foundation for Health Research and Education, Middleton, Wisconsin

William M. Reynolds
University of British Colombia

The problem of identification and treatment of depression in primary care patients is increasingly recognized as an important health care issue (Attkisson & Zich, 1990; Depression Guideline Panel, 1993a, 1993b; Eisenberg, 1992). Although primary care physicians are the main providers of treatment for depression (Shapiro et al., 1984), rates of undetected depression in primary care patients have been found to range as high as 60% (Schulberg & Burns, 1988; Spitzer et al., 1994). The Epidemiologic Catchment Area (ECA) study found 45% of patients diagnosed with an affective disorder had sought treatment from a primary care physician for a *nonpsychiatric* medical problem in the prior 6 months (Shapiro et al., 1984). Often these patients present with somatic symptoms suggestive of a medical condition while volunteering few psychological complaints (Kroenke, Jackson, & Chamberlin, 1997; Schulberg & Burns, 1988).

Several other factors contribute to the underrecognition of depression by primary care physicians, such as unfamiliarity with diagnostic criteria, uncertainty about specific questions to elicit mental health symptoms, and time limitations in busy office practices (Orleans, George, Houpt, & Brodie, 1985; Rost, Smith, Matthews, & Guise, 1994). Also, patients too often fail to report symptoms of depression due to the stigma associated with having a "mental illness" (Depression Guideline Panel, 1993b) and their uncertainty about the appropriateness of talking about emotional problems in a primary care setting.

Unrecognized and untreated mental disorders result in substantial disability (Broadhead, Blazer, George, & Tse, 1990) and reduced quality of life (Wells et al., 1989), are associated with increased health care utilization (Henk, Katzelnick, Kobak, Greist, & Jefferson, 1996; Johnson, Weissman, & Klerman, 1992), and cost billions of dollars to society each year (Greenberg, Stiglin, Finkelstein, & Berndt, 1993). Given the high rate of primary care patients presenting with depression, and the fact that often there is an established relationship between the primary care physician and the patient (as well as with his or her family), the primary care physician is in a unique position to identify and treat patients suffering from depression (Attkisson & Zich, 1990). Although initial studies found that screening for depression in primary care patients did not typically result in better clinical outcomes than usual care (see Schade, Jones, & Wittlin, 1998, for a review), more recent data have shown that identification and treatment of depression in primary care can significantly reduce symptomatology, disability, and health care utilization, and improve quality of life (Katzelnick, Kobak, Greist, Jefferson, & Henk, 1997; Katzelnick, Simon, Pearson, Manning, Helstad, Henk, & Kobak, 1997). A valid and reliable depression screener would help the primary care physician to identify the depressed primary care patient, and a good symptom rating scale would help the physician to more effectively monitor the patient's response to treatment in order to guide the treatment intervention.

The Hamilton Depression Inventory (Reynolds & Kobak, 1995a, 1995b) was developed as a self-report, paper-and-pencil and computer-administered measure that emulates and extends the clinician-administered Hamilton Depression Rating Scale (HAMD; Hamilton, 1960, 1967). The HAMD was one of the first symptom rating scales developed to quantify the severity of depressive symptomatology. First introduced by Max Hamilton in 1960, it has since become the most widely used and accepted outcome measure for the evaluation of depression. It was included in the National Institute of Mental Health's Early Clinical Drug Evaluation program (ECDEU) Assessment Manual (Guy, 1976), in its attempt at providing a uniform battery of assessments for use in psychotropic drug evaluation. As a result, it has become the standard outcome measure used in clinical trials of new antidepressant medications presented to the Food and Drug Administration (FDA) by pharmaceutical companies for approval of new drug applications. It was also the primary outcome measure in the National Institute of Mental Health (NIMH) collaborative studies comparing pharmacotherapy with psychotherapy for the treatment of depression (Elkin et al., 1989), and is often the standard against which other depression rating scales are validated (Carroll, Feinberg, Smouse, Rawson, & Greden, 1981; Montgomery & Asberg, 1979; Reynolds & Kobak, 1998). The scale has been translated into European (Fava, Kellner, Munari, & Pavan, 1982; Hamilton, 1986; Ramos-Brieva & Cordero-Villafafila, 1988), and Asian (Kim, 1977) languages. The psychometric properties of the scale have been well documented (see Hedlund & Vieweg, 1979, for a review), and a meta-analysis found it more sensitive in measuring change due to treatment (both drug and psychotherapy) than several self-rated scales (Edwards et al., 1984; Lambert, Hatch, Kingston, & Edwards, 1986).

Hamilton (1960, 1967) reported that the scale was not intended for use as a diagnostic instrument, but was designed for measuring symptom severity in patients who have already been diagnosed as depressed. As in all symptom rating scales, all the exclusion and inclusion criteria required for a diagnosis are not necessarily evaluated. Nonetheless, using various cutoff scores, the scale has shown good properties as a "screener"; that is, it has demonstrated high levels of sensitivity and specificity in identifying those likely to have a diagnosis of major depression and thus warranting further evaluation (Reynolds, Kobak, & Greist, 1992a). The sensitivity and specificity of the HAMD in distinguishing between diagnostic groups have also been examined (Reynolds et al., 1992a; Riskind, Beck, Brown, & Steer, 1987; Tamburrino et al., 1997; Thase, Hersen, Bellack, Himmelhoch, & Kupfer, 1983). Others have incorporated the HAMD into or have extracted HAMD scores out of structured diagnostic interviews such as the Diagnostic Interview Schedule (DIS; Whisman et al., 1989) and the Schedule for Affective Disorders and Schizophrenia (SADS; Endicott, Cohen, Nee, Fleiss, & Sarantakos, 1981).

The HAMD was designed to be administered by a trained clinician using a semistructured clinical interview. The standard version of the HAMD consists of 17 "items," each of which is rated on either a 5-point (0–4) or a 3-point (0–2) scale, with the latter being used in cases where quantification was felt to be either difficult or impossible (see Table 13.1). In general, on the 5-point scale, the ratings are: 0 = absent, 1 = doubtful to mild, 2 = mild to moderate, 3 = moderate to severe, and 4 = very severe. A rating of 4 is usually reserved for extreme symptoms. On the 3-point scale, the ratings are: 0 = absent, 1 = probable or mild, and 2 = definite. The scale originally contained items for diurnal variation, depersonalization/derealization, paranoia, and obsessional symptoms. Hamilton later dropped these items, as they did not adequately measure depression severity or occurred too infrequently to add to the scale's utility (Hamilton, 1974).

Several of the items consist of a constellation of individual "symptoms," all of which should be considered in determining the items' final ratings. For example, for item 1, "Depressed Mood," Hamilton suggested evaluating feelings of sadness, as well as pessimism, hopelessness, and a tendency to cry, as a way to gauge depressed

TABLE 13.1

HDI Item Congruence With 17-Item Clinician HAMD and With *DSM–IV* Diagnostic Criteria, Melancholic Subtype, and Associated Features of Major Depressive Disorder

DSM–IV Diagnostic Criteria		HDI Question	Clinician HAMD Question
1.	Depressed mood	1a, 1b, 1c, 1d	1
2.	Loss of interest/pleasure	7a, 14	7, 14
3.	Weight/appetite loss	12, 17a, 17b, 17c	16
4a.	Insomnia: initial, mid, late	4a 4b, 5a, 5b, 6a, 6b	4, 5, 6
4b.	Hypersomnia	18	Not assessed
5a.	Psychomotor retardation	8	8
5b.	Psychomotor agitation	9	9
6.	Fatigue, loss of energy	13a	13
7a.	Guilt/worthlessness	2	2
7b.	Worthlessness	21	Not assessed
8.	Indecisiveness	23	Not assessed
9.	Suicidal ideation/behavior	3	3
DMS–IV Melancholic Features			
1.	Distinct depressed mood	1a, 1b	1
2.	Lack of mood reactivity	1c	Not assessed
3.	Diurnal mood variation	1e	Not assessed
4.	Excessive guilt	2	2
5.	Early morning awakening	6a, 6b	6
6.	Pervasive loss of interest	7a	7
7.	Marked psychomotor retardation	8	8
8.	Marked psychomotor agitation	9	9
9.	Significant weight loss	17a, 17b	16
DSM–IV Associates Features			
1.	Work impairment	7a	7
2.	Psychic anxiety	10a, 10b	10
3.	Somatic anxiety	11a, 11b, 11c, 11d	11
4.	Somatic, general	13b	13
5.	Hypochondriasis	15a, 15b	15
6.	Helplessness	19	Not assessed
7.	Hopelessness	22	1

mood. Both the frequency and severity of each symptom should be considered in rating each item, and ratings should be based on a change from the patient's "usual self" due to depression (e.g., if a person never had much interest in sex, one would not count current low interest at present, unless the current low interest is even lower than the person's usual baseline). The time frame on which the ratings are based is typically the past week, in order to assess current severity apart from temporary or minor fluctuations.

Hamilton provided only general guidelines as to the administration and scoring of the scale. No standardized probe questions were provided to elicit information from patients, and no behaviorally specific guidelines were developed for determining each item's rating. In order to improve the interrater reliability of the scale, several sets of guidelines were developed by a diverse group of researchers (Bech, Kastrup, & Rafaelsen, 1986; Kobak, Schaettle, Katzelnick, & Simon, 1995; Miller, Bishop, Norman, & Maddever, 1985; Potts, Daniels, Burnham, & Wells, 1990; Whisman et al., 1989; Williams, 1988). As a result, raters trained at the same site using the same set of guidelines have achieved adequate interrater reliability. However, interrater reliability between raters at different sites has been difficult to achieve due to the use of different sets of guidelines and differences in clinical training and experience (Hooijer et al., 1991).

In addition, training raters is a time-consuming process. Even when raters undergo extensive reliability training, adequate interrater reliability is often not obtained. For example, in a recent reliability training for a multisite clinical trial (Demitrack, Faries, DeBrota, & Potter, 1997), the difference in maximum and minimum total HAMD scores (full scale range 0–52) obtained from 86 raters from 32 sites evaluating the same patients on videotape presentations varied from a spread of 14 points in the best case, to a spread of 21 points in the worst case. This occurred in spite of training that included an overview of interview methodology, a detailed review of anchor points, a review of the customized interview guide, and review and discussion of videotaped interviews.

Even with fully structured interviews, problems with interrater reliability have been found. In one study, clinicians failed to ask up to 5% of the required questions (Fairbairn, Wood, & Fletcher, 1959), and in another, incorrect diagnoses were made on as many as 10% of patients because of clinician branching errors and misapplication of the scoring algorithm (Kobak et al., 1997a).

To address these and other issues, we developed a self-report version of the HAMD, called the Hamilton Depression Inventory (HDI; Reynolds & Kobak, 1995a). The HDI is designed to emulate the clinician-administered version and provide parallel scores and item content. The HDI is available in two formats: paper-and-pencil and desktop computer (PC) administration. The items in the paper-and-pencil and desktop computer-administered versions are identical. As described later, we also enhanced the HDI to reflect current diagnostic criteria and contemporary descriptions of depression. A score summary report and a more detailed clinical interpretive report are provided using the HDI software available from the publisher.

Two versions of the HDI are available. The full-scale version consists of 23 items that evaluate symptoms of depression according to current diagnostic criteria. It also allows for the derivation of a 17-item version that corresponds to the original HAMD described by Hamilton. There is also a 9-item HDI Short Form that is useful for screening purposes or where time or other restraints preclude the use of the longer version.

The HDI may be used in a wide range of clinical and research applications. The full-scale HDI is particularly useful in the primary care setting. There are several reasons for this recommendation. First, the full-scale HDI covers symptom domains of depression consistent with specifications for major depressive disorder in *DSM–IV*. Although it does not provide a diagnosis, the cutoff score is reasonably accurate in identifying individuals who may demonstrate a depressive disorder. Second, the flexible response format, either paper-and-pencil or computer administration, with computer scoring options available for both formats, allows each clinic to select the format that is most appropriate for its clients. Third, the HDI includes several computer scoring programs that provide either a brief scoring report or a detailed interpretive report of between 7 and 10 pages. Described next are the scale's psychometric data and its use in screening, treatment planning, treatment monitoring, and treatment evaluation.

OVERVIEW OF THE HAMILTON DEPRESSION INVENTORY

Goals of Development

In developing the HDI, we focused on four primary goals. The first was to develop a self-report paper-and-pencil and computer-administered version of the HAMD that was consistent with (i.e., equivalent to) the clinician-administered version. Our goal was to have both the item content and the scores obtained parallel those obtained with the clinician-administered version. One psychometric issue requiring attention when adapting a clinician-administered test to another form of administration (e.g., computer or paper and pencil) is that factors associated with the mode of administration may result in the inability to generalize normative and validity data from the original test to the alternative version (Hofer & Green, 1985). Our goal was to demonstrate the equivalence of the HDI with the clinician version from the perspective of cutoff scores, rank order data, mean scores, variances, and item homogeneity.

Second, we wanted to update the HDI to be consistent with current definitions of depression. The original HAMD was developed 38 years ago, prior to the development of modern diagnostic criteria. Thus, we expanded the HDI to parallel current symptoms associated with major depression as outlined in the current *Diagnostic and Statistical Manual of Mental Disorders,* 4th edition (*DSM–IV*; American Psychiatric Association, 1994).

Third, we wanted the scale to reflect a more complete and more precise evaluation of depressive symptomatology than is typically obtained in paper-and-pencil self-report measures. In this way, the HDI differs from other self-report measures of depression, such as the Beck Depression Inventory (BDI; Beck, Ward, Mendelson, Mock, & Erbaugh, 1961) and the Self-Report Depression Scale (SRDS; Zung, 1965) in that several questions (as opposed to just one) are asked in rating each item. For example, as previously discussed, in rating item 1 (depressed mood), feelings of sadness, crying, and pessimism are evaluated, and both the frequency and severity of the symptom are assessed. Answers to all these questions are then processed by an empirically derived scoring algorithm to obtain the final score for that item. In this way, the HDI obtains a more thorough evaluation of each item, and is more similar to how a clinician would probe, using branching logic as appropriate. For example, if the frequency of a symptom is reported to be "not at all," the interview then skips over the severity probe for that symptom.

Fourth, we wanted to increase both the reliability and the clinical utility of the scale. The former was attained by establishing a consistent set of questions for obtaining information and a consistent and empirically based scoring algorithm for determining each item's rating. This insures that the entire domain of each symptom is covered with all persons, and that the basis for determining scores does not vary from rater to rater. The clinical utility of the scale was increased by (a) the self-report format, which overcomes the problem of training interviewers, as well as the cost and effort of clinician time in administering and scoring the scale, and (b) identification of a subset of items to constitute a short form, which allows for use in clinical or research settings where time or other issues preclude the use of the full scale.

The computer-administered version offers several additional advantages, such as the elimination of data entry and scoring, immediate availability of results, and easier utilization of branching logic. In addition, patients are often more honest with the computer or prefer it when disclosing information of a sensitive nature, such as alcohol and drug use (Lucas et al., 1977; Skinner & Allen, 1983; Turner et al., 1998), suicidal ideation (Greist et al., 1973; Petrie & Abell, 1994), sexual behavior (Greist & Klein, 1980; Turner et al., 1998), and social anxiety (Katzelnick et al.,1995; Kobak et al., 1997).

Initial Development and Psychometric Data: Computer Version

The items for the preliminary form of the HDI were written to parallel the 17 item domains of the clinician HAMD. Originally, a total of 52 questions were developed to evaluate these 17 items; 10 of the 17 items utilize more than one question in determining the score for that item. These items were then pilot tested in a sample of 61 depressed outpatients via desktop computer (Kobak, Reynolds, Rosenfeld, & Greist, 1990). Items with a correlation of less than .50 with the corresponding item on the clinician version were revised or dropped, resulting in a final set of 37 questions that evaluated the 17 item domains specified by Hamilton.

Our initial investigation was designed to evaluate the viability of a self-report version of the HAMD. Of particular interest was the determination of equivalence between the computer form and clinician-administered HAMD. After our pilot study, we evaluated the 17-item computer version in a sample of 97 adults who were given both the computer-administered HDI and the clinician-administered HAMD in a counterbalanced order (Kobak et al., 1990). The sample consisted of patients with a Research Diagnostic Criteria (RDC; Spitzer, Endicott, & Robins, 1978) diagnosis of major depression ($n = 52$), minor depression ($n = 20$), and community controls ($n = 25$). Diagnoses were made using the Schedule for Affective Disorders and Schizophrenia (SADS; Endicott & Spitzer, 1978).

The desktop computer version begins by asking patients for their name and demographic data, and by giving some brief instructions on the computer interview. To answer each question, patients press a numbered key from 0 to 4 on the computer keyboard. The program has error checking built in so that numbers out of range cannot be entered. Patients can change an answer or return to a previous question with different keystrokes. After completing the interview, patients are instructed to return to the clinician and inform him or her that they are finished. Numeric and graphical summaries of present and previous interviews are available immediately.

The clinician-administered HAMD was administered using training procedures and administration and scoring guidelines developed by William M. Reynolds. These guidelines have been used in clinical research for the past 12 years, and included scoring items to the half point for greater reliability and accuracy.

The internal consistency reliability (coefficient alpha) was .91 for the computer version and the median item-to-total scale correlation was .62, suggesting a high degree of internal consistency reliability. The correlation between the computer and clinician HAMD was high [$r(95) = .96$, $p < .0001$], suggesting a high degree of criterion-related validity. The mean score difference between the computer and clinician HAMD was nonsignificant [.10 of a point, $t(96) = .41$, $p = ns$]. The computer version correlated highly with the Beck Depression Inventory (BDI; Beck et al., 1961; $r = .93$), providing evidence of convergent validity. The computer-administered version was successful in discriminating between patients with major and minor depression, as well as discriminating patients with either major or minor depression from non-psychiatric controls [$F(2, 94) = 214.62$, $p < .0001$]. The clinical sensitivity of the computer HAMD was also examined using cutoff scores to differentiate patients with major depression from non-psychiatric controls. Using a cutoff score of 17, the specificity (true negatives) of the computer HAMD was 100%, and the sensitivity was 94%. No order effects were found.

Given the positive results of this study, we created the Hamilton Depression Inventory (Reynolds & Kobak, 1995a) by revising our original set of items and expanding the items to evaluate additional symptoms of depression that are specified by current definitions of depression. We also developed this measure to be administered in a paper-and-pencil as well as computer format to provide scores on the expanded form that conforms to *DSM-IV* symptoms of major depression as well as a score based on the 17 items corresponding to those on the clinician HAMD. In addition, we developed a short form of the HDI for use in screening, as well as a melancholia subscale that provides additional clinical information. Toward these efforts we evaluated the psychometric properties of these scales and subscales. These research findings are summarized later in this chapter.

HDI Full Scale

The 17 items described by Hamilton covered many of the *DSM-IV* symptoms associated features of major depressive episode (American Psychiatric Association, 1994, pp. 320–323, 345–347). However, the original 17 items did not cover all the *DSM-IV* symptoms and features of major depressive episode and dysthymia, having no specific items for indecisiveness, worthlessness, detachment, helplessness, hopelessness, or social isolation, or the atypical symptoms of hypersomnia or increased appetite. In addition, the original 17 items did not provide information on *DSM-IV* subtypes, such as major depression with melancholia, which is useful information for treatment planning. Thus, the HDI was developed to include items evaluating these domains.

To evaluate these new domains, an additional 8 items were developed, resulting in a 25-item measure. Statistical analyses of these items resulted in dropping two of these new items: social isolation (an associated feature in *DSM-IV*) and weight gain. Statistical analyses of these items found low item-to-total scale correlation coefficients ($r < .20$), low factor loadings in an exploratory factor analysis, and a low rate of endorsement. Thus, the final version of the HDI consisted of 23 items that are evaluated with 38 questions. The number of questions used in determining each item's rating varies, as do the content and number of response options for each question. Answers to individual questions are processed by an empirically derived scoring algorithm to yield scores for each of the 23 items. The scoring algorithm uses weighted means of the questions to derive each item's final score. The final score for each item is consistent with the range for that particular item described by Hamilton, that is, either 0–4 or 0–2.

Table 13.1 contains a list of the *DSM–IV* symptoms of major depressive disorder and melancholic features and the corresponding HDI items evaluating these domains. This expanded version allows for a more comprehensive evaluation of depression consistent with modern diagnostic criteria while retaining the original 17 HAMD items. The HDI requires a fifth-grade reading level, and takes about 10 min to complete.

HDI–17

The items in the 17-item HDI scale are contained within the full-scale, 23-item version, and are thus obtained by calculating a subscore rather than a separate administration. We retained the 17-item version as a separate subscale with separate validation data in order to make more accurate comparisons to the 17-item clinician HAMD, and to provide HDI scale scores consistent with and parallel to the 17-item clinician HAMD.

HDI–Melancholia Subscale (HDI–Mel)

As previously described, the HDI–Mel subscale consists of nine items that are part of the full-scale HDI (Table 13.1). The melancholia scale evaluates the presence of melancholic features as defined in *DSM–IV* (American Psychiatric Association, 1994). Several investigators have examined subscales derived from the HAMD that are indicative of a melancholic subtype (Bech et al., 1986; Kovacs, Rush, Beck, & Hollon, 1981; Thase et al., 1983; Zimmerman, Coryell, Pfohl, & Stangl, 1986). With the advent of *DSM–IV* in 1994, these features and their significance were further defined. The clinical implications of melancholic features are described in *DSM–IV* and include the increased likelihood to respond to antidepressant medication, the decreased likelihood to have a premorbid personality disorder, lack of a clear precipitant of their current depressive episode, and a decreased likelihood of responding to placebo medication. Melancholic features are more often associated with older patients, more common in inpatients versus outpatients, and are frequently associated with several biological markers, such as dexamethasone nonsuppression, hyperadrenocorticism, reduced rapid eye movement latency, and abnormal tyramine challenge and dichotic listening tests (American Psychiatric Association, 1994, p. 384).

HDI Short Form

Although the full-scale HDI offers a comprehensive evaluation of depressive symptomatology, clinical and research settings are often limited by time and other constraints, making use of the full-scale HDI unfeasible. The HDI short form (HDI–SF) provides a valid and reliable depression screener for these situations. Several writers have performed factor analytic and logistic studies of the 17-item HAMD in order to identify a subset of items that provide a global measure of depression severity that is useful as a "unidimensional" index of overall severity (Bech et al., 1975, 1981; Bech, Allerup, Reisby, & Gram, 1984; Gibbons, Clark, & Kupfer, 1993; Maier, Philipp, & Gerken, 1985; Riskind et al., 1987).

The criteria for selection of items for the HDI short form included high item-to-total-scale correlation coefficients and the ability to distinguish between persons with major depression, other psychiatric disorders, and nonpsychiatric community controls. Based on a preliminary analysis, nine items were chosen: HDI items 1 (depressed mood), 3 (suicide), 7 (loss of interest/work impairment), 10 (psychic anxiety), 13 (fatigue/somatic-general), 19 (helplessness), 21 (worthlessness), 22 (hopelessness), and 23 (indecisiveness). An analysis of variance found these items had the highest F values in distinguishing between the three diagnostic categories (all F 200.00, $p < .0001$). A discriminant function analysis between persons with major depression and community controls found eight of these items demonstrated Wilks's lambda values of .200 to .466 with $F(1,256)$ values ranging from 1024.8 to 293.8. Although the suicide item was somewhat less discriminating between groups [Wilks's lambda = .594, $F(1,256) = 174.3$], it was included on the short form due to its clinical significance. All nine items showed high item-to-total correlation coefficients with the full-scale HDI, ranging from .63 to .87. The HDI–SF items also showed considerable overlap with the short-form items identified on the clinician HAMD by other researchers (Bech et al., 1975, 1981, 1984; Gibbons et al., 1993; Maier et al., 1985; Riskind et al., 1987).

PSYCHOMETRIC PROPERTIES OF THE HDI

Normative Data

Normative (standardization) data for the HDI were based on a nonreferred community sample of 510 adults (235 male and 271 female) between 18 and 89 years of age (18–24 = 16%; 25–39 = 38%; 40–64 = 34%; and over 65 = 12%). The sample was 84.6% White, 5.3% African American, 4.5% Asian, 4.5% Hispanic, and 1.1% of other ethnicity. Raw scores were linearly transformed into standard scores (i.e., T-scores) and percentile ranks. Normative data for the full-scale HDI, as well as for the 17-item and 9-item short form and melancholia subscale, are available in the user manual for the entire standardization sample as well as separately for males and females (Reynolds & Kobak, 1995a). The authors, however, note that the absolute value of the HDI score is more meaningful than a normative comparison, and that normative data should not be used as the sole basis for score interpretation. No significant differences were found in full scale HDI scores in comparisons involving age ($F = 1.87, p > .05$) or ethnicity ($F = 1.65, p > .10$). A small but statistically significant difference was found for gender, with females scoring 1.18 points higher ($t = 2.37, p < .05$). Similar results were found for the 17-item and 9-item short form.

A useful strategy for interpretive purposes is the examination of cutoff scores denoting clinically significant levels of depressive symptomatology. Cutoff scores for the full scale HDI, as well as the 17-item and 9-item short form and melancholia subscale, were empirically derived from samples of normal community adults and psychiatric outpatients with major depression. As cutoff scores were chosen that maximized sensitivity (i.e., minimized false negatives), normative data may be used in conjunction with cutoff scores in score interpretation. Use of cutoff scores is described further in the section on interpretive strategies.

Reliability and Validity Data

Data on the reliability and validity of the HDI were based on a sample of 921 adults (396 males and 521 females), including a nonreferred community sample (n = 510), psychiatric outpatients (n = 313), and college students (n = 98). Participants were between 18 and 89 years of age (mean = 38.28, SD = 15.38) and were distributed across a wide range of age groups (18–24 = 23%; 25–39 = 36%; 40–64 = 33%; and over 65 = 9%). The sample was 83.8% white, 4.6% African American, 6.9% Asian, 3.1% Hispanic, and 1.6% of other ethnicity. This sample is representative of a cross section of individuals likely to be evaluated with the HDI.

Reliability.   The reliability of the HDI was examined from several perspectives, including internal consistency (Cronbach's [1951] coefficient alpha), test–retest, item homogeneity in the form of item-to-total score correlation coefficients, and estimates of the standard error of measurement. Coefficient alpha (roughly the equivalent to the mean of all possible split-halves) was chosen as the most appropriate measure of internal consistency, as the item content of the HDI is not necessarily randomly distributed.

A summary of the reliability information for the entire development sample on all three forms of the HDI and the melancholia subscale is presented in Table 13.2. As shown in Table 13.2, internal consistency is high (over .90) for all forms. This is especially noteworthy for the nine-item short form, in that the lower number of items would typically tend to reduce the reliability coefficient. The internal consistency of the HDI was also examined separately for the psychiatric outpatient sample. Similar results were found, with a coefficient alpha of .89 for the full scale HDI. Overall, the internal consistency results support the item homogeneity of the HDI.

TABLE 13.2

HDI Reliability Estimates and Standard Error of Measurement (*SEM*) for the Total Development Sample (n = 921) and for Psychiatric Outpatients Only (n = 313)

Form	Sample	r	r_{ii}	Mdn r_{it}	Range r_{it}	SEM
HDI–23	Total sample	.931	.358	.57	.26–.84	2.81
	Psychiatric outpatients	.890	.250	.49	.21–.79	3.47
HDI–17	Total sample	.897	.328	.53	.23–.82	2.41
	Psychiatric outpatients	.850	.246	.40	.28–.73	2.90
HDI–SF	Total sample	.924	.924	.74	.59–.85	1.66
	Psychiatric outpatients	.880	.880	.48	.41–.79	2.07
HDI–Mel	Total sample	.818	.314	.51	.22–.79	1.66
	Psychiatric outpatients	.755	.234	.45	.03–.71	2.32

Note. Symbols are: r, coefficient alpha reliability; r_{ii}, mean interitem correlation; Mdn r_{it}, median item–total scale correlation. From Reynolds and Kobak (1995a). Reprinted with permission.

Further support for the item homogeneity of the HDI is provided by the high median item-to-total correlation coefficients and mean interitem correlation coefficients found on all forms (Table 13.2). An examination of individual items in the whole development sample found high correlation coefficients for 20 of the 23 items (i.e., between .43 and .84), moderate correlation coefficients for 2 items (insight and hypersomnia; .34 and .39, respectively), and a low correlation for 1 item (weight loss, .26). The low correlation for weight loss can be partially explained by the low rate of endorsement for this item, as well as its low mean score (0.18). The latter resulted in restricted variance for the item, thus attenuating the correlation. Rehm and O'Hara (1985) found similar results on the clinician HAMD.

An examination of individual items on the HDI short form found high item-to-total correlation coefficients for all the items (range = .59 to .85). This high degree of item homogeneity suggests the short form possesses psychometric characteristics similar to the 17- and 23-item versions. Overall, the results support the item homogeneity of the HDI, indicating it is a reliable measure of a relatively homogenous construct of depression. This supports the use of a total HDI score as a reliable indicator of depression severity.

In addition to internal consistency reliability, test–retest reliability was also examined in a subsample of 189 participants. This subsample included both community (n = 110) and psychiatric (n = 79) participants, and had demographic characteristics that were roughly similar to the development sample. The mean retest interval was 6.2 days (range 2 to 9 days, mode 7 days). All retesting was done prior to any treatment intervention. The test–retest reliability coefficient of .954 was found for both the full-scale and 17-item HDI, .930 for the HDI short form, and .926 for the melancholia subscale. The results indicate a high degree of rank-order stability on all forms of the HDI. Mean score changes were small (1.14, .83, .61, and .51 for full-scale, 17-item, 9-item, and melancholia HDI scales, respectively), but significant (t = 4.77, 4.69, 3.77, and 3.75, respectively; $p < .001$ for all comparisons). Although statistically significant due to the large sample size, these changes were not clinically significant (e.g., roughly equivalent to about a 10th of a standard deviation). Given the potential for random fluctuation when evaluating a state (vs. a trait) construct such as depression, the results are particularly strong. These findings supports the use of the HDI as an outcome measure, as changes in scores associated with nonintervention factors (i.e., error variance) were minimal.

Overall, the results support the reliability of the HDI. As reliability (i.e., the stability or consistency of a test measure) is a precondition for validity (i.e., how well a test actually measures what it purports to measure), the results provide a strong foundation for the examination of the validity of the HDI.

Validity. According to the *Standards for Educational and Psychological Testing* (American Educational Research Association, 1985), validity refers to "the appropriateness, meaningfulness, and usefulness of the specific inferences made from test scores," and "test validation is the process of accumulating evidence to support such inferences" (p. 9). The validity of the HDI was examined from a number of perspectives, including (a) content validity, (b) criterion (i.e., concurrent) validity, (c) construct validity, in the form of convergent and discriminant validity, and (d) clinical validity in the form of HDI scores differentiating between contrasted groups, and in the sensitivity and specificity of HDI cutoff scores. Given the many research investigations documenting the validity of the clinician HAMD, demonstrating the equivalence of the HDI to the clinician version provides additional validation support.

Content validity refers to the extent to which a test adequately represents or samples the domain it purports to measure. The current standard for the classification of depression is the *Diagnostic and Statistical Manual for Mental Disorders* (*DSM–IV*; American Psychiatric Association, 1994). The *DSM–IV* attempts to define and describe the symptoms of depression from an empirical basis while remaining neutral regarding etiology and atheoretical in nature (American Psychiatric Association, 1994, p. xviii). As shown in Table 13.1, the HDI evaluates the main symptoms of depression as defined by *DSM–IV*, as well as many of the associated features described in the manual.

Content validity may also be inferred by item-to-total scale correlation coefficients. Although it does not measure whether the entire domain of the construct of depression is evaluated, it does indicate how well each of the items covaries with sum of the remaining items. Items that are a significant part of the construct they are measuring should co-vary with the overall score for that construct. Given the high internal consistency of the HDI, each of the items thus contributes in a meaningful way to the total score. From this perspective, item-to-total scale correlation coefficients provide additional statistical support of content validity.

As described in the *Standards for Educational and Psychological Testing* (American Educational Research Association, 1985), types of validity are not mutually exclusive, but tend to overlap conceptually. Thus, further evidence of content validity is also provided in the sections that follow on contrasted groups validity and the ability of HDI items to differentiate between persons with major depression, other psychiatric disorders, and nonreferred community adults.

Criterion-related validity refers to how well a scale's score predicts performance on an outside measure of the same construct. *Concurrent validity*, a type of criterion validity, refers to how well the scale predicts scores on a related measure given at the same time (i.e., concurrently). For test validation purposes, there is typically a "gold standard" measure against which the new scale is compared, one that is widely used and accepted, and whose psychometric properties have been well established. Given that the clinician HAMD is one of the standards for the evaluation of depressive symptomatology and that our purpose was to demonstrate the equivalence between the self-report HDI and the clinician HAMD, the clinician HAMD was chosen as the criterion for the criterion-related validity studies that follow.

To examine the criterion-related concurrent validity of the HDI, a subsample of 403 adults (male = 174, female = 229) were given both the HDI and the clinician-administered HAMD in a counterbalanced order in a single session. Participants ranged in age from 18 to 89 years (mean = 38.43, *SD* = 13.04), and were from diverse ethnic backgrounds (Caucasian = 86.4%; African American = 7.1%; Asian = 2.3%; Hispanic = 2.8%; other ethnicity = 1.4%). Participants had a *DSM–III–R* diagnosis of major depression (*n* = 135), other psychiatric disorder (*n* = 151), or were community controls with no current psychopathology (*n* = 117). Diagnoses were confirmed using the Structured Clinical Interview for the *DSM–III–R* (SCID) (Spitzer, Williams, Gibbon, & First, 1988), modified to assess for current psychopathology only, except for those disorders that carry a lifetime diagnosis (e.g., bipolar disorder). Both the SCID and clinician HAMD interviews were conducted by one of nine research coordinators who received extensive training on the administration and scoring of the interviews, or by the first author, who conducted the majority (58%) of the interviews. Interviewers were blind to participants' HDI scores. Participants were also given a number of other self-report measures to examine convergent validity and discriminant validity, which are discussed in a later section.

The correlation coefficients between the 17-item clinician HAMD and all versions of the HDI were very high, (.941, .945, .910, and .912 for the full scale, 17-item, 9-item short form, and HDI–Mel, respectively, all $p < .001$), providing strong evidence for the criterion-related validity of the HDI. Of particular interest is the high validity coefficient for the 9-item short form, providing support for its utility for screening and research purposes. Overall, the results indicate that the HDI and HAMD share a high degree of score variance and provide supportive evidence for criterion-related validity of the HDI.

In addition to the correlation between scores on the HDI and HAMD, the mean score difference between the two instruments was examined. As the HDI was developed to provide scores that parallel the clinician HAMD, this examination is of particular importance. The mean score obtained on the entire sample on the 17-item HAMD ($M = 12.83$, $SD = 8.60$) was only .33 of a point different from the mean score obtained with the 17-item HDI ($M = 13.16$, $SD = 8.75$), $t(402) = 2.28, p < .05$. Again, although the comparison was statistically significant due to the large sample size associated with 402 degrees of freedom, the magnitude of the effect was small, and the difference was clinically insignificant. The variances associated with each of the measures also were similar.

The *construct validity* of the HDI was examined from the perspective of convergent and discriminant validity, and the diagnostic efficacy of HDI cutoff scores. *Convergent validity* was established by examining the relationship between the HDI and scores on other measures of the same construct (i.e., depression), as well as related constructs (i.e., suicidal ideation, hopelessness, self-esteem, anxiety). One would expect high correlation coefficients with scales measuring the same construct, and moderate correlation coefficients with similar constructs. As previously noted, the criterion validity data presented previously comparing the HDI to the HAMD (the current "gold standard") also provide evidence for construct validity. As further evidence of construct validity, we examined the relationship between HDI scores and scores on the Beck Depression Inventory (BDI; Beck et al., 1961). We also examined the relationship between scores on the HDI and scores on scales measuring related constructs. These included the Beck Hopelessness Scale (BHS.; Beck, Weissman, Lester, & Trexler, 1974), Adult Suicidal Ideation Questionnaire (ASIQ; Reynolds, 1991), Beck Anxiety Inventory (BAI; Beck, Epstein, Brown, & Steer, 1988), and Rosenberg Self-Esteem Scale (RSES; Rosenberg, 1965).

The correlation coefficients between the HDI and convergent validity measures are presented in Table 13.3. The relationship between the BDI and all forms of the HDI were high, ranging from .91 to .93 ($p < .0001$); the correlation coefficient between the BDI and the HDI-Mel was .89 ($p < .0001$). The results presented in Table 13.3 support the convergent validity of the HDI as a measure of depression severity. Also shown in Table 13.3 are the correlation coefficients between the HDI and measures of constructs that are associated with depression. As would be expected, moderately high correlation coefficients were found between the HDI and these measures, providing further support for the construct validity of the HDI.

In order to evaluate whether the high correlation coefficients between these measures are specific to depression as opposed to a general level of emotional distress, a multiple regression analysis was performed with the HDI as the dependent variable. The standardized beta coefficients indicate the amount of variance associated with each of the independent variables. Results found the largest standardized beta coefficient was with the BDI (.582), confirming that the majority of the variance was attrib-

TABLE 13.3
Correlation Coefficients Between HDI and Related Measures
of Psychological Distress for the Total Sample

Measure	n	HDI	HDI-17	HDI-SF	HDI-Mel
Beck Depression Inventory (BDI)	764	.93***	.91***	.92***	.89***
Beck Hopelessness Scale (BHS)	482	.78***	.72***	.81***	.73***
Adult Suicidal Ideation Questionnaire (ASIQ)	895	.66***	.63***	.69***	.61***
Beck Anxiety Inventory (BAI)	483	.77***	.77***	.72***	.69***
Rosenberg Self-Esteem Scale (RSES)	625	−.68***	−.63***	−.73***	−.65***
Marlowe-Crowne Social Desirability Scale–Short Form (MCSDS-SF)	486	−.37***	−.35***	−.37***	−.39***

Note. From Reynolds and Kobak (1995a). Reprinted with permission.
***$p < .001$.

utable to the relationship between the HDI and BDI, a measure of depression. Only a small amount of variance was attributable to the other measures, with beta coefficients ranging from .01 (ASIQ) to .26 (BAI). Similar results were found when the clinician HAMD was substituted in the regression equation for the BDI, with an even larger beta of .68 ($p < .0001$) found for amount of variance attributed to the HAMD.

Construct validity was also determined by examining the *clinical efficacy* of HDI cutoff scores. These empirically derived cutoff scores are used as a rough threshold to determine a "clinically relevant" level of depressive symptomatology (i.e., symptoms that result in some degree of impairment in the person's life). The degree to which cutoff scores accurately place individuals into correct diagnostic categories is another measure of the clinical validity of the HDI.

Using a cutoff score of 19, the full-scale (23-item) HDI demonstrated a *sensitivity* of 99.3%; that is, the HDI correctly identified 99.3% of persons who had been diagnosed with major depression on the SCID. The same cutoff score demonstrated a *specificity* of 95.9%; that is, the HDI correctly identified 95.9% of the persons who did not have any diagnosis on the SCID. The *positive predictive value* (PPV) (i.e., the percentage of persons identified by a test as having a specific characteristic that actually have that characteristic) was also examined. This is important, as it provides an indication of the clinical utility of the test (i.e., a test that has a high rate of false positives may still be highly sensitive, but of little practical value). The PPV of the full-scale HDI using a cutoff of 19 was 86.9% which is high, and addresses the problem of poor PPV that has been reported in the literature with past depression screeners (Campbell, 1987). The *negative predictive value* (NPV) of a cutoff score of 19 was 99.8%; that is, using this cutoff score, almost no subjects who were classified as not depressed by the HDI were actually depressed. The kappa and phi coefficients associated with a cutoff score of 19 were also high (.905 and .908, respectively), suggesting the clinical utility of this cutoff score.

Similar analyses were performed on the 17-item HDI and the 9-item HDI short form using cutoff scores of 15 and 10, respectively. Results are presented in Table 13.4. High levels of sensitivity and specificity were found across HDI forms, with all values greater than .95. High values were also found for PPV, chi-square, phi, and kappa coefficients. Overall, the results demonstrate a high degree of association between HDI cutoff scores and the diagnosis of major depression, supporting the clinical efficacy of the HDI. Although the HDI is not intended as a diagnostic instrument, the clinical utility of HDI cutoff scores have shown to be valuable in identifying persons with a significant (i.e., clinical) level of depressive symptomatology.

TABLE 13.4
Clinical Utility of HDI Cutoff Scores to Differentiate Among Psychiatric
Outpatients With Major Depression and Normal Community Controls

HDI Version	Maximum Score	Cutoff Score	Sensitivity	Specificity	PPP	χ^2	φ	κ
HDI Full Scale	73	19	99.3	95.9	86.9	536.14***	.908***	.905
HDI-17	52	15	95.7	96.7	88.7	525.65***	.899***	.898
HDI-SF	33	10	97.1	97.1	90.1	546.58***	.917***	.916

Note. PPP, positive predictive power: the proportion of persons who are identified by the HDI as clinical depressed (i.e., who score at or above the cutoff score) who actually have a diagnosis of major depression. From Reynolds and Kobak (1995a). Reprinted with permission.
***p < .001.

The *clinical validity* of the HDI was examined from the perspective of contrasted groups validity (Wiggins, 1973), also known as *criterion group validity* (Edwards, 1970). This refers to the ability of a test to differentiate between groups of people known to have different levels of the construct under examination. The contrasted groups validity for all three forms of the HDI and the HDI–Mel was examined by comparing mean score differences between persons with major depression, persons with other psychiatric disorders, and community controls. This comparison is a rigorous test of contrasted groups validity in that persons with other psychiatric disorders often have some degree of comorbid depressive symptomatology. The ability of the HDI to differentiate between these groups is strong evidence for the validity and clinical utility of the scale. As shown in Table 13.5, highly significant differences were found between the three diagnostic groups on all forms of the HDI. Persons with major depression had nearly double the HDI scores of persons with other psychiatric diagnoses, and the scores were nearly four standard deviations above the community

TABLE 13.5
Contrasted Groups Validity of the HDI, HDI-17, HDI-SF, and HDI-Mel

HDI Form	Community (n = 510) (1)	Other Psychiatric Diagnoses (n = 173) (2)	Major Depression (n = 140) (3)	F	Group Comparison
HDI					
Mean	7.29	16.66	30.93		
SD	5.64	8.28	7.13	747.64***	3 > 2 > 1
HDI-17					
Mean	5.71	12.29	22.13		
SD	4.22	6.09	5.10	664.07***	3 > 2 > 1
HDI-SF					
Mean	3.14	8.30	16.70		
SD	3.00	4.54	3.88	838.62***	3 > 2 > 1
HDI-Mel					
Mean	3.34	7.03	13.10		
SD	2.82	3.94	3.12	548.64***	3 > 2 > 1

Note. Scheffe post hoc comparisons computed with p < .01. From Reynolds and Kobak (1995a). Reprinted with permission.
***p > .001.

controls. The results provide strong support for the contrasted groups validity and clinical utility of the HDI as a measure of the severity of depressive symptomatology.

BASIC INTERPRETIVE STRATEGY

In clinical applications, assessment of depressive symptomatology is typically from the perspective of current definitions of depression and diagnostic criteria. As such, the full-scale HDI is recommended as the standard format. In situations (typically research settings) where there is a need for scores consistent with the clinician HAMD, the 17-item scores may be extracted from the full-scale HDI format. In situations where time is limited, or when a brief screener is desired, the HDI short form may be used. In general, the full-scale HDI provides the most complete evaluation of depressive symptomatology by virtue of assessing the a widest range of symptoms.

Interpretation of the HDI consists of examination of the following seven elements: validity check, HDI raw score and cutoff score, HDI Melancholia Checklist, comparisons with normative data, HDI critical items, major depression checklist, and examination of individual items.

Validity Check

Before making any clinical decisions or recommendations based on HDI results, the HDI protocol should be checked for signs of invalid responding. Reasons for invalid responding include (a) attempts to minimize or exaggerate symptoms, or (b) a lack of compliance with the evaluation process resulting in cursory responding. The latter may be examined on the computer-administered version by examining the time it took to administer the HDI. A very short response time may indicate that the subject answered the questions without reading the items. Some individuals may have trouble reading or understanding the questions, but may be reticent to inform the examiner. In some cases, an invalid response set may be due to extreme distress or psychological disorganization.

At least 19 of the 23 HDI items should be completed to be considered a valid administration (this is not applicable for the computer-administered HDI, as items cannot be skipped). The clinician should also check the HDI answer sheet for unusual patterns of responding, such as endorsing the same response to all items (with the exception of 0), or a consistent pattern of responses, such as alternating responses (e.g., 1, 2, 1, 2, 1, 2). Such response patterns are rare in valid protocols and indicate the likelihood of an invalid response set.

Comparing items that evaluate opposite symptoms is another check for an invalid protocol. For example, items 4–6 (insomnia) can be compared with item 18 (hypersomnia), and item 8 (psychomotor retardation) can be compared with item 9 (psychomotor agitation). In most cases, high scores on these pairs of opposites symptoms are unlikely and may suggest an invalid response to the HDI.

Another indication of invalid responding on the paper-and-pencil version is the completion of items that should have been skipped. Unlike the computer version, where the computer does the branching and only administers items that are appropriate, the paper-and-pencil version instructs respondents to skip follow-up questions when the response to the initial question was negative (e.g., if the response to item 1a, frequency of depressed mood, is "not at all," the person is instructed to skip over the follow-up question regarding severity). A consistent pattern of failure to do this may indicate an invalid response set.

Finally, blank items, particularly the suicide item, should be checked as an indication of potential difficulty. The clinician should ask the client to complete the missing item, and follow up by exploring the reasons for skipping the item. This process is facilitated by the HDI critical items form, discussed later.

Raw Score and Cutoff Scores

The first step in interpreting valid HDI scores should involve comparing the raw score to the HDI cutoff score. Cutoff scores are used to indicate the presence of a clinically significant level of depressive symptomatology. Cutoff scores were derived from a number of psychometric perspectives, including frequency distributions of the community sample, sensitivity, specificity, predictive power, and hit rate. Statistical analyses (i.e., chi-square, phi coefficient, and kappa) were computed to identify cutoff scores that differentiate between depressed outpatients and nondepressed community controls. Because one uses of the HDI is to screen for clinical levels of depression, the HDI cutoff scores were chosen to maximize sensitivity (i.e., minimize false negatives, while retaining acceptable specificity), and are thus conservative in this regard.

For the full-scale HDI, the range of possible scores is 0 to 73. In actual clinical use, scores above 50 are rare. As many of the HDI items involve several questions that are then averaged according to a weighted scoring algorithm, total raw scores may not be an integer. We chose to retain these raw scores and round them to the nearest half point in order retain accuracy.

The average HDI scores in the community sample was 7, and the mean score for outpatients with a diagnosis of major depression was 31. A cutoff score of 19 is suggested to denote a clinical level of depressive symptomatology on the full-scale HDI. In the community sample, this corresponds to the 96th percentile, a T-score of 71, and is about two standard deviations above the mean. Persons scoring at or above the cutoff should be referred for further evaluation and possible treatment. Clinicians desiring higher levels of sensitivity may adjust the cutoff scores according to the normative data provided in the test manual (Reynolds & Kobak, 1995a).

For the HDI–17, scores may range from 0 to 52, with scores above 35 being relatively rare. The recommended cutoff score on the HDI–17 is 15. This corresponds to the 97th percentile of the community sample and a T-score of 71. The mean score for psychiatric outpatients with major depression was 22, with only 4.3% scoring below the cutoff score of 15. The mean score in the community sample on the HDI–17 was approximately 6. Again, the cutoff score was intended to maximize sensitivity for screening purposes, and thus is slightly less than the cutoff of 17 used in some, but not all, antidepressant outcome studies (Dunlop, Dornseif, Wernicke, & Potvin, 1990; Paykel, 1979).

The HDI–SF score range is 0 to 33. As a brief screener in clinical and research settings, a cutoff score of 10 is recommended. This corresponds to the 97th percentile of the community sample and a T-score of 72. Although the HDI–SF is not intended to replace the full-scale HDI, it does provide a valid and reliable screening tool for clinical and research applications.

After examination of cutoff scores, raw scores may also be interpreted for levels of severity. Table 13.6 provides a general guide for the interpretation of raw scores.

TABLE 13.6
Descriptions of Clinical Severity Levels of Depressive
Symptomatology Associated With HDI Scores

Form	Range of Scores	Clinical Description
HDI	0–13.5	Not depressed
	14.0–18.5	Subclinical
	19.0–25.5	Mild
	26.0–32.5	Moderate
	33.0–39.5	Moderate to severe
	40.0	Severe
HDI–17	0–9.5	Not depressed
	10.0–14.5	Subclinical
	15.0–19.5	Mild
	20.0–24.5	Moderate
	25.0–29.5	Moderate to severe
	30.0	Severe
HDI–SF	0–6.0	Not depressed
	6.5–8.5	Subclinical
	9.0–12.5	Mild
	13.0–16.5	Moderate
	17.0–20.5	Moderate to severe
	21.0	Severe

Note. Descriptions associated with HDI score ranges are general guidelines to suggest levels of clinical severity. These descriptions should not be considered a formal classification of HDI scores or diagnostic groupings. From Reynolds and Kobak (1995a). Reprinted with permission.

Scores may be classified as *not depressed, subclinical, mild, moderate, moderate to severe,* and *severe*. These score ranges are based on clinical interpretation and are provided as general interpretive guidelines, but are not intended to provide formal classifications or diagnostic groupings.

Melancholic Features

Examination of the HDI–Mel score provides an indication as to the extent to which the client reports features of melancholia as outlined in *DSM–IV*. A cutoff score of 16 is suggested as an indication of a clinical level of melancholic symptoms. Although the HDI–Mel scale was not intended to provide a diagnosis of the melancholic subtype, it does provide a measure of the extent to which the person's current depression is associated with melancholic features.

Normative Data

A secondary interpretive perspective may be gained by comparison of raw scores with normative data. This provides information as to the significance of the raw score, particularly in clients who have clinical levels of depression. Normative data allows comparisons using percentile ranks and standard scores. This evaluation should be considered secondary to the comparison of raw scores to cutoff scores, as depression assessment is more similar to a criterion-referenced orientation than to a norm-referenced orientation.

Critical Items

Seven HDI items have been identified as particularly useful in interpreting the HDI, as they demonstrate particular utility in differentiating persons with major depression from other diagnostic groups, or are particularly important due to the serious nature of the item. These items consist of items 1 (depressed mood), 3 (suicide), 7 (loss of interest), 13 (fatigue, general somatic), 21 (worthlessness), 22 (hopelessness), and 23 (indecisiveness). A score of 2 or greater on these items should be considered significant. Persons endorsing three or more critical items but scoring below the cutoff should nonetheless receive further evaluation. Conversely, persons who score above the cutoff but low on most of the critical items should be evaluated as possible false positives. Occasionally, persons without clinical depression but with other psychiatric disorders or certain medical conditions with a lot of somatic complains exceed the cutoff score. Examination of the critical items, particularly item 1 (depressed mood), can help identify these individuals. In general, persons endorsing three or more critical items should receive further evaluation regardless of their HDI raw score. A score of 1 or greater on item 3 (suicide) should *always* be followed up on, given the serious nature of suicidal ideation and behavior.

HDI Major Depression Checklist

The HDI contains items that evaluate the nine symptoms that constitute the A criteria of a major depressive episode as currently defined by *DSM–IV* diagnostic criteria. These symptoms include depressed mood, loss of interest/pleasure, weight loss, insomnia/hypersomnia, psychomotor agitation/retardation, fatigue, worthlessness/guilt, indecisiveness, and suicidal ideation/behavior. *DSM–IV* requires a minimum of five of the nine symptoms to be present for a diagnosis of major depressive episode, one of which must be depressed mood or loss of interest/pleasure. A score of 2 or greater on an item is considered above the threshold. The checklist is provided for descriptive purposes, and is not intended to constitute a formal diagnosis of depression, as the latter involves other inclusion and exclusion criteria not evaluated by the HDI (or any symptom rating scale). However, cases where either item 1 or item 7 is endorsed and four or more other symptoms are endorsed clearly warrant further evaluation of the remaining diagnostic criteria to confirm the presence of a diagnosis of major depressive episode or another affective disorder.

Examination of Individual Items

Examination of individual items provides useful information for the clinician. For example, clients who endorse several of the endogenous symptoms of depression may be particularly appropriate referrals for antidepressant treatment, whereas clients who more heavily endorse the more cognitive items such as hopelessness, helplessness, and low self-esteem may be appropriate candidates for cognitive interventions. Item 3 (suicide) should *always* be examined. This item on the clinician HAMD has been shown to correlate highly with other measures of suicidal ideation and behavior (Bulik, Carpenter, Kupfer, & Frank, 1990; Reynolds, 1991; Reynolds, Kobak, & Greist, 1993; Reynolds, Kobak, Greist, Jefferson, & Tollefson, 1993).

USE OF THE HDI FOR SCREENING DEPRESSION IN PRIMARY CARE

Screening for depression in primary care patients has been cited as an important part of an effective overall health care plan (Eisenberg, 1992). Depression is the most common psychiatric symptom in primary care patients (American Psychiatric Association, 1995), with prevalence rates of major depression in primary care between 6% and 8% (Depression Guideline Panel, 1993c). Although depression is usually recognized in patients with clear-cut and prominent symptoms (Eisenberg, 1992), depression is overlooked in the majority of primary care patients who have this disorder (Kessler, Cleary, & Burke, 1985; Schulberg & Burns, 1988; Spitzer, 1994). Given the high prevalence rates, low detection rates, and the availability of effective treatments and treatment guidelines, screening for depression in primary care patients seems warranted. This may take the form of routine screening (e.g., as part of an annual physical exam), or may be initiated when the physician has reason to suspect depression may be present.

Three types of scales are typically used in an initial assessment process: *screeners*, *diagnostic instruments*, and *symptoms rating scales*. A *screener* identifies persons who are likely to have a disorder and thus warrant further evaluation. Diagnostic instruments, such as the SCID, SADS, and PRIME–MD (Spitzer et al., 1994), provide such an evaluation in order to confirm the diagnosis. *Symptom rating scales* provide an indication as to the severity of symptoms associated with the disorder, as well as a general accounting of which symptoms are present. They also are useful as change measures to monitor treatment outcome.

The Agency for Health Care Policy and Research (AHCPR) recently developed a set of clinical practice guidelines for the identification and treatment of depression in primary care patients (Depression Guideline Panel, 1993a, 1993b, 1993c). The AHCPR guidelines suggest a stepwise process to facilitate the identification and treatment of depression in primary care, consisting of:

1. Vigilance to the symptoms of depression.
2. Screening of those individuals suspected of having the disorder.
3. A diagnostic interview to confirm the presence of the disorder in those screening positive.
4. A complete medical history and physical examination to rule out symptoms caused by general medical illnesses or other conditions.
5. Development of a treatment plan.

For the screening phase, self-report questionnaires were cited as a "low cost, but valuable, case-finding tool to help clinicians better detect currently depressed patients" (Depression Guideline Panel, 1993a, p. 75). The HDI has psychometric properties that enable it to serve the dual functions of both a screener and a symptom rating scale. As a screener, it identifies individuals with a clinically significant level of depressive symptomatology, and thus likely to have a diagnosis of depression. Such individuals warrant more in-depth evaluation to confirm the diagnosis. As a symptom rating scale, it provides an in-depth evaluation of both the type and severity of symptoms currently present. As suggested by the AHCPR guidelines, the HDI (and other scales evaluating symptom severity) should be used in conjunction with a careful diagnostic interview, as the latter confirms the presence of a disorder, whereas the former indicates the severity of the disorder. Several diagnostic interviews have been recently developed specifically for use by primary care physicians, including PRIME–MD (Spitzer et al., 1994) and the Symptom Driven Diagnostic System for Primary Care (SDDS–PC; Broadhead et al., 1995). Computer-administered versions of both these diagnostic interviews are available that can be administered directly to patients (Kobak et al., 1997a, 1997b; Weissman et al., 1998).

Depressed primary care patients often present with multiple somatic symptoms suggestive of a medical condition while volunteering few psychological complaints (Kessler et al., 1985; Schulberg & Burns, 1988). A set of symptoms have been identified that are common in depressed primary care patients (American Psychiatric Association, 1994, p. 323; Depression Guideline Panel, 1993c, p. 2.) These include: (a) pain (e.g., abdominal, headache, or other body aches); (b) low energy or excessive fatigue; (c) sexual difficulties, such as problems with desire or functioning (e.g., anorgasmia in women or erectile dysfunction in men); and (d) anxiety, phobias, or excessive worry over physical health. Patients presenting with these symptoms where an organic cause cannot be found warrant screening for depression with the HDI. In addition, several primary risk factors for depression have been identified. These include: (a) prior episodes of depression; (b) family history of depressive disorder; (c) prior suicide attempts; (d) female gender; (e) age of onset under 40 years; (f) postpartum period; (g) medical comorbidity; (h) lack of social support; (i) stressful life events; and (j) current alcohol or substance abuse (Depression Guideline Panel, 1993a, p. 73). Patients with these risk factors who present with one or more of the symptoms commonly found in depressed primary care patients are at increased risk of having depression, and warrant screening with the HDI.

Once a patient has been screened with the HDI, a decision needs to be made as to whether further evaluation with a diagnostic interview is warranted. As previously mentioned, any of the following response profiles indicate follow-up evaluation with a diagnostic interview is indicated:

1. Scoring above or near the cutoff score.
2. A score of 2 or greater on three or more critical items, regardless of total score.
3. Cases where either item 1 (depressed mood) or item 7 (loss of interest) is endorsed, and four or more other *DSM–IV* symptoms are endorsed (three or more other symptoms if both items 1 and 7 are endorsed).
4. Persons scoring 1 or greater on item 3 (suicide).

Patients who screen positive on the HDI and who meet criteria for a mood disorder on a follow-up diagnostic interview need to be evaluated to determine if the mood disorder is primary or secondary to another medical condition or other cause. The mood disorder would be secondary if it is a direct physiological consequence of a specific general medical condition (American Psychiatric Association, 1994). Approximately 10% to 15% of major depressive conditions are caused by a general medical illness (typically autoimmune, neurologic, metabolic, infectious, oncologic, and endocrine disorders) or other conditions (e.g., substance abuse, concurrent medication, other nonmood psychiatric disorders) (Depression Guideline Panel, 1993c). AHCPR guidelines suggest that a complete medical history (review of systems) and physical examination be performed to identify and treat the medical illness or condition before initiating treatment. If the depression persists after treatment of the associated condition, then treatment is indicated. Often patients become depressed as a psychological reaction to having a general medical condition. For example, a patient with cancer may become clinically depressed as a reaction to the diagnosis, pain, or incapacity. In these cases, the depression should be considered an independent disorder and treatment should proceed (Depression Guideline Panel, 1993c). Clinically significant depressive symptomatology exists in approximately 12% to 16% of patients with a nonpsychiatric medical condition (Depression Guideline Panel, 1993a).

Often patients who exceed the cutoff score on the HDI and are found to have a mood disorder also have a comorbid nonmood psychiatric disorder. Alcohol abuse is particularly common in primary care, with prevalence rates ranging from 3% to 20% (Johnson et al., 1995). Most studies have found that alcoholism is rarely a result of primary depression, occurring in less than 5% of depressed patients (Depression Guideline Panel, 1993a). On the other hand, a series of studies have found that between 10% and 30% of patients with alcoholism develop depression (Depression Guideline Panel, 1993a; Petty, 1992). The ECA study found that persons with alcoholism were nearly twice as likely to meet criteria for major depressive disorder than those without alcoholism (Helzer & Pryzbeck, 1988). The AHCPR guideline recommended discontinuing the use of alcohol first, then reevaluating the depression after 4 to 8 weeks. If the depression is still present, then proceed with treatment. However, in some cases, concurrent treatment may be indicated, particularly with patients who have melancholic features or suicidal ideation. Patients with comorbid alcohol abuse who score above the cutoff on the HDI melancholic subscale or who endorse suicidal ideation (HDI item 3) warrant consideration for concurrent treatment.

Other nonmood psychiatric disorders that frequently co-occur with depression in primary care patients are anxiety disorders (panic, generalized anxiety disorder [GAD], and obsessive compulsive-disorder [OCD]) and eating disorders. Depressive symptoms often accompany anxiety disorders, and the reverse is also true as well. In the case of panic disorder, this comorbidity results in greater impairment than does either disorder alone (Coryell et al., 1998), and the suicide rate of panic patients with depression disorder is twice that of patients with panic alone (Johnson, Weissman, & Klerman, 1990). Thus, screening patients for depression is strongly suggested by the AHCPR for patients complaining of symptoms of anxiety (Depression Guideline Panel, 1993a). If the comorbid disorder is OCD or an eating disorder, AHCPR guidelines suggest treating those disorders first; if it is GAD, treat the depression first. In the case of comorbid panic, treatment focus is determined by which is more severe, longest standing by history, or runs in the patient's family (Depression Guideline Panel, 1993a, p. 44). However, in all cases, the severity of the comorbid depression may require concurrent treatment of the affective symptoms, particularly if vegetative and motivational symptoms are present. Examination of the HDI–Mel score as well as the HDI critical items provides information that will help in this determination.

Subthreshold depression is also common in primary care patients (Olfson et al., 1996), and is nonetheless still debilitating. Wells and colleagues (1989) found that primary care and other specialty patients with depressive symptomatology but who were below diagnostic threshold for major depression had poorer social and role functioning, more days spent in bed, and lower ratings of well-being than patients with several other chronic medical conditions. Similarly, Spitzer et al. (1995) found that primary care patients with subsyndromal depression had significantly greater impairment in social, role, and physical functioning than patients with no mental disorder. Other studies have found subthreshold depression to be associated with more work days lost (Broadhead et al., 1990; Johnson et al., 1992; Wells et al., 1989), increased financial and household strain and social irritability (Judd, Paulus, Wells, & Rapaport, 1996), and more lifetime suicide attempts (Howarth, Johnson, Klerman, & Weissman, 1992). Even when controlling for demographics and other psychiatric comorbidity, subthreshold depression in primary care patients was associated with high rates of disability, and resulted in a 7.7 times increased risk for marital distress and 2.5 times increased risk for work loss (Olfson et al., 1996).

Thus, when using the HDI for screening depression in primary care patients, even cases falling at or near the cutoff scores should be examined. Although they may be subthreshold for a diagnosis of major depression, primary care patients with lower HDI scores are likely to meet criteria for dysthymia, depression in partial remission, or depression not otherwise specified. These subthreshold disorders are associated with significant impairment, and warrant treatment intervention (Depression Guideline Panel, 1993a). Cutoff scores for differentiating clinical from subclinical levels of depressive symptomatology may also be adjusted by one point in primary care patients, thus increasing the sensitivity of the scale for detecting subthreshold disorders in this population (see Table 13.6). Particular attention should be paid to elevated scores on HDI items 4 through 6 (initial, middle, and late insomnia) and 13 (fatigue), as these are the most common symptoms in subsyndromal depression (Judd et al., 1996). It should be noted that the empirical evidence for the efficacy of antidepressant intervention in patients with subthreshold depression is not as extensive as with major depression, although substantial evidence does support its efficacy in this subgroup (see Howland, 1991, for a review)

A syndrome of mixed subthreshold anxiety and depression (i.e., symptoms of both disorders but failure to meet full criteria of either a mood or an anxiety disorder) has been identified that commonly presents in primary care setting (American Psychiatric Association, 1994, p. 723). This syndrome has been recognized by the International Classification and Diagnosis System, Version 10 (ICD–10), and is currently a proposed category for consideration in *DSM–IV*. Barrett, Barrett, Oxman, and Gerber (1988) found rates of 4.1% for this disorder in rural primary care patients. Although treatment guidelines are still under consideration for this subtype, it is nonetheless associated with significant distress and/or impairment (Liebowitz et al., 1990). Thus, patients screening at or near the cutoff score who have prominent symptoms of anxiety (e.g., HDI items 9 [psychomotor agitation], 10 [psychological anxiety], and 11 [somatic anxiety]) may warrant treatment intervention, even if they fail to meet formal criteria for a mood disorder.

Item 3 (suicide) should *always* be examined, and persons with a score of 1 or greater should always receive follow-up evaluation. Not all persons who feel suicidal are depressed, and thus this item may be elevated even in those without a high level of depressive symptomatology. Suicidal ideation has been found to be prominent in patients with other psychiatric disorders, such as panic disorder (Weissman, Klerman, Markowitz, & Ouellette, 1989), social phobia (Cox, Direnfeld, Swinson, & Norton, 1994), and obsessive-compulsive disorder (Reynolds, Kobak, & Greist, 1992b), often when there is no comorbid diagnosis of depression. An examination of item 22 (hopelessness) should also be examined in conjunction with item 3, as the relationship between hopelessness and suicide has been well established and is often a better predictor of suicidal intent than depression (Beck, Kovacs, & Weissman, 1975; Beck, Brown, Berchick, Stewart, & Steer, 1990).

The HDI can help in determining the appropriate level of care. A score of 3 on item 3 (suicide) indicates the person is thinking about suicide and has a plan, and a score of 4 indicates a recent suicide attempt. Careful follow-up is warranted to determine if the person is currently at risk of harming him- or herself and if hospitalization is required. Patients scoring 3 on item 7b (work performance) indicate impairment at a level where simple self-care, such as washing and bathing, is difficult, and a score of 4 indicates the person reports being unable to care for him- or herself at all. In such cases, partial or full hospitalization may be indicated. Delusional thinking in the form of somatic delusions is captured on item 15a, and the presence of psychosis should be evaluated. The HDI total scale score as a reflection of overall symptom severity may also be considered in choosing the appropriate level of care.

The HDI may also be useful in determining the appropriate therapeutic approach. Persons scoring above the cutoff on the HDI–Mel scale demonstrate a clinical level of melancholic features. The *DSM–IV* reports that persons with these features are more likely to respond to antidepressant medications, and are thus good candidates for this type of treatment intervention (American Psychiatric Association, 1994, p. 384). They are also less likely to have a clear precipitant to their current episode and less likely to have a premorbid personality disorder, further indicating a somatic approach to treatment. Traditionally, the concept of melancholia has been used to indicate a more "endogenous" or biologically based depression, although the concept has been the focus of much debate (Nelson, Mazure, & Jatlow, 1990; Nelson, Mazure, Quinlan, & Jatlow, 1984; Price, Nelson, Charney, & Quinlan, 1984; Zimmerman, Black, & Coryell, 1989). *DSM–IV* focuses on the clinical implications of melancholia and does not provide any etiological interpretations.

Among patients with a diagnosis of depression, patients with atypical features (i.e., hypersomnia, increased appetite, mood reactivity, leaden paralysis, and rejection sensitivity) have shown preferential response to certain classes of drugs, such as monoamine oxidase inhibitors (Liebowitz et al., 1988; Thase, Carpenter, Kupfer, & Frank, 1991). These features have been recognized as important clinical information, and have been included in the *DSM–IV*. HDI items 1c (mood reactivity), 8 (psychomotor retardation), and 18a and 18b (hypersomnia) evaluate these domains, and warrant examination for treatment planning. Patients with atypical features typically have an earlier age of onset of their first depressive episodes, and their episodes tend to follow a more chronic, less episodic course, with only partial recovery between major episodes (American Psychiatric Association, 1994, p. 385). As such, patients with atypical features may be candidates for long-term, supportive psychotherapy, or interventions aimed at preventing relapse. In such cases, referral to a mental health clinician is indicated in addition to pharmacologic intervention.

Cognitive-behavior therapy (CBT) is one of the most well-validated treatments for depression (Beck, 1991; Hollon, Shelton, & Loosen, 1991). Persons scoring high on HDI items associated with the cognitive symptoms of depression are particularly appropriate candidates for this type of therapy, and referral to a mental health clinician offering this type of treatment may be indicated. In particular, items 22 (hopelessness), 21 (worthlessness), 19 (helplessness), and 2 (guilt) are symptoms domains that are amenable to a cognitive intervention. As recommended by Beck and colleagues (Beck, Rush, Shaw, & Emory, 1979), patients with severe behavioral or motivational deficits might benefit more from an initial treatment approach that focuses on behavioral interventions, in order to restore the patient's functioning (p. 117). Elevated scores on items 7a (loss of interest/pleasure), 7b (work difficulty), 8 (psychomotor retardation), and 13a (fatigue) indicate that a behavioral approach initially might be indicated. Beck et al. (1979) and others (Lewinsohn, Antonuccio, Steinmetz, & Teri, 1984; Teri & Lewinsohn, 1982) suggested such interventions as activity scheduling and pleasant and unpleasant activities monitoring as techniques that are useful in this situation.

A large National Institute of Mental Health (NIMH)-sponsored study found cognitive-behavioral therapy (CBT) to be as efficacious as drug therapy (imipramine) for mild cases of depression (defined as a score of less than 20 on the clinician-administered Hamilton Depression Scale), whereas for more severe cases, drug intervention was superior (Elkin et al., 1989), although some have disputed this difference on methodological grounds (Jacobson & Hollon, 1996). Other studies have found CBT to be as efficacious as pharmacotherapy in moderate to severe depression (see Hollon et al., 1991, for a review). Current treatment guidelines developed by the AHCPR (Depression Guideline Panel, 1993b) and the American Psychiatric Association (American Psychiatric Association, 1993) do not recommend CBT alone for severe cases of major depression. As our validation studies have found the clinician-administered HAMD to be comparable to the HDI, those wishing to follow those guidelines may use a score of 20 on the 17-item version as the cut point.

Results of the HDI may be shared with the patient as part of working collaboratively with the patient in developing a treatment plan, be that treatment within the primary care setting, or referral to a behavioral health clinician. This collaborative approach to treatment planning helps foster the "therapeutic alliance," an important component for successful treatment outcome. Reviewing results may be used as a way of building rapport with the patient, and as a springboard into a fuller discussion of symptoms and issues from the patient's perspective.

Use of the HDI for Treatment Monitoring

Once a treatment plan has been established, the HDI may be used as a gauge to monitor the effectiveness of the treatment intervention. Although the standard time frame of the HDI is the past 2 weeks, patients may be instructed to evaluate their symptoms over the past week in order to evaluate changes more precisely. Given the high 1-week test–retest reliability of the HDI, changes found are likely to be associated with the treatment intervention rather than measurement error. Hamilton described the 1-week interval as a valid time frame for assessing change with the HAMD (Hamilton, 1967).

Clinical practice guidelines for the treatment of major depression in primary care were recently developed by the U.S. Department of Health and Human Services Agency for Health Care Policy and Research (AHCPR; Depression Guideline Panel, 1993). These guidelines identify three stages in the treatment of depression. The *acute* stage is aimed at removing all depressive symptoms. If a relapse occurs within 6 months of remission, a relapse is declared. The *continuation* phase is aimed at preventing this relapse. Once a patient has been asymptomatic for 6 months, a recovery is declared. Once a recovery is declared, treatment for most patients may be stopped. The *maintenance* phase follows recovery, and is aimed at preventing a recurrence of depression. Recurrences occur in 50% of cases within 2 years after continuation treatment (NIMH, 1985). Thus, for some patients, continued monitoring and relapse prevention intervention may be warranted during this phase. Given these guidelines, we recommended that the HDI be administered weekly during the acute phase of treatment, and monthly during the continuation and maintenance phases. Clinician discretion should be used to adjust the frequency of administration up or down as warranted by clinical judgment. For clinical purposes, a patient may be considered in remission by examining scores on the HDI Major Depression Checklist. If none of the nine *DSM–IV* items are scored higher than 1 and the total HDI score is below 10, the patient may be considered clinically in remission.

Some patients may have clinically meaningful improvement while not obtaining full remission. The determination of whether changes in HDI scores are clinically meaningful is a complex undertaking that is a function of the original level of depressive symptomatology, nature of the depressive disorder, and nature and extent of the treatment regime. There is no hard and fast single rule for specifying an absolute change score criterion for significant change. One criterion that has been used in many pharmacological treatment outcome studies with the HAMD is a reduction in scores of 50% over the course of treatment. Given the similarities in basic content and assessment metric between the HDI and HAMD, it is reasonable to view a 50% reduction in score as clinically meaningful. In most cases of individuals with depression, such a reduction will result in the individual demonstrating a posttreatment score below the cutoff score on the HDI or HDI–17.

Another perspective on change would be to view a change in standard scores (*T*-scores) of 1½ standard deviations, or 15 *T*-score points, as clinically meaningful. Thus, an individual with a *T*-score of 90 on the HDI who posttreatment manifests a standard score of 75*T*, although still demonstrating a mild clinical level of depressive symptomatology, may be viewed as having shown a clinically significant reduction in HDI scores.

A third perspective on whether clinically meaningfull change has occurred was suggested by Jacobsen and Truax (1991). They propose the Reliable Change (RC) index as a way of determining whether change reflects "more than the fluctuations of an imprecise measuring instrument" (Jacobsen & Truax, 1991, p. 14). The RC index is the difference between two scores at two points in time, divided by the standard error of difference. If the resulting value of time 2 minus time 1 is ±1.96, one can be 95% confident that real change has occurred. Thus, a decrease of 4.4 in the full-scale HDI score, or 3.2 on the HDI–17, from time 1 to time 2 would indicate statistically reliable improvement, whereas an increase of 4.4 or 3.2, respectively, would indicate statisticalliy reliable deterioration.

According to Jacobson and Truax (1991), *clinically* significant change is that in which the change in score is both statistically reliable and, in the case of improvement, moves the patient to either within two standard deviations from the mean of the "normal" (nondepressed) population, at least two standard deviations away from the dysfunctional (depressed) population mean, or closer to the mean of normal population than that of the dysfunctional population. Although not addressed by Jacobson and Truax, one can assume that clinically significant deterioration would require a statistically reliable score change that moves the patient to either within two standard deviations from the mean of the depressed population, at least two standard deviations away from the nondepressed population mean, or closer to the mean of that depressed population than to that of the nondepressed population.

It is important to note that these guidelines are broad suggestions for the evaluation of changes in HDI and HDI–17 scores. A similar perspective may be taken for the

HDI–SF, although this measure should be used with caution for the evaluation of treatment outcome as a function of reduced item coverage. The criterion of 50% reduction in score described earlier may also be useful when applied to the HDI–Mel subscale, particularly in cases of more endogenous depression where antidepressant medications are the primary mode of treatment. The examination of change in specific symptom-content domains such as cognitive or somatic symptoms is not suggested given the more limited reliability of such scores.

Symptoms of depression may improve at different rates, depending on the type of treatment intervention. For example, DiMascio et al. (1979) found that antidepressant therapy had its effect mainly on vegetative symptoms, such as sleep (HDI items 4, 5, 6, and 18) and appetite (HDI items 12 and 17), with improvements occurring early in treatment, often within the first week. Interpersonal psychotherapy, on the other hand, had its effect mainly on mood (HDI item 1), suicidal ideation (HDI item 3), and work and interests (HDI item 7), with these effects occurring later in treatment, usually at 4 to 8 weeks. Similarly, Rush, Kovacs, Beck, Weissenburger, and Hollon (1981) found patients treated with cognitive therapy had improvements in hopelessness (HDI item 22) and mood (HDI item 1) that generally preceded improvements in vegetative symptoms. Monitoring of differential symptom change by examination of these items, as well as scores on the HDI–Mel scale and HDI critical items, can serve as a guide for treatment focus. Improvement in cognitive symptoms without a similar improvement in vegetative symptoms after a course of cognitive therapy of adequate duration may indicate the need for the addition of antidepressant therapy. The reverse may also be true.

Ongoing monitoring of treatment informs the clinician as to whether the interventions chosen are effective. In the case where there is no progress being made, the therapist may wish to reevaluate the treatment plan and identify reasons for the lack of progress. Depression often follows a fluctuating course, and patients sometimes get worse during the course of treatment. Particular attention should be paid to item 3 (suicide) and appropriate follow-up taken any time this item is endorsed. If psychotherapy alone has been chosen, the AHCPR guidelines suggest a switch to medication if the psychotherapy is completly ineffecitve by 6 weeks or if it does not result in nearly a full symptomatic remission within 12 weeks. For patients treated with medication alone, they suggest a reevaluation of both the diagnosis and the adequacy of the medication if there has been only a minimal response or less by 6 weeks (assuming adequate dosage was achieved) (Depression Guideline Panel, 1993b). A more recent study found that patients who were never at least minimally improved by the end of 4 weeks of treatment were unlikely to eventually respond to that medication (Quitkin et al., 1996). An improvement of less than 20% on the HDI may be used to approximate minimal improvement.

One final note is warranted on the use of the HDI for outcomes assessment. As previously mentioned, different symptoms of depression may respond at different rates, depending on the treatment and symptom (DiMascio et al., 1979; Rush et al., 1981). As such, before making conclusions as to the efficacy of an intervention, one should wait until the standard course of treatment recommended for the intervention is attained. For example, Rush et al. (1981) found that with cognitive therapy, changes in cognitive symptoms such as hopelessness preceded improvements in vegetative symptoms. Before determining that a cognitive intervention has been ineffective for vegetative symptoms, one should not perform the final outcome measurement until the proper duration of treatment has been administered, according to the guidelines of the intervention. The HDI includes items evaluating both of these domains, allowing for the examination of vegetative and cognitive symptoms separately.

The computer-administered HDI is particularly useful for ongoing clinical assessment. Patients may take the computer interview in the waiting room while waiting to see the clinician. The results are scored automatically and a report is available to the clinician to review prior to the session. Computer administration eliminates the time and costs involved in administration and scoring by staff members. Such a situation was set up by the first author at an outpatient community mental health clinic in conjunction with a study of a computerized diagnostic screener (Kobak et al., 1997b). A desk with a desktop computer and printer was set up in the patient waiting room. Patients were instructed to arrive a few minutes prior to the start of each session and take the computer HDI. Results were reviewed and filed in the patient's chart (APA ethical guidelines require that computer-administered assessments filed in charts be clearly labeled that the data were obtained by computer administration; American Psychological Association, 1986). Objective data on positive changes over time served as reinforcers in therapy, and often helped to counteract patient's negative thinking that they would never get any better. Patients enjoyed taking the computer interview, and objected on the few occasions when it was not administered due to time or other constraints. The computer-administered form of HDI has been used as an outcome measure in several clinical drug trials (Kobak, Greist, Jefferson, Katzelnick, & Schaettle, 1996; Kobak, Greist, Jefferson, Reynolds, & Tollefson, 1994) and was the primary outcome measure in a study of the treatment of depressed high utilizing medical patients by primary care physicians in a large health maintenance organization (HMO) (Katzelnick, Kobak, Jefferson, Greist, & Henk, 1997).

STRENGTHS AND LIMITATIONS OF USE
OF THE HDI IN PRIMARY CARE SETTINGS

Newman, Ciarlo, and colleagues discussed the 11 criteria identified by the National Institute of Mental Health as important to consider when choosing an outcome measure (Newman & Ciarlo, 1994). These criteria fell under five general headings: applications, methods and procedures, psychometric features, cost, and utility. Although these guidelines were developed for evaluating the strengths and limitations of outcome measures in psychiatric settings, they provide a useful framework for evaluating measures for use in the primary care setting as well. What follows is a brief overview of how the HDI addresses these concerns.

Criterion 1: Applications. This addresses the concern that the measure used is appropriate for the group being studied, that it adequately evaluates the symptom domain of that group, and that it is independent of the treatment provided. The evidence provided previously in this chapter provides support for the HDI as an appropriate outcome measure of depressive symptomatology. It has been used successfully in the primary care setting (Katzelnick, Kobak, et al., 1997). Its construct and content validity document that it adequately samples the domain of depressive symptomatology. It has been the primary outcome measure used in pharmacological depression trials for the past 30 years. The validation sample adequately samples both genders, and consists of a wide range of ages and ethnicity. It is appropriate for the evaluation of severity and change in depressive symptomatology independent of treatment modality, and the clinician version has been used to evaluate both pharmacological and psychological interventions (Elkin et al., 1989).

Criterion 2: Simple, Teachable Methods and Procedures.   The HDI provides an in-depth user manual with explicit instruction on the administration and interpretation of the scale. The computer-administered version provides a separate manual containing software documentation and a number for technical support. The HDI is intended for use by qualified professionals (e.g., physicians, mental health professionals) who have some knowledge of adult psychopathology, current diagnostic schemas, and the nature of depressive disorders in adults.

Criterion 3: Psychometric Features.   The psychometric features of the HDI are well documented from several perspectives (Reynolds & Kobak, 1995a, 1995b). In addition, the psychometric data on the clinician HAMD may be inferred to also apply to the HDI, by virtue of the demonstration of equivalence of the two forms. Newman and Ciarlo (1994) discussed the value of "objective referents," that is, standardized, concrete examples of each level of a symptom evaluated by the scale. The HDI addresses the limitations of the clinician version in this regard by providing behavioral descriptors whenever possible. For example, in rating insomnia, both the number of hours it takes to fall asleep and the number of days per week the problem occurs are evaluated. Regarding the use of multiple respondents, the HDI is more limited in this regard than the clinician HAMD, in that the clinician may use information from other sources, such as family, in determining ratings.

Newman and Ciarlo (1994) also discussed the advantages and disadvantages of using multiple perspectives. Physicians using the HDI should incorporate additional information obtained from other perspectives in making clinical decisions. Such an approach is also encouraged by the AHCPR guidelines (Depression Guideline Panel, 1993b, p. 78).

Criterion 4: Costs.   The HDI is cost-effective compared to the clinician-administered version. The computer-administered version of the HDI provides screening and outcomes data without requiring any clinician involvement in the administration or scoring of the test. Furthermore, a detailed interpretive report is also available from the HDI Computer Scoring Program. This program also saves clinician time and can be easily integrated into a word-processing file for editing and inclusion into the clinician's case report.

Criterion 5: Utility.   The NIMH guidelines cite as an asset the ability of test results to be understood by a nonprofessional audience, enabling all who have an interest in outcomes to take advantage of the information. The HDI provides general descriptions of score values in terms understandable to the non-professional (see Table 13.6). The HDI also provides graphic and narrative reports and computerized scoring as recommended by the panel. The HDI has clinical utility in case planning, ongoing treatment monitoring, and outcomes evaluation. Computer administration enables the collection and processing of data without burden to the clinician or support staff. As previously discussed, the HDI measures the construct of depression consistent with current definitions, and it is thus compatible for use in evaluating outcomes from a variety of treatment approaches. The clinician HAMD has been used as an outcome measure to evaluate a diverse range of treatment interventions utilized for treating depression, including medication, cognitive therapy, and interpersonal psychotherapy (Elkin et al., 1989).

CASE STUDY

The following case study is provided as an example for interpreting the HDI. It is an actual clinical case, with a pseudonym and minor changes in demographic data to insure anonymity. The HDI Summary Sheet and individual item score summary table for this case are included in Fig. 13.1 and 13.2 for illustration purposes. A complete interpretive report is also generated, but is not reproduced here.

The case illustration is that of Paula, a 28-year-old unmarried nursing assistant with a high school education. Paula was screened for depression as part of a pilot study examining the impact of the identification and primary care treatment of depressed high-utilizing patients (Katzelnick et al., 1997). Paula has a history of renal colic and recent active significant gastrointestinal (GI) complaints, including weight loss and diarrhea. She was previously referred to a gastroenterologist, who performed an upper and lower GI endoscopy. He was unable to come up with a diagnosis for her chronic GI complaints. She also has a possible seizure disorder, for which her neurologist suspected a possible psychiatric etiology.

Paula reported a several-year history of mood disorder and anxiety. She complained of increasing sleep disturbance, feelings of depression and anxiety, a lack of interests in doing things, some mild tearfulness, weight loss, and GI complaints. She has had no prior psychiatric evaluation or treatment. She was administered the PRIME–MD, and received diagnoses of major depressive disorder and anxiety disorder NOS.

Paula was administered the HDI on a laptop computer in her primary care physician's office. Paula's Form HS Summary Sheet is presented in Fig. 13.1. Paula obtained a score of 19.5 on the full-scale HDI, which is slightly above the cutoff score of 19. This raw score is in the 97th percentile and equivalent to a T-score of 72. On the HDI-17, Paula obtained a score of 17.5, which is slightly above the cutoff of 15.0 used to indicate a clinical level of depressive symptomatology, and is in the 98th percentile. Paula received a score of 8.0 on the HDI–Mel. This score is well below the cutoff score of 16.0 for this subscale, indicating that Paula's depression does not fit the melancholic subtype.

Paula's self-report on the HDI was consistent with her psychiatric diagnosis. On the HDI Major Depression Checklist, which lists the nine primary symptoms of major depressive disorder, Paula received a criterion-level score of 2.0 or higher on four of the nine criteria (depressed mood, loss of interest, insomnia, and fatigue). For a diagnosis of major depression, five of the nine DSM–IV symptoms must be evident nearly every day for at least a 2-week period. On the PRIME–MD clinical interview, her physician also rated a fifth symptom, psychomotor agitation, as present.

Paula's HDI symptom profile is typical of that found in depressed primary care patients. She endorsed both insomnia (items 4 through 6) and fatigue (item 13), the two most common symptoms of the subsyndromal type of depression typically found in primary care patients (Judd et al., 1996). She also scored high on other symp-

Hamilton Depression Inventory

Form HS Summary Sheet

by William M. Reynolds, PhD and Kenneth A. Kobak, PhD

Name Paula White Date 11/10/94 ID 2139 Sex F

Race W Age 28 Education 12 years Occupation Nursing Assistant

	Raw score	Recommended cutoff score	At or above cutoff score	T score	%ile	Appendix table
HDI	19.5	19.0	No (yes)	72	97	A-1
HDI-17	17.5	15.0	No (yes)	76	98	B-1
HDI-Mel	8.0	16.0	(No) yes	67	92	C-1

HDI Major Depression Checklist

DSM-IV Symptom	HDI Items or Question(s)			Score
1. Depressed mood	1	→		2.0
2. Loss of interest/pleasure	7a	→		2.0
3. Weight loss	17	→		0
4. Insomnia/hypersomnia	4	1.3		
	5	1.3		
	6	2.0		
	18	0	(Enter highest of four scores) →	2.0
5. Psychomotor retardation/agitation	8	0		
	9	0	(Enter highest of two scores) →	0
6. Fatigue or loss of energy	13a	→		2.0
7. Worthlessness or guilt	2	1		
	21	0	(Enter highest of two scores) →	1.0
8. Indecisiveness	23	→		0
9. Suicidal ideation/behavior	3	→		0
			Number of scores 2.0 or higher:	4

PAR Psychological Assessment Resources, Inc.
P.O. Box 998/Odessa, Florida 33556/Toll-Free 1-800-331-TEST

9 8 7 6 5 4 3 2 1 Reorder #RO-2885 Printed in the U.S.A.

FIG. 13.1. Paula's Form HS Summary Sheet.

toms that have been identified as common in primary care depression, such as psychological and somatic anxiety (items 10 and 11), hypochondriasis (item 15), and pain (muscle aches and headaches, questions 11d and 13b, respectively). She has several of the features identified by the AHCPR guidelines as risk factors for depression in primary care patients, including female gender, age of onset under 40, and medical comorbidity.

HDI INDIVIDUAL ITEM SCORE SUMMARY TABLE

Item	Symptom	Item score	Score range	Clinical level	Response time
1	Dysphoria	2.0	0-4	Yes	28.3
2	Excessive/feelings of guilt	1.0	0-4	No	13.0
3	Suicidal ideation or attempt	0.0	0-4	No	2.3
4	Insomnia (early)	1.3	0-2	No	5.0
5	Insomnia (middle)	1.3	0-2	No	1.0
6	Insomnia (late)	2.0	0-2	Yes	3.0
7	Loss of interest/poor work performance	2.0	0-4	Yes	9.1
8	Psychomotor retardation	0.0	0-4	No	2.2
9	Psychomotor agitation	0.0	0-4	No	0.8
10	Anxiety-psychological	2.0	0-4	Yes	7.1
11	Anxiety-somatic	2.0	0-4	Yes	21.0
12	Loss of appetite	0.0	0-2	No	7.4
13	Somatic fatigue, muscle-ache	2.0	0-2	Yes	9.4
14	Somatic-genital/libido	0.0	0-2	No	18.4
15	Hypochondriasis	2.0	0-4	Yes	12.0
16	Loss of insight	0.0	0-2	No	11.9
17	Weight loss	0.0	0-2	No	12.0
18	Hypersomnia	0.0	0-2	No	2.3
19	Helplessness	0.0	0-3	No	3.6
20	Detachment-depersonalization	0.0	0-4	No	4.6
21	Feelings of worthlessness	0.0	0-4	No	3.2
22	Pessimism - hopelessness	2.0	0-4	Yes	2.3
23	Indecision	0.0	0-4	No	2.5

FIG. 13.2. Paula's HDI individual item score summary table.

Her scores on the three insomnia items (e.g., items 4, 5, and 6) were 1.3, 1.3, and 2.0, respectively, indicating persistent troubles with falling asleep, waking during the night, and early morning awakening. According to guidelines described by Hamilton (1960, 1967), items rated on a 0 to 2 scale represent symptoms that are difficult to quantify. Thus, a score of 2 indicates both the certainty that the symptom exists and that it is significantly severe. Her score of 1.3 on initial and middle insomnia indicates frequent difficulty with these problems (3 to 5 nights a week) or a moderately severe nature (up to 1 hr). Paula's score of 2 on terminal insomnia (i.e., early morning awakening) indicated her insomnia was persistent (e.g., almost every night) and significantly intense (e.g., for more than an hour every night).

Paula's HDI protocol also indicated her depressive episode was complicated by clinically significant comorbid anxiety. Her score on the HDI item 10 (psychic anxiety) was 2.0, indicating a moderate level of anxiety that was present about half the time. In a related manner, her score of 2.0 on item 15 (hypochondriasis) indicates that she feels very worried about her health. Although she has sought medical help for her complaints, no medical explanation was established. Other significant aspects of the current episode include significant feelings of hopelessness, as indicated by a score of 2.0 on item 22, and loss of interest and pleasure in things, reflected by a score of 2 on item 7. Both of these symptoms are HDI critical items. She denied any suicidal ideation.

Paula was started on 25 mg of nortriptyline with instructions to increase by 25 mg no sooner than every 3 days for a total maximum dose of 75 mg. A tricyclic antidepressant was chosen rather than a selective serotonin reuptake inhibitor (SSRI) because of her major GI symptoms. Her primary care physician also explained the possible relationship between her chronic GI complaints and her symptoms of major depression and anxiety.

Paula was seen again in 1 week. She did not increase the dose because of daytime somnolence, although this side effect had then worn off. She reported her sleep had dramatically improved and that she was quite happy about this. Her 17-item HDI score was now 13.5. She also reported feeling less ruminative, less worried, and more relaxed. Her dose was increased to 50 mg/day. After a month of treatment, her 17-item HDI score dropped to 5.5. She reported a significant improvement in her bowels. She remained on a dose of 50 mg. After 2 months of treatment, her HDI score was 6.2, and she reported a resolution of her chronic diarrhea. At the end of 6 months of treatment Paula's HDI score was 2.4. Her scores on all the HDI critical items were zero, with only some mild subclinical symptoms of anxiety remaining. Her physician planned to continue with her treatment.

CONCLUSIONS

The HDI, as a computer-administered and paper-and-pencil version of the HAMD, builds on a strong foundation for the assessment of depression in primary care patients. The HDI may be used in a range of clinical applications, such as for screening, treatment planning, treatment monitoring, and measuring treatment outcomes. The various forms of the HDI increase its utility, making it an appropriate instrument for both clinical and research purposes. The full-scale form of the HDI evaluates domains consistent with current diagnostic symptoms of depression. The HDI differs from traditional self-report measures in that it emulates a clinical interview by asking several questions in evaluating each symptom domain, weighs the answers to the questions in arriving at a final score, and uses branching logic. Unlike clinicians, the HDI is consistent and does not vary from person to person in terms of the questions asked, nor in the scoring algorithm used to determine item ratings.

Depression is a serious illness, associated with significant disability and decreased quality of life (Broadhead et al., 1990; Hays, Wells, Sherbourne, Rogers, & Spitzer, 1995). Estimates of those with severe depression who die of suicide are as high as 15% (American Psychiatric Association, 1994, p. 340). The good news is, great advances have been made in both the treatment and public awareness of depression and its impact. Increased efforts are being made in the screening of depressed individuals (Baer et al., 1995), and in the empirical evaluation of treatment interventions (Elkin et al., 1989). The HDI provides a psychometrically sound and clinically useful tool for both of these purposes. The rise in HMOs has resulted in the inclusion of marketplace factors into the clinical care of patients. Although this has caused some concern and resistance, the measurement of treatment outcomes may provide new opportunities for improved clinical care. The measurement of outcomes provides clinicians and patients with more information on which they can mutually make more informed treatment decisions. Systematic data gathering can inform which treatments work for which patients under what conditions. Psychometrically sound outcome measures such as the HDI can provide a tool by which patients, clinicians, and managed care providers can search together for what Minichiello and Baer (1994) referred to as "the bottom line: what works." The final result is improved clinical care for patients.

REFERENCES

American Educational Research Association, American Psychological Association, & National Council on Measurement in Education. (1985). *Standards for educational and psychological testing.* Washington, DC: American Psychological Association.

American Psychiatric Association. (1987). *Diagnostic and statistical manual of mental disorders* (3rd ed., rev.). Washington, DC: Author.

American Psychiatric Association. (1993). Practice guideline for major depressive disorder in adults. *American Journal of Psychiatry, 150* (suppl. 4).

American Psychiatric Association. (1994).*Diagnostic and statistical manual of mental disorders* (4th ed.). Washington, DC: Author.

American Psychiatric Association. (1995). *Diagnostic and statistical manual of mental disorders, fourth edition, primary care version (DSM–IV–PC).* Washington, DC: Author.

American Psychological Association. (1986). *Guidelines for computer-based tests and interpretations.* Washington, DC: Author.

Attkisson, C. C., & Zich, J. M. (1990). Depression screening in primary care: clinical needs and research challenges. In C. C. Attkisson & J. M. Zich (Eds.), *Depression in primary care: Screening and detection* (pp. 3–11). New York: Routledge.

Baer, L., Jacobs, D. G., Cukor, P., O'Laughren, J., Coyle, J. T., & Magruder, K. M. (1995). Automated telephone screening for depression. *Journal of the American Medical Association, 273,* 1943–1944.

Barrett, J. E., Barrett, J. A., Oxman, T. E., & Gerber, P. D. (1988). The prevalence of psychiatric disorders in a primary care practice. *Archives of General Psychiatry, 45,* 1100–1106.

Bech, P., Allerup, P., Gram, L. F., Reisby, N., Rosenberg, R., Jacobsen, O., & Nagy, A. (1981). The Hamilton Depression Scale: Evaluation of objectivity using logistic models. *Acta Psychiatrica Scandinavica, 63,* 290–299.

Bech, P., Allerup, P., Reisby, N., & Gram, L. F. (1984). Assessment of symptom change from improvement curves on the Hamilton Depression Scale in trials with antidepressants. *Psychopharmacology, 84,* 276–281.

Bech, P., Gram, L. F., Dein, E., Jacobsen, O., Vitger, J., & Bolwig, T. G. (1975). Quantitative rating of depressive states. *Acta Psychiatrica Scandinavica, 51,* 161–170.

Bech, P., Kastrup, M., & Rafaelsen, O. J. (1986). Mini-compendium of rating scales for states of anxiety, depression, mania, schizophrenia with corresponding DSM-II syndromes. *Acta Psychiatrica Scandinavica, 73,* 5–37.

Beck, A. T. (1991). Cognitive therapy: A 30-year retrospective. *American Psychologist, 46,* 368–375.

Beck, A. T., Brown, G., Berchick, R. J., Stewart, B. L., & Steer, R. (1990). Relationship between hopelessness and ultimate suicide: A replication with psychiatric outpatients. *American Journal of Psychiatry, 147,* 190–195.

Beck, A. T., Epstein, N., Brown, G., & Steer, R. A. (1988). An inventory for measuring clinical anxiety: Psychometric properties. *Journal of Consulting and Clinical Psychology, 56,* 893–897.

Beck, A. T., Kovacs, M., & Weissman, A. (1975). Hopelessness and suicidal behavior: An overview. *Journal of the American Medical Association, 234,* 1146–1149.

Beck, A. T., Rush, A. J., Shaw, B., & Emory, G. (1979). *Cognitive therapy of depression.* New York: Guilford Press.

Beck, A. T., Ward, C., Mendelson, M., Mock, J., & Erbaugh, J. (1961). An inventory for measuring depression. *Archives of General Psychiatry, 4,* 561–571.

Beck, A. T., Weissman, A., Lester, D., & Trexler, M. (1974). The measurement of pessimism: The Hopelessness Scale. *Journal of Consulting and Clinical Psychology, 42,* 861–865.

Broadhead, W. E., Blazer, D. G., George, L. K., & Tse, C. K. (1990). Depression, disability days, and days lost from work in a prospective epidemiologic survey. *Journal of the American Medical Association, 264,* 2524–2528.

Broadhead, W. E., Leon, A. C., Weissman, M. M., Barrett, J. E., Blacklow, R. S., Gilbert, T. T., Keller, M. B., Olfson, M., & Higgins, E. S. (1995). Development and validation of the SDDS–PC screen for multiple mental disorders in primary care. *Archives of Family Medicine, 4,* 211–219.

Bulik, C. M., Carpenter, L. L., Kupfer, D. J., & Frank, E. (1990). Features associated with suicide attempts in recurrent major depression. *Journal of Affective Disorders, 18,* 29–37.

Campbell, T. L. (1987). Is screening for mental health problems worthwhile in family practice? An opposing view. *Journal of Family Practice, 25,* 184–187.

Carroll, B. J., Feinberg, M., Smouse, P. E., Rawson, S. G., & Greden, J. F. F. (1981). The Carroll Rating Scale for Depression: I. Development, reliability and validation. *British Journal of Psychiatry, 138,* 194–200.

Coryell, W., Endicott, J., Andreasen, N. C., Keller, M. B., Clayton, P. J., Hirschfeld, R. M., Scheftner, W. A., & Winokur, G. (1988). Depression and panic attacks: The significance of overlap as reflected in follow-up and family study data. *American Journal of Psychiatry, 145,* 293–300.

Cox, B. J., Direnfeld, D. M., Swinson, R. P., & Norton, G. R. (1994). Suicidal ideation and suicide attempts in panic disorder and social phobia. *American Journal of Psychiatry, 151,* 882–887.

Cronbach, L. J. (1951). Coefficient alpha and the internal structure of tests. *Psychometrika, 16,* 297–334.

Demitrack, M. A., Faries, D., DeBrota, D., & Potter, W. Z. (1997). The problem of measurement error in multisite clinical trials. *Psychopharmacology Bulletin, 33,* 513.

Depression Guideline Panel. (1993a). *Depression in primary care: Volume 1. Detection and diagnosis. Clinical practice guidelines, Number 5* (AHCPR Publication No. 93-0550). Rockville, MD: U.S. Department of Health and Human Services.

Depression Guideline Panel. (1993b). *Depression in primary care: Volume 2. Treatment of major depression. Clinical practice guidelines, Number 5* (AHCPR Publication No. 93-0551). Rockville, MD: U.S. Department of Health and Human Services.

Depression Guideline Panel. (1993c). *Depression in primary care: Detection, diagnosis, and treatment. Clinical practice guidelines, Number 5* (AHCPR Publication No. 93-0552). Rockville, MD: U.S. Department of Health and Human Services.

DiMascio, A., Weissman, M. M., Prusoff, B. A., Neu, C., Zwilling, M., & Klerman, G. L. (1979). Differential symptom reduction by drugs and psychotherapy in acute depression. *Archives of General Psychiatry, 36,* 1450–1456.

Dunlop, S. R., Dornseif, B. E., Wernicke, J. F., & Potvin, J. H. (1990). Pattern analysis shows beneficial effects of fluoxetine treatment in mild depression. *Psychopharmacology Bulletin, 26,* 173–180.

Edwards, A. L. (1970). *The measurement of personality traits by scales and inventories.* New York: Holt, Reinhart, & Winston.

Edwards, B. C., Lambert, M. J., Moran, P. W., McCully, T., Smith, K. C., & Ellingson, A. G. (1984). A meta-analytic comparison of the Beck Depression Inventory and the Hamilton Rating Scale for Depression as measures of treatment outcome. *British Journal of Clinical Psychology, 23,* 93–99.

Eisenberg, L. (1992). Treating depression and anxiety in primary care: Closing the gap between knowledge and practice. *New England Journal of Medicine, 326,* 1080–1083.

Elkin, I., Shea, M. T., Watkins, J. T., Imber, S. D., Sotsky, S. M., Collins, J. F., Glass, D. R., Pilkonis, P. A., Leber, W. R., Docherty, J. P., Fiester, S. J., & Parloff, M. B. (1989). National Institute of Mental Health treatment of depression collaborative research program. *Archives of General Psychiatry, 46,* 971–983.

Endicott, J., Cohen, J., Nee, J., Fleiss, J., & Sarantakos, S. (1981). Hamilton Depression Rating Scale: Extracted from regular and change versions of the Schedule for affective disorders and schizophrenia. *Archives of General Psychiatry, 38,* 98–103.

Endicott, J., & Spitzer, R. L. (1978). A diagnostic interview: The Schedule for Affective Disorders and Schizophrenia. *Archives of General Psychiatry, 35,* 837–844.

Fairbairn, A. S., Wood, C. H., & Fletcher, C. M. (1959). Variability in answers to a questionnaire on respiratory symptoms. *British Journal of Preventive and Social Medicine, 13,* 175–193.

Fava, G. A., Kellner, R., Munari, F., & Pavan, L. (1982). The Hamilton Depression Rating Scale in normals and depressives: A cross cultural validation. *Acta Psychiatrica Scandinavica, 66,* 27–32.

Gibbons, R. D., Clark, D. C., & Kupfer, D. J. (1993). Exactly what does the Hamilton Depression Rating Scale measure. *Journal of Psychiatric Research, 27,* 259–273.

Greist, J. H., Gustafson, D. H., Stauss, F. F., Rowse, G. L., Laughren, T. P., & Chiles, J. A. (1973). A computer interview for suicide-risk prediction. *American Journal of Psychiatry, 130,* 1327–1332.

Greist, J. H., & Klein, M. H. (1980). Computer programs for patients, clinicians, and researchers in psychiatry. In J. B. Sydowski, J. H. Johnson, & T. A. Williams (Eds.), *Technology in mental health care delivery systems* (pp. 161–181). Norwood, NJ: Ablex.

Guy, W. (1976). *ECDEU assessment manual for psychopharmacology, revised* (Publication ADM 76-338). Rockville, MD: National Institute of Mental Health, U.S. Department of Health, Education, and Welfare.

Hamilton, M. (1960). A rating scale for depression. *Journal of Neurology, Neurosurgery and Psychiatry, 23,* 56–62.

Hamilton, M. (1967). Development of a rating scale for primary depressive illness. *British Journal of Social and Clinical Psychiatry, 6,* 278–296.

Hamilton, M. (1974). General problems of psychiatric rating scales (especially for depression). In P. Pichot (Ed.), *Modern problems of pharmacopsychiatry: Vol. 7. Psychiatric measurements in psychopharmacology* (pp. 125–138). Basel: Karger.

Hamilton, M. (1986). The Hamilton Rating Scale for Depression. In N. Sartorius & T. A. Ban (Eds.), *Assessment of depression* (pp. 143–152). Berlin: Springer-Verlag.

Hays, R. D., Wells, K. B., Sherbourne, C. D., Rogers, W., & Spritzer, K. (1995). Functioning and well-being outcomes of patients with depression compared with chronic general medical illnesses. *Archives of General Psychiatry, 52,* 11–19.

Hedlund, J. L., & Vieweg, B. W. (1979). The Hamilton Rating Scale for Depression: A comprehensive review. *Journal of Operational Psychiatry, 10,* 149–161.

Helzer, J. E., & Pryzbeck, T. R. (1988). The co-occurence of alcoholism with other psychiatric disorders in the general population and its impact on treatment. *Journal of Studies on Alcohol, 49,* 219–224.

Henk, H. J., Katzelnick, D. J., Kobak, K. A., Greist, J. H., & Jefferson, J. W. (1996). Excess medical costs associated with depression. *Archives of General Psychiatry 53,* 899–904.

Hofer, P. J., & Green, B. F. (1985). The challenge of competence and creativity in computerized psychological testing. *Journal of Consulting and Clinical Psychology, 53,* 826–838.

Hollon, S. D., Shelton, R. C., & Loosen, P. T. (1991). Cognitive therapy and pharmacotherapy for depression. *Journal of Consulting and Clinical Psychology, 59,* 88–99.

Hooijer, C., Zitman, F. G., Griez, E., van Tilburg, W., Willemse, A., & Dinkgreve, M. A. H. M. (1991). The Hamilton Depression Rating Scale (HDRS): Changes in scores as a function of training and version used. *Journal of Affective Disorders, 22,* 21–29.

Howarth, E., Johnson, J., Klerman, G. L., & Weissman, M. (1992). Depressive symptoms as relative and attributable risk factors for first-onset major depression. *Archives of General Psychiatry, 49,* 817–823.

Jacobson, N. S., & Hollon, S. D. (1996). Cognitive-behavior therapy versus pharmacotherapy: Now that the jury's returned its verdict, it's time to present the rest of the evidence. *Journal of Consulting and Clinical Psychology, 64,* 74–80.

Jacobson, N. S., & Truax, P. (1991). Clinical significance: A statistical approach to defining meaningful change in psychotherapy research. *Journal of Consulting and Clinical Psychology, 59,* 12–19.

Johnson, J. G., Spitzer, R. L., Williams, J. B. W., Kroenke, K., Linzer, M., Brody, D., deGruy, F., & Hahn, S. (1995). Psychiatric comorbidity, health status, and functional impairment associated with alcohol abuse and dependence in primary care patients: Findings of the PRIME MD–1000 study. *Journal of Consulting and Clinical Psychology, 63,* 133–140.

Johnson, J., Weissman, M. M., & Klerman, G. L. (1990). Panic disorder, comorbidity, and suicide attempts. *Archives of General Psychiatry, 47,* 805–808.

Johnson, J., Weissman, M. M., & Klerman, G. L. (1992). Service utilization and social morbidity associated with depressive symptoms in the community. *Journal of the American Medical Association, 267,* 1478–1483.

Katzelnick, D. J., Kobak, K. A., Greist, J. H., Jefferson, J. W., & Henk, H. J. (1997). Effect of primary care treatment of depression on service use by patients with high medical expenditures. *Psychiatric Services, 48,* 59–64.

Katzelnick, D. J., Kobak, K. A., Greist, J. H., Jefferson, J. W., Mantle, J. M., & Serlin, R. C. (1995). Sertraline for social phobia: A double-blind, placebo-controlled crossover study. *American Journal of Psychiatry, 152,* 1368–1371.

Katzelnick, D. J., Kobak, K. A., Jefferson, J. W., Greist, J. H., & Henk, H. J. (1997). Effect of primary care treatment of depression on service use by patients with high medical expenditures. *Psychiatric Services, 48,* 59–64.

Katzelnick, D. J., Simon, G. E., Pearson, S. D., Manning, W. G., Helstad, C. P., Henk, H. J., & Kobak, K. A. (1997, December). *CARE study: Impact of the step-wise depression management program for depressed high utilizers in three HMOs.* Paper presented at the American College of Neuropsychopharmacology, 36th Annual Meeting, Waikoloa, HI.

Kessler, L. G., Cleary, P. D., Burke, J. D., Jr. (1985). Psychiatric disorders in primary care: Results of a follow-up study. *Archives of General Psychiatry, 42,* 583–587.

Kim, K. I. (1977). Clinical study of primary depressive symptoms. Part 1: Adjustment of Hamilton's rating scale for depression. *Neuropsychiatry, 16,* 36–60.

Kobak, K. A., Greist, J. H., Jefferson, J. W., Katzelnick, D. J., & Schaettle, S. C. (1996, May). *Computerized assessment in clinical drug trials.* Paper presented at the National Institute of Mental Health, New Clinical Drug Evaluation Unit, 36th Annual Meeting, Boca Raton, FL.

Kobak, K. A., Greist, J. H., Jefferson, J. W., Reynolds, W. M., & Tollefson, G. D. (1994). *The computer adminis-tered Hamilton Depression Rating Scale in a double-blind study of fluoxetine vs imipramine in agitated depres-sion.* Unpublished manuscript.

Kobak, K. A., Reynolds, W. R., Rosenfeld, R., & Greist, J. H. (1990). Development and validation of a com-puter administered Hamilton Depression Rating Scale. *Psychological Assessment, 2,* 56–63.

Kobak, K. A., Schaettle, S. C., Greist, J. H., Jefferson, J. W., Katzelnick, D. J., Dottl, S. L. (1998). Computer In-terview Assessment of Social Phobia in a Clinical Drug Trial. *Depression & Anxiety, 7,* 97–104.

Kobak, K. A., Schaettle, S., Katzelnick, D. J., & Simon, G. (1995). *Guidelines for the Hamilton Depression Rat-ing Scale: Modified for the depression in primary care study.* Madison, WI: Dean Foundation.

Kobak, K. A., Taylor, L. V., Dottl, S. L., Greist, J. H., Jefferson, J. W., Burroughs, D., Mantle, J. M., Katzelnick, D. J., Norton, R., Henk, H. J., & Serlin, R. C. (1997a). A computer-administered telephone in-terview to identify mental disorders. *Journal of the American Medical Association, 278,* 905–910.

Kobak, K. A., Taylor, L. V., Dottl, S. L., Greist, J. H., Jefferson, J. W., Burroughs, D., Katzelnick, D. J., & Mandell, M. (1997b). Computerized diagnostic assessment in an outpatient community mental health clinic. *Psychiatric Services, 48,* 1048–1057.

Kovacs, M., Rush, A. J., Beck, A. T., & Hollon, S. D. (1981). Depressed outpatients treated with cognitive therapy or pharmacotherapy: A one-year follow-up. *Archives of General Psychiatry, 38,* 33–39.

Kroenke, K., Jackson, J. L., & Chamberlin, J. (1997). Depressive and anxiety disorders in patients present-ing with physical complaints: Clinical predictors and outcome. *American Journal of Medicine, 103,* 339–347.

Lambert, M. J., Hatch, D. R., Kingston, M. D., & Edwards, B. C. (1986). Zung, Beck, and Hamilton Rating Scales as measures of treatment outcome: A meta-analytic comparison. *Journal of Consulting and Clinical Psychology, 54,* 54–59.

Lewinsohn, P. M., Antonuccio, D. O., Steinmetz, J. L., & Teri, L. (1984). *The coping with depression course: A psychoeducational intervention for unipolar depression.* Eugene, OR: Castalia.

Liebowitz, M. R., Hollander, E., Schneier, F., Campeas, R., Fallon, B., Welkowitz, L., Cloitre, M., & Davies, S. (1990). Anxiety and depression: Discrete diagnostic entities? *Journal of Clinical Psychopharmacology, 10*(suppl.), 61S–65S.

Liebowitz, M. R., Quitkin, F. M., Stewart, J. W., McGrath, P. J., Harrison, W., Markowitz, J. S., Rabkin, J. G., Tricamo, E., Goetz, D. M. D. M., & Klein, D. F. (1988). Antidepressant specificity in atypical depression. *Archives of General Psychiatry, 45,* 129–137.

Lucas, R. W., Mullin, P. J., Luna, C. B. X., & McInroy, D. C. (1977). Psychiatrists and a computer as interro-gators of patients with alcohol-related illnesses: A comparison. *British Journal of Psychiatry, 131,* 160–167.

Maier, W., Philipp, M., & Gerken, A. (1985). Dimensions of the Hamilton Depression Scale. *European Ar-chives of Psychiatry and Neurological Sciences, 234,* 417–422.

Miller, I. W., Bishop, S., Norman, W. H., & Maddever, H. (1985). The modified Hamilton Rating Scale for Depression: Reliability and validity. *Psychiatry Research, 14,* 131–142.

Minichiello, W. E., & Baer, L. (1994). Managed care: Our behavioral imperative. *Behavior Therapist, 17,* 22.

Montgomery, S. A., & Asberg, M. (1979). A new depression scale designed to be sensitive to change. *British Journal of Psychiatry, 134,* 382–389.

Nelson, J. C., Mazure, C., Quinlan, D. M., & Jatlow, P. I. (1984). Drug-responsive symptoms in melancholia. *Archives of General Psychiatry, 41,* 663–668.

Nelson, J. C., Mazure, C. M., & Jatlow, P. I. (1990). Does melancholia predict response in major depression? *Journal of Affective Disorders, 18,* 157–165.

Newman, F. L., & Ciarlo, J. A. (1994). Criteria for selecting psychological instruments for treatment out-come assessment. In M. E. Maruish (Ed.), *The use of psychological testing for treatment planning and out-comes assessment* (pp. 98–108). Mahwah, NJ: Lawrence Erlbaum Associates.

NIMH Consensus Development Conference Statement. (1985). Mood disorders: Pharmacologic preven-tion of recurrences. *American Journal of Psychiatry, 142,* 469–476.

Orleans, C. T., George, L. K., Houpt, J. L., & Brodie, H. K. H. (1985). How primary care physicians treat psy-chiatric disorders: A national survey of family practitioners. *American Journal of Psychiatry, 142,* 52–57.

Paykel, E. S. (1979). Predictors of treatment response. In E. S. Paykel & A. Coppen (Eds.), *Psychophar-macology of affective disorders* (pp. 193–220). Oxford, England: Oxford University Press.

Petrie, K., & Abell, W. (1994). Responses of parasuicides to a computerized interview. *Computers in Human Behavior, 10,* 415–418.

Petty, R. (1992). The depressed alcoholic: Clinical features and medical managment. *General Hospital Psy-chiatry, 14,* 458–464.

Price, L. H., Nelson, J. C., Charney, D. S., & Quinlan, D. M. (1984). The clinical utility of family history for the diagnosis of melancholia. *Journal of Nervous and Mental Disease, 172,* 5–11.

Potts, M. K., Daniels, M., Burnam, M. A., & Wells, K. B. (1990). A structured interview version of the Hamilton Depression Rating Scale: Evidence of reliability and versatility of administration. *Journal of Psychiatry Research, 24,* 335–350.

Quitkin, F. M., McGrath, P. J., Stewart, J. W., Ocepek-Welikson, K., Taylor, B. P., Nunes, E., Deliyannides, D., Agosti, V., Donovan, S. J., Petkova, E., & Klein, D. F. (1996). Chronological milestones to guide drug change. When should clinicians switch antidepressants? *Archives of General Psychiatry, 53,* 785–792.

Ramos-Brieva, J. A., & Cordero-Villafafila, A. (1988). A new validation of the Hamilton Rating Scale for Depression. *Journal of Psychiatric Research, 22,* 21–28.

Rehm, L. P., & O'Hara, M. W. (1985). Item characteristics of the Hamilton Rating Scale for Depression. *Journal of Psychiatric Research, 19,* 31–41.

Reynolds, W. M. (1991). *Adult Suicidal Ideation Questionnaire: Professional manual.* Odessa, FL: Psychological Assessment Resources.

Reynolds, W. M., & Kobak, K. A. (1995a). *Hamilton Depression Inventory: A self-report version of the Hamilton Depression Rating Scale. Professional manual.* Odessa, FL: Psychological Assessment Resources.

Reynolds, W. M., & Kobak, K. A. (1995b). Development and validation of the Hamilton Depression Inventory: A self-report version of the Hamilton Depression Rating Scale. *Psychological Assessment 7,* 472–483.

Reynolds, W. M., & Kobak, K. A. (1998). *Reynolds Depression Screening Inventory: Professional manual.* Odessa, FL: Psychological Assessment Resources.

Reynolds, W. R., Kobak, K. A., & Greist, J. H. (1992a, August). *Diagnostic utility of the Hamilton Depression Rating Scale.* Paper presented at the annual meeting of the American Psychological Association, Washington, DC.

Reynolds, W. R., Kobak, K. A., & Greist, J. H. (1992b, June). *Suicidal behavior in outpatients with panic disorder, obsessive compulsive disorder and major depression.* Paper presented at the International Conference on Suicidal Behavior, Pittsburgh, PA.

Reynolds, W. M., Kobak, K. A., & Greist, J. H. (1993, March). *The Adult Suicidal Ideation Questionnaire: Psychometric characteristics with psychiatric outpatients.* Paper presented at the annual meeting of the Society for Personality Assessment, San Francisco, CA.

Reynolds, W. M., Kobak, K. A., Greist, J. H., Jefferson, J. W., & Tollefson, G. D. (1993, May). *Fluoxetine versus imipramine: Changes in suicidal ideation.* Paper presented at the annual meeting of the American Psychiatric Association, San Francisco, CA.

Riskind, J. H., Beck, A. T., Brown, G., & Steer, R. A. (1987). Taking the measure of anxiety and depression: Validity of the reconstructed Hamilton scales. *Journal of Nervous and Mental Disease, 175,* 474–479.

Rosenberg, M. (1965). *Society and the adolescent self-image.* Princeton, NJ: Princeton University Press.

Rost, K., Smith, R., Matthews, D. B., & Guise, B. (1994). The deliberate misdiagnosis of major depression in primary care. *Archives of Family Medicine, 3,* 333–337.

Rush, A. J., Kovacs, M., Beck, A. T., Weissenburger, J., & Hollon, S. D. (1981). Differential effects of cognitive therapy and pharmacotherapy on depressive symptoms. *Journal of Affective Disorders, 3,* 221–229.

Schade, C. P., Jones, E. R., & Wittlin, B. J. (1998). A ten-year review of the validity and clinical utility of depression screening. *Psychiatric Services, 49,* 55–61.

Schulberg, H. C., & Burns, B.J. (1988). Mental disorders in primary care: Epidemiologic, diagnostic, and treatment research directions. *General Hospital Psychiatry, 10,* 79–87.

Shapiro, S., Skinner, E. A., Kessler, L. G., Von Korff, M., German, P. S., Tischler, G. L., Leaf, P. J., Benham, L., Cottler, L., & Regier, D. A. (1984). Utilization of health and mental health services. Three epidemiologic catchment area sites. *Archives of General Psychiatry, 41,* 971–978.

Skinner, H. A., & Allen, B. A. (1983). Does the computer make a difference? Computerized versus face-to-face versus self-report assessment of alcohol, drug, and tobacco use. *Journal of Consulting and Clinical Psychology, 51,* 267–275.

Spitzer, R. L., Endicott, J., & Robins, E. (1978). Research diagnostic criteria: Rationale and reliability. *Archives of General Psychiatry, 35,* 773–782.

Spitzer, R. L., Kroenke, K., Linzer, M., Hanh, S. R., Williams, J. B. W., deGruy, F. V., Brody, D., & Davies, M. (1995). Health-related quality of life in primary care patients with mental disorders. Results from the PRIME–MD 1000 study. *Journal of the American Medical Association, 274,* 1511–1517.

Spitzer, R. L., Williams, J. B. W., Kroenke, K., Linzer, M., deGruy, F. V., Hanh, S. R., Brody, D., & Johnson, J. G. (1994). Utility of a new procedure for diagnosing mental disorders in primary care: The PRIME–MD 1000 study. *Journal of the American Medical Association, 272,* 1749–1756.

Spitzer, R. L., Williams, J. B., Gibbon, M., & First, M. B. (1988). *Structured Clinical Interview for DSM–III–R.* New York: New York Psychiatric Institute.

Tamburrino, M. B., Nagel, R. W., Lynch, D. J., Smith, M. K., Ali, O. M., & Narayan, R. A. (1997, May). *Depression screening: Ham–D compared with PRIME–MD.* Paper presented at the American Psychiatric Association 150th Annual Meeting, San Diego, CA.

Teri, L., & Lewinsohn, P. M. (1982). Modification of the pleasant and unpleasant events schedules for use with the elderly. *Journal of Consulting and Clinical Psychology, 50,* 444–445.

Thase, M. E., Carpenter, L., Kupfer, D. J., & Frank, E. (1991). Atypical depression: Diagnostic and pharmacologic controversies. *Psychopharmacology Bulletin, 27,* 17–22.

Thase, M. E., Hersen, M., Bellack, A. S., Himmelhoch, J. M., & Kupfer, D. J. (1983). Validation of a Hamilton subscale for endogenomorphic depression. *Journal of Affective Disorders, 5,* 267–278.

Turner, C. F., Ku, L., Rogers, S. M., Lindberg, L. D., Pleck, J. H., & Sonenstein, F. L. (1998). Adolescent sexual behavior, drug use, and violence: Increased reporting with computer survey technology. *Science, 280,* 867–873.

Weissman, M. M., Broadhead, W. E., Olfson, M., Sheehan, D. V., Hoven, C., Conolly, P., Fireman, B. H., Farber, L., Blacklow, R. S., Higgins, E. S., & Leon, A. C. (1998). A diagnostic aid for detecting (DSM–IV) mental disorders in primary care. *General Hospital Psychiatry, 20,* 1–11.

Weissman, M. M., Klerman, G. L., Markowitz, J. S., & Ouellette, R. (1989). Suicidal ideation and suicide attempts in panic disorder and attacks. *New England Journal of Medicine, 321,* 1209–1214.

Wells, K. B., Stewart, A., Hays, R. D., Burnam, M. A., Rogers, W., Daniels, M., Berry, S., Greenfield, S., & Ware, J. (1989). The functioning and well-being of depressed patients: Results from the Medical Outcomes Study. *Journal of the American Medical Association, 262,* 914–919.

Whisman, M. A., Strosahl, K., Fruzzetti, A. E., Schmaling, K. B., Jacobson, N. S., & Miller, D. M. (1989). A structured interview version of the Hamilton Rating Scale for Depression: Reliability and validity. *Psychological Assessment, 1,* 238–241.

Wiggins, J. S. (1973). *Personality and prediction: Principles of personality assessment.* Reading, MA: Addison-Wesley.

Williams, J. B. W. (1988). A structured interview guide for the Hamilton Depression Rating Scale. *Archives of General Psychiatry, 45,* 742–747.

Zimmerman, M., Black, D. W., & Coryell, W. (1989). Diagnostic criteria for melancholia: The comparative validity of DSM–III and DSM–III–R. *Archives of General Psychiatry, 46,* 361–368.

Zimmerman, M., Coryell, W., Pfohl, B., & Stangl, D. (1986). Validity of the Hamilton Endogenous Subscale: An independent replication. *Psychiatry Research, 18,* 209–215.

Zung, W. W. K. (1965). A self-rating depression scale. *Archives of General Psychiatry, 12,* 63–70.

Tools to Improve the Detection and Treatment of Depression in Primary Care

Teresa L. Kramer
G. Richard Smith
University of Arkansas for Medical Sciences

Despite 35 years of focused attention on detection and treatment, depression in its various forms continues to plague our society. In 1996, the World Health Organization, Harvard School of Public Health, and the World Bank ranked depression as the fourth leading cause of disease burden worldwide. By the year 2020, depression is projected to be the second leading cause of disease burden for both men and women, behind only ischemic heart disease. Unipolar depression was already identified in 1990 as the leading cause of disability in the world (Murray & Lopez, 1996).

Depression affects physical, role, and social functioning; leads to a disproportionately large number of bed days; results in high medical utilization rates; and in the United States alone, is associated with more than 20,000 suicides annually (American Psychiatric Association, 1994; Greenberg, Stiglin, Finkelstein, & Berndt, 1993a, 1993b; Kessler & Frank, 1997; Kouzis & Eaton, 1994; Mintz, Mintz, Arruda, & Hwang, 1992; Von Korff, Ormel, Katon, & Lin, 1992; Wells et al., 1989). Wells et al. (1989) also found that the only chronic medical condition comparable to depression in lower functioning and patient well-being was current heart conditions. Rost, Fortney, Zhang, and Smith (in press) found that 28% of depressed primary care patients in their study contemplated suicide without once discussing depression with a health professional. Greenberg et al. (1993a) estimated the economic cost to this country for all forms of depression to be approximately $44 billion annually. Of this estimate, 85%, or roughly $38 billion, is for major depressive disorder (MDD). This amount does not include the adverse effects of pain and suffering or other quality-of-life issues.

There is growing evidence that rates of depression are increasing while age of onset is decreasing (American Psychiatric Association, 1994; Keller, Lavori, Beardslee, Wunder, & Ryan, 1991; Klerman & Weissman, 1989, 1992; Madianos & Stefanis, 1992; Regier et al., 1993; Robins & Regier, 1991). Currently, 1 in 20 people experiences major depression in any given year (Bland, 1997). The lifetime risk for MDD is 10% to 25% for women and 5% to 12% for men. The point prevalence of depression in primary care settings has been estimated from 5% to 9% for women and from 2% to 3% for men (American Psychiatric Association, 1994).

PROBLEMS IN DETECTING AND TREATING
DEPRESSION IN PRIMARY CARE

Although the detection and management of depression have traditionally fallen within the realm of the mental health setting, changes in the structure and financing of medical care have increased the need for addressing this disorder in primary care settings. Generally, more than half of all patients who receive some type of mental health care do so in a primary care setting (Wells et al., 1989). Consequently, primary care physicians are often the point of first contact for most emotionally distressed patients. Findings demonstrate, however, that there is a serious problem with detection, diagnosis, and treatment of this pervasive disorder within this setting.

For example, only one half to one third of primary care patients are recognized by their physicians as depressed (Jones, Badger, Ficken, Leeper, & Anderson, 1987; Linn & Yager, 1984; Perez-Stable, Miranda, Munoz, & Ying, 1990; Rost et al., 1998; Zung, Magill, Moore, & George, 1983). Underrecognition has remained a constant phenomenon since the 1980s (Coyne, Schwenk, & Fechner-Bates, 1995; Keller et al., 1992; Klerman & Weissman, 1989). Rost et al. (1998) found that 32% of primary care patients with current major depression went undetected for up to 1 year. They also found these patients were more likely than those detected to report more emotional and physical role limitations and higher disability days.

Of those who are diagnosed, the same one third to one half are inaccurately diagnosed (Katon, 1987; Ormel, Koeter, van den Brink, & van de Willige, 1991; Rost, Smith, Matthews, & Guise, 1994; Wells et al., 1989). One study indicated that two-thirds of patients with depression who commit suicide have visited a physician in the month immediately preceding the suicide (Barraclough, Bunch, Nelson, & Sainsbury, 1974). There are also numerous studies published that suggest that depressed patients with comorbid physical problems may have poorer outcomes over time (e.g., Covinsky, Fortinsky, Palmer, Kresevic, & Landefeld, 1997; Katon, 1987; Katzelnick, Kobak, Greist, Jefferson, & Henk, 1997; Von Korff et al., 1992).

Even when patients are accurately diagnosed as depressed, treatment may be lacking or insufficient. For example, Zung and King (1983) found that of identified depressed patients who did receive treatment, 64% improved over a 4-week period, but that many of these identified patients were not treated. Jones et al. (1987) found that inappropriate treatment was given in one fifth of the cases in their study. Wells, Katon, Rogers, and Camp (1994) found that 39% of patients taking an antidepressant medication used an inappropriately low dose. Furthermore, less than one third of depressed outpatients used antidepressant medications at all. In yet another study, Katon et al. (Katon, Von Korff, Lin, Bush, & Ormel, 1992; Katon et al., 1997) found that the visit frequency of usual care of primary care patients is far below that recommended in the Agency for Health Care Policy and Research (AHCPR) Depression Guidelines (Depression Guideline Panel, 1993a). Rost, Williams, Wherry, and Smith (1995) found that only 11% of depressed patients received pharmacologic treatment concordant with AHCPR guidelines. These findings are notable because Rost et al. (in press) also found that subjects receiving AHCPR guideline-concordant treatment between the index visit and follow-up were significantly more likely to be in remission at follow-up than subjects who did not. In this same study, 80% of depressed individuals visited a primary care physician during the course of a year, yet only 40% of those identified received treatment; of those who remained undetected, 45.8% reported suicidal ideation during the course of the year following baseline. Likewise,

Linn and Yager (1980) found that only 12% of the patients in their medical record sample received any type of treatment for depression. Eisenberg (1992) found that only about one in three people with major depression receive antidepressant medications and specific psychotherapies, in spite of the fact that these treatments have been shown to be efficacious.

Indications suggest that both the patient and the provider contribute to this problem of underdetection and undertreatment. Patients may not recognize the symptoms and report only physical manifestations, underestimate the severity, be restricted to treatment access, not follow treatment when recommended, be reluctant to see a mental health provider because of stigma, or lack adequate insurance (Depression Guideline Panel, 1993b). Providers have other reasons for misdiagnosing or not detecting depression. For instance, they may not have received adequate education about psychiatric diagnoses in medical school or not have enough time to evaluate and treat depression (Brody & Larson, 1992; Rost, Humphrey, & Kelleher, 1994; Rost, Smith, Matthews, & Guise, 1994). Physicians may also use alternate diagnoses (e.g., fatigue/malaise, insomnia, headache or anxiety) due to concerns about the stigma associated with depression, patient resistance to being "labeled" as depressed, fear of future reprisals or nonreimbursement from third-party payers, or some combination of these (Rost, Smith, Matthews, & Guise, 1994).

In summary, although primary care physicians should be our best source for early detection and effective treatment of depression, previous research has demonstrated otherwise. Katon et al. (1995) showed that a multifaceted primary care intervention improves not only adherence to psychotropic medications but also satisfaction with care. The purpose of this chapter is to present several tools to assist in the detection and assessment of treatment outcomes for depressed patients in a primary care setting. Development, uses, strengths, and limitations of these tools are discussed and recommendations are provided for interventions.

PRELIMINARY CONSIDERATIONS

Before proceeding with a description of our assessment tools for depression, it is important to provide specific information about the clinical features of this disorder. Because patients with mental health problems may present with a variety of complaints in a primary care setting, depression may not always be the most obvious diagnosis. This information, coupled with the self-report measures discussed in this chapter, can help the provider in identifying depression in his or her setting.

Major Depressive Disorder

Increasing the rates of detection and recommending appropriate treatments for depression in primary care patients are pivotal to improving outcomes for patients. Detection involves knowledge of the disorder, including the diagnostic criteria and key features.

MDD is an episodic condition lasting 6 months or longer if untreated. The disorder can occur as a single episode or recur multiple times during an individual's lifetime. Recurrences may occur at any time and, in severe cases, recurrences may be as frequent as once per year. Patients with MDD have a 2-week or longer history of depressed mood or loss of interest and pleasure in life. This nearly constant depressed mood is associated with a number of symptoms such as weight change, sleep difficulties, psychomotor agitation or retardation, fatigue, feelings of worthlessness, impaired concentration, and/or thoughts of death or suicide. A description of the *DSM–IV* criteria for MDD is presented later in this chapter.

Disease-Specific Considerations

There are two general kinds of outcome domains in mental health—generic and disease-specific. The first is relevant to all patients, regardless of their presenting problems or diagnostic history, and may include medical or psychiatric problems. The second is relevant to a specific health condition, such as depression, diabetes, or asthma. An advantage of disease-specific measures—the topic of this chapter—is that they are directly relevant to clinical care. In other words, screening instruments for a specific disorder, such as depression, guide the clinician toward additional assessment methods, whereas more in-depth diagnostic tools can provide feedback regarding initial symptom severity or, later, the outcomes of care.

At present, there is a wide choice of disorder-specific measures for depression with little consensus on which measure is best. Most of these measures focus on symptom severity, sentinel indicators, and/or general functioning. Recent measures of symptom severity have been based on the *DSM–IV* and include sentinel indicators for depression such as suicidal intentions and attempts, as well as medication side effects. Functioning measures for depression include areas such as social relationships that are not adequately assessed by generic social functioning measures, number of bed days, and amount of medical utilization.

There are also a number of comorbid conditions known to affect the presence, severity, and prognosis of depressive symptoms. These conditions are covered later when case-mix variables are discussed.

New Instruments to Detect Depression

Adequate screening of patients, knowledge of diagnostic criteria, information about appropriate treatment interventions, and efficient delivery of those services were all identified by the AHCPR (Depression Guideline Panel, 1993a, 1993b) as necessary for significant reductions in depressive symptoms, improvement in functioning, and overall decreases in medical care costs. These guidelines point out the need for screeners and updated diagnostic interviews that promote an increase in detection by identifying high-risk patients. Those health care professionals responsible for their care may then further evaluate identified patients. However, in order for screeners to be widely incorporated into clinical care, they should be brief, easily scored, and sensitive across diverse patient populations. Many instruments meet only a few of these criteria (Beck, Ward, Mendelson, Mock, & Erbaugh, 1961; Boyd, Weissman, Thompson, & Myers, 1982; Hamilton, 1960; Radloff, 1977; Robins, Helzer, Croughan, & Ratcliff, 1981; Rost, Burnam, & Smith, 1993; Rush, Gullion, Basco, Jarrett, & Trivedi, 1996; Spitzer, Williams, Gibbon, & First, 1992; Zimmerman, Coryell, Corenthal, & Wilson, 1986; Zung, 1965).

The result of AHCPR's recommendations was the development of a new set of instruments to improve detection and diagnosis of depressive disorders and to measure patient outcomes. Researchers at the University of Arkansas for Medical Sciences

(UAMS), along with experts from RAND Corporation, created three of these instruments: the Screener, the D–ARK, and the DOM. The Screener consists of either two or three items and is designed to identify patients at high-risk for a depressive disorder. The researchers also developed an 11-item instrument for detecting and diagnosing major depression called the Depression Arkansas Scale (D–ARK). The third tool is a comprehensive module; called the Depression Outcomes Module (DOM), it incorporates the Screener and the D–ARK, as well as a patient baseline assessment, a clinician baseline assessment, a patient follow-up assessment, and a medical record review.

Each of these tools assesses the presence of depressive symptoms primarily from the patient's perspective. They have been developed to be user-friendly and related only to depression, not to any other psychiatric disorders. They are also grounded in scientific methodology with established psychometric properties. Each has been used in a variety of settings, including primary care, to detect, monitor, and improve the care of depressed patients.

THE DEPRESSION SCREENER

The Depression Screener, consisting of two or three items, depending on the version used, will identify 83% to 94% of general medical patients and 89% to 93% of mental health care patients who have had a psychiatric diagnosis of a depressive disorder within the previous year (Rost et al., 1993). Because some patients will screen positive without having the disorder, the actual diagnosis of a depressive disorder requires further evaluation by a clinician or through the administration of some other diagnostic tool. The Screener is particularly useful for primary care providers to assist in the detection of depression. In a study of 631 patients in 21 rural primary care practices, 248 (39.3%) were identified as being at high risk for depression using the Screener (Rost et al., 1995). Figures from other primary care specialties range from 12% to 19% (Booth, Stewart, & Kramer, 1997; Stewart, Booth, & Kramer, 1997).

Development of the Screener

One approach to increasing detection of depression is to identify high-risk patients who should be more intensively evaluated. Requirements for a screener include: (a) high sensitivity to current major depression and (b) positive predictive value that would insure that at least one third of those testing positive at the first stage of screening would subsequently test positive at the second stage (Burnam, Wells, Leake, & Landsverk, 1988).

Developers of the Screener used data from the Epidemiological Catchment Area (ECA) research project, in which the Diagnostic Interview Schedule (DIS; Robins et al., 1981) and *DSM–III–R* diagnostic information were used to assess for the presence of depression (among other psychiatric diagnoses). Because questions regarding depressive symptoms were asked in only three of the five sites, developers used only data obtained from Los Angeles, Baltimore, MD, and Piedmont, NC. The groups were also divided into two subsamples, consisting of individuals who utilized outpatient services for a medical problem in the preceding 6 months and individuals who utilized outpatient services for a mental health problem in the preceding 6 months.

TABLE 14.1
Items Constituting the Two- and Three-Item Screeners
for Depressive Disorders and Scoring

Source	Item Number	Two-Item	Three-Item	Item Content
DIS072	1	X	X	In the past year, have you had 2 weeks or more during which you felt sad, blue or depressed, or when you lost all interest or pleasure in things that you usually cared about or enjoyed? (YES = 1; NO = 0)
DIS073	2a	X	X	Have you had 2 years or more in your life when you felt depressed or sad most days, even if you felt okay sometimes? (YES — ASK2b; NO = 0 — SKIP 2b)
CES–D	2b			Have you felt depressed or sad much of the time in the past year? (YES = 1; NO = 0)
CES–D1	3		X	How much of the time during the past week did you feel depressed? (LESS THAN ONE DAY = 0; 1–2 DAYS = 1; 3–4 DAYS = 2; 5–7 DAYS = 3)

Scoring

Three-Item Screener: Either DIS072 = 1 or (DIS073a = 1 and DIS073b = 1) in the past year, plus CESD1 = 1 or more as defined above. Two-Item Screener: Either DIS072 = 1 or (DIS073a = 1 and DIS073b = 1) in the past year.

Note. From Rost, Burnam, and Smith (1993). Adapted with permission.

Building on an earlier study (i.e., Burnam et al., 1988), Rost et al. (1993) used stepwise multiple logistic regression analysis to select the best subset of the original eight items for the Screener. Two of the original eight items were from the DIS, and the remaining six were from the Center for Epidemiological Studies Depression Scale (CES-D; Radloff, 1977). The research team reviewed the logistic regression coefficients and removed the items that contributed least to the accurate prediction of those at high-risk for depression. The result was a three-item Screener consisting of two DIS items and an item from the CES–D, regarding how much of the time during the past week respondents felt depressed. A two-item Screener consisting of questions 1 and 2 was developed with sensitivity and specificity established as well.

Questions composing both the two- and three-item Screener are listed in Table 14.1. As evidenced, both Screeners include *DSM–III* criteria. DIS criteria reflected *DSM–III* definitions because the ECA database used in this study predated the release of *DSM–III–R*; however, *DSM–III–R* as well as *DSM–IV* criteria for depressive disorders are very similar to *DSM–III* criteria.

Basic Psychometric Properties

The sensitivity of a screener is the proportion of true positive cases that the screener correctly detects, that is, the percentage of individuals identified as depressed who are truly depressed. The specificity of a screener is the proportion of true negative cases that it correctly detects, that is, the percentage of individuals who are not identified as depressed who truly are not depressed. The positive predictive value (PPV) is defined as the proportion of positive screenings that correctly identifies those at

TABLE 14.2
Psychometric Properties of Two- and Three-Item Depression Screeners

	Total				Mental				Medical			
	Sens	Spec	PPV	NPV	Sens	Spec	PPV	NPV	Sens	Spec	PPV	NPV
Two-item Screener												
Los Angeles	91	91	23	99	93	78	39	99	94	90	24	99
Baltimore	83	92	21	99	92	71	27	99	92	92	17	99
Piedmont	90	93	14	99	89	81	23	99	92	92	17	99
Three-item Screener	81	95	33	99	82	87	49	97	80	95	33	99

Note.   Total = total population; Mental = mental health subsample; Medical = medical subsample; Sens = sensitivity; Spec = specificity; PPV = positive predictive value; NPV = negative predictive value. From Rost, Burnam, and Smith (1993). Adapted with permission.

risk for a depressive disorder. The negative predictive value (NPV) is the proportion of negative screenings that correctly identifies those people who are not at risk for a depressive disorder (Wassertheil-Smoller, 1995).

Table 14.2 shows that nonweighted scoring of three of the items in the original eight-item screener item pool resulted in estimates of 80% to 82% sensitivity and 87% to 95% specificity to a DIS diagnosis of depressive disorder in the last year. (The range reflects variations in the two subsamples of individuals receiving medical versus mental health services in the past 6 months.) Ranges for the PPV indicate that 33% to 49% of patients identified by the Screener as depressed are actually depressed, whereas the NPV indicates that 97% to 99% of patients identified by the Screener as not depressed actually are not.

Basic Interpretive Strategy

When a patient screens positive on the Screener (refer to Table 14.1), it is an indication that he or she may be suffering from a depressive disorder. Development of the Screener was based on criterion for MDD and for dysthymia; therefore, it is impossible to determine, solely on the results of the Screener, whether the patient actually meets criteria for major depression, dysthymia, or a depressive episode of a bipolar affective disorder. The depressive disorder may also coexist with another primary or secondary psychiatric diagnosis, such as substance abuse, psychosis, or dementia, to name a few. In addition, the Screener can only identify the presence of a recent—but not necessarily current—depressive disorder. Therefore, care should be taken to further evaluate the patient's symptoms to rule out other possibilities before treatment is initiated.

Implementation

As a Stand-Alone Instrument.   The two- or three-item depression Screener can be used independently of other measures with significant sensitivity in detecting a depressive disorder. Primary care providers may incorporate the Screener into routine clinical practice to identify patients at risk for depression prior to the clinical interview and/or physical examination. This process will assist the provider in assessing a patient's mental health status and will provide a starting point for interviewing the patient further about his or her emotional functioning. Providers may also use the Screener on an aggregate level to determine the prevalence of depression in their patient population. These data may be helpful in developing treatment guidelines, educating providers about the comorbidity of medical problems and depression in their clinics, and demonstrating the relationship between mental and physical health treatment and outcomes.

With Other Instruments/Procedures.   The two- or three-item depression Screener can also be used in combination with other instruments. In fact, the two-item Screener has long been incorporated into a version of the SF–36 Health Survey (Ware, Snow, Kosinski, & Gandek, 1993), which assesses general physical and mental health status, as well as signaling the provider that the patient may have an increased risk for depression. Clinicians who are interested in investigating treatment effectiveness may also wish to incorporate the Screener into a larger assessment battery to identify patients who are depressed to further evaluate their mental health status and monitor those conditions that affect outcomes. For example, in one primary care setting, providers were interested in the relationship between health status in diabetic patients and presence of a depressive disorder, resulting in a study that assessed diagnostic-specific symptoms of diabetes in combination with a depressive screener. As seen in Table 14.3, patients who screened positive for a depressive disorder reported more diabetic symptoms and worse general functioning on the SF–36 (Stewart et al., 1997). The Screener can also be used in conjunction with the D–ARK and the DOM (as described in the following sections).

Potential Issues in Implementation.   Because the Screener is designed to identify patients at risk for a depressive disorder, the tool can not be used as a final assessment measure. It must be used in combination with a clinical interview or other assessment instruments in order to conclusively determine the diagnosis or rule out

TABLE 14.3
Medical Outcomes Comparing Patients Screening
Positive and Negative for Symptoms of Depression

Group	Depression Screener Positive	Depression Screener Negative	p Value
All patients (n = 300)	18.7%	81.3%	
Follow-up (n = 46)	23.9%	76.1%	
No follow-up (n = 254)	17.7%	82.3%	
SF–36	(n = 56)	(n = 244)	
Diabetes score	2.08		.0001
Physical functioning	43.54	66.95	.0001
Role – physical	25.59	66.29	.0001
Bodily pain	44.59	67.11	.0001
General health	41.73	59.87	.0001
Vitality	33.63	55.46	.0001
Social functioning	50.89	83.25	.0001
Role – emotional	41.07	77.80	.0001

Note.   Reprinted with permission from Center for Outcomes Research and Effectiveness, Little Rock, AR.

other possibilities. For example, the patient may be taking medications that are associated with depressive symptoms.

Guidelines for Decision Making

Figure 14.1 demonstrates the steps to follow when the Screener identifies a potentially depressed patient. As mentioned earlier, patients who screen positive may not meet full criteria for MDD, but instead may have only mild or transient symptoms of a depressive disorder, meet criteria for dysthymia, or be experiencing a depressive episode of bipolar affective disorder. By the same token, there may be some patients who do not screen positive—due to minimization or denial of symptoms on a self-report— who would clearly meet the full criteria of MDD. In most cases, providers would be well advised to follow the algorithm in Fig. 14.1, based on AHCPR guidelines.

Provision of Feedback to Patient

If results on the Screener are positive, feedback to the patient should be provided, particularly if the provider conducts a more formal assessment or administers a second depression instrument. This feedback can consist of a general observation, such as "I noticed on this questionnaire that you've been feeling kind of down lately," to a more specific query, such as, "Your responses indicate you might be feeling somewhat depressed lately. Can you tell me more about that?" Such open-ended statements tend to be less threatening to the patient, and can then lead to a more in-depth discussion of specific symptoms. Again, feedback can be provided as the clinical interview proceeds, in a relationship-building manner.

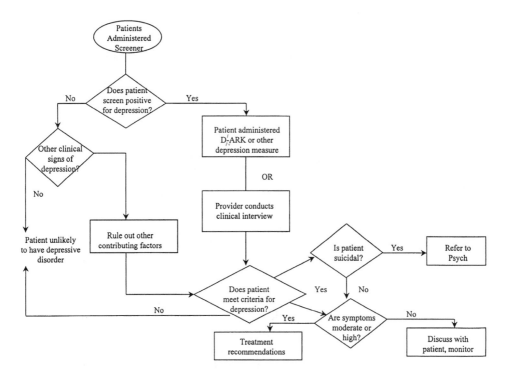

FIG. 14.1.   Evaluation pathway, based on AHCPR guidelines.

Use as an Instrument for Population Monitoring

General Considerations. The Screener can only be used as a tool for generally monitoring changes in a clinical population. Because of its dichotomous approach to a depressive disorder (positive or negative), the Screener is most useful when combined with other measures or aggregated for a patient population. For example, a provider may want to demonstrate changes in the rates of depressive disorder in a patient population over time as a result of an educational intervention to improve the detection of depression in his/her practice. Patients would be assessed for a depressive disorder using the Screener prior to the intervention and again at 2 to 3 months following the intervention. By comparing the results of the Screener to the medical record, a provider could then determine whether the proportion of patients diagnosed had increased as a result of more careful evaluation.

Implementation Issues. Magruder-Habib, Zung, and Feussner (1990) demonstrated that routine use of a depression screener might improve physician recognition of depression and increase initiation of treatment. This is, of course, dependent on the proper use of the Screener and development of specific guidelines within a practice for further assessing and treating such patients. Administration of the Screener will not be helpful to the patient or provider unless the results are integrated into routine practice guidelines.

Strengths and Limitations of Screening in Primary Care Settings

Cost Constraints. Hough et al. (1990) presented two considerations — high sensitivity and cost-effectiveness — in the clinical use of screening scales. High sensitivity is a desirable attribute because it results in the identification of persons needing care. This consideration was one of the primary objectives in developing a screening instrument for depression. Cost-effectiveness is also an issue, particularly in primary care where the average time a provider spends with patients is 13 min (Schappert, 1994). By initially screening only high-risk patients, the Screener helps to identify those who should be further assessed and to what extent, thereby improving care without excessive burden to the provider.

Ease of Use. The Screener takes 1 min to complete and can be filled out by most patients. Because there are only two or three items, scoring can be easily accomplished by office staff within minutes and the chart flagged for cases requiring further attention.

Clinical Utility. As previously indicated, the Screener can detect patients at high risk for a depressive disorder, but contains limited information for providers about the severity, etiology, and prognosis of symptoms. Therefore, use of the Screener should always be considered in conjunction with other assessment tools or provider-initiated assessments and treatment-monitoring protocols.

Summary

Findings from the Medical Outcomes Study (MOS) (Wells, Goldberg, Brook, & Leake, 1988) and others (Greenberg et al., 1993a; Kessler & Frank, 1997; Kouzis & Eaton, 1994; Von Korff et al., 1992) demonstrate that depressed patients report impairment across several domains of general functioning and well-being that are as great as patients with major chronic medical problems such as heart disease (Wells, Rogers, Burnam, Greenfield, & Ware, 1991). In addition, the impairment related to depression may have an effect independent of and additive to problems related to medical conditions, warranting an assessment to better understand which patients have depression co-occurring with their medical diagnosis and how that affects overall outcomes (Booth et al., 1997). Because findings demonstrate that the brief, hand-scored Screener may be useful to identify patients in community, medical, and mental health settings who are at high risk for having recently experienced a depressive disorder, clinicians may wish to incorporate screeners into their batteries to identify patients who are at high risk for comorbid conditions that adversely affect outcomes. This brief Screener provides clinicians with an efficient, inexpensive way to begin this diagnostic process.

THE DEPRESSION–ARKANSAS SCALE (D–ARK)

Although the two- and three-item Screeners increase detection by identifying those patients at high risk for MDD, the Depression–Arkansas Scale (D–ARK) is a tool for both diagnosing depression and evaluating severity of the disorder. This instrument is a brief yet comprehensive and valid self-report measure that is available for use without a fee.

The D–ARK is a tool developed by the Centers for Mental Healthcare Research at the University of Arkansas for Medical Sciences (UAMS). It is designed to diagnose depression based on *DSM-IV* criteria, and to quantify the severity for each of the symptoms. Originally conceptualized as a diagnostic and symptom severity component of the Depression Outcomes Module (DOM), the D–ARK has since been used independently in a number of settings. As a result of its performance, it has been endorsed by the Foundation for Accountability (FACCT Staff, 1996) and the Scientific Advisory Board of the Medical Outcomes Trust as part of their initiatives to identify state-of-the-science measures for MDD. The Outcomes Roundtable has also endorsed the D–ARK scale as a reliable and valid measure to compare the performance of healthcare systems and services in the treatment of MDD.

Development of the D–ARK

Several scales have been developed and validated to diagnose MDD and/or depression severity. However, none meet all the prescribed criteria for a multipurpose, inexpensive, user-friendly measure (Smith et al., 1998). For example, the depression section of the Structured Clinical Interview for the *DSM-III-R* (SCID; Spitzer et al., 1992) is brief, but requires administration by a trained clinician and has not been updated for *DSM-IV* criteria. The Diagnostic Interview Schedule (DIS; Robins et al., 1981) can assess for caseness and does measure severity, but contains 44 items and requires trained interviewers. The Inventory to Diagnose Depression (IDD; Zimmerman et al., 1986) assesses for symptom severity and caseness, has 22 items, but is only available for a fee. The Beck Depression Inventory (BDI; Beck et al., 1961), the Hamilton Depression Rating Scale (HDRS; Hamilton, 1960), and the Center for Epidemiologic Studies Depression Scale (CES-D; Radloff, 1977) assess severity, but not caseness, and are somewhat lengthy (Boyd et al., 1982). The Inventory of Depressive Symptomatology (IDS; Rush et al., 1996) is a 30-item scale measuring depression severity and incorporating *DSM-IV* criteria. There are two forms currently available, the IDS-C (to be completed by the clinician) and the IDS-SR (a self-report instrument to be completed by the patient). Despite its strong psychometric properties and availability to the public, the IDS does not assess caseness and is somewhat lengthy.

The D-ARK was developed using 20 items. (See Appendix A for the scoring algorithm and Table 14.4 for the items.) Following administration of these items to 44

TABLE 14.4
Comparison Between the D-ARK and *DSM-IV* Criteria for Major Depression

D-ARK Items	DSM-IV Criteria
1. How often in the past 4 weeks have you felt depressed, blue or in low spirits for most of the day?	Depressed mood. Depressed mood (sometimes irritability in children and adolescents) most of the day, nearly every day.
2. How often in the past 4 weeks did you have days in which you experienced little or no pleasure in most of your activities?	Loss of interest/pleasure. Markedly diminished interest or pleasure in almost all activities most of the day, nearly every day (as indicated either by subjective account or observation by others of apathy most of the time).
3. How often in the past 4 weeks has your appetite been either less than usual or greater than usual?	Weight/appetite change.
4. In the past 4 weeks, have you gained or lost weight without trying to?	Weight/appetite change.
5. How often in the past 4 weeks have you had difficulty sleeping or trouble with sleeping too much?	Insomnia or hypersomnia
6. In the past 4 weeks, has your physical activity been slowed down or speeded up so much that people who know you could notice?	Psychomotor agitation/retardation
7. In the past 4 weeks, have you felt more tired out or less energetic than usual?	Fatigue/loss of energy
8. In the past 4 weeks have you felt worthless or been bothered by feelings of guilt?	Worthlessness
9. In the past 4 weeks, have you had trouble thinking, concentrating, or making decisions?	Difficulty concentrating
10. How often have you thought about death or suicide in the past 4 weeks?	Recurrent thoughts of death/suicide ideation
11. In the past 4 weeks, have you thought about a specific way to commit suicide?	Recurrent thoughts of death/suicide ideation

Note. In order to meet the criteria for major depression, at least 5 of the 11 symptoms must be present during the same period. At least (a) depressed mood or (b) loss of interest or pleasure *must* be present. Symptoms are present most of the day nearly daily for at least 2 weeks. In addition, the symptoms do not meet criteria for a mixed episode and cause clinically significant distress or impairment in social, occupational, or other important areas of functioning. The symptoms are also not due to the direct physiological effects of a substance or a general medical condition and are not better accounted for by bereavement (i.e., after the loss of a loved one). The symptoms persist for longer than 2 months or are characterized by marked functional impairment, morbid preoccupation with worthlessness, suicidal ideation, psychotic symptoms, or psychomotor retardation (American Psychiatric Association, 1994).

subjects, the 9 items that correlated the lowest with the total score were omitted. As a result, the scale is based on 11 items, with responses on symptoms ranging from 1 (*not at all*) to 4 (*a lot*).

Consistency With *DSM–IV* Criteria

As can be seen in Table 14.4, the D–ARK identifies patients whose current symptoms meet the *DSM–IV* criteria for major depression. These criteria were chosen, in part, because the Health Care Financing Administration (HCFA) and many third-party payers accept these criteria for reimbursements.

Psychometric Properties

The D–ARK scale has been designed to provide the highest possible sensitivity and specificity when compared to the depression section of the SCID (Spitzer et al., 1992). Early versions of the scale achieved a 100% sensitivity with a specificity of 77.8% at baseline assessment in a specialty care population (Rost, Smith, Burnam, & Burns, 1992; Smith, Burnam, Burns, Cleary, & Rost, 1994).

In the specialty care patients, test–retest reliability for severity of depressive symptoms measured 1 week apart had a correlation coefficient of $r = 0.87$ ($p < 0.0001$). The two-item measure of suicidality was somewhat less reliable at retest ($r = 0.56$). The internal consistency for the depression severity scale was high (alpha coefficient of .87; Rost et al., 1992; Rush et al., 1996). Item to scale correlation ranges from .53 to .88 ($p \leq .0001$).

Two later studies were conducted to develop and test the validity of the most recent edition of the D–ARK using *DSM–IV* criteria. Using the IDD (Zimmerman et al., 1986), 32 of the original 44 participants, who were mental health patients recruited by their clinicians, were identified as depressed. Their mean D–ARK score was 54.4 ($SD = 17.1$) with a range of 30.2 to 100. The mean score for the nondepressed patients was 15.0 ($SD = 10.5$) with a range from 0 to 36.4. As Table 14.5 shows, the D–ARK demonstrated high internal reliability (Cronbach's alpha = .92) and a high correlation with the IDD criterion measure (kappa = .89). There was also a strong and significant relationship between the severity measure of the IDD and the D–ARK ($r = .89$; $n = 38$; $p \leq .001$).

In the second study, 54 participants were recruited: 22 from three hospital-based clinics at the Veterans Administration Medical Center (VAMC) in Little Rock, Arkansas; 21 from the Adult Outpatient Clinic of the Department of Psychiatry at UAMS; and 11 nonpatients. A total of 29 met criteria for depression based on the SCID, with a mean score on the D–ARK of 56.4 ($SD = 14.7$) and a range from 30.3 to 87.9. The mean score for nondepressed patients was 13.8 ($SD = 9.8$), with a range from 0 to 33. The D–ARK continued to demonstrate high reliability, as shown in Table 14.5 (Cronbach's alpha = .90; $n = 54$), and a 94% concordance rate with the SCID. A correlation of .94 ($n = 24$; $p < .001$) was obtained between the IDD and the D–ARK measures of severity.

D–ARK Scoring

The scoring algorithm has recently been revised. (See Appendix A for the scoring algorithm.) Basically, the D–ARK is scored for the presence (1) or absence (0) of major depression. The D–ARK also provides a severity measure ranging from 0 to 100, with 100 being the most severe.

TABLE 14.5
Validity of the D–ARK

	Preliminary Study (n = 44)	Replication Study (n = 54)
Internal reliability	.92	.90
Correlation with IDD	.89	.94
Severity		
IDD case identification		
Sensitivity	.91	1.00
Specificity	.83	.81
PPV	.94	.67
NPV	.77	1.00
Kappa	.72	.70
Concordance rates with IDD	89%	52%
SCID case identification		
Sensitivy	—	.93
Specificity	—	.96
PPV	—	.96
NPV	—	.92
Kappa	—	.89
Concordance rates with SCID	—	94%

Note. Data from the Center for Outcomes Research, and Effectiveness.

Basic Interpretive Strategy

The D–ARK provides information as to the presence of major depression in adult patients, as well as severity of individual *DSM–IV* symptoms and a total severity score.
Because the sensitivity of the D–ARK is so high, most patients with depression can be
accurately detected with this instrument. Detection requires presence of at least one
of the first two symptoms (i.e., depressed mood and/or loss of interest or pleasure) in
addition to three more symptoms (i.e., weight/appetite change; insomnia or
hypersomnia; psychomotor agitation/retardation; fatigue/loss of energy; worthlessness; difficulty concentrating; recurrent thoughts of death/suicide ideation). Although cut points have not been identified to establish mild, moderate, or severe
symptoms, it is reasonable to assume that a score of over 70 suggests severe impairment. Providers should also check the two suicidal items on the D–ARK (questions
10 and 11) whenever the instrument is administered.

Implementation

As a Stand-Alone Instrument. The D–ARK differentiates between major depression and other depressive disorders. Although this screener can be used as a baseline
assessment (as it is with the DOM), it can also stand alone to be used in the primary
care setting to detect MDD. When used in conjunction with a follow-up evaluation,
levels of symptom severity, social functioning, and bed days can be compared with
patient baseline responses.

Independently, the D–ARK can be administered with minimal patient burden in
primary care or mental health settings, in person, by mail, or over the telephone. Responses to individual items can be examined immediately by the clinical staff and/or
provider and noted for further evaluation.

The scoring of the D–ARK does require some computational effort, but can be incorporated into a format that facilitates scoring and reporting. In addition, efforts are currently underway by the authors of this chapter to develop a web site where providers can enter the D–ARK responses of a patient and immediately receive an individualized report. If used in the health care setting, the instrument should be scored and reviewed by a clinical specialist prior to the patient leaving the office. If the instrument is used as a screening tool or follow-up assessment over the telephone, personnel should be provided with specific instructions to respond to patients who indicate they are depressed and/or are experiencing suicidal ideation.

With Other Instruments/Procedures. The D–ARK Scale can be administered with generic measures of mental or physical health, such as the SF–36 (Ware et al., 1993) and/or with other tools designed to assess diagnostic-specific symptoms of a medical condition. In this manner, an individual patient's progress can be assessed as well as aggregate patient responses to treatment. The D–ARK Scale has also been included in the Depression Outcomes Module (DOM; Smith et al., 1994), which, in addition to baseline caseness and severity of depression, measures types of care, outcomes of care, and patient characteristics for case-mix or risk adjustment.

Commonly Used Adjuncts. In the primary care setting, a system may be developed for patients to complete the three-item Screener described earlier. If this screening is positive, patients may complete the D–ARK. If results of the D–ARK indicate the presence of depression, the provider should inquire further into the patient's mental health status and initiate appropriate treatment recommendations.

If the D–ARK is being used in conjunction with the Depression Outcomes Module (DOM), additional questions will be asked pertaining to general health status, number of bed days, sociodemographic characteristics, and psychiatric history. This will provide a very in-depth profile of the patient, which can then be used for diagnostic and prognostic considerations.

Potential Issues in Implementation. The D–ARK can be administered to all patients in a practice or a particular health care plan as part of a periodic health status assessment to differentiate major depression from other depressive disorders. This instrument can be used as a baseline assessment (as it is with the DOM). It can also stand alone to be used in the primary care setting to detect major depression so that providers have accurate information about the prevalence of depression in their settings to further identify appropriate treatment approaches and potential costs for these treatments. In addition, the D–ARK can be used in conjunction with a patient follow-up assessment to determine the effectiveness of treatment and estimate costs for such improvements.

Guidelines for Decision Making

To assess diagnostic status, remission, and relapse in an accountability-oriented measurement system, the following need to be obtained:

1. The treatment diagnosis from the clinical setting.
2. A measurement system that generates diagnosis near the time of initiation of treatment.
3. Diagnostic status at follow-up, usually at 3 or 6 months.

Once a patient has been identified as depressed through administration and scoring of the D–ARK, his or her psychiatric status can be formally determined through a clinical interview. In particular, patient responses to individual items, especially the two pertaining to suicidality, should be further investigated so that an appropriate treatment plan and/or referral can be initiated. Thereafter, patient symptoms can be assessed at regular intervals to ascertain the degree of improvement.

Based on AHCPR guidelines, a decision tree for treatment has been developed for use in primary care by clinicians and researchers at UAMS. As shown in Fig. 14.2, the guidelines call for adequate screening and evaluation followed by appropriate treatment in the form of medication and/or psychotherapy by a generalist or specialist. Various levels of treatment (e.g., hospitalization) may also be recommended depending on the patient's symptom severity.

Provision of Feedback to the Patient

The D–ARK is self-administered and easily scored. As with the Screener, providers can discuss item responses with patients as part of the clinical interview. If the D–ARK is administered over time, it can be used as a way of checking in with the patient as treatment proceeds.

Use as an Instrument for Treatment Monitoring

Wells et al. (1988) stressed the importance of a program of systematic review of the treatment actually received by depressed patients in a wide variety of settings. The most commonly used indicators for disease progression of MDD are remission, relapse, severity reduction, and absence or reduction in suicidal ideation (Depression

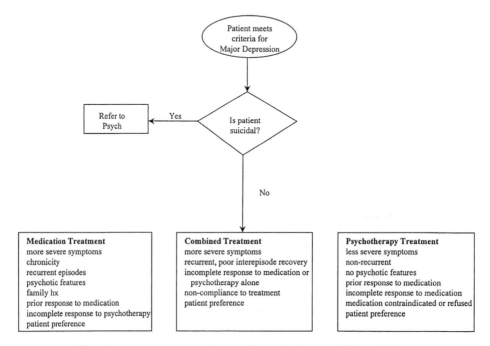

FIG. 14.2.   Acute treatment phase pathway, based on AHCPR guidelines.

Guideline Panel, 1993b). The D–ARK can provide information on all of these indicators in an efficient and timely manner.

Because the D–ARK has only recently been revised, information on the reliable change index is not yet available. However, earlier revisions did show sensitivity to clinical change. For example, in an investigation of remission of depression at follow-up (as assessed by patient reports and the SCID), it has been found to be 67% sensitive and 73% specific to the disorder (Smith et al., 1998). The measure of treatment and case-mix variables as well as disease severity was accurate enough to discriminate between patients who received medication at therapeutic levels and those who did not.

In clinical settings, patients who remit also report higher functioning. Changes in depression symptoms also correlated strongly with three general measures of health: change in bed days ($r = 0.56$, $p < .005$), change in social functioning ($r = 0.52$, $p < .01$), and change in emotional functioning ($r = 0.47$, $p < .01$).

Research has shown that most patients treated with medication begin to respond within 4 weeks and full symptom remission usually occurs within 8 weeks (Wells et al., 1994). Patients receiving psychotherapy typically begin to respond in 5 to 6 weeks, and full symptom remission is usually observed within 12 weeks (Depression Guideline Panel, 1993a, 1993b; Keller, 1988). The D–ARK can assist providers to some extent in predicting treatment response. For example, patients who report significant symptoms of depression may be less likely to remit within 8 weeks, particularly if a clinical interview or the DOM indicates a history of prior episodes, early age of onset, comorbid medical complications, and/or failure to respond to treatment in the past. On the other hand, patients with milder symptoms may remit over time with minimal treatment intervention.

Strengths

Cost Constraints. Although copyrighted by UAMS, the D–ARK is available for unlimited public use as long as fees are not charged to the patient for its use and the instrument is not used commercially.

Ease of Use. The D–ARK has only 11 items, is self-administered, and takes approximately 3 min to complete. Therefore, it requires minimal effort from patients and no additional burden to the provider for administration.

Clinical Utility. The D–ARK has demonstrated high sensitivity and specificity but, as with any other mental health tool, requires clinical intervention as an adjunct to the assessment process. Until further refinement of the severity scale can be conducted, the D–ARK is not appropriate for use as a treatment guide. In other words, scores on the D–ARK cannot be used yet to determine what type of treatment the patient should receive.

Limitations. Validity studies done on the D–ARK are limited by their focus on settings in which Caucasians and individuals of middle age were predominant. This may limit the generalizability of the scale to other groups, such as culturally diverse individuals and/or the elderly.

Summary

The D–ARK was developed by the Centers for Mental Healthcare Research at UAMS to diagnose MDD based on specific criteria of the *DSM–IV*. This self-administered, 11-item instrument is also designed to quantify depression severity for each of the *DSM–IV* symptoms, based on a scale of 1 to 4, with the exception of the last item that assesses the presence or absence of a suicidal plan. The diagnostic measure is dichotomous, with 0 indicating no MDD and 1 indicating a positive diagnosis. The D–ARK severity measure ranges from 0 to 100, with 100 being the most severe. Independently, this scale can be administered with minimal patient burden in primary care or mental health settings, by mail or over the telephone. This scale has also been included in the DOM (Smith, Ross, & Rost, 1996), which, in addition to baseline caseness and severity of depression, measures types of care, outcomes of care, and patient characteristics for case mix or risk adjustment.

THE DEPRESSION OUTCOMES MODULE (DOM)

Health care today is a market driven primarily by managed care. Payers and other stakeholders are now also making decisions that were once strictly within the domain of the physician. These choices can profoundly affect the patient's care and well-being. Because of this shift, an increased need for patient and systems data has developed so that more information is available to make informed judgments, justify clinical decisions, and demonstrate accountability. Developing tools that routinely monitor outcomes of the care provided is not a new endeavor; however, the process has become more important in this era of cost containment and quality conscientiousness.

In the 1990s, a cooperative research and development effort was established to create diagnostic-specific tools to be incorporated into an outcomes management system (OMS) by UAMS, Centers for Mental Healthcare Research. Where randomized controlled trials yield results in a "perfect" world, outcome systems assess what occurs in the real world. The systems are designed to monitor or enhance patient care and the quality of services. These systems can also include claims data, treatment authorizations, scheduling, use of pharmacy services, and costs of procedures. Therefore, the data collected can be applied to the actual setting in which outcomes occur and have an immediate impact on the care provided to the patient (Ellwood, 1988).

Interdisciplinary researchers, clinicians, and government and professional organizations were brought together to develop these tools, one of which was to be used specifically in the treatment of depression. The panel of experts was challenged to identify disease-specific outcomes that might be affected by treatment; types of treatment routinely provided for depressive disorder; and patient characteristics that influence either the type of treatment or its outcome.

Depression was one of the earliest targeted psychiatric disorders because of its high prevalence and devastating effects. The OMS allows monitoring of critical data in a standardized manner that can help determine whether differences in patient characteristics (e.g., disease severity) account for differences in treatment intensity or whether greater treatment intensity effects higher rates of patient improvement. By administering measures at baseline, periodically throughout treatment, and at follow-up intervals, providers can document changes over time. An estimate of treatment effect can then be calculated (Bartlett, 1997). Measures can be used in routine practice and in settings such as primary care, where most of the depressed patients are presenting.

The DOM is a comprehensive yet relatively brief and validated measure for outcomes assessment for MDD. The first version of the module, the Depression TyPE Specification, was developed as part of UAMS's and InterStudy's work with OMS. Subsequently, the module was revised several times following field and validity studies (Rost et al., 1992; Smith et al., 1994, 1998). The DOM was implemented in a number of health care delivery systems and managed care organizations to improve care, enhance quality, and increase accountability. The module is available for noncommercial use as long as patients are not charged for its application and no electronic derivatives are created.

The DOM has five components. The Screener takes 1 min to complete; the Patient Baseline Assessment takes 20 min to complete; the Clinician Baseline Assessment takes less than 2 min to complete; the Patient Follow-up Assessment takes 20 min to complete; and the Medical Record Review takes about 20 min to complete, but requires substantially less time when patient records are computerized.

Development of the DOM

A multidisciplinary panel of experts from various institutions convened to identify the clinical and treatment issues relevant for depressed patients. These issues became part of a measurement set that was tested, validated, and combined into the depression module. Hence, the DOM consists of diagnostic criteria, general functioning measures, prognostic variables influencing outcomes over time, and data regarding the treatment process.

More specifically, the Patient Baseline Assessment is comprised of 80 items, including the D–ARK and the SF–36 (Ware et al., 1993). This initial assessment also includes measures of social functioning, productivity, and bed days. Prognostic characteristics that were identified as predictive of outcomes include:

- Symptom severity.
- Comorbid psychiatric conditions (alcoholism, substance abuse, and dysthymia).
- Comorbid physical conditions.
- Family history of depression or alcoholism.
- Previous psychiatric hospitalizations.
- Previous psychiatric episodes and age of onset.
- Degree of social support.

The Clinician Baseline Assessment evaluates patient diagnostic status from the clinicians' perspective, ruling out other related disorders such as bereavement and bipolar disorder. Information is also collected on psychotropic medications prescribed or adjusted at the initial visit and referral information provided to the patient, if applicable.

Because the DOM is designed to assess the effectiveness and outcomes of care, a patient follow-up is recommended. Containing 53 items, this measure may be administered to the patient as early as 3 months after baseline. Disease-specific outcomes are evaluated, including depression diagnosis and severity, as well as general physical and mental health functioning. The patient also reports on type and extent of treatment received since baseline and on his or her compliance with these treatment recommendations.

The Medical Record Review is considered an optional component to the DOM. It includes 11 items regarding treatment, such as dosages of psychotropic medication, frequency of care in the medical and mental health settings, type of mental health treatment, emergency-room visits, and hospitalizations. If patient records are computerized or extracted from an administrative database, this portion of the DOM may take only minutes to complete.

Basic Psychometric Properties

Because the D–ARK is included in the DOM, the reliability and validity coefficients detailed in the previous section for the depression diagnosis and severity apply. In addition, the DOM contains the SF–36 Health Survey, the psychometric properties of which have already been established (Ware & Sherbourne, 1992; Ware et al., 1993, 1995).

Other items contained within the DOM were derived from existing instruments. For example, on the Patient Baseline Assessment, the question on previous psychiatric history is from the National Health Interview Survey (National Center for Health Statistics, 1989). Items regarding social support, social functioning, and productivity measures (bed/disability days) are derived from the Medical Outcomes Study (Tarlov et al., 1989). Two questions concerning dysthymia and five additional ones concerning comorbidity for substance abuse were adapted for use from the DIS (Robins et al., 1981). Items created specifically for the DOM were also tested prior to their inclusion in the instrument.

Reliability and Validity

The Screener portion of the DOM has been tested in the community as well as with medical and mental health patient samples for its ability to detect those at high risk for a depressive disorder within the last year. As has already been discussed, the sensitivity of the three-item Screener was 91% with a 91% specificity. The positive predictive value was 23%; the negative predictive value was 99% (refer to Table 14.2).

Comparing the DOM against the Depression Section of the SCID (Spitzer et al., 1992) results in high sensitivity and specificity. The symptom severity scale demonstrates good internal consistency with a Cronbach's alpha of .92. Diagnosis of MDD using the DOM results in 100% sensitivity and 81% to 96% specificity compared with the SCID (Spitzer et al., 1992) depression section. Comparing the SCID (Spitzer et al., 1992) analysis to patient reports, remission of MDD at follow-up has 67% sensitivity and 73% specificity. The measure of treatment variables, case-mix characteristics, and disease severity was accurate enough to discriminate between those who did and those who did not receive effective pharmacological treatment.

Test–retest reliability in a rural primary care setting was 0.85 ($p < .001$) for the DOM, and when comparing it to the DIS yielded a Pearson correlation of .63. The question regarding suicidality had a test–retest Kappa of .70 ($p < .001$) and validity of Kappa = .42 ($p = .03$) when compared with the DIS.

Basic Interpretive Strategy

Various components of the DOM can be used to better understand the patient's overall functioning. Because the DOM contains the D–ARK, depression diagnosis and severity can be determined and interpreted as indicated in a previous section. In addition, the DOM provides information on risk for substance abuse and prognostic indicators. Such information is critical to developing a comprehensive treatment plan, while keeping in mind patient characteristics that may impede recovery.

Implementation

As a Stand-Alone Instrument.   The Screener and the D–ARK are both instruments that can be used alone to detect those at high risk for MDD and to diagnose those with MDD respectively, whereas the DOM is a series of data collection measures that provide significantly more information on the clinical status and progress of patients in treatment. However, the DOM should only be administered when it has been established that the patient meets criteria for depression or there is a strong suspicion that the patient has a depressive disorder. Because of its length and more detailed questions, patients need to be asked by the provider to complete the DOM. This includes an explanation of the assessment and instructions regarding follow-up. Providers should encourage participants to complete the instrument as they would any other diagnostic test recommended by the provider. In this way, patient improvement (or lack thereof) can be traced over time with rich, detailed information available on depression as well as other areas of functioning.

With Other Instruments and Procedures.   Often the Screener or D–ARK is used to determine whether a patient should complete the DOM as part of his or her full evaluation. Because the DOM is designed to assess a number of symptoms and functional impairments related to depression, it is somewhat lengthy to be administered with any other instruments, particularly in a primary care setting. However, providers who are interested in specific aspects of care or patient perspectives on access, quality, or care given by the provider or clinical staff may wish to augment the DOM with additional questions pertaining to these areas.

Potential Issues in Implementation.   The DOM was not designed to serve as a screener or brief assessment tool in any setting. As part of a larger OMS, it provides extensive information at the individual and aggregate patient levels, requiring a sophisticated protocol for data collection, scoring, and analysis. In implementing the DOM, providers should outline the criteria or trigger for selecting patients, the mechanisms for scoring the patient responses, the process whereby feedback is provided to providers and patients, and the procedures for follow-up.

Guidelines for Decision Making

Determination of Need for Behavioral Health Intervention.   Once the diagnosis and severity of depression have been established, treatment recommendations should follow AHCPR guidelines, as outlined in the previous section. One primary advantage of the DOM is that it allows the provider to monitor whether guideline-concordant care has been recommended and/or initiated and associate patient outcomes with the type of care provided. For example, is the patient with moderate to severe depression receiving therapeutic doses of an antidepressant medication? Has he or she been referred to a mental health specialist? Was the patient compliant with these instructions?

Determination of Most Appropriate Intervention. AHCPR guidelines outline essential care processes for the treatment of major depression. Basically, patients with MDD should receive pharmacotherapy, psychotherapy, electroconvulsive therapy, or some combination of these treatments, depending on the severity of symptoms. The guidelines describe recommended dosages and frequency of these treatments, as outlined in the previous section (Depression Guideline Panel, 1993a).

Specific Treatment Recommendations. The DOM provides information on the health status of the individual patient, particularly the level of overall impairment. This information, combined with the guidelines, can assist the provider in developing specific treatment parameters; however, specific pathways of care coinciding with the DOM's results have not yet been developed.

Prediction of Treatment Outcome. Based on a thorough review of the literature and guidance from the DOM's expert panels, a number of variables were identified that have the potential to affect a depressed patient's response to treatment. These variables interact to form a complex array of case-mix factors that influence not only the care provided but also the outcomes of that care. Currently, no formal algorithm exists for combining these preexisting conditions into a formal model for predicting recovery. However, providers can use the information to generally determine the patient's initial health status and prognosis for improvement.

Provision of Feedback to Patient

As with the Screener and the D–ARK, patients should receive feedback about their initial symptom levels and changes in symptoms over time. This feedback can be accomplished by discussing individual items on the DOM (e.g., the amount of time spent in bed) or by examining profiles of the D–ARK or SF–36 (Ware et al., 1993) from baseline to follow-up. In cases where there is little or no improvement, providers should openly discuss this lack of progress with patients and develop alternative treatment plans accordingly.

Use as an Instrument for Treatment Monitoring

General Considerations. The DOM assesses the types of care received for MDD, the outcomes of that care, and the patient characteristics that influence outcome. It not only collects information from the physician, but also includes data collected from the patient.

Guidelines for Decision Making. Assessment of information regarding disease management information in an accountability system allows providers to compare care provided with an accepted standard such as AHCPR or best-practice guidelines. Assessment of disease management permits aggregate population, subgroup, or individual patient monitoring of care. The DOM provides a data collection tool to assist in the management of this information. No other comprehensive assessment tool for MDD exists.

How Often to Monitor. The DOM employs a simple case-finding strategy that requires that all patients in the primary care setting periodically complete the two- or three-item Screener described earlier. Patients who screen positive for depressive disorder should be identified to the providers responsible for their care and begin participation in the DOM protocol. Baseline data from the patient should be collected as soon as the depression assessment is complete, whether that occurs as the result of a screener or a clinical interview. Follow-up assessment of patients using the DOM is recommended at 3-month intervals, until the patient is in remission (i.e., fewer number of feelings of depression for at least 1 month). The 3-month follow-up period was recommended by the expert panel, given that most depressed patients do not show significant signs of improvement before then.

Use of Reliable Change (RC) Index. As indicated, the D–ARK adequately measures change over time and can differentiate patients who receive guideline-concordant care from those who do not. There have also been numerous studies published on the SF–36's ability to measure clinical change over time (Ware et al., 1993; Ware & Sherbourne, 1992).

Strengths

The DOM can be used to explore patterns in the relationships between patient characteristics, treatment, and outcomes, without the need for specific training to administer the instrument. Key constructs are measured with sufficient reliability and validity to detect clinical improvements resulting from different treatments. These strengths of the DOM allow clinicians to use outcomes data to maximize the effectiveness of treatment. Clinicians can also make informed treatment decisions based on the data collected in a particular setting. Additionally, the outcomes of similar treatments delivered in different settings (primary care vs. outpatient mental health) can be evaluated.

Cost Constraints. The DOM is protected under copyright and is available for unlimited free use, provided that there is no charge associated with its administration. To that end, UAMS permits unlimited reproduction and distribution of the module by the public for nonprofit, educational, or research purposes. However, any commercial use, including the creation of electronic versions or other derivative works of the module for sale, constitutes a violation of the copyright of the university, unless prior authorization has been granted in writing. At the time of this writing, plans are being developed for a free Internet-based resource to facilitate the use of the DOM.

Ease of Use. The Patient Baseline Assessment and the Patient Follow-up Assessment of the DOM require 20 min each to complete. This is one reason why the D–ARK may be preferable under certain circumstances where time limits are a constraint for detection of depression, as is the case in many primary care settings. All segments of the DOM are self-administered, except for the Medical Records Review. If necessary, the DOM can either be mailed or administered over the phone.

Limitations

Because of the DOM's length, patients may resist completing the instrument in the office unless the purpose of the assessment is fully explained by the provider. Additional limitations include the burden imposed by the larger OMS, requiring extra staff time for scoring the DOM, tracking patients for follow-up, and generating reports regarding individual and aggregate patient status. It is therefore recommended that primary care providers interested in establishing an OMS for depression consult with professionals experienced in implementing this type of quality improvement project, so that it meets the needs of the clinical setting in which patient care is provided.

Summary

The DOM assesses the types of care received for MDD, the outcomes of that care, and the patient characteristics that influence outcome. The DOM not only collects information from the physician, but also includes data collected from the patient. The DOM is useful in most psychiatric and primary care settings and is very adaptable.

The DOM includes the D–ARK scale, which represents the diagnostic component of this module. It also includes the SF–36 (Ware et al., 1993) to assess functioning and mental and physical health status.

SUMMARY

Because major depression is a common but often unrecognized and undertreated disorder in primary care, it is important to identify tools that will aid in the detection and care of depressed patients. With the onslaught of managed care dictating the parameters and costs of treatment, it is also paramount that providers develop innovative ways of monitoring outcomes in their practices for depressed patients, who are often the most expensive and difficult general medical patients to treat.

The tools recommended in this chapter can be used in the primary care setting to improve detection, treatment, and outcomes of depressed patients. The depression Screener will identify high-risk patients who may require further assessment and intervention. The D–ARK, a brief, self-report scale, will provide severity ratings for *DSM–IV* symptoms and will indicate those patients endorsing enough MDD symptoms to meet full criteria for the disorder. Finally, the DOM can be administered as part of a comprehensive OMS to monitor the processes and outcomes of care and evaluate practice alterations that result from the information provided.

In each case, providers will improve the quality of care for patients by enhancing the knowledge of individual patients as well as their entire clinical population and implementing guidelines, intervention programs, and educational supplements aimed at reducing the rate of depression in their settings.

ACKNOWLEDGMENTS

The authors acknowledge J. Eileen Gharapour, BA, for her contributions to this chapter.

APPENDIX A
D–ARK Diagnostic and Severity Scoring (See Table 14.4 for D–ARK items.)

D–ARK Diagnostic Scoring

For Part A: If respondent scores Questions 1 or 2 greater than or equal to 2, then PART A = 1.
For Part B: Score individual items as follows:
  If Question 1 is greater than or equal to 2, Criterion 1 = 1.
  If Question 2 is greater than or equal to 2, Criterion 2 = 1.
  If Question 3 is greater than or equal to 2, *or*
    Question 4 is greater than or equal to 2, Criterion 3 = 1.
  If Questions 5–9 are greater than or equal to 3, Criteria 4–8 = 1 each.
  If Question 10 is greater than or equal to 3, *or*
    Question 11 = 2, Criterion 9 = 1.

If the total of Criteria 1–9 is greater than or equal to 5, then PART B = 1.
If Part A = 1 and Part B = 1, then the respondent meets the criteria for depression.

D–ARK Severity Scoring

Recode Questions 1–10 as 0 to 3. If Question 11 = 1, then Question 11 = 0. If Question 11 = 2, then
  Question 11 = 3.
Calculate the mean of Questions 1–11; multiple by 33.33. This product is the severity score.
If Question 10 is missing *or* two or more questions are missing, do not score Severity.

Note. The D–ARK is available for unlimited free public use. If fees are charged, then licensing arrangements must be made with the copyright holder. For more information, please write to the Department of
Psychiatry, Center for Outcomes Research and Effectiveness (CORE), 5800 W. 10th Street, Little Rock, AR
72204, or phone (501) 660-7500.

REFERENCES

American Psychiatric Association. (1994). *Diagnostic and statistical manual of mental disorders* (4th ed.).
  Washington, DC: Author.
Barraclough, B., Bunch, J., Nelson, B., & Sainsbury, P. (1974). A hundred cases of suicide: Clinical aspects.
  British Journal of Psychiatry, 125, 355–373.
Bartlett, J. (1997). Treatment outcomes: The psychiatrist's and health care executive's perspectives. *Psychi-
  atric Annals, 27,* 100–103.
Beck, A. T., Ward, C. H., Mendelson, M., Mock, J. E., & Erbaugh, J. K. (1961). An inventory for measuring
  depression. *Archives of General Psychiatry, 5,* 462–467.
Bland, R. C. (1997). Epidemiology of affective disorders: A review. *Canadian Journal of Psychiatry, 42,*
  367–377.
Booth, B., Stewart, M. K., & Kramer, T. L. (1997). *Depressive disorders in patients with low back pain.* Unpub-
  lished manuscript.
Boyd, J. H., Weissman, M. M., Thompson, W. D., & Myers, J. K. (1982). Screening for depression in a com-
  munity sample. *Archives of General Psychiatry, 39,* 1195–1200.
Brody, D. S., & Larson, D. B. (1992). The role of primary care physicians in managing depression. *Journal of
  General Internal Medicine, 7,* 243–247.
Burnam, M. A., Wells, K. B., Leake, B., & Landsverk, J. (1988). Development of a brief screening instrument
  for detecting depressive disorders. *Medical Care, 26,* 775–789.
Covinsky, K. E., Fortinsky, R. H., Palmer, R. M., Kresevic, D. M., & Landefeld, C. S. (1997). Relation be-
  tween symptoms of depression and health status outcomes in acutely ill hospitalized older persons.
  Annals of Internal Medicine, 126, 417–425.
Coyne, J. C., Schwenk, T. L., & Fechner-Bates, S. (1995). Nondetection of depression by primary care physi-
  cians reconsidered. *General Hospital Psychiatry, 17,* 3–12.
Depression Guideline Panel. (1993a). *Depression in primary care: Volume 2. Treatment of major depression.
  Clinical practice guideline, Number 5* (AHCPR Publication No. 93-0551). Rockville, MD: U.S. Department
  of Health and Human Services, Public Health Service, Agency for Health Care Policy and Research.

Depression Guideline Panel. (1993b). *Depression in primary care: Volume 1. Detection and diagnosis. Clinical practice guideline, Number 5* (AHCPR Publication No. 93-0550). Rockville, MD: U.S. Department of Health and Human Services, Public Health Service, Agency for Health Care Policy and Research.

Eisenberg, L. (1992). Treating depression and anxiety in primary care: Closing the gap between knowledge and practice. *New England Journal of Medicine, 326,* 1080–1084.

Ellwood, P. M. (1988). Outcomes management: A technology of patient experience [Shattuck Lecture]. *New England Journal of Medicine, 318,* 1549–1556.

FAACT Staff. (1996). Accountability action. *Foundation for Accountability (FACCT), 1,* 1–13.

Greenberg, P. E., Stiglin, L. E., Finkelstein, S. N., & Berndt E. R. (1993a). The economic burden of depression in 1990. *Journal of Clinical Psychiatry, 54,* 405–418.

Greenberg, P. E., Stiglin, L. E., Finkelstein, S. N., & Berndt E. R. (1993b). Depression: A neglected major illness. *Journal of Clinical Psychiatry, 54,* 419–424

Hamilton, M. (1960). A rating scale for depression. *Journal of Neurology, Neurosurgery and Psychiatry, 23,* 56–62.

Hough, R. L., Landsverk, J. A., & Jacobson, G. F. (1990). The use of psychiatric screening scales to detect depression in primary care patients. In C. C. Attkisson & J. M. Zich (Eds.), *Depression in primary care: Screening and detection* (pp. 139–154). New York: Routledge.

Jones, R. L., Badger, L. W., Ficken, R. P., Leeper, J. D., & Anderson, R. L. (1987). Inside the hidden mental health network: Examining mental health care delivery of primary care physicians. *General Hospital Psychiatry, 9,* 287–293.

Katon, W. (1987). The epidemiology of depression in medical care. *International Journal of Psychiatry in Medicine, 17,* 93–111.

Katon, W., Von Korff, M., Lin, E., Bush, T., & Ormel, J. (1992). Adequacy and duration of antidepressant treatment in primary care. *Medical Care, 30,* 67–76.

Katon, W., Von Korff, M., Lin, E., Unutzer, J., Simon, G., Walker, E., Ludman, E., & Bush, T. (1997). Population-based care of depression: Effective disease management strategies to decrease prevalence. *General Hospital Psychiatry, 19,* 169–178.

Katon, W., Von Korff, M., Lin, E., Walker, E., Simon, G., Bush, T., Robinson, P., & Russo, J. (1995). Collaborative management to achieve treatment guidelines. Impact on depression in primary care. *Journal of the American Medical Association, 273,* 1026–1031.

Katzelnick, D. J., Kobak, K. A., Greist, J. H., Jefferson, J. W., & Henk, H. J. (1997). Effect of primary care treatment of depression on service use by patients with high medical expenditures. *Psychiatric Services, 48,* 59–64.

Keller, M. B. (1988). Undertreatment of major depression. *Psychopharmacology Bulletin, 24,* 75–80.

Keller, M. B., Lavori, P. W., Beardslee, W. R., Wunder, J., & Ryan, N. (1991). Depression in children and adolescents: New data on "undertreatment" and a literature review on the efficacy of available treatments. *Journal of Affective Disorders, 21,* 163–171.

Keller, M. B., Lavori, P. W., Mueller, T. I., Endicott, J., Coryell, W., Hirschfield, R. M. A., & Shea, T. (1992). Time to recovery, chronicity, and levels of psychopathology in major depression. *Archives of General Psychiatry, 49,* 809–816.

Kessler R. C., & Frank R. G. (1997). The impact of psychiatric disorders on work loss days. *Psychological Medicine, 27,* 861–873.1.

Klerman, G. L., & Weissman, M. M. (1989). Increasing rates of depression. *Journal of the American Medical Association, 261,* 2229–2235.

Klerman, G. L., & Weissman, M. M. (1992). The course, morbidity, and costs of depression. *Archives of General Psychiatry, 49,* 831–834.

Kouzis, A. C., & Eaton, W. W. (1994). Emotional disability days: Prevalence and predictors. *American Journal of Public Health, 84,* 1304–1307.

Linn, L. S., & Yager, J. (1984). Recognition of depression and anxiety by primary physicians. *Psychosomatics, 25,* 593–600.

Linn, L. S., & Yager, J. (1980). The effect of screening, sensitization and feedback on notation of depression. *Journal of Medical Education, 55,* 942–949.

Madianos, M. G., & Stefanis, C. N. (1992). Changes in the prevalence of symptoms of depression and depression across Greece. *Social Psychiatry & Psychiatric Epidemiology, 27,* 211–219.

Magruder-Habib, K., Zung, W. W. K., & Feussner, J. R. (1990). Improving physicians' recognition and treatment of depression in general medical care: Results from a randomized clinical trial. *Medical Care, 28,* 239–250.

Mintz J., Mintz L. I., Arruda M. J., & Hwang S. S. (1992). Treatments of depression and the functional capacity to work. *Archives of General Psychiatry; 49,* 761–768.

Murray, C. J. L., & Lopez, A. D. (Eds.). (1996). *Summary of the Global Burden of Disease: A Comprehensive Assessment of Mortality and Disability from Diseases, Injuries, and Risk Factors in 1990 and Projected to 2020.* World Health Organization. Boston: Harvard University Press.

National Center for Health Statistics. (1989). *Current estimates from the US National Health Interview Survey* (ICPSR; NCHS 9403; Publication Series 10 No. 176 90-154; RA 445 N38 1989 (LC)). Washington, DC: U.S. Government Printing Office.

Ormel, J., Koeter, M. W. J., van den Brink, W., & van de Willige, G. (1991). Recognition, management, and course of anxiety and depression in general practice. *Archives of General Psychiatry, 48,* 700–706.

Perez-Stable, E. J., Miranda, J., Munoz, R. F., & Ying, Y. (1990). Depression in medical outpatients: Underrecognition and misdiagnosis. *Archives of Internal Medicine, 150,* 1083–1088.

Radloff, L. S. (1977). The CES-D scale: A self-report depression scale for research on the general population. *Applied Psychological Measure, 1,* 385–401.

Regier, D. A., Narrow, W. E., Rae, D. S., Manderscheid, R. W., Locke, B. Z., & Goodwin, F. K. (1993). The de facto US mental and addictive disorders service system: Epidemiologic Catchment Area prospective 1-year prevalence rates of disorders and services. *Archives of General Psychiatry, 50,* 85–94.

Robins, L. N., Helzer, J. E., Croughan, J., & Ratcliff, K. S. (1981). National Institute of Mental Health Diagnostic Interview Schedule. *Archives of General Psychiatry, 38,* 381–389.

Robins, L. N., & Regier, D. A. (Eds.). (1991). *Psychiatric disorders in America.* New York: Free Press.

Rost, K., Burnam, M. A., & Smith, G. R. (1993). Development of screeners for depressive disorders and substance disorder history. *Medical Care, 31,* 189–200.

Rost, K., Fortney, J., Zhang, M., & Smith, G. R. (in press). Treatment of depression in rural Arkansas: Policy implications for improving care. *Journal of Rural Health.*

Rost, K., Humphrey, J., & Kelleher, K. (1994). Physician management preferences and barriers to care for rural patients with depression. *Archives of Family Medicine, 3,* 409–414.

Rost, K., Smith, G. R., Matthews, D. B., & Guise, B. (1994). The deliberate misdiagnosis of major depression in primary care. *Archives of Family Medicine, 3,* 333–337.

Rost, K., Smith, G. R., Burnam, M. A., & Burns, B. J. (1992). Measuring the outcomes of care for mental health problems: The case of depressive disorders. *Medical Care, 20,* MS266–MS273.

Rost, K., Williams, C., Wherry, J., & Smith, G. R. (1995). The process and outcomes of care for major depression in rural family practice settings. Journal of Rural Health, 11, 114–121.

Rost, K., Zhang, M., Fortney, J., Smith, J., Smith, G. R., & Coyne, J. (1998). Persistently poor outcomes of undetected major depression in primary care. *General Hospital Psychiatry, 20,* 12–20.

Rush, J. A., Gullion, C. M., Basco, M. R., Jarrett, R. B., & Trivedi, M. H. (1996). The Inventory of Depressive Symtomatology (IDS): Psychometric properties. *Psychological Medicine, 26,* 477–486.

Schappert, S. M. (1994). National Ambulatory Medical Care Survey: 1991 Summary. *Vital & Health Statistics–Series 13: Data from the National Health Survey,* 1–110.

Smith, G. R., Burnam, M. A., Burns, B. J., Cleary, O. D., & Rost, K. (1994). *Major Depression Outcomes Module.* Little Rock: University of Arkansas.

Smith, G. R., Kramer, T. L., Hollenberg, J. A., Mosley, C. L., Ross, R. L., & Burnam, M. A. (1998). *Validity of the Depression–Arkansas (D–ARK) Scale: A tool for primary and specialty care.* Manuscript submitted for publication.

Smith, G. R., Ross, R. L., & Rost, K. M. (1996). Psychiatric outcomes module: Depression (DOM). In L. I. Sederer & B. Dickey (Eds.), *Outcomes assessment in clinical practice* (pp. 82–84). Baltimore, MD: Williams & Wilkins.

Spitzer, R. L., Williams, J. B. W., Gibbon, M., & First, M. (1992). The Structured Clinical Interview for DSM-III-R (SCID) 1: History, rationale, and description. *Archives of General Psychiatry, 49,* 624–629.

Stewart, M. K., Booth, B., & Kramer, T. L. (1997). *Depressive disorders in patients with diabetes mellitus.* Unpublished manuscript.

Tarlov, A. R., Ware, J. E., Greenfield, S., Nelson, E. C., Perrin, E., & Zubkoff, M. (1989). The Medical Outcomes Study: An application of methods for evaluating the results of medical care. *Journal of the American Medical Association, 262,* 925–930.

Von Korff, M., Ormel, J., Katon, W., & Lin, E. H. B. (1992). Disability and depression among high utilizers of health care—A longitudinal analysis. Archives of General Psychiatry, 49, 91–100.

Ware, J., Jr., Kosinski, M., Bayliss, M. S., McHorney, C. A., Rogers, W. H., & Raczek, A. (1995). Comparison of methods for the scoring and statistical analysis of the SF-36 health profile and summary measures: Summary of results from the Medical Outcomes Study. *Medical Care, 33,* AS264–AS279.

Ware, J., Jr., & Sherbourne, C. D. (1992). The MOS 36-item short-form health survey (SF-36): 1. Conceptual framework and item selection. *Medical Care, 30,* 473–483.

Ware, J. E., Jr., Snow, K. K., Kosinski, M., & Gandek, B. (1993). *SF–36 Health Survey manual and interpretation guide*. Boston: New England Medical Center, Health Institute.

Wassertheil-Smoller, S. (1995). *Biostatistics and epidemiology: A primer for health professionals* (2nd ed.). New York: Springer-Verlag.

Wells, K. B., Goldberg, G., Brook, R., & Leake, B. (1988). Management of patients on psychotropic drugs in primary care clinics. *Medical Care, 26,* 645–656.

Wells, K. B., Katon, W., Rogers, B., & Camp, P. (1994). Use of minor tranquilizers and antidepressant medications by depressed outpatients: Results from the Medical Outcomes Study. *American Journal of Psychiatry 151,* 694–700.

Wells, K. B., Rogers, W., Burnam, M. A., Greenfield, S., & Ware, J. E., Jr. (1991). How the medical comorbidity of depressed patients differs across health care settings: Results from the Medical Outcomes Study. *American Journal of Psychiatry, 148,* 1688–1696.

Wells, K. B., Stewart, A., Hays, R. D., Burnam, M. A., Rogers W., Daniels, M., Berry, S., Greenfield, S., & Ware, J. (1989). The functioning and well-being of depressed patients: Results from the Medical Outcomes Study. *Journal of the American Medical Association, 262,* 914–919.

Zimmerman, M., Coryell, W., Corenthal, C., & Wilson, S. (1986). A self-report scale to diagnose major depressive disorder. *Archives of General Psychiatry, 43,* 1076–1081.

Zung, W. W. K. (1965). A self-rating depression scale. *Archives of General Psychiatry, 12,* 63–70.

Zung, W. W. K., & King, R. E. (1983). Identification and treatment of masked depression in a general medical practice. *Journal of Clinical Psychiatry, 44,* 365–368.

Zung, W. W. K., Magill, M., Moore, J. T., & George, D. T. (1983). Recognition and treatment of depression in a family medical practice. *Journal of Clinical Psychiatry, 44,* 3–6.

Geriatric Depression Scale

Forrest Scogin
Noelle Rohen
Elaine Bailey
University of Alabama

The Geriatric Depression Scale (GDS) is a widely used instrument developed in the early 1980s as a measure of geriatric depressive symptomatology. It is a measure well suited for use as a screening and/or monitoring instrument in primary care settings where qualities such as brevity, sensitivity, and specificity are valued. A relatively extensive literature on the GDS is reviewed in this chapter, accompanied by suggestions for its use. Our opinion is that use of the GDS in primary care settings would improve the detection of depression among older adults. This is an important and worthwhile goal for at least a couple of reasons. First, depression has been reliably associated with increase health care use (Callahan, Hui, Nienaber, Musick, & Tierney, 1994). Second, geriatric depression is a treatable disorder (Friedhoff, 1994).

OVERVIEW

The development of the GDS was motivated by the perception that existing self-report measures of depression were lacking when used with older adults (e.g., Jarvik, 1976; Kane & Kane, 1981; Salzman & Shader, 1978). The most frequently expressed concerns were with somatic symptoms of depression, including energy, sex, sleep, and gastrointestinal difficulties, as these tended to be unreliable indicants of depression when evaluated in elders. Other concerns included the confusion often engendered by the multiple-response format of extant instruments, especially with older adults experiencing mild to moderate cognitive impairment. The lack of norms for older adults was frequently expressed as a shortcoming as well. These concerns coincided with the maturation of the field of geriatric mental health to the point that investigators were ready to develop a self-report depression instrument specifically geared for older adults.

Development

The results of initial development efforts of the GDS were detailed in articles published in the early 1980s. A group of investigators at Stanford University and the Palo Alto Veteran's Administration Medical Center, led by T. L. Brink and Jerome Yesavage, published these initial studies. The first (Brink et al., 1982) reported in rather truncated fashion the development of the scale. The second (Yesavage et al., 1983) is a much more detailed version of the same initial development and validation and is reviewed for the purposes of this chapter.

The development of the GDS began with the generation of 100 questions that experts in geriatric psychiatry believed might be useful in detecting depression among older adults. An effort was made to include items that covered the range of depressive phenomena, including loss, cognitive complaints, somatic complaints, and self-image. A yes/no response format was chosen based on the experiences of the authors with multiple-response formats. They observed that multiple-response formats often confused elderly patients. The 100 items were administered to 47 persons 55 years of age or older who either were community dwelling with no complaints of depression or were hospitalized for depression. The authors used a bootstrapping strat-

TABLE 15.1
Geriatric Depression Scale

Choose the best answer for how you felt over the past week.

1. Are you basically satisfied with your life?	yes/no
2. Have you dropped many of your activities and interests?	yes/no
3. Do you feel that your life is empty?	yes/no
4. Do you often get bored?	yes/no
5. Are you hopeful about the future?	yes/no
6. Are you bothered by thoughts you can't get out of your head?	yes/no
7. Are you in good spirits most of the time?	yes/no
8. Are you afraid that something bad is going to happen to you?	yes/no
9. Do you feel happy most of the time?	yes/no
10. Do you often feel helpless?	yes/no
11. Do you often get restless and fidgety?	yes/no
12. Do you prefer to stay at home, rather than going out and doing new things?	yes/no
13. Do you frequently worry about the future?	yes/no
14. Do you feel you have more problems with memory than most?	yes/no
15. Do you think it is wonderful to be alive now?	yes/no
16. Do you often feel downhearted and blue?	yes/no
17. Do you feel pretty worthless the way you are now?	yes/no
18. Do you worry a lot about the past?	yes/no
19. Do you find life very exciting?	yes/no
20. Is it hard for you to get started on new projects?	yes/no
21. Do you feel full of energy?	yes/no
22. Do you feel that your situation is hopeless?	yes/no
23. Do you think that most people are better off than you are?	yes/no
24. Do you frequently get upset over little things?	yes/no
25. Do you frequently feel like crying?	yes/no
26. Do you have trouble concentrating?	yes/no
27. Do you enjoy getting up in the morning?	yes/no
28. Do you prefer to avoid social gatherings?	yes/no
29. Is it easy for you to make decisions?	yes/no
30. Is your mind as clear as it used to be?	yes/no

Note. From Yesavage et al. (1983). Reprinted with permission.

egy to select items whereby those items evidencing the best correlation to the total score were retained for further validation. The rationale provided for this strategy was that the 100 items generated would provide the best measure of the geriatric depression construct. A decision to select 30 items was made, presumably to minimize fatigue effects. The item-to-total correlations ranged from .47 to .83. Interestingly, the 12 items related to somatic concerns were not selected based on this procedure; that is, the item-to-total correlations for these items were not in the top 30. Table 15.1 contains the 30 items that comprise the GDS.

The next step in the development of the GDS involved cross-validation with a new set of participants. Forty community-dwelling nondepressed elders and 60 older adults in treatment for depression comprised the sample. The depressed sample was divided into mild ($n = 26$) and severe ($n = 34$) cases based on the number of depressive symptoms evidenced. Participants were administered the Hamilton Rating Scale for Depression (HRSD; Hamilton, 1967), the Zung Self-rating Scale for Depression (SDS; Zung, 1965), and the GDS in random order.

Consistency and reliability estimates for the GDS were impressive. The alpha coefficient was .94, split-half reliability was also .94, and test–retest reliability over a 1-week interval was .85. Validity was examined by using the classifications of nondepressed, mildly depressed, and severely depressed as between-subjects variables, and then comparisons of the scores obtained on the GDS, HRSD, and SDS were made. Scores on each of the measures reliably distinguished the three grades of severity, suggesting discriminate validity. Concurrent validity for the GDS was explored by correlating total scores from the three instruments. The GDS correlated at .84 with the SDS and at .83 with the HRSD. These correlations were suggestive of concurrent validity.

Yesavage and colleagues also suggested a cutoff score of 11 for identifying depression (i.e., 0–10 nondepressed, ≥11 depressed). This cut score yielded sensitivity (the ability to correctly classify depressed patients) and specificity (the ability to correctly classify "normal" patients) rates of 84% and 95%, respectively.

The results of this initial validation study were encouraging. The GDS demonstrated adequate reliability and validity, although the methods of this study did not permit the demonstration of superiority to other measures of depression. This article serves as the cornerstone of GDS literature and is the most frequently referenced study pertaining to the scale.

Short Form

Another significant event in the history of the GDS was the development of a short form. The rationale in developing a short form was that if 30 items were good, 15 would be better, particularly in terms of ease of administration. Sheikh and Yesavage (1986) selected the 15 items best correlated with the total score using data from the initial validation study. Cross-validation of these items was undertaken with 35 participants, 18 nondepressed and 17 in treatment for depression or dysthymia. Participants completed both the long and short forms of the measure, and correlational analyses indicated strong association ($r = .84$). It is not clear if corrections were made for part–whole inflation of the correlation. The 15 items that comprise the short form of the GDS are displayed in Table 15.2. More specific information on the GDS short form is provided in a later section of this chapter.

TABLE 15.2
Geriatric Depression Scale (Short Form)

Choose the best answer for how you felt over the past week:

1. Are you basically satisfied with your life?   yes/no
2. Have you dropped many of your activities and interests?   yes/no
3. Do you feel that your life is empty?   yes/no
4. Do you often get bored?   yes/no
5. Are you in good spirits most of the time?   yes/no
6. Are you afraid that something bad is going to happen to you?   yes/no
7. Do you feel happy most of the time?   yes/no
8. Do you often feel helpless?   yes/no
9. Do you prefer to stay at home, rather than going out and doing new things?   yes/no
10. Do you feel you have more problems with memory than most?   yes/no
11. Do you think it is wonderful to be alive now?   yes/no
12. Do you feel pretty worthless the way you are now?   yes/no
13. Do you feel full of energy?   yes/no
14. Do you feel that your situation is hopeless?   yes/no
15. Do you think that most people are better off than you are?   yes/no

Note. From Sheik and Yesavage (1986). Reprinted with permission.

DISEASE-SPECIFIC CONSIDERATIONS

Much of the literature on the GDS addresses the utility of the scale when used with special populations. Specifically, studies have examined GDS applications with dementia patients, older adults in medical settings including nursing homes and rehabilitation centers, and general outpatient mental health settings. Research on the GDS in primary health care settings is somewhat limited; nonetheless, we extrapolate from the available literature and our experiences in using the GDS to provide recommendations for use in these settings.

Older adults with cognitive impairments are the population for whom depression assessment is most vexing. Not surprisingly, then, the most frequently studied area in the GDS literature is the utility of the instrument with mild and moderate dementia cases. Investigators have also explored the important issue of the utility of the GDS in detecting the dementia syndrome of depression, the condition formerly known as pseudodementia. In one of the best studies of the use of the GDS with cognitively impaired elders, Parmalee, Lawton, and Katz (1989) found little attenuation of psychometric properties when the scale was used with mildly and moderately impaired institutionalized elders. Factor analysis suggested a unidimensional scale, consistent with the use of an overall summary score. Agreement with clinical diagnoses of depression was also relatively good except when evaluating lower, less severe levels of depression. Using 11 as the cut score, sensitivity was rather low. Based on this finding, Parmalee et al. (1989) suggested using a more liberal cut score when screening for depression, an issue to which we return in a later portion of this chapter.

Another study of the use of the GDS with dementia patients reached a less positive conclusion. Burke, Houston, Boust, and Roccaforte (1989) tested the utility of the GDS with mild Alzheimer's dementia patients ($n = 72$) and older adults with no evidence of cognitive impairment ($n = 70$). The authors concluded the scale was a useful screener with the intact group but not so with the dementia patients. Using signal detection analyses, the GDS was no better than chance at identifying depressed from nondepressed dementia patients. Significant weaknesses in this investigation were that the criterion was a clinical diagnosis of either major depression or not, apparently made without the aid of a structured interview, and with no report of reliability of diagnoses. Despite these limitations, the results of this study suggest strong caution in the use of the GDS with cognitively impaired elders.

In a slightly different twist on the same problem, Feher, Larabee, and Crook (1992) attempted to identify factors attenuating the validity of the GDS with demented patients. Persons with mild to moderate dementia who were not evidencing major depression comprised the sample ($n = 83$). Major depression was excluded to avoid the diagnostic quagmire of the dementia syndrome of depression. These authors concluded that the GDS was valid with mild to moderate dementia cases, but the validity was attenuated for elders who lacked self-awareness of cognitive deficits. Self-awareness was operationally defined as the total score difference on a memory assessment questionnaire filled out by the patient and by an informant. With this caveat, the authors recommend use of the GDS with mildly and moderately demented older adults.

Ward, Wadsworth, and Peterson (1994) examined the validity of the GDS with male dementia patients. Patients were read the GDS as well as several other measures of psychopathology and were clinically interviewed. The GDS demonstrated good concurrent validity and internal consistency, which led the authors to recommend the scale as "probably the self-report instrument of choice with both normal and cognitively impaired elderly patients" (p. 10).

It is intuitive that the GDS will be less useful as the degree of cognitive impairment increases, but a pragmatic question is the point at which the scale loses validity. McGivney, Mulvihill, and Taylor (1994) addressed this question by administering the GDS and the Mini-Mental State Exam (MMSE) and by obtaining psychiatric diagnoses. Sixty-six newly admitted nursing home residents were the participants. These investigators found that sensitivity and specificity estimates were considerably attenuated in patients with MMSE scores of 14 or less. The authors noted that diagnosing depression in older adults with more severe cases of dementia (i.e., MMSE < 15) remains problematic.

Shah and colleagues (Shah, Phongsathorn, George, Bielawska, & Katona, 1992) examined sensitivity and specificity rates for the GDS in demented and intact respondents as part of a study of psychiatric conditions in continuing care geriatric patients. The data from this study suggested that raising the cut score from 10 to 12 gave optimal sensitivity (75%) and specificity (73%) for both demented and nondemented respondents. They also found strong test–retest reliability for the GDS over a 1-week interval for both groups of patients. These authors reached the conclusion that demented patients provide answers to GDS questions that are not random, are accurate, and have stability.

Finally, Burke, Nitcher, Roccaforte, and Wengel (1992) reported the results of a study improving on their group's 1989 study by using prospective clinical diagnoses of depression as the criterion rather than chart reviews. Participants were 182 patients evaluated at an outpatient geriatric assessment center. The patients were divided into two groups: cognitively intact ($n = 67$) and impaired ($n = 115$), based on an MMSE cut score of 24. Burke and his colleagues found that the GDS was efficient with cognitively impaired patients. They attribute the difference in finding to the improvement in the criterion variable and to the fact that the GDS and the clinical diagnosis were contiguous.

The bottom line on the use of the GDS with dementia patients seems to be the following. For mild and moderate cases of dementia, the GDS performs well as a self-report measure of depression severity. This is particularly true if MMSE scores are no less than 15 and questions are administered orally for those patients who have difficulty with reading. This is encouraging, given that many service providers, especially those with limited backgrounds in aging, may be reluctant to use screening devices with impaired elders. Depression is so often unrecognized that the use of any screening instrument can only aid in detection and ultimately treatment. For interested readers, a more broad-ranging review of the literature on the assessment of depression in cognitively impaired respondents is provided by Katz and Parmalee (1994).

DEVELOPMENT OF A SHORT-FORM GDS

A spate of articles has appeared since Sheikh and Yesavage (1986) selected the 15 items for the GDS short form (GDS–SF). In one of the first validation efforts, Cwikel and Ritchie (1988) administered the GDS–SF to 20 depressed and 20 matched community control older adults. Using a cutoff score of 7 yielded sensitivity of 70% and specificity of 75%, which the authors believed were not sufficient to warrant recommendation of the scale as a diagnostic instrument. Instead they sensibly suggested that the GDS–SF be used as a screener to detect possible cases in need of further evaluation.

Lesher and Berryhill (1994) directly compared the long and short forms of the GDS with 72 patients at a geropsychiatric unit. The correlation between the two was .89, which was very similar to the .84 reported by Sheikh and Yesavage (1986). With a cut score of 7, the short form evidenced sensitivity of .83 and specificity of .73, values quite similar to those shown for the long form (GDS–LF). Lesher and Berryhill (1994) concluded that use of the GDS–LF is not warranted because the GDS–SF yields nearly identical information.

Herrmann et al. (1996) evaluated the GDS–SF in 116 older adult outpatients from an affective disorders clinic. A clinician-rated measure of depression severity served as the criterion against which the scale was evaluated. The correlation of the GDS–SF and the clinician-rated depression severity was .78. Optimal sensitivity (85%) and specificity (74%) were obtained with a cut score of 5. The authors note that with an average administration time of about 6 min, the GDS–SF represents a significant advance in the screening of late-life depression.

Steiner et al. (1996) examined the psychometric properties of four shortened measures of well-being in community dwelling elders. The GDS–SF was administered to 414 persons, 75 years of age and older. Cronbach's alpha, an estimate of internal consistency, was .78 and test-retest reliability ($n = 48$) was .85. The authors compared these values to those obtained in other studies of the GDS–LF and concluded that the GDS–SF has comparable psychometric properties. They also divided the sample into age groups of 75–79, 80–84, and 85 years and above and found test–retest reliability to hold across the age groups. Steiner and colleagues maintained that the time savings achieved justified use of the shortened version.

A study clearly relevant to the focus of this chapter was conducted by D'Ath, Katona, Mullan, Evans, and Katona (1994). These investigators examined the utility of the GDS–SF in older adult primary care attenders. The article noted the underdetection and undertreatment of geriatric depression that tends to occur in primary care settings. Participants were 194 patients visiting their general practitioners. Assignment to "caseness" of depression was made on the basis of a cutscore of 5. Item-to-total correlations were significant for all 15 items, and the item "Do you feel your life is empty?" was most discriminating in terms of caseness. In an interesting addendum, respondents were also asked how acceptable they found the GDS–SF. A total of 88% found it to be "very acceptable," 89% found it to be "not at all stressful," and 88% found it "not at all difficult."

The authors also explored the possibility of making the short form even shorter. A 10-item (see Table 15.3) and a 4-item scale (see Table 15.4) were created based on the most discriminating items. Correlations with the GDS–SF (15 items) were .97 and .89, respectively. Sensitivity and specificity estimates were attenuated but acceptable for the 10- and 4-item versions. The authors conclude that use of the 4-item scale deserves special consideration as a minimal screening procedure in light of their finding that sensitivity was 93% with a cut score of 1. D'Ath and colleagues noted that the GDS–LF has not received widespread application in primary care settings because physicians perceive the scale to be too long.

As the final salvo on this issue, Mahoney et al. (1994) compared the diagnostic efficiency of a single question about depression to the GDS–LF. Community-dwelling Veterans Affairs patients ($n = 55$) seen in an 8-month period for intake or annual checkup were asked "Do you often feel sad or depressed?" and were given the 30-item GDS in alternating order on the same visit. The criterion was a structured clinical interview diagnosis of a depressive disorder. Unexpectedly, the single item, which incidentally is not a GDS item, performed as well as or even a bit better than the GDS in identifying depressed versus nondepressed patients. Sensitivity and specificity rates were, respectively, .69 and .90 for the single item and .54 and .93 for

TABLE 15.3
Geriatric Depression Scale (SF–10)

Choose the best answer for how you felt over the past week:

1. Are you basically satisfied with your life?	yes/no
2. Have you dropped many of your activities and interests?	yes/no
3. Do you feel that your life is empty?	yes/no
4. Are you afraid that something bad is going to happen to you?	yes/no
5. Do you feel happy most of the time?	yes/no
6. Do you often feel helpless?	yes/no
7. Do you feel you have more problems with memory than most?	yes/no
8. Do you feel full of energy?	yes/no
9. Do you feel that your situation is hopeless?	yes/no
10. Do you think that most people are better off than you are?	yes/no

Note. From D'Ath et al. (1994). Reprinted by permission.

TABLE 15.4
Geriatric Depression Scale (SF–4)

Choose the best answer for how you felt over the past week:

1. Are you basically satisfied with your life?	yes/no
2. Do you feel that your life is empty?	yes/no
3. Are you afraid that something bad is going to happen to you?	yes/no
4. Do you feel happy most of the time?	yes/no

Note. From D'Ath et al. (1994). Reprinted by permission.

the GDS. This study was based on a small sample, and relatively few of the participants were depressed. Nonetheless, we suspect these results would replicate in a larger sample. The lesson in this study is that to identify depression one must ask about depression.

In summary, the GDS–SF is a viable alternative to the 30-item full scale. Circumstances in which brevity is a prime consideration are well suited to the GDS–SF. Follow-up evaluation with a clinical interview or more extensive self-report assessment is suggested if the 15-, 10-, or 4-item short forms (or single depression question) suggest possible depressive symptoms.

ALTERNATE ADMINISTRATION TECHNIQUES

Older adults can present limitations that require nontraditional questionnaire administration strategies. For example, visual or manual dexterity problems may require examiner-assisted responding that departs from the clipboard, pencil, sit-alone prototype. Many of the studies reviewed for this chapter included data collected by oral administration of the GDS. But there are other alternatives that have been empirically evaluated: telephone administration and the use of collateral sources.

Telephone Administration

Oral administration of the GDS by an examiner via telephone is an extension of the examiner-assisted literature presented previously. There are several potential uses of telephone administrations; they include checkups for ongoing treatments, large-scale screening for epidemiological studies, and recruitment for clinical trials. Two studies were published recently addressing this form of administration. Burke, Roccaforte, Wengel, Conley, and Potter (1995) gave the GDS–LF to 101 patients on three occasions: by telephone several days prior to a face-to-face assessment, again during the assessment, and by telephone several days after the assessment. The criterion used in this study was the diagnosis of depression by a geriatric psychiatrist. There was substantial agreement between the two telephone administrations and between the initial telephone administration and the face-to-face administration. Using a cut score of 11, sensitivity and specificity rates of 86% and 70%, respectively, were found for clinical diagnosis of depression. These results led Burke et al. to recommend the "GDS–T" for research and clinical applications where appropriate.

Morishita et al. (1995) compared telephone and in-person administration of the GDS–LF with 31 community-dwelling older adults. Order of administration was counterbalanced and separated by 2 weeks. The correlation of the two administrations was .90. The authors noted that the average time of telephone administration was 11.5 min, making the GDS–T an efficient means to estimate depression severity.

These studies on the use of the GDS via telephone administration may seem rather pedestrian, but they have significant applied importance. For non-mental health providers such as nurses or primary care physicians, the telephone GDS can provide a simple and quick assay of the geriatric patient for depression identification or monitoring. This of course should not become a substitute for face-to-face contact, but in situations in which traditional assessment is difficult or impossible, the GDS–T is an appealing alternative.

Collateral Sources

A second alternate administration study addressed an equally important topic: the use of collateral sources in assessing geriatric depression. Persons evidencing moderate and severe dementia are routinely evaluated exclusively or conjointly via a collateral source. Nitcher, Burke, Roccaforte, and Wengel (1993) evaluated the utility of a collateral source GDS with 170 outpatients at a geriatric assessment clinic. The collateral source GDS (GDS–CS) consisted of the 30 items of the GDS in which the pronoun "they" was substituted for "you" (e.g., "Are they basically satisfied with their life?"). In brief, Nitcher et al. found moderate correlation between the GDS–CS and GDS ($r = .42$). Both were found to correspond to clinical diagnoses of depression. Perhaps the most interesting finding of this study was the consistent endorsement of more GDS symptoms by collateral sources. As a consequence, the score that resulted in optimal sensitivity and specificity on the GDS–CS was 21. The authors conclude that the GDS–CS can be a useful instrument but that a higher cutoff point should be used due to the tendency for overendorsement.

USE AS A SCREENER

The GDS has great potential for use as a depression screener. The use of screeners in primary care is desirable for a number of reasons. Major depression is a relatively common disorder among the elderly. Prevalence rates of 3% for major depression and 15% for significant depressive symptoms have been reported (Friedhoff, 1994), making depression the most common mental health problem from which older adults suffer. Unfortunately, symptoms of older individuals' underlying mental health problems are often either ignored, misdiagnosed, or are simply attributed to the inevitability of the "aging process" and then left untreated (Butler, Lewis & Sunderland, 1991). Friedhoff (1994) elaborated:

> Because of the many physical illnesses and social and economic problems of elderly patients, individual health care providers often conclude that depression is a normal consequence of these problems, an attitude often shared by the patients themselves. All of these factors conspire to make the illness underdiagnosed and, more importantly, undertreated. (p. 494)

Underdiagnosis of depression by the general practitioner can be a serious problem given that elderly people prefer to seek help from their general practitioner (Robinson, 1998), and that the most common provider of depression treatment is the primary care physician (Narrow, Reigier, Rae, Manderscheid, & Locke, 1993).

Because of the role that the primary care physician plays in the detection and treatment of depression in the elderly, accurate screening for depression is critical. Such screening can be accomplished quite effectively using the GDS. The GDS is in our opinion the screening instrument of choice for geriatric depression. It has all the desirable qualities; it is brief, it is well-tolerated by patients, it is cost-efficient in that it only costs as much as the paper on which it is printed, and it exhibits high sensitivity and reliability across a variety of populations. For these reasons in particular, it is well suited for use in busy primary care settings.

To assess for depression among older adults in a primary care setting, we suggest using the following sequential approach. First, include the GDS or GDS–SF as a screener administered annually to patients aged 60 years and older, or administer it more frequently if there is reason to believe the patient may be depressed. This may easily be accomplished in a short period while the patient is waiting to see the physician. Although many patients will be able to fill out the GDS without assistance, some may need extra assistance. Patients who are unable to read the questionnaire may need a staff member or family member to read the items to them. To avoid unnecessary frustration on the part of the patient, office staff should ask at the time the questionnaire is handed out if the patient would like to have the items read aloud to them. Similarly, some patients may lack the necessary manual dexterity to circle answers to the questionnaire; office staff should offer to assist with this step as well. In the event that a patient expresses resistance to filling out the GDS, an effort should be made by the office staff to explain to the patient that the questionnaire simply assists the doctor in determining how best to help the patient. Because resistance may stem from a concern about inability to read, comprehend, or answer the items, staff should reassure the patient that the form only takes a few minutes to complete, and the staff would be happy to read the items to the patient and circle the answers for them if desired. In the event that a patient is known to be or believed to be moderately to severely cognitively impaired, the GDS should be completed by a collateral source as well as or instead of by the older adult.

The cutoff score on the measure should be set low to maximize sensitivity; we recommend a cutoff score of 7 on the GDS, and 3 on the GDS–SF. By setting a low cutoff, few false negatives will occur (i.e., failures to identify that a patient is depressed), and false positives (incorrect identification by the screener of nondepressed patients as depressed) can be identified during the office visit itself. The exception to this guideline is with collateral source administration; in this case, due to collateral sources' tendency to overreport depressive symptoms, the cut score may be set higher—we recommend 17.

If the older patient scores above the cutoff on the screener, a semistructured clinical interview focusing on depression should be administered with the goal of establishing and distinguishing mood disorder diagnoses including major depression, dysthymic disorder, depressive disorder not otherwise specified, adjustment disorder with depressed features, minor depression, and mixed anxiety and depression. The *Diagnostic and Statistical Manual of Mental Disorders*, 4th edition (*DSM–IV*; American Psychiatric Association [APA], 1994) provides criteria for each of these depressive spectrum disorders. The Diagnostic Interview Schedule (DIS; Robins & Helzer, 1985) and the Structured Clinical Interview for *DSM* (SCID; Spitzer, Williams, Gibbon, & First, 1992) provide useful frameworks for this type of diagnostic interview. Both generate information on current and past disorders and allow subtyping of depressive disorders, which may affect the decision of as to what treatment modality is most appropriate. Unfortunately, both are time-consuming, require extensive training to administer properly, and may assess for more disorders than of interest to the physician. It may be more useful in a primary care setting for physicians to become familiar with the types of questioning used in these instruments, and tailor to their practice a succinct but thorough line of questioning aimed at determining *DSM–IV* diagnoses.

If more detailed information is desired, the Hamilton Rating Scale for Depression (HRSD; Hamilton, 1967) or the Geriatric Depression Rating Scale (GDRS; Jamison & Scogin, 1992) can be administered to provide a quantitative severity rating. The

HRSD is the classic instrument for estimating depression severity; generally, scores of 10 or above indicate at least mild depression among older and younger patients, and scores of 17 or above almost always result in a patient meeting *DSM–IV* criteria for a depressive diagnosis (Scogin & McElreath, 1994). The GDRS was created with the intent of combining the format of the HRSD with the content of the GDS, to deemphasize the somatic items that can make depressive diagnosis problematic in older adults. Although this scale is still in development, initial psychometric evaluations suggest that it exhibits acceptable internal consistency, and good concurrent validity with the HRSD, GDS, and the Beck Depression Inventory (BDI; Beck, Ward, Mendelson, Mock, & Erbaugh, 1961). Sensitivity and specificity estimates compare favorably with the HRSD. The GDRS may require less experience and training to administer reliably than does the HRSD. A score of 20 on the GDRS suggests the presence of at least mild to moderate depression severity.

If the follow-up interview indicates the presence of a depressive disorder, treatment with antidepressant medication may certainly be appropriate. As noted in the NIH Consensus Development Conference (Friedhoff, 1994), the decision may be less obvious if a person exhibits less severe depressive symptomatology. The important point is made, however, that less severe depression negatively impacts quality of life and is associated with increased risk of health problems as well as with development of more severe depression. Therefore, depressive symptoms should not be considered a normal part of aging; instead, they should be given prompt attention by the clinician. Discussion of treatment options with the patient is warranted, and referral to a psychotherapist may be appropriate.

When an older patient has been diagnosed with a depressive disorder, the question arises as to whether it is best to provide treatment in the primary care office or to refer to a mental health clinician. Some patients will refuse to take antidepressant medication, or may simply express a preference for another mode of treatment; in fact, a survey conducted by Rokke and Scogin (1995) found that older adults reported a preference for psychotherapy over drug therapy for depression. In the event that a patient is opposed to drug therapy, discussion with the patient regarding their preferences for treatment should be a key to determining an appropriate referral.

If a patient does not express a treatment preference, a combination of approaches may hold the best potential for outcome. Specifically, we would recommend a combination of pharmacotherapy, which can be provided by the primary care physician or a psychiatrist, and psychotherapy provided by a qualified psychotherapist. Although the effectiveness of antidepressant treatment has been well researched and documented, a significant percentage of those treated respond only partially to treatment or fail to respond altogether. It has been reported that a third of patients treated with an initial trial of antidepressants will not respond (Thase, 1997). Elderly patients may be even less treatment responsive than younger people (Thase & Rush, 1995). By the time patients have failed to respond to several different medications, the response rate per trial may be as low as 15% to 25% (Thase & Rush, 1995). Fava and Davidson (1996) reported similar figures in a meta-analysis of 36 antidepressant therapy trials; 12% to 15% of the patients exhibited only a partial response to therapy, and 19% to 34% exhibited nonresponse. Studies focusing on elderly people report similar figures; initial trial nonresponse rates as high as 40% have been reported for elderly patients (Flint & Rifat, 1996).

Fortunately, research is suggesting that improved response rates can be attained using a combination of pharmacotherapy and psychotherapy. Miller, Bishop, Norman, and Keitner (1985) augmented pharmacotherapy with cognitive behavioral therapy (CBT) in 6 inpatient drug-resistant adult females, and found that a majority of them substantially improved. Scott (1992) treated 16 chronically depressed adult patients with CBT and a pharmacotherapy regimen in a hospital setting, and reported response rates of 69%.

In outpatient settings, Fava, Savron, Grandi, and Rafanelli, (1997) treated 19 antidepressant treatment-resistant adult patients with a combination of antidepressants and CBT. All exhibited a significant decrease in depression scores after therapy, and 12 were judged to be in remission. At a 2-year follow-up, only 1 had relapsed. In an outpatient setting with an elderly population, Wilson, Scott, Abou-Saleh, Burns, and Copeland (1995) compared lithium augmentation to CBT as an adjunct to antidepressant therapy, and found CBT to be effective but lithium to be no more effective than placebo. Thompson and Gallagher-Thompson (1994), in a treatment study with older adults, compared desipramine alone, CBT alone, and the combination of the two. They found that participants receiving the combination and participants receiving CBT alone improved to a greater degree than did those receiving desipramine alone. They concluded that CBT is an effective treatment for depression in the elderly, and that the combination of pharmacotherapy and CBT may be particularly effective for patients who do not respond completely to antidepressants or psychotherapy.

Once the decision has been made to refer a patient out for psychotherapy, the type of therapy referral ought to be considered. Cognitive-behavior therapy is an appealing treatment approach for use with pharmacotherapy as an initial combination treatment, or as an augmentation strategy in cases in which residual symptoms of depression remain a problem. CBT may be well suited for elders because they experience more unchangeable negative life events including deteriorations in health, change of status in family and community, and death of loved ones. CBT facilitates the development of a more adaptive view of oneself and the situations in which one finds oneself (Gallagher-Thompson & Thompson, 1995). Additionally, CBT can increase a patient's sense of self-efficacy; it can increase coping ability through its management of paralyzing cognitive distortions; and it can enhance medication compliance through the implementation of behavioral techniques designed to facilitate adherence to a treatment regimen (Thase, 1997). Cognitive-behavior therapy is one of the most extensively researched psychotherapies; it has been found to be at least as effective as antidepressant medication in the treatment of acute episodes of depression, and may be more effective in the prevention of future episodes (Dobson, 1989; Hollon, Shelton, & Loosen, 1991; Robinson, Berman, & Neimeyer, 1990). Numerous research studies have demonstrated that CBT ranks as one of the most effective interventions for treating depression in the aging population (Gallagher-Thompson & Thompson, 1995; Scogin & McElreath, 1994). In their meta-analytic review, Scogin and McElreath (1994) found CBT for geriatric depression to have a substantial effect size ($d = .85$) relative to control conditions.

MONITORING

After a carefully chosen treatment regimen has been implemented, consideration must turn to the monitoring of the patient's progress. Given the rates cited earlier for incomplete response to a single trial of antidepressants, it is clear that effective monitoring will be important to establish the potential need for use of alternative treatment strategies. The GDS can prove to be an ideal instrument, particularly because it can be administered reliably and validly by telephone. This offers the physician the choice to monitor patients outside of regularly scheduled appointments if deemed necessary. Certainly, at the least, the GDS or GDS–SF should be administered each time the patient returns for medication checks or adjustments, or for other health consultations.

The determination of when a patient has responded sufficiently to a medication or when an alternative strategy is warranted can be a difficult one to make. An alternative strategy is very likely to be warranted when a patient demonstrates residual symptoms of depression following an adequate trial of antidepressant treatment that continue to warrant a diagnosis of a mood disorder, or that meet criteria for a mood disorder in partial remission as defined by the *DSM–IV*. This possibility is suggested when a patient scores 7 or above on the GDS, or 3 or above on the GDS–SF, and should be followed up as indicated previously with a semistructured clinical interview.

When a patient responds favorably to an intervention or to a combination of interventions, it is necessary for the physician to monitor and attempt to prevent relapse or recurrence. This is particularly important given that fewer than one third of elderly experience a positive outcome (i.e., no relapse) after 1- to 3-year follow-ups (Murphy, 1994). Evidence suggests that treatment should continue for at least 6 months after the patient's depression has remitted, and this period should be extended to 12 months of continued treatment if the person has experienced previous episodes (Friedhoff, 1994).

CASE STUDY

What follows is a fictionalized case we have created to illustrate our notions about the use of the GDS in primary care settings. The case represents a composite of features we have seen in our work with older adults.

Mrs. L. is a 72-year-old retired secretary who is widowed and living on her own but requires some assistance from her daughter in activities of daily living. Tasks such as looking up telephone numbers, completing insurance forms, and others requiring visual acuity prove difficult for Mrs. L. She also reports having a poor appetite and admits meal preparation is difficult. She eats more when her daughter delivers prepared meals. Despite her daughter's efforts to prepare bland food, Mrs. L. still complains of frequent nausea and indigestion. She has three children, two daughters and one son, but only one daughter lives nearby and assists her when needed. Mrs. L. has scheduled an appointment with her primary care physician to evaluate her frequent complaints of nausea and indigestion. Additionally, Mrs. L.'s daughter has been concerned that something else may be bothering Mrs. L. Lately she has seemed less energetic and less interested in her usual enjoyments. Because Mrs. L.'s vision is poor, her daughter has driven her to the appointment and has remained to assist her if necessary.

The nurse, in reviewing the patient's charts, notes that Mrs. L. has not been evaluated for depression in over a year, and decides this will be a good opportunity to do so. She presents Mrs. L. with a clipboard holding the GDS–SF and a pencil and asks Mrs. L. to take a few minutes to complete the form. The nurse explains the questionnaire is given annually to patients to help the doctor decide how best to help them.

The nurse explains to Mrs. L. that to complete the form, she needs to read each question and circle "yes" or "no" depending on how she has felt in the past week. She then asks Mrs. L. if she would like any assistance reading the form or circling her responses. Mrs. L. indicates that her vision makes reading difficult but that her daughter can read the questions to her. Because her arthritis limits her manual dexterity, Mrs. L.'s daughter circles the items for her as well.

The nurse is aware that Mrs. L. has begun to experience some cognitive impairment in the past few years; her chart notes that she sometimes becomes confused and feels easily overwhelmed by tasks she could previously perform on her own. The nurse waits a couple of minutes to ensure that Mrs. L. is able to respond to the questionnaire without difficulty. In the event that Mrs. L. is unable to understand and accurately respond to the items, the nurse will advise Mrs. L.'s daughter to answer them for her mother. Fortunately, Mrs. L. has no difficulty answering "yes" or "no" to each of the items as long as her daughter reads them to her, although she occasionally notes that answering "yes" or "no" is too limited, and expresses a desire to explain her answers. The nurse assures her that she will have such an opportunity when she talks with the doctor.

The nurse notices that some of the items seem to be emotionally difficult for Mrs. L. to answer in the presence of her daughter, and similarly that her daughter seems uncomfortable asking her mother some of the items. She addresses their discomfort by suggesting they leave blank any items that they don't wish to complete, and says that Mrs. L. and the nurse can finish completing the questionnaire in the doctor's office.

In reviewing Mrs. L.'s responses on the GDS–SF, the physician notes that she has endorsed several items indicative of depression, including feeling that her life is empty, often feeling helpless and worthless, and that she has dropped many of her activities and interests. Her total score is a 7, which exceeds the recommended cut score of 3 and warrants a follow-up interview. The physician has familiarized herself with the types of questions asked in the major depression section of the SCID and at this time asks Mrs. L. similar questions aimed at obtaining a *DSM–IV* diagnosis in a succinct fashion. This interview indicates that Mrs. L. in fact has experienced five of the nine symptoms listed in the *DSM–IV* as indicative of major depression, and has experienced them continuously for the last couple of months. She spontaneously reports feeling lonely and isolated, and frustrated over the limitations posed by her failing health.

Mrs. L.'s daughter mentions that Mrs. L. hasn't seemed herself lately, that she has been less talkative, less enthusiastic about participating in family functions, and has not been as energetic as she usually is. Mrs. L. had routinely come to her daughter's home for the Sunday noon meal, but had recently stopped attending, stating she was "too tired." The family members have not been overly concerned because they have attributed these changes to her age. Her physician wonders if her gastrointestinal complaints may be related to the depression.

Treatment for depression is clearly indicated for Mrs. L., so the physician discusses with her recommendations for a combination treatment of pharmacotherapy and psychotherapy. She explains that the antidepressant will most likely help to improve Mrs. L.'s mood and other symptoms, although it may take several weeks or longer to take effect. The physician explains that the psychotherapist will offer support to Mrs. L., offer her a chance to discuss what is bothering her, and assist her in evaluating her thoughts and feelings regarding the changes she is experiencing in relation to her health and growing older. The physician explains that the therapy and medication will complement each other to give her the best chance of reducing or eliminating her depression. Mrs. L. expresses an interest in both, so she is prescribed an appropriate antidepressant and referred to a psychotherapist the physician regularly uses who specializes in cognitive behavioral therapy for depression.

Mrs. L. returns in a month for a medication check, and completes the GDS for treatment monitoring; on this administration, she scores a 5. She reports that she still feels poorly; her endorsement of many of the same items as before reinforces her report. The physician has also received a report from the psychotherapist that corroborates Mrs. L.'s assessment. However, she says she is enjoying her therapy sessions and likes her therapist, and acknowledges that she is feeling better about some things. Her daughter mentions that the therapist has been working with Mrs. L. to increase the number of pleasant activities in which she engages, and has begun to address Mrs. L.'s feelings of worthlessness through exercises designed to increase her sense of mastery. The therapist encouraged Mrs. L. to return to her volunteer work at the Public Library and to use humor to cope with her occasional memory lapses and visual problems. Together, Mrs. L. and her therapist perused catalogs and chose implements such as specialty magnifying glasses, faucet adapters, and timer devices that increased Mrs. L.'s comfort and independent functioning. Mrs. L. seems to be responding well to these techniques. The physician commends her for her work with the therapist, and reminds her that the medication takes some time to produce noticeable results but that she should notice improvements in mood in the next few weeks. She reminds her to take the medication as prescribed and not to discontinue, even if she begins to feel better, without first consulting with her. She encourages Mrs. L. or her daughter to call her if they do not note significant improvement in the next few weeks.

One month later, the nurse calls Mrs. L. to follow up on her progress by telephone. Using the GDS–SF, the nurse finds that Mrs. L.'s symptoms have decreased markedly — only two symptoms are endorsed, and she reports feeling happier, spending more time with family and friends, and feeling positively about the future. She expresses a desire to discontinue the medication, but the nurse instructs her to continue taking it until she sees the physician again, explaining that it is best to continue the medication for several months to prevent relapse.

Mrs. L. continues her psychotherapy for a 20-week course, and at the end of that time her symptoms of depression have remitted. The psychotherapist offers Mrs. L. strategies to practice in an effort to prevent relapse and reoccurence, and Mrs. L. practices these regularly. Mrs. L. was encouraged to continue using her good sense of humor to cope with her physical limitations, as well as to focus on new skills she now has time to explore. During this time, Mrs. L.'s physician continues to monitor her systematically using the GDS–SF, and eventually discontinues Mrs. L.'s pharmacotherapy when she deems it appropriate. Because of Mrs. L.'s past experience with depression, her physician will continue to screen her for depression using the GDS–SF at every visit.

SUMMARY AND CONCLUSIONS

Geriatric depression is a common problem affecting a substantial percentage of older patients in primary care settings. Because older patients express a preference to seek help from primary care physicians, and because geriatric depression is commonly underdiagnosed, accurate screening for depression is crucial. The GDS provides an inexpensive, quick, easy, and reliable way to regularly screen patients age 60 years and over. And, the GDS provides flexibility in that it may be administered over the telephone or through the use of collateral sources.

We recommend use of the GDS or the GDS-SF as an annual screener in older patients; administration should be more frequent if the physician suspects that a patient is depressed. Administration of the screener should be followed up in cases in which depressive symptoms are indicated; this may be accomplished through the use of a semistructured clinical interview. When a depressive disorder has been diagnosed, treatment with antidepressant medication and/or a referral for psychotherapy is indicated. In cases in which depressive symptomatology is present but the criteria for a depressive disorder are not met, the discussion of treatment options with the patient is recommended. Once treatment has been implemented, the GDS may further be used to monitor patients' progress, and/or in the attempt to prevent relapse or recurrence. We recommend that patients be monitored through administration of the GDS at each consecutive visit, and by telephone between visits if deemed necessary by the physician.

REFERENCES

American Psychiatric Association. (1994). *Diagnostic and statistical manual of Mental disorders* (4th ed.). Washington, DC: Author.

Beck, A. T., Ward, C. H., Mendelson, M., Mock, J., & Erbaugh, J. (1961). An inventory for measuring depression. *Archives of General Psychiatry, 4,* 561–571.

Brink, T. L., Yesavage, J. A., Lum, O., Heersema, P. H., Adey, M., & Rose, T. L. (1982). Screening tests for geriatric depression. *Clinical Gerontologist, 1,* 37–43.

Burke, W. J., Houston, M. J., Boust, J. S., & Roccaforte, W. H. (1989). Use of the Geriatric Depression Scale in dementia of the Alzheimer type. *Journal of the American Geriatrics Society, 37,* 856–860.

Burke, W. J., Nitcher, R. L., Roccaforte, W. H., & Wengel, S. P. (1992). A prospective evaluation of the Geriatric Depression Scale in an outpatient geriatric assessment center. *Journal of the American Geriatric Society, 40,* 1227–1230.

Burke, W. J., Roccaforte, W. H., Wengel, S. P., Conley, D. M., & Potter, J. F. (1995). The reliability and validity of the Geriatric Depression Rating Scale administered by telephone. *Journal of the American Geriatric Society, 43,* 674–679.

Butler, R. N., Lewis, M., & Sunderland, T. (1991). *Aging and mental health* (4th ed.) New York: Merrill.

Callahan, C. M., Hui, S. L., Nienaber, N. A., Musick, B. S., & Tierney, W. M. (1994). Longitudinal study of depression and health services use among elderly primary care patients. *Journal of the American Geriatrics Society, 42,* 833–838.

Cwikel, J., & Ritchie, K. (1988). The Short GDS: Evaluation in a heterogeneous multilingual population. *Clinical Gerontologist, 8,* 63–71.

D'Ath, P., Katona, P., Mullan, E., Evans, S., & Katona, C. (1994). Screening, detection and management of depression in elderly primary care attenders: The acceptability and performance of the 15 Item Geriatric Depression Scale (GDS15) and the development of short versions. *Family Practice – An International Journal, 11,* 260–266.

Dobson, K. (1989). A meta-analysis of the efficacy of cognitive therapy for depression. *Journal of Consulting and Clinical Psychology, 57,* 414–419.

Fava, M. & Davidson, K. G. (1996). Definition and epidemiology of treatment-resistant depression. *Psychiatric Clinics of North America, 19,* 179–200.

Fava, G. A., Savron, G., Grandi, S., & Rafanelli, C. (1997). Cognitive-behavioral management of drug-resistant major depressive disorder. *Journal of Clinical Psychiatry, 58,* 278–282.

Feher, E. P., Larrabee, G. J., & Crook, T. H. (1992). Factors attenuating the validity of the Geriatric Depression Scale in a dementia population. *Journal of the American Geriatrics Society, 40,* 906–909.

Flint, A. J., & Rifat, S. L. (1996). The effect of sequential antidepressant treatment on geriatric depression. *Journal of Affective Disorders, 36,* 95–105.

Friedhoff, A. J. (1994). Consensus panel report. In L. S. Schneider, C. F. Reynolds, B. D. Lebowitz, & A. J. Friedhoff (Eds.), *Diagnosis and treatment of depression in late life: Results of the NIH Consensus Development Conference.* Washington, DC: American Psychiatric Press.

Gallagher-Thompson, D., & Thompson, L. W. (1995). Psychotherapy with older adults in theory and practice. In B. Bonger & L. Beutler (Eds.), *Comprehensive textbook of psychotherapy* (pp. 357–379). New York: Oxford University Press.

Hamilton, M. (1967). Development of a rating scale for primary depressive illness. *British Journal of Social and Clinical Psychology, 6,* 278–296.

Herrmann, N., Mittman, N., Silver, N., Shulman, K., Busto, U. A., Shear, N., & Naranjo, C. A. (1996). A validation study of the Geriatric Depression Scale Short Form. *International Journal of Geriatric Psychiatry, 11,* 457–460.

Hollon, S. D., Shelton, R. C., & Loosen, P. T. (1991). Cognitive therapy and pharmacotherapy for depression. *Journal of Consulting and Clinical Psychology, 59,* 88–99.

Jamison, C., & Scogin, F. (1992). Development of an interview-based geriatric depression rating scale. *International Journal of Aging and Human Development, 35,* 193–204.

Jarvik, L. (1976). Aging and depression: Some unanswered questions. *Journal of Gerontology, 31,* 324–326.

Kane, R. A., & Kane, R. L. (1981). *Assessing the elderly: A practical guide to measurement.* Boston: Lexington Books.

Katz, I. R., & Parmalee, P. A. (1994). Depression in elderly patients in residential care settings. In L. S. Schneider, C. F. Reynolds III, B. D. Lebowitz, & A. J. Friedhoff (Eds.), *Diagnosis and treatment of late life depresson: Results of the NIH Consensus Development Conference* (pp. 437–462). Washington, DC: American Psychiatric Press.

Lesher, E. L., & Berryhill, J. S. (1994). Validation of the Geriatric Depression Scale–Short form among inpatients. *Journal of Clinical Psychology, 50,* 256–260.

Mahoney, J., Drinka, T. J. K., Abler, R., Gunter-Hunt, G., Matthews, C., Gravenstein, S., & Carnes, M. (1994). Screening for depression: Single question versus GDS. *Journal of the American Geriatrics Society, 42,* 1006–1008.

McGivney, S. A., Mulvihill, M., & Taylor, B. (1994). Validating the GDS depression screen in the nursing home. *Journal of the American Geriatric Society, 42,* 490–492.

Miller, I. W., Bishop, S. B., Norman, W. H., & Keitner, G. I. (1985). Cognitive-behavioural therapy and pharmacotherapy with chronic, drug-refractory depressed inpatients: A note of optimism. *Behavioural Psychotherapy, 13,* 320–327.

Morishita, L., Boult, C., Ebbit, B., Rambel, M., Fallstrom, K., & Gooden, T. (1995). Concurrent validity of administering the Geriatric Depression Scale and the physical functioning dimension of the SIP by telephone. *Journal of the American Geriatrics Society, 43,* 680–683.

Murphy, E. (1994). The course and outcome of depression in late life. In L. S. Schneider, C. F. Reynolds, B. D. Lebowitz, & A. J. Friedhoff (Eds.), *Diagnosis and treatment of depression in late life: Results of the NIH Consensus Development Conference* (pp. 81–97). Washington, DC: American Psychiatric Press.

Narrow, W. E., Reigier, D. A., Rae, D. S., Manderscheid, R. W., & Locke, B. Z. (1993). Use of services by persons with mental and addictive disorders: Findings from the National Institute of Mental Health Epidemiologic Catchment Area Program. *Archives of General Psychiatry, 50,* 95–107.

Nitcher, R. L., Burke, W. J., Roccaforte, W. H., & Wengel, S. P. (1993). A collateral source version of the Geriatric Depression Rating Scale. *American Journal of Geriatric Psychiatry, 1,* 143–152.

Parmalee, P. A., Lawton, M. P., & Katz, I. R. (1989). Psychometric properties of the Geriatric Depression Scale among the institutionalized aged. *Psychological Assessment, 1,* 331–338.

Robins, L. N., & Helzer, J. E. (1985). *Diagnostic Interview Schedule: Version III–A.* St. Louis, MO: Washington University School of Medicine.

Robinson, P. (1998). Behavioral health services in primary care: A new perspective for treating depression. *Clinical Psychology: Science and Practice, 5,* 77–89.

Robinson, L. A., Berman, J. S., & Neimeyer, R. A. (1990). Psychotherapy for the treatment of depression: A comprehensive review of controlled outcome research. *Psychological Bulletin, 108,* 30–49.

Rokke, P. D., & Scogin, F. (1995). Depression treatment preferences in younger and older adults. *Journal of Clinical Geropsychology, 1,* 243–257.

Salzman, C., & Shader, R. I. (1978). Depression in the elderly: Relationship between depression, psychologic defense mechanisms and physical illness. *Journal of the American Geriatrics Society, 26,* 253–260.

Scogin, F. & McElreath, L. (1994). Efficacy of psychosocial treatments for geriatric depression: A quantitative review. *Journal of Consulting and Clinical Psychology, 62,* 69–74.

Scott, J. (1992). Chronic depression: Can cognitive therapy succeed when other treatments fail? *Behavioural Psychotherapy, 20,* 25–36.

Shah, A., Phongsathorn, V., George, C., Bielawska, C., & Katona, C. (1992). Psychiatric morbidity among continuing care geriatric inpatients. *International Journal of Geriatric Psychiatry, 7,* 517–525.

Sheik, J. I., & Yesavage, J. A. (1986). Geriatric Depression Scale (GDS): Recent evidence and development of a shorter version. *Clinical Gerontologist, 5,* 165–173.

Spitzer, R. L., Williams, J. B. W., Gibbon, M., & First, M. (1992). The Structured Clinical Interview for DSM–III–R (SCID): History, rationale, and description. *Archives of General Psychiatry, 49,* 624–629.

Steiner, A., Raube, K., Stuck, A. E., Aronow, H. U., Draper, D., Rubenstein, L. Z., & Beck, J. C. (1996). Measuring psychosocial aspects of well-being in older community residents: Performance of four short scales. *Gerontologist, 36,* 54–62.

Thase, M. E. (1997). Psychotherapy of refractory depressions. *Depression and Anxiety, 5,* 190–201.

Thase, M. D., & Rush, J. A. (1995). Treatment-resistant depression. In F. E. Bloom & D. J. Kupfer (Eds.), *Psychopharmacology: The fourth generation of progress* (pp. 1081–1097). New York: Raven Press.

Thompson, L. W., & Gallagher-Thompson, D. (1994, August). *Comparison of desipramine and cognitive/behavioral therapy for the treatment of late-life depression: A progress report.* Paper presented at the 102nd Annual Convention of the American Psychological Association, Los Angeles.

Ward, L. C., Wadsworth, A. P., & Peterson, L. P. (1994). Concurrent validity of measures of anxiety, depression, and somatization in elderly, demented, male patients. *Clinical Gerontologist, 15,* 3–13.

Wilson, K. M., Scott, M., Abou-Saleh, M., Burns, R., & Copeland, J. M. (1995). Long-term effects of cognitive-behavioural therapy and lithium therapy on depression in the elderly. *British Journal of Psychiatry, 167,* 653–658.

Yesavage, J. A., Brink, T. L., Rose, T. L., Lum, O., Huang, V., Adey, M., & Leirer, V. O. (1983). Development and validation of a geriatric depression screening scale: A preliminary report. *Journal of Psychiatric Research, 17,* 37–49.

Zung, W. W. K. (1965). A self-rating depression scale. *Archives of General Psychiatry, 12,* 63–70.

Using the Beck Anxiety Inventory in Primary Care

Robert J. Ferguson
Dartmouth Medical School

Anxiety disorders are the most prevalent of behavioral health problems in the United States, with more Americans affected by anxiety disorders than substance abuse or depression (Robins et al., 1984). Approximately 10% of individuals will endure an anxiety disorder in their lifetime (Wittchen & Essau, 1991). However, despite their relatively high numbers, the majority of individuals suffering significant anxiety do not seek evaluation and treatment from psychologists, psychiatrists, or other mental health specialists; rather, they tend to seek services through primary care or medical specialty clinics (Boyd, 1986; Katon et al., 1990). Indeed, individuals with anxiety disorders utilize medical services at rates higher than individuals without problematic anxiety (Carter & Maddock, 1992; Katon et al., 1990). Unfortunately, many patients with anxiety disorders are misdiagnosed or not detected at all in the primary care setting, which then leads to reduced patient function, compromised quality of life, and unnecessary or redundant use of medical services. In view of this, using a valid and reliable measure of anxiety in the primary care setting to aid detection of anxiety disorders makes eminent sense. One such tool is the Beck Anxiety Inventory (BAI).

The BAI is a brief 21-item measure of common anxiety symptoms. Its design was intended as a research and clinical measure of anxiety that minimized content overlap with measures of depression (Beck, Epstein, Brown, & Steer, 1988; Beck & Steer, 1993). Historically, many anxiety scales, such as the Hamilton Anxiety Rating Scale-Revised (HARS-R; Riskind, Beck, Brown, & Steer, 1987) and the State-Trait Anxiety Inventory (STAI; Spielberger, Gorsuch, & Lushene, 1970), correlated highly with self-report measures of depression, thus suggesting high symptom/content overlap (Beck et al., 1988; Dobson, 1985; Gotlib & Cane, 1989; Mountjoy & Roth, 1982; Prusoff & Klerman, 1974; Riskind et al., 1987; Snaith & Taylor, 1985; Tanaka-Masumi & Kameoka, 1986). Over the past decade, studies on the BAI strongly suggest it discriminates well between anxiety and depressive symptoms. This has direct implications for primary care. The fast-paced environment of primary care medicine demands quick, reliable assessment that can aid diagnosis and improve therapeutic decision making in the realm of behavioral health problems. Because of its apparent discriminant validity, the BAI can help distinguish anxiety problems from depressed mood, thus reducing diagnostic or therapeutic error.

Although the BAI has great potential in screening for anxiety disorders and measuring anxiety severity in primary care, it is not infallible. For example, the BAI may tend to measure panic attack symptoms more than generalized anxiety (Cox, Cohen, Direnfeld, & Swinson, 1996a), thereby complicating interpretations of the total score and clouding decisions of whether to treat or not to treat. Emphatically, this chapter is not a substitute for appropriate training in administration and interpretation of the BAI as described by the American Psychological Association's *Standards for Educational and Psychological Tests* (1985). Use of the BAI, and other psychological measurement tools, requires clinical experience and expertise in responding to a wide variety of patient complaints that can accompany BAI responses. Clinicians should be sensitive to the limits and strengths of the BAI and interpret the BAI information as one part of an overall assessment of patient presentation, not as a comprehensive assessment in and of itself. Thus, this chapter emphasizes that individuals who use the BAI in primary care be adequately trained.

The BAI can be conveniently implemented in a variety of clinical settings. It is short, easily understood by most patients, and can be administered in both self-report and oral formats. The BAI content consists of 14 items that represent physiological symptoms such as numbness and tingling, dizziness, and sweating, and 7 other items representing "subjective" symptoms such a fear of the worst happening, fear of losing control, or feeling scared. Respondents are instructed to rate each item on a 0 to 4 Likert type-rating scale with the following anchors:

0 = *Not at all.*
1 = *Mildly. It did not bother me much.*
2 = *Moderately. It was very unpleasant but I could stand it.*
3 = *Severely. I could barely stand it.*

Ratings are for "the past week, including today." Written administration is generally 5 to 10 minutes, whereas oral administration is generally 10 minutes. Verbatim instructions for oral administration are published on p. 4 of the BAI test manual (Beck & Steer, 1993). Oral instructions can be used for phone administration, which is a convenient way to conduct follow-up assessments in primary care practice. The scale produces a total score that is a sum of item ratings and can range from 0 to 63. The general interpretation of scores is guided by recommendations in the BAI test manual. These guidelines are based on the original anxiety disorder sample used in establishing test norms (Beck et al., 1988) and are outlined in Table 16.1.

However, these interpretive ranges are not based on studies of BAI sensitivity and specificity in anxiety populations, nor are they based on nonclinical samples selected

TABLE 16.1
BAI Scores and Severity Ranges as Described by Beck and Steer (1993)

BAI Score	Severity Range
0–7	Minimal
8–15	Mild
16–25	Moderate
26–63	Severe

to reflect demographic characteristics of the U.S. population. Such studies have been published since the latest edition of the BAI manual published in 1993, and this brings into question the validity of the preceding interpretive categories. This is discussed later in the Basic Interpretive Strategy portion of this chapter, and it is suggested that that section be considered as an interpretive guide when using the BAI in primary care practice.

OVERVIEW

Summary of Development

When Beck and colleagues set out to develop the BAI, they noted that tests designed to measure anxiety were constructed primarily with items that reflected an underlying theory of anxiety and clinical experience (Beck et al., 1988). For example, the STAI based much of its development on the theory that anxiety is the affective response when there is a perceived or actual discrepancy between external demands and coping resources (Speilberger et al., 1970). As a result, individual items were selected to fit with this theory—not on each item's potential for distinguishing anxiety from other affective states such as depression. Thus, the question of discriminant validity was addressed only after the final anxiety measure was identified. Beck and colleagues contended that by constructing anxiety measures in this fashion, the natural consequence was a number of anxiety scales that correlated highly with measures of depression (Beck et al., 1988).

In contrast to previous methods, the BAI was developed by selecting individual items that maximally represented anxiety phenomena, but maximally discriminated anxiety from depression (Anastasi, 1986; Jackson, 1970). The steps of BAI development were based on a three-step procedure outlined by Jackson (1970). These steps were:

1. Reduction of items from a large initial pool.
2. Analysis of an interim scale including reliability and validity analyses (the interim BAI was 37 items).
3. Establishment of psychometric properties on the final scale (i.e., the 21-item BAI).

The total sample utilized by Beck et al. (1988) consisted of 1,086 patients (456 men, 630 women; mean age = 36.02, SD = 12.27) who were seeking treatment for anxiety disorders at the Center for Cognitive Therapy in Philadelphia.

Step 1, scale development (item reduction), involved 810 patients who responded to a list of 86 items with 0 to 3 Likert type ratings. The items were derived from three previously developed anxiety instruments: the Anxiety Checklist, the *Physician's Desk Reference* Checklist, and the Situational Anxiety Checklist (Beck et al., 1988). Twenty items were eliminated due to redundancy or high similarity with one another, and 19 additional items were eliminated on the basis of repeated principal component factor analyses. Items with depression symptom overlap were dropped. The remaining 47-item scale was further reduced to 37 items on the basis of criterion-based validity analyses, such as mean score comparisons "between diagnostic and other criterion groups," that is, depressed groups versus anxious groups (see Beck et al., 1988, p. 895).

In step 2, BAI development, 116 patients completed the 37-item interim scale. The authors then conducted validity and reliability analyses that lead to the 21-item scale (these analyses are not detailed in the original manuscript of Beck et al., 1988, but may be obtained through writing the authors). In step 3, 160 patients completed the final 21-item scale. Analyses indicated the BAI had strong internal consistency (coefficient alpha = .92) and item-to-total score correlations ranging from .30 to .71 (median = .60). Eighty-six patients completed the 21-item scale 1 week apart with a test–retest coefficient of .75, thereby demonstrating reasonable stability. More psychometric findings of this sample and other samples reported elsewhere in the literature are reported later in the Basic Psychometric Information section.

Available Norms

The majority of reported BAI norms are based on samples of individuals with *DSM–III–R* and *DSM–IV* Axis I anxiety disorder diagnoses of young to middle-aged adults (Antony, Purdon, Swinson, & Downie, 1997; Beck et al., 1988; Fydrich, Dowdall, & Chambless, 1992). There are other studies reporting mean BAI scores, variability, and psychometic properties on various nonclinical samples such as university and medical students (Dent & Salkovskis, 1986; Osman, Kopper, Barrios, Osman, & Wade, 1997) and community adult samples (Dent & Salkovskis, 1986; Osman, Barrios, Aukes, Osman, & Markway, 1993). There are at least two known publications reporting BAI psychometric properties and mean scores on older adult populations, including older individuals in primary care (Wetherell & Arean, 1997) and older adults seeking outpatient psychiatric services (Kabacoff, Segal, Hersen, & Van Hasselt, 1997). However, only one known publication to date reports BAI responses of a sample of individuals selected to resemble the general demographic characteristics of the U.S. population (Gillis, Haaga, & Ford, 1995). In essence, Gillis et al. reported "normal" responses to which BAI scores from other subsamples (e.g., primary care patients) may be compared. Reported means and standard deviations of various BAI respondent samples and their sample characteristics are summarized in Table 16.2.

Basic Interpretive Strategy

A useful way to interpret a patient's BAI score is to compare the obtained score with the average score of a sample of individuals from a given population. For instance, if a patient reports to the primary care clinic with recurrent panic attacks over the 2 previous weeks and scores a 20 on the BAI, that score can be compared to the average of a group of nonclinical volunteers. This basic interpretive strategy, known as *norm-referenced interpretation*, is recommended for the BAI, particularly if it is used to help identify individuals with problematic anxiety in primary care. This strategy emphasizes use of actuarial statistics to aid detection of problem anxiety and thus improves clinical judgement and accountability (Wilson, 1998).

In norm-referenced interpretation, the basic question that is asked with respect to the patient's test score is, "Is the score within or outside the normal scoring range?" Because patients with anxiety disorders are generally expected to score higher on the BAI than patients without anxiety disorders, a BAI score obtained from someone

TABLE 16.2

Reported BAI Means and Standard Deviations Across Various Study Samples

Study	Group							
	NC	PDA	PD	Any PD	GAD	SOC	OCD	SP
Antony, Purdon, Swinson, and Downie (1997)	3.43 (3.59) n = 49			25.78 (14.25) n = 82		19.48 (12.43) n = 96	18.48 (11.78) n = 85	12.42 (9.06) n = 96
Beck and Steer (1993) and Beck et al. (1988)	15.88 (11.81) n = 16	27.27 (13.11) n = 95	28.81 (13.46) n = 93		18.83 (9.08) n = 90	17.77 (11.64) n = 44	21.69 (12.42) n = 26	
Creamer, Foran, and Bell (1995)	13.1 (9.6) n = 326							
Cox, Cohen, Direnfeld, and Swinson (1996)				26.86 (14.01) n = 157				
Fydrich, Dowdall, and Chambless (1992)		28.29 (14.29) n = 21	22.22 (12.21) n = 9					
Gillis, Haaga, and Ford (1995)	6.6 (8.1) n = 242							
Osman, Barrios, Aukes, Osman, and Markway (1993)	11.54 (10.26) n = 225							
Wetherell and Arean (1997)	9.5 (10.0) n = 197							

Note. NC, normal control group; PDA, panic disorder with agoraphobia; PD, panic disorder; any PD, panic disorder with and without agoraphobia; GAD, generalized anxiety disorder; SOC, social phobia; OCD, obsessive compulsive disorder; SP, specific phobia.

513

with an anxiety disorder would fall at the high end of a distribution of BAI scores obtained from a nonclinical sample. Table 16.3 lists possible BAI scores and their estimated percentile rank equivalents based on the distribution of community sample scores reported by Gillis et al. (1995). Instructions on how to use Table 16.3 for BAI test score interpretation are provided.

Table 16.3 was constructed in the following manner: BAI raw scores were converted to standard z-scores based on the BAI overall sample mean (of raw scores) and standard deviation reported by Gillis et al. (1995; z = raw score $- M/SD$). They found an overall BAI mean score for a sample of 242 adult volunteers of 6.6, with a standard deviation of 8.1. Each z-score thus indicates where a given BAI raw score falls on this distribution of BAI scores in terms of standard deviation units. Corresponding percentile rank equivalents on the theoretical "normal curve" distribution of standard scores or z-scores are listed in the far right column.

TABLE 16.3
Normative BAI Values and Percentile Rank Equivalents Based
on a Community Sample Matched to 1990 U.S. Census
Data Reported by Gillis, Haaga, and Ford (1995)

BAI Raw Score	z-Score (Number of SDs from Mean)	Percentile Equivalent
0	−.82	21
1	−.69	25
2	−.57	30
3	−.44	32
4	−.32	37
5	−.20	42
6	−.07	47
7	.05	53
8	.17	58
9	.30	61
10	.42	66
11	.54	70
12	.67	75
13	.79	79
14	.91	83
15	1.04	86
16	1.20	87
17	1.30	90
18	1.41	92
19	1.53	94
20	1.65	95
21	1.78	96
22	1.90	97
23	2.03	98
24	2.20	98
25	2.30	99
26	2.40	99
27	2.52	99
28	2.64	99.2
29	2.77	99.4
30	2.89	99.5
—	—	—
63	6.96	99.99

To illustrate, a BAI raw score of 20 produces a z-score of 1.65 when using the mean and standard deviation reported by Gillis et al. (20 − 6.6/8.1 = 1.65), or 1.65 standard deviations above the mean. At 1.65 standard deviation units above the mean, 95% of BAI scores fall below this in the distribution of community volunteer BAI scores. In other words, a BAI score of 20 is higher than 95% of BAI scores in the community sample. Problematic anxiety or an anxiety disorder is therefore highly likely for this patient. By contrast, a patient scoring 10 on the BAI may be above the mean of 6.6, but this score is at about the 66th percentile, well within the normal range of BAI scores.

The use of norm-referenced test interpretation is useful in detection of anxiety problems and allows for clinicians and patients to put symptoms in perspective with regard to the "average" individual. The key to norm-referenced test interpretation is that normative samples be obtained that approximate the demographic characteristics of the target population. Age, gender, and racial proportions should be about the same in the sample as the greater population. Until 1995, there were no BAI norms available in a reasonably large nonclinical sample of adults that reflected the U.S. population base. One nonclinical sample obtained by Dent and Salkovskis (1986) in England was cited in the BAI test manual. Although the sample was sufficient in size (243 volunteers), the average age was 23 years, likely due to the fact that 85% of participants were students. Also, 68% of the sample were women, which is not reflective of the general population male-to-female ratio. By contrast, Gillis et al. (1995) obtained a sample carefully selected to match 1990 U.S. census data across race, gender, income, and age range. The final sample closely reflected census data, which was 51% female, ranged in age from 18 to 65 years, and was 85% Caucasian. No differences on the BAI were observed across income, sex, or race variables, although younger participants (ages 18 to 44) scored higher ($M = 7.3$, $SD = 8.4$) than older participants ($M = 4.4$, $SD = 6.3$), $t (240) = 2.9$, $p < .01$ (Gillis et al., 1995).

Table 16.3 is a useful BAI interpretive guide, but precisely what BAI score indicates problematic anxiety or an anxiety disorder is not yet clearly defined. To date there is only one known published empirical study investigating sensitivity, specificity, and overall diagnostic efficiency of the BAI (Kabacoff et al., 1997). Although of high quality, this study was conducted with patients age 55 years or older ($M = 65.86$, $SD = 8.54$) seeking psychiatric services and thus limits generalizability to other adult population segments.

Based on Table 16.3, criterion scores and corresponding interpretive statements are outlined in Table 16.4. Beside each interpretive statement is a rationale for using the criterion score. Table 16.4 is presented here as a set of guidelines for making clinical decisions based BAI results, but is not based on facts gleaned from BAI sensitivity and specificity data in primary care. Clinicians are thus urged to exercise discretion when using Table 16.4.

Some final points of caution on norm-referenced test interpretation are worth noting. First, although norm-referenced interpretation of the BAI can indicate where an individual's BAI score lies on the distribution of normal scores, it cannot say with predictive certainty whether the individual has an anxiety disorder. Any psychological test's ability to discriminate individuals with or without anxiety disorders depends on the base rates of anxiety disorders in the population in question (Kabacoff et al., 1997). Base rates in outpatient psychological services for anxiety disorders may differ from those in the primary care sector. Second, when comparing an individual patient score to an average score of a normative sample, the patient demographic characteristics should reasonably match those of the normative group. It would not

TABLE 16.4
Interpretive Statements on BAI Scoring Ranges Based on Normative
BAI Scores Reported by Gillis, Haaga, and Ford (1995)

BAI Criterion Score	Interpretive Statement	Rationale for Criterion Score
0–10	Normal scoring range	See Table 16.1
11–14	High-normal scoring range	Score is still within one standard deviation of the normal mean, but some individuals with anxiety disorders such as specific phobia can score in this range
15	Suggests a likelihood of problematic anxiety or presence of anxiety disorder	86th Percentile, a little over one standard deviation above normal mean
20	Strongly suggests the presence of problematic anxiety or anxiety disorder	95th Percentile, within the top 5% of BAI scores
23	Highly likely problematic anxiety or anxiety disorder is present	98th Percentile of BAI scores; within top 2% of scores

be valid, for example, to compare a 12-year-old male patient's score on the BAI to the normative data presented in Table 16.3, because the age range for Table 16.3 data was from 18 to 65 years, a distinctly adult sample. Nevertheless, when these factors are taken into consideration, the norm-referenced interpretive strategy presented here can aid clinicians in the actuarial detection and treatment of problematic anxiety, rather than relying solely on their clinical judgement.

Basic Psychometric Information

The BAI has excellent psychometric properties based a number of published studies on various clinical and nonclinical samples. Here is a review of BAI reliability and validity research.

Internal Consistency Reliability. Studies reporting the BAI's internal consistency have been highly favorable. Reliability coefficients reported (Cronbach's coefficient alpha) have generally ranged from .90 to .94, indicating that 90% of variability in BAI scores among test takers is due to true score variability. In the original test sample, Beck et al. (1988) reported an alpha of .92 among 160 outpatients with various anxiety disorders. Similarly, Fydrich et al. (1992) reported an alpha of .94 with a sample of adult outpatients with mixed anxiety disorders. In other clinical samples, Kabacoff et al. (1997) reported Cronbach's alpha to be .90 among 217 elderly (age $M =$ 65.86; $SD = 8.54$) psychiatric outpatients diagnosed with anxiety disorders. Wetherell and Arean (1997) reported an alpha of .92 among elderly, indigent, general medical patients. Cox et al. (1996a) reported a coefficient alpha of .93 among 157 outpatients with panic disorder with and without agoraphobia. In student samples, Osman et al. (1997) reported an alpha of .90 among 350 college undergraduates, whereas Creamer, Foran, and Bell (1995) reported an alpha of .91 among 326 college undergraduates.

Test–Retest Reliability. BAI test scores have been demonstrated to remain stable over time. Because it is a self-report measure of symptoms within a 1-week time frame, the BAI tends to be better suited as an instrument assessing anxiety states rather than anxiety as a trait that is stable over long time frames (Creamer et al., 1995;

Fydrich et al., 1992). Over a 7-day test–retest period, Beck et al. (1988) reported a correlation of .75 in the original test sample. Similarly, Fydrich et al. (1992) reported a 7-day test–retest coefficient of .73 among an outpatient sample of individuals with anxiety disorders. However, when the time frame is extended, the test–retest correlation lowers slightly to .67 (Fydrich et al., 1992). Among 326 undergraduate students, a test–retest correlation of .62 was reported by Creamer et al. (1995) over a 7-week period. In summary, the BAI demonstrates good stability over time, but is also sensitive to changes in reported anxiety symptoms, an important factor when considering the BAI as a measure of outcome.

Item-to-Total Score Correlations. With regard to other indexes of reliability, Beck et al. (1988) reported corrected item-to-total score correlations ranging from .30 to .71 in the original test sample. Kabacoff et al. (1997) reported item-to-total score correlations ranging from .37 to .69 among anxious elderly outpatients, whereas Wetherell and Arean (1997) reported item-to-total score correlations of .48 to .70 among elderly general medical outpatients. Finally, Creamer et al. (1995) reported item-to-total correlations found among their college undergraduate sample ranging from .31 to .64. Thus, the BAI has good interitem correlation and tends to measure a consistent cluster, or anxiety construct, with regularity across clinical and nonclinical samples.

Content Validity. The BAI was constructed such that selected items would not correlate with items of self-report inventories of depression. As stated previously, Beck and colleagues appeared to have succeeded in attaining this objective. However, in so doing, a majority of the BAI's item content (14 of 21 items) reflects primarily psychophysiological symptoms of anxiety. Consequently, recent data suggest that the BAI is more a self-report measure of psychophysiological rather than affective or cognitive aspects of anxiety (Cox, Cohen, Direnfeld, & Swinson, 1996a, 1996b; Creamer et al., 1995). Indeed, patients with panic disorder with or without agoraphobia tend to score higher on the BAI than patients with other anxiety disorders (Fydrich et al., 1992; Kabacoff et al., 1997; Antony et al., 1997; see Table 16.2). This is likely due to the fact that in the original test sample, patients with panic disorder were more highly represented than patients with other anxiety disorders (about 40% prevalence of panic disorder vs. 19% prevalence of other anxiety disorders; Beck et al., 1988; Cox et al., 1996b). Construction of the BAI may thus have been slanted toward anxiety features more closely associated with panic than with worry or rumination. Nevertheless, because of the high internal consistency coefficients obtained in research on the BAI, the test is highly content valid. In summary, the BAI appears to be a measure of anxiety content that is not confounded with depression or other negative affect measures, but tends to be more sensitive to psychophysiological rather than other aspects of anxiety.

Construct and Discriminant Validity. If the BAI is a valid measure of anxiety, it should correlate more strongly with tests of anxiety (convergent validity) than with tests of depression (discriminant validity). By and large, this has been the case. Beck et al. (1988) reported moderate correlations with other anxiety measures, such as the Hamilton Anxiety Rating Scale (HARS; $r = .51$) and the Cognitive Check List–Anxiety scale (CCL–A; $r = .51$). By contrast, the BAI only correlated with the Hamilton Rating Scale for Depression (HRSD) at only .25 and the CCL–Depression scale at .22, which suggests good discrimination. The BAI was found to correlate moderately with the

Beck Depression Inventory (BDI; $r = .48$). However, a principal-component factor analysis conducted with BAI and BDI items combined into one test demonstrated that only one BAI item, "terrified," loaded on a depression factor as a secondary loading. Together, these results suggest that the BAI and BDI measure separate phenomena despite correlated total scores.

Other studies of anxiety-disordered samples are consistent with these findings. Fydrich et al. (1992) produced a multitrait, multimethod matrix where the BAI correlated with the Trait ($r = .58, p < .001$) and the State ($r = .47, p < .01$) versions of the STAI. Similarly, Kabacoff et al. (1997) reported correlations of .52 and .44 between the BAI and STAI-State and -Trait scales, respectively, among elderly patients with anxiety disorders. Fydrich et al. (1992) did find the BAI to correlate with the BDI moderately ($r = .50, p < .001$). However, the BAI correlated less strongly with daily depression diary ratings ($r = .38, p < .05$), suggesting the BAI discriminates anxiety from depression. Further, in a nonclinical sample of 326 students, Creamer et al. (1995) found the BAI to correlate with the BDI moderately ($r = .54$), but both the State and Trait scales of the STAI had stronger correlations with the BDI ($r = .74$ and .77, respectively). The difference between these coefficients was significant ($p < .001$), suggesting BAI superiority to the STAI in discrimination between anxiety and depression symptoms.

The BAI was not designed to discriminate between psychiatric diagnoses, but there is evidence that individuals with anxiety disorders will score significantly higher on the BAI than individuals without an anxiety disorder. Beck et al. (1988) reported a variety of between-groups comparisons among individuals with anxiety disorders alone, anxiety disorders and comorbid depression, and a normal control group. Results indicated higher BAI scores in the anxiety disorder groups than the depressed and normal groups. For example, individuals with an anxiety disorder produced a mean BAI score of 24.59 ($SD = 11.41$), whereas individuals with major depression produced a mean BAI score of 13.27 ($SD = 8.36, p < .01$). The normal control group ($n = 16$) produced a mean BAI score of 15.88 ($SD = 11.81$). In addition, Kabacoff et al. (1997) reported significant differences in mean BAI total scores between those older individuals meeting diagnostic criteria for an anxiety disorder ($M = 21.75, SD = 13.11$) and those who did not [$M = 14.44, SD = 10.93; t(215) = 4.38, p < .00001$]. Antony et al. (1997) also reported similar findings, and inspection of Table 16.2 suggests that individuals with anxiety disorders will score higher on the BAI than individuals without anxiety disorders across various samples. This suggests the BAI can aid in detection of problematic anxiety or anxiety disorders in a primary care.

Factorial Validity. The BAI demonstrates good overall factorial validity. The bulk of factor analytic data gleaned to date suggests the BAI is a solid, internally consistent measure of anxiety and not confounded with measurement of other affective states. There are three broad conclusions drawn regarding factor analytic research of the BAI:

1. In general, most factor analyses of the BAI find two- and four-factor solutions, with three-factor solutions found when other measures (depression, other anxiety scales) are added to BAI items.
2. Factors uncovered by analyses generally do not correlate with factors reflecting depressive symptoms when depression measures are included in analyses.
3. BAI factors are generally consistent with item content reflecting physiological characteristics of anxiety and, to a lesser extent, cognitive and behavioral aspects of anxiety.

These findings are briefly reviewed.

Beck et al. (1988) reported the first BAI exploratory principal component factor analysis among outpatients with anxiety disorders ($n = 160$). This resulted in a two-factor solution. Factor I comprised somatic items such as "numbness," "feeling hot," "dizzy or lightheaded," and "sweating," and Factor II, or subjective symptoms, loaded high with items such as "fear of the worst happening" and "fear of dying." These factors were correlated ($r = .56$), supporting alpha coefficient findings of good internal consistency for the entire scale. Beck et al. (1988) also conducted a factor analysis that added the BDI as a means of establishing discriminant validity. A four-factor solution was obtained, with three BAI item factors and a depression factor. As stated earlier, only one BAI item loaded on the depression factor ("terrified"), which was a secondary loading, indicating the BAI items discriminate anxiety and depression content well.

Other factor analyses of the BAI have been conducted on samples of outpatients with anxiety disorders. These analyses, again, generally suggest that the BAI predominantly measures psychophysiological aspects of anxiety, and subjective/cognitive aspects of anxiety to a lesser degree. For instance, Beck and Steer (1993) in the BAI test manual reported a cluster analysis on BAI responses of 393 patients with mixed anxiety disorders that included diagnoses of panic disorder with and without agoraphobia, social phobia, obsessive-compulsive disorder, and generalized anxiety disorder. Four item clusters or subscales were identified. These were labeled neurophysiological, panic, autonomic, and subjective. Patients with panic disorder scored higher on the panic subscale than the other anxiety disorder patients, suggesting that these subscales could help in distinguishing differential response patterns to the BAI among different anxiety disorder groups. However, to date, these subscales have not been tested for internal consistency and stability across various patient populations.

Cox et al. (1996a) combined the BAI items with those of the Panic Attack Questionnaire (PAQ), a measure of panic symptom intensity, to address the question of whether or not BAI items were distinct from panic items. The BAI and PAQ were administered to patients meeting *DSM–IV* criteria for panic disorder with and without agoraphobia. What Cox et al. (1996a) found was a three-factor solution in which each factor included dizziness-related items, cardiorespiratory-related items, and catastrophic cognition items. Both the PAQ and BAI items loaded equally on the factors, suggesting the BAI was an anxiety measure not distinct from a measure of panic.

Despite the psychophysiological leanings of the BAI's content, a consistent finding among factor-analytic studies of the BAI among anxiety disorder populations is a "subjective" or cognitive factor (e.g., Cox et al., 1996a). Kabacoff et al. (1997) conducted a principal-component factor analysis of the BAI with 154 elderly patients with anxiety disorders. Similar to the original factor analysis reported by Beck et al. (1988), a two-factor solution was found with both somatic and subjective symptoms. The factor structure identified by Kabacoff et al. (1997) was nearly identical to the factor structure reported by Beck et al. (1988) and accounted for 84% of the variance in BAI scores. Factor I, the "somatic" subscale, had a coefficient alpha of .89. Factor II, the "subjective" subscale (items 4, 9, 10, 14, 16, and 17), had a coefficient alpha of .86. Patients with anxiety disorders scored higher on these subscales than those without anxiety disorders.

In summary, factor-analytic investigations of the BAI among anxiety-disordered populations demonstrate that it tends to measure physiological and subjective aspects of anxiety, but with more sensitivity to the measurement of the physiological components.

THE BAI AS A SCREENING INSTRUMENT

General Considerations

As a screening instrument for detection of anxiety and anxiety disorders in primary care, the BAI holds great promise. It is an unparalleled practical instrument. It is brief, easily and quickly scored, and there is a host of research data (much of which is discussed in this chapter) that supports its validity and reliability. It allows for immediate feedback to patients and practitioners. However, two points of caution should be kept in mind:

1. The BAI is a face-valid self-report instrument, making the validity of its results subject to the patient's motivation to honestly and accurately report their experience.
2. The BAI may not be sensitive to detecting anxiety disorders where psychophysiological arousal is not a prominent feature. Examples of this might include specific phobia or subtypes of social phobia.

Therefore, the accuracy with which the BAI will detect anxiety disorders in primary care screening is contingent on practitioner knowledge of patient motives for self-report, and his or her knowledge of *DSM–IV* diagnostic criteria for anxiety disorders.

Relevant Psychometric Support

Consistency With **DSM-IV** *Criteria.*   As stated previously, relevant literature on the BAI suggests that the instrument is weighted more as a measure of psychophysiological symptoms associated with anxiety rather than cognitive/worry aspects of anxiety (e.g., Cox et al., 1996a; Fydrich et al., 1992). As such, the BAI overlaps highly with *DSM–IV* criteria for panic attack and panic disorder (with and without agoraphobia). However, when the BAI was developed, *DSM–III–R* was the current diagnostic manual for mental disorders. The *DSM–III–R* diagnostic criteria for Generalized Anxiety Disorder (GAD) listed seven symptoms that were also listed as panic symptoms. Cox et al. (1996b) noted that these seven symptoms are items on the BAI, making the BAI a reasonable index of GAD symptom severity as GAD was defined at that time. These symptoms are shortness of breath, trembling, accelerated heart rate, dizziness, sweating, nausea (indigestion), and hot flashes or chills. Cox et al. (1996b) also pointed out that this symptom list of autonomic hyperactivity was dropped from the revised GAD diagnostic criteria in *DSM–IV* (Brown, Barlow, & Liebowitz, 1994), rendering the BAI "even more closely linked with panic attacks in the current psychiatric nomenclature" (Cox et al., 1996b, p. 960). In light of these observations, the BAI appears to be closely associated with *DSM–IV* criteria for panic disorder when diagnostic categories are considered.

Diagnostic Efficiency Statistics. Diagnostic efficiency of the BAI in adult primary care patients is not well established. Two studies on BAI diagnostic efficiency have been conducted, both of which are cited in this chapter. However, one study targeted a sample of elderly psychiatric outpatients (Kabacoff et al., 1997), whereas the other study, although targeting a broad age range of patients (20–77 years), examined the diagnostic efficiency of a short version of the BAI for use in primary care (BAI–PC). In the first study, Kabacoff et al. (1997) selected a sample of elderly adults seeking outpatient behavioral health services in a university-based outpatient clinic. Patients were diagnosed with anxiety disorders using the Structured Clinical Interview for *DSM–III–R* (SCID–P; Spitzer, Williams, Gibbon, & First, 1988). As reported earlier, the authors did not report a BAI cutoff score that would provide optimal predictive accuracy regarding who would or would not have an anxiety disorder. Further, the cutoff scores they did identify were based on a base rate of anxiety disorder diagnosis of 29%. Because base rates can statistically affect diagnostic efficiency of psychological measures, it is important to note the base rate of anxiety disorders or problematic anxiety in the population with which one works. Base rates in primary care practices can vary. For example, Philbrick, Connelly, and Wofford (1996) found rates of anxiety disorders at about 12.3% in rural primary care practice, whereas Fifer et al. (1994) reported a base rate of anxiety disorders at about 33% in primary care.

In the second study on BAI diagnostic efficiency, Beck et al. (1997) reported promising findings on the BAI–PC among 56 primary care patients ages 20–77 years. The authors found the BAI–PC to have a sensitivity of 85% and specificity of 81%, with overall diagnostic efficiency of 82% for identifying patients with panic disorder, GAD, or both disorders. Use of the anxiety and mood modules of the Primary Care Evaluation of Mental Disorders (PRIME–MD) determined GAD and/or panic disorder diagnosis in that study. Coefficient alpha of the BAI–PC was reported at .90. These findings lend support to the BAI–PC as an internally consistent and accurate diagnostic screening instrument for GAD and panic disorder in primary care. Nevertheless, because its other psychometric characteristics, such as sensitivity to change over time, are as yet to be investigated in a large and diagnostically diverse primary care sample, the BAI–PC should not be substituted for the full BAI at present. Further, because the full BAI is only 13 items longer than the BAI–PC, and because the BAI is a better researched outcome measure of clinical anxiety, the BAI remains a solidly practical instrument for screening purposes in primary care.

Implementation

As a Stand-Alone Instrument. When using the BAI in primary care as a screening device, three findings stand out:

1. The BAI appears to discriminate well between clinical anxiety and depression.
2. It can identify individuals for whom psychophysiological arousal is problematic, such as those with panic disorder.
3. The BAI may not as easily identify anxiety problems where cognitive symptoms or avoidance behavior play a significant role (e.g., GAD, social phobia).

The BAI's limits on identifying anxiety symptoms of cognitive rumination and avoidance behavior should be carefully considered. The clinician should be well versed in recognizing other anxiety disorders, such as specific phobia, obsessive-compulsive disorder (OCD), and posttraumatic stress disorder (PTSD). It is strongly recommended that when patients score in the "high normal range" as seen in Table 16.4, the primary care physician or other practitioner query the patient directly about symptoms of worry, rumination, or avoidance behavior.

Use With Other Instruments and Procedures. If problematic anxiety or an anxiety disorder is suspected (e.g., a BAI score over 15), there are several lines of clinical procedure to take. First, the primary care physician or other clinician should inquire about a history of anxiety disorders or treatment by other physicians, psychologists, or other health care practitioners. This question will narrow down diagnostic possibilities. If the patient reports no history of anxiety treatment, the clinician should ask the patient to describe the anxiety problem. Practitioners can assist the patient with questions presented in Table 16.5. These questions are aimed at five general problem areas associated with various anxiety disorders: panic disorder, GAD, PTSD, OCD, and social phobia. The reason for this line of inquiry is that these disorders and their variations are associated with high rates of medical utilization (DiBartolo, Hofmann,

TABLE 16.5
Sample Clinical Questions for Five Anxiety Problem Areas

Anxiety Problem Area	Clinical Question(s)
Panic and agoraphobia	• Have you had sudden unexpected periods of intense physical symptoms and a feeling you were going to die? Have you experienced symptoms such as a pounding heart, shortness of breath, and dizziness? I'm talking about a panic or anxiety attack.
	• How long did the symptoms take to become intense? (Look for <10 min.)
	• Have you changed your behavior because of these attacks, such as avoiding activities outside the home because you are concerned of other attacks?
GAD	• Are you a worrier?
	• Do you worry excessively, or more than you believe you need to?
	• About what percent of the day are you worried, nervous, and tense? (>50%?)
PTSD	• Have you ever had any stressful or traumatic experiences, where your life or someone else's life was threatened, or serious injury resulted? I'm talking about things like being in an auto accident, or fire, being assaulted, either physically or sexually, or have you ever been in combat?
	• Do you have memories of these events that intrude, or interrupt activities?
	• Any distressing dreams since the event?
	• Are you jumpy, or easily startled?
	• Have you ever had any experiences of reliving the event, such as a feeling like "being there" or a "flashback?"
	• Any physical reactions, such as rapid heart beat, shortness of breath, or sweating, when you are in situations that remind you of the event?
OCD	• Do you have thoughts that recur that are nonsensical but repeat themselves again and again? These can be thoughts such as concerns of contamination or filth, a need to check door locks or electrical appliances, or that you might shout an obscenity in public?
	• Do you find yourself wanting to repeat an act over and over again, even though you do not want to repeat it? I'm talking about actions such as repetitive cleaning or hand washing, repeated checking, arranging, or counting?
Social phobia	• Do you ever have strong feelings of anxiety or shyness in social situations where you could be evaluated by others?
	• Do you have strong feelings of anxiety in situations where you believe you could do something to embarrass or humiliate yourself?

& Barlow, 1995; Katon et al., 1990). Once again, knowledge of the *DSM–IV* anxiety disorders criteria is critical to determine the appropriate treatment course or to whom referral should be made.

Another method of obtaining additional clinical information on the nature and intensity of problem anxiety is the use of other anxiety measures. The Penn State Worry Questionnaire (PSWQ) is a brief, valid, and highly reliable instrument that measures the cognitive components of GAD (Meyer, Miller, Metzger, & Borkovec, 1990). This can be administered and quickly scored when GAD is suspected, and it is a reliable measure of outcome. Also, the PTSD Check List (PCL; Weathers, Litz, Herman, Huska, & Keane, 1993) is a measure of intensity and frequency of PTSD symptoms for patients with anxiety problems related to experiencing trauma such as assault, past or current abuse, natural disaster, combat, and motor vehicle or other accident trauma. The PCL also has been found to have strong diagnostic efficiency (.90) among motor vehicle accident victims (Blanchard, Jones-Alexander, Buckley, & Forneris, 1996). The Padua Inventory, a brief measure of OCD symptoms and their intensity, has also been developed (Burns, 1995). Finally, a self-report measure of agoraphobic avoidance is also available (Oest, 1990). Other instruments are available in a number of resources (Corcoran & Fischer, 1987).

While supplementing the BAI in primary care practice with other anxiety instruments, the instruments should be properly implemented under the supervision or guidance of those licensed to administer them and interpret results, usually a licensed psychologist. The psychological consultant can also help make decisions of parsimony and identify only the most essential and pragmatic measures. The goal in primary care is to use minimal detection and intervention measures, not to provide comprehensive assessment and treatment — that is the purview of specialty mental health.

Guidelines for Decision Making

Determination of Need for Behavioral Intervention.   Using the guidelines just detailed in the screening process, the BAI score can help determine need for behavioral intervention. To activate behavioral intervention or consultation, there are two criteria to consider: (a) BAI score within or above the "high normal" range as seen in Table 16.4, and (b) the patient reports anxiety complaints addressed in Table 16.5. In general, if a patient meets one or both of these criteria, a behavioral health consultation or intervention for anxiety is warranted. Many individuals may not meet either criterion, but this does not rule out behavioral methods as a means of addressing the presenting problem. A good rule of thumb for primary behavioral health consultation is, "when in doubt, consult " (Strosahl, 1996).

Determination of the Most Appropriate Intervention.   Determining the most appropriate treatment depends on the anxiety problem. Suffice it to say that a score on the BAI alone cannot determine what the most appropriate clinical intervention should be, nor can a BAI score predict treatment outcome. For example, individuals with social phobia, on average, score lower than panickers on the BAI, presumably because the BAI is more sensitive to autonomic-related anxiety problems (see Table 16.2). Socially anxious individuals may thus be overlooked in the fast pace of primary care if the BAI is the only screen for problem anxiety used. However, social phobia can be debilitating if left untreated. The bottom-line message here is to verbally inquire about other anxiety problems (e.g., past psychological trauma, social phobia, obsessions or compulsions), in addition to the BAI results. If anxiety is an acute reaction to stress, then a behavioral health consultation may not be necessary at first visit. Conversely, if a patient scores extremely high on the BAI and reports a greater than 5-year history of problematic, untreated anxiety with poor functioning and/or coexisting depression, then referral to a psychologist, psychiatrist, or qualified counselor outside of primary care is likely the best course of action.

Provision of Feedback to the Patient

Because the BAI is quickly scored, results can be immediately discussed with patients. It is recommended that the scoring ranges and normative percentile equivalents be discussed with patients. An example of feedback on an initial visit might be as follows:

> You have scored a 17 on the Beck Anxiety Inventory, our standard measure of anxiety symptoms. This score suggests that the anxiety symptoms are intense, and we expect about 90% of individuals will score lower than the score you have. While this score is "not off the charts" — the scale does go up to 63 — it does indicate we should look more closely at your anxiety so that we may help you manage it.

It is helpful to point out to patients that although the BAI is a valid and highly reliable measure of clinical anxiety, it will not capture entirely the patient's experience. However, in an imperfect world, it is one the best and most practical methods of establishing an objective index of anxiety symptoms. Further, patients should be told that the BAI score at the first appointment can act as a measure to which subsequent administrations of the BAI may be compared.

USE AS AN INSTRUMENT FOR TREATMENT MONITORING

General Considerations

Because of its brevity and ease in scoring, the BAI is ideal for anxiety treatment monitoring in primary care. The BAI is also sensitive to change over time (Beck et al., 1988; Crits-Cristoph & Connolly, 1997; Fydrich et al., 1992). Successive BAI scores, after an initial baseline score is obtained in the screening phase, can help determine effectiveness of treatments. Subsequent BAI administrations and obtained BAI scores thus should be fed back to patients in order for patients to view progress. Indeed, this is in itself a therapeutic process and reinforces self-care behaviors that enhance anxiety management.

However, when implementing the BAI as an outcome measure in primary care, there are several considerations that cannot be overlooked. First, as repeated throughout this chapter, the BAI tends to measure physiological aspects of anxiety and does not tap into assessment of avoidance behavior or severe cognitive symptoms (e.g., worries or obsessions). Benchmarking improvement in these symptoms should be done by methods other than the BAI. Second, the BAI is not a measure of self-reported function, but rather of symptoms. Thus, the BAI cannot provide information about the impact of anxiety symptoms on role function in social, occupational, and familial domains. Third, when implementing any psychometric instrument in the medical setting, it must be made clear from the outset why using outcome measures benefits the practice and patient care. Too often, psychometric measures are applied with no forethought into why measuring a behavioral phenomenon is important to the organization and those it serves. The result of poor planning is a poor organizational attitude toward the measure, unwillingness among staff and patients to value the data, and thus poor and unreliable outcome data are produced.

In summary, using the BAI in practice should be well planned and its goals well articulated before it is used. When this is done, the implementation will become routine and smooth, and it will likely increase patient satisfaction through purveying a sense that all health concerns are being addressed and effectiveness of treatment is being objectively monitored.

Relevant Psychometric Support

The BAI has been demonstrated to be sensitive to change as affected by treatment (see Crits-Christoph & Connolly, 1997), making it a good choice as an anxiety treatment outcome measure. Using the BAI as a primary dependent variable, studies on the efficacy of various psychological treatments for GAD produced effect sizes ranging from .85 to 1.63 (Crits-Christoph & Connolly, 1997). Crits-Cristoph, Conolly, Azarian, Crits-Christoph, and Shappell (1996) also reported a pre- to posttreatment effect size of 1.99 using the BAI as a dependent variable in GAD treatment. Further, although the BAI has demonstrated sensitivity to change, it also has been demonstrated to be stable over time in untreated samples (see Beck & Steer, 1993). Internal consistency, factorial validity, and test–retest stability data on the BAI presented earlier in this chapter illustrate the sound psychometric properties of the BAI. Because of its sensitivity to change, its high internal consistency, and its strong test–retest reliability in untreated samples, the BAI is a psychometrically sound measure of treatment outcome.

Implementation Problems

There are two potential problems that could affect using the BAI in primary care. In fact, these problems are of concern for any organization using psychometric outcome data (Berman, Rosen, Hurt, & Kolarz, 1998). These are: (a) expense of implementing the BAI in the primary care, and (b) data management concerns. With respect to expense, costs for BAI implementation will be in terms of both monetary expense for the instrument itself, and staff time in administering, scoring, and managing data. In 1998, the BAI was listed by its publisher, the Psychological Corporation, at $104.50 for a set of 100 BAI record forms. The BAI manual costs $25.50. Costs of managing BAI data will vary depending on organizational need. For example, the BAI may be used by individual clinicians with individual patients, or used to build a continual computer database on multiple patients and providers. The former type of use simply involves individual clinicians administering and scoring the instrument and providing feedback for patients. The latter strategy will be more expensive, and is more appropriate if large group practices want to demonstrate need and effectiveness of anxiety interventions for reimbursement purposes. For example, a practice may want to demonstrate to a contracted managed care company that early detection and treatment of anxiety problems reduce medical utilization and offset costs of reimbursement for anxiety treatment. Whether used for individual patients or across aggregate segments of the practice, the BAI can vary in expense of implementation. Good planning on use of the BAI is necessary if the benefits of using the BAI are to outstrip its costs.

Questions that must be answered before implementing the BAI might include: Do we need to measure anxiety in our population? If we measure anxiety, how will we use that information to improve care? *How* will we improve care, and do we have the resources to help anxious patients? After answering these questions, identifying a system to distribute, collect, and manage BAI data should be well planned. It is recommended that all staff (physicians, nursing staff, and administrative assistants) be educated as to why measurement of anxiety in some or all patients is important. Instruction on how to help patients complete measures, and scoring instructions for all clinicians who have direct patient care responsibilities will also be helpful. Individual practices will have different goals in the use of the BAI; thus no one system of BAI administration and data collection is the "right" way. Identifying the reasons for using the BAI and how the data will be used in a practical way is prerequisite, however. If these matters are addressed, problems of implementation should be minimal.

Guidelines for Decision Making

On deciding to continue, discontinue, or change treatment based on repeated BAI administrations, three key points may prove helpful. These are: (a) specifying the treatment goal(s), (b) identifying a specific time frame for the treatment, and (c) use of the Reliable Change Index (RCI; Jacobson & Truax, 1991). With respect to determining an anxiety treatment goal, there are two types to consider. First, there is a symptom goal as measured by the BAI, and second, a *functional* goal. A functional goal is one that involves the reduction or elimination of an observable and measurable behavior that impairs vocational, social, or other function. Identifying treatment goals prior to treatment is a collaborative effort between the patient and clinician. Such collaboration will enhance treatment adherence and help clarify when satisfactory resolution of the anxiety problem is achieved. A symptom goal can be a normal BAI score (≤ 14; see Table 16.2). An example of a functional goal can be the elimination of agoraphobic avoidance of one or more situations (e.g., stores or public transportation), or elimination of emergency-room visits for panic. If both symptom and functional goals are achieved, the patient and clinician can discontinue treatment. If one goal but not the other is achieved, treatment may be changed to focus on the other goal, discontinued if the patient finds results satisfactory, or simply continued until both functional and BAI (symptom) goals are achieved.

In setting a time frame for a treatment intervention, the patient and clinician should consider a long enough interval to see satisfactory results. Most anxiety disorders do not evolve rapidly (with the exception of acute stress disorder, or adjustment disorder with anxiety), and thus treatment will not reverse effects of anxiety rapidly. A realistic time frame should be emphasized. Because the BAI is an assessment of symptoms over the week prior to BAI completion, administration of the BAI should be done at a frequency of no greater than once per week.

Finally, the RCI is a statistic that was devised as a method to determine if differences in pre- and posttreatment test scores are due to a true change in the psychological construct being measured (e.g., anxiety), or if the change is simply due to chance (Jacobson & Truax, 1991). In other words, it determines if the change in pre- to posttreatment test scores is statistically significant. This has important implications for treatment outcome: It provides a guideline for determining whether to stop or continue treatment. If the patient's pre–post treatment difference in BAI scores exceeds the magnitude of the RCI, then the change in BAI scores is significant. Based on data provided in the BAI manual (Beck & Steer, 1993), the RCI value computed is 17 (see Lambert et al., 1996, for computation instructions). That is, a change of 17 or more BAI points is needed in order for the change to be considered significant. Note, however, that for mild anxiety this may not be practical because many baseline BAI scores obtained in primary care may be 17 or below. Therefore, using the goal of a BAI score within the normal range in conjunction with the RCI is advised when making treatment decisions.

DISEASE-SPECIFIC CONSIDERATIONS

Physiological symptoms associated with highly anxious states, especially panic attacks, can often be associated with either general medical conditions or direct effects of a substance. In turn, these problems can inflate the scores of the BAI because the BAI is most sensitive to autonomic symptoms of anxiety. To adjust for score inflation, reviewing basic information about patient history is critical. For example, most anxiety disorders have an onset from late adolescence to mid thirties, although this can vary widely (American Psychiatric Association, 1994). DiBartolo et al. (1995) pointed out that if atypical symptoms accompany anxiety complaints or panic attacks "such as vertigo, amnesia, headaches, slurred speech, loss of consciousness, and loss of bladder or bowel control," substance use or a medical cause should be investigated (p. 136). This is particularly so in cases of onset of troublesome autonomic symptoms before mid-adolescence and/or after age 45 years. DiBartolo et al. (1995) also pointed out that problematic anxiety is not a mutually exclusive event from a medical problem and one cannot automatically rule out the other. Panic disorder, for example, can often co-occur with a general medical condition (Jacob & Lilienfeld, 1991), and simply identifying and treating the medical condition will not necessarily address panic. In general, a thorough history and medical examination reviewing neurological, endocrine, and other systems is sound practice despite BAI score.

Specific medical disorders known to spawn panic and other anxiety symptoms (and hence, inflate BAI scores) include hypo- and hyperthyroidism, pheochromocytoma, hypoglycemia, and cardiac conditions such as arrhythmias, bacterial endocarditis, and mitral valve prolapse (DiBartolo et al., 1995; Jacob & Lilienfeld, 1991). In addition, intoxication with stimulants such as amphetamine, cocaine, caffeine, and so on and cannabis intoxication can spawn symptoms that are reflected by the BAI. Also, barbiturate, benzodiazepine, or alcohol withdrawal can influence BAI scores because autonomic agitation is one result of withdrawal. If symptoms persist after 4 weeks of withdrawal from substances, panic disorder or other anxiety problems can be given stronger consideration. Toxicology laboratory reports, oral glucose testing, urinalysis for urine catecholamine, and thyroid-stimulating hormone (TSH) testing can identify or rule out medical conditions contributing to symptoms reported on the BAI (DiBartolo et al., 1995).

STRENGTHS AND LIMITATIONS
OF USE IN PRIMARY CARE SETTINGS

An obvious strength of using the BAI in primary care is its simplicity and ease of scoring. It is readily adaptable to the rapid pace of primary care. Patients can clearly understand its content and instruction, and clinicians can quickly become familiar with scoring procedures. By contrast, one limitation of the BAI for some practices is its costs, both for purchase of the instrument and management of data. Stated earlier, clear planning in clinical, fiscal, and operational domains as to how the BAI will benefit patient care and the practice is necessary if successful implementation is to be achieved. Having a behavioral health consultant in the primary care practice can be a large help with development of care policies and practices that will make the expense of the BAI and data management worthwhile.

Purchase of the BAI is restricted to qualified individuals. This is another potential limitation of using the BAI in primary care. The reason for selling restrictions is that the BAI, although a seemingly simple paper-and-pencil test, is a psychometric instrument that has been carefully developed for use with patients. Norms have been established, and thus data produced by individual patients or groups of patients should be interpreted by those with a clear understanding of what the norms mean. The Psychological Corporation regards the BAI as a "C-Level" instrument, which means it reserves the right not to release the instrument to individuals who do not verify licensure, certification, or training consistent with the expectations outlined in the American Psychological Association's *Standards for Educational and Psychological Testing* (1985). However, if the behavioral health consultant in the primary care practice is a psychologist, physician, or counselor with requisite training in psychometric assessment, this will pose no problem in purchase of the BAI.

CASE STUDIES

Examples of how the BAI is useful in screening and tracking anxiety problems in primary care are presented here. One case illustrates a brief intervention designed to deter recurrent panic attacks and panic disorder; another case demonstrates the use of the BAI with individuals who have medical problems complicated by anxiety.

Case 1

The first case is of a healthy, 25-year-old Caucasian male law student who initially presented to the Emergency Department (ED) with acute chest pain. The chest pain had a sudden onset in the evening during study activity and was accompanied by shortness of breath, bilateral parasthesias, dizziness, and unreality. Symptoms had peaked in intensity within 5 min of onset (*DSM–IV* panic attack criteria requires peak intensity in 10 min or less), and he immediately attributed symptoms to heart attack. Importantly, the patient's father was reported as having suffered similar panic symptoms at middle age when the patient was a preadolescent. The patient's father received no treatment for panic and was often frightened of the attacks. The patient recalled his father as modeling obvious fear during panic attacks, contributing to the patient's fear of anxiety symptoms. To compound this learning history, the patient's father had suffered angina symptoms within 2 months of the patient's presentation and a coronary obstruction was detected. These events contributed to the patient's cognitive distress about his symptoms and escalated fear and sympathetic arousal through confusing panic with acute cardiac distress.

A regular ED workup was completed with normal electrocardiogram (EKG) and normal cardiovascular findings. The patient was discharged home. He made an appointment in General Internal Medicine to follow up and establish care with a primary care physician 2 days later. The patient was still experiencing limited symptom and full panic attacks and was avoiding exercise and physical exertion.

The primary care physician detected no neurological, endocrine, or cardiovascular abnormalities. He was prescribed alprazolam (Xanax) at 0.25 mg t.i.d., and an appointment with the behavioral health specialist (R.F.) and physician was made for several days later. In the behavioral health visit with the physician, a brief behavioral and psychiatric history was taken, an educational intervention was administered, and a behavioral prescription was made. The patient's BAI score at this consultation meeting was 32. The patient had no previous psychiatric history but had learned about panic vicariously through his father's experience. Despite this, he knew little about the nature and physiology of panic, and had many misconceptions about the dangerousness of symptoms and their causes. The educational intervention consisted of a 15- to 20-min talk on the causes of panic, the physiology underlying uncomfortable symptoms, and why panic attacks seemingly "come out of the blue" based on behavioral theory (Barlow, 1988). The patient was provided a written booklet on this topic, which is under current development along with the educational intervention (Ferguson, 1998). The intent of the educational intervention is to teach patients the underlying mechanisms of uncomfortable bodily sensations in order deter catastrophic interpretations of symptoms, and to reduce avoidance of activities where panic is feared. Finally, the patient was given brief instruction in breathing relaxation, and was encouraged to increase aerobic activity (a goal of 2 days a week of brief jogging) and reduce caffeine intake. A gradual taper of alprazalam dosing was also prescribed because long-term outcome with benzodiazepine treatment of panic is poor (Otto, Pollack, & Sabatino, 1996).

In a phone follow-up after 1 week, the patient had not experienced any full panic attacks, was not avoiding or missing law school activity, and was completing relaxation and aerobic exercises. At 2 months, the patient's BAI score was 11 and he was panic free (Fig. 16.1). The change in pre–post BAI scores exceeded the RCI of 17, indicating clinically significant decrease in anxiety symptoms. His verbal report was that he thought of anxiety symptoms as less threatening and safe, given his age and health status, and that managing stress with applied breathing relaxation, sound exercise, and diet habits helped reduce anxious anticipation of sudden panic attack. The initial ED visit cost $247 and a follow-up primary care physician (PCP) visit cost $47, for a total of $294 (not counting lab tests). The behavioral health consultation cost $64 for a ½-hr intervention with brief assessment. The cost savings in the short term are obvious. However, they are more dramatic considering that multiple ED visits for unexplained chest pain are likely for many patients with panic anxiety (Katerndahl & Realini, 1995). Fortunately in this case, development of full panic disorder was averted, and unknown but likely cost savings were realized in terms of future medical utilization, scholastic productivity, and quality of life.

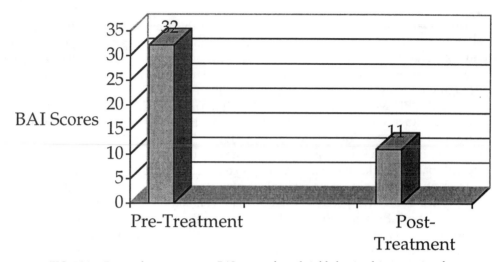

FIG. 16.1. Pre- and posttreatment BAI scores for a brief behavioral intervention for acute panic attacks in a 25-year-old male. Note that the pretreatment score of 32 is within the 99th percentile of BAI scores among a community sample (see Table 16.2). The posttreatment score, 11, is within one standard deviation of the community sample mean (70th percentile), or within the normal range. This satisfies the treatment goal of a normal BAI score. In addition, pre-to-post BAI score change was greater than 17, indicating statistically significant or "reliable" change, suggesting treatment outcome was not due to natural fluctuation of BAI scores.

Case 2

The next case is presented to illustrate the interaction of problematic generalized anxiety with medical illness, and how the BAI is a useful tool to screen for anxiety and measure treatment outcome. The patient, a 65-year-old, divorced, retired woman, was referred to the behavioral health consultant after discussing problematic worry and tension with her primary care physician. Ten years previous, the patient under went many life changes that included retirement and a cerebellar stroke. The stroke resulted in vertigo that would appear and disappear. She also developed nocturnal panic attacks and limited symptom panic attacks in anticipation of difficulty with movement, interacting with others, or times when she worried. Predating these problems, the patient admitted to being a perfectionist and being "a worrier," which are features consistent with GAD. However, at the time of initial consultation, she did not meet full *DSM–IV* criteria for GAD. She also struggled with hypertension that was a contributing factor to the stroke. Despite antihypertension medications, her blood pressure was higher than desired by her physician.

At baseline, the patient's BAI score was 24, and this alerted the primary care providers to treat the anxiety problem. Moreover, her mean systolic and diastolic blood pressure readings were 160/90 based on her home monitoring records. A four-session (½ hr per session) behavior therapy plan involving applied relaxation training and brief cognitive therapy was implemented. The patient was taught progressive muscle relaxation in the office with instructions audiotaped by the behavioral consultant. She rehearsed with the audiotape daily, and an applied strategy of cue-controlled relaxation (a brief-relaxation of 30 sec to 3 min) was added at the next session. The intent of cue-controlled relaxation is to help patients cultivate lower baseline arousal, regardless of external stressors. In other words, patients are in-

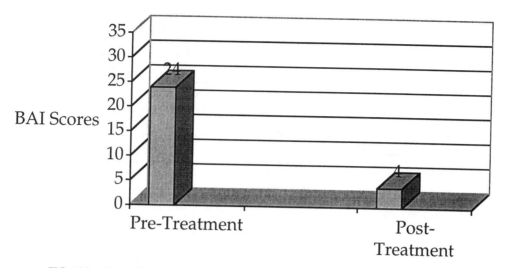

FIG. 16.2. Pre- and posttreatment BAI scores of a 65-year-old female with features of generalized anxiety disorder, hypertension, and who was status post cerebellar stroke. Similar to Fig. 16.1, the pretreatment score was in the 98th percentile with a posttreatment score in the normal range, meeting the treatment goal of a normal BAI score. Again, the pre-to-post change was statistically significant (>17 BAI points), indicating a reliable pre- to posttreatment change.

structed to not wait for stress to increase, but rather "beat it to the punch" by cultivating lower overall arousal. The last sessions were devoted to cognitive restructuring, or the process of helping the patient identify and modify beliefs and cognitions that unnecessarily produce increased anxiety and arousal.

At 1-month follow-up, the patient's BAI score was 4, representing a normal range score and a statistically significant change from the baseline of 24, exceeding the RCI of 17 (Fig. 16.2). Moreover, the patient's systolic and diastolic blood pressure average over 3 days of monitoring prior to the follow-up visit was 130/75 (Fig. 16.3). Both treatment goals—BAI score reduction to a normal range and a behavioral/physiological goal of blood pressure reduction—were met. Treatment was terminated and the patient was scheduled for her annual physical, at which time she would complete the BAI again. In the interim, she was instructed to maintain daily practice of the cue-controlled relaxation and cognitive strategies and weekly practice of progressive muscle relaxation.

This case serves to illustrate that complex medical problems can be addressed efficiently with evidenced-based behavioral medicine procedures in primary care. The BAI efficiently captured anxiety symptom distress and change over time, and thus served to guide treatment cessation or continuation decisions. Maintenance of therapeutic change can also be easily indexed over long-term follow-up in routine primary care.

SUMMARY

The BAI is a practical and sound psychometric measure of anxiety symptoms. Strengths of the BAI include its clarity, brevity, and ease of scoring, which make it readily adaptable to the brisk pace of primary care practice. Chief among its weak-

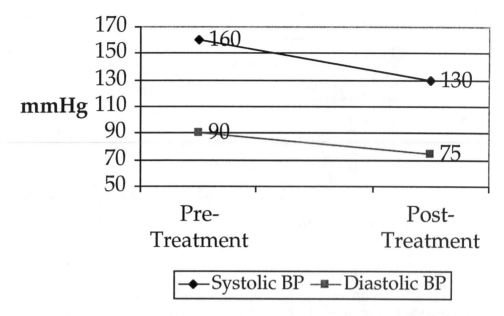

FIG. 16.3.   Pre- and posttreatment systolic and diastolic blood pressure averages for a
65-year-old female with generalized anxiety disorder features and hypertension.

nesses is that studies of its content indicate the BAI is more sensitive to panic symptoms and the psychophysiological arousal aspects of anxiety disorders and problems. In light of this, clinicians are advised to query patients about cognitive
symptoms of anxiety such as anticipatory worry, and behavioral symptoms such as
avoidance behavior that interferes with function.

The BAI is a commercially available measure and thus will be an expense with
which primary care practices will have to contend. Time in managing BAI data is also
an expense. These matters are common to all practices in an era of proving to health
care consumers that the practice is using evidenced-based treatments, and that the
health care delivered is worth the price. Thus, in using the BAI, practice managers
must determine if anxiety is worth identifying and treating (most studies say it is if
long-term medical savings are to be realized), and then plan exactly how the BAI will
be used to improve care.

This chapter outlines some methods of using the BAI that can be useful. However,
each primary care setting will have unique clinical, operational, and fiscal demands
on it, and no one method is the best for all primary care practices. Nevertheless, problematic anxiety that goes undetected and untreated contributes to overall poor health
and unnecessary health care expense, and puts modern primary care practices at risk,
especially those in capitated payer systems. Systematic use of the BAI for both anxiety screening and measurement of treatment outcome is a sound start in addressing
problem anxiety in the primary care setting.

REFERENCES

American Psychiatric Association. (1994). *Diagnostic and statistical manual of mental disorders* (4th ed.).
     Washington, DC: Author.

American Psychological Association. (1985). *Standards for educational and psychological testing*. Washington, DC: Author.

Anastasi, A. (1986). Evolving concepts of test validation. *Annual Review of Psychology, 37*, 1–15.

Antony, M. M., Purdon, C., Swinson, R. P., & Downie, F. (1997, November). *Beck Anxiety Inventory across the anxiety disorders and individuals from a community sample*. Poster session presented at the annual meeting of the Association for the Advancement of Behavior Therapy, Miami, FL.

Barlow, D. H. (1988). *Anxiety and its disorders: The nature and treatment of anxiety and panic*. New York: Guilford Press.

Beck, A. T., Epstein, N., Brown, G., & Steer, R. A. (1988). An inventory for measuring clinical anxiety: Psychometric properties. *Journal of Consulting and Clinical Psychology, 56*, 893–897.

Beck, A. T., & Steer, R. A. (1993). *The Beck Anxiety Inventory manual*. San Antonio, TX: Psychological Corporation.

Beck, A. T., Steer, R. A., Ball, R., Ciervo, C. A., & Kabat, M. (1997). Use of the Beck Anxiety and Depression Inventories in primary care with medical outpatients. *Assessment, 4*, 211–219.

Berman, W. H., Rosen, C. S., Hurt, S. W., & Kolarz, C. M. (1998). Toto, we're not in Kansas anymore: Measuring and using outcomes in behavioral health care. *Clinical Psychology: Science and Practice, 5*, 115–133.

Blanchard, E. B., Jones-Alexander, J., Buckley, T. C., & Forneris, C. A. (1996). Psychometric properties of the PTSD Checklist (PCL). *Behavior Research and Therapy, 34*, 669–673.

Boyd, J. H. (1986). Use of mental health services for the treatment of panic disorder. *American Journal of Psychiatry, 143*, 1569–1574.

Brown, T. A., Barlow, D. H., & Liebowitz, M. R. (1994). The empirical basis for generalized anxiety disorder. *American Journal of Psychiatry, 151*, 1272–1280.

Burns, G. L. (1995). *Padua Inventory – Washington State University Revision*. Pullman, WA: Author. (Available from G. Leonard Burns.)

Carter, C. S., & Maddock, R. J. (1992). Chest pain in generalized anxiety disorder. *International Journal of Psychiatry in Medicine, 22*, 291–298.

Corcoran, K., & Fischer, J. (1987). *Measures for clinical practice: A sourcebook*. New York: Free Press.

Cox, B. J., Cohen, E., Direnfeld, D. M., & Swinson, R. P. (1996a). Does the Beck Anxiety Inventory measure anything beyond panic attack symptoms? *Behavior Research and Therapy, 34*, 949–954.

Cox, B. J., Cohen, E., Direnfeld, D. M., & Swinson, R. P. (1996b). Reply to Steer and Beck: Panic disorder, generalized anxiety disorder, and quantitative versus qualitative differences in anxiety assessment. *Behavior Research and Therapy, 34*, 959–961.

Creamer, M., Foran, J., & Bell, R. (1995). The Beck Anxiety Inventory in a non-clinical sample. *Behavior Research and Therapy, 33*, 477–485.

Crits-Christoph, P., & Connolly, M. B. (1997). Measuring change in patients following psychological and pharmacological interventions: Anxiety disorders. In H. H. Strupp, L. M. Horowitz, & M. J. Lambert (Eds.), *Measuring patient changes in mood, anxiety, and personality disorders* (pp. 155–188). Washington, DC: American Psychological Association.

Crits-Christoph, P., Connolly, M. B., Azarian, K., Crits-Christoph, K., & Shappell, S. (1996). An open trial of brief supportive-expressive psychotherapy in the treatment of generalized anxiety disorder. *Psychotherapy, 33*, 418–430.

Dent, H. R., & Salkovskis, P. M. (1986). Clinical measures of depression anxiety and obsessionality in nonclinical populations. *Behavioral Research and Therapy, 24*, 689–691.

DiBartolo, P. M., Hofmann, S. G., & Barlow, D. H. (1995). Psychosocial approaches to panic disorder and agoraphobia: Assessment and treatment issues for the primary care physician. *Mind/Body Medicine, 1*, 133–143.

Dobson, K. S. (1985). The relationship between anxiety and depression. *Clinical Psychology Review, 5*, 307–324.

Ferguson, R. J. (1998). *Cognitive-behavioral prevention of recurrent panic attacks*. Unpublished manuscript.

Fifer, S. K., Mathias, S. D., Patrick, D. L., Mazonson, P. D., Lubeck, D. P., & Buesching, D. P. (1994). Untreated anxiety among adult primary care patients in a health maintenance organization. *Archives of General Psychiatry, 51*, 740–750.

Fydrich, T., Dowdall, D., & Chambless, D. L. (1992). Reliability and validity of the Beck Anxiety Inventory. *Journal of Anxiety Disorders, 6*, 55–61.

Gillis, M. M., Haaga, D. A. F., & Ford, G. T. (1995). Normative values for the Beck Anxiety Inventory, Fear Questionnaire, Penn State Worry Questionnaire, and Social Phobia and Anxiety Inventory. *Psychological Assessment, 5*, 450–455.

Gotlib, I. H., & Cane, D. B. (1989). Self-report assessment of depression and anxiety. In P. C. Kendall & D. Watson (Eds.), *Anxiety and depression: Distinctive and overlapping features* (pp. 131–169). New York: Academic Press.

Jackson, D. N. (1970). A sequential system for personality scale development. In C. D. Spielberger (Ed.), *Current topics in clinical and community psychology* (Vol. 2, pp. 61–96). New York: Academic Press.

Jacob, R. G., & Lilienfeld, S. O. (1991). Panic disorder: Medical assessment and psychological assessment. In J. R. Walker, G. R. Norton, & C. A. Gross (Eds.), *Panic disorder and agoraphobia: A comprehensive guide for the practitioner* (pp. 16–102). Pacific Grove, CA: Brooks/Coles.

Jacobson, N. S., & Truax, P. (1991). Clinical significance: A statistical approach to defining meaningful change in psychotherapy research. *Journal of Consulting and Clinical Psychology, 59,* 12–19.

Kabacoff, R. I., Segal, D. L., Hersen, M., & Van Hasselt, V. B. (1997). Psychometric properties and diagnostic utility of the Beck Anxiety Inventory and State-Trait Anxiety Inventory with older adult psychiatric outpatients. *Journal of Anxiety Disorders, 11,* 33–47.

Katerndahl, D. A., & Realini, J. P. (1995). Where do panic attack sufferers seek care? *Journal of Family Practice, 40,* 237–243.

Katon, W., Von Korff, M., Lin, E., Lipscomb, P., Russo, J., Wagner, E., & Polk, E. (1990). Distressed high utilizers of medical care: DSM-III-R diagnosis and treatment needs. *General Hospital Psychiatry, 12,* 335–362.

Lambert, M. J., Hansen, N. B., Umpress, V., Lunnen, K., Okiishi, J., & Burlingame, G. M. (1996). *Administration and scoring manual for the OQ-45.* Stevenson, MD: American Professional Credentialing Services, LLC.

Meyer, T. J., Miller, M. L., Metzger, R. L., & Borkovec, T. D. (1990). Development and validation of the Penn State Worry Questionnaire. *Behavior Research and Therapy, 28,* 487–495.

Mountjoy, C. Q., & Roth, M. (1982). Studies in the relationship between depressive disorders and anxiety states. *Journal of Affective Disorders, 4,* 127–147.

Oest, L. (1990). The Agoraphobia Scale: An evaluation of its reliability and validity. *Behavior Research and Therapy, 28,* 323–329.

Osman, A., Barrios, F. X., Aukes, D., Osman, J. R., & Markway, K. (1993). The Beck Anxiety Inventory: Psychometric properties in a community population. *Journal of Psychopathology and Behavioral Assessment, 15,* 287–297.

Osman, A., Kopper, B. A., Barrios, F. X., Osman, J. R., & Wade, T. (1997). The Beck Anxiety Inventory: Reexamination of factor structure and psychometric properties. *Journal of Clinical Psychology, 53,* 7–14.

Otto, M. W., Pollack, M. H., & Sabatino, S. A. (1996). Maintenance of remission following cognitive behavioral therapy for panic disorders: Possible deleterious effects of concurrent treatment. *Behavior Therapy, 27,* 473–482.

Philbrick, J. T., Connelly, J. E., & Wofford, A. B. (1996). The prevalence of mental disorders in rural office practice. *Journal of General Internal Medicine, 11,* 9–15.

Prusoff, B., & Klerman, G. (1974). Differentiating depressed from anxious neurotic outpatients. *Archives of General Psychiatry, 30,* 302–308.

Riskind, J., Beck, A. T., Brown, G., & Steer, R. A. (1987). Taking the measure of anxiety and depression: Validity of the reconstructed Hamilton scales. *Journal of Nervous and Mental Disease, 174,* 129–136.

Robins, L. N., Helzer, J. E., Weissman, M. M., Orvaschel, H., Gruenberg, F., Burke, J. D., & Regier, D. A. (1984). Lifetime prevalence of psychiatric disorders at three sites. *Archives of General Psychiatry, 41,* 949–959.

Snaith, R. P., & Taylor, C. M. (1985). Rating scales for depression and anxiety: A current perspective. *British Journal of Clinical Pharmacology, 19,* 17s–20s.

Spielberger, C. D., Gorsuch, R. L., & Lushene, R. (1970). *STAI manual.* Palo Alto, CA: Consulting Psychologists Press.

Spitzer, R. L., Williams, J. B. W., Gibbon, M., & First, M. B. (1988). *Structured clinical interview for DSM-III-R-Patient version (SCID-P 6/1/88).* New York: Biometrics Research Department, New York State Psychiatric Institute.

Strosahl, K. (1996). Confessions of a behavior therapist in primary care: The odyssey and the ecstasy. *Cognitive and Behavioral Practice, 3,* 1–28.

Tanaka-Matsumi, J., & Kameoka, V. A. (1986). Reliabilities and concurrent validities of popular self-report measures of depression, anxiety, and social desirability. *Journal of Consulting and Clinical Psychology, 54,* 328–333.

Weathers, F. W., Litz, B. T., Herman, D. S., Huska, J. A., & Keane, T. M. (1993, November). *The PTSD Checklist: Reliability, validity, and diagnostic utility.* Paper presented at the annual meeting of the International Society for Traumatic Stress Studies, San Antonio, TX.

Wetherell, J. L., & Arean, P. A. (1997). Psychometric evaluation of the Beck Anxiety Inventory with older medical patients. *Psychological Assessment, 9,* 136–144.

Wilson, G. T. (1998). Manual-based treatment and clinical practice. *Clinical psychology: Science and practice, 5,* 363–375.

Wittchen, H. U., & Essau, C. A. (1991). The epidemiology of panic attacks, panic disorder, and agoraphobia. In: J. R. Walker, G. R. Norton, & C. A. Ross (Eds.), *Panic disorder and agoraphobia: A comprehensive guide for the practitioner* (pp. 103–149). Pacific Grove, CA: Brooks/Cole.

Self-Administered Alcoholism Screening Test (SAAST)

Leo J. Davis
Mayo Clinic and Mayo Foundation

Screening for alcoholism in primary care settings has obvious relevance to health care because this disorder has been found to coexist with, or be causative of, numerous physical and mental disorders. In addition, alcoholism is a disorder in and of itself, requiring no other physical or psychiatric disorder to be present for a diagnosis to be made. It is a relatively common disorder, yet paradoxically it is underdiagnosed in primary care settings. To the surprise of many, it is a treatable disorder, yet scarcely 10% of alcoholics undergo formal treatment. Although considered a hidden disorder, it nonetheless can be detected with a relatively high degree of confidence in a setting where its prevalence is 10% or greater.

The diagnosis of alcoholism is, to a large extent, a behavioral diagnosis. Although many advanced cases of alcoholism present classic physical signs, the majority of alcoholics do not show other than fleeting physical or laboratory evidence of their disorder. Until such time as the spectrum of alcoholism can be confidently diagnosed by means of laboratory tests or physical findings, behavioral techniques (in the present case, a questionnaire) hold sway.

The Self-Administered Alcoholism Screening Test, or SAAST, is perhaps representative of a large number of brief measures that originated as paper-and-pencil tests, or structured interviews. The advantages of paper-and-pencil administration are well established, and include little or no professional staff involvement, low cost, and brevity. Current refinements of such measures include computer administration, scoring, and interpretation. Choice of a particular measure out of the many available should revolve around the relevance of the measure to the particular setting in which it will be used. In view of its origin in a large outpatient medical center, the SAAST merits serious consideration for use in other health care settings.

OVERVIEW

Summary of Development

The SAAST is a derivative of the Michigan Alcohol Screening Test, or MAST (Selzer, 1967, 1971), with items added relating to health care concerns. It was developed by

Swenson and Morse (1975) as a self-administered questionnaire instead of the inter-viewer-administered format then in use with the MAST. In its current form, it con-sists of 37 items that are responded to in yes–no fashion (Table 17.1). Two methods of scoring are utilized: (a) a total score format, which is the sum of the items responded to in the "alcoholic" direction, and (b) a short-form total, which is the weighted sum of responses to 9 items of the original 37 items that have been found through research

TABLE 17.1
SAAST–I Items

---

1. Do you have a drink now and then?
   (If you never drink alcoholic beverages, and have no previous experiences with drinking, do not con-tinue this questionnaire.)
   If you don't drink now, did you stop drinking because of problems with alcohol?
   (If you *do* drink now, leave this item blank.)
2. Do you feel you are a normal drinker? (That is, drink no more than average.)[a]
3. Have you ever awakened the morning after some drinking the night before and found that you could not remember a part of the evening?
4. Does your spouse ever worry or complain about your drinking?
   Do close relatives ever worry or complain about your drinking?[a]
5. Can you stop drinking without a struggle after one or two drinks?
6. Do you ever feel guilty about your drinking?
7. Do friends or relatives think you are a normal drinker?
8. Are you always able to stop drinking when you want to?[a]
9. Have you ever attended a meeting of Alcoholics Anonymous (AA) because of your drinking?
10. Have you gotten into physical fights when drinking?
11. Has your drinking ever created problems between you and your wife, husband, parents or other near relative?[a]
12. Has your wife, husband or other family member ever gone to anyone for help about your drinking?
13. Have you ever lost friendships because of your drinking?
14. Have you ever gotten into trouble at work because of your drinking?
15. Have you ever lost a job because of your drinking?
16. Have you ever neglected your obligations, your family, or your work for two or more days in a row because of drinking?
17. Do you ever drink in the morning?[a]
18. Have you ever felt the need to cut down on your drinking?[a]
19. Have there been times in your adult life when you found it necessary to completely avoid alcohol?
20. Have you ever been told you have liver trouble? Cirrhosis?
21. Have you ever had Delirium Tremens (D.T.s)?
22. Have you ever had severe shaking, heard voices or seen things that weren't there after heavy drink-ing?
23. Have you ever gone to anyone for help about your drinking?
24. Have you ever been in a hospital because of your drinking?
25. Have you ever been told by a doctor to stop drinking?[a]
26. Have you ever been a patient in a psychiatric hospital or on a psychiatric ward of a general hospital?
   (If the answer to #26 is NO, skip to #28)
27. If you answered YES to #26, was drinking part of the problem that resulted in your hospitalization?[a]
28. Have you ever been a patient at a psychiatric or mental health clinic or gone to any doctor, social worker or member of the clergy for help with any emotional problem?
   (If the answer to #28 is NO, skip to #30.)
29. If you answered YES to #28, was your drinking part of the problem?
30. Have you ever been arrested, even for a few hours, because of drunken behavior (not driving)?
31. Have you ever been arrested, even for a few hours, because of driving while intoxicated?[a]
32. Has either of your parents ever had problems with alcohol?
33. Have any of your brothers or sisters ever had problems with alcohol?
34. Has your husband or wife ever had problems with alcohol?
35. Have any of your children ever had problems with alcohol?

---

[a]Items that constitute the nine-item short form.

to possess most of the predictive power contained in the total score format. Two of these 9 items were found to possess considerable discriminatory power, and thus were given extra weighting in computing the short-form total. With these exceptions, all items scored in the "alcoholic" direction count one point toward the total score in their respective formats.

Clinical experience with the SAAST suggested that a parallel form be developed that could be administered to a significant other of the target patient. This was felt to be necessary in order to counter the tendency for persons with alcoholism to minimize or otherwise distort their alcohol use. This parallel form was designated SAAST-II to distinguish it from the original SAAST, or SAAST-I. A manual that discusses the development and use of the SAAST in considerable detail is available (Colligan, Davis, & Morse, 1990).

Large-scale evaluation of the measure began in the late 1970s, and norms were developed in the years following. Briefly, a score of 7 or more on the total score form of the SAAST-I would suggest the presence of alcoholism; a score of 4 or more on the short form of the SAAST-I would also suggest alcoholism.

The SAAST-I possesses adequate reliability, and the specificity of the instrument is quite high when sensitivity is set at appropriate levels (Davis, Hurt, Morse, & O'Brien, 1987). As with any measure, discriminatory accuracy degrades when the measure is used in a population in which the prevalence of alcoholism is substantially lower than in the validation sample.

It is important to emphasize that both the SAAST-I and SAAST-II are screening instruments. Thus, a score of 7 or more on the total score forms and 4 or more on the short forms should alert the clinician to the *possible* presence of alcoholism in the patient. Establishing the diagnosis of alcoholism requires the use of confirmatory procedures, such as an extensive clinical interview with both the patient and knowledgeable informants, as well as laboratory and physical examination findings.

USE AS A SCREENER

The SAAST-I and SAAST-II are used most appropriately as screening instruments . They should never be substituted for confirmatory procedures such as were just discussed. The following points should be considered if a decision is made to use the SAAST or any similar instrument for screening purposes.

Population Bias

It is very important to use a screening device in the population for which it is intended. For example, the SAAST was developed in a large upper midwestern outpatient medical center with a predominantly white, middle-class patient group. Ethnicity was largely northern European in origin. Responses to a brief questionnaire regarding alcohol use are going to reflect attitudes and behaviors that do not precisely overlap with those held by other socioeconomic groups. For example, a study by Davis, Offord, Colligan, and Morse (1991) found that alcoholism screening tests derived from the Minnesota Multiphasic Personality Inventory (MMPI) show very little item overlap. This presumably reflected the divergent characteristics of the samples on which the various measures were developed. Other factors to consider are age and gender. A study by Davis and Morse (1987a) demonstrated that men and women alcoholics display statistically significant differences in responding to various symptom clusters on the SAAST. Men alcoholics are more likely to report socially disruptive behavior than women alcoholics, whereas female alcoholics are much more likely to report emotional consequences of drinking than male alcoholics. Obviously, if items are omitted in a screening test that have relevance for the target population, many potential alcoholics will be missed.

A form of population bias that is associated with many screening techniques concerns the standardization sample. The usual procedure in the standardization and validation of a screening measure consists in identifying (in this instance) a group of well-diagnosed alcoholics, and contrasting their responses to a questionnaire with the responses of a group of nonalcoholics. The fact that the alcoholics are usually identified as such by some sort of independent procedure (clinical interview, laboratory tests, etc.) prior to being administered the screening test in question may change their behavior significantly. Thus, such identified patients may respond in a way different from persons with alcoholism who have not yet been labeled as such. Yet it is this last group for which the screening test in question is being developed. In this way, the standardization sample may differ from the population in which the test is employed.

Prevalence of Disorder

One of the key factors to consider in the use of any alcoholism screening procedure is the prevalence of the disorder in the target population. The issue of prevalence of disorder was brought to the attention of psychologists over 42 years ago by Meehl and Rosen (1955). These investigators used the term *base rate* to describe what epidemiologists and others refer to as *prevalence*. Among other conclusions, they pointed out that, "In some circumstances, notably when the base rates of the criterion classification deviate greatly from a 50 per cent split, use of a test sign having slight or moderate validity will result in an *increase* of erroneous clinical decisions" (p. 215). This would be true in the case of the SAAST if it were employed in a setting where the prevalence is quite low (e.g., less than 1%) or quite high (e.g., 90%)

Operating Characteristics

Sensitivity and Specificity.   In order to understand the effect that prevalence has on the accuracy of detection, it is necessary to consider the related concepts of *sensitivity* and *specificity*. As Baldessarini, Finklestein, and Arana (1983) noted, "There is an important, but not always appreciated, interaction between the diagnostic power of even a highly efficient (sensitive and specific) test and the *prevalence* of an index diagnosis in the population being tested or screened" (p. 569). Sensitivity is defined as "the probability of correct diagnosis of 'positive' cases", and specificity is defined as "the probability of correct diagnosis of 'negative' cases" (Yerushalmy, 1947, p. 1435). (Positive and negative cases are determined by whatever standard is appropriate for the disease under consideration. In the paper by Yerushalmy, positive cases were those showing X-ray evidence that suggested the presence of tuberculosis, and negative cases were those without such evidence.) Although sensitivity and specificity (along with the false-negative and false-positive rates) are generally considered to be constants that are established during the standardization phase of the development of a screening instrument, this is true only as long as the test administration procedures used in the field are not significantly different from those used in the standardization phase.

The usual method of presenting the concepts of sensitivity and specificity (as well as positive and negative predictive power, which are discussed later) is through use of a 2 × 2 table (e.g., see Baldessarini et al., 1983, p. 571). It should be noted that estimates of sensitivity and specificity depend on the criteria used to establish the "gold standard," and that these estimates would possibly change if a different set of criteria were used. For example, the SAAST was standardized using *DSM–III* criteria, and this needs to be taken into account when using *DSM–III–R* and *DSM–IV* diagnostic schemes.

In the case of screening tests such as the SAAST, high sensitivity is desirable, even with somewhat limited specificity, especially if test results are negative. If test results are positive, there is a likelihood of an appreciable number of false positive cases, which may then require further evaluation. However, in situations where the prevalence of alcoholism is moderately low, the preponderance of results will be negative.

The major validation study of the SAAST was reported by Davis et al. (1987). A discriminant analysis was performed on SAAST results of 1,156 patients (520 alcoholics and 636 nonalcoholics). With sensitivities set at 90% and 95%, respectively, specificities for the total score format were 97.8%, and 96.4%, respectively. Discriminatory accuracy in this idealized sample is high in large part because of the high percentage of well-studied alcoholics (45%) in the study. The values chosen for sensitivity in this study are in line with the earlier recommendation that screening tests should be highly sensitive.

Positive and Negative Predictive Power. Recent recognition of the effect of prevalence of disorder on discriminatory accuracy of tests and measures has led to increased emphasis on consideration of the *predictive power* of these tests and measures. Although sensitivity and specificity are important operating characteristics, in theory they do not vary with changes in prevalence of disorder. Positive and negative predictive power, however, are significantly effected by such changes and provide us with strong evidence of the efficacy of our tests and measures in our target populations. Griner, Mayewski, Mushlin, and Greenland (1981) defined positive and negative predictive power as follows: "(1) Given a positive test, what is the probability that the disease is present? (2) Given a negative test, what is the probability that the disease is not present?" (p. 565). If the results of the SAAST validation study reported by Davis et al. (1987) are used as an example, with sensitivity and specificity set at 90% and 97.8%, respectively, positive predictive power is 97%, and negative predictive power is 92%. But this assumes a prevalence rate of 45% (the percentage of well-studied alcoholics in this idealized study). However, if a prevalence rate of 10% is assumed, the positive and negative predictive powers drop to 82% and 99%, respectively. Furthermore, if the SAAST were used in a population where the prevalence of alcoholism is only 1%, the positive predictive power drops to only 29%, while the negative predictive power is virtually 100%. In this instance, more correct decisions would be made if the test was discarded and all patients were declared to be nonalcoholic!

Although the 1% prevalence figure just used is extreme, the example illustrates the difficulties inherent in screening for disorders that are rare in the target population. A prevalence estimate of 5% would not be unrealistic in a general medical subpopulation of older women, for example. In such a case, a positive test result would be truly positive only about two-thirds of the time. A situation in which two out of three test positive cases are truly positive might be acceptable in some clinical settings but not in others. A decision to screen for alcoholism in such a situation would depend on a number of other factors, such as the expense involved in screening in the first place, and the expense involved in applying confirmatory procedures (such as clinical interviews, laboratory testing, etc.) to all cases with a positive test score, including the false-positive cases. Another factor would be the availability of proper alcoholism treatment facilities. Griner et al. (1981) identified four important considerations where screening for disorder is concerned:

> First, the disease in question should be common enough to justify the effort to detect it. Secondly, it should be accompanied by significant morbidity if *not* treated. Thirdly, effective therapy must exist to alter its natural history. Finally, detection and treatment of the presymptomatic state should result in benefits beyond those obtained through treatment of the early *symptomatic* patient. (p. 559)

Reliability

The reliability of the SAAST was computed as part of a study on its discriminatory accuracy (Davis et al., 1987). Kuder-Richardson 20 (K-R 20: for dichotomous items) yielded a reliability coefficient of .81 for the total sample and .84 for the alcoholic sample, indicating adequate internal consistency for screening purposes.

Relative Operating Characteristic Analysis

Cut points have been associated for a long time with various tests and measurements. Usually, this has been in the form of a single score that separates the "normal" subject from the "abnormal." Unfortunately, a single cut point does not allow for changes in the population being evaluated, nor for changes in selection policy. For example, a cut point of 7 on the SAAST is the usual one chosen, but a policy that emphasizes the necessity for identifying most patients with alcoholism might require that a cut point of 5 or 6 be used. However, a lower cut point would produce a higher number of false positives, all of whom would have to be evaluated. The point is that cut points should be chosen that are in line with the screening policy of the facility using the particular test or measure.

The choice of cut point is facilitated by use of relative operating characteristic or receiver operating characteristic (ROC) curve methodology (Cleary, Bush, & Kessler, 1987; Griner et al., 1981; Swets, 1988). This technique is derived from signal detection theory and attempts to find a particular "signal" (correct diagnosis) against a background of "noise" (diagnostic error). From the ROC curve, a choice of cut point can be made which optimizes the current selection policy. In considering the ROC curve, it is important to realize that increasing the true positive rate ("hits") increases the false positive rate ("misses"), and that decreasing one decreases the other. A primary care setting is one in which a limited chemical dependency staff might want to raise the cut point, and thereby increase the likelihood that a patient identified as probably alcoholic is in fact alcoholic. This also has the benefit of decreasing the number of false positive cases, which would then have to be evaluated by an already overloaded staff. The problem here, of course, is that a larger number of alcoholics will go undetected.

Relevant Psychometric Support

The SAAST has been used in a variety of settings to detect individuals who are likely to have alcoholism. The following is a review of relevant research conducted on various patient samples.

General Medical Patients. This is the area of greatest use of the SAAST. Swenson and Morse (1975) developed the SAAST as a medically oriented revision of the Michigan Alcoholism Screening Test, or MAST (Selzer, 1967, 1971). Items were added to the MAST that inquired into medical aspects of a patient's alcohol use, as well as items pertaining to the use of alcohol in the family. Items from the MAST and new items were modified so they could be completed by patients as a paper-and-pencil screening test. Subjects included 100 patients already diagnosed as having alcoholism (70 males; 30 females), and 100 psychiatric and general medical patients (31 males; 69 females), none of whom had been admitted for alcoholism treatment or had admitted an alcohol problem. Using an arbitrary cut point of 10, the SAAST correctly identified 90 of the alcoholics, including 6 of the control group whose histories were strongly suggestive of the presence of alcoholism. Sixteen of the alcoholic group were counted as false negatives, but only 3 in the control group were counted as false positives. The authors concluded that "This self-administered alcoholism screening test can be used effectively to detect the presence of alcoholism" (p. 206).

Although the study by Swenson and Morse did not use a large enough sample to be considered a proper validation study, it did suggest that potential usefulness of the SAAST with medical patients. A later study by Hurt, Morse, and Swenson (1980) reported on the administration of the SAAST to 1,002 patients receiving medical examinations. This study did not use control and contrast samples, but was done to gain more experience with the use of the SAAST in a general medical population. Two findings of note were that 142 (14%) of the patients refused to complete the SAAST, and another 42 (4%) turned in an incomplete SAAST. Another 132 (13%) patients indicated on the SAAST that they were nondrinkers. Of the 686 (69%) drinkers, 36 (5% of drinkers) obtained a SAAST score of 7 to 9, whereas 18 (3% of drinkers) obtained a score of 10 or greater. In order to provide verification of the test results, the medical records of patients chosen at random from each of these groups were scrutinized. The authors concluded that "the SAAST is an effective tool for the detection of alcoholism and that it can be used in the general medical setting." (p. 365).

A study by Davis et al. (1987) represents the formal validation of the SAAST in a general medical population. This study used patient data from the study by Hurt et al. (1980) and added a contrast group of patients who had been classified according to *DSM–III* criteria and had undergone inpatient treatment for alcoholism. The final validation sample consisted of 1,156 patients (520 alcoholics and 636 nonalcoholics). The appropriateness of placement in the control group was investigated by a computer search of all patient records for alcoholism/alcohol abuse, or alcohol-related diseases. As a result, 47 of the patients in this group had evidence of alcoholism or chronic alcohol abuse and were placed in the contrast (alcoholic) group. Stepwise discriminant function analysis was performed on the total score, a nine-item version, and a two-item version of the SAAST. With sensitivity set at 90%, a score of 7 or greater yielded a specificity of 98% for the total score version. A score of 4 or greater on the nine-item version yielded a specificity of 99%, when set at the same sensitivity level. A finding of note was that two items ("Do close relatives ever worry or complain about your drinking?" and "Have you ever felt the need to cut down on your drinking?") correctly classified 81% of alcoholics and 96% of nonalcoholics. These two items represent half of the items on the popular CAGE questionnaire (Mayfield, McLeod, & Hall, 1974).

Special Populations

The SAAST has been used with specific patient and nonpatient groups. The following is a survey of studies that have been performed on these groups.

Spouses of Alcoholics.   Because of the well-known tendency for alcoholics to minimize the problematic aspects of their drinking, Morse and Swenson (1975) administered the SAAST to the spouses or nearest relative of alcoholic patients, and to the alcoholism counselor of these same patients. The spouse or nearest relative and the alcoholism counselor were asked to rate the patient. Fifty patients were the subjects of this study, along with 45 spouses, 3 daughters, 1 mother, and 1 sister. On the basis of patient response to the SAAST, 42 (85%) of the 50 patients were correctly diagnosed as having alcoholism. However, if the SAAST ratings of the patients by the spouses or significant others were used, 45 (90%) of the patients were correctly diagnosed. The authors concluded that the spouse or close relative of an alcoholic patient can be a source of valid information about the patient's alcoholism. This opinion is contrasted with that of Guze, Tuason, Stewart, and Picken (1963), who found that only 41% of their cases could be correctly diagnosed on the basis of information obtained from relatives. However, Morse and Swenson thought that the Guze et al. study was based on a sample that differed in important ways from their own sample.

Davis and Morse (1987b) attempted to replicate the findings of the Morse and Swenson study using 240 patient–collateral pairs. The SAAST was administered to the patient, and a collateral was asked to complete an SAAST on the patient. All 240 patients (181 men) had been admitted to an inpatient alcoholism treatment program and were diagnosed as alcoholic according to *DSM–III* criteria. Patients who were diagnosed as abusing or being dependent on other drugs were excluded. The collaterals included 181 spouses, 13 parents, 18 friends, 16 children, and 12 others. A score of 7 or greater on the SAAST was considered to be indicative of the presence of alcoholism. Collateral ratings on the SAAST suggested alcoholism 98% of the time, whereas patient ratings of their own drinking behavior yielded a correct classification 97% of the time. Conjoint patient–collateral classification was correct 95% of the time. There were no cases in which both patient and collateral agreed that the patient was nonalcoholic. Furthermore, when the items of the SAAST were composed into clusters of similar content, it was found that the highest percent of agreement (88%) occurred on items relating to alcohol problems in the family (parents, siblings, children), and the lowest percent agreement (68%) was in the area of loss of control, which is a primary component in the diagnosis of alcoholism. The relative lack of concordance on this component may be due to the nature of the items that comprise it, because they have to do with the internal state of the drinker. Thus, "loss of control" may not be as readily observable by another individual.

The use of the SAAST with collaterals of patients with alcoholism suggested a format specifically designed to be administered to spouses and others who know the patient well. The original SAAST items were reworded to focus on the target patient rather than the respondent, and the test was retitled SAAST–II to distinguish it from the original form, now titled SAAST–I. The SAAST–II uses the same cut points as the SAAST–I, and the interpretive statements associated with the obtained scores are the same.

Loethen and Khavari (1990) administered the SAAST and the Khavari Alcohol Test (KAT) to a total of 170 inpatients and outpatients. All of the patients had received a diagnosis of alcohol dependence according to *DSM–III–R* criteria. Ninety-nine of the patients volunteered collaterals, and the remaining 71 patients did not. Fifty-five of the collaterals were contacted and filled out a KAT and a SAAST. The authors concluded that:

(1) The alcoholics' self-reports were in impressive agreement with those of their corresponding collaterals: (2) the self-report of patients who did not volunteer collaterals and those who volunteered collaterals were not different for the two groups, and (3) there is a positive correlation between the group with collaterals and the one without collaterals. (p. 758).

Psychiatric Patients. In the past, alcoholism has been thought of as symptomatic of an underlying psychiatric disorder. However, modern conceptions of alcoholism treat it as an independent disorder. Both *DSM–IV* and ICD–9 classification systems adhere to this point of view.

A study by Pristach, Smith, and Perkins (1993) involved the administration of the SAAST to 236 (122 men) acutely ill psychiatric patients. The study asked the following questions:

(1) Can acutely ill psychiatric inpatients complete a self-administered questionnaire (the SAAST) shortly after admission? (2) do patients from different diagnostic subgroups vary in their response to the SAAST? (3) can alcohol abuse be detected in acutely ill psychiatric inpatients using the SAAST? (4) do patients give reliable and consistent answers on SAAST questions posed at different times during an acute psychiatric admission? (p. 79).

Of the 41 patients who did not complete an initial SAAST, 13 refused, and the remaining 28 could not do so because of because of "uncontrolled behavior or disorganized mental state" (p. 80). Twenty-one of the patients who did not complete an initial SAAST received a schizophrenia diagnosis. The investigators did not find that different diagnostic subgroups varied significantly in their response to the SAAST. Furthermore, they found that the SAAST "is useful for the detection of alcohol abuse and dependence in acutely ill psychiatric patients, especially when used in conjunction with the clinical interview" (p. 86). Lastly, the patients were found to be consistent in responding to individual items (coefficient alpha = .92).

In an attempt to identify individuals enrolled in a methadone maintenance program at high risk for alcoholism, Cohen, McKeever, Cohen, and Stimmel (1977) administered a modified version of the SAAST to 30 patients enrolled in a methadone maintenance program who showed signs of severe alcoholism ("Alcoholic group"), 30 patients enrolled in a methadone maintenance program who did not exhibit signs or symptoms of alcoholism ("Control group"), and 80 consecutive admissions to the same program during a 6-month period ("Admission group"). The SAAST was modified by the inclusion of five additional validity questions, which differed only slightly in form and content from five questions already in the SAAST. The Alcoholic group had a mean SAAST score of 14.03 (range: 4–23), the Control group mean score was 3 (range: 0–7), and the Admission group mean score was 5.17 (range: 0–22). Of the 21 patients in the admission group who had an SAAST score of 8 or more, 12 were judged to be excessive drinkers, whereas only 5 of 59 patients who scored below 8 were so judged, and only 1 of the 59 was discharged because of excessive drinking. The authors concluded:

> Early identification of the individual most likely to develop difficulties with alcohol consumption once enrolled in methadone maintenance is therefore of prime importance. The evidence presented in this current study indicates that the modified SAAST is able to satisfactorily provide this discrimination. The use of this questionnaire, when combined with a comprehensive rehabilitative program, may serve to diminish the prevalence of alcoholism in persons maintained on methadone maintenance. (p. 266).

Coronary Care Patients. Juergens et al. (1993) studied the concordance between clinician diagnosis of alcoholism and SAAST results in 544 patients (371 men) admitted to a coronary care unit. Overall, 9.6% of the patients (11.1% of men; 6.4% of women) obtained scores on the SAAST greater than or equal to 7. However, SAAST and clinician results were in agreement on the possible presence of alcoholism in only 43% of the cases thought to have the disorder. From these results, the investigators concluded that "No one test should be relied on exclusively. . . . The purpose of a screening procedure is to identify patients for a more in-depth evaluation" (p. 70). Furthermore, the authors commented that the SAAST was well received by the patients in this sample. This is supported by the overall completion rate for the SAAST of 90%, and by a completion rate of 97% for those patients who were in the hospital when the SAAST was administered.

Alcoholism in Physicians. Noting that little information was available on the prevalence of alcohol abuse/dependence in physicians, Niven, Hurt, Morse, and Swenson (1984) administered the SAAST to 399 physicians attending a continuing medical education program. The SAAST questionnaires were randomly distributed and were filled out anonymously. The respondents were classified into one of four groups, depending on their scores: (a) nondrinkers; (b) those with SAAST scores <7; (c) those with SAAST scores from 7 to 9; and (d) those with SAAST scores ≥10. Forty-nine of the physicians (12%) indicated they were nondrinkers; 320 (81%) obtained scores <7; 21 (5%) obtained scores from 7 to 9; and 9 (2%) obtained scores of 10 or more. The investigators concluded that the SAAST results obtained in this sample of physicians are similar to those obtained in a general medical sample, suggesting that the prevalence of alcohol abuse/dependence does not differ in the two groups.

Alcoholism and Psoriasis. Morse, Perry, and Hurt (1985) administered the SAAST to 99 patients with disabling psoriasis, and 99 controls who had dermatologic disorders other than psoriasis. Both groups were hospitalized for treatment of their disorders, and were matched for age and sex. Ten of the psoriasis patients obtained SAAST scores ≥7, whereas only 2 control patients obtained such scores. Independent record review suggested alcoholism in 1 additional psoriasis patient and 1 control patient. It was noted that 10 of the 11 psoriasis patients with SAAST scores suggestive of alcoholism were males, but this finding was of borderline statistical significance. The authors concluded:

Our study suggests a higher rate of alcoholism, as defined by NCA criteria and by higher SAAST scores, among hospitalized, psoriatic male patients than among control patients hospitalized for other dermatologic diseases. These findings are consistent with anecdotal reports and our clinical impression that there is some correlation between the two disorders. (p. 398).

Gender and Age.   Early work with alcoholism screening tests focused on male subjects. As Wilsnack and Beckman (1984) noted:

Until quite recently women received little specific attention in research on alcohol problems. In a search of the literature published between 1929 and 1970, Sandmaier (1980) found only 28 English-language studies of alcoholic women. Higher rates of problem drinking and alcoholism among men than women, underrepresentation of women in popular clinical research settings (e.g., VA or state hospitals), and lack of any special interest in women's alcohol problems on the part of predominantly male researchers may all have contributed to the neglect of women as subjects of alcohol-related research. (p. ix)

The development of the SAAST has been undertaken with this caveat in mind. Swenson and Morse (1975) included both women alcoholics and nonalcoholic controls in their initial presentation of the SAAST. In the Hurt et al. (1980) study of 1,002 general medical patients, 635 were women. The formal validation study of the SAAST by Davis et al. (1987) included 119 alcoholic and 402 nonalcoholic women. Because the alcoholic sample in this study contained mostly men, and the nonalcoholic sample consisted mostly of women, separate analyses were performed for men and women. It was found that discriminatory accuracy was essentially equal for men and women, although more items entered the discriminant function for women (13 for women 45 years old or younger and 11 for women older than 45) than for men (7 for each age group).

However, clinical experience with both men and women alcoholics suggests that the symptom patterns differ on the basis of gender and age. Davis and Morse (1987a) analyzed the SAAST records of 437 men and 146 women undergoing inpatient evaluation and treatment for alcoholism. A principal components factor analysis of the SAAST item responses yielded six interpretable components: (I) loss of control, (II) occupational and social disruption, (III) physical consequences (of drinking), (IV) emotional consequences (of drinking) and requests for help, (V) concern on the part of others, and (VI) family members with alcohol problems. Males alcoholics were significantly more likely to display occupationally and socially disruptive behaviors (component II), as well as eliciting more concern on the part of others (component V). Women were more likely to admit to emotional consequences and request help (component IV), to report loss of control (component I), and to report alcohol problems in their families (component VI). Younger alcoholics (age ≤45 years) were significantly more likely to admit to loss of control, to engage in occupationally and socially disruptive behavior, to experience emotional consequences and request help, and to obtain higher total scores on the SAAST. Older alcoholics were significantly higher in reporting physical consequences of drinking (component III). These results suggest that although men and women alcoholics may obtain similar total scores on the SAAST, or any other similar screening instrument, the patterns of reported drinking behavior may be quite different Although caution is advised in using a screening test for anything other than screening purposes, the availability of SAAST results prior to consultation provides the health care provider with material that can serve as leading questions in the evaluation of a patient's alcohol use.

Cross-Cultural Studies.   The application of the SAAST to Spanish-speaking individuals has been the objective of two studies that have appeared in the literature. The first is a study by de la Fuente et al. (1982) in which a Spanish version of the SAAST was administered to 121 alcoholics, 150 randomly selected medical patients, and "41 non-alcoholic, healthy subjects" (p. 1). All 121 patients from the first group were correctly identified as alcoholic and 21 patients from the second group were so classified. The authors concluded that the CUAAL (The Spanish version of the SAAST) "can be a useful aid to help clinicians with the early detection of alcoholism" (p. 1).

The second study, by Davis, de la Fuente, Morse, Landa, and O'Brien (1989), asked the following questions:

> a) Does the SAAST yield the same level of discriminatory accuracy in a Mexican sample as it does in a predominantly middle-class sample from the United States (Rochester, MN)? (b) Do the same items provide most of the discriminant accuracy in the two cultures? and (c) Is the factor structure of the SAAST for diagnosed alcoholics similar in the two cultures? (p. 224).

SAAST results from 304 (191 alcoholics) subjects were employed in a stepwise discriminant analysis. This analysis yielded a nine-item discriminant function that was comparable to that obtained in the Rochester sample reported on by Davis et al. (1987). In addition, five of the nine items appeared in both the Mexican sample and the Rochester sample, including the two most powerful predictors ("Do close relatives ever worry or complain about your drinking?" and "Have you ever felt the need to cut down on your drinking?"). A principal-components analysis yielded six components, but only four of these were similar to the six obtained in the Rochester sample.

IMPLEMENTATION

Use as a Stand-Alone Instrument

The SAAST was designed to be used routinely in a health care setting. The most common format is a paper-and-pencil questionnaire, consisting of 35 numbered questions (with 2 additional branching questions), which are responded to in yes–no fashion (see Table 17.1). The questionnaire can usually be completed in 5 min or less. Typically, the questionnaire is prefaced with text that explains that a patient's alcohol use is an important aspect of a medical examination and that a report based on the SAAST will be included in the patient's medical history. An envelope is included with the questionnaire in which the SAAST can be sealed and returned to the person who presented it to the patient. The SAAST is intended for use with adult medical patients, and its use should be restricted to individuals 18 years of age of older.

Once the SAAST is completed it can be easily scored by nonprofessional staff. Scoring templates are available that overlay the SAAST questionnaire. A number of output formats are possible One is a simple report that indicates the score obtained by the patient, plus a statement as to which drinking category this places the patient into. A more elaborate report might include key items endorsed by the patient that can serve as interview cues for health care providers. For some years, a computer-generated report has been used at the Mayo Clinic. This report uses summary information from the SAAST as a basis for suggesting various follow-up options, such as a clinical interview with a chemical dependency professional or suitable laboratory tests that might be obtained (e.g., SGOT, MCV). In addition, the report prints out critical item statements endorsed by the patient that deserve special attention.

A more recent innovation has been the use of computer software that permits computer administration, scoring, and report generation of the SAAST. This innovation was based on a study by Davis and Morse (1991) that investigated the equivalence of paper-and-pencil and computer-administered formats of the SAAST. One hundred ninety-nine patients were administered both computerized and paper-and-pencil versions of the test in counterbalanced order. When the patients were categorized (by test results) into alcoholic and nonalcoholic groups, agreement between the two formats was 95% for both the total score and short-form versions of the SAAST. It was concluded that the two formats are equivalent and that computerized administration and scoring of the SAAST is a cost-effective measure. Furthermore, computerized administration allows for branching statements to be inserted, which allow for more detailed assessment of specific aspects of drinking behavior, as well as for elimination of inappropriate or redundant questions.

Use With Other Instruments or Procedures

Any screening measure is best viewed as a means of identifying "maybes" and obviously needs to be followed up by a confirmatory procedure if it is to have any clinical utility. The "gold standard" for alcohol abuse/dependence is the clinical interview, using criteria developed under *DSM-III*, *DSM-III-R*, or *DSM-IV* guidelines, especially if conducted by someone with extensive experience in the field of chemical dependency. Although laboratory tests are helpful, many studies document the large numbers of false-negative and false-positive results generated by laboratory tests. Even the clinical interview is subject to error (especially false-negative errors) when patients minimize their alcohol use or knowledgeable collaterals are not available. However, it is likely that the majority of patients with alcohol problems *will* provide reliable information. Clinical experience suggests that patients with significant alcohol problems will typically reject the idea that they are alcoholic, yet will be remarkably candid about their drinking behavior. In essence, they have not made the association between their drinking behavior and the diagnosis of alcoholism.

The SAAST can serve a useful function in the clinical interview. It can provide lead statements endorsed by the patient that can facilitate entry into the patient's drinking history. Items from the SAAST that have proven to be highly discriminating are item 18, "Have you ever felt the need to cut down on your drinking?," and item 4a, "Do close relatives ever worry or complain about your drinking?" Endorsement of either or both of these items significantly increases the likelihood of alcoholism. But inquiry into positive responses to these items is important because many patients cut down on their drinking during certain critical periods of their lives (e.g., pregnant women) or are related to individuals whose disapproval of drinking does not reflect the cultural norm.

Because knowledgeable collaterals often provide the most accurate information about the drinking behavior of the patient, use of the SAAST–II is strongly recommended when a collateral is present. The SAAST–II is especially useful when the clinician suspects that the patient is denying significant aspects of his or her alcohol use.

Potential Issues in Implementation

Problems in implementing the SAAST are few and can be listed under the following headings: (a) cost, (b) patient acceptance, (c) staff acceptance, (d) drug of dependence, (e) prior history of active alcoholism, and (f) screening hits and misses.

Cost.   The SAAST is not expensive. Paper-and-pencil tests can be printed in large numbers at low cost, and computer administration and scoring can almost eliminate the cost of scoring and preparing a report. Perhaps the major question concerning cost is, "Who pays?" Patients who are nondrinkers would justifiably resent being charged for a test that for them is irrelevant. Drinkers, on the other hand, might resist paying for a test that would represent an invasion of their privacy. This issue spills over into the problem of patient acceptance.

Patient Acceptance.   In most of the studies done with the SAAST, a small number of patients refuse to fill out the test, and are free to do so without providing a reason. However, the majority of patients readily accept the proposition that one's alcohol use can lead to medical consequences and thus is a medical issue. The point is that refusals are rare, but they do occur and should be accepted without question.

Staff Acceptance.   For reasons that may be similar to those behind patient refusal to answer questions about their alcohol use, professional staff may feel that inquiry into this area is not a legitimate medical issue but rather a moral or social issue to be addressed by others. Another concern that health care professionals have is the difficulty in dealing with a patient who is in denial concerning his or her drinking. Attempts to inquire into drinking behavior can often be met with expressions of anger and resentment on the part of the patient. Health care professionals are understandably reluctant to broach the topic when it can be so easily avoided.

Drug of Dependence.   The SAAST is a screening test for alcoholism and not a screening test for drugs in general. Attempts to develop a SAAST-like screening test for other drugs have not been successful due to the wide scope that such a test would have to have. Such a test would need to assess both licit and illicit drugs, and it is difficult to develop questions that address such a broad range of drug behaviors. However, patients who have or have had abuse/dependence problems with other drugs often respond to the SAAST in terms of these other drugs. Brief questioning is usually sufficient to clear up the confusion.

Prior History of Active Alcoholism.   Patients who have a history of alcoholism but are now recovering often respond to the SAAST as though they were still actively using. This is in large part a function of the format of the questions, which are usually phrased as "have you ever . . . ?" In order to correctly identify patients in recovery, the following question was added to the SAAST: "If you don't drink now, did you stop drinking because of problems with alcohol?" Occasionally, patients will answer "no" to this question because they stopped drinking for reasons other than problematic use. Such reasons could include a concern with the long-term effects of alcohol use on health, the role model implications for children of adult alcohol use, or that the use of alcohol violates a moral or ethical code.

Screening Hits and Misses. This issue has been addressed in other parts of this chapter but bears repeating here, because it affects implementation. The SAAST (or any other screening instrument) is not a perfect predictor, and therefore false-positive and false-negative rates can be expected to be something other than zero. It is important to recognize that either can be maximized or minimized, depending on policies adopted in a particular clinical setting. In an earlier part of this chapter it was pointed out that the cut point that has been used in research studies is not sacred and can be changed to meet the needs of the setting. For example, setting a low cut point will significantly reduce the number of false-negative cases, but will increase the false-positive ones. This, however, may swamp the resources of clinical staff who evaluate chemical dependency issues. Conversely, setting a higher cut point would produce a higher false-negative rate, and many patients with significant alcohol problems would go unevaluated and untreated.

Guidelines for Decision Making

Guidelines for SAAST use are fairly simple. A total score of 7 or more would indicate probable alcoholism and would typically call for confirmatory evaluation. But, as noted earlier, the cut point of 7 is not sacred and may be modified as experience dictates. If further evaluation indicates that a diagnosis of alcoholism is merited, then various treatment modalities need to be considered. Prior to the advent of managed care, inpatient treatment of alcoholism lasting almost a month was considered the norm. However, the chemical dependency field has undergone considerable revamping in recent years, and today outpatient treatment of some form is the standard. Such treatment is programmatic in nature and consists of lectures, individual and group counseling, reading, and multimedia materials.

CASE HISTORIES

The following case histories do not represent specific individuals, but are instead composites that the author has encountered in the alcoholism field

Case 1

The patient is a 45-year-old college-educated male, married, with three children. His spouse is 42 years old, and his three daughters are 14, 12, and 9 years old. He works as a middle manager for a large corporation. This is his first visit to this particular outpatient medical clinic, which has a provider relationship with his corporation.

As part of this patient's workup, he is asked to fill out the SAAST–I questionnaire, which is presented to him via computer. After it is electronically scored and a report is printed, it becomes a part of his medical record. The clinician who conducts his initial examination notes that he has obtained a total score of 5 on the SAAST, but that his short form score is 4 (the screening cut point for probable alcoholism) and he has endorsed two highly discriminating items: "Do close relatives ever worry or complain about your drinking?" and "Have to ever felt the need to cut down on your drinking?" As part of his examination, he is asked about these items. He states that his wife has complained in the past about his drinking, but he dismisses this as her bias because she drinks very little herself. However, to appease her, he has cut back on his alcohol intake for short periods of time. When asked if he thinks that he might have a problem with alcohol he denies it quite emphatically. The clinician suspects that the patient may be minimizing his alcohol use and its consequences, so she asks if he would give his permission for his wife to fill out a SAAST–II. He reluctantly agrees, saying that it is totally unnecessary and a waste of time.

The patient's spouse fills out a SAAST–II, and gives the patient a total score of 15, which is well within the alcoholism range. Because of the discrepancy, the clinician arranges for a family interview, and includes the children. With the patient present, the family describes behavior that is consistent with severe alcoholism. Among the behaviors cited are frequently coming home late after work in an intoxicated state, two drunken driving citations in the past 3 years, arguments over his drinking, verbally abusive behavior toward the spouse and children while intoxicated, and frequent attempts to "go on the wagon" after a drinking episode. Initially, the patient denies the behavior, but the accumulated evidence gradually brings him to admit that he has a serious problem with alcohol and has had for many years. He agrees to be seen by the clinic chemical dependency specialist and to follow the recommendations that are made following that visit.

Case 2

This 32-year-old housewife and mother of two school-age children comes in for her annual medical examination, and is asked to take the SAAST–I, which is now being routinely administered to all adult patients. She takes the paper-and-pencil version, which is then scored by clinic personnel and a report is prepared. She obtains a total score of 12 and a short-form score of 5. When interviewed, she admits that she has become increasingly concerned about her drinking, but has been afraid to seek help or consultation. She says that she has been drinking at home for years, usually after her husband leaves for work and her children for school. Initially, she would have an afternoon drink after she finished her housework, but noted that her intake gradually increased to the point where she was having five to six drinks a day. She had always drank vodka because she didn't want the smell of alcohol on her breath. Over the years she became aware that there were periods in her day that she could not remember (blackouts), routine tasks were being left undone, her mood became more and more depressed, and she would try to relieve this with alcohol. She recalls one occasion when she fell down a short flight of stairs after drinking and broke her ankle (she told her family that she had tripped on a toy left by one of the children). She made many attempts to stop drinking, only to return to it within a short time. She recalls that on one or two occasions, she considered "ending it all" because it was the only way she knew of to stop drinking.

The interviewing clinician referred this patient to a chemical dependency specialist, who, in addition to taking a complete chemical use history, interviewed the family members. The husband said he thought his wife would have a drink on occasion but was unaware of her excessive daily use. The specialist recommended a short period of inpatient treatment for the patient, followed by intensive outpatient treatment.

SUMMARY

The increasing recognition of alcoholism as a significant health care issue also highlights the importance of instruments for detecting its presence. The SAAST is one such instrument that has been applied in general medical settings. This inexpensive and easy-to-administer questionnaire has been shown to have adequate reliability and validity when administered to a variety of patient samples. Patient acceptance has been good when the use of alcohol is looked at as a health care issue. Patient endorsement of test items on the SAAST has been found to be an excellent starting point for a clinician interview. As long as the SAAST is viewed as a screening instrument and with the realization that published cut points are not cast in stone, it should be given serious consideration for use in health care settings.

REFERENCES

Baldessarini, R. J., Finklestein, M. D., & Arana, G. W. (1983). The predictive power of diagnostic tests and the effect of prevalence of illness. *Archives of General Psychiatry, 40,* 569–573.

Cleary, P. D., Bush, B. T., & Kessler, L. G. (1987). Evaluating the use of mental health screening scales in primary care settings using receiver operating characteristic curves. *Medical Care, 25 (Supplement),* S90–S98.

Cohen, A., McKeever, W., Cohen, M., & Stimmel, B. (1977). The use of an alcoholism screening test to identify the potential for alcoholism in persons on methadone maintenance. *American Journal of Drug and Alcohol Abuse, 4,* 257–266.

Colligan, R. C., Davis, L. J., & Morse, R. M. (1990). *The Self-Administered Alcoholism Screening Test (SAAST): A user's guide.* Rochester, MN: Mayo Foundation.

Davis, L. J., de la Fuente, J. R., Morse, R. M., Landa, E., & O'Brien, P. C. (1989). Self-Administered Alcoholism Screening Test (SAAST): Comparison of classificatory accuracy in two cultures. *Alcoholism: Clinical and Experimental Research, 13,* 224–228.

Davis, L. J., Hurt, R. D., Morse, R. M., & O'Brien, P. C. (1987). Discriminant analysis of the Self-Administered Alcoholism Screening Test. *Alcoholism: Clinical and Experimental Research, 11,* 269–273.

Davis, L. J., & Morse, R. M. (1987a). Age and sex differences in the responses of alcoholics to the Self-Administered Alcoholism Screening Test. *Journal of Clinical Psychology, 43,* 423–430.

Davis, L. J., & Morse, R. M. (1987b). Patient-spouse agreement on the drinking behaviors of alcoholics. *Mayo Clinic Proceedings, 62,* 689–694.

Davis, L. J., & Morse, R. M. (1991). Self-Administered Alcoholism Screening Test: A comparison of conventional versus computer-administered formats. *Alcoholism: Clinical and Experimental Research, 15,* 155–157.

Davis, L. J., Offord, K. P., Colligan, R. C., & Morse, R. M. (1991). The CAL: An MMPI alcoholism scale for general medical patients. *Journal of Clinical Psychology, 47,* 632–646.

de la Fuente, J., Guiterrez, L., Rivero, F., Tsao, G., Rokind, M., & Kerschenobich, D. (1982). Early detection of alcoholism in a hospital population. *Revista de Investigacion Clinica, 34,* 1–6.

Griner, P. F., Mayewski, R. J., Mushlin, A. I., & Greenland, P. (1981). Selection and interpretation of diagnostic tests and procedures. *Annals of Internal Medicine, 94,* 559–570.

Guze, S. B., Tuason, V. B., Stewart, M. A., & Picken, B. (1963). The drinking history: A comparison of reports by subjects and their relatives. *Quarterly Journal of Studies on Alcohol, 24,* 249–260.

Hurt, R. D., Morse, R. M., & Swenson, W. M. (1980). Diagnosis of alcoholism with a self-administered alcoholism screening test. *Mayo Clinic Proceedings, 55,* 365–370.

Juergens, S. M., Hurt, R. D., Offord, K. P., Zarling, K. K., Kemke, K. K., Anderson, L. L., Fredrickson, P. A., & Miller, F. A. (1993). Alcoholism in a coronary care unit population. *Journal of Addictive Diseases, 12,* 57–76.

Loethen, G. J., & Khavari, K. A. (1990). Comparison of the Self-Administered Alcoholism Screening Test (SAAST) and the Khavari Alcohol Test (KAT): Results from an alcoholic population and their collaterals. *Alcoholism: Clinical and Experimental Research, 14,* 756–760.

Mayfield, D., McLeod, G., & Hall, P. (1974). The CAGE questionnaire: Validation of a new alcoholism screening instrument. *American Journal of Psychiatry, 131,* 1121–1123.

Meehl, P. E., & Rosen, A. (1955). Antecedent probability and the efficiency of psychometric signs, patterns, or cutting scores. *Psychological Bulletin, 52,* 194–216.

Morse, R. M., Perry, H. O., & Hurt, R. D. (1985). Alcoholism and psoriasis. *Alcoholism: Clinical and Experimental Research, 9,* 396–399.

Morse, R. M., & Swenson, W. M. (1975). Spouse response to a self-administered alcoholism screening test. *Journal of Studies on Alcohol, 36,* 400–405.

Niven, R. G., Hurt, R. D., Morse, R. M., & Swenson, W. M. (1984). Alcoholism in physicians. *Mayo Clinic Proceedings, 59,* 12–16.

Pristach, C. A., Smith, C. M., & Perkins, C. (1993). Reliability of the Self-Administered Alcoholism Screening Test (SAAST) in psychiatric inpatients. *Journal of Addictive Diseases, 12,* 77–88.

Selzer, M. L. (1967). Problems encountered in the treatment of alcoholism. *Michigan Medical Center Journal, 33,* 58–63.

Selzer, M. L., (1971). The Michigan Alcoholism Screening Test: The quest for a new diagnostic instrument. *American Journal of Psychiatry, 127,* 89–94.

Swenson, W. M., & Morse, R. M. (1975). The use of a self-administered alcoholism screening test (SAAST) in a medical center. *Mayo Clinic Proceedings, 50,* 204–208.

Swets, J. A. (1988). Measuring the accuracy of diagnostic systems. *Science, 240,* 1285–1293.

Wilsnack, S. C., & Beckman, L. J. (1984). *Alcohol problems in women: Antecedents, consequences and intervention.* New York: Guilford Press.

Yerushalmy, J. (1947). Statistical problems in assessing methods of medical diagnosis, with special reference to X-ray techniques. *Public Health Reports, 62,* 1432–1449.

Screening for Cognitive Impairments in Primary Care Settings

George J. Demakis
Elmhurst College and Evanston Hospital, Evanston, Illinois

Michael G. Mercury
Jerry J. Sweet
Evanston Hospital and Northwestern University Medical School, Evanston, Illinois

The ability to perform and interpret cognitive screening evaluations is essential for clinicians in primary care, particularly those working with older patients. For example, a patient may present complaining of memory loss, or the clinician may detect possible confusion in a patient who has not been diagnosed with dementia. This chapter addresses the outpatient office and bedside evaluation of patients suspected of a developing or progressing dementia. Cognitive impairments other than diffuse degenerative dementia include isolated cognitive impairments due to focal lesions, trauma, delirium, and mental retardation (Royall, 1996). However, these conditions generally are readily distinguishable from an ongoing dementing process by history and physical examination, and are not discussed further here.

Many studies have attempted to define normal cognition in older patients. Although there are some discrepancies among the studies, there seems to be general agreement that patients show decreased learning efficiency and slower information-processing speed. A syndrome termed *benign senescent forgetfulness* describes patients who have difficulty with recall, especially names and dates, which can be facilitated with cues and a recognition format. Even though not a prodrome for degenerative dementia, consistent with incidence data, some of these patients develop dementia over time.

If patients present with memory or cognitive symptoms that are not attributable to normal aging or benign senescent forgetfulness, then they may have a more serious cognitive disorder, such as a progressive dementia. There are many etiologies for dementia, some of which may warrant a thorough workup. Much attention has been given to the potentially treatable dementias. Drug toxicity and depression can cause a dementia type syndrome and because of treatability should be carefully evaluated. Other etiologies for reversible dementias include alcoholism, hypothyroidism, vitamin B12 deficiency, metabolic disorders, and a wide variety of other medical problems. These are generally detected through history taking, physical examination, and brief screening lab work. Surgically treatable lesions are less common and include normal pressure hydrocephalus, subdural hematoma, and brain tumors. Generally, such conditions are evaluated with neuroimaging studies.

However, most dementias are not considered reversible. Of these, the most frequently diagnosed is Alzheimer's disease, which causes up to 60% of cases of dementia in the elderly. Alzheimer's disease is a progressive disease characterized by the cardinal feature of memory impairment (especially rapid forgetting) and one or more of the following features of cortical dysfunction: aphasia, apraxia, agnosia, and impaired executive functioning (American Psychiatric Association, 1994). Vascular dementia (often referred to as "multi-infarct dementia) has been thought of as the second most frequently encountered dementing disorder and is estimated by autopsy to account for approximately 20% of cases. Autopsy studies have also demonstrated that 15% to 20% of cases have a combination of Alzheimer's disease and vascular disease (Jellinger, 1976; Tomlinson, Blessed, & Roth, 1970).

Lewy body dementia presents as a symptom complex of visual hallucinations, Parkinsonism, and dementia characterized by rapid progression and fluctuations in the severity of the dementia, of alertness, and of attention. Lewy bodies have been found in up to 25% of autopsy cases (McKeith et al., 1996) and may actually account for more cases of dementia than vascular dementia. Other causes of dementias include other neurological diseases, such as progressive supranuclear palsy, Pick's disease, Parkinson's disease, Huntington's disease, and prion diseases, such as Creutzfeldt–Jacob disease.

PREVALENCE OF COGNITIVE IMPAIRMENT IN THE PRIMARY CARE SETTING

Dementia is, and will remain, a major public health concern for decades to come. As the number of people over age 65 years rises, the number of cases of dementia will also rise. Additionally, the fastest growing segment of our population is the group age 85 and older, which also has the highest incidence of dementia. Because women have a longer life expectancy than men, many more women are likely to be affected than men. Dementia is relatively infrequent in the 65- to 75-year-old group, affecting 3% to 11% of community-dwelling adults over 65 years of age (Fleming et al., 1995), and becoming increasingly prevalent with age. Surveys have estimated dementia in people aged 85 and older to be in the range of 25% to 35% (National Institute of Aging, 1995). An even higher figure was found by Evans et al. (1989), who reported that 47.2% of people over the age of 85 had Alzheimer's disease.

Given the fact that dementia is not uncommon, particularly among the "oldest old" patients, it is important for all clinicians to be able to realize that debilitating memory loss is *not* part of normal aging and that it is a disease process that warrants evaluation, just as much as chest pain or bleeding does. The following review can serve to guide the clinician in the use of brief testing to guide diagnosis, further workup, and treatment. We wish to be explicit at the outset that brief screening for brain-based cognitive impairment is never meant to substitute for thorough neurological and neuropsychological examinations, when the latter are indicated. Rather, brief cognitive screening is intended to assist in the accurate identification of those instances in which more thorough evaluation by specialists (i.e., neurologists, neuropsychologists) either can be ruled out as unnecessary because a patient is obviously normal or so severely impaired as to obviate more thorough investigation, or is indicated clinically because questions regarding degree or type of impairment and/or etiology. Further, brief cognitive screening is generally not helpful in distinguishing acute versus chronic conditions or in identifying localized brain disorder.

BRIEF PSYCHOMETRIC INSTRUMENTS USED IN SCREENING FOR COGNITIVE IMPAIRMENT

Mini-Mental Status Examination (MMSE)

Purpose

The Folstein Mini-Mental Status Examination (MMSE; Folstein, Folstein, & McHugh, 1975) was developed to establish a brief, objective, quantitative screening instrument that could be used to assess cognitive ability of patients on a neurogeriatric ward, including serial testing across hospital admissions or physician visits. The MMSE has been useful for quantitifying estimates of severity of cognitive impairment, serially documenting change, and teaching residents a method of cognitive assessment. Folstein et al. (1975) described the MMSE as being divided into two parts. The first part examines orientation, memory, and attention; the second part examines naming, repetition, following a three-step verbal command and a one-step written command, writing a sentence, and copying two intersecting pentagons. A score of 23 or less has been accepted as a general cutoff for cognitive impairment. Based on the notion of an average person, severity of impairment has been classified as mild, 18 to 23, and severe, 0 to 17 (Tombaugh & McIntyre, 1992).

Relevant Reliability Information

A review by Tombaugh and McIntyre (1992) reported internal consistency alpha levels ranging from .54 with a sample having 8 or more years of education to .96 for a sample of medical patients. The lower alphas may reflect sample characteristics and the fact that MMSE item heterogeneity is necessary in order to measure several cognitive processes. Tombaugh and McIntyre (1992) also examined test–retest reliability and found that in studies with test–retest intervals of less than 2 months, reliability fell between .80 and .95. Lower reliability coefficients have also been reported, and these authors conclude that in longitudinal studies, small changes in scores should be interpreted with caution.

Relevant Validity Information

Concurrent Validity. Tombaugh and McIntyre (1992) reviewed several studies of correlations of the MMSE with cognitive screening tests, intelligence and memory tests, and neuropsychological tests. They reported the following correlations: .70 to .90 for cognitive screening tests; .78 for the Wechsler Adult Intelligence Scale (WAIS) Verbal IQ and .66 for WAIS Performance IQ; "moderate to high" correlations with the Wechsler Memory Scale (WMS); and "modest to high" correlations with cognitive tests.

Convergent and Divergent Validity. Tierney, Szalai, Snow, Fisher, and Dunn (1997) examined the convergent and divergent validity of the MMSE Attention, Memory, and Copy items. Correlational analyses confirmed convergent validity, but not divergent validity, for these three items. The Naming item was not sensitive to impairment in naming abilities. They concluded that performance on each MMSE item should not be interpreted as measuring performance on the respective cognitive domain. Rather, the MMSE may best be used for reflecting level of general cognitive impairment.

Discriminant Validity. Tombaugh and McIntyre (1992) examined the sensitivity and specificity of the MMSE in 25 studies that used a cutoff score of 23. Sensitivity for dementia was found to increase with high levels of cognitive impairment. Although a high sensitivity was found in individuals with an MMSE score of 15 or less, sensitivity when the MMSE score was 20 or greater was only 44% and 68% in two studies. There was greater sensitivity among hospital and clinic patients versus community-dwelling elderly, leading the reviewers to hypothesize a greater degree of impairment in the former samples. Tombaugh and McIntyre (1992) also found lower sensitivity (21% to 76%) for neurology and psychiatry patients. They cited two reasons for this lower sensitivity: (a) reliance on verbal items resulting in a relative insensitivity to right-hemisphere problems, and (b) relative insensitivity of verbal items to mild cognitive changes. Alpert et al. (1995), using an alternate form of the MMSE (last item was to copy a clock face instead of intersecting pentagons), found that it was not affected by depression severity when used with otherwise healthy volunteer outpatients (age range 18 to 65) suffering from major depression.

In reviewing studies, Tombaugh and McIntyre (1992) found moderate to high specificity. Level of specificity was directly related to the control group used (e.g., psychiatric patients as controls lowered specificity) and to demographics (especially education and age; Crum, Anthony, Bassett, & Folstein, 1993). MMSE scores were directly related to education level; that is, individuals with lower education (less than 9 years) tend to score lower. Cross-sectional and longitudinal studies seem to support the idea that education represents a psychometric bias. There is also concern that because lower education is associated with certain biological risk factors associated with vascular dementia (e.g., hypertension, obesity, increased serum cholesterol), it may also represent a risk factor, and correcting for age may actually mask this relationship. MMSE scores are inversely related to age such that they decrease with increasing age (beginning about age 55 and accelerating after age 75). Although a psychometric bias, age also represents a risk factor for dementia. Tombaugh and McIntyre (1992) also noted Galasko, Corey-Bloom, and Thal's (1991) finding that rate of deterioration in Alzheimer's disease is independent of age, which further complicates the relationship of age and MMSE score.

According to Tombaugh and McIntyre (1992), MMSE gender differences are not meaningful. There appear to be some race/ethnicity and social class differences on the MMSE, but these observations are complicated by the use of translated versions of the test and by studies showing no differences. One study by Weiss, Reed, Kligman, and Abyad (1995) raised the possible significance of reading level to MMSE scores, but further research is necessary due to several limitations of this study including selection bias and failure to examine the possibility of dementia independently.

Tangalos et al. (1996) examined the use of the MMSE in an internal medicine practice at the Mayo Clinic in Rochester, Minnesota. Age and education but not sex influences were also demonstrated. Age and education cutoffs were thus determined with an 82% sensitivity and 98% specificity in their dementia and control group. However, the sensitivity and specificity were based on a population with a base rate of 45% (the rate within the studied groups), which was much higher than the actual base rate of .1. Thus, the authors suggested that the MMSE is not appropriate for general, routine screening of patients, but instead should be limited to specific populations with higher base rates (e.g., 10%). Examples of such populations would be those presenting with memory complaints or those residing in assisted care facilities. The suggestion was made that future studies are needed to investigate the sensitivity and specificity of longitudinal change in scores, which, if adequate, would argue for use of the MMSE in patient groups with lower base rates. Longitudinal change was also examined, and it was found that a change of 3 points or less over 4 years was within normal limits.

These modifiers of sensitivity and specificity are best addressed by identifying relevant factors (especially education and age) and examining the MMSE score both in terms of the conventional cutoff of 23 (with mild impairment 18–23, severe impairment 0–17) and the recommended education- and age-corrected cutoff.

Relevant Normative Data

Crum et al. (1993) collected data on the MMSE on 18,056 participants, aged 18 years and older, selected by probability sampling from the National Institute of Mental Health Epidemiologic Catchment Area Program. Participants represented a normative sample from their respective communities (New Haven, CT; Baltimore, MD; St. Louis, MO; Durham, NC; Los Angeles, CA). As such, cognitively normal and abnormal individuals were included; means, standard deviations, medians, and percentile scores were presented. Lower scores by elderly participants were hypothesized to represent cohort and disease effects, rather than the effect of aging, because items on the MMSE are thought to represent crystallized intelligence (Cummings, 1993). An inverse relationship was found between MMSE score and age, and a direct relationship was found between MMSE score and education. MMSE scores were not distributed normally. Limitations identified by the authors included nonresponders (although statistical methods were used to match U.S. age, sex, and race distributions); minor variations regarding correct answers across sites (e.g., using the higher score from serial 7s or spelling "world" backward—which varies from Folstein's original directions); administration at home, which could have resulted in higher scores; some age-education strata had small numbers which may limit reliability; and there was no clinical examination of participants to evaluate distribution of scores without cognitively compromised individuals.

Additionally, a Mayo study (Tangalos et al., 1996) reported age and education norms based on 3,513 elderly patients (aged 60 to 102) who were undergoing general medical examinations. Participants were residents of Olmsted County, including Rochester, Minnesota, which could limit generalizability. Similar to Crum et al. (1993), Tangalos et al. also found the same inverse relationship with age and direct relationship with education. They found that 4 or more points in total MMSE score were necessary in order for "substantial deterioration rather than chance fluctuation" (p. 835) over 1 to 4 years.

Cossa, Sala, Musicco, Spinnler, and Ubezio (1997) compared scoring methods (i.e., raw scores versus age and education corrected) in an epidemiological study of the Italian version of the MMSE on 829 inhabitants over age 59 years of a small town in northern Italy. They found that age- and education-corrected scoring resulted in a false negative rate of 28.5%, compared to 14.3% with the original raw score method. An observed increase in specificity (6.3%) and in positive predictive value (18.9%) did not offset a doubling of the false negative rate. The Cossa et al. results could be viewed as challenging the generally accepted notion in neuropsychology of correcting for age and education. However, the generalizability of these findings on an Italian sample to Americans is problematic.

Strengths and Limitations

Strengths. The MMSE is a widely recognized and frequently used instrument. It is also a well-studied and brief instrument. It takes 5 to 10 min to administer, which makes it appropriate for use at bedside or office visit. It is objective in that it has a standardized administration and norm-based data, and it is quantitative in that it yields a numeric score and thus lends itself to statistical analysis and research. It has adequate psychometric properties.

Limitations. The MMSE is limited by its purpose, specifically, that it is a brief, objective, quantitative screening instrument (Folstein et al., 1975) not meant to replace the neuropsychological exam. Although the MMSE is the most frequently used cognitive screening test (Tangalos et al., 1996; Tombaugh & McIntyre, 1992), it is not as widely accepted by clinicians as it is by researchers.

The evaluation of patient performance traditionally is limited to a single score; a cutoff of 23 or lower has been used with the MMSE to indicate the need for further investigation of an individual's cognitive status. The instrument does not provide diagnostic information.

Additional limitations of the MMSE include possible ceiling effects or lower sensitivity for patients with higher education and more false positives with older, less educated patients. The MMSE is insensitive to individuals with right-hemisphere lesions who perform similarly to controls. Because it has only one nonverbal item (intersecting pentagons), it is not easily administered to patients with aphasia (who may appear to perform poorly because of the language demands, but are not necessarily demented). It cannot distinguish left-hemisphere from diffuse-hemispheric disease. There is no internal evaluation of mood, which, especially in the elderly, can affect cognitive functioning.

MMSE administration often has been taught casually, with the result being that clinicians have not always followed the standardized administration (e.g., asking patients to name the parts of a watch, rather than the watch itself). Another problem has been that the cutoff score has been interpreted as diagnostic for the presence of dementia, rather than indicative for the need for further assessment. Proper instruction in the appropriate administration and interpretation of this instrument will ensure its integrity in the medical setting.

Recommendations

The MMSE is the most frequently used screening test of mental status and can be useful in screening for cognitive impairment and change over time. It has been very well studied and has adequate reliability and validity. It allows a standardized approach to the testing of mental status in 5 to 10 min. A cutoff of 23 has often been used, with severity of impairment classified as 18–23 for mild and 0–17 for severe. However, norms based on demographic variables (education and age) are available (see Crum et al., 1993, and Tangalos et al., 1996) and are recommended when interpreting results. A decline of 4 or more points in 1 to 4 years appears to suggest substantial deterioration.

Research supports convergent, but not divergent, validity for attention, memory and copy subtests. The naming subtest is not sensitive to naming difficulties. If evaluation of naming ability is viewed as an important aspect of the screening process, a different screening test should be used or a naming test added.

The overall score appears to provide an adequate appraisal of *general* cognitive functioning. However, the MMSE is highly verbal and thus is inappropriate for patients with aphasia. In keeping with the idea that screening measures are not useful with localized disorders, the MMSE has not been useful with, and is not recommended for, right-hemisphere disorders. Sensitivity and specificity have been found to be highest with inpatients and clinic patients with base rates of brain dysfunction 10% or above.

As a screening test the MMSE does not provide a diagnosis, and may need to be followed by more detailed neurological and/or neuropsychological evaluation. The MMSE is appropriate as part of a short mental status battery and should be supplemented with other tests, such as the Clock Drawing test and a measure of mood.

Clock Drawing

Purpose

The Clock Drawing test is another frequently used screening test for evaluation of cognitive status. It has several advantages. It is easily administered, can be easily interpreted, and represents a cognitive capacity that research indicates should be preserved through age 90 years (Cahn & Kaplan, 1997). Clock drawing has been described as measuring visuospatial skills (Sunderland et al., 1989), constructional skills (Suhr, Grace, Allen, Nadler, & McKenna, 1998), temporoparietal function (Wolf-Klein, Silverstone, Levy, & Brod, 1989), constructional apraxia (Mendez, Ala, & Underwood, 1992), and planning and abstraction (Freedman et al., 1994). Use of the Clock Drawing test has been hampered by a lack of consensus regarding administration and scoring. Differences in administration revolve around the instructions used and whether a time is specified. Freedman et al. (1994) reviewed these differences; some of these points are elaborated next.

Instructions to the patient typically approximate "Draw the face of a clock. Make it large and put in all the numbers." Some believe that the instructions should not specify a time as part of the initial directions because knowing the time might influence how the subject proceeds with number placement. Others prefer to specify a standard time, in order to make the procedure more uniform across patients.

The next issue involves whether one asks the patient to draw the circle or whether one provides a pre-drawn circle (e.g., Wolf-Klein et al., 1989). Freedman et al. (1994) suggested that one provide a predrawn circle if the patient produces no circle or a circle that is distorted or too small.

Drawing of the clock is yet another issue. Freedman et al. (1994) pointed out that the command condition is especially sensitive to temporal lobe and frontal dysfunction. There is greater demand on language skills for comprehension of the verbal instructions (left temporal lobe) and on memory (right and left temporal) for recalling what a clock looks like and for remembering instructions regarding time setting. The frontal lobe is important for executive functioning. Approaching the task differently by requesting that the patient copy a picture of a clock makes the task more dependent on perceptual functions and can be expected to be more sensitive to parietal-lobe dysfunction.

One can also require both the command and the copy conditions and compare the patient's performance. Freedman et al. (1994) cited the following examples: A patient with a parietal lesion in the right hemisphere may draw an acceptable clock to a verbal command, but omit the numbers in the lower left of a clock drawn in the copy condition. On command, a patient with a right temporal lesion may draw numbers poorly spaced and without a circle serving as the edge of the clock face, whereas the same patient's copy may be adequate.

As indicated earlier, a separate issue is whether to ask the patient to place the hands pointing to a specific time. Wolf-Klein et al. (1989) did not use a time. Lezak (1995) advocated for requesting a specific time because of the added information that can be obtained. Freedman et al. (1994) discussed numerous specific clock times in order of apparent sensitivity in detecting abnormality; from most to least, these times are: "10 after 11," "20 after 8," "20 to 4," and "3 o'clock."

A different and major issue with Clock Drawing is lack of a consensual scoring method. Freedman et al. (1994) identified three approaches: (a) informal, qualitative appraisal of the drawing, (b) a process oriented approach (Werner, 1937, 1956), and (c) a quantitative approach, of which there are several (e.g., Rouleau, Salmon, Butters, Kennedy, & McGuire, 1992; Spreen & Strauss, 1991; Sunderland et al., 1989; see also Suhr et al., 1998). The qualitative approach varies from a clinician's informal appraisal of the appropriateness of the clock to a set of specific criteria as identified by Rouleau et al. (1992): clock size, graphic difficulties, stimulus-bound responses, conceptual deficits, spatial/planning deficits, and perseverations. Using these criteria, Suhr et al. (1998) found differences between lesion groups (right- vs. left-hemisphere stroke, cortical vs. subcortical). The process approach based on Werner (1937, 1956) uses detailed observation of how the patient proceeds through the clock drawing in order to generate hypotheses about intact and impaired abilities, based on present understanding of brain–behavior relationships (Freedman et al., 1994). Quantitative methods of scoring have, in general, proved less helpful in this instance, because a global score does not add to the identification of the numerous possible difficulties that the patient is experiencing.

An extensive study of clock drawing techniques was undertaken by Freedman et al. (1994). In a normative study, 348 volunteers aged 20 to 90 years from the Metropolitan Toronto area were given three clock conditions in a fixed order: free-drawn, predrawn, and "examiner clocks." These took approximately 6 to 10 min to administer. Interrater reliability was found to be high. The free-drawn condition consisted of asking the participant to draw a clock and place all the numbers on it. Once that part of the task was satisfied, they were asked to place the hands at a specified time (quarter to seven). In the predrawn condition, participants were given a predrawn circle and asked to put the numbers in it and to set the time at 5 after 6. In the examiner clocks condition, the participants were given three sheets of paper, each with a predrawn clock with all the numbers on it. They were then asked to set the following times: 20 after 8, 10 after 11, and 3 o'clock.

In the Freedman et al. study, a set of "critical" responses highly likely to occur in healthy volunteers were identified by consensus for "objective" scoring purposes.

All conditions were scored for the categories of hands (6 critical items in free- and pre-drawn, 8 total in examiner clocks) and center (i.e., a center drawn from which clock hands extend, 1 critical item in free- and pre-drawn, 3 total in examiner clocks). Additionally, the free-drawn and predrawn clocks were scored for numbers (6 critical items) and the free-drawn clock was scored for the circle (2 critical items) produced. Total score for each condition was 15 for the free-drawn clock, 13 for the predrawn clock, and 11 for each of the examiner clocks. Means and standard deviations are provided for total clock scores.

Relevant Reliability Information

Suhr et al. (1998) examined interrater reliability using six separate quantitative scoring systems and found acceptable reliability (range .92 to .98) in all but one. The Rouleau et al. (1992) qualitative scoring system had an interrater reliability ranging from .73 to 1.00.

Relevant Validity Information

Construct Validity. Freedman et al. (1994) examined clock scores derived through different administration approaches with selected neuropsychological test scores by a principal-components analysis followed by an orthogonal Varimax rotation of the intercorrelation matrices. The total clock score loaded on Factor 2, along with Rey–Osterrieth Complex Figure, copy; WAIS–R Block Design score; and Wisconsin Card Sorting Test's number of perseverative responses.

Discriminant Validity. Wolf-Klein et al. (1989) reported a sensitivity of 86.7% for Alzheimer's Disease and a specificity of 92.7%. Freedman et al. (1994) found that a cutoff of less than 28 for the total score identified 85% of demented participants, with 18% false positives. A cutoff of less than 12 for the free-drawn clock identified 78% of demented patients, also with 18% false positives. Age was significantly correlated with clock drawing with the greatest decrease in scores occurring after age 70. Means and standard deviations were presented for each clock condition for seven age ranges ($n = 348$) and for normals ($n = 176$) compared to participants with Alzheimer's disease ($n = 13$), Parkinson's disease with dementia ($n = 14$), and Parkinson's disease without dementia ($n = 20$). Qualitative features and longitudinal data were also reviewed in this very useful study.

Relevant Normative Data

Freedman et al. (1994) examined the clock drawings of 348 volunteers from Toronto, ranging in age from 20 to 90, and subdivided the participants' results into seven age groups and attempted to identify critical items that "spoil" clock performance. These investigators found that after age 70 performance decreased on a quantitative measure, with errors involving proportion of hands and placement of the minute hand. When scores of subjects in the 70–79 and the 80+ years group were compared, no group differences were noted. Cahn and Kaplan (1997), using Rouleau's method of scoring, investigated 237 individuals from the Rancho Bernardo Study population (Criqui, Barrett-Connor, & Austin, 1978) and found no decline through age 90. They noted that the Freedman et al. participants, as volunteers, may have represented a selection bias.

Strengths and Limitations

Strengths. As a screening tool, clock drawing has several advantages in that it is easily administered, can be easily interpreted, and represents an ability that research indicates should be preserved through age 90 (Cahn & Kaplan, 1997). Clock drawing has been described as measuring visuospatial ability, at least, and may, depending upon which instructional set if provided, also evaluate executive function.

Limitations. The Clock Drawing test is limited by a lack of consensus of administration and scoring. Differences in administration revolve around (a) the instructions used, (b) whether to provide a circle within the which the clock face can be drawn, (c) whether to provide a clock to copy, (d) whether to specify a time to depict on the clock face, and, if so, (e) which time to specify.

Recommendations

The Clock Drawing test is a brief screening test of visuospatial, constructional, and planning skills. The results can be used to generate diagnostic hypotheses that can be tested further within a neuropsychological evaluation. A lack of consensus exists regarding administration. There are both qualitative interpretation and quantitative scoring approaches. In general, studies indicate acceptable interrater reliability, validity, and sensitivity and specificity. It is recommended that readers consider the extensive review of clock drawing techniques and scoring by Freedman et al. (1994), as it provides the most useful information to date.

Mattis Dementia Rating Scale (DRS)

Purpose

The DRS was developed to (a) provide a brief measure of cognitive status in individuals with known cortical impairment, particularly diffuse dementia; (b) track the cognitive decline in dementia; and (c) accurately assess cognitive ability at lower ability levels (Mattis, 1988). To accomplish these goals, 36 items traditionally used in mental status assessment were compiled into five subscales that could be easily administered to a wide range of patients. The subscales are Attention (8 items), Initiation/Perseveration (11 items), Construction (6 items), Conceptualization (6 items), and Memory (5 items). The test also yields a total composite score. The DRS utilizes a screen and metric approach to save time. With this approach, an initial difficult screening item is administered and if it is failed, easier metric items are then administered. If the screen item is passed, the metric items are skipped and considered correct, thereby saving time.

Relevant Reliability Information

Coblentz et al. (1973) evaluated test–retest reliability of the DRS. One-week test–retest reliability in a sample of Alzheimer's patients ranged from a high of .97 for the total score to a low of .61 for the Attention subscale. Practice effects were minimal, with score increases on retesting all below one third of a standard deviation. Gardner, Oliver-Munoz, Fisher, and Empting (1981) examined split-half reliability of the DRS in a small sample of patients with "organic brain syndrome or senile dementia" and found it to be .90. In a more recent study, Smith et al. (1994) examined Cronbach's alpha for the DRS total score and each subscale in a large sample of demented patients. Internal consistency was .84 for the total score, above .70 for Construction, Conceptualization, and Memory, .65 for Attention, and .45 for Initiation/Perseveration. The lower internal consistency for the Initiation/Perseveration is not surprising given that the test assesses diverse abilities, including semantic fluency, phoneme production, motor sequencing, and graphomotor performance. The authors noted that because many of the easier items on scales were not administered and are therefore not free to vary, these internal consistency estimates may be inflated and should be viewed as the upper estimates of DRS reliability.

Relevant Validity Information

Construct Validity.   Woodard, Salthouse, Godsall, and Green (1996) performed a series of confirmatory factor analyses on the DRS in a large homogenous sample of patients with probable or possible Alzheimer's disease. They tested several possible factor structures and found that the best fit was with four factors — Construction, Conceptualization, Memory, and a separate factor with both the Attention and Initiation/Perseveration subscales. The authors acknowledge that the loading of these last two subscales on one factor may be a statistical artifact. However, Woodward et al. (1996) tested other factor-analytic models, including a two-factor model proposed by Kessler, Roth, Kaplan, and Goode (1994) and a three-factor model by Colantonio, Becker, and Huff (1993), that did not fit the data as well.

Convergent and Divergent Validity.   Marson, Dymek, Duke, and Harrell (1997) examined relationships between DRS subscales and well-established criterion measures in a sample of mild and moderate Alzheimer's patients. Although each subscale was correlated with several criterion measures (both related and unrelated), four of five were most strongly correlated with the predicted criterion measure. For instance, correlations between the WMS–R Verbal Memory factor and the subscales were as follows: .69 for Memory, .57 for Initiation/Perseveration and Construction, .43 for Attention, and .20 for Construction. Only the Construction subscale was not the most strongly related to its criterion measure (Block Design of the WAIS).

Instead of the actual subscales, Woodard et al. (1996) examined the convergent and divergent validity of the four factors derived from factor analysis just described with a wide-range of neuropsychological tests. They found that although several tests correlated with three or four different factors (e.g., Animal Fluency, Digit Span, and the WRAT–R Reading), some evidence of convergent validity was obtained. For instance, Logical Memory of the Wechsler Memory Scale–Revised was significantly correlated with only the Memory factor, whereas Block Design was only related to the Construction factor. In a broader view, Smith et al. (1994) found the DRS total score to be highly related to Mayo Clinic version of the WAIS–R FSIQ (.73), VIQ (.75), and PIQ (.57).

Concurrent Validity.   DRS performance has also been compared to well-established clinical markers of dementia severity. Shay et al. (1991) administered the DRS to controls and Alzheimer's patients whose dementia severity was rated on the 4-point Consensus Dementia Rating scale (CDR). The CDR is based on clinician judgment of patient competence in six categories of general cognitive and behavioral functioning (Hughes, Berg, Danziger, Coben, & Martin, 1982). Comparing controls and mild dementia patients, discriminant function analyses of the DRS total score accurately classified 100% of controls and 92% of mild dementia patients. Comparing mild and moderate dementia, 92% of the mild dementia patients and 71% of the moderately demented patients were correctly classified.

Discriminant Validity. Paulsen et al. (1995) administered the DRS to patients with Huntington's and Alzheimer's disease at various levels of dementia severity. Severity ranges were mild (average DRS = 129), moderate (average DRS = 117), and severe (average DRS = 102). Although matched on severity, Alzheimer's patients performed significantly worse than Huntington's patients on the Memory subscale at each stage, whereas Huntington's patients performed significantly worse on the Initiation subscale at each stage. Huntington's patients with moderate and severe dementia also performed more poorly than Alzheimer's patients on the Construction subscale. Groups did not differ on the Attention or Conceptualization subscales. Paolo, Tröster, Glatt, Hubble, and Koller (1995b) compared Alzheimer's and Parkinson's patients matched on DRS total score and found that Alzheimer's patients performed more poorly on the Memory subscale and Parkinson's patients performed more poorly on the Construction subscale. Taken together, these studies indicate that the DRS is differentially sensitive to the patterns of cognitive dysfunction typically associated with cortical and subcortical dementias.

In the DRS manual, a study by Montgomery and Costa (1983b) is presented using a total score cutoff of 123 in a sample of depressed and demented patients. None of the depressed patients scored below this cutoff, but 12% of the "psychologically disordered" patients, 36% of the focal brain damage patients, and 62% of the demented patients did. In a more sophisticated study, Monsch et al. (1995) evaluated the ability of the DRS to discriminate between Alzheimer's patients and controls. Using the optimal cutoff score determined from receiver operating curve analyses for the DRS total (less than or equal to 130), sensitivity (true positives) was 97% and specificity (true negatives) was 99%. Classification rates for the subscales were as follows: Initiation/Perseveration (93%), Memory (93%), Attention (71%), Construction (73%), and Conceptualization (69%). A modified DRS with only the Memory and Initiation/Perseveration subscales yielded a sensitivity of 98% and specificity was 98%. These latter findings corroborate previous research suggesting that memory and verbal fluency impairments are among the few hallmarks of cognitive decline in Alzheimer's disease.

Green, Woodard, and Green (1995) also used the DRS to discriminate between patients diagnosed with probable Alzheimer's or vascular dementia and normal controls. With a total DRS score of 133 used as the cut point, sensitivity was 95% and specificity was 100%. Vangel and Lichtenberg (1995) found somewhat lower rates when cognitively impaired versus cognitively intact patients (67% of whom were African Americans) on a geriatric physical medicine and rehabilitation service were evaluated. A DRS total cutting score of 125 yielded a sensitivity of 85% and a specificity of 90%. Notably, neither of these studies provides information regarding utility with psychiatric patients.

Relevant Normative Data

In the DRS manual, Mattis (1988) presented frequency distributions and recommended cutoffs (2 SDs below the mean) based on 85 normal community-dwelling elderly subjects, ranging from 65 to 81 years old. These data are from Montgomery and

Costa (1983a). Means, standard deviations, percentiles, and nonnormalized T-scores are also presented from the Coblentz et al. (1973) study on 30 Alzheimer's patients. Formal diagnostic statistics are not presented. In a more recent Austrian study, Schmidt et al. (1994) presented age (50–59, 60–69, and 70–80 years old) and education (4–9, 10–13, and 14 and above years) stratified normative data in a sample of 1,001 health volunteers. Unfortunately, these authors only provided the total DRS score and did not provide individual subscale scores.

Influence of Sociodemographic Factors

Several studies have demonstrated effects of age and education on the DRS. For instance, Schmidt et al. (1994) found age and years of education to be significantly related to the DRS total score in a normal sample. Yet, these mean differences between age and education groups do not appear clinically significant. For instance, individuals with 4 to 9 years of education scored an average of 140 on DRS total score and those with a college degree or higher scored 142; individuals 50–59 years of age scored 142, whereas those aged 70–80 scored 140. In neurologically impaired samples, age and education have been found to be significantly, but modestly, related to DRS total score. For instance, Smith et al. (1994) found correlations with age and education that accounted for approximately 9% of the variance in DRS total scores, and Vangel and Lichtenberg (1995) found that age accounted for only 7% of the variance. Paolo, Tröster, Glatt, Hubble, and Koller (1995a) found age, but not education or gender, to account for a larger portion of the variance (20%) in DRS total score in a large sample of normals. Yet, age-sensitive cutoffs developed from these norms were not appreciably better in discriminating between Parkinson's and Alzheimer's patients and controls. These authors concluded that only one cutoff (DRS total score less than or equal to 130) is necessary for individuals 50 years old or older. In general, although the DRS appears related to age and education, the relationship does not appear strong enough to warrant use of age- or education-adjusted cutoffs.

Use in Monitoring Course of Impairment

Salmon, Thal, Butters, and Heindel (1990) examined the MMSE, Information–Memory–Concentration (see next section), and the DRS in a 3-year longitudinal study of Alzheimer's disease. They found that the tests were equally sensitive to decline in the early to middle stages of Alzheimer's disease, but that the DRS was maximally sensitive to decline in severely demented patients. For instance, for severely impaired patients, the annual rate of cognitive decline was greater than for mildly impaired patients on the DRS, but not on the other measures. Salmon et al. (1990) concluded that this was because the DRS has more easy items and that the cognitive skills necessary to complete them are preserved until late in the disease. In a quite different design, Tröster, Moe, Vitiello, and Prinz (1994) longitudinally examined three groups of patients — normals, patients at risk for dementia, and patients diagnosed with dementia. At-risk patients had similar DRS scores as controls, but the presence of a memory disorder was verified by a significant other. At 4- to 6-year follow-up examination, 13% of the patients moved from the at-risk to the demented group. The Memory subscale predicted at-risk group follow-up diagnoses with 75% accuracy. This finding should be interpreted cautiously, however, given the small sample sizes (only 30 patients were followed across time and only 4 moved from at risk to demented).

Relationship to Daily Functioning

Nadler, Richardson, Malloy, Marran, and Brinson (1993) examined the relationship between the DRS and the Occupational Therapy Evaluation of Performance and Support, a measure that assesses hygiene, safety, medication, cooking, money management, and community utilization. The DRS total score accounted for a modest amount of the variance (27%–41%) for the daily skills, except cooking. Of the individual subtests, Initiation/Perseveration and Memory were most closely correlated to daily skills, suggesting the importance of these cognitive abilities in daily life. Vitaliano et al. (1984) demonstrated that the DRS total score was related to the Record of Independent Living, a measure that includes both maintaining (e.g., feeding, washing, etc.) and higher functioning (e.g., reading, writing, hobbies, etc.) activities. The magnitude of these relationships was not addressed.

Strengths and Limitations

Strengths. Considerable research has demonstrated that the DRS has favorable psychometric properties in both normals and demented subjects, can accurately discriminate between Alzheimer's patients and normal controls and between Alzheimer's and Parkinson's patients, and is related to daily functioning.

Compared to several other brief screening measures, the DRS samples a wider range of cognitive abilities. For instance, while it may take up to 15 or 20 min longer to administer than the MMSE, it provides significantly more useful qualitative information about a patient's neuropsychological functioning.

The DRS is better than other screening instruments in assessing and tracking patients with moderate to severe dementia. By including simpler metric items, it allows even severely impaired patients to get some items correct and thus lessens the likelihood of floor effects. As such, the DRS is also probably the best screening measure available to assess the longitudinal progression of dementia.

Limitations. Norms presented in the manual are inadequate (discussed earlier) and potentially misleading. For instance, on p. 22 of the manual, percentiles and nonnormalized T-scores for the DRS total score and subtests are presented for an Alzheimer's, not a normal control, sample. If used in a mixed clinical sample, these T-scores are likely to overestimate patients' cognitive functioning. Nevertheless, with the considerable research available on the DRS, there are other alternatives. We recommend use of the more extensive norms and cutoffs presented in the well-designed study of Monsch et al. (1995).

The DRS assesses semantic fluency and other important aspects of language, such as naming, repetition, and comprehension, but these are not scored separately and appear on the Initiation/Perseveration subtest. This is problematic given that linguistic deficits are a hallmark of Alzheimer's and may be among the first signs of the disease. Formal assessment of comprehension would also provide useful information for competency questions.

The screen and metric format of the DRS (on all subtests except Memory) has not yet been evaluated. For instance, if the screens are too difficult, they waste time because the following metric items must be administered; if they are too easy and subjects cannot pass the metric items, cognitive functioning may be overestimated and a false negative decision may be made. Research thus needs to assess the relationship of screen and metric items, as has already been accomplished with the Neuro-behavioral Cognitive Screen Examination (see later discussion).

As is the case with most cognitive screening measures, the DRS does not have an alternative form, which can make test–retest issues problematic, particularly if the time between assessments is short. However, given that the DRS is designed for use in a dementia population, within which memory disorder is prominent, this may be less an issue than it is with other neuropsychological tests designed for less impaired populations.

Although it can discriminate successfully between Alzheimer's and normals, the Initiation/Perseveration subtest should be interpreted cautiously. This subtest has the lowest internal consistency (.45) and consists of various different tasks, including semantic fluency, alternating motor sequencing, and graphomotor design. The tasks do not contribute equally to the total Initiation/Perseveration score, as indicated by the fact that semantic fluency tasks can contribute up to 76% of this subtest's total score. As of result of this particular subtest's organization, it is probably better to interpret the individual items, rather than the subtest as a whole.

Recommendations

The DRS is one of the most widely used dementia assessment instruments. It is particularly useful for tracking cognitive deterioration in degenerative dementias, as it has some relatively simple items that even moderately to severely demented patients can get correct. It is typically not indicated for use in younger patients or patients with other neurological disorders (e.g., head injury). We recommend that the more extensive norms and impairment cutoffs presented in Monsch et al. (1995) be used. This study also suggests that the Memory and Initiation/Perseveration subscales are the most sensitive to dementia. In all, this is a good screening instrument that can provide data on an individual's basic memory, attention, construction, conceptualization, and initiation abilities in an efficient manner.

The Neurobehavioral Cognitive Status Examination (NCSE)

Purpose

The Neurobehavioral Cognitive Status Examination is a brief, individually administered cognitive screening instrument (Kiernan, Mueller, Langston, & Van Dyke, 1987; Northern California Neurobehavioral Group, 1988; now distributed as *Cognistat* by Psychological Assessment Resources, Inc.). It is designed to assess the following domains: level of consciousness, orientation, attention, language, constructional ability, memory, calculations, and reasoning. Language has three scored subsections—comprehension, repetition, and naming; spontaneous speech is assessed, but not scored. Reasoning includes subsections of similarities and judgment. All but the level of consciousness, orientation, and memory scales are given in a screen and metric format; only if the initial screen item is failed are the subsequent metric items administered. Each scale is rated as average, mildly impaired, moderately impaired, or severely impaired. In cognitively intact individuals, the NCSE takes less than 5 min to administer. In cognitively impaired patients, administration time may take up to 25 to 40 min.

Relevant Reliability Information

No reliability data is presented in the NCSE manual and, to our knowledge, this has yet to be documented. Kiernan et al. (1987) noted that because normals tend to perform perfectly on the NCSE and there is little variability among their scores, test-retest reliability is not likely to be meaningful in normals. Because of the screen and metric format, internal consistency and split-half reliability analyses may also be suspect because all items may not be administered and are therefore not free to vary.

Relevant Validity Information

Validity of the Screen–Metric Format.   Kiernan et al. (1987) found that approximately 20% of a neurologically normal population fail each screen. In a mixed sample of psychiatric patients, Logue, Tupler, D'Amico, and Schmitt (1993) found considerable variability in screen item failure rate, but very high levels of failure for Construction (90%), Similarities (95%), and Judgment (86%) screens. They suggested that the screens saved little time (as they were designed to do), as most patients needed to complete the metric items. They unfortunately did not report performance on the screen compared to the metric items—an analysis necessary to determine the validity of screen items. Particularly problematic would be a false-negative error in which a patient could pass the more difficult screen item, but fail the following easier metric items. Marcotte, van Gorp, Hinkin, and Osato (1997) performed such analyses in a mixed sample of neuropsychological patients by administering screen and metric items, regardless of whether the screen item was passed. Results indicated that the false negative rate varied from 0 to 15%, with the highest rate for Attention and Similarities (13% and 15%, respectively). Similarly, Oehlert et al. (1997) found false negative rates ranging from 1% (Construction) to 11% (Calculation). Taken together, these false negative rates suggest that clinicians should administer the entire test, given the relatively small investment of time needed to enhance the accuracy of the NCSE.

Concurrent Validity.   Marcotte et al. (1997) also assessed the relationships between each NCSE scale and a commonly used "gold standard" of that neuropsychological construct. For instance, the standard measure for attention was WAIS–R Digit Span and the standard for memory was the sum of words learned on trials 1–5 of the CVLT. All correlations were statistically significant and ranged from .40 to .83, but only three scales (Similarities, Naming, and Construction) explained more than 50% of the variance in the associated neuropsychological test. Unfortunately, no divergent correlations were reported. In a psychiatric sample, Logue et al. (1993) intercorrelated the various scales and found that scales tapping similar constructs were not necessarily highly correlated. For instance, relatively low correlations were obtained between language scales (Repetition, Naming, and Comprehension) and reasoning scales (Similarities and Judgment). Yet some of the highest correlations were found between dissimilar scales, including Repetition and Similarities and Naming and Constructions.

Concurrent validity has also been evaluated by comparing impairment on the NCSE with other measures. For instance, Marcotte et al. (1997) assessed the relationship between impairment on the NCSE scales and impairment on construct-related neuropsychological tests. Impairment on the NCSE was failure on at least one screen item, whereas impairment on the neuropsychological tests was defined as performance 1.5 standard deviations below well-established control group means. Kappa rates (agreement on impairment with chance taken into account) were generally low (.31–.69), raising questions about the NCSE subtests' ability to accurately assess domain-specific cognitive impairment. In a similar study, Fals-Stewart (1997) compared impairment on the NCSE and the Neuropsychological Screening Battery (NSB). The NSB includes, among others, such well-known tests as the Trail-Making Tests, Rey–Osterrieth Complex Figure, Multilingual Aphasia Examination, and components of the Wechsler Memory Scales. Using performance on the NSB as the criterion for impairment, the NCSE had low sensitivity (36%) but much higher specificity (86%). In all, these studies caution against use of individual NCSE scales to delineate a specific area of neuropsychological dysfunction.

Discriminant Validity. Several studies have shown that performance on the NCSE conforms to established deficit patterns in various patient groups. Osmon, Smet, Winegarden, and Gandhavadi (1992) found that a small group of unilaterally damaged patients performed significantly worse than an orthopedic control group. Compared to controls, left-hemisphere patients performed more poorly on the Comprehension, Naming, Memory, and Similarities scales; right-hemisphere patients performed worse on the Naming and Construction scales. No significant differences were observed between left- and right-hemisphere patients. Logue et al. (1993) confirmed the cognitive deficits known to exist in psychiatric patients, as they performed below the standardization sample on all scales. Particular impairment was noted on Orientation and Memory scales for young patients (20–39 years old) who scored 2.50 SDs below the standardization sample on Orientation and 4.60 Sds below on Memory. In a sample of mildly traumatically brain-injured patients, Blostein, Jones, Buechler, and Vandongen (1997) found that Memory was the most commonly affected scale and that the Glasgow Coma Scale (GCS), but not computed axial tomography (CAT) scan results, predicted NCSE outcome. For instance, patients with GCS scores of 13/14 were more likely to demonstrate NCSE impairment as compared to patients with a GCS score of 15 (75% vs. 37%).

The cutoff for impairment suggested in the NCSE manual is impaired performance on any scale. Using this cutoff based on age-adjusted norms in a sample of demented patients and elderly controls, Drane and Osato (1997) found 100% sensitivity, but only 30% specificity. This yielded an unacceptably high rate (70%) of false-positive errors. When the cutoff was altered to two impaired scales, sensitivity remained 100% and specificity improved to 80%. In a separate study, using the cutoff of one impaired scale, Schwamm, Van Dyke, Kiernan, Merrin, and Mueller (1987) compared the classification accuracy of the NCSE to the MMSE and the Cognitive Capacity Screening Instrument (CCSI). For 30 patients with documented brain lesions, the NCSE's sensitivity was 93%, the MMSE's sensitivity was 67%, and the CCSI's sensitivity was 47%. Because this study did not have a control group, specificity could not be determined.

Mitrushina, Abara, and Blumenfeld (1994) used the NCSE to differentiate between hospitalized psychiatric patients with or without a history of "organic" pathology. In accord with the manual, performance on each scale was rated as *average* (1), *mildly impaired* (2), *moderately impaired* (3), or *severely impaired* (4). A cutoff score of 13 (obtained by summing these ratings) maximized diagnostic efficiency and resulted in a sensitivity of .72 and a specificity of .73. In a more sophisticated study, Engelhart, Eisenstein, and Meininger (1994) performed receiver operating curve (ROC) analyses on a large set of mixed neurological and psychiatric patients. For neurological subjects, sensitivity was 93%, but specificity was only 56%.

Relevant Normative Data

Kiernan et al. (1987) presented data on NCSE performance of healthy individuals in young (average age = 28.2 years), old (average age = 50.8 years) and geriatric (average age = 77.6 years) samples. Data presented included means and standard deviations of all scales. Similar data were presented for neurosurgical patients with documented brain lesions. Logue et al. (1993) presented means and standard deviations of 8 age groups (ranging in age from 15–19 to 80–92 years) of psychiatric patients.

Strengths and Limitations

Strengths. Some research indicates that the NCSE can discriminate accurately between psychiatric patients with and without brain dysfunction and between demented patients and normal elderly controls. However, these findings were not based on recommended cutoffs in the manual (i.e., one impaired scale), but rather cutoffs derived from their respective samples. Until more comprehensive norms are developed, we recommend that clinicians develop their own cutoffs (based on local patient samples)

Compared to other screening instruments, the NCSE taps a wider range of cognitive abilities, yet still remains relatively quick and easy to administer. For instance, it is the only well-known cognitive screening instrument to assess reasoning skills via both similarities and judgment; language skills are also assessed through a range of various measures, including fluency (not scored), repetition, naming, and comprehension.

Limitations. Despite the attractive findings just summarized, the psychometric properties of the NCSE have yet to be fully established, and considerably more research is needed before it can be confidently used. For instance, neither internal nor test–retest reliability has yet to be established.

Although the NCSE's scales assess a range of neuropsychological abilities, they do not appear to accurately assess the neuropsychological ability in question. This is confirmed via correlational studies, as well as comparison of impairment on NCSE scales and well-established neuropsychological tests. Thus, we recommend that clinicians use performance across the whole test as the most sensitive marker of impairment and interpret the scales cautiously. We should note, however, that given the time constraints and obviously limited scope of screening instruments, it is probably unfair to expect them to perform as well as more traditional neuropsychological measures.

We were able to locate only one study (Drane & Osato, 1997) that examined performance of demented patients on the NCSE. Given that many neuropsychological referrals are for dementia, considerably more research on performance patterns of these patients and the utility of this measure in dementia needs to be established.

The screen and metric system of the NCSE should be used cautiously (see Oehlert et al. 1997). Several studies have shown that if the whole test is given without regard for performance on the screen, an unacceptably high number of patients will pass the screen but fail the metrics (false-negative error). Given the current research demonstrating high false-negative errors, we recommend giving the entire test to minimize false negatives.

Because of the screen–metric format, the amount of time between verbal learning and recall is unstandardized, potentially confounding individual comparisons on the Memory scale. For instance, patients who pass the Language and Construction screens have a shorter delay interval than those who are administered screen and metric items. Standardization of the delay period would be useful.

Recommendations

Although sometimes lacking psychometric support, the NCSE assesses a wider range of cognitive abilities than other screening instruments. For instance, it assesses reasoning skills with similarities and judgment items and a range of language skills, including fluency (not scored), repetition, naming, and comprehension. We recommend norms provided by Kiernan et al. (1987), although these should be viewed as a starting point because they are limited to normal patients (of various ages) and a poorly defined group of neurosurgical patients with "brain lesions." We further recommend that the entire test be administered because of questions of the accuracy of the screen–metric format. Also, based on the Drane and Osato (1997) study, the impairment cutoff should be changed from one to two scales. In all, the NCSE appears to need further empirical support before it can be used confidently, but it has some psychometric support and assesses a broad range of cognitive abilities while still remaining brief. Compared to other screening instruments, the NCSE also appears more relevant for patients of various ages and with various neurological disorders.

Blessed Dementia Scale (BRS)

Purpose

The Blessed Dementia Scale is a two-part scale, with a rating scale of patients' functional behavioral changes during the past 6 months in several areas (e.g., personal, social, domestic domains) and a brief mental status component, known as the Blessed Information–Memory–Concentration Test (BIMCT), that consists of 26 commonly used mental status questions and items (Blessed, Tomlinson, & Roth, 1968). The BIMCT consists of three parts: an orientation section; a memory section that includes personal (school attended), remote (date of World War II), and new learning (recall a new name and address 5 min later) items; and a concentration section that consists of repeating the months backward and counting from 1 to 20 forward and backward. This measure requires a collateral source to verify personal memory information, such as school attended and name of employer, and has a total score (most impaired) of 37. The rating scale component of the Blessed has been know by various names, including the Dementia Rating Scale, the Dementia Score, and Part I of the Blessed Dementia Rating Scale. Following Lezak (1995), we refer to it as the Blessed Rating Scale (BRS). In addition to these two Blessed tests, a six-item mental status test abstracted from the BIMCT has also been developed, but because of the limited data on this test we do not review it here.

As noted, the BRS requires that a caregiver who knows the patient well rate functional behavioral change, as well as personality and emotional changes. Most of the items are rated as present or absent, but three items about eating, dressing, and sphincter control are weighted according to severity, yielding a total possible score of 28 for the most severe impairment. Eastwood, Lautenschlaeger, and Corbin (1983) indicated that a score below 4 is not impaired, 4 to 9 is mildly impaired, and 10 or higher is moderately to severely impaired.

Relevant Reliability Information

Using a modified BRS, Villardita and Lomeo (1992) found acceptable test–retest reliability of .88 across a 1-week retest interval for patients with probable Alzheimer's disease. The modification was to rate each item on a 0 (absence of symptom) to 4 (greatest severity) scale, yielding a total score of 88. The same study found test–retest reliability of .89 for the BIMCT. Cole (1990) assessed interrater reliability on the BRS by having two trained clinical psychologists administer it on successive days to the same caretaker of a demented patient. The correlation between raters was only .59 for the total BRS score, but was even lower for some items (e.g., .04 for "Increased rigidity" and .06 for "Hilarity in inappropriate situations"). To improve BRS reliability, Cole suggested that vague items be clarified, several complex items be simplified into subcomponents, and interviewers undergo training before using the instrument. To our knowledge, this important issue has yet to be further examined.

Relevant Validity Information

Construct Validity.   In order to more fully comprehend the decline in Alzheimer's disease, Stern, Hesdorffer, Sano, and Mayeux (1990) factor analyzed the BRS and found it to be comprised of four separate factors—cognitive, personality, apathy, and basic self-care. These factors were judged to have good face validity and were later useful in predicting decline in Alzheimer's, but no further analyses were conducted on these factors.

Concurrent and Divergent Validity.   In the original study on the BRS, Blessed, Tomlinson, and Roth (1968) found correlations of .77 and −.59 between mean senile plaque count at postmortem and BRS and BIMCT scores, respectively. The demented patients also had significantly higher mean number of plaques compared to depressed, delirious, and medically ill patients. Villardita and Lomeo (1992) found scores on the BRS to correlate highly with the MMSE (−.73), the BIMCT (.70), and the Cognitive Capacity Screening Examination (−.72).

Discriminant Validity.   Using the *DSM–III* as the criterion for dementia diagnosis, Erkinjuntti, Hokkanen, Sulkava, and Palo (1988), found the BRS to have a sensitivity of 90% and a specificity of 84% in discriminating between demented patients and neurologically normal controls. These findings were based on a cutoff of 4. Although they did not statistically discriminate between mild, moderate, and severe dementia (as rated by a neurologist), each of these patient groups performed significantly different from one another, with mild patients performing best and severe patients worst.

Normative Data

To our knowledge, normative data have not been presented.

Influence of Sociodemographic Variables

Little data pertaining to the effect of variables such as age and education on the BRS has been reported. A nonsignificant correlation between the BIMCT and education was obtained by Schmitt, Ranseen, and DeKosky (1989).

Monitoring Course of Impairment

In several different samples of Alzheimer's patients with various demographic backgrounds and disease severities (Katzman et al., 1988), the mean *annual* rate of change on the BIMCT was 4.4 (*SD* = 3.6). Although the individual rate of decline was variable, severely demented patients (BIMCT = 24–33) tended to decline at a slower rate, perhaps due to a ceiling effect. Davis, Morris, and Grant (1990) compared performance on the BRS and the BIMCT with dementia staging on the CDR. Not surprisingly, there was a clear linear relationship between both tests and dementia, as scores progressively increased with dementia severity. Unfortunately, no diagnostic efficiency statistics were presented. Bowen et al. (1996) found that among many potential predictors the BRS had the strongest association with shortened survival in a longitudinal design of patients with probable Alzheimer's disease. Patients with severe versus mild BRS impairment were 2.7 times more likely to die over the course of the study. Median time to retest for all patients was 3.3 years.

Strengths and Limitations

Strengths. Compared to other mental status examinations, the Blessed offers a unique approach because (if both components are administered) it assesses collateral perception of patient decline and the patients' cognitive functioning. Collateral report may be particularly important given that demented patients are often unreliable historians and, sometimes even relatively early in the disease process, may suffer from anosognosia.

Although more research is needed, studies have indicated that the BRS is sensitive to the presence of cognitive deficits in dementia and that the BIMCT is sensitive to the cognitive decline in dementia. As might be anticipated by content alone, the BRS is highly correlated with the MMSE, BIMCT, and the CCSI. We should note that the body of research on the various Blessed tests is not as developed as the mental status measures described previously.

Limitations. As a brief screening measure, the BMICT provides little useful information beyond a patient's level of performance. It essentially taps only orientation, attention and memory, whereas the similarly brief MMSE taps these functions, as well as several aspects of language and praxis. In other words, the clinician can get more information from other measures without significantly more time investment.

Despite the apparent attractiveness of the BRS, low interrater reliability is cause for concern and, as Cole (1990) suggested, may signal that the items need to be rewritten and/or simply changed. For instance, some of the lowest correlations between raters were for items that would likely be vague and perhaps confusing to the layperson (e.g., increased rigidity).

Although an essential part of the BRS, we should note that the collateral source format requires, at the very least, fairly detailed medical records and, ideally, a collateral well known to the patient. These resources may not be reasonably available on every patient; thus, the BRS probably needs to be administered in conjunction with at least the BIMCT, if not some other cognitive measure, to provide the most accurate assessment of a patient's current functional level.

Recommendations

The BRS assesses dementia in two ways—caregiver report of patients' functional behavioral change in the past 6 months, and a brief mental status component (BIMCT) that consists of 26 commonly used mental status questions and items. Although caregiver report is a potentially attractive feature of this instrument, it suffers from occasional ambiguous language and lacks interrater reliability. Until these items are improved, caregiver report on this instrument should be viewed cautiously. Although the mental status component appears to be sensitive to cognitive impairment in dementia, it only assesses attention, memory, and orientation and provides little useful information beyond a patient's level of performance. Thus, for approximately the same time investment, we recommend that one of the other screening measures discussed in this chapter be used.

Delirium Rating Scale (DelRS)

Purpose

The Delirium Rating Scale (DelRS; Trzepacz, Baker, & Greenhouse, 1988) is a 10-item scale that rates patients on the following symptoms: onset of symptoms, perceptual disturbances, hallucinations, delusions, psychomotor behavior, cognitive status during testing, physical disorder, sleep–wake cycle, lability of mood, and variability of symptoms. To make the ratings, the clinician uses all available information, including family reports, medical history and tests, nursing observations, and mental status examination. Items are rated on various scales (usually 0–3 or 0–4) and the total (most impaired) score is 32. Features thought to be phenomenologically more characteristic of delirium (i.e., types of perceptual disturbances, hallucinations, delusions) are ascribed higher point values. Because delirium fluctuates, the DRS rating should be based on the patient's presentation during the previous 24-hr period.

Relevant Reliability and Validity Information

In a mixed geriatric sample of delirious, demented, and psychiatric patients, Rockwood, Goodman, Flynn, and Stolee (1996) found the DRS to have excellent internal consistency (.90) with variable kappa corrected interrater reliabilities. Most of the kappa coefficients ranged from .50 to .72, but outliers were hallucinations (1.0) and delusions (.30). Trzepacz, Baker, and Greenhouse (1988) found an interrater reliability of .97 for the total score in a sample of demented, schizophrenic, and control subjects. Using the same subjects, Trzepacz and Dew (1995) factor analyzed the DRS and found that two factors accounted for most of the variance; factor 1 consisted of sleep-wake cycle, psychomotor behavior, delusions, cognition, and mood lability items, and factor 2 comprised temporal onset of symptoms, symptom variability, and perceptual disturbance items. This basic factor structure was replicated in a sample of delirious and demented-delirious patients (Trzepacz et al., 1998).

In terms of validity, Rockwood et al. (1996) found the DelRS to have adequate concurrent validity, as it was strongly related to the MMSE (−.78) and the Barthel Index (−.63). This same research group also found it to accurately discriminate between delirium (determined by *DSM–III* criteria) and the mixed group of geriatric patients described above. With a cutoff of 7.5, the DelRS has a sensitivity of 90% and a specificity of 82%. Using receiver operating characteristics, Rosen et al. (1994) found that a cutoff of 10 had a sensitivity of 94% and a specificity of 82% in a sample of delirious (again identified by *DSM–III–R* criteria), demented, and psychiatric patients.

Strengths and Limitations

Strengths. According to Inouye (1994), the DelRS meets the essential criteria for usefulness in diagnosing delirium: validated specifically for use in delirium, capable of distinguishing delirium from dementia, assessment of multiple features of delirium, and feasible for use with delirious patients. In addition, based on relatively limited research, the DelRS has favorable psychometric properties, including good internal consistency and generally good interrater reliability.

Limitations. The DelRS does not explicitly recognize an important, and perhaps defining, feature of delirium—disturbance of consciousness with its attendant inattention. Although an individual item assesses a given aspect of cognitive status, it may include almost all aspects of cognitive functioning, including inattention, memory disturbance, verbal perseverations, disorientation, and so on. In comparison, other delirium scales and *DSM–IV* criteria explicitly examine attention independently, as it is a defining feature of delirium (see Inouye, 1994).

To our knowledge, research has yet to examine serial ratings on the DelRS. This would appear to be an important area of investigation to establish the validity of the DelRS, given the waxing and waning nature of delirium. For instance, we might expect that once a patient no longer meets DSM criteria for delirium, his or her DelRS score would improve.

Recommendations

Of the many delirium rating scales available, the DelRS has many attractive features, including the fact that it was specifically validated for use in delirium, can discriminate delirium from dementia, and assesses multiple cognitive and behavioral features of delirium. Based on research, we recommend an approximate cutoff score of 7–10; the exact number may be influenced by local norms. Nonetheless, this measure appears to have better psychometric support than other delirium measures and is feasible for use with delirious patients. We should note that as a rating scale the DelRS should be used, if feasible, in conjunction with a brief cognitive screening measure to provide the most extensive and accurate view of a patient's status.

CONCLUSION

With the aging of the U.S. population, dementia and other age-related cognitive impairments are likely to become even greater issues for clinicians of various types working in the primary care settings. As evident within this chapter and at various points throughout this text, clinicians in primary care settings have a wide variety of choices to make with regard to screening instruments used to detect cognitive impairments. As depicted in Table 18.1, the available measures differ in content, format, extent and strength of supporting literature, and clinical effectiveness. The majority of screening instruments were not intended to detect, and generally fail to detect, localized cognitive impairments. Moreover, the American Psychological Association appointed a taskforce that recently published guidelines for the evaluation of dementia and age-related cognitive decline (American Psychological Association Presidential Task Force, 1998). Among their 10 guidelines, the task force noted the importance of standardized psychological and neuropsychological tests that assess a range of cognitive functions, including memory, attention, perceptual and motor skills, language, visuospatial abilities, and problem solving and executive function. Brief

TABLE 18.1
Summary of Information Pertaining to Commonly Used Mental Status Examinations

Test	Domains Assessed	Time to Administer (min)	Normative Information	Reliability	Validity
BRS	Informant rating of behavioral changes and limited mental status (orientation, attention, memory)	5–15	See Blessed et al. (1968); needs further development.	Generally good, but interrater is suspect	Limited
Clock Drawing	Visuospatial, constructional, and planning	2–10	Varies with adminstration format (e.g., Freedman et al., 1994; Cahn & Kaplan, 1997)	Good interrater, but no test–retest	Good, but may vary with format
DelRS	Rating of behavioral and cognitive symptoms of delirium; information can be obtained from sources other than patient	5–15	See Trzepacz et al. (1998) for delirious and demented patents.	Adequate interrater, but no test–retest	Good
DRS	Attention, memory, initiation/perseveration, construction, conceptualization	15–45	See Monsch et al. (1995) for more extensive norms and cutoffs than found in the manual	Good	Good
MMSE	Global cognitive impairment	5–10	See Tombaugh and McIntyre (1992), Crum et al. (1993), and Tangalos et al. (1996)	Good	Good
NCSE	Attention, language, construction, memory, calculations, reasoning	5–40	See Kiernan et al. (1987); local norms may be best	Not established	Good

Note. BRS = Blessed Rating Scale (Blessed et al., 1968), DelRS = Delirium Rating Scale (Trzepacz et al., 1988), DRS = Mattis Dementia Rating Scale (Mattis, 1988), MMSE = Mini-Mental Status Examination (Folstein et al., 1975), NCSE = Neurobehavioral Cognitive Status Examination (Kiernan et al., 1987).

screening and mental status measures, such as those discussed within this chapter, may not assess all of these functions. In fact, as the task force pointed out, screening measures will at times not be sufficient to establish a diagnosis. Instead, screening measures provide a brief, objective, and, depending on the instrument, reliable and valid method of assessing some of these cognitive functions. The best of the general mental status measures reviewed in this chapter are able to detect moderate to severe diffuse degenerative dementias, and in some instances (e.g., DelRS), delirium. Primary care clinicians who desire evaluation of specific and localized cognitive impairments or who desire an elaborate understanding of complex neuropsychological functions and relatively mild conditions will need to rely on close collaborative relationships with neurologists and clinical neuropsychologists. Brief cognitive screening measures are not intended to provide such information.

REFERENCES

Alpert, J. E., Uebelacker, L. A., McLean, N. E., Abraham, M., Rosenbaum, J. F., & Fava, M. (1995). The Mini-Mental State Exam among adult outpatients with major depressive disorder. *Psychotherapy & Psychosomatics, 63,* 207–211.

American Psychiatric Association. (1994). *Diagnostic and statistical manual of mental disorders* (4th ed.). Washington DC: Author.

American Psychological Association Presidential Task Force on Assessment of Age-Consistent Memory Decline and Dementia. (1998). Guidelines for the evaluation of dementia and age-related cognitive decline. *American Psychologist, 53,* 1298–1303.

Blessed, G., Tomlinson, B. E., & Roth, M. (1968). The association between quantitative measures of dementia and of senile change in the cerebral grey matter of elderly subjects. *British Journal of Psychiatry, 114,* 797–811.

Blostein, P. A., Jones, S. J., Buechler, C. M., & Vandongen, S. (1997). Cognitive screening in mild traumatic brain injuries: Analysis of the Neurobehavioral Cognitive Status Examination when utilized during initial trauma hospitalization. *Journal of Neurotrauma, 14,* 171–177.

Bowen, J. D., Malter, A. D., Sheppard, L., Kukull, W. A., McCormick, W. C., Teri, L., & Larson, E. B. (1996). Predictors of mortality in patients diagnosed with probable Alzheimer's disease. *Neurology, 47,* 433–439.

Cahn, D. A., & Kaplan, E. (1997). Clock drawing in the oldest old. *Clinical Neuropsychologist, 11,* 96–100.

Coblentz, J. M., Mattis, S., Zingesser, L. H., Kasoff, S. S., Wisniewski, H. M., & Katzman, R. (1973). Presenile dementia: Clinical aspects and evaluation of cerebrospinal fluid dynamics. *Archives of Neurology, 29,* 299–308.

Colantonio, A., Becker, J. T., & Huff, F. J. (1993). Factor structure of the Mattis Dementia Rating Scale among patients with probable Alzheimer's disease. *The Clinical Neuropsychologist, 7,* 313–318.

Cole, M. G. (1990). Interrater reliability of the Blessed Dementia Scale. *Canadian Journal of Psychiatry, 35,* 328–330.

Cossa, F. M., Sala, S. D., Musicco, M., Spinnler, H., & Ubezio, M. C. (1997). Comparison of two scoring systems of the Mini-Mental State Examination as a screening test for dementia. *Journal of Clinical Epidemiology, 50,* 961–965.

Criqui, M. H., Barrett-Connor, F., & Austin, M. (1978). Differences between respondents and non-respondents in a population-based cardiovascular disease study. *American Journal of Epidemiology, 108,* 367–372.

Crum. R. M., Anthony, J. C., Bassett, S. S., & Folstein, M. F. (1993). Population-based norms for the Mini-Mental State Examination by age and education level. *Journal of the American Medical Association, 269,* 2386–2391.

Cummings, J. (1993). Mini-Mental State Examination: Norms, normals, and numbers. *Journal of the American Medical Association, 269,* 2420–2421.

Davis, P. B., Morris, J. C., & Grant E. (1990). Brief screening tests versus clinical staging in senile dementia of the Alzheimer type. *Journal of the American Geriatrics Society, 38,* 129–135.

Drane, D. L., & Osato, S. S. (1997). Using the Neurobehavioral Cognitive Status Examination as a screening measure for older adults. *Archives of Clinical Neuropsychology, 12,* 139–143.

Eastwood, M. R., Lautenschlaeger, E., & Corbin, S. (1983). A comparison of clinical methods for assessing dementia. *Journal of the American Geriatrics Society, 31,* 342–347.

Engelhart, C., Eisenstein, N. & Meininger, J. (1994). Psychometric properties of the Neurobehavioral Cognitive Status Exam. *Clinical Neuropsychologist, 8,* 405–415.

Erkinjuntti, T., Hokkanen, L., Sulkava, R., & Palo, J. (1988). The Blessed Dementia Scale as a screening test for dementia. *International Journal of Geriatric Psychiatry, 3,* 267–273.

Evans, D. A. , Funckenstein, H. H., Albert, M. S., Scherr, P. A., Cook, N. R., Chown, M. J., Hebert, L. E., Hennekens, C. H., & Taylor, J. O. (1989). Prevalence of Alzheimer's disease in a community population of older persons. *Journal of the American Medical Association, 262,* 2551–2556.

Fals-Stewart, W. (1997). Detection of neuropsychological impairment among substance-abusing patients: Accuracy of the Neurobehavioral Cognitive Screening Examination. *Experimental and Clinical Psychopharmacology, 5,* 269–276.

Fleming, K. C, Adams, A. C., & Peterson, R. C. (1995). Dementia: Diagnosis and evaluation. *Mayo Clinic Proceedings, 70,* 1093–1107.

Folstein, M. F., Folstein, S. E., & McHugh, P. R. (1975). Mini-Mental State, a practical method for grading the cognitive state of patients for the clinician. *Journal of Psychiatric Research, 12,* 189–98.

Freedman, M., Leach, L., Kaplan, E., Winocur, G., Shulman, K. I., & Delis, D. C. (1994). *Clock Drawing: A neuropsychological analysis.* New York: Oxford University Press.

Galasko, D., Corey-Bloom, J., & Thal, L. J. (1991). Monitoring progression in Alzheimer's disease. *Journal of the American Geriatric Society, 39,* 932–942.

Gardner, R., Oliver-Munoz, S., Fisher, L., & Empting, L. (1981). Mattis Dementia Rating Scale: Internal reliability study using a diffusely impaired population. *Journal of Clinical Neuropsychology, 3,* 271–275.

Green, R. C., Woodard, J. L., & Green, J. (1995). Validity of the Mattis Dementia Rating Scale for detection of cognitive impairment in the elderly. *Journal of Neuropsychiatry, 7,* 357–360.

Hughes, C. P., Berg, L., Danziger, W. L., Coben, L. A., & Martin, R. L. (1982). A clinical scale for the staging of dementia. *British Journal of Psychiatry, 140,* 566–572.

Inouye, S. K. (1994). The dilemma of delerium: Clinical and research controversies regarding diagnosis and evaluation of delirium in hospitalized elderly medical patients. *American Journal of Medicine, 97,* 278–288.

Jellinger, K. (1976). Neuropathological aspects of dementias resulting from abnormal blood and cerebrospinal fluid dynamics. *Acta Neurologica Belgica, 76,* 83–102.

Katzman, R., Brown, T., Thal, L. J., Fuld, P. A., Aronson, M., Butters, N., Klauber, M. R., Wiederholt, W., Pay, M., Renbing, X., Ooi, W. L., Hofstetter, R., & Terry, R. D. (1988). Comparison of rate of annual change of mental status score in four independent studies of patients with Alzheimer's disease. *Annals of Neurology, 24,* 384–389.

Kessler, H. R., Roth, D. L., Kaplan, R. F., & Goode, K. T. (1994). Confirmatory factor analysis of the Mattis Dementia Rating Scale. *Clinical Neuropsychologist, 8,* 451–461.

Kiernan, R. J., Mueller, J., Langston, W., & Van Dyke, C. (1987). The Neurobehavioral Cognitive Status Examination: A brief but differentiated approach to cognitive assessment. *Annals of Internal Medicine, 107,* 481–485.

Lezak, M. L. (1995). *Neuropsychological assessment* (3rd edition). New York: Oxford.

Logue, P. E., Tupler, L. A., D'Amico, C., & Schmitt, F. A. (1993).The Neurobehavioral Cognitive Status Examination: Psychometric properties in use with psychiatric inpatients. *Journal of Clinical Psychology, 49,* 80–89.

Marcotte, T. D., van Gorp, W., Hinkin, C. H., & Osato, S. (1997). Concurrent validity of the Neurobehavioral Cognitive Status Exam subtests. *Journal of Clinical and Experimental Neuropsychology, 19,* 386–395.

Marson, D. C., Dymek, M. P., Duke, L. W., & Harrell, L. E. (1997). Subscale validity of the Mattis Dementia Rating Scale. *Archives of Clinical Neuropsychology, 12,* 269–275.

Mattis, S. (1988). *Dementia Rating Scale: Professional manual.* Odessa, FL: Psychological Assessment Resources.

McKeith, I. G., Galasko, D., Kosaka, K., Perry, E. K., Dickson, D. W., Hansen, L. A., Salmon, D. P., Lowe, J., Mirra, S. S., Byrne, E. J., Lennox, G., Quinn, N. P., Edwardson, J. A., Ince, P. G., Bergeron, C., Burns, A., Miller, B. L., Lovestone, S., Collerton, D., Jansen, E. N. H., Ballard, C., de Vos, R. A. I., Wilcock, G. K., Jellinger, K. A., & Perry, R. H. (1996). Consensus guidelines for the clinical and pathologic diagnosis of dementia with Lewy Bodies (DLB): Report of the consortium on DLB International Workshop, *Neurology, 47,* 1113–1124.

Mendez, M. F., Ala, T., & Underwood, K. L. (1992). Development of scoring criteria for the clock drawing task in Alzheimer's disease. *Journal of the American Geriatrics Society, 40,* 1095–1099.

Mitrushina, M., Abara, J., & Blumenfeld, A. (1994). The Neurobehavioral Cognitive Status Examination as a screening tool for organicity in psychiatric patients. *Hospital and Community Psychiatry, 45,* 252–256

Monsch, A. U., Bondi, M. W., Salmon, D. P., Butters, N., Thal, L. J., Hansen, L. A., Wiederholt, W. C., Cahn, D. A., & Klauber, M. R. (1995). Clinical validity of the Mattis Dementia Rating Scale in detecting dementia of the Alzheimer type: A double cross-validation and application to a community-dwelling sample. *Archives of Neurology, 52,* 899–904.

Montgomery, D. M., & Costa, L. (1983a). *Neuropsychological test performance of a normal elderly sample.* Paper presented at the International Neuropsychological Society meeting. Mexico City, Mexico.

Montgomery, D. M., & Costa, L. (1983b). *Concurrent validity of the Mattis Dementia Rating Scale.* Paper presented at the International Neuropsychological Society meeting, Lisbon.

Montorio, I., & Izal, M. (1996). The Geriatric Depression Scale: A review of its development and utility. *International Psychogeriatrics, 8,* 103–112.

Nadler, J. D., Richardson, E. D., Malloy, P. F., Marran, M. E., & Brinson, M. E. (1993). The ability of the Dementia Rating Scale to predict everyday functioning. *Archives of Clinical Neuropsychology, 8,* 449–460.

National Institute of Aging. (1995). *Alzheimer's Disease: Unraveling the mystery* (NIH Publication No. 95-3782). Washington, DC: Author.

Northern California Neurobehavioral Group. (1988). *Manual for the Neurobehavioral Cognitive Status Examination.* Fairfax, CA: Author.

Oehlert, M. E., Hass, S. D., Freeman, M. R., Williams, M. D., Ryan, J. J., & Sumerall, S. W. (1997). The Neurobehavioral Cognitive Status Examination: Accuracy of the "screen-metric" approach in a clinical sample. *Journal of Clinical Psychology, 53,* 733–737.

Osmon, D. C., Smet, I. C., Winegarden, B., & Gandhavadi, B. (1992). Neurobehavioral Cognitive Status Examination: Its use with unilateral strike patients in a rehabilitation setting. *Archives of Physical Medicine and Rehabilitation, 73,* 414–418.

Paolo, A. M., Tröster, A. I., Glatt, S. L., Hubble, J. P., & Koller, W. C. (1995a). Influence of demographic variables on the Demential Rating Scale. *Journal of Geriatric Psychology and Neurology, 8,* 38–41.

Paolo, A. M., Tröster, A. I., Glatt, S. L., Hubble, J. P., & Koller, W. C. (1995b). Differentiation of the dementias of Alzheimer's and Parkinson's disease with the Dementia Rating Scale. *Journal of Geriatric Psychology and Neurology, 8,* 184–188.

Paulsen, J. S., Butters, N., Sadek, J. R., Johnson, S. A., Salmon, D. P., Swerdlow, N. R., & Swenson, M. R. (1995). Distinct cognitive profiles of cortical and subcortical dementia in advanced illness. *Neurology, 45,* 951–956.

Rockwood, K., Goodman, J., Flynn, M., & Stolee, P. (1996). Cross-validation of the Delirium Rating Scale in older patients. *Journal of the American Geriatrics Society, 44,* 839–842.

Rosen, J., Sweet, R. A., Mulsant, B. H., Rifai, A. H., Pasternak, R., & Zubenko, G. S. (1994). The Delirium Rating Scale in a psychogeriatric inpatient setting. *Journal of Neuropsychiatry, 6,* 30–35.

Rouleau, I., Salmon, D. P., Butters., N., Kennedy, C., & McGuire, K. (1992). Quantitative and qualitative analyses of clock drawings in Alzheimer's and Huntington's disease. *Brain and Cognition, 18,* 70–87.

Royall, D. R. (1996). Dementia. In D. R. Reuben, T. T. Yoshikawa, & R. W. Besdine (Eds.), *American Geriatrics Society geriatrics review syllabus: A core curriculum in geriatric medicine: Book I. Syllabus, annotated references and appendix* (3rd ed., pp. 105–114). Dubuque, IA: Kendall/Hunt.

Salmon, D. P., Thal, L. J., Butters, N., & Heindel, W. C. (1990). Longitudinal evaluation of dementia of the Alzheimer type: A comparison of 3 standardized mental status examinations. *Neurology, 40,* 1225–1230.

Schwamm, L. H., Van Dyke, C., Kiernan, R. J., Merrin, E. L., & Mueller, J. (1987). The neurobehavioral cognitive status examination: Comparison with the cognitive capacity screening examination and the Mini-Mental State Examination in a neurosurgical population. *Annals of Internal Medicine, 107,* 486–491.

Schmidt, R., Freidl, W., Faxekas, F., Reinhart, B., Grieshofer, P., Koch, M., Eber, B., Schumacher, M., Polmin, K., & Lechner, H. (1994). The Mattis Dementia Rating Scale: Normative data from 1,001 healthy volunteers. *Neurology, 44,* 964–966.

Schmidt, F. A., Ranseen, J. D., & DeKosky, S. T. (1989). Cognitive mental status examinations. In F. J. Pirozzolo (Ed.), *Clinics in geriatric medicine* (Vol. 5, No. 3, pp. 545–564). Philadelphia: W. B. Saunders.

Shay, K. A., Duke, L. W., Conboy, T., Harrell, L. E., Callaway, R., & Folks, D. G. (1991). The clinical validity of the Mattis Dementia Rating Scale in staging Alzheimer's dementia. *Journal of Geriatric Psychiatry and Neurology, 4,* 18–25.

Smith, G. E., Ivnik, R. J., Malec, J. F., Kokmen, E., Tangalos, E., & Petersen, R. C. (1994). Psychometric properties of the Mattis Dementia Rating Scale. *Assessment, 1,* 123–131.

Spreen, O., & Strauss, E. (1991). *A compendium of neuropsychological tests*. New York: Oxford University Press.

Stern, Y., Hesdorffer, D., Sano, M., & Mayeux, R. (1990). Measurement and prediction of functional capacity in Alzheimer's disease. *Neurology, 40*, 8–14.

Suhr, J., Grace, J., Allen, J., Nadler, J., & McKenna, M. (1998). Quantitative and qualitative performance of stroke versus normal elderly on six clock drawing systems. *Archives of Clinical Neuropsychology, 13*, 495–502.

Sunderland, T., Hill, J. L., Mellow, A. M., Lawlor, B. A., Gundersheimer, J., Newhouse, P. A., & Grafman, J. F. (1989). Clock drawing in Alzheimer's Disease: A novel measure of dementia severity. *Journal of the American Geriatrics Society, 37*, 725–729.

Tangalos, E. G., Smith, G. E., Ivnik, R. J., Peterson, R. C., Kokmen, E., Kurland, L. T., Offord, K. P., & Parish, J. E. (1996). The Mini-Mental State Examination in general medical practice: Clinical utility and practice. *Mayo Clinic Proceedings, 71*, 829–837.

Tierney, M. C., Szalai, J. P., Snow, W. G., Fisher, R. H., & Dunn, E. (1997). Domain specificity of the subtests of the Mini-Mental State Exam. *Archives of Neurology, 54*, 713–716.

Tombaugh, T. N., & McIntyre, N. J. (1992). The Mini-Mental State Examination: A comprehensive review. *Journal of the American Geriatrics Society, 40*, 922–935.

Tomlinson, B. E., Blessed, G., & Roth, M. (1970). Observations on the brains of demented old people. *Journal of Neurological Sciences, 11*, 205–242.

Tröster, A. I., Moe, K. E., Vitiello, M. V., & Prinz, P. N. (1994). Predicting long-term outcome in individuals at risk for Alzheimer's disease with the Dementia Rating Scale. *Journal of Neuropsychiatry and Clinical Neurosciences, 6*, 54–57.

Trzepacz, P. T., & Dew, M. A. (1995). Further analyses of the Delirium Rating Scale. *General Hospital Psychiatry, 17*, 75–79.

Trzepacz, P. T., Baker, R. W., & Greenhouse, J. (1988). A symptom rating scale for delirium. *Psychiatry Research, 23*, 89–97.

Trzepacz, P. T., Mulsant, B. H., Dew, M. A., Pasternak, R., Sweet, R. A., & Zubenko, G. S. (1998). Is delirium different when it occurs in dementia? A study using the delirium rating scale. *Journal of Neuropsychiatry and Clinical Neurosciences, 10*, 199–204.

Vangel, S. J., & Lichtenberg, P. A. (1995). Mattis Dementia Rating Scale: Clinical utility and relationship with demographic variables. *Clinical Neuropsychologist, 9*, 209–213.

Villardita, C., & Lomeo, C. (1992). Alzheimer's disease: Correlational analysis of three screening tests and three behavioral scales. *Acta Neurologica Scandanivica, 86*, 603–608.

Vitaliano, P. P., Breen, A. R., Russo, J., Albert, M., Vitiello, M. V., & Prinz, P. N. (1984). The clinical utility of the Dementia Rating Scale for assessing Alzheimer patients. *Journal of Chronic Disease, 37*, 743–753.

Weiss, B. D., Reed, R., Kligman, E. W., & Abyad, A. (1995). Literacy and performance on the Mini-Mental State Exam. *Journal of the American Geriatrics Society, 43*, 807–810.

Werner, H. (1937). Process and achievement: A basic problem of education and developmental psychology. *Harvard Educational Review, 7*, 353–368.

Werner, H. (1956). Microgenesis and aphasia. *Journal of Abnormal and Social Psychology, 52*, 343–353.

Wolf-Klein, G. P., Silverstone, F. A., Levy, A. P., & Brod, M. S. (1989). Screening for Alzheimer's disease by clock drawing. *Journal of the American Geriatrics Society, 37*, 730–736.

Woodard, J. L., Salthouse, T. A., Godsall, R. E., & Green, R. C. (1996). Confirmatory factor analysis of the Mattis Dementia Rating Scale in patients with Alzheimer's disease. *Psychological Assessment, 8*, 85–91.

Using the SF–36 Health Survey in Primary Care

Harry P. Wetzler
Physician and Clinical Outcomes Specialist; Bainbridge Island, WA

Donald L. Lum
Family Practice and Emergency Physician; Northfield, MN

Dwana M. Bush
Integrative Health Institute; Atlanta, GA

Medical students are told, "Listen to patients, they will tell you the diagnosis." Today, however, a number of factors reduce physicians' listening time. These include shorter appointments in the name of "efficiency" and more emphasis on "objective" findings such as laboratory tests and imaging results. Yet patients are not fundamentally interested in tests or X-ray pictures. They want to be understood, feel good, and function well. If these concerns are not addressed, patient satisfaction suffers, root problems are often missed, and, most important, patient health status is not improved.

Patient–physician communication is a two-way street. Physicians must listen and patients must be willing to talk about their problems. In a Louis Harris poll (Koop, 1998, p. 58), 25% of more than 1,000 responding patients said they were reluctant at times to talk to their doctors about a health problem. This is especially true in sensitive areas such as sexual dysfunction and behavioral health, where patients are virtually the only source of information, and it is important to facilitate communication. Questionnaires and surveys have been found to promote information flow, and it is possible to measure seemingly subjective concepts such as well-being and functional capacity accurately.

One of the hallmarks of primary care is a concern for the whole person as opposed to the constituent organs or systems. This whole-person emphasis leads naturally to the Short Form with 36 questions (SF–36), a measure of overall health. Counts of visits or procedures or laboratory test results do not assess what is most important to patients and are inadequate measures of quality or health. This sentiment has existed for over 40 years; Lembcke (1952) stated it clearly: "The best measure of quality is not how well or how frequently a medical service is given, but how closely the result approaches the fundamental objectives of prolonging life, relieving distress, restoring function and preventing disability" (p. 276).

Distress, function, and disability are subjective concepts that are often termed quality of life or subjective health status (Leplège & Hunt, 1997). Although professionals may assess distress, function, and disability, it is widely accepted that patients are a crucial source of information. Indeed, a number of studies have found considerable discordance between patient and physician assessments. Jachuck, Brierly, Jachuck, and Willcox (1982) found that doctors considered every one of 75 patients on hypertensive therapy as improved because blood pressure was controlled. However, only 48% of the patients felt improved and 8% felt worse. Patient-based assessments are not intended to replace traditional clinical measures; rather, they complement them by providing insights heretofore unavailable or gained more efficiently.

Increasingly, effectiveness studies include patient-based measures. One of the first was a study of men with mild to moderate hypertension to determine the effects of captopril, methyldopa, and propranolol on their quality of life (Croog et al., 1986). After a 24-week treatment period, all three groups had similar blood pressure control, and the treatment groups were similar in scores for sleep dysfunction, visual memory, and social participation. However, patients taking captopril as compared with patients taking methyldopa scored significantly higher on measures of general well-being, and had fewer side effects and better scores for work performance, visual motor functioning, and measures of life satisfaction. Patients taking propranolol also reported better work performance than patients taking methyldopa.

The SF–36 is a self-administered generic health profile including eight scales:

1. Physical Function (PF).
2. Role Physical (RP).
3. Bodily Pain (BP).
4. General Health (GH).
5. Vitality (VT).
6. Social Function (SF).
7. Role Emotional (RE).
8. Mental Health (MH).

Physical, role, and social functioning scales measure functional status, and the bodily pain, mental health, and vitality scales are well-being measures. The SF–36 is called a generic measure because the scales are neither age, gender, disease, nor treatment specific. Each of the SF–36 scales is scored on a 0 (worst) to 100 (best) basis. Thus, a score of 0 represents the worst level of health for each scale, and 100 is the best possible for each scale. However, the scales have a different number of levels, and they are ordinal rather than interval scales (i.e., a score of 100 is better than 50 but not necessarily twice as good). Table 19.1 summarizes the number of items, possible levels, and the meaning of low and high scores for each scale. The two role scales have fewer levels and are thus coarser measures.

The eight SF–36 scales represent a compromise between brevity and comprehensiveness, and their selection was not easy. John Ware, Jr., PhD, the principal developer, faced two difficult choices in developing the SF–36. The first choice, which health concepts to include, was the most difficult. Ware, Snow, Kosinski, and Gandek (1993, p. 3:4) said,

> The most difficult task in developing the SF–36 was the selection of a subset of 8 health concepts from the more than 40 concepts and scales studied in the MOS [Medical Outcomes Study]. Among those seriously considered, but not chosen, were measures of health distress, sexual functioning, family functioning, and sleep adequacy.

TABLE 19.1

Information About SF-36 Health Status Scales

Concepts	Number of Items	Number of Levels	Meaning of Scores	
			Low	High
Physical Function	10	21	Limited a lot in performing all physical activities including bathing or dressing due to health	Performs all types of physical activities including the most vigorous without limitations due to health
Role Physical	4	5	Problems with work or other daily activities as a result of physical health	No problems with work or other daily activities as a result of physical health
Bodily Pain	2	11	Very severe and extremely limiting pain	No pain or limitations due to pain
General Health	5	21	Evaluates personal health as poor and believes it is likely to get worse	Evaluates personal health as excellent
Vitality	4	21	Feels tired and worn out all of the time	Feels full of pep and energy all of the time
Social Function	2	9	Extreme and frequent interference with normal social activities due to physical or emotional problems	Performs normal social activities without interference due to physical or emotional problems
Role Emotional	3	4	Problems with work or other daily activities as a result of emotional problems	No problems with work or other daily activities as a result of emotional problems
Mental Health	5	26	Feelings of nervousness and depression all of the time	Feels peaceful, happy, and calm all of the time

Note. From Ware, Snow, Kosinski, and Gandek (1993). Reprinted with permission.

The second difficult choice for Ware et al. was whether to construct new scales. The SF–36 was developed for use in the Medical Outcomes Study (MOS), a quasi-experimental study of variations in physician practice styles and patient outcomes in different health care delivery systems. However, many scales had been developed for a prior study, the Health Insurance Experiment (see the next section). For the SF–36, new scales were constructed to measure five of the eight concepts.

The SF–36 has been used in over 1200 studies encompassing a wide variety of medical, surgical, and behavioral conditions. An annotated bibliography of studies from 1988 through 1996 is available (Manocchia et al., 1998). In keeping with modern information technology, there is an SF–36 web site on the Internet, www.SF–36.com.

OVERVIEW

Summary of Development

The SF–36 has roots in the Health Insurance Experiment (HIE), a randomized trial designed to address two key questions in health care financing: (a) How much more medical care will people use if it is free, and (b) what are the consequences for their health? The HIE included scales for measuring a broad array of functional status and well-being concepts for adults and children. These scales were based on a multidimensional model of health.

Some HIE participants refused to complete the lengthy health surveys used in that study. To prevent loss to follow-up, a very short 5-min telephone survey was developed. This short survey improved cooperation and provided preliminary data supporting the use of short scales. Although the early experience with the short survey was promising, there were two unanswered questions after the HIE: (a) Can methods of data collection and scale construction such as those used in the HIE work in sicker and older populations, and (b) can more efficient scales be constructed?

HIE data were collected from 1974 to 1982, and the MOS began enrolling patients in the mid 1980s. The first large-scale use of a comprehensive short-form general health survey was an 18-item instrument used in a 1984 national survey conducted by Louis Harris and Associates (Montgomery & Paranjpe, 1985, cited in Ware et al., 1993). In 1986, two items were added, creating the SF–20, which was used in the MOS. Following Ellwood's Shattuck Lecture to the Massachusetts Medical Society and its publication in the *New England Journal of Medicine* in June 1988, there was increased demand for an improved short form. A developmental SF–36 was released in 1988, and the standardized version was first used in the fall of 1990.

Variant Forms

At least two variants of the SF–36 are in use. First is the Health Status Questionnaire (HSQ), distributed by the Health Outcomes Institute (InterStudy's successor) in Bloomington, Minnesota (now a part of StratisHealth). The HSQ is identical to the SF–36 except that it has three items added to screen for depression (Rost, Burnam, & Smith, 1993, p. 192). The Rand Corporation released the Rand–36, which is identical to the SF–36 in content but uses simple summation scoring for the general health and bodily pain scales. Conversely, Ware recommended more complex methods including weighting certain responses. We are not aware of published studies comparing the scoring alternatives, but Ware et al. (1993, p. 6:22) said that the standard Bodily Pain scoring produces means that are 2 to 4 points lower.

The standard SF–36 uses a 4-week recall period when asking about function or well-being (i.e., "During the past 4 weeks, have you had . . ."). When studying acute conditions, with frequent observations, a shorter recall period is more appropriate so there will be no recall overlap across administrations. The *acute version* of the SF–36 has a 1-week recall period. In a study of 142 participants (60% female, average age 39 years) in a clinical trial of an asthma medication, the acute form scales met the requirements for scoring by simple summation, were not skewed excessively, were internally consistent, and the correlations between the scales were similar to those for the standard SF–36 (Keller et al., 1997). The data indicated that although the acute form was more sensitive than the standard to change in health status associated with changes in acute symptoms, acute scale scores may not be comparable to national norms derived from the standard, particularly for those scales that assess frequency of health events during a specified time period.

In 1994, Ware, Kosinski, and Keller introduced two new summary scales for physical and mental health after factor analysis revealed that the eight SF–36 scales define distinct physical and mental health clusters. The new scales were found to be generalizable because the SF–36 scale intercorrelations are very similar across populations. The physical and mental summaries explain 80% to 85% of the reliable variance in the eight SF–36 scales. The summary scales are scored using norm-based methods whereby each scale is forced to have a mean of 50 and standard deviation of 10 in the U.S. population. Another important feature of the summary scales is that they have a much greater number of levels. For instance, the Physical Function scale has 21 different possible scores (0, 5, 10, . . . , 95, 100), whereas the Physical Component Summary (PCS) scale has 567 levels and the Mental Component Summary (MCS) scale has 493 levels. Thus, the measurements are much more precise for individuals.

Generally, estimating more scales requires more items. Because there are only two summary scales, the question arose as to how well these scales could be generated from a shorter questionnaire. Ten items from six of the eight SF–36 scales account for at least 90% of the variance in both of the summary scales. Adding two more items provides even better estimates of the summary scale scores and makes it possible to produce a profile of the eight SF–36 scales. The resulting SF–12 is an excellent tool for group or population estimates, but it is too coarse for use in assessing individual patients.

One possible difficulty in interpreting the SF–36 is that the scales each have different averages. To foster comparability, Ware has suggested standardizing each of the eight scales using a mean of 50 and standard deviation 10 in the fashion used for the mental and physical summaries. Although our experience has been that clinicians quickly learn the meaning of individual scale scores, more comparable scales may facilitate the learning process. The choice of the norm is not firmly established. It seems most reasonable to use U.S. averages (listed later), but averages for certain clinical populations might be more appropriate in some circumstances.

In September 1996, the developers of the SF–36 announced version 2 with changes in the content and layout, including:

1. Improvements in some instructions and questions to make the wording more familiar and less ambiguous.

2. An improved layout for questions and answers that reduces missing data.
3. Greater comparability with translations widely used in the United States and in developed countries.
4. Five-levels in place of dichotomous response choices for seven items in the two role functioning scales.

The last point is particularly important because in standard version 1 the role functioning scales are quite coarse, with only five or four possible levels in the Role Physical and Role Emotional scales, respectively. The changes increase the number of levels fourfold and substantially reduce the variance of each scale. Reduced variance increases the reliability of the scales.

The SF–36 has been used in a number of countries outside the United States, and extensively in the United Kingdom. In the United Kingdom, although translation per se was not required, six items needed minor changes (Brazier et al., 1992). For example, "block" is not recognized as a distance measure in the United Kingdom. Thus, the United Kingdom version uses "half a mile" and "100 yards" instead. As part of the International Quality of Life Assessment Project, translations of the SF–36 are being tested in more than 40 countries.

Available Norms

In contrast with many psychological tests where norms are often available prior to widespread use, most health status measures do not have population-based norms. The SF–36 is a noteworthy exception. From October through December 1990, the National Opinion Research Center conducted the National Survey of Functional Health Status (NSFHS) in a representative sample of the noninstitutionalized U.S. population, aged 18–94. Respondents were drawn from the sample frames of the 1989 and 1990 General Social Survey (GSS), which has been conducted annually for over 20 years.

NSFHS respondents were randomly assigned to a postal survey (80%) or a computer-assisted telephone interview (20%). Only 10% of the postal respondents were not located, and 12% of the telephone respondents could not be found. The overall response rate was 77.1%. Comparisons between the respondents to the NSFHS and those of the general U.S. population from the National Center for Health Statistics support the representativeness of the NSFHS sample. The norms in Table 19.2 are from the

TABLE 19.2
SF-36 Norms for the General U.S. Population and a Sample of Primary Care Patients

Scale	U.S. Population	Primary Care
Physical Function	84.2	85.7
Role Physical	81.0	73.3
Bodily Pain	75.2	70.4
General Health	72.0	73.0
Vitality	60.9	56.1
Social Function	83.3	80.5
Role Emotional	81.3	75.3
Mental Health	74.7	71.3

Note. The data in column 1 are from Ware, Snow, Kosinski, and Gandek (1993, p. 10). Reprinted with permission.

"mixed mode" survey, and may be slightly higher (but less than 2 points) than those from a totally self-administered sample due to bias due to live telephone interviewers (McHorney, Kosinski, & Ware, 1994). Table 19.2 also lists norms for a primary care sample from Atlanta Family Medicine in Atlanta, Georgia. The primary care sample has an average age of 41.6 years and is 60% female. The Role Physical scale is 7.7 points less in the primary care sample compared to the U.S. population, and the Role Emotional scale is 6.0 points less. The other scales differ by a maximum 4.8 points.

Jenkinson, Coulter, and Wright (1993) published normative data for adults aged 18–64 years in the United Kingdom. The mean scores closely parallel those in Table 19.2 in each age- and gender-specific group. In a study of British civil servants, Hemingway, Nicholson, and coworkers (1997) found significant age-adjusted differences by employment grade, with worse health in the lower grades.

Although there have been no comparable nationwide attempts to gather normative data on people with clinical conditions, numerous studies have looked at patients with various problems. One study reported average scores for patients with urinary incontinence, prostate cancer, chronic obstructive pulmonary disease (COPD), acquired immune deficiency syndrome (AIDS), fibromyalgia, and hyperlipidemia. Patients with prostate cancer and hyperlipidemia had scores comparable with normative data from healthy persons. Those with the other conditions had lower scores, but the lowest averages were a function of the condition. For example, hospitalized patients with AIDS had the lowest General Health and Social Function scores, but those with COPD had the lowest Role Physical, Role Emotional, and Mental Health scores (Schlenk et al., 1998).

The American Medical Group Association's Outcomes Consortia began collecting data on patients with various conditions in 1992. Scores for patients with asthma, diabetes, hip replacement (pre-op) and sleep disorder are listed in Table 19.3. Note that the hip replacement patients are about 20 years older on the average, which may contribute to their lower Vitality scores (Kania, 1996; Labanowski & Kania, 1996).

Basic Psychometric Information

Psychometrics is the science of measurement of human behavior and traits. Generally, psychometrics is considered to have two basic domains: one concerning indi-

TABLE 19.3

Health Status Questionnaire Scale Scores for Patients With Asthma, Depression, Diabetes, Hip Replacement (Pre-Op), and Sleep Disorder

Scale	Asthma	Depression	Diabetes	Hip Replacement	Sleep Disorder
Physical Function	77.4	71.6	68.7	28.3	78.8
Role Physical	64.9	44.4	60.9	16.8	65.2
Bodily Pain	76.2	58.8	68.4	30.0	60.4
General Health	58.7	52.9	54.6	64.9	61.9
Vitality	53.8	40.1	51.3	44.2	70.2
Social Function	62.9	57.2	68.5	53.8	44.5
Role Emotional	81.0	38.9	72.5	59.1	66.9
Mental Health	72.4	46.3	70.9	70.5	63.5

Note. The data in column 2 are SF–36 scores from Ware, Snow, Kosinski, and Gandek (1993, p. 10). Reprinted with permission.

ces or measures of personal behavior, and the other involving testing and examination. To some extent, the SF–36 bridges these domains.

The SF–36 has excellent psychometric properties. Three aspects of a test or survey are usually included in psychometric assessment — reliability, sensitivity, and validity. Reliability is the extent to which results are reproducible or consistent with repeated measures and accurate in terms of conformity with a standard. Sensitivity or responsiveness to change is the extent to which change is detected when it actually occurs. Hays and Hadorn (1992) argued that responsiveness is an aspect of validity and not a separate dimension. Validity is the extent to which a test measures what it is designed to measure. It is critical to note that a scale should not be considered "valid" or "invalid" or "reliable" or "unreliable." It is better to think in terms of relative degrees of validity, reliability, or sensitivity, where more is known as additional data accumulate. It is also important to recognize that there are no "gold standards" that can be used to determine the true value for any of these psychometric properties.

Reliability.   Ware and colleagues' (1993, p. 7:1) definition of reliability actually encompasses two domains: consistency and accuracy. Because accuracy is actually an aspect of validity (Feinstein, 1987, p. 143), we emphasize consistency in what follows. Consistency is the capacity of a test to give the same result — whether correct or incorrect — on repeated administration to a person under the same conditions. It addresses the question, "Can I believe this particular measurement?" No physician would treat a patient for hypertension based on only one blood pressure measurement. Normal systolic blood pressure (BP) can vary by as much as 60 mm Hg (excluding exercise), and normal diastolic BP by up to 40 mm Hg over 24 hr. Two systolic BP measurements are usually adequate, but three are often needed for a stable diastolic assessment (Pearce, Evans, Summerson, & Rao, 1997). The reason for repeating measurements is that measurement error or biological variation may yield a spuriously high reading. Indeed, W. E. Deming, the quality control expert, stated, "There is no true value of anything" (Deming, 1986, p. i). From a statistical standpoint, any measurement in an individual should be considered a *sample* from an underlying distribution for that person. As such, these observations have a sampling distribution with a mean and standard deviation. Most measures in humans have bell-shaped distributions. Narrower or tighter distributions reflect more consistency and reliability.

Blood pressure measurements can be repeated with little difficulty, and previous determinations do not highly influence subsequent measures. However, it is impossible to repeat the SF–36 on the same person under the same conditions over a short period of time where previous testing does not influence later testing (test independence). However, using psychometric theory it is possible to estimate the width of the sampling distribution for SF–36 scales in individuals. It is known as the *standard error of measurement* and is described subsequently.

Two measures of reliability are commonly used — test–retest reliability and internal consistency reliability. Test–retest reliability is determined by comparing the results from the same test on different occasions. There is an inherent problem here because it is necessary to have some interval between the measurements, and true change may occur during the interval. Test–retest reliability is often not studied and has not been reported for the MOS. Two-week SF–36 test–retest reliability was measured in primary care patients in the United Kingdom where the coefficients ranged from .60 to .81 with a median of .76 (Brazier et al., 1992). Nerenz, Repasky, Whitehouse, and Kahkonen (1992) reported correlations between baseline and 6-month fol-

TABLE 19.4
Measures of SF–36 Internal Consistency in the General
U.S. Population and a Sample of Primary Care Patients

Scale	U.S. Population	Primary Care
Physical Function	.94	.92
Role Physical	.89	.88
Bodily Pain	.88	.80
General Health	.83	.81
Vitality	.87	.89
Social Function	.63	.85
Role Emotional	.81	.83
Mental Health	.82	87

Note. The data in column 1 are from Ware, Snow, Kosinski, and Gandek (1993, p. 7). Reprinted with permission.

low-up scores ranging from .43 for Bodily Pain to .90 for Physical Function in a sample of patients with diabetes. Six months is a long interval for assessing test–retest reliability; however, Nerenz's findings generally corroborate those from the United Kingdom.

A more common measure of reliability is internal consistency. This is the degree to which answers to similar items are consistent. Cronbach's alpha (α, often called "coefficient alpha") is the most widely used measure of internal consistency. Higher alpha scores (the range is 0 to 1) indicate greater internal consistency reliability, and scales with more items usually have higher alpha scores. Internal consistency has been measured in many studies of the SF–36. Table 19.4 shows the measures of internal consistency (Cronbach's alphas) for the SF–36 in the U.S. general population and a primary care sample in Atlanta, Georgia. All values except that for Social Function in the U.S. population equal or exceed .8. Comparable values were obtained from general population (Jenkinson et al., Coulter, & Wright, 1993) and primary care (Brazier et al., 1992) samples in the United Kingdom.

Interpretation of these values depends on the intended comparisons. Comparisons among individuals or across tests on the same individual require high reliability (>.90); comparisons between diagnostic, treatment, or population groups require values of .70 or more (Nunnally & Bernstein, 1994).

Interpreting measurements in individuals requires the *standard error of measurement (SEM)*, which is calculated using the formula

$$SEM = s \times (1 - \alpha)^{1/2}$$

where s is the standard deviation for the scale in a group sample, and α is Cronbach's or coefficient alpha (note that both of these values, s and α, also have sampling error). The *SEM* can be used to construct confidence intervals for individual scores. For example, a 95% confidence interval for an SF–36 score is the score $\pm 1.96 \times SEM$. Confidence intervals become smaller as alpha increases, although the rate of decrease is quite gradual until alpha exceeds .9. Thus, greater internal consistency and reliability result in scores with smaller confidence intervals. More confidence can be placed in these scores, and it is easier to detect change with them.

Confidence intervals are often misinterpreted. A 95% confidence interval does *not* mean there is a 95% probability that the true score lies in the interval. It means that if it were possible to repeat the measurement 100 times without changing the circumstances of measurement (a practical impossibility), then at least 95 of the 95% confidence intervals generated from those measurements would include the true score, which is actually impossible to know.

Confidence intervals are created by adding (for the upper limit) and subtracting (for the lower limit) a multiple of th *SEM* from the observed SF–36 score. Table 19.5 lists 90% and 95% confidence interval values for individual measurements for each of the SF–36 scales for the U.S. general population and a primary care sample from Atlanta Family Medicine. The values for the U.S. and primary care samples in Table 19.5 are quite similar except for Bodily Pain and Social Function. The discrepancies for these two scales arise from different reliabilities in the two populations. The Bodily Pain reliability (Cronbach's alpha) in the U.S. population is .88, but only .80 at Atlanta Family Medicine. Conversely, the values for Social Function are .63 and .85, respectively.

For screening, one must use the initial score as the best estimate, although suspicious scores should be questioned because mistakes may occur in either answering or scoring (see the later section on interpretation). Over time, however, repeated observations usually provide more stable estimates. Indeed, Meyer and colleagues (1994) reported that many patients are very consistent and define their own norms. They went on to say that after three or four observations one can often recognize pattern changes and define the individual's response to illness and other events that affect health.

Sensitivity.   Sensitivity or responsiveness addresses the question, "If change actually occurs, will this instrument detect it?" Clinicians recognize change and want to know whether tools like the SF–36 will corroborate their observations. Of course, if they do not, then the clinician could be wrong, but they don't like to admit error. One requirement for increased sensitivity is more gradations in a measure. Thus, if a measure has only "yes" and "no" alternatives, then it is possible for a person to change from "mostly yes" to "slightly yes" but still have the same test result. An item with more response options would be more likely to detect change and provide more information. The Physical Function, General Health, Vitality, and Mental Health scales have more levels (see Table 19.1) and should be more sensitive.

TABLE 19.5
SF–36 Confidence Interval Values for Individual SF–36 Measurements

Scale	U.S. Population		Primary Care	
	90%[a]	95%[b]	90%	95%
Physical Function	10.2	12.3	10.2	12.1
Role Physical	18.7	22.6	21.6	25.7
Bodily Pain	12.4	15.0	18.0	21.4
General Health	14.7	17.6	14.3	17.1
Vitality	13.0	15.6	12.2	14.6
Social Function	21.3	25.7	15.5	18.5
Role Emotional	23.2	28.0	25.4	30.3
Mental Health	12.0	14.0	11.4	13.5

Note.   The data in columns 1 and 2 are from Ware, Snow, Kosinski, and Gandek (1993, p. 7). Reprinted with permission.
[a]90% Confidence interval equals 1.64 *SEM*s.
[b]95% Confidence interval equals 1.96 *SEM*s.

Although there are no criterion measures of sensitivity, the *effect size* and *standardized response mean* are commonly used to express an instrument's change scores in a standardized way. These scores enable one to compare the sensitivity of the different SF–36 scales and with different instruments. The effect size is the mean change divided by the baseline standard deviation. Effect sizes of 0.2, 0.5, and 0.8 or more are generally considered to indicate small, moderate, and large differences, respectively. The standardized response mean is the mean change divided by the standard deviation of change. It is not appropriate to compare effect sizes and standardized response means directly. One aspect of responsiveness that has received little attention is *variability*. Murawski and Miederhoff (1998) found substantial variation in responsiveness of instruments depending on the specific application, although the SF–36 was not included in their study. In a large study in the United Kingdom, Hemingway and coworkers (1997) concluded that the SF–36 is sensitive to changes in general populations.

Validity. Validity deals with the questions, "What is this actually measuring?" and "How much confidence can I place in conclusions drawn from these scales?" No one disputes that a yardstick measures length. Length is tangible and there is no confusion. Health status is intangible, and there is no universally accepted "gold standard" or criterion measure that can be used for calibration. As a result, a number of alternatives for assessing validity have come into use. These include face, content, construct, criterion, convergent, divergent, and predictive validity. The SF–36 was subjected to a deliberate validation strategy, and massive evidence attests to its validity. Some of this evidence is described in the next few paragraphs.

Face validity is whether, on the surface, the items appear to measure the intended attributes. Clearly, this is highly subjective, but if an instrument does not pass this test, then it is probably doomed regardless of its latent quality. For instance, using shoe size to measure depression would lack face validity. More subtly, face validity includes what Feinstein (1987) termed "focus of interpersonal exchange." An example of the wrong interpersonal exchange focus would be using items about physical function that elicit responses about general public opinion instead of individual personal capability. For instance, asking "Is climbing stairs a good measure of physical function?" asks for an opinion and lacks a personal anchor. To our knowledge the face validity of the SF–36 has never been questioned.

Content validity refers to whether there are any gaps or omissions in the items or concepts measured. Another aspect is the inclusion of unsuitable items. The SF–36, which uses eight scales to measure health status, could be criticized as incomplete. Yet the authors' intent was to develop a short form, and compromises were necessary. Ware et al. (1993, p. 8:3), acknowledged the limitations by writing, "sexual functioning . . . is a good candidate for inclusion in questionnaires that supplement the eight SF–36 scales." It is impossible to create a brief, all-encompassing measure of health status. The operational question is whether the SF–36 has useful content, and we are convinced that it does.

Construct validity is perhaps the most difficult aspect of validity to understand. This is not because the concept is that difficult to comprehend, but rather due to terminology. Clinicians use constructs but call them *diseases* or *severity* or *excess* instead. Each of these words denotes a mental synthesis of observations that conforms with a theory. The eight scales in the SF–36 are *constructs* in that they represent concepts or dimensions of health status. Likewise, depression is a mental health construct. One approach to assessing construct validity is to test the difference between two groups

TABLE 19.6
Percentages of Primary Care Patients With Ceiling and Floor SF–36 Scores

Scale	Ceiling (%)	Floor (%)
Physical Function	38.8	0.5
Role Physical	58.9	14.6
Bodily Pain	25.1	0.7
General Health	8.4	0.2
Vitality	1.2	1.8
Social Function	46.1	0.9
Role Emotional	64.8	14.3
Mental Health	1.9	0.1

with known differences. The fact that patients with psychiatric illness have lower Mental Health scores compared to patients with minor medical conditions attests to the construct validity of the Mental Health scale.

"Ceiling" and "floor" effects also impact SF–36 validity. A ceiling effect occurs when there is insufficient discrimination at the highest level. Thus, if two people score 100 on a scale and there is an important difference in that concept between the two people, the ceiling effect masks the difference. Similarly, a floor effect occurs at the lowest level for zero scores that mask differences. Table 19.6 shows the percentage of respondents in the Atlanta Family Medicine primary care sample with scores at the upper (ceiling) or lower (floor) extremes. Although there are substantial ceiling and floor effects on some of the scales, the Mental Health and Vitality scales—the most important in psychological assessment—have very little ceiling or floor bias.

Basic Interpretive Strategy

Doctors Dwana Bush and Donald Lum, pioneers in the real-time clinical use of health status data, have developed an interpretive approach called *health status graph assessment*. Health status graph assessment is a standardized, structured approach to interpreting health status measures, determining the underlying reasons for low scores, and negotiating a health plan with the patient in the exam room. In their work, Bush and Lum discovered that the use of graph assessment is an important new clinical tool for the care of individual patients and defined populations. In addition to original use in their primary care practices in Atlanta, Georgia, and Northfield, Minnesota, respectively, the graph assessment was introduced and disseminated to a growing number of primary practice environments throughout the United States. Its purpose is to assist the clinician to build the clinician–patient relationship, support clinical decision making, and enhance provider and health care team productivity. Graph assessment can provide a critical bridge for the transmission of unique "patient stories" into standardized clinical data.

Based on currently available and valid quality-of-life questionnaires and measures such as SF–36 and its variant, the HSQ, health status graph assessment uses the patient-generated answers to the health status assessment and the visual cues of the graph as the starting point for a focused patient interview. The graph assessment interview consists of a standard set of interpretations and questions to engage the patient to discover the reasons for low or suboptimal health status measures. The patient responses enable a rapid "word picture" of physical and mental health functioning to be developed in the context of the patient's presenting problem(s). This clinical context — the connection of the patient problem to physical and emotional functioning — in turn assists the clinician to take and negotiate more timely and effective diagnostic or therapeutic actions with the patient. In addition, a trend assessment can identify the patient's perspective on what made the difference in that person's physical and psychological health based on two or more graphs over time.

The Health Status Graph Assessment[1]:

• Builds the clinician–patient relationship by engaging both the clinician and the patient in a dialogue to discover the reasons for low health status measures. This reflective listening tool results in the patient feeling that he or she is heard. It also provides consistency and continuity of listening and documentation in an era of medicine when the patient experiences frequent changes in providers.

• Supports clinical decision making by arriving at a more comprehensive picture of the patient from both physical and emotional health perspectives and focusing in on the relevant reasons for poor functioning for a given clinical situation, which may or may not relate to the original complaint, and allows for a negotiation and consensus to take place between clinician and patient about next steps, diagnostic or therapeutic.

• Enhances productivity by the use of a standardized, easy to master, structured interview technique to obtain 20–30 min of clinical history in 2–10 min (time-efficient); timely consideration of alternate reasons, symptoms, or problems (hidden or unstated patient agendas); and possible changes in ordering, sequencing, or reduction of tests, treatments or other interventions.

Although it is appropriate for use in all primary care patient encounters, Bush and Lum have found that health status graph assessment is particularly helpful for patients with multiple complaints, ill-defined symptoms such as fatigue, gastrointestinal complaints and chest pain, chronic pain, chronic disease management, depression screening, elective surgery, health maintenance/wellness, and patients with a history of high utilization. They have both used condition-specific screeners such as the Beck Anxiety Scale and Zung and D–ARK Depression Scales on the basis of abnormal low mental health or role emotional scale scores.

Health status graph assessment involves four basic steps: (a) explain the health status measures to the patient, (b) identify and confirm low measures, (c) ask the essential questions for each low measure, and (d) apply the answers to support clinical decision(s). Bush and Lum have found that the rigorous use of scripted interpretations and questions facilitates learning graph assessment.

The health status graph assessment contains five key components that apply to each individual SF–36 scale, as well as summary scales:

1. *Interpretation* is the interviewer's explanation of the meaning of the score for a particular scale to the patient in the context of that patient's score.
2. *Clarifying question* is the open-ended, standardized inquiry to determine the patient's perception for a low score (impaired functioning) or a high score (wellness).

---

[1]The Health Status Graph Assessment section is copyright 1998 by Dwana M. Bush and Donald L. Lum. Reprinted with permission.

3. *Patient response* is the feedback by the patient for the reasons for low or high scores or trends (changes in measure scores over time). These responses are categorized as spontaneous or prompted and are documented directly on the graph.

4. *Clinical action* is a range of one or more clinical decisions which are taken by the interviewer as a consequence of the Patient Response. These may be

   • Prioritized in order of problem type, importance, or urgency.
   • Categorized in a number of different ways (diagnosis/assessment, treatment—drug or nondrug, specialist referral, cost, time, etc.).
   • Customized according to the interests and priorities of the clinician.

5. *Clinical trend* is the subsequent and/or serial determination of the patient perspective of what has made the difference in changes in physical or psychological health overtime.

The graph assessment interview helps the primary care clinician or health care team to learn the patient's perception of the cause of his or her functional impairment, and thus serves as a "compass" to guide in developing a care plan more likely to improve function and patient satisfaction. The trend interview helps to identify the patient's perception of reasons for improvement or decline in his or her physical or psychosocial functioning over time as measured by multiple graphs. If the trended data change exceeds the confidence level on any scale or the physical or mental health summary scales, interview with the patient can reveal the patient's perception of what has contributed to the interval change in health status.

In conclusion, health status graph assessment can be applied across the spectrum of care for individual patients. Individual "snapshot" health status graph assessments have been demonstrated to be very useful for more comprehensive and rapid diagnosis, initiation of treatment, and patient satisfaction. When combined with the sequential use of condition-specific screeners for psychological problems in the subset of primary care patients with low mental health scores, graph assessment becomes a common initial pathway for primary care clinicians and behavioral health specialists to view the patient from the other complementary aspects of mental and physical health functioning, respectively. Trend assessments are currently be applied to demonstration projects in chronic disease management such as diabetes, treatment monitoring, and outcomes management at both the individual patient and defined population level. Bush and Lum continue to explore the wider application of this tool in primary care to identify and manage behavioral health problems such as depression and anxiety as important comorbidities to chronic disease and contributors to daily office visits for episodic care.

USE AS A SCREENER

In 1957, the Commission on Chronic Illness (p. 45) defined screening as:

the *presumptive* identification of *unrecognized* disease or defect by the application of tests, examinations, or other procedures which can be applied *rapidly* to sort out apparently well persons who *probably* have a disease from those who *probably do not*. A screening test is not intended to be diagnostic. [italics added]

The last sentence in the definition is very important because screening does not yield final diagnoses; people who appear likely to have the disease need further evaluation to arrive at a final diagnosis.

Numerous studies have found that many psychosocial problems—depression, anxiety disorders, alcohol abuse, eating disorders, somatization—are overlooked in routine medical care. Primary care clinicians need simple but valid and reliable tools to assist them in finding these disorders efficiently. This is especially true in managed care where primary care visits are often limited to 15 min or even less. With reduced time to spend with each patient, the clinician's "listening time" is usually the first casualty. Clinicians have found that the SF–36 enhances the listening and history taking process.

Although the SF–36 will usually be administered to individuals one at a time, primary care clinicians can also use it to begin to assess their practice *population*. Populations or groups provide a context whereby clinicians can determine whether hypothetical trends are true. For example, if a clinician suspects an increase in anxiety disorders, then it would be possible to review SF–36 trends over time and the attendant follow-up diagnostic data. Indeed, using the SF–36 in primary care should be considered one part of a screening program consisting of diagnostic and treatment components. The screening part includes the screening instrument(s) and schedule for their use, as well as the procedures for evaluation of those who screen positive.

Screening tests also have validity and reliability properties. Validity for a screening test refers to how accurately the test categorizes people. Validity has two components: sensitivity and specificity. *Sensitivity* is defined as the ability of a test to identify correctly those who have the disease or disorder (note this is a different use of "sensitivity" than given previously). *Specificity* is the ability of a test to identify correctly those who *do not* have the disease or disorder.

Reliability is the extent to which a screening test gives consistent results when the test is performed more than once on the same individual under the same conditions. Reliability does not guarantee high sensitivity or specificity, but an unreliable test usually does not have sufficient sensitivity or specificity to be of practical value.

Relevant Psychometric Support

*Consistency With **DSM–IV/ICD–9 Criteria.*** The SF–36 is a measure of general or overall health and does not place people in specific diagnostic categories. Yet the eight scales make it possible to reach preliminary conclusions about possible problems and diagnoses. The most helpful scales for psychological assessment are Mental Health, the two role scales, Role Physical and Role Emotional, and Vitality. Patients with low Mental Health scores (to be defined subsequently) definitely have more behavioral health problems, ranging from major depression to subsyndromal and undifferentiated difficulties. Scores on the role scales are often useful in determining the extent to which a problem may interfere with work or homemaking activities.

SF–36 and Clinical Depression. The depression screening properties of the SF–36 were assessed in the MOS. SF–36 surveys were self-administered as part of a two-stage process that used a short form of the Center for Epidemiologic Studies Depression

Scale (CES–D) and then the National Institute of Mental Health Diagnostic Interview Schedule (DIS) for the final diagnosis. Sensitivity and specificity are a function of the *criterion of positivity* — the score threshold used to classify the results. Lower positivity criteria (i.e., lowering the Mental Health score required for a positive screen) increase specificity but reduce sensitivity. Receiver operating curve (ROC) analysis combines sensitivity and specificity in an effort determine an optimal cutoff for positivity. In the MOS, the best all-around cutoff for Mental Health in screening for clinical depression was 52 or below, which had a sensitivity of 66.8% and a specificity of 86.2% (Ware, 1994). The best all-around cutoff for the Mental Component Summary score was 42 or less, which had a sensitivity and specificity of 73.7% and 80.6%, respectively.

It is not possible to determine which patients are clinically depressed using SF–36 information only. However, it is possible to calculate the expected percentage of depressed patients for a given prevalence (proportion of all patients who are depressed), sensitivity, and specificity. The *positive predictive value* is the percentage of those who screen positive who actually have the condition of interest. When a condition has a low prevalence, screening tests do not work as well. If a test with a sensitivity of 74% and specificity of 81% is used in a population with a 15% prevalence of depression, 40% of those screening positive can be expected to be diagnosed with depression after further evaluation. If the prevalence of depression is 30%, then 62% of those screening positive can be expected to be depressed.

In the MOS, SF–36 data were collected for research, and clinicians did not have real-time access to the results. At Atlanta Family Medicine, where the primary care physician had the results before seeing the patient, a Mental Health score of 60 or less was found to correlate empirically with a higher prevalence of psychosocial problems. In this population, 27.0% of patients had initial Mental Health scores of 60 or less, and 27.4% had Mental Component Summary scores of 42 or below. However, the two criteria do not identify the same group of patients needing further evaluation. As seen in Table 19.7, just over 12% of the sample had discordant classifications based on the different criteria. Approximately one third were positive on one or both criteria.

Combining the Positive Predictive Value with the data in Table 19.7 reveals that although only about 40% of those in the group with Mental Health score ≤60 or Mental Component Summary score ≤42 will be depressed, approximately 80% of the depressed people will be found in that group (assuming 15% overall prevalence of depression). Secondary screening is needed to identify those who are actually depressed. A number of depression screeners are described in this book.

SF–36 and Other Psychosocial Problems.   Of the 60% with low Mental Health or Mental Component Summary scores who are not depressed, many will have other diagnoses such as anxiety or panic disorders, phobias, or somatization. Other screen-

TABLE 19.7
Percentage of Patients Screening Positive for
Clinical Depression by Two SF–36 Criteria

Mental Component Summary	Mental Health Score		
	≤60	>60	Total (%)
≤42	21.0	6.3	27.4
>42	5.9	66.7	72.6
Total (%)	27.0	73.0	100.0

ers are available for these disorders. Some of the patients with low Mental Health or Mental Component Summary scores will not have a *DSM–IV* diagnosis. Yet just because diagnostic criteria are not met does not mean there is nothing wrong or that the patient should be ignored. Sherbourne, Jackson, Meredith, Camp, and Wells (1996) reported that up to 73% of primary care patients perceived unmet needs for care for personal or emotional problems. Further research is needed to understand patients with low Mental Health or Mental Component Summary scores. We are convinced that patients identified using either threshold are candidates for further evaluation and treatment.

Implementation

The SF–36 should be used with other instruments (serial screening) because it leads to improved efficiency in secondary screening, and the results for every patient are useful in patient education and monitoring. Implementation in busy office practices involves a number of issues that must be addressed to achieve success.

Perhaps the most important potential SF–36 implementation issue is acceptance by clinicians. Many clinicians believe the SF–36 duplicates existing information. This has not been the case. In this respect the words of Meyer et al. (1994, p. 277) are very instructive:

> When we began this work, we wondered whether we already knew what the SF–36 would tell us about our patients. We did not. Health status surveillance has done more than give quantitative expression to our intuition. The activity reveals new information, and the information it reveals is qualitatively different from the assessments that we otherwise make in the care of our patients. In retrospect, our belief that we already assessed functional status implicitly in the course of the routine clinical encounter was very naive.

Clinicians have consistently found that the SF–36 provides new insights efficiently. Another objection clinicians may raise concerns the act of measuring human attributes that are usually considered part of the "art" of medicine. Often this objection is rooted in fear that such measurements threaten the already diminished core of humanistic clinical art that was a major attraction for entering primary care. Feinstein (1987, pp. 1–2) considered this dilemma and offered the following insight:

> In the current climate of technology and science, the artful citation of important human phenomena is regarded as soft data. These soft citations are used for all the distresses, discomforts, and other sensations that constitute clinical symptoms, as well as for the anxiety, gratification, love, hate, sorrow, joy, and other important human reactions that occur in both sickness and health. Nevertheless, when competing scientifically with the hard data derived from technologic forms of measurement, the soft clinical information may be overlooked or deliberately ignored. . . . These omissions produce major flaws in the art and science of patient care, as well as the education of clinicians.

We firmly believe the SF–36 is scientifically sound and can enhance clinical art by playing an important role in assessment and prognostication, decision making, and treatment monitoring.

Prior experiences in a group practice environment indicate that clinical mentoring and coaching are important and viable approaches to rapidly disseminating and learning new cognitive skills such as health status graph assessment. Memos, paper guideline formats, and one-shot continuing medical education conferences have been shown to have little or no impact on the adoption of new clinical practice skills or behaviors. Mentoring and coaching are complementary processes. Mentoring is learning that is relationship based, whereas coaching is an active process for transferring a defined set of skills. Both clinical mentors and coaches must be respected, experienced, enthusiastic, and available to be effective champions, for trust is a critical element in relationship-based learning. Importantly, identification and selection of such clinical teachers should be done from the internal ranks of clinicians within a clinical organization for the sake of credibility and to make the costs of training feasible. In addition, administration and managers must actively sponsor and support the necessary change management and face the inevitable obstacles to successful learning, dissemination, and implementation of such new skills by the mentors and their clinician-learners. Proactive attention to time management, competing clinical projects or innovations, and financial disincentives will pave the way for success. Coaching and mentoring programs also need flexibility in format and delivery. This is very important because cookie-cutter, one-size-fits-all approaches just do not succeed with a diverse group of clinician-learners. For example, some clinicians prefer to have a coaching session occur in a half day with multiple patients and graphs, whereas others prefer to have it spread over a week with one graph a day. Some clinicians love a video format; others hate it.

When primary care providers start using the SF–36, they will not be as efficient in seeing patients, and it is important to schedule fewer patients. This is particularly true if the coaching time is concentrated direct observation with clinical coach and clinician. Although such a schedule affects "productivity," the alternative is provider and patient frustration. Other coaching variations include selecting patient scenarios of particular interest to the clinician, restricting the number of patients with health status assessments for a given time period, and spreading the active coaching period to several days or a week. These latter options can decrease the disruption to regular office routine, but work best when the clinical mentor/coach is on site. Previous training experience has demonstrated that clinicians will become comfortable after 10 to 20 graph assessments. It is advisable for the clinician to have access to an experienced clinical mentor (optimally the same coach) for the first month after the initial coaching period.

Administration of the instrument is another important consideration. Most patients can complete the SF–36 in 6 to 10 min, and schedules need to be set up to accommodate the extra time. A variety of data capture methods are available ranging from forms completed manually to optical scanning and touchscreen. The simplest approach is to have patients complete the form with a pen or pencil. Virtually all clinicians doing real-time SF–36 analysis use automated data capture and scoring. Readers should consult the chapter entitled "Integrating Behavioral Health Assessment With Primary Care Services" (chap. 5) for information on systems and vendor selection. Those contemplating purchasing systems are strongly encouraged to try any system on a number (25 or more) of patients before purchase. Because the list of SF–36 commercial vendors changes frequently, readers should visit the SF–36 web site for the most up-to-date information.

In addition to hardware and software, there is a critical need for staff orientation and training. Although the SF–36 is quite simple, staff must understand how it fits in the care process and support its use. Training need not be lengthy but it is crucial. Understanding is greatly facilitated if staff members complete the SF–36 and receive a scored report. In addition to staff training, one or more staff members must be delegated to perform data collection and processing. This includes giving forms to patients or orienting them to a device such as a touchscreen computer, answering questions, scanning forms (if applicable), and attaching printouts to charts.

The SF–36 items are widely available. However, the phrase "SF–36" is trademarked by the Medical Outcomes Trust and the scoring rules are copyrighted by John E. Ware, Jr. Commercial users of the SF–36 trademark or scoring are expected to pay royalties. Use of the Health Status Questionnaire (HSQ) from the Health Outcomes Institute and of the Rand–36 is royalty free.

A critical implementation issue to address in advance is disposition of patients who screen "positive." Primary care clinicians should anticipate that as many as one third of patients will have Mental Health scores less than or equal to 60. Although Mental Health score ≤60 should not be the sole criterion in SF–36 interpretation, it is a point of departure. In any event, patients with unforeseen problems will be found, and it is imperative to manage them with a minimum of disruption. Often managed care dictates will prevail, but there are some cautions here. Some managed care contracts have behavioral health "carve-outs" that mandate referral. A few require patients to call an 800 number to make arrangements for behavioral or mental health care. This may be better than ignoring results, but we believe that primary care clinicians should try to manage most of the problems that will be uncovered using the SF–36.

Although primary care clinicians have the knowledge and skill to manage most of the psychosocial problems found as a result of using the SF–36, administrative constraints may make it difficult to provide proper care. In some cases there is a knee-jerk reaction where the clinician thinks, "If I touch it, I'm dead for 30 minutes" because the proverbial "can of worms" will be opened. Unfortunately, today's reimbursement climate militates against managing these problems properly, and these issues and problems are often swept under the rug. The problem with this, however, is that patients continue to suffer unnecessarily if root problems are not addressed. In addition, these patients often become "frequent flyers" with numerous visits and no progress, where the cost savings are illusory and actually mask poor quality.

In some instances it is necessary to refer patients to a mental or behavioral health specialist. However, it is important to recognize that many patients who screen "positive" via the SF–36 will have undifferentiated problems that may frustrate specialists. New ways to deal with these patients and their problems are needed.

Guidelines for Decision Making

Because the SF–36 may uncover such a wide variety of problems and diagnoses, it is impossible to give specific guidelines for all the possibilities. However, there are principles regarding appropriate intervention and use of guidelines that need review.

Need for Behavioral Health Intervention. There are some cases where behavioral health intervention is the most appropriate course. These include overt psychoses, suicidal behavior, bipolar disorder, and some substance use disorders. Furthermore, in some instances financial or organizational arrangements may dictate behavioral health referral. Again, we emphasize that patients' health, rather than finances or organizational convenience, should be the guiding factor. We are optimistic that more widespread use of the SF–36 and adjunctive instruments and the consequent understanding of patients' overall health can lead to arrangements designed for the overall benefit of most patients.

Determining the Most Appropriate Intervention.   Primary care clinicians have two basic intervention alternatives: continuing treatment themselves, or referral. The most appropriate course depends on the clinician's skill and interests, the nature of the problem, workload, and payment arrangements. Although payment arrangements are not a medical consideration, and ideally should not enter into treatment planning, they often do and cannot be ignored.

Primary care clinicians vary in their interest and skill in treating patients with psychosocial or behavioral health problems. Obviously, clinicians with little interest in or skill with these problems should refer patients. However, most patients have less severe problems that should be treated in primary care. There is better continuity of care, and the primary care clinician is more aware of the patient's overall situation. Moreover, Burnum (1982) noted that most depressed patients have major physical disease, and virtually all have many baffling physical symptoms requiring skilled diagnostic acumen.

Specific Treatment Recommendations.   Specific treatment recommendations depend on the diagnosis. There are few user-friendly behavioral medicine guidelines for primary care. Although guidelines have been criticized as "cookbooks" that infringe on clinicians' autonomy, we believe there is excessive variation that works to the detriment of many patients. There are always exceptions, and these need to be handled individually. However, it is incumbent on clinicians as professionals to learn from each patient, particularly those who do not match the guideline description, so that treatment science can advance.

The Agency for Health Care Policy and Research (AHCPR) sponsored development of a guideline for major depression that has been used widely and adapted by many organizations (Depression Guideline Panel, 1993). Whenever a guideline is adopted, even one with a prestigious background, local clinicians need to be involved in reviewing and making needed local adaptations. Clinicians have strong aversions to guidelines that are "not invented here," and if their opposition is not apparent, they will often covertly scuttle guidelines perceived as external dictates. Another negative aspect of guidelines is that they are difficult to use. Most are either lengthy or buried in lengthy tomes. Thus, practice reorganization and improved information systems (including decision support) are badly needed.

Guidelines do not exist for patients who screen positive and have ill-defined or subsyndromal problems with no specific DSM–IV/ICD–9 diagnoses. Yet these people are ill or hurting and need help. Some of these patients will have subthreshold depression, and there is a suggestion that even "inadequate" antidepressant therapy may be beneficial (Simon et al., 1995). Results from the MOS indicate that patients with mild or subthreshold depression have an increased risk of developing major depression (Wells, Sturm, & Sherbourne, 1996). Anxiety is another common finding in this group. Hales and colleagues (1997) recently proposed a guideline for anxiety disorders.

In the final analysis, some patients will not fit into any discrete diagnostic category. For these patients, and indeed most of those who do have diagnoses, primary care and most of medicine are often not well suited to help. Medical care is organized to screen for, triage, and treat acute illnesses that can be cured with short-term management. Many patients identified with the SF-36 will have a relapsing or chronic illness that needs a different approach. To bring this about Wagner, Austin, and Von Korff (1996) stated that changes are needed in four areas: physician practice, patient education, expert support systems, and information systems. Perhaps the crux of the issue is that physicians must make a commitment to treating these patients.

The patients we are talking about are demanding and frustrating. They are the ones who elicit piloerective responses (and deleted expletives) when they appear on the daily schedule. Most of these patients cannot be "cured" in the traditional sense, and the physician–patient relationship is crucial for their improvement. Physicians need to recognize that a significant "dose of the doctor" is required along with empathy for the patient's circumstances, patient and family education, and supportive caring. In the short term, these patients require more time, but initial studies are promising in terms of positive cost-effectiveness (Katon et al., 1997). To some extent, primary care clinicians must navigate between needing a diagnosis for reimbursement, differential reimbursement for behavioral or mental disorders, and the needs of patients who are often demanding and frustrating. The SF-36 is not a panacea in this context, but it is a useful tool.

One promising method advocated by Seifert and Otteson (1994) uses a health educator called a *health coordinator* to help patients develop effective coping strategies and tactics. The health coordinator is not a counselor or therapist. Rather, the health coordinator is an educator who works with patients to identify and develop what Seifert and Otteson term *life management skills*—especially in the area of stress management. A health coordinator was employed at Atlanta Family Medicine for 2 years with considerable success. However, despite the fact that many patients were willing to pay out of pocket for the service, long-term economic viability could not be achieved. More positively, Robinson and coworkers (1997) found that a majority of primary care patients with depression read booklets and watched a video as part of a randomized trial evaluating a new model for treating depression. In a randomized controlled trial, Rubenstein et al. (1995) found that computer-generated screening results accompanied by management and resource suggestions resulted in better outcomes. Finally, there are other perhaps controversial treatments such as mindful meditation that might be useful for some of these patients.

Prediction of Treatment Outcome. There are four basic outcome categories: cure, improvement but with occasional relapses, no change, and decline. Every patient wants to know the outlook. Prediction is also implicit in scheduling follow-up. As in all medical prognoses, group predictions are more accurate than those for individuals. In the MOS, 42% of depressed patients had better Mental Component Summary scores after one year; 40% were the same; and 18% were worse (Ware et al., 1994, p. 8:36). Physical Component Summary scores changed very little in this group, but this may be due to potential shortcomings in the summary scoring system as pointed out by Simon, Revicki, Grothaus, and Von Korff (1998). Data from Atlanta Family Medicine suggest that most (62%) patients with initial Mental Health scores less than or equal to 60 improve within 60 to 90 days. However, about 8% were worse and nearly a third were unchanged. Using a Mental Health cutoff score invokes regression to the mean phenomena, and more study is needed of the natural history of subsyndromal illness.

TABLE 19.8
Six-Month Effect Sizes for Patients With Low Initial
Mental Health Scores and Hip Replacement Patients

Scale	$MH \leq 60$	Hip Replacement
Physical Function	0.03	0.85
Role Physical	0.26	0.82
Bodily Pain	0.12	1.30
General Health	0.21	0.01
Vitality	0.60	0.61
Social Function	0.59	0.59
Role Emotional	0.79	0.26
Mental Health	1.35	0.26

In terms of effect sizes, Table 19.8 shows effect sizes corresponding to scale score changes for patients with initial Mental Health scores of 60 or less from the Atlanta primary care sample. Effect sizes for patients 6 months after hip replacement are shown for comparison. As expected, the patients with low initial Mental Health scores have large changes in that score, but negligible change in Physical Function. The situation is reversed for hip replacement patients, although they do not experience the same magnitude of change.

Feedback to Patients

Patients like to be asked for their views on their health, but they also want feedback. Whenever patients complete a SF–36 or similar instrument, the results should be discussed with the patient as soon as possible. Ideally, the discussion follows the Basic Interpretive Strategy. A printed report for the patient to keep is also useful. The best format for printed reports for the patient is not known. Much ado has been made over putting normative data on graphic reports. We have found, however, that clinicians rapidly learn how to interpret scale scores. Even more important, patients become their own controls, decreasing the need for external norms. Regardless of the format of the report, the most important aspect of feedback is the timing—immediate point-of-care interpretation by the clinician is best.

It is also possible to give patients more detailed booklets that explain the SF–36 and the scales in addition to providing the patient's scores and normative comparisons. Our opinion is that most patients will not read the booklet, making this a largely wasted effort. In this context, there is no substitute for human interaction. However, it may be possible to use interactive video technology to provide patients with additional information tailored to their particular situation.

Although we are convinced of the net benefit of using the SF–36 in primary care, there are some potential drawbacks. Screening always produces false positives (those who have a positive test but not the condition of interest) and false negatives (ill people with a negative test result). False positives need secondary screening or diagnostic evaluation, which entails use of time, possible expense, and probably anxiety. Thus, it is important for those dealing with patients with "positive" results to not have an alarmist approach or tone. Patients who screen positive should be told about the need for additional screening in a matter-of-fact and reassuring way. One of the benefits of newer technology will be the capability to integrate primary and secondary screening seamlessly. Clinicians will still need to verify results in person, but the need to administer additional forms or questionnaires will be avoided. False negatives receive reassurance that is incorrect. Much of the error with false negatives can be reduced by using the SF–36 periodically in all patients using a schedule that depends on previous scores (i.e., more frequent administration in those with lower scores).

System Feedback

System feedback is needed because patients will inevitably "fall through the cracks" in busy primary care practices. Thus, some needing screening will be missed, and follow-up will not occur as needed for others. Tickler files and reminder systems are useful in this regard. System feedback is also needed to refine screening criteria and thresholds. For instance, if too many people are "positive," and overwhelm the practice, then the positivity criteria may need to be adjusted temporarily until the volume can be accommodated.

TREATMENT MONITORING

After the initial SF–36 assessment, patients must be monitored to assess improvement. In essence, a control system with a feedforward loop, where prior information informs the future, is created. After each measurement, the new data are assessed and a decision is made about changing the treatment (which may be "watchful waiting").

Psychometric Issues

Like all measurement tools, the SF–36 has measurement error. The challenge is to separate true change from random fluctuations or noise. The implications of measurement error and the associated confidence intervals for individual treatment monitoring are that if there are only two measurements, then considerable numerical change must occur to be highly confident that true change has taken place. For instance, if the initial Mental Health score is 40, then the next score must be 54 or more in order to be 95% confident that a positive change has occurred. If the score changes by 12 points, there is a 90% probability of a real change (see Table 19.5).

As mentioned in the screening section, patients tend to be consistent and define their own norms. Statistically, if scores are relatively stable over a number of measurements, then less change is needed to yield a true change. Statistical process control (SPC) charts are the best way to assess individual measurements over time. SPC theory (Committee E-11 on Quality and Statistics, 1995) indicates that if three consecutive measurements are exactly the same, then a 4-point change is significant at the 95% confidence level. On the Mental Health scale, if two scores are the same, then SPC calculations show that a 10-point change is significant at the 95% level.

One of the benefits of the SF–36 in primary care is that it has scales for physical as well as mental health. The Physical Function scale has the highest reliability of all the scales, and in young people particularly, any score below 100 in the absence of obvious contributing pathology should elicit inquiry from the clinician. Similarly, if a young person's Physical Function score goes down by 5 points or more, the reason should be ascertained. The same considerations apply to the Role Physical and Role Emotional scales, except the change values are 25 and 33, respectively.

Implementation

Treatment monitoring is synonymous with *follow-up testing*. The major issue is obtaining the data. Most people do not like to go to the doctor. Moreover, when they have improved and are feeling better, they are even less inclined to visit. Thus, considerable bias may be associated with follow-up data obtained only in the office. This is not to say that follow-up data should not be obtained in the office setting. The goal is to maximize follow-up data capture and standardize intervals. This involves using different modes of data collection.

In addition to the data collection modes described previously, two additional modes are frequently used in follow-up assessment: mail and telephone. Each has different benefits and costs. Postal questionnaires are used frequently in survey research. Their principal advantages are familiarity and low initial cost. However, response rates are frequently low and the follow-up needed to improve response rates is costly. In some instances motivated groups have higher response rates. Thus, if the clinician emphasizes the importance of completing postal questionnaires, response rates are usually higher. One drawback of postal questionnaires is that someone must process them, either scanning them or performing manual data entry.

Telephone data capture has great promise. Many people have negative thoughts about this mode because of all the unsolicited telemarketing calls they receive. Again, if patients are told about the calls and their importance is emphasized, the telephone has proven to be an excellent way to gather data. If live interview is used, there is a bias (McHorney et al., 1994) as well as higher cost. A more promising avenue is to have a live operator make the initial contact and then transfer the respondent to an automated system. The initial costs of telephone data capture are higher than mail, but when response rates and the total staff costs and burden of the mail mode are calculated, the telephone is attractive, particularly if volumes are high. One drawback of the telephone is the length of the SF–36. It usually takes about 12 to 15 min to complete via telephone. This can be shortened if the respondent has the questionnaire and just has to press the buttons indicating their answers. Telephone and fax follow-up were used in the first case study described later in this chapter.

Decision Guidelines

The main decisions needed in treatment monitoring are monitoring frequency, changing interventions, and when to discontinue treatment.

Monitoring Frequency. As with any clinical problem, monitoring frequency should be tailored to the patient's situation. SF–36 scores are one indicator; patients with lower scores indicative of more severe conditions should receive more frequent follow-up. Cost and respondent burden are also considerations. Unfortunately, payers will not reimburse separately for SF–36 administration. This may change as its efficacy and utility continue to be demonstrated. In capitation situations where prevention of serious problems and hospitalization has direct economic implications, it may be easier to justify the cost. Respondent burden refers to the time and effort required of patients to complete the questionnaire. Patients generally like to complete the

SF–36. However, after they have done it many times, some become resistant. If this occurs, a personal statement from the clinician about its importance usually makes a difference. Planned developments that will shorten the questionnaire will be helpful in this regard.

Changing Interventions and Discontinuing Treatment. We do not recommend using the SF–36 alone to make decisions regarding treatment initiation, changes, or cessation. Changing interventions or discontinuing treatment depends on clinical response and perhaps specific measures such as those discussed in other chapters of this book. One factor to keep in mind is that many behavioral conditions have cycles of remission and relapse or chronicity. Accordingly, even though a specific episode may remit or seem cured, we recommend periodic use of the SF–36, although the frequency can be reduced to every 6 to 12 months.

Feedback

As with screening, there are two major feedback concerns: providing information to patients about their own results, and obtaining information on system performance.

To Patients. Graphic presentation of SF–36 results is very effective and facilitates dialogue between patient and clinician. Graphs make it easy to see trends in scale scores. There are examples in the case studies presented later in this chapter. Some practices use newsletters to communicate with patients. Although it is usually inappropriate to use actual patient data in a newsletter, it is useful to present the concept and goals of the SF–36. In addition, summary information about practice performance can make interesting reading.

System Feedback. Screening, treatment, and monitoring are part of a continuum where feedback is needed to improve processes based on longer term and more definitive outcomes. The key is linking processes and outcomes because improving outcomes is the goal but processes are the tools that must be used to affect outcomes. To date the SF–36 has been used in busy primary care settings where research support has been lacking. Focused studies are needed to determine the system measures and feedback modalities that will be most useful in creating improvement.

In addition to monitoring and improving care processes for individual patients, the care system must be assessed. Those who screen "positive" by whatever criteria need follow-up, and some loss to follow-up is inevitable. However, by monitoring and studying follow-up numbers and patterns, it is possible to improve. One simple aspect of this effort is a need for practice staff to generate periodic summary reports. Practice summary data should be reviewed at least quarterly, and monthly if volume is sufficient.

DISEASE-SPECIFIC CONSIDERATIONS

The SF–36 is sensitive to most diseases and disorders (see Table 19.3). As a result, users need to consider comorbid conditions in interpreting SF–36 findings. Group comparisons may need to be adjusted to produce more meaningful results.

Comorbid Diseases and Disorders

There are a number of issues in dealing with comorbidities. First, many people have more than one comorbid condition. Second is severity of various comorbidities. Finally, there is the problem of ascertainment. Seemingly, the primary care physician would be the best source of knowledge, but time constraints usually make it impossible to obtain physician input. We have found that a simple comorbidity score derived from a patient completed checklist strikes a useful balance among the competing data priorities. It is simple, and there is a monotonic relationship between the number of diseases or conditions and SF-36 scale scores. The Health Outcomes Institute has a checklist that has been used extensively. Katz, Chang, Sangha, Fossel, and Bates (1996) found that a questionnaire measure of comorbidity was reproducible and valid and offered practical advantages over medical record based assessment of comorbidity. The Duke Severity of Illness Checklist (Parkerson, Broadhead, & Tse, 1993) includes severity data but requires staff input. In the future it should be possible to automate comorbidity data (Parkerson, Hammond, & Yarnall, 1994).

Risk Adjustment Procedures

Inevitably, there will be comparisons between individuals or groups. Because everyone is unique and groups may differ due to factors such as age, gender, and socioeconomic status, these comparisons are fraught with the age-old "apples and oranges" problem. *Risk adjustment* is a generic term for a number of techniques that makes it possible to compensate to some extent for differences. Stratification is the simplest approach. For example, younger people have higher Physical Function scores. Comparing groups with different age mixes could be misleading even if there were no other differences. One solution is to compare the different age groups from each group separately. It is impossible to make overall comparisons using this method, but it usually provides useful information. If overall comparisons are required, then statistical techniques such as direct adjustment or analysis of covariance may be used. Beyond simple adjustment, it is best to obtain the advice of a statistical expert because the techniques involve a number of assumptions that may invalidate the results. Iezzoni (1997) compiled a useful monograph on risk adjustment. It is important to bear in mind that no adjustment method can compensate for all underlying differences. The best comparisons come from prospective interventions in randomized groups.

STRENGTHS AND LIMITATIONS OF USE IN PRIMARY CARE SETTINGS

One of the SF-36's major strengths is that it measures a broad continuum of health, physical as well as mental. Thus, it can be used to monitor all patients age 14 years and over who are literate and mentally competent. Further discussion of its strengths and limitations needs to include scientific, cost, and ease-of-use issues.

Scientific Issues

The SF-36 has been used in more clinical studies and programs than any other health status instrument. Although its qualities and characteristics vary depending on the clinical condition, it is robust and broadly applicable, having been demonstrated to be reliable, sensitive, and valid in a wide number of conditions. Existing and planned studies will continue to add to an already impressive amount of knowledge regarding its capabilities.

The SF–36 developers are continuing to refine and develop the instrument. Version 2 was mentioned previously and significantly improves the two role functioning scales. The two greatest scientific needs, however, are better sensitivity and specificity for screening, and tighter confidence intervals for follow-up. The instrument needs fundamental changes to accomplish these goals. One promising approach uses item response theory.

Briefly, item response theory uses an algorithm to determine the next question based on the answer to the previous question. Thus, if a person says he or she can walk a mile without difficulty, then asking about walking a block should be unnecessary. An item pool is developed and the desired confidence interval is specified in advance — more responses are needed to reduce the confidence interval. Furthermore, it is possible to base the initial item on patient information such as demographic data or previous questionnaire results. For instance, if the respondent is 20 years old, then the first Physical Function item should involve the most difficult task — vigorous activity in the current SF–36 — unless there is previous information indicating the person had difficulty with that. Item response-based instruments will definitely produce smaller confidence intervals and eliminate the ceiling and floor effects (Bjorner & Ware, 1998). The impact on screening sensitivity and specificity will need study, although it stands to reason that more precise measurement should be helpful.

The Health Status Graph Assessment also needs careful assessment, ideally in a randomized clinical trial. The findings of Rubenstein et al. (1995) are encouraging, but more research is needed to determine the effectiveness of Health Status Graph Assessment. One of the keys to success is training and mentoring clinicians. The training need not be lengthy but it must be accomplished, and clinicians starting out need to be able to discuss cases and questions with an experienced clinician. In preparation for a randomized trial, methods for teaching and mentoring clinicians need to be refined. The ultimate question is whether use of the SF–36 increases SF–36 scores and improves other clinical measures.

Determining the best treatment for a given patient will need ongoing research. Illnesses such as depression will continue to be studied. However, minor depression and subsyndromal conditions have great impact on large numbers of people and need more investigation. A final avenue for scientific inquiry is follow-up intervals and algorithms. Currently, physicians must rely primarily on their intuition to set follow-up intervals. This is an area where large databases with information from many practices would be useful. Combined with standard clinical data, SF–36 data will yield new process-outcome insights and provide clinicians with new ways to learn from their patients.

Cost and Reimbursement Issues

There are direct and indirect costs of using the SF–36 in primary care. Direct costs are those that must be paid to actually produce graphs and reports. These consist of hardware (computers, printers, etc.), software (computer programs), and incidentals such as paper. These costs are not inconsequential, but they are tractable and depend mostly on the number of SF–36s processed. Per member per month (pmpm) costs can also be estimated.

Indirect costs are more difficult to estimate. These include staff time and the effect on patient throughput. Initially, using the SF–36 will slow the clinician down. After the clinician learns to use the SF–36, then some patients will require more time in the beginning especially. This increase will be offset by fewer visits overall and better health. Unfortunately, payers now pay for health care and not health. We look forward to a change where "productivity" will be viewed not in terms of the number of patients seen or procedures done but the improvements in a valid measure of health.

Reimbursement also needs to be addressed. Employers pay for most of the medical care in the United States. A recent study in the United Kingdom (Stewart-Brown & Layte, 1997) suggested that emotional problems account for twice as much work disability as do physical problems. The irony here is that payers are so stingy with behavioral health by ignoring it or demanding cost-benefit studies to support reimbursement policy changes. At this time, solid evidence is lacking and a new generation of studies is needed to provide cost-benefit data (Simon & Katzelnick, 1997). Contrast these demands with policies for reimbursing "physical" illness where most claims are reimbursed with little or no question.

Patient scheduling is also a cost issue. For example, if clinicians are limited to 10-min sessions, then it is virtually impossible to provide adequate care. The authors are convinced that clinicians need flexibility to, say, substitute a 30-min session for three symptom-focused or "Band-Aid" sessions of 10 min each. More study is needed to assess optimal time allocations and reimbursement arrangements.

Ease of Use

At this point in time, it is not easy to administer and score the SF–36. Scanners were a significant advance over manual processing, but significant staff time is required to make sure forms are completed properly and the scanning produces reasonable results. Touchscreen and interactive voice may offer significant advantages for easier data capture. Technology is evolving rapidly and will solve many of these problems.

Obtaining SF–36 scores is only the "front end" of the assessment, intervention, feedback, and learning process. To be most useful, SF–36 data need to be integrated with other clinical data. Currently, the only automated data in most physician offices are diagnostic data on claims, and SF–36 and claims software are usually not integrated. Thus, data must be combined manually for analysis. Electronic medical records will eliminate most of this difficulty, but more widely accepted data standards are needed before electronic records will gain further acceptance.

Follow-up data are the final issue. Most early users have stumbled on follow-up data capture. Better tracking and monitoring systems are needed, but the incentives are also lacking. As long as practices must defray SF–36 costs internally, then follow-up will continue to be marginal.

CASE STUDIES

Case 1

Functional health status measurement used as a "whole person vital sign" allowed a primary care physician (PCP) and a woman with profound chronic fatigue to have new conversations about an old problem in order create solutions in partnership with other health care providers. Her fatigue was multifactorial, due to depression and nasal obstruction. Serial use of SF–36 and Zung depression scales from 1994 to 1996 allowed the primary care physician to effectively treat the patient's depression while simultaneously diagnosing and treating her sleep disorder, which was caused by nasal obstruction and required two procedures to correct. It is noteworthy that the patient's Vitality score improved to 50 after the first sinus procedure and to 80 after the second surgery, and she was free of fatigue. Interestingly, the patient's insurance plan would not pay for the second procedure. The patient was so convinced that the second surgery would be beneficial that she assumed a loan to pay for the procedure herself.

L.S. is a 28-year-old architecture student with a history of debilitating fatigue since 1985. Table 19.9 contains a time line of significant events in this patient's care. During the 27-month interval described next, 11 SF–36s were obtained, but only 3 of these are mentioned and graphed in this case study. Likewise, some office visits are not mentioned.

August 23, 1994. The physician had had a telephone conference with the patient's mother 1 month earlier. The patient had been diagnosed with chronic fatigue syndrome by an internist at an academic medical center 9 years earlier. L.S. had a remote history of bingeing every day without purging and gained 25 pounds after 1 year. She weighed 125 pounds 4 years ago. Her mother stated that her daughter "sleeps a lot and hides out." Although the patient finished a master's degree in architecture, she was too debilitated to even interview for jobs. A 30-min exam was scheduled.

Although her primary complaint was fatigue especially after exercise and in mid-afternoon, L.S. also expressed concerns about irregular menses, which were 36–40 days apart, lasting 4–5 days and accompanied by hand and knee pain. She also acknowledged worry about stress, work, relationships, and money. The primary care physician noted that L.S. had seen multiple providers in the past, including two endocrinologists and two psychiatrists in addition to the academic medical center evaluation in another state (see Table 19.9).

Past medical history was significant for mononucleosis in 1989, giant-cell tumor of the hand in 1990, and negative TB skin test in 1993. Surgery included tumor excision in 1990 and cervical cryotherapy in 1991. L.S. reported allergies/intolerances to Trazodone. Her current medications included Prozac 20 mg qd × 6 months and Doxepin 25 mg hs × 4 years. The family history was remarkable in that her father had rheumatoid arthritis and depression, and her mother had an unstable back that was fused in 1993; she also had interstitial cystitis.

Physical exam revealed weight 174 pounds, height 5 feet 4 inches, temperature 98.1°F, and blood pressure 110/70; the exam was otherwise normal except for mild obesity. Lab tests, including urinalysis, complete blood count, Pap smear, rheumatoid factor, FANA, thyroid, and sedimentation rate, were all normal.

The initial SF–36 results for this date are shown in Fig. 19.1. All scores are quite low for a 28 year old, and Vitality is markedly reduced. The summary scores are not shown on the graph, but the Physical Component Summary score was one-half standard deviation below the U.S. population average, and the Mental Component Summary score was two standard deviations below average.

Because of the low mental health score, the Beck anxiety scale and Zung depression scale were automatically administered by a medical assistant. The Beck scale in-

TABLE 19.9

Time Line of Health Events for Patient L.S.

Date	VT	MH	Zung Depression	Beck Anxiety	Health Events
1985					Evaluation in academic medical center—
					Diagnosis: chronic fatigue syndrome;
					Start antidepressant 1
					Psychiatrist 1 changes to antidepressant 2
					Endocrinologist 2
					Psychiatrist 2 changes to antidepressant 3
1993 June	(Began at this practice)				
August					Initial office visit; old records requested
1994 May					Follow-up for fatigue; TRH stimulation test; continue antidepressant 4
August	15	48	Moderate-marked	Minimal-moderate	Practice began using scanner for SF-36
					Complete exam with SF-36; self-care plan 1
October					Referral to infectious disease specialist 2
					Referral to endocrinologist 3
November					Sleep study 1 revealed nasal obstruction
December					Referral to ENT
1995 January	20	32	Moderate-marked	Minimal-moderate	Nasal surgery 1; change to antidepressant 5
April	50	72	Normal	Normal	Sleep study 2
June	55	72			Referral to psychiatrist 3; change to antidepressant 6; add Ritalin
December					Nasal surgery 2
February			Normal	Normal	Self-care plan 2
1996 November	88	94	Normal	Normal	Phone/fax follow-up; patient continues on antidepressant 6 and Ritalin

612

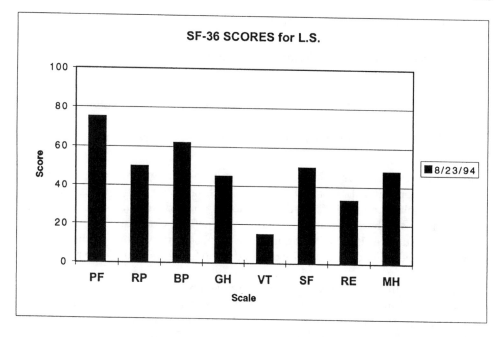

FIG. 19.1.   Patient L.S., initial SF–36 graph.

dicated minimal to moderate anxiety, whereas the Zung scale indicated moderate to marked depression.

The primary care physician (PCP) used the health status graph assessment interview to interpret the measures to the patient and ask clarifying questions to find the reasons for low scores. Based on SF–36 graph assessment and depression and anxiety screeners, the doctor negotiated the following health plan with the patient:

- Fatigue for 9 years: make appointments with infectious disease specialist in October 1994 and endocrinologist in September 1994.
- Myalgias/joint pain: check labs, change medications, consider future need for physical therapy.
- Irregular menses: check thyroid.
- Exercise deficiency: walk 20 minutes 4 times a week.
- Weight: decide optimal weight maintenance goal at follow-up visit in November 1994.
- Feelings of depression and sadness: acknowledge these simply as feelings and steer away from labeling a "diagnosis" as though it would be lifelong. Instead, the focus was placed on working to increase the patient's Vitality measure.

Responding to the question about her general health perception, the patient stated that she wanted to improve her overall health, mainly in the areas of weight and exercise. Specifically, she contracted with the doctor to do the following in the next 12 months:

1. Get control of my overeating and fast food diet; develop a well-balanced normal eating pattern based on moderation.
2. Achieve and maintain optimal body weight—130–135 lbs.

3. Implement a new exercise program that would help me lose weight and increase my overall muscle tone.

Finally, I want to work with my doctors to find a treatment plan for my fatigue that I can live with long-term.

The physician's clinical management strategy was to see the patient every 2 to 3 months until things were resolved. Frequent contact was a key element of patient's care. This is why one-time academic medical center mega-workups often do not help.

January 30, 1995. Reason for visit was follow-up of fatigue and a new complaint of possible depression. L.S. stated she was "feeling down, different from fatigue, don't like myself much, and it's hard for me to get going during the day." Sleep studies done in November 1994 showed nasal obstruction. Consequently, patient had surgery on January 4, 1995, to straighten her nasal septum. Although the ear–nose–throat (ENT) specialist did not do the turbinates, he felt she should have recovered in 4 weeks.

At this point, the primary care physician revised her assessment and wondered if patient was still clinically depressed. L.S. had made no progress on exercise and was not doing the work of job hunting. Beck and Zung scales were still abnormal and unchanged. The patient was started on Paxil, 20 mg daily, for fatigue and depression.

The septoplasty and antidepressant effects as well as the patient's "self-care plan" were checked with the Health and Disease Questionnaire (HDQ), which consists of the SF–36 and a tool called the Life Management Skills Questionnaire. To improve her life management skills, L.S. was referred to the health coordinator for a 50-min session to create her own self-care plan and to contract for follow-up on her life management strategy.

March 22, 1995. The patient complained of fatigue and concern about side effects of the antidepressant. Although the patient was feeling very good, she was concerned about "yawning on Paxil." She was sleeping 10–11 hours per day, but only occasionally satisfied.

As seen in Fig. 19.2, SF–36 scores for this date were improved on all scales, although Vitality continued low at 50. Beck anxiety scale and Zung depression scales were normal.

The PCP concluded that fatigue and depression were improved, but L.S. wanted to change to either Zoloft or Effexor. Clinician also decided to recheck sleep study to reevaluate sleep disorder because depression was clearly better but fatigue was not totally resolved. The patient was referred to a psychiatrist for further management of antidepressant therapy. She saw the third psychiatrist in June 1995, and developed a medication strategy including gradual changes in antidepressants and emphasizing those that avoid fatigue; Ritalin was also started.

February 14, 1996. L.S. was seen for follow-up of fatigue and an annual checkup. Although she was sometimes tired all day, yawning, unable to concentrate, and slept 12 or more hours a day, Ritalin and the second nasal surgery in December 1995 made her much better. When asked about reasons for improvement, she stated her improvement was due first to nasal surgery, second Ritalin, third new job, and fourth antidepressant. Her current medications included Ritalin 10 mg bid and Zoloft 50 mg

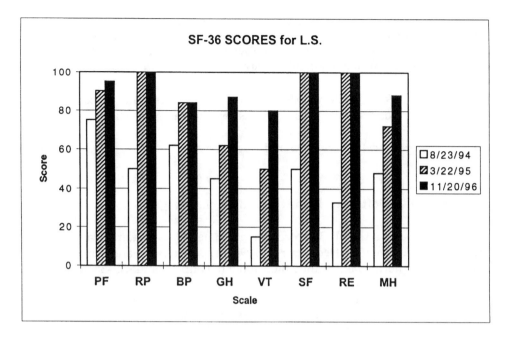

FIG. 19.2. Patient L.S., three sets of SF–36 results.

qd. Patient stated, "I'm feeling good; feel a lot better; my sleep pattern is better. When I'm awake I feel awake; I have a good social life."

PCP's assessment: some daytime sleepiness and yawning; OK to observe; doing so much better. Fatigue—dramatically better. Continue Zoloft and Ritalin.

The patient's 12-month goals were:

> Now that my fatigue sleep disorder is under control, I would like to focus on my physical well-being. For me this means losing weight, lowering my cholesterol, and being more physically active, increasing muscle tone and strength. I need to develop a plan to achieve these goals in a way that fits with my life-style.

Five-year goals were:

> I would like to find myself physically, emotionally, and economically secure. I would like to feel that my physical health is at its optimum. This includes fatigue, sleep, weight, emotional, and physical strength. I would like to look back at these 5 years and feel I've been at my best—not just struggling to get there.

L.S. concluded:

> As far as my medical experience, I look back with disappointment at all the doctors who just told me that I was depressed. I knew that my fatigue and sleep patterns were not normal and they were a major frustration in my life, so of course I had symptoms of depression, but it was a result of, not a cause of, my physical state. I wanted to find the true cause and treat it directly. It was frustrating to have the doctors throw drugs at me without really finding the problem that they were treating. As a result, none of the medications really worked. Sometimes they helped, but I never felt that they were truly the right solution. My family doctor really listened and tackled the problem of diagnosis

logically—ruling out possible causes one at a time until we found the true cause and a true solution. Other doctors were content to have me on medications even if they helped only a little. My doctor helped me find the answers for me and my body and my problem so I could be healthy and as a result, happy.

November 20, 1996.   Follow-up SF–36 was faxed to patient and a phone interview was conducted. Positive events as perceived by the patient were:

- Nasal surgery in January 1995 and December 1995.
- Ritalin.
- A job in a field I enjoy.
- Prompted—Zoloft helps keep worry in check.

Figure 19.2 shows the SF–36 scores for this date. All are dramatically improved and essentially normal. On December 23, 1996, the Beck anxiety and Zung depression scales were also normal. L.S. commented about the impact of the SF–36 in her care:

I just had doctor after doctor tell me, "It's just depression, all in your head." Initially, I was taken aback by [my family doctor] asking me to fill out surveys. I thought, "I can tell you what's wrong." I had done it so many times with all the other doctors before. But it helped her ask me more questions back in areas I didn't even think of. With the way my family doctor communicated with me, I was no longer isolated by one specialist here and one specialist there. Everyone was communicating together, and that was very satisfying to me.

L.S. was treated for bronchitis on July 10, 1998. An SF–36 on that date was essentially unchanged from the December 1996 assessment.

Case 2

In this case, generic health-related quality-of-life or health status assessment was integrated into the diagnostic process during an episodic visit for a patient who had consulted other health care providers in the same group about multiple complaints.

June 10, 1996.   P.D. is a 42-year-old computer graphics company employee who presented to the office with multiple medical complaints. Her primary complaints were sudden onset of weakness, palpitations, and mild fast breathing for 1 hr earlier in the day. The patient also complained of intermittent lower abdominal pain and low back pain for at least 1 year. In addition, she had had a recent illness of "flu" with some mild nausea and vomiting and fatigue 2 weeks ago. P.D. also mentioned some occasional flushing and expressed a concern about menopause. Further questioning revealed that she had three episodes of the same primary complaint in the prior 2 months and admitted to varying degrees of feeling anxious or worried.

P.D. completed an SF–36 at the beginning of the visit in the waiting room, and the graph (Fig. 19.3) was available after the initial history was obtained. Interpretation of the SF–36 results for this date pointed to abnormally low scores across the board in both physical and mental health dimensions, in particular a Mental Health score of 48 and Vitality of 20.

Based on the scripted health status graph assessment questions, the patient revealed that she attributed her limitations in her usual and daily activities to the phys-

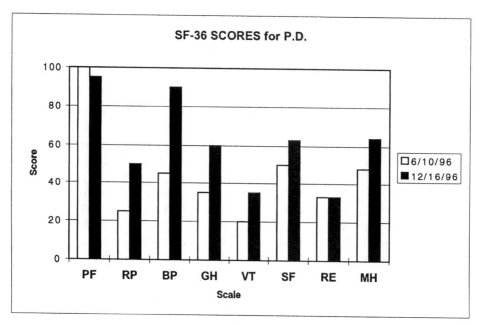

FIG. 19.3. Patient P.D., initial and follow-up SF–36 results.

ical symptoms of pain as well as "weakness." Furthermore, she ascribed her pain source to 60% lower abdomen and 40% low back. P.D. said her limitations in daily activities due to emotional health concerns were due to being worried. She also stated that her low energy levels might be due to 70+ hours of work per week. The health negotiation to improve her general health was to "resolve all her symptoms in the last several months, to make sure that nothing is significantly wrong, and increase energy levels so that [she] could enjoy life more."

Her past medical history was significant for remote peptic ulcer. She had been taking Prilosec for the past month. P.D. previously denied any black tarry stools or diarrhea, and she had had infrequent bowel movements in the past. She had recently been to the local emergency room for abdominal pain with a negative laboratory workup including urinalysis, hemogram, and serum chemistries including glucose, blood urea nitrogen (BUN), creatinine, sodium, and potassium. Abdominal plain films were also negative. She was signed out as abdominal pain of uncertain etiology. There was no history of major surgery and no allergies. P.D. did not smoke, and drank less than one glass of wine a week. A chart review revealed a normal thyroid-stimulating hormone (TSH) level to rule out thyroid disease during a health maintenance visit 1 year earlier.

The combined data from the SF–36 and subsequent graph assessment led the PCP to suspect that the dizziness and other nonspecific symptoms could be secondary to panic/anxiety, probably due to ongoing concerns. In addition, low back pain and lower abdominal pain were suspected to represent possible irritable bowel syndrome. The initial plan and strategy at the end of the 30-min visit was to decrease patient stress by resolving outstanding issues through the use of colonoscopy and a complete physical exam in 4 weeks. She was started on Imipramine for panic symptoms and possible reactive depression.

Four weeks later, P.D. was seen for a comprehensive physical exam. She reported that her episodes of palpitations, weakness, and sweating had decreased significantly since starting Imipramine. P.D. was only having occasional epigastric pain, but experienced constipation over the last 10 days. Imipramine was increased to 100 mg per day. She underwent colonoscopy with negative findings 1 week later.

December 16, 1996.   P.D. was not seen in follow-up until 6 months later because of a job change in the interim. She had continued on Imipramine. A repeat SF–36 and graph assessment were done. The SF–36 results for this date are presented in Fig. 19.3.

Although P.D. experienced occasional anxiety symptoms and worry, she felt significantly improved overall. The trend assessment revealed that she attributed her mental health improvement to "thinking more clearly, no longer worrying, and taking more control of my life." She felt that her improvement in physical health was related to eating much better, taking vitamins, and decreased physical symptoms of anxiety because she could readily recognize them at an early stage. Indeed, she was having rare episodes of lower abdominal pain, back pain, or constipation. When prompted about medication, she acknowledged that Imipramine had also been important.

Addendum.   Although there was definite improvement on most of the scales, many of the scores (see Fig. 19.3), particularly Role Physical, General Health, Vitality, Social Function, and Role Emotional, are low for a 42-year-old person. Additional follow-up is needed to help P.D. maintain or improve on these gains. This is exactly the kind of person who needs periodic attention and SF–36 assessment (at least every 6 months) to monitor status. Although it is not possible to cure every ailment, everyone has a "personal best" to which they can aspire. Medicine's major challenge is to help people reach their personal best level of health.

SUMMARY

The SF–36 is a generic or whole-person health status instrument consisting of eight scales that assess most of the important dimensions of health status. The scales include Physical Function (PF), Role Physical (RP), Bodily Pain (BP), General Health (GH), Vitality (VT), Social Function (SF), Role Emotional (RE), and Mental Health (MH). Each scale is scored on a 0 to 100 basis; 100 always represents the most favorable result.

The SF–36 can provide significant help for busy primary care clinicians. It facilitates and focuses listening and can be viewed as a vital sign or laboratory test. With eight scales it covers the mental-physical health continuum and is reliable, sensitive, and valid. Patients like to complete the SF–36 and feel that it shows a concern for their viewpoint and feelings; most patients can complete it in 8 min or less.

Over 1200 studies have included the SF–36, and it has been tested in over 40 countries. Norms are available for the overall U.S. population and for age and gender subgroups. Although true norms are not available for patients with various diseases and conditions, comparative data are available for a large number of maladies.

A variety of techniques can be used to capture SF–36 data and report the results. New technology involving touchscreen devices and hand-held computers promises to reduce patient and staff burdens. Physicians considering using the SF–36 should do a careful assessment of their own situations and the various possibilities. It is imperative to train office personnel and conduct small pilot tests to iron out the inevitable bugs that accompany any new activity.

When patients complete their first SF–36, it is a screening tool that is especially useful for detecting psychosocial problems. However, it does not provide definitive diagnostic information, and secondary screeners or more definitive evaluative tests must be used. Bush and Lum have developed an interpretive approach for the SF–36 called *health status graph assessment*. Health status graph assessment is a standardized, structured approach to interpreting health status measures, determining the underlying reasons for low scores, and negotiating a health plan with the patient in the exam room. Graph assessment can provide a critical bridge for the transmission of unique "patient stories" into standardized clinical data.

Although this is appropriate for use in all primary care patient encounters, Bush and Lum have found that health status graph assessment is particularly helpful for patients with multiple complaints, ill-defined symptoms such as fatigue, gastrointestinal complaints and chest pain, chronic pain, chronic disease management, depression screening, elective surgery, health maintenance/wellness, and patients with a history of high utilization. Health status graph assessment involves four basic steps: (a) explain the health status measures to the patient, (b) identify and confirm low measures, (c) ask the essential questions for each low measure, and (d) apply the answers to support clinical decision(s). Bush and Lum found that the rigorous use of scripted interpretations and questions facilitate learning graph assessment.

Although the SF–36 will detect most patients with depression, it is not specific for depression. A Mental Health score of 60 or less has been found to correlate with a high prevalence of psychosocial distress. Depending on the underlying prevalence of depression in a practice population, approximately 30% to 50% of those with low Mental Health scores will be depressed. Those who are not depressed may have other disorders such as anxiety or somatization. However, many will not have specific diagnoses according to *DSM-IV*. Yet most of these patients have high utilization rates and low scores on other scales.

The medical care system is not configured to help patients with subsyndromal or subthreshold problems. New techniques involving education are promising. Two impediments to helping these patients are physicians' dislike of them and administrative and reimbursement constraints. Many of these patients are frustrating and will never be cured in the traditional sense. The goal should be to care for them and recognize that they can be helped even if there is no cure. Enabling physicians in this role will require changes by physicians and system changes. Physicians using the SF–36 and health status graph assessment achieve more success with these patients and derive greater satisfaction from their work. However, these inroads will not occur in a context of 10-min appointment blocks. The entire incentive system needs to change to reward improving health instead of just delivering health care.

Even though early experience with the SF–36 is promising, more study is needed to determine its true value in primary care. Pilot studies are needed to refine effective teaching methods and implementation procedures. New developments in the instrument itself promise increased precision and accuracy. Combined with standard clinical data, SF–36 data will yield new process-outcome insights and provide clinicians with new ways to learn from and help their patients achieve their personal best level of health.

ACKNOWLEDGMENT

This chapter is dedicated to Milton H. Seifert, Jr., MD.

REFERENCES

Bjorner, J. B., & Ware, J. E. (1998). Using modern psychometric methods to measure health outcomes. *Medical Outcomes Trust Monitor, 3*(2), 12–17.

Brazier, J. E., Harper, R., Jones, N. M. B., O'Cathain, A., Thomas, K. J., Usherwood, T., & Westlake, L. (1992). Validating the SF–36 Health Survey questionnaire: New outcome measure for primary care. *British Medical Journal, 305,* 160–164.

Burnum, J. F. (1982). Diagnosis of depression in a general medical practice: Observations on "lack of pizzazz," the "blahs," and other complaints. *Postgraduate Medicine, 72*(3), 71–73, 76.

Bush, D. M., & Lum, D. L. (1998). *The health status graph assessment.* Unpublished manuscript.

Commission on Chronic Illness. (1957). *Chronic illness in the United States, Vol. 1.* Cambridge, MA: Commonwealth Fund, Harvard University Press.

Committee E-11 on Quality and Statistics. (1995). *Manual on presentation of data and control chart analysis* (6th ed.). Philadelphia, PA: American Society for Testing and Materials.

Croog, S. H., Levine, S., Testa, M. A., Brown, B., Bulpitt, C. J., Jenkins, D., Klerman, G. L., & Williams, G. H. (1986). The effects of hypertensive therapy on the quality of life. *New England Journal of Medicine, 314,* 1657–1664.

Deming, W. E. (1986). Foreword. In W. A. Shewhart, *Statistical method from the viewpoint of quality control* (pp. i–ii). New York: Dover.

Depression Guideline Panel. (1993). *Depression in primary care: Clinical practice guideline.* Rockville, MD: U.S. Department of Health and Human Services, Public Health Service, Agency for Health Care Policy and Research.

Feinstein, A. (1987). *Clinimetrics.* New Haven, CT: Yale University Press.

Hales, R. E., Hilty, D. A., & Wise, M. G. (1997). A treatment algorithm for the management of anxiety in primary care practice. *Journal of Clinical Psychiatry, 58*(suppl 3), 76–80.

Hays, R. D., & Hadorn, D. (1992). Responsiveness to change: An aspect of validity, not a separate dimension. *Quality of Life Research, 1,* 73–75.

Hemingway, H., Nicholson, A., Stafford, M., Roberts, R., & Marmot, M. (1997). The impact of socioeconomic status on health functioning as assessed by the SF–36 questionnaire: The Whitehall II study. *American Journal of Public Health,* 1484–1490.

Hemingway, H., Stafford, M., Stansfeld, S., Shipley, M., & Marmot, M. (1997). Is the SF–36 a valid measure of change in population health? Results from the Whitehall II study. *British Medical Journal, 315,* 1273–1279.

Iezzoni, L. I. (Ed). (1997). *Risk adjustment for measuring health care outcomes* (2nd ed.). Ann Arbor, MI: Health Administration Press.

Jachuck, S. J., Brierly, H., Jachuck, S., & Willcox, P. M. (1982). The effect of hypotensive drugs on the quality of life. *Journal of the Royal College of General Practitioners, 32* (February), 103–105.

Jenkinson, C., Coulter, A., & Wright, L. (1993). Short form 36 (SF–36) health survey questionnaire: Normative data for adults of working age. *British Medical Journal, 306,* 1437–1440.

Kania, C. (1996). The Health Status Questionnaire—A three consortium update. *Quality Source, 4*(1), 1–7.

Katon, W., Von Korff, M., Lin, E., Unützer, J., Simon, G., Walker, E., Ludman, E., & Bush, T. (1997). Population-based care of depression: Effective disease management strategies to decrease prevalence. *General Hospital Psychiatry, 19,* 169–178.

Katz, J. N., Chang, L. C., Sangha, O., Fossel, A. H., & Bates, D. W. (1996). Can comorbidity be measured by questionnaire rather than medical record review? *Medical Care, 34,* 73–84.

Keller, S. D., Bayliss, L. S., Ware, J. E., Hsu, M. A., Damiano, A. M., & Goss, T. F. (1997). Comparison of responses to SF–36 Health Survey questions with one-week and four-week recall periods. *Health Services Research, 32,* 367–384.

Koop, C. E. (1998). Patient-provider communication and managed care. *Group Practice Journal, 47*(5), 57–58.

Labanowski, M., & Kania, C. (1996). Insomnia and health. *Quality Source, 4*(1), 14–16.

Lembcke, P. A. (1952). Measuring the quality of medical care through vital statistics based on hospital service . . . appendectomy. *American Journal of Public Health, 42,* 276.

Leplège, A., & Hunt, S. (1997). The problem of quality of life in medicine. *Journal of the American Medical Association, 278,* 47–50.

Manocchia, M., Bayliss, L. S., Connor, J., Keller, S. D., Shiely, J. C., Tsai, C., Voris, R. A., & Ware, J. E. (1998). *SF-36 health survey annotated bibliography: Second edition (1988–1996).* Boston: Health Assessment Lab.

McHorney, C. A., Kosinski, M., & Ware, J. E. (1994). Comparisons of the costs and quality of norms for the SF-36 health survey collected by mail versus telephone interview: Results from a national survey. *Medical Care, 32,* 551–567.

Meyer, K. B., Espindle, D. M., DeGiacomo, J. M., Jenuleson, C. S., Kurtin, P. S., & Davies, A. R. (1994). Monitoring dialysis patients' health status. *American Journal of Kidney Diseases, 24,* 267–279.

Murawski, M. M., & Miederhoff, P. A. (1998). On the generalizability of statistical expressions of health related quality of life instrument responsiveness: A data synthesis. *Quality of Life Research, 7,* 11–22.

Nerenz, D. R., Repasky, D. P., Whitehouse, F. W., & Kahkonen, D. M. (1992). Ongoing assessment of health status in patients with diabetes mellitus. *Medical Care, 30,* MS112–MS124.

Nunnally, J. C., & Bernstein, I. H. (1994). *Psychometric theory* (3rd ed.). New York: McGraw-Hill.

Parkerson, G. R., Broadhead, W. E., & Tse, C. K. J. (1993). The Duke Severity of Illness Checklist (DUSOI) for measurement of severity and comorbidity. *Journal of Clinical Epidemiology, 46,* 379–393.

Parkerson, G. R., Hammond, W. E. & Yarnall, K. S. (1994). Feasibility and potential clinical usefulness of a computerized severity of illness measure. *Archives of Family Medicine, 3,* 968–974.

Pearce, K. A., Evans, G. W., Summerson, J., & Rao, J. S. (1997). Comparisons of ambulatory blood pressure monitoring and repeated office measurements in primary care. *Journal of Family Practice, 45,* 426–33.

Robinson, P., Katon, W., Von Korff, M., Bush, T., Simon, G., Lin, E., & Walker, E. (1997). The education of depressed primary care patients: What do patients think of interactive booklets and a video? *Journal of Family Practice, 44,* 562–571.

Rost, K., Burnam, M. A., & Smith, G. R. (1993). Development of screeners for depressive disorders and substance disorder history. *Medical Care, 31,* 189–200.

Rubenstein, L. V., McCoy, J. M., Cope, D. W., Barrett, P. A., Hirsch, S. H., Messer, K. S., & Young, R. T. (1995). Improving patient quality of life with feedback to physicians about functional status. *Journal of General Internal Medicine, 10,* 607–614.

Schlenk, E. A., Erien, A., Dunbar-Jacob, J., McDowell, J., Engberg, S., Sereika, S. M., Rohay, J. M., & Bernier, M. J. (1998). Health-related quality of life in chronic disorders: A comparison across studies using the MOS SF-36. *Quality of Life Research, 7,* 57–65.

Seifert, M. H., & Otteson, O. J. (1994). *Health care that works: A plan for transforming our national health care system.* Spring Park, MN: M. D. Publishing.

Sherbourne, C. D., Jackson, C. A., Meredith, L. S., Camp, P., & Wells, K. B. (1996). Prevalence of comorbid anxiety disorders in primary care outpatients. *Archives of Family Medicine, 5,* 27–35.

Simon, G. E., & Katzelnick, D. J. (1997). Depression, use of medical services and cost-offset effects. *Journal of Psychosomatic Research, 42,* 333–344.

Simon, G. E., Lin, E. H. B., Katon, W., Saunders, K., Von Korff, M., Walker, E., Bush, T., & Robinson, P. (1995). Outcomes of "inadequate" antidepressant treatment. *Journal of General Internal Medicine, 10,* 663–670.

Simon, G. E., Revicki, D. A., Grothaus, L., & Von Korff, M. (1998). SF-36 summary scores: Are physical and mental health truly distinct? *Medical Care, 36,* 567–572.

Stewart-Brown, S., & Layte, R. (1997). Emotional health problems are the most important cause of disability in adults of working age: A study in the four counties of the old Oxford region. *Journal of Epidemiology and Community Health, 51,* 672–675.

Wagner, E. H., Austin, B. T., & Von Korff, M. (1996). Organizing care for patients with chronic illness. *Milbank Quarterly, 74,* 511–543.

Ware, J. E., Jr., Kosinski, M., & Keller, S. D. (1994). *SF-36 physical and mental health summary scales: A user's manual.* Boston: Health Institute, New England Medical Center.

Ware, J. E., Jr., Snow, K. K., Kosinski, M., & Gandek, B. (1993). *SF-36 health survey manual and interpretation guide.* Boston: Health Institute, New England Medical Center.

Wells, K. B., Sturm, R., & Sherbourne, C. D. (1996). *Caring for depression.* Cambridge, MA: Harvard University Press.

The Primary Care Assessment Survey: A Tool for Measuring, Monitoring, and Improving Primary Care

Alison Murray
Dana Gelb Safran
The Health Institute, Boston

Primary care has been defined as "the provision of integrated, accessible health care services by clinicians who are accountable for addressing a large majority of personal health care needs, developing a sustained partnership with patients, and practicing in the context of family and the community" (Institute of Medicine, [IOM] 1996). A noteworthy feature of this and previous definitions of primary care is that primary care is defined in terms of characteristics of the care itself, rather than in terms of characteristics of the clinicians who provide it (e.g., generalist, specialist, physician, nurse practitioner) or the setting in which it is provided.

The Primary Care Assessment Survey (PCAS) is a brief, validated, patient-completed questionnaire designed to operationalize this definition of primary care (Safran et al., 1998a). The survey is intended for performance measurement and quality improvement at the individual physician, group practice, health plan, or delivery system level. The PCAS provides an assessment of seven domains of primary care through 11 summary scales, as follows: access (financial and organizational), continuity (relationship duration, visit-based), comprehensiveness ("whole-person" knowledge of the patient, preventive counseling), integration of care, quality of the clinical interaction (clinician-patient communication, thoroughness of physical examinations), interpersonal treatment, and trust (Safran et al., 1998a). Figure 20.1 illustrates the seven domains and 11 summary scales that comprise the PCAS.

All concepts in the PCAS are measured in the context of a specific clinician–patient primary care relationship, and reference the entirety of that relationship (i.e., they are not visit specific). This is consistent with the IOM definition (Institute of Medicine, 1996) and our own definitional study results (Safran, 1994), which emphasize primary care to be predicated on a sustained clinician–patient relationship. A single screener item is used to determine whether the respondent has an established relationship with a primary clinician (or team of primary clinicians). Only those indicating such a relationship complete the remaining PCAS items. The PCAS was developed for use in a general adult population, although a pediatric version of the questionnaire has been developed.

FIG. 20.1.   Essential attributes of primary care measured by the Primary Care Assessment Survey (PCAS).

This chapter begins by providing an overview of the rationale for using patient-provided information to assess primary care performance. It then describes the development of the PCAS and summarizes its measurement properties, some current uses of the PCAS for quality assessment and improvement, and practical information about its use.

OVERVIEW

Why Use Patient-Provided Information About Care?

With the increasing emphasis on quality assessment and continuous quality improvement, patients have emerged as an important source of information about health care. Patient-provided information about health care has important strengths and limitations that must be taken into account in designing a quality assessment initiative and interpreting data from it.

With respect to primary care quality assessment, there are four salient strengths of patient-provided information. First, patient-provided data are generally less expensive to obtain than comparable data from other sources (e.g., health plan administration, physician, other health staff; Davies and Ware, 1988). Second, because no documentation of performance on many defining elements of primary care currently exists in administrative data collection systems, information must be obtained either by observation of the primary care process (which would be both costly and intrusive) or from its participants (i.e., patient, clinician, plan). In this case, patients have less motivation to distort ratings and reports than would sources who are directly involved in and accountable for care.

Third, the reliability and validity of patient-provided information concerning important elements of care, including access, continuity, and interpersonal treatment have been extensively documented (Aday & Anderson, 1975; Aday, Anderson, & Fleming, 1980; Brown & Adams, 1992; Davies et al., 1986; Gerbert & Hargreaves, 1986; Office of Technology Assessment, 1988; Sox, Margulies, & Sox, 1981; Ware et al., 1976). For example, studies have shown that patients' assessments of the interpersonal aspects of care accord with assessments made by trained observers of the medical encounter (DiMatteo et al., 1980; Stiles, 1979). Moreover, patient reports about specific occurrences related to their care (e.g., whether a test was performed, a treatment recommended, a particular clinician seen) have been shown to be highly accurate—in fact, as accurate as physicians' reports about these occurrences (Brown & Adams, 1992; Davies & Ware, 1988; Gerbert & Hargreaves, 1986; Lewis, 1988; Montano & Phillips, 1995; Zapka et al., 1995).

Patient assessments of technical quality of care are the sole exception, and represent an important limitation of patient-provided information concerning health care. With respect to the technical quality of care, evidence concerning the reliability and validity of patient-provided information is mixed. On the one hand, patients have been shown to appropriately discriminate between encounters judged by physicians to differ in the quality of medical history taking and physical examination (Davies & Ware, 1988; Ware, 1978). On the other hand, there is evidence that patients' ratings of technical quality of care are influenced by the amount of care received (i.e., more is better) and by the interpersonal treatment (Davies, Ware, Brook, Peterson, & Newhouse, 1986; Gerbert & Hargreaves, 1986; Office of Technology Assessment, 1988; Sox et al., 1981; Ware et al., 1976). For this reason, as noted earlier, the PCAS includes only a limited assessment related to technical quality (i.e., an item concerning thoroughness of physical examination for which the reliability and validity of patient-provided information has been established).

A final advantage of patient-provided information about care is that patients' assessments of their care have been linked to important outcomes of care, including patients' adherence to medical advice, utilization and care-seeking behavior (including disenrollment from a physician's practice or a health plan), and self-assessed health outcomes (Safran et al., 1998d; Ware & Davies, 1983a). Studies of adherence, for example, have demonstrated that it is positively associated with effective clinician-patient communication (DiMatteo, 1994; DiMatteo et al., 1993; Smith, Polis, & Hadac, 1981), continuity in the clinician–patient relationship (Becker, Drachman, & Kirscht, 1974; Charney et al., 1967), and humane interpersonal treatment (Eraker, Kirscht, & Becker, 1984; Francis, Korsch, & Morris, 1969). More recently, a study using the PCAS reaffirmed the relationship of each of these with adherence, but suggested that patients' trust in their physician and the physician's comprehensive knowledge of the patient supersede all other factors in the strength of their relationship to adherence (Safran et al., 1998d). With all other factors held constant, adherence rates were nearly three times higher in primary care relationships characterized by very high levels of trust and "whole-person" knowledge than in those with very low levels.

PCAS scales were also significant predictors of patient satisfaction with their physician, and of patients' self-reported changes in overall health during the previous 4 years.

In summary, patient-provided information about care represents considerably more than a simplistic marker of patient satisfaction. A substantial body of empirical research demonstrates that patients can reliably report about and evaluate numerous essential aspects of health care. Moreover, in addition to providing an accurate portrayal of the patient's health care experience, patient-provided information about care predicts important outcomes of care. In this way, patients' assessments of health care are distinguished from assessments of other services that people are asked to evaluate. Unlike an airline passenger, for example, whose assessment of the service received on a flight has no bearing on the probability that his plane will crash, a patient's assessment of the care he or she receives is directly linked to whether his or her metaphorical "plane" will crash. The link is through patient behaviors that are influenced by the patient's experience in the care setting, particularly by the quality of relationships established with clinicians.

Development of the PCAS

The idea for the PCAS originated in earlier work by Safran, Tarlov, and Rogers (1994), which operationalized the Institute of Medicine's (1978) original definition of primary care. That definition of primary care, which was one of the first formal definitions of primary care in the United States, articulated five essential and defining characteristics of primary care: accessibility, comprehensiveness, coordination, continuity, and accountability. Using data from the Medical Outcomes Study, Safran et al. (1994) measured each of these attributes, and compared performance on them across three models of health insurance represented in the study (indemnity insurance, independent practice association [IPA]/network-model health maintenance organizations [HMOs], and staff/group-model HMOs), and across medical specialties. The results highlighted the approach to be a meaningful way to characterize primary care performance, and to identify and compare the primary care performance profiles across different groups of providers, settings, and delivery systems.

In 1994, the Institute of Medicine Committee on the Future of Primary Care proposed the revised definition of primary care noted at the beginning of the chapter. Most of the characteristics referenced are consistent with those named in the past (Alpert & Charney, 1973; Institute of Medicine, 1978; Millis, 1966; Starfield, 1992). However, two features named by the IOM are new and noteworthy. The first is the assertion that primary care requires a sustained partnership with patients. The second is the specification that primary care occurs in the context of family and the community. Although past definitions have consistently stressed the importance of continuity in primary care, the term *sustained partnership* clarifies that it is continuity of the clinician–patient relationship that is required. Moreover, by specifying that primary care occurs *in the context of family and the community*, the definition makes explicit the importance of a "whole-person" orientation in primary care practice.

The naming of these additional attributes accords with findings from the definitional study by Safran (1994), which were presented to the IOM Committee as it was formulating its revised definition. The work by Safran included a series of 90-min interviews with generalist physicians, in order to elicit their view of the defining and essential characteristics of primary care. The overwhelming majority of physicians interviewed highlighted both the notion of "sustained partnership" and of a "whole-person" orientation as central to primary care. The following excerpts illustrate the physicians' view that primary care is predicated on a sustained physician-patient relationship:

> Well, continuous care is the notion. Maybe that's a better word than ongoing. But the whole idea is that it's *not* episodic around the problem. The commitment is long-term. Which enables you to use time. One of the biggest differences between primary care and a specialist, is that a specialist is asked to answer a question at a point in time. And they, therefore, have a certain pressure to do everything they know how to do to answer that question at that point in time. A primary care physician has the luxury of following things over time, and letting time be a diagnostic help, rather than an impediment and a challenge. It's a big, big difference, and an important one.

> The other piece of continuous care is that it's a commitment to the patient that you're going to be there tomorrow and the next day. That you're—the whole thing is—what you do now is going to be building for everything you're going to be doing in the future.

> Being someone's primary care doctor is like a marriage.

And the importance of a "whole-person" orientation in primary care is well illustrated by these excerpts:

> How much do I need to know? The more I know about what's going on in a patient's life, the more likely I am to be able to help that patient.

> It's not enough just to have a very strong medical knowledge of physiology and anatomy. You've got to understand the psychosocial. And I think for primary care, that's an important part of training. Because you can miss a lot of issues and not understand them unless you're very sensitive to psychosocial issues of the person, and the person in their family and their community. . . . So it's not by organ system or age. We have a general knowledge of who the person is."

> I think to be a primary care physician, you just have to look beyond a person's organ systems. It shouldn't be, you know, from the chin to the knees.

Defining Features of the PCAS

The PCAS was developed to measure primary care in accordance with the definitional work by Safran (1994) and the definition of primary care proposed by the IOM Committee on the Future of Primary Care (Institute of Medicine, 1996). The PCAS contains 51 questions used to score 11 summary scales. The 51 PCAS items take an average of 7 min to complete in a self-administered format. The survey rates a fifth-grade reading level on the Flesch–Kincaid reading ease index, an algorithm based on the number of words per sentence and the number of syllables per 100 words (Flesch, 1951; Kincaid, Fishbourne, Rogers, & Chissom, 1975). The PCAS was developed for use in a general adult population, although a pediatric version of the questionnaire has been developed.

Consistent with results of the definitional study by Safran (1994) and the IOM definition of primary care (Institute of Medicine, 1994), all PCAS concepts are measured in the context of a specific clinician–patient primary care relationship, and reference the entirety of that relationship (i.e., not visit specific). A single screener item is used to determine whether the respondent has an established relationship with a primary clinician (or team of primary clinicians). Only those indicating such a relationship complete the remaining PCAS items. In some cases, evaluation programs using the PCAS have adapted it to evaluate the performance of a primary care team, rather than of a primary clinician. The PCAS is easily adapted in this way. However, to date, most applications of the PCAS have chosen to maintain the focus on performance of the primary clinician and have fielded a parallel set of items (not formally part of the PCAS, but available with it) to assess the performance of other members of the primary care team.

Each PCAS scale corresponds to one of the defining elements of primary care named in the IOM definition of primary care (Institute of Medicine, 1996). As with definitions of primary care, the assessment methodology encompasses both *distinguishing* features of primary care (i.e., elements that are essential and unique to primary care) and *shared* features (i.e., elements that are essential to primary care but not unique to it). For purposes of measuring primary care performance, all essential characteristics—both distinguishing and shared—should be assessed (Institute of Medicine, 1978, 1994; Starfield, 1992).

Table 20.1 summarizes the item content for each PCAS scale. The items include a combination of report-format questions (i.e., questions that ask patients to report specific information about their care) and rating-format (evaluative) questions (i.e., questions that ask patients to evaluate some aspect of their care, for example, on a scale ranging from *excellent* to *very poor*). All PCAS scales range from 0 to 100 points, with higher scores indicating more of the underlying attribute.

The PCAS was pilot tested in 1995. The first large-scale fielding of the PCAS occurred in 1996, in a federally funded study designed to compare the primary care performance of five forms of managed care, ranging from managed indemnity insurance to staff-model HMOs. In that study, a survey that included the PCAS, along with 56 supplementary questions, was mailed to a random sample of Massachusetts state employees, stratified by health plan, age, and area of residence (Safran et al., 1998a). A standard three-step mail survey protocol (Dillman, West, & Clark, 1994) yielded a response rate of 68.5% (7,204 respondents). The vast majority of respondents (89.5%) reported having a primary physician (Safran et al., 1998a). Of these, 87% named a generalist physician (general internist, family physician, or general practitioner). These findings regarding the percentage of patients who identify a primary physician and the role of subspecialists as primary physicians for a portion of patients are in keeping with those from other studies of U.S. adults (Aiken et al., 1979; Smith & Buesching, 1986; Spiegel, Rubinstein, Scott, & Brook, 1983). Data from that study provided the basis for comprehensive testing of the measurement properties of the PCAS, detailed next.

MEASUREMENT PERFORMANCE OF THE PCAS

Two stages of analysis were used to evaluate the measurement properties of the PCAS scales. In the first stage, Safran et al. (1998a) tested five scaling assumptions that must be satisfied for Likert's method of summated rating scales to be appropriately applied. This stage of analysis was applicable only to the seven scales comprised of multiple evaluative items (Table 20.1), where Likert's scaling method was used. In the second stage, all 11 scales were assessed for data completeness, score dis-

TABLE 20.1

Descriptive Characteristics and Content of the Primary Care Assessment Survey (PCAS) Scales

Scale	Number of Item[a]	Response Format	Item Content
Financial Access	2	Rating	Assessment of the amount of money patient pays for doctor visits, and for prescribed treatments.
Organizational Access	6	Rating	Ability to get through to the physician's office by telephone, to get a medical appointment when sick, and to obtain information by telephone, punctuality of appointments, convenience of office location, and convenience of office hours.
Longitudinal Continuity	1	Report	Duration of patient's relationship with primary physician.
Visit-Based Continuity	2	Report	How often patient sees primary physician (not an assistant or partner) for routine checkups, and for appointments when sick.
Contextual Knowledge of the Patient	5	Rating	Primary physician's knowledge of patient's medical history, responsibilities at work, home or school, principal health concerns, values, and beliefs.
Preventive Counseling	7	Report	Whether primary physician has discussed the following with patient: smoking, alcohol use, seat belt use, diet, exercise, stress, safe sex.[b]
Integration	6	Rating	Assessment of primary physician's role in coordinating and synthesizing care received from specialists and/or while patient was hospitalized.
Communication	6	Rating	Thoroughness of primary physician's questions about symptoms, attention to what patient says, clarity of explanations and instructions, and advice and help in making decisions about care.
Physical Exams	1	Rating	Thoroughness of primary physician's physical examinations of patient.
Interpersonal Treatment	5	Rating	Primary physician's patience, friendliness, caring, respect and time spent with patient.
Trust	8	Rating	Assessment of primary physician's integrity, competence, and role as the patient's agent.

[a]The PCAS includes 51 items: 49 items listed here and 2 screener items (not listed). Only patients who respond affirmatively to the first screener item (indicate having a primary clinician or team of primary clinicians) complete the remaining PCAS items. Only patients who report having received specialty and/or hospital care (second screener item) complete the items in the "integration" scale.

[b]These topics correspond to seven behavioral risks that the U.S. Preventive Services Task Force (1989) recommends every primary physician address with every adult patient, regardless of age, sex, race, ethnicity, or other personal characteristics. Attention to preventive care has been suggested as a useful proxy for comprehensiveness of care, given the difficulty of otherwise monitoring and quantifying all services and treatments provided.

tribution characteristics, and interscale correlations. All analyses were conducted in the combined population and replicated in 16 population subgroups defined according to age, sex, race, years of education, household income, and health status. Subgroup analyses were conducted to assure that measures performed adequately across varied segments of the population.

The results suggest that the PCAS has excellent measurement properties and that it performs consistently well across varied sectors of the population. Details of the methods and results of these analyses are summarized in the following sections.

Tests of Likert Scaling Assumptions

Seven PCAS scales are scored based on Likert's method of summated rating scales. The Likert method assumes that item responses in each scale can be summed without standardization or weighting (Likert, 1932). Five scaling assumptions must be met for this form of item aggregation to be appropriate. These assumptions are:

1. That each item correlates substantially with its hypothesized scale (item-convergent validity).
2. That items within a scale correlate more substantially with their hypothesized scale than with any other scale (item-discriminant validity).
3. That items within a scale have approximately equal means and variances (equal item variance).
4. That all items in a scale contribute approximately the same proportion of information about the underlying concept (equal item–scale correlations).
5. That scores be reproducible and reliable (score reliability).

Revised Multitrait Attribute Program, a microcomputer software application for psychometric testing, was used to test these five assumptions in the seven multi-item evaluative scales (Hays & Hayshi, 1990).

Results from tests of five scaling assumptions are summarized in Table 20.2 and described in the sections that follow. For a more complete report about these results, see Safran et al. (1998a).

Item-Convergent Validity. This scaling assumption is evaluated on the basis of item–scale correlations (i.e., each item with its hypothesized scale). Item-convergent validity is supported if, after correcting for overlap (i.e., estimating the item–scale correlation with the item removed from its hypothesized scale) (Howard & Forehand, 1962), an item correlates at .30 or greater with its hypothesized scale. All PCAS item–scale correlations (corrected for overlap) well exceeded the accepted minimum (.30) in the combined population and all population subgroups (Safran et al., 1998a). The vast majority of item-scale correlations (86.5%) were greater than .60 (Table 20.2).

Item-Discriminant Validity. This scaling assumption was tested by contrasting each item's correlation to its hypothesized scale (corrected for overlap) with its correlation to all other scales. Steiger's *t*-test for dependent correlations was used to test the significance of the difference between two item–scale correlations (Steiger, 1980). Scaling success is expressed as a percentage and indicates how often items within a

TABLE 20.2
Tests of Likert Scaling Assumptions, Total Analytic Sample

Scale	Range of Item–Scale Correlations[a] (Assumptions 1, 4)	Item Scaling Tests (Assumption 2) Success/Total[b]	Scaling Success Rate (%)	Measures of Equal-Item Variance (Assumption 3) Scott's Homogeneity[c]	Intraclass Correlation[d]	Cronbach's Alpha (Assumption 5)
Financial Access	.67–.67	22/22	100.0	.67	.67	.81
Organizational Access	.42–.69	66/66	100.0	.46	.46	.84
Contextual Knowledge of Patient	.63–.85	55/55	100.0	.69	.69	.92
Integration	.63–.86	66/66	100.0	.66	.67	.92
Communication	.68–.90	66/66	100.0	.77	.78	.95
Interpersonal Treatment	.78–.92	55/55	100.0	.81	.81	.95
Trust	.49–.73	87/88	98.9	.43	.44	.86

[a]Range of correlations between items and their hypothesized (parent) scale correlated for overlap.

[b]Each item in each scale is tested to assure that its correlation with the hypothesized (parent) scale is substantially greater than its correlation with any other (nonparent) scale. In this ratio, the denominator represents the total number of item–scale correlations tested (i.e., all items in the scale tested against all scales). The numerator represents the number of these correlations for which the items in the scale correlate significantly higher with the parent scale than with any other scale. The scaling success rate translates this ratio into a percentage; 100% represents perfect scaling success.

[c]Average interitem correlation for standardized items (mean = 0, SD = 1).

[d]Average of interitem correlations.

scale correlate significantly more with their hypothesized scale than with any other scale. One hundred percent represents perfect scaling success.

Six of the seven multiitem scales achieved 100% scaling success, indicating that all items in these scales correlated substantially more highly with their hypothesized scale than with any other scale (Table 20.2). The Trust scale achieved 98.9% scaling success because of one item that correlated equally with another scale (Contextual Knowledge). The item was retained because its inclusion in the Trust scale was supported by other theoretical and psychometric standards (Safran et al., 1998a). Scaling success rates were similarly high in each of the 16 population subgroups.

Equal Item Variance. The assumption of equal item variance was tested through a combination of visual inspection of item means and variances, and use of two statistics computed by multitrait analysis—Scott's coefficient of homogeneity (Scott, 1968) and the intraclass correlation coefficient. If the intraclass correlation coefficient is equal to Scott's homogeneity ratio, then items in a scale are judged to have approximately equal variances.

Equal item variance was well supported for all multiitem scales. Item means differed by less than 0.4 point and item standard deviations differed by less than 0.3 point (Safran et al., 1998a). The intraclass correlation coefficient and Scott's homogeneity ratio were approximately equal to one another for each scale, providing further indication of equal item variance (Table 20.2).

Equal Item–Scale Correlations. The assumption of equal item-scale correlations is tested by computed item–scale correlations (corrected for overlap) for each scale, and inspecting the range of correlations obtained for all items in a scale. A narrow range indicates support for equal item–scale correlations.

All PCAS scales demonstrated a relatively narrow range of item-scale correlations (Table 20.2). Two scales (Organizational Access and Trust) had wider ranges because of a single item in each which were low outliers in correlation with their parent scales. These items were retained because they were supported as important items by other psychometric indicators (Safran et al., 1998a).

Score Reliability. Two measures of reliability were used to test this fifth scaling assumption: Cronbach's alpha coefficient, and test–retest reliability. Cronbach's alpha coefficient (Cronbach, 1970) measures the internal consistency reliability of a scale (i.e., the degree to which the items that comprise a scale measure the same underlying concept). An alpha coefficient of at least .70 is recommended for group-level comparisons (Nunnelly & Bernstein, 1994). Data for test–retest analyses were obtained by administering a second (abbreviated) survey to a random sample of respondents ($n = 500$). The second survey contained eight PCAS items and nine supplementary items (including an item to assess the number of medical visits made since completing the initial survey). Test–retest reliability was assessed with a Pearson correlation coefficient for each PCAS item administered in both surveys. The sensitivity of the results to the time interval between test and retest, and to the occurrence of additional visits between test and retest, was assessed.

All scales exceeded the established standard for internal consistency reliability for group-level comparisons (Cronbach's alpha of .70) (Nunnelly & Bernstein, 1994). Alpha coefficients ranged from .81 (financial access) to .95 (communication, interpersonal treatment) in the combined population (Table 20.2) and were similarly high across all population subgroups. Table 20.3 presents estimates of test–retest reliability

TABLE 20.3

Item-Level Test–Retest Correlations for Eight PCAS Items by Number of Intervening Medical Visits

	Intervening Visits			Length of Retest Interval	
Rating Items	None (n = 111)	One or more (n = 152)		Shorter Than Median (5–13 weeks) (n = 165)	Median[a] (14 weeks) (n = 109)
Appointment Wait (ORG1)	.70	.52		.64	.48
Office Wait (ORG2)	.65	.66		.66	.65
Doctors Office Location (ORG5)	.61	.57		.63	.48
Hours Open (ORG6)	.58	.57		.55	.62
Amount you pay for visit (FIN1)	.58	.72		.72	.60
Amount you pay for medication (FIN2)	.68	.71		.68	.72
See regular doctor for routine care (CONTV1)	.72	.64		.71	.52
See regular doctor when sick (CONTV2)	.74	.75		.80	.60
Median (all items)	.67	.65		.65	.62

[a]The median and maximum time interval between receipt of test and retest surveys was 14 weeks. The 14-week interval occurred among those who responded most promptly to the initial survey.

for the eight PCAS items administered twice to a subset of respondents. Overall, item-level correlations were higher among patients with no intervening visits than among patient with at least one intervening visit (median correlation .67 and .65, respectively), and higher among patients with shorter time intervals between surveys than among those with longer intervals (median correlation .65 and .62, respectively).

Evaluations Performed on All Scales

Three features of measurement performance were assessed for all 11 PCAS scales: data completeness, score distribution characteristics, and interscale correlations. Completeness of data is an important criterion by which to evaluate a scale and/or survey in that substantial amounts of missing data may suggest that items are difficult to understand or that respondents find them objectionable. Score distribution characteristics are important in that for a scale to yield meaningful information, either as a dependent or independent variable, sufficient variability of responses must be obtained. Indicators of score distributions include skewness, range, and percentage of respondents with the lowest possible score (floor) and highest possible score (ceiling). Finally, comparing interscale correlations with scale score reliability (alpha coefficients) provides a means of assessing the uniqueness of the concepts measured by each scale. That is, to the extent that a scale's alpha coefficient exceeds its correlation with any other scale, there is evidence of unique reliable variance measured by that scale. Establishing evidence for the distinctiveness of each scale is important for the interpretability of scale scores and, in practical terms, helps justify the value of scaling and reporting each separately.

Completeness of Data. Completeness of data was assessed by computing the percentage of item-level missing data for each of the items used in scoring the 11 PCAS scales. In addition, for each scale, we computed the percentage of respondents (combined population and 16 subgroups) for which a score was computable (i.e., individual responded to at least half of the scale items). Missing value rates for all PCAS items were low, ranging from 0.0 to 4.2%. The percentage of the population with computable scores ranged from 98.3 to 99.9 in both the combined population and the subgroups. The high data completeness rates indicate the acceptability of the survey content and length to respondents.

Features of Score Distributions. All evaluative scales were negatively skewed, indicating distributions with more positive ratings of primary care. The full range of possible scores (0 to 100) was observed for all scales except one (Trust). This suggests that the full range of response choices offered within each scale's constituent items was meaningful to respondents. The percentage of respondents scoring at the floor and ceiling was acceptably low for all multi-item evaluative scales. The most substantial ceiling effects occurred for the report format continuity scales and the single-item evaluative measure (Thoroughness of Physical Exams), due to the smaller number of response categories (levels) in these measures (Safran et al., 1998a).

Correlations Among Scales. In all cases, PCAS scale Cronbach's alpha coefficients substantially exceed the scale's correlation with all other scales. Approximately half of scale–scale correlations (26 of 55) were less than .36. The highest scale–scale correlation occurred between communication and interpersonal treatment (.86), although the alpha coefficients for both were substantially higher (.95). The findings support the value and importance of separately measuring and interpreting the concepts reflected in the 11 PCAS scales.

USING THE PCAS IN QUALITY ASSESSMENT AND IMPROVEMENT

The PCAS is designed for performance measurement and quality improvement at the individual physician, group practice, health plan, or delivery system level. The following sections provide examples of its use in (a) identifying patient groups for whom primary care, as measured by the PCAS, differs from other patient groups, (b) profiling individual clinicians and medical groups, and (c) comparing the primary care performance of health plans and of different models of health insurance (plan types).

Identifying Differences in the Care Received by Different Patient Populations

The PCAS can be used to measure and compare the quality of primary care rendered to different patient populations and population subgroups, and to identify populations for whom one or more aspects of primary care requires improvement. In this way, a practice, clinic, or health plan could use the instrument to determine how well it is meeting the needs of various population subgroups—elderly patients, minority patients, patients with chronic illness—and to identify areas requiring improvement for one or more patient groups. For example, the director of a medical group practice might find the PCAS a valuable tool in determining how well patients with asthma are being served by the group's primary care clinicians, and in determining whether asthma patients report sufficient continuity with and access to their primary clinician, and whether integration of care is adequate.

In the research setting, the PCAS has been used to compare the primary care received by racial minorities with that received by Caucasian patients. Taira et al. compared the PCAS scores of Caucasian, Asian, African American, and Latino patients (Taira et al., 1997). The study found that the PCAS scores of minority patients—particularly Asian patients—differed significantly from those of Caucasian patients. Moreover, the study found that PCAS score differences among racial groups increased as income decreased.

The study findings indicate the need for further research into the underlying reasons for differences in PCAS scores of patients in different racial groups. Possible explanations range from the hypothesis that different cultures have different norms around assessment, and therefore have a different rating tendency; to the hypothesis that racial minorities receive similar treatment from physicians, but that this standard of care does not meet their needs, which may be greater, more complicated, or different from those to which the practice is geared; to the hypothesis that the standard of care received by racial minorities actually differs from that received by Caucasians. The latter hypothesis is somewhat supported by the finding that minority patients' responses to both report- and rating-format questions differed from those of Caucasian patients. Reports are generally considered more objective indicators than ratings, in that reports reflect the patient's account of what happened (e.g., how many days it took to obtain an appointment at their physician's office), whereas ratings incorporate the patient's assessment of what happened (e.g., excellent, good, fair, poor), which is influenced by how well it met their individual expectations (Davies & Ware, 1988).

Similarly, another study by Taira et al. employed the PCAS to examine the type and amount of behavioral risk factor counseling received by patients in different income groups (Taira, Safran, Seto, Rogers, & Tarlov, 1997). That study found that rates of behavioral risk counseling differed in ways that were associated with patients' income level. For example, rates of counseling about smoking were significantly higher among low-income patients who smoked than among high-income smokers, whereas rates of counseling about exercise were significantly higher among high-income patients who reported not exercising than among low-income patients at risk in this area. The study also found that low-income patients were significantly more likely to report having attempted to change their behavior based on physician advice. This study illustrates how patient-provided information about the quality and content of discussions in the examining room (which are otherwise nearly impossible to capture) can help clinicians to uncover potential blind spots in their practice and develop strategies to address them.

In these ways, the PCAS can serve as a valuable tool in identifying subgroups of patients who are reporting a lower level of care than the general population. However, it is then up to the clinician, practice, or other user of the instrument to determine how and why these differences arise, and to address them. But a cautionary note is warranted. Although these and other findings that identify statistically significant differences in PCAS scores associated with patient race, income, or other sociodemographic characteristics are important, and must be followed up in order to identify the basis for their occurrence, it is important to note that patients' sociodemographic characteristics (including age, sex, race, education, and household income) account for only 3% of the variance in PCAS scores (Safran et al., 1998b). This accords with other empirical studies, which consistently find patients' sociodemographic characteristics to be limited predictors of their assessments of their care (Attkisson & Pascoe, 1983; Davies & Ware, 1988; Davies et al., 1986; Ware et al., 1976; Ware, Snyder, Wright, & Davies, 1983b). Thus, in applying the PCAS for performance assessment and quality improvement, it is necessary to begin to formulate interpretive guides by which we can consider not only the statistical significance of observed differences, but also the clinical and practical significance of these differences. Much work to develop these interpretive metrics is underway and is described later in the chapter.

Profiling Clinicians and Groups

The PCAS is also designed as a tool for profiling the performance of clinicians and health care organizations, and providing feedback about multiple specific and important aspects of the care provided to patients. Although some aspects of care that are assessed by the PCAS are substantially influenced by the practice site, organization, or health plan (e.g., organizational access, visit-based continuity), other aspects are more directly controlled by the individual clinician interacting with the individual patient (e.g., interpersonal treatment, thoroughness of physical exams, preventive counseling, contextual "whole-person" knowledge of the patient). The following sections detail several initiatives in which the PCAS has been or is being used to profile the performance of individual clinicians or clinician groups.

Case Study.   In 1995, the PCAS was pilot tested in a large primary care practice in the Boston area (Safran, Rogers, Lieberman, & Kosinski, 1995). The group consisted of both full-time and part-time general internists delivering primary care to adults. The goal of the assessment was to identify areas for improvement at the group practice level (aggregated results), with a secondary goal of providing feedback to individual physicians about their performance. For each physician in the practice, approximately 20 patients completed the PCAS. Study participants included a convenience sample drawn from each physician's recent appointment log going back as far as needed to identify the requisite number of patients. A mail survey protocol was used. This consisted of an initial mailing, a reminder postcard mailed 1½ weeks later, a second survey mailed to nonrespondents, and a reminder phone call to a portion of remaining nonrespondents. The response rate was 66%.

Aggregated primary care performance results were presented to the practice. As illustrated in Fig. 20.2, the summary results of the 11 PCAS scales showed that the group's relative strengths were in the areas of interpersonal treatment and the quality of the clinical interaction (Thoroughness of Physician Examinations, and Physician-Patient Communication). The group scored lower in the areas of Longitudinal Continuity (relationship duration), Organizational Access to Care, and Behavioral Risk Counseling.

The results of the lower scoring scales were examined in more detail:

Relationship duration (Longitudinal Continuity) was found to be low because there had been a recent addition of several new physicians to the group, who were beginning to build their practice. The more tenured physicians had much higher continuity.

Analysis of report-format and rating-format item pairs was used to further evaluate the group's relatively poor Organizational Access score. Figure 20.3 provides an illustration of this pairing, in this case showing patients' reports about the length of time they typically wait for their appointment to begin and their rating of that aspect of their care. The results highlighted that a wait up to about 10 min was acceptable to patients, but that longer waits were less so. Although the office management and cli-

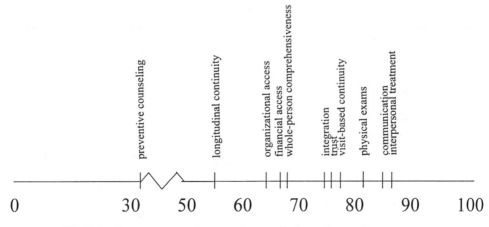

FIG. 20.2.   Primary care performance in a medical practice: attribute summary.

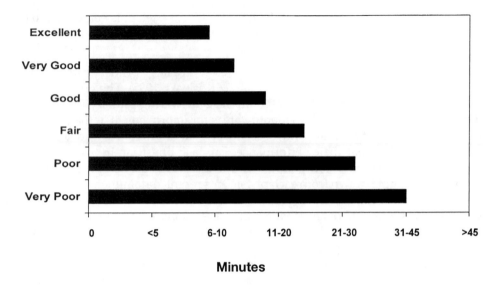

FIG. 20.3.   Amount of time spent in the waiting room.

nicians might disagree with 10 min as a threshold of tolerance on patients' part, it was information regarding patients' expectations. They could either attempt to meet these expectations or to change them.

Results of the organizational access evaluation also demonstrated that patients were having difficulty with phone access to the office. A new phone system was put in place by the office management to rectify this problem. Lastly, results showed that patients of physicians who had fewer than three clinics per week experienced substantial difficulty reaching their physicians by telephone to discuss a medical problem or question. This feedback was given to both the office management and individual physicians, so that improvement could be made in this area.

Results of the PCAS were also used to improve rates of behavioral risk counseling in the practice. The behavioral risk counseling scale of the PCAS assesses each of seven behavioral risk factors (smoking, alcohol use, diet, exercise, seat belt use, stress, and safe sex) that the U.S. Preventive Task Force recommends that primary care physicians address with all adult patients (U.S. Preventive Services Task Force, 1989). In addition, the survey included items from the Behavioral Risk Factor Survey (Carter Center of Emory University & Health Risk Appraisal Program, 1991) to determine patients' current behavioral risk status in each area. Results from this practice demonstrated that physicians were doing little in the way of behavioral-risk counseling, even among patients whose self-reported behaviors classified them as at risk. Moreover, physicians' behavioral risk counseling was not well adapted to patients' associated levels of risk. Results were particularly poor in the area of seatbelt use. With this issue called to clinicians' attention, the group substantially increased attention given to the topic of seatbelt use with patients, and received a commendation from the National Highway Traffic Safety Administration (NHTSA) for its work.

A final area for improvement was found in the Contextual (Whole-Person) Knowledge scale. An item in this scale revealed that the patients did not feel that their primary physician would know what they would want done for them in the event that they were in a coma or unable to communicate their treatment preferences. This finding led to an education program for physicians within the practice about the discussion of advanced directives with patients.

Information about individual-level performance was also provided to physicians within the practice. An example profile is illustrated in Fig. 20.4. For each scale, the length of the bar indicates the range of scores the physician received. The vertical line through the bar indicates the practice-wide average. The remaining notation indicates the physician's own average score, and whether it was statistically significantly different from the group average. Physicians who scored below the group average on a given scale were provided with the item-level results so that they could better determine what factors were driving their below-average score. For example, a doctor who scored significantly below the group average on Communication might find that his weakness lay in the thoroughness with which he was questioning patients about their symptoms and explaining their treatment (communication items 1 and 3). This physician could then target these specific behaviors for improvement.

As this case study demonstrates, the PCAS provides a broad and multidimensional assessment of primary care performance, and of the quality of the primary care relationship. Although no follow-up assessments were used in this case, the following example illustrates how the PCAS may be used to monitor changes in performance, particularly those that may result from improvement programs undertaken by a practice or health plans. This allows for a form of continuous quality improvement.

Other Initiatives Using the PCAS to Profile Clinician Performance. The PCAS is currently being used in three large-scale initiatives that will profile clinician performance. In the first, the PCAS is being used in conjunction with an intervention designed to improve the performance of several pediatric group practices in the northeastern United States. In particular, the program will train clinicians in skills needed

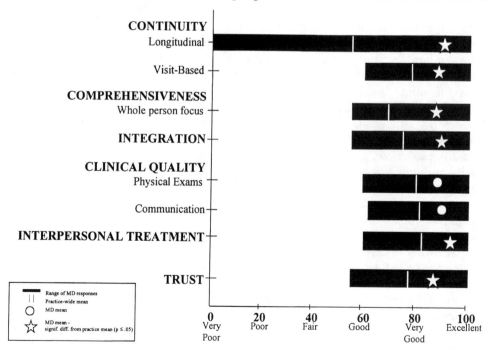

FIG. 20.4. Physician profile, doctor 24 (n = 22).

to improve the quality of their relationships with patients and office staff. In this project, the PCAS is being used to assess the baseline (preintervention) status of the practices and to measure whether improvements occur in response to the intervention. For each clinician in each practice, a sample of 70 patients who have recently been seen at the practice will be invited to complete the PCAS. The survey will be administered by mail, with repeated follow-up of nonrespondents. Completion of the PCAS by 40 or more patients per physician is targeted. Similar to the case study described earlier, each clinician will receive a summary profile based on the information received from his or her patients. A practice-wide profile will also be generated. After receiving these profiles, the clinicians will participate in an intensive training program, focused on skill-building in the area of communication and other components of relationship quality with patients. Two months after the course, the PCAS will again be administered to a sample of 70 patients who have recently been seen at the practice. Changes in performance, as measured by the 11 PCAS scales, will be reported for individual clinicians and for the practice as a whole. Subsequently, the PCAS will be used by the practices as a routine form of quality assessment and improvement planning.

A second study using the PCAS to profile clinician performance involves a comparison of the primary care provided by nurse practitioners with that provided by generalist physicians. The investigators developed a Spanish translation of the PCAS for use in this study. The Columbia University School of Nursing is conducting the study under a grant from the United Hospital Fund. The issue is of particular interest in New York, where a statute allows nurse practitioners to practice more independently than is allowed in most other states. The study participants were drawn from patients attending the urgent care center or two emergency departments of Columbia Presbyterian Medical Center, which serves a low-income, immigrant community. Patients who reported having no regular source of care and who agreed to participate in the study were randomly assigned to either a new primary care practice, run entirely by nurse practitioners, or one of five existing primary care practices, run by general internists. Study participants completed a brief survey at baseline, and at 6 months and 2 years postbaseline. Follow-up surveys included assessments of patients' functional health status, evaluation of their care (including the PCAS), health care utilization, and medication use. In addition, patients with any of three chronic diseases (hypertension, asthma, diabetes) were followed with an additional disease-specific survey instrument, as well as certain physiologic measures (e.g., blood pressure, peak flow, glycosolated hemoglobin). Results will be used to profile the quality and outcomes of care among patients of generalist physicians with those of nurse practitioners.

The National Primary Care Research and Development Centre (NPCRDC) in Britain adapted the PCAS for use in quality assessment in medical practices nationwide. The British version of the instrument, entitled the General Practice Assessment Survey (GPAS), was used in Great Britain in a nationwide quality assessment initiative entitled the QUASAR Study (Quality Assessment: Systemic Application of Review criteria). The study was designed to profile practice groups rather than individual physicians. In each of six geographically dispersed health authority areas in North Thames, the northwest, and the southwest regions of England, 10 practices were randomly selected. A strategy of stratified sampling was used to ensure that the practices represented the national distribution of practices in terms of partnership size, proportion of practices receiving deprivation payments, and proportion of training practices. The evaluation combines measures of organizational structure (e.g., staff characteristics, skill mix, and teamwork in a practice), process (e.g., chronic disease management performance indicators), and outcome (e.g., patient evaluations of care, the GPAS). QUASAR results will provide insight into the relationship between team characteristics, chronic disease management strategies, and primary care performance as measured by the GPAS. Results of the study at the practice level will only be released to the practices themselves. Physicians' opinions on the value of the different quality measures will also be reported. Data collection for this study concluded in December 1998 and preliminary results were expected in mid 1999. Beginning in early 1999, the NPCRDC planned to make the GPAS available to any primary care group in Britain for quality monitoring and improvement. Demand for the instrument has been high.

Health Plan and Delivery System Assessment

The PCAS and its precursor from the Medical Outcomes Study (MOS) have also been used to compare the primary care performance of different health plans and different forms of health insurance (plan types). More recently, the PCAS has begun being used in studies that seek to identify specific organizational and financial characteristics of health plans that influence primary care performance.

Using MOS data (1986–1988), which included a precursor to the PCAS, Safran et al. (1994) identified significant differences in performance on core dimensions of primary care among each of three plan types: indemnity insurance, IPA/network-model HMO, and staff/group-model HMO. The study found that each plan type had a unique profile of strengths and weaknesses, and that no single plan type excelled in all areas. Financial access was a strength of the two prepaid systems, whereas organizational access and continuity were highest in the indemnity insurance system. Coordination of care was highest in staff/group-model HMOs, whereas comprehensiveness (measured as the portion of the patient's care received from the primary physician) was lowest there.

More recently, the PCAS has been used to compare the primary care performance of five models of managed care: managed indemnity insurance, point of service (POS), IPA/network-model HMO, group-model HMO, and staff-model HMO. The study population included adults employed by the Commonwealth of Massachusetts and enrolled in any of 12 health plans offered to employees. Once again, a unique profile of strengths and weaknesses was observed for each plan type, although unlike the MOS results, this study suggested one plan type (managed indemnity) whose scores on most measures were significantly higher than the other plan types, and one plan type (staff-model HMO) whose scores on most measures were significantly lower than the other plan types (Safran et al., 1998c).

In an effort to identify specific features of plans that might account for the plan-type differences in performance, the study also examined the relationship of specific organizational and financial characteristics of plan to primary care performance. Plan characteristics examined included physician payment (salary, capitation, fee-for-service), financial incentives and criteria, use of physician profiling, and use of practice guidelines. Of these, physician payment was most substantially related to primary care performance, as measured by the PCAS (Safran et al., 1998c).

As public and private purchasers of health insurance, and individual patients, increasingly demand information with which to compare the quality of care provided by different health care organizations, health plans, and delivery systems, studies using the PCAS demonstrate its ability to meaningfully differentiate among providers and to highlight the relative strengths and weaknesses in the performance of each. In this way, those using the PCAS to choose a doctor, health plan, or organization can prioritize those areas of primary care most important to them, and those using it for performance improvement can readily set priorities and monitor change.

IMPLEMENTATION

This section provides a brief overview of of implementation guidelines and of factors to consider in using the PCAS for research or quality improvement. The section includes discussion of other assessment instruments that can serve as useful adjuncts to the PCAS, practical considerations related to administering the PCAS, and methods for interpreting scores and score differences.

Using the PCAS With Other Instruments

The PCAS can be used as a stand-alone instrument or supplemented with other batteries of items. As a stand-alone instrument, the PCAS provides detailed information about each of seven defining features of primary care: access, continuity, comprehensiveness, integration, clinical interaction, interpersonal treatment, and patient trust. In cases where summary information about the relative strengths and weaknesses of performance along these dimensions is all that is required, using the PCAS as a stand-alone assessment is a useful approach.

In most cases, though, it is valuable to supplement the PCAS with other batteries of items that characterize the patient population being surveyed and/or to monitor outcomes of care. At a minimum, it is helpful to field the PCAS with a set of items that characterize the respondent's sociodemographic profile (e.g., age, sex, race, employment status, insurance status, household income, marital status).

It is also very often advantageous to include a battery of items that measure the respondent's functional health status, as well as to enumerate any chronic medical conditions or permanent disabilities. One reason that measures of functional health are an important complement to the PCAS is that they allow one to monitor health outcomes if used longitudinally in the population. The 12-item and 36-item short-form health surveys are well-validated functional health status assessment batteries that are easily incorporated with the PCAS (Ware & Sherbourne, 1992; Ware, Kosinski, & Keller, 1996). In some cases, including a disease-specific assessment battery of symptoms and/or functioning may also be desirable.

Another useful adjunct is a behavioral risk factor assessment tool, such as the Carter Center's Behavioral Risk Factor Survey (Carter Center of Emory University & Health Risk Appraisal Program, 1991), which allows one to measure and monitor patients' health-risk behaviors. Monitoring changes in these behaviors is another appropriate form of outcomes assessment in primary care.

Finally, for several of the PCAS rating-format items, there are report-format items that have been developed and that are extremely useful supplements. Although these report-format items are not necessary to score the 11 PCAS summary scales, they provide valuable and specific information that may guide interpretation of the rating-based responses. An example of the use of these rating-report pairs was described earlier (case study) and illustrated in Fig. 20.3. Although the quality assessment field continues to debate whether report- or rating-format items are preferable for quality assessment, we contend that their use together is better than using either in isolation. Used together, report- and rating-format item pairs provide specific information about the patients' health care experiences (reports), along with a basis for determining how acceptable these experiences are to patients (ratings). In this way, the item pairs make it possible to identify aspects of care most in need of improvement, from patients' perspectives, and to identify the nature of the changes that patients desire.

As noted earlier, an important limitation of the PCAS, and of patient-based assessment methods generally, is the ability to evaluate technical aspects of care (e.g., adequacy and appropriateness of tests performed, accuracy of diagnoses, appropriateness of treatments). Assessment of this domain almost certainly requires other data sources (Davies et al., 1986; Gerbert & Hargreaves, 1986; Office of Technology Assessment, 1988; Sox et al., 1981; Ware et al., 1976). Both the Columbia University and British studies, described earlier, provide examples of how other data sources can be used in conjunction with the PCAS to assess clinical parameters and technical quality of care.

Administering the PCAS

The PCAS was developed in a format that allows respondents to self-administer the questionnaire. The 51 items needed to scale the 11 PCAS measures are written at a fifth-grade reading level, as assessed by the Flesch–Kincaid reading ease index (an algorithm based on the number of words per sentence and the number of syllables per 100 words) (Flesch, 1951; Kincaid et al., 1975). Pilot data revealed that adults complete the self-administered questionnaire in an average of 7 min (Safran et al., 1995). Although no single short-form version of the PCAS has been developed or validated, substantial work has been done to identify the subsets of items from each scale that, together, account for the majority of the scale variance, and those that best differentiate among physicians. Information about these subsets of items is available to registered users of the PCAS (http://www.rogersa.com/pcas/index.html).

In most cases, administering the survey by mail is preferred to administering it in other settings. Mailed questionnaires provide a sense of anonymity that can be extremely important in cases such as this, where respondents are asked to provide information that they may view as private. Where the PCAS is used for practice-based performance assessment, the simplicity and cost savings of disseminating the survey package in the medical office may be tempting. However, we advise against it. Evidence concerning social desirability response bias (i.e., the tendency to refrain from giving responses that suggest a negative or critical point of view) suggests that office-based distribution of the PCAS may inhibit patients' willingness to openly criticize aspects of their care that they are dissatisfied with. Patients who receive the questionnaire in the medical office may have a heightened concern that their specific information will be made known to their physician or to other members of the practice and thus may be less forthcoming. The British QUASAR study will conduct a formal test of this issue, by comparing responses to surveys administered by mail (majority of the study) with those from a small sample disseminated in medical practices.

Regardless of whether the survey is administered by mail, in the practice setting, or elsewhere, assuring patients' confidentiality is critical. In the case of mailed questionnaires, the letter inviting the patient's participation must clearly indicate how confidentiality will be maintained, and assure them that no one (including their physician) will be given information about their individual responses. This reassurance should also be included on a sheet within the survey booklet, preceding the actual questions.

When administering the PCAS by mail, we recommend a multistage protocol for mail surveys (Dillman, 1978). At a minimum, this should include an initial mailing of the questionnaire with a cover letter; a reminder postcard mailed within a few weeks of the initial mailing; and a second full mailing (questionnaire and cover letter) to nonrespondents. Using this method, we have consistently obtained response rates greater than 60%. If telephone follow-up is affordable, it is a useful way to increase response rates further. Using an interviewer as the primary mode of administering the PCAS (i.e., by telephone or in person) may be preferred under certain circumstances or with certain populations (e.g., with literacy or vision problems). The higher cost and greater tendency for social desirability response bias are concerns that must be taken into account with these interviewer-administered modes.

The quality and appearance of the survey package are important to response rates — especially when the survey is administered by mail. Issues such as clear formatting, adequate font size for the age group being studied, and overall survey length are important. Including a postage-paid return envelope and a telephone number that the respondent can call with questions are vital. The importance of the cover letter content and stationery should not be underestimated. Deciding who the letter should come from (i.e., who is inviting the patient to participate) and crafting a letter that will compel the patient's interest in participating are critical to the success of the initiative.

The sampling strategy for initiatives using the PCAS will depend substantially on the focus of the assessment (e.g., individual clinicians, medical groups, health plans) and the overall objectives. For purposes of profiling individual clinician performance using the PCAS, approximately 50 questionnaires completed by patients of each clinician is recommended. At this level, the assessment will have 80% power to detect performance differences among physicians of 8 points or more (8 points represents approximately twice the observed standard deviation [SD] of differences between physicians, or .4 SD of the measure). Because there tends to be less variability between practice groups, sites, and health plans than there is between physicians, a larger number of patients per entity is recommended when comparing groups, sites, or plans. Plan-based comparisons, for example, require completed questionnaires from approximately 250 patients per plan. This affords 80% power to detect 4-point differences between plans (4 points represents approximately twice the observed SD of differences between plans or .20 SD of the measure).

Scoring and Interpreting Results

A detailed scoring document, along with a computer program to score the 11 PCAS scales, is provided to registered users of the PCAS. Details about scoring are not included here. Readers can receive a copy of the instrument by completing the user's agreement available through the web site of the Primary Care Assessment Program at the Health Institute (http://www.rogersa.com/pcas/index.html).

The remainder of this section addresses methods for interpreting PCAS scores and profiling results. Inevitably, in using any assessment tool, one reaches the important moment of needing to understand what the measurement results mean. In the case of the PCAS, one will ask: What does this particular score in this population indicate? And what magnitude of score differences (between groups of patients, between doctors, between health plans) should be considered important?

We summarize four strategies useful in interpreting PCAS scores and score differences: (a) use of information linking PCAS performance to specific outcomes of care; (b) use of normative data from other populations; (c) use of report-rating item pairs; and (d) use of statistical standards.

Linking PCAS Scores to Outcomes of Care.   One extremely useful means of interpreting PCAS scores and score differences is to examine their relationship to important outcomes of care. For example, one might wish to know the extent to which the observed level of performance on access or continuity or communication predicts favorable health outcomes or patient retention in a practice.

A study by Safran et al. (1998d) provides initial evidence about the relationship between the PCAS scales and three important outcomes of care. The study examined the degree of association between each PCAS scale and each of three outcomes: patients' adherence to their primary physician's advice, satisfaction with their physician, and self-reported health outcomes. Each of the PCAS scales was significantly related to each outcome ($p < .05$). In examining the *relative* strength of each scale's relationship with each outcome, the study found that physicians' comprehensive ("whole-person") knowledge of patients and patients' trust in their physician were most strongly associated with their adherence to the physician's advice. With other factors equal, adherence rates were 2.6 times higher among patients with comprehensive knowledge scores in the 95th percentile compared with 5th percentile (44% adherence vs. 16.8% adherence). Figure 20.5 illustrates these findings. A comparable

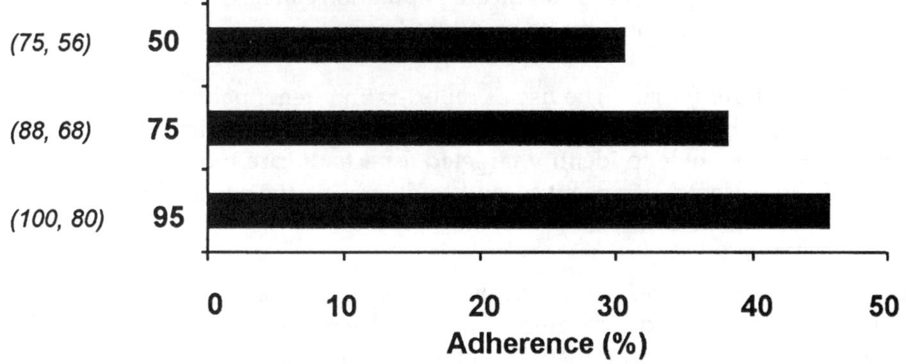

Adherence scores derived from multivariate regression results. Model adjusts for patients' sociodemographic characteristics and health status. Results reflect levels of adherence as trust and comprehensive contextual knowledge scores are sytstematically varied, holding all other variables constant at their mean.

FIG. 20.5.   Level of adherence by trust and comprehensiveness contextual knowledge.

relationship was observed between patient trust in their physician and adherence to that physician's advice.

With respect to satisfaction, trust was the single leading correlate. The likelihood of complete satisfaction was 87.5% for patients with 95th percentile trust scores compared with 0.4% for patients with 5th percentile trust scores.

Finally, although all PCAS scales were significantly related to patients' self-reported health improvements over the preceding 4 years ($p < .05$), five scales were the leading correlates of this outcome measure: integration of care, thoroughness of physical examinations, communication, comprehensive knowledge of patients, and trust.

A limitation of the study is that it was based on cross-sectional data, thereby precluding determination of the sequencing of effects (e.g., what is causing what). However, several large-scale longitudinal studies are now underway and are designed to provide detailed information about the extent to which performance on dimensions measured by the PCAS drives outcomes of care. In this way, using the PCAS, it will ultimately be possible to indicate to a physician or practice, for example, that at their current level of communication or patient trust, they can expect adherence rates that are approximately 40%, or that they can expect 20% disenrollment from the practice over the next 6-month period. Similar types of outcome projections, based on PCAS profiles, will be available to health plans and delivery systems.

Using Normative Data From Other Populations. Another means of interpreting PCAS scores and score differences is to compare them to the scores obtained in other populations. As the PCAS gains use in research and quality improvement initiatives, the database from which to draw such normative information is increasing. At present, several large databases afford information against which to benchmark PCAS scores of adults in any of several population subgroups defined according to a variety of sociodemographic and health characteristics. For example, an employer undertaking an assessment of the primary care provided through the health plans contracted by the company could compare its results to those of insured, employed adults in Massachusetts ($n = 7,204$), and even compare its plan-level performance to plan-level performance in Massachusetts. Similarly, a national study of Medicare quality (AHCPR grant number RO1 HS09622) that is using the PCAS will yield data that can serve as norms of primary care performance among elderly Americans, against which specific sectors of the Medicare population can be compared, and with which changes in performance can be monitored over time.

Report-Rating Item Pairs. The use of report-rating items pairs for interpretive purposes was described earlier. Used in conjunction with one another, report-rating item pairs make it possible to identify targeted aspects of care most in need of improvement, from patients' perspectives, and to determine the specific nature of the changes that patients desire.

Statistical Approaches to Interpretation. Finally, traditional statistical methods are useful in interpreting score differences observed across segments of the population, or across physicians, health plans, or other units of observation. As is typical in evaluative work, measures of statistical significance indicate the extent to which the observed level of variability among groups is likely to have occurred by chance, as opposed to as a result of "true" differences across the groups. In assessing individual clinician performance with PCAS data, for most scales, a 4-point difference in two clinicians' average scores should be considered important, and an 8-point difference should be considered substantial. This computation is based on the standard deviation of differences observed among physicians, which is approximately 4 points for most PCAS scales. In other words, an 8-point difference represents the magnitude of performance differences observed between the average physician in a group and a physician at the extreme high (or low) end of that group. The sample size recommendations cited earlier (completed questionnaires from 50 patients per clinician) derive from these computations. With 50 observations per clinician, if a physician's performance is truly 4 points better than a group, that physician's PCAS scores will be higher than the group's 98% of the time, and will be higher by an amount that is statistically significant 55% of the time. As noted earlier, research that is presently underway will clarify the extent to which differences that are statistically significant should be considered *clinically* significant — that is, whether they are linked to differences in outcomes of care.

In the case of health plan comparisons, a 2-point difference in the average score of plans should be considered important, and a 4-point difference in average scores of plans should be considered substantial. These computations derive from a measure of the standard deviation of differences observed among health plans. A 4-point difference in the average score of plans is akin to differences observed between the average plan and the highest (or lowest) performing plan in a large-scale, multiplan study (Safran et al., 1998c).

SUMMARY

An unprecedented rise in the demand for information about health care quality and for tools with which to measure quality continues nationwide. The demand is fueled partly by public- and private-sector purchasers of health insurance, including employers, who want to assure the value being received for their expenditures. It is also fueled by a public increasingly desiring information with which to make good health care choices, particularly in the face of the continuing drive for cost containment that causes many to worry about whether their providers will have the incentives and ability to give them the best available care. And it is fueled by health care organizations and clinicians who want to continuously improve the quality of care that they provide and who recognize that this requires measuring and monitoring performance on many dimensions of care.

In this context, the Primary Care Assessment is a valuable tool, capable of providing patients, clinicians, health care organizations, purchasers, and policymakers with information about several important elements of quality. The Primary Care Assessment Survey profiles performance on seven defining characteristics of primary care using information provided by patients. The PCAS advances substantially beyond previous patient-based assessment tools, including our own, by measuring features of care not previously assessed, including the physician's contextual (whole-person) knowledge of the patient, the patient's trust in the physician, and the physician's integration (coordination and synthesis) of the patient's care.

The PCAS provides a detailed assessment of performance on each of the characteristics that are considered to define primary care and to be essential to it. Consistent with definitions of primary care, performance is measured in the context of a specific clinician–patient primary care relationship, and references the entirety of that relationship (i.e., not visit specific). The PCAS has been shown to have excellent measurement properties, and to perform consistently well across population subgroups defined according to sociodemographic and health characteristics.

In both research and practice, the PCAS has been shown to effectively identify population subgroups for whom there are specific weaknesses or gaps in the quality of primary care being received, and to discriminate between the performance of individual clinicians, clinical groups, health plans, or delivery systems on essential features of primary care. This chapter has highlighted numerous quality assessment and improvement initiatives that are using the PCAS for these purposes. In the northeastern United States, a practice-based initiative is applying the PCAS as a tool to measure and monitor performance through a series of interventions designed to improve patient care. At Columbia University, researchers are using the PCAS, in conjunction with several other indicators of health care quality, to compare the performance of nurse practitioners and generalist physicians in primary care roles. In Great Britain, the PCAS has been adapted (GPAS) and is being applied in practice-based assessments and improvement planning nationwide. In our own work, we continue applying the PCAS as a tool for determining whether organizational characteristics and financial incentives in health care delivery influence the quality of primary care.

Finally, we continue to examine the relationship between primary care performance, as measured by the PCAS, and important outcomes of care. With the establishment of specific linkages between primary care performance and outcomes, the value of the information provided by the PCAS will be amplified. Not only will the instrument afford patients, clinicians, health care organizations, purchasers, and policymakers a detailed performance profile on essential and defining features of primary care, but it will also serve as a prognostic indicator of the outcomes that can be anticipated, given a particular level of primary care performance. That is, through results of longitudinal studies now underway, one can expect that it will ultimately be possible for clinicians, practice groups, and health plans to project any of several important outcomes of care based on their current PCAS performance profile. In addition, by identifying specific features of primary care, from among many, that are most predictive of outcomes, this work will guide priority setting for quality improvement initiatives. As these linkages between primary care performance and outcomes are elucidated, it is possible that the PCAS will prove to be one of the most versatile and informative assessment tools available.

ACKNOWLEDGMENTS

The Primary Care Assessment Survey was conceived of, developed, and validated in collaboration with a gifted and dedicated team of research scientists that included Alvin R. Tarlov, MD, William H. Rogers, PhD, John E. Ware, PhD, Mark Kosinski, MA, and Deborah Taira, ScD, MPP. We are indebted to each of these individuals for their innumerable contributions and their partnership in developing the instrument, and applying it in research to improve health care quality and outcomes. The authors also acknowledge Jana E. Montgomery and Hong Chang, PhD. for their important contributions to several of the studies reported in this chapter. Finally, we are grateful to the Henry J. Kaiser Family Foundation's Functional Outcomes Program, which funded the initial research and development of the PCAS, and to the Agency for Health Care Policy and Research, which funded the study of Health Care Delivery Systems & Primary Care Performance (RO1 HS08841) that is the basis for many of the research findings summarized here and reported elsewhere in greater detail.

REFERENCES

Aday, L. A., & Andersen, R. (1975). *Access to Medical Care*. Ann Arbor, MI: Health Administration Press.

Aday, L. A., Andersen, R., & Fleming, G. V. (1980). *Health care in the U.S.: Equitable for whom?* Beverly Hills, CA: Sage.

Aiken, L. H., Lewis, C. E., Craig, J., Mendenhall, R. C., Blendon, R. J., & Rogers, D. E. (1979). The contribution of specialists to the delivery of primary care: A new perspective. *New England Journal of Medicine, 300*(24), 1363–1370.

Alpert, J., & Charney, E. (1973). *The education of physicians for primary care*. Washington, DC: U.S. Department of Health, Education, and Welfare.

Attkisson, C. C., & Pascoe, G. C. (1983). Patient satisfaction in health and mental health services. *Evaluation and Program Planning, 6*(3,4), 185–210.

Becker, M. H., Drachman, R. H., & Kirscht, J. P. (1974). A field experiment to evaluate various outcomes of continuity of physician care. *American Journal of Public Health, 64*(11), 1062–1070.

Brown, J. B., & Adams, M. E. (1992). Patients as reliable reporters of medical care process. *Medical Care, 30*(5), 400–411.

Carter Center of Emory University & Health Risk Appraisal Program. (1991). *Healthier people version 4.0*. Atlanta, GA: Carter Center of Emory University.

Charney, E., Bynum, R., Eldridge, D., Frank, D., MacWhinney, J. B., McNabb, N., Scheirer, A., Sumpter, E. A., & Iker, H. (1967). How well do patients take oral penicillin? A collaborative study in private practice. *Pediatrics, 40*, 188–195.

Cronbach, L. (1970). *Essentials of psychological testing*. New York: Harper and Row.

Davies, A. R., & Ware, J. E. (1988). Involving consumers in quality of care assessment. *Health Affairs, Spring*, 33–48.

Davies, A. R., Ware, J. E., Brook, R. H., Peterson, J. R., & Newhouse, J. P. (1986). Consumer acceptance of prepaid and fee-for-service medical care: Results from a randomized controlled trial. *Health Services Research, 21*(3), 429–452.

Dillman, D. A. (1978). *Mail and telephone surveys: The total design method*. New York: John Wiley.

Dillman, D. A., West, K. K., & Clark, J. R. (1994). Influence of an invitation to answer by telephone on response to census questionnaires. *Public Opinion Quarterly, 58*, 557–568.

DiMatteo, M. R. (1994). Enhancing patient adherence to medical recommondations. *JAMA, 271*(1), 79–83.

DiMatteo, M. R., Taranta A., Friedman, H. S., Prince, L. M. (1980). Predicting patient satisfaction from physicians' nonverbal communication skills. *Medical Care, 18*, 376–387.

DiMatteo, M. R., Sherbourne, C. D., Hays, R. D., Ordway, L., Kravitz, R. L., McGlynn, E. A., Kaplan, S., & Rogers, W. H. (1993). Physicians' characteristics influence patients' adherence to medical treatment: results from the Medical Outcomes Study. *Health Psychology, 12*(2), 93–102.

Eraker, S. A., Kirscht, J. P., & Becker, M. H. (1984). Understanding and improving patient compliance. *Annals of Internal Medicine, 100*(2), 258–268.

Flesch, R. (1951). *How to test readability*. New York: Harper & Brothers.

Francis, V., Korsch, B. M., & Morris, M. J. (1969). Gaps in doctor-patient communication: Patients' response to medical advice. *New England Journal of Medicine, 280*(10), 535–540.

Gerbert, B., & Hargreaves, W. A. (1986). Measuring physician behavior. *Medical Care, 24*, 838–847.

Hays, R., & Hayshi, T. (1990). Beyond internal consistency: Rationale and user's guide for Multitrait Analysis Program (MAP) on the microcomputer. *Behavioral Research Methods, Instruments, and Computers, 22*, 167.

Howard, K., & Forehand, G. (1962). A method for correcting item-total correlations for the effect of relevant item inclusion. *Educational Psychological Measures, 22*, 731.

Institute of Medicine. (1978). *Report of a study: A manpower policy for primary health care*. Washington, DC: National Academy of Sciences.

Institute of Medicine. (1996). Defining primary care. In M. Donaldson, K. Yordy, K. Lohr, & N. Vanselow (Eds.), *Primary care: America's health in a new era* (p. 31). Washington, DC: National Academy Press.

Kincaid, J. P., Fishbourne, R. P., Rogers, R., & Chissom, B. S. (1975). *Derivation of new readability formulas (Automated Readability Index, Fog Count, and Flesch Reading Ease Formula) for Navy enlisted personnel* (Navy Research Branch Report No. 8-75).

Lewis, C. E. (1988). Disease prevention and health promotion practices of primary care physicians in the United States. *American Journal of Preventive Medicine, 4,* 9-16.

Likert, R. (1932). A technique for the measurement of attitudes. *Archives of Psychology, 140,* 1-55.

Millis, J. S. (1966). *The Millis Commission report.* Chicago: American Medical Association.

Montano, D. E., & Phillips, W. R. (1995). Cancer screening by primary care physicians: A comparison of rates obtained from physician self-report, patient survey, and chart audit. *American Journal of Public Health, 85*(6), 795-800.

Nunnelly, J., & Bernstein, I. (1994). *Psychometric theory* (3rd ed.). New York: McGraw-Hill.

Office of Technology Assessment. (1988). *The quality of medical care: Information for consumers* (U.S. Congress Report No. OTA H386). Washington, DC: U.S. Government Printing Office.

Safran, D. G. (1994). *Defining primary care. A background paper prepared for the Insititue of Medicine Committee on the Future of Primary Care.* Boston: New England Medical Center.

Safran, D. G., Kosinski, M., Taira, D. A., Rogers, W. A., Ware, J. E., Lieberman, N., & Tarlov, A. R. (1998a). The Primary Care Assessment Survey: Tests of data quality and measurement performance. *Medical Care, 35*(5), 728-739.

Safran, D. G., Rogers, W. H., Lieberman, N., & Kosinski, M. (1995). *The Primary Care Assessment Survey: A tool for improvement, overview of a practice-based performance assessment.* Boston: Health Institute, New England Medical Center.

Safran, D. G., Rogers, W. H., Montgomery, J. E., Murray, A., Chang, H., & Tarlov, A. R. (1998b, November). *Integrating measures of socioeconomic characteristics of patients and their environments into primary care research.* Paper presented at the 126th annual meeting of the American Public Health Association, Washington, DC.

Safran, D. G., Rogers, W. H., Tarlov, A. R., Montgomery, J. E., Taira, D. A., Invi, T., Kosinski, M., & Ware, J. E. (1998c). Organization and financial characteristics of health plans: Do they affect primary care performance. *Journal of General Internal Medicine, 13*(supplement): 66.

Safran, D. G., Taira, D. A., Rogers, W. H., Kosinksi, M., Ware, J. E., & Tarlov, A. R. (1998d). Linking primary care performance to outcomes of care. *Journal of Family Practice, 47*(3), 213-220.

Safran, D. G., Tarlov, A. R., & Rogers, W. H. (1994). Primary care performances in fee-for-service and pre-paid health care systems: Results from the Medical Outcomes Study. *Journal of the American Medical Association, 271*(20), 1579-1586.

Scott, W. (1968). Attitude measurement. In G. Lindzey and E. Aronson (Eds.), *Handbook of social psychology* (Vol. 2). Reading, MA: Addison-Wesley.

Smith, C. K., Polis, E., & Hadac, R. R. (1981). Characteristics of the initial medical interview associated with patient satisfaction and understanding. *Journal of Family Practice, 12*(2), 283-288.

Smith, W. G., & Buesching, D. (1986). Measures of primary medical care and patient characteristics. *Journal of Ambulatory Care Management, 9*(1), 49-57.

Sox, H. C., Margulies, I., & Sox, C. H. (1981). Psychologically mediated effects of diagnostic tests. *Annals of Internal Medicine, 95*(6), 680-685.

Spiegel, J. S., Rubenstein, L. V., Scott, B., & Brook, R. H. (1983). Who is the primary physician? *New England Journal of Medicine, 308*(20), 1208-1212.

Starfield, B. (1992). *Primary care: Concept, evauation and policy.* New York: Oxford University Press.

Steiger, J. (1980). Tests for comparing elements of a correlation matrix. *Psychological Bulletin, 87,* 245-251.

Stiles, W. B. (1979). Dimensions of patient and physician roles in medical screening interviews. *Social Science and Medicine, 13a,* 335-341.

Taira, D., Safran, D. G., Seto, T. B., Rogers, W. H., Kosinski, M., Ware, J. E., Lieberman, N., & Tarlov, A. R. (1997). Asian-American patient ratings of physician primary care performance. *Journal of General Internal Medicine, 12*(April), 237-242.

Taira, D. A., Safran, D. G., Seto, T. B., Rogers, W. H., & Tarlov, A. R. (1997). The relationship between patient income and physician discussion of health risk behaviors. *Journal of the American Medical Association, 278*(17), 1412-1417.

U.S. Preventive Services Task Force. (1989). *Guide to clinical preventive services: An assessment of the effectiveness of 169 interventions.* Baltimore, MD: Williams & Wilkins.

Ware, J. E. (1978). Effects of differences in quality of care on patient satisfaction. *Proceedings of the 17th Annual Conference on Research in Medical Education,* Washington, DC.

Ware, J. E., & Davies, A. R. (1983). Behavioral consequences of consumer dissatisfaction with medical care. *Evaluation and Program Planning, 6,* 291–297.

Ware, J. E., Kosinski, M., & Keller, S. D. (1996). A 12-item short-form health survey: Construction of scales and preliminary tests of reliability. *Medical Care, 34*(3), 220–233.

Ware, J. E., & Sherbourne, C. D. (1992). The MOS 36-item short-form health survey (SF–36) I. Conceptual framework and item selection. *Medical Care, 30*(6), 473–483.

Ware, J. E., Snyder, M. K., & Wright, W. R. (1976). Part B: Results regarding scales constructed from the patient satisfaction questionnaire and measure of other health perceptions. In *Development and Validation of Scales to Measure Patient Satisfaction with Health Care Services, I* (NTIS Publication No. PB 288–330).

Ware, J. E., Snyder, M. K., Wright, W. R., & Davies, A. R. (1983). Defining and measuring patient satisfaction with medical care. *Evaluation and Program Planning, 6,* 247–263.

Zapka, J., Palmer, R. H., Hargreaves, W. A., Nerenz, D., Frazier, H., & Warner, C. (1995). Relationships of patient satisfaction with experience of system performance and health status. *Journal of Ambulatory Care Management, 18,* 73–83.

The Difficult Doctor Patient Relationship Questionnaire

Steven R. Hahn
Albert Einstein College of Medicine and Jacobi Medical Center, Bronx, New York

The Difficult Doctor Patient Relationship Questionnaire (DDPRQ; Hahn, Thompson, Stern, Budner, & Wills, 1994; Hahn et al., 1996) is a self-report instrument completed by physicians and other medical providers after an encounter with a patient that is designed to identify patients whose care is experienced as difficult (Hahn et al., 1994). It has long been recognized that some patients are experienced by their medical providers as difficult to care for. Physician-experienced difficulty has typically been ascribed to the patient; therefore patients who are experienced as difficult are often described as "difficult," "frustrating," or "problem" patients. Patients experienced as difficult are thought to be relatively common and have health-related outcomes that make them of special concern. They are thought to be high utilizers of health care service, dissatisfied with the care they receive, cause physician burn-out and dissatisfaction, and have poorer treatment outcomes than patients who do not cause difficulty in the doctor–patient relationship.

Although empirical studies using the DDPRQ have determined that much of what creates difficulty in the doctor–patient relationship can indeed be explained by characteristics of the patient, the phrase *patients experienced as difficult* better represents the fact that the difficulty that is the object of our study is experienced by and belongs to the physician. The phrase *patients experienced as difficult* also makes it clear that both parties participate in generating the difficulty. Despite this advantage, the phrase *patients experienced as difficult* is cumbersome and the term *difficult patient* is used interchangeably with it in this chapter, with the understanding that the true locus of the difficulty lies in the relationship, not in the patient exclusively.

Past efforts to describe and understand difficult patients, although substantial, have been severely hampered by lack of a methodology for reliably identifying patients experienced as difficult so that they can be empirically studied. The Difficult Doctor Patient Relationship Questionnaire was developed to remedy that deficit (Hahn et al., 1994). The original DDPRQ consists of 30 Likert items completed by the physician after an encounter with the patient. The DDPRQ–10 consists of 10 of those

30 items, and was developed for use in the PRIME–MD 1000 Study discussed elsewhere in this volume (chap. 6; also see Hahn et al., 1996).

CHARACTERISTICS OF PATIENTS EXPERIENCED AS DIFFICULT

Prior to the development of the DDPRQ, our understanding of patients experienced as difficult was based on thoughtful descriptive work that relied on an intuitive understanding of the types of patients who generate negative emotional responses in their providers. Abrasive personality styles, multiple and confusing physical symptoms, and the presence of mental disorders were the most prominently discussed patient characteristics thought to be associated with difficulties in the doctor–patient relationship. Attitudes toward behavioral and psychological issues, communications skills, and inclusion of the patient in decision making were the physician characteristics identified as relevant to difficulty in the doctor–patient relationship.

Abrasive Personality Styles and Personality Disorders

Groves's (1978) classic article, "Taking Care of the Hateful Patient," identified four behavioral personality styles experienced as difficult: (a) the dependent clinger, (b) the help-rejecting complainer, (c) the entitled demander, and (d) the self-destructive denier. These patient behaviors, described in more detail later, all provoke strong negative reactions in physicians. The *dependent clinger* is a bottomless pit of neediness who overwhelms with multiple, insoluble problems. The *help-rejecting complainer* demands relief for problems, but creates tremendous frustration by finding all the offered treatments to be inadequate or harmful. The *entitled demander* angrily insists on special treatment and uses intimidation to ensure the physician's attention. Entitled demanders evoke fear, anger, and, subsequently, guilt and shame for the almost inevitable rejection and counterattack that are provoked in the physician. *Self-destructive deniers* generate feelings of helplessness and guilt by eliciting and then frustrating the physician's consequently ambivalent efforts to change the patient's self-destructive health-related behaviors. Most difficult patients display one or a combination of these behavioral traits. Although never empirically tested, many students of the difficult doctor–patient relationship have found Groves's categories to be extremely useful.

Kahana and Bibring (1964) contributed an important discussion of the ways in which different personality traits affect an individual's behavioral and emotional responses to illness. Their treatise addressed the relationship between personality type and illness behavior within the range of normal behaviors rather than in patients with personality disorders. Their descriptions of the "meaning of illness" and consequent adaptational responses of patients with different personality types are also useful in understanding what happens in the nonnormal extremes of the difficult doctor–patient relationship. Schwenk, Marquez, Lefever, and Cohen (1989) also demonstrated that an "abrasive behavioral style" (i.e., less than a full-blown personality disorder) was a major determinant of physician-experienced difficulty in a study of patients identified as "the most difficult that day." Other descriptive works

on the effect of frankly pathological personality disorders on patient care acknowledge the difficulty created for the physician (Lipsitt, 1970; Oldham, 1994).

Psychiatric Disorders

Psychopathology has long been identified as a cause of difficulty in the doctor–patient relationship, a conclusion taken largely on faith and personal conviction rather
than empirical study. Prior to the development of the DDPRQ there were few empirical studies of the association and none that combined study of a general medical population with both a reliable method of identifying the difficult patient and valid
methods for assessing mental disorders.

Investigations characterized by one or two of these criteria have generally confirmed the hypothesis. Goodwin, Goodwin, and Kellner (1979) found that anxiety,
hostility, depression, and organic impairment of mental status were characteristics of
the "most disliked" among 22 patients with systemic lupus erythematosis. Novack
and Landau (1985) evaluated 52 "problem patients" referred to a medical psychological consultation clinic and found that 49 had symptoms meeting criteria for a
DSM–III diagnosis. Among the most common were psychogenic pain disorder
(31%), conversion disorder (17%), major depressive disorder (15%), and panic disorder (7%). Lin et al. (1991) evaluated 251 health maintenance organization (HMO) patients who were psychologically distressed high utilizers of medical care. These patients had high levels of mood and anxiety disorders and somatoform symptoms.
Those among the distressed high utilizers that were experienced as frustrating by
their providers had particularly high levels of somatoform symptoms and generalized anxiety. Sharpe et al. (1994) found that patients who were rated as "difficult to
help" had higher symptom scores on the Hospital Anxiety and Depression Scale.

Somatoform and Physical Symptoms

Multiple physical symptoms, especially somatoform symptoms, have been identified
as a potent cause of difficulty in the doctor–patient relationship. Because physical
symptoms are more prevalent in patients with a variety of nonsomatoform mental
disorders, the independent effects of physical symptoms and co-occurring psychopathology have been difficult to assess. Nevertheless, the association between physical symptoms and physician-experienced difficulty is so strong that it deserves attention independently of comorbid psychopathology.

Most discussion of the relationship between physician-experienced difficulty and
somatization has been provided as a passing comment in general discussions of the
management of somatization (e.g., Kaplan, Lipkin, & Gordon, 1988; Smith, Monson,
& Ray, 1986). A few studies have used empirical methods to study difficulty and
somatization. Schwenk, Marquez, Lefever, and Cohen (1989) assessed perceived difficulty with 205 patients cared for by 22 family physicians who rated 40 patient characteristics considered to be associated with difficulty. They found two factors among
these items that collectively accounted for 35% of the total variance: "interpersonal
difficulty" (discussed earlier in the section on personality style) and "medical uncertainty." Items that loaded on the medical uncertainty factor clearly reflected the physician's response to multiple, vague, and probably somatoform physical complaints
(e.g., "the patient's medical problems are difficult to solve," "the patient has many
problems," "the patient's complaints have no apparent cause").

McGaghie and Whitenack (1982) developed a physician rating scale designed to identify "problem" patients. Despite problems with the method used to select patients for study (described later), their observations confirmed the association of multiple complaints lacking in pathophysiological cause with physician experienced difficulty. Lin et al. (1991), in the study described earlier, demonstrated that high levels of physical symptoms differentiated the frustrating patients among high utilizers even when the presence of mood disorders did not. Drossman (1978) described a variety of mental disorders, characterized by a tendency to present somatically, that are associated with the "problem patient."

Characteristics of Physicians and Difficulty in the Doctor–Patient Relationship

Considerably less attention has been focused on the physician's contribution to difficulty in the doctor-patient relationship. Numerous studies have identified deficits in clinician communication skills and assumed or implied that these produced difficulty for the physician as well as the patient (Hall, Roter, & Katz, 1988; Korsch, Gozzi, & Francis, 1968). Anstett (1980) explicitly addressed the need to expand physicians' usual focus on biomedical issues to include psychosocial dimensions such as attention to the meaning of the illness for the patient, the patient's expectations and wishes, and the patient's coping style. O'Dowd (1988) conducted an informal study of "heartsink patients" in a general practice and observed that getting more psychosocial information about the patient made doctor's heart sink less by reducing insecurity about clinical management. Merrill, Laux, and Thornby (1987) found that an abrasive personal style and multiple symptoms consistently generated negative feelings in all of the 81 physicians they assessed but that physicians with low self-esteem were particularly vulnerable to difficult responses.

Previous Efforts to Quantify Difficulty in the Doctor–Patient Relationship

The DDPRQ was developed to identify the subgroup of patients that physicians experience as difficult so that empirical research on the characteristics, needs, and management of difficult patients could be performed. Prior to the development of the DDPRQ only one attempt had been made to create such an instrument (McGaghie & Whitenack, 1982). In that study 24 of the participating patients were selected because their physicians identified them as having at least one of three characteristics: multiple symptoms across physical systems, excessive demands for care and attention, and/or being sickness prone with a low threshold for complaint. A comparison group was composed of 25 patients who had none of these characteristics. Physician ratings of the 15 items of the Patient Description Questionnaire (PDQ) were assessed for internal consistency reliability (Cronbach's alpha = .91), test–retest reliability at 8 weeks (Cronbach's alpha = .90, correlation coefficient of initial and follow up scores r = .88), and the ability to discriminate between the preselected problem and control group patients (t-test for difference in mean PDQ scores was significant at $p < .0001$).

Although the PDQ has good psychometric characteristics, the small sample size and the use of a preselected group of "problem patients" characterized by only three features create a risk that other types of problem patients might not be assessed as ef-

fectively. This concern may be heightened by the authors' emphasis on objective patient behaviors rather than physician's subjective responses in creating PDQ items.

THE DDPRQ: OVERVIEW

General Considerations and Description of the DDPRQ

The DDPRQ was developed to identify patients experienced as difficult by their providers, assess the degree of difficulty experienced, and identify the component parts
of difficulty. It was designed to assess difficulty from the point of view of the physician about a particular patient during a specific visit. The DDPRQ is a self-report
questionnaire using 6-point Likert-type questions anchored by "not at all" and "a
great deal." It is available in two versions: the original 30-item DDPRQ (DDPRQ–30)
and a 10-item version (DDPRQ–10) (Hahn, 1996). The DDPRQ is completed by the
physician after seeing the patient and takes from 30 sec (DDPRQ–10) to less than 3
min (DDPRQ–30) to complete.

DDPRQ–30 Development

Setting: Patients and Providers. The DDPRQ was developed in the General
Medical and Adult Primary Care Clinics of Jacobi Medical Center (then known as
Bronx Municipal Hospital Center). Both clinics served a patient population with a
mean age of 65 years and low socioeconomic status. Two-thirds of patients were female, 35% White, 34% African American, and 29% Latino. The clinics were staffed by
attending physicians, internal medicine residents, and nurse practitioners. Individual clinicians provide continuity of care to their patient in these clinics.

Item Development. Construction of the DDPRQ–30 began with a pool of 57
items that reflected difficult patient behaviors and physicians' subjective responses
to patients (Hahn et al., 1994). Content for these items was derived from the models
of previous investigators described earlier and the investigators' clinical experience.
Groves's model of four different types of "hateful patients" (Groves, 1978) figured
heavily in constructing items, as did the principle that somatization was a critical
component of physician experienced difficulty. Factor and item analysis was performed on physician and nurse practitioner ratings of 92 patient encounters. Thirty
items were selected for use in the final version of the DDPRQ–30 (see Table 21.1).

Distribution of scores, factor analysis, and assessment of reliability. To assess reliability
and factor composition, the DDPRQ–30 was completed by 54 clinicians after encounters with 224 patients. Completed data were obtained on 204 subjects. The
DDPRQ–30 had an internal consistency reliability (Cronbach's alpha) of .96 in this
sample. The distribution of DDPRQ scores is a skewed curve with a long tail in the
range of higher scores (Fig. 21.1). The tail of the curve contains approximately 20% of
the population and begins at one standard deviation above the mean. A principal-component varimax rotation factor analysis revealed five factors (Table 21.1).
These factors demonstrate an intuitive internal consistency of theme: Factor 1 consists of 14 items, half of which describe "demanding irritating" patient behavior, that
is, patients who are demanding, draining, manipulative, time-consuming, and have

TABLE 21.1

Difficult Doctor Patient Relationship Questionnaire Items and Factor Loadings

		Factor Loading				
Item Number	Questionnaire Item	Factor 1	Factor 2	Factor 3	Factor 4	Factor 5
	Factor 1: The Demanding Irritating Patient					
9	How demanding was this patient today?	.82	.32	.10	-.06	-.02
11	How "draining" is this patient?	.81	.26	.21	.02	-.06
13	How manipulative is this patient?	.74	.30	.17	.16	.27
8	To what extent are you frustrated by this patient's "vague" complaints?	.72	.41	.24	.01	.02
14	How tense did you feel when you were with this patient today?	.72	.32	.15	.09	.04
10	How time consuming is caring for this patient?	.71	.06	.24	-.06	-.02
22	Does this patient overreact to symptoms or problems?	.70	.28	-.02	.10	.17
3	How unreasonable were this patient's expectations today?	.69	.32	.19	.00	.04
24	How angry did you feel while seeing this patient today?	.66	.34	.16	.21	-.10
1	How difficult is this patient's personality?	.65	.42	.21	.25	.15
23	How much would you like to transfer this patient to another primary provider?	.64	.55	.04	.26	.07
12	Do you find yourself secretly hoping that this patient will not return?	.63	.55	.02	.28	.05
5	How "frustrating" do you find this patient?	.61	.44	.34	.21	-.08
28	Does this patient present minor problems?	.59	.22	.07	-.12	.32

658

Factor 2: Physician Dysphoria

17	* How much are you looking forward to this patient's next visit after seeing this patient today?	.39	**.80**	.30	.04	.08
15	* Overall, how enjoyable is caring for this patient?	.38	**.77**	.21	.13	.13
6	* How upbeat did you feel after seeing this patient today?	.25	**.76**	.16	.11	.03
18	* How pleased are you with your working relationship with this patient?	**.44**	**.75**	.25	.12	-.03
25	* Overall, how positive do you feel about caring for this patient?	**.47**	**.71**	.28	.15	.03
2	* How enthusiastic do you feel about caring for this patient?	.19	**.68**	.25	.01	**.40**
20	* How at ease did you feel when you were with this patient today?	.29	**.62**	.13	.00	-.04
7	How negative did you feel about the visit?	**.49**	**.62**	.01	.22	-.09
21	How hopeless do you feel about helping this patient?	.34	**.48**	.25	.27	-.19

Factor 3: Compliance and Communication

16	* Does this patient understand your explanations of medical information?	.15	**.48**	**.68**	-.08	-.10
27	To what extent does this patient neglect health related self-care, e.g. diet, hygiene?	.15	.05	**.61**	**.50**	.17
29	How difficult is it to communicate with this patient?	.37	.31	**.59**	.06	-.17
26	* How compliant is this patient?	.17	**.41**	**.59**	.16	.21

Factor 4: The Self-Destructive Patient

4	To what extent does this patient have health related problems from drug or alcohol abuse?	-.12	.18	-.02	**.80**	-.02
30	How self-destructive is this patient?	**.40**	.10	.38	**.67**	.11

Factor 5: The Seductive Patient

19	How seductive is this patient?	.05	.02	-.01	.06	**.86**

Note. Each item is answered on a 6-point Likert scale where 1 = *not at all* and 6 = *a great deal*. Items marked with asterisks are scored in reverse. Values ≥ .40 shown boldface. Reprinted from *Journal of Clinical Epidemiology, 47*, Hahn, S. R., Thompson, K. S., Stern, V., Budner, N. S., & Wills, T. A., The difficult doctor–patient relationship: Somatization, personality and psychopathology, pp. 647–658, Copyright © 1994, with permission from Elsevier Science.

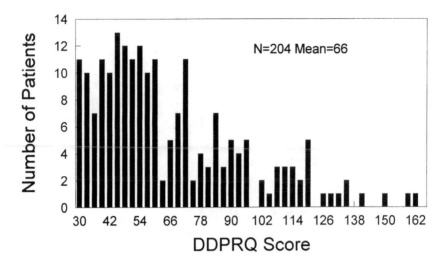

FIG. 21.1.   Distribution of DDPRQ scores. Reprinted from *Journal of Clinical Epidemiology*, 47, Hahn, S. R., Thompson, K. S., Stern, V., Budner, N. S., & Wills, T. A., The difficult doctor–patient relationship: Somatization, personality and psychopathology, pp. 647–658, Copyright © 1994, with permission from Elsevier Science.

unreasonable expectations. The other items on this factor describe awareness of a wish to get rid of the patient (i.e., "Do you find yourself secretly hoping that this patient won't return?" and "How much would you like to transfer this patient to another primary provider?") or feelings of anger and frustration.

The second factor consists of nine items, all of which reflect negative subjective responses to the patient. Six of these items are reverse scored; that is, they are phrased so that agreement endorses positive feelings about the experience of caring for the patient and difficult patients evoke a rejection of the statement (e.g. "How much are you looking forward to this patient's next visit after seeing this patient today?"). Other descriptors in Factor 2 items that are rejected by physicians caring for difficult patients include being enjoyable, feeling upbeat, pleased, positive, enthusiastic, and at ease. Directly endorsable items on this factor include feeling negative about the visit and being hopeless about helping the patient. In short, there is nothing good about patients who score high on Factor 2, which we have labeled *physician dysphoria*.

The third factor, *compliance and communication*, contains items reflecting clarity in communication with the patient and the patient's acceptance of the medical model. Patients who score high on Factor 3 are "noncompliant," neglect self-care, and cannot communicate with the provider in terms consistent with the biomedical model.

The fourth factor contains two items specifically related to alcohol and drug abuse and to self-destructive behavior prominent in patients with substance abuse. Patients who neglect self-care also score high on Factor 4, the *self-destructive patient* factor. One item that loaded highest on the compliance and communication factor (3) also loaded on this one, presumably because of the self-destructive nature of extreme disregard of self-care. It is noteworthy that being self-destructive also loaded relatively highly on Factor 1, the demanding irritating patient factor.

The final factor, Factor 5 or *the seductive patient*, consists of one item: "How seductive is this patient?" This item did not perform very well in the original derivation sample, possibly due to the large age and cultural differences between the patients and the providers (the mean age of the clinic population was 65, and many of the providers were young residents). The item was retained because it is theoretically important and might prove useful in other patient populations where fewer demographic differences may make seductive patient behavior more likely or problematic.

Factor scores are best expressed as the mean of all the individual items so that subscales can be compared numerically. Each factor subscale has a theoretical range of 1 to 6, and scores of 3.5 or higher would indicate that a patient is predominantly experienced as having the cluster of characteristics embodied in the factor.

Determining the Cutpoint for Difficulty. Although it may be meaningful to distinguish degrees of difficulty in the doctor–patient relationship, in common parlance and in the literature it is common for patients to be classified dichotomously as difficult and not difficult. Although there is no external gold standard that can be used to set a cutoff point for DDPRQ scores, the distribution of DDPRQ scores and factor scores can be used to rationalize a threshold for dichotomous classification. Most clinicians will find it difficult to rank order the degree of difficulty of patients that they would not include in the general category of "difficult patients". On the other hand, most clinicians have little difficulty ranking the difficulty of patients who they would label as difficult. Physician-experienced difficulty is not a continuum from pleasurable to difficult, and "degree of difficulty" is a meaningful concept only for the categorically difficult patient. The distribution curve of the DDPRQ appears to follow this intuitive pattern. As noted earlier, the distribution of DDPRQ scores is a skewed curve; approximately 20% of the population lies in a high-scoring tail that begins at 90, one standard deviation above the mean. The majority of patients, with scores less than 90, lie to the left of the tail and are among the undifferentiated not difficult; the difficult patients are spread, according to their degree of difficulty, within the tail of the curve from 91 to 160.

Ninety-eight percent of the patients who scored above 90 on the DDPRQ scored 3.5 or higher on the *physician dysphoria* (Factor 2) subscale, indicating that they produced significant negative emotional responses in their providers. Ninety-nine percent of patients who were *demanding and irritating* (scores of 3.5 or higher on factor 1) scored 90 or above. Thus, a cut point of 90 will classify virtually all "demanding and irritating" patients as difficult, and no patient will be classified as difficult unless the person produces a predominantly negative emotional response in the provider.

Assessment of Validity: Methods. Because there is no "gold standard" for the difficult patient, the validity of an instrument like the DDPRQ can only be established through face or construct validity, and convergent validity (i.e., correlation with other measures theoretically associated with physician experienced difficulty). To assess validity, a chart review was performed on a sample of 112 of the 224 patient encounters collected in the reliability phase (stratified by DDPRQ–30 score to ensure equal representation of difficult and nondifficult patients). In addition, 154 patients were asked to participate, and 113 (73%) completed questionnaire-based interviews and chart reviews. Charts were abstracted for patient demographics, utilization, general medical and psychiatric diagnoses, and medications. The number of physical symptoms recorded in the patient's chart over the previous 3 years that were either stated to be somatoform by the provider or judged to be so by the chart reviewer was counted. Patients completed the General Health Questionnaire (GHQ), a self-report questionnaire designed to detect psychopathology, and the Personality Diagnostic Questionnaire–Revised (PDQ–R), a self-report questionnaire designed to assess personality pathology. Patients' providers completed the DDPRQ-30 and a Practitioner Psychopathology Diagnostic Questionnaire that reported the provider's assessment of the presence and clinical impact of psychopathology. The provider's gender, type of clinician (physician or adult nurse practitioner, resident or attending), year of graduation from medical school if a resident, and full- versus part-time status if an attending were noted.

Assessment of Validity: Results. The DDPRQ development study demonstrated that the characteristics that determine physician-experienced difficulty transcend superficial demographic characteristics. Patients' age, gender, race, and marital status did not distinguish between difficult and not difficult patients. Nor were there any differences in the proportion of patients experienced as difficult among different types of clinicians (first-, second-, third-, and fourth-year medical residents, nurse practitioners, full- and part-time attending physicians).

In contrast to demographic characteristics, their was a strong relationship between *major (Axis I) psychopathology* and physician-experienced difficulty. Psychopathology was examined using the three previously described indices of psychopathology: (a) the General Health Questionnaire ($n = 101$), (b) the number and types of psychopathology noted in the patient's chart ($n = 208$), and (c) provider-reported psychopathology recorded on the PPDQ ($n = 107$). Total GHQ score was significantly associated with total DDPRQ-30 score ($r = .25$, $p = .01$). The mean GHQ score was significantly higher in patients who were classified as difficult by the DDPRQ-30 ($t_{99} = 2.55$, $p = .01$). Seventy percent of difficult patients met GHQ criteria for at least mild psychopathology, compared with 28% of not difficult patients (absolute increase in risk of being experienced as difficult 42.5%, 95% CI = 14.1%–72.4%).

The total number of *active charted psychiatric diagnoses* correlated positively with DDPRQ-30 score ($r = .35$, $p < .001$). Half of all difficult patients had at least one psychiatric diagnosis noted in the chart compared to 26% of not difficult patients (absolute increase in risk 23.8%, 95% CI = 6.9%–40.7%). Patients with no, one, and two or more charted psychiatric diagnoses showed a consistent increase in mean DDPRQ score ($F_{2,205} = 6.49$, $p = .01$).

Providers rated the severity of psychopathology on the PPDQ as absent, mild subclinical, and clinically significant. DDPRQ-30 scores showed a significant increase across these three categories ($r = .47$, $p < .001$). Differences in mean scores for the three groups were significant ($F_{2,104} = 15.0$, $p < .001$).

The relationship between difficulty and *personality (Axis II) pathology* was assessed using the PDQ-R. Forty-four percent of subjects met criteria for subthreshold personality "types," and 12% met criteria for a personality type and had a positive index of distress, thus meeting criteria for a personality disorder. Eight of the nine difficult patients who completed the PDQ-R met criteria for a personality type, compared with only 39% of not difficult patients (95% CI for the difference of 49.7% = 26.5%–72.9%). Total PDQ-R score, also an index of personality pathology, correlated with DDPRQ score ($r = .20$, $p = .06$) and was significantly higher for difficult patients ($t_{86} = 2.12$, $p = .04$).

Difficult patients had an average of 3.4 *somatoform symptoms* (95% CI 2.6–4.1) recorded in the chart over a three year period compared with 1.4 symptoms (95% CI 1.2–1.6) for not difficult patients ($p < .001$). The total number of somatoform symptoms correlated positively with DDPRQ scores ($r = .43$, $p < .001$). Although the mean number of *medical illnesses* was not associated with DDPRQ scores, the presence of any of a number of classically *psychosomatic illnesses* was. Patients with irritable bowel syndrome, migraine, chronic pain, and other syndromes labeled by the provider as psychosomatic had a mean DDPRQ score of 75.6 (95% CI 65.0–86.3) compared with 64.1 (95% CI 60.2–68.0).

Patients who scored high on the DDPRQ were likely to have more than one of the five characteristics of difficult patients (somatization, abrasive personality, charted psychopathology, physician-detected psychopathology, and high GHQ scores). A cumulative score with a range of 0–5 computed by dichotomizing each of these variables had a mean of 3.3 among difficult patients (95% CI = 2.2–4.5), compared to 1.1 among not difficult patients (95% CI = 0.86–1.4). Eighty-nine percent of difficult patients had two or more indices; by comparison, only 29% of not difficult patients had two or more (95% CI for the 60% difference in the percentage of patients with two or more vs. less than two characteristics was 37%–83%).

Development of the DDPRQ-10

Although the 30-item DDPRQ takes less than 3 min to complete and is acceptable to physicians, even 3 min may be excessive in the time-pressured clinical environment. The 30-item's high Cronbach's alpha and the high level of correlation between the five factors of the DDPRQ-30 suggested that a shorter version might capture the most important characteristics of physician-experienced difficulty more efficiently. The 10-item DDPRQ (DDPRQ-10; see Fig. 21.2) was created by stepwise forward re-

DDPRQ-10

Date ___ ___ / ___ ___ / ___ ___   Patient Number ___ ___ ___ ___ ___ ___ ___

   Study Number ___ ___ ___   M.D. Code ___ ___ ___

		Not At All					A Great Deal
1.	How much are you looking forward to this patient's next visit after seeing this patient today?	1	2	3	4	5	6
2.	How "frustrating" do you find this patient?	1	2	3	4	5	6
3.	How manipulative is this patient?	1	2	3	4	5	6
4.	To what extent are you frustrated by this patient's vague complaints?	1	2	3	4	5	6
5.	How self-destructive is this patient?	1	2	3	4	5	6
6.	Do you find yourself secretly hoping that this patient will not return?	1	2	3	4	5	6
7.	How at ease did you feel when you were with this patient today?	1	2	3	4	5	6
8.	How time consuming is caring for this patient?	1	2	3	4	5	6
9.	How enthusiastic do you feel about caring for this patient?	1	2	3	4	5	6
10.	How difficult is it to communicate with this patient?	1	2	3	4	5	6

CIRCLE THE APPROPRIATE NUMBER

FIG. 21.2. The DDPRQ-10.

gression on the original 30-item version. The DDPRQ–10 has an R^2 of .96 with original instrument and a Cronbach's alpha of .88. As with the DDPRQ–30, each of the 10 items has a 6-point Likert scale, giving the DDPRQ–10 a range of 10 to 60. A cut point of 30 classified 20% of the derivation sample as difficult; and Kroenke (1999), in their study of 500 walk-in patients, reconfirmed the utility of a cut point of 30, and of dichotomization of patients as difficult versus not difficult, rather than three groups of "difficult," "average," and "satisfying."

EPIDEMIOLOGY AND CHARACTERISTICS OF DIFFICULT PATIENTS AND THEIR DOCTORS

To further study patient characteristics associated with physician-experienced difficulty, the DDPRQ–10 was added to the PRIME–MD 1000 Study, a mental health survey of primary care patients performed to develop the PRIME–MD, a brief case-finding and diagnostic instrument for use in the primary care setting (discussed in chap. 6 and Spitzer et al., 1994). Other investigators have also used the DDPRQ to study the epidemiology and characteristics of difficult patients. The results of these investigations are presented in conjunction those of the PRIME–MD 1000 Study.

Demographic and Patient Care Characteristics and Difficulty

The DDPRQ–10 was added to the PRIME–MD 1000 Study protocol about halfway through the study and administered to 627 of the 1,000 patients in the study. The mean age of the patients was 57 years; 62% were female; 52% were White, 33% Black, and 11% Hispanic. College graduates accounted for 24% of the patients. As in the DDPRQ development study, no univariate association was observed between these demographic variables and DDPRQ–10 scores. In their study of 68 women with either fibromyalgia or rheumatoid arthritis, Walker, Katon, Keegan, Gardner, and Sullivan (1997) found that the 29 single patients had higher DDPRQ–10 scores than the 39 married patients (31.1 ± 9.0 vs. 24.4 ± 9.7, $p < .01$). Age was not associated with physician-experienced difficulty, and ethnicity was not studied. Jackson and Kroenke's (1999) study of 500 walk-in patients confirmed the lack of association between DDPRQ-measured difficulty and demographic characteristics.

Fifteen percent (96) of the PRIME–MD 1000 Study patients were experienced as difficult based on a DDPRQ–10 scores of 30 or higher. Although the prevalence of difficult patients ranged from 11% to 21% at the four different clinical sites ($p = .08$) and mean DDPRQ–10 scores were significantly different at the four sites (range 18 to 22, $p < .001$), these differences were eliminated after correcting for the prevalence of difficult patient characteristics described later.

Physician familiarity with the patient does have an influence on physician-experienced difficulty. Patients who were "not at all known" to the provider were less likely to be difficult than patients who were "somewhat" and "well known" (7%, 18%, and 17%, respectively, $p = .010$). Jackson and Kroenke (1999) found the prevalence of difficult encounters in 500 walk-in visits made by nondemented patients to the Walter Reed Army Medical Center with a chief complaint of a physical symptom other than an upper respiratory tract infection (URI) was 15%. This observation sug-

TABLE 21.2
The Difficult Doctor Patient Relationship Questionnaire, 10-Item Version (DDPRQ-10)

Item	Percent of Patients Rated Difficult by Item[a]	
	Difficult Subjects (n = 96)	Not Difficult Subjects (n = 531)
1. How much are you looking forward to this patient's next visit after seeing this patient today?[b]	74	9
2. How "frustrating" do you find this patient?	90	6
3. How manipulative is this patient?	44	2
4. How difficult is it to communicate with this patient?	40	5
5. To what extent are you frustrated by this patient's vague complaints?	68	6
6. How self-destructive is this patient?	29	3
7. Do you find yourself secretly hoping that this patient will not return?	52	2
8. How at ease did you feel when you were with this patient today?[b]	49	8
9. How time consuming is caring for this patient?	81	34
10. How enthusiastic do you feel about caring for this patient?[b]	74	9

Note.   Each item is scored on a six point scale: 1 = *not at all*, 6 = *a great deal*. The DDPRQ–10 score equals the sum of the ten items. All χ^2 comparisons were significant at <.001. From Hahn et al. (1996). Reproduced with permission.

[a]Response were dichotomized by coding raw scores of 4 through 6 on each item as difficult (after reversing for direction of items 1, 8, 10).

[b]Item was reversed for scoring.

From Hahn, S. R., Kroenke, K., Spitzer, R. L., Brody, D., Williams, J. B. W., Linzer, M., & deGruy III, F. V. (1996). The difficult patient: Prevalence, psychopathology, and functional impairment. *Journal of General Internal Medicine, 11*, 1–8. Reprinted by permission of Blackwell Science.

gests that physician-experienced difficulty may be more common in walk-in settings, given that these patients are not likely to be known to their provider.

Table 21.2 shows the percentage of difficult and not difficult patients whose physicians endorsed each of the DDPRQ–10 items positively (4–6 on the 6-point Likert scale used for DDPRQ items). With the exception of being time-consuming, all of the other difficult characteristics assessed by the DDPRQ–10 were endorsed positively in less than 10% of not difficult patients; 34% of not difficult patients were notably time-consuming. In contrast, 90% of difficult patients evoked feelings of frustration, 81% were time-consuming, physicians experienced a lack of enthusiasm in providing care to three-quarters, and they were secretly hoping that half wouldn't return. In comparison to not difficult patients, patients experienced as difficult were much more manipulative, difficult to communicate with, afflicted with vague complaints, and self-destructive.

Axis I Psychopathology: Mood, Anxiety, and Somatoform Disorders and Alcohol Abuse/Dependence

In contrast to demographic characteristics, a strong association was observed between the presence of mental disorders and physician-experienced difficulty. Difficult patients were almost twice as likely to have a PRIME–MD diagnosis as were not difficult patients (67% vs. 35%, $p < .001$), and 25% of patients with mental disorders were experienced as difficult compared to only 8.5% of those without a mental disorder. The typical difficult patient had 1.8 mental disorders whereas not difficult patients had a mean of 0.7 mental disorder ($p < .001$).

Physician-experienced difficulty increased with the severity of mental disorders present. As shown in Fig. 21.3, the percentage of patients experienced as difficult and mean difficulty scores were greatest in patients whose symptoms met criteria for *DSM–III–R* diagnoses, and decreased in a stepwise fashion for patients with subthreshold diagnoses, psychiatric symptoms but no diagnosis, and no symptoms of psychiatric disorders. Among the 11 *DSM–III–R* diagnoses (shown in Table 21.3) that were present in at least 4% of the study sample, 6 were associated with an increased risk of physician-experienced difficulty: multisomatoform, dysthymic, generalized anxiety, major depressive and panic disorders, and probable alcohol abuse or dependence. After adjustment by analysis of variance for the comorbidity of the six difficult diagnoses, three remained independently associated with difficulty: multisomatoform disorder, probable alcohol abuse or dependence, and panic disorder ($p < .001$ for the first two, and .052 for panic). The association between difficulty and major depression approached significance after correction for comorbidity ($p = .068$).

Other investigators using the DDPRQ have confirmed the association between Axis I pathology and difficulty. Jackson and Kroenke (1999) found that the presence of either an anxiety or mood disorder increased the likelihood of physician experienced difficulty (odds ratio = 2.4, 95% CI = 1.5–3.9). Using a Dutch translation of the DDPRQ-10, Wiefferink, De Best-Waldhober, and Mellenbergh (1998) also found that difficulty score correlated with evidence of anxiety and depression. Walker et al. (1997) found that in patients with fibromyalgia and rheumatoid arthritis, DDPRQ score correlated with the presence of current dysthymia and agoraphobia, and lifetime panic, obsessive-compulsive, and somatization disorders.

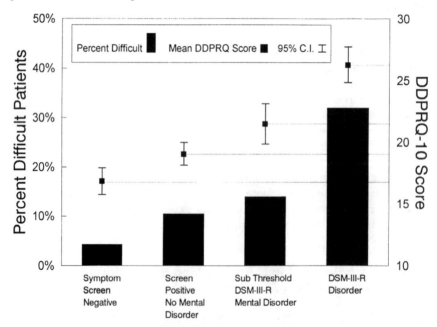

FIG. 21.3. Percentage of patients experienced as difficult (left *y*-axis) and mean DDPRQ-10 scores (with 95% confidence intervals), for patients with no symptoms of mental disorders, symptoms but no disorder, subthreshold mental disorders, and *DSM–III–R* mental disorders, diagnosed using the PRIME-MD. From Hahn, S. R., Kroenke, K., Spitzer, R. L., Brody, D., Williams, J. B. W., Linzer, M., & deGruy III, F. V. (1996). The difficult patient: Prevalence, psychopathology, and functional impairment. *Journal of General Internal Medicine, 11*, 1–8. Reprinted by permission of Blackwell Science.

TABLE 21.3
Association Between Mental Disorders and the Likelihood
of Being Experienced as Difficult in 627 Primary Care Patients

| Mental Disorder (% Total Sample) | Percent of Patients Experienced as Difficult | | Adjusted Odds Ratio* |
	Disorder Present	Disorder Absent	
Diagnostic Modules			
Any Diagnosis (40)	25	8	3.5 (2.1–6.0)[†]
Any Somatoform Disorder (14)	46	10	8.9 (4.8–16.6)[†]
Any Mood Disorder (26)	28	11	2.9 (1.7–4.8)[†]
Any Anxiety Disorder (21)	30	12	2.8 (1.6–4.8)[†]
Specific Diagnoses			
Multisomatoform Disorder (8)	54	12	12.3 (5.9–25.8)[†]
Panic Disorder (4)	56	14	6.9 (2.6–18.1)[†]
Dysthymia (8)	40	13	4.2 (2.0–8.7)[†]
Generalized Anxiety Disorder (8)	36	14	3.4 (1.7–7.1)[†]
Major Depression (12)	31	13	3.0 (1.8–5.3)[†]
Probable Alcohol Abuse or Dependence (5)	29	15	2.6 (1.01–6.7)[‡]
Depression in Partial Remission/Recurrence (5)	30	14	2.1 (0.9–2.4)
Binge Eating Disorder (4)	31	15	2.2 (0.8–1.7)
Somatoform Disorder Not Otherwise Specified (4)	29	15	1.5 (0.5–3.3)
Minor Depression (8)	19	15	1.2 (0.6–2.6)
Anxiety Not Otherwise Specified (11)	19	15	1.1 (0.5–2.2)

*Odds ratio adjusted by logistic regression for age, gender, minority status, number of physical illnesses, clinical site, amount of school and familiarity with the patient. Because of missing data on control variables, $n = 568$ for odds ratios.

†$p \leq .001$.

‡$p \leq .05$.

From Hahn, S. R., Kroenke, K., Spitzer, R. L., Brody, D., Williams, J. B. W., Linzer, M., & de Gruy III, F. V. (1996). The difficult patient: Prevalence, psychopathology, and functional impairment. *Journal of General Internal Medicine, 11*, 1–8. Reprinted by permission of Blackwell Science, Inc.

Physical and Somatoform Symptoms

Physical symptoms are the most powerful and consistent predictors of difficulty in the doctor–patient relationship. In the PRIME–MD 1000 Study, DDPRQ–10 scores correlated with the overall number of physical symptoms and the number of symptoms judged to be somatoform ($r = .39$ and $.37$ respectively, $p < .001$). In Jackson and Kroenke's (1999) study, the presence of 5 or more of the 15 symptoms on the PRIME–MD Patient (screening) Questionnaire was associated with increased risk of being experienced as difficult (odds ratio 1.9, 95% CI = 1.1–3.1). A self-report symptom severity of 6 or greater out of 10 was also a predictor of patients experienced as difficult (odds ratio = 1.6, 95% CI = 1.0–2.4). No specific symptom was strongly associated with difficulty, but dermatological, otolaryngolic, and genitourologic symptoms were less likely to be associated with physician-experienced difficulty.

Physical Illnesses

The number of patients' medical illnesses was not associated with difficulty in either the PRIME–MD 1000 Study or in Jackson and Kroenke's study of walk-in patients. However, in the PRIME–MD 1000 Study, DDPRQ–10 scores were higher in patients with a variety of "psychosomatic" or "functional" disorders: irritable bowel syndrome (27 vs. 21, $p < .001$), tension headaches (28 vs. 20, $p < .001$), fibromyalgia (32 vs. 21, $p < .001$), and premenstrual complaints (28 vs. 21, $p = .011$). In the study by Walker et al. (1997), patients with fibromyalgia had significantly higher scores than did those with rheumatoid arthritis (31.4 ± 9.9 vs. 22.5 ± 9.2, $p < .001$).

Personality Style and Pathology

As mentioned earlier, an abrasive personality style as measured by the PDQ–R was strongly associated with difficulty in the original instrument development study. Personality pathology was not assessed in the PRIME–MD 1000 Study. However, Walker et al. (1997) assessed a variety of personality characteristics in their study. They found that the NEO Neuroticism scale, which measures worry, tension, loneliness, and helplessness (Costa & McCrae, 1980), was positively correlated with DDPRQ–10 score ($r = .42$, $p < .001$). In addition, a measure of adjustment to chronic illness (the Appraisal of Diabetes Scale; Carey et al., 1991) demonstrated that patients who perceive a loss of control because of chronic illness are more likely to be experienced as difficult.

Physician Characteristics and Difficulty in the Doctor–Patient Relationship

Results of the PRIME–MD 1000 Study confirmed the findings observed in DDPRQ development: Physician gender, age, years of training, and type of training (internal medicine vs. family practice) were not associated with the mean DDPRQ–10 scores of physicians' practices. There was no interaction between physician and patient gender and difficulty.

Jackson and Kroenke (1999) made similar observations, and explored interactions between physician and patient age and ethnicity in addition to gender interaction, finding no association with physician experienced difficulty. Assessment of the relationship of physician characteristics and the prevalence of patients experienced as difficult in their practice is complicated by the fact that the formation of a doctor–patient relationship is probably not independent of the extent to which a physician is disposed to experience difficulty. As a result, certain physicians are likely to accumulate difficult patients in the their practice, whereas other physicians are likely to have fewer patients experienced as difficult. Thus, in the PRIME–MD 1000 Study, physicians who rated themselves as more interested than their peers in psychiatric diagnosis had higher mean patient difficulty scores in their practices than did physicians who reported being less interested than their peers (21.6 vs. 16.2, $n = 27$ physicians, $p = .003$). In fact, there was a trend for the more psychiatrically interested physicians to have a higher prevalence of the "difficult" psychiatric diagnoses in their practices.

Jackson and Kroenke's (1999) study contributed a great deal to our understanding of the relationship of physician characteristics with physician-experienced difficulty by examining physicians' responses to arbitrarily assigned patients in a walk-in setting, thus eliminating the possible segregation of difficult patients to specific physicians. They also employed the Physician Belief Scale, a 32-item questionnaire measuring attitudes toward psychosocial aspects of patient care (Ashworth, Williamson, & Montanco, 1984), a more reliable and valid instrument than the one-item question used in the PRIME–MD 1000 Study. Using a cut point of 70 to distinguish physicians with a negative attitude toward psychosocial issues ($n = 17$) from those with a positive attitude ($n = 21$), they found that the psychosocially sympathetic physicians experienced 8% of the randomly assigned patients as difficult compared to 23% of the patients seen by physicians with a negative attitude towards psychosocial care ($p < .001$).

Characteristics Associated With Difficulty

All studies indicate that physician-experienced difficulty is multifactorial and that many of the variables associated with difficulty are themselves highly intercorrelated. For this reason multivariate analyses have been used to identify a parsimonious set of patient physician, and clinical features that can explain physician experienced difficulty. In the PRIME–MD 1000 Study, a three-stage forward regression was used. In the first stage patient demographic characteristics, clinical site, and physician's familiarity with the patient accounted for 4.8% of the variance in difficulty score. In the second stage the six "difficult diagnoses" and other patient characteristics that had univariate association with difficulty scores were entered in a stepwise fashion. The number of mental disorders, the number of somatoform symptoms, the total number of physical symptoms, the presence of multisomatoform disorder, and probable alcohol abuse or dependence accounted for 23% of the variance. The presence of the other four "difficult diagnoses" made no additional contribution to explaining difficulty. This is no doubt due in part to the strong correlation between mood and anxiety disorders and physical symptoms (Kroenke et al., 1994). In the third stage of the analysis, physicians' self-assessed interest in psychiatric diagnosis (the one physician characteristic that demonstrated univariate association with DDPRQ–10 scores) was entered and explained an additional 5.6% of the variance in difficulty score. Collectively, this combination of patient and physician characteristics accounted for 33% of the variance in DDPRQ–10 scores.

Jackson and Kroenke (1999) used a logistic regression on the patient and physician characteristics assessed in their study expressed as dichotomous variables. Four were independently associated with physician-experienced difficulty: the presence of a depressive or anxiety disorder, five or more physical symptoms, self-rated symptom severity of 6 or greater (on a 10-point scale), and negative physician attitude toward psychosocial issues. Collectively, these four variables accounted for 34% of the variance in DDPRQ–10 scores. The proportion of doctor–patient interactions with 0, 1, 2, 3, and 4 of these characteristics that were experienced as difficult were 3%, 8%, 18%, 23%, and 47%, respectively.

The following conclusions regarding physician experienced difficulty may be drawn from these studies:

1. Physician-experienced difficulty is associated with Axis I psychopathology: depression, anxiety, somatoform disorders, and alcohol abuse or dependence.
2. Physician-experienced difficulty is associated with Axis II personality pathology.
3. Physician-experienced difficulty is associated with somatization and multiple physical symptoms.
4. Negative physician attitudes toward psychosocial issues increase the likelihood that any patient will be experienced as difficult.

5. A general interest in psychiatric diagnosis may be associated with a higher prevalence of patients experienced as difficult in a physician's practice.

HEALTH-RELATED OUTCOMES AND PHYSICIAN-EXPERIENCED DIFFICULTY

Patients experienced as difficult have also been noted to have poorer health-related quality of life, utilize more health care services, and be more dissatisfied with the care they receive. These outcomes are particularly important in today's health care marketplace. The DDPRQ has contributed to our understanding of the relationship between physician-experienced difficulty and health-related quality of life, utilization, and satisfaction.

Health-Related Quality of Life

Difficult patients had lower scores on all six dimensions of the Medical Outcomes Study Short Form–20 (MOS SF–20), a measure of health-related quality of life (HRQL) that was employed in the PRIME–MD 1000 Study ($p < .003$ on all six scales). After adjusting for number of mental disorders, only the Pain subscale demonstrated a significant difference between patients experienced as difficult and not difficult, suggesting that much of impairment in HRQL can be attributed to the more severe psychopathology found in difficult patients. Difficult patients also reported 11 disability days in the 3 months preceding assessment, compared to only 4 days for not difficult patients ($p < .0001$). Much of this difference could be accounted for by adjusting for mental disorders, but a significant difference remained (8.8 vs. 4.5, $p = .03$). Using a shorter version of the MOS, Jackson and Kroenke (1999) found a significant difference in HRQL between difficult and not difficult patients on initial encounters in a walk-in clinic, but not at 2-week and 3-month follow-up evaluations.

Patient Satisfaction

In the PRIME–MD 1000 Study, 52% of difficult patients rated the care they had received during the previous 3 months as excellent and 15% rated it fair to poor, compared to 79% and 6%, respectively, for not difficult patients. The difference in satisfaction ratings could be accounted for by adjusting for the number of mental disorders in difficult and not difficult patients. Jackson and Kroenke (1999) also found significantly more difficult patients to be somewhat or very dissatisfied with physicians' technical competence, bedside manner, explanation of treatment, and time spent with the physician (no objective difference in visit length was observed). Patients who were experienced as difficult were also more likely to have unmet expectations for care immediately and 2 weeks after their walk-in visit.

Utilization

Difficult patients in the PRIME–MD 1000 Study reported 2.4 visits to their physician in the preceding 3 months and 0.49 emergency department visits, compared to 1.5 and .25 for not difficult patients ($p = .022$ and .03, respectively). The difference in visits to the emergency department could be accounted for by adjusting for the presence of mental disorders, whereas the difference in doctor visits decreased but remained significant ($p = .036$). The Jackson and Kroenke study assessed utilization during 3 months before and 3 months after the walk-in visit and found that patients experienced as difficult made more visits in the 3 follow-up months (4 vs. 2, $p = .004$) and during the 6 months bracketing the index visit (5.5 vs. 4, $p = .002$).

These data suggest that patients classified as difficult by the DDPRQ represent a population that is worthy of attention not only because of the distress they cause their providers, but also because of their measurably worse health-related outcomes. Furthermore, the fact that much of the discrepancy in outcomes can be explained by the prevalence of psychopathology in patients experienced as difficult suggests that identification and treatment of psychopathology in difficult patients may have a significant effect on these important health-related outcomes.

USE OF THE DDPRQ IN PRIMARY CARE

The DDPRQ is a new tool that was designed primarily for research. To date, empirical study using the DDPRQ has been limited to epidemiological investigations. However, the ability of the DDPRQ to identify a unique population of patients with utilization and outcome characteristics of great interest in health services management, and the fact that this population of patients is of compelling interest to the physicians who care for them, make the DDPRQ an instrument with a variety of additional potential applications. Physicians' natural interest in experiencing less difficulty gives an interventional strategy focused explicitly on this population a distinct advantage in eliciting physician participation and enthusiasm.

The DDPRQ in Research

Patients experienced as difficult remain an inadequately understood group of patients with unique health care needs. Issues that deserve further attention include:

1. Variation in prevalence of patients experienced as difficult in:
   a. Different reimbursement settings.
   b. Different specialties and subspecialities.
2. The effect of difficulty on health care utilization patterns including:
   a. Referral rates and outcomes.
   b. Medication use.
   c. Laboratory testing.
   d. Procedure rates and complications.
3. The effect of difficulty on disease specific outcomes.
4. Patient satisfaction and difficulty:
   a. Concordance between physician experienced difficulty and patient satisfaction.
   b. Interactions between difficulty, satisfaction, and utilization.
5. Studying the physician's contribution to difficulty:
   a. Identifying the characteristics of physicians who experience patients as difficult.

> b. Identifying the characteristics of physicians who accumulate difficult pa-
>   tients in their practice.
> 6. Interventional studies:
>   a. Providing special services to address the three clinical characteristics of dif-
>   ficult patients:
>   i. Axis I psychopathology.
>   ii. Abrasive personality styles (Axis II).
>   iii. Somatization.
>   b. Providing training to physicians in managing the difficult clinical charac-
>   teristics of patients experienced as difficult.
>   c. Providing special training for physicians who are more likely to experience
>   patients as difficult.

The DDPRQ in Clinical Practice

With the exception of some of the educational applications of the DDPRQ and one
study in which the DDPRQ-10 was used as an outcome for intervention, both addressed later, all discussion of the use of the DDPRQ in clinical practice is specula-
tive. The following thoughts are therefore offered as suggestions.

Guidelines for Management Decisions.   Clinical use of the DDPRQ in the management of individual patients would be predicated on the benefit of alerting the clinician to the fact that the patient is being experienced as difficult. Although this
might seem superfluous because the physician should already know that the patient
is difficult, in truth physicians do not explicitly or consciously recognize or label their
experience in this way. There are a variety of reasons for this. The "difficulty" exists
as an internal emotional experience that physicians have not been taught to consider
as useful clinical data. In fact, as part of the "hidden curriculum" of professional
training, physicians learn to suppress awareness of a variety of emotional experiences that might interfere with effective functioning. These include reactions to unpleasant odors, horrible wounds, expressions of pain, and their own fear and anxiety
in the face of life-threatening emergencies or technically unfamiliar medical situations.

Some negative emotional responses have a unique reason for being suppressed:
those that are associated with guilt or shame. There is nothing shameful in having a
negative emotional and visceral response to a horrible wound (although communicating that response to a patient would be countertherapeutic). On the other hand, secretly wishing that a self-destructive alcoholic with active esophageal bleeding who is
intoxicated, vomiting blood all over you and your colleagues, and receiving massive
transfusions during the fourth such admission in as many months would simply "get
it over with and die," is a thought that can generate intolerable guilt.

This guilt is produced despite the fact that under the circumstances described, the
thought is common, understandable, and virtually normal. The internal, guilty response to the initial primitive emotional reaction generates an immediate disavowal
of the thought. That disavowal then prevents the wish "that the patient would get it
over with and die" from becoming conscious enough to be examined. In fact the
whole sequence—initial primitive emotional response, guilt, suppression of the
awareness of the primitive impulse—remains largely automatic and unconscious. As
a result, the important distinction between having a feeling, thought, or impulse, and
acting on it is incompletely realized. Furthermore, the physician is denied the oppor-

tunity to examine the initial emotional response and recognize that such feelings are common, understandable, and essentially normal.

Although this psychological strategy may prevent acting out the impulse to allow the patient to die, or worse to facilitate that death, it cannot prevent the very common anger, even rage, that is experienced in caring for these patients. These are the patients who were, in more arrogant, less politically correct days, openly referred to as SPAS, which is an anagram for Subhuman Piece of Sh‑‑. (The language is expressed without euphemism because it is important for the reader to appreciate the intensity of emotional reaction that can accompany caring for many difficult patients.) Almost inevitably the physician's anger and rage are felt by the patient through subtler communications such as an angry tone of voice, facial expression, discourteous cursory interactions, self-righteous admonitions to change their ways, or open statements of moral disgust or disdain.

Throughout this encounter, the physician would rarely realize that he or she is caring for a "difficult patient." It is even more unlikely that the physician will focus on the fact that this patient's clinical presentation can be understood in terms of a combination of: (a) Axis I psychopathology for which there is likely to be a specific treatment that can offer some benefit, and (b) an abrasive personality style for which there are effective management strategies, if not treatments (other difficult patients also create difficulty by somatizing, as discussed earlier). Typically, the uneducated experience of the difficult patient is overwhelming, opaque, and not intuitively understood as being composed of distinguishable components, each of which can be addressed.

One of the most striking characteristics of the DDPRQ–10 is that physicians actually like to fill it out. When the instrument is presented to professional audiences, the item "How much are you secretly hoping that the patient will not return?" inevitably evokes the laughter of relief that accompanies the revelation of a slightly guilty "secret" that everyone actually knows, but no one has the courage to acknowledge. The fact that the DDPRQ exists and is being used in a formal research protocol or as a clinical tool accomplishes, to some extent, the two cardinal components of a destigmatizing intervention: normalization and universalization.

In addressing any socially undesirable behavior, such as the presence of negative or hateful feelings toward patients, it is critical to create an environment in which the socially undesirable behavior can be acknowledged without too much shame, guilt, or other injury to self-esteem. Limited and conditional normalization and universalization are keys to creating such an environment. Normalization takes the basic form, "Under these circumstances, it would be normal for a person to feel _____." Universalization takes the basic form, "Under these circumstances, almost everyone feels _____." Although the presence of an item implying that one might feel like never seeing a patient again does not explicitly state that the feeling is normal or universal under any or all circumstances, it does imply that under some circumstances such a reaction would be both normal and common.

Thus the experience of filling out a DDPRQ has the potential of validating the presence of negative emotional responses, destigmatizing the feeling to some extent by implying that they may be normal and common under some circumstances, thus permitting acknowledgment, discussion, and examination of the physician's response. When associated with the theoretical model of difficulty, completing the DDPRQ can transform dimly perceived, consciously and unconsciously rejected clinical data (i.e., the subjective experience of difficulty) into a much more definable, analyzable, and manageable clinical problem.

There is no doubt that transforming a difficult encounter from an overwhelming, emotionally distressing, and opaque experience requires much more than the experience of completing a DDPRQ alone. A systematic and relatively sophisticated analysis and intervention addressing the component characteristics of physician-experienced difficulty, described later, is required. The DDPRQ can be a trigger to begin this process and can make its own destigmatizing contribution in the manner just described. Although the author has observed this effect, it has not been empirically tested. It is also not known whether this transformation can become an internalized behavior after using the DDPRQ on a number of occasions so that the recognition and effective clinical consideration of the patient's difficulty will be triggered without having to complete a DDPRQ.

Use With Other Evaluation Data and Behavior Intervention

Identifying a patient encounter as difficult should trigger an assessment of the three characteristics of patients who are experienced as difficult: Axis I psychopathology, personality pathology (Axis II), and somatization. It is beyond the scope of this chapter to address the assessment and management of these three domains. However, the reader is directed to "Evaluation of Mental Disorders with the PRIME–MD" (chap. 6, this volume) for a more detailed discussion of methods for evaluating Axis I pathology and somatization.

Axis I Psychopathology.   The first step in the evaluation of patients experienced as difficult is to determine the presence of Axis I psychopathology. The PRIME–MD is a brief self-report screen and structured physician interview instrument designed for case-finding and diagnosing mental disorders in the primary care setting. It consists of two parts: a patient self-report screen with 25 questions (the Patient Question or PQ) and a Clinician Evaluation Guide (CEG) divided into five modules. The modules enable clinicians to diagnose mood, anxiety, alcohol, eating, and somatoform disorders in primary care. The PQ is used to determine which if any of the five modules should be administered. The PRIME–MD has demonstrated validity and acceptance in the primary care setting. The chapter on the PRIME–MD in this volume (chap. 6) contains a more complete discussion of the management and treatment of the disorders that can be diagnosed using the PRIME–MD, including the role of psychiatric and behavioral health clinicians.

Somatization.   The PRIME–MD is designed to diagnose multisomatoform disorder, a diagnosis that is made when there are (a) three or more physical symptoms present for which there is an inadequate organic explanation, (b) a history of such symptoms over a period of years, and (c) functional disability because of those symptoms. As mentioned earlier, the odds of being experienced as difficult are 12 times greater when multisomatoform disorder is present than in its absence, and 28% of patients experienced as difficult met criteria for this disorder. A variety of approaches have been suggested for addressing somatization in the primary care setting. Those most commonly recommended in the literature are detailed in chap. 6 on the PRIME–MD (see especially Table 6.7).

One approach, less commonly discussed but most effective in the author's experience, is to use a family systems approach (Hahn, 1997). This approach assumes that somatization is generated and sustained by the effect it has on changing the patient's relationships with others in their family system. This is accomplished by enabling *the patient and the family* to meet their needs through the patient's acceptance of the "sick role" as described by Talcott Parsons and others.

According to Parsons (1958), the sick role is understood as a series of rules that govern the way in which individuals are to behave and be treated when they are ill. A patient in the sick role is entitled to dispensation from normal expectations of role functioning and to special treatment and assistance from others. In exchange, the person is expected to adhere to medical treatment, try to get better, and feel ashamed about and not like being in the sick role. The sick role has very powerful social, economic, practical, and emotional effects, and its attribution is therefore carefully controlled.

Physicians play a key role in the creation of the sick role, both informally when patients report to their family members what the doctor said about their condition and imply or state how the family should respond, and formally as in the common requirement of a physician's documentation in determinations of disability, sick days, insurance reimbursements, and so on. This role can put the physician in the middle of conflicts between patients and their families and other parts of their social system. Patients will often present to physicians in a way that induces an alliance that compensates for conflicts in the patient's social system, often unbeknownst to the physician (Hahn, Feiner, & Bellin, 1998). When such a "compensatory alliance" is being enacted, the normal expectation that the patient is requesting diagnosis and treatment for a medical symptom is subverted by the family's need to alter interpersonal relationships in an effort to cope with family conflict and dysfunction. It is for this reason that many somatizing difficult patients act as though they don't really want to get well.

Further complicating the physician's dilemma is the fact that in almost all social milieus the sick role is considered to be less legitimate if the illness is a mental illness or a psychological problem. Thus the psychosomatic hypothesis (i.e., that physical symptoms are due to psychological stress or problems) is incompatible with the patient's and family's need to justify the sick role with a physical disorder. Empirical evidence for somatizers' need to avoid attributing dysfunction to or basing the sick role on a psychiatric disorder was provided by data from the PRIME–MD 1000 Study: Patients with somatoform disorders showed better mental functioning on the MOS SF–20 than did patients with no mental disorders at all, despite reporting the most impairment in general functioning of any group of patients (Spitzer et al., 1995)

The strategy required to address somatoform presentations is to redirect attention away from the physical symptom onto the underlying interpersonal and family systems problems *without* drawing an explicit connection between physical symptoms and psychological distress. This process can be accomplished in four stages, discussed at greater length in the PRIME–MD chapter (chap. 6) and by Hahn (1997):

1. *Analyze*: Explore the family system by performing a "genogram-based interview" using a family tree diagram as an aid and organizing device for exploring the patient's interpersonal relationships. In this stage it is important to help the patient express the emotions that are associated with difficult relationships or situations; in other words, "bring the pain in to the room."

2. *Reframe*: Direct attention toward the difficult and emotionally charged issues that are explored during the genogram-based interview as an alternative and additional focus — for example, "It seems to me that in addition to your [somatoform complaints], the difficult and painful problems you have just described are also worthy of attention." Reframing does *not* require establishing any connection between the physical complaints and the interpersonal stress. The patient *does not* have to accept the psychosomatic hypothesis.

3. *Empathically witness*: Provide empathic support to the patient as you bare witness to the important interpersonal problems they have described — for example, "I am very impressed with how well you are doing despite all of the problems you have been dealing with."

4. *Refer*: After bringing the patient's interpersonal relationships and the emotional distress associated with them into the room, and reframing attention to those problems as a concern that is as important as the somatoform complaints, the physician can refer the patient (and family) for therapy.

Completion rates for referrals from primary care to mental health specialists for somatoform problems have a notoriously high failure rate. Given the role that we believe somatization plays in the family's attempts to cope with their problems, and the fact that accepting the psychosomatic hypothesis delegitimizes the sick role, resistance to accepting a referral for mental health care services is understandable. For this reason "bringing the pain into the room" is necessary to make the suggestion of psychotherapy compelling. Reframing in a way that avoids the psychosomatic hypothesis is also critical because it is important to not deprive the patient and family of their current coping strategy. Empathic witnessing is a necessary antidote to the narcissistic injury inherent in a referral for treatment of a stigmatizing or socially undesirable condition (i.e., a mental disorder).

This strategy also has the virtue of defining a clear limit to the primary care provider's therapeutic agenda: It is not the purpose of this approach to "do therapy" or to "fix" the problem, only to establish a new therapeutic agenda that can be pursued by other clinicians who have specific skills and treatment resources. These structural features are necessary to give primary care providers some confidence that their forays into the patient's psychosocial problems will not be a counterproductive opening of either "Pandora's box" or a "can of worms."

Personality Pathology.   The third characteristic of patients experienced as difficult is an abrasive interpersonal style or frank personality pathology. As noted earlier, abrasive behavior does not have to rise to the level of a diagnosable personality disorder in order to have a deleterious effect on the doctor patient relationship. At the outset it is important to note that the primary care clinician's objective is to "manage" personality pathology, not to treat or change the patient's personality. The goal of management is to minimize the effect of the patient's problematic behavior on the therapeutic alliance, on the decision-making process, and on the physician's distress.

One model for managing abrasive personality styles is based on understanding the characteristic pattern of interaction of difficult patient behavior with physicians' emotional and behavioral responses that was introduced earlier. According to this model, the fundamental features of the interaction are:

1. The difficult patient's abrasive behaviors produce a "primitive emotional response" in the physician that is frequently well established before any higher level awareness of negative feelings occur.

2. The physician's feelings are painful and negative for two reasons: First, feelings such as anger or rage are negative and painful in themselves. Second, and more telling, because physicians believe that they should not have negative feelings toward patients, the primitive emotional response generates guilt and shame.

3. Because the guilt and shame are painful, awareness of the negative feelings, and the guilt and shame along with it, is suppressed. As a consequence physicians are not fully conscious of their own feelings and are not able to monitor the effect of the suppressed feelings on their behavior.

4. The physician's "reflex behavioral response" is the end result of the suppressed primitive emotional response. Because physicians avoid awareness of their true feelings, the physician can only rely on his or her relatively simplistic formal concepts of how physicians should behave (i.e., respectful, patient, complete if not caring). These formal characteristics, which are relatively easy to monitor, do a reasonably good job of preventing destructive acting out of the primitive emotional responses but do not succeed in preventing the communication of negative emotions in tone of voice, a more aloof and cold demeanor, and so on.

5. Because the patient's behavior is so stereotypical for them, the physician's reflex behavioral response is also stereotypical. It is also similar to that of everyone whose relationship to the patient has some structural similarity to the relationship with the physician. Therefore, the physician's reflex behavioral response is familiar to the patient and anticipated, and the patient's counterresponse is a well-rehearsed routine. In fact the abrasive personal style is powerful because it evokes reflex behavioral responses that are countertherapeutic and further enmesh the physician by intensifying the negative emotional response, generating more guilt, more suppression, more countertherapeutic reflex responses, which the patient seconds in an escalating negative vicious cycle, until the system falls apart with some kind of doctor–patient blow-up.

The solution to this situation lies in physicians developing insight into their own experience and modifying their own behavior:

1. The physician must accept that doctors, like anyone else, can have negative and even hateful reactions to abrasive behavior. This requires an ability to use introspection and achieve emotional honesty. The injury to self-esteem that can accompany accepting negative feelings that are inconsistent with a naive self-image of professional altruism requires, among other things, an understanding of the moral difference between having a feeling and acting on it.

2. Physicians must learn to identify their primitive emotional responses and identify their reflex reaction to those emotions. They must understand the countertherapeutic effect of their reflex behavior and develop an alternative strategy based on the patient's emotional needs. For example, instead of responding to an "entitled demander's" demands for care and attacks on one's competence with a reflex attempt to set limits "because that is how we take care of all our patients," the physician should join with the patient by assuring the person that he or she is *entitled to*

the very best possible care," and that "in order for you to receive the very best possible care, the following circumstances [i.e., limits] need to be created" (e.g., "What we need to do is make a scheduled appointment when there is enough time and your chart is available so that you can receive the care to which you are entitled").

It should be clear from the preceding discussion that managing abrasive personality styles requires growth in areas of skills and knowledge that are not typically addressed in the training of physicians. It requires a willingness to develop insight into the clinician's own inner life and emotional responses, the ability to perform honest emotional introspection, and the ability to trace the relationships between feelings and action. Furthermore, it requires some insight into the complex and counter-intuitive motivations of the most difficult individuals encountered in any walk of life. Finally, it requires the ability to accomplish this introspection and understanding while enduring the confusing emotional stress of a difficult situation. Perhaps the most unique aspect of this challenge is that it requires treating physicians, rather than patients alone, as objects of change.

INTEGRATED CARE FOR PATIENTS EXPERIENCED AS DIFFICULT

Real-World Applications

Because of the unique evaluation and treatment needs of difficult patients, the author created a special clinic to which patients experienced as difficult are referred. In this clinic patients are evaluated using the PRIME–MD (Spitzer et al., 1994), supplemented as needed, to assess Axis I psychopathology. A family systems assessment and intervention is performed using a genogram-based interview (Hahn, 1997). Finally, the physician's primitive emotional reaction to the patient and the physician's reflex behavioral response are analyzed. The hidden emotional needs that are being enacted in the patient's abrasive behavior is identified.

Based upon these evaluations, recommendations for psychopharmacological interventions and referrals for behavioral and psychotherapeutic interventions are made. The core family systems issue is identified and named, attention is reframed toward the problems discovered, the patient is empathically supported in efforts to deal with problems, and these observations and actions are used to help the patient understand the need for psychotherapy when appropriate. An alternative physician response that meets the patient's hidden emotional need while controlling the doctor–patient interaction is developed and tested in the interview.

Finally, these interventions are transformed into recommendations that are communicated to the referring physician. The challenge in providing the referring physician with this information is to capture and translate the therapeutic effect achieved by the new doctor–patient relationship created in the consultation. This is particularly difficult with the emotional content of the family systems intervention and the alternative behaviors designed to address the patient's abrasive personal style. Ideally, all primary care physicians should be able to perform this three-part intervention themselves. However, at the present time it seems clear that assistance and consultation from behavioral health specialists, psychiatrists, and quasi-subspecialized primary care providers will be required for all physicians during their training, and for many physicians throughout their careers.

The DDPRQ in Medical Education: Interventions With the Physician

Perhaps one of the most fruitful arenas for using the DDPRQ is in training physicians. The DDPRQ, especially the hand-scored version of the DDPRQ-10, can be used by physicians to identify the patients who are experienced as difficult in their own practice for use in case-based educational interventions. The author has had excellent experiences using the DDPRQ in case-based educational interventions with primary care internal medicine residents and faculty. Using patients experienced as difficult as the basis of clinical training offers several advantages:

- The characteristics of difficult patients (i.e., Axis I and II psychopathology and somatization) are core issues for primary care curricula, and will predictably be present in patients selected using the DDPRQ.
- Physicians are uniquely motivated to learn how to improve their ability to treat patients experienced as difficult so that they can decrease their own distress.
- Patients experienced as difficult will be of unique interest to the health care delivery system because of their high utilization and low satisfaction with health care services. Using the DDPRQ to target this population may help improve systems outcomes. This benefit should be an effective rationale for obtaining administrative support for in-service education.
- Providers who are more likely to experience patients as difficult (not the same as physicians who have more difficult patients in their panel of patients) can be targeted for specific intervention.

STRENGTHS AND LIMITATION OF THE DDPRQ

Relevance

The DDPRQ identifies a population of patients that is relevant to today's concerns with health care utilization, patient satisfaction, and physician burn-out and satisfaction. The DDPRQ can be used to aid in the management of individual patients who are experienced as difficult, with populations of difficult patients within a system, and with physicians who have more of a problem with difficulty or related quality indicators such as patient satisfaction and utilization.

The DDPRQ positive patient is also relevant to many educational agendas that have been endorsed by institutional and expert opinion leaders. Specifically, the DDPRQ can be used to enhance skills and knowledge in the management of Axis I and II psychopathology, somatization, doctor–patient and doctor–patient–family communications, and the doctor–patient relationship itself.

Procedures

Administration of the DDPRQ is simple, requiring little more than the form itself. The hand-scored DDPRQ-10 can easily be completed at the end of an encounter so that interventions can be initiated before the patient leaves the clinical setting. The

30-item DDPRQ takes longer than the 10-item version, but its factor scores may prove useful, particularly in interventional studies. The DDPRQ poses some unique concerns regarding confidentiality because of the critical nature of the information recorded.

Objective Referents

The DDPRQ by its very nature and purpose measures internal emotional experiences for which there are no gold standards or criteria. Each item in the DDPRQ describes a specific emotional state or characteristic of patients. The cutoff point used to identify patients experienced as difficult has considerable support from convergent validity, and the very high internal consistency reliability that the DDPRQ has demonstrated speaks favorably toward the generalizability of results obtained with the instrument.

Use of Multiple Respondents

In research settings the DDPRQ is typically completed by only one physician. However, it would be both possible and useful in some instances to have the same patient rated by multiple providers. Data are not available on the concordance of different providers caring for the same patient, nor are there data on the effect of different kinds of doctor–patient relationships, such as primary care provider versus specialist/consultant versus mid-level provider or health educator.

Treatment Linkages

As discussed at length earlier, strong arguments can be made that patients experienced as difficult should receive specific evaluation and (as appropriate) treatment for Axis I and II psychopathology and somatization.

Psychometric Strength

As discussed earlier, the DDPRQ has excellent internal consistency reliability and strong construct and convergent validity. It can be counted on to identify a similar cohort of patients in different clinical settings, and indeed in more than one culture and language (see, e.g., Wiefferink et al., 1998).

Low Measure Costs Relative to Its Uses

The DDPRQ is extremely inexpensive to use. It requires a few minutes or less of provider time and is simple to analyze.

Understanding by Nonprofessional Audiences

The use of the DDPRQ with nonprofessional audiences presents some unique challenges. For the reasons mentioned earlier, it is often difficult for physicians to acknowledge the negative feelings they experience caring for patients in general, and especially so with regard to individual patients. Recent attention to problems in the doctor–patient relationship in the lay press has demonstrated that the public is capable of understanding the validity of this issue without condemning physicians. Nonprofessionals involved in health systems management should have little difficulty understanding and accepting the concepts behind the DDPRQ and data produced. On the other hand, presenting information on physician-experienced difficulty regarding a specific patient could be destructive, and is not envisaged as a part of clinical care.

Easy Feedback and Uncomplicated Interpretation

Taking into account the preceding caveats, presenting and interpreting DDPRQ results are relatively straightforward. It does not require sophisticated interpretation and can easily be presented as a dichotomous categorical variable or total score.

Usefulness in Clinical Services

The utility of the DDPRQ in clinical services remains to be empirically established. The DDPRQ has considerable potential for improving the care of a unique population of patients with special health care needs and predictably undesirable outcomes.

Compatibility With Clinical Theories and Practices

The DDPRQ is based on a broad theoretical foundation compatible with standard clinical practice. Some of the treatment recommendations discussed earlier require skills that are not widely disseminated in primary care practice. The family systems assessment interventions and strategies for managing personality pathology will be familiar to some behavioral health specialists, but not necessarily those who currently work with primary care providers.

SUMMARY AND CONCLUSIONS

The DDPRQ is a new instrument that can reliably identify a group of patients whose care is experienced as difficult by physicians. The construct validity of the instrument has been established by demonstrating strong associations between characteristics that have long been associated with physician experienced difficulty. The instrument classifies 11% to 20% of primary care patients as difficult using a cut point that has been shown to distinguish between patients with difficult characteristics and those without. The DDPRQ score can also be used as a continuous measure.

The instrument is available in two formats: the DDPRQ–30, a 30 item version that requires 3 to 5 min to complete, and a 10-item version, the DDPRQ–10, requiring less than 1 min. The hand-scored version of the DDPRQ–10 has reversed numeration for the Likert responses that require reversal prior to calculating the total score, thus facilitating rapid assessment. The DDPRQ has been translated into Dutch.

The DDPRQ was designed as a research tool to permit empirical study of a population of patients whose care physicians experience as difficult. Prior to the development of the DDPRQ, study of the difficult patient was limited to anecdote, descriptive discourse, or evaluation of idiosyncratically assembled cohorts. The DDPRQ has been used in a number of studies and has proven to be an effective and reliable research tool.

Patients experienced as difficult are an important group to study because they are more likely to have psychopathology, use health care services disproportionately, and are less satisfied with the care they receive. Physician-experienced difficulty also takes its toll on physician morale and job satisfaction. Further study of the epidemiology, determinants, and effective strategies for the management of difficult patients is needed. The physician characteristics that predispose to experiencing patients as difficult should also receive more attention. Health care systems and educational interventions can take advantage of physicians' high levels of interest in obtaining help in caring for their difficult patients. The DDPRQ can be used to identify difficult patients in learners' practices to use as material for case-based learning or to direct clinical supervision in the skills required to manage patients experienced as difficult.

REFERENCES

Anstett, R. (1980). The difficult patient and the physician–patient relationship. *Journal of Family Practice, 11,* 281–286.

Ashworth, C. D., Williamson, P., & Montanco, D. (1984). A scale to measure physician beliefs about psychosocial aspects of patient care. *Social Science and Medicine, 19,* 1235–1238.

Carey, M. P., Jorgensen, R. S., Weinstock, R. S., Sprafkin, R. P., Lanatiga, L. J., Carnricke, C. L. M., Baker, M. T., & Meisler, A. W. (1991). Reliability and validity of the appraisal of diabetes scale. *Journal of Behavioral Medicine, 14,* 43–51.

Costa, P. T., & McCrae, R. R. (1980). Influences of extroversion and neuroticism on subjective well-being: Happy and unhappy people. *Journal of Personality and Social Psychology, 38,* 668–678.

Drossman, D. A. (1978). The problem patient: Evaluation and care of medical patients with psychosocial disturbances. *Annals of Internal Medicine, 88,* 366–372.

Goodwin, J. M., Goodwin, J. S., & Kellner, R. (1979). Psychiatric symptoms in disliked medical patients. *Journal of the American Medical Association, 241,* 1117–1120.

Groves, J. E. (1978). Taking care of the hateful patient. *New England Journal of Medicine, 298,* 883–887.

Hahn, S. R. (1996). *The Difficult Doctor Patient Relationship Manual: DDPRQ-30, DDPRQ-10, and DDPRQ-10H.* Available from Dr. Steven R. Hahn, MD, Ambulatory Care Service, Jacobi Medical Center, Bronx, NY 10461.

Hahn, S. R. (1997). Working with specific populations: Families. In M. D. Feldman & J. F. Christensen (Eds.), *Behavioral medicine in primary care: A practical guide* (pp. 57–71). Stamford, CT: Appelton & Lange.

Hahn, S. R., Feiner, J. S., & Bellin, E. H. (1988). The doctor–patient–family relationship: A compensatory alliance. *Annals of Internal Medicine, 109,* 884–889.

Hahn, S. R., Thompson, K. S., Stern, V., Budner, N. S., & Wills, T. A. (1994). The difficult doctor–patient relationship: Somatization, personality and psychopathology. *Journal of Clinical Epidemiology, 47,* 647–658.

Hahn, S. R., Kroenke, K., Spitzer, R. L., Brody, D., Williams, J. B. W., Linzer, M., & deGruy III, F. V. (1996). The difficult patient: Prevalence, psychopathology, and functional impairment. *Journal of General Internal Medicine, 11,* 1–8.

Hall, J. A., Roter, D. L., & Katz, N. R. (1988). Meta-analysis of correlates of provider behavior in medical encounters. *Medical Care, 26,* 657–672.

Jackson, J. L., & Kroenke, K. (1999). Difficult patient encounters in the ambulatory clinic: Clinical predictors and outcomes. *Archives of Internal Medicine, 159,* 1069–1075.

Kahana, R. J., & Bibring, G. L. (1964). Personality types in medical management. In N. Zinberg (Ed.), *Psychiatry in medical practice* (pp. 108–123). New York: International University Press.

Kaplan, G., Lipkin, M., Jr., & Gordon, G. H. (1988). Somatization in primary care: Patients with unexplained and vexing medical complaints. *Journal of General Internal Medicine, 3,* 177–190.

Korsch, B. M., Gozzi, E. K., & Francis, V. (1968). Gaps in doctor–patient communication. I: Doctor–patient interaction and patient satisfaction. *Pediatrics, 42,* 855–871.

Kroenke, K., Spitzer, R., Williams, J. B. W., Linzer, M., Hahn, S. R., deGruy, F. V. III, & Brody, D. (1994). Physical symptoms in primary care: Predictors of psychiatric disorders and functional impairment. *Archives of Family Medicine, 3,* 774–779.

Lin, E. H. B., Katon, W., Von Korff, M,. Bush, T., Lipscomb, P., Russo, J., & Wagner, E. (1991). Frustrating patients: Physician and patient perspectives among distressed high users of medical services. *Journal of General Internal Medicine, 6,* 241–246.

Lipsitt, D. R. (1970). Medical and psychological characteristics of "crocks." *International Journal of Psychiatry in Medicine, 1,* 15–25.

McGaghie, W. C., & Whitenack, D. C. (1982). A scale for measurement of the problem patient labeling process. *Journal of Nervous and Mental Disorders, 170,* 598–604.

Merrill, J. M., Laux, L., & Thornby, J. I. (1987). Troublesome aspects of the patient–physician relationship: A study of human factors. *Southern Medical Journal, 80,* 1211–1215.

Novack, D. H., & Landau, C. (1985). Psychiatric diagnoses in problem patients. *Psychosomatics, 26,* 853–858.

O'Dowd, T. C. (1998). Five years of heartsick patients in general practice. *British Medical Journal, 297,* 528–530.

Parsons, T. (1958). Definitions of health and illness in the light of American values and social structure. In E. G. Jaco (Ed.), *Patients, physicians, and illness* (pp. 165–187). Glencoe: The Free Press.

Schwenk, T. L., Marquez, J. T., Lefever, D., & Cohen, M. (1989). Physician and patient determinants of difficult physician–patient relationships. *Journal of Family Practice, 28,* 59–63.

Sharpe, M., Mayou, R., Seagroatt, V., Surawy, C., Warwick, C., Bulstrode, C., Dawber, R., & Lane, D. (1994). Why do doctors find some patients difficult to help? *Quarterly Journal of Medicine, 87,* 187–193.

Smith, G. R., Monson, R. A., & Ray, D. C. (1986). Patients with multiple unexplained symptoms: Their characteristics, functional health, and health care utilization. *Archives of Internal Medicine, 146,* 69–72.

Spitzer, R. L., Kroenke, K., Linzer, M., Hahn, S. R., Williams, J. B. W., deGruy, F. V. III, Brody, D., & Davies, M. (1995). Health-related quality of life in primary care patients with mental disorders: Results from the PRIME–MD 1000 Study. *Journal of the American Medical Association, 274,* 1511–1517.

Spitzer, R. L., Williams, J. B. W., Kroenke, K., Linzer, M., deGruy, F. V. III, Hahn, S. R., Brody, D., & Johnson, J. G. (1994). Utility of a new procedure for diagnosing mental disorders in primary care: The PRIME–MD 1000 Study. *Journal of the American Medical Association, 272,* 1749–1756.

Walker, E. A., Katon, W. J., Keegan, D., Gardner, G., & Sullivan, M. (1997). Predictors of physician frustration in the care of patients with rheumatological complaints. *General Hospital Psychiatry, 19,* 315–323.

Wiefferink, C. H., De Best-Waldhober, M., & Mellenbergh, G. J. (1998). Moeilijke patiënten in huisartspraktijk: De validering van de Nederlandse verse van de DDPRQ [Difficult Doctor-Patient Relationship Questionnaire in the Netherlands]. *Tijdshrift voor Gezondheidswetenschappen, 76,* 298–304.

III

PRIMARY AND BEHAVIORAL HEALTH CARE INTEGRATION PROJECTS

Improving Care for a Primary Care Population: Depression as an Example

Patricia Robinson
Kirk Strosahl
Mountainview Consulting Group Inc.
Moxee, Washington

Health care providers who work in primary care settings provide numerous services to patients troubled by mental and behavioral impairments (Shapiro et al., 1984). Primary care physicians spend almost one quarter of their work week providing direct treatment for psychiatric conditions (Howard, 1992). In fact, more mental health services are delivered in the primary care setting than in any other health care setting in America (Knesper & Pagnucco, 1987; Magil & Garrret, 1988). During the past decade, primary care providers have begun to partner with mental health providers to improve outcomes in what has been called the de facto mental health system in America (Regier, Goldberg, & Taube, 1978). Group Health Cooperative of Puget Sound has a 13-year history of integrating behavioral health services into the primary care treatment setting. This pioneering health care system has developed models for general behavioral health consultation service (Strosahl, 1996, 1997) and programmatic treatment of depression (Robinson, Wischman, & Del Vento, 1996).

Depression merits close attention from psychologists who plan to partner with primary care in clinical or research roles because it is (a) the most frequently encountered mental disorder in primary care, (b) recurrent, and (c) associated with severe physical, social, and work role impairment (Wells et al., 1989). Epidemiological studies suggest that rates of depression have increased in America over the past two decades. Results of the Epidemiologic Catchment Area (ECA) Study, conducted in the 1980s with 20,000 adults aged 18 years and older, suggested a lifetime prevalence for major depressive disorder of 7.8 (Narrow, Regier, Rae, Manderscheid, & Locke, 1993). In 1990–1991, the National Co-Morbidity Study of adults aged 18–55 years found a lifetime prevalence of 17.1% for major depressive episode. The corresponding rate for 12-month prevalence was 10.3% (Kessler et al., 1994). In a study involving over 75,000 primary care patients, Zung, Broadhead, and Roth (1993) found that 20.9% were experiencing clinically significant depressive symptoms. In a clinic providing primary care to indigent patients, Rucker, Fye, and Cygan (1986) found that 32% of the patients were moderately to severely depressed. Azocar (1994) screened women's public health clinic waiting rooms and found 37% to have some type of mood disorder (21% major depression, 14.5% minor depression, 14.5% dysthymia).

Depression is common among older patients and patients who suffer from chronic diseases. In one study, a quarter of patients over age 65 years met criteria for depression at the time of hospital admission for a medical illness. Depression troubles between 25% and 50% of patients who suffer chronic illnesses, such as cancer, diabetes mellitus, multiple sclerosis, Parkinson's disease, and stroke (Ness & Finlayson, 1996). Primary care providers experience firsthand the extent to which depression compounds successful medical management of patients with chronic diseases. Depressed patients are expensive patients, and they are often dissatisfied with their care (Hall, Milburn, Roter, & Daltroy, 1998). Although depressed primary care patients suffer from chronic illnesses at rates similar to nondepressed patients, depressed patients have been found to report lower scores on perceived physical health and poorer mental health status than nondepressed patients (Jeffries, Scarinci, Reid, Jones, & Brantley, 1998). Relative to nondepressed patients, depressed patients have been found to have higher outpatient charges, specifically in the areas of lab and x-ray charges (Ness & Finlayson, 1996).

The primary care setting is rich with possibilities for the behavioral health clinician and researcher. Behavioral health specialists can complement primary care providers in developing and delivering multidisciplinary services to improve depression outcomes. This big picture/little picture perspective applies to other high-prevalence disorders in primary care, such as diabetes, chronic pain, and addiction disorders. In this chapter, we provide a brief review of literature relevant to designing integrated programmatic treatment for depression and make specific recommendations to guide the work of others. The term *integrated* refers to programs that support patient care by a team of primary care providers and behavioral health professionals who share common assessment methods and treatment goals and work side by side. We present information about the Integrated Program (IP) (Robinson et al., 1996), as it is an example of an evidence-based programmatic treatment for depression in primary care. The IP serves as a model for developing and evaluating behavioral health programs for high prevalence primary care populations. The primary care setting supports the scientist practitioner model (Hayes, 1987) and attention to population needs as well as individual needs. Our suggestions derive from over a decade of collaborative clinical work and research efforts, and our intention is to support others in successful explorations of integrated behavioral health work (Strosahl, 1998).

THE BASICS OF ADDRESSING DEPRESSION IN PRIMARY CARE

Although literature concerning the prevalence, causes, and treatments of depression is abundant (our program development effort began with a review of 3,700 abstracts), the literature concerning assessment and treatment in the primary care setting is much more limited. Here, only a handful of properly conducted studies are available to guide program development efforts (Katon et al., 1995, 1996; Miranda & Munoz, 1994; Mynors-Wallace, Gath, Lloyd-Thomas, & Tomlinson, 1995; Schulberg et al., 1996). Agency for Health Care Policy and Research (AHCPR) guidelines for treating depression in primary care assume that treatments with demonstrated efficacy in specialty settings will also be effective in the primary care setting (Depression Guideline Panel, 1993a, 1993b). This assumption has yet to be verified, and health care resources are not vast enough to extend the specialty model for treating depression to the primary care setting. In this chapter, we assume an underpinning philosophy of integrated health and behavioral health services within the primary care team environment, and we focus on research conducted in the primary care setting. More detailed information about the recommended model of integrated care is available elsewhere (Strosahl, 1996, 1997, 1998).

Population Management as a Service Philosophy

In developing a systematic treatment program, key decisions include selection of a model of care, the relative role of patient education versus psychotherapy, and the role of prevention in the management of the target problem. Of course, any treatment programs that are contemplated should have empirically demonstrated clinical effectiveness and be time effective as well. Population management is an ideal service philosophy for the primary care setting. Population management refers to the broader context of managing an at-risk population, such as depressed primary care patients. Typically, a population-based care approach seeks to expand the penetration of services into the population. This generally requires services to be flexibly designed and highly transportable. The success of primary prevention programs and patient education models is a classic example of the population management philosophy in action. Perhaps more importantly, assessment of program indicators tends to rely more on "aggregate data" than on clinical outcome data. For example, many employer purchasers are interested in the percentage of their work force that is put on a depression-related disability by a health care system during any given year. Preferential contracting status may be given to health care vendors who demonstrate lower population rates of depression-related disability. Similarly, process of care indicators may be used at the system level to "infer" the quality of care that is given at the individual case level. In the HEDIS (Health Plan–Employer Data Information Set) "report card" on health plans, there are two specific indicators of program "quality" in regards to depression: (a) the percentage of hospitalized depressed patients seen for an outpatient mental health visit within 7 days of hospital discharge and (b) the percentage of depressed patients who are rehospitalized for depression within a 90-day period after their initial discharge. These program indicators are difficult to use as clinical outcome indicators, but at a population level can be highly revealing about the performance of a depression management system.

The Primary Care Team Culture

Primary care providers work in a team. Team members may play multiple roles. The behavioral health consultant in primary care is an ancillary member of the primary care team (Robinson et al., 1996). The specifics of team composition and competencies vary significantly both from team to team and from clinic to clinic. The first 6 months of work in the primary care context will help the behavioral health consultant identify the team dynamics within the clinic and plan assessment strategies that use them optimally. Whatever the variation among teams, they have in common the fact that they are the hub of the wheel for the patient in today's health care system.

The Meaning of Primary.   Regardless of the presenting problem, an episode of care begins and ends in primary care. The relationship between the patient and the primary care provider often is a long-term one. The primary care provider is in a key position for detecting signs and symptoms of escalating psychological distress. The use of simple, straight-forward assessment instruments makes detection a concrete exercise that is easily within the skill and competency range of most primary care providers. Assessment by primary care providers can also help patients evaluate functioning and maintain behavior changes associated with an episode of effective psychological and psychiatric care.

Multidisciplinary Assessment and Treatment.   Provider roles may differ from team to team. It is best to recognize and capitalize on variations in strengths and interests among primary care providers. A medical receptionist on one team may have a strong interest in depression and take the lead in assessment for the team. This role might be played by a nurse on another team. A behavioral health consultant who takes the time to meet with the practice team is in a stronger position to advise the team on how to use its unique talents to improve care to depressed patients.

Local Experts.   In some cases, behavioral health clinicians will spend only part of their work week in the primary care clinic. The clinician who teaches others to be experts on the assessment and treatment of depression extends the effectiveness of assessment and treatment initiatives in a multiplicative fashion. We have found it helpful to create a team of depression experts in each clinic. This team includes a physician or physician assistant, nurse, and pharmacist.

The Fast Work Pace.   Time is of the essence in primary care. Educating patients about time limitations and ways to make the most of a visit is a vital endeavor. Pamphlets that encourage patients to review critical information and to write out ideas and questions prior to the appointment are very helpful. Providers can also find relief from time pressures by using available technologies in lieu of direct contact.

Phone-call follow-ups can be initiated when appointments are unfilled or patients fail to show. Phone calls are often acceptable to patients because they save the patient time. Phone calls need to be brief and targeted. A call can be used to intensify treatment efforts during active treatment or to support a written relapse prevention plan during the maintenance phase of treatment.

Computers can also support the provider extender approach. Software programs that encourage coordination of care (e.g., e-mail), provider reminders for tracking and follow-up, and development of personalized messages for patients are commonly available. Psychiatrists and pharmacists can work together to develop programs that alert physicians to unfilled antidepressant prescriptions in a timely manner. Computers can also be used to evaluate outcomes for individual providers, clinics, and an entire system.

Recognition and Screening

There is a controversy in the literature concerning the extent to which integrated programs need to increase physician recognition of depression and other mental disorders, and behavioral health providers need to think through the complexities of this dilemma. Several studies suggest that primary care physicians in office settings fail to diagnose and treat more than half of the patients who are suffering from common mental disorders (Borus, Howes, Devina, Rosenberg, & Livingston, 1988; Ormel, Koeter, van den Brink, & van de Willige, 1991; Rydon, Redmon, Sanson-Fisher, & Reid, 1992; Schulberg & Burns, 1988). On the other hand, Simon, Von Korff, Wagner, and Barlow (1995) and Simon and colleagues (1995) found that doctors tended to correctly discriminate between depressed patients who were more impaired by their mental disorder and less likely to improve without treatment and those with lesser impairments and a greater likelihood of spontaneous recovery. Coyne (1994) also found that undetected depressed primary care patients were more mildly depressed, less obviously symptomatic, demonstrated higher functioning, and were less likely to have a history of mental health outpatient or hospital treatment. Overrecognition and overtreatment could add cost without adding value (Von Korff, et al., 1998). Rates of recognition need to be evaluated, watched over time, and considered in the light of system resources.

In our experience at Group Health, the presence of behavioral health services in the primary care setting appears to be associated with increased recognition rates. The old adage that we "recognize what we can treat" probably holds true in the care of depressed primary care patients. Passive screening, including use of posters, pamphlets, and program announcements, can boost recognition in clinics where population data suggest underrecognition. The presence of a one-page announcement on an exam room bulletin board concerning a class for patients wanting to improve the quality of their lives may prompt patients to initiate discussions about depression and treatment. Given that at least half of the depressed people in America who receive mental health care do so through their primary care provider (Narrow et al., 1993), accurate and timely recognition of depression is an important factor in health care today.

Provider Variation

Providers vary in their patient panels and practice styles. Although some physicians excel in the diagnosis and treatment of patients with mental disorders, others have little or no interest in this area. Some physicians have older patient panels, and some younger. Some have a concentration of patients with a particular medical diagnosis (e.g., diabetes). Physician practice style also appears to be related to patient outcomes (Bertakis et al., 1996). Assessment strategies need to be consistent among all primary care providers and, indeed, throughout the health care system. Primary care providers of all skill levels, on-site behavioral health consultants, and outpatient mental health clinic staff need to use the same assessment materials. Although depression assessments may be more extensive and sophisticated when externally located specialists are involved, the basic assessment approach needs to remain consistent with all patients. When the method of assessment is consistent, results can be entered into computerized records that can reflect outcomes for individual patients, for clinics, and for the entire system. Patients benefit from visual displays of assessment results, which are easily generated by today's electronic medical records. If all providers in a system use the same assessment approach, providers who are less likely to recognize depression become more skillful. Providers who tend to see mild depression as moderate will learn to delay costly treatment and provide less intensive patient education and monitoring as an alternative. Consistency is powerful.

Linking Assessment and Treatment

The best cost, clinical, and satisfaction outcomes will be achieved by programs that closely link assessment and treatment. This may seem obvious, but there are many examples of depression screening programs where appropriate treatment services either do not exist or are not linked to assessment in any systematic way. For example, mildly depressed patients need to be treated differently from moderately depressed patients. The moderately depressed patient can make a choice between an effective counseling-based treatment, such as cognitive-behavioral therapy, or antidepressant therapy. Severely depressed patients may require more intensive cognitive-behavioral treatment and medicines in combination in order to avoid unnecessary hospitalizations. Although mildly depressed patients may not need antidepressant therapy or traditional counseling services, many will benefit from a low-intensity, patient education approach. This might include teaching the patient to self-monitor and to make small changes in daily schedules to promote a better mood state. Psychoeducational interventions help patients recognize the importance of repeat assessments over time and behavioral change in response to assessment results.

SCREENING AND ASSESSMENT SYSTEMS

As health care systems embrace the trend toward primary care-based behavioral health care, they will face numerous decisions concerning the development of an outcome measurement system. In this section, we identify key issues in designing a system that is consistent with today's health care system resources, in sync with the culture of primary care, and focused on using providers strengths and remediating weaknesses. We also identify needs of subpopulations of depressed primary care patients that have historically been underdiagnosed and undertreated.

The Bigger Picture: Single- or Multidimensional Outcomes Assessment

The assessment of response to depression treatment is a central component of any effective population management program. Conventional definitions of clinical outcome have relied almost exclusively on measures of symptom severity and meeting diagnostic criteria for remission, whereas the behavioral health care marketplace of the future will require an expansion of this definition. It will be useful to examine some of the more recent trends toward multidimensional assessment of depression outcomes.

Symptom Severity.   Measuring the severity of depression symptoms before and after treatment is an age-old outcomes assessment strategy; as are structured clinical interviews to determine whether a patient no longer meets diagnostic criteria for a particular depression syndrome. For example, at Group Health, we employ an Interactive Voice Response (IVR) system to screeen for depression screening. Our IVR approach has been scientifically established as having very high concurrent validity with other well-known self-report measures of depression. The severity tool is administered at baseline, at 4 weeks, and at 8 weeks to assess response to the acute phase of treatment. There are numerous depression severity measures available on the market today. They are all highly intercorrelated; there does not appear to be a "gold standard" self-report measure for use in primary care.

Health Status. Along with clinical response to treatment, there is growing interest and emphasis on the impact behavioral interventions have on general health status and medical services utilization. Perhaps the best known measure in this area is the SF–36 (Wells et al., 1989), a measure of general health, physical impairment, emotional well-being, and social role impairment. At Group Health, we employ the SF–12, a shortened form of the SF–36, as a central measure in the pre- and posttreatment assessment package.

Work Performance and Disability. Employer purchasers are increasingly interested in learning about not only clinical symptom relief and changes in health status, but also the effect that depression treatment has on work performance. These indicators include work absenteeism, tardiness, lost production, or disability days. Typically, these data are presented in aggregate form when reporting to purchasers on the success of a depression management program. Not surprisingly, depression management programs that emphasize an early, aggressive disability prevention and return-to-work philosophy are in great demand There are several fairly elaborate scientific measures of disability behavior, but often a "quick and dirty" assessment is sufficient. At Group Health, the depression battery consists of specific questions about number of missed work days in the last month, the number of days arriving late or leaving early from work because of depression, and the degree to which depression is interfering with normal work productivity.

Consumer Satisfaction. The contemporary "triad" of quality clinical care involves good clinical and functional outcomes (including health status and work/social role), minimum cost to treat, and high levels of consumer satisfaction. Consumer satisfaction addresses the issue of service quality within a depression care program. How quickly are patients able to get through to schedule an initial appointment? Are patient's generally satisfied with their appointment times and frequency of contacts? Does the provider treat the patient with respect and dignity? Does the provider appear to coordinate the patient's care with other health care professions? These indicators are often thought to be isomorphic with clinical outcomes; that is, patients who get better are satisfied and those that get worse are dissatisfied. However, research at Group Health suggests this is not the case. In a large sample of clients receiving mental health services, the observed correlation between adjusted outcome scores and consumer satisfaction rating scales was only .32. Although this is a significant relationship, it suggests that only 5% to 10% of the variation in consumer satisfaction is accounted for by observed clinical outcomes. Any primary care-based depression treatment program should have consumer satisfaction assessments as a core element of the outcomes assessment battery.

Intent-to-Treat Success Rates. Traditionally, researchers have ignored the problem of treatment dropouts in research studies by conducting statistical analyses only on "treatment completers" or creating estimated endpoint scores using regression analysis. A more important contemporary approach in programmatic treatment of depression is the intent-to-treat analysis, which includes every patient who is enrolled in a program. Those that drop out are counted as treatment failures. At a program level, that patient will need to be treated again by another primary care provider. Intent-to-treat analyses reveal a stunningly low success rate of most treatments for depression, even in the specialty mental health setting. Therefore, an effective primary care-based program for treating depression must be capable of retaining patients. Although the patient completion rate (over 90%) for the Integrated Program (Katon et al., 1996; Robinson et al., 1996) seems like a peripheral statistical result, it is in fact a major program success indicator. Because of its extraordinarily high retention and treatment compliance rates, the IP may well be superior to most forms of specialty mental health treatment for depression.

Relapse Rates. Depression is a recurrent condition. About 50% of patients who have a single episode will have a recurrence within 2 years. The rate is higher for patients treated solely with antidepressants. It is lower in patients who are treated with cognitive therapy or interpersonal therapy alone, or in combination with antidepressants. Measuring relapse is a central feature of effective primary care based treatment programs. A relapse means that "rework" occurs. The same treatment has to be delivered over again. This costs behavioral health and primary care providers time and money. Typically, patients should be monitored for at least 2 years after successful initial treatment. Relapse can be defined as either (a) developing the full-blown symptoms of the same depressive disorder, or (b) developing another disorder that requires additional treatment. At Group Health, we define relapse as seeking additional unplanned behavioral health services, where the service code reflects a depressive disorder, whether or not it is the same disorder that was noted during the index treatment regime.

Make the System Simple

Depression is the most common mental problem in primary care. Assessment methods that are simple and straightforward help primary care providers expand diagnostic screening to include behavioral and cognitive symptoms. Primary care providers work in 10- and 15-min units of time. Although primary care visits with depressed patients are slightly longer than visits with nondepressed patients, they are less than half as long as patient visits with psychiatrists (Olfson & Klerman, 1992). Patients readily agree to completing simple self-report inventories in the waiting area prior to an appointment, and providers agree readily to using simple structured interviews to increase their accuracy and efficiency in diagnosis and treatment planning. Simplicity also supports communication among providers.

Manuals for psychiatric classification were designed for the mental health setting. They are not "user-friendly" for primary care providers. The *Diagnostic and Statistical Manual of Mental Disorders*, 4th Edition (American Psychiatric Association, 1994), is a large and complex volume. Several major efforts are currently underway to adapt the *DSM–IV* (American Psychiatric Association, 1994) and other standard diagnostic approaches for use in primary care. The PRIME–MD is one such instrument designed for the primary care setting. It provides an assessment approach for depression and other commonly occurring mental disorders in primary care. PRIME–MD results are consistent with *DSM–III–R* criteria (Spitzer et al., 1994). Other user-friendly diagnostic systems include the Duke Anxiety–Depression Screener (Duke A–D) (Parkerson, 1996) and the International Classification and Diagnosis System, Primary Care Version 10 (ICDS–PC) (Lamberts, Wood, & Hofmans-Okkes, 1993). The ICDS–PC includes brief suggestions of efficacious treatments along with shortened, more clinically oriented diagnostic descriptors. Health care systems may develop and cross-validate their own depression detection tools. A brief screener with follow-up questions for patients scoring positively is a time-effective strategy for primary care. Whooley, Avins, Miranda, and Browner (1997) found that a two-question instrument was 96% sensitive for detecting major depression. Figure 22.1 presents the assessment tool used in the Integrated Program (Robinson et al., 1996). Most patients complete this instrument in less than 5 min.

Develop Awareness of Physical and Psychological Symptoms

Given their emphasis on the detection and treatment of physical symptoms, primary care providers may need assistance in recognizing the psychological symptoms of depression. Educational strategies for PCP's may include simple mnemonic strategies, such as acronyms or use of prescription pads that list key symptoms of depression. Large-scale studies suggest that primary care patients tend to report a predominance of cognitive and behavioral symptoms of depression. Jacobs, Kopans, and Reizes (1995) screened 40,000 patients for depression in 1992 and 1993. Ninety-one percent of the 40,000 patients who scored positive for moderate or severe depression suffered from the following symptoms: difficulty in getting things done, feeling hopeless about the future, difficulty in making decisions, feeling worthless and not needed, and no longer enjoying the things that used to be enjoyable. Less than half of this large group of community-dwelling adults were identified by primary care providers as having endorsed significant physical symptoms associated with depression. Assessment efforts need to help primary care providers place adequate emphasis on the behavioral and cognitive symptoms of depression.

Use Structured Interviews and an Interactive Format

Provider interviews can be structured by patient provision of self-report data designed to help the provider and patient collaboratively plan treatment. Structured interviews help change provider behavior over time and enhance consistency among providers. Most patients are willing to "begin treatment in the waiting room" by responding to brief questionnaires designed to assess symptoms. Patients need to know that their completion of such questionnaires will allow their direct contact time with the provider to focus more exclusively on critical treatment planning issues. When assessment results link to specific treatment protocols and structured interviews, primary care providers are more likely to use assessments results. In the Integrated Program (Robinson et al., 1996), the patient screening tool for depression is folded into an a larger behavioral health protocol, with a menu of treatment options. A copy of the first page of the "Coping Plan" is presented in Fig. 22.2 to illustrate how assessment can be used in a format that structures patient-physician interactions about treatment.

Monitor Provider Performance

Only a small number of behavioral providers are trained in primary care behavioral health during graduate training (Brantley & Applegate, 1998). Although the number of primary care providers who receive training in behavioral health counseling is

Patient:	Provider(s):

Dear Patient: Please respond to the following questions. If you need help with any of the questions, ask your doctor or nurse.

Mark an "X" by any symptom that has troubled you *more days than not* during the past ☐ one or ☐ two (*check one*) week(s).	Today's Date	Return Visit Date
1. Anger or Irritability—often during the day	☐	☐
2. Sadness—often during the day	☐	☐
3. Sleep Problems: ☐ too much; ☐ slow to go to sleep; ☐ waking in middle of night; ☐ early morning waking	☐	☐
4. Interest Problems—a lack of interest in others and in activities you usually enjoy	☐	☐
5. Guilt, self critical thoughts, feeling inadequate or worthless	☐	☐
6. Energy Problems—tired most of the time	☐	☐
7. Concentration Problems	☐	☐
8. Appetite Changes: ☐ significantly greater; ☐ significantly less; ☐ weight gain; ☐ weight loss	☐	☐
9. Psychomotor Problems: ☐ very "slowed down" or ☐ very "speeded up"	☐	☐
10. Pain Problems—more aches and more pain	☐	☐
11. Suicidal Thoughts	☐	☐
12. Sexual interest change	☐	☐

How often have you used the following coping strategies in the past ☐ one or ☐ two (*check one*) week(s).

0 = Not at all; 1 = Once; 2 = Several times; 3 = Almost Daily; 4 = Daily

1. Participating in pleasurable activities _____ _____

2. Participating in activities that boost your confidence _____ _____

3. Simply being aware of an uncomfortable thought, feeling, or emotion without struggling with it _____ _____

4. Participating in activities that help you relax _____ _____

5. Using problem-solving techniques for problems you're having in life such as problems with your job or relationships _____ _____

6. Noticing negative thoughts and replacing them with more realistic thoughts _____ _____

7. Participating in creative activities _____ _____

FIG. 22.1. Integrated Program depression assessment tool.

IP Coping Plan—Page 1

Name

Dear Patient: Your answers to the following questions will assist you and your primary care provider in developing a helpful treatment plan.

---

1. What is the major problem you would like help with?

2. What do you think is **causing** your problem? (Check all that apply.)
   ☐ Physical disorder or illness; ☐ Stress; ☐ Other

   Describe cause(s):

3. Which of the following do *you* think is or might be **helpful**? (Check all that apply.)
   ☐ Medications; ☐ Lifestyle adjustments; ☐ Other

   Describe:

4. If you have read the booklets, "*Seven Ways to Cope*" or "*Using Medications Successfully*," what questions do you have about them?

5. If you have ever had a period of depression before, **what helped** you start to feel better then?

6. List the activities or thoughts that have helped you feel a little better in the past two weeks, no matter how brief the time that you felt better (for example, visiting a friend or going for a walk).

7. List the activities you'd be doing or the thoughts you'd be having if you started to feel a little bit better in the coming week.

FIG. 22.2. The IP coping plan.

growing, both primary care providers and behavioral health consultants who partner with them may slide back to early patterns of practice under pressure. Programs that monitor and provide feedback to providers in a positive manner are most likely to retain their integrity over time.

Consider the Needs of Special Populations

Compared to depressed patients seen in the mental health clinic specialty system, depressed primary care patients are likely to be older and less educated (Waxman, Carner, & Blum, 1983). They are also more likely to be married and of ethnically diverse backgrounds. Depressed primary care patients have worse physical health, more physical and psychophysiological symptoms, and more pain than depressed patients seeking care in mental health clinics. The primary care provider's emphasis is on evaluating the whole person, and many depressed primary care patients have a somatic focus. Assessment strategies need to address language and cultural barriers to better recognition. For example, older adults may be more likely agree to having "the blues" than to being "depressed." Male patients may present with more irritability than female patients. Assessment strategies also need to address the physical health issues presented by patients as well. For example, behavioral health providers can assist the primary care team by evaluating the role of depression in a chronic pain patient's presentation.

Use Multilevel Cut Points to Trigger Appropriate Types of Care

Several studies at Group Health have suggested that primary care providers tend to overprescribe antidepressant medications to patients with milder symptoms of depression (Katon et al., 1995, 1996). This is a costly problem because there is no clear evidence demonstrating that antidepressant therapy is effective for mild depression. An assessment approach that is capable of discriminating between mild and moderate to severe levels of depression can reduce overprescribing.

Build Economic Considerations Into Program Design

Economic factors are a major consideration in designing integrated assessment and treatment programs. Assessment and outcomes monitoring strategies must be economically feasible and should be continuously evaluated in terms of improved outcomes, cost-effectiveness, and medical cost offsets. Both increased cost-effectiveness and medical cost savings may be realized with efforts to improve depression outcomes in primary care. One of the first studies to look specifically at treatment of depression in primary care did find a significant cost-effectiveness effect (Von Korff et al., 1998). This finding will likely support mental health administrators who want to deploy some of their resources to the primary care arena. More substantial medical cost offsets may be noted when longer follow-up time periods are explored (cf. Strosahl & Sobel, 1996, for a review).

Cost savings are more likely to be realized when programs encourage efficiency on the part of the patient and provider. Providers can orient patients to self-assessment and emphasize its value in maintaining treatment gains and preventing future episodes of depression. Positive contingencies for the individual patient also include provision of provider attention and reinforcement for critical self-management skills, such as anticipating and planning for stresses, successful employment, and so forth.

Cost rewards for the system may also be built into depression assessment and treatment programs. Most patients are motivated to find nonmedical strategies for managing depression. More than half of the patients identified as having probable major depression and as being good candidates for antidepressant therapy in two large primary care studies were found to actually have subsyndromal depression (Robinson et al., 1996). A period of watchful waiting and basic behavioral education is much less expressive than a regimen of antidepressant therapy that continues for months or years. Structured depression assessments including mnemonics, such as ASSIGECAPPSS (i.e., Anger, Sadness/Sleep, Interest loss, Guilt, Energy loss, Concentration difficulty, Appetite change, Psychomotor problems, Pain, Suicidal thoughts, Sexual interest change), and a depression severity tool can help providers match patients to specific treatment options.

Improved assessment and treatment may also assist the system in obtaining ongoing contracts with employers, who see decreased disability costs when patients receive care in a system providing integrated services. The single largest potential source of system-level cost savings is preventing the recurrence of depression in a patient who already has had an episode of depression. At Group Health, we estimate that an episode of depression costs approximately $1,300.00. For every 100 episodes we prevent, we can completely fund 5,200 hours of behavioral consultation in primary care. This is equivalent to almost 2½ full-time behavioral health positions for a year. Many programmatic options are possible for the prevention of relapse in recurrent conditions, such as those employed in the Integrated Program (Robinson et al., 1996).

AN INFORMATICS INFRASTRUCTURE

Many technologies are available that can increase ease, efficiency, and clinical accuracy of primary care-based assessment efforts. Technology can facilitate the process of collecting data at multiple time points and can be used to inform the care management process for the individual. It also supports efficient evaluation of progress toward health care system initiatives concerning change in provider or patient behaviors pertinent to management of depressed patients. Additionally, technological advances may support use of collected data to benefit care for the individual and to evaluate the effectiveness of program initiatives for the entire population of depressed primary care patients.

Use Alternative Technologies

Computers can be combined with other technologies to increase accuracy and efficiency. Patients who prefer e-mail to telephonic assessments can provide assessment information through e-mail. Patients who prefer to provide assessment information at the clinic can come early for appointments and enter assessment information into computers with touchscreens, often referred to as "point of view" boxes. Large-screen formats may be particularly helpful for older patients with visual impairments. Java-based web charts currently under development offer maximum flexibility and information for providers as well as administrators of health care (*Healthcare Intranet Report*, 1998).

Form a Registry

Using the computer for assessment facilitates the scientist-practitioner model (Richard, 1998). Building an automated depression registry supports consistent follow-up and continuity of care management over time. It also permits individual and systematic evaluation of initiatives designed to improve outcomes for a significant population. When patients are entered into a registry, they can easily be notified of follow-up assessments, new research findings concerning depression, and changes to existing treatment programs within the health care system. Systems can evaluate systemwide goals through use of a registry (e.g., increase in percentage of patients with mild symptoms who participate in a second assessment 1 month after identification; reduction in percentage of patients with recurrent episodes within 1 year of treatment).

Use an Interactive Voice Response System

Research suggests that computer-based interviews are superior to face-to-face interview in promoting participant self-disclosure (Lock & Gilbert, 1995). One of the most promising technological innovations in the field of behavioral informatics is the use of interactive voice response technology, sometimes referred to as IVR. IVR systems allow administration of assessment protocols in an automated phone survey format. IVR systems have numerous advantages over traditional data collection methods. First, assessment data are collected, scored, and profiled in "real time." This means providers can have virtually instantaneous access to depression screening results, self-report diagnostic checklists, and so forth. Second, IVR surveys are virtually error free, once operational. Third, IVR systems can be accessed 24 hours a day by any patient who has access to a touch-tone telephone. Although one might worry about the acceptability of automated phone interviews, experience at Group Health suggests that consumers like the anonymity, brevity (typical surveys take 15 min or less), and user-friendly, structured nature of such systems. At Group Health, depressed primary care patients can be asked to complete an IVR survey that assesses health status, social/work role functioning, coping skills, and depression symptoms, all in less than 8 min. These data are automatically scored and faxed back to the behavioral health clinician in real time. Finally, apart from the significant initial capital costs to purchase IVR hardware, there is very little ongoing maintenance and, because no paper forms are involved, personnel costs associated with collecting, managing, scoring, and profiling assessment results are minimal.

Scanable forms and point of view (POV) hand-held computers are a less desirable, although commonly used, alternative to interactive voice response systems. They are a popular means of collecting, scoring, and managing data. Be aware, however, that scanning and point of view technology requires the purchase, maintenance, and periodic replacement of hardware, is supported by complicated and error-prone software, and requires a locally based "host" computer to store, manage, and analyze data. For these reasons, the long-term costs of such systems generally exceed the up-front costs of installing an interactive voice system. Given the real-time efficiency, lower support cost, and greater capacity of interactive voice technology, we recommend pursuing that option whenever it is economically feasible to do so.

PHILOSOPHICAL ISSUES IN DEPRESSION MANAGEMENT PROGRAM DESIGN

Treatment needs to grow from a theoretical model. The medical model suggests that depression is an illness. Given this model, the logical treatment for depression is pharmacological. It is not surprising that primary care physicians write 80% of the antidepressant prescriptions in the United States (Olfson & Klerman, 1987, 1992, 1993). The biopsychosocial model present an alternative approach that is more "user friendly." This model will support basic behavioral health education in primary care, while still allowing for prescription of antidepressant medicines. The biopsychosocial model works well in primary care. It provides a rationale for assessment and treatment of physical, behavioral, and mental symptoms of depression. The model "validates" all of the promising psychotherapeutic treatments, as well as the role that antidepressants may play in treatment. The biopsychosocial model suggests to patients and providers that both counseling and medication treatments are effective singly and in combination. Patients and providers can select a specific course of treatment based on the patient's unique symptom presentation and personal preferences. The model encourages patients and providers to focus treatment on all aspects of depression and to consider alternative treatments. In this way, the biopsychosocial model encourages support of the physician's pharmacological treatment by the behavioral health consultant and the behavioral health consultant's behavioral treatment by the primary care provider. Behavioral health education about depression and psychological coping strategies that moderate mood becomes the foundation of treatment for all patients when the biopsychosocial model is used in initiating treatment (see Robinson et al., 1996, for a broader discussion of this approach).

The model is the template for all patient and provider education. Figure 22.3 provides a visual aid that patients and primary care providers, including behavioral health consultants, can use to collaboratively develop individual treatment plans. Using this model as the template for treatment planning empowers assessment efforts by patients and providers, as well as changes to the original treatment plan. This model also supports education concerning the relapse prevention strategies that will follow successful treatment.

The brief context of primary care requires that psychotherapeutic interventions be delivered with an educational focus. An educational focus helps the behavioral health consultant avoid the more time-consuming work of psychotherapy per se. A patient education management model is acceptable to most patients, and a variety of educational materials can be offered, ranging from briefs pamphlets to short workbooks.

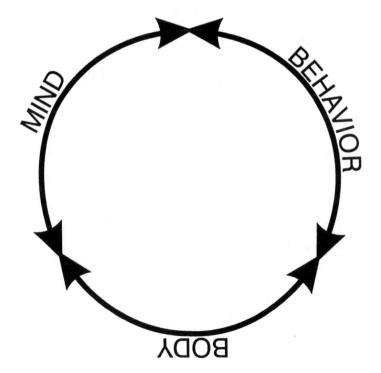

FIG. 22.3. Biopsychosocial model of depression.

An educational approach fits the fast pace that both primary care and behavioral health providers maintain in primary care. Critical messages can be delivered clearly even under significant time constraints. Written materials, audiotapes, and video-tapes may supplement and reinforce key educational messages delivered in office or phone visits. An educational model helps the behavioral health consultant avoid the "take charge" role of the outpatient psychotherapist. The role of a behavioral health consultant is to assist with assessment and treatment planning and to return the pa-tient (smarter and more skillful) to the primary care team for ongoing care. Use of ac-tive coping strategies and improvement in quality of life are key components of an educational approach to depression management.

Focusing on self-management supports evolution of the patient–physician rela-tionship in the direction of greater collaboration. Many providers struggle when pa-tients expect longer term treatment that is no longer financially feasible. Providers welcome programs that empower them to address the "ethical challenges" resulting from insurers' demand for patients and providers to balance value issues in health care (Sabin & Pearson, 1998, p. 15). There are unavoidable ambiguities and uncertain-ties inherent in providing care for individual members of a population within the constraints of a budget. Providers need to give clear messages that address these un-certainties and that fit seamlessly into clinical routines. An education approach helps providers respond to patients in a nondefensive manner. Use of an educational model encourages the patient to become an active participant in treatment. Patient and physician interactions are shifted from angry indignation and paternalism to-ward personal responsibility and equality. With a recurrent disorder such as depres-sion, this is a necessary and powerful shift in perspective for the patient.

Depression management programs need to teach prevention. Patient mastery of assessment strategies and specific coping skills paves the way for the concept of re-lapse prevention. The basic biopsychosocial model is an ideal way to introduce re-lapse prevention. Patients can identify behavioral, physical, or cognitive symptom changes that would signal a need for increased attention to coping plans, including potential restarting of antidepressant therapy. The Integrated Program (Robinson et al., 1998) suggests use of a written document that is supported for a 6-month period by the primary care physician and the behavioral health clinician. This includes peri-odic structured self-assessments of depression symptoms and associated severity levels. Another possibility is to have a behavioral health clinician become involved in developing a relapse prevention plan after the patient responds to antidepressant therapy.

GUIDELINES FOR DESIGNING DEPRESSION MANAGEMENT PROGRAMS

With adaptations, several psychosocial treatments, as well as pharmacological treat-ment efforts, can improve outcomes for treatment of depression in the primary care setting. Brown and Schulberg (1995) provided an excellent review of 18 randomized clinical trials assessing the efficacy of psychosocial treatments in primary care. Eight of the 18 studies reviewed focused on the treatment of depressed patients. On the bright side, most have studied the use of traditional mental health specialty treat-ments with primary care patients. These treatments are not logistically feasible or cost effective options in most primary care settings. Several recent studies focused on innovative primary care treatments of depression (Katon et al., 1995, 1996; Miranda & Munoz, 1994; Mynors-Wallace et al., 1995; Schulberg et al., 1996; Schulberg et al., 1998). Cognitive-behavioral therapy, interpersonal therapy, problem-solving therapy, and pharmacotherapy combined with brief cognitive-behavioral treatment are promising treatments for depression in the primary care setting. Pharmacological treatments can be made more effective by assessment programs that help providers identify the best candidates for pharmacological treatment and address barriers to successful adherence.

Use an Evidence-Based Care Approach

Treatments validated in settings other than primary care may or may not be feasible or effective in primary care. In a large clinical trial, Schulberg and his colleagues (1996) established that standardized pharmacotherapy and psychotherapy are significantly more effective than a primary care physician's usual care in resolving episodes of major depression. Their treatments were designed to be consistent with AHCPR guidelines concerning specialty treatment. Protocols of interpersonal and pharmacological treatments were developed to be consistent with protocols for which efficacy was established in the traditional mental health setting. The interpersonal psychotherapy condition involved patient attendance at 16 weekly sessions of individual therapy at the primary care clinic and four monthly appointments during the last 4 months of treatment. Drop out rates were high prior to and after the start of the study. Forty-five percent of the pharmacotherapy and 50% of the psychotherapy patients completed active and continuation treatment phases (Schulberg et al., 1998). This type of treatment package would not be feasible or cost-effective in most primary care systems. Schulberg et al. (1998) also found that treatment type (medication vs. psychotherapy) was unrelated to the clinical course among the more severely depressed primary care patients.

Another early effort to map out a treatment for primary care involved use of on-site experts to diagnosis patients and advise providers about treatment. Katon, Von Korff, Lin, Bush, and Ormel (1992) placed liaison psychiatrists in primary care clinics to see physician-referred patients directly for an evaluation. After the evaluation, the psychiatrist provided the physician with a written summary, including a diagnosis and suggestions for treatment. This minimally integrated "one-shot" approach failed to improve clinical outcomes.

In order for treatments to be effective, they must be sufficiently intensive, integrated, and feasible. Feasibility criteria include acceptability to the patient and availability of resources for large-scale dissemination of the treatment. Although some of the treatment regimens empirically validated in trials involving mental health outpatients may be effective in primary care research studies, their effectiveness in day-to-day care may be limited by their considerable costs and low acceptability to patients.

Problem Solving Works

Mynors-Wallace et al. (1995) found that primary care providers could apply standardized, structured psychotherapy protocols to improve care to depressed primary care patients. They compared a brief problem-solving treatment delivered by primary care physicians to a combined clinical management and antidepressant treatment protocol. Both were superior to usual care, and both involved less than 4 hours of provider time over a 6-week period. Mynors-Wallace et al. (1995) concluded that physician-delivered problem-solving therapy was as effective as antidepressant therapy for patients with major depression. Further, patients who received problem-solving treatment tended to be more satisfied with care and were more likely to complete treatment than patients receiving antidepressant medications. Problem-solving therapy may be well suited for the primary care setting because it is simple and straightforward and because patients are often struggling with specific life circumstance problems (Robinson et al., 1994, 1997).

Antidepressant Therapy Works

Over half of the patients seen for depression in primary care clinics receive antidepressant therapy (Olfson & Klerman, 1987). Unfortunately, patients often fail to adhere to medications, and primary care providers tend to prescribe antidepressants at dosages that are lower than recommended by guidelines (Katon et al., 1992; Olfson & Klerman, 1993; Simon et al., 1993). A third problem with primary care antidepressant treatment is that physicians often prescribe medications to patients with milder forms of depression, even though evidence documenting efficacy of pharmacological treatment for minor depression is lacking (Elkin et al., 1989; Katon et al., 1995).

Behavioral health consultants who work in primary care can improve pharmacological treatment efforts by engaging in specific forms of assessment and intervention. Behavioral health consultants can help patients started on antidepressants by using assessments that identify specific obstacles to adherence. For example, a patient's beliefs about medication may influence adherence behavior significantly. In the Integrated Care Program, the Medication Assessment Questionnaire helps behavioral health or primary care providers quickly evaluate a patient's past history, current preferences, current fears about side effects, and beliefs pertinent to use of an antidepressant. Beliefs are assessed quickly in a checklist format, where patients indicate endorsement of statements such as "I should be able to get by without using these kinds of drugs," "I could get addicted," and "My family would not want me to use these kinds of drugs." Consultants can also help by developing educational materials that help other primary care providers work directly on adherence behaviors, including development of specific behavioral plans for coping with anticipated side effects.

Combined Behavioral and Antidepressant Therapy Works

During the early 1990s, two randomized clinical trials at Group Health evaluated multifaceted interventions designed to develop and test models of care that would be feasible and effective in improving outcomes with depressed primary care patients. Both studies involved placing mental health professionals on site in selected primary care clinics, training primary care providers in behavioral health protocols, providing patients with written educational materials, and changing the system of care to maximize coordination and collaboration between primary care providers and on-site behavioral health providers. Both models employed a biopsychosocial model that supported cognitive behavioral and antidepressant treatment. The first model employed liaison psychiatrists and the second, health psychologists. These studies resulted in the development of an integrated care model that can be implemented in other health maintenance organizations and, indeed, in numerous health care system arrangements. We discuss this dissemination model in the last section of the chapter and refer to it as the Integrated Program (IP). In this section, we discuss the two trials that informed the development of the IP. The first research model is referred to as the Liaison Psychiatry model and the second research model as the Integrated Program model.

The Liaison Psychiatry model included providing patients with educational booklets and a video prior to special half-hour appointments with primary care physicians. Patients and physicians discussed the educational materials and planned specific written medication and behavioral health interventions in the special visit. Patients were seen by primary care physicians 2 weeks later. Between the first and second appointments with the primary care physician study, patients saw a liaison psychiatrist. Most patients saw the on-site psychiatrist for a second visit in week 4 of the intensive treatment protocol. A small group of patients continued to see liaison psychiatrists for up to 10 visits. In addition to providing direct patient care, liaison psychiatrists also provided consultation and training to primary care physicians and surveyed automated pharmacy data concerning patient refills of prescribed antidepressants. When a patient did not refill at the expected time, the psychiatrist notified the primary care physician or nurse concerning the failed refill, and the primary care team phoned the patient to update the treatment plan.

The Liaison Psychiatry model resulted in improvements on several outcome measures. Patients with major and minor depression who participated in the program were significantly more likely than usual care controls to take antidepressant medications at adequate dosages as recommended by AHCPR guidelines for treatment of depression in primary care (Katon et al., 1995). The intervention program also improved satisfaction with care and clinical outcomes in patients with major, but not minor, depression. The program was acceptable to patients and primary care providers. In a poststudy survey, over 80% of the primary care physicians stated that the multifaceted intervention greatly increased their satisfaction in treating depression. Lin et al. (1995) conducted a poststudy investigation of the prescribing practices of participating physicians and found that providers tended to return to previous prescribing patterns after the study ended and all aspects of the intervention were removed from the clinic. Thus, improvements in the process and outcome of care associated with the Liaison Psychiatry model appear to be dependent on continued presence of on-site mental health staff and use of strategic educational materials designed to change the process of care.

The Integrated Program model involved deploying health psychologists into the primary care setting to relieve the burden of care on the primary care team while still keeping the team in the loop. In this approach, patients were offered a choice concerning number of visits with the psychologist. The basic program required four weekly, 30 minute visits during active treatment and four brief phone-call follow-ups initiated by the psychologist at 2, 4, 12, and 24 weeks after patient completion of active treatment. Phone calls were focused on the patient's adherence to a behavioral relapse prevention plan developed collaboratively with the patient in the last active treatment visit. The enhanced program included two additional clinic visits with the psychologist. The initial visit with the psychologist was 1 hr and subsequent visits were 30 min in length. Total direct treatment time between the patient and behavioral consultant ranged from 2.5 to 3.5 hr of contact, and active treatment ended within 4 to 6 weeks of referral.

The Integrated Program (IP) behavioral treatment was based on multimodal therapy (Lazarus, 1992), social learning theory (Lewinsohn, Antonuccio, Breckenridge, & Teri, 1984), cognitive theory (e.g., Rush, Beck, Kovacs, & Hollon, 1977), and psychological acceptance theory (Hayes, 1987). Additionally, development of skill work exercises in the intervention treatment was influenced by the works of Gath (1993), Jacobowski and Lange (1978), Jacobson (1986), and Kabat-Zinn (1990). A 125-page manual supported implementation of the intervention treatment.

Psychologists were responsible for the following: (a) provision of written and verbal instruction in use of coping skills; (b) assessment, education, and planning about benefits and side effects of medication; and (c) collaborative development of weekly behavioral experiments tailored to patient psychosocial needs. Patients used self-assessment techniques, including a symptom checklist and the Beck Depression Inventory–Short Form (Beck & Beck, 1972), and actively participated in behavioral and medication planning. During and between intervention treatment visits, psychologists worked with both primary care physicians and the consulting liaison psychiatrist to assist with medication starts, switches, dose changes, augmentations, and stops. Psychologists also conferred with the liaison psychiatrist regarding medications in brief weekly staff meetings conducted by phone or in the clinic. The psychologist or primary care physician could refer complex patients for a direct medication consultation with the psychiatrist consultant.

In all intervention treatment visits, the behavioral consultant and patient worked together to plan behavioral experiments to improve quality of life in one or more areas of daily living. A written relapse prevention plan, called the Progress Plan, was developed in the final contact and served as the basis for telephone checks during the follow-up phase of treatment. Brief chart notations regarding behavioral and medication treatment plans and the patient's Progress Plan were given to the primary care physician on the same day of the visit and then placed in the medical chart. Primary care providers were encouraged to reinforce intervention treatment materials in medical contacts with the patient.

The Integrated Program model resulted in significant improvements on depression outcome measures for patients with major depression (Katon et al., 1996). Significant results were also obtained for patients with minor depression, but were less robust. Patient rates of using coping strategies targeted in the intervention increased significantly for intervention patients with minor depression at all follow-ups and for intervention patients with major depression at the early follow-up. This finding is noteworthy in that recent research has documented an association between use of active coping strategies and severity of depression (Burns & Nolen-Hoeksema, 1991). Patients who received the Integrated Program also tended to use medications more consistently than usual care controls later in the treatment process. Specifically, both major and minor depressives who received the intervention were more likely to report use of medications during the third month of treatment. Finally, patients with major and minor depression who participated in the Integrated Program were much more likely than control patients to be following a relapse prevention plan at the 4-month follow-up.

Of the two models, the Integrated Program (IP) model appears to be the most feasible. This model involved brief treatment that supported treatment options already available in the primary care setting. Eighty-eight percent of the patients referred to the program completed the basic program, which involved four sessions and development of a relapse prevention plan supported by the primary care team. Of the 72 patients who attended at least the first IP visit, 94% completed the program. The program attempted to adjust level of intensity of care to lessen treatment costs. Only 6 of the 77 patients (7.8%) referred to the IP were seen directly by the Liaison Psychiatrist for medication consultation. Telephone follow-up appeared to be acceptable to patients, and psychologists made a mean of 4.1 telephone calls to patients who completed the IP. Patients who received the Integrated Program were consistently more satisfied with treatment than usual care controls at all follow-ups. All participating physicians preferred the Integrated Program to specialty mental health treatment for their depressed patients, and 88% indicated that IP materials were easy to use in follow-up visits with patients. Cost studies suggest that the Collaborative Care model and the Integrated Care model result in a mental health cost offset and a significant net cost effectiveness over "usual care" (Von Korff et al., 1998).

The Integrated Program Is a Clinically Effective Model

The Integrated Program (IP) (Robinson et al., 1996) is a population-based, evidence-based treatment program that is designed for depressed primary care patients. This program is derived from the findings of the two pioneering studies at Group Health (evaluating the Integrated Program intervention; Katon et al., 1996) discussed earlier, as well as from years of clinical experience in primary care. The IP defines (a) new methods for assessment and clinical management by primary care providers and (b) brief, on-site assessment and treatment by mental health providers. The IP addresses treatment needs for all patients, ranging from minor, transitory depression to severe, longer term depression. All providers work collaboratively and give theoretically consistent information to patients. The IP subscribes to a biopsychosocial theory of depression that justifies pharmacological treatment or psychotherapeutic treatment or both. Assessment approaches are thorough yet brief, and linked to treatment goals. Patient education materials include 20-page, pamphlet-sized workbooks provided in photocopy-ready form for busy practitioners (Robinson et al., 1996) and a more complete, 100-page workbook, *Living Life Well: New Strategies for Hard Times* (Robinson, 1996). Treatment formats include both individual care and group psychoeducational programs (Robinson et al., 1998).

Several changes in basic service delivery protocols can make the Integrated Program more cost-effective than was observed in the randomized field trial that initially tested the treatment protocols. First, telephone follow-ups may be used with select patient groups in lieu of clinic visits. Second, the physician-extender model used successfully with medical patients may be applied to behavioral health treatments in the primary care setting. Specifically, social workers and master's level therapists may deliver services under the supervision of more highly trained and costly mental health providers. A third strategy involves adjusting level of care to severity of illness. In the Integrated Program, patients with minor and major depression should not receive equally intensive treatments. "Watchful waiting" combined with the behaviorally focused patient education approach is preferred for patients with minor depression, thereby increasing the overall cost-effectiveness of the IP with lessening clinical impact. Patient's who are assessed to be deteriorating in mood and behavioral functioning can be stepped up to more intensive module-based IP curriculum that is used to treat major depression.

SUMMARY

The primary care setting is fertile ground for assessing and treating psychological disorders. Depression is a particularly important target because it is an extremely common disorder in primary care and a costly one. Depression is second to cardiovascular disease in terms of time lost from work (Ness & Finlayson, 1996). Unfortunately, less than half of depressed patients with coexisting medical illness are diagnosed, and only 30% of these receive appropriate treatment (Richardson, 1993). There are many assessment methods available to help improve diagnosis and many promising treatments. Some treatments can be delivered effectively and exclusively by primary care providers (e.g., problem-solving therapy and pharmacotherapy). Others require on-site behavioral health clinicians (Katon et al., 1995, 1996). The primary care setting has unique features, and behavioral health specialists are most likely to succeed if they design programs that build on the strengths of the primary care providers and use models developed specifically for the primary care setting from empirical studies and best practice settings.

Researchers can have a field day in primary care. A priority is the evaluation of behavioral activation strategies implemented by primary care providers and behavioral health providers working in integrated efforts. Behavioral activation strategies have demonstrated clinical efficacy equal to more complex cognitive strategies (Jacobson et al., 1996), and they are easily disseminated and consistent with "naturalistic" primary care provider interventions. Additionally, researchers should evaluate the effects of treating depressed patients on a long-term basis. Less than 11% of outcome studies in process in 1994 incorporated follow-up assessments from 3 to 12 months after the treatment episode (American Psychiatric Association, 1994). Without such long-term studies, we may pursue programs that yield short-term benefits but are long-term failures. Only long-term studies are capable of evaluating the ability of behavioral and psychiatric interventions to produce durable effects. Finally, the medical cost-offset literature continues to be plagued by major conceptual and methodological problems. Ultimately, the integration of behavioral health programs for depression into primary care relies on a convincing data-based demonstration that such services save medical dollars in the intermediate to longer term. Researchers could dramatically advance the cause of integrated services by developing more sophisticated methods for detecting medical cost offsets.

REFERENCES

American Psychiatric Association. (1994). *Diagnostic and statistical manual of mental disorders* (4th ed.). Washington, DC: Author.

Azocar, P. (1994, July). *Depression prevalence in primary care.* Paper presented at the National Institute of Mental Health Conference on Treatment of Medical Disorders in General Medical Settings, McLean, VA.

Beck, A. T., & Beck, R. W. (1972). Screening depressed patients in family practice: A rapid technique. *Postgraduate Medicine, 52,* 81–85.

Bertakis, K. D., Callahan, E. J., Helms, L. J., Azari, R., Robbins, J. A., & Miller, J. (1996). *Physician practice styles and patient outcomes: Differences between family practice and general internal medicine.* Manuscript submitted for publication.

Borus, J. F., Howes, M. J., Devina, N. P., Rosenberg, R., & Livingston, W. W. (1988). Primary health care providers' recognition and diagnosis of mental disorders in their patients. *General Hospital Psychiatry, 10,* 317–321.

Brantley, P. J., & Applegate, B. W. (1998). Training behavior therapists for primary care. *The Behavior Therapist, 21,* 74–76.

Brown, C., & Schulberg, H. C. (1995). The efficacy of psychosocial treatments in primary care: A review of randomized clinical trials. *General Hospital Psychiatry, 17,* 414–424.

Burns, D. D., & Nolen-Hoeksema, S. (1991). Coping styles, homework compliance, and the effectiveness of cognitive-behavioral therapy. *Journal of Consulting and Clinical Psychology, 59,* 305–311.

Coyne, J. (1994, September). *Detection of depression in depressed primary care patients.* Paper presented at the National Institute of Mental Health conference on Treatment of Mental Disorders in General Medical Settings, McLean, VA.

Depression Guideline Panel. (1993a). *Depression in primary care: Vol. 1. Detection and diagnosis.* (Clinical Practice Guideline No. 5, AHCPR Publication No. 93-0550). Rockville, MD: U.S. Department of Health and Human Services, Public Health Service, Agency for Health Care Policy and Research.

Depression Guideline Panel. (1993b). *Depression in primary care: Vol. 2. Treatment of major depression* (Clinical Practice Guideline No. 5, AHCPR Publication No. 93-0551). Rockville, MD: U.S. Department of Health and Human Services, Public Health Service, Agency for Health Care Policy and Research.

Elkin, E., Shea, M. T., Watkins, J. T., Imber, S. D., Sotsky, S. M., Collins, J. F., Glass, D. R., Pikonis, P. A., Leber, W. R., Docherty, J. P., Fiester, S. J., & Parlaff, M. B. (1989). National Institute of Mental Health Treatment of Depression Collaborative Research Program: General effectiveness of treatments. *Archives of General Psychiatry, 46,* 971–982.

Gath, D. (1993). *A manual for problem solving treatment in the general medical setting.* Unpublished manuscript.

Hall, J. A., Milburn, M. A., Roter, D. L., & Daltroy, L. H. (1998). Why are sicker patients less satisfied with their medical care? Tests of two explanatory models. *Health Psychology, 17,* 70–75.

Hayes, S. C. (1987). A contextual approach to therapeutic change. In N. Jacobson (Ed.), *Psychotherapists in clinical practice: Cognitive and behavioral perspectives* (pp. 327–387). New York: Guilford.

Healthcare Intranet Report. (1998). Kaiser's Java-based WebChart. 8–10 January.

Howard, K. I. (1992). The psychotherapeutic service delivery system. *Psychotherapy Research, 2,* 164–180.

Jacobowski, P., & Lange, A. J. (1978). *The assertive option: Your rights and responsibilities.* Champaign, IL: Research Press.

Jacobs, D. G., Kopans, B. S., & Reizes, J. M. (1995). Revaluation of depression: What the general practitioner needs to know. *Mind/Body Medicine, 1,* 17–22.

Jacobson, N. (1986). *A conflict resolution manual for couples.* Unpublished manuscript.

Jacobson, N. S., Dobson, K. S., Truax, P. A., Addis, M. E., Koerner, K., Gollan, J. K., Gortner, E., & Prince, S. E. (1996). A component analysis of cognitive-behavioral treatment for depression. *Journal of Consulting and Clinical Psychology, 64,* 295–304.

Jefries, S. K., Scarinci, I. C., Reid, P. A., Jones, G. N., & Brantley, P. J. (1998, March). *Major depression and health outcomes among low-income individuals.* Poster session presented at the annual meeting of the Society for Behavioral Medicine, New Orleans, LA.

Kabat-Zinn, J. (1990). *Full catastrophe living: Using the wisdom of your body and mind to face stress, pain, and illness.* New York: Hyperion.

Katon, W., Von Korff, M., Lin, W., Bush, T., & Ormel, J. (1992). Adequacy and duration of antidepressant treatment in primary care. *Medical Care, 30,* 67–76.

Katon, W., Robinson, P. Von Korff, M., Lin, E., Bush, T., Ludman, E., Simon, G., & Walker, E. (1996). A multifaceted intervention to improve treatment of depression in primary care. *Archives of General Psychiatry, 53,* 924–932.

Katon, W., Von Korff, M., Lin, E., Walker, E., Simon, G., Bush, T, Robinson, P., and Russo, J. (1995). Collaborative management to achieve treatment guidelines: Impact on depression in primary care. *Journal of the American Medical Association, 273,* 1026–1031.

Kessler, R. C., McGonagle, K. A., Zhao, S., Nelson, C., Hughes, M., Eshelman, S., Wittchen, H. U., & Kendler, K. S. (1994). Lifetime and 12-month prevalence of DSM–III–R psychiatric disorders in the United States. *Archives of General Psychiatry, 51,* 8–19.

Knesper, D. J., & Pagnucco, D. J. (1987). Estimated distribution of effort by providers of mental health services to U.S. adults in 1982 and 1983. *American Journal of Psychiatry, 144,* 883–888.

Lamberts, H., Wood, M., & Hofmans-Okkes, I. (1993). *The international classification of primary care in the European Community with a multilanguage layer.* Oxford, England: Oxford University Press.

Lazarus, A. (1992). The multimodal approach to the treatment of minor depression. *American Journal of Psychotherapy, XIV,* 50–57.

Lewinsohn, P. M., Antonuccio, D. O., Breckenridge, J. S. & Teri, L. (1984). *The coping with depression course: A psychoeducational intervention for unipolar depression.* Eugene, OR: Castalia.

Lin, E., Von Korff, M., Katon, W., Bush, T., Simon, G., Walker, E., & Robinson, P. (1995). *Achieving guidelines for the treatment of depression in primary care: Training model vs. reorganization of service delivery.* Presented at the Eighth Annual NIMH International Research Conference on Mental Health Problems in the General Health Care Sector, McLean, Virginia, 7–9 September, 1994.

Locke, S. D., & Gilbert, B. O. (1995). Method of psychological assessment, self-disclosure, and experiential differences: A study of computer, questionnaire, and interview assessment formats. *Journal of Social Behavior and Personality, 10,* 255–263.

Magil, M. K., & Garrett, R. W. (1988). Behavioral and psychiatric problems. In R. B. Tayler (Ed.), *Family medicine* (3rd ed., pp. 534–562). New York: Springer-Verlag.

Miranda, J., & Munoz, R. F. (1994). Intervention for minor depression in primary care patients. *Psychosomatic Medicine, 56,* 136–141.

Mynors-Wallace, L., Gath, D. H., Lloyd-Thomas, A. R., & Tomlinson, D. (1995). Randomized controlled trial comparing problem solving treatment with amitriptyline and placebo for major depression in primary care. *British Medical Journal, 310,* 441–446.

Narrow, W. E., Regier, D. A., Rae, D. S., Manderscheid, R., & Locke, B. Z. (1993). Use of services by persons with mental and addictive disorders: Findings from the National Institute of Mental Health Epidemiologic Catchment Area Program. *Archives of General Psychiatry, 50,* 95–107.

Ness, R. E., & Finlayson, R. E. (1996). Management of depression in patients with coexisting medical illness. *American Family Physician, 53,* 2125–2133.

Olfson, M., & Klerman, G. L. (1992). The treatment of depression: Prescribing practices of primary care physicians and psychiatrists. *Journal of Family Practice, 35,* 627–635.

Olfson, M., & Klerman, G. L. (1993). Trends in the prescription of psychotropic medications: The role of physician specialty. *Medical Care, 31,* 559–564.

Ormel, J., Koeter, M. W. J., van den Brink, W., & van de Willige, G. (1991). Recognition, management, and course of anxiety and depression in general practice. *Archives of General Psychiatry, 48,* 700–706.

Parkerson, G. R. (1996). *User's guide for the Duke Health Profile (Duke).* Durham, NC: Duke University Medical Center.

Regier, D. A., Goldberg, I. D., & Taube, C. (1978). The de facto U.S. mental health service system. *Archives of General Psychiatry, 35,* 685–693.

Richard, D. C. S. (1998). Computers in the 21st century: Challenge to behavioral assessment and behavior therapy. *The Behavior Therapist, 20,* 186–188.

Richardson, E. (1993). Treatment of acute depression. *Psychiatric Clinic of North America, 16,* 461–178.

Robinson, P. (1996). *Living life well: New strategies for hard times.* Reno, NV: Context Press.

Robinson, P. (1998). *The quality of life class: Impact of a primary care behavioral health group.* Manuscript submitted for publication.

Robinson, P., Bush, T., Von Korff, M., Katon, W., Lin, E., Simon, G. E., & Walker, E. (1994). Primary care physician use of cognitive behavioral techniques with depressed patients. *Journal of Family Practice, 40,* 352–357.

Robinson, P., Bush, T., Von Korff, M., Katon, W., Lin, E., Simon, G. E., & Walker, E. (1997). The education of depressed primary care patients: What do patients think of interactive booklets and a video? *Journal of Family Practice, 44,* 562–571.

Robinson, P., Wischman, C., & Del Vento, A. (1996). *Treating depression in primary care: A manual for primary care and mental health providers.* Reno, NV: Context Press.

Rucker, L., Fye, E. B., & Cygan, R. W. (1986). Feasibility and usefulness of depression screening in medical outpatients. *Archives of Internal Medicine, 146,* 729–731.

Rush, A. J., Beck, A. T., Kovacs, M., & Hollon, S. (1977). Comparative efficacy of cognitive therapy and pharmacotherapy in the treatment of depressed outpatients. *Cognitive Therapy Research, 1,* 17–38.

Rydon, P., Redman, S., Sonson-Fisher, R. W., & Reid, A. L. A. (1992). Detection of alcohol-related problems in general practice. *Journal for the Study of Alcoholism, 58,* 197–202.

Sabin, J. E., & Pearson, S. D. (1998). Patient–clinician trust: The learning curve of communication. *HMO Practice, 12,* 14–16.

Schulberg, H. C., & Burns, B. J. (1988). Mental disorders in primary care: Epidemiologic, diagnostic, and treatment research directions. *General Hospital Psychiatry, 10,* 79–87.

Schulberg, H., Block, M., Madonia, M., Scott, C., Rodriguez, E., Imber, S., Perel, J., Lave, J., Houck, P., & Coulehan, J. (1996). Treating major depression in primary care practice: Eight-month clinical outcomes. *Archives of General Psychiatry, 153,* 1293–1300.

Shapiro, S., Skinner, E., Kessler, L., Von Korff, M., German, P., Tischler, G., Leaf, P., Benham, L., Cottler, L., & Regier, D. (1984). Utilization of mental health services. *Archives of General Psychiatry, 41,* 971–978.

Simon, G., Von Korff, M., Wagner, E. H., & Barlow, W. (1993). Patterns of antidepressant use in community practice. *General Hospital Psychiatry, 15,* 399–408.

Simon, G., Lin, E. H. B., Katon, W., Saunders, K., Von Korff, M., Walker, E., Bush, T., & Robinson, P. (1995). Outcomes of "inadequate" antidepressant treatment. *Journal of General Internal Medicine, 10,* 663–670.

Spitzer, R. L., Williams, J. B., Kroenke, K., Linzer, L., deGruy, F. V., Hahn, S. R., Brody, D., & Johnson, J. G. (1994). Utility of a new procedure for diagnosing mental disorders in primary care: The PRIME–MD 1000 Study. *Journal of the American Medical Association, 272,* 1749–1756.

Strosahl, K. (1996). Primary mental health care: A new paradigm for achieving behavioral health integration. *Behavioral Healthcare Tommorow, 5,* 93–96.

Strosahl, K. (1997). Building integrated primary care behavioral health delivery systems that work: A compass and a horizon. In N. Cummings, J. Cummings, & J. Johnson (Eds.), *Behavioral health in primary care: A guide for clinical integration* (pp. 37–60). Madison, CT: International Universities Press.

Strosahl, K. (1998). Integrating behavioral health and primary care services: The primary mental health care model. In A. Blount (Ed.), *Integrated primary care: The future of medical and mental health collaboration* (pp. 139–166). New York: W. W. Norton.

Strosahl, K., & Sobel, D. (1996). Behavioral health and the medical cost offset effect: Current status, key concepts and future applications. *HMO Practice, 10,* 156–162.

Von Korff, M., Katon, W., Bush, T., Lin, E. H. B., Simon, G., Saunders, K., Ludman, E., Walker, E., & Unutzer, J. (1998). Treatment costs, cost offset and cost-effectiveness of collaborative management of depression. *Psychosomatic Medicine, 60,* 143–149.

Waxman, H. M., Carner, E. A., & Blum, A. (1983). Depressive symptoms and health service utilization among the community elderly. *Journal of the American Geriatric Society, 31,* 417–420.

Wells, K. B., Stewart, A., Hays, R. D., Burnam, A., Rogers, W., Daniels, M., Berry, S., Greenfield, S., & Ware, J. (1989). The functioning and well-being of depressed patients: Results from the Medical Outcomes Study. *Journal of the American Medical Association, 262,* 914–919.

Whooley, M. A., Avins, A. L., Miranda, J., & Browner, W. S. (1997). Detecting depression with two questions. *Journal of Family Practice, 45,* 376.

Zung, W. W. K., Broadhead, W. E., & Roth, M. E. (1993). Prevalence of depression in primary care. *Journal of Family Practice, 37,* 337–344.

A Case Study: The Kaiser Permanente Integrated Care Project

Arne Beck
Carolee Nimmer
Kaiser Permanente, Rocky Mountain Division

Psychiatric disorders are associated with significant morbidity, disability, and cost. The estimated 1990 cost of depression in the United States was $44 billion, with only $12.4 billion spent on actual treatment; the remaining cost was attributed to inadequate treatment, lowered job productivity, lost income from missed work days, and suicide (Franco, 1995). A study of health maintenance organization (HMO) primary care patients found that those with *DSM–III–R* anxiety or depressive disorders had 91% higher medical utilization costs at baseline assessment than patients without these disorders, and that these cost differences persisted after adjustment for medical morbidity (Simon, Von Korff, & Barlow, 1995). Other research has demonstrated that patients with anxiety or depressive disorders reported "reduced functioning levels within ranges that would be expected for patients with chronic physical diseases, such as diabetes and congestive heart failure" (Fifer et al., 1994, p. 740).

In addition, anxiety and depressive disorders are prevalent in primary care (estimated at 15%), yet are often unrecognized and untreated (Katon, 1996; Simon et al., 1995; Wells et al., 1989). Despite the gaps in detection and treatment of these disorders, the locus of treatment for depression and other common psychiatric disorders is increasingly primary care. It has been estimated that up to 60% of patients with diagnosable psychiatric disorders seek help through primary care providers, not mental health professionals (Barsky & Borus, 1995). Reasons for this shift include patients' perceived barriers to access for mental medical services and the stigma associated with seeking such services. Moreover, up to 50% of patients referred to mental health specialists do not complete the referral (Schulberg, 1991; Schulberg et al., 1993). Because of the increasing shift of treatment for psychiatric disorders to primary care, and the recognized gaps in physician knowledge about detecting and effectively treating these disorders, mental health policy experts argue that quality improvement efforts in primary care are needed (Sturm & Wells, 1995).

One response to the call for increasing the quality of treatment for psychiatric disorders is the collaborative care model, in which mental health providers are located in the same office as primary care providers and share the treatment of these patients.

Collaborative activities include consultation, coordination of treatment plans, joint or alternating sessions with patients, physician and patient education, patient follow-up for medication adherence and symptom assessment, and monthly case conferences focusing on difficulties with treatment that physicians may encounter (McDaniel, Campbell, & Seaburn, 1996; Pace, 1995).

A growing literature supports the effectiveness of these models for reducing symptom severity, offsetting medical services utilization and its associated costs, and improving appropriate dosage of and adherence to antidepressant medication (Bray & Rogers, 1995; Katon, 1996; Katon & Gonzales, 1994; Katon et al., 1995; Leahy, Galbreath, Powell, & Shinn, 1994; Mumford, Schlesinger, Glass, Patrick, & Cuerdon, 1984; Pace, 1995; Pace, Chaney, Mullins, & Olson, 1995; Pallak, Cummings, Dorken, & Henke, 1993). A review of the literature on collaborative care indicates that incorporating mental health treatment into the primary care system leads to better care, better outcomes, and greater cost-effectiveness, especially for those patients who would not access mental health services outside of their primary care department (McDaniel et al., 1996). Similar results are reported by Lareau and Nelson (1994), whose survey of British physicians demonstrated that a liaison practice with mental health professionals resulted in lower costs, easier access, and reduced number of psychotropic medications. Studies have also demonstrated increased provider satisfaction with collaborative models (Muchnick, Davis, Getzinger, Rosenberg, & Weiss, 1993).

Evidence for the effectiveness of integrated care created interest among a small group of mental health providers and researchers within Kaiser Permanente's Rocky Mountain Division (KPRMD). This group, called the working group on collaborative care, set as its primary goal the implementation of a pilot integrated care program in KPRMD. Funding for the program was sought and awarded from KPRMD's internal Research and Development (R&D) fund. The implementation of and preliminary results from this integrated care project are described in this chapter.

THE INTEGRATED PRIMARY AND BEHAVIORAL HEALTH CARE PROGRAM

Kaiser Permanente Rocky Mountain Division (KPRMD) is a group-model HMO providing comprehensive primary and specialty care to more than 335,000 members in the Denver and Boulder metropolitan areas, and a relatively new provider network model in the Colorado Springs metropolitan area. KPRMD has 14 outpatient facilities, including 4 outpatient mental health clinics. Inpatient services are provided primarily by two contract hospitals, Saint Joseph Hospital in Denver, and Lutheran Hospital in Wheat Ridge. Because it is an integrated health care delivery system, KPRMD captures patient-level encounter data in mainframe computer administrative databases, including (a) outpatient visits, (b) pharmacy, (c) emergency room (ER) visits, (d) membership status and demographics, (e) hospitalization, (f) lab tests and results, and (g) imaging tests.

Impetus for Development

Three separate events led to the development of the KPRMD integrated care project. The first was related to a Depression in Primary Care program developed jointly by the Behavioral Health and Pharmacy Departments. The program provided educational materials and training to help physicians increase the detection and appropriate treatment of depression. This program resulted in a growing awareness of the number of patients in primary care with a wide variety of mental health issues who were unwilling to act on a referral to the Behavioral Health Department. Some of these patients had minor to moderate depression, but others had severe depression or comorbid psychopathology. As the communication about the types of disorders being seen in primary care improved, so did the awareness that this was a population that would be unlikely to seek treatment within the Behavioral Health Department. Physicians often described these patients as time-consuming because they were repeat visitors with vague somatic complaints that at times did not respond to medical intervention. Some physicians were aware of their patients' psychosocial concerns but felt hard pressed to address these in the time allotted for a primary care visit.

The second event was the development and successful implementation of a program for patients without health insurance who were seen at the University Hospital in Denver. This program, called CU Care, was provided by Kaiser Permanente and the University of Colorado Health Sciences Center. David Price, MD, a family practice physician, developed this project and included psychology graduate student interns as part of an integrated care treatment model to meet the needs of this indigent population. The interns worked directly with the patients but also spent time consulting with the physicians on developing comprehensive treatment plans for the patients. The program was highly successful in providing treatment for anxiety and depression in a population that was unlikely to follow through with treatment at a mental health facility.

The third event was the increase in managed health and mental health care companies in the Colorado area. With this increase, the need to provide a truly integrated health care service became more important. Potential subscribers indicated a strong interest in a health care company that could demonstrate the integration of all health services to decrease overall health care costs and ensure that patients were being treated for the appropriate health care problems. Employer groups are well informed about the high costs of untreated depression and anxiety and requested evidence of collaboration and integration between behavioral health and primary care. As a group-model HMO, KPRMD is in a position to demonstrate a competitive edge in the ability not only to share information and provide consultation between mental health and primary care, but also to provide the best possible care by addressing patients' psychosocial and medical needs simultaneously.

Steps to Development of the Program

Several mental health providers formed an interest/working group on collaborative care. They reviewed the growing psychological literature on collaborative care models, attended conferences, and networked with mental health providers in other managed care organizations. At the same time, they began working with the R&D department to draft a proposal for funding a collaborative care study to implement within KPRMD. In addition, this group developed a partnership with the physician in charge (PIC) at one of KPRMD's medical offices. The PIC is the physician manager for a medical office and, in combination with the nursing supervisor and nursing staff, is the key decision maker for implementing new service delivery models in the medical offices. The PIC expressed an interest in having the providers and nurses at his medical office participate in research projects. Moreover, he and the staff were receptive to the idea of testing an integrated care model, recognizing the relatively high prevalence of depression among patients attending the medical office.

Selection of a Model of Collaborative Care. Several models for integrated service delivery were discussed in the development of the program—a consultative model, a collaborative model, and an integrated model.

In the past, the behavioral health department had been physically located at the medical clinics and had attempted to establish a consultative model. The consultative model at this time involved a mental health provider being available to the internal medicine/family practice staff for immediate consultation by telephone, and quarterly educational sessions on mental health issues. This model met with limited success, primarily due to lack of strong relationships between providers in the different departments. The lack of structure and the lack of training with both mental health and medical personnel also contributed to the limited success of the model. Mental health providers often perceived the calls from primary care providers (PCPs) as an attempt to shift the responsibility for a patient onto the mental health department and did not provide optimal care for the patient. This perception had a negative impact on the relationship between providers in the two departments.

The collaborative model that was considered developed from other managed health companies who placed a mental health provider in the medical clinic for a limited period of time each week (4 to 8 hr). This model was reported to be working well for other managed care companies. The model allowed the providers to develop a relationship and to consult and work together on selected cases. The primary drawback of this model was the limited amount of time to provide for learning between the providers. The collaborative model presented the risk of developing into a difficult-case conference/referral model. For medical providers who were less sophisticated in the area of psychosocial issues, this model might have relatively little impact because the providers might not access the service for any of their patients.

At one small medical clinic, the mental health and internal medicine/family practice departments developed a very strong working relationship. The model that this group of providers adopted informally over time was an integrated model. The primary care physicians would frequently call the mental health providers to come into one of their visits with a patient to discuss the behavioral health concerns. The two departments developed a style of relating that involved sharing cases and curbside consultation on both behavioral health and medical issues. Close daily contact played a strong role in the natural development of the model. This model was also used at CU Care. The success of these two programs suggested that an integrated model of care with providers from each department feeling a part of the same team met the needs of the organization better than a consultative or collaborative model.

The key components of the integrated model included:

1. The development of a strong relationship between the providers on the integrated team.
2. A clear understanding of the roles of each team member.
3. The development of an understanding and respect for each other's culture.
4. A structure that encouraged sharing cases and mutual consultation to provide the best care for patients.

5. Commitment on the part of management and providers to devote time, space, and resources to the program.

6. Collection of data to feed back into the integrated care system to allow for adjustments and changes to the program, and to monitor patient outcomes.

The working group kept in mind that a model for a collaborative team must be developed by the team working with one another to best meet the demands of the patient population, the characteristics of the clinic, and preferences of the professionals involved.

Obstacles and Solutions to Collaboration.   A truly integrated approach to health care is a radical change in service delivery for most medical and mental health professionals, and represents a significant shift in organizational structure as well. The following obstacles to implementing the integrated care program were identified in the literature and discussed at length by the working group.

1. *Physical space.* For collaboration to work, providers need to be in close physical proximity, and mental health providers need some minimal space other than exam rooms to meet with patients (Bray & Rogers, 1995; McDaniel, Hepworth, & Doherty, 1993). The site chosen, the Aurora Centrepoint facility, was recently built and had extra offices, which removed the physical space obstacle.

2. *Financial structures.* It has been suggested that health care organizations need to adopt a perspective of savings/expenses occurring across the board and over the long range rather than in the short-term and limited to one department or another, particularly in regard to high-utilizing patients. In most collaborative studies, mental health costs increase, whereas medical, surgical, and pharmacy costs decrease (Bray & Rogers, 1995; Katon, 1996; McDaniel et al., 1993). Assessment of health services utilization was therefore a requirement for determining program cost effectiveness.

3. *Language/culture.* Language and/or cultural differences may contribute to lack of clear communication between disciplines and with patients and their families. Physicians and psychologists need education and time with each other in order to be able to understand each other's professional languages, and to communicate cohesively to patients and families. Increased comfort with other professionals will result in more effective and efficient collaboration, and is likely to be most beneficial to the patient (Glenn, 1987). We therefore purposefully built in lead time for the mental health providers to become acculturated into the medical facility.

4. *Theoretical models.* There is a divergent focus on the scientific method in each discipline's training, with primary care physicians typically focused on the application of concrete scientific findings, and psychologists experienced in science as a methodology, and therefore more focused on methods and processes. Understanding of each other's theoretical base, as well as a respect for the differences, can help providers overcome this obstacle (Pace, 1995).

5. *Time constraints.* Psychologists in primary care settings need to be prepared to have briefer periods of time with patients, and to respect physicians' time constraints (McDaniel et al., 1996). This point was continually emphasized by PCPs and the nursing staff who prided themselves on efficiently managing patient flow in a busy medical office.

Key Components of the Model Selected.   The model selected was based on the interest and availability of the mental health providers. It was designed to have two part-time psychologists providing full-time coverage on site at the medical office. Their time was structured to be able to provide curbside consultation 50% of the time and direct patient treatment 50% of the time.

IMPLEMENTATION OF THE PROGRAM

The working group applied for and received internal funding from KPRMD's Research and Development fund to implement the integrated care program.

Overall Plan for Program Implementation

A task force comprised of behavioral health, medicine, and research and development personnel met to carefully review the program implementation process. The task force met on a weekly basis for 2 hr. The task force attempted to address the program from three different perspectives: the patient's, the medical staff's, and the behavioral health provider's. Specific areas of focus included training of professional and support staff, selection of mental health providers, medical record confidentiality issues, and general integrated program characteristics.

Training of Professional and Support Staff

The task force initially addressed major issues with the professional and support staff: creating a culture to encourage integration, managing dangerous patients, developing a crisis system to handle behavioral health crises, and creating a strong liaison system back to the behavioral health department. Later the task force focused on more minor but important issues: development of a check-in system for patients, ordering equipment and supplies for the behavioral health providers to see patients and to record data from clinical interviews, and a workable referral system to the behavioral health department for urgent or complicated cases. Input was solicited from the medical and behavioral health staff to identify barriers and problems to implementation of the program. The mental health providers were selected for the special assignment 4 weeks before the program was expected to be fully functional, to give time to familiarize themselves with the medical office, staff, and procedures.

Selection of Mental Health Providers

The behavioral health provider positions for this project were advertised witin the department. Two 24-hr-per-week positions were funded through the research and development grant. Temporary replacement providers were hired to take over the providers' normal clinic duties while they were on special assignment. The criteria for selecting the two providers included: (a) interest and experience in working with a medical patient population, (b) interest in and knowledge of integrated care models, (c) ability to adapt practice style to a medical practice setting, and (d) research and data collection experience. The providers were prescreened by the task force and then, if appropriate, scheduled for the final interview with the internal medicine/family practice department chief.

The most important factor in the training of professional staff was to develop a spirit of collaboration and respect for the different disciplines. The task force was acutely aware that if the mental health staff came into the medical unit with a program to "sell," the true spirit behind the program would be lost. Every effort was made to reinforce the idea that the program would be developed as a collaboration between the medical and mental health providers. The task force added the mental health providers and representatives from the medical staff, including the PIC and nursing supervisor. The group spent time discussing the difference in cultures and the need to adapt mental health treatment to the medical culture. They emphasized the need to continue to find ways to integrate the two services so that they appeared to be seamless to the patient. Medical providers on the unit varied in how often they utilized their mental health colleagues. The task force identified ways to encourage consultation. Over time, it became increasingly clear that the collaborative relationship was the cornerstone of both medical and mental health provider training, as well as the development of the integration of care.

Medical Record Confidentiality Issues

The confidentiality of a patient's mental health record was preserved in the program by using the already existing mental health section in the medical record to write progress notes. This section of the medical record was created to communicate to medical personnel who share a patient with the behavioral health department. Typically, diagnostic, critical incident, and medication information is written on purple paper and sent to the medical records department. These notes are then placed in a special section at the back of the medical chart. The special section and the purple paper prevent these notes from being copied when a patient's medical information is released. The mental health providers working in the medical clinic kept brief progress notes on the patients they evaluated and treated and placed these notes on purple paper to be filed in the behavioral health section of the chart.

Billing and Reimbursement Issues. Because KPRMD is a group-model HMO that tracks patient encounters but does not generate claims, billing for services was not a significant issue. A policy was developed for waiving patient copays for participating in the study.

Other Implementation Issues. The biggest concern expressed by the PCPs was keeping the clinic running smoothly and not putting PCPs behind schedule by introducing a time-consuming psychiatric assessment procedure into the clinic. From the mental health department manager's perspective, one of the more difficult challenges was splitting mental health provider clinical time between the primary care facility and the mental health department while ensuring adequate clinical support in the mental health department. This issue became more critical later when our data showed that the majority of the integrated care patients had not been seen in mental health. It therefore became increasingly clear that we were using mental health resources to treat a newly identified patient population, rather than offsetting potential mental health department utilization by identifying and intervening with patients in the primary care setting.

Another issue was that although the project focus was on improving outcomes for patients with depression and/or anxiety, mental health providers were available for consultation and treatment of other cases, such as posttraumatic stress disorder (PTSD), somatoform disorder, bipolar disorder, and chronic pain. This availability had to be carefully negotiated so that the mental health providers could accomplish their primary goals for the project without being overwhelmed by other consultative demands.

Integrated Program Characteristics

Two half-time mental health providers were available on site to work with primary care providers. Mental health providers were expected to spend approximately 50% of their time in direct treatment and the other 50% in such collaborative activities as "curbside consults" with primary care providers, coordinating treatment plans, and regular conferences to discuss difficult cases as well as team issues. Additional duties/roles for the mental health providers included patient education, coordinating referrals to the mental health department, and tracking and follow-up of patients initiated on treatment in order to assess progress and adherence to treatment regimens.

Consultation/liaison with off-site psychiatrists at the nearest mental health department was available on a regular basis for discussing questions and problems around psychotropic medications (e.g., indications for one medication over another, appropriate dosing, continuation, tapering, risks for elderly patients with polypharmacy, etc.). Clinical pharmacy services were also involved in monitoring medication dosage and duration, as well as offering patient education on side effects associated with different medications.

Patient enrollment occurred through physician referral, based on a high index of suspicion for the disorders in question. Patients were asked to complete the Shedler Quick PsychoDiagnostics Panel (QPD Panel), an automated mental health test that patients can self-administer. The QPD Panel screens for nine psychiatric disorders and requires only 6 min (on average) to complete. Additionally, patients completed the Zung depression and anxiety scales, and the SF–12 to assess health, functional status, and medical comorbidities. Patients meeting criteria for depression, anxiety, and/or panic, as assessed through the diagnostic instruments, were recruited and their consent was obtained for participating in the study. Patients with "subthreshold" disorders (i.e., presence of clinically significant symptoms, but not meeting all of the *DSM–IV* criteria for diagnosis) were also included. Subthreshold assessment was based on out-of-range scores reported by the QPD for the diagnostic categories in question.

Treatments

Treatment guidelines for depression were developed by the Treatment of Depression in Primary Care Task Force at KPRMD. These guidelines were based on Agency for Health Care Policy and Research (AHCPR) guidelines for treatment of depression in primary care. Treatment guidelines for anxiety/panic were developed by KPRMD's Benzodiazepine Task Force. Task force members were comprised of clinical staff from the behavioral health, primary care, and pharmacy departments.

Depression. The treatment options of psychotherapy (short-term cognitive or interpersonal), antidepressant medications, or both were offered for patients with depression at the collaborative care site. A shared decision-making method was used to involve patients with minor to moderate depression in their treatment decisions, because psychotherapy and antidepressant medications for these patients have shown equivalent efficacy (Antonuccio, 1995). Patients were provided with education materials developed by AHCPR. Because of the established efficacy of antidepressant medications for patients with severe depression, use of these medications was encouraged, although psychotherapy could also have been chosen.

Anxiety/Panic. Treatment for anxiety and panic disorders was conducted according to guidelines recently developed by the Benzodiazepine Task Force, entitled "Guidelines for the Management of Anxiety Disorders, Insomnia, and Alcohol Withdrawal in Primary Care." These guidelines encompass both pharmacologic and nonpharmacologic treatments (e.g., relaxation techniques, cognitive-behavioral therapy). The guidelines also address treatment for comorbid anxiety and depression, which is prevalent in primary care.

THE ROLE OF PSYCHOLOGICAL TESTING
IN THE INTEGRATED PROGRAM

There were two purposes for using psychological testing instruments in the integrated care program. The first was to assist providers with more objective assessment of psychiatric disorders in their patients. The second was to provide data to determine patient eligibility for the integrated care program, and to evaluate the symptom severity and functional status of patients after receiving treatment.

Instrumentation

The instruments described next were selected for several purposes. First, they had to be self-reports and relatively quick to complete in order to gain provider acceptance. Second, the initial assessment instrument needed to provide both symptom-specific and diagnostic information. The Shedler Quick PsychoDiagnostics Panel (QPD) was selected for this purpose. Third, instruments were required to provide severity scores in order to track symptom reduction over time. Finally, instruments were selected to cover both the disorders of interest and more general functional impairment, physical and mental, that might have been associated with these disorders.

Shedler Quick PsychoDiagnostics Panel (QPD). The Shedler QPD Panel is a self-report psychiatric screening and assessment tool administered on a small hand-held computer tablet. It uses a series of true/false questions with branching logic to assess symptom severity and make a diagnosis for the following disorders: major depressive episode, dysthymic disorder, generalized anxiety disorder, panic disorder, obsessive-compulsive disorder, somatization, bulimia nervosa, and alchohol/substance abuse. It also assesses suicide risk and identifies cases of possible bipolar disorder. The QPD was chosen as the principle assessment instrument because:

1. It provides real-time, summarized data for the clinician to use in his or her practice.
2. It requires no provider data input.
3. It assesses the full range of common psychiatric disoders.
4. It showed high patient acceptance in its prior use.
5. It takes an average of 6 min for patients to complete.
6. It scores data electronically and creates a database that can be linked to patient encounter data from our administrative databases.

A detailed description of the development and validation of the QPD is provided in an earlier chapter of this volume (chap. 8).

Several months prior to implementing the integrated care program at the Aurora Centerpoint facility, we installed the QPD Panel for PCPs to use in patient assessment. A few of these providers had already expressed interest in obtaining a valid screening and assessment tool for psychiatric disorders. To paraphrase one of the physicians, "I would like a tool to assess my patients' emotional vital signs." After providing a demonstration of the QPD Panel and getting agreement among providers to use the instrument, we held training sessions for the physician, nurse practioner, nursing staff, and front desk staff on using the QPD Panel and interpreting the results. During this pilot test phase, we actively sought feedback from the PCPs on the utility of the instrument and ideas for any modifications. The principal feedback was that the test report should list the specific symptoms that led to a diagnosis, in addition to providing *DSM–IV* diagnoses and symptom severity scores. This information could then be quickly reviewed by the provider and discussed with the patient. The author of the QPD Panel worked with us to incorporate this suggestion, and the providers appeared to readily accept and use the QPD Panel in their practices. An example of a QPD printout is found in Appendix A. PCPs also told us that regular feedback on the characteristic symptoms associated with psychiatric disorders sensitized them to looking for these symptoms in their patients.

Because of the PCPs' extensive experience using the QPD Panel in clinical practice, there was no learning curve once the integrated care project was launched.

Four months into the project, we downloaded the QPD Panel data from the computer tablets, performed statistical analyses, and presented the results to the staff and at a larger regional quality assurance meeting. In both cases, the data generated considerable interest.

Zung Depression and Anxiety Scales.   These instruments were used for the integrated care project to provide symptom severity data for comparison with the QPD Panel depression and anxiety modules. We believed it important to obtain these data from a more widely used instrument than the QPD Panel in order to further assess convergent validity with the QPD Panel and to examine how the QPD Panel compared to the Zung scales with regard to assessing symptom remission over time.

SF–12.   The SF–12 Health Survey was chosen as a brief measure of functional impairment. It produces Physical and Mental Component Summary scores with norm-based means of 50 ($SD = 10$). We were specifically interested in whether patients with psychiatric disorders would also show impairment in physical functioning.

Administration Procedure

PCPs administered the QPD Panel when they encountered a patient whom they suspected had a psychiatric disorder. This procedure was employed instead of general screening of patients in the waiting room for several reasons. First, general screening for depression and other common psychiatric disorders is not currently recommended (U.S. Preventive Services Task Force, 1996). Second, we believed that general screening would be difficult logistically, as well as costly. Finally, our assumption was that with the experience of the integrated care model and the availability of on-site psychologists and a standard assessment tool, the PCPs would increase their detection of psychiatric disorders in their patients. Interestingly, their sensitivity to detecting disorders was increased as much by continual use of the QPD Panel as it was by consultation and collaboration with the psychologists.

Providers developed various methods of administering the QPD Panel. Some would give it in the exam room to patients who were suspected of having depression or anxiety. While the patient was completing the QPD, the provider would go on to see another patient and return to get the QPD results in 10 min. Other providers would typically have a nurse administer the QPD to a patient as well as obtain the printed results. Many providers would review and interpret the results with their patients, finding that patients often viewed the results as a second opinion.

Because the PCPs had used the QPD for 4 months prior to the beginning of the integrated care project, no training was necessary to familiarize them with the tool. In addition, the QPD was generally accepted as useful to the PCPs for sorting out the type(s) and severity of psychiatric disorders in their patients or to simply provide a "second opinion" that would confirm their assessment. Most important, the QPD did not require substantial additional time on the part of the PCP because it is a self-report instrument.

Means of Scoring and Providing Test Feedback to the Provider

Once the patient completed the QPD Panel, the provider or nurse would place the computer tablet on a small docking station that was connected to a printer. A test report was sent to the printer automatically, as soon as the QPD Panel computer tablet was placed on the docking station. The printout provided three types of diagnostic information in an easy-to-use format: (a) symptom severity scores, (b) specific DSM–IV diagnoses, and (c) the symptoms that led to the diagnoses. Data were permanently stored in the computer tablets until they were downloaded to a computer for analysis.

Patient Enrollment

Once the QPD Panel results were available and indicated the presence of a psychiatric disorder, the PCP referred the patient to the on-site psychologist. This process was typically met with agreement by the patient because their PCP had already suspected the patient had depression or anxiety and had then confirmed it with the QPD Panel. Most of these patients were in enough distress that the immediate availability of the psychologist was viewed as a significant benefit provided by the HMO.

Upon referral to the psychologist, the patient was interviewed briefly and introduced to the research project coordinator, who administered the baseline data collection protocol, including a consent form for participating in the study, demographic items, the SF–12, and Zung Depression and Anxiety scales. Once the patient completed the instruments, the psychologist informed him or her of the available treatment options and asked for a choice for initial therapy. The psychologist often initiated brief counseling at this visit. He or she then scheduled follow-up visits at regular intervals over the next 6 weeks. The psychologist had an average of three visits per patient during this time.

Aside from using the QPD Panel to assess patients' psychological status, there was no formal score-based guideline to determine which patients should be referred to mental health (as opposed to treated in the integrated care program). Referral decisions were made instead by the integrated care psychologists based on their clinical interview with the patient. Referral criteria used by the psychologists included assessment of lethality, psychosis, and complex and/or difficult cases (e.g., bipolar disorder, posttraumatic stress disorder).

Patients Served by the Integrated Care Program

The program was targeted at patients with depression and/or anxiety. Specific patient-inclusion criteria were adults age 18 years or older with clinically significant levels of depression, anxiety, and/or panic, as assessed by the QPD Panel. Patients were excluded from the study if they: (a) screened positive on the QPD Panel for current alcohol and substance abuse, (b) planned to disenroll from Kaiser Permanente within the next 12 months, (c) had difficulty speaking English, (d) showed symptoms of psychosis or dementia, or (e) had a terminal illness. The characteristics of patients in the program are described in detail in the evaluation section that follows.

EVALUATION OF THE INTEGRATED PROGRAM

Because the integrated care program was supported through an internal research and development grant, a comprehensive evaluation was required and an evaluation plan was developed.

Overview of Program Evaluation

The goal of the project was to implement and evaluate the effectiveness of a model of integrated care between mental health and primary care providers, for the treatment of depressive and anxiety/panic disorders. The primary objectives were:

1. To improve outcomes for patients in primary care settings who have depressive or anxiety/panic disorders. Improved outcomes were measured by symptom reduction and improved functioning following treatment.
2. To more actively involve patients in treatment decisions, such as choosing cognitive-behavioral therapy and/or medications, by using a shared decision-making approach to such decisions.

3. To increase patient satisfaction with the quality of care for the disorders identified.

Secondary objectives were:

1. To demonstrate guidelines-concordant pharmacotherapy for patients with depression as assessed by adequate continuation of therapy at recommended dosages.
2. To explore the possible reduction of costs associated with unnecessary medical services utilization related to depressive, anxiety, and panic disorders by providing more timely and appropriate mental health treatment.

Although an evaluation design comparing integrated care to usual care at a comparison clinic would have provided a more rigorous test of the program, this design was not feasible for logistical reasons. Asking providers in a usual care clinic to conduct psychological testing and enrollment of patients would have been difficult without also providing mental health services, and would have introduced an intervention that deviated from usual care. Therefore, for an assessment of symptom reduction, we focused only on the integrated care patients, using a comparison of changes in symptoms for integrated care patients over three time points: at enrollment, at 3 months, and at 6 months.

The measurement of primary care resource utilization that is currently being conducted will include a matched control group selected from several comparison clinics. Patients will be matched on age, gender, length of membership in the program, and a diagnosis of depression within approximately the same time period as that for the integrated care patients. Because the assessment of health care utilization is to take place over 18 months, complete data are not yet available.

Evaluation Measures

The primary test of the intervention effect was symptom remission at the three follow-up intervals for higher severity patients. Follow-up assessment conducted at 1-, 3-, and 6-month intervals included the QPD, the Zung Depression and Anxiety scales, and SF–12 Mental and Physical Component Summary scores to assess symptom remission and functional improvement. A repeated-measures analysis of variance with a linear contrast term was used to assess symptom reduction from baseline to 3 months. Other analyses included a description of the distribution of patient treatment choices between pharmacotherapy, psychotherapy, or both. Patient satisfaction with care was measured at 3 months using Likert-type scales.

Additional data to be analyzed for the project include pharmacotherapy continuation and adequacy of dosing and medical services utilization. These data will be obtained from KPRMD's automated pharmacy and encounter databases.

Evaluation Results

The evaluation of the integrated care program is not yet complete. However, preliminary data on symptom reduction, patient treatment choices, and patient satisfaction with care are available and are discussed next.

In total, 290 patients were screened with the QPD over approximately 9 months. Of these screened patients, 113 consented to and were enrolled in the study. Many of the patients not enrolled did not meet study inclusion criteria because they had additional psychiatric comorbidities that required additional specialty care referral. For example, 114 patients were initially assessed with the QPD and referred to the psychologist, but were subsequently diagnosed with PTSD and excluded from the study. These patients did receive treatment, typically through referral to the mental health department.

Patient Demographics.   Table 23.1 shows the demographic characteristics of the integrated care patients. The average age was 41.04 years ($SD = 12.69$). The majority of the patients were female (78%), White (74%), with at least some college education or more (67%), employed full time (73%), and married (60%).

Medical Comorbidities.   The most frequently reported medical comorbidities in this patient population included arthritis or rheumatism (23%), hypertension (22%), sciatica or chronic back pain (20%), asthma (14%), and angina (10%).

TABLE 23.1
Demographics

Characteristic	n (N = 113)	%
Gender		
Male	25	22%
Female	88	78%
Race		
Black	13	12%
Hispanic	11	10%
White	83	74%
Asian	2	2%
Other	3	3%
Education		
Eighth grade or less	1	1%
Some high school	6	5%
High school graduate	30	27%
Some college	46	41%
College graduate	25	22%
Postgraduate	5	4%
Employment		
Full time	82	73%
Part time	8	7%
Retired	8	7%
Unemployed	1	1%
Homemaker	8	7%
Temporary medical leave	3	3%
Permanently disabled	2	2%
Student	1	1%
Marital Status		
Married	68	60%
Separated	7	6%
Divorced	26	23%
Widowed	2	2%
Never married	10	9%

TABLE 23.2
Baseline and Symptom Severity Data

Parameter	n	%
Diagnostic data from QPD panel		
Major depressive disorder	56	52%
Generalized anxiety disorder	41	38%
Panel disorder	30	28%
Obsessive-compulsive disorder	17	16%
Number of diagnoses per patient from QPD panel		
None	38	34%
One	34	30%
Two	21	19%
Three	12	11%
Four	8	7%
Out-of-range (clinically significant) scores from QPD Panel		
Major depressive disorder	88	82%
Generalized anxiety disorder	87	81%
Panel disorder	36	33%
Obsessive-compulsive disorder	20	19%

Baseline Psychological Assessment Results. Table 23.2 shows the baseline QPD Panel diagnostic and symptom severity data for the patient sample. The most common diagnosis was major depressive episode (52%), followed by generalized anxiety disorder (38%), panic disorder (28%), and obsessive-compulsive disorder (16%). However, there was considerable psychiatric comorbidity among these patients, as evidenced by the finding that 37% had two or more of these diagnoses. In addition, the vast majority of patients had out-of-range symptom severity scores for depression and anxiety (82% and 81%, respectively), which was expected because inclusion criteria for the study were clinically significant levels of depression and/or anxiety.

Shared Decision-Making Treatment Preferences. Initial treatment choices for patients with depression were assessed in the clinical interview at baseline. Forty-four (39%) preferred cognitive-behavioral psychotherapy, 63 (56%) preferred a combination of psychotherapy and antidepressants, and 2 (2%) preferred antidepressants. This latter finding was surprisingly low.

Symptom Remission. Figures 23.1 through 23.3 show symptom reduction between baseline and 3-month follow-up assessment on the Zung and QPD Depression and Anxiety scales, and the SF–12 Mental and Physical Component Summary scores. The Zung and QPD measures indicate that patients' scores at baseline were in the moderately severe range. At 3 months, clinically and statistically significant reductions in symptoms on these measures were observed. Similarly, significant improvements in the Mental Component Summary score of the SF–12 were observed from baseline to 3 months. However, the Physical Component Summary score was stable over this time period, with a mean score ranging from 45 to 47. Caution should be exercised in interpreting these results because they are based on a subsample of the data, because not all of the 3-month follow-up interviews have been completed.

Patient Satisfaction. Tables 23.3 through 23.5 display patients' responses to the satisfaction items. Table 23.3 shows that between 85% and 95% of patients agreed or

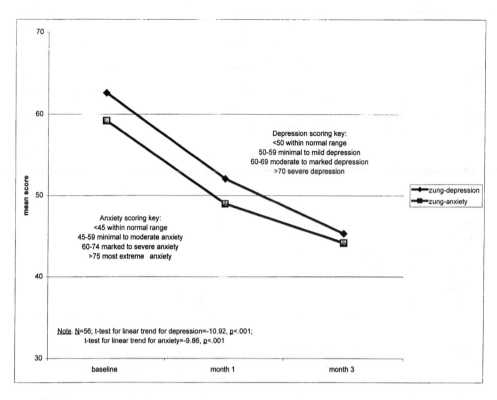

FIG. 23.1. Kaiser Permanente Rocky Mountain Division Integrated Care Project, Zung Depression and Anxiety scores.

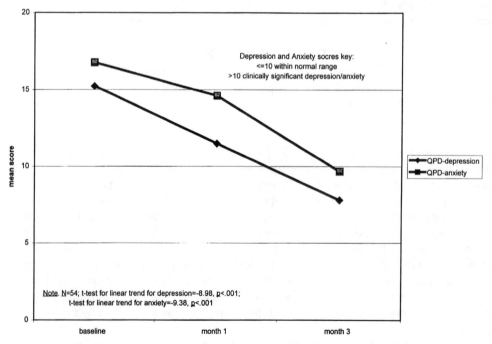

FIG. 23.2. Kaiser Permanente Rocky Mountain Division Integrated Care Project, QPD Panel Depression and Anxiety scores.

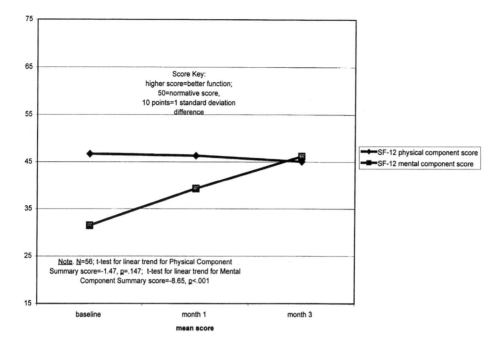

Score Key:
higher score=better function;
50=normative score,
10 points=1 standard deviation
difference

SF-12 physical component score
SF-12 mental component score

Note. N=56; t-test for linear trend for Physical Component
Summary score=-1.47, p=.147; t-test for linear trend for Mental
Component Summary score=-8.65, p<.001

baseline   month 1   month 3

mean score

FIG. 23.3.   Kaiser Permanente Rocky Mountain Division Integrated Care Project, SF–12 Physical and Mental Component Summary scores.

TABLE 23.3
Patient Satisfaction Ratings

Item	Strongly Agree	Agree	Uncertain	Disagree/ Strongly Disagree
I am very satisfied with the medical care I receive here.	53%	39%	5%	3%
I think my doctor or provider should know about the emotional issues I am dealing with.	57%	38%	5%	0%
I have a say in the type of treatment I choose for my personal problems.	52%	42%	3%	3%
The health care professionals here have shown ongoing concern about my personal and emotional well-being.	49%	36%	8%	7%
The mental health professional I saw was available for questions or appointments when I needed them.	47%	48%	2%	3%

Note.   N = 61.

strongly agreed with items related to general satisfaction with care for their emotional problems by the physician or mental health professional. Table 23.4 shows that 75% of patients rated the health care available to them at Kaiser for their personal or emotional problems as either very good or excellent. In addition, 89% reported that the care they received definitely or probably helped them deal more effectively with their personal and emotional problems. Most patients (96%) also indicated that they would recommend this program to a friend in need of similar help.

High levels of patient satisfaction were also seen regarding pharmacotherapy (see Table 23.5). The majority of patients were somewhat or very satisfied with (a) the ex-

TABLE 23.4
Patient Satisfaction Ratings

Item	Poor	Fair	Good	Very Good	Excellent
How would you rate the health care available to you at Kaiser for personal or emotional problems?	0%	10%	15%	39%	36%

	Definitely Yes	Probably Yes	Uncertain	Probably Not	Definitely Not
Has the care you received at Kaiser helped you deal more effectively with your personal and emotional problems?	66%	23%	10%	2%	0%
If a friend were in need of similar help, would you recommend our program to him or her?	80%	16%	2%	0%	2%

Note.   N = 61.

TABLE 23.5
Satisfaction With Antidepressant Information

Satisfaction Ratings of:	Very Satisfied	Somewhat Satisfied	Neither Satisfied nor Dissatisfied	Somewhat Dissatisfied	Very Dissatisfied
The explanation you were given about why antidepressants were prescribed	82%	16%	0%	0%	2%
The information you were given about how to take your antidepressant medication	77%	16%	2%	2%	2%
The information you were given on what to expect and how to deal with side effects	68%	28%	2%	2%	0%

Note.   N = 44.

planation they were given about why antidepressants were prescribed (98%), (b) the information they were given about how to take their medication (93%), and (c) the information they were given on what to expect and how to deal with side effects (96%).

Additional data on pharmacotherapy continuation at adequate doses and health services utilization rates are currently being analyzed. Regarding the latter, assessment of the cost of the integrated care program, and the anticipated offset of medical services utilization, were and continue to be issues for discussion. Integrated care, like other new models of care being evaluated at KPRMD, has been challenged to demonstrate its cost-effectiveness through a combination of improving quality of care and reducing costs through reducing unnecessary medical services utilization.

Qualitative/Anecdotal Data.   In addition to the data obtained from standard measures, the psychologists made several observations about the patients' and providers' responses to the integrated care program. The first was that patients were generally quite pleased to be able to access mental health services at their primary care facility. Many commented that this removed some of the stigma of visiting the mental health department. Also, patients expressed satisfaction with the immediate access to a mental health professional after having been diagnosed with depression and/or anxiety. This was especially true during the times when appointment access in the mental health department was longer than patients would have preferred. A second observation by the psychologists was that patients were "primed" to engage in treatment after having been assessed by their PCP and given the QPD. Their level of motivation to improve was high, and the psychologists, being immediately available to engage the patient in treatment, felt that this immediacy increased their treatment effectiveness. Third, the psychologists noted that significant patient improvement was evident with a relatively small number of visits, typically between three and four. Finally, several PCPs noted that through the use of the QPD and consultation with the psychologists, their diagnostic accuracy for anxiety and depression increased.

SUMMARY AND FUTURE DIRECTIONS FOR THE INTEGRATED PROGRAM

Although the integrated care program was successful in demonstrating symptom remission, patient satisfaction, and provider acceptance, more widespread implementation of the program will likely be based on a cost analysis and evidence for medical services utilization offset. These analyses have not been completed. One option under consideration is to transfer some mental health providers from the mental health department to primary care settings. However, our findings showed that majority of patients diagnosed and treated for psychiatric disorders in the integrated care program had not been seen in the mental health department, nor would they be likely to complete a referral to this department. Therefore, transferring mental health providers to primary care would address an unmet need for behavioral health services in primary care rather than offset the demand for services in the mental health department.

On a more optimistic note, momentum is building for integrated care programs in managed care organizations from the regulatory sector. The National Commtittee for Quality Assurance (NCQA) now requires evidence that managed care organizations implement integrated care, and there is increasing pressure from employer groups for managed care to provide integrated care.

In addition, our work in integrated care continues at KPRMD. Currently we are enrolling patients in another integrated care program at a larger hub facility. Again, the program is funded through a grant, in this case from the Kaiser Permanente Garfield Memorial Fund, a central research and development funding source in the Kaiser Permanente Program Office. Also, one of our mental health departments moved its physical location to a medical office, offering a natural laboratory for implementing and evaluating integrated care.

The combination of encouraging results from research and demonstration projects in integrated care, and promising cost offset data, will increase the likelihood of making integrated care a permanent component of our delivery system. However, we view integrated care as one part of a larger set of primary care-based approaches to care for patients with psychiatric disorders that include telephone-based behavioral consultation, case management follow-up, and group treatment models. Inextricably linked with all of these care models is the use of standard patient assessment instruments for clinical management, referral decisions, and outcomes assessment.

APPENDIX A

Shedler QPD Panel (Quick Psycho-Diagnostics Panel), Shedler Technologies, LLC

Physician Copy

Physician:	Dr. John Doe		
Patient:	Smith, Joe	Sex:	M
Ref No:	117588193	Age:	27
Date:	2/8/95		

Diagnostic Report

	Results		Reference
Test	within range	out of range	Range
Depression		21	0–10
Anxiety	8		0–10
Panic Disorder	2		0–8
OCD	0		0–3
Bulimia	0		0–4
Alcohol/Substance Abuse	3		0–6
Somatization	6		0–11

Notes: Patient appears to meet *DSM-IV* criteria for Major Depressive Episode. PATIENT EXPRESSES SUICIDAL IDEATION.

Patient:	Smith, Joe
Ref No:	117588193

Depressive Symptoms

—Depressed mood, nearly every day, 2 weeks or longer duration
—Diminished interest or pleasure in activities
—Appetite loss
—Weight loss
—Insomnia
—Fatigue, loss of energy
—Feelings of worthlessness or guilt
—Poor Concentration
—Hopelessness
—Suicidal ideation: answered true to "I have thoughts about killing myself."

REFERENCES

Antonuccio, D. (1995). Psychotherapy versus medication for depression: challenging the conventional wisdom with data. *Professional Psychology: Research and Practice, 26,* 574–585.

Barsky, A., & Borus, J. (1995). Somatization and medicalization in the era of managed care. *Journal of the American Medical Association, 274,* 1931–1933.

Bray, J., & Rogers, J. (1995). Linking psychologists and family physicians for collaborative practice. *Professional Psychology Research and Practice, 26,* 132–138.

Fifer, S. K., Mathias, S. D., Patrick, D. L., Mazonson, P. D., Lubeck, D. P., & Buesching, D. P. (1994). Untreated anxiety among adult primary care patients in a health maintenance organization. *Archives of General Psychiatry, 51,* 740–750.

Franco, R. (1995). The added costs of depression to medical care. *Pharmacoeconomics, 7,* 284–291.

Glenn, M.(1987). Structurally determined conflicts in health care. *Family Systems Medicine, 5,* 413–427.

Katon, W. (1996). Collaborative care: Patient satisfaction, outcomes, and medical cost-offset. *Family Systems Medicine, 13,* 351–365.

Katon, W., & Gonzales, J. (1994). A review of randomized trials of psychiatric consultation-liaison studies in primary care. *Psychosomatic Medicine, 35,* 268–278.

Katon, W., Von Korff, M., Lin, E., Walker, E., Simon, G. E., Bush, T., Robinson, P., & Russo, J. (1995). Collaborative management to achieve treatment guidelines: Impact on depression in primary care. *Journal of the American Medical Association, 273,* 1026–1031.

Lareau, M., & Nelson, E. (1994). The physician and licensed mental health professional team: Prevalence and feasibility. *Family Systems Medicine, 12,* 37–45.

Leahy, D., Galbreath, L., Powell, D., & Shinn, M. (1994). Medical family therapy casebook: A case of collaboration HMO style. *Family Systems Medicine, 12,* 437–439.

McDaniel, S., Campbell, T., & Seaburn, D. (1996). Principles for collaboration between health and mental health providers in primary care. *Family Systems Medicine, 13,* 283–298.

McDaniel, S., Hepworth, J., & Doherty, W. (1993). *Medical family therapy: A biopsychosocial approach to families with health problems.* New York: Basic Books.

Muchnick, S., Davis, B., Getzinger, A., Rosenberg, A., & Weiss, M. (1993). Collaboration between family therapy and health care: An internship experience. *Family Systems Medicine, 11,* 271–279.

Mumford, E., Schlesinger, H., Glass, G., Patrick, C., & Cuerdon, T. (1984). A new look at evidence about reduced cost of medical utilization following mental health treatment. *American Journal of Psychiatry, 141,* 1145–1158.

Pace, T. (1995). Psychological consultation with primary care physicians: Obstacles and opportunities in the medical setting. *Professional Psychology Research and Practice, 26,* 123–131.

Pace, T., Chaney, J., Mullins, L. & Olson, R. (1995). Psychological consultation with primary care physicians: Obstacles and opportunities in the medical setting. *Professional Psychology: Research and Practice, 26,* 123–131.

Pallak, M., Cummings, N., Dorken, H., & Henke, C. (1993). Managed mental health, medicaid, and medical cost offset. *New Directions for Mental Health, 59,* 27–40.

Schulberg, H. C. (1991). Mental disorders in the primary care setting: Research priorities for the 1990's. *General Hospital Psychiatry, 13,* 156–164.

Schulberg, H. C., Coulehan, J. L., Block, M. R., Lave, J., Rodrizuez, E., Scott, C. P., Madonia, M. J., Imber, S., & Perel, J. (1993). Clinical trials of primary care treatment for major depression: Issues in design, recruitment and treatment. *International Journal of Psychiatry Medicine, 23,* 29–42.

Simon, G. E., Von Korff, M., & Barlow, W. (1995). Health care costs associated with depressive and anxiety disorders in primary care. *American Journal of Psychiatry, 152,* 352–356.

Sturm, R., & Wells, K. (1995). How can the care for depression become more cost-effective? *Journal of the American Medical Association, 273,* 51–58.

U.S. Preventive Services Task Force. (1996). *Guide to clinical preventive services* (2nd ed.). Baltimore, MD: Williams & Wilkins.

Wells, K. B., Hays, R. D., Burnam, M. A., Rogers, W., Greenfield, S., & Ware, J. E. (1989). Detection of depressive disorder for patients receiving prepaid or fee-for-service care. *Journal of the American Medical Association, 262,* 3298–3302.

The INOVA Primary Behavioral Health Care Pilot Project

Leonard Goldstein
Integrated Behavioral Care, Springfield, Virginia

Boris Bershadsky
University of Minnesota School of Public Health

Mark E. Maruish
United Behavioral Health, Minneapolis, Minnesota

This chapter describes the evolution, implementation, and results from the INOVA Primary Behavioral Health Care Pilot Project. The project was built around the concept of *primary behavioral health care,* which may be defined as the effective diagnosis and treatment of behavioral disorders that are often seen in the primary care setting and that can be effectively treated in the primary care arena. It thus represents an integration of behavioral health care with primary care medicine. Primary behavioral health care includes a number of participants—primary care physicians (PCPs), psychiatrists, nurse practitioners/physician assistants, and other mental health professionals. The setting theoretically is the entire health care delivery system, workplace, and home and community, but for this project was the primary care office.

The rationale for and benefits of integrating behavioral health care services in primary care settings were discussed extensively in Maruish's introductory chapter (chap. 1) and other chapters in this book. Therefore, they are not repeated here. Suffice it to say that:

1. A large portion of patients who seek services from primary care providers experience significant psychological distress or symptomatology.
2. Primary care providers, in general, are not sufficiently skilled to identify or provide appropriate treatment to these patients.
3. Consequently, patients with behavioral health problems consume a large portion of the available primary care resources.
4. Identifying and adequately treating the behavioral health problems of primary care patients in the primary care setting has been shown to result in significant cost savings.
5. Consultation, liaison, and educational services offered by behavioral health professionals can be instrumental in ensuring the success of these intervention efforts in the primary care setting.

The primary goal of the INOVA project was to demonstrate that on-site integration of behavioral healthcare services in primary care practices will result in more effective and efficient means of treating or otherwise dealing with patients who may be problematic for the primary care provider than those that are currently employed in primary care practices. Problematic patients included high medical resource utilizers, patients presenting with significant psychiatric symptomatology (either primary or secondary to a physical health condition), patients being managed on psychoactive drugs, or patients who otherwise may be suspected of being in need of behavioral health assessment and/or intervention.

The project consisted of two phases. The first phase was designed to yield baseline measures of patients' behavioral health status, as well any changes therein at 3 months after an initial objective assessment. The second phase involved the same baseline and follow-up procedures as in the first phase. During this phase, the primary care provider had psychological test results available to aid in the assessment, monitoring, and disposition of patients requiring behavioral health intervention. In addition, an on-site behavioral health consultant was available to the primary care staff for consultation and short-term intervention. It was hypothesized that as a result of the procedures and practices introduced into the existing practice of participating clinics during Phase II of the project, the collected data would reflect one or more of the following:

1. An increase in patients' self-reported, overall level of psychological functioning/well-being.
2. A reduction in medical resource utilization.
3. An increase in patients' level of satisfaction with services received.
4. An increase in the PCPs' level of satisfaction with the behavioral health services provided to their patients.

ORGANIZATIONAL PARTICIPATION

This project represented a collaborative effort of a number of organizations, including INOVA Health System (IHS), Fairfax Family Practice Centers, INOVA Affiliated Practices (Mount Vernon Family Medicine), Northern Virginia Psychiatric Group, Group Practice Affiliates, Integrated Behavioral Care, and Strategic Advantage, Inc. (a Magellan Health Services company). INOVA Health System (IHS) is an integrated delivery system in the Washington, DC, metropolitan area. Based in northern Virginia, INOVA includes four acute care hospitals, nursing homes, home care, and primary care practices (the INOVA Affiliated Practices). INOVA also owns a small health plan with a network of more than 1,000 physicians. Fairfax Family Practice Centers (FFPC) is a large, nationally known practice in northern Virginia. Like the INOVA Affiliated Practices, FFPC has numerous capitated arrangements with health plans.

Group Practice Affiliates (GPA, a subsidiary of Magellan Health Service) is a national behavioral physician practice management company. GPA and a subsidiary of IHS are partners in a limited liability company that manages Northern Virginia Psychiatric Group (NVPG) and Integrated Behavioral Care (IBC). NVPG, formed in 1977, is a multidisciplinary psychiatric group with several sites and 24 clinicians. IBC is a regional behavioral care network that covers Maryland, the District of Columbia, and Virginia. It is built around 25 multidisciplinary groups. Strategic Advantage, Inc. (SAI), another subsidiary of Magellan Health Services, offers expertise in the development and implementation of treatment outcomes instrumentation and technology.

Gaining internal acceptance for the project was accomplished primarily through the senior author's participation on numerous INOVA physician board meetings, INOVA Medical Management Task Forces, and long-standing referral relationships. IBC and INOVA approved funding for the Primary Behavioral Health Care Pilot Project. INOVA affiliated family practices had agreed to participate after reviewing the proposal and meeting with INOVA and IBC/NVPG team members. In addition, Strategic Advantage, Inc. (SAI), agreed to provide consultation about study design, screening tools, and immediate scoring services for some of the required instrumentation (i.e., SA–45 and SF–12), as well as data entry and analysis services.

METHODOLOGY

Participants

Eligible participants included male and female adults (18 years and older) seeking primary care services at the Vienna, VA, office of the FFPC under capitated health care contracts. All agreed to participate in a two-phased project designed to investigate the benefits of making available on-site psychological screening, consultation, and time-limited intervention services in primary care settings. Each study phase was designed to include both baseline and 3-month post baseline follow-up assessments.

The initial design of the study sought to enlist the participation of at least 200 eligible patients (100 for Phase I and 100 for Phase II) from each of three FFPC clinics, for a grand total of 600 patients. Difficulties in enlisting patient participation led to a revised objective of 100 participants for Phase I and 100 participants for Phase II, all of which were seen at the Vienna clinic only.

Instrumentation

Several instruments were selected for use in the primary care project.

Symptom Assessment–45 Questionnaire (SA–45). The SA–45 (Strategic Advantage, Inc. [SAI], 1998) is a symptom checklist that asks respondents to indicate on a 5-point Likert scale (*Not at all* to *Extremely*) how much each of 45 psychiatric symptoms has bothered them during the previous 7 days. Responses to the SA–45 items yield separate area *T*-scores (hereafter referred to as *T*-scores) on each of nine symptom domain scales: Anxiety (ANX), Depression (DEP), Obsessive-Compulsive (OC), Somatization (SOM), Phobic Anxiety (PHO), Hostility (HOS), Interpersonal Sensitivity (INT), Paranoid Ideation (PAR), and Psychoticism (PSY). Also, two summary indices — the Positive Symptom Total (PST) and Global Severity Index (GSI) — are scored from the responses to all 45 items. According to the SA–45 *Manual*, a score of 60*T* (one standard deviation above the mean) or higher on any symptom domain or summary index suggests the presence of symptom domain problem(s) warranting further evaluation (SAI, 1998). Although primarily developed for treatment outcomes measurement, the SA–45 also has demonstrated utility as a psychological screening and treatment monitoring instrument. The SA–45 is more fully discussed in chapter 10 of this volume.

During Phase II of the study (discussed later), the SA–45 was scored via the Strategic Advantage, Inc. (SAI) Infinifax fax-back scoring and reporting system. Using the Infinifax system, the SA–45 was faxed to SAI, computer scored, and then a printed report of the results was sent back to the primary care office within 5–10 min. The Infinifax report includes a table indicating the raw score, T-score, percentile, item responses, and missing items for each of the nine symptom domain scales, as well as the raw scores, T-scores, and percentiles for the GSI and PST indices. It also presents a brief, computer-generated interpretation of the results.

Symptom Assessment–24 Questionnaire (SA–24). The SA–24 (SAI, 1996) is a 24-item short form of the SA–45 that provides a predicted T-score for the SA–45 GSI. It was developed for use in outcomes studies requiring only a measure of overall level of psychological distress rather than more symptom domain-specific data. It thus met the requirements of the follow-up portions of the study. In a addition, because all five Depression scale items are included in this short form, the SA–45 Depression scale T-score can be derived from the SA–24 administration.

SF–12 Health Survey. The SF–12 (Ware, Kosinski, & Keller, 1995) is a self-report, 12-item abbreviated version of the SF–36 Health Survey (SF–36; Ware, Snow, Kosinski, & Gandek, 1993) developed to yield predicted T-scores for the SF–36 Mental Component Summary (MCS) and Physical Component Summary scales (PCS; Ware, Kosinski, & Keller, 1994). The T-score for each scale is obtained by applying a scale-specific set of regression weights to all 12 items, summing the resulting products, and adding a constant. Thus, each item contributes to the score of both the MCS scale and the PCS scale. The MCS scale provides a broad assessment of depressive symptomatology and limitations of social and work functioning due to emotional factors. The PCS is sensitive to general health concerns and limitations in social and work functioning due to physical problems. Unlike the SA–45 and SA–24, scores of $40T$ (one standard deviation below the mean) or lower suggest the presence of problems that warrant further evaluation.

As with the SA–45, the SF–12 was scored and a report of results was transmitted via the SAI Infinifax system faxback system during Phase II of the study.

Resource Utilization Form. This patient-completed form consists of six questions pertaining to the patient's use of healthcare services during the previous three months. Specifically, respondents are asked to indicated the number of medically related emergency room visits, inpatient days, and outpatient visits during the indicated time period. Similarly, they are asked to indicate the number of emergency room visits, inpatient days, and outpatient visits related to mental health or substance use problems during those same three months.

Patient Tracking Form. This five-item form was designed to be completed by the primary care provider after each office visit. The five yes–no items provide a broad summary of the patient's behavioral health status at the time of the visit and any prescribed interventions made during the visit.

Patient Satisfaction Form.   This 18-item Likert rating instrument asks respondents to indicate their level of satisfaction with the care they have received from both medical and behavioral health care providers. A portion of the items ask about general aspects of the care they have received, and the remainder ask about the patient's satisfaction with specific aspects of care.

Provider Satisfaction.   This 13-item Likert rating scale asks primary care providers to indicate their level of satisfaction with the care given to their patients by mental health and substance abuse care providers. As with the patient satisfaction form, the provider satisfaction form consists of items that ask about satisfaction with both general and specific aspects of care, including communication with the behavioral health care provider.

Procedures

Pre-Phase-I Provider Satisfaction Measurement.   Prior to the beginning of Phase I patient data gathering, the provider satisfaction instrument was administered to FFPC providers practicing at the Vienna clinic and other FFPC clinics in order to obtain a baseline measure of the preproject level of satisfaction with the behavioral health care services that their patients had been receiving.

Phase I.   Consecutive adult (18 years and older) primary care patients covered by capitated health care plans were invited to participate in the project during their office visit. Eligible patients who agreed to participate during the 4-week enrollment period signed a consent form agreeing to the conditions of the study, including permission for the study team to contact them by telephone for follow-up assessment. The participants then completed the SA–45, SF–12, and resource utilization forms prior to being seen by their primary care provider. The completed forms were handed back to the clinic support staff, collected weekly by a project coordinator, and later submitted to SAI for data entry and scoring. Providers did not have access to the data gathered at that time. Thereafter, providers were instructed to complete the patient tracking form following each visit.

During a 5-week period surrounding the 3-month postbaseline assessment endpoint, each subject was contacted by telephone by one of two behavioral health providers for administration the SA–24 and the patient satisfaction form, and readministration of the SF–12 and resource utilization form.

Phase II.   The baseline and follow-up assessment instruments and procedures were the same as those in Phase I but with two additional features. First, the results of the SA–45 and SF–12 baseline assessment were made available to the patient's primary care provider no later than 7 days after the instruments were administered. The provider, at his or her discretion, could make use of these findings to assist identifying patients that should be referred for evaluation for behavioral health problems. Second, a behavioral health professional was on site at the FFPC Vienna office two to five days of the week for 4 hours each day, from the beginning of Phase II baseline data gathering until 3 months after the last patient enlisted completed the Phase II baseline assessment. While on site, the behavioral health professional oversaw the baseline assessment and Infinifax scoring processes, and made herself available to primary care providers for consultation and for brief treatment of referred patients.

Post-Phase-II Provider Satisfaction Measurement.   Near or at the completion of Phase II patient data gathering, the provider satisfaction instrument was administered again.

Data Analyses

Baseline and follow-up data gathered during both Phase I and Phase II of the project were analyzed in a manner so as to test the four hypotheses stated earlier. Additional analyses to conducted to investigate the validity and utility of the SA–45, SF–12, and other data gathering tools in primary care settings.

RESULTS

Sample Characteristics

The Phase I baseline sample consisted of 39 males and 87 females. Although all patients initially agreed to participate in the follow-up assessment, only 30 males and 67 females actually completed the 3-month telephone interview (see Table 24.1). The baseline patients who completed the follow-up interview were compared to those who did not on several intake variables to determine if any systematic bias might have accounted for those who failed to complete the study. *t*-tests for equality of means for independent samples were used to determine if there were significant differences between the two subsamples on age, gender, and numerous SA–45 and SF–12 scores (e.g., *T*-scores, significant elevations on individual scales and sets of scales) reported at baseline. Of these variables, significant differences were found between the two groups with regard to the percent of patients with an MCS score at or below 40T ($p = .04$), and the percent with a Hostility scale score of 70T or greater ($p = .05$).

Phase II consisted of 40 males and 65 females. One hundred and five baseline patients initially agreed to participate in the follow-up assessment, but only 28 males

TABLE 24.1
Gender and Age-Range Frequencies for Phase I
and Phase II Baseline and Follow-Up Samples

	Phase I		*Phase II*	
	Baseline	*Follow-Up*	*Baseline*	*Follow-Up*
Age (years)				
18–34	55	40	44	24
35–44	30	22	31	27
45–54	20	17	19	16
55–64	14	11	5	4
65–74	4	4	4	4
75+	3	3	1	1
Unknown	0	0	1	1
Gender				
Male	39	30	40	28
Female	87	67	65	48
Total *N*	126	97	105	76

Note.   There were no statistically significant demographic differences ($p < .05$) between phases.

and 48 females actually completed the three-month telephone interview (see Table 24.1). There were no significant differences between Phase I and Phase II patients in terms of gender or age. Differences between Phase II patients who underwent both baseline and follow-up assessment and those who were assessed only at baseline were not performed.

Phase I Baseline and Follow-Up Results

Provider Satisfaction. The preproject mean ratings for each of the 13 items assessing the Vienna clinic and other INOVA providers' satisfaction with behavioral health care services for their patients are presented in Table 24.2. On average, both the FFPC Vienna providers and other providers who completed these ratings rated behavioral health care services in the fair to poor range just prior to the project.

The percent of providers giving a response indicative of satisfaction with each of the 13 measured aspects of behavioral healthcare is indicated in Table 24.3. No more than one third of the Vienna providers gave a satisfactory rating to any of the 13 items prior to the beginning of the project. With one exception, this was also true of the other INOVA providers.

SA–45/SA–24. Although the range of reported level of symptom severity was quite broad, the mean baseline *T*-score for each of the 11 SA–45 symptom domain scales and summary indices fell within one standard deviation of the SA–45's nonpatient mean *T*-score of 50 (see Table 24.4). (The relatively high Phobic Anxiety and Psychoticism mean *T*-scores [59*T*] reflect the particular aspects of the nonpatient norms whereby on either scale, a *T*-score of greater than 60 can occur if the respondent answers *a little bit* to just one item.). Follow-up SA–24 *T*-scores and standard deviations for the Depression scale and predicted GSI were quite similar to those found on baseline assessment.

SF–12. As with the SA–45/SA–24 findings, Table 24.4 also reveals that the mean baseline SF–12 MCS and PCS *T*-scores were within one standard deviation of the mean, with individual scores also showing a wide range of variability. Also, SF–12 follow-up data were quite similar to the baseline data.

Resource Utilization. Comparison of the mean resource utilization data of those patients who were assessed at both baseline and follow-up indicates decreases in the use of medical and mental health services from the 3-month period prior to baseline assessment, compared to the 3-month period following baseline assessment (see Table 24.5). However, only the decrease in mean medical emergency room visits was significant. Moreover, with the exception of medical outpatient visits, both pre- and postbaseline 3-month utilization rates of medical and behavioral resources were extremely low or nonexistent.

Patient Tracking. There was inconsistent compliance from providers in completing the five patient-tracking questions after each clinic visit. For this reason, the tracking data obtained were not analyzed, and a decision was made to exclude this form from Phase II of the project.

TABLE 24.2
Average Provider Satisfaction Ratings

Provider Satisfaction Item	Vienna Pre-Phase I		Vienna Post-Phase II		Other INOVA Pre-Phase I	
	n	Mn	n	Mn	n	Mn
1. Your access to managed care companies.	6	1.7	7	2.4	30	1.8
2. Appointment access and availability for the patient.	6	2.0	7	3.6**	30	2.3
3. Your access to the treating provider by telephone.	7	1.3	7	3.4†	31	1.7
4. Receiving information from the treating provider on a timely basis.	7	1.9	7	3.1	33	1.6
5. Receiving clear and legible information from the treating provider.	7	2.3	7	3.0	33	1.9
6. Summary information of visits, including medication monitoring.	7	2.0	7	3.0	32	1.5
7. Notification of admission and discharge to a higher level of care.	5	1.2	7	2.7*	28	1.6
8. Patient access to emergency services.	6	2.2	7	3.1**	30	2.3
9. Quality of outpatient mental health services.	6	2.2	7	3.6**	29	2.3
10. Quality of outpatient substance abuse services.	2	NA	7	3.6	23	2.0
11. Quality of inpatient mental health services.	2	NA	7	3.0	26	2.7
12. Overall effectiveness of services provided to referred patients.	7	2.0	7	3.6*	31	2.1
13. Overall integration of primary care, MH, and SA services.	7	1.4	7	3.3**	32	1.3

Note. $1 = Poor, 2 = fair, 3 = good, 4 = very good, 5 = excellent.* Satisfaction defined as an item rating of *good, very good,* or *excellent.* Comparison of pre-Phase I and post-Phase II results not possible because of an inability to match cases from one administration to the next. NA indicates that sample is too small to provide meaningful statistics. Other INOVA Pre-Phase I refers to other INOVA PCPs completing the provider satisfaction form prior to the start of Phase I but not practicing in the Vienna office. Changes in Vienna pre-Phase I and Vienna post-Phase II test for significance of difference. MN, mean.

*$p < .03$.

**$p < .01$.

†$p < .002$.

TABLE 24.3

Percent of Providers Indicating Satisfaction With Aspects of MH/SA Patient Care at Pre-Phase I and Post-Phase II

Provider Satisfaction Item	Vienna Pre-Phase I		Vienna Post-Phase II		Other INOVA Pre-Phase I	
	n	%	n	%	n	%
1. Your access to managed care companies.	6	17	7	43	30	23
2. Appointment access and availability for the patient.	6	33	7	100**	30	33
3. Your access to the treating provider by telephone.	7	0	7	71†	31	13
4. Receiving information from the treating provider on a timely basis.	7	29	7	57	33	12
5. Receiving clear and legible information from the treating provider.	7	29	7	71	33	21
6. Summary information of visits, including medication monitoring.	7	14	7	71	32	16
7. Notification of admission and discharge to a higher level of care.	5	0	7	71*	28	18
8. Patient access to emergency services.	6	17	7	86**	30	40
9. Quality of outpatient mental health services.	6	33	7	100**	29	31
10. Quality of outpatient substance abuse services.	2	NA	7	100	23	22
11. Quality of inpatient mental health services.	2	NA	7	86	26	54
12. Overall effectiveness of services provided to referred patients.	7	14	7	86*	31	29
13. Overall integration of primary care, MH, and SA services.	7	14	7	86**	32	9

Note. $1 = Poor$, $2 = fair$, $3 = good$, $4 = very good$, $5 = excellent$. Satisfaction defined as an item rating of $good$, $very good$, or $excellent$. Comparison of pre-Phase I and post-Phase II results not possible because of an inability to match cases from one administration to the next. NA indicates that sample is too small to provide meaningful statistics. Other INOVA Pre-Phase I refers to other INOVA PCPs completing the provider satisfaction form prior to the start of Phase I but not practicing in the Vienna office. Change in Vienna pre-Phase I and Vienna post-Phase II test for significance of difference.

$^*p < .03$.
$^{**}p < .01$.
$^†p < .002$.

TABLE 24.4
Mean SA–45, SA–24, and SF–12, T-Scores for Phase I and Phase II Baseline and Follow-Up Samples

| | Phase I | | | | | | | Phase II | | | | | | |
| | Baseline | | | Follow-Up | | | | Baseline | | | Follow-Up | | |
Scale	n	Mean	SD	n	Mean	SD		n	Mean	SD	n	Mean	SD
SA–45													
GSI	126	49.21	8.97	97	47.77	8.93		105	48.87	9.07	76	48.70	8.65
PST	126	48.78	9.43					105	48.45	10.30			
ANX	126	53.56	7.82					105	53.54	7.77			
DEP	125	53.06	6.64	97	52.16	6.37		105	52.07	6.62	77	51.82	6.56
OC	126	51.52	7.63					102	51.95	8.46			
SOM	126	54.37	7.09					104	54.15	7.80			
PHO	126	59.32	2.89					105	59.90	3.64			
HOS	126	55.68	5.46					104	55.44	5.22			
INT	125	52.05	5.45					105	52.69	5.89			
PAR	126	51.20	7.35					105	50.85	5.61			
PSY	126	59.26	2.57					105	59.11	2.74			
SF–12													
MCS	113	51.47	8.60	84	52.21	8.76		104	51.33	10.16	68	52.02	8.68
PCS	113	51.02	9.29	84	49.73	10.20		104	48.46	9.06	68	50.15	7.99

Note. GSI, Global Severity Index; PST, Positive Symptom Total; ANX, Anxiety; DEP, Depression; HOS, Hostility; INT, Interpersonal Sensitivity; OC, Obsessive-Compulsive; PAR, Paranoid Ideation; PHO, Phobic Anxiety; PSY, Psychoticism; SOM, Somatization; MCS, Mental Component Summary; PCS, Physical Component Summary. Greater degree of impairment indicated by higher T-scores on the SA–45 scales and lower T-scores on the SF–12. Only GSI (based on SA–24), DEP, MCS, and PCS were measured at follow-up. No significant differences between Phase I and Phase II baseline scores.

TABLE 24.5
Phase I and Phase II Baseline and Follow-Up Resource Utilization Using Paired Samples

| | Phase I | | | | | | | | Phase II | | | | | | | |
| | Baseline | | | Follow-Up | | | | Baseline | | | Follow-Up | | |
Type of Utilization	n	Mean	SD	n	Mean	SD	n	Mean	SD	n	Mean	SD
Medical ER visits	89	0.09	0.29	89	0.01*	0.11	74	0.15	0.63	74	0.04	0.20
Medical inpatient days	87	0.17	0.85	87	0.06	0.23	74	0.11	0.54	74	0.08	0.40
Medical outpatient visits	88	1.74	1.98	88	1.74	1.97	74	1.89	2.21	74	2.04	2.13
MH/SA ER visits	88	a	a	88	a	a	74	0.01	0.12	74	a	a
MH/SA inpatient days	88	a	a	88	a	a	74	0.01	0.12	74	a	a
MH/SA outpatient visits	88	0.47	2.70	88	0.28	1.23	73	0.04	0.26	73	0.11	0.94

Note. Results are those of patients who provided utilization data at both baseline and follow-up.

[a]Values not computed because all patient responses were zero.

*Difference between Phase I baseline and follow-up significant at $p < .05$. No other significant baseline-to-follow-up changes for either Phase I or Phase II, nor differences in the mean change from baseline to follow-up *between* phases for any utilization variable, are indicated.

Patient Satisfaction. In contrast to the providers' preproject satisfaction with behavioral health services, the vast majority of patients assessed at the 3-month fol-low-up indicated satisfaction with the all measured aspects of the services they had received from the Vienna clinic during the 3 months following their baseline assess-ment (see Table 24.6). There were no significant expressed satisfaction differences be-tween Phase I and Phase II patients on any of the 18 items. Of particular note is the fact that 93.8% of Phase I patients and 96% of Phase II patients expressed satisfaction with the overall care and treatment they received at the Vienna clinic, and 94.7% of Phase I patients and 96% of Phase II patients indicated that they would recommend the Vienna clinic to someone else.

Phase II Baseline and Follow-Up Results

Provider Satisfaction. Provider ratings on each of the satisfaction items in-creased by the end of the project, with ratings falling, on average, into the good to very good range (see Table 24.2). There were, in fact, statistically significant increases in ratings pertaining to the following: their patients' access to behavioral health pro-viders and emergency services, the providers' telephone access to the treating pro-vider, the quality and overall effectiveness of behavioral health services provided to their referred patients, notification of their patients' admission to higher levels of be-

TABLE 24.6
Percent of Phase I and Phase II Patients Indicating
Satisfaction With Aspects of Service Delivery

Patient Satisfaction Item	Phase I		Phase II	
	n	*%*	*n*	*%*
1. I did not need the treatment that I received.	91	8.8[a]	73	6.8
2. This treatment helped me with my problems.	94	90.4	74	86.5
3. The treatment met my expectations.	95	89.5	74	7.8
4. I am satisfied with the quality of services I received.	95	89.5	75	90.7
5. I would recommend Vienna Clinic to someone else.	95	94.7	75	96.0
6. Ease of access.	96	95.8	75	94.7
7. Waiting time for services provided.	97	91.8	75	80.0
8. The explanation of your diagnosis.	95	87.4	72	90.3
9. The explanation of your options for treatment and follow-up.	93	87.1	69	91.3
10. The explanation of the side effects that might occur with your medications.	76	84.2	51	88.2
11. The explanation of the test and medical procedures you received.	80	92.5	56	89.3
12. Our clinical staff's response to your emotional needs.	81	91.4	64	93.8
13. Our clinical staff's response to your physical needs.	96	93.8	75	93.3
14. The extent to which our clinical staff listened and answered your questions.	97	88.7	75	96.0
15. The clinical staff's knowledge and ability.	96	94.8	75	97.3
16. The extent to which Vienna Clinic involved your family in your treatment.	38	97.4	15	100
17. The overall care and treatment you received.	97	93.8	75	96.0
18. In general I had enough time with the care providers at Vienna Clinic.	96	92.7	75	93.3

Note. Satisfaction on items 1–5 defined as a response of either *strongly agree* or *agree*. Satisfaction on items 6–17 defined as a response of *excellent, very good,* or *good*. Satisfaction on item 18 defined as a response of *yes*. For items 6–18, patients who answered N/A (not applicable) were excluded from analyses. No significant differences in expressed satisfaction on individual item between phases. *n*, total number of patients responding to item; %, percent of total number of patients indicating satisfaction on the item.

[a]Item scored in direction reverse to that of all other items, thus accounting for the low percent.

havioral health care, and overall integration of primary and behavioral healthcare services.

Similarly, the percent of providers giving a satisfactory rating increased for each of the 13 items, with a great majority of providers (71% or more) giving a satisfactory rating to 11 of the items (see Table 24.3). Only with regard to access to managed care companies (43%) and receiving information from the treating behavioral health care provider (57%) was this not the case.

SA–45/SA–24. Phase II mean baseline GSI, PST, and symptom domain *T*-scores were not significantly different from those found for the Phase I sample (see Table 24.4). Also, the difference between baseline and follow-up GSI and DEP *T*-scores in Phase II were quite comparable to that in Phase I.

SF–12. As with the SA–45/SA–24, Phase II mean baseline MCS and PCS *T*-scores were not significantly different from those found for the Phase I sample (see Table 24.4), and the difference between baseline and follow-up MCS and PCS *T*-scores in Phase II was very similar to that in Phase I.

Resource Utilization. There were small, insignificant changes in mean values for each of the six resource utilization variables from baseline to follow-up in Phase II (see Table 24.5). Also, the mean baseline-to-follow-up utilization changes noted in Phase I were not significantly different from the mean baseline-to-follow-up changes in Phase II for any of these same utilization variables.

Patient Satisfaction. Generally, 86% or more of the patients completing the Phase II follow-up interview indicated satisfaction with most of the measured aspects of care (see Table 24.6). However, the change in the percent of patients indicating satisfaction in Phase II was not significantly different from that found in Phase I for any of the 18 items. Notable is that the percent satisfied with the waiting time for services dropped from 92% in Phase I to 80% in Phase II; in addition, the percent of patients indicating satisfaction with the extent to which the clinical staff listened to and answered their questions rose from 89% in Phase I to 96% in Phase II.

Additional Analyses

In an effort to further explore the potential benefits of integrated behavioral health care and the utility of the study instruments in a primary care setting, the data collected during Phase I and Phase II at the Vienna clinic were subjected to additional analyses.

Comparison of Number of Medical and Behavioral Health Outpatient Visits at Phase I and Phase II. Further examination of resource utilization reported by the project participants revealed findings somewhat different from those resulting from the analysis of paired patient data (i.e., data only from those Phase I and Phase II patients who completed the utilization at both baseline and follow-up; see Table 24.5). Also, instead of considering differences in mean units of utilization from Phase I and Phase II for each of the six resource variables, the present analysis considered the proportion of the patients who reported no utilization of a given resource to the proportion of patients who reported one or more units of utilization of that same resource, from Phase I to Phase II.

The results of these analyses revealed significant differences in follow-up data proportions between Phase I to Phase II for only the medical outpatient visit and mental health/substance abuse outpatient visit variables. As indicated in Table 24.7, the percent of patients who reported one or more medical outpatient visits increased significantly from the Phase I follow-up assessment to the Phase II follow-up assessment. At the same time, the percent of patients reporting one or more mental health/substance abuse outpatient visits decreased significantly from Phase I follow-up to Phase II follow-up.

Percent of Sample Classified as Impaired Using SA–45 and SF–12 Variables. An indication of the utility of the SA–45 and SF–12 in identifying behavioral health problems in primary care settings is the rate at which respondents are classified as having a psychological problem or experiencing a level of distress or impairment warranting further evaluation. That is, how closely does the test-based rate of classification match that which is known or has been reported in the literature? For the purpose of this study, a T-score of 60 or greater on SA–45 scales and indices, or a T-score of 40 or less on the SF–12 variables were used as impairment classification cutoffs. Both cutoffs identify scores one standard deviation or more away from the nonpatient mean in the direction of impairment.

Table 24.8 presents the rate at which members of the baseline and follow-up samples were classified as experiencing a significant level of general distress or impairment. Using the standard $60T$ or greater criterion, GSI scores classified about 16% of the baseline sample and 14% of the follow-up sample as requiring further evaluation in Phase I. These rates dropped to 11% and 12%, respectively, in Phase II. Using this same criterion, the PST classified approximately 14% of the baseline sample in Phase I and 17% in Phase II. In contrast, approximately 13% of the baseline sample and 11% of the follow-up sample were classified as requiring evaluation when the one standard deviation cutoff ($40T$ or less) was applied to Phase I MCS scores. These rates increased slightly to 15% and 12%, respectively, in Phase II. In Phase I, PCS results indicated that 13% of the baseline sample and 16% of the follow-up sample reported physical problems and limitations suggesting the need for further evaluation. Although the Phase II PCS follow-up sample impairment classification decreased slightly to 13%, the baseline classification rate PCS classification rate jumped to 23%.

TABLE 24.7
Phase I and Phase II Medical and Mental Health/Substance
Abuse Outpatient Resource Utilization at Follow-Up

	Phase I		Phase II	
Utilization Variable	*n*	*%*	*n*	*%*
Medical outpatient visits	96		77	
Patients reporting no visits	35	36.5	15	19.5
Patients reporting 1 or more visits	61	63.5	62	80.5*
MH/SA outpatient visits	97		77	
Patients reporting no visits	90	92.8	76	98.7
Patients reporting 1 or more visits	7	7.2	1	1.3*

*Change from Phase I to Phase II significant at $p < .05$.

TABLE 24.8
Classification of Phase I and Phase II Baseline and Follow-Up Samples Using SA–45 and SF-12 T-Score Cutoff Criteria

| | Phase I | | | | | | Phase II | | | | | |
| | Baseline | | | Follow-Up | | | Baseline | | | Follow-Up | | |
Classification Variable	N	n	%	N	n	%	N	n	%	N	n	%
GSI ≥ 60T	126	20	15.9	97	14	14.4	105	12	11.4	76	9	11.8
PST ≥ 60T	126	18	14.3				105	18	17.1			
1+ Symptom domain scales ≥60T	126	61	48.4				105	57	54.3			
1+ Symptom domain scales ≥70T	126	15	11.9				105	18	17.1			
ANX ≥ 60T	126	25	19.8				105	20	19.0			
DEP ≥ 60T	125	21	16.8	97	15	15.5	105	15	14.3	77	7	9.1
OC ≥ 60T	126	22	17.5				102	17	16.7			
SOM ≥ 60T	126	32	25.4				94	28	26.9			
PHO ≥ 60T	126	19	15.1				105	23	21.9			
HOS ≥ 60T	126	19	15.1				104	14	13.5			
INT ≥ 60T	125	18	14.4				105	19	18.1			
PSY ≥ 60T	126	22	17.5				105	19	18.1			
MCS ≤ 40T	113	15	13.3	84	9	10.7	104	16	15.4	68	8	11.8
PCS ≤ 40T	113	15	13.3	84	13	15.5	104	24	23.1	68	9	13.2

Note. GSI, Global Severity Index; PST, Positive Symptom Total; ANX, Anxiety; DEP, Depression; HOS, Hostility; INT, Interpersonal Sensitivity; OC, Obsessive-Compulsive; PHO, Phobic Anxiety; PSY, Psychoticism; SOM, Somatization; MCS, Mental Component Summary; PCS, Physical Component Summary. Only GSI (based on SA–24), DEP, MCS, and PCS data were available for both baseline and follow-up samples. N is number in total sample; n, number of total sample meeting classification cutoff; %, percent of total sample meeting classification cutoff.

Baseline impairment classification rates based on combined and individual SA–45 symptom domain scale elevations varied from those obtained from the SA–45 and SF–12 summary scales. As indicated in Table 24.8, 48% of the Phase I baseline sample and 54% of the Phase II baseline sample met the classification criterion of one or more SA–45 symptom domain scales equal to or greater than 60T. These rates fell to about 12% and 17%, respectively, when the classification cutoff score was raised to 70T (i.e., two standard deviations above the mean). Applying the 60T cutoff to each of eight symptom domain scales (excluding Paranoid Ideation) at baseline, classification rates ranged from 14% for Interpersonal Sensitivity to 25% for Somatization in Phase I, and from 14% for Hostility to 27% for Somatization in Phase II. Along with Somatization, the individual scales representing symptom domains commonly presenting in primary care settings are Depression and Anxiety. These scales yielded Phase I and Phase II baseline classification rates of 17% and 20%, respectively, in Phase I; in Phase II, the rates dropped slightly to 14% and 19%, respectively.

Comparison of Resource Utilization of Impaired Versus Unimpaired Patients. To further study the potential effects of patient-reported psychological and physical health status on the use of health care resources, standard impairment classification criteria were applied to SA–45 and SF–12 variables that were measured at both the baseline and follow-up assessments of Phase I and Phase II (GSI, DEP, MCS, PCS). The mean units of the utilization variable (e.g., number of medical outpatient visits) for each of the two subsamples formed by each classification process (e.g., those patients with GSI ≥ 60 and those patients with GSI < 60; those patients with MCS ≤ 40 and those patients with MCS > 40) were compared. The results of these comparisons are presented in Table 24.9.

Examination of Table 24.9 reveals only six occurrences of significant mean differences in resource utilization. They were as follows:

1. Phase I baseline patients with MCS > 40 indicated more medical emergency room visits than Phase I baseline patients with MCS ≤ 40.
2. Phase I baseline patients with PCS > 40 indicated more medical room visits than Phase I baseline patients with PCS ≤ 40.

TABLE 24.9
Mean Medical and Psychiatric Resource Utilization by Impaired and
Unimpaired Subsamples Classified by GSI, DEP, MCS, and PSC Scale Cutoffs

| | Phase I | | | | Phase II | | | |
| | Baseline | | Follow-Up | | Baseline | | Follow-Up | |
	n	Mean	n	Mean	n	Mean	n	Mean
Med. ER								
GSI ≥ 60	20	0.05	14	0.00	10	0.10	9	0.11
GSI < 60	98	0.07	83	0.01	89	0.20	67	0.30
DEP ≥ 60	20	0.05	15	0.00	13	0.13	7	0.00
DEP < 60	97	0.07	82	0.01	86	0.20	70	0.04
MCS ≤ 40	15	0.00*	9	0.00	14	0.21	8	0.13
MCS > 40	91	0.09	75	0.01	84	0.19	60	0.02
PCS ≤ 40	14	0.00*	13	0.00	23	0.39	9	0.00
PCS > 40	92	0.09	71	0.01	75	0.13	59	0.03

(Continued)

TABLE 24.9
(Continued)

	Phase I				Phase II			
	Baseline		Follow-Up		Baseline		Follow-Up	
	n	Mean	n	Mean	n	Mean	n	Mean
Med. inpatient								
GSI ≥ 60	20	0.00	14	0.07	10	0.10	9	0.33
GSI < 60	96	0.16	83	0.05	89	0.09	67	0.05
DEP ≥ 60	20	0.00	15	0.07	13	0.08	7	0.57
DEP < 60	95	0.16	82	0.05	86	0.09	70	0.04
MCS ≤ 40	15	0.00	9	0.00*	14	0.07	8	0.50
MCS > 40	89	0.17	75	0.07	84	0.10	60	0.03
PCS ≤ 40	14	0.00	13	0.08	23	0.00	9	0.11
PCS > 40	90	0.17	71	0.06	75	0.12	59	0.09
Med. outpatient								
GSI ≥ 60	20	1.90	14	2.29	10	1.30	9	2.33
GSI < 60	98	1.69	82	1.57	88	1.98	67	1.97
DEP ≥ 60	20	1.65	15	2.27	13	2.00	7	2.71
DEP < 60	97	1.70	81	1.57	85	1.89	70	1.99
MCS ≤ 40	15	0.67*	9	2.11	14	2.29	8	2.75
MCS > 40	91	1.90	74	1.68	83	1.87	60	1.88
PCS ≤ 40	14	1.86	12	2.75	23	3.04*	9	1.67
PCS > 40	92	1.71	71	1.55	74	1.58	59	2.03
Psy. ER								
GSI ≥ 60	20	0.00	14	0.00	10	0.10	9	0.00
GSI < 60	97	0.00	83	0.00	89	0.00	67	0.00
DEP ≥ 60	20	0.00	15	0.00	13	0.08	7	0.00
DEP < 60	96	0.00	82	0.00	86	0.00	70	0.00
MCS ≤ 40	15	0.00	9	0.00	14	0.07	8	0.00
MCS > 40	90	0.00	75	0.00	84	0.00	60	0.00
PCS ≤ 40	14	0.00	13	0.00	23	0.00	9	0.00
PCS > 40	91	0.00	71	0.00	75	0.01	59	0.00
Psy. inpatient								
GSI ≥ 60	20	0.00	14	0.00	10	0.10	9	0.00
GSI < 60	97	0.00	83	0.00	89	0.00	67	0.00
DEP ≥ 60	20	0.00	15	0.00	13	0.08	7	0.00
DEP < 60	96	0.00	82	0.00	86	0.00	70	0.00
MCS ≤ 40	15	0.00	9	0.00	14	0.07	8	0.00
MCS > 40	90	0.00	75	0.00	84	0.00	60	0.00
PCS ≤ 40	14	0.00	13	0.00	23	0.00	9	0.00
PCS > 40	91	0.00	71	0.00	75	0.01	59	0.00
Psy. outpatient								
GSI ≥ 60	20	0.50	14	0.17	10	0.10	9	0.00
GSI < 60	97	0.33	83	0.86	88	0.16	67	0.12
DEP ≥ 60	20	0.45	15	0.17	13	0.92	7	0.00
DEP < 60	96	0.34	82	0.80	85	0.04	70	1.11
MCS ≤ 40	15	0.40	9	0.00*	14	0.71	8	0.00
MCS > 40	90	0.00	75	0.35	83	0.06	60	0.00
PCS ≤ 40	14	0.29	13	1.23	23	0.43	9	0.00
PCS > 40	91	0.35	71	0.14	74	0.07	59	0.14

Note. GSI, Global Severity Index; DEP, Depression; MCS, Mental Component Summary; PCS, Physical Component Summary. For each of the six treatment settings, significance of difference was tested between the mean units of those classified as impaired to those classified as unimpaired by each of the four scales, in each of the baseline and follow-up assessments of Phase I and Phase II.

*$p < .01$.

3. Phase I follow-up patients with MCS > 40 indicated more medical inpatient days than Phase I baseline patients with MCS ≤ 40.

4. Phase I baseline patients with MCS > 40 indicated more medical outpatient visits than Phase I baseline patients with MCS ≤ 40.

5. Phase II baseline patients with PCS ≤ 40 indicated more medical outpatient visits than Phase II baseline patients with PCS > 40.

6. Phase I follow-up patients with MCS > 40 indicated greater utilization of psychiatric outpatient treatment than Phase I follow-up patients with MCS ≤ 40.

Prediction of Follow-Up Resource Utilization Overall Patient Satisfaction From SA–45, SF–12, and Utilization Variables. Phase I and Phase II data were further analyzed to determine if variables important to testing the study's hypotheses could be predicted from other variables derived from the study instruments. Specifically, attempts were made to arrive at regression equations that would allow for the prediction of resource utilization and overall patient satisfaction. These efforts resulted in the derivation of two linear regression equations: one for the prediction of outpatient medical resource utilization and one for the prediction of overall patient satisfaction (item 17) during the follow-up assessment. The equation for the prediction of the medical outpatient resource utilization is:

$$\text{FRU3C} = -1.37 + 0.035\text{BHOST} + 0.36\text{BPCST40} + 0.285\text{Phase}$$

where FRU3C is the number of medical outpatient visits; BHOST is the SA–45 Hostility *T*-score at baseline; BPCST40 is 1 if the SA–12 baseline PCS *T*-score is less than or equal to 40, and 0 if the baseline SA–12 PCS *T*-score is greater than 40; and Phase is 1 if predicting Phase I utilization, and 2 if predicting Phase II utilization.

The equation for the prediction of overall patient satisfaction is as follows:

$$\text{FSAT17} = -0.694 + 0.045\text{BHOST} + 0.087\text{BRU3}$$

where FSAT17 is the satisfaction rating for item 17 of the patient satisfaction form; BHOST is the baseline SA–45 Hostility *T*-score; and BRU3 is the number of medical outpatient visits reported at baseline.

Correlation Between SA–45 and SF–12 Variables. Correlations between and among the scales of the SA–45 and the SF–12, using combined Phase I and Phase II baseline data, were computed as a means of further validating the use of these instruments in primary care settings. The pattern of correlations presented in Table 24.10 is as would be expected for these two tests: All 11 SA–45 variables correlated significantly with each other and with the SF–12 MCS scale ($p < .01$); the MCS scale did not correlate with SF–12 PCS scale; and even though some were significant, the correlations between the PSC scale and the SA–45 scales were much lower than those found for the MCS and the SA–45 variables.

Correlations Between Patient Satisfaction Variables. Intercorrelations among the 18 patient satisfaction items were computed in order to explore the possibility of findings that might reveal additional information on the various aspects of the services offered by the Vienna clinic. For this analysis, the patient satisfaction data from

TABLE 24.10

Combined Phase I and Phase II Baseline Intra- and Interscale Correlations of SA–45 and SF-12 Variables

Scale	GSI	PST	ANX	DEP	OC	SOM	PHO	HOS	INT	PAR	PSY	MCS
PST	.97**											
ANX	.83**	.80**										
DEP	.79**	.74**	.66**									
OC	.80**	.79**	.62**	.64**								
SOM	.69**	.65**	.49**	.37**	.51**							
PHO	.51**	.54**	.49**	.29**	.37**	.33**						
HOS	.63**	.61**	.51**	.53**	.47**	.33**	.31**					
INT	.83**	.81**	.71**	.63**	.64**	.46**	.51**	.57**				
PAR	.74**	.72**	.54**	.52**	.47**	.40**	.41**	.51**	.68**			
PSY	.45**	.48**	.37**	.37**	.33**	.21**	.35**	.42**	.42**	.49**		
MCS	-.65**	-.61**	-.62**	-.67**	-.59**	-.29**	-.25**	-.49**	-.55**	-.43**	-.34**	
PCS	-.20**	-.19**	-.16*	-.05	-.08	-.35**	-.17*	-.11	-.11	-.15*	-.02	-.06

Note. Based on samples of 214–231 outpatients.

*p < .05.

**p < .01.

Phase I and Phase II were combined for this purpose because results reported earlier indicated that there were no significant differences between the mean Phase I and Phase II ratings on any of the items.

With relatively few exceptions, these interitem correlations, presented in Table 24.11, are statistically significant and fall within the moderate to high range. In general, those items measuring satisfaction with the clinical staff's listening and responding to the patients' physical, emotional, and informational needs correlated quite highly with each other and with the overall satisfaction item (item 17). Among the lowest correlations were those between the item measuring satisfaction with the amount of time spent with the provider (item 18) and the other patient satisfaction items. Six of these 17 correlations were insignificant.

SUMMARY AND DISCUSSION

The INOVA Integrated Behavioral Health Care Pilot Project was undertaken to explore the possible benefits of integrating on-site behavioral health care services—psychological testing, consultation, and brief therapy—into FFPC primary care clinics. It was thought that the on-site availability of these services would lead to improved psychological outcomes, decreases in medical resource utilization, an increase in patients' satisfaction with the total care provided by the FFPC clinics, and an increase in FFPC providers' satisfaction with the behavioral health services provided to their referred patients. The data obtained during Phase I (control period) and Phase II (behavioral health integration period) of the project revealed both expected and unexpected findings.

Primary Findings

The Phase I sample did not differ significantly from the Phase II sample in any of the following: age or gender; patient-reported baseline psychological symptom severity or functional limitation; patient-reported change in psychological symptom severity or functional limitation 3 months postbaseline; patient-reported medical or behavioral resource utilization at baseline; or patient satisfaction with any of the measured clinical or nonclinical aspects of the provided care. In addition, except for the decline in average number of medical emergency room visits from baseline to follow-up in Phase I, patient-reported change in medical and behavioral resource utilization from baseline to 3 months postbaseline for paired subsamples was not statistically significant in either Phase I or Phase II.

At the same time, significant Phase I to Phase II differences in provider-reported satisfaction were found on many of the measured aspects of behavioral health care services. Specifically, during Phase II, the providers were more satisfied with appointment access and availability for the patient; telephone access to the treating provider; notification of admission to and discharge from a higher level of care; patients' access to emergency services; and the quality of outpatient mental health services provided to their patients. In addition, there were significant increases in the primary care providers' satisfaction with both the overall integration and the effectiveness of behavioral health care services offered to their patients. Finally, although not statistically significant, there were increases in the providers' satisfaction with the other

TABLE 24.11

Interitem Correlations of Satisfaction Variables Computed From Combined Phase I and Phase II Data

Item	1	2	3	4	5	6	7	8	9	10	11	12	13	14	15	16	17
2	-.15																
3	-.36**	.29**															
4	-.43**	.25**	.68**														
5	-.32**	.23**	.53**	.77**													
6	-.29**	.10	.27**	.33**	.38**												
7	-.11	.13	.24**	.30**	.44**	.51**											
8	-.30**	.27**	.60**	.58**	.61**	.48**	.46**										
9	-.28**	.23**	.55**	.62**	.59**	.46**	.42**	.80**									
10	-.20*	.17	.50**	.43**	.54**	.47**	.44**	.61**	.68**								
11	-.36**	.25**	.50**	.55**	.63**	.56**	.42**	.75**	.76**	.71**							
12	-.27**	.31**	.48**	.46**	.47**	.58**	.50**	.60**	.61**	.61**	.63**						
13	-.29**	.24**	.49**	.52**	.56**	.61**	.54**	.75**	.72**	.63**	.75**	.73**					
14	-.32**	.23**	.46**	.59**	.67**	.58**	.55**	.78**	.75**	.59**	.81**	.68**	.82**				
15	-.37**	.33**	.52**	.62**	.63**	.60**	.53**	.79**	.75**	.56**	.73**	.67**	.81**	.84**			
16	-.24	.24	.52**	.54**	.53**	.57**	.42**	.80**	.83**	.79**	.80**	.66**	.72**	.83**	.80**		
17	-.33**	.27**	.55**	.69**	.66**	.53**	.45**	.80**	.76**	.58**	.77**	.60**	.74**	.82**	.82**	.79**	
18	.01	.01	.05	.16*	.30**	.14	.33**	.17	.29**	.26**	.32**	.11	.30**	.35**	.25**	.17	.22**

Note. Based on samples of 48–172 patients. Negative correlations between item 1 and all other items reflect the fact that unlike all other items, a "disagree" response to item 1 indicates satisfaction.

*p < .05.
**p < .01.

measured aspects of behavioral health care services. All in all, the primary care providers' perception of and satisfaction with the behavioral health care services that referred patients received greatly improved during the time a behavioral health care provider was available for on-site consultation and brief treatment.

Further analysis of the project data revealed several interesting findings. First, a substantial proportion of the patients being seen at the Vienna clinic appear to be experiencing a significant level of psychological distress. Using a GSI score of 60T or greater to classify patients as requiring further evaluation resulted in the identification of 16% of the baseline sample and 14% of the follow-up sample in Phase I, and 11% and 12% in Phase II, respectively. Phase I baseline and follow-up rates of about 13% and 11%, respectively, were achieved when an SF–12 MCS T-score of 40 or less was the criterion. These rates increased slightly to 15% and 12%, respectively, during Phase II. Although both the GSI- and MCS-based rates are still much lower than the 25% to 39% rates reported in the literature using various other instruments and methodologies for the classification of the presence of any diagnosable or subthreshold disorder (Johnson et al., 1995; Kessler et al., 1994; Kobak et al., 1997; Locke & Larsson, 1997), baseline classification rates increased dramatically to 48% in Phase I and 54% in Phase II when one or more symptom domain scales with a T-score of 60 or greater was used as the criterion.

Use of score elevations (≥60T) on individual primary care-relevant SA–45 symptom domain scales (Depression, Anxiety, Somatization) resulted in classification rates that varied in their consistency with the prevalence rates reported in the literature for related disorders or problems in primary care settings. The Phase I and Phase II baseline Anxiety scale elevation classification rates (20% and 19%, respectively) are fairly consistent with the 13% to 24% anxiety disorder rates reported by Johnson et al. (1995), Kobak et al. (1997), and Kessler et al. (1994). The 17% and 15% baseline classification rates obtained using the Depression scale 60T cutoff during Phase I and Phase II, respectively, are generally lower than the mood disorder rates reported by these same authors, but they are fairly consistent with Zung, Broadhead, and Roth's (1993) 21% finding. The same cutoff applied to the Somatization scale scores resulted in a 25% and 27% classification rates for Phase I and Phase II, respectively. These are higher than the 14% rate reported by Johnson et al. for somatoform disorders but much lower that the 50%+ rate reported by Locke and Larsson (1997) for the presence of the defense mechanism of somatization. Unfortunately, the accuracy of the classifications could not be verified because the required corroborating data were not collected as part of this project.

It had been expected that the percent of patients reporting psychological distress from baseline to follow-up would be significantly lower in Phase II than in Phase I as a result of the availability of the behavioral health services. In fact, no significant change difference in baseline to follow-up change was found between the two phases. The reason for this may lie in the fact that the conditions actually did not change substantially in Phase II. Investigation of the slow rate of enlisting patient participation in Phase II revealed implementation problems. Instead of testing all eligible patients during the Phase II baseline period, only those who were specifically referred by providers for assessment were administered the project instruments. Consequently, the use of the instrumentation as an ordered "lab test" instead of as a general baseline screener may have resulted in the selection of biased sample during Phase II. Moreover, when they were administered, the SA–45 and SF–12 frequently were not immediately scored by the Infinifax scoring system.

In addition, limited access to the clinic's fax machine often resulted in the scoring of these instruments at an off-site location, sometimes days after their administration. As a result, providers may not have had access to up-to-date assessment information on the day the patient was being seen. Finally, anecdotal reports suggest that the behavioral health clinician was not utilized to her full capacity. It thus would appear that Phase I and Phase II presented similar conditions for patients and providers, and that under neither condition were the providers able to adequately manage those cases in need of behavioral health intervention.

When the Phase I and Phase II data from all patients who completed the follow-up resource utilization assessment (not just those who also completed the baseline assessment, as was the case reported earlier) were considered, it was found that the percent of patients reporting at least one outpatient medical visit during the 3-month follow-up period increased significantly from Phase I to Phase II. At the same time, there was a significant decrease in the number of patients reporting at least one outpatient mental health/substance abuse visit during the same 3-month follow-up period. These unexpected findings may reflect increased sensitivity/attention to behavioral health problems stemming from their participation in the project, as well as the particular characteristics of the Vienna providers. Because of their training in dealing with behavioral health issues, these providers are more apt to treat patients with behavioral health problems themselves rather than to refer them to a behavioral health care provider. Moreover, the on-site availability of behavioral health care backup during Phase II may have facilitated this; on the other hand, the reported underutilization of the behavioral health consultant would not support this.

The medical and psychiatric resource utilization of subsamples of patients classified as impaired or unimpaired based on GSI, DEP, MCS, and PCS T-scores was rather curious. Significant resource utilization differences between the impaired and unimpaired groups emerged only when the classification was based on the SF–12 MCS and PCS scales (see Table 24.9). More importantly, in four of the six comparisons in which this occurred, patients scoring in the unimpaired ranged (i.e., T-score > 40) of the SF–12 MCS scale reported more utilization than those scoring in the impaired ranged. Thus, a Phase I "normal" range MCS score was more likely associated with more medical emergency room visits, inpatient days and outpatient visits, and psychiatric outpatient visits than a score falling into the impaired range. A similar finding was noted for Phase I impaired-range PCS subsamples and medical emergency room visits. Closer to expectations, an impaired-range PCS in Phase II was associated with greater medical outpatient visits. It is difficult to arrive at possible reasons for the MCS findings, but perhaps they are a function of the particular samples that participated in the project. Alternately, they may indicate that the MCS and PCS scales are indeed related to medical resource utilization in primary care patients. Regardless, replication of this study with larger and different samples would help clarify the matter.

Additional Findings

Two findings that emerged from the application of more sophisticated statistical techniques may have implications for identifying potentially problematic patients early on. Patients with high SA–45 Hostility (HOS) scale T-scores and an SF–12 Physical Components Summary (PCS) scale T-score less than or equal to 40 at baseline have a higher probability of having more medical outpatient visits than those without these scores. In addition, the higher the baseline HOS T-score, the more likely it is that the patient will report dissatisfaction with overall care and treatment. Thus, it may be worthwhile to be sensitive to the needs of patients exhibiting these patterns of scores at the beginning of an episode of care.

Finally, the correlations among and between the SA-45 and SF-12 scales and indices, along with the means and standard deviations obtained from the results of Phase I and Phase II baseline and follow-up samples, support the use of these instruments for measuring psychological symptom severity and functional status in primary care settings. In addition, the intercorrelations of the patient satisfaction items are generally quite high and significant. Unsurprisingly, items relating to the provider's skill and sensitivity and response to patient needs generally showed the strongest relationships with the overall satisfaction item (item 17).

Limitations of the Project

Project design limitations as well as implementation and other problems that were encountered during the course of the project likely played a significant role in the outcome of the study. First, a number of problems arose during the implementation of the project. Foremost among them was the fact that only 231 patients from the Vienna clinic participated in the study. The project design originally called for a total of 600 patients (100 Phase I and 100 Phase II patients from three different clinics).

Unanticipated problems in either enlisting the cooperation of other primary care sites or starting the project at these sites on a timely basis, as well as other circumstances, significantly limited the ability to gather the needed data. For example, a second site agreed to participate in project. The staff at this site is not as sophisticated as the Vienna staff in dealing with behavioral health problems and thus is probably more typical of primary care practices in general. Unfortunately, it was also involved in a consolidation of practices at the time of the study, and the demands placed on the administrative staff were already approaching the maximum level. Because the site was unable to both keep up with the daily demands of a busy practice and devote the time that was needed for involvement in the project, the data gathering that began at the second site was slowed and eventually discontinued. A third site also was invited to participate in the study. Although interested in participating in the project, this site had to decline the invitation for reasons similar to those of the second site. Consequently, the results of the project reflect the effect of the intervention at only one relatively atypical primary care site, thus limiting the generalizability of the findings. Also, the relatively small sample size substantially decreased the likelihood of obtaining the expected statistically significant findings.

Staff compliance with the study's methodology presented other types of problems. The underutilization of behavioral assessment and consultative resources was discussed earlier. In addition, during Phase I, the providers were inconsistent in their completion of the patient tracking form. For this reason, the form was not a part of the Phase II instrumentation. Thus, important information relating to whether the patient was receiving behavioral health treatment or was referred for this type of treatment during a specific visit was not obtained.

Finally, two other aspects of the project may have limited its success. One is the fact that the physicians at the Vienna clinic have been exposed to several opportunities for training focused on the detection and treatment of behavioral health disorders in primary care settings. Their training in dealing with these problems likely has made them feel more competent and confident in their ability to manage patients presenting with these problems, and thus they may be less likely to refer many of these types of patients to behavioral health care specialists for treatment. As noted earlier, this might explain the increased utilization of medical outpatient services during Phase II. In addition, the fact that the project focused on short-term (3-month) changes may have impacted the utilization findings. Tracking of medical and behavioral health utilization resources over a longer period of time (e.g., 6 months, 1 year) might have yielded different findings.

CONCLUSIONS AND RECOMMENDATIONS

Although some of the results of the Primary Behavioral Health Care Pilot Project were unexpected, the project as a whole is supportive of the development and implementation of a more controlled study of the impact of integrated behavioral healthcare services in primary care settings. The lessons learned and experience gained from the implementation of and findings from the current project, combined with the basic project design and methodology that was initially developed, should provide the opportunity to better demonstrate how integrated behavioral health care can result in more efficient and cost-effective services to patients requiring mental health or substance abuse treatment. Specifically, the following are recommended:

1. Maintain the basic two-phase pilot project design, instrumentation, and methodology.

2. Enlist the participation of several clinics before the beginning of the project.

3. Begin Phase I at each clinic simultaneously. Similarly, begin Phase II at each clinic simultaneously.

4. Obtain data on at least 100 Phase I patients and 100 Phase II patients from each participating clinic.

5. Ensure that provider and support staff are aware of all study-related expectations of them, and that they consistently comply with these expectations. For example, providers should complete the patient tracking form after each visit with a study participant. Support staff should solicit each consecutive, eligible patient for their consent to participate in the study until the sample quota is complete; this should be done even if in Phase II the provider is only interested in the results of specific members of the sample. In addition, the provision of more intense training in the use of the behavioral health resources provided in Phase II would be imperative.

6. Ensure that potential logistical problems (e.g., during Phase II, availability of office space for the behavioral health provider, and access to a fax machine for immediate scoring of the SA–45 and SF–12) are addressed prior to beginning the project.

Primary care practices are fast-paced, high-intensity settings where time is at a premium and the demands placed on both clinical and administrative staff members are significant. Any attempt to integrate behavioral health care services into a primary care setting places yet another set of demands on the staff. The obstacles are not insurmountable, but successful integration of medical and behavioral services will require the coordinated efforts of dedicated staff at all levels, in the design and implementation of a program that will work best in the constraints of their particular setting.

REFERENCES

Johnson, J. G., Spitzer, R. L., Williams, J. B., Kroenke, K., Linzer, M., Brody, D., deGruy, F., & Hahn, S. (1995). Psychiatric comorbidity, health status, and functional impairment associated with alcohol abuse and dependence in primary care patients: Findings of the PRIME MD–1000 study. *Journal of Consulting and Clinical Psychology, 63,* 133–140.

Kessler, L. G., McGonagle, K. A., Shanyang, Z., Nelson, C. B. Hughes, M., Eshleman, S., Wittchen, H. U., & Kendler, K. S. (1994). Lifetime and 12-month prevalence of DSM–III–R psychiatric disorders. *Archives of General Psychiatry, 51,* 8–19.

Kobak, K. A., Taylor, L. V., Dottl, S. L., Greist, J. H., Jefferson, J. W., Burroughs, D., Mantle, J. M., Katzelnick, D. J., Norton, R., Henk, H. J., & Serlin, R. C. (1997). A computer-assisted telephone interview to identify mental disorders. *Journal of the American Medical Association, 278,* 905–910.

Locke, S. E., & Larsson, K. M. (1997). Clinical presentation, screening, and treatment of somatization in primary care. In J. D. Haber & G. E. Mitchell (Eds.), *Primary care meets mental health: Tools for the 21st century* (pp. 179–191). Tiburon, CA: CentraLink.

Strategic Advantage, Inc. (1996). *Symptom Assessment–24 Questionnaire (SA–24).* [Unpublished psychological test instrument.]

Strategic Advantage, Inc. (1998). *Symptom Assessment–45 Questionnaire (SA–45) technical manual.* Toronto: Multi-Health Systems.

Ware, J. E., Jr., Kosinski, M., & Keller, S. D. (1994). *SF–12 physical and mental health summary scales: A user's manual* (3rd ed.). Boston: Health Institute, New England Medical Center.

Ware, J. E., Jr., Kosinski, M., & Keller, S. D. (1995). *SF–12: How to score the SF–12 physical and mental health summary scales* (2nd ed.). Boston: Health Institute, New England Medical Center.

Ware, J. E., Jr., Snow, K. K., Kosinski, M., & Gandek, B. (1993). *SF–36 Health Survey manual and interpretation guide.* Boston: Health Institute, New England Medical Center.

Zung, W. K., Broadhead, W. E., & Roth, M. E. (1993). Prevalence of depressive symptoms in primary care. *Journal of Family Practice, 37,* 337–344.

IV

FUTURE DIRECTIONS

Future Directions in Psychological Assessment and Treatment in Primary Care Settings

Kenneth A. Kobak
James C. Mundt
David J. Katzelnick
Healthcare Technology Systems, Madison, Wisconsin

It's the year 2010 and many changes have occurred in psychological assessment and treatment. Following the treatment process of two members of a large health plan, Mr. A and Ms. D, illustrates some of the advances that have occurred.

Mr. A is a 55-year-old man who has a long history of coronary artery disease and stable angina and who also has a family history of depression. He is in the Health Plan's registry for cardiac disorders and is followed by a chronic disease treatment coordinator for his coronary artery disease. Once put in the cardiac registry, the combination of a family history of depression and cardiac disease place him at high risk of developing depression, so he receives depression educational materials from the health plan to help decrease the risk of his developing depression. These educational materials include information about the nature of depression, warning signs, simple self-help preventive measures such as exercise and activity scheduling, and a self-assessment for depression. All these materials are available "online." During what feels like a long January, Mr. A decides to complete the computer-administered depression questionnaire. He finds that he has many of the symptoms of major depression, including sleep disturbance, decreased appetite, and poor concentration. As a result, he contacts his treatment coordinator, who sets up a more comprehensive computer-administered mental health evaluation via interactive video.

Mr. A screens positive for the presence of major depression on the mood module of the mental health evaluation, which then automatically branches to a symptom severity measure to evaluate depression severity. The severity assessment indicates he has had a moderate level of major depression for at least the past 2 months. The results of all assessments are immediately (and automatically) transmitted to the cardiac treatment coordinator, who also coordinates treatment of depression. Based on the results of the psychological assessments he received, and because this is his first episode of depression, the treatment coordinator follows established clinical guidelines and arranges for him to see his primary care physician, who receives all the testing information in a brief, standardized report. In preparation for Mr. A's visit with his primary care physician, the treatment coordinator also sends Mr. A a video to watch outlining in more detail some of the treatment options available. A few days later he sees his primary care physician, who also treats his cardiac illness.

Mr. A has worked with his primary care physician for years and, as suggested by the treatment coordinator, brings his wife along for the visit. After reviewing the psychological assessments with Mr. A, his doctor confirms that he has major depression and describes the different treatment options available, including psychotherapy and medication. Based on Mr. A's genetic evaluation and the results from his computer-administered psychological assessment, as well as information generated from the larger health plan treatment outcomes database, his primary care physician is able to give him accurate probabilities of responding to each of the treatment alternatives. Mr. A is very motivated to get better but has a limited amount of time, and some concerns about taking medication. He opts to enroll in a self-help treatment program administered by interactive video, where the computer will design cognitive and behavioral assignments to decrease his depressive symptoms.

As with all depressed patients in the Health Plan, he is registered in the Depression Registry and has regularly scheduled outcome assessments done by the computer via interactive video, with the results transmitted immediately to his treatment coordinator and primary care physician. Mr. A finds the interactive video cognitive behavior therapy program extremely helpful, and his depression severity outcome scores rapidly decrease over the next 6 weeks. He returns to see his primary care physician, who encourages him to continue his work with the self-help program and to then begin the relapse prevention program. At 6-month intervals for the next 2 years, he is evaluated for depression by video assessment and tracked by his treatment coordinator, who continues to stay involved in treating his cardiac illness.

A second patient, Ms. D, is a 46-year-old woman with no chronic medical problems and who is experiencing a significant change in her mood and her ability to function following a difficult divorce. She finds herself unable to function at work and is getting increasingly irritated with her teenage children. Finally, on the way home from work one day, she has the strong desire to drive her car off a bridge. Thinking about her children, she decides instead to drive to the Health Plan emergency room. She is rapidly triaged to the mental health specialist in the emergency room, and while waiting for the mental health specialist, she completes a brief computer-administered diagnostic screening. On the suicide assessment, Ms. D acknowledges strong suicidal thoughts and a suicidal plan. After a more complete psychological assessment, it is determined that she has severe major depression with acute suicidal thoughts and that a brief inpatient hospitalization is most appropriate.

Once she is settled on the inpatient unit, more detailed psychological testing indicates a second psychiatric diagnosis, obsessive-compulsive disorder (OCD). After meeting with her psychiatrist and treatment team, it is determined that she has had obsessive-compulsive disorder for over 25 years and that her attempts to decrease germs and contamination in the house were a major stressor that led to her divorce. Ms. D finds this explanation very reassuring, especially after she discovers that her depression and obsessive-compulsive disorder are both quite treatable. Based on the results of her testing and genetic makeup evaluation, she begins a combination treatment with a new pharmaceutical that begins working within 2 days, along with exposure and response prevention treatment for her OCD. This is initiated by a behavior therapist and continued via an interactive video program. Ms. D leaves the hospital 3 days later, after repeat testing shows that her suicidal risk has dramatically decreased and her symptoms are beginning to resolve. She is enrolled in the Depression Registry and meets her depression treatment coordinator in the hospital.

As an outpatient, she begins follow-up treatment with a psychiatrist for the acute phase of treatment. She is monitored by systematic outcome assessments that she completes at home via video assessment, the results of which are reviewed by her psychiatrist and treatment coordinator. At this point, her care is transferred to the primary care setting and the same depression treatment coordinator follows her progress via the bimonthly outcome assessments. Not only are her clinical symptoms improving but her quality of life and productivity have also dramatically improved.

Following 1 year of treatment with medication, her primary care physician, in consultation with her psychiatrist and depression treatment coordinator, tapers her medication. She continues her relapse prevention programs for depression and OCD. Her depression treatment coordinator contacts her every 6 months to be sure that she continues in remission, and makes recommendations to her primary care physician as appropriate.

Throughout Mr. A's and Ms. D's treatment, all of the data from their psychological assessments, physician visits, pharmacy visits, and medical claims are collected in the same Health Plan database. Plan members have control over the level of security of each of the pieces of information and who can get access to their medical records. Only medical personnel with the correct passwords can access sensitive information. The primary care physician and mental health specialist each receive aggregate information on the clinical outcomes of their patients on a monthly basis. These are all case adjusted to compensate for various patient variables that may impact outcome. The Health Plan is able to use their data on the improved health of their population to attract additional employers and members to join their plan.

These hypothetical scenarios, although currently in the realm of science fiction, are less speculation than educated guess at how clinical tools and practices, many of which already exist, may come to be integrated to provide a more comprehensive, systematic approach to patient and service management than is presently realized. The basic triad of patient screening, accurate diagnosis, and outcome monitoring is fundamental to providing quality patient care. These provide the building blocks for developing effective, evidence-based treatment. However, the breadth and depth of knowledge required to make informed decisions (including individual and demographic risk factors, expertise in standardized clinical diagnostic interviews and symptom severity measures, guidelines for managing treatment, and the interactions among and between such factors) exceed any reasonable expectations of front-line primary care physicians. Not only is it unrealistic to expect, or hope, that physicians could perform these functions within the constraints of a managed care environment, it is unnecessary.

Decades of research have demonstrated that interactive information systems, allowing immediate access to comprehensive knowledge bases and programmed to execute complex, modifiable algorithms using these databases and information specific to given individuals, can reliably improve patient care and treatment outcome. More than 20 years ago, McDonald (1976) found that even a simple protocol-based computer reminder to physicians dealing with simple clinical events, such as elevated blood pressure, increased physician responses to such events twofold. The increased computing speed and capabilities made available since that time have produced many wide-ranging applications designed to facilitate better delivery of health care. However, systematic integration and application of such systems have lagged well behind their potential. The remainder of this chapter explores the current "state of the art" of these innovations and identifies future directions in this area.

In order to more fully delineate the future role of psychological assessment in primary care, it is first necessary to define the *context*, that is, the model of mental health care delivery that will likely (i.e., ideally) exist in the future. After the model is defined, we illustrate how psychological assessment fits within that model. Some of the methods described already exist, whereas others have yet to be developed.

A FUTURE MODEL FOR PRIMARY CARE

The arrival of managed care has resulted in the increased emphasis on primary care as a more efficient way to provide and coordinate care. O'Connor, Solberg, and Baird (1998) pointed out that the immense costs associated with the failure to provide prevention services and the failure to successfully treat chronic diseases suggest that future primary care models will need to focus on improvement in these two areas. Psychiatric disorders are both chronic and amenable to prevention intervention, and thus fall within the focus of this domain. Current models of primary care are still focused on "providing episodic care, and . . . manage chronic diseases and preventive services in the same way: one patient and one visit at a time" (O'Connor et al., 1998, p. 63). The current model for the interaction between the patient in the community, in primary care, and in mental health speciality is illustrated in Fig. 25.1. As can be seen, the current model involves little overlap between the three systems, and little standardized infrastructure to facilitate coordination between the three systems. This

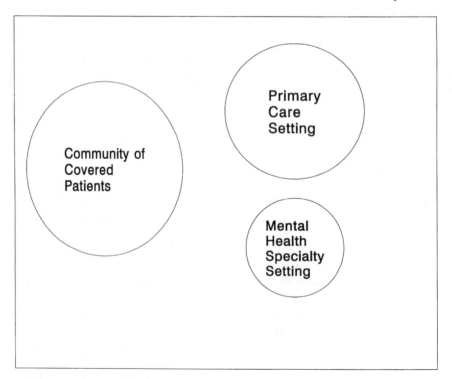

FIG. 25.1. Current model of patient interaction in the community, primary care, and mental health specialty.

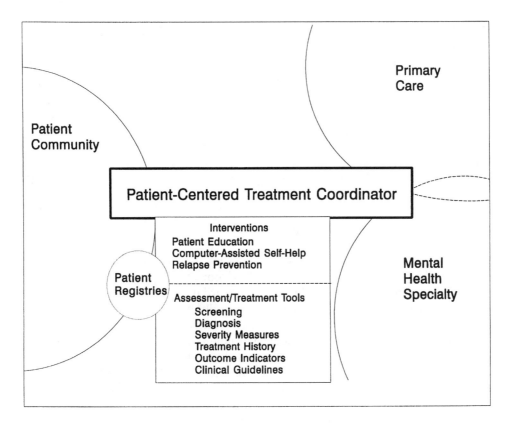

FIG. 25.2. An alternative model of patient interaction.

leads to suboptimal care as patients pass from one system to another, with the transmission of valuable information either unavailable or not in a usable form.

An alternative model has been proposed by O'Connor et al. (1998) that combines innovations in information technology (i.e., clinical databases) while incorporating the concepts of continuity of care, ongoing relationships with patients, and patient autonomy and responsibility. An expanded version of this model is presented in Fig. 25.2. This new model consists of formalized structures that allow for facilitation of communication and coordination of care between primary care and mental health specialty, as well as serving as a bridge between the patient community and the health care system as a whole. It allows for the more effective coordination of treatment of psychiatric patients with medical comorbidity, as well as integrated treatment of patients with more than one medical problem. The proposed model integrates the tools described by O'Connor et al. (1998), as well as some new methodologies we describe next.

At the hub of this new model are the two main components that coordinate the treatment delivery system as a whole and act as the "glue" that holds the system together: (a) a patient-centered treatment coordinator and (b) a comprehensive computerized health management system. This second component, the comprehensive computerized health management system, consists of three elements:

1. A large set of databases, including patient registries for various diseases, patient histories, empirically derived treatment guidelines, and systemwide infor-

mation gathering for continuing development of effective disease management and treatment guidelines.

2. Computer-administered patient assessments, including screeners, diagnostic instruments, and outcomes measures (e.g., symptom severity rating scales, quality of life measures, disability scales, patient satisfaction measures).
3. Computer-administered treatment interventions, prevention programs, and patient educational materials (including telephone reminders and outreach).

What follows is a review of what currently exists in these domains, as well as how these innovations may be implemented in the future for those that do not currently exist, or exist only in a preliminary form (see Fig. 25.2).

Patient-Centered Treatment Coordinator

The patient-centered treatment coordinator serves the function of integrating and overseeing all aspects of patient health care. The coordinator prevents the fragmentation of care, and monitors patients' progress toward expected outcomes. The role of treatment coordinator is relatively new and rapidly evolving in U.S. medical systems. Training of physicians in the present medical model focuses on acute treatment of illnesses, at which the American medical system is outstanding. The treatment of chronic illnesses in the United States (such as depression), however, is more problematic; fewer than 30% of patients with chronic illnesses in the United States receive long-term treatment consistent with treatment guidelines (Melfi et al., 1998). The institution of treatment guidelines and continuous quality improvement programs has had a modest impact on this problem, but there has been a general recognition that a change in the underlying system is necessary for major change to occur.

Once treatment guidelines have been established, it is critical to set up tracking systems that monitor whether patients are completing visits on schedule, are complying with treatment regimens, and are responding to treatment, in order to determine whether modification of treatment plans is needed. Tracking systems can alert treatment providers to the need to institute interventions if the patient falls off the anticipated response curve. Even if physicians were willing to take on this longitudinal tracking role, it would not be cost-effective. Nurses that collaborate directly with physicians on day-to-day care have difficulty finding the time to track the patients who should be, but are not, coming in, when the waiting room is already overflowing with patients requesting immediate care today. To fill in this gap, the role of treatment coordinator has been invented.

The treatment coordinator role is a modification of what has traditionally been viewed as the role of case managers. Case managers have been assigned to patients with very significant needs that cross specialties, especially when patients may not be capable of navigating the medical and social systems themselves. The treatment coordinator role is different in that these people are responsibile for monitoring a larger but less critically ill population who have chronic illnesses. Treatment coordinators must be experts in understanding the computerized database systems containing health service utilization and clinical outcome data from psychological evaluations. They must also be able to understand and integrate information from the patient registries and to effectively communicate information to patients and physicians in the clinic. Their role transcends the traditional divisions of the community population, primary care treatment population, and inpatient population. This allows them to provide continuity of care across these divisions (as was the case in our example of Ms. D) and allows for the optimal possibility of keeping patients out of the hospital and at high functioning in the community.

By bringing both population-based and individual patient information together to coordinate programs and services, effective treatment coordination is both evidence based and outcome focused. This approach attempts to optimize client self-care, diminish fragmentation of care across the continuum of providers and services, and use scarce resources in a cost-effective manner, with the goal of enhanced quality of life and increased patient satisfaction (Erickson, 1997; Girard, 1994; Weiss, 1998).

Precedent for this type of treatment coordinator already exists for treating mental disorders in primary care. The University of Pittsburgh Psychiatric–Primary Care Nurse Practitioner program focuses on training nurses to function as case managers for psychiatric problems in primary care settings (Dyer, Hammill, Regan-Kubinski, Yurick, & Kobert, 1997). Also, Katzelnick, Simon, Pearson, Manning, Helstad, Henk, and Kobak (1997) developed a disease management program for identifying and treating depression in primary care. The model utilizes a treatment coordinator who telephones patients after 2 weeks (the time patients are most likely to discontinue a new trial of antidepressant medication) in order to monitor (and encourage) compliance and to evaluate any side effects. The model also includes a telephone contact at 10 weeks, to insure evaluation of treatment response. In a multicenter study conducted at three large health maintenance organizations (HMOs), patients in the depression management program had significantly lower Hamilton Depression Scores than patients receiving usual care (Katzelnick, Simon, et al., 1997). The role of the treatment coordinator was instrumental in keeping patients in treatment long enough for effective treatment to occur.

A study by Atkinson (1996) found that using a case manager approach for seriously mentally ill patients resulted in earlier hospitalizations at less serious stages, reduced length of stay, higher functioning, improved self-care skills, and improvement in obtaining and receiving medical care. Similarly, a program using a patient care coordinator on a neuroscience unit resulted in positive outcomes in terms of length of stay, costs, and patient and staff satisfaction (Counsell, Guinn, & Limbaugh, 1994). Thus, when used in coordination with computerized medical information systems, the case manager is a powerful tool to insure comprehensive and cost-effective treatment and improved patient care.

Computer Databases

The second component of the hypothesized model is a comprehensive computerized health arrangement system. The first element of this component is computer databases. Quality health care involves a tremendous amount of information processing. Computerized databases can facilitate the assessment and treatment of mental disorders in primary care through several mechanisms, including disease-specific computerized patient registries for mental disorders (and other diseases), computerized patient histories, computer-generated treatment plans (based on empirical data), and systemwide data collection and outcomes monitoring for improving disease management and treatment guidelines.

Computerized Patient Registries. A concept central to the proposed model for enhanced primary care treatment is the identification and registration of special patient populations that could benefit from specific treatment interventions, prevention efforts, or patient education programs. Such individuals could be entered into these computerized registries based on treatment history, current diagnosis, or identified risk factors, and provided access to programs designed to proactively address current or potential medical problems. For example, patients entered into a depression registry could be monitored regularly at intervals that have been found effective for early detection of depression in order to reduce severity or to prevent relapse. Depression is often a chronic disorder, with cycles of remission and exacerbation. Computerized prevention and education programs (examples of which are discussed in more detail later) could be made available to patients in the registry. Such programs could include routine computer-administered self-monitoring to identify relapse or onset of a depressive episode.

Because the patient registries, medical histories, and treatment guidelines databases are all computerized, they can can compliment and interact with each other in order to provide more comprehensive and effective care. For example, Mr. A, our hypothetical case discussed at the beginning of this chapter, was in the cardiac registry, and his computerized medical history indicated a strong family history of depression. The computerized treatment outcomes guidelines for depression would identify such patients as having increased risk for developing depression following a cardiac event. As a result, Mr. A was proactively given information and self-help materials on depression to decrease his risk of developing depression. He also was provided access to a computer-administered self-monitoring system, in order to identify when and if his depression levels become severe enough to warrant treatment intervention. Programs such as this would not only minimize the suffering of patients with psychiatric disorders through more comprehensive, better integrated care, but would also reduce service utilization costs through earlier identification and treatment of problems while they are less severe and more easily addressed. Patients with depression have been found to be high utilizers of nonpsychiatric medical services (Henk, Katzelnick, Kobak, Greist, & Jefferson, 1996; Katon et al., 1990; Widmer & Cadoret, 1979).

Development of computer-based patient registries to expand knowledge of particular diseases is not a new idea. For example, a registry of Alzheimer's patients using common outcome measures was developed in the late 1980s (Morris et al., 1988), and has contributed greatly to increasing our understanding of the disease, its progression, and associated risk factors. Typically, such registries are incorporated into large, often nationally funded, basic research projects from which it is hoped information pertinent to developing effective prevention or treatment strategies can be derived. Less frequently, such registries are used interactively to influence and optimize ongoing treatment interventions. A notable example consistent with the type of patient registry use proposed in this chapter is that of Loeser, Zvagulis, Hercz, and Pless (1983), who developed a computerized immunization registry for a defined population of public clinics and private practitioners. Ninety-three percent of providers agreed to participate. The registry identified a prospective cohort of newborns that were at "high risk" for overdue immunizations. After 1 year, the immunization rates in audited groups improved significantly.

O'Connor et al. (1998) described how a hypothetical registry (similar to the one described by Loeser et al., 1983) could be used for immunizations, mammograms, and sigmoidoscopies. The registry could be checked monthly by the treatment coordinator or secretary who identifies clinic patients due for particular needs. A letter then would be sent to the patients to come in for services, and if a patient did not follow through, a letter would be placed in the patient's chart to remind the provider of the issue at the next clinic visit, even if for an unrelated reason. A similar procedure could be implemented for depression in primary care.

Computerized Patient Histories. As discussed previously, patient medical and psychiatric histories are an essential part of a integrated computerized information system. In the earliest investigation of the initial use of computers for obtaining medical histories, Slack and Van Cura (1968) found that patients responded positively to the experience. However, caution was advised in interpreting the findings, given the novelty of computers at that time. In the future, these histories could be obtained directly from the patient by computer.

In addition to saving clinician time, computer-administered medical histories are thorough and complete. Computers never fail to ask the required questions as clinicians often do. For example, in one study, physicians missed or failed to record 35% of the information obtained by a computer-administered medical history (Simmons & Miller, 1971). In addition, patients may be more likely to disclose information of a sensitive nature to a computer than to a clinician. In a study by Carr and Ghosh (1983), psychiatric inpatients reported an average of 5½ more items of information on a computerized psychiatric history than on a clinician interview, including having a criminal record (reported on computer but not clinician in 26% of patients), blackouts from drinking (23%), impotence (20%), being fired (17%), and suicide attempts (17%). As discussed in more detail later, dozens of studies have investigated both the subjective responses to computer-based interrogation and the comparability of data obtained using such methods relative to live interviews. The consensus that has emerged indicates patients typically have favorable impression of computer-administered assessments and may actually prefer it to clinician interviews in some circumstances (see Kobak, Greist, Jefferson, & Katzelnick, 1996, for a review).

Primary care patients with depression often present with multiple somatic symptoms suggestive of a medical condition while volunteering few psychological complaints (Kessler, Cleary, & Burke, 1985; Schulberg & Burns, 1988). A set of symptoms, including (a) pain (e.g., abdominal, headache, or other body aches), (b) low energy or excessive fatigue, (c) sexual difficulties, such as problems with desire or functioning (e.g., anorgasmia in women or erectile dysfunction in men), and (d) anxiety, phobias, or excessive worry over physical health has been identified that is common in depressed primary care patients (American Psychiatric Association, 1994, p. 323; Depression Guideline Panel, 1993c, p. 2.) Patients presenting with these symptoms where an organic cause cannot be found warrant screening for depression. Such information can be obtained by computerized medical histories, which can trigger evaluation by a computerized depression screener (described in more detail later).

In addition to the identification of somatic symptoms indicative of depression, a computerized medical history can help insure that questions regarding the primary risk factors for depression have been administered. These include: (a) prior episodes of depression, (b) family history of depressive disorder, (c) prior suicide attempts, (d) female gender, (e) age of onset under 40 years, (f) postpartum period, (g) medical comorbidity, (h) lack of social support, (i) stressful life events, and (j) current alcohol or substance abuse (Depression Guideline Panel, 1993a, p. 73). Patients with these risk factors can be identified by the computerized medical history and incorporated into the disease management database. Patients with identified risk factors presenting with one or more of the common depression symptoms would warrant further screening. Such screening could be done through computer-administered evaluations of depression (described later in this chapter).

Computer-Administered Treatment Guidelines.   A successful computerized health management system should incorporate treatment guidelines to help clinicians select the most appropriate treatment for an individual patient. The Agency for Health Care Policy and Research (AHCPR) developed a set of clinical practice guidelines for the identification and treatment of depression in primary care patients (Depression Guideline Panel, 1993a, 1993b, 1993c). A computerized health management system could use information obtained through the computerized medical history and computerized outcomes database in order to guide the physician in determining the most appropriate course of treatment, using AHCPR guidelines. For example, information obtained from the computer-administered medical history can help identify previous trials of antidepressant medications for a specific patient, the presence or absence of comorbid medical conditions, and any concurrent medications the patient is taking for those conditions. The outcomes database can identify whether previous antidepressant trials were successful or not, as well as the level of severity of the current episode. This information, in conjunction with AHCPR guidelines, would be useful in generating a recommended course of action for a individual patient. For example, patients who did not respond previously to a certain class of medication may be tried initially on a different class. Comorbid medical conditions may also dictate the type of antidepressant chosen. The computerized database can evaluate all these factors in generating a suggested treatment plan, and can collect data regarding treatment outcome. In the case of Mr. A, our example at the beginning of this chapter, his moderate level of depression, absence of psychotic symptoms, and the fact that his depression was not chronic or recurrent indicated either medication or cognitive therapy as viable treatment options. If his depression were more severe, recurrent, or associated with psychotic features (or if a previous response to psychotherapy was not successful), AHCPR guidelines would advise against prescription of psychotherapy alone.

Another advantage of the computerized management system is that empirical data will be gathered over the course of time that will help to modify and improve the disease specific treatment guidelines. In a pilot study at Dartmouth (Wasson, O'Connor, James, & Olmstead, 1992), ongoing monitoring of patients with unstable angina pectoris resulted in the identification of specific sets of symptoms and electrocardiography changes that help predict imminent myocardial infarction. Although similar types of predictions have been difficult in psychiatry in predicting suicide due to low base rates, ongoing outcomes evaluation can help inform and improve treatment guidelines by providing continuous input into the database. The increase in information should help improve predictions in terms of matching specific interventions with specific patient profiles. Such information can be shared across HMOs and may produce increasingly accurate and individualized guidelines for case management (Selby, 1997).

Before leaving this section on computer databases, it is worth noting a study by Balas and colleagues (1996), who completed a comprehensive review of 98 randomized, controlled trials of clinical information systems in medical practice. They were able to identify four generic information interventions that were "active ingredients" of systems that made a significant difference in family medicine:

1. Physician reminders, typically used to improve the provision of preventive care by computer-generated reminders on encounter forms. These include reminders for screenings, such as mamograms and other cancer screening, as well as immunization reminders.
2. Patient prompts/reminders, such as computer-generated telephone or mail reminders, typically, for preventive screening or immunization.
3. Computer-assisted treatment planners, including computer algorithms to assist decision making concerning drug dosages.
4. Interactive patient education, instruction, and therapy.

Computer-Administered Psychological Assessments

The intrusion of the marketplace into the clinical care of patients has met with substantial resistance, but it may herald new opportunities for improved clinical care. Increasing concern with the costs and benefits of treatments has resulted in a renewed emphasis on outcomes measurement. However, the increased information provided through outcomes measurements will help clinicians (and their patients) make more informed treatment decisions, thus improving the quality of patient care.

In addition to outcomes measurement, there are several other types of psychological assessments that are useful in primary care. Generally, these assessments fall under four broad categories: (a) *symptom rating scales*, used to measure symptom severity at the onset of treatment as well as to monitor a patients response to treatment, including side effects; (b) *screeners*, used to screen large numbers of people in order to identify a subset who are likely to have a disorder, and thus warrant more in-depth follow-up assessment with diagnostic interviews (often shortened versions of symptom rating scales serve as screeners); (c) *diagnostic interviews*, which serve to confirm the diagnosis in patients; and (d) *quality of life and patient satisfaction scales*, used to evaluate the impact of the disease and the success of the intervention on the patient's overall functioning, apart from disease-specific symptoms.

The Agency for Health Care Policy and Research (AHCPR) suggested a stepwise process to facilitate the identification and treatment of depression in primary care (Depression Guideline Panel, 1993a). These steps mirror the classes of rating scales described earlier. The first step begins with vigilance to the symptoms of depression, followed by screening of those individuals suspected of having the disorder; a diagnostic interview to confirm the presence of the disorder in those screening positive; a complete medical history and physical examination to rule out symptoms caused by general medical illnesses or other conditions; and finally, development of a treatment plan. This stepwise approach is applicable to other psychological disorders in addition to depression.

Although the value of psychological assessment in primary care is apparent, the use of psychological assessment in primary care has been limited for several reasons, including lack of expertise and training in the use of these scales, and the time and cost involved in their administration and scoring. Valid and reliable computer-administered psychological assessments provide a solution to these problems. Such assessments are cost-effective, are always available, and provide feedback immediately for the physician (and the patient) to review. Several studies have found patients are often more honest with the computer or prefer it to clinicians when disclosing information of a sensitive nature, such as alcohol and drug use (Lucas, 1977; Skinner & Allen, 1983; Turner et al., 1998), suicidal ideation (Petrie & Abell, 1994; Greist et al., 1973), sexual functioning (Greist & Klein, 1980; Turner et al, 1998), and social anxiety (Katzelnick et al., 1995; Kobak, Schaettle, Greist, Jefferson, Katzelnick, & Dottl, 1998). Computer administration frees physicians to focus their attention on weighing the available information, forming relationships with their patients, and making mutually informed treatment decisions. Several computer-administered versions of the types of assessments described earlier have been developed. What follows is a brief overview of this literature.

Symptom Rating Scales. Symptom rating scales identify salient aspects of the disorder, measure the severity of symptoms associated with specific disorders, and are used to measure change in symptoms over time. Symptom rating scales are not intended to provide diagnoses because they do not necessarily cover all the symptoms required to make a diagnosis, often contain items not directly germane to the diagnosis, and do not necessarily evaluate all the inclusion and exclusion criteria required for a diagnosis (Zimmerman et al., 1986). Many symptom rating scales have been adapted to desktop computer administration, and many have also been adapted for administration over the telephone by computer using interactive voice response (IVR), discussed later. These include the most widely used clinician-administered scales for the assessment of depression (Hamilton Depression Rating Scale, HAMD; Ancill, Rogers, & Carr, 1985; Carr, Ancill, Ghosh, & Margo, 1981; Kobak, Reynolds, Rosenfeld, & Greist, 1990), anxiety (Hamilton Anxiety Scale; HAS; Kobak, Reynolds, & Greist, 1993), obsessive-compulsive disorder (Yale–Brown Obsessive-Compulsive Scale, Y–BOCS; Baer, Brown-Beasley, Sorce, & Henriquess, 1993; Rosenfeld et al., 1992), and social phobia (Liebowitz Social Anxiety Scale and the Brief Social Phobia Scale; Kobak, Schaettle, et al., 1998). Clinician-administered rating scales adapted for computer-administration are programmed to obtain the same information a clinician would obtain during a clinical interview. Generally, each of these interviews begins with a brief introduction and a practice question. Patients are instructed to press keys on the computer keyboard corresponding to their response choice for a given item. Standard options include the ability to return to the previous questions, change answers, or discontinuing the interview at any time. Branching is based on patient response, and some programs allow patients to enter text for greater specificity (e.g., identifying most troublesome obsessive thoughts or most feared social situation). Validation studies have found these scales to have a high correlation (equivalency) with scores obtained using the clinician-administered versions (Kobak et al., 1990, 1993; Kobak, Schaettle, et al., 1998; Rosenfeld et al., 1992), with small mean score differences between the two forms of administration. These scales have been used both in clinical drug trials and as the primary outcome measure in a study evaluating the treatment of depression in high-utilizing primary care patients (Katzelnick, Kobak, Greist, Jefferson, & Henk, 1997a).

Interactive voice response (IVR) technology presents new opportunities for expanding the utility of computerized clinical assessment. Although desktop administration has certain advantages over clinician administration, it still requires the use of on-site computer hardware and software and that the patient be physically present, often solely for the purpose of evaluation. To improve the availability and clinical utility of these assessments, these symptom rating scales have been adapted for administration over the telephone using IVR technology (Dottl et al., 1998; Kobak,

Greist, Hirsch, Marks, & Baer, 1998; Kobak, Greist, Jefferson, & Katzelnick, 1998a; Kobak, Greist, Katzelnick, & Jefferson, 1998). This method permits the patient to dial a toll-free phone number and listen to questions read by the computer over the telephone, and then respond by pressing keys on the touch-tone telephone. IVR administration makes possible remote longitudinal assessment of patients 24 hours a day, 7 days a week, thus allowing physicians to monitor patient status between visits. Information entered into the system is stored and processed immediately, making it available for immediate review by the physician and/or the treatment coordinator. Such accessability allows more precise monitoring of treatment response, and real-time registration of any difficulties patients might be experiencing.

In one application of IVR technology, a nationwide telephone assessment program (TAP) was recently implemented using the IVR Y–BOCS (Greist et al., 1997). The program was designed to help physicians monitor treatment response of patients being treated for obsessive-compulsive disorder. Patients phoned a toll-free number and completed the IVR version of the Y–BOCS. Results were faxed or mailed to the patient's physician, who used the information to monitor the patient's response to treatment and modify treatment plans, if appropriate. The program also tracked the name and dose of any medication the patient was receiving for OCD, and obtained the patient's global impression of change since starting treatment (e.g., very much improved, much improved, minimally improved, no change, minimally worse, much worse, very much worse). Patient confidentiality was maintained by using a unique personal patient identification number (PIN) and self-selected passwords. Mailed reports contained the patient's name, but faxed reports included only the patient's PIN number, so that only the physician could determine the identity of the patient. Over 1,600 patients enrolled in this service, and over 2,000 calls were made.

The availability of "real-time" data via IVR not only improves patient care but in some cases can save lives. For example, in a recent clinical trial using the IVR version of the HAMD (Kobak, Greist, Jefferson, & Katzelnick, 1998b), the computer was programmed to automatically page a physician if a patient indicated a significant risk for committing suicide. In one case the page was generated, and the physician tried to phone the patient, with no success. The physician decided to call 911. The emergency team found the patient unconscious, the result of an attempted suicide via overdose. The patient was rushed to the emergency room and survived.

Several studies have found patients prefer disclosing ideas of suicide to a computer rather than to a clinician. In one study (Petrie & Abell, 1994), 150 patients hospitalized for a recent suicide attempt preferred the computer over the clinician 52% to 17%, with 30% having no preference. The preference for the computer grew larger as the level of suicidal ideation increased. In another study, a desktop diagnostic interview (PRIME–MD, discussed later in this chapter) was administered to 272 patients presenting to a large, urban, emergency room with low-acuity, nonpsychiatric complaints. Recent suicidal ideation was found in 28 patients, and 3 received acute psychiatric intervention (Risser, Biros, Hodroff, Kobak, & Mandell, 1997). Clearly, the computer is a valuable tool to help clinicians proactively identify and intervene with patients having active suicidal intent.

Screeners. Obtaining an accurate diagnosis involves a considerable amount of clinician time. In practical terms, it does not make sense to perform full evaluations on all subjects in order to identify a small subset of patients who have a particular psychiatric disorder. The purpose of a screener is to provide a time- and cost-efficient tool for identifying those patients who are most likely to have a disorder, in order to focus more in-depth follow-up assessments on only those patients warranting it.

As previously discussed, symptom rating scales are often used as screeners, by utilizing cutoff scores. Depression is one of the most common psychiatric problems found in primary care patients. The most widely used clinician-administered depression scale is the Hamilton Depression Rating Scale (HAMD; Hamilton, 1960). Although it was originally developed to measure depression severity in patients already diagnosed with depression, it has been found to possess good diagnostic utility. In one study of 570 adults, a cutoff score of 17 on the 17-item HAMD correctly identified 95% of patients with a SCID (Structured Clinical Interview for the *DSM*) diagnosis of major depression, with none of the control subjects incorrectly identified as depressed (Reynolds, Kobak, & Greist, 1992).

Although the full 17-item HAMD administered by clinicians shows good psychometric properties as a screener, the full scale takes too long to administer to have practical value to physicians in primary care practice. Shortened versions of the HAMD have been developed for both desktop and IVR administration that retain its psychometric properties for screening purposes, while requiring less patient (and no clinician) time. A nine-item version of the HAMD (described in a previous chapter of this book) has been developed for self-administration by either paper and pencil or desktop computer (Reynolds & Kobak, 1995a, 1995b). In a mixed sample of 650 clinical and nonclinical adults, a cutoff score of 10 demonstrated a sensitivity of 97.1% and specificity of 95.9%; that is, it correctly identified 97.1% of persons who had been diagnosed with major depression on the SCID, and did not identify as depressed 95.9% of the persons who did not have any such diagnosis on the SCID.

Sensitivity and specificity are important characteristics of a screening instrument, but do not fully characterize instrument utility for practical application, because they may be influenced by base-rate occurrences of the disorder. Two additional indices that are important for evaluating the clinical utility of an instrument are the *positive predictive value* (PPV) and the *negative predictive value* (NPV). The PPV is the percentage of positive screens that actually have the disorder screened for, and the NPV is the percentage of negative screens not having the disorder. That is, the PPV and NPV represent an estimate of the probablity that a given screening result is an accurate classification for a given individual.

The PPV of the nine-item HAMD using a cutoff of 10 was 90.1%, which is high, and addresses the problem of poor PPV that has been reported in the literature with past depression screeners (Campbell, 1987). The *negative predictive value* (NPV) of a cutoff score of 10 was 99.2%; that is, using this cutoff score, almost no subjects who were classified as not depressed by the HDI were actually depressed.

A short form of the HAMD has also been developed for IVR administration (Mundt et al., 1998). The scale consists of the 6 HAMD items identified by Bech and colleagues as providing a global measure of depression severity that is useful as a "unidimensional" index of overall severity (Bech et al., 1981; Beech, Allerup, Reisby, & Gram, 1984; Bech et al., 1975). These include items 1 (mood), 2 (guilt), 7 (work and interests), 8 (psychomotor retardation), 10 (psychic anxiety), and 11 (somatic anxiety). The 6-item HAMD had a correlation of .96 with the full scale, 17-item HAMD, and had an internal consistency of .88. In a sample of 367 subjects (a mix of primary care patients, psychiatric patients, and community controls), a score of 8 on the 6-item IVR HAMD had a sensitivity of 95% and a specificity of 93% in distinguishing subjects with major depression from community controls. The positive predictive value was 89%, and the negative predictive value was 97%, making it a practical tool that has few false positives.

Side-Effects Monitoring. Another potential application of IVR-administered rating scales as part of a computerized health management program is for the monitoring of medication side effects. Most patients being treated for depression in primary care fail to receive treatment of adequate dose and/or duration (Katzelnick, Kobak, Greist, Jefferson, & Henk, 1997b; Simon et al., 1995; Wells et al., 1989). The highest discontinuation rate is typically in the first 2 weeks of treatment, due to side effects. The ability to follow up with patients during this period in order to address this issue is critical in terms of increasing the likelihood of patients ultimately receiving adequate treatment. An IVR system that monitors side effects, when used in conjunction with a treatment coordinator, can identify patients having problems, address their concerns, and make adjustments, if necessary.

IVR side-effects monitoring has been implimented in several settings. The State of Rhode Island, in collaboration with the National Institute of Mental Health (NIMH), developed a computerized system for monitoring white blood counts in patients taking clozapine (Freyer, 1991). Medical directors of community mental health centers telephoned a computer at NIMH and entered an access code, a patient code, and the results of the patient's blood tests. Computerized feedback then told the director the results of the previous week's blood test, and whether or not the patient could continue in treatment.

Another computer software program for managing information on side effects is Systematic Assessment for Treatment-Emergent Events (SAFTEE; Clyde, 1986). SAFTEE is a structured interview schedule developed by the National Institute of Mental Health to systematically evaluate side effects of medications in clinical trials (Rabkin & Markowitz, 1986). SAFTEE is designed to evaluate treatment-emergent side effects in either a general or systematic way. The SAFTEE software is a database that collects and manages information obtained by the SAFTEE interview. Unlike traditional database systems, it has the flexibility of creating file structures that contain different numbers of questions and answers for each patient.

Diagnostic Interviews. Once a patient has been identified as likely to have a psychiatric disorder (either by screener or a symptom rating scale), the primary care physician must confirm the diagnosis through a diagnostic interview. This has been a vexing problem, in that the literature consistently reports that the majority of primary care patients with mental disorders go undetected and untreated (Schulberg & Burns, 1988; Kessler et al., 1985). Several factors contribute to this problem, such as unfamiliarity with diagnostic criteria, uncertainty about specific questions to elicit mental health symptoms, and time limitations in busy office practices (Orleans, George, Houpt, & Brodie, 1985; Rost, Smith, Matthews, & Guise, 1994).

Several diagnostic interviews have been recently developed specifically for use by primary care physicians, including the Primary Care Evaluation of Mental Disorders (PRIME-MD; Spitzer et al., 1994) and the Symptom Driven Diagnostic System for Primary Care (SDDS-PC; Broadhead et al., 1995). Computer-administered versions of these diagnostic interviews are available for direct self-administration to patients (Kobak et al., 1997; Weissman et al., 1998). Although not intended as a substitute for clinician judgment, the computer-administered diagnostic interview can be a useful and time-saving tool for primary care physicians. Physicians can use the computer to gather complete information that they can then use to follow up with the patient to confirm or disconfirm the diagnosis. The computer has the advantage of not having any time constraints on its schedule, and never forgets to ask required questions. For example, in a validation study of the PRIME–MD administered by IVR technology (Kobak et al., 1997), 200 outpatients (including 80 primary care patients) were given both clinician- and IVR-administered versions of the PRIME–MD. A standardized, structured diagnostic interview (i.e., the SCID; First, Spitzer, Williams, & Gibbon, 1995) was also given by a separate clinician and was used as the "gold standard" against which both the clinician and the IVR versions of the PRIME–MD were compared for accuracy. A review of the data found that 10% of the clinician PRIME–MD diagnosis were incorrect due to misapplication of the scoring algorithm. Another interesting finding was that patients reported twice as much alcohol abuse to the computer than they did to either of the clinician interviewers. This is consistent with the literature, in that patients often report higher rates of behaviors of a sensitive or embarrassing nature to the computer versus a clinician (see Kobak et al., 1996, for a review).

The feasibility of the computer-administered version of the Symptom Driven Diagnostic System for Primary Care (SDDS–PC) was evaluated in 1,001 primary care patients coming for routine care in a large HMO (Weissman et al., 1998). Although not self-administered by the patient, the SDDS–PC prompts the clinician to ask questions presented on the computer screen and automatically guides the clinician through the appropriate branching according to the *DSM–IV* scoring algorithm. The interviewer records the patients' response directly into the computer. At the end of the interview, the computer generates a one-page diagnostic summary of the results. Subjects complete a brief questionnaire prior to the interview, which determines which questions the computer will generate. Following the interview, the results are given to the primary care physician, who then uses the information to make a diagnosis. In this evaluation, patients were reinterviewed and rediagnosed 96 hr later by a mental health professional (MHP) who was blind to the computer information and primary care physician diagnosis. The agreement between primary care and mental health diagnoses were moderate, with kappa values ranging from .43 for major depression, to .38 for panic disorder, to .28 for GAD and .28 for OCD. The physician diagnosed as positive more cases than the MHP, although in 84% of those rated physician positive and mental health professional negative, the mental health professional rated the patient as symptomatic, but just under threshold. Ninety-two percent of primary care physicians said the computer-generated summary helped them understand their patients' psychiatric problems, and 64% said they would use the procedure in their practice.

As previously discussed, the use of computer-administered diagnostic interviews in primary care is intended to provide information to the physicians, not to replace them. The model used in the SDDS–PC study was a good example. The physician made the final diagnosis based on a follow-up interview, but was guided by more comprehensive and complete information. The model could be expanded by patients completing the interview directly, either via desktop computer, IVR, or on the Internet, and providing a summary of the results to their physician to assist in diagnosis and treatment planning.

A third diagnostic interview that has been adapted to computer administration is the MINI (Mini-International Neuropsychiatric Interview; Sheehan et al., 1998). The MINI was developed jointly by a group of psychiatrists and clinicians from both the

United States and Europe. Although not developed specifically for primary care physicians, the MINI was designed to provide a brief (15 min) structured interview for multicenter clinical trials and epidimiology studies. A high concordance has been found between diagnoses obtained by the clinician-administered MINI and those found by more lengthy, semistructured clinical interviews (i.e., the SCID in the United States, and the Composite International Diagnostic Interview [CIDI] in Europe). Although no validation data on the computer-administered version were reported, the authors stated that both an IVR version (which has been integrated into a triage interview for primary care) and a Internet version are available (Sheehan et al., 1998).

Quality-of-Life Scales. Quality of life is becoming an increasingly important dimension to evaluate for accreditation and licensing agencies, and is an important component of the computerized health management program. Quality-of-life (QOL) scales are designed to evaluate, from the patient's point of view, the extent to which the patient feels satisfied with his or her level of functioning in various life domains. QOL scales provide another perspective by which to gauge treatment success. One of the more widely used quality of life measures is the SF-36 Health Survey (Ware, 1993). The scale consists of 36 items, yielding scores on eight subscales: physical functioning, social functioning, bodily pain, general mental health, role limitations due to emotional problems, role limitations due to physical functioning, vitality, and general health perception. More recently, new scoring algorithms with the 36 items yielded two new summary scales: one for physical funcioning and one for mental functioning.

A 12-item version of the SF-36 (called the SF-12) was developed by Ware and his colleageus (Ware, Kosinski, & Keller, 1995). It was thought that a 12-item version could estimate the two summary components (physical and mental) with fewer items. The SF-12 evaluates four of the eight components contained in the 36 item version: physical functioning, role emotional, role physical, and mental health.

A IVR version of the SF-12 was reported by Millard and Carver (1999). They compared scores on live versus IVR administration of the SF-12 in 229 patients with low back pain. They found the two methods produced similar results on the physical component subscale, but higher scores on the mental component were found with the IVR. The study is limited methodologically by the fact that none of the subjects received both interviews. In addition, the 36-item version was recently adapted to IVR administration by Healthcare Technology Systems for use in a outcome study of asthma patients. No outcome data are yet available, as the trial is in progress.

In summary, we believe that computer-administered assessment is an essential part of a computerized health management system. Such information is vital for clinicians to more effectively identify patients needing intervention, evaluate symptom severity, develop treatment plans, monitor outcomes, and develop and improve treatment guidelines. Although no fully integrated computerized health management system as we describe it currently exists, some initial exploratory studies have been done. Kaiser Permanente of Northern California recently developed a optically scanned questionnaire to monitor the psychiatric outpatients of 20 clinicians at intake and following treatment (Hunkeler, Westphal, & Williams, 1995). The majority of clinicians reported using the information obtained most of the time, 75% found it "very" or "somewhat helpful," and 44% said the reports alerted them to specific areas needing focus or to things they might otherwise have missed. Four clinicians

(25%) used them to validate their own diagnosis. Although the use of computer-administered assessments in primary care is in its infancy, it is a methodology that affords great opportunities to improve the quality of patient care within the context of a well-designed primary care-mental health intervention model.

One example that incorporates several features of our model has been pilot tested in the field of diabetes control (Meneghini, Albisser, Goldberg, & Mintz, 1998). They used an IVR system (called the *electronic case manager* or ECM) that diabetic patients phoned daily to report self-measured glucose levels or hypoglycemic symptoms. The ECM also provided 24-hr assistance in adjusting daily insulin, automatically generated a standardized medical report, and provided an electronic medical record. In a study with 184 patients, over 45,000 calls were received in the first year. Prevalence of diabetes-related crises decreased approximately threefold ($p < .005$), with a statistically significant reduction in hemoglobin A1c (HbA1c) at 6 months ($p < .024$) and 12 months ($p < .044$). Clinic visits in managing complex diabetes were reduced approximately twofold ($p < .0001$), and there was a marked reduction in the amount of time spent on the telephone with patients. This pilot provides evidence that the model may not only increase treatment outcome and improve patient care, but can do so in a cost-effective manner.

Computer-Administered Treatment, Prevention, and Education

Computer-administered treatment, prevention, and patient education programs are an important component of future computerized health management systems for managing psychiatric disorders in primary care. For some disorders, the future is now. Several systems addressing a diverse range of chronic medical and psychiatric conditions have been developed and investigated. For the most part, these systems have been implemented in small, stand-alone pilot projects to evaluate concept feasibility. The challenge for the future is to integrate systems demonstrating efficacy and cost efficiency into the broader context of routine health care services. As previously discussed, such integration would be facilitated greatly by the creation of patient registries that would permit linkages of condition-specific programs to the patient populations served by these programs, and by treatment coordinators who can coordinate and manage patient care. A sampling of the types of computer programs that have been developed and tested in particular patient populations is presented next. This overview is intended to provide examples of the types of computer programs available, and is not a comprehensive review of such programs (see Marks, Shaw, & Parkin, 1998, for a more comprehensive overview).

Computer-Assisted Treatment Programs: An Overview. Empirical evaluation of psychotherapy for treating mental disorders has received renewed interest. Treatments have been manualized, specific components identified as active treatments, and outcomes empirically documented using rigorous double-blind trials (Beck, 1991; Elkin et al., 1989; Hollon, Shelton, & Loosen, 1991; Jacobson et al., 1996). Two of the most well-documented treatments in regard to efficacy have been cognitive therapy for depression (Beck, 1991) and behavior therapy for obsessive-compulsive disorder (Kobak, Greist, Jefferson, Katzelnick, & Henk, 1998). Although the efficacy of these treatments is now well established, the availability of trained cognitive or behavior therapists exceeds the demand (Greist, 1989). The eclectic treatment of these disorders in the field often lacks the important elements that make cognitive or behavior therapy work. For example, in a naturalistic study of "real-world" treatments of anxiety disorders, Goisman and colleagues (1993) found that in vivo exposure was only offered to 28% of person with OCD. In addition, the quality of the initial assessments performed was often inadequate, with only 40% of therapists developing a list of the feared (i.e., trigger) situations.

Computer-administered behavior therapies offer patients increased access to these types of therapies at reasonable cost and at a time and place convenient for the patient. Computer-assisted treatment programs are not intended to replace clinician-administered therapy, but to provide self-help tools for patients to use, either alone or in conjunction with clinician psychotherapy. As was the case with Mr. A, our example at the beginning of the chapter, some patients prefer psychotherapy to medications, may not have the time to come to treatment, or may opt for self-help due to the (unfortunate) stigma associated with seeing a psychotherapist. The computer-administered treatments incorporate outcome measures that permit clinicians to monitor a patient's progress, possibly freeing their time to concentrate on more difficult cases.

The roots of computer-administered psychotherapy date back to 1966, when Weizenbaum (1966) developed a computer program (ELIZA) that simulated Rogerian psychotherapy. The author developed the program primarily to demonstrate the capacity of the computer to perform text manipulations, so it was never clinically tested (nor did the author believe in the ethical acceptability of computer use for this purpose). Also that year, Colby, Watt, and Gilbert (1966) developed programs that allowed patients to communicate with the computer free-form, with the computer providing therapist-like responses (e.g., clarifying, reflecting, questioning, etc.). Most users felt frustrated by the computer's failure to answer pertinent questions.

Computer-Administered Treatment of Depression. More recently, Selmi and colleagues developed a computer-administered cognitive-behavioral treatment program for depression (Selmi, Klein, Greist, Sorrell, & Erdman, 1990). Described as "experimental and psychoeducational in nature," the program consists of six to eight 40- to 50-min sessions over a 6-week period, following the protocol for outcome studies prepared by Beck and colleagues (Beck, Rush, Shaw, & Emory, 1979). The program is administered on a desktop computer and consists of ongoing evaluation with the Beck Depression Inventory (BDI; Beck, Ward, Mendelson, Mock, & Erbaugh, 1961), an explanation of the cognitive theory of depression, identification of major complaints, homework assignments, and reviews of progress and self-tests. In a validation study, Selmi et al. (1990) randomly assigned 36 mildly to moderately depressed outpatients to either computer-administered cognitive therapy, clinician-administered cognitive therapy, or a wait-list control. Patients in both the computer and clinician therapy conditions improved significantly more than controls, and gains were maintained at 2-month follow-up.

Another self-care program for depression, called COPE (Osgood-Hynes et al., 1998), was developed for mild to moderate depression. COPE combines 7 self-help booklets with 11 IVR telephone calls that help patients work through one of three modules: Constructive Thinking, Pleasant Activities, and Assertive Communication. Each of these components has been shown to be effective in treating depression. The calls reinforce the homework suggestions provided in the booklets and conduct auditory practice role-plays to strengthen newly acquired skills. Treatment recommendations and feedback are given to the patients based on their responses during the phone call. Patients are free to choose the order, length, and pace of the program. Rating scales are administered periodically via IVR during the course of treatment to monitor progress and provide feedback. The program also contains a videotape describing depression and its treatment.

An open validation study of COPE was recently conducted at three sites (Boston; Madison, Wisconsin; and London, UK) with 41 mildly to moderately depressed outpatients (Osgood-Hynes et al., 1998). All 41 patients completed the self-assessment phase of the program, and 68% completed the entire program. An intent-to-treat analysis found a significant reduction in depression (as reflected on HAMD scores), as well as a decrease in overall impairment (as reflected on Work and Social Adjustment scale scores; Marks, 1986). Interestingly, there was a strong correlation ($r = .56, p < .001$) between the number of calls made and the amount of improvement. Eighty percent (12/15) of patients who thought COPE was "logical" prior to entering the study were treatment responders (defined as a 50% reduction in HAMD score), whereas none of the 5 patients who thought it was either "okay," "not that logical," or "not at all logical" were responders. Thus, it is important to carefully consider the patient's acceptance when integrating self-help materials in a health management program. Those who are reluctant to participate in or feel negatively toward this type of intervention might be best offered other alternatives. However, even if only a modest percentage of patients choose to participate in such programs, improved patient care may result. Primary care physicians may prescribe self-help treatments like COPE to interested patients in addition to medication, as some patients may be willing to do self-help but not require or accept a referral for psychotherapy.

Computer-Administered Treatment for OCD. Another IVR-administered self-help program that has been evaluated is BT STEPS (Greist et al., 1998). BT STEPS is a self-help behavior therapy program that uses a manual and IVR phone calls to help patients complete exposure and response prevention (ERP) for the treatment of obsessive-compulsive disorder (OCD). ERP has long been found to an effective treatment for OCD, with effect sizes comparable to those of serotonergic antidepressants (Kobak, Greist, Jefferson, Katzelnick, & Henk, 1998). In addition, studies have found ERP to be effective even when patients perform it without the help of a therapist and outside of a clinic (Marks, et al., 1988).

BT STEPS consists of nine parts or "steps," each involving reading a chapter in the manual and then calling the computer. The first four steps consist of an explanation of how to use the IVR system, education about the treatment model (ERP) and OCD, self-assessment, identification of triggers that are associated with their obsessions or compulsions, symptom and trigger ratings, and identification of potential friends or family members who may act as coaches or "cotherapists" with the patient. The final five steps involve developing a treatment plan, setting treatment goals, developing ERP tasks, choosing coping statements, implementing the treatment plan, and ongoing monitoring of results with feedback, identification of problems, tips on problem solving, and modifications to the plan, as the patient progresses through treatment. New goals are generated with each success, as patients work their way up their self-generated hierarchy, and from short-term to long-term treatment goals. The final step involves relapse prevention and how to maintain gains and how to anticipate and deal with setbacks.

BT STEPS has been evaluated in three clinical trials. The first was a open study involving 40 subjects recruited from three sites (Madison, Wisconsin; Boston; and London, UK). The trial consisted of a one-week evaluation period, followed by 12 weeks of treatment. Following the 12-week treatment phase, patients were allowed to access the system for up to 22 weeks. The subjects continued to use the system for an average of 15.6 weeks after the trial (the final visit in this extension phase is called "endpoint"). Patients were required to meet diagnostic criteria for OCD, to score at least 16 or higher on the Y–BOCS (i.e., mild to moderate severity), and have a score of 8 or higher on the Y–BOCS compulsions subscale. Subjects could be admitted with scores below 16 on the Y–BOCS if their compulsions subscale score was greater than 10. Patients were excluded if they had 10 hr or more of prior ERP for OCD. Thirty-five of the 40 patients (87.5%) completed the assessment phase, and 50% went on to do the treatment module, with 42.5% completing two or more ERP sessions (called "ERP completers").

In total, 1,781 calls were made to the system, 72% of which occurred outside of usual office hours (i.e., Monday to Friday, 9 a.m. to 5 p.m.). Ratings on the amount of discomfort that triggers caused decreased significantly by week 4, and remained so through the end of the trial and extension phase. Ratings on work and social adjustment improved significantly by week 8, and remained improved from that point on. Subjects' Y–BOCS scores were significantly improved after 8 weeks and at endpoint, but not at the end of the 12-week treatment phase. Patients who did between 2 and 20 ERP sessions had significantly lower endpoint Y–BOCS scores than those doing 0 to 1 ERP session. Of the 28 patients with available data, 17 (61%) rated themselves "much" or "very much improved" at endpoint.

A second study of BT STEPS, which included limited clinician involvement, was conducted with 23 United Kingdom patients. The second study had several purposes. First, we wanted to check the robustness of the findings in a new sample of patients. Second, we wanted to see how patients fared with clinician-guided care subsequent to BT STEPS. Third, we wanted to see if the addition of a "personal touch" would help improve outcome. In this trial, the coordinator signed feedback sheets that were faxed to subjects following IVR calls, brief written praise for progress was added, and suggestions on which sections of the manual to reread were given for those having difficulty. Subjects could only call the coordinator with technical questions on how to use the IVR system, and were referred to their manual or referring clinician with clinical questions.

Eighteen of the 23 patients completed the self-assessment section, and 12 completed the self-treatment module. A significant reduction was found on both the Y–BOCS and Work and Social Adjustment scale scores for those who completed more than one ERP task ($p < .001$. The number of ERP sessions correlated highly with the degree of improvement on the Y–BOCS score ($r = .62, p = .001$). Finally, there was no significant difference in the amount of change found in this study (with limited clinician involvement) and the amount of change found in study 1.

In light of the findings of studies 1 and 2, a randomized, multicenter, controlled clinical trial was recently completed, comparing the efficacy of the computer-automated BT STEPS program, live therapist-delivered behavior therapy, and a relaxation control condition. This trial included 200 patients randomly assigned to a 10-week treatment condition following a 2-week pretreatment assessment period. Results of this study are currently being analyzed.

Computer-Administered Treatment for Panic Disorder.   Computer programs have been developed and tested for treating patients suffering from a variety of other anxiety disorders. Newman, Kenardy, Herman, and Taylor (1997) evaluated the efficacy of treating panic disorder using a four-session treatment protocol augmented with palmtop computers carried by patients that allowed them to practice principles of cognitive-behavioral treatment (CBT). Palmtop computers have the advantage of allowing continuous, unobtrusive collection of data on treatment adherence, as well as evaluating the impact of treatment in the client's natural setting. The study compared palmtop treatment to a standard 12-session CBT without computer augmentation. Both treatment conditions were effective in reducing fear and panic symptoms, but no difference was found between the treatment conditions. The computer-assisted CBT with fewer clinician–client contact hours was over $500 less expensive to administer, including the cost of the computer, than the more extended CBT. Not only is this treatment approach equally effective, but it also provides a wealth of daily self-monitoring data that can be used by therapists to track client progress and allows for regular, computer-guided practice of CBT skills away from the therapist's office. A similar program has been developed by the same authors for the treatment of generalized anxiety disorder (Newman, Consoli, & Taylor, in press).

Virtual Reality.   Therapeutic techniques for graded exposure to anxiety-provoking situations, such as flying, are particularly well suited to computer graphics applications. Using virtual reality technology, exposure to simulated heights was effective in reducing anxiety, avoidance, and distress associated with heights (Rothbaum, et al., 1995). These techniques have been incorporated into simulated airplane experiences with similar success (North, North, & Coble, 1997; Rothbaum, Hodges, Watson, Kessler, & Opdyke, 1996). Carlin, Hoffman, and Weghorst (1997) successfully integrated tactile stimulation with visual inputs in a virtual reality application for treating spider phobia. The success of such pilot studies promises expanded development of such applications for treating phobias and may also provide the methodological tools needed to evaluate the efficacy of different treatment approaches, both standard human-administered therapies and those based on computer-automated approaches (Kirby, 1996). Given the current capacity of relatively inexpensive home video devices, such as Nintendo-type systems, to deliver very-high-quality computer-generated graphics, as well as the rapidly expanding capabilities of the Internet to deliver similar quality images, animations, and video, it is not difficult to envision such programs being made widely available to special patient populations (patient registries) as a value-added, cost-effective, treatment option in a managed care environment.

Computer-Assisted Prevention.   One way that computers can help in the area of prevention is in reminding patients to monitor their symptoms to catch relapse, or in generating reminders to patients to follow through on treatment recommendations. Such a system has been used in areas outside of psychiatry. For example, many diabetic patients regularly fail to monitor their glucose or adhere to recommended diet or exercise guidelines despite the demonstrated value of early intervention and prevention services for such patients. Piette and Mah (1997) used an automated voice messaging system to inquire about diabetic symptoms, problems with glucose monitoring and foot care, adherence to medication, and diet schedules. They also gave patients opportunities to hear health promotion materials pertaining to diabetic eye care, foot care, cardiovascular health, and management of sick days. Patient responses indicating severe or urgent conditions prompted a live follow-up call by a health care professional to discuss status. The system inquired about diabetic symptoms prognostic of poor glucose control and adverse health outcomes, problems with glucose monitoring and foot care, and adherence to medication and diet schedules. All but 1 of the 65 study participants found the automated voice messaging system helpful and easy to use, and 89% of these patients indicated that they would like to continue to receive such calls in the future. Seventy-seven percent indicated that such services would increase their satisfaction with their health care.

Computer-Assisted Prevention in the Elderly. Another area where computers may play a prominent preventive role is in managing the health care needs of the elderly. America's aging population presents a current and growing challenge to health care delivery systems. The integration of technology with service delivery systems can help meet the challenges. Transportation becomes increasingly difficult for the aged, making it desirable to extend services out of the clinics and into patient homes using telecommunications. Such services have included telephone reviews of medications, joint pain, and other symptoms of chronic medical conditions with nonmedical personnel that demonstrated significant gains in physical functioning and decreased pain at 1-year follow-up without significantly increasing the overall costs of providing health care (Weinberger, Tierney, Cowper, Katz, & Booher, 1993). Use of computer-automated telephone technology could likely drive the costs of such telephone interventions down further.

Depressive symptoms in later life is a major public health problem (NIH Consensus Panel, 1992). The vast majority of elderly patients with depression do not present to mental health professionals, in spite of the increased functional morbidity and rates of suicide and suicidal ideation in the elderly (Conwell, 1994; Gurland, 1994). Several screeners have been developed specifically for the identification of depression in the elderly (Yesavage et al., 1983). The availability of such screeners via IVR and the incorporation of such screeners in the disease management system would help with the identification and ultimate treatment of depressed elderly primary care patients.

The elderly population also faces other significant health risks, such as the development of Alzheimer's disease. About 4 million Americans presently suffer from Alzheimer's disease, and less than one in four receives treatment. Over $100 billion dollars is spent annually on Alzheimer's, which has a prevalence of roughly 15% among persons over 65 years. Promising treatments that appear to arrest or slow the progressive deterioration are available and others are being developed (Peskind, 1998), but the unfortunate present reality is that the cognitive and functional losses are permanent and irreversible. The most critical element to maximizing the benefits of current treatment options is the initiation of treatment as early as possible following disease onset (Duncan & Siegal, 1998). Greater public education and effective screening are critical to such efforts. Various dementia screening instruments have been developed and validated (Fillenbaum, 1988; Hill et al., 1993; Pfeffer, Afifi, & Chance, 1987; Pfeffer et al., 1981); however, research into potential computer automation of such processes for public screening is just beginning.

Computer technology has been incorporated into programs designed to directly enhance the quality of life of long-term care residents (Carlin et al., 1997), and telephone-based programs designed to provide support and information to care givers

of Alzheimer's patients—the "second victims" of the disease—are being implemented (Beck et al., 1961; Carr et al., 1981; Depression Guideline Panel, 1993b). These
caregivers, often family members of the Alzheimer's patient, are at greatly increased
risk for developing mental heath problems in response to the emotional loss, increased responsibilities, and social isolation. Peer-support networks, telephone-accessed informational lectures, and automated bulletin boards provide such caregivers a link to the outside world as well as a connection to others with common
experiences.

Computer-Administered Prevention in Alcohol Abuse.   The medical and social
impact of alcohol-related problems in America is enormous, accounting for more
than 15% of all health care costs and 100,000 deaths annually (O'Connor &
Schottenfeld, 1998). Clearly, patients with current or past alcohol or other drug disorders represent an "at risk" population. Risk of relapse is greatest immediately following treatment discharge, with the majority of treatment clients who relapse doing so
within the first 6 months. Relapse prevention is a fundamental issue in alcoholism
treatment (Gordis, 1989), because roughly 90% of treated alcoholics experience at
least one relapse within a 4-year period following treatment.

The concept of using telephones and technology to facilitate recovery and prevent
relapse among alcohol and other drug abusers is not new. Programs were established
in the 1960s and 1970s to investigate the utility of follow-up outreach telephone therapy with alcoholics (Catanzaro & Green, 1970). Most subjects liked receiving calls
from a counselor every 2 weeks following treatment discharge, wanted them to continue, and perceived them as good treatment; however, there was little evidence that
the intervention was effective (Fitzgerald & Mulford, 1985). Similarly, others
(Heather, Kissoon-Singh, & Fenton, 1990) have found that recovering patients make
poor use of opportunities to provide telephone progress reports as a means to assist
the natural recovery processes among problem drinkers. The historically marginal
impact and mixed reactions of such patients to these types of programs provides an
interesting context for examining the potential uses and possible benefits of computer-automated data collection.

Although valid measures of treatment outcome can be obtained reliably using live
telephone interviews (Breslin, Sobell, Sobell, Buchan, & Kwan, 1996), it has been repeatedly demonstrated that use of interactive computers for assessing alcohol and
drug problems increases response candor and self-disclosure. Since initial investigations in the 1970s to the present day, comparisons of the data obtained and evaluations of patient reactions to both methods of patient interviewing have demonstrated
methodological benefits of computerized interviews (Erdman, Klein, & Greist, 1983;
Hile & Adkins, 1997; Lucas, Mullin, Luna, & McInroy, 1977; Skinner & Allen, 1983;
Turner et al., 1998). These findings strongly suggest that increased automation of assessment and treatment procedures might perform better at detecting and preventing relapse than has been experienced using live telephone interviewers. Alemi et al.
(1994) directly investigated the potential utility of an interactive voice response telephone system for treatment outcome/relapse monitoring. They asked recovering
drug users and alcoholics to report weekly experiences associated with relapse to a
computer automated telephone system after discharge from treatment. Over 70% of
the participants indicated that the reporting process alone was useful in reducing
their drug use, and 61% reported that the automated interview encouraged them to
discuss their experiences and feelings with their counselors.

Prospective monitoring of alcohol consumption on a daily basis has successfully been implemented using IVR technology, with an overall response rate of 93% over an initial 16-week study period (Searles, Perrine, Mundt, & Helzer, 1995) and a 98% response rate in a recent 2-year study (J. Searles, personal communication, 1998). These studies support the feasibility of using this technology to prospectively monitor drinking-related activities. Many of the subjects that participated in these studies indicated that the reporting process increased their awareness of alcohol consumption patterns and that such awareness had motivated them to reevaluate their alcohol consumption, considering or attempting to reduce their drinking. Such effects are consistent with treatment interventions that include self-monitoring of drinking-related behaviors and thoughts (Marlatt, 1985; Sobell, Sobell, Bogardis, Leo, & Skinner, 1992) and could easily be built into adaptive computer-driven protocols for self-help programs specifically designed for early-stage alcohol and drug abusers (Barber, 1991).

Computer-Assisted Prevention: Smoking Cessation. If the future model of preventative care is the identification of at-risk patient populations for targeting educational and self-help support programs, as proposed in this chapter, then clearly the future is here regarding current trends toward reducing tobacco use. From government-sponsored educational materials and advertising to the wide-ranging pharmaceutical commercialization of smoking cessation products, the campaign to reduce the adverse economic and health consequences of smoking is in full swing. Self-help programs increase the efficacy of pharmacotherapy and are preferred by a majority of smokers (Fiore et al., 1990). Many such programs are standardized, providing a "one-size-fits-all" approach to smoking cessation. Personal telephone counseling sessions, in conjunction with self-help quit materials, have been demonstrated to influence abstinent outcome rates in a dose-related fashion (Curry, McBride, Grothaus, Louie, & Wagner, 1995; Zhu et al., 1996). Similarly, a self-help IVR smoking cessation program advertised through work site health promotions, print media, and radio found that of 571 smokers, 35% quit smoking while using the program and 14% remained abstinent 6 months after their initial call. These percentages increase substantially (68% and 22%, respectively) for smokers who called the system five or more times (Schneider, Schwartz, & Fast, 1995). Patients interacting with such IVR systems can provide information that allows personal tailoring of context-relevant messages, which has also been shown to increase effectiveness in a family practice setting (Strecher et al., 1994). By incorporating regular computer assessments of mood within such individualized self-help programs, other factors that may pose a risk to patient well-being, such as development of depression (Borrelli et al., 1996), may be detected early on.

Regular tobacco use is not uncommon among drug abusers, particularly alcohol abusers. Within the integrated treatment model proposed, those patients enrolled in a alcohol or drug relapse prevention aftercare program could be given access to telephone-based smoking cessation programs. It has been shown that such programs can be effective in promoting smoking-related behavioral change in this patient population (Schneider et al., 1995).

Computerized Information and Support: The CHESS Programs. Researchers at the University of Wisconsin have developed a series of interactive, computer-based systems to provide support to people facing health-related crises (Gustafson, Bosworth, Hawkins, Boberg, & Bricker, 1992). The programs, called CHESS (Comprehensive Health Enhancement Support System), were developed to improve access to health services to those who would otherwise find such access difficult due to psychological, social, economic, or geographic barriers. CHESS programs have been developed for five areas: AIDS/HIV infection, breast cancer, sexual assault, academic crisis, and adult children of alcoholics. A study of CHESS was conducted in 204 patients with HIV infection (Gustafson et al., 1999). Subjects were randomized to receive CHESS computers in their homes for 3 to 6 months; controls received no intervention. CHESS subjects reported improved quality of life compared to controls. They also reported spending less time during ambulatory care visits, and experienced fewer and shorter hospitalizations. The CHESS program can serve as a model for future implementations in other disorders, such as those psychiatric disorders most commonly found in primary care.

The Internet as a Source of Health Information.   Without doubt, the World Wide Web (the web) is one of the fastest growing sources of health-related information (Huang & Alessi, 1999). With access to the Internet available to anyone with a library card and given the exponential growth of home computers and other devices with Internet connectivity, literally thousands of web sites providing health-related information and services are available with very little effort—and virtually no oversight or regulation. Comprehensive MEDLINE searches of the scientific literature are facilitated through the National Library of Medicine's web site (http://www.ncbi.nlm.nih.gov/PubMed/) as easily as the "cure for cancer" can be purchased online in exchange for a valid credit card number (Bond, 1998). At present, legitimate professional organizations honestly concerned about public health issues and education vie elbow to elbow with professional confidence artists concerned about early retirement, for the attention of needy, and in some cases desperate, patients seeking information and help. Although the potential exists for developing systems to rate the validity and accuracy of information available at different medical-related web sites, it is not clear whether the impact of such systems would be beneficial or not (Jadad & Gagliardi, 1998). It is unlikely that the informational content of web-site postings is likely to be subject to regulatory constraints anytime in the near future. Thus, it will likely fall on service provider networks such as managed care organizations to "legitimate" links through their own web sites to web sites of recognized, respected organizations, such as the Alzheimer's Association or the American Cancer Society, and exclude links to sites of poor or indeterminate informational quality.

Although such legitimating mechanisms could be useful in assisting patients to discriminate between potential sources of information available on the web, it can do little to reduce access to less reputable web sites promoted through unregulated "chat room" referrals, unsolicited electronic mail promotions, or haphazard web browsing. Consequently, it is likely that the World Wide Web as a primary mechanism for legitimate patient education will continue to be a dubious source of general medical information for the foreseeable future. It is more likely that proactive, preventative health programs involving patient education and treatment specific to identified patient populations will require development of outreach programs sponsored by provider organizations and accessible only by registered users.

Within the context of the expanded primary care model advanced in this chapter, there are several ways in which the World Wide Web could be called into service to facilitate more comprehensive care efficiently. Many health care providers already maintain web sites that provide links to patient education pages that provide general preventive health information. Within the framework described in this chapter, it can easily be envisioned that patients providing an identification number could be linked to look-up tables in the existing patient registries and be provided access to disorder-specific information. Those participating in self-treatment programs could be provided graphical feedback regarding their progress and treatment history, and in fact many of the types of programs envisioned or described in this chapter (such as the exposure and desensitization programs for anxiety disorders that utilize graphical materials) could be administered through a web-based interface. As the web becomes increasingly accessible to broader segments of the population, many of the regular monitoring and patient screening functions proposed earlier, as well as the routine acquisition of medical history used by primary and specialty providers at intake, could be obtained from patients using the convenience and privacy of their home computers. Obviously, a primary concern of web-based data collection and information access is the issue of patient privacy and confidentiality. This is a fundamental concern across all of the electronic information systems envisioned throughout this chapter, and the solutions to such concerns are likely to be adapted from similar security issues and concerns driven by the rapid expansion of electronic commerce.

Finally, Balas and colleagues (1997) examined the "telemedicine" literature to evaluate the evidence for the efficacy of distance technologies. Eighty clinical trials were identified, and independent reviewers evaluated the nature and quality of the methodology and its effect on health care outcome. They found six different categories of interventions: computerized communication; telephone follow-up and counseling; telephone reminders; interactive telephone systems; after-hours telephone access; and telephone screening. Of the 80 trials, 61 analyzed provider-initiated communication with patients, and 50 reported positive outcome, improved performance, or significant benefits. Balas et al. concluded that distance medicine technologies improve continuity of care by improving access to and coordinating of care, and that the results document the benefit of this methodology in facilitating communication between physicians and patients.

CONCLUSIONS

The examples just given are but a few of the patient groups with sufficiently common problems and concerns for which specially designed programs providing support, education, regular monitoring, and treatment could facilitate long-term health and quality of life. Such programs could be automated using current technology, providing built-in safeguards for notification to appropriate health care staff upon either patient request or indications of deteriorating medical status. Such programs could be efficiently administered with the potential to reduce overall service costs relative to the current practice of episodic care in response to patient-initiated concerns. They hold great potential as resources for patients sharing common concerns and difficulties, and could go far toward addressing the need to increase coverage for clinical preventative services as part of health insurance, proposed as an objective in the forthcoming *Healthy People 2010 Objectives* (http://web.health.gov/healthypeople/2010fctsht.htm). Obviously, prior to the creation and implementation of such registries, mechanisms for identifying and enrolling patients appropriate to the registries must be established. Hence there is a need for comprehensive medical histories and electronic medical records.

The future is uncertain, and this vision of 2010 mental health care may look like "tomorrow-land" at a former World's Fair site. What is clear is that behavioral mental health care will look very different from today and that psychological assessment will play an increasingly major role. Many of the elements described in the model already exist. Our challenge is to provide the right information to the right person at the right time. Resources will continue to be limited, and technology will need to play an active role to make psychological testing results widely available. The largest challenge is maintaining confidentiality for sensitive psychological information and only using this data for the client's benefit. Technology can empower us to provide better care for ourselves, improve communication between providers, and allow clinicians to have more time with their clients, building the human bond that will always be a key to healing.

REFERENCES

American Psychiatric Association. (1994). *Diagnostic and statistical manual of mental disorders* (4th ed.). Washington, DC: Author.

Alemi, F., Stephens, R., Parran, T., Llorens, S., Bhatt, P., Ghadiri, A., & Eisenstein, E. (1994). Automated monitoring of outcomes: Application to treatment of drug abuse. *Medical Decision Making, 14,* 180–187.

Ancill, R. J., Rogers, D., & Carr, A. C. (1985). Comparison of computerised self-rating scales for depression with conventional observer ratings. *Acta Psychiatrica Scandinavica, 71,* 315–317.

Atkinson, M. M. (1996). Psychiatric clinical nurse specialists as intensive case managers for the seriously mentally ill. *Seminars for Nurse Managers, 4,* 130–136.

Baer, L., Brown-Beasley, M. W., Sorce, J., & Henriquess, A. I. (1993). Computer-assisted telephone administration of a structured interview for obsessive-compulsive disorder. *American Journal of Psychiatry, 150,* 1737–1738.

Balas, E. A., Austin, S. M., Mitchell, J. A., Ewigman, B. G., Bopp, K. D., & Brown, G. D. (1996). The clinical value of computerized information services: A review of 98 randomized clinical trials. *Archives of Family Medicine, 5,* 271–278.

Balas, E. A., Jaffrey, F., Kuperman, G. J., Boren, S. A., Brown, G. D., Pinciroli, F., & Mitchell, J. A. (1997). Electronic communication with patients: Evaluation of distance medicine technology. *Journal of the American Medical Association, 278,* 152–159.

Barber, J. G. (1991). Microcomputers and prevention of drug abuse. *M.D Computing, 8,* 150–155.

Bech, P., Allerup, P., Gram, L. F., Reisby, N., Rosenberg, R., Jacobsen, O., & Nagy, A. (1981). The Hamilton Depression Scale: Evaluation of objectivity using logistic models. *Acta Psychiatrica Scandinavica, 63,* 290–299.

Bech, P., Allerup, P., Reisby, N., & Gram, L. F. (1984). Assessment of symptom change from improvement curves on the Hamilton Depression Scale in trials with antidepressants. *Psychopharmacology, 84,* 276–281.

Bech, P., Gram, L. F., Dein, E., Jacobsen, O., Vitger, J., & Golwig, T. G. (1975). Quantitative rating of depressive states: correlation between clinical assessment, Beck's self-rating scale and Hamilton's objective rating scale. *Acta Psychiatric Scandinavica, 51,* 161–170.

Beck, A. T. (1991). Cognitive therapy. A 30-year retrospective. *American Psychologist, 46,* 368–375.

Beck, A.T., Rush, A. J., Shaw, B. F., & Emory, G. (1979). *Cognitive therapy of depression.* New York: Guilford Press.

Beck, A. T., Ward, C., Mendelson, M., Mock, J., & Erbaugh, J. (1961). An inventory for measuring depression. *Archives of General Psychiatry, 6,* 561–571.

Bond, H. (1998, March). Accuracy of medical information on the internet. *Young Physicians,* pp. 12–14.

Borrelli, B., Niaura, R., Keuthen, N. J., Goldstein, M. G., DePue, J. D., Murphy, C., & Abrams, D. B. (1996). Development of major depressive disorder during smoking-cessation treatment. *Journal of Clinical Psychiatry, 57,* 534–538.

Breslin, C., Sobell, L. C., Sobell, M. B., Buchan, G., & Kwan, E. (1996). Aftercare telephone contacts with problem drinkers can serve a clinical and research function. *Addication, 91,* 1359–1364.

Broadhead, W. E., Leon, A., Weissman, M. M., et al. (1995). Development and validation of the SDDS–PC screen for multiple mental disorders in primary care. *Archives of Family Medicine, 4,* 211–219.

Campbell, T. L. (1987). Is screening for mental health problems worthwhile in family practice? An opposing view. *Journal of Family Practice, 25,* 184–187.

Carlin, A. S., Hoffman, H. G., & Weghorst, S. (1997). Virtual reality and tactile augmentation in the treatment of spider phobia: A case report. *Behaviour Research and Therapy, 35,* 153–158.

Carr, A. C., & Ghosh, A. (1983). Response of phobic patients to direct computer assessment. *British Journal of Psychiatry, 142,* 60–65.

Carr, A. C., Ancill, R. J., Ghosh, A., & Margo, A. (1981). Direct assessment of depression by microcomputer. *Acta Psychiatric Scandinavica, 64,* 415–422.

Catanzaro, R. J., & Green, W. G. (1970). WATS telephone therapy: New follow-up technique for alcoholics. *American Journal of Psychiatry, 126,* 1024–1027.

Clyde, D. J. (1986). SAFTEE: Data system for side effect assessment scale. *Psychopharmacology Bulletin, 22,* 287.

Colby, K. M., Watt, J. B., & Gilbert, J. B. (1966). A computer method of psychotherapy. Preliminary communication. *Journal of Nervous and Mental Disease, 142,* 148–152.

Conwell, Y. (1994). Suicide in elderly patients. In L. S. Schneider, C. F. Reynolds III, B. D. Lebowitz, & A. J. Friedhoff (Eds.), *Diagnosis and treatment of depression in late life* (pp. 347–418). Washington, DC: American Psychiatric Press.

Counsell, C. M., Guin, P. R., & Limbaugh, B. (1994). Coordinated care for the neuroscience patient: Future directions. *Journal of Neuroscience Nursing, 26,* 245–250.

Curry, S. J., McBride, C., Grothaus, L. C., Louie, D. & Wagner, E. H. (1995). A randomized trial of self-help materials, personalized feedback, and telephone counseling with nonvolunteer smokers. *Journal of Consulting and Clinical Psychology, 63,* 1005–1014.

Depression Guideline Panel. (1993a). *Depression in primary care: Volume 1. Detection and diagnosis* (Clinical Practice Guidelines No. 5, AHCPR Publication No. 93-0550). Rockville, MD: U.S. Department of Health and Human Services.

Depression Guideline Panel. (1993b). *Depression in primary care: Volume 2. Treatment of major depression* (Clinical Practice Guidelines No. 5, AHCPR Publication No. 93-0551). Rockville, MD: U.S. Department of Health and Human Services.

Depression Guideline Panel. (1993c). *Depression in primary care: Detection, diagnosis, and treatment* (Clinical Practice Guidelines No. 5, AHCPR Publication No. 93-0552). Rockville, MD: U.S. Department of Health and Human Services.

Dottl, S. L., Taylor, L. vH., Kobak, K. A., Greist, J. H., Mundt, J., Jefferson, J. W., Katzelncik, D. J., Schaettle, S., & Davidson, J. R. T. (1998, June). *Computer-assisted, telephone-administered version of the brief social phobia scale.* Paper presented at the meeting of the National Institute of Mental Health, New Clinical Drug Evaluation Unit, 38th Annual Meeting, Boca Raton, FL.

Duncan, B. A., & Siegal, A. P. (1998). Early diagnosis and management of Alzheimer's disease. *Journal of Clinical Psychiatry, 59*(suppl. 9), 15–21.

Dyer, J. G., Hammill, K., Regan-Kubinski, M. J., Yurick, A., & Kobert, S. (1997). The psychiatric-primary care nurse practitioner: A futuristic model for advanced practice psychiatric-mental health nursing. *Archives of Psychaitric Nursing, 11,* 2–12.

Elkin, I., Shea, R., Watkins, J. T., Imber, S. D., Sotsky, S. M., Collins, J. F., Glass, D. R., Pilkonis, P. A., Leber, W. R., Docherty, J. P., Fiester, S. J., & Parloff, M. B. (1989). National Institute of Mental Health treatment of depression collaborative research program: General effectiveness of treatments. *Archives of General Psychiatry, 46,* 971–982.

Erdman, H., Klein, M. H., & Greist, J. H. (1983). The reliability of a computer interview for drug use/abuse information. *Behavior Research Methods & Instrumentation, 15,* 66–68.

Erickson, S. M. (1997). Managing case management across the continuum: An organized response to managed care. *Seminars for Nurse Managers, 5,* 124–128.

Fillenbaum, G. G. (1988). The Oars multidimensional functional assessment questionnaire. In G. G. Fillenbaum (Ed.), *Multidimensional Functional Assessment of Older Adults* (pp. 7–12). Hillsdale, NJ: Lawrence Erlbaum Associates.

Fiore, M. C., Novotny, T. E., Pierce, J. P. Giovino, G. A., Hatziandreu, E. J., Newcomb, P. A., Surawicz, T. S., & Davis, R. M. (1990). Methods used to quit smoking in the United States. *Journal of the American Medical Association, 263,* 2760–2765.

First, M. B., Spitzer, R. L., Williams, J. B., & Gibbon, M. (1995). *Structured Clinical Interview for DSM–IV Axis I Disorders – Patient edition (SCID–I/P, version 2.0).* New York: New York State Psychiatric Institute.

Fitzgerald, J. L., & Mulford, H. A. (1985). An experimental test of telephone aftercare contacts with alcoholics. *Journal of Studies on Alcohol, 46,* 418–424.

Freyer, F. J. (1991, 21 July). Mentally Ill gain access to new treatment. *Providence Sunday Journal,* pp. C1, C5.

Girard, N. (1994). The case management model of patient care delivery. *AORN Journal, 60,* 403–405, 408–412, 415.

Goisman, R. M., Rogers, M. P., Steketee, G. S., et al. (1993). Utilization of behavioral methods in a multicenter anxiety disorders study. *Journal of Clinical Psychiatry, 54,* 213–218.

Goodman, C. C., & Pynoos, J. A. (1990). A model telephone information and support program for caregivers of Alzheimer's patients. *The Gerontologist, 34*(4), 553–556.

Gordis, E. (1989). Alcohol alert: Relapse and craving. *National Institute on Alcohol Abuse and Alcoholism, 6* (PH 277), 1–5.

Greist, J. H. (1989). Computer-administered behavior therapies. *International Review of Psychiatry, 1,* 267–274.

Greist, J. H., Gustafson, D. H., Stauss, F. F., Rowse, G. L., Laughren, T. P., & Chiles, J. A. (1973). A computer interview for suicide-risk prevention. *American Journal of Psychiatry, 130,* 1327–1332.

Greist, J. H., Jefferson, J. W., Wenzel, K., Kobak, K. A., Bailey, T., Katzelnick, D. J., Hagerson, S. J., & Dottl, S. L. (1997). Telephone assessment program: Efficient patient monitoring and clinician feedback. *MD Computing, 14,* 382–387.

Greist, J. H., & Klein, M. H. (1980). Computer programs for patients, clinicians, and researchers in psychiatry. In J. B. Sidowski, J. H. Johnson, & T. A. Williams (Eds.), *Technology in mental health care delivery systems* (pp. 161–182). Norwood, NJ: Ablex.

Greist J. H., Marks, I. M., Baer, L., Parkin, R., Manzo, P., Mantle, J. M., Wenzel, K. W., Spierings, C. J., Kobak, K. A., Dottl, S. L., Bailey, T. M., & Forman, L. (1998). Home self-exposure therapy of obsessive compulsive disorder using a manual and a computer-conducted telephone interview: A US–UK study. *MD Computing, 15,* 149–157.

Gurland, B. J. (1994). The range of quality of life: Relevance to the treatment of depression in elderly patients. In L. S. Schneider, C. F. Reynolds III, B. D. Lebowitz, & A. J. Friedhoff (Eds.), *Diagnosis and treatment of depression in late life* (pp. 61–80). Washington, DC: American Psychiatric Press.

Gustafson, D. H., Bosworth, K., Hawkins, R. P., Boberg, E. W., & Bricker, E. (1992). CHESS: A computer-based system for providing information, referrals, decision support and social support to people facing medical and other health-related crises. *Proceedings of the Annual Symposium on Computer Applications in Medical Care,* 161–165.

Gustafson, D. H., Hawkins, R., Boberg, E., Pingree, S., Serlin, R. E., Graziano, F., & Chan, C. L. (1999). Impact of a patient-centered, computer-based health information/support system. *American Journal of Preventive Medicine, 16,* 1–9.

Hamilton, M. (1960). A rating scale for depression. *Journal of Neurology, Neurosurgery and Psychiatry, 23,* 56–62.

Heather, N., Kissoon-Singh, J., & Fenton, G. W. (1990). Assisted natural recovery from alcohol problems: Effects of a self-help manual with and without supplementary telephone contact. *British Journal of Addiction, 85,* 1177–1185.

Henk, H. J., Katzelnick, D. J., Kobak, K. A., Greist, J. H., & Jefferson, J. W. (1996). Excess medical costs associated with depression. *Archives of General Psychiatry 53,* 899–904.

Hile, M. G., & Adkins, R. E. (1997). Do substance abuse and mental health clients prefer automated assessments? *Behavior Research Methods, Instruments, & Computers, 29,* 146–150.

Hill, L. R., Klauber, M. R., Salmon, D. P., Yu, E. S. H., Liu, W. T., Zhang, M., & Katzman, R. (1993). Functional status, education, and the diagnosis of dementia in the Shanghai survey. *Neurology, 43,* 138–145.

Hollon, S. D., Shelton, R. C., & Loosen, P. T. (1991). Cognitive therapy and pharmacotherapy for depression. *Journal of Consulting and Clinical Psychology, 59,* 88–99.

Huang, M. P., & Alessi, N. E. (1999). Developing trends of the world wide web. *MD Computing, 50,* 31–41.

Hunkeler, E. M., Westphal, J. R., & Williams, M. (1995). Developing a system for automated monitoring of psychiatric outpatients: A first step to improve quality. *HMO Practice, 9,* 162–167.

Jacobson, N. S., Dobson, K. S., Truax, P. A., Addis, M. E., Koerner, K., Gollan, J. K., Gortner, E., & Prince, S. E. (1996). A component analysis of cognitive-behavioral treatment for depression. *Journal of Consulting and Clinical Psychology, 64,* 295–304.

Jadad, A. R., & Gagliardi, A. (1998). Rating health information on the Internet: Navigating to knowledge or to babel? *Journal of the American Medical Association, 279,* 611–614.

Katon, W., Von Korff, M., Lin, E., Lipscomb, P., Russo, J., Wagner, E., & Polk, E. (1990). Distressed utilizers of medical care (DSM–III–R): Diagnoses and treatment needs. *General Hospital Psychiatry, 12,* 355–362.

Katzelnick, D. J., Kobak, K. A., Greist, J. H., Jefferson, J. W., & Henk, H. J. (1997a). Effect of primary care treatment of depression on service use by patients with high medical expenditures. *Psychiatric Services, 48,* 59–64.

Katzelnick, D. J., Kobak, K. A., Greist, J. H., Jefferson, J. W., & Henk, H. J. (1997b). Predictors of adequate dose and duration of antidepressant medication for depression in a HMO. *Psychopharmacology Bulletin, 33,* 534.

Katzelnick, D. J., Kobak, K. A., Greist, J. H., Jefferson, J. W., Mantle, J. M., & Serlin, R. C. (1995). Sertraline for social phobia: A double-blind, placebo-controlled crossover study. *American Journal of Psychiatry, 152,* 1368–1371.

Katzelnick, D. J., Simon, G. E., Pearson, S. D., Manning, W. G., Helstad, C. P., Henk, H. J., & Kobak, K. A. (1997, December). *CARE Study: Impact of the step-wise depression management program for depressed high utilizers in three HMOs.* Paper presented at the meeting of the American College of Neuropsychopharmacology, 36th Annual Meeting, Waikoloa, HI.

Kessler, L. G., Cleary, P. D., & Burke, J. D., Jr. (1985). Psychiatric disorders in primary care: Results of a follow-up study. *Archives of General Psychiatry, 42,* 583–587.

Kirkby, K. C. (1996). Computer-assisted treatment of phobias. *Psychiatric Services, 47,* 139–142.

Kobak, K. A., Greist, J. H., Hirsch, J., Marks, I., & Baer, L. (1998, June). *Decision support using computer-administered symptom rating scales: Computerized assessment of obsessive-compulsive disorder via interactive voice response technology.* Paper presented at the meeting of the Psychiatric Society for Informatics, Toronto, Canada.

Kobak, K. A., Greist, J. H., Jefferson, J. H., & Katzelnick, D. J. (1996). Computer-administered clinical rating scales: A review. *Psychopharmacology, 127,* 291–301.

Kobak, K. A., Greist, J. H., Jefferson, J. W., & Katzelnick, D. J. (1998a, June). *Validation of a computerized Hamilton Depression Rating Scale administered by telephone via interactive voice response.* Paper presented at the meeting of the National Institute of Mental Health, New Clinical Drug Evaluation Unit, 38th Annual Meeting, Boca Raton, FL.

Kobak, K. A., Greist, J. H., Jefferson, J. W., & Katzelnick, D. J. (1998b, June). *The utility of the IVR Hamilton Depression Rating Scale in a multi-site depression trial: A feasability study.* Paper presented at the meeting of the National Institute of Mental Health, New Clinical Drug Evaluation Unit, 38th Annual Meeting, Boca Raton, FL.

Kobak, K. A., Greist, J. H., Jefferson, J. W., Katzelnick, D. J., & Henk, H. J. (1998). Behavioral versus pharmacological treatment of obsessive compulsive disorder: A meta-analysis. *Psychopharmacology, 136,* 205–216.

Kobak, K. A., Greist, J. H., Katzelnick, D. J., & Jefferson, J. W. (1998, June). *Validation of a computerized version of the Hamilton Anxiety Scale administered over the telephone via interactive voice response (IVR).* Paper presented at the meeting of the American Psychiatric Association, 151st Annual Meeting, Toronto, Canada.

Kobak, K. A., Reynolds, W. M., & Greist, J. H. (1993). Development and validation of a computer-administered version of the Hamilton Anxiety Scale. *Journal of Consulting and Clinical Psychology, 5,* 487–492.

Kobak, K. A., Reynolds, W. M., Rosenfeld, R., & Greist, J. H. (1990). Development and validation of a computer-administered version of the Hamilton Depression Rating Scale. *Journal of Consulting and Clinical Psychology, 2,* 56–63.

Kobak, K. A., Schaettle, S. C., Greist, J. H., Jefferson, J. W., Katzelnick, D. J., & Dottl, S. L. (1998). Computer interview assessment of social phobia in a clinical drug trial. *Depression & Anxiety, 7,* 97–104.

Kobak, K. A., Taylor, L. V., Dottl, S. L., Greist, J. H., Jefferson, J. W., Burroughs, D., Mantle, J. M., Katzelnick, D. J., Norton, R., Henk, H. J., & Serlin, R. C. (1997). A computer-administered telephone interview to identify mental disorders. *Journal of the American Medical Association, 278,* 905–910.

Loeser, H., Zvagulis, I., Hercz, L., & Pless, I. B. (1983). The organization and evaluation of a computer-assisted, centralized immunization registry. *American Journal of Public Health, 73,* 1298–1301.

Lucas, R. W. (1977). A study of patients' attitudes to computer interrogation. *International Journal of Man-Machine Studies, 9,* 69–86.

Lucas, R. W., Mullin, P. J., Luna, C. B. X., & McInroy, D. C. (1977). Psychiatrists and a computer as interrogators of patients with alcohol-related illnesses: A comparison. *British Journal of Psychiatry, 131,* 160–167.

Marks, I. M. (1986). *Behavioural psychotherapy.* Bristol: John Wright.

Marks, I. M., Lelliott, P., Basoglu, M. Noshirvani, H. Monteiro, W. W., Cohen, D., & Kasvikis, Y. (1988). Clomipramine, self-exposure and therapist-aided exposure for obsessive-compulsive rituals. *British Journal of Psychiatry 152*, 522–534.

Marks, I. M., Shaw, S., & Parkin, R. (1998). Computer-aided treatments of mental health problems. *Clinical Psychology: Science and Practice, 5*, 151–170.

Marlatt, G. A. (1985). Situational determinants of relapse and skill-training interventions. In G. A. Marlatt & J. R. Gordon (Eds.), *Relapse prevention: Maintenance strategies in the treatment of addictive behaviors* (pp. 71–127). New York: Guilford Press.

McConatha, D., McConatha, J. T., Dermigny, R. (1994). The use of interactive computer services to enhance the quality of life for long-term care residents. *The Gerontologist, 34*(4), 553–556.

McCormick, W. C., Kukull, W. A., van Belle, G., Bowen, J. D., Teri, L., Larson, E. B. (1994). Symptom patterns and comorbidity in the early stages of Alzheimer's disease. *Journal of the American Geriatrics Society, 42*, 517–521.

McDonald, C. J. (1976). Protocol-based computer reminders: The quality of care and the non-perfectability of man. *New England Journal of Medicine, 295*, 1351–1355.

Melfi, C. A., Chawla, A. J., Croghan, T. W., Hanna, M. P., Kennedy, S., & Sredl, K. (1998). The effects of adherence to antidepressant treatment guidelines on relapse and recurrence of depression. *Archives of General Psychiatry, 55*, 1128–1132.

Meneghini, L. F., Albisser, A. M., Goldberg, R. B., & Mintz, D. H. (1998). An electronic case manager for diabetes control. *Diabetes Care, 21*, 591–596.

Millard, R. W., & Carver, J. R. (1999). Cross-sectional comparison of live and IVR administration of the SF-12. *American Journal of Managed Care, 5*, 153–159.

Morris, J. C., Mohs, R. C., et al. (1988). Consortium to Establish a Registry for Alzheimer's Disease (CERAD) clinical and neuropsychological assessment of Alzheimer's disease. *Psychopharmacology Bulletin, 24*(4), 641–652.

Mundt, J. C., Kobak, K. A., Taylor, L. V. H., Mantle, J. M., Jefferson, J. W., Katzelnick, D. J., & Greist, J. H. (1998). Administration of the Hamilton Depression Rating Scale using interactive voice response technology. *MD Computing, 15*, 31–39.

Newman, M. G., Consoli, A. J., & Taylor, C. B. (in press). A palmtop computer program for the treatment of generalized anxiety disorder. *Behavior Modification.*

Newman, M. G., Kenardy, J., Herman, S., & Taylor, C. B. (1997). Comparison of palmtop-computer-assisted brief cognitive-behavioral treatment to cognitive-behavioral treatment for panic disorder. *Journal of Consulting and Clinical Psychology, 65*, 178–183.

NIH Consensus Development Panel on Depression in Late Life. (1992). Diagnosis and treatment of depression in late life. *Journal of the American Medical Association, 268*, 1018–1024.

North, M. M., North, S. M., & Coble, J. R. (1997). Virtual reality therapy for fear of flying [Letter to the editor]. *American Journal of Psychiatry, 154*, 130.

O'Connor, P. G., & Schottenfeld, R. S. (1998). Patients with alcohol problems. *New England Journal of Medicine, 338*, 592–602.

O'Connor, P. J., Solberg, L. I., & Baird, M. (1998). The future of primary care: The enhanced primary care model. *Journal of Family Practice, 47*, 62–67.

Orleans, C. T., George, L. K., Houpt, J. L., & Brodie, H. K. H. (1985). How primary care physicians treat psychiatric disorders: A national survey of family practitioners. *American Journal of Psychiatry, 142*, 52–57.

Osgood-Hynes, D. J., Greist, J. H., Marks, I. M., Baer, L., Heneman, S. W., Wenzel, K. W., Manzo, P. A., Parkin, J. R., Spierings, C. J., Dottl, S. L., & Vitse, H. M. (1998). Self-administered psychotherapy for derpession using a telephone-accessed computer system plus booklets: An open U.S.–U.K. study. *Journal of Clinical Psychiatry, 59*, 358–365.

Peskind, E. R. (1998). Pharmacologic approaches to cognitive deficits in Alzheimer's disease. *Journal of Clinical Psychiatry, 59*(Suppl. 9), 22–27.

Petrie, K., & Abell, W. (1994). Responses of parasuicides to a computerized interview. *Computers in Human Behavior, 10*, 415–418.

Pfeffer, R. I., Afifi, A. A., & Chance, J. M. (1987). Prevalence of Alzheimer's disease in a retirement community. *American Journal of Epidemiology, 125*, 420–436.

Pfeffer, R. I., Kurosaki, T. T., Harrah, C. H., Chance, J. M., Bates, D., Detels, R., Filos, S., & Butzke, C. (1981). A survey of diagnostic tools for senile dementia. *American Journal of Epidemiology, 114*, 515–527.

Piette, J. D., & Mah, C. A. (1997). The feasibility of automated voice messaging as an adjunct to diabetes outpatient care. *Diabetes Care, 20*, 15–21.

Rabkin, J. G., & Markowitz, J. S. (1986). Side effect assessment with SAFTEE: Pilot study of the instrument. *Psychopharmacology, 22*, 389–396.

Reynolds, W. M., & Kobak, K. A. (1995a). *Hamilton Depression Inventory: A self-report version of the Hamilton Depression Rating Scale. Professional manual.* Odessa, FL: Psychological Assessment Resources.

Reynolds, W. M., & Kobak, K. A. (1995b). Development and validation of the Hamilton Depression Inventory: A self-report version of the Hamilton Depression Rating Scale. *Psychological Assessment, 7,* 472–483.

Reynolds, W. R., Kobak, K. A., & Greist, J. H. (1992, August). *Diagnostic utility of the Hamilton Depression Rating Scale.* Paper presented at the meeting of the American Psychological Association, 100th Annual Convention, Washington, DC.

Risser, J., Biros, M., Hodroff, M., Kobak, K. A., & Mandell, M. (1997, October). *Prevalence of unsuspected psychiatric disease in emergency department patients.* Paper presented at the meeting of the American College of Emergency Physicians, Scientific Assembly, San Francisco, CA.

Rosenfeld, R., Dar, R., Anderson, D., et al. (1992). A computer administered version of the Yale–Brown Obsessive Compulsive Scale. *Psychological Assessment, 4,* 329–332.

Rost, K., Smith, R., Matthews, D. B., & Guise, B. (1994). The deliberate misdiagnosis of major depression in primary care. *Archives of Family Medicine, 3,* 333–337.

Rothbaum, B. O., Hodges, L. F., Kooper, R., Opdyke, D., Williford, J. S., & North, M.. (1995). Effectiveness of computer-generated (virtual reality) graded exposure in the treatment of acrophobia. *American Journal of Psychiatry, 152,* 626–628.

Rothbaum, B. O., Hodges, L., Watson, B. A., Kessler, C. D., & Opdyke, D. (1996). Virtual reality exposure therapy in the treatment of fear of flying: A case report. *Behaviour Research and Therapy, 34,* 477–481.

Schneider, S. J., Schwartz, M. D., & Fast, J. (1995). Computerized, telephone-based health promotion: I. Smoking cessation program. *Computers in Human Behavior, 11,* 135–148.

Searles, J. S., Perrine, M. W., Mundt, J. C., & Helzer, J. E. (1995). Self-report of drinking using touch-tone telephone: Extending the limits of reliable daily contact. *Journal of Studies on Alcohol, 56,* 375–382.

Schulberg, H. C., & Burns, B. J. (1988). Mental disorders in primary care: Epidemiologic, diagnostic, and treatment research directions. *General Hospital Psychiatry, 10,* 79–87.

Selby, J. V. (1997). Linking automated databases for research in managed care settings. *Annals of Internal Medicine, 127,* 719–724.

Selmi, P. M., Klein, M. H., Greist, M. H., Sorrell, S. P., & Erdman, H. P. (1990). Computer-administered cognitive-behavioral therapy for depression. *American Journal of Psychiatry, 147,* 51–56.

Sheehan, D. V., Lecrubier, Y., Sheehan, K. H., Amorim, P., Janavs, J., Weiller, E., Hergueta, T., Baker, R., & Dunbar, G. C. (1998). The Mini-International Neuropsychiatric Interview (M.I.N.I.): The development and validation of a structured diagnostic psychiatric interview for DSM–IV and ICD–10. *Journal of Clinical Psychiatry, 59 (suppl. 20),* 22–33.

Simon, G. E., Lin, E. H. B., Katon, W., Saunders, K., Von Korff, M., Walker, E., Bush, T., & Robinson, P. (1995). Outcomes of "inadequate" antidepressant treatment. *Journal of General Internal Medicine 10,* 663–670.

Simmons, E. M., & Miller, O. W. (1971). Automated patient history-taking. *Hospitals, 45,* 56–59.

Skinner, H. A., & Allen, B. A. (1983). Does the computer make a difference? Computerized versus face-to-face versus self-report assessment of alcohol, drug, and tobacco use. *Journal of Consulting and Clinical Psychology, 51,* 267–275.

Slack, W. V., & Van Cura, L. J. (1968). Patient reaction to computer-based medical inteviewing. *Computers and Biomedical Research, 1,* 527–531.

Smyth, K. A., & Harris, P. B. (1993). Using telecomputing to provide information and support to caregivers of persons with dementia. *The Gerontologist, 33*(1), 123–127.

Sobell, M. B., Sobell, L. C., Bogardis, J., Leo, G. I., & Skinner, W. (1992). Problem drinkers' perceptions of whether treatment goals should be self-selected or therapist-selected. *Behavior Therapy, 23,* 43–52.

Spitzer, R. L., Williams, J. B., Kroenke, K., et al. (1994). Utility of a new procedure for diagnosing mental disorders in primary care. The PRIME–MD 1000 study. *Journal of the American Medical Association, 272,* 1749–1756.

Strecher, V. J., Kreuter, M., Boer, D.-J. D., Kobrin, S., Hospers, H. J., & Skinner, C. S. (1994). The effects of computer-tailored smoking cessation messages in family practice settings. *Journal of Family Practice, 39,* 262–270.

Turner, C. F., Ku, L., Rogers, S. M., Lindberg, L. D., Pleck, J. H., & Sonenstein, F. L. (1998). Adolescent sexual behavior, drug use, and violence: Increased reporting with computer survey technology. *Science, 280,* 867–873.

Ware, J. E. (1993). *SF–36 Health Survey. Manual and Interpretation Guide.* Boston, MA: Health Institute, New England Medical Center.

Ware, J. E., Kosinski, M., & Keller, S. D. (1995). *SF–12: How to score the SF–12 Physical and Mental Health Summary Scales.* Boston: Health Institute, New England Medical Center.

Wasson, J. H., O'Conner, G. T., James, D. H., & Olmstead, E. M. (1992). A physician-completed patient registry system: Pilot results for unstable angina in the elderly. The Northern New England Cardiovascular Disease Study Group and the Dartmouth Primary Care COOP. *Journal of General Internal Medicine, 3,* 298–303.

Weinberger, M., Tierney, W. M., Cowper, P. A., Katz, B. P., & Booher, P. A. (1993). Cost-effectiveness of increased telephone contact for patients with osteoarthritis. A randomized, controlled trial. *Arthritis and Rheumatism, 36,* 243–246.

Weiss, M. E. (1998). Case management as a tool for clinical integration. *Advanced Practice Nursing Quarterly, 4,* 9–15.

Weissman, M. M., Broadhead, W. E., Olfson, M., Sheehan, D. V., Hoven, C., Conolly, P., Fireman, B. H., Farber, L., Blacklow, R. S., Higgins, E. S., & Leon, A. C. (1998). A diagnostic aid for detecting (DSM–IV) mental disorders in primary care. *General Hospital Psychiatry, 20,* 1–11.

Weizenbaum, J. (1966). ELIZA—A computer program for the study of natural language communication between man and machine. *Communication of the Association for Computing Machinery, 9,* 36–45.

Wells, K. B., Hays, R. D., Burnam, M. A., Rogers, W., Greenfield, S., & Ware, J. E. (1989). Detection of depressive disorder for patients receiving prepaid or fee-for-service care: Results from the Medical Outcomes study. *Journal of the American Medical Association, 262,* 3298–3302.

Widmer, R. B., & Cadoret, R. J. (1979). Depression in family practice: Changes in pattern of patient visits and complaints during subsequent developing depression. *Journal of Family Practice, 9,* 1017–1021.

Yesavage, J. A., Brink, T. L., Rose, T. L., Lum, O., Huang, V., Adey, M., & Leirer, V. O. (1983). Development and validation of a geriatric depression screening scale: A preliminary report. *Journal of Psychiatric Research, 17,* 37–49.

Zhu, S.-H., Stretch, V., Balabanis, M., Rosbrook, B., Sadler, G., & Pierce, J. P. (1996). Telephone counseling for smoking cessation: Effects of single-session and multiple-session interventions. *Journal of Consulting and Clinical Psychology, 64,* 202–211.

Zimmerman, M., Coryell, W., Wilson, S., et al. (1986). Evaluation of symptoms of major depressive disorder: Self-report vs clinician ratings. *Journal of Nervous and Mental Disorders, 174,* 150–153.

Author Index

A

Abara, J., 571, *581*
Abashian, S. W., 315, *333*
Abel, J. L., 382, *388*
Abell, W., 428, *459*, 774, 775, *794*
Abeloff, M., 318, 326, *328*, *329*, *330*
Abler, R., 497, *507*
Abou-Saleh, M., 502, *508*
Abraham, M., 558, *579*
Abrams, D. B., 787, *791*
Abyad, A., 558, *582*
Academy of Psychosomatics Medicine, 2, 5, 8, 9, 10, 13, *38*
Achenbach, T. M., 100, *111*
Acuda, S. W., 373, *388*
Adams, A. C., 556, 564, *580*
Adams, M. E., 625, *649*
Adams, S. G., Jr., 382, *387*
Aday, L. A., 625, *649*
Addis, M. E., 708, *709*, 780, *792*
Adey, M., 492, *506*, *508*, 785, *796*
Adkins, R. E., 786, *792*
Ae Lee, M., 312, 313, *328*
Afifi, A. A., 785, *794*
Agency for Health Care Policy and Research, 156, *186*
Agosti, V., 449, *460*
Aiken, L. H., 628, *649*
Ala, T., 561, *581*
Albert, M. S., 139, *145*, 556, 568, *580*, *582*
Albisser, A. M., 780, *794*
Alemi, F., 786, *790*
Alessi, N. E., 788, *792*
Alexander, F., 376, *387*
Ali, O. M., 424, *461*
Allen, B. A., 428, *460*, 774, 786, *795*
Allen, J., 561, 562, 563, *582*
Allerup, P., 431, *456*, 776, *790*
Allison, T. G., 115, 134, *145*, 299, 310, 322, *328*
Allred, L. J., 323, *330*
Alovis, N., 325, *333*
Alpert, J. E., 558, *579*, 626, *649*
Altamura, A. C., 373, *388*
Altemeier, W., 95, *112*
Alter, C. L., 23, 26, *38*

Alvarado, M. L., 135, *145*
Amaro, H., 157, *186*
Amenson, C. S., 311, *328*
American Academy of Pediatrics, 94, 95, *111*
American Educational Research Association, 433, 434, *456*
American Presidential Task Force, 578, *579*
American Psychiatric Association, 97, 98, 99, *111*, 277, 295, 298, *328*, 375, 382, *387*, 409, 412, *416*, 427, 429, 430, 434, 442, 443, 445, 446, 447, 455, *456*, 463, 474, *487*, 500, *506*, 527, *532*, 556, *579*, 694, 708, *708*, 771, *790*
American Psychological Association, 10, *38*, 94, *111*, 356, *371*, 450, *456*, 510, 528, *533*
Ames, S. C., 375, 384, *387*
Amick, B. C., 118, *149*
Amodei, N., 135, *145*
Amorim, P., 778, *779*, *795*
Anastasi, A., 511, *533*
Ancill, R. J., 774, 786, *790*, *791*
Andersen, R., 625, *649*
Andersen, S. M., 236, *247*, 277, *296*
Anderson, D. J., 307, 312, 322, 332, 396, *420*, 774, *795*
Anderson, D. R., 68, *88*
Anderson, J., 141, *148*
Anderson, L. L., 546, *553*
Anderson, R., 193, 194, *247*
Anderson, R. L., 118, *148*, 464, *488*
Anderson, S. M., 118, 119, *145*
Andreasen, N. C., 213, *247*, 444, *457*
Andresen, E. M., 408, *416*
Andrews, G., 31, *38*
Aneshensel, C. S., 116, *152*, 407, *417*
Anfinson, T. J., 133, *145*
Angel, R., 407, *418*
Angst, J., 311, *328*
Anstett, R., 656, *682*
Anthony, J., 140, *149*
Anthony, J. C., 192, *251*, 297, *332*, 558, 559, 561, 563, 578, *579*
Antonuccio, D. O., 447, *459*, 706, *710*, 721, *732*
Antony, M. M., 512, 513, 517, 518, *533*
Appelbaum, S. A., 34, *38*
Applegate, B. W., 407, 412, *420*, 695, *709*
Arana, G. W., 125, *145*, 540, 541, *553*
Areans, P. A., 512, 513, 516, 517, *534*

Armitage, J. M., 321, *330*
Arndt, S., 213, *247*
Arnett, H. L., 101, *113*
Arnold, M. B., 378, *387*
Aroian, K. J., 303, *328*
Aronow, H. U., 496, *508*
Arons, B. S., 156, *186*, 195, *248*
Aronson, M., 575, *580*
Arrington, M. E., 198, 201, 216, *249*
Arruda, M. J., 463, *488*
Asberg, M., 424, *459*
Ashcroft, G. W., 392, *419*
Ashworth, C. D., 668, *682*
Asnis, G. M., 307, 311, *334*
Atkinson, C. C., 93, *113*
Atkinson, H., 322, *328*
Atkinson, M. M., 769, *790*
Attala, J. M., 157, *186*
Attkisson, C. C., 52, 53, *89*, 409, *421*, 423, *456*, 636, *649*
Aukes, D., 512, 513, *534*
Austin, B. T., 603, *621*
Austin, M., 563, *579*
Austin, S. M., 772, *790*
Austin, T., 48, *91*
Avins, A. L., 214, 241, *252*, 695, *711*
Azari, R., 391, *417*, 691, *708*
Azarian, K., 525, *533*
Azocar, P., 687, *708*

B

Badger, L. W., 118, *148*, *150*, 193, 194, *247*, 464, *488*
Baer, B. A., 302, *331*
Baer, L., 455, *456*, *459*, 774, 775, 781, 782, *790*, *792*, *793*, *794*
Baider, L., 320, *328*
Bailey, K. R., 115, 134, *145*, 299, 310, 322, *328*
Bailey, T. M., 775, 782, *792*
Baird, M. A., 23, 25, *39*, 45, 72, 84, *88*, *89*, 766, 767, 770, *794*
Bairnsfather, L. E., 118, *146*
Baker, F., 141, 142, *145*
Baker, J., 193, *248*
Baker, M. T., 668, *682*
Baker, R., 778, 779, *795*
Baker, R. W., 576, 578, *582*
Balabanis, M., 787, *796*
Balas, E. A., 772, 789, *790*
Baldessarini, R. J., 125, *145*, 540, 541, *553*
Ball, R., *184*, 385, *387*, 395, 396, 398, 401, 404, *416*, *417*, 521, *533*
Ballard, C., 556, *580*
Ballard, T. J., 158, *186*
Ballenger, J. C., 307, *329*
Balleweg, B. J., 396, *420*
Barber, J. G., 787, *790*
Barker, L. R., *90*, 193, *251*
Barlow, D. H., 156, *186*, 195, *248*, 385, *387*, 520, 522, 527, 529, *533*
Barlow, W., 57, 64, *90*, 192, *247*, 392, *420*, 691, 704, *711*, 713, *733*
Barraclough, B., 464, *487*
Barrett, J., 12, 13, *38*, 194, *250*
Barrett, J. A., 115, 116, *145*, 213, *247*, 279, *296*, 307, *329*, 445, *456*

Barrett, J. B., 213, *247*
Barrett, J. E., 115, 116, *145*, 279, *296*, 307, *329*, 443, *456*
Barrett, P. A., 222, *251*, 603, 609, *621*
Barrett-Connor, F., 563, *579*
Barros, F., 373, *389*
Barrios, F. X., 512, 513, 516, *534*
Barsky, A. J., 7, *38*, 54, *87*, 128, 136, *151*, *152*, 192, 206, 209, *253*, 409, *417*, 713, *732*
Bartlett, J., 481, *487*
Barton, D., 322, *332*
Basco, M. R., 466, 474, 475, *489*
Basha, I., 216, *247*
Basoglu, M., 782, *794*
Bassett, S. S., 558, 559, 561, 563, 578, *579*
Bastine, R., 404, *419*
Bates, D., 785, *794*
Bates, D. W., 608, *620*
Baum, A., 378, *387*
Bayles, K., 138, *145*
Bayliss, L. S., 586, 587, *620*, *621*
Bayliss, M. S., 482, *489*
Beamesderfer, A., 395, 397, *416*
Beardslee, W. R., 463, *488*
Bech, P., 133, *145*, 426, 430, 431, *456*, 776, *790*
Beck, A. T., 127, 128, 132, 133, 137, *145*, *146*, 150, *151*, *184*, 236, *247*, 279, 285, 287, *296*, 385, *387*, 393, 394, 395, 396, 397, 398, 401, 402, 403, 404, 405, 407, *416*, *417*, *418*, *419*, 420, 424, 427, 429, 430, 431, 435, 445, 446, 447, 448, *456*, *459*, 460, 466, 474, *487*, 501, *506*, 509, 510, 511, 512, 513, 516, 517, 518, 519, 521, 524, 525, 527, *533*, *534*, 706, *708*, *710*, 780, 781, 786, *790*
Beck, J. C., 496, *508*
Beck, R. W., 132, *145*, 394, *416*, 706, *708*
Becker, J. T., 565, *579*
Becker, M. H., 625, *649*
Beckman, L. J., 547, *554*
Bedrosian, R. C., 403, *417*
Behar, L. B., 101, *111*
Beitman, B. D., 216, *247*
Belizan, J. M., 373, *389*
Belkin, B. M., 259, *275*
Bell, R., 513, 516, 517, 518, *533*
Bell, R. A., 131, *149*, 310, *332*
Bellack, A. S., 424, 430, *461*
Bellin, E. H., 675, *682*
Belyea-Caldwell, S., 311, *332*
Benham, L., 52, *90*, 192, *252*, 423, *460*, 687, *711*
Benjamin, A. H., 306, 321, *329*
Benkert, O., 307, *329*
Bennett, R. T., 315, *329*
Bennett, S. E., 314, *329*
Bensen, S., 285, 287, *296*
Benson, F., 139, *146*
Benson, H., 10, 18, 23, 26, *39*, 53, 55, *89*, 307, *329*
Berchick, R. J., 445, *456*
Berg, G., 141, *146*
Berg, L., 141, *146*, 565, *580*
Berger, M. E., 95, *113*
Berger, R. E., 373, *387*
Berghuis, J. P., 373, *387*
Bergeron, C., 556, *580*
Berhard, M., 140, 141, *148*
Berman, J. S., 502, *507*
Berman, W. H., 525, *533*

Berndt, E. R., 463, 473, *488*
Bernier, M. J., 589, *621*
Bernstein, I. H., 591, *621*
Bernstein, K., 632, *650*
Berry, S. D., 154, *186*, 192, *252*, 392, *421*, 423, 444, 445, *461*, 463, 464, *490*, 687, 691, *711*
Berryhill, J. S., 496, *507*
Bershadsky, B., 336, 337, 339, 340, 358, *371*
Bertakis, K. D., 391, *417*, 691, *708*
Berwick, D. M., 46, *87*, 127, 128, *149*, *151*, 409, *417*
Best, A. M., 138, 139, 140, *148*
Best-Castner, S., 134, *152*
Beusterien, K. M., *185*
Beutler, L. E., 316, *332*
Bhardwaj, S., 319, *333*
Bhatt, P., 786, *790*
Bibring, G. L., 654, *682*
Bieber, J., 336, 337, 339, 340, 358, *371*
Bielawska, C., 140, *147*, 495, *508*
Bien, T. H., 155, 157, *186*
Bijur, P. E., 95, *114*
Binns, H. J., 97, *112*
Bird, J., 193, *248*
Bires, J. A., 95, *113*
Biros, M., 775, *795*
Birtchnell, J., 128, *146*
Bishop, S., 426, *459*
Bishop, S. B., 501, *507*
Bishop, S. J., 101, *111*, *113*
Bjorner, J. B., 609, *620*
Black, D. W., 446, *461*
Blacklow, R. S., *185*, 200, *250*, 443, *456*, *461*, 777, 778, *796*
Blackstock, J., 140, *147*
Blanchard, C. G., 134, *152*
Blanchard, E. B., 523, *533*
Bland, R. C., 463, *487*
Blazer, D. G., 9, *41*, 53, 54, *87*, 192, *251*, 443, 445, *456*
Blendon, R. J., 628, *649*
Blessed, G., 142, *146*, 556, 573, 574, 578, *579*, *582*
Block, A., 392, 412, *420*
Block, M. R., *184*, 223, 237, 239, *251*, 392, 410, 412, *417*, *420*, 688, 703, *711*, 713, 733
Bloom, J. R., 57, *90*
Blostein, P. A., 571, *579*
Blount, A., 72, 77, *88*
Blow, F., 238, 241, 246, *252*
Blum, A., 697, *711*
Blumenfeld, A., 571, *581*
Blumenthal, J. A., 321, *331*
Boberg, E. W., 787, 788, *792*
Bobula, J. A., 119, *149*, 237, *250*
Bodison, D., 7, *39*, 279, *296*
Boer, D. -J. D., 787, *795*
Boes, J. L., 131, *150*, *184*
Bogardis, J., 787, *795*
Bohachick, P., 321, *329*
Boland, R., 193, 236, *251*
Boleloucky, Z., 304, *329*
Bolwig, T. G., 431, *456*
Bond, H., 788, *790*
Bondi, M. W., 566, 568, 569, 578, *581*
Bone, L. R., 221, *250*
Booher, P. A., 785, *796*
Booker, S., 135, *148*
Booth, B., 467, 470, 473, *487*, *489*

Bopp, K. D., 772, *790*
Borduin, C. M., 314, *334*
Boren, S. A., 789, *790*
Borgquist, L., 115, *148*, 192, *248*
Borkovec, T. D., 523, *534*
Borrelli, B., 787, *791*
Borrelli, D. J., 311, *329*
Borus, J. F., 5, 7, *38*, 127, *149*, 213, *253*, 277, *296*, 691, *709*, 713, *732*
Borysenko, J., 53, 55, *89*
Bosworth, K., 787, *792*
Bottler, L., 192, *252*
Boudreaux, E. D., 375, 379, 383, 384, *387*
Boult, C., 498, *507*
Boust, J. S., 494, *506*
Bowen, J. D., 575, *579*,
Bowers J. D., *794*
Bowman, F. M., 236, *247*
Boyce, W. T., 95, *114*
Boyd, J. H., 115, *150*, 297, 299, 310, *332*, 466, 474, *487*, 509, *533*
Boyd, S. C., 318, *333*
Boyle, R. B., 47, *90*
Boyle, R. G., 47, *88*
Braiman, S., 132, *151*
Braith, J. A., 311, *332*
Brandt, J., 142, *151*
Brantley, P. J., 375, 379, 381, 382, 383, 384, 385, *387*, *388*, *389*, 407, 410, 412, *420*, 688, 695, *709*
Brater, D. C., 136, *146*
Bray, J., 714, 717, *732*
Brazier, J. E., 588, 590, 591, *620*
Breckenridge, J., 306, *333*
Breckenridge, J. S., 706, *710*
Breen, A. R., 568, *582*
Breiter, H. J., 399, *417*
Breitner, J. C., 142, *151*
Brems, C., 325, *331*
Brent, D., 95, *111*
Breslau, N., 410, 411, *417*
Breslin, C., 786, *791*
Bricker, E., 787, *792*
Bridges, K., 116, *146*, 194, *247*, 299, *329*
Brierly, H., 584, *620*
Brill, P. L., 11, 15, 26, 27, 33, *41*, 257, 259, 260, 270, *275*
Brink, T. L., 492, *506*, *508*, 785, *796*
Brink, W., 54, *89*
Brinson, M. E., 568, *581*
BrintzenhofeSzoc, K. M., 134, *152*
Britt, M., 136, *150*
Broadhead, E., 153, 155, *185*, *187*
Broadhead, W. E., 7, 8, *41*, 200, 222, *250*, *251*, 391, 392, 393, *421*, 443, 445, *456*, *461*, 608, *621*, 687, *711*, 756, *760*, 777, 778, *791*, *796*
Brockington, I. F., 214, *248*
Brod, M. S., 561, 562, 563, *582*
Brodie, H. K. H., 118, *149*, 194, *250*, 423, *459*, 777, *794*
Brody, D. S., 7, 8, 31, *39*, *41*, 154, 155, 156, *184*, *186*, 191, 196, 197, 202, 208, 209, 210, 211, 216, 218, 219, 221, 226, 234, 235, 241, 246, *247*, *248*, 249, *250*, *252*, 280, *296*, 423, 442, 443, 444, *458*, *460*, 465, *487*, 653, 654, 664, 665, 667, 669, 675, 678, *682*, *683*, 694, *711*, 756, *760*
Bromet, E. J., 194, *248*
Bronson, D., 277, *296*

Brook, R., 473, 478, *490*
Brook, R. H., 625, 628, 636, 643, *649, 650*
Brooks, J. D., 415, *417*
Brown, B., 303, *329*, 584, *620*
Brown, C., *417*, 702, *709*
Brown, G., 133, *150*, 424, 431, 435, 445, *456, 460*, 509,
        510, 511, 512, 513, 516, 517, 518, 519, 524,
        533, 534
Brown, G. D., 772, 789, *790*
Brown, G. K., 394, 396, 404, *417*
Brown, G. W., 378, 386, *387*
Brown, J., 396, *420*
Brown, J. B., 625, *649*
Brown, R. L., 312, *329*
Brown, T. A., 520, *533*, 575, *580*
Brown-Beasley, M. W., 774, *790*
Browner, W. S., 214, 241, *252*, 695, *711*
Bruce, M. L., 393, *417*
Brunton, S. A., 374, *387*
Bryer, J. B., 311, *329*
Buchan, G., 786, *791*
Buchan, I., 237, *248*
Buckley, T. C., 523, *533*
Buckner, J. C., 312, 324, *329*
Budd, M., 53, 55, *89*
Budenz, D., 403, *417*
Budman, S. H., 127, *149*
Budner, N. S., 201, 205, 206, 219, 226, 231, *248*, 653,
        657, *659*, *682*
Buechler, C. M., 571, *579*
Buesching, D. P., 118, *152*, 392, *420*, 521, *533*, 628, *650*,
        713, *732*
Bulik, C. M., 137, *146*, 312, *329*, 441, *457*
Buller, R., 307, *329*
Bulpitt, C. J., 303, *329*, 584, *620*
Bulstrode, C., 655, *683*
Bunch, J., 464, *487*
Bunney, W. E., 318, *333*
Burke, J., 118, 119, *150*
Burke, J. D., Jr., 7, 41, 94, 97, *112*, 115, 117, 118, 119, 145,
        146, 150, 192, 193, 213, 236, 237, *249, 251,
        252*, 297, 299, 310, *332, 333*, 373, *388*, 442,
        443, *458*, 509, *534*, 771, 777, *793*
Burke, J. R., 142, *151*
Burke, K. C., 373, *388*
Burke, W. J., *185*, 494, 495, 498, 499, *506, 507*
Burlingame, G. M., 527, *534*
Burnam, A., 140, *147*, 192, *251*, 392, *421*, 687, 691, *711*
Burnam, M. A., 8, *41*, 128, *146, 184*, 192, 201, 202, *248*,
        252, 259, *275*, 423, 426, 444, 445, *460, 461*,
        463, 464, 466, 467, 468, 469, 473, 475, 477,
        479, 481, *487, 489, 490*, 586, *621*, 733, 777,
        796
Burns, A., 556, *580*
Burns, B. J., 7, *39, 41*, 52, *88*, 95, 97, 100, 101, 102, 103,
        111, *112*, 117, 118, 119, *146, 150, 184*, 194,
        213, 236, 237, *248, 251, 252*, 277, 279, *296*,
        423, 442, 443, *460*, 475, 477, 481, 489, 691,
        703, *710*, 771, 777, *795*
Burns, D. D., 706, *709*
Burns, G. L., 523, *533*
Burns, J., 9, 12, 13, 18, 21, *38*
Burns, R., 502, *508*
Burnum, J. F., 602, *620*
Burroughs, D., 31, *40*, 203, 221, 229, 241, *249*, 426, 443,
        450, *459*, 756, *760*, 777, 778, *793*

Burrows, G. D., 307, *329*
Burton, R. H., 194, *248*
Bush, B. T., 542, *553*
Bush, D. M., 595, *620*
Bush, T. M., 55, 56, *89, 184*, 223, 224, 236, 237, 238,
        239, 242, 249, 250, 375, 389, 391, *418*, 464,
        465, *488*, 602, 603, *620, 621*, 655, 656, *683*,
        688, 691, 694, 698, 703, 704, 705, 706, 707,
        708, 709, 710, 711, 714, 733, 777, *795*
Buss, R. R., 375, 382, *387, 388*
Busto, U. A., 496, *507*
Butcher, J. N., 28, 34, *38*
Butler, R. N., 499, *506*
Butters, N., 562, 563, 566, 567, 568, 569, 575, 578, *580*,
        581
Butzke, C., 785, *794*
Bynum, R., 625, *649*
Byrne, E. J., 556, *580*
Bystritski, A., 322, *332*

C

Cabral, H., 157, *186*
Cadoret, R. J., 770, *796*
Cahn, D. A., 561, 563, 564, 566, 568, 569, 578, 579, *581*
Cahn, T. S., 306, 321, *329*
Cahn, W., 307, 311, *334*
Caine, E. D., 53, *88*, 409, *419*
Callahan, C. M., 136, *146*, 491, *506*
Callahan, E. J., 391, *417*, 691, *708*
Callaway, R., 565, *581*
Callon, E. B., 375, *387*
Calucin, R. Q., 118, *152*
Cameron, O. G., 307, 312, 313, *328, 329*
Camp, P., 464, *490*, 599, *621*
Campbell, T., 65, 72, *89*, 714, 717, *733*
Campbell, T. L., 196, *247*, 373, 374, 375, *387*, 436, *457*,
        776, *791*
Campeas, R., 445, *459*
Cane, D. B., 509, *534*
Cannon, W. B., 376, *388*
Carmack, C., 375, *387*
Carey, K. B., 324, *329*
Carey, M. P., 324, *329*, 668, *682*
Carlin, A. S., 784, 785, *791*
Carlson, G., 395, *420*
Carner, E. A., 697, *711*
Carnes, M., 497, *507*
Carney, R. M., 68, *88*
Carnricke, C. L. M., 131, *147*, 297, *330*, 668, *682*
Carpenter, J. T., 320, *332*
Carpenter, L. L., 137, *146*, 312, *329*, 441, 446, *457, 461*
Carr, A. C., 771, 774, 786, *790, 791*
Carr, E. W., 134, *152*
Carrington, P., 307, *329*
Carroll, B. J., 424, *457*
Carter Center of Emory University, 638, 642, *649*
Carter, C. S., 509, *533*
Carter, W. B., 408, *416*
Carver, J. R., 779, *794*
Cataldo, M. R., 96, 104, *112*
Catanzaro, R. J., 786, *791*
Cathebras, P., 193, 194, *251*
Cattell, R., 305, *331*
Catz, S. L., 379, 383, 384, *387*

Caudill, M., 10, 18, 23, 26, *39*
Cavanaugh, D., 320, *333*
Celia, D. F., 319, *333*, 402, *418*
Cervantes, P., 407, *419*
Chamberlin, J., 216, 241, *249*, 423, *459*
Chambless, D. L., 512, 513, 516, 517, 518, 520, 524, *533*

Chan, C. L., 788, *792*
Chance, J. M., 785, *794*
Chandrashekar, C. R., 373, *388*
Chaney, J., 714, *733*
Chang, G., 135, *146*
Chang, H., 636, *650*
Chang, L. C., 608, *620*
Chao, D. V. K., 200, *250*
Chapman, J., 319, *331*
Charap, P., 137, *151*
Charney, D. S., 377, *388*, 446, *460*
Charney, E., 625, 626, *649*
Chawla, A. J., 768, *794*
Cherkin, D. C., 192, *247*
Chessare, J. B., 96, *112*
Chiles, J. A., 136, *146*, 306, 321, *329*, 428, *457*, 774, *792*
Chissom, B. S., 627, 643, *650*
Chong, M., 128, *146*
Choquette, K. A., 305, *329*
Chown, M. J., 556, *580*
Christiansen, J., 137, *149*, 312, *332*
Christoffel, K., 97, *112*
Christophersen, E. R., 95, 100, 101, 103, *111*
Christy, W., 118, *150*, 298, *333*, 397, 405, 409, 410, 412, 413, 414, *420*
Ciarcia, J. J., 7, *38*
Ciarlo, J. A., 239, *250*, 371, 372, 450, 451, *459*
Ciervo, C. A., 385, *387*, 395, 396, 398, 401, 404, *417*, 521, *533*
Clancy, J., 137, *149*, 307, 312, 313, *332*
Clark, C. A., 116, *152*
Clark, D. A., 127, 128, *151*
Clark, D. C., 431, *457*
Clark, E., 142, *149*
Clark, J. R., 628, *649*
Clark, L. A., 144, *151*, 313, *329*
Clark, V. A., 131, *147*, 407, *417*
Clark, W., 221, *247*
Clarke, K., 68, *88*
Clarke, M., 141, *148*
Clarke-Stewart, K. A., 94, *111*
Clayton, P. J., 444, *457*
Cleary, O. D., 475, 477, 481, *489*
Cleary, P. A., 305, *330*, 336, *372*
Cleary, P. D., 119, *148*, 193, 194, *248*, *249*, 442, 443, *458*, 542, *553*, 771, 777, *793*
Cloitre, M., 445, *459*
Clyde, D. J., 777, *791*
Coben, L. A., 565, *580*
Coble, J. R., 784, *794*
Coblentz, J. M., 564, 567, *579*
Cochran, C. D., 131, *146*
Cocke, T. B., 381, *387*
Coffey, P., 315, *329*
Coggins, D. R., 118, *150*
Cohen, A., 545, *553*
Cohen, B., 55, *89*
Cohen, D., 782, *794*
Cohen, E., 510, 513, 516, 517, 519, 520, *533*

Cohen, J., 286, *296*, 316, *329*, 424, *457*
Cohen, L. J., 312, *329*
Cohen, M., 545, *553*, 654, 655, *683*
Cohen, P., 100, *113*
Cohen, S., 376, 377, 378, *388*
Cohen-Cole, S. A., 193, 220, *248*
Colantonio, A., 565, *579*
Colby, K. M., 781, *791*
Cole, J., 307, *329*
Cole, K. A., 90, 193, *251*
Cole, M. G., 574, 575, *579*
Cole, S., 12, 13, 14, 23, 26, *38*
Collaborative care requires new approaches, says internist, 18, 20, *38*
Collerton, D., 556, *580*
Colligan, R. C., 539, *553*
Collings, G. H., 307, *329*
Collins, J. F., 424, 447, 451, 452, 455, *457*, 704, *709*, 780, *791*
Commerford, K., 374, *389*
Commission on Chronic Illness, 119, *146*, 349, *371*, 596, *620*
Committee E-11 on Quality and Statistics, 605, *620*
Comstock, G. W., 131, *146*
Conboy, T., 565, *581*
Cone, D., 320, *333*
Conley, D. M., 185, 498, *506*
Connelly, J. E., 241, *251*, 521, *534*
Conners, C. K., 100, *113*
Connolly, M. B., 524, 525, *533*
Connor, J., 586, *621*
Connors, L., 53, *88*
Conoley, J. C., 184
Conolly, P., 443, *461*, 777, 778, *796*
Consoli, A. J., 784, *794*
Conwell, Y., 185, 409, *419*, 785, *791*
Cook, B. L., 313, *332*
Cook, N. R., 556, *580*
Cooper, A. F., 128, *148*
Cooper, B., 298, *331*
Cooper, J. E., 305, *334*
Cooper-Patrick, L., 185
Cope, D. W., 222, *251*, 603, 609, *621*
Copeland, J. M., 502, *508*
Corbin, S., 574, *580*
Corcoran, K., 523, *533*
Cordero-Villafafila, A., 424, *460*
Corenthal, C., 466, 473, 475, *490*
Corey-Bloom, J., 558, *580*
Coryell, W., 312, *329*, 430, 444, 446, *457*, *461*, 464, 466, 473, 475, *488*, *490*, 774, *796*
Cossa, F. M., 559, *579*
Costa e Silva, J. A., 192, *251*
Costa, J. A., 373, *388*
Costa, L., 566, *581*
Costa, P. T., 668, *682*
Costello, A. J., 95, *111*
Costello, E. J., 94, 95, 97, *111*
Cottler, L., 52, *90*, 423, *460*, 687, *711*
Coulehan, J. L., 223, 237, 239, *251*, 392, 410, 412, *417*, *420*, 688, 703, *711*, 713, *733*
Coulter, A., 589, 591, *620*
Counsell, C. M., 769, *791*
Covi, L., 119, *146*, 299, *330*, 335, *372*
Covinsky, K. E., 464, *487*
Cowper, P. A., 785, *796*

Cox, B. J., *185*, 445, *457*, 510, 513, 516, 517, 519, 520, *533*
Cox, C., *185*
Cox, D., 409, *419*
Coyle, J. T., 455, *456*
Coyne, J. C., 54, *88*, 192, 194, *248*, *252*, 379, 381, 383, 388, 392, 393, 408, 409, 410, 411, 412, 413, *417*, *418*, *419*, 464, *487*, 691, *709*
Craig, J., 628, *649*
Craig, T. J., 318, *329*
Craven, J. L., 132, *146*, 194, 233, *251*
Creamer, M., 513, 516, 517, 518, *533*
Criqui, M. H., 563, *579*
Crits-Christoph, P., 524, 525, *533*
Croghan, T. W., 768, *794*
Cromer, W. W., 102, 103, *111*
Cronbach, L. J., 288, *296*, 432, *457*, 632, *649*
Croog, S. H., 303, *329*, 584, *620*
Crook, T., 138, 142, *150*
Crook, T. H., 495, *506*
Crotty, M. T., *184*
Crough, M. A., 118, *146*
Croughan, J., *332*, *419*, 466, 467, 473, 482, *489*
Crowe, R. R., 307, *332*
Crum, R. M., *185*, 558, 559, 561, 563, 578, *579*
Csernansky, J., 141, *147*
Cubic, B., 382, *388*
Cuerdon, T., 714, *733*
Cukor, P., 455, *456*
Cummings, J. L., 72, *88*, 139, *146*, 559, *579*
Cummings, N. A., 57, 72, *88*, 714, *733*
Curry, S. J., 787, *791*
Curry, W., 48, *91*
Curtis, G. C., 307, 312, *329*
Cutlip, Q., 382, *388*
Cwikel, J., 496, *506*
Cygan, R. W., 687, *710*
Cyr, M. G., 135, *146*

D

Dahlstrom, W. G., 28, *38*, 415, *417*
Dakof, G., 379, *388*
Dalack, G. W., 238, 241, 246, *252*, 373, 374, *388*
Daltroy, L. H., 688, *709*
Damiano, A. M., 587, *620*
D'Amico, C., 570, 571, 572, *580*
Dammers, P. M., 382, *387*
Daniels, M., 192, *252*, 392, *421*, 423, 426, 444, 445, *460*, *461*, 463, 464, *490*, 687, 691, *711*
Danziger, W. L., 141, *146*, 565, *580*
Dar, R., 774, *795*
D'Ath, P., 496, 497, *506*
Davidoff, F., 156, *186*, 195, *248*
Davidson, J. R. T., 774, *791*
Davidson, K. G., 501, *506*
Davies, A. R. 7, *41*, 592, 599, *621*, 624, 625, 636, 643, *649*, *651*
Davies, M., 100, *113*, 132, *151*, 154, 155, 156, *186*, 202, 209, 211, 213, 235, 241, *250*, *252*, *253*, 392, *420*, 444, *460*, 675, *683*
Davies, R., 377, 378, *388*
Davies, S., 445, *459*
Davies, S. O., 311, *332*
Davis, B., 714, *733*

Davis, K., 95, *114*
Davis, L. J., *185*, 539, 541, 542, 543, 544, 547, 548, 549, *553*
Davis, P. B., 575, *579*
Davis, R. M., 787, *792*
Davis, T. C., 118, *146*
Davis, T. F., 56, 82, *88*
Davison, M. L., 336, 337, 339, 340, 358, *371*
Dawber, R., 655, *683*
De Best-Waldhober, M., 666, 680, *683*
de la Fuente, J. R., 548, *553*
de Vos, R. A. I., 556, *580*
Deahl, M., 128, *146*
Deardorff, W. W., 400, *417*
DeBrota, D., 426, *457*
DeGiacomo, J. M., 592, 599, *621*
deGruy, F. V., III, 7, 8, *39*, 52, 57, *72*, *88*, 154, 155, 156, *184*, *186*, 191, 193, 194, 196, 197, 202, 208, 209, 210, 211, 216, 218, 219, 221, 226, 234, 235, 241, 246, *247*, *248*, 249, *250*, *252*, 253, 280, *296*, 392, *420*, 423, 442, 443, 444, *458*, *460*, 653, 654, 664, 665, 667, 669, 675, 678, *682*, *683*, 694, *711*, 756, *760*
Dein, E., 431, *456*, 776, *790*
DeKosky, S. T., 575, *581*
Del Vecchio, P., 15, 17, *38*
Del Vento, A., 687, 688, 689, 694, 695, 698, 699, 701, 707, *710*
deLeon, M., 138, 142, *150*
Delgado, A., 140, 141, *148*
Delgado, P. L., 225, 227, *248*
D'Elia, L., 142, *149*
Delis, D. C., 561, 562, 563, 578, *580*
Deliyannides, D., 449, *460*
DellaPietra, L., 33, *38*, 119, *146*, 299, 310, 318, *330*, 349, 350, 353, *372*
DeLongis, A., 379, *388*
Deming, W. B., 590, *620*
Demitrack, M. A., 426, *457*
Demotts, J., 396, *420*
DeNour, A. K., 320, *328*
Dent, H. R., 512, 515, *533*
Depression Guideline Panel, 215, 221, 225, 227, *248*, 399, 403, *417*, 423, 442, 443, 444, 445, 447, 449, 451, *457*, 464, 465, 466, 478, 479, 484, *487*, 488, 602, *620*, 689, *709*, 771, 772, 773, 786, *791*
Depression still undertreated despite efforts to redress, 10, 13, 16, *38*
DePue, J. D., 787, *791*
Dermigny, R., *794*
Derogatis, L. R., 29, 33, *38*, 115, 117, 118, 119, 130, 131, 144, 145, *146*, *147*, 297, 298, 299, 301, 302, 304, 305, 306, 307, 308, 309, 310, 318, 326, *328*, *329*, *330*, 335, 336, 349, 350, 353, *371*, 372, 396, 407, *417*
Derogatis, M. F., 119, *146*, 306, *330*, 396, 407, *417*
DeRosear, L., 216, *247*
DeSoto, C. B., 323, *330*
Detection of psychological disorders unrelated to outcomes, 12, 13, 16, 28, *38*
Detels, R., 785, *794*
Deutch, A. Y., 377, *388*
Devina, N. P., 691, *709*
Devins, N. P., 277, *296*
Devlin, M., 202, *252*

Devlin, M. J., *334*
Dew, M. A., 194, *248*, 321, *330*, 576, 578, *582*
Deyo, R. A., 192, *247*
DiBartolo, P. M., 522, 527, *533*
Dick, J., 140, *147*
Dickey, B., 30, 35, *39*, *41*, 128, 132, *147*, *150*
Dickson, D. W., 556, *580*
DiClemente, C. C., 47, 69, *90*, 225, 228, *251*
Dietz, L. S., 381, 382, *387*
Dill, D. L., *185*
Dillman, D. A., 628, 644, *649*
DiMascio, A., 449, *457*
DiMatteo, M. R., 625, *649*
Dinkgreve, M. A. H. M., 426, *458*
Directions: Anxiety costs, 9, *39*
Direnfeld, D. M., 445, *457*, 510, 513, 516, 517, 519, 520, *533*
Dismuke, S. E., 116, *150*
Dittus, R. S., 136, *146*
Dixon, K., 19, 21, *39*
Dobie, R., 325, *333*
Dobler-Mikola, A., 311, *328*
Dobson, K. S., 399, *417*, *502*, *506*, 509, *533*, 708, *709*, 780, *792*
Docherty, J. P., 318, *333*, 424, 447, 451, 452, 455, *457*, 704, *709*, 780, *791*
Doherty, W., 717, *733*
Doherty, W. J., 23, 25, *39*, 72, 84, *88*
Dohrenwend, B. P., 116, *147*, 237, *248*, 378, 383, *388*, *390*
Dohrenwend, B. S., 378, *388*
Dolan, S., 137, *151*, 312, *333*
Dolinsky, A., 132, *151*
Donaldson, M. S., 4, *39*
Dongier, M., 324, *330*
Donovan, S. J., 449, *460*
Dorken, H., 714, *733*
Dornseif, B. E., 439, *457*
Dorwart, R. A., 36, *39*
Dottl, L., 203, 221, 229, 241, *249*
Dottl, S. L., 31, *40*, 426, 443, 450, *459*, 756, 760, 774, 775, 777, 778, 781, 782, *791*, *792*, 793, *794*
Douglass, A., 238, 241, 246, *252*
Dowdall, D., 512, 513, 516, 517, 518, 520, 524, *533*
Downie, F., 512, 513, 517, 518, *533*
Dowrick, D., 237, *248*
Doyle, G., 141, *147*
Dozier-Hall, D., 134, *152*
Drachman, R. H., *649*
Drane, D. L., 571, 572, 573, *580*
Draper, D., 496, *508*
Dreher, H., 7, *39*
Driever, M., 374, *389*
Drinka, T. J. K., 497, *507*
Drossman, D. A., 326, *330*, 656, *682*
Drotar, D., 98, 99, 102, 103, 104, *111*, *114*
Drude, K., 131, *150*, 310, *333*
Duke, L. W., 565, *580*, *581*
Dulcan, M. K., 95, *111*
Dunbar, G. C., 778, 779, *795*
Dunbar-Jacob, J., 589, *621*
Duncan, B. A., 785, *791*
Duncan-Jones, P., 413, *417*
Dunlop, S. R., 439, *457*
Dunman, R. S., 84, *88*
Dunn, E., 558, *582*

Dunn, L. O., 194, *248*
Dunn, R. L., 68, *88*
Dunn, S., 141, *147*
DuPont, R. L., 307, *329*
Dusseault, K., 101, *111*
Dworkin, M., 311, *331*
Dworkin, S. F, 115, *151*, 297, *333*
Dworkind, M., 193, 194, *249*, *251*, 411, *418*
Dyer, H. R., 379, *389*
Dyer, J. G., 769, *791*
Dymek, M. P., 565, *580*

E

Eastwood, M. R., 574, *580*
Eaton, W. W., 463, 473, *488*
Ebbit, B., 498, *507*
Eber, B., 567, *581*
Ebrahim, S., 142, *148*
Eckerle, D., 104, *111*
Edelbrock, C., 95, *111*
Eden, D. T., 131, *149*
Edmunds, M., 4, 14, 17, 20, *39*
Edwards, A. L., 437, *457*
Edwards, B. C., 403, 404, *417*, 424, *457*, *459*
Edwards, D., 141, *146*
Edwards, R. K., 374, *387*
Edwardson, J. A., 556, *580*
Efforts to integrate with primary care, 18, 26, *39*
Ehrhardt, A. A., 322, *334*
Eisen, S. V., 132, *147*, *185*
Eisenberg, L., 155, 156, *186*, 415, *418*, 423, 442, *457*, 465, *488*
Eisenstein, E., 786, *790*
Eisenstein, N., 571, *580*
Eisert, D. C., 100, *111*, *114*
Eldridge, D., 625, *649*
Elkin, B., 704, *709*
Elkin, I., 424, 447, 451, 452, 455, *457*, 780, *791*
Ellingson, A. G., 403, 404, *417*, 424, *457*
Ellwood, P. M., 480, *488*
Elstein, A. S., H. S., 126, *151*
Emery, G., 394, *417*
Emmelkamp, P. M. G., 386, *390*
Emory, G., 446, 447, *456*, 781, *790*
Employers' health costs held down in 1997, 3, *39*
Empting, L., 564, *580*
Ende, J., 221, *250*
Endicott, J., 156, *186*, 194, 195, *248*, *252*, 410, *418*, *420*, 424, 428, 444, *457*, *460*, 464, *488*
Engberg, S., 589, *621*
Engelhart, C., 571, *580*
Englen, R. G., 103, *112*
Enns, M. W., *185*
Enterline, J. P., 131, *152*, 306, 310, *334*
Epstein, N., 435, *456*, 509, 510, 511, 512, 513, 516, 517, 518, 519, 524, *533*
Eraker, S. A., 625, *649*
Erbaugh, J. K., 132, *146*, 236, *247*, 279, *296*, 393, 405, 407, *417*, 427, 429, 435, *456*, 466, 474, *487*, 501, *506*, 781, 786, *790*
Erdman, H. P., 781, 786, *791*, *795*
Erickson, S. M., 769, *791*
Erien, A., 589, *621*
Erikkson, J., 133, *147*

Erkinjuntti, T., 574, *580*
Eschleman, S., 391, *418*
Escobar, J. I., 140, *147*, 201, 202, *248*
Eshleman, S., 6, *39*, 192, *249*, 687, *709*, 756, *760*
Espindle, D. M., 592, 599, *621*
Essau, C.A., 509, *534*
Evans, C., 128, *146*, 277, *296*
Evans, D. A., 556, *580*
Evans, G. W., 590, *621*
Evans, S., 496, 497, *506*
Evers-Szostak, M., 96, 103, 106, *112*
Ewigman, B. G., 772, *790*
Ewing, J. A., 200, *248*
Eyberg, S. M., 100, *112, 113*

F

FAACT Staff, 473, *488*
Fabb, W. E., 200, *250*
Fairbairn, A. S., 426, *457*
Fairbum, C. G., 305, *332*
Falconer, J. J., 378, *388*
Fallon, B., 445, *459*
Fallstrom, K., 498, *507*
Fals-Stewart, W., 571, *580*
Faragher, E., 193, *248*
Faravelli, C., 375, *388*
Farber, L., 155, 157, 158, *185, 186*, 443, *461*, 777, 778, *796*
Farber, N. J., 33, *41*, 136, 137, *149*, 192, *253*
Faries, D., 426, *457*
Farmer, A., 214, *248*
Farnot, U., 373, *389*
Fast, J., 787, *795*
Fauman, M. A., 118, *147*
Faust, D., 140 141, *147*
Faustman, W., 141, *147*
Fava, G. A., 424, *457*, 502, *506*
Fava, M., 501, *506*, 558, *579*
Favero, R. V., 405, *419*
Fawzy, F. I., 57, *88*
Fawzy, N. W., 57, *88*
Faxekas, F., 567, *581*
Fechner-Bates, S., 54, *88*, 192, 194, *248, 252*, 392, 393, 409, 410, 411, 412, *417, 418*, 464, *487*
Feher, E. P., 495, *506*
Feightner, J. W., 407, *418*
Feinberg, M., 424, *457*
Feiner, J. S., 675, *682*
Feinstein, A., 590, 593, 599, *620*
Felice, M. E., 98, 99, *114*
Fenton, G. W., 786, *792*
Ferguson, R. J., 529, *533*
Ferris, S., 138, 142, *150*
Fetting, J. H., 131, *147*, 152, 297, 306, 310, *330, 334*
Feussner, J. R., 209, 237, *250*, 472, *488*
Fichter, M. M., 313, *332*
Ficken, J., 27, 32, 33, *39*, 335, 353, *372*
Ficken, R. P., 118, *148*, 193, 194, *247*, 464, *488*
Fiester, S. J., 424, 447, 451, 452, 455, *457*, 704, *709*, 780, *791*
Fife, M., 319, *333*
Fifer, S. K., 392, *420*, 521, *533*, 713, *732*
Figueroa, S., 238, 241, 246, *252*
Filer, S., 118, *152*

Fillenbaum, G. G., 785, *791*
Filos, S., 785, *794*
Fineberg, H. V., 126, *151*
Finkelstein, S. N., 125, *145*, 463, 473, *488*
Finklestein, M. D., 540, 541, *553*
Finlayson, R. E., 688, 708, *710*
Finn, S. E., 356, 364, *372*
Finney, J. W., 96, 104, *112*
Fiore, M. C., 787, *792*
Fireman, B. H., 443, *461*, 777, 778, *796*
First, M. B., 192, 195, 206, 213, *252*, 253, 285, *296*, 434, *460*, 466, 473, 475, 482, *489*, 500, *508*, 521, *534*, 792
Firth, J., 307, *333*
Fischer, H. L., 103, *112*
Fischer, J., 523, *533*
Fischer, L. R., 56, 82, *88*
Fishback, D., 142, *147*
Fishbourne, R. P., 627, 643, *650*
Fisher, D. G., 325, *331*
Fisher, L., 564, *580*
Fisher, P., 100, *113*
Fisher, R. H., 558, *582*
Fitzgerald, J. L., 786, *792*
Fitzgibbon, M., 402, *418*
Flaker, G., 216, *247*
Flaum, M., 213, *247*
Fleiss, J. L., 412, *420*, 424, *457*
Fleming, G. V., 625, *649*
Fleming, K. C., 556, 564, *580*
Flesch, R. A., 410, *418*, 627, 643, *649*
Fleshner, M., 377, *389*
Fletcher, C. M., 426, *457*
Flett, G. L., 394, *420*
Flint, A. J., 501, *506*
Flynn, M., 576, *581*
Fogel, B., 140, 141, *147*
Fogleman, B. S., 116, *150*
Foley, M., 322, *331*
Folkman, S., 377, 378, 379, *388, 389*
Folks, D. G., 565, *581*
Follette, W. C., 317, *331*, 360, *372*
Folstein S., 140, *147*
Folstein, M. F., 140, 142, *147, 150, 151*, 557, 558, 559, 560, 561, 563, 578, *579, 580*
Foran, J., 513, 516, 517, 518, *533*
Ford, C. V., 373, *388*
Ford, D. E., 135, *147,185*, 221, *247*
Ford, E. D., 54, *88*
Ford, G. T., 512, 513, 514, 515, 516, *533*
Forehand, G., 630, *649*
Foreman, M., 141, *147*
Forman, L., 782, *792*
Forrieris, C. A., 523, *533*
Forsyth, B., 95, 97, *112*
Forsythe, A., 140, *147*, 201, 202, *248*
Fortinsky, R. H., 464, *487*
Fortney, J., 463, 464, *489*
Fossel, A. H., 608, *620*
Fox, B. H., 318, *333*
Frame, P. S., 196, *248*
Francis, V., 625, *649*, 656, *682*
Franco, K., 277, *296*
Franco, R., 713, *732*
Frank, B., 446, *461*
Frank, D., 625, *649*

Frank, E., 137, *146,* 312, *329,* 441, *457*
Frank, R., 4, 9, *9,* 14, 17, 20, *41,* 118, *150,* 298, *333,* 397,
      405, 409, 410, 412, 413, 414, *420*
Frank, R. G., 463, 473, *488*
Frankenburg, W. K., 100, *112*
Frasure-Smith, N., 57, *88*
Frazier, H., 625, *651*
Frazier, P. A., 314, *330*
Fredrickson, P. A., 546, *553*
Freedheim, K. D., 96, *113*
Freedland, K. E., 68, *88*
Freedman, M., 561, 562, 563, 578, *580*
Freeling, P., 194, *248*
Freeman, A., 193, *248*
Freeman, M. A., 19, *39*
Freeman, M. R., 570, 572, *581*
Freidl, W., 567, *581*
Frerichs, R. R., 131, *147,* 407, *417*
Freyer, F. J., 777, *792*
Fricchione, G. L., 325, 327, *330*
Fricton, J. R., 79, *88*
Fried, L. E., 157, *186*
Friedhoff, A. J., 491, 499, 501, 503, *507*
Friedman, H. S., 625, *649*
Friedman, M. J., 377, *388*
Friedman, R., 10, 18, 23, 26, *39*
Friend, R., 311, *332*
Froom, J., 156, *186,* 195, *248*
Fruzzetti, A. E., 424, 426, *461*
Fuld, P. A., 575, *580*
Fulop, G., 116, 137, *147,* 151
Funabiki, D., 400, *417*
Funckenstein, H. H., 556, *580*
Furher, R., 138, 141, *147*
Fydrich, T., 512, 513, 516, 517, 518, 520, 524, *533*
Fye, E. B., 687, *710*

G

Gage, L. W., 374, *388*
Gagliardi, A., 788, *793*
Galasko, D., 556, 558, *580*
Galbreath, L., 714, *733*
Gallagher, D., 306, *333,* 395, *418*
Gallagher-Thompson, D., 502, *507, 508*
Galton, F., 128, *147*
Gandek, B., 30, *41,* 342, *372,* 470, 481, 482, 484, 485,
      486, *490,* 584, 585, 586, 587, 588, 589, 590,
      591, 592, 593, *621,* 738, *760*
Gandhavadi, B., 571, *581*
Gandhi S., 141, *148*
Ganguli, M., 118, *150,* 298, *333,* 397, 405, 409, 410, 412,
      413, 414, *420*
Gany, F., 137, *151*
Garbin, M. G., 395, 396, 404, *417*
Garcia, C., 373, *389*
Gardner, G., 664, 666, 668, *683*
Gardner, R., 564, *580*
Garner, D. M., 311, 325, *333*
Garrett, R. W., 415, *419,* 687, *710*
Garrett, V. D., 382, *388*
Garrison, B., 395, *420*
Garvey, M. J., 137, *149,* 312, 313, *332*
Gask, L., 236, *247,* 248
Gaskin, S., 193, 194, *247*

Gath, D. H., 56, *89,* 375, *389,* 688, 691, 703, 704, 706,
      709, 710
Gau, G. T., 115, 134, *145,* 299, 310, 322, *328*
Gawinski, B. A., 72, *90*
Gaydos, G. R., 382, *387*
Gazmararian, J. A., 158, *186*
Geissner, E., 313, *332*
Gelenberg, A. J., 225, 227, *248*
Geller, G., 221, *250*
George, C., 495, *508*
George, D. T., 118, 119, *152,* 237, *253,* 464, *490*
George, L. K., 7, *39,* 115, 118, *149,* 150, *194, 250,* 279,
      296, 299, 310, *332,* 423, 443, 445, 456, *459,*
      777, *794*
Gerber, P. D., 115, 116, *145,* 213, *247,* 279, *296,* 307,
      329, 445, *456*
Gerbert, B., 625, 643, *649*
Gerety, M. B., 214, 237, 241, *250,* 392, 400, 401, *419*
Gerken, A., 431, *459*
German, P., 52, *90,* 118, 119, 140, *149,* 150, 192, 213,
      236, 237, *252,423, 460,* 687, *711,*
Gershenson, D. M., 319, *333*
Geschwind, N., 139, *149*
Getzinger, A., 714, *733*
Ghadiri, A., 786, *790*
Ghinelli, F., 323, *331*
Ghoneim, M. M., 307, *332*
Ghonheim, M. M., 131, *149*
Ghosh, A., 771, 774, 786, *791*
Giambra, L. M., 402, *418*
Gibbon, M., 192, 194, 195, 206, 213, *252, 253,* 285, *296,*
      434, *460,* 466, 473, 475, 482, *489,* 500, *508,*
      521, *534, 792*
Giese-Davis, J., 318, *331*
Gift, A. G., 306, *330*
Gilbar, O., 319, *330*
Gilbert, B. O., 700, *710*
Gilbert, J. B., 781, *791*
Gilbert, T., *185,* 200, *250*
Gilbert, T. T., 443, *456*
Gillis, J. S., 375, *388*
Gillis, M. M., 512, 513, 514, 515, 516, *533*
Gilmer, T. D., 47, *88*
Gingrich, R., 135, *148*
Ginsberg, B., 137, *151*
Giovino, G. A., 787, *792*
Girard, N., 769, *792*
Gladis, M., *334*
Glajchen, M., 134, *152*
Glaser, R., 378, *388*
Glass, D. R., 424, 447, 451, 452, 455, *457,* 704, *709,* 780,
      791
Glass, G., 714, *733*
Glass, R. M., 195, *248*
Glassman, A. H., 57, *88*
Glatt, S. L., 566, 567, *581*
Glazer, W., 324, *333*
Glenn, M., 717, *733*
Gloyd, S. V., 241, *250*
Godsall, R. E., 565, *582*
Goetsch, V. L., 382, *388*
Goetz, D. M., 446, *459*
Goetz, R. R., 323, *331*
Goetzel, R. Z., 68, *88*
Goisman, R. M., 781, *792*
Gold, M. S., 259, *275*

Goldberg, D. P., 116, 131, *146, 147, 148,* 191, 192, 193, 194, 236, 237, 247, *248, 249, 251,* 299, *329*
Goldberg, G., 473, 478, *490*
Goldberg, I. D., 52, *90,* 94, 97, *112,* 116, 117, *150,* 277, *296,* 391, *419,* 687, *710*
Goldberg, R. B., 780, *794*
Goldberger, E., 137, *151,* 312, *333*
Goldfarb, A., 140, 142, *148*
Golding, J. M., 8, *41,* 140, *147,* 201, 202, *248*
Goldman, P. A., 128, *151,* 409, *417*
Goldsmith, M., 135, *147*
Goldstein, L., 342, 343, 350, 351, 352, 356, *372*
Goldstein, M., 156, *186,* 195, *248*
Goldstein, M. G., 787, *791*
Gollan, J. K., 708, *709,* 780, *792*
Golwig, T. G., 776, *790*
Gonzales, J., 714, *733*
Goode, K. T., 565, *580*
Gooden, T., 498, *507*
Goodman, C. C., *792*
Goodman, J., 576, *581*
Goodwin, F. J., 53, *88*
Goodwin, F. K., 8, 12, *40,* 52, *90,* 145, *150,* 192, *251,* 463, *489*
Goodwin, J. M., 655, *682*
Goodwin, J. S., 655, *682*
Gordis, E., 786, *792*
Gordon, B. N., 103, *113*
Gordon, G. H., *249,* 655, *682*
Gordon, L. U., 376, 377, 378, *388*
Goreczny, A. J., 381, 382, *387,388*
Gorman, J. M., 156, *186,* 195, *248,* 322, *334*
Gorsuch, R. L., 509, 511, *534*
Gortner, E., 708, *709,* 780, *792*
Goss, T. F., 587, *620*
Gotay, C. C., 134, *148,* 320, *331*
Gotlib, I. H., 400, *418,* 509, *534*
Gould, J. W., 132, *150,* 395, *419*
Gouvier, W. D., 382, *388*
Gozzi, E. K., 656, *682*
Grace, J., 561, 562, 563, *582*
Grafman, J. F., 561, 562, *582*
Graham, J. R., 28, *38*
Graham, P. J., 101, *113*
Gram, L. F., 431, *456,* 776, *790*
Grands, S., 502, *506*
Grant, E., 575, *579*
Grant, I., 322, *328*
Grant, J. R., 315, *333*
Grassi, L., 320, 323, *331*
Gravenstein, S., 497, *507*
Graziano, F., 788, *792*
Greden, J. F., 313, *328*
Greden, J. F. F., 424, *457*
Green, B. F., 427, *458*
Green, J., 395, 420, 566, *580*
Green, R C., 565, 566, *580, 582*
Green, W. G., 786, *791*
Greenberg, E., 115, *150,* 297, *333*
Greenberg, P. E., 463, 473, *488*
Greenfield, S., 154, *186,* 192, *252,* 392, *421,* 423, 444, 445, *461,* 463, 464, 473, 482, *489, 490,* 687, 691, *711, 733,* 777, *796*
Greenfield, T. K., 409, *421*
Greenfields, S., 259, *275*
Greenhouse, J., 576, 578, *582*

Greenland, P., 541, 542, *553*
Greist, J. H., 8, 31, 32, *39, 40,* 192, 203, 221, 229, 241, *248, 249,* 423, 424, 426, 428, 441, 443, 445, 450, *457, 458, 459, 460,* 464, *488,* 756, *760,* 770, 771, 774, 775, 776, 777, 778, 780, 781, 782, 786, *791, 792, 793, 794, 795*
Greist, M. H., 781, *795*
Grembowski, D., 57, *91*
Griel, R., 305, *334*
Grieshofer, P., 567, *581*
Griez, E., 426, *458*
Griffith, B. P., 321, *330*
Griger, M. L., 327, *332*
Griner, P. F., 541, 542, *553*
Grinker, R. R., 378, *388*
Grissom, G. R., 11, 15, 26, 27, *41,* 184, 257, 259, *275*
Gritz, E. R., 319, *334*
Grob, M. C., 132, *147, 185*
Grosby, H., 133, *145*
Grothaus, L. C., 223, *252,* 603, *621,* 787, *791*
Groves, J. E., 654, 657, *682*
Gruenberg, F., 509, *534*
Gruman, J., 48, *91*
Grunberg, N., 378, *387*
Guarnaccia, C. A., 383, *390*
Guarnaccia, P. J., 407, *418*
Guertin, J. E., *185*
Guide, B., 195, *251*
Guiloff, R., 140, *147*
Guin, P. R., 769, *791*
Guise, B., 423, *460,* 464, 465, *489,* 777, *795*
Guiterrez, L., 548, *553*
Gullion, C. M., 466, 474, 475, *489*
Gundersheimer, J., 561, 562, *582*
Gunn, W. B., 72, *90*
Gunter-Hunt, G., 497, *507*
Gurland, B. J., 785, *792*
Gustafson, D. H., 428, *457,* 774, 787, 788, *792*
Guth, D., *184,* 385, *387,* 396, 398, 401, 404, *416*
Guthrie, D., 156, *186,* 195, *248*
Guthrie, M., 326, *334*
Guy, W., 424, *457*
Guze, S. B., 544, *553*

H

Haaga, D. A. F., 411, *418,* 512, 513, 514, 515, 516, *533*
Haber, J. D., 3, 14, 17, 20, 23, 26, 28, 31, *39, 40,* 72, *88*
Habert, B. A., 115, *150*
Habert, M., 299, 325, *333*
Hadac, R. R., 625, *650*
Hadigan, C. M., *334*
Hadorn, D., 590, *620*
Hagerson, S. J., 775, *792*
Haggerty, R. J., 94, *112,* 373, *389*
Haglund, R., 141, *148*
Hahn, S. R., 7, 8, 31, *39, 41,* 154, 155, 156, *184, 186,* 191, 196, 197, 201, 202, 205, 206, 208, 209, 210, 211, 216, 218, 219, 221, 222, 226, 231, 234, 235, 241, 244, 246, *247, 248, 249, 250, 252, 253,* 280, *296,* 392, 420, 423, 442, 443, 444, *458, 460,* 653, 654, 657, 659, 664, 665, 667, 669, 674, 675, 678, *682, 683,* 694, *711, 756, 760*
Hain, J., 193, *248*
Hajek, V., 139, *148*

Hale, W. D., 131, *146*
Hales, R. E., 602, *620*
Hall, J. A., *90*, 193, *251*, 656, *682*, 688, *709*
Hall, P., 544, *554*
Halvorson, G., 47, *88*
Hamer, M. E., 321, *331*
Hamilton, M., 133, *148*, 407, *418*, 424, 425, 447, 457, 458, 466, 474, *488*, 500, *507*, 776, *792*
Hamlett, K. W., 102, *112*
Hammen, C. L., 400, 401, 402, 403, 404, 405, *418*
Hammill, K., 769, *791*
Hammond, W. E., 608, *621*
Hampton, C., 311, *332*
Hankin, J., 7, *39*, 117, *150*
Hanley, J. A., 126, *148*
Hanna, M. P., 768, *794*
Hannum, A., 318, *331*
Hansen, L. A., 556, 566, 568, 569, 578, *580*, *581*
Hansen, N. B., 527, *534*
Hansom, J., 315, *334*
Hansson, L., 115, *148*, 192, *248*
Harding, K., 318, *331*
Hargreaves, W. A., 625, 643, *649*, *651*
Harper, R., 588, 590, 591, *620*
Harrah, C. H., 785, *794*
Harrell, L. E., 565, *580*, *581*
Harrington, J. B., 409, *418*
Harris, P. B., *795*
Harrison, W., 311, *332*, 446, *459*
Harrop-Griffiths, J., 315, 325, *333*, *334*
Hart, R. P., 138, 139, 140, *148*
Harthorn, B. H., 118, 119, *145*, 277, 236, 247, 296
Hartman, J., 193, 194, 247
Hartung, J., 33, *41*, 192, *253*
Hasin, D., 202, *252*
Hass, S. D., 570, 572, *581*
Hasset, T., 323, *333*
Hatch, D. R., 424, *459*
Hatfield, A. K., 318, *331*
Hathaway, S. R., 405, *418*
Hatziandreu, E. J., 787, *792*
Haven, C., 443, *461*
Hawkins, C., 47, 48, *90*
Hawkins, N. C., 377, 378, *388*
Hawkins, R. P., 787, 788, *792*
Hawton, K., 116, *148*
Hayes, R. D., 392, *421*
Hayes, S. C., 688, 706, *709*
Hays, R. D., 154, *186*, 192, 206, 209, *252*, 259, 275, 423, 444, 445, 455, *458*, *461*, 463, 464, *490*, 590, *620*, 625, 630, *649*, 687, 691, *711*, *733*, 777, *796*
Hayshi, T., 630, *649*
Health care spending, 3, *39*
Health Enhancement Research Organization (HERO) Research Committee, 68, *88*
Healthcare Intranet Report, 699, *709*
Heather, N., 786, *792*
Hebert, L. E., 556, *580*
Hedemark, N., 9, *41*
HEDIS, 49, *89*
Hedlund, J. L., 133, *148*, 424, *458*
Hedlund, S. C., 134, *152*
Heerlein, A., 404, *419*
Heersema, P. H., 492, *506*
Heiligenstein, J. H., 223, *252*

Heindel, W. C., 567, *581*
Heinrich, R. L., 21, *40*, 50, 56, 57, 71, 77, 81, 82, 84, 85, 86, *88*, *89*, *90*
Heirnan, J. R., 373, *387*
Hellman, C. J., 53, 55, *89*
Helms, L. J., 391, *417*, 691, *708*
Helms, M. J., 142, *151*
Helsing, K. J., 131, *146*
Helstad, C. P., 424, 452, *458*, 769, *793*
Helzer, J. E., 115, *150*, 192, 214, *248*, *251*, 297, 332, 333, 419, 444, *458*, 466, 467, 473, 482, *489*, 500, *507*, 509, *534*, 787, *795*
Hemingway, H., 589, 593, *620*
Henark-Zolten, K., 101, *113*
Henderson, S., 413, *417*
Hendon, A., 101, *113*
Hendrichs, M., 297, *330*
Hendrie, H. C., 136, *146*
Hendriks, V. M., 324, *333*
Heneman, S. W., 781, 782, *794*
Heninger, G. R., 84, *88*
Henk, H. J., 8, 31, *39*, *40*, 192, 203, 221, 229, 241, *248*, 249, 423, 424, 426, 443, 450, 452, *458*, *459*, 464, *488*, 756, 760, 769, 770, 774, 777, 778, 780, 782, *792*, *793*
Henke, C., 714, *733*
Hennekens, C. H., 556, *580*
Henning, K., 315, *329*
Henrichs, M., 131, *147*
Henriquess, A. I., 774, *790*
Hepworth, J., 717, *733*
Hercz, L., 770, *793*
Hergueta, T., 778, 779, *795*
Herman, D. S., 523, *534*
Herman, S., 784, *794*
Hermann, R. C., 35, *41*
Hernandez, J., 314, *331*
Herndon, J., 319, *333*
Herrmann, N., 496, *507*
Hersen, M., 424, 430, *461*, 512, 515, 516, 517, 518, 519, 521, *534*
Hertzog, C., 407, *418*
Hesdorffer, D., 574, *582*
Hickok, L. R., 315, *334*
Hickson, G., 95, *112*
Higgins, E. S., 11, 12, 15, *39*, 443, 456, *461*, 777, 778, *796*
Hile, M. G., 786, *792*
Hill, J. L., 561, 562, *582*
Hill, L. R., 785, *792*
Hiller, W., 313, *332*
Hillier, V. F., 131, *148*, 191, 236, *248*
Hilty, D. A., 602, *620*
Himmelhoch, J. M., 424, 430, *461*
Hinkin, C. H., 570, *580*
Hinrich, J. V., 131, *149*, 191, 236, *248*
Hirsch, J., 774, 775, *793*
Hirsch, S. H., 222, *251*, 603, 609, *621*
Hirschfeld, R. M. A., 145, *150*, 156, *186*, 192, 195, *248*, *251*, 444, 457, 464, *488*
Hodges, L. F., 784, *795*
Hodroff, M., 775, *795*
Hoeper, E. W., 117, 119, *148*, *150*, 237, *249*
Hofer, P. J., 427, *458*
Hoffman, H. G., 784, 785, *791*
Hofmann, S. G., 522, 527, *533*

Hofmans-Okkes, I., 695, *709*
Hofstetter, R., 575, *580*
Hogan, M., 4, 14, 17, 20, *39*
Hohmann, A. A., 52, 53, *89, 93, 113*
Hokkanen, L., 574, *580*
Holahan, C. J., 379, *388*
Holahan, C. K., 379, *388*
Holden, E. W., 104, *112*
Holland, J. C., 319, 320, *332, 333*
Holland, J. F., 319, *333*
Hollander, E., 445, *459*
Hollander, O., 135, *148*
Hollenberg, J. A., 473, 479, 481, *489*
Hollon, S. D., 401, 402, 403, 404, 405, *417, 418, 419,*
        430, 446, 447, 448, *458, 459, 460,* 502, *507,*
        706, *710,* 780, *792*
Holm, L., 315, *334*
Holmes, T. H., 53, *89,* 377, 378, *388*
Holzer, C. E., III, 297, *332*
Hooijer, C., 426, *458*
Hopkins, T. B., 135, *148*
Hoppe, R. B., 220, *252*
Horne, R. L., 202, *252*
Horowitz, L. M., 302, *331*
Horst, T., 14, *39*
Horvath, M., 304, *329*
Horwath, E., 391, *418*
Horwitz, S. M., 95, 97, *112*
Hospers, H. J., 787, *795*
Houck, P., 688, 703, *711*
Houck, P. K., 223, 237, 239, *251*
Houck, P. R., *417*
Hough, R. L., 7, *39,* 279, *296,* 472, *488*
Houpt, J. L., 118, *149,* 194, *250,* 423, *459,* 777, *794*
Houston, M. J., 494, *506*
Hoven, C., 777, 778, *796*
Howanitz, E., 325, 327, *330*
Howard, K. I., 11, 15, 26, 27, *41,* 256, 257, 259, 260, 270,
        275, 316, *332,* 630, *649,* 687, *709*
Howard, M. T., 396, *420*
Howarth, E., 445, *458*
Howe, B. A., 314, *334*
Howes, M. J., 213, *253,* 277, *296,* 691, *709*
Hsu, M. A., 587, *620*
Huang, M. P., 788, *792*
Huang, V., 492, *508,* 785, *796*
Hubble, J. P., 566, 567, *581*
Hudson, C. J., 312, *329*
Hueston, W. J., 192, *249*
Huff, F. J., 565, *579*
Hughes, C. P., 565, *580*
Hughes, H. M., 314, *329*
Hughes, M. D., 6, *39,* 192, *249,* 391, 409, *418,* 687, *709,*
        756, *760*
Hughson, A. V. M., 128, *148*
Hui, S. L, 136, *146,* 491, *506*
Humphrey, J., 194, *251,* 465, *489*
Hunkeler, E. M., 779, *792*
Hunt, S., 583, *621*
Hurley, J. R., 305, *331*
Hurley, L. K., 96, 103, *112*
Hurry, M. J., 382, *390*
Hurt, R. D., *185,* 539, 543, 546, 547, *553, 554*
Hurt, S. W., 525, *533*
Husaini, B. A., 409, *418*
Huska, J. A., 523, *534*

Husum, B., 133, *145*
Hwang, S. S., 463, *488*
Hyun, C. D., 57, *88*

I

Iezzoni, L. I., 366, *372,* 608, *620*
Iker, H., 625, *649*
Illback, R. J., 94, *112*
Imber, S. D., 223, 237, 239, *251,* 424, 447, 451, 452,
        455, 457, 688, 703, 704, *709, 711,* 780, *791*
Impara, J. C., *185*
Ince, P. G., 556, *580*
Ingram, R. E., 401, 402, 403, 404, 405, *418*
Inouye, S. K., 577, *580*
Institute for International Research, 7, *39*
Institute of Medicine, 623, 626, 627, 628, *649, 650*
Invi, T., 641, 647, *650*
Isaac, M., 373, *388*
Isham, G., 47, 48, 51, *89, 90*
Israel, Y., 135, *148*
Ivnik, R. J., 558, 559, 560, 561, 565, 567, 578, *581, 582*
Izal, M., *581*

J

Jachuck, S. J., 584, *620*
Jackson, C. A., 599, *621*
Jackson, D. N., 511, *534*
Jackson, J. L., 216, 241, *249,* 423, *459,* 664, 666, 667,
        668, 669, 670, *682*
Jacob, R. G., 527, *534*
Jacobowski, P., 706, *709*
Jacobs, D. G., 455, *456,* 695, *709*
Jacobs, J., 140, 141, *148*
Jacobs, K. W., 402, *418*
Jacobsen, O., 431, *456,* 776, *790*
Jacobson, N. S., 424, 426, 447, 448, *458, 461*
Jacobson, G. F., 472, *488*
Jacobson, M. S., 317, *331*
Jacobson, N. S., 144, *148,* 317, *331,* 360, 361, 364, 365,
        369, *372,* 526, 527, *534,* 706, 708, *709,* 780,
        792
Jadad, A. R., 788, *793*
Jaffrey, F., 789, *790*
Jagger, C., 141, *148*
James, D. H., 772, *796*
Jamison, C., 500, *507*
Jamison, K. R., 53, *88*
Janavs, J., 778, 779, *795*
Janca, A., 373, *388*
Jandorf, L., 325, 327, *330*
Jansen, E. N. H., 556, *580*
Jarrett, R. B., 466, 474, 475, *489*
Jarvik, L., 142, *149,* 491, *507*
Jatlow, P. I., 446, *459*
Jefferson, J. W., 8, 31, 32, *39, 40,* 192, 203, 221, 229,
        241, 248, *249,* 423, 424, 426, 428, 441, 443,
        450, *458, 459, 460,* 464, *488,* 756, *760,* 770,
        771, 774, 775, 776, 777, 778, 780, 782, 791,
        792, 793, 794
Jefries, S. K., 688, *709*
Jellinek, M. S., 100, 101, *111, 112*
Jellinger, K. A., 556, *580*
Jenkins, C. D., 303, *329*
Jenkins, D., 584, *620*

Jenkins, L., 193, *248*
Jenkins, R., 7, 16, *39*
Jenkinson, C., 589, 591, *620*
Jenks, S. F., 193, *249*
Jenuleson, C. S., 592, 599, *621*
Jitapunkul, S., 142, *148*
Johndrow, D. A., 97, *113*
Johnson, A., 319, *333*
Johnson, C. A., 382, 384, *389*
Johnson, D. P., 406, *420*
Johnson, J., 132, *151*, 298, *331*, 391, *418*, 423, 444, 445, *458*
Johnson, J. G., 7, 8, 31, *39*, *41*, *184*, 191, 196, 197, 208, 209, 210, 211, 221, 234, 241, 246, *249*, *252*, 280, *296*, 323, *331*, 423, 442, 443, 444, *458*, *460*, 664, 678, *683*, 694, *711*, 756, *760*
Johnson, J. H., 384, *389*
Johnson, J. N., 72, *88*
Johnson, M. E., 325, *331*
Johnson, S. A., 566, *581*
Johnstone, A., 237, *249*
Johnstone, B. G. M., 319, *331*
Jones, E. R., 424, *460*
Jones, G. N., 375, 379, 381, 382, 383, 384, 385, *387*, *388*, *389*, 407, 410, 412, *420*, 688, *709*
Jones, L. R., 118, *148*
Jones, M. L., 315, *334*
Jones, N. M. B., 588, 590, 591, *620*
Jones, R. L., 464, *488*
Jones, S. J., 571, *579*
Jones-Alexander, J., 523, *533*
Jones-Webb, R. J., 407, *418*
Joost, J. C., 96, *112*
Jorgensen, R. S., 668, *682*
Joukama, M., 192, *249*
Judd, B., 141, *148*
Judd, L. L., 145, *150*, 192, *251*
Juergens, S. M., 546, *553*
Junger, F., 119, 145, *152*

K

Kabacoff, R. I., 512, 515, 516, 517, 518, 519, 521, *534*
Kabat, M., 385, *387*, 395, 396, 398, 401, 404, *417*, 521, *533*
Kabat-Zinn, J., 706, *709*
Kaemmer, B., 28, *38*
Kahana, R. J., 654, *682*
Kahkonen, D. M., 590, *621*
Kahn, R., 140, 142, *148*
Kahn, R. S., 307, 311, *334*
Kaiser, H. E., 305, *331*
Kalikow, K., 132, *151*
Kameoka, V. A., 400, *420*, 509, *534*
Kamerow, D. B., 116, *148*, 299, *331*
Kamlet, M., 9, *41*
Kane, J., 213, *253*
Kane, M. T., 133, *148*
Kane, R. A., 491, *507*
Kane, R. L., 336, 337, 339, 340, 358, *371*, 491, *507*
Kania, C., *620*
Kanner, A. D., 381,383, *388*
Kanoy, K. W., 103, 105, *112*, *113*
Kaplan, E., 561, 562, 563, 564, 578, *579*, *580*
Kaplan G., *249*, 655, *682*
Kaplan, R. F., 565, *580*

Kaplan, S., 625, *649*
Karlsson, H., 192, *249*
Karmarck, T., 378, *388*
Karno, M., 115, 140, *147*,*150*, 201, 202, *248*, 297, 299, 310, *332*
Kashner, M. T., 7, *41*
Kashner, T. M., 55, *89*, *90*, 201, *252*
Kasoff, S. S., 564, 567, *579*
Kastrup, M., 426, 430, *456*
Kasvikis, Y., 782, *794*
Kaszniak, A., 138, *145*
Katerndahl, D. A., 529, *534*
Kathol, R. G., 133, *145*
Katon, W. J., 7, *39*, 53, 55, 56, 57, 64, *89*, *91*, 115, 116, 145, *148*, 155, 156, 158, *184*, *186*, 192, 193, 213, 221, 223, 224, 236, 237, 238, 239, 242, 247, *249*, *250*, *251*, *252*, 277, *296*, 299, 310, 311, 313, 315, 325, 326, *331*, *333*, *334*, 373, 375, *388*, *389*, 391, 415, *418*, 463, 464, 465, 473, *488*, *489*, 490, 509, 523, *534*, 602, 603, *620*, *621*, 655, 656, 664, 666, 668, *683*, 688, 691, 694, 698, 703, 704, 705, 706, 707, 708, 709, 710, *711*, 713, 714, 717, 733, 770, 777, *793*, *795*
Katona, C., 495, 496, 497, *506*, *508*
Katona, P., 496, 497, *506*
Katz, B. P., 785, *796*
Katz, I. R., 494, 496, *507*
Katz, J. N., 608, *620*
Katz, N. R., 656, *682*
Katzelnick, D. J., 8, 31, 32, *39*, *40*, 64, *89*, 192, *248*, 423, 424, 426, 428, 443, 450, 452, *458*, *459*, 464, *488*, 610, *621*, 756, *760*, 769, 770, 771, 774, 775, 776, 777, 778, 780, 782, *791*, *792*, *793*, *794*
Katzelnick, R., 203, 221, 229, 241, *249*
Katzman, R., 564, 567, 575, *579*, *580*, 785, *792*
Kaye, A. L., 311, *332*
Keane, T. M., 523, *534*
Kedward, H. B., 298, *331*
Keegan, D., 664, 666, 668, *683*
Keith, B. R., 97, *113*
Keitner, G. I., 501, *507*
Kelleher, K., 194, *251*, 465, *489*
Keller, A. M., 95, *113*
Keller, M. B., 156, *186*, 195, *248*, 443, 444, *456*, *457*, 463, 464, 479, *488*
Keller, S. D., 30, *41*, 342, 368, 372, 586, 587, 598, 603, *620*, *621*, 642, *651*, 738, *760*, 779, *796*
Kelley, M. L., 101, *113*
Kellner, R., 314, *331*, 424, *457*, 655, *682*
Kemke, K. K., 546, *553*
Kempf, E. J., 128, *149*
Kempt, J., 324, *331*
Kenardy, J., 784, *794*
Kendall, P. C., 133, *148*, 401, 402, 403, 404, 405, *418*
Kendler, K. S., 6, *39*, 391, *418*, 687, *709*, 756, *760*
Kendler, R. S., 192, *249*
Kennedy, C., 562, 563, *581*
Kennedy, C. A., 322, *331*
Kennedy, C. J., 322, *328*
Kennedy, S., 768, *794*
Kerber, C., 214, 237, 241, *250*, 392, 400, 401, *419*
Kern, D. E., *90*, 193, *251*
Kerner, S. A., 402, *418*
Kerschenobich, D., 548, *553*

Kessler, C. D., 784, 795
Kessler, H. R., 565, 580
Kessler, L. G., 6, 7, 39, 52, 90, 118, 149, 192, 193, 237,
    249, 252, 279, 296, 423, 442, 443, 458, 460,
    542, 553, 687, 711, 756, 760, 771, 777, 793
Kessler, R. C., 192, 249, 376, 377, 378, 388, 391, 418,
    463, 473, 488, 687, 709
Keuthen, N. J., 787, 791
Khadivi, A., 311, 334
Khavari, K. A., 545, 554
Kian, D. T., 319, 333
Kick, H., 404, 419
Kiecolt-Glaser, J. K., 378, 388
Kiernan, R. J., 569, 570, 571, 572, 573, 578, 580, 581
Kilroy, V., 119, 146
Kim, K. I., 424, 458
Kincaid, J. P., 627, 643, 650
King, D. A., 53, 88, 185, 409, 419
King, K. M., 307, 330
King, R. E., 464, 490
Kingston, M. D., 424, 459
Kirby, S., 140, 150
Kirkby, K. C., 784, 793
Kirmayer, L. F., 193, 194, 251
Kirmayer, L. J., 193, 194, 249, 311, 331, 411, 418
Kirscht, J. P., 625, 649
Kissoon-Singh, J., 786, 792
Klag, M. J., 135, 147
Klauber, M. R., 566, 568, 569, 575, 578, 580, 581, 785,
    792
Kleber, H. D., 311, 324, 333, 334
Klein, A. A., 132, 147
Klein, D. F., 446, 449, 459, 460
Klein, L. E., 118, 119, 140, 150, 213, 236, 237, 252
Klein, M. H., 428, 457, 774, 781, 786, 791, 792, 795
Kleinman, P. H., 324, 331
Klerman, G. L., 127, 149, 155, 186, 206, 209, 253, 298,
    303, 307, 329, 331, 332, 391, 418, 423, 444,
    445, 449, 457, 458, 461, 463, 464, 488, 509,
    534, 584, 620, 694, 700, 704, 710
Kligman, E. W., 558, 582
Klinkman, M. S., 52, 55, 89, 194, 235, 246, 249
Knesper, D. J., 687, 709
Knight, R. G., 407, 418
Kobak, K. A., 8, 31, 32, 39, 40, 192, 203, 221, 229, 241,
    248, 249, 285, 296, 423, 424, 426, 428, 429,
    431, 432, 436, 437, 439, 440, 441, 443, 445,
    450, 451, 452, 458, 459, 460, 464, 488, 756,
    760, 769, 770, 771, 774, 775, 776, 777, 778,
    780, 782, 791, 792, 793, 794, 795
Kobert, S., 769, 791
Kobrin, S., 787, 795
Koch, M., 567, 581
Koerner, K., 708, 709, 780, 792
Koeter, M. W. J., 54, 89, 277, 296, 305, 331, 334, 780,
    792, 691, 710
Kohn, R., 193, 236, 251
Kokman, E., 558, 559, 560, 561, 565, 567, 578, 582, 581
Kolarz, C. M., 525, 533
Koller, W. C., 566, 567, 581
Koocher, G. P., 103, 113
Koop, C. E., 583, 620
Kooper, R., 784, 795
Koot, H. M., 305, 334
Kopans, B. S., 695, 709
Kopper, B. A., 512, 516, 534

Kopta, S. M., 257, 275, 316, 332
Kornblith, A. B., 319, 333
Kornetsky, C., 311, 329
Korsch, B. M., 625, 649, 656, 682
Korten, A., 192, 250
Korzon, A., 319, 333
Kosaka, K., 556, 580
Kosinski, M., 30, 41, 342, 368, 372, 470, 481, 482, 484,
    485, 486, 489, 490, 584, 585, 586, 587, 588,
    589, 590, 591, 592, 593, 598, 603, 606, 621,
    623, 625, 628, 630, 632, 634, 635, 637, 641,
    642, 643, 645, 647, 650, 651, 738, 760, 779,
    796
Kouzis, A. C., 463, 473, 488
Kovacs, M., 137, 145, 403, 419, 430, 445, 448, 456, 459,
    460, 706, 710
Kraemer, H. C., 57, 90
Kramer, J. J., 184
Kramer, M., 115, 118, 119, 140, 149, 150, 236, 237, 252,
    297, 299, 310, 332
Kramer, P. D., 116, 150
Kramer, T. L., 467, 470, 473, 479, 481, 487, 489
Krames, L., 394, 420
Krantz, D. S., 378, 388
Krause, M. S., 257, 275
Kravitz, R. L., 625, 649
Kresevic, D. M., 464, 487
Kreuter, M., 787, 795
Kroenke, K., 7, 8, 31, 39, 41, 53, 89, 154, 155, 156, 184,
    186, 191, 196, 197, 198, 201, 202, 203, 208,
    209, 210, 211, 216, 218, 219, 221, 226, 234,
    235, 241, 246, 247, 248, 249, 250, 252, 253,
    280, 296, 373, 385, 388, 392, 420, 423, 442,
    443, 444, 458, 459, 460, 653, 654, 664, 665,
    666, 667, 668, 669, 670, 675, 678, 682, 683,
    694, 711, 756, 760, 777, 778, 795
Krosesler, D., 325, 327, 330
Kruger, A., 115, 151, 297, 333
Ku, L., 428, 461, 774, 786, 795
Kuhn, W. F., 131, 149, 310, 332
Kukull, W. A., 575, 579, 794
Kuperman, G. J., 789, 790
Kupfer, D. J., 137, 146, 312, 329, 424, 430, 431, 441,
    446, 457, 461
Kuppenheimer, M., 137, 151, 312, 333
Kurland, L. T., 558, 559, 560, 561, 578, 582
Kurosaki, T. T., 785, 794
Kurtin, P. S., 592, 599, 621
Kushner, M., 216, 247
Kuzma, M. A., 33, 41, 136, 137, 149, 192, 253
Kwan, E., 786, 791

L

Labanowski, M., 620
Lacey, J. I., 376, 389
Lai, K. Y. C., 200, 250
Lailert, C., 142, 148
Lambert, M. J., 394, 403, 404, 417, 419, 424, 457, 459,
    527, 534
Lamberts, H., 695, 709
Landa, E., 548, 553
Landau, C., 655, 683
Landefeld, C. S., 464, 487
Landsverk, J. A., 128, 140, 146, 147, 467, 468, 472,
    487, 488
Lane, D., 655, 683

Lange, A. J., 706, *709*
Langer, A., 373, *389*
Langston, W., 569, 570, 572, 573, 578, *580*
Lareau, M., 714, *733*
Larnberti, J. W., 216, *247*
Larrabee, G. J., 495, *506*
Larson, D. B., 52, 53, *89, 93, 113*, 221, *247, 465, 487*
Larson, E., 140, *151*
Larson, E. B., 575, *579, 794*
Larsson, K. M., 6, 7, 20, 33, 40, 756, *760*
LaRue, A., 142, *149*
Laufer, S. T., 131, *149*, 310, *332*
Laughren, T. P., 428, *457, 774, 792*
Lautenschlaeger, E., 574, *580*
Laux, L., 656, *683*
Lave, J., 223, 237, 239, *251*, 688, 703, *711*, 713, *733*
Lave, J. R., 392, *420*
Lavigne, J. V., 97, *112*
Lavori, P. W., 463, 464, *488*
Lawlor, B. A., 561, 562, *582*
Lawton, M. P., 494, *507*
Layte, R., 610, *621*
Lazar, J. B., 145, *150*
Lazar, J. N., 192, *251*
Lazarus, A., 706, *710*
Lazarus, R. S., 377, 378, 379, 381, 383, *388, 389*
Lazev, A., 241, *253*
Lazorick, S., 158, *186*
Leach, L., 561, 562, 563, 578, *580*
Leaders predict integration of MH, primary care by 2000, 17, *40*
Leaf, J., 52, *90*
Leaf, P. J., 95, 97, *112*, 192, *252*, 297, *332*, 393, *417*, 423, *460*, 687, *711*
Leahy, D., 714, *733*
Leake, B., 128, *146*, 467, 468, 473, *487, 490*
LeBaron, S., 96, *112*
Leber, W. R., 424, 447, 451, 452, 455, *457*, 704, *709*, 780, *791*
Lebovits, A., 137, *151*, 319, *333*
Lechner, H., 567, *581*
Lecrubier, Y., 192, *251*, 778, 779, *795*
Leeper, J., 193, 194, *247*
Leepek, J. D., 118, *148*, 464, *488*
Lefever, D., 654, 655, *683*
Lehrer, P. M., 307, *329*
Lehtinen, V., 192, *249*
Leidy, N. K., 374, *388*
Leirer, V. O., 492, *508*, 785, *796*
Leitenberg, H., 315, *329*
Lelliott, P., 782, *794*
Lembcke, P. A., 583, *620*
Lenihan, P., 141, *147*
Lennox, G., 556, *580*
Leo, G. I., 787, *795*
Leon, A. C., 155, 157, 158, *185, 186*, 443, *456, 461*, 777, 778, *791, 796*
Leothen, G. J., 545, *554*
Leplege, A., 583, *621*
LeResche, S. K., 115, *151*
Leserman, J., 326, *330*
Lesher, E. L., 140, *149*, **496,** *507*
Lesko, L. M., 320, *332*
Lesperance, F., 57, *88*
Lesser, A. L., 236, *248*
Lesser, I. M., 307, *329*

Lester, D., 397, *417*, 435, *456*
Leung, T., 200, *250*
Levenson, J. L., 138, 139, 140, *148*
Leventhal, J. M., 95, 97, *112*
Levine, D., 135, *147*
Levine, D. M., 221, *250*
Levine, E. G., 320, *332*
Levine, S., 303, 322, *329, 332*, 584, *620*
Levy, A. P., 561, 562, 563, *582*
Lewinsohn, P. M., 311, *328*, 410, *419*, 447, *459, 461*, 706, *710*
Lewis, C. C., 95, *113*
Lewis, C. E., 625, 628, *649, 650*
Lewis, M., 499, *506*
Lezak, M. L., 562, 573, *580*
Libow, L., 138, 142, *149*
Lichtenberg, P. A., 566, 567, *582*
Liddell, D. L., 137, *151*
Lieberman, J. A., III, 155, 156, *186*
Lieberman, N., 623, 628, 630, 632, 634, 635, 637, 643, *650*
Liebowitz, M. R., 311, *332*, 445, 446, *459*, 520, *533*
Lief, A., 377, *389*
Likert, R., 630, *650*
Lilienfeld, S. O., 527, *534*
Lilimperi, D. R., 237, *250*
Limbaugh, B., 769, *791*
Lin, E. H. B., 53, 55, 56, 64, *89, 91*, 115, 116, 145, *148, 184*, 192, 223, 224, 236, 237, 238, 239, 242, *249, 250, 252*, 299, 310, 313, 326, *331, 463*, 464, 465, 473, *488, 489*, 509, 523, *534*, 602, 603, *620, 621*, 655, 656, *683*, 688, 691, 694, 698, 703, 704, 705, 706, 707, 708, *709, 710*, 711, 714, *733*, 770, 777, *793, 795*
Lin, W., 391, *418*, 703, 704, *709*
Lindberg, L. D., 428, *461*, 774, 786, *795*
Linden, W., 57, *89*
Lindner, J. E., 131, *149*, 310, *332*
Lipman, R. S., 299, *330*
Line, E., 375, *389*
Link, D., 96, *112*
Linn, L. S., 116, 118, 119, *149*, 237, *250*, 464, 465, *488*
Linzer, L., 694, *711*
Linzer, M., 7, 8, 31, *39, 41*, 154, 155, 156, *184, 186*, 191, 196, 197, 202, 208, 209, 210, 211, 216, 218, 219, 221, 226, 234, 235, 241, 246, *247, 248*, *249, 250, 252, 253*, 280, 296, 392, 420, 423, 442, 443, 444, *458, 460*, 653, 654, 664, 665, 667, 669, 675, 678, *682, 683*, 756, *760*
Lipkin, M., Jr., 13, 14, 15, *40*, 220, *249, 251*, 655, *682*
Lipman, R. S., 119, *146*, 335, *372*
Lipowski, Z. J., 54, 55, *89*
Lipschutz, R. C., 392, *420*
Lipscomb, P., 115, 116, 145, *148*, 299, 310, 313, 326, *331*, 509, 523, *534*, 655, 656, *683*, 770, *793*
Lipsitt, D. R., 4, 19, 20, 23, *40*, 655, *683*
Lipton, D. S., 324, *331*
Lir, E., 464, *488*
Lish, J. D., 33, *41*, 136, 137, *149*, 192, *253*, 259, *275*
Liskow, B., 323, 324, *332*
Little, M., 101, *113*
Littlefield, C., 132, *146*, 194, 233, *251*
Litz, B. T., 523, *534*
Liu, W. T., 785, *792*
Livingston, W. W., 277, *296*, 691, *709*
Llorens, S., 786, *790*

Lloyd-Thomas, A. R., 56, *89*, 375, *389*, 688, 691, 703, 704, *710*
Lnatiga, L. J., 668, *682*
Locher, J. W., 134, *152*
Locke, B. Z., 8, 12, *40*, 52, *89*, *90*, 115, 131, *150*, 297, 299, 310, 311, *332*, 334, 406, 409, 421, 463, 489, 499, *507*, 687, 691, *710*
Locke, S. D., 700, *710*
Locke, S. E., 6, 7, 9, 20, 33, *40*, 756, *760*
Loeser, H., 770, *793*
Logue, P. E., 570, 571, 572, *580*
Lohr, K. N., 4, *39*
Lomeo, C., 574, *582*
Long, N., 101, *113*
Loosen, P. T., 446, 447, *458*, 502, *507*, 780, *792*
Lopes, C. E., 323, *330*
Lopez, A. D., 463, *489*
Lorenz, A. D., 72, *90*
Louie, D., 787, *791*
Louria, D. B., 322, *331*
Lovallo, W. R., 375, *389*
Lovelace, patients reap rewards, 10, *40*
Lovestone, S., 556, *580*
Lowe, J., 556, *580*
Lowry, J. L., 316, *332*
Lubeck, D. P., 392, 420, 521, 533, 713, *732*
Lucas, R. W., 428, *459*, 774, 786, *793*
Lucas, S. F., 56, 66, 67, 82, *88*, *89*
Luce, R. D., 122, *149*
Ludman, E., 55, 56, *89*, 223, 224, 238, 242, *249*, 391, 418, 464, *488*, 603, 620, 688, 691, 694, 698, 703, 706, 707, 708, 709, *711*
Lueger, R., 256, *275*
Luft, H. S., 45, *89*
Lum, D. L., 137, *151*, 312, 333, 595, *620*
Lum, O., 492, *506*, *508*, 785, *796*
Luna, C. B. X., 428, *459*, 785, *796*
Lunnen, K., 527, *534*
Lush, D. T., 33, *41*, 136, 137, *149*, 192, *253*
Lushene, R., 509, 511, *534*
Lustman, 403, *419*
Lutz, L., 194, *250*
Lutz, W., 257, 260, 270, *275*
Lynch, D. J., 424, *461*
Lynch, T. R., 95, *113*
Lyness, J. M., 53, *88*, 185, 409, *419*

M

Mabe, P. A., 100, *111*
MacDonald, D. I., 116, *148*, 299, *331*
Mack, J., 236, *247*
MacWhinney, J. B., 625, *649*
Maddever, H., 426, *459*
Maddock, R. J., 509, *533*
Madianos, M. G., 463, *488*
Madonia, M. J., 184, 223, 237, 239, *251*, 392, 412, 417, 420, 688, 703, *711*, 713, *733*
Madri, J. J., 126, *149*
Magil, M. K., 415, *419*, 687, *710*
Magill, M., 118, 119, *152*, 237, *253*, 464, *490*
Magruder-Habib, K. M., 209, 221, 237, *247*, *250*, 455, 456, 472, *488*
Mah, C. A., 784, *794*
Mahoney, J., 497, *507*
Maier, S. F., 377, *389*

Maier, W., 307, *329*, 431, *459*
Main, D., 194, *250*
Mainous, A. G., 192, *249*
Makoui, S., 323, *331*
Malec, J. F., 325, *332*, 565, 567, *581*
Maling, M., 256, *275*
Malloy, P. F., 568, *581*
Malmgren, J. A., 408, *416*
Malt, U. F., 131, *149*
Malter, A. D., 575, *579*
Mamon, J. A., 221, *250*
Managed care execs face the providers, 11, *40*
Mandell, M., 443, 450, *459*, 775, *795*
Mandell, W., 312, 324, *329*
Manderscheid, R. W., 8, 12, *40*, 52, *89*, *90*, 463, 489, 499, *507*, 687, 691, *710*
Mandry, C., 382, *387*
Mangelsdorff, A. D., 53, *89*, 198, 201, 216, *249*, 373, 385, *388*
Mann, J. D., 315, *333*
Manning, W. G., 47, *88*, 424, 452, *458*, 769, *793*
Manocchia, M., 586, *621*
Mantel, J. M., 31, *40*, 203, 221, 229, 241, *249*, 426, 428, 443, *458*, *459*, 756, *760*, 774, 776, 777, 778, 782, *792*, *793*, *794*
Manzo, P. A., 781, 782, *792*, *794*
Marcotte, T. D., 570, *580*
Marcus, M. D., 202, *252*
Marcus, S. C., 53, *90*
Marek, R. G., 156, *186*, 195, *248*
Margo, A., 774, 786, *791*
Margulies, I., 625, 643, *650*
Marion, D., 257, *275*
Markowitz, J. S., 311, *332*, 445, 446, *459*, 461, 777, *794*
Marks, I. M., 774, 775, 780, 781, 782, *792*, *793*, *794*
Marks, J. S., 158, *186*
Markush, R. E., 405, *419*
Markway, K., 512, 513, *534*
Marlatt, G. A., 787, *794*
Marmot, M., 589, 593, *620*
Marquez, J. T., 654, 655, *683*
Marran, M. E., 568, *581*
Marsden, C., 140, *147*
Marson, D. C., 565, *580*
Martin, H., 356, 364, *372*
Martin, R. L., 565, *580*
Martinovich, Z., 256, 257, 260, 270, *275*
Maruish, M. E., *184*, 335, 336, 337, 339, 340, 342, 343, 350, 351, 352, 356, 358, *371*, *372*
Mashberg, D. E., 320, *332*
Master, N., 128, *146*
Mathias, S. D., 118, *152*, 521, *533*, 713, *732*
Matthew, J., 194, *250*
Matthews, C., 497, *507*
Matthews, D. B., 195, *251*, 423, 460, 464, 465, *489*, 777, *795*
Matthews, E. J., 311, *329*
Matthews, K., 392, *419*
Mattis, S., 564, 566, 567, 578, *579*, *580*
Mauksch, L. B., 72, *90*
Maurer, T. A., 156, *186*, 195, *248*
Maurice, J., 57, *89*
Maviglia, M. A., 241, *250*
Maxwell, A., 193, 194, *247*
May, P. A., 241, *250*
Mayeux, R., 574, *582*

Mayewski, R. J., 541, 542, *553*
Mayfield, D., 544, *554*
Mayou, R., 655, *683*
Mazonson, P. D., 521, *533, 713, 732*
Mazure, C. M., 375, *389, 446, 459*
McArdle, C. S., 128, *148*
McArthur, J., 140, *150*
McBeth, C. D., 318, 326, *330*
McBride, C., 787, *791*
McCain, A. P., 101, *113*
McCarter, T. G., 135, *148*
McCarthy, E. A., 321, *331*
McCartney, J. R., 141, *149*, 193, 236, *251*
McCarty, D., 4, 14, 17, 20, *39*
McClelland, C. Q., 95, *113*
McClelland, D. C., 53, 55, *89*
McClelland, M., 118, *150*, 277, *296*, 298, *333*, 397, 405,
        409, 410, 412, 413, 414, *420*
McClure, S. Y., 106, *112*
McConatha, D., *794*
McConatha, J. T., *794*
McCormick, W. C., 575, *579, 794*
McCoy, J. M., 222, *251*, 603, 609, *621*
McCullough, J. P., 311, *332*
McCully, T., 403, 404, *417, 424, 457*
McCune, K. J., 311, *332*
McCutchan, J. A., 322, *328*
McDaniel, S. H., 23, 25, *39*, 65, 72, *84, 88, 89*, 373, 374,
        375, 386, 387, *389, 714, 717, 733*
McDonald, C. J., 765, *794*
McDonald, W. M., 142, *151*
McDougal, M., 139, *149*
McDowell, J., 589, *621*
McElreath, L., 501, 502, *507*
McEvoy, L. T., 214, *248*
McGae, R. R., 668, *682*
McGaghie, W. C., 656, *683*
McGee, R., 407, *418*
McGivney, S. A., 495, *507*
McGlynn, E. A., 154, *186*, 625, *649*
McGonagle, K. A., 6, *39*, 192, *249*, 391, *418*, 687, *709,
        756, 760*
McGrath, G., 236, *247*
McGrath, P. J., 311, *332*, 446, 449, *459, 460*
McGuire, K., 562, 563, *581*
McHorney, C. A., 482, *489*, 589, 606, *621*
McHugh, P., 140, *147*
McHugh, P. R., 557, 560, 578, *580*
McInerny, T. K., 94, 97, *112*
McInroy, D. C., 428, *459, 786, 793*
McIntire, D. D., 96, *112*
McIntyre, N. J., 557, 558, 560, 578, *582*
McKeever, W., 545, *553*
McKeith, I. G., 556, *580*
McKenna, M., 561, 562, 563, *582*
McKinley, J. C., 405, *418*
McKnight, G. T., 381, 382, *387, 388*
McLean, N. E., 558, *579*
McLeod, G., 544, *554*
McNabb, N., 625, *649*
McNair, D. M., 404, *419*
McNeil, B. J., 126, *148, 151*
Meehl, P. E., 123, *149*, 540, *554*
Mehan, D. J., 410, *420*
Meininger, J., 571, *580*
Meisler, A. W., 324, *329*, 668, *682*

Melek, S. P., 10, 11, 26, *40*
Melfi, C. A., 768, *794*
Melisaratos, N., 131, *147*, 299, 318, *330*
Mellenbergh, G. J., 666, 680, *683*
Mellow, A. M., 561, 562, *582*
Menaber, N. A., 491, *506*
Mendelson, M., 132, *146, 236, 247, 279, 296*, 393, 405,
        407, *417*, 427, 429, 435, *456, 466, 474, 487*,
        501, *506*, 781, 786, *790*
Mendenhall, R. C., 628, *649*
Mendez, M. F., 561, *581*
Meneghini, L. F., 780, *794*
Mental Health Parity Act, 4, *40*
Meredith, L. S., 153, 155, 156, 157, *187*, 599, *621*
Merikangas, K. R., 297, *334*
Mermelstein, R., 378, *388*
Merrill, J. M., 656, *683*
Merrin, E. L., 571, *581*
Merritt, K. A., 97, *113*
Mesibov, G. B., 105, *113*
Messe, M., 319, *333*
Messer, K. S., 222, *251*, 603, 609, *621*
Messick, S., 123, *149*, 304, *332*
Mesulam, M., 139, *149*
Metha, M. P., 131, *149*
Metz, C. E., 126, *149*
Metzger, D. S., 307, 324, *333*
Metzger, R. L., 523, *534*
Meyer, J., 141, *148*
Meyer, J. K., 307, *330*
Meyer, K. B., 592, 599, *621*
Meyer, R., 156, *186*, 195, *248*
Meyer, R. J., 373, *389*
Meyer, T. J., 523, *534*
Miechenbaum, D., 385, *389*
Miederhoff, P. A., 593, *621*
Milburn, M. A., 688, *709*
Millar, T., 193, 236, 247, *248*
Millard, R. W., 779, *794*
Miller, A. B., 324, *331*
Miller, B. L., 556, *580*
Miller, D. M., 424, 426, *461*
Miller, F. A., 546, *553*
Miller, I. W., 426, *459*, 501, *507*
Miller, J., 391, *417*, 691, *708*
Miller, L. S., 9, *40*
Miller, M. L., 523, *534*
Miller, N. S., 259, *275*
Miller, O. W., 771, *795*
Miller, R. H., 7, *39, 45, 89*, 279, *296*
Miller, R. S., 194, *250*
Miller, S. T., 116, *150*
Miller, T. D., 115, 134, *145*, 299, 310, 322, *328*
Miller, V., 135, *148*
Miller, W. R., 155, 157, *186*
Millions with mental illnesses benefit from new
        federal rules, 4, *40*
Millis, J. S., 626, *650*
Millman, R. B., 324, *331*
Milne, S., 392, *419*
Mine, E. D., *185*
Minichiello, W. E., 455, *459*
Mintz, D. H., 780, *794*
Mintz, J., 463, *488*
Mintz, L. I., 463, *488*

Miranda, C. T., 373, *388* 464, *489,* 688, 695, 703, *710,*
        711
Miranda, J., 7, *40,* 52, 53, *89,* 93, *113,* 214, 241, *252,*
Mirra, S. S., 556, *580*
Mitchell, C. M., 326, *330*
Mitchell, G. E., 3, 14, 17, 20, 23, 26, 28, 31, *39, 40,* 72, *88*
Mitchell, J., 202, *252*
Mitchell, J. A., 772, 789, *790*
Mitchell, J. B., 116, *150*
Mitchell, J. V., *184*
Mitrushina, M., 571, *581*
Mittman, N., 496, *507*
Mock, J., 132, *146,* 427, 429, 435, *456,* 501, *506,* 781, 786,
        790
Mock, J. E., 393, 405, 407, *417,* 466, 474, *487*
Moe, K. E., 567, *582*
Moffett, L. A., 305, *332*
Mohs, R. C., 770, *794*
Monroe, S. M., 379, *389*
Monsch, A. U., 566, 568, 569, 578, *581*
Monson, R. A., 55, *90,* 201, *252,* 655, *683*
Montanco, D., 668, *682*
Montano, D. E., 625, *650*
Monteiro, W. W., 782, *794*
Montgomery, D. M., 566, *581*
Montgomery, J. E., 636, 641, 647, *650*
Montgomery, S. A., 424, *459*
Montiel, O. M., 214, 237, 241, *250,* 392, 400, 401, *419*
Montorio, I., *581*
Moore, J. T., 118, 119, *149,* 152, 237, *250,* 253, 464, *490*
Moore, R. D., 221, *250*
Moran, P. W., 394, 403, 404, *417, 419,* 424, *457*
Moras, K., 257, 260, 270, *275*
Moreland, K. L., 31, *40*
Morgan, T. M., 407, *417*
Morishita, L, 498, *507*
Morris, J. C., 575, *579,* 770, *794*
Morris, J. L., 379, *389*
Morris, M. J., 625, *649*
Morrow, G., 297, *330*
Morrow, G. R., 131, *147*
Morse, R. M., *185,* 538, 539, 541, 542, 543, 544, 546,
        547, 548, 549, *553, 554*
Mortel, K., 141, *148*
Moses, J., 141, *147*
Mosley, C. L., 473, 479, 481, *489*
Mosley, T. H., 382, 384, *389*
Mosser, G., 48, *89*
Mossman, D., 127, 128, *149, 151*
Moulton, A. W., 135, *146*
Mountjoy, C. Q., 509, *534*
Mouton-Simien, P., 101, *113*
Muchnick, S., 714, *733*
Mueller, J., 569, 570, 571, 572, 573, 578, *580, 581*
Mueller, T. I., 464, *488*
Mukerji V., 216, *247*
Mulford, H. A., 786, *792*
Mullan, E., 496, 497, *506*
Mullin, P. J., 428, *459,* 786, *793*
Mullins, L., 714, *733*
Mulrow, C. D., 214, 237, 241, *250,* 392, 400, 401, *419*
Mulsant, B. H., 576, 577, 578, *581, 582*
Mulvey, T., 193, 236, *251*
Mulvihill, M., 495, *507*
Mumford, E., 714, *733*
Mumma, G. H., 320, *332*

Munari, F., 424, *457*
Mundt, J. C., 774, 776, 787, *791, 794, 795*
Mungas, D., 139, *149*
Munoz, R., 7, *40*
Munoz, R. F., 464, *489,* 688, 703, *710*
Murawski, M. M., 593, *621*
Murphy, C., 787, *791*
Murphy, E., 503, *507*
Murphy, G. E., 403, *419*
Murphy, J. M., 100, 101, *111, 112, 113,* 127, 128, *149,*
        151, 409, *417*
Murphy, L. B., 97, *113*
Murphy, L. O., 95, *113*
Murray, A., 636, *650*
Murray, C. J. L., 463, *489*
Mushlin, A. I., 541, 542, *553*
Musicco, M., 559, *579*
Musick, B. S., 491, *506*
Myers, J. K., 115, 116, *150, 151,* 297, 299, 310, *332,* 410,
        411, *417, 419,* 466, 474, *487*
Myers, P., 10, 18, 23, 26, *39*
Mynors-Wallace, L., 688, 691, 703, 704, *710*
Mynors-Wallis, L. M., 56, *89*

N

Nadler, J. D., 561, 562, 563, 568, *581, 582*
Nael, S., 326, *334*
Nagel, R. W., 424, *461*
Nagy, A., 431, *456,* 776, *790*
Naranjo, C. A., 496, *507*
Narayan, R. A., 424, *461*
Narens, L., 122, *149*
Narrow, N. E., 8, 12, *40,* 52, *89, 90,* 259, *275,* 463, *489,*
        499, *507,* 687, 691, *710*
Nathan, R. G., 118, *146*
National Center for Health Statistics, 482, *489*
National Committee for Quality Assurance, 19, *40,*
        49, *89*
National Institute of Aging, 556, *581*
National Institute of Mental Health, 202, *250*
Nearly 40 percent of older suicide victims, 9, 13, *40*
Nee, J., 424, *457*
Neff, J. A., 409, *418*
Neimeyer, R. A., 325, *332,* 502, *507*
Nelson, B., 464, *487*
Nelson, C., 687, *709*
Nelson, C. B., 6, *39,* 192, *249,* 391, *418,* 756, *760*
Nelson, E., 714, *733*
Nelson, E. C., 482, *489*
Nelson, J. C., 446, *459, 460*
Nerenz, D. R., 590, *621,* 625, *651*
Ness, D. E., 221, *250*
Ness, R. E., 688, 708, *710*
Nesse, R. M., 307, 312, *329*
Nestler, E. J., 84, *88*
Nettlebladt, P., 115, *148,* 192, *248*
Neu, C., 449, *457*
Neuhauser, D., 126, *151*
Neutra, R. R., 126, *151*
Newberry, P., 409, 413, *421*
Newcornb, P. A., 787, *792*
Newhouse, J. P., 625, 636, 643, *649*
Newhouse, P.A., 561, 562, *582*
Newman, F. L., 239, *250,* 364, 371, 372, 450, 451, *459*

Newman, M. G., 784, *794*
Ng, F. S., 200, *250*
Niaura, R., 787, *791*
Nicholson, A., 589, *620*
Nickel, E. J., 323, 324, *332*
Nickel, R. E., 100, *114*
Nielson, A. C., 116, *149*, 277, *296*, 400, 405, *419*
Nies, G., 395, *418*
NIH Consensus Panel, 785, *794*
NIMH Consensus Development Conference Statement, 447, *459*
NIMH official cites high cost of schizophrenia, 9, *40*
Nitcher, R. L., 495, 499, *506, 507*
Niven, R. G., 546, *554*
Noel, T. K., *185*, 409, *419*
Noh, S., 192, *252*
Nolen-Hoeksema, S., 706, *709*
Norcross, J. C., 47, 69, *90*, 225, 228, *251*
Nordstrom, G., 115, *148*, 192, *248*
Norman, W. H., 426, *459*, 501, *507*
Norris, S. W., 311, *332*
North, M., 784, *795*
North, M. M., 784, *794*
North, S. M., 784, *794*
Northern California Neurobehavioral Group, 569, *581*
Northouse, L. L., 318, *332*
Norton, G. R., 445, *457*
Norton, H. J., 203, 221, 229, 241, *249*
Norton, L., 319, *333*
Norton, R., 31, *40*, 426, 443, *459*, 756, *760*, 777, 778, *793*
Noshirvani, H. 782, *794*
Novack, D. H., 655, *683*
Novotny, T. E., 787, *792*
Noyes, R., 137, *149*, 307, 312, 313, *329, 332*
Nunes, E., 449, *460*
Nunnally, J., 123, *149*, 302, *332*, 406, *419*, 591, *621*, 632, *650*
Nyez, G. R., 117, 119, *148, 150*, 194, 237, *248, 249*

O

O'Cathain, A., 588, 590, 591, *620*
Ocepek-Welikson, K., 449, *460*
O'Conner, G. T., 772, *796*
O'Connor, P. G., 786, *794*
O'Connor, P. J., 45, 47, 48, 62, 69, *88, 89, 90*, 766, 767, 770, *794*
O'Donnell, W. E., 323, *330*
O'Dowd, T. C., 656, *683*
Oehlert, M. E., 570, 572, *581*
Oest, L., 523, *534*
Office of Technology Assessment, 625, 643, *650*
Offord, K. P., 539, 546, 553, 558, 559, 560, 561, 578, *582*
O'hara, M. N., 131, *149*
O'Hara, M. W., 433, *460*
Ohio study documents cost-offsets, 10, *40*
Okiishi, J., 527, *534*
Okkes, I., 52, 55, *89*
Olaman, S., 407, *418*
O'Laughren, J., 455, *456*
Oldehinkel, T., 192, *250*
Olfson, M., 11, *40*, 53, *90*, 155, 157, 158, *185, 186*, 194, 200, *250*, 443, *456, 461*, 694, 700, 704, *710*, 777, 778, *796*

Oliver, J. M., 400, *419*
Oliver-Munoz, S., 564, *580*
Olmstead, E. M., 772, *796*
Olmsted, M. P., 311, 325, *333*
Olsen, T., 79, *88*
Olson, R., 714, *733*
O'Malley, P. G., 241, *250*
Ooi, W. L., 575, *580*
Opdyke, D., 784, *795*
Oppenheim, S., 311, *334*
Ordway, L., 625, *649*
Orleans, C. T., 118, *149*, 194, *250*, 423, *459*, 777, *794*
Orlinsky, D. E., 257, *275*
Ormel, J., 7, *41*, 53, 54, 64, *89, 91*, 184, 192, *250, 251*, 252, 277, *296*, 392, 420, 463, 464, 473, *488*, 489, 691, 703, 704, *709, 710*
Orvaschel, H., 115, *150*, 192, *251*, 297, *332, 333*, 509, *534*
Osato, S. S., 570, 571, 572, 573, *580*
Osgood-Hynes, D. J., 781, 782, *794*
Oski, F. A., 95, *114*
Osman, A., 512, 513, 516, *534*
Osman, J. R., 512, 513, 516, *534*
Osmon, D. C., 571, *581*
Ostroff, J. S., 320, *332*
Otkay, J. S., 7, *39*
Otteson, O. J., 603, *621*
Ottinger, D. R., 103, *113*
Otto, M. W., 529, *534*
Ouellette, R., 445, *461*
Overman, C., 142, *151*
Oxman, T. E., 115, 116, *145*, 213, *247*, 279, *296*, 307, *329*, 445, *456*
Ozminkowski, R. J., 68, *88*

P

Pace, T., 714, 717, *733*
Pace, T. M., 401, *421*
Pagnucco, D. J., 687, *709*
Pajer, K. A., 54, 56, *90*
Palacios, J., 407, *419*
Palermo, T. M., 101, *114*
Pallak, M. S., 335, 372, 714, *733*
Palmateer, L., 141, *149*
Palmer, R. H., 625, *651*
Palmer, R. M., 464, *487*
Palo, J., 574, *580*
Pang, A. H. T., 200, *250*
Panico, S., 156, *186*, 195, *248*
Pantell, R. H., 95, *113*
Paolo, A. M., 566, 567, *581*
Parchman, M. L., 401, *421*
Parikh, R. M., 131, *149*
Parish, J. E., 558, 559, 560, 561, 578, *582*
Parker, J. D. A., *185*
Parker, S., 95, *114*
Parker, T., 241, *250*
Parkerson, G. R., 222, *251*, 608, *621*, 694, *710*
Parkin, J. R., 781, 782, *794*
Parkin, R., 780, 782, *792, 794*
Parloff, M. B., 424, 447, 451, 452, 455, *457*, 704, *709*, 780, *791*
Parmalee, P. A., 494, 496, *507*
Parran, T., 786, *790*
Parrish, R., 95, *113*

Parsons, T., 675, *683*
Pascoe, G. C., 636, *649*
Pastemak, R., 576, 577, 578, *581, 582*
Paster, V. S., 94, *113*
Pathak, D., 314, *331*
Patrick, C., 714, *733*
Patrick, D. L., 57, *91*, 326, *330*, 408, *416*, 521, *533*, 713, *732*
Patsdaughter, C. A., 303, *328*
Patten, C. A., 115, 134, *145*, 299, 310, 322, *328*
Paul, E., 140, *147*
Paulsen, J. S., 566, *581*
Pavan, L., 424, *457*
Pay, M., 575, *580*
Paykel, E. S., 194, *248*, 251, 439, *459*
Payne, T. H., 384, *389*
Peacock, E. J., 378, *389*
Pearce, K. A., 590, *621*
Pearson, S. D., 424, 452, *458*, 702, *710*, 769, *793*
Peck, A., 140, 142, *148*
Pecknold, J. C., 307, *329*
Peek, C. J., 20, 21, 22, 23, *40*, 50, 56, 57, 66, 67, 71, 77, 81, 82, 84, 85, 86, *88, 89, 90*
Penaman, D., 297, *330*
Penick, E., 323, 324, *332*
Penman, D., 131, *147*
Penn, J. V., 193, 236, *251*
Penzien, D. B., 382, 384, *389*
Perconte, S. T., 327, *332*
Perel, J., 223, 237, 239, *251*, 688, *703, 711*
Peres, J., 713, *733*
Peretz, T., 320, *328*
Perez-Stable, E. J., 7, *40*, 464, *489*
Perkins, C., 545, *554*
Perloff, M., 319, *333*
Perrin, E., 482, *489*
Perrin, J., 95, *112*
Perrine, M. W., 787, *795*
Perry, E. K., 556, *580*
Perry, H. O., 546, *554*
Perry, R. H., 556, *580*
Peskind, E. R., 785, *794*
Peters, L., 31, *38*
Peterson, C. D., 415, *417*
Peterson, J. R., 625, 636, 643, *649*
Peterson, L. P., 495, *508*
Peterson, R. C., 556, 558, 559, 560, 561, 564, 565, 567, 578, *580, 581, 582*
Petkova, E., 449, *460*
Petrakes, S., 241, *250*
Petrie, K., 428, *459*, 774, 775, *794*
Petrik, N., 396, *420*
Petty, R., 444, *459*
Peveler, R. C., 305, *332*
Pfeffer, R. I., 785, *794*
Pfeiffer, E., 140, 141, *149*
Pfohl, B., 430, *461*
Philbrick, J. T., 241, *251*, 521, *534*
Philipp, M., 431, *459*
Philips, B. G., 321, *331*
Phillips, K., 156, *186*, 195, *248*
Phillips, W. R., 625, *650*
Phoenix, C., 319, *331*
Phongsathorn, V., 495, *508*
Physicians report problems in finding mental health specialists, 16, *40*

Piacentini, J., 100, *113*
Piasetsky, S., 131, *147*, 297, *330*
Picken, B., 544, *553*
Pierce, J. P., 787, *792, 796*
Pierce, W. E., 237, *249*
Piersma, H. L., 131, *150, 184*
Piette, J. D., 784, *794*
Pilkonis, P. A., 424, 447, 451, 452, 455, *457*, 704, *709, 780, 791*
Pinciroli, F., 789, *790*
Pincus, H. A., 11, *40*, 53, *90*, 116, *148*, 299, *331*
Pingree, S., 788, *792*
Pini, S., 192, *250*
Plake, B. S., *185*
Plant, M. A., 193, 194, *247*
Platt, J. J., 307, 324, *333*
Plaud, J. J., 384, *389*
Pleck, J. H., 428, *461*, 774, 786, *795*
Plemel, D., 396, *420*
Plescia, G., 33, *41*, 136, 137, *149*, 192, *253*
Pless, I. B., 94, *112*, 770, *793*
Plichta, S., 157, 158, *186*
Polinsky, M. L., 134, *152*
Polis, E., 625, *650*
Polk, E., 115, 116, 145, *148*, 299, 310, 313, 326, *331*, 509, 523, *534*, 770, *793*
Pollack, M., 140, 142, *148*
Pollack, M. H., 529, *534*
Pollack, S., 115, *150*, 299, 325, *333*
Polmin, K., 567, *581*
Polvin, J. H., 439, *457*
Pope, H. G., Jr., 213, *253*
Pope, M. K., 382, *388*
Pottenger, M., 311, *334*, 406, 409, *421*
Potter, J. F., 498, *506*
Potter, W. Z., 426, *457*
Potts, M. K., 426, *460*
Powell, B. J., 323, 324, *332*
Powell, D., 714, *733*
Powell, F. C., 407, *420*
Price, L. H., 446, *460*
Price, T. R., 54, *90*, 131, *149*
Priest, R. G., 194, *251*
Prince, L. M., 625, *649*
Prince, S. E., 708, *709, 780, 792*
Prinz, P. N., 567, 568, *582*
Pristach, C. A., 545, *554*
Pritchett, E. L. C., 321, *331*
Prochaska, J. O., 47, 69, *90*, 225, 228, *251*
Pronk, N. P., 47, 48, 62, 69, *88, 89, 90*
Prusoff, B., 409, 413, *421*, 509, *534*
Prusoff, B. A., 307, 311, *332, 334*, 406, 409, *421*, 449, *457*
Pryzbeck, T. R., 444, *458*
Public Health Service Agency for Health Care Policy and Research, 374, 375, *389*
Purdon, C., 512, 513, 517, 518, *533*
Putnam, S. M., 220, *251*
Pynoos, J. A., *792*

Q

Quinlan, D. M., 446, *459, 460*
Quinn, N. P., 556, *580*
Quitkin, F. M., 311, *332, 333*, 446, *459, 460*

R

Rabalais, J., 382, *387*
Rabkin, J. G., 311, 322, 323, *331, 332*, 334, 446, *459*, 777, *794*
Raczek, A., 482, *489*
Raczynski, J. M., 320, *332*
Radenhausen, R., 305, *332*
Radloff, L. S., 131, *150*, 385, *389*, 405, 406, 407, 408, 409, *419*, 466, 468, 474, *489*
Radloff, S. L., 191, 236, *251*
Rae, D. S., 8, 12, *40*, 52, *89, 90*, 115, *150*, 259, 275, 297, 299, 310, *332*, 463, *489*, 499, *507*, 687, 691, *710*
Rafaelsen, O. J., 426, 430, *456*
Rafaelson, L., 133, *145*
Rafanelli, C., 502, *506*
Rahe, R. H., 53, *89*, 378, *388*
Raich, P., 319, *333*
Raju, M., 12, 13, 14, 23, 26, *38*
Rambel, M., 498, *507*
Rameizl, P., 142, *150*
Ramirez, G., 214, 237, 241, *250*, 392, 400, 401, *419*
Ramos-Brieva, J. A., 424, *460*
Ramsay, J. O., 407, *419*
Rand, E. H., 118, *150*, 193, 194, *247*
Rangwani, S., *185*
Ranieri, W. F., 307, 324, *333*
Rankin, J. G., 135, *148*
Ranseen, J. D., 575, *581*
Rao, B. M., 194, *248*
Rao, J. S., 590, *621*
Rapee, R. M., 385, *387*
Rapoport, J., 132, *151*
Rapp, S. R., 136, *150*
Rappaport, N. B., 381, 382, *387*
Rappo, P. D., 99, *113*
Raskin, A., 405, 407, *419*
Ratcliff, K. S., *332, 419*, 466, 467, 473, 482, *489*
Raube, K., 496, *508*
Ravenstorf, D., 317, *331*
Rawson, S. G., 424, *457*
Ray, C. G., 3, 8, 12, *40*
Ray, D. C., 55, *90*, 201, *252*, 655, *683*
Realini, J. P., 529, *534*
Reaume, W. M., 131, *150*
Redman, S., 691, *710*
Redmon, S., 277, *296*
Reed, R., 558, *582*
Regan-Kubinski, M. J., 769, *791*
Regier, D. A., 8, 12, *40*, 52, *89, 90*, 97, *111*, 115, 116, *117*, 145, *150*, 192, *251, 252*, 259, 275, 277, *296*, 297, 299, 310, *332, 333*, 391, *419*, 423, *460*, 463, *489*, 509, *534*, 687, 691, *710, 711*
Rehm, L. P., 433, *460*
Reid, A. L. A., 277, *296*, 691, *710*
Reid, P. A., 688, *709*
Reifler, B., 140, *151*
Reigier, D. A., 499, *507*
Reiman, E. M., 228, *251*
Reinhart, B., 567, *581*
Reisberg, B., 116, 138, 142, *150*
Reisby, N., 431, *456*, 776, *790*
Reisinger, K. S., 95, *113*
Reizes, J. M., 695, *709*
Remien, R. H., 322, 323, *331, 334*

Renbing, X., 575, *580*
Repasky, D. P., 590, *621*
Rettew, D. C., 137, *151*, 312, *333*
Revenstorf, D., 360, *372*
Revicki, D. A., 223, *252*, 603, *621*
Reynolds, W. M., 132, *150*, 285, *296*, 341, *372*, 395, *419*, 424, 426, 428, 429, 431, 432, 435, 436, 437, 439, 440, 441, 445, 450, 451, *459, 460*, 774, 776, 793, *795*
Rhoades, H. M., 131, *150*, 407, 412, *419*
Rice, D. P., 9, *40*
Rich, M. W., 68, *88*
Richard, D. C. S., 699, *710*
Richardson, E., 708, *710*
Richardson, E. D., 568, *581*
Richardson, L. A., 95, *113*
Richman, D. D., 322, *328*
Richman, N., 101, *113*
Richmond, J. B., 94, *113*
Richter, P., 404, *419*
Rickels, K., 119, *146*, 299, 302, 304, 326, *330*, 334, 335, *372*
Rief, W., 313, *332*
Rieger, D., 100, *113*
Rifai, A. H., 577, *581*
Rifat, S. L., 501, *506*
Rifkin, A., 307, *329*
Righi, R., 323, *331*
Riley, A. W., 96, 104, *112*
Riskind, J. H., 133, *150*, 424, 431, *460*, 509, *534*
Risser, J., 775, *795*
Ritchie, K., 138, 141, *147*, 496, *506*
Rivero, F., 548, *553*
Robbins, J., 391, *417*
Robbins, J. A., 691, *708*
Robbins, J. M., 193, 194, *249, 251*, 311, *331*, 411, *418*
Robbins, L. N., 297, 299, 310, *332*
Roberts, C. S., 134, *152*, 320, *333*
Roberts, M. A., 145, *150*
Roberts, M. C., 97, 102, 103, *113*
Roberts, R., 589, *620*
Roberts, R. E., 131, *150*, 407, 410, 411, 412, *419*
Roberts, W. C., 311, *332*
Robins, E., 410, *420*, 428, *460*
Robins, L. N., 115, *150*, 192, 214, *248, 251*, 297, *333*, *419*, 463, 466, 467, 473, 482, *489*, 500, *507*, 509, *534*
Robinson, E. A., 100, *113*
Robinson, G. E., 311, 325, *333*
Robinson, H., 307, *329*
Robinson, L. A., 502, *507*
Robinson, M., 137, *151*
Robinson, P., 55, 56, *89*, 184, 223, 224, 237, 238, 239, *249*, 375, *389*, 391, *418*, 465, *488*, 499, *507*, 602, 603, *621*, 687, 688, 689, 691, 694, 695, 698, 699, 701, 702, 703, 704, 705, 706, 707, 708, 709, 710, 711 714, 733, 777, *795*
Robinson, R. G., 54, *90*, 131, *149*
Robinson-Blake, R., 4, 14, 17, 20, *39*
Roca, R. P., *90*, 140, *150*, 193, *251*
Roccaforte, W. H., *185*, 494, 495, 498, 499, *506, 507*
Rock, A., 302, 304, *330*, 335, *372*
Rockwood, K., 576, *581*
Rodin, G. M., 132, *146*, 194, 233, *251*
Rodriguez, E., *184*, 223, 237, 239, *251*, 392, 412, *417*, *420*, 688, 703, *711*, 713, *733*

Rodriguez, G., 384, *389*
Rogentine, D. S., 318, *333*
Rogers, B., 464, *490*
Rogers, D., 774, *790*
Rogers, D. E., 628, *649*
Rogers, J., 714, 717, *732*
Rogers, M. P., 781, *792*
Rogers, R., 141, *148*, 627, 643, *650*
Rogers, S. M., 428, *461*, 774, 786, *795*
Rogers, W., 192, *252*, 259, *275*, 392, 421, 423, 444, 445, *458, 461*, 463, 464, 473, *490*, 687, 691, *711*, *733*, *777*, *796*
Rogers, W. A., 623, 628, 630, 632, 634, *650*
Rogers, W. H., 154, *186*, 482, *489*, 625, 626, 635, 636, 637, 641, 643, 645, 647, *649, 650*
Roghman, K. J., 94, 97, *112*
Rohay, J. M., 589, *621*
Rokind, M., 548, *553*
Rokke, P. D., 501, *507*
Rolnick, S. J., 48, *90*
Romano, J. M., 397, *420*
Rome, L. P., 96, *113*
Roose, S. P., *334*
Rosbrook, B., 787, *796*
Rose, T. L., 492, *506, 508*, 785, *796*
Rosen, A., 123, *149*, 540, *554*
Rosen, C. S., 525, *533*
Rosen, J., 577, *581*
Rosenbaum, J. F., 558, *579*
Rosenberg, A., 714, *733*
Rosenberg, M., 374, *389*, 435, *460*
Rosenberg, R., 277, *296*, 431, *456*, 691, *709*, 776, *790*
Rosenberg, S. E., 302, *331*
Rosenblatt, J. E., 318, *333*
Rosenfeld, R., 428, *459*, 774, *793, 795*
Rosenthal, R. H., 116, *150*
Rosenthal, T. L., 116, *150*
Rosetti, K., 320, *333*
Ross, A. W., 100, *112, 113*
Ross, J., 156, *186*, 195, *248*
Ross, R., L., 473, 479, 480, 481, *489*
Rost, K. M., 7, *41*, 55, *89, 90, 184*, 194, 195, 201, *251*, *252*, 423, *460*, 463, 464, 465, 466, 467, 468, 469, 475, 477, 480, 481, *489*, 586, *621*, 777, *795*
Rosti, G., 320, *331*
Roter, D. L., *90*, 193, *251*, 656, *682*, 688, *709*
Roth, D. L., 565, *580*
Roth, L. H., 321, *330*
Roth, M. E., 7, 8, *41*, 142, *146*, 153, 155, *187*, 391, 392, 393, *421*, 509, *534*, 556, 573, 574, 578, *579*, *582*, 687, *711*, 756, *760*
Rothbaum, B. O., 784, *795*
Rothman, I., 373, *387*
Rouleau, I., 562, 563, *581*
Rounsaville, B. J., 307, 324, *332, 333*
Rouse, B. A., 6, 8, 9, *40*
Routh, D. K., 103, *113*
Rovner, B. W., *185*
Rowland, C., 118, *152*
Rowse, G. L., 428, *457*, 774, *792*
Roy, M. J., 241, *250*
Royall, D. R., 555, *581*
Roy-Byrne, P. P., 7, *39*, 155, 156, 158, *186*, 311, 313, *331*
Royce, D., 131, *150*, 310, *333*
Ruben, H. L., 311, *334*

Rubenstein, L. V., 222, *251*, 603, 609, *621*, 628, *650*
Rubenstein, L. Z., 496, *508*
Rubman, S., 382, 384, *389, 390*
Rucker, L., 687, *710*
Rush, A. J., 223, *251*, 394, 403, *417, 419*, 430, 446, 447, 448, *456, 459, 460*, 706, *710*, 781, *790*
Rush, J. A., 466, 474, 475, *489*, 501, *508*
Rush, W. A., 47, 48, *88, 89*
Russo, J., 115, 116, 145, *148, 184*, 223, 224, 237, 239, 249, 299, 310, 313, 315, 325, 326, *331, 333*, 334, 465, *488*, 509, 523, *534*, 568, *582*, 655, 656, *683*, 688, 698, 703, 704, 705, 708, *709*, 714, *733*, 770, *793*
Rutherford, L. E., 138, 139, 140, *148*
Rutigliano, P. J., 144, *147*
Rutman, D., 139, *148*
Rutter, C. M., 57, *91*, 236, *250*
Rutz, W., 259, *275*
Ryan, J. J., 570, 572, *581*
Ryan, N., 463, *488*
Rydon, P., 277, *296*, 691, *710*

S

Sabatino, S. A., 529, *534*
Sabin, J. E., 702, *710*
Sacco, W. P., 399, *419*
Sadek, J. R., 566, *581*
Sadish, W. R., 116, *150*
Sadler, G., 787, *796*
Safran, D. G., 623, 625, 626, 627, 628, 630, 632, 634, 635, 636, 637, 641, 643, 645, 647, *650*
Saia, T. L., 382, *387*
Saini, J., 68, *88*
Sainsbury, P., 464, *487*
Sakai, C., 325, *333*
Sala, S. D., 559, *579*
Salkovskis, P. M., 512, 515, *533*
Salmon, D. P., 562, 563, 566, 567, 568, 569, 578, *580*, *581*, 785, *792*
Salthouse, T. A., 565, *582*
Saltzman, L. E., 158, *186*
Salzman, C., 491, *507*
Sanchez-Graig, M., 135, *148*
Sanderman, R., 386, *390*
Sangha, O., 608, *620*
Sano, M., 574, *582*
Sanson-Fisher, R. W., 277, *296*
Santor, D. A., 407, 408, 410, *419*
Sarantakos, S., 424, *457*
Sarasor, I. G., 384, *389*
Saravay, S. M., 115, *150*, 299, 325, *333*
Sartorius, N., 192, *251, 252*, 305, *334*
Sato, T., 7, *40*
Sauer, H., 404, *419*
Saul, M., 118, *150*, 277, *296*, 298, *333*, 397, 405, 409, 410, 412, 413, 414, *420*
Saunders, K. W., 236, *250*, 602, *621*, 691, 698, 707, *711*, 777, *795*
Savron, G., 502, *506*
Sayetta, R. B., 406, *420*
Scarinci, I. C., 375, 384, *387*, 407, 410, 412, *420*, 688, *709*
Schade, C. P., 424, *460*
Schaefer, A., 396, *420*
Schaefer, C., 381, 383, *388*

Schaeffer, J., 48, *91*
Schaettle, S. C., 426, 450, *458, 459,* 774, *791, 793*
Schaeufelle, J., 96, *112*
Schain, W., 319, *334*
Schappert, S. M., 198, 201, *251,* 472, *489*
Schauben, L. J., 314, *330*
Scheftner, W. A., 444, *457*
Scheirer, A., 625, *649*
Scher, H., 139, *148*
Scherr, P. A., 556, *580*
Schilling, R., 192, *249*
Schleifer, S. J., 319, *333*
Schlenk, E. A., 589, *621*
Schlesinger, H., 714, *733*
Schmale, A. H., 297, *330*
Schmale, A. M., 131, *147*
Schmaling, K. B., 424, 426, *461*
Schmidt, F. A., 575, *581*
Schmidt, R., 567, *581*
Schmitt, F. A., 570, 571, 572, *580,*
Schneider, S. J., 787, *795*
Schneier, F., 445, *459*
Schoen, C., 95, *114*
Schoenborn, C. A., 94, *114*
Schonfeld, W. H., 392, *420*
Schottenfeld, R. S., 786, *794*
Schover, L. R., 319, *333*
Schroeder, C. S., 103, 105, 106, *112, 113*
Schuckit, M., 141, *148*
Schulberg, H. C., 7, *39,* 41, 54, 56, *90,* 118, *150,* 184, 192,
    194, 213, 223, 237, 239, *248, 249, 251,* 277,
    296, 298, 321, *330, 333,* 375, *388,* 392, 397,
    405, 409, 410, 412, 413, 414, 415, *417, 418,*
    420, 423, 442, 443, *460,* 688, 691, 702, 703,
    709, 710, 711, 713, *733,* 771, 777, *795*
Schumacher, M., 567, *581*
Schumann, W. B., 104, *112*
Schurman, R. A., 116, *150*
Schwab-Stone, M., 100, *113*
Schwamm, L. H., 571, *581*
Schwartz, G., 324, *330*
Schwartz, M. D., 787, *795*
Schwartz, S. M., 138, 139, 140, *148*
Schwenk, T. L., 54, *88,* 156, *186,* 192, 194, 195, 196, 200,
    248, 251, 252, 392, 393, 409, 410, 411, 412,
    413, *417, 418,* 464, *487,* 654, 655, *683*
Scmid, L., 216, *247*
Scogin, F., 500, 501, 502, *507*
Scott, B., 628, *650*
Scott, C. P., 223, 237, 239, *251,* 392, 412, *420,* 688, 703,
    711, 713, *733,*
Scott, J., 502, *507*
Scott, M., 502, *508*
Scott, W., 632, *650*
Seaburn, D., 714, 717, *733*
Seaburn, D. B., 65, 72, *89, 90,* 373, 374, 375, *387*
Seagroatt, V., 655, *683*
Seale, J. P., 135, *145*
Searles, J. S., 787, *795*
Sederer, L. I., 35, *41,* 128, *150*
Segal, D. L., 512, 515, 516, 517, 518, 519, 521, *534*
Seifert, M. H., 603, *621*
Selby, J. V., 772, *795*
Selby-Harrington, M. L., 95, *113*
Selden, D. R., 3, 12, *41*
Seligeon, D., 131, *149,* 310, *332*

Selmi, P. M., 781, *795*
Seltzer, A., 117, *150*
Selye, H., 376, *389*
Selzer, M. L., 537, 543, *554*
Sereika, S. M., 589, *621*
Serlin, R. C., 31, *40,* 203, 221, 229, 241, *249,* 426, 428,
    443, *458, 459,* 756, *760,* 774, 777, 778, *793*
Serlin, R. E., 788, *792*
Sessler, C. N., 138, 139, 140, *148*
Seto, T. B., 635, 636, *650*
Seuzler, M., 313, *332*
Seville, J. L., 315, *333,* 384, *389*
Shader, R. I., 491, *507*
Shaffer, D., 100, *113,* 132, *151*
Shah, A., 495, *508*
Shanyang, Z., 6, *39,* 756, *760*
Shapiro, D. A., 307, *333*
Shapiro, P. A., 57, *88*
Shapiro, S., 7, *39, 41,* 52, *90,* 118, 119, *150,* 192, 213,
    236, 237, *252,* 279, *296,* 423, *460,* 687, *711*
Shappell, S., 525, *533*
Sharfstein, S. S., 156, *186,* 195, *248*
Sharp, J. W., 134, *152*
Sharp, L., 95, *113*
Sharpe, M., 655, *683*
Shaw, B., 446, 447, *456*
Shaw, B. F., 394, *417,* 781, *790*
Shaw, S., 780, *794*
Shay, K. A., 565, *581*
Shea, M. T., 424, 447, 451, 452, 455, *457,* 704, *709*
Shea, R., 780, *791*
Shea, T., 464, *488*
Shear, M. K., *417*
Shear, N., 496, *507*
Shedler, J., *184,* 285, 287, *296*
Sheehan, D. V., 155, 157, 158, *185, 186,* 443, *461,* 777,
    778, 779, *795, 796*
Sheehan, J. P., 374, *389*
Sheehan, K. H., 778, 779, *795*
Sheik, J. I., 493, 494, 496, *508*
Shelton, R. C., 446, 447, *458,* 502, *507,* 780, *792*
Sheppard, L., 575, *579*
Sherbourne, C. D., 30, *41,* 153, 155, 156, 157, *187,* 455,
    458, 482, 485, *489,* 599, 602, *621,* 625, 642,
    649, 651
Shiely, J. C., 586, *621*
Shinn, M., 714, *733*
Shipley, M., 593, *620*
Shmuely-Dulitzki, Y., *185*
Sholomskas, D., 311, *334,* 406, 409, *421*
Shore, D., 142, *151*
Shrout, P. E., 131, *151,* 408, 412, *420*
Shugart, M. A., 97, *111*
Shugerman, A., 193, *248*
Shulman, K. I., 496, *507,* 561, 562, 563, 578, *580*
Sias, C. R., 375, *387*
Siegal, A. P., 785, *791*
Siegel, J. M., 384, *389*
Sloane, P. D., 373, 374, *389*
Smith, C. K., 374, *389*
Sighinolfi, L., 323, *331*
Silberfield, M., 319, *331*
Silimperi, D. R., 119, *149*
Silver, N., 496, *507*
Silversmith, D., 336, 337, 339, 340, 358, *371*
Silverstone, F. A., 561, 562, 563, *582*

Simeone, C., 68, *88*
Simmons, E. M., 771, *795*
Simmons, M. E., 400, *419*
Simmons, R. G., 321, *330*
Simon G. E., 7, *41*, 52, 53, 54, 55, 56, 57, 64, *89, 90, 91, 184,*
    193, 223, 224, 236, 237, 238, 239, 242, 249, 250,
    251, 252, 311, *333,* 375, *389,* 391, 392, 415, *418,*
    420, 424, 426, 452, *458, 459,* 464, 465, *488,* 602,
    603, 610, *620, 621,* 688, 691, 694, 698, 703, 704,
    705, 706, 707, 708, *709,* 710, *711,* 713, 714, *733,*
    769, 777, *793, 795*
Simons, A. D., 403, *419*
Sipkoff, M. Z., 10, *41*
Sireling, L. I., 194, *248*
Skinner, C. S., 787, *795*
Skinner, E. A., 52, *90,* 118, 119, 140, *149, 150,* 192, 213,
    236, 237, *252,* 423, *460,* 687, *711*
Skinner, E. A.,
Skinner, H., 7, *41*
Skinner, H. A., 428, *460,* 774, 786, *795*
Skinner, W., 787, *795*
Skurnick, J. H., 322, *331*
Slack, W. V., 771, *795*
Slau, J., 319, *334*
Slymen, D. J., 307, *332*
Smet, I. C., 571, *581*
Smith, C., 140, *150,* 236, *248*
Smith, C. K., 625, *650*
Smith, C. M., 545, *554*
Smith, D. C., 128, *148*
Smith, E. D., 134, *152*
Smith, E. E., 96, *113*
Smith, G. E., 558, 559, 560, 561, 565, 567, 578, *581, 582*
Smith, G. R., 55, *90,* 201, *252,* 463, 464, 465, 466, 467,
    468, 469, 473, 475, 477, 479, 480, 481, *489,*
    586, *621,* 655, *683*
Smith, J., 464, *489*
Smith, K. C., 403, 404, *417,* 424, *457*
Smith, M. K., 424, *461*
Smith, P. M., 134, *152*
Smith, R. C., 195, 220, *251, 252,* 423, *460,* 777, *795*
Smith, R. G., Jr., 7, *41*
Smith, S. S., 136, *150*
Smith, W. G., 628, *650*
Smith-Wilson, R., 131, *152,* 306, 310, *334*
Smolinski, M., 413, *417*
Smouse, P. E., 424, *457*
Smucker, W. D., 95, *113*
Smyth, K. A., *795*
Snaith, R. P., 509, *534*
Snow, K. K., 30, *41,* 342, *372,* 470, 481, 482, 484, 485,
    486, *490,* 584, 585, 586, 587, 588, 589, 590,
    591, 592, 593, *621,* 738, *760*
Snow, W. G., 558, *582*
Snowden, L. R., 407, *418*
Snyder, M. K., 625, 636, 643, *651*
Snyder, S., 117, *151*
Sobel, D. S., 10, 18, 23, 26, *39,* 53, *90,* 373, *389,* 698, *711*
Sobell, L. C., 786, 787, *791, 795*
Sobell, M. B., 786, 787, *791, 795*
Solberg, L. I., 45, *89,* 766, 767, 770, *794*
Solomon, A., 411, *418*
Soltzman, R. K., 214, *248*
Somoza, E., 127, 128, *149, 151*
Sonenstein, F. L., 428, *461,* 774, 786, *795*
Sonson-Fisher, R. W., 691, *710*

Sorce, J., 774, *790*
Sorrell, S. P., 781, *795*
Sotsky, S. M., 424, 447, 451, 452, 455, *457,* 704, *709,*
    780, *791*
Sox, C. H., 625, 643, *650*
Sox, H. C., 625, 643, *650*
Spar, J., 142, *149*
Specter, S. A., 322, *328*
Speechley, K. N., 95, 97, *112*
Spencer, P. M., 131, *147,* 299, *330,* 336, *372*
Sperry, L., 11, 15, 26, 27, 33, *41,* 257, 259, 275
Spiegel, D., 57, *90*
Spiegel, J. P., 378, *388*
Spiegel, J. S., 628, *650*
Spielberger, C. D., 509, 511, *534*
Spierings, C. J., 781, 782, *792, 794*
Spilker, B., 128, *151*
Spinnler, H., 559, *579*
Spitz, A. M., 158, *186*
Spitzer, R. L., 7, 8, 31, *39, 41,* 154, 155, 156, *184, 186,*
    191, 192, 194, 195, 196, 197, 202, 203, 206,
    208, 209, 210, 211, 213, 216, 218, 219, 221,
    226, 234, 235, 241, 246, 247, *248,* 249, 250,
    252, 253, 280, 285, *296,* 392, 410, *418, 420,*
    423, 428, 434, 442, 443, 444, *457, 458, 460,*
    466, 473, 475, 482, *489,* 500, *508,* 521, *534,*
    653, 654, 664, 665, 667, 669, 675, 678, *682,*
    683, 694, *711,* 756, *760,* 777, 778, *792, 795*
Spitznagel, R. L., 214, *248*
Spivey, L., 236, *248*
Sprafkin, R. P., 668, *682*
Spreen, O., 562, *582*
Springer, A., 382, *387*
Spritzer, K., 455, *458*
Squires, J., 100, *114*
Squires, R. W., 115, 134, *145,* 299, 310, 322, *328*
Sredl, K., 768, *794*
Srikiatkhachorn, A., 142, *148*
Stabler, B., 102, 103, *112, 114*
Stafford, M., 589, 593, *620*
Stancin, T., 101, *114*
Standiford, C., 238, 241, 246, *252*
Stangl, D., 430, *461*
Stansfeld, S., 593, *620*
Staples, W. P., 95, *113*
Starfield, B., 626, 628, *650*
Starkstein, S. E., 54, *90*
Starr, L. B., 54, *90*
State of Minnesota Employees Consumer Satisfac-
    tion Survey Results, 49, *90*
Stauss, F. F., 428, *457,* 774, *792*
Steele, J. J., 236, *248*
Steer, R. A., 127, 128, 132, 133, *145, 150, 151, 184,* 307,
    323, 324, *333,* 385, *387,* 394, 395, 396, 398,
    401, 402, 404, 405, *416, 417, 420,* 424, 431,
    435, 445, *456, 460,* 509, 510, 511, 512, 513,
    516, 517, 518, 519, 521, 524, 525, 527, *533,*
    534
Stefanis, C. N., 463, *488*
Steffens, D. C., 142, *151*
Steiger, J., 630, *650*
Steinberg, M. D., 115, *150,* 299, 325, *333*
Steiner, A., 496, *508*
Steinmetz, J. L., 447, *459*
Steinwald, B., *185*
Steketee, G. S., 781, *792*

Stelovich, S., 14, *41*
Stephens, R., 786, *790*
Stern, A., 137, *151*
Stern, J. D., 134, *148*, 320, *331*
Stern, V., 201, 205, 206, 219, 226, 231, *248*, 653, 657, 659, *682*
Stern, Y., 574, *582*
Steward, J. W., 311, *332*
Stewart, A., 140, *147*, 192, *252*, 259, *275*, 392, *421*, 423, 444, 445, *461*, 463, 464, *490*, 687, 691, *711*
    Stewart, A. L., 35, *41*, 154, *186*, 206, 209, *252*
Stewart, B. L., 445, *456*
Stewart, D., 95, *112*
Stewart, J. W., 311, *333*, 446, 449, *459*, *460*
Stewart, M. A., 544, *553*
Stewart, M. K., 467, 470, 473, *487*, *489*
Stewart-Brown, S., 610, *621*
Stiglin, L. E., 463, 473, *488*
Stiles, W. B., 625, *650*
Stimmel, B., 545, *553*
Stokes, E. J., 221, *250*
Stolee, P., 576, *581*
Stoltzman, R., 297, *332*
Stone, R. H., 409, *418*
Stosssel, C., 57, *89*
Stoudemire, A., 9, *41*
Strain, J. J., 116, 117, 137, 140, 141, *147*, *148*, *151*, 319, *333*
Strategic Advantage, Inc., 29, *41* 335, 336, 346, 348, 349, 351, 354, 361, *372*, 737, 738, *760*
Strauman, T. J., 313, *333*
Strauss, E., 562, *582*
Strecher, V. J., 787, *795*
Street, J. H., 192, *247*
Stretch, V., 787, *796*
Strober, M., 395, *420*
Strosahl, K. D., 4, 5, 8, 22, *41*, 52, 53, 61, 66, *91*, 136, *146*, 424, 426, *461*, 523, *534*, 687, 688, 689, 698, *711*
Stuck, A. E., 496, *508*
Stunkard, A. D., 202, *252*
Sturgeon, J., 319, *331*
Sturm, L., 104, *111*
Sturm, R., 10, 12, 16, *41*, 153, 155, 156, 157, *187*, 602, *621*, 713, *733*
Sturner, R. A., 100, *111*
Suelzer, M., 137, *149*, 312, *332*
Suhr, J., 561, 562, 563, *582*
Sulkava, R., 574, *580*
Sullivan, M., 664, 666, 668, *683*
Sullivan, M. D., 311, 325, *331*, *333*
Sumerall, S. W., 570, 572, *581*
Summerson, J., 590, *621*
Sumpter, E. A., 625, *649*
Sunde, S., 241, *250*
Sunderland, T., 499, *506*, 561, 562, *582*
Surawicz, T. S., 787, *792*
Surawy, C., 655, *683*
Sutcliffe, S. B., 319, *331*
Swain, M. A., 318, *332*
Swedo, S. E., 137, *151*, 312, *333*
Sweeney, J. A., 402, *418*
Sweet, R. A., 576, 577, 578, *581*, *582*
Swenson, M. R., 566, *581*
Swenson, W. M., *185*, 538, 543, 544, 546, 547, *553*, *554*
Swerdlow, N. R., 566, *581*

Swets, J. A., 126, *151*, 542, *554*
Swindle, R., 199, 241, *250*
Swinson, R. P., 510, 512, 513, 516, 517, 518, 519, 520, *533*, 307, *329*, 445, *457*
Szalai, J. P., 558, *582*

T

Tacchini, G., 373, *388*
Tafforeau, G., 259, *275*
Taira, D. A., 623, 625, 628, 630, 632, 634, 635, 636, 641, 645, 647, *650*
Takeichi, M., 7, *40*
Takeuchi, D. T., 393, *417*
Talajic, M., 57, *88*
Tamburino, M., 277, *296*
Tamburrino, M. B., 424, *461*
Tan, A. W. H., 47, 69, *88*, *90*
Tanahashi, N., 141, *148*
Tanaka, S., 319, *333*
Tanaka-Matsumi, J., 400, *420*, 509, *534*
Tangalos, E. G., 558, 559, 560, 561, 565, 567, 578, *581*, *582*
Tanielian, T. L., 53, *90*
Taranta, A., 625, *649*
Tarlov, A. R., 482, *489*, 623, 625, 626, 628, 630, 632, 634, 635, 636, 641, 645, 647, *650*
Taube, C. A., 52, *90*, 116, 117, *150*, 277, *296*, 391, *419*, 687, *710*
Tawaklna, T., 141, *148*
Taylor, B., 495, *507*
Taylor, B. P., 449, *460*
Taylor, C. B., 784, *794*
Taylor, C. M., 509, *534*
Taylor, J. O., 556, *580*
Taylor, L. H., 203, 221, 229, 241, *249*
Taylor, L. V. H., 31, *40*, 426, 443, 450, *459*, 756, *760*, 774, 776, *777*, 778, *791*, 793, *794*
Taylor, L. V. H., 774, 776, *791*, *794*
Taylor, S. E., 298, *334*
Tee, C. K. J., 608, *621*
Teesson, M., 31, *38*
Teitelbaum, M. L., 118, 119, *150*, 213, 236, 237, *252*, *252*
Tejeda, M. J., 364, *372*
Tellegen, A. M., 28, *38*, 144, *151*
Templeton, B., 193, *247*
Teri, L., 140, *151*, 398, 410, *419*, *420*, 447, *459*, *461*, 706, *710*, *794*
Terman, J. S., 311, *333*
Terman, M., 311, *333*
Terry, R. D., 575, *580*
Test, M. A., 312, *329*
Testa, M. A., 303, *329*, 584, *620*
Teti, L., 575, *579*
TeVelde, A., 68, *88*
Thadani, I., 141, *147*
Thal, L. J., 558, 566, 567, 568, 569, 575, 578, *580*, *581*
Thase, M. D., 501, *508*
Thase, M. E., 156, *186*, 195, *248*, 424, 430, 446, *461*, 501, 502, *508*
Thomas, J. L., 407, 410, 412, *420*
Thomas, K. J., 588, 590, 591, *620*
Thomason, B. T., 379, *389*
Thompson, D., 410, *417*
Thompson, J., 53, *90*, 118, *149*

Thompson, K. S., 201, 205, 206, 219, 226, 231, *248*, 653, 657, 659, *682*
Thompson, L. W., 306, *333*, 395, *418*, 502, *507*, *508*
Thompson, M. E., 321, *330*
Thompson, R. J., 97, *113*
Thompson, T. L., 221, *247*
Thompson, W. D., 116, *151*, 311, *334*, 466, 474, *487*
Thornby, J. I., 656, *683*
Thorson, J. A., 407, *420*
Thyer, B. A., 307, 312, *329*
Tiemens, B. G., 7, *41*
Tierney, M. C., 558, *582*
Tierney, W. M., 136, *146*, 491, *506*, 785, *796*
Tietze, P., 193, 194, *247*
Till, J. E., 319, *331*
Timmerman, I. G. H., 386, *390*
Tischler, G., 687, *711*
Tischler, G. L., 7, *39*, 52, *90*, 192, *252*, 279, *296*, *332*, 423, *460*
Todd, T., 324, *331*
Tollefson, G. D., 441, 450, *459*, *460*
Tombaugh, T. N., 557, 558, 560, 578, *582*
Tomlinson, B., 142, *146*
Tomlinson, B. E., 556, 573, 574, 578, 579, *582*
Tomlinson, D., 56, *89*, 375, *389*, 688, 691, 703, 704, *710*
Tonigan, J. S., 155, 157, *186*
Tonsager, M. E., 356, 364, *372*
Toomey, T. C., 315, *333*
Trexler, L., 397, *417*
Trexler, M., 435, *456*
Tricamo, E., 446, *459*
Trivedi, M. H., 466, 474, 475, *489*
Tross, S., 319, *333*
Troster, A. I., 566, 567, *581*, *582*
Truax, P. A., 144, *148*, 317, *331*, 360, 361, 364, 365, 369, *372*, 448, *458*, 526, 527, *534*, 708, *709*, 780, *792*
Tryon, R. C., 304, *333*
Trzepacz, P. T., 576, 578, *582*
Tsai, C., 586, *621*
Tsao, G., 548, *553*
Tse, C. K., 222, *251*, 443, 445, *456*
Tuason, V. B., 544, *553*
Tulley, R., 381, 382, *387*
Tuma, J. M., 96, *114*
Tupler, L. A., 570, 571, 572, *580*
Turner, C. F., 428, *461*, 774, 786, *795*
Turner, J. A., 397, *420*
Turner, R., 118, 119, *150*
Turner, R. J., 192, *252*
Turner, R. W., 213, 236, 237, *252*
Turner, T., 315, *329*

U

U.S. Preventive Services Task Force, 200, 215, *252*, 629, 638, *650*, 723, *733*
Ubezio, M. C., 559, *579*
Uebelacker, L. A., 558, *579*
Uhlenhuth, E. H., 119, *146*, 299, *330*
Ulchaker, M. M., 374, *389*
Umpress, V., 527, *534*
Underwood, K. L., 561, *581*
Unutzer, J., 57, *91*, 224, 242, *249*, 464, *488*, 603, *620*, 691, 698, 707, *711*
Ureno, G., 302, *331*

Usala, P. D., 407, *418*
Usherwood, T., 588, 590, 591, *620*
Ustun, T. B., 192, *250*, *251*, *252*

V

Vachon, 324, *330*
Valenstein, M., 238, 241, 246, *252*
Van Alstine, J., 407, *418*
van Belle, G., *794*
Van Casteren, T., 259, *275*
Van Cura, L. J., 771, *795*
van de Willige, G., 277, *296*, 464, 489 , 691, *710*
van den Brink, W., 277, *296*, 305, *334*, 464, *489*, 691, *710*
van der Enoe, J., 305, *334*
Van der Veken, J., 259, *275*
Van Dorsten, B., 382, *388*
Van Dyke, C., 569, 570, 571, 572, 573, 578, *580*, *581*
van Gorp, W., 570, *580*
Van Hasselt, V. B., 512, 515, 516, 517, 518, 519, 521, *534*
Van Hook, M. P., 393, *420*
Van Korff, M., 7, *41*, 391, *418*, 509, 523, *534*, 687, 688, 691, 694, 698, 703, 704, 705, 706, 707, 708, *709*, *710*, *711*, 770, 777, *793*, *795*
Van Oyde, P., 259, *275*
van Tilburg, W., 426, *458*
Vandongen, S., 571, *579*
Vangel, S. J., 566, 567, *582*
VanKammen, D. P., 318, *333*
VanPraag, H. M., 307, 311, *334*
Vanselow, N. A., 4, *39*
Vecchio, T. J., 123, 124, *151*
Veitia, M. C., 375, *387*
Veltum, L. G., 382, *388*
Vemon, S. W., 407, 412, *419*
Verboncoeur, C. J., 392, *420*
Verhulst, F. C., 305, *334*
Verloin duGruy, F., 7, 31, *41*
Vernon, S. W., 131, *150*, 410, 411, *419*
Victora, C., 373, *389*
Vieweg, B. W., 424, *458*
Vieweg, M. D., 133, *148*
Villar, J., 373, *389*
Villardita, C., 574, *582*
Villasenor, V. S., 302, *331*
Vitaliano, P. P., 568, *582*
Vitger, J., 431, *456*, 776, *790*
Vitiello, M. V., 567, 568, *582*
Vitse, H. M., 781, 782, *794*
Voegler, M. E., 106, *112*
Vogelsang, G., 140, *150*
Volk, R. J., 401, *421*
von Knorring, L., 259, *275*
Von Korff, M., 48, 52, 53, 54, 55, 56, 57, 64, *89*, 90, 91, 115, 116, 118, 119, 140, 145, *148*, *149*, *150*, *151*, *184*, 192, 193, 213, 223, 224, 236, 237, 238, 239, 242, *249*, *250*, *251*, *252*, 297, 299, 310, 311, 313, 326, *331*, *333*, 375, *389*, 392, 415, *420*, 423, *460*, 463, 464, 465, 473, *488*, *489*, 602, 603, *620*, *621*, 655, 656, *683*, 713, 714, *733*
Voris, R. A., 586, *621*
Vredenberg, K., 394, *420*

W

Wadden, T., 202, *252*
Wade, T., 512, 516, *534*
Wadsworth, A. P., 495, *508*
Wagenaar, H., 30, *39*
Waggoner, C. D., 381, 382, *387*
Wagner, 299, 310, 313, 326, *331*
Wagner, E. H., 48, *91*, 115, 116, 145, *148*, 223, *252*, 509,
          523, *534, 603, 621,* 655, 656, *683,* 691, 704,
          711, 770, 787, *791 793*
Wahler, H. J., 385, *390*
Walinder, J., 259, *275*
Walker, C. E., 103, *114*
Walker, E., 57, *91, 184,* 223, 224, 237, 238, 239, 242, *249,*
          375, *389,* 391, *418,* 464, 465, *488,* 602, 603,
          620, 621, 688, 691, 694, 698, 703, 704, 705,
          706, 707, 708, *709, 710, 711,* 714, *733, 777,*
          795
Walker, E. A., 55, 56, *89,* 236, *250,* 315, *334,* 664, 666,
          668, *683*
Walsh, B., 132, *151*
Walsh, B. T., *334*
Wang, H., 319, *334*
Ward, C., 132, *146,* 236, 247, 427, 429, 435, *456,* 781,
          786, *790*
Ward, C. H., 279, *296,* 393, 405, 407, *417,* 466, 474, *487,*
          501, *506*
Ward, J. H., 336, *372*
Ward, L. C., 495, *508*
Ware, J. E., Jr., 30, 35, *41,* 92, 154, *185, 186,* 206, 209,
          222, *252,* 259, *275,* 342, 368, *372,* 392, 409,
          417, 421, 423, 444, 445, *461,* 463, 464, 470,
          473, 481, 482, 484, 485, 486, *489, 490,* 584,
          585, 586, 587, 588, 589, 590, 591, 592, 593,
          598, 603, 606, 609, *620, 621,* 623, 624, 625,
          628, 630, 632, 634, 635, 636, 641, 642, 643,
          645, 647, *649, 650, 651,* 687, 691, *711, 733,*
          738, *760, 777,* 779, *795, 796*
Warner, C., 625, *651*
Warwick, C., 655, *683*
Wasserman, J., 68, *88*
Wassertheil-Smoller, S., 469, *490*
Wasson, J. H., 772, *796*
Waters, W. F., 382, *388, 390*
Watkins, L. R., 377, *389*
Watkins, J. T., 424, 447, 451, 452, 455, *457,* 704, *709,*
          780, *791*
Watson, B. A., 784, *795*
Watson, C. G., 396, *420*
Watson, D., 144, *151,* 313, *329*
Watt, J. B., 781, *791*
Waxman, H. M., 697, *711*
Weathers, F. W., 523, *534*
Weaver, M. T., 96, *112*
Weghorst, S., 784, 785, *791*
Weiller, E., 778, 779, *795*
Weinberger, H. L., 95, *114*
Weinberger, M., 785, *796*
Weinschel, B., 115, *150,* 299, 325, *333*
Weinstein, M. C., 126, 127, 128, *149, 151,* 409, *417*
Weinstock, R. S., 668, *682*
Weisberg, I., 95, *113*
Weisner, C., 4, 14, 17, 20, *39*
Weiss, B. D., 558, *582*
Weiss, L., 396, *421*

Weiss, M. E., 714, *733,* 769, *796*
Weissenburger, J., 448, *460*
Weissman, A., 137, *145,* 397, *417,* 435, 445, *456*
Weissman, C., 313, *332*
Weissman, M. M., 115, 116, *150, 151,* 155, 157, 158,
          185, 186, 200, *250,* 297, 298, 307, 311, 324,
          331, 332, 333, 334, 391, 406, 409, 410, 411,
          413, *417, 418, 419, 421,* 423, 443, 444, 445,
          449, *456, 457, 458, 461,* 463, 464, 466, 474,
          487, 488, 509, *534,* 777, 778, *791, 796*
Weizenbaum, J., 781, *796*
Welb, K., 713, *733*
Welkowitz, L., 445, *459*
Wellisch, D. K., 319, *334*
Wells, C., 138, *151*
Wells, K. B., 8, 10, 12, 16, *41,*128, *146,* 153, 154, 155,
          156, 157, *186, 187,* 192, *252,* 259, *275,* 392,
          421, 423, 426, 444, 445, 455, *458, 460, 461,*
          463, 464, 467, 468, 473, 478, *487, 490,* 599,
          602, *621,* 687, 691, *711, 733, 777, 796*
Welsh, K. A., 142, *151*
Wender, E. H., 95, *114*
Wengel, S. P., *185,* 495, 498, 499, *506, 507*
Wenzel, K. W., 775, 781, 782, *792, 794*
Werner, H., 562, *582*
Werner, J., 404, *419*
Wernicke, J. F., 439, *457*
Werthman, M. J., 30, *41*
Wesson, L., 105, *113*
West, K. K., 628, *649*
Westefeld, J. S., 137, *151*
Westlake, L., 588, 590, 591, *620*
Westphal, J. R., 779, *792*
Wetherell, J. L., 512, 513, 516, 517, *534*
Wetzel, R. D., 403, *419*
Wetzler, S., 307, 311, *334*
Whelihan, W., 140, *149*
Whelton, P. K., 135, *147*
Wherry, J., 464, 467, *489*
Whisman, M. A., 424, 426, *461*
Whitaker, A., 132, *151*
White, S., 104, *111*
Whitehouse, F. W., 590, *621*
Whitenack, D. C., 656, *683*
Whitmer, R. W., 68, *88*
Whooley, M. A., 214, 241, *252,* 695, *711*
Wider, A., 299, *334*
Widmer, R. B., 770, *796*
Wiebe, D. J., 382, *388*
Wiederholt, W. C., 566, 568, 569, 575, *578, 580, 581*
Wiefferink, C. H., 666, 680, *683*
Wienschel, B., 325, *333*
Wiggins, J. S., 304, *334,* 437, *461*
Wilber, C. H., 324, *333*
Wilcock, G. K., 556, *580*
Wildman, B. G., 95, *113*
Wilkinson, G., 128, *146*
Willcox, P. M., 584, *620*
Willemse, A., 426, *458*
Williams, C., 464, 467, *489*
Williams, D. E., 115, 134, *145,* 299, 310, 311, 322, *328,*
          334
Williams, G. H., 303, *329,* 584, *620*
Williams, J. B. W., 7, 8, 31, *39, 41,* 133, *151,* 154, 155,
          156, *184, 186,* 191, 192, 194, 195, 196, 197,
          202, 203, 206, 208, 209, 210, 211, 213, 216,

218, 219, 221, 226, 234, 235, 241, 246, 247, 248, 249, 250, 252, 253, 280, 285, 296, 322, 323, 331, 334, 392, 420, 423, 426, 434, 442, 443, 444, 458, 460, 461, 466, 473, 475, 482, 489, 500, 508, 521, 534, 653, 654, 664, 665, 667, 669, 675, 678, 682, 683, 694, 711, 756, 760, 777, 778, 792, 795
Williams, J. F., 135, 145
Williams, J. W., 392, 400, 401, 419
Williams, J. W., Jr., 214, 237, 241, 250
Williams, M., 779, 792
Williams, M. D., 570, 572, 581
Williams, P., 126, 131, 148, 149
Williams, S., 407, 418
Williams, T., 277, 296
Williams, T. A., 116, 149, 400, 405, 419
Williamson, J. M., 314, 334
Williamson, P., 668, 682
Williege, G., 54, 89
Williford, J. S., 784, 795
Wills, T. A., 201, 205, 206, 219, 226, 231, 248, 653, 657, 659, 682
Wilsnack, S. C., 547, 554
Wilson, G. T., 512, 534
Wilson, J. L., 96, 114
Wilson, J. M., 119, 145, 152
Wilson, K. M., 502, 508
Wilson, S., 466, 473, 475, 490, 774, 796
Winegarden, B., 571, 581
Wing, J. K., 305, 334
Wing, R., 202, 252
Winocur, G., 561, 562, 563, 578, 580
Winokur, A., 326, 334
Winokur, G., 444, 457
Wischman, C., 687, 688, 689, 694, 695, 698, 699, 701, 707, 710
Wise, M. G., 298, 334, 602, 620
Wise, R. N., 375, 390
Wise, T. N., 115, 117, 145, 147, 297, 298, 310, 330
Wisniewski, H. M., 564, 567, 579
Witmer, L., 96, 114
Wittchen, H. U., 6, 39, 192, 249, 251, 391, 418, 509, 534, 687, 709, 756, 760
Wittlin, B. J., 424, 460
Wittrock, D. A., 384, 389
Wiznitzer, M., 305, 334
Wofford, A. B., 241, 251, 521, 534
Wolf, D., 117, 151
Wolf-Klein, G. P., 561, 562, 563, 582
Wolraich, M. L., 98, 99, 114
Wong, P. T. P., 378, 389
Wong, P. W. K., 241, 250
Wong, R. K. H., 241, 250
Wood, C. H., 426, 457
Wood, L. W., 307, 329
Wood, M., 695, 709
Wood, R. J., 128, 152
Wood, W., 319, 333
Woodard, J. L., 565, 566, 580, 582
Woodworth, R. S., 128, 152
Woody, G. E., 324, 331
Woolfolk, R. L., 307, 329
Worakul, P. 142, 148
Worobey, J. L., 407, 418
Worrall, G., 407, 418
Woznicki, R. M., 325, 327, 330

Wright, E. J., 131, 149
Wright, L., 96, 102, 113, 114, 589, 591, 620
Wright, W. R., 625, 636, 643, 651
Wunder, J., 463, 488
Wyatt, R., 142, 151
Wyatt, R. J., 156, 186, 195, 248
Wyshak, G., 136, 152, 192, 206, 209, 253

Y

Yaffe, M. J., 193, 194, 249, 251, 311, 331, 411, 418
Yager, J., 116, 118, 119, 149, 237, 250, 464, 465, 488
Yager, T. J., 131, 151, 408, 420
Yancy, W. S., 94, 114
Yanovski, S., 202, 252
Yarnall, K. S., 608, 621
Yelin, E., 118, 152
Yerushalmy, J., 540, 554
Yesavage, J. A., 492, 493, 494, 496, 506, 508, 785, 796
Yeung, O. C. Y., 200, 250
Ying, Y., 7, 40, 464, 489
Yopenic, P. A., 116, 152
Yordy, K. D., 4, 39
Young, J. E., 403, 417
Young, K. T., 95, 114
Young, R. T., 222, 251, 603, 609, 621
Yu, E. S. H., 785, 792
Yurick, A., 769, 791

Z

Zabora, J. R., 131, 134, 152, 306, 310, 334
Zagami, E. A., 326, 330
Zalaquett, C. P., 128, 152
Zapka, J., 625, 651
Zarin, D. A., 53, 90
Zarling, K. K., 546, 553
Zarro, V. J., 135, 148
Zautra, A. J. 383, 390,
Zeltzer, L., 96, 112
Zervas, I., 325, 327, 330
Zhang, M., 463, 464, 489, 785, 792
Zhao, S., 192, 249, 391, 418, 687, 709
Zhiming, M., 326, 330
Zhu, S. -H., 787, 796
Zich, J. M., 409, 421, 423, 456
Zill, N., 94, 114
Zimmerman, M., 33, 41, 136, 137, 149, 155, 156, 187, 192, 253, 430, 446, 461, 466, 473, 475, 490, 774, 796
Zingesser, L. H., 564, 567, 579
Zitman, F. G., 426, 458
Zito, J. M., 53, 90
Zrull, J., 277, 296
Zubenko, G. S., 576, 577, 578, 581, 582
Zubkoff, M., 482, 489
Zuckerman, B., 157, 186
Zung, W. W. K., 7, 8, 41, 118, 119, 152, 153, 155, 187, 191, 206, 209, 236, 237, 250, 253, 279, 296, 368, 372, 391, 392, 393, 405, 421, 427, 461, 464, 466, 472, 488, 490, 493, 508, 687, 711, 756, 760
Zuroff, D. C., 407, 419
Zvagulis, I., 770, 793
Zweifler, A. J., 373, 374, 388
Zwilling, M., 449, 457

Subject Index

A

Abrasive personality styles, *see* Personality styles
Abuse, 157–158
Accreditation, 159
Accuracy
    Neurobehavioral Cognitive Status
        Examination, 570
    PRIME-MD 1000 study, 207, 208, 210
    SF-36 Health Survey, 590
    Shedler Quick PsychoDiagnostics Panel, 287
Actuarial samples, 300
Acute/chronic care, 67–68
ADHD, *see* Attention deficit hyperactivity disorder
Adherence rates, 625, 645
Administration
    Beck Depression Inventory instruments, 402
    COMPASS–PC, 258
    Daily Stress Inventory, 382–383
    Difficult Doctor Patient Relationship
        Questionnaire, 679–680
    Kaiser Permanente Integrated Care Project,
        722
    Primary Care Assessment Survey, 643–644
    PRIME-MD, 217
Adolescent community norm, 300
Adolescents
    pediatric psychologists, 108
    Symptom Checklist 90 Revised/Brief
        Symptom Inventory, 137, 312,
        314–315
    Symptom Assessment-45 Questionnaire, 339
Adult Suicidal Ideation Questionnaire (ASIQ), 435,
        436, *see also* Suicidal ideation; Suicide
AF, *see* Atrial fibrillation
Age
    Dementia Rating Scale, 567
    Mini-Mental Status Examination, 558, 559,
        560
    Self-Administered Alcoholism Screening Test
        screening, 547–548
    SF-36 Health Survey norms, 589
Age-range frequency, 740
Agency for Health Care Policy and Research
    (AHCPR) guidelines
    depression screening

Beck Depression Inventory instruments, 403
Depression Outcomes Module, 483–484
detection, 464, 466–467, 471
Hamilton Depression Inventory, 442–443,
    444, 447, 449
Kaiser Permanente Integrated Care Project,
    720
management program, 703, 704
primary care, 688–689
SF-36 Health Survey, 602
future of primary health care, 772
inadequacies in behavioral health treatment,
    16
AHCPR, *see* Agency for Health Care Policy and Re-
    search
AIDS, *see* Autoimmune Disease Syndrome
AIDS-related complex (ARC), 322
Alcohol abuse/dependence
    future of primary health care, 786–787
    Hamilton Depression Inventory, 444
    prevalence in primary care, 157
    PRIME-MD, 200, 201, 220, 228–229
    screening, 135
    Shedler Quick PsychoDiagnostics Panel
        validity, 286–287, 288
    Symptom Checklist-90-Revised/Brief
        Symptom Inventory applications,
        323–325
Alternate forms reliability, 303, *see also*
    Psychometric properties; Reliability
Alzheimer's disease
    Blessed Dementia Scale, 575
    characterization, 556
    clock drawing validity, 563
    Dementia Rating Scale, 565, 566, 567, 568
    future of primary health care, 785–786
    Geriatric Depression Scale, 494
    patient registries, 770
    screening, 139, 142
American Psychiatric Association (APA), 16, 94
Analogue scale, 318, 319
Analysis of variance (ANOVA), 380
Anorexia nervosa, 228
ANOVA, *see* Analysis of variance
Antidepressants, see also Depression; Medication
    COMPASS–PC case study, 272

depression management program, 701,
704–707
dosage and problems in depression detection,
464
elderly, 501–502
Hamilton Depression Inventory, 446, 449
Kaiser Permanente Integrated Care Project,
730
PRIME-MD, 226, 227, 228
Antisocial Personality Disorder (ASP), 324
Anxiety disorders
comorbidity of depression, 194
COMPASS–PC, 264
cost, 10
Difficult Doctor Patient Relationship
Questionnaire-10, 666
Hamilton Depression Inventory, 444
Kaiser Permanente Integrated Care Project,
721
misdiagnosis by physicians, 117
prevalence, 7, 156–157, 298
PRIME-MD, 200, 201, 211, 227–228
screening tests, 133
Shedler Quick PsychoDiagnostics Panel,
285–286, 287, 292
Symptom Assessment-45 Questionnaire, 347
Symptom Checklist-90-Revised/Brief
Symptom Inventory, 310–313
Anxiety scale, 357, 368
APA, see American Psychological Association
ARC, see AIDS-related complex
Area T-scores, 337–338, see also Scores/scoring;
T-scores
Area under the curve (AUC), 127, 305
Artificial intelligence, 281
ASIQ, see Adult Suicidal Ideation Questionnaire
ASP, see Antisocial Personality Disorder
Assessment, see Evaluation
benefits/costs and behavioral health
conditions, 158–161
criteria for selection, 163–166
defining process, 166–167
depression management programs, 690, 691,
694–695
Hamilton Depression Inventory, 450
Kaiser Permanente Integrated Care Project,
727
resources requirements for behavioral health
assessments, 170
screening for psychiatric disorders, 128–130
stress, 375, 378–379
Atrial fibrillation (AF), 321
Attention deficit hyperactivity disorder (ADHD),
106
Attention impairment, 139
AUC, see Area under the curve
Autoimmune deficiency syndrome (AIDS), 322–323,
589
Axis I psychopathology, 665–667, 669, 674

B

BAI, see Beck Anxiety Inventory
Barthel Index, 576

Base rate, 121, 123–125, 540
BASIS-32, see Behavior and Symptom Identification
Scale
BDI, see Beck Depression Inventory
BDI-IA, see Beck Depression Inventory-IA
BDI-II, see Beck Depression Inventory II
BDI-PC, see Beck Depression Inventory Primary
Care
BDPRS, see Brief Derogatis Psychiatric Rating Scale
Beck Anxiety Inventory (BAI)
case studies, 528–531
disease-specific considerations, 527
Hamilton Depression Inventory validity,
435, 436
interpretative strategy, 512, 514–516
norms, 512, 513
psychometric properties, 516–520
screening, 520–524
strengths/limitations, 528
summary of development, 511–512
treatment monitoring, 524–527
Beck Anxiety Scale, 595, 611, 613, 616
Beck Depression Inventory (BDI)
Beck Anxiety Inventory validity, 518
Center for Epidemiologic Studies
Depression Scale validity, 407
COMPASS–PC, 261
computer version, 429
consistency of measures with DSM-IV,
399–400, 520
depression severity in elderly, 501
diagnostic efficiency, 399–401
guidelines for clinical decisions, 403
Hamilton Depression Inventory, 427, 435,
436
history of scales, 393–395
implementation issues, 401–402
interpretative strategy, 397–398
psychometric characteristics, 395–396
screening, 132, 134, 137, 398–399
treatment monitoring, 403–405
Beck Depression Inventory IA (BDI-IA), 394,
395–396, see also Beck Depression Inventory
Beck Depression Inventory II (BDI-II), 394, 404, see
also Beck Depression Inventory
Beck Depression Inventory Primary Care (BDI-PC),
395, 400–401, 404, see also Beck Depression Inventory
Beck Hopelessness Scale (BHS), 137, 396, 435, 436
Behavior, negative, 106
Behavior and Symptom Identification Scale (BA-
SIS-32), 132–133
Behavior Checklist, 101
Behavioral health care
changes and delivery, 3–4
disorder prevalence, 6–8
integration with primary medical care, 4
interventions and reduction in medical
morbidity/mortality, 57
models of integrated primary services, 22
outcomes management, 259
problems
dissatisfaction and integrated medical
delivery, 58–61

presentation in medical frame of reference, 53–54
treatment in primary facilities, 55–57
report cards, 365–366
as specialty, 63–65
Behavioral health conditions
assessment benefits/costs, 158–161
impact, 154–155
prevalence, 155–158
Behavioral therapy, 704–707
Benign senescent forgetfulness, 555, see also Alzheimer's Disease
Benzodiazepines, 228
BHS, see Beck Hopelessness Scale
Bias, 129, 558, 564
Billing, 719
BIMCT, see Blessed Information-Memory-Concentration Test
Binge eating, 228, see also Eating disorders
Biologic stress syndrome, 376
Biological perspective, etiological stress models, 376–377
Biopsychosocial care continuum, 21–22
Biopsychosocial model, 700–702
Bipolar disorder, 227, 311, see also Depression
Blessed Dementia Scale (BRS), 142, 573–576
Blessed Information-Memory-Concentration Test (BIMCT), 573
Blood pressure, 531, 532, 590
BMI, see Body Mass Index
Body Mass Index (BMI), 375
Bonferroni adjustment, 396
Bootstrapping strategy, 492–493
Breast cancer, 318–319, see also Cancer
Brief Derogatis Psychiatric Rating Scale (BDPRS), 300
Brief Screening Inventory (BSI), see also Symptom Checklist 90/Brief Symptom Inventory
behavioral health care assessment, 29
screening for psychiatric disorders, 130–131, 134, 137
Symptom Assessment-45 Questionnaire validity, 341
Bromocriptine, 324
BRS, see Blessed Dementia Scale
BSI, see Brief Screening Inventory
BSI-18, 310
BT STEPS, 782–783
Bulimia nervosa, 228, 288, 289, see also Eating disorders
Buspirone, 228

C

CAGE questionnaire, 135, 167
Cancer, 57, 134, 306, 444
Capitation, 46, 67
Cardiology, 321–322, 378
Carter Center's Behavioral Risk Factor Survey, 642
Carve-outs, 49
Case finding
PRIME-MD, 196, 236–237, 238–239
screening distinction, 119
Case managers, 768
Case studies
Beck Anxiety Inventory, 528–531

behavioral health assessment program, 179–183
Geriatric Depression Scale, 503–505
Hamilton Depression Inventory, 452–455
Primary Care Assessment Survey quality assessment, 637–639
PRIME-MD, 243–245
Self-Administered Alcoholism Screening Test, 551–552
SF-36 Health Survey, 610–618
Symptom Assessment-45 Questionnaire, 367–369
Caseness, 130, 309
CBCL, see Child Behavior Checklist
CBT, see Cognitive-behavior therapy
CCL-A, see Cognitive Check List-Anxiety Scale
CCSE, see Cognitive Capacity Screening Examination
CCSI, see Cognitive Capacity Screening Instrument
CDR, see Consensus Dementia Rating Scale
CEG, see Clinician Evaluation Guide
Ceiling effects, 594, 609
Center for Epidemiologic Studies Depression Scale (CES-D)
consistency with DSM-IV criteria, 411–412
development, 405–406
implementation issues, 412–413
interpretative strategy, 408–409
psychometric characteristics, 406–408
screening, 409–411
SF-36 Health Survey correlation, 597–598
short form, 408
screening for psychiatric disorders, 131, 134, 136
treatment planning, 413
Cervical cancer, 319, see also Cancer
CES-D, see Center for Epidemiologic Studies Depression Scale
Chemical dependency, 10
Child Behavior Checklist (CBCL), 100
Chronic illness, 68, 768
Chronic obstructive pulmonary disease (COPD), 589
Chronic pain, 315
Chronic stress, 375
Chula Mental Test (CMT), 142
Classification errors, 126
Classification scheme, 98–100
CLF, see Current life functions
Clinic leadership, 176–177
Clinical child psychology, 108
Clinical depression, see Depression
Clinical implementation, see Implementation, clinical
Clinical interview, see Interview
Clinical services, 243, 681
Clinical utility
depression screener, 472
Depression-Arkansas Scale, 479
Hamilton Depression Inventory, 428, 436, 437
Clinical validity, 433, 437, see also Validity
Clinician Baseline Assessment, 481
Clinician Evaluation Guide (CEG), see also Primary Care Evaluation of Mental Disorders (PRIME-MD)

diagnosis of axis I psychopathology and difficult patient identification, 674
PRIME-MD
    administration, 213, 216, 219–221
    mood module, 199
    similarity to PPQ, 203
    structured interview, 200, 238
Clinician performance, *see* Performance, clinician
Clinics, 69–71, 84–85, *see also* HealthPartners
Clock drawing, 561–564
Cluster analysis, 336–337
CMT, *see* Chula Mental Test
Coaching, 182, 600
Cocaine abuse, 324, *see also* Substance abuse
Coding, 55
Coefficient alpha, 475, *see also* Psychometric properties
    BDI-II validity, 396
    Beck Anxiety Inventory, 516
    Brief Symptom Inventory, 303
    Center for Epidemiologic Studies Depression Scale validity, 406
    Dementia Rating Scale, 565
    depression outcomes module, 482
    Difficult Doctor Patient Relationship Questionnaire, 657, 663–664
    Geriatric Depression Scale short-form, 496
    Hamilton Depression Inventory, 432
    Mini-Mental Status Examination, 557
    Patient Description Questionnaire, 656
    Primary Care Assessment Survey, 632
    SF-36 Health Survey, 591
    Symptom Assessment-45 Questionnaire, 339
    Symptom Checklist-90-Revised reliability, 302
Cognitive Capacity Screening Examination (CCSE), 141
Cognitive Capacity Screening Instrument (CCSI), 571
Cognitive Check List-Anxiety Scale (CCL-A), 517
Cognitive impairment
    Geriatric Depression Scale, 495, 496
    prevalence, 556–557
    screening, 137–142
        Blessed Dementia Scale, 573–576
        clock drawing, 561–564
        Delirium Rating Scale, 576–577
        Mattis Dementia Rating Scale, 564–567
        Mini-Mental Status Examination, 557–561
        monitoring course, 567–569
        Neurobehavioral Cognitive Status Examination, 569–573
Cognitive Test for Delirium (CTD), 139–140
Cognitive-behavior therapy (CBT), 446–447, 449, 502, 784
Collaborative model, 21–22, 716, 717
Collaborative relationships, 56, 97, 102
Collaborative team model, 103
Collaborative-care interventions, 237–238, 239
Collateral sources, 499
Comanagement, effective, 20
Communication, 107–108, 193, 656, 660
Community nonpatient norm, 300
Community resources, 179
Comorbidity

behavioral health care disorders in primary care settings, 7–8
instrumentation for behavioral health care assessment, 30
medical, 158, 726, 772
nonmood psychiatric disorders and depression screening, 444
psychiatric disorders and primary medical disorders, 115, 116, 299
SF-36 Health Survey, 608
treatment decision making, 225
COMPASS-PC
    basic interpretive strategy, 264–265
    case study, 270–272
    creation, 259
    decision making guidelines, 267–269
    development criteria, 257–259
    developmental history, 255–256
    disease-specific considerations, 269
    future directions, 270
    office procedure, 265
    outcomes management, 256
        versus outcomes measurement, 259
    phase and dose-response theories, 256–257
    psychometric properties, 259–264
    strengths and limitations, 269–270
    treatment progress report, 266–267
Compensatory alliance, 675
Competing demands model, 235
Competition, 49, 159
Completeness of data, 634
Comprehensive Health Enhancement Support System (CHESS) programs, 787–788
Computer
    depression management program, 699–700
    future of primary health care, 769–773
    Hamilton Depression Rating Scale and development of form, 428–429
    PRIME-MD, 203
    psychological assessment, 31–32
    Shedler Quick PsychoDiagnostics Panel, 281, 284
    why they don't work in primary care, 284
Concurrent validity, *see also* Psychometric properties; Validity
    Beck Depression Inventory, 395
    Blessed Dementia Scale, 574
    Center for Epidemiologic Studies Depression Scale, 407
    Dementia Rating Scale, 565– 566
    Geriatric Depression Scale, 493
    Hamilton Depression Inventory, 433, 434
    Mini-Mental Status Examination, 557
    Neurobehavioral Cognitive Status Examination, 570–571
    weekly stress inventory, 384
Confidence interval, 591–592
Confidentiality issues, 643–644, 719–720
Consensus Dementia Rating (CDR) Scale, 565
Consensus Development Panel on Depression in Late Life, 12–13
Consistency, *see also* Internal consistency; Psychometric properties
    Center for Epidemiologic Studies Depression Scale, 411–412

DSM-IV criteria and Beck Depression Inventory instruments, 399, 400, 520

Geriatric Depression Scale, 493

management of depression-related disorders by primary care providers, 691

Construct validity, *see also* Psychometric properties; Validity

Beck Anxiety Inventory, 517–518

Blessed Dementia Scale, 574

clock drawing, 563

Dementia Rating Scale, 565

Hamilton Depression Inventory, 433, 435, 436

SF-36 Health Survey, 593

Symptom Checklist–90–Revised, 304

Consultation

integrated behavioral health providers, 67

medical by pediatric psychologists, 104

–liaison psychiatry, 5–6, 217, 237–238

Consultative case management, 22

Consumer satisfaction, 693

Content validity, 433, 434, 517, 593, *see also* Psychometric properties; Validity

Continuous quality improvement (CQI), 36

Convergent validity, *see also* Psychometric properties; Validity

daily stress inventory, 382

Dementia Rating Scale, 565

Hamilton Depression Inventory, 435

Mini-Mental Status Examination, 558

Primary Care Assessment Survey, 630

Shedler Quick PsychoDiagnostics Panel, 287

Copayment, 14, *see also* Reimbursement

COPD, *see* Chronic obstructive pulmonary disease

COPE, 781–782

Coping, 315, 706

Coping plan, 695, 697

Core scales, 257

Cornell Medical Index, 299

Coronary artery disease, 134–135

Coronary care patients, 546

Corticosteroids, 378

Cost-effectiveness effect, 698

Cost-offset ambiguities, 26

Costs

Beck Anxiety Inventory, 525–526

behavioral health assessments, 8, 9, 161, 166

Brief Symptom Inventory, 306

COMPASS–PC, 259

depression management program, 698–699, 700

depression outcomes module, 485

Depression-Arkansas Scale, 479

Difficult Doctor Patient Relationship Questionnaire, 680

Hamilton Depression Inventory, 451

PRIME-MD, 215, 241–242

Self-Administered Alcoholism Screening Test, 550

SF-36 Health Survey, 606, 609–610

Symptom Assessment–45 Questionnaire, 366

Counseling, 701

CQI, *see* Continuous quality improvement

Criteria of positivity, 598

Criterion group validity, 437

Criterion scores, 515, 516, *see also* Scores/scoring

Criterion-oriented validity, 307, *see also* Psychometric properties; Validity

Criterion-related validity, *see* Concurrent validity

Crohn's disease, 382

Cronbach's alpha, *see* Coefficient alpha

Cross-cultural studies, 548

Cross-validation, 339, 340–341, 493

CS, *see* Current symptoms

CTD, *see* Cognitive Test for Delirium

Cultural differences, 23

Current life functions (CLF), 257, 259, 260, 262, 263, 266–267, *see also* COMPASS–PC

Current symptoms (CS), 257, 259, 260, 261, 262, 266–267, *see also* COMPASS–PC

Cut off criteria, 748, 749, 750–751

Cutoff scores, *see also* Scores/scoring

Center for Epidemiologic Studies Depression Scale interpretation, 409, 410, 412

Geriatric Depression Scale, 493

Hamilton Depression Inventory, 431–432, 436, 439–440, 441

Self-Administered Alcoholism Screening Test screening, 542

Cutoff value, 126, 127

Cutpoint, 698

for difficulty, 661

D

Daily functioning, 568

Daily stress inventory (DSI)

administration/interpretation, 382–383

development, 379–380

norms, 380–381

psychometric information, 381–382

–weekly stress inventory (WSI)

clinical implementation, 385

etiological models of stress, 376–378

overview, 373–376

stress assessment, 378–379

summary, 385–386

Daily work flow, 360

D-ARK, *see* Depression Arkansas Scale

Data

Beck Anxiety Inventory, 526

behavioral health assessments, 166, 170–174

pilot program, 181–182

PRIME-MD 1000 study, 205–207

Shedler Quick PsychoDiagnostics Panel, 291–294

Symptom Assessment–45 Questionnaire, 338, 364

DDPRQ, *see* Difficult Doctor Patient Relationship Questionnaire

Decision making

Beck Anxiety Inventory, 523–524, 526–527

Beck Depression Inventory instruments, 403

COMPASS–PC, 267–270

Depression Outcomes Module, 483–484

Depression-Arkansas Scale, 477–478

future of health care delivery, 48

Hamilton Depression Inventory, 443

PRIME-MD, 222–226

Self-Administered Alcoholism Screening Test, 551

SF-36 Health Survey, 601–604, 606–607

Symptom Assessment–45 Questionnaire, 348, 354–356, 360–362
Symptom Checklist 90 Revised/ Brief Symptom Inventory interpretation, 308
Delirium screening, 138
Delirium Rating Scale (DelRS), 576–577
DelRS, *see* Delirium Rating Scale
Delusional thinking, 446
Demanding irritating patient, 657, 660, 661
Dementia, 138, 495, 555–556
Dementia of Alzheimer's Type Inventory (DAT), 139
Dementia Rating Scale (DRS), 564–567
Demographics, patient, 726, *see also* Kaiser Permanente Integrated Care Project
Dependent clinger, 654
Depression
    Beck Anxiety Inventory, 509
    Brief Symptom Inventory, 306
    clinical misdiagnosis, 117
    comorbidity, 138, 228
    COMPASS–PC, 264
    cost, 10
    detection rates, 193
    future of primary health care, 770, 771, 781–782, 785
    Hamilton Depression Inventory, 442–450
    Hamilton Depression Rating Scale, 424
    inadequate detection, 12–13
    Kaiser Permanente Integrated Care Project, 721, 732
    linking assessment and treatment, 692
    medical conditions correlation, 392
    pilot behavioral health assessment program, 181
    population management as service philosophy, 688
    presentation in medical frame of reference, 54
    presenting problem in childhood, 106
    prevalence, 7, 156–157
    primary care
        depression-Arkansas scale, 473–480
        depression-outcomes module, 480–486
        preliminary considerations, 465–467
        problems in detection and treatment, 464–465
        provider variation, 691
        recognition and screening, 33, 467–473, 690–691
        severity measurement and assessment, 692–693
        team culture, 689–690
        underrecognition by providers, 423
    screener
        age and generalizability, 123
        decision-making guidelines, 471
        development, 467–468
        feedback, 471
        implementation, 469–471
        interpretative strategy, 469
        psychometric properties, 468–469
        strengths and limitations, 472
        tests, 131, 132, 133, 135–136
        use as instrument for population monitoring, 472
    SF-36 Health Survey, 597–598

Shedler Quick PsychoDiagnostics Panel, 282–283, 287, 292
Symptom Assessment–45 Questionnaire, 347
Symptom Checklist–90–Revised/ Brief Symptom Inventory interpretation, 308, 311–312, 313
Depression Adjective Checklist, 402
Depression-Arkansas Scale (D-Ark), 181
    consistency with DSM-IV criteria, 474, 475
    decision making, 477–478
    development, 473–475
    feedback, 478
    implementation, 476–477
    interpretative strategy, 476
    psychometric properties, 475, 476
    scoring, 475
    SF-36 Health Survey correlation, 595
    strengths/limitations, 479
    treatment monitoring, 478–479
Depression-dejection scale, 396
Depression management program, 693, 700–702
Depression Outcomes Module (DOM)
    decision making, 483–484
    Depression-Arkansas Scale administration, 477
    development, 481–482
    feedback, 484
    implementation, 483
    interpretative strategy, 483
    limitations, 486
    psychometric properties, 482
    reliability and validity, 482
    strengths, 485
    treatment monitoring, 484–485
Depression scales, 368–369
Derogatis Psychiatric Rating Scale (DPRS), 300, 326–327
Derogatis family of symptom checklists, 29
Detection, behavioral health disorders
    instruments for depression, 466–467
    primary care settings, 235–239
        complexity of issues, 54–55
        depression by providers, 393
        inadequacies, 12–13
        treatment, 55
        PRIME-MD study, 213
    rates of mental disorders, 193
Development
    Symptom Assessment–45 Questionnaire, 335–336, 337
    Beck Anxiety Inventory, 511–512
    Center for Epidemiologic Studies Depression Scale, 405–406
    Daily Stress Inventory, 379–380
    Depression Outcomes Module, 481–482
    depression screener, 467–468
    Depression-Arkansas Scale, 473
    Difficult Doctor Patient Relationship Questionnaire-30, 657–663–664
    Geriatric Depression Scale short form, 496–498
    Kaiser Permanente Integrated Care Project, 714–718
    Primary Care Assessment Survey, 626–627
    SF-36 Health Survey, 586
    Weekly Stress Inventory, 383–384

Developmental criteria, 257–259, *see also* COM-PASS–PC
Developmental history, 255–256, *see also* COMPASS–PC
Dexamethasone suppression test (DST), 125, 311
Diabetes, 154, 382, 780, 784–785
Diagnosis
   early and cost of behavioral health care, 10
   efficiency
      Beck Depression Inventory instruments, 398, 399, 521
      Center for Epidemiologic Studies Depression Scale, 410, 412
      Geriatric Depression Scale short-form, 497
      Hamilton Depression Inventory, 435
      Symptom Assessment–45–Questionnaire, 351
   future of primary health care, 777–779
   incomplete and recognition of problems unique to psychiatric disorders, 117
   PRIME-MD, 207–208, 210, 214, 222, 239
   Self-Administered Alcoholism Screening Test screening, 544–545
Diagnostic and severity scoring, 487
Diagnostic and Statistical Manual of Mental Disorders-III-Revised (DSM-III-R), 666
Diagnostic and Statistical Manual of Mental Disorders-IV (DSM-IV)
   Center for Epidemiologic Studies Depression Scale, 411
   Beck Depression Inventory instruments, 399–400, 520
   Depression-Arkansas Scale, 474, 475
   depression management programs, 694
   Hamilton Depression Inventory/Rating Scale, 425
   SF-36 Health Survey, 597
Diagnostic and Statistical Manual of Mental Disorders–PC (DSM-PC), 97, 98–100
Diagnostic Interview Schedule (DIS), 402, 473–474, 500, 598
Diagnostic Interview Schedule for Children (DISC), 100
Diagnostic Interview Schedule for the DSM-IV (DIS-IV), 410
DIAMOND Project, 62, 73–76
Difficult Doctor Patient Relationship Questionnaire (DDPRQ)
   characteristics of patients experienced as difficult, 654–657
   characterization, 653–654
   considerations and description, 657
   development, 657–664
   epidemiology and characteristics of difficult patients and their doctors, 664–670
   health-related outcomes and physician-experienced difficulty, 670–671
   integrated care for patients experienced as difficult, 678–679
   strengths/limitations, 679–681
   use in primary care, 671–678
Difficult Doctor Patient Relationship Questionnaire (DDPRQ-10), 205, 219, see also Difficult Doctor Patient Relationship Questionnaire

Difficult patients, 654–657
Dimensions scores, 308, *see also* Scores/scoring
Direction, 265, *see also* COMPASS–PC
DIS, *see* Diagnostic Interview Schedule
DISC, *see* Diagnostic Interview Schedule for Children
Discriminant validity, *see also* Validity
   Beck Anxiety Inventory, 510, 517–518
   Blessed Dementia Scale, 574
   clock drawing, 563
   Daily Stress Inventory, 382
   Dementia Rating Scale, 566
   Hamilton Depression Inventory, 435
   Mini-Mental Status Examination, 558–559
   Neurobehavioral Cognitive Status Examination, 571–572
   Primary Care Assessment Survey, 630, 632
   screening for psychiatric disorders, 127
Disease
   building health care systems, 49–50
   -specific considerations
      Beck Anxiety Inventory, 527
      COMPASS–PC, 269
      depression, 466
      Geriatric Depression Scale, 494–496
      PRIME-MD, 233–235
      SF-36 Health Survey, 607–608
      Symptom Assessment–45–Questionnaire, 366
   -specific outcomes, 481–482
DIS-IV, *see* Diagnostic Interview Schedule for the DSM-IV
Disincentives, 14
Distress style, 307
Divergent validity, 558, 565, 574, *see also* Validity
DOM, *see* Depression Outcomes Module
Domains of monitoring, 143–144
Doorknob questions, 14
Dose-response theory, 256, 257
DPRS, *see* Derogatis Psychiatric Rating Scale
Drop out rate, 703
DRS, *see* Dementia Rating Scale
Drugs, *see also* Substance abuse
   Beck Depression Inventory instruments, 404
   future of primary health care, 787
   interactions and comorbidity of psychiatric and primary medical disorders, 115
   Symptom Checklist–90–Revised/ Brief Symptom Inventory, 311, 324–325
   toxicity and dementia etiology, 555
DSI, *see* Daily stress inventory
DSM-III-R, *see* Diagnostic and Statistical Manual of Mental Disorders-III-Revised
DSM-IV, *see* Diagnostic and Statistical Manual of Mental Disorders-IV
DSM-PC, *see* Diagnostic and Statistical Manual of Mental Disorders–PC (DSM-PC)
DST, *see* Dexamethasone suppression test
Dualism, 13–14
DUKE A-D, *see* Duke Anxiety-Depression Screener
Duke Anxiety-Depression Screener (DUKE A-D), 694
Duke Severity of Illness Checklist, 608
Dysthymic disorder, 391

E

Eating disorders, 200, 202, 228, 444
ECA, *see* Epidemiologic Catchment Area
ECM, *see* Electronic case manager
Economics, depression management, 698–699
ECT, *see* Electroconvulsive therapy
Education
    behavioral health care assessments, 178–179,
        182
    Dementia Rating Scale, 567
    Difficult Doctor Patient Relationship
        Questionnaire, 679
    future of primary health care, 780–789
    philosophical issues in depression
        management program, 701–702
    primary care settings and PRIME-MD, 229,
        236, 239
    programs and assessment of behavioral
        health care disorders, 16–17
    psychometric bias and Mini-Mental Status
        Examination, 558, 559, 560
Effect size, 593
Elderly patients
    depression, *see also* Geriatric Depression Scale
    detection and suicide, 12–13
    presentation in medical frame of reference, 54
    prevalence, 688
        screening and suicide, 136
    future of primary health care, 785–786
Electroconvulsive therapy (ECT), 227
Electronic case manager (ECM), 780
ELIZA, 781
E-mail, 699
Empathy, 676
Employers, 61
Entitled demander, 654
Environment, 377, 378
Epidemiologic Catchment Area (ECA), 115, 423, 687
Epidemiologic screening model, 121–122
Epidemiology, 664–670, *see also* Difficult Doctor Pa-
        tient Relationship Questionnaire
Epinephrine, 378
Episodic care, 216
Equal item variance, 632
Equal item-scale correlations, 632, 633
ERP, *see* Exposure and response prevention
Errors, 129, 164, 605
Ethnicity, 314, 431, 434
Etiological stress models, 376–378
Evaluation, *see also* Assessment
    behavioral health assessment tools, 163
    children for pediatric psychology practice,
        107
    Difficult Doctor Patient Relationship
        Questionnaire, 674
    Kaiser Permanente Integrated Care Project,
        724–731
    pathway and depression screener, 471
    PRIME-MD, 215–217, 221–222
    principles and screening for psychiatric
        disorders, 122–123
    Symptom Assessment–45 Questionnaire, 348, 363,
        364
    Symptom Checklist 90 Revised/Brief
        Symptom Inventory, 316

Event inventory, 383–384
Event score, 379, 380, 381, 382
Evidence-based care, 703
Exclusion criteria, 169
Expectations, realistic, 105
Experts, 690, 703
Exposure and response prevention (ERP), 782–783
External forces, 19
Extracted Hamilton Depression Rating Scale
        (XHDRS), 136
Eyberg Child Behavior Inventory, 100

F

FACCT, *see* Foundation for Accountability
Face validity, 593, *see also* Validity
Factor analysis
    Difficult Doctor Patient Relationship
        Questionnaire-30, 657–661
    Geriatric Depression Scale, 494
Factorial validity, 518–520, *see also* Validity
False positives/negatives, 33, 551
Family systems method, 674–676
Family, 109, 157–158, 225
Family-system analysis, 231–232
Feasibility criteria, 703
Feedback
    Beck Anxiety Inventory, 524
    Depression Outcomes Module, 484
    Depression-Arkansas Scale, 478
    Difficult Doctor Patient Relationship
        Questionnaire, 681
    Kaiser Permanente Integrated Care Project,
        723
    patient and use of depression screener, 471
    PRIME-MD study, 232–233, 243
    SF-36 Health Survey, 604–605, 607
    Symptom Assessment–45 Questionnaire, 356,
        364–365
Field testing, 285
Financial considerations
    benefits of behavioral health assessments,
        159–160
    collaborative model of Kaiser Permanente
        Integrated Care Project, 717
    integration of primary and behavioral
        health care services, 17, 18–19
    pediatric psychologists, 109–110
First-order change, 46
Five-factor model, 407
Flight or fight response, 376
Floor effects, 594, 609
FOCUS screening, 264, 265, 267
Follow-ups, 606, 616, 690
Foundation for Accountability (FACCT), 159
Four-factor structure model, 407–408
Free-standing behavioral care, 22
Free-standing medical care, 21
Frequency of monitoring, *see* Monitoring
FROMAJE, 142
Functional impairment, 218
Future
    COMPASS–PC, 270
    health care delivery, 45–52
    HealthPartners, 85–86

Kaiser Permanente Integrated Care Project, 731
psychological assessment and treatment in primary care settings
  case study, 763–766
  computer databases, 769–773
  computer-administered psychological assessments, 773–780
  computer-administered treatment, prevention, and education, 780–789
  patient-centered treatment coordinator, 768–769
Shedler Quick PsychoDiagnostics Panel, 292, 294

G

GAD, see Generalized anxiety disorder
GAF, see Global Assessment of Functioning
GAS, see General adaptation syndrome
Gatekeepers, 77, 117–119
GCS, see Glasgow Coma Scale
GDRS, see Geriatric Depression Rating Scale
GDS, see Global Deterioration Scale
GDS-SF, see Geriatric Depression Scale short-form
Gender
  INOVA Primary Behavioral Health Care Pilot Project, 740
  Mini-Mental Status Examination, 558
  patient factors influencing detection of mental disorders, 194
  Self-Administered Alcoholism Screening Test screening, 540, 547–548
  SF-36 Health Survey norms, 589
  Symptom Checklist–90–Revised, 300, 322
General adaptation syndrome (GAS), 376
General Health Questionnaire (GHQ)
  Difficult Doctor Patient Relationship Questionnaire-30, 661, 662
  psychiatric disorders diagnosis, 119
  screening for psychiatric disorders, 131
  Symptom Checklist–90–Revised, 305
General Practice Assessment Survey (GPAS), 640–641
General Social Survey (GSS), 588
Generalizability, 123, 300
Generalized Anxiety Disorder (GAD), see also Anxiety disorders
  Beck Anxiety Inventory, 520–522
  Hamilton Depression Inventory, 444
  Symptom Checklist–90–Revised/ Brief Symptom Inventory, 313
Generic care process, five-step, 72–76
Genogram-based interview, see Interview, genogram-based
Geriatric Depression Rating Scale (GDRS), 500–501
Geriatric Depression Scale (GDS)
  alternate administration techniques, 498–499
  case study, 503–505
  development, 492–493
  disease-specific considerations, 494–496
  monitoring, 502–503
  screening, 499–502
  short form, 493–494
    development, 496–498

Geriatric Depression Scale short-form (GDS-SF), 496–498
Geriatric patients, 138, see also Elderly patients
GHQ, see General Health Questionnaire
Glasgow Coma Scale (GCS), 571
Global Assessment of Functioning (GAF), 194
Global Deterioration Scale (GDS), 138, 142
Global scores, 307–308, see also Scores/scoring
Global Severity Index (GSI)
  Brief Symptom Inventory, 303, 309
  Symptom Assessment–45 Questionnaire, 337
    behavioral health care report cards, 365
    case study, 368, 369
    INOVA Primary Behavioral Health Care Pilot Project, 737, 738, 748, 749, 750–751, 756
    interpretation, 347
    validity compared to SF-12, 343, 344
  Symptom Checklist–90–Revised, 299, 303, 309
    applications, 319
    HIV/AIDS infections, 323
    suicide screening, 312
Goals
  Beck Anxiety Inventory, 526
  behavioral health assessments, 171, 180
  Hamilton Depression Inventory, 427–428
  INOVA Primary Behavioral Health Care Pilot Project, 736
  primary care clinics and behavioral health integration, 70–71
  Symptom Assessment–45 Questionnaire, 336
GPAS, see General Practice Assessment Survey
Graph assessment, 181
Group Health, 77, see also HealthPartners
GSI, see Global Severity Index
GSS, see General Social Survey
Guidelines
  behavior health assessments, 173, 178
  depression management program, 702–707
  diagnosis of pediatric psychological problems, 99
  implementation and inadequacies in treating behavioral health disorders, 16
Guilt, 672, 677

H

HAMD, see Hamilton Depression Rating Scale
Hamilton Anxiety Rating Scale (HARS), 517
Hamilton Anxiety Scale (HAS), 133, 136
Hamilton Depression Inventory (HDI)
  background and use, 423–427
  case study, 452–455
  full scale, 429–430, 439
  goals of development, 427–428
  interpretative strategy, 438–441
  melancholia subscale, 430, 435
  psychometric data: computer version, 428–429
  psychometric properties, 431–438
  screening depression in primary care settings, 442–450

17-item version, 430
short form, 430–432
strengths and limitations, 450–452
Hamilton Depression Inventory-17 (HDI-17), 430, 439, 440
Hamilton Depression Inventory–Melancholia Subscale (HDI-Mel), 430, 435
Hamilton Depression Inventory short form (HDI-SF), 430–431, 439, 440
Hamilton Depression Rating Scale (HAMD), 424, 775, 776
Hamilton Depression Rating Scale (HDRS), 402, 413, 425–426
Hamilton Psychiatric Rating Scale for Anxiety, 396
Hamilton Rating Scale (HRS), 407
Hamilton Rating Scale for Depression (HRSD)
    BDI-IA, 396
    Beck Anxiety Inventory, 404, 517
    Beck Depression Inventory, 395
    depression severity in elderly, 500–501
    Geriatric Depression Scale, 493
    screening for psychiatric disorders, 133
Hardware, 171, 284–285
HARS, see Hamilton Anxiety Rating Scale
HAS, see Hamilton Anxiety Scale
Hassles Scale, 383, 384
Hateful patients, 657
HCFA, see Health Care Financing Administration
HDI, see Hamilton Depression Inventory
HDI-17, see Hamilton Depression Inventory-17
HDI-Mel, see Hamilton Depression Inventory-Melancholia Subscale
HDI-SF, see Hamilton Depression Inventory short form
HDRS, see Hamilton Depression Rating Scale
Health care
    building for future, 49–50
    cost, 3
    delivery evolution, 45–49
    organization and population screening, 167
    utilization, 212
    venders and management of depression-related disorders, 689
Health Care Financing Administration (HCFA), 159
Health coordinators, 603
Health Insurance Experiment (HIE), 586
Health Maintenance Organization (HMO), 3, 641
Health management system, 767–768
Health plan delivery system, 641–642
Health psychologists, 374, 705–706
Health status graph assessment, 594–596, 609, 613
Health Status Questionnaire (HSQ), 181, 182, 586, 589
Healthpartners
    behavioral health interventions and hospitalization, 57
    first pilot, 78–80
    historical context, 77–78
    integrated behavioral health and wider organization, 82–84
    mainstreaming the pilots: what mattered at each clinic, 84–85
    need to move from pilot to mainstream, 81–82
    tasks for the future, 85–86
    theme deserving of variations, 80–81
    vertical integration of health care systems, 62

Health-related outcomes, 670–671, see also Outcomes
Health-related Quality of Life (HRQL), see also Quality of life
    patients experienced as difficult, 670
    impact of behavioral health conditions, 155
    PRIME-MD study, 209, 211–212, 222
Heart attacks, 57
HEDIS report, 689
Help-rejecting complainer, 654
Heterosexuals, 322
HIE, see Health Insurance Experiment
High Sensitivity Cognitive Screen (HSCS), 141–142
Hip-pocket consultation, 70
HIV, see Human immunodeficiency virus
HMO, see Health Maintenance Organization
Hodgkins disease, 319–320
Homosexuals, 322, 323
Hopkins Symptom Checklist (HSCL), 299
Horizontal/vertical integration, 61–62
Hormones, stress, 378
Hospital Anxiety and Depression Scale, 655
Hostility, 347, 355
Hostility scale, 357, 368
HPA, see Hypothalamic-pituitary-adrenocortical axis
HRDS, see Hamilton Rating Scale for Depression
HRQL, see Health-related Quality of Life
HRS, see Hamilton Rating Scale
HRSD, see Hamilton Rating Scale for Depression
HSCL, see Hopkins Symptom Checklist
HSCS, see High Sensitivity Cognitive Screen
HSQ, see Health Status Questionnaire
Human immunodeficiency virus (HIV), 322–323
Huntington's disease, 566
Hypertension, 321
Hypnotics, 228
Hypochondriasis, 202
Hypothalamic-pituitary-adrenocortical (HPA) axis, 376–377
Hypothesis matrix, 305

I

I/E score, see Impact/event score
IBD, see Inflammatory bowel disease
IBQ, see Illinois Behavior Questionnaire
ICD-10, see International Classification and Diagnosis System, Version 10
ICDS-PC, see International Classification and Diagnosis System, Primary Care Version 10
IDD, see Inventory to Diagnose Depression
IDS, see Inventory of Depressive Symptomatology
Illinois Behavior Questionnaire (IBQ), 319
Illness, meaning, 654
Imipramine, 447
Immune system, 378
Immunization registry, 770
Impact score, 379, 380, 381, 382, see also Scores/scoring
Impact/event (I/E) score, 379, 380, 381, 382–383, see also Scores/scoring
Implementation
    Beck Anxiety Inventory, 521–523
        problems, 525–526

Beck Depression Inventory instruments, 401–402
behavioral health assessment programs, 162
    pilot, 180–183
Center for Epidemiologic Studies Depression Scale, 412–413
Daily And Weekly Stress Inventory, 385
Depression Outcomes Module, 483
depression screener, 469–471
Depression-Arkansas Scale, 476–477
Kaiser Permanente Integrated Care Project, 718–721
Primary Care Assessment Survey, 642–647
Self-Administered Alcoholism Screening Test, 548–551
SF-36 Health Survey, 599–601, 606
Symptom Assessment-45 Questionnaire, 352–354, 358–360
Independent functions model, 103
Indirect functions model, 103
Individual responses, 348, see also Symptom Assessment-45 Questionnaire
Individual symptoms, 308, see also Symptom Checklist-90-Revised/Brief Symptom Inventory
Infinifax scoring system, 756, see also Scoring/scoring
Inflammatory bowel disease (IBD), 326
Informatics infrastructure, 699–700
Information, 105, 164, 166
Information systems, 48, 176
INOVA Primary Behavioral Health Care Pilot Project
    analyses, 747–754, 755
    findings, 757–758
    limitations, 758–759
    methodology, 737–740
    organizational participation, 736–737
    Phase I baseline, 741–746
    Phase II baseline, 746–747
    primary findings, 754, 756–757
    sample characteristics, 740–741
Institute of Medicine (IOM), 4
Instruments, disorder-specific, 33
Insurance, 50, 110
Integrated behavioral health, see also Healthpartners
    concept and distinctions, 65–67
    HealthPartners, 82–84
    primary care, see Integrated service delivery
    provider role, 66–67
Integrated model, 716
Integrated pediatric model, 102–105
Integrated Program (IP) model
    depression assessment, 695, 696
    Kaiser Permanente Integrated Care Project
        characteristics, 720
        psychological testing, 721–724
    model of depression management
        clinical effectiveness, 707
        guidelines in design, 705–707
        philosophical issues, 702
Integrated service delivery
    primary and behavioral health care integration: distinctions and concepts, 4, 61–69
    engaging primary care clinics: selecting a focus, 69–71

future health care delivery, 45–52
HealthPartners experience, 77–86, see also HealthPartners
improving the care and care system, 44–45
primary and behavioral health care services
    barriers, 23, 26
    impetus for integration, 17–19
    models, 21–25
    qualities of care, 19–21
    theme with variations, 71–76
    why integrate medical and behavioral health care
        dissatisfaction with status quo, 58–61
        review of relevant findings, 52–57
Integrated specialty consultation, 22
Integrating behavioral health assessment/primary care services
    additional resources, 177–179
    case study, 179–183
    cost and benefits, 158–161
    designing the process, 161–169
    educating providers and staff, 179, 180
    impact of behavioral health conditions, 154–155
    prevalence of behavioral health conditions, 155–158
    resources required, 169–174
    roles and responsibilities for providers and staff, 174–177
Integration team, roles, 174–175
Intent-to-treat, 693–694, 782
Interactive Voice Response (IVR)
    computer-administered PRIME-MD, 203, 221
    depression management program, 692, 700
    future of primary health care, 774–777, 779, 787
Interdisciplinary care models, 108
Internal consistency, see also Consistency; Psychometric properties
    Beck Anxiety Inventory, 516, 517, 525
    Brief Symptom Inventory, 303
    Center for Epidemiologic Studies Depression Scale, 406
    Dementia Rating Scale, 565
    Depression Outcomes Module, 482
    Difficult Doctor Patient Relationship Questionnaire, 657, 680
    estimate in reliability, 302
    Geriatric Depression Scale, 495
    Hamilton Depression Inventory, 432
        computer version, 429
    Mini-Mental Status Examination, 557
    Neurobehavioral Cognitive Status Examination, 570
    Patient Description Questionnaire, 656
    Primary Care Assessment Survey, 632
    SF-36 Health Survey, 590, 591
    Symptom Assessment-45 Questionnaire, 339
    Symptom Checklist 90 Revised, 302
International Classification and Diagnosis System, Primary Care Version 10 (ICDS-PC), 694–695
International Classification and Diagnosis System, Version 10 (ICD-10), 192, 445
Internet, 788–789

Interpersonal sensitivity, 347, 355
Interpretative strategies
    BDI-II, 397–398
    BDI-PC, 398
    Beck Anxiety Inventory, 512, 514–516
    Beck Depression Inventory, 397
    Center for Epidemiologic Studies Depression
        Scale, 408–409
    COMPASS–PC, 264–265
    Daily Stress Inventory, 382–383
    depression outcomes module, 483
    depression screener, 469
    Depression-Arkansas Scale, 476
    Hamilton Depression Inventory, 438–441
    Primary Care Assessment Survey, 644–647
    PRIME-MD study, 243
    SF-36 Health Survey, 594–596
    Symptom Assessment–45 Questionnaire, 338,
        345–348
    Symptom Checklist–90–Revised/
        Brief Symptom Inventory 307–309
Interrater correlation, 426, see also Psychometric
    properties
Interrater reliability, 574, 576, see also Psychometric
    properties; Reliability
Interscale correlations, 340, see also Psychometric
    properties
Intervention
    Beck Anxiety Inventory, 523
    depression management program, 701
    future of primary health care, 772–773
    PRIME-MD, 223
    SF-36 Health Survey, 601–602
    Symptom Assessment–45 Questionnaire, 354
Intervention effects, 725
Interviews
    cognitive impairment screening, 142
    genogram-based, 675, 676
    physician style and detection of mental
        disorders, 15, 193
    PRIME-MD study, 205–206, 207
    Self-Administered Alcoholism Screening
        Test, 549
    structured, 695
    telephone and alcoholism recovery, 786
Invalid response set, 438–439
Inventory of Depressive Symptomatology (IDS), 474
Inventory of Small Life Events (ISLE), 383
Inventory to Diagnose Depression (IDD), 474
IOM, see Institute of Medicine
IP, see Integrated Program model
ISLE, see Inventory of Small Life Events
Item
    content and Primary Care Assessment
        Survey, 628, 629
    development
        Difficult Doctor Patient Relationship
            Questionnaire-30, 657, 660–661
        Shedler Quick PsychoDiagnostics Panel, 283,
            284
    missing and Symptom Assessment–45
        Questionnaire, 338, 346
Item-to-score correlations, 517, see also Psychometric
    properties
IVR, see Interactive Voice Response

J

JAS, see Jenkins Activity Scale
JCAHO, see Joint Commission on Accreditation of
    Healthcare Organizations
Jenkins Activity Scale (JAS), 313
Job satisfaction, 160
Joint Commission on Accreditation of Healthcare
    Organizations (JCAHO), 159

K

Kaiser Permanente Integrated Care Project
    evaluation of program, 724–731
    implementation, 718–721
    integrated primary and behavioral health
        care program, 714–718
    role of psychological testing, 721–724
    Shedler Quick PsychoDiagnostics panel, 732
    summary of future directions, 731
KAT, see Khavari Alcohol Test
Khavari Alcohol Test (KAT), 545

L

Laboratory report, 281–283, see also Shedler Quick
    PsychoDiagnostics Panel
Laboratory screening, 133
Language, 717
Learning systems, 270
Legal counsel, 177
Legislation, 3–4
Length of stay (LOS), 325–326
Length of treatment, 359
LES, see Life Events Survey
Lewy body dementia, 556
Liability, 160
Liaison psychiatry model, 705
Life events inventory, 375
Life Events Survey (LES), 384
Life Management Skills Questionnaire, 614
Lifetime prevalence rate, 6
Lifetime risk, 463
Likert scaling assumptions, 628, 630, 631
Limitations, see Strengths/limitations
Linguistic deficits, 569
Live events, 378
Logistic regression analysis, 305, 312, 669
LOS, see Length of stay

M

Mainstream, 81–82, see also Healthpartners,
Major depressive disorder (MDD), see also Depres-
    sion
    Beck Depression Inventory instruments,
        399–401
    clinical features, 465–466
    economic costs, 463
    Hamilton Depression Inventory, 441
    prevalence rate, 391
    PRIME-MD, 226, 227
    psychosocial stressors relation, 375
    sequential screening for low base rates, 125

Shedler Quick PsychoDiagnostics Panel, 282
Mammograms, 770
Managed care, 3, 159, 641, *see also* Health Mainte-
    nance Organization
Management decisions, 672–674, *see also* Decision
    making
Marijuana, abuse, 324, *see also* Substance abuse
Masked depression, 194, *see also* Depression
MAST, see Michigan Alcohol Screening Test
MCS, see Mental Component Summary
MDD, *see* Major depressive disorder
Medical conditions, misdiagnosis, 139
Medical consultation-liaison models, 108
Medical history, 771
Medical Outcomes Study (MOS), 154, 473, 626
Medical Outcomes Study Short Form (MOS-SF), 670
Medical Outcomes Study Short Form Health Sta-
    tus-20 (SF-20), 209, 211
Medical Outcomes Study Short Form Health Sta-
    tus-36 (SF-36), 222
Medical Outcomes Study Short Form Health Status
    (SF-36/SF-12), 30
Medical records, 48, 719–720
Medical subspecialty care, 216–217
Medication, *see also* Individual entries
    COMPASS–PC, 258, 267, 272, 274
    Hamilton Depression Inventory, 449
    SF-36 Health Survey case study, 614–616
    Symptom Assessment–45 Questionnaire, 355, 369
MEDLINE, 788
Melancholia, 440, 425, 446
Mental Component Summary (MCS)
    INOVA Primary Behavioral Health Care Pilot
        Project, 738, 741, 744, 747, 750–752,
        756
    Kaiser Permanente Integrated Care Project,
        727, 729
    SF-36 Health Survey, 587, 598, 599
    Symptom Assessment–45 Questionnaire,
        342–343, 369
Mental disorders
    detection, 192–195
    Difficult Doctor Patient Relationship
        Questionnaire, 665–667
    patient-centered treatment coordinator, 769
    prevalence and health-related outcomes, 192
    primary care as de facto system and why
        integration is needed, 52–53
    PRIME-MD, 233–234
Mental Health Index (MHI), 259, 260, 262–264,
    266–268, 270, *see also* COMPASS–PC
Mental Health Professional (MHP), 205–206, 207, 778
Mental health providers, 718–719, 720
Mental health screening tests, 278–280
Mental Status Questionnaire (MSQ), 142
Mentoring, 600
Mercer Survey, 3
Methadone, 324, 545
MHI, *see* Mental Health Index
MHQ, *see* Middlesex Hospital Questionnaire
Michigan Alcohol Screening Test (MAST), 537–538
Middlesex Hospital Questionnaire (MHQ), 304
MINI, *see* Mini-International Neuropsychiatric In-
    terview
Mini-International Neuropsychiatric Interview
    (MINI), 778–779

Mini-Mental State Examination (MMSE)
    depression diagnosis compared with
        Geriatric Depression Scale, 495,
        496
    screening for cognitive impairment,
        140–141, 557–561
Minnesota Multiphasic Personality Inventory-2
    (MMPI-2), 304, 311, 405, 539
Minnesota Multiphasic Personality Inventory-2
    (MMPI-2), 28
Minnesota Multiphasic Personality Inventory De-
    pression (MMPI-D) Scale, 395, 396
Misdiagnosis, depression, 465
MMPI, *see* Minnesota Multiphasic Personality In-
    ventory
MMPI-2, *see* Minnesota Multiphasic Personality In-
    ventory-2 (MMPI-2)
MMPI-D, *see* Minnesota Multiphasic Personality
    Inventory Depression
MMSE, *see* Mini-Mental State Examination
Monitoring
    alcohol abuse and computer-assisted
        treatment, prevention, education,
        786–787
    Beck Anxiety Inventory, 524–527
    Beck Depression Inventory instruments,
        403–405
    Blessed Dementia Scale, 575
    COMPASS–PC, 256, 267–268
    Dementia Rating Scale, 567–569
    Depression Outcomes Module, 484–485
    Depression-Arkansas Scale, 478
    future of primary health care, 777, 784
    Geriatric Depression Scale, 502–503
    Hamilton Depression Inventory, 447–450
    population using depression screener, 472
    PRIME-MD, 233
    provider performance and depression
        management, 695, 697
    psychiatric disorders in primary care
        populations, 142–144
    psychological assessment and treatment
        planning, 35
    role of assessment in primary care settings,
        27
    SF-36 Health Survey, 605–607
    side effects monitoring, 777
    Symptom Assessment–45 Questionnaire,
        356–362
    Symptom Checklist– 90–Revised/
        Brief Symptom Inventory,
        315–317
Monoamine oxidase inhibitors, 227, 446
Mood disorders
    BDI-PC, 401
    Difficult Doctor Patient Relationship
        Questionnaire, 666
    Hamilton Depression Inventory, 443, 444
    identification by primary care providers, 393
    PRIME-MD, 200, 201, 211, 227
        clinician evaluation guide, 220
    Shedler Quick PsychoDiagnostics Panel
        validity, 285–286
Mood stabilization, 226
Morbidity, 57, 118
Mortality, 57

MOS, *see* Medical Outcomes Study
MOS-SF, *see* Medical Outcomes Study Short Form
MSQ, *see* Mental Status Questionnaire
Multi-infarct dementia, 556, *see also* Dementia
Multiple respondents, 680
Multivariate analyses, 669

N

National Committee for Quality Assurance (NCQA), 19, 49, 159
National Comorbidity Survey, 192
National Health and Nutrition Examination Survey (NHAMES-I), 406
National Primary Care Research and Development Centre (NPCRDC), 640–641
National Survey of Functional Health Status (NSFHS), 588
Natural killer (NK) cells, 378
NCQA, *see* National Committee for Quality Assurance
NCSE, *see* Neurobehavioral Cognitive Status Examination
NCSS, *see* Nonclinical staff support condition
Negative feelings, 677
Negative predictive value (NPV), 436, 469, 541–542, 776, *see also* Psychometric properties
Neurobehavioral Cognitive Status Examination (NCSE), 569–573
Neuropsychological functioning, 29–30
Neuropsychological Screening Battery (NSB), 571
NHAMES-I, *see* National Health and Nutrition Examination Survey
NK, *see* Natural killer cells
Nocturnal worsening, 139, *see also* Dementia
Nonsupport condition, 238
Nonclinical staff support condition (NCSS), 238
Nonmood psychiatric disorders, 444
Nonpatient groups, 337, 544–545, 547–548
Nonprofessional audience, 242–243, 680–681
Norepinephrine, 378
Normative data
    Blessed Dementia Scale, 574
    Center for Epidemiologic Studies Depression Scale, 406
    clock drawing, 563
    Dementia Rating Scale, 566–567
    Hamilton Depression Inventory, 431–432, 440
    Mini-Mental Status Examination, 559–560
    Neurobehavioral Cognitive Status Examination, 572
    Primary Care Assessment Survey, 646
    Symptom Assessment–45 Questionnaire, 337, 350–351
    Symptom Checklist 90 Revised, 300–301
Norm-referenced interpretation, 512, 515
Norms
    Beck Anxiety Inventory, 512, 513, 514
    Daily Stress Inventory, 380–381
    Self-Administered Alcoholism Screening Test, 539
    SF-36 Health Survey, 588–589
    Symptom Checklist–90–Revised/ Brief Symptom Inventory, 300–301
    Weekly Stress Inventory, 383, 384
NOS, *see* Not otherwise specified

Nosologic depression, 399
Not otherwise specified (NOS), 201, 202, 391
NPCRDC, *see* National Primary Care Research and Development Centre
NPV, *see* Negative predictive value
NSB, *see* Neuropsychological Screening Battery
NSFHS, *see* National Survey of Functional Health Status
Nursing staff, 175
Nursing support condition (RN), 238

O

Objective referents, 240, 680
Obsessive-compulsive disorder
    Beck Anxiety Inventory, 522
    future of primary health care, 775, 780–781, 782–784
    Hamilton Depression Inventory, 444
    PRIME-MD, 201
    Shedler Quick PsychoDiagnostics Panel validity, 286
    Symptom Assessment–45 Questionnaire, 347
Obsessive-compulsive scale, 368
Occupational Therapy Evaluation of Performance and Support, 568
OCD, *see* Obsessive-compulsive disorder
Odds ratio, 238
Oncology, 318–321, *see also* Cancer
Operating characteristics, 209, 540–542
Opioid peptides, 378
Organic mental disorder (OMD), 137–138
Organizations, 159–161, 736–737
Outcomes
    assessment
        Shedler Quick PsychoDiagnostics Panel, 291
        depression, 692–694
        Hamilton Depression Inventory, 449
    management, 35–36, 256, 259
Outpatient care, 104, 747–748

P

Padua Inventory, 523
PAIS, *see* Psychological Adjustment to Illness Scale
Panic Attack Questionnaire (PAQ), 519
Panic disorder (PD)
    Beck Anxiety Inventory, 510, 520, 522, 529, 530
    future of primary health care, 784
    Hamilton Depression Inventory, 444
    Kaiser Permanente Integrated Care Project, 721
    prevalence in primary care, 156
    PRIME-MD, 200, 227, 228
    Shedler Quick PsychoDiagnostics Panel, 286
    Symptom Checklist–90–Revised/ Brief Symptom Inventory, 311, 312
PAQ, *see* Panic Attack Questionnaire
Parallel care delivery systems, 58, 59, 60, 61
Paranoid ideation, 347, 355
Parents, pediatric primary care, 96
Parkinson's disease, 563, 566, 567
Pathways, disease-specific, 178
Patient Description Questionnaire (PDQ), 656

Patient(s)
   behavioral health assessments, 173, 176, 182
   COMPASS–PC, 270, 271
   current model of interaction in primary and
         mental health care, 766
   detection of mental disorders, 194
   demanding irrational, 657, 660, 661
   elderly, *see* Elderly patients
   hateful, 657
   health-related   outcomes   and
         physician-experienced difficulty, 670
   INOVA Primary Behavioral Health Care Pilot
         Project, 739
      Phase I, 746
      Phase II, 747
      prediction from phases I/II, 752, 754
      primary findings, 754
      tracking form, 738, 741
   integrated delivery service, 68
   Kaiser Permanente Integrated Care Project,
         723–724, 727, 729–730
   psychiatric, 545–546, 571
   primary care
      future, 771–772, 784
      physician communication, 583
      providers and identification of at-risk, 167
      stress impact, 373
      why use patient-provided information, 624–626
   Primary Care Assessment Survey assessment of
         populations, 635–636
   PRIME-MD, 207, 217–219, 225
   psychological assessment and identification of
         characteristics, 35
   resistance barriers to integrated primary and
         behavioral health care services, 23
   selection criteria, 168–169
   Self-Administered Alcoholism Screening
         Test, 543–544, 545–547, 550
   self-destructive, 659, 660
   service/access perspective and specialty
         behavioral health care model, 64
   Shedler Quick PsychoDiagnostics Panel,
         290–291
   Symptom Assessment-45 Questionnaire, 360–361
   value of questionnaires, 162, 164, 166
Patient problem questionnaire (PPQ), 202–203
Patient Questionnaire (PQ)
   administration, 219, 238
   diagnosis of Axis I psychopathology and
         difficult patient identification, 674
   PRIME-MD, 197–200, 209
Patterned response, 346
Pattern-matching algorithms, 283
PCAS, see Primary Care Assessment Survey
PCL, *see* PTSD Check List
PCP, *see* Primary care provider
PCS, *see* Physical Component Summary
PD, *see* Panic disorder
PDI-PC, consistency, 399, 400
PDQ, *see* Patient Description Questionnaire
PDQ-R, *see* Personality Diagnostic Question-
      naire-Revised
Pearson correlation coefficient, 632
Pediatric primary care, integrating behavioral health
      care

characteristics of psychology practice,
      106–108
current trends in identifying behavioral
      issues, 97–101
justification for integration, 93–97
providing care, 101–105
setting up a psychology practice, 108–111
Pediatric psychologist, 96, 103–104, 109
Pediatric psychology practice
   characteristics of and primary care settings,
      106–108
   setting up, 108–111
Pediatric service delivery, 94–96
Pediatric Symptom Checklist (PSC), 101
Pediatricians, 95
Penn State Worry Questionnaire (PSWQ), 523
Perceived Stress Scale (PSS), 378
Perceived value, 212–213
Percentile conversions, 337–338
Perceptions, 193–194
Performance
   clinician, 636–641, 644
   depression management, 693, 695, 697
Personal Data Sheet, 128
Personal identification number (PIN), 775
Personality Diagnostic Questionnaire-Revised
      (PDQ-R), 661, 662, 668
Personality disorders, 654–655
Personality pathology, 676–678
Personality style, 654–655, 668, 676–677
Pharmacists, 176
Pharmacotherapy, 729–730
Phase theory, 256–257
Phobias, 156
Phobic anxiety, 348
Physical Component Summary (PCS)
   INOVA Primary Behavioral Health Care
      Pilot Project, 738, 741, 744, 747,
      750–752
   Kaiser Permanente Integrated Care Project,
      727, 729
   SF-36 Health Survey, 587
   Symptom Assessment-45 Questionnaire validity
      compared to SF-12, 343, 369
Physical disorders, 233–234, 667–668
Physical space, 717
Physical symptoms, 218, 655, 667, 695
Physician(s)
   Difficult Doctor Patient Relationship
      Questionnaire, 656, 659, 660, 661,
      668–669
   mental disorder detection, 192–194
   –patient relationship, 230–231
   PRIME-MD, 226, 238
   psychiatric disorder recognition, 117–119
   Self-Administered Alcoholism Screening
      Test screening, 546
   Shedler Quick PsychoDiagnostics Panel,
      289–290
Physician Belief Scale, 668–669
Physician in charge (PIC), 715
Physiological perspective, stress, 378
PIC, *see* Physician in charge
Pilot program, 78, *see also* HealthPartners
Pilot sample, 283

Pilot testing, 173–174, 181, *see also* Behavioral health
    assessments
PIN, *see* Personal identification number
Point of view (POV) boxes, 264, 265, 699, 700
Population
    depression
        needs of special and management, 697–698
        screening, 167, 472
        service philosophy, 689
    future of primary health care, 47, 770
    primary care
        addressing depression, 688–692
        design guidelines for depression
            management program, 702–707
        informatics infrastructure, 699–700
        philosophical issues in depression
            management program design,
            700–702
        screening and assessment systems, 692–699
    Self-Administered Alcoholism Screening Test
        screening, 539–540
Positive predictive value (PPV), *see also*
    Psychometric properties
    depression screener, 468–469
    future of primary health care, 776–777
    Hamilton Depression Inventory, 436
    Self-Administered Alcoholism Screening Test
        screening, 541–542
    SF-36 Health Survey, 598
Positive Symptom Distress Index (PSDI), 299, 303,
    307, 312
Positive Symptom Total (PST)
    Brief Symptom Inventory, 303, 307–308
    Symptom Assessment–45 Questionnaire
        case study, 369
        interpretation, 347
        INOVA Primary Behavioral Health Care Pilot
            Project, 737, 738, 748, 749
        validity, 343, 344
        summary of development, 337
    Symptom Checklist–90–Revised, 299,
        307–308
Postal questionnaires, 606, 628, 643–644
Postpartum problems, 311
Posttraumatic stress disorder (PTSD), 201, 522
POV, *see* Point of view boxes
PPDQ, *see* Practitioner Psychopathology Diagnostic
    Questionnaire
PPQ, *see* Patient Problem Questionnaire
PPV, *see* Positive predictive value
PQ, *see* Patient questionnaire
Practitioner Psychopathology Diagnostic Question-
    naire (PPDQ), 662
Prediction
    Center for Epidemiologic Studies Depression
        Scale, 409
    Primary Care Assessment Survey, 625
    PRIME-MD 1000 study, 208, 210
    screening tests for psychiatric disorders, 122,
        123–126
    Self-Administered Alcoholism Screening
        Test, 551
    Shedler Quick PsychoDiagnostics Panel, 286
    Symptom Assessment–45 Questionnaire, 356, 363

Symptom Checklist–90–Revised/
    Brief Symptom Inventory
    interpretation, 308
Preschool Behavior Questionnaire, 101
Present State Examinations (PSE), 305
Pretherapy therapy, 67
Prevalence
    alcoholism, 540
    cognitive impairment in primary care
        setting, 556–557
    depression, 391
    major depressive disorder, 463
    psychiatric and anxiety disorders, 297–298
    rates and results of PRIME-MD study, 207
Prevention
    computer-assisted in elderly, 784–785
        future of primary health care, 780–789
    philosophical issues in depression
        management program, 702
Preventive Services Task Force, 215
Primary care
    Beck Anxiety Inventory, 521
    behavioral health care delivery, 44–45,
        52–55, 57
    clinics, 69–71
    definition, 4–5
    Difficult Doctor Patient Relationship
        Questionnaire-30, 671–678
    Geriatric Depression Scale, 499–500
    model, 45–46
    partnership, 20–21
    physicians, 193
    population, *see* Population, primary care
    PRIME-MD, 215–216, 235–239
    Symptom Assessment–45 Questionnaire,
        342–344, 348–349
    Symptom Checklist–90–Revised/
        Brief Symptom Inventory,
        309–314
Primary Care Assessment Survey (PCAS)
    characterization, 623–624
    defining features, 627–628
    development, 626–627
    implementation, 642–647
    measurement performance, 628–635
    quality assessment and improvement,
        635–642
    why use patient-provided information
        about care, 624–626
Primary Care Evaluation of Mental Disorders
    (PRIME-MD)
    background, 192–195
    case study, 243–245
    characterization, 195–203
    depression diagnosis, 694
    Difficult Doctor Patient Relationship
        Questionnaire
    diagnosis, 674–676
    epidemiology comparison, 664, 665, 667, 668
    disease-specific considerations, 233–235
    future of primary health care, 777, 778
    impact of behavioral health conditions, 154
    improving detection of behavioral health
        disorders, 235–239
    instrumentation for behavioral health care
        assessment, 31–32

prevalence of depression and anxiety, 156–157
strengths and limitations, 239–243
use for screening behavioral health disorders
administration of individual components, 219–221
candidates for evaluation, 215–217
guidelines for decision making, 222–226
patient characteristics, 217–219
prediction of treatment outcomes, 232
providing feedback of results, 232–233
specific treatment recommendations, 226–232
use with other evaluation data, 221–222
who should administer, 217
use in treatment monitoring, 233
validation by 1000 study, 203–214
Primary care provider (PCP)
behavioral health assessments 159–161, 182, 166–167
benefits, 159–161
education, 179
impact of conditions, 154
roles and responsibilities, 175
COMPASS–PC, 270
Geriatric Depression Scale, 499
Kaiser Permanente Integrated Care Project, 722, 723
knowledgeability and inadequacies in treating behavioral health disorders, 15
management of depression-related disorders, 689–690, 691
PRIME-MD study, 204–205, 217
satisfaction, 739, 741, 742, 743, 746–747, 754
Symptom Assessment–45 Questionnaire, 348–349
Primary mental health care, 22–23
PRIME-MD, see Primary Care Evaluation of Mental Orders
Problem drinking, 201, see also Alcohol abuse/dependence
Problem identification, 34, 70, 104–105
Problem-solving therapy, 703–704
Process approach, 562
Prochaska-DiClemente model, 228, 229, 230
Procrustes method, 305
Progress Plan, 706
Provider satisfaction, see Primary care provider
PSC, see Pediatric Symptom Checklist
PSDI, see Positive Symptom Distress Index
PSE, see Present State Examinations
Pseudodementia, 138, see also Dementia
Psoriasis, 546–547
PSS, see Perceived Stress Scale
PST, see Positive Symptom Total
PSWQ, see Penn State Worry Questionnaire
Psychiatric disorders
diagnosis using revised Symptom Checklist–90/Brief Symptom Inventory, 298
difficult patient characteristics, 655
monitoring in primary care, 142–144
prevalence rate in population, 297
recognition of unique problems, 116–117
screening tests, 128–133
Psychiatric Inpatient/Outpatient Norm, 300
Psychiatric patients, see Patient(s), psychiatric

Psychiatric screening, 128
Psychological Adjustment to Illness Scale (PAIS), 134
Psychological assessment
computer-administered and future of primary health care, 773–780
role in primary care settings, overview and general considerations, 26–28
tool
outcomes management, 35–36
treatment planning, 34–35
Psychological distress, 298, 357
Psychological perspective, stress, 377–378
Psychological symptoms, 28–29, 157, 695
Psychological tests, 27, 721–724
Psychometric bias, see Bias
Psychometric principles, 122–123
Psychometric properties
Beck Anxiety Inventory, 516–520
Beck Depression Inventory, 395–396
Center for Epidemiologic Studies Depression Scale, 406–408
COMPASS–PC, 259–264
Daily Stress Inventory, 381–382
Depression Outcomes Module, 482
depression screener, 468–469
Depression-Arkansas Scale, 475, 476
Difficult Doctor Patient Relationship Questionnaire, 657, 680
Geriatric Depression Scale, 493, 495, 496, 498
Hamilton Depression Inventory, 431–438, 451
Self-Administered Alcoholism Screening Test, 540–542
SF-36 Health Survey, 589–594
Shedler Quick PsychoDiagnostics Panel, 287–288
Symptom Assessment–45 Questionnaire, 339–341, 350–352
treatment monitoring, 357–358
Psychometric strength, 241
Psychometric support, 543–548, 597–599
Psychosocial assessment, 27
Psychosocial problems, 373–374, 598–599
Psychosomatic hypothesis, 675
Psychosomatic illness, 663
Psychotherapy, 226
Psychoticism, 348
scale, 357
PTSD Check List (PCL), 523
PTSD, see Posttraumatic stress disorder

Q

Qualitative approach, 562
Qualities, integrated care, 19–21
Quality Assessment, 624, 635–642
Quality Assessment: Systemic Application of Review Criteria (QUASAR), 640–641, 643
Quality of care, 159
Quality of life (QOL), 31, 144, 298
scales, 779–780
Quantitative approach, 362
QUASAR, see Quality Assessment: Systemic Application of Review Criteria

R

Race/ethnicity, 558, 635, 657
RAND Medical Outcomes Study, 12
Rand-36, 586, 601
Raskin Rating Scale, 407, 413
Rate of onset of symptoms, 139
Rating, clinician, 128–130
RC, *see* Reliable Change Index
RCI, *see* Reliable change index
RDC, *see* Research Diagnostic Criteria
Readability, questionnaires, 164
Reading ability, 367, 379
Reading level, 258, 627, 643
Receiver operating curve (ROC) analysis
    BDI-II, 397–398
    Dementia Rating Scale, 566
    Neurobehavioral Cognitive Status
        Examination, 571–572
    psychiatric disorder screening, 126–128
    SF-36 Health Survey, 598
    Symptom Checklist–90–Revised, 305
Recommendations
    Blessed Dementia Scale, 576
    clock drawing, 564
    Delirium Rating Scale, 577
    Dementia Rating Scale, 569
    INOVA Primary Behavioral Health Care Pilot
        Project, 759–760
    Mini-Mental Status Examination, 560–561
    Neurobehavioral Cognitive Status
        Examination, 573
Recovery, 316–317, 369, 448
Reductionism, 13–14
Referral resources, 177–178
Referrals
    criteria and inadequacies in treating
        behavioral health disorders, 16
    family-systems approach and difficult
        patient identification, 676
    pediatric psychology practice, 106, 107
    treatment   recommendations   and
        PRIME-MD, 227
Referred-care interventions, 237–238, 239
Reflex behavioral response, 677
Reframing, 676
Registries, 699, 769–771
Rehabilitation, 257
Reimbursement
    barriers to integrated primary and behavioral
        health care services, 23, 26
    disincentive and of mental disorder
        detection, 194–195
    pediatric treatment of psychological
        problems of children, 98, 99
    policies and roles of clinic leadership, 176–177
    primary care settings
        behavioral health problems, 55
        psychological assessment, 27
    SF-36 Health Survey, 609–610
Relapse rate, 230, 694, 706, 727
Relative operating characteristic analysis, 542
Reliability, *see also* Psychometric properties
    Beck Anxiety Inventory, 516–517
    Beck Depression Inventory, 395
    behavioral health assessments, 166

Blessed Dementia Scale, 574
Brief Symptom Inventory, 304
Center for Epidemiologic Studies
    Depression Scale, 406–407
characterization, 301–302
clock drawing, 563
COMPASS–PC, 260, 261, 263, 268–269
Daily Stress Inventory, 381
Delirium Rating Scale, 576–577
Dementia Rating Scale, 564–565
Depression Outcomes Module, 482
Difficult Doctor Patient Relationship
    Questionnaire, 657
Geriatric Depression Scale, 493
Hamilton Depression Inventory, 428,
    432–433
Mini-Mental Status Examination, 557
Neurobehavioral Cognitive Status
    Examination, 570
Patient Description Questionnaire, 656
Primary Care Assessment Survey, 625, 632,
    634
screening for psychiatric disorders, 121, 122
Self-Administered Alcoholism Screening
    Test, 539, 542
SF-36 Health Survey, 590–592, 597
Symptom Assessment–45 Questionnaire,
    339–340
Symptom Checklist–90–Revised, 302–303
Weekly Stress Inventory, 384
Reliable Change (RC) Index
    Beck Anxiety Inventory, 526, 527
    depression outcomes module, 485
    Hamilton Depression Inventory, 448
    Symptom Assessment–45 Questionnaire, 358,
        360
    Symptom Checklist–90–Revised/
        Brief Symptom Inventory,
        316–317
Remediation, 256–257
Remission, 448
Remoralization, 256
Renal disease, end-stage, 325
Reporting technology, 171–172
Reports, aggregate, 292, 293
Research Diagnostic Criteria (RDC), 192, 410, 428
Resources
    behavioral health assessments
        additional, 177–179
        constraints and benefits, 160–161
        requirements, 169–174
    stewardship, 47, 51, 57
    utilization, 343, 344
        form, 738, 741, 745, 747, 748, 750–751
Response theory, 376, 377
Risk
    adjustment, 365–366, 269, 608
    behavioral health and chronic illness, 68
    counseling, 636, 638
    disease and building health care systems, 50
    future of health care delivery, 48
    screening, 136, 771–772
Risk adjuster, 363
River Valley Clinic, 179–183
RN, *see* Nursing support condition
ROC, *see* Receiver operating curve analysis

Rogerian psychotherapy, 781
Rosenberg Self-Esteem Scale (RSES), 435, 436
RSES, *see* Rosenberg Self-Esteem Scale

S

SA-24, *see* Symptom Assessment-24
SA-45, *see* Symptom Assessment–45 Questionnaire
SAAST, *see* Self-Administered Alcoholism Screening Test
SADS, *see* Schedule for Affective Disorders and Schizophrenia
SAFTEE, *see* Systematic Assessment for Treatment-Emergent Events
SAM, *see* Stress Appraisal Measure
Sample characteristics, 740–741
Sample size, 204
SAMSHA, *see* Substance Abuse and Mental Health Services Administration
Satisfaction measurement, 739–740, 746
Satisfaction survey, 289–291
Scale correlations, 634–635
Scale for Suicide Ideation, 396
Schedule for Affective Disorders and Schizophrenia (SADS), 402
Schedule of Recent Experience (SRE), 378
Schizophrenia, 545
SCI, *see* Spinal-cord injury
SCID, *see* Structured Clinical Interview of DSM
Scientific issues, 608–609
SCL-90, *see* Symptom Checklist-90
SCL-90-R, *see* Symptom Checklist-90-Revised
Score distribution, 634, 657
Scores/scoring
    BDI-II interpretation, 397–398
    Beck Anxiety Inventory, 510, 514, 515, 516
    Beck Depression Inventory, 397, 414
    behavioral health care assessment, 32
    Center for Epidemiologic Studies Depression Scale, 408–409, 414
    COMPASS–PC, 261
    Depression-Arkansas Scale, 475, 477
    Geriatric Depression Scale, 493
    Hamilton Depression Inventory, 429
    INOVA Primary Behavioral Health Care Pilot Project, 737, 738, 756–757
    Kaiser Permanente Integrated Care Project, 723
    method, 559–560, 562
    patient questionnaires, 164
    Primary Care Assessment Survey, 644–646
    SF-36 Health Survey, 584–586, 605
    Shedler Quick PsychoDiagnostics Panel, 281, 288
    Symptom Assessment–45 Questionnaire, 338
    systems, 170–171
Scott's coefficient of homogeneity, 632
SCREENER instrument, 137
Screening
    at-risk patients by primary care providers, 164
    Beck Anxiety Inventory, 520–524
    Beck Depression Inventory instruments, 398–399
    BSI-18, 310

Center for Epidemiologic Studies Depression Scale, 409–411
depression-related disorders, 690–691, 692–699
future of primary health care, 775–777
Geriatric Depression Scale, 499–502
Hamilton Depression Inventory, 424, 442–450
pediatric psychological problems, 100
Primary Care Assessment Survey, 627–628
primary care provider and inadequacies in treating behavioral health care disorders, 15
PRIME-MD, 196
psychiatric disorders in primary care
    concept, 119–121
    epidemiologic model, 121–122
    problem of low base rates, 123–125
    psychometric and evaluative principles, 122–123
    receiver operating characteristic analysis, 126–128
    recognition, 116–119
    sequential: technique for low base rates, 125–126
    special issues, 133–142
    tests, 128–133
psychological assessment as tool, 32–35
role of assessment in primary care settings, 27
Self-Administered Alcoholism Screening Test, 539–540
SF-36 Health Survey correlation, 596–605
Shedler Quick PsychoDiagnostics Panel, 280–281
Symptom Assessment–45 Questionnaire, 349–356
Symptom Checklist–90–Revised/ Brief Symptom Inventory, 309–310
tests and why doctors do not use for mental health, 278–280
Screen-metric format, 570, 573
SDDS-PC, *see* Symptom-Driven Diagnostic System for Primary Care
SDS, *see* Zung Self-rating Depression Scale
Secondary disorders, 234
Second-order change, 46
Seductive patient, 659, 660–661
Self-Administered Alcoholism Screening Test (SAAST)
    case study, 551–552
    development, 537–539
    implementation, 548–551
    screening
        operating characteristics, 540–542
        population bias, 539–540
        prevalence of disorder, 540
        psychometric support, 543–548
        reliability, 542
        relative operating characteristic analysis, 542
Self-destructive deniers, 654
Self-esteem, 656
Self-management, 702
Self-Report Depression Scale (SRDS), 427

Self-report forms, 197–200, 202–203
Self-report inventory, 128–130
Sensitivity, *see also* Psychometric properties
  BDI-PC, 398
  Beck Anxiety Inventory, 525
  Brief Symptom Inventory, 306
  Center for Epidemiologic Studies Depression
    Scale, 410
  clock drawing, 564
  COMPASS–PC, 260
  Dementia Rating Scale, 566
  Depression Outcomes Module, 482
  depression screener, 468, 469
  Depression-Arkansas Scale, 475
  diagnostic efficiency of BDI-PC, 401
  Geriatric Depression Scale, 495, 498, 500
    short-form, 496, 497–498
  Hamilton Depression Inventory, 424, 436
  Mini-Mental Status Examination, 559
  PRIME-MD 1000 study, 207, 208, 209, 210, 214,
    241
  screening tests for psychiatric disorders, 126,
    127, 130, 132
  Self-Administered Alcoholism Screening
    Test, 540–541, 543
  SF-36 Health Survey, 590, 592–593, 597, 598
  Shedler Quick PsychoDiagnostics Panel, 286,
    287
  Symptom Assessment–45 Questionnaire, 340,
    351–352, 358
Separate care delivery systems, 58, 59, 60, 61
Sequential screening, 125–126
Serotonin reuptake inhibitor (SSRI), 227, 228, 369
Service satisfaction measures, 31
SES, *see* Socioeconomic status
Sexual abuse, 314, *see also* Abuse
Sexual victimization, 314–315
SF-12 Health Survey (SF-12)
  future of primary health care, 779
  INOVA Primary Behavioral Health Care Pilot
    Project, 738
    correlation with SA-45 variables, 752, 753
    Phase I, 741, 744
    Phase II, 747
    primary findings, 756
    sample classification as impairment, 748
  Kaiser Permanente Integrated Care Project,
    722
  Symptom Assessment–45 Questionnaire, 342
SF-12, *see* SF-12 Health Survey
SF-20, *see* Medical Outcomes Study Short Form
  Health Status-20
SF-36, *see* Medical Outcomes Study Short Form
  Health Status-36
SF-36 Health Survey
  case studies, 610–618
  characterization, 583–586
  depression, 693
  Depression Outcomes Module, 482
  depression screener use, 470
  Depression-Arkansas Scale administration, 477
  disease-specific considerations, 607–608
  future of primary health care, 779
  interpretative strategy, 594–596
  norms, 588–589
  psychometric properties, 589–594

screening, 596–605
  strength/limitations, 608–610
  summary of development, 586
  treatment planning, 605–607
  variant forms, 586–588
Shame, 677
Shedler QPD panel, *see* Shedler Quick
  PsychoDiagnostics panel
Shedler Quick PsychDiagnostics panel (Shedler
  QPD panel)
  data reporting, 291–294
  Kaiser Permanente Integrated Care Project,
    720, 721–722, 723, 725, 727, 728
  laboratory report, 281–283
  outcome assessment, 291
  patient satisfaction, 290–291
  physician acceptance, 289–290
  summary, 294–295
    test development, 283–285
  use as screener, 280–281
  validity, 285–289
  why doctors do not use mental health
    screening tests, 278–280
Short form, 394, 408, 493, 494, 521
Short Portable Mental Status Questionnaire
  (SPMSQ), 141
Sick role, 675
Side effects monitoring, *see* Monitoring
Sigmoidoscopy, 770
Signal detection analysis, 494
Smokers/nonsmokers, 306, 320, 375, 787
Social class, 558
Social phobia, 522
Social Readjustment Rating Scale (SRRS), 378
Social system, 222
Sociodemographic factors, 567, 575
Socioeconomic status (SES), 241, 407
Software, 171, 283
Somatic complaints, 6–7, 116–117
Somatic illness, 9
Somatic symptom superhighway, 52–53
Somatic symptoms, 443, 771
Somatization
  difficult patient identification, 655, 674–676
  disorders, 55, 201–202
  Shedler Quick PsychoDiagnostics Panel, 289
  Symptom Assessment–45 Questionnaire, 348,
    368
Somatoform disorders
  Difficult Doctor Patient Relationship
    Questionnaire, 662
  PRIME-MD, 201–202, 211, 230–231, 234–235
    clinician evaluation guide, 220
  Symptom Checklist–90–Revised/
    Brief Symptom Inventory,
    310–314
Space, 110, 174
SPC, *see* Statistical control process
Spearman–Brown correlation, 406
Specialists, 177–178
Specialty behavioral health care model, 63
Specific-conflict hypothesis, 376
Specificity, *see also* Psychometric properties
  BDI-PC, 398, 401
  Beck Depression Inventory instruments, 402

Center for Epidemiologic Studies Depression
  Scale, 409, 410
clock drawing, 564
Dementia Rating Scale, 566
Depression Outcomes Module, 482
depression screener, 468, 469
Depression-Arkansas Scale, 475
Geriatric Depression Scale, 495, 498, 500
  short-form, 496, 497–498
Hamilton Depression Inventory, 424, 436
Mini-Mental Status Examination, 558, 559
PRIME-MD 1000 study, 207, 208, 209, 210
screening tests for psychiatric disorders, 126,
  130
Self-Administered Alcoholism Screening Test
  screening, 540–541, 543
SF-36 Health Survey correlation, 597, 598
Shedler Quick PsychoDiagnostics Panel, 286,
  287
Symptom Assessment–45 Questionnaire, 340, 351
Spinal-cord injury (SCI), 325
SPMSQ, see Short Portable Mental Status Question-
  naire
Spouses of alcoholics, 544–545
SRDS, see Self-Report Depression Scale
SRE, see Schedule of Recent Experience
SRRS, see Social Readjustment Rating Scale
SSRI, see Serotonin reuptake inhibitor
Staff, 167, 360, 550
Stage of readiness to change, 229–230
STAI, see State-Trait Anxiety Inventory
Stand-alone instrument
  Beck Anxiety Inventory, 521–522
  Beck Depression Inventory instruments,
    401–402
  Depression Outcomes Module, 483
  depression screener, 469–470
  Depression-Arkansas Scale, 476–477
  Primary Care Assessment Survey, 642
  Self-Administered Alcoholism Screening
    Test, 548–549
  Symptom Assessment–45 Questionnaire,
    341–342, 352–353
Standard error of measurement, 590, 591
Standardized response mean, 593
State-Trait Anxiety Inventory (STAI), 134, 518
Statistical control process (SPC), 605
Steiger's t-test, 630
Stigma, mental illness, 14
Strengths/limitations
  Beck Anxiety Inventory, 528
  Beck Depression Inventory/Center for
    Epidemiologic Studies Depression
    Scale, 413–415
  Blessed Dementia Scale, 575–576
  clock drawing, 564
  COMPASS–PC, 269–270
  Delirium Rating Scale, 577
  Dementia Rating Scale, 568–569
  Depression Outcomes Module, 485–486
  depression screener, 472
  Depression-Arkansas Scale, 479
  Difficult Doctor Patient Relationship
    Questionnaire, 679–681
  Hamilton Depression Inventory in primary
    care settings, 450–452

INOVA Primary Behavioral Health Care
    Pilot Project, 758–759
  Mini-Mental Status Examination, 560
  Neurobehavioral Cognitive Status
    Examination, 572–573
  Primary Care Assessment Survey, 646
  PRIME-MD, 239–243
  SF-36 Health Survey, 608–610
  Shedler Quick PsychoDiagnostics Panel,
    288–289
  Symptom Assessment–45 Questionnaire,
    366–367
  Symptom Checklist–90–Revised/
    Brief Symptom Inventory,
    327–328
Streptococcal infections, 373
Stress Appraisal Measure (SAM), 378
Stress
  disorders and cost of behavioral health care,
    10
  etiological models, 376–378
  management and pediatric psychologists, 105
  psychosocial and illness onset in primary
    care settings, 373
Stroke Unit Mental Status Examination (SUMSE),
    139
Structural intervention, 239
Structure Clinical Interview for DSM (SCID)
  BDI-PC, 401
  Beck Depression Inventory instruments, 402
  COMPASS–PC, 262
  depression diagnosis in elderly, 500
  diagnosis of mental disorders, 195, 203, 206
  future of primary health care, 776
  Shedler Quick PsychoDiagnostics Panel,
    285, 286
Structure/formatting, 258
Structured interviews, see Interviews, structured
Subjective well-being (SWB), 257, 259, 260, 262,
    266–267
Substance Abuse and Mental Health Services Ad-
    ministration (SAMHSA), 6, 8–12
Substance abuse
  Brief Symptom Inventory validity, 306
  inadequacies in identification and
    treatment, 14
  Shedler Quick PsychoDiagnostics Panel
    validity, 286–287
  Symptom Checklist–90–Revised/
    Brief Symptom Inventory
    applications, 323–325
Substance abuse/dependence disorder, 6
Subthreshold disorders, 444–445
Success rates, 693–694
Suicidal ideation, 282, 397, 445–446, 732
Suicide, 136–137, 312–314, 392
SUMSE, see Stroke Unit Mental Status Examination
Superventricular tachycardia, 321
Support staff, 175–176, see also Staff
Support/leadership, 180
SWB, see Subjective well-being
Sympathetic-adrenal medullary system, 376–377
Symptom Assessment-24 (SA-24), 738, 741, 744, 747
Symptom Assessment–45 Questionnaire (SA-45)
  area T-score and percentile conversions,
    337–338

basic interpretative strategy, 345–348
case study, 367–369
clinical applications, 362–364
comparability of stand-alone and SCL-90
    extracted versions, 341–342
corrections for missing item responses, 338
development background, 335–336
disease-specific considerations, 366
general considerations for use in primary care
    settings, 348–349
INOVA Primary Behavioral Health Care Pilot
    Project, 737–738
    correlation with SF-12 variables, 752, 753
    Phase I, 741, 744
    Phase II, 747
    primary findings, 756
    sample classification as impairment, 748, 750
normative data, 337
psychometric considerations, 339–341
screening, 349–356
strengths and limitations in primary care
    settings, 366–367
summary and conclusions, 369–371
summary of development, 336–337
treatment monitoring, 356–362
treatment outcomes assessment, 362–366
validity in primary care settings, 342–344
Symptom Checklist–90–Revised (SCL-90-R),
    326–327
Symptom Checklist–90–Revised (SCL-90-R)/Brief Symp-
    tom Inventory (BSI)
    advantages and limitations, 327–328
    applications in specialized medical settings
        alcohol and substance abuse, 323–325
        cardiology, 321–322
        HIV/AIDS, 322–323
        oncology, 318–321
        other medical populations, 325–326
    characterization, 299–300
    impact of comorbidity, 299
    interpretation, 307–309
    medical settings, 297–298
    norms and normative samples, 300–301
    primary care populations, 309–314
    psychiatric disorders and psychological
        distress, 298
    reliability and validity, 301–307
    sexual victimization, 314–315
    treatment monitoring, 315–317
Symptom checklist, 269, 274
Symptom Checklist-90 (SCL-90)
    BDI-IA validity, 396
    behavioral health care assessment, 29
    Center for Epidemiologic Studies Depression
        Scale validity, 407
    screening for psychiatric disorders, 130–131,
        134, 137
    Symptom Assessment–45 Questionnaire validity
        comparison, 341, 353
Symptom Checklist-90–extracted Symptom Assess-
    ment–45 Questionnaire, 341–342
Symptom distress, 346–347
Symptom domain scales, 347–348, 367, 368
Symptom rating scales, 774–775
Symptom severity, 209, 692–693, 727

Symptom-Driven Diagnostic System for Primary
    Care (SDDS-PC), 777
Syndromal depression, 398, see also Depression
System feedback, 605, 607, see also Feedback
Systematic Assessment for Treatment-Emergent
    Events (SAFTEE), 777
Systematic collaboration, 23, 24–25

T

TAP, see Telephone assessment program
Team-based care, 48–49
Teamwork, 51, 65
Telemedicine, 789
Telephone, 498, 606, 644, 690
Telephone assessment program (TAP), 775
Telephone Interview for Cognitive Status, 142
Temporal mandibular disorder (TMD), 78–80
Testis cancer, 319–320, see also Cancer
Test-retest reliability, see also Psychometric proper-
    ties
    BDI-IA, 396
    BDI-II, 396
    BDI-PC, 396
    Beck Anxiety Inventory, 516–517, 525
    Beck Depression Inventory, 395
    Bless Information-Memory-Concentration Test,
        574
    Brief Symptom Inventory, 303
    Center for Epidemiologic Studies
        Depression Scale, 406–407, 408
    Dementia Rating Scale, 564
    Depression Outcomes Module, 482
    Depression-Arkansas Scale, 475
    estimate in reliability, 302
    Geriatric Depression Scale, 493, 495, 496
    Hamilton Depression Inventory, 432
    Mini-Mental Status Examination, 557
    Patient Description Questionnaire, 656
    Primary Care Assessment Survey, 632, 633,
        634
    SF-36 Health Survey, 590
    Symptom Assessment–45 Questionnaire, 339,
        340, 357, 359, 360–361, 369
    Symptom Checklist–90–Revised, 302–303
    Weekly Stress Inventory, 384
Theoretical models, 717
Theory development, 256
Third-party payers, 258
Three-factor model, 407
Three-part model of consultation, 102
Time issues, 160–161, 212–213, 719
Time of monitoring, 143, see also Monitoring
Tinnitus, 325
TMD, see Temporal mandibular disorder
Toddler Behavior Screening Inventory, 101
TPR, see Treatment Progress Report
Tracking, 173, 768
Traditional specialty referral model, 64
Training, 95, 104, 279, 679, 718
Transition stress, 51
Transplants, 321
Treatment
    behavioral health care problems by primary
        care providers, 12–17
    coordinator, 767, 768–769

depression management program, 691, 700–701, 703–707
Depression Outcomes Module, 484
intervention, 446
Kaiser Permanente Integrated Care Project, 720–721
pediatric psychology practice, 107
primary care
    future, 768, 770, 772–773, 780–789
    mental disorders, 55–57
    psychiatric disorders, 143–144
    PRIME-MD study, 223–232, 240–241
psychological assessment, 34–35
    of children, 95–96
SF-36 Health Survey, 602–603, 607
Symptom Assessment–45 Questionnaire, 354–356, 361–362
Treatment monitoring
    Beck Anxiety Inventory, 524–527
    Beck Depression Inventory instruments, 403–405
    Center for Epidemiologic Studies Depression Scale, 413
    Depression Outcomes Module, 484–485
    Depression-Arkansas Scale, 478
    Geriatric Depression Scale, 503
    Hamilton Depression Inventory, 447–450
    PRIME-MD, 233
    SF-36 Health Survey, 605–607
    Symptom Assessment–45 Questionnaire, 356–362
    Symptom Checklist–90–Revised/ Brief Symptom Inventory, 315–317
Treatment outcome
    depression outcomes module, 484
    Primary Care Assessment Survey, 625, 645–646
    PRIME-MD, 232
    psychosocial stressors and disease in primary care settings, 374
    SF-36 Health Survey, 603–604
    Symptom Assessment–45 Questionnaire, 362–366
Treatment Progress Report (TPR), 264, 265, 266–267, 273, 271
Tricyclics, 227
True/false tests, 280–281, 283
T-score, see also Psychometric properties; Scores/scoring
    daily stress inventory, 380–381
    Dementia Rating Scale limitations, 569
    Hamilton Depression Inventory, 431, 439, 448
    INOVA Primary Behavioral Health Care Pilot Project, 738
    Symptom Assessment–45 Questionnaire, 339, 350–351, 353
        behavioral health care report cards 365
        case study 368, 369
        changes and treatment monitoring 357
        clinical decision making 360–362
        interpretation, 346, 347–348
        validity compared to SF-12, 343, 344
    Symptom Checklist–90–Revised/Brief Symptom Inventory, 307

U

Underrecognition, depression, 464, see also Depression
Unhealthy behaviors, 68–69
Unipolar depression, 311, see also Depression
User friendliness, 284, 285
Utilization assessment, 670

V

Validation sample, 450–451
Validity, see also Psychometric properties
    Beck Anxiety Inventory, 517–520
    Beck Depression Inventory, 395
    behavioral health assessments, 166
    Blessed Dementia Scale, 574
    Brief Symptom Inventory, 306–307
    Center for Epidemiologic Studies Depression Scale, 407–408
    characterization, 304
    clock drawing, 563
    COMPASS–PC, 260, 261
    Daily Stress Inventory, 381–382
    Delirium Rating Scale, 576–577
    Dementia Rating Scale, 565–566
    Depression Outcomes Module, 482
    Depression-Arkansas Scale, 475, 476
    Difficult Doctor Patient Relationship Questionnaire, 661–663, 680
    Geriatric Depression Scale, 493, 495
    Hamilton Depression Inventory, 433–439
    Mini-Mental Status Examination, 557–560
    Neurobehavioral Cognitive Status Examination, 570–572
    patient-provided information, 625
    PRIME-MD 1000 study, 203–214, 241
    screening for psychiatric disorders, 121, 122, 123, 126
    Self-Administered Alcoholism Screening Test screening, 541, 545
    SF-36 Health Survey, 590, 593–594, 597
    Shedler Quick PsychoDiagnostics Panel, 285–289
    Symptom Assessment–45 Questionnaire, 340–341, 345–346
    Symptom Checklist 90 Revised, 304–306
Variability, 593, see also SF-36 Health Survey
Variant forms, 586–588
Variations, behavioral health integration, 71–76
Varimax rotation, 407, 657–659, see also Psychometric properties
Vascular dementia, 566, see also Dementia
Virtual reality, 784

W

WAIS, see Wechsler Adult Intelligence Scale
Warning signs, suicide, 137
Watson Wyatt Worldwide Study, 3
Wechsler Adult Intelligence Scale (WAIS), 557, 570, 565
Wechsler Memory Scale (WMS), 557, 565
Wechsler Memory Scale-III, 29
Weekly stress inventory (WSI), 383*387

Weight loss, 397
Weight gain, 375
WHO, *see* World Health Organization
WMS, *see* Wechsler Memory Scale
Work performance, 693
Workload, 107
Workplace productivity, 10
World Health Organization (WHO), 120–121, 373
World Wide Web, 788–789
WSI, *see* Weekly Stress Inventory

X

XHDRS, *see* Extracted Hamilton Depression Rating
        Scale

Y

YASR, *see* Young Adult Self-Report
Yes/no format, 492
Young Adult Self-Report (YASR), 305

Z

Z-scores, 514, 515, *see also* Scores/scoring
Zung Anxiety Scale, 209, 722, 725, 727, 728
Zung Self-Rating Depression Scale (SDS)
    BDI-IA, 396
    Beck Depression Inventory, 395, 402
    diagnosis of psychiatric disorders, 119
    Geriatric Depression Scale, 493
    Kaiser Permanente Integrated Care Project,
            722, 725, 727, 728
    pilot behavioral health assessment program,
            181
    prevalence of behavioral health disorders, 7
    PRIME-MD 1000 study, 209
    SF-36 Health Survey, 595, 611, 613, 616